Women's Health in Primary Care

WOMEN'S HEALTH IN PRIMARY CARE

Editor

Jo Ann Rosenfeld, M.D.
Associate Professor of Family Practice
Bristol Family Practice Center
East Tennessee State University, James H. Quillen College of Medicine
Bristol, Tennessee

Special Considerations for Nurse Practitioners and Physician Assistants written by

Nancy Alley, RN.C., F.N.P., Ph.D.
Associate Professor of Family and Community Nursing
Associate Dean
East Tennessee State University, College of Nursing
Johnson City, Tennessee

Assistant Editors

Louise S. Acheson, M.D., M.S.
Associate Professor of Family Medicine
Case Western Reserve University
    School of Medicine
University Hospitals of Cleveland
Cleveland, Ohio

Jacqelyn B. Admire, M.S.P.H.
Assistant Director of Scientific Activities
American Academy of Family Physicians
Kansas City, Missouri

Editor: *Jonathan Pine*
Managing Editor: *Leah Hayes*
Production Coordinator: *Marette Magargle-Smith*
Copy Editor: *Susan Sfarra*
Designer: *Silverchair Science & Communications, Inc.*
Cover Designer: *Silverchair Science & Communications, Inc.*
Typesetter: *Peirce Graphic Services, Inc.*
Printer: *R.R. Donnelley*
Binder: *R.R. Donnelley*

Printed in the United States of America

First Edition,

Library of Congress Cataloging-in-Publication Data

Women's health in primary care / editor, Jo Ann Rosenfeld ; special considerations for nurse practitioners and physician assistants written by Nancy Alley ; assistant editors, Louise S. Acheson, Jacqelyn B. Admire.
    p.   cm.
    Includes index.
    ISBN 0-683-07366-4
    1. Women—Diseases.   2. Women—Health and hygiene.   3. Primary care (Medicine)   I. Rosenfeld, Jo Ann.
II. Alley, Nancy.   III. Acheson, Louise S.   IV. Admire, Jacqelyn B.
    [DNLM: 1. Women's Health.   2. Primary Health Care.   WA 309 W8735 1997]
RC 48.6.W645   1997
616'.0082—dc20
DNLM/DLC
for Library of Congress   96-13729
                                                                                                                        CIP

97 98 99
1 2 3 4 5 6 7 8 9 10

This book is dedicated to my parents and my children.
Jo Ann Rosenfeld

Preface

"Why are women the opposite sex? They are more like men than any other creature on earth."
—Dorothy Sayers

In an ideal world, this book would not be necessary. Women would not be the "opposite" sex. However, women and their health concerns have often, unfortunately, been considered as certainly different, alternate, and less important imitations of those of men. Over time, women's health concerns have not always merited the time, concern, involvement, research, and regard that they deserve. Thus, this book has been developed for all primary health care providers—physicians, nurse practitioners, and physician assistants—as a comprehensive guide to the whole life cycle of women's health. It has been written by primary care providers who work with women daily. It is intended for the primary care provider who plans to take the opportunity to give women and their health the attention they require.

This book has been written with four principles in mind. First, women and their concerns cannot be fit into the pattern of men's concerns, especially when we truly do not know where that fit is accurate and where it is inadequate, because of the lack of woman-inclusive research. Women's issues will be examined in light of the available research and with the position that these are important problems for women. Hopefully, more studies that chronicle women's health over time, like the Nurses' Health Study, will give us answers to many of the questions to which we now have no solid answers.

Secondly, women can only be understood in the context of their particular place in their life, family, culture, and society. The provider must take the time to learn about where every woman fits in her life cycle and in her family. A 60-year-old woman can be at the apex of a career, retired and caring for an older spouse, or raising her toddler-grandchildren.

Thirdly, medicine and health care providers cannot generalize for all women, any more than women can be considered shadows of men. Individuality is the rule. Each woman has different needs and plans. Each woman faces adolescence, widowhood, motherhood, or death differently. Although some women may have some symptoms during menopause, it cannot be generalized that all women will react, or will react similarly, to those symptoms. The provider must learn both how women differ and are similar to men, and how they differ from each other.

Lastly, medicine cannot be "practiced" on women. It is possible for the provider and woman to work together to help her find and maintain good health in a sensitive, noninvasive, individualistic way. This book hopes to support such an application of the medical and psychologic sciences for the health of all women and each woman.

Primary care providers, in their continuing care of women throughout their life, should and do continue to care for women during pregnancy and delivery. Care of the woman in pregnancy and in labor should not be compartmentalized; it should be a seamless connection with the care of the whole woman and the whole family. The care of the woman who is pregnant will be found in many chapters in this book. However, this book cannot hope to measure the whole depths of the discussion of pregnancy and delivery, but attempts to consider philosophy, care, and how the pregnant woman is affected by other considerations and problems.

The key to this book is comprehension, both in scope and understanding. We have created a book that spans the widest breadth of considerations of women's concerns and problems. We have dealt with more than women's diseases, including also health promotion and concerns throughout her life. Health promotion is an inclusive and extensive task that takes the cooperation and coordination of the woman, her provider, and often her family and society.

We have sought to examine the totality of women's lives, both the traditional medical and the less customary psychological and social concerns. Women are more than gynecologic organs that need monitoring. The diseases women face are much wider than just those that affect the genitourinary system. We have striven to examine the available research and to observe its validity, in light of a model of a woman until now seldom revealed and recognized, as an individual with particular tendencies and with individual and valid responses. Hopefully, in this way, the provider can come to understand, appreciate, consider, and work with women to promote health.

Jo Ann Rosenfeld, M.D.
Bristol, Tennessee

Acknowledgments

To my parents for their support and belief, and to my colleagues and residents for their tolerance and help.

Contributors

Abby Goulder Abelson, M.D.
Assistant Clinical Professor of Medicine
Division of Rheumatology
Case Western Reserve University School
of Medicine
University Hospitals of Cleveland
Cleveland, Ohio

Louise S. Acheson, M.D., M.S.
Associate Professor of Family Medicine
Case Western Reserve University School
of Medicine
University Hospitals of Cleveland
Cleveland, Ohio

Beth A. Alexander, M.D., M.S.
Professor of Family Practice
Michigan State University, College of
Human Medicine
East Lansing, Michigan

Nancy Alley, RN.C., F.N.P., Ph.D.
Associate Professor of Family and
Community Nursing

Associate Dean
East Tennessee State University, College
of Nursing
Johnson City, Tennessee

Janice Anderson, M.D.
Coordinator, Obstetrics and Gynecology
Curriculum
Forbes Family Practice Residency Program
Forbes Health System
Pittsburgh, Pennsylvania

Kathryn M. Andolsek, M.D., M.P.H.
Clinical Professor of Community and
Family Medicine
Program Director, Family Medicine
Residency Program
Duke University Medical Center
Durham, North Carolina

Kay A. Bauman, M.D., M.P.H., A.B.F.P.
Associate Professor of Family Practice
University of Hawaii, John A. Burns
School of Medicine
Honolulu, Hawaii

Diane K. Beebe, M.D.
Associate Professor and Residency Director
Department of Family Medicine
Lakeland Family Medicine Teaching Center
University of Mississippi Medical Center
Jackson, Mississippi

Kathleen L.B. Beine, M.D.
Clinical Assistant Professor of Family
   Medicine
East Tennessee State University
James H. Quillen College of Medicine
Johnson City, Tennessee

Reid B. Blackwelder, M.D.
Assistant Professor of Family Medicine
East Tennessee State University
James H. Quillen College of Medicine
Kingsport, Tennessee

Ann J. Brown, M.D.
Assistant Professor of Medicine
Duke University Medical Center
Durham, North Carolina

Carol M. Buchter, M.D.
Assistant Professor of Medicine
Division of Cardiology
Case Western Reserve University School
   of Medicine
Director, Heart Failure Evaluation and
   Treatment Program
University Hospitals of Cleveland
Cleveland, Ohio

Sandra K. Burge, Ph.D.
Associate Professor of Family Practice
University of Texas Health Science Center
San Antonio, Texas

Rima J. Couzi, M.D., M.H.S.
Senior Clinical Fellow in Oncology
The Johns Hopkins Oncology Center
The Johns Hopkins University School of
   Medicine
Baltimore, Maryland

Bickley Craven, M.D.
Assistant Professor of Family Medicine
East Tennessee State University
James H. Quillen College of Medicine
Kingsport, Tennessee

Nancy E. Davidson, M.D.
Associate Professor of Oncology
The Johns Hopkins Oncology Center
The Johns Hopkins University School
   of Medicine
Baltimore, Maryland

Joann Falkenburg, M.D.
Instructor in Family Practice
Bristol Family Practice Center
East Tennessee State University
James H. Quillen College of Medicine
Bristol, Tennessee

Linda Frazier, M.D., M.P.H.
Associate Professor of Community and
   Family Medicine
Duke University Medical Center
Durham, North Carolina

Valerie J. Gilchrist, M.D.
Professor of Family Medicine
Northeastern Ohio University College
   of Medicine
Rootstown, Ohio
Associate Director, Family Practice
   Center
Aultman Hospital
Canton, Ohio

Karen L. Hall, M.D.
Associate Professor and Director of Resi-
   dency Training
Department of Community Health and
   Family Medicine
University of Florida College of
   Medicine
Gainesville, Florida

Diane M. Harper, M.D., M.P.H.
Associate Professor of Community and
  Family Medicine
University of Missouri
Kansas City School of Medicine
Kansas City, Missouri

Deborah G. Haynes, M.D.
Clinical Assistant Professor of Family and
  Community Medicine
University of Kansas School of Medicine,
  Wichita
Wichita, Kansas

Marybeth Hendricks-Matthews, Ph.D.
Associate Professor of Preventive Medicine
  and Community Health
Virginia Commonwealth University
Medical College of Virginia
Richmond, Virginia
Associate Clinical Professor of Family
  Medicine
·University of Virginia, School of Medi-
  cine
Charlottesville, Virginia

Laurie L. Hornberger, M.D., F.A.A.P.
Assistant Professor of Pediatrics
University of Missouri, Kansas City School
  of Medicine
Section of Adolescent Medicine
Children's Mercy Hospital
Kansas City, Missouri

William J. Hueston, M.D.
Assistant Professor of Family Medicine
University of Wisconsin Medical School
Madison, Wisconsin

Thomas J. Johnson, Ph.D.
Assistant Professor of Psychology
Indiana State University, School of Arts
  and Sciences
Terre Haute, Indiana

Rick D. Kellerman, M.D.
Associate Professor of Family and
  Community Medicine
University of Kansas School of Medicine,
  Wichita
Wichita, Kansas
Director, Smoky Hill Family Practice
  Residency Program
Salina, Kansas

Tina M. Kenyon, M.S.W., A.C.S.W.
Community Education Initiative
  Coordinator
New Hampshire-Dartmouth Family
  Practice Residency
Dartmouth Medical School
Hanover, New Hampshire
Concord Hospital
Concord, New Hampshire

Mitchell S. King, M.D.
Director, Family Practice Residency
  Program
St. Francis Hospital of Evanston
Evanston, Illinois

Jean L. Kristeller, Ph.D.
Associate Professor of Psychology
Indiana State University, School of Arts
  and Sciences
Terre Haute, Indiana

Diane J. Madlon-Kay, M.D.
Clinical Assistant Professor of Family and
  Community Medicine
University of Minnesota Medical School
St. Paul Ramsey Medical Center
St. Paul, Minnesota

Gail S. Marion, PA-C
Assistant Professor of Family and
  Community Medicine
Wake Forest University, Bowman Gray
  School of Medicine
Winston-Salem, North Carolina

Joy Melnikow, M.D., M.P.H.
Assistant Professor of Family Practice
University of California, Davis, School of
    Medicine
Sacramento, California

Lisa Nadler, M.D.
Assistant Clinical Professor of Community
    and Family Medicine
Associate Residency Director
Duke University Medical Center
Durham, North Carolina

Hilde Lindemann Nelson, M.D.
Director, Center for Applied and Profes-
    sional Ethics
University of Tennessee, College of Arts
    and Sciences
Knoxville, Tennessee

Robert E. Nesse, M.D.
Associate Professor of Family Medicine
Mayo Medical School
Vice Chairman, Department of Family
    Medicine
Mayo Clinic
Rochester, Minnesota

Patsy Parker, M.D.
Clinical Associate Professor of Family
    Practice
University of Minnesota Medical School
Medical Director, Women's Health Care
    Associates
Minneapolis, Minnesota

Zelda L. Powers, M.Ed.
Social Worker and Licensed Professional
    Counselor
Department of Family Medicine
Bristol Family Practice Center
East Tennessee State University
James H. Quillen College of Medicine
Bristol, Tennessee

Jerilynn C. Prior, M.D., F.R.C.P.C.
Professor of Medicine
Division of Endocrinology
University of British Columbia
Vancouver Hospital and Health Sciences
    Centre
Vancouver, British Columbia, Canada

Kara J. Quan, M.D.
Fellow in Cardiology
Department of Internal Medicine
Case Western Reserve University School
    of Medicine
University Hospitals of Cleveland
Cleveland, Ohio

Jo Ann Rosenfeld, M.D.
Associate Professor of Family Practice
Bristol Family Practice Center
East Tennessee State University, James H.
    Quillen College of Medicine
Bristol, Tennessee

Miriam B. Rosenthal, M.D.
Associate Professor of Psychiatry and
    Reproductive Biology
Case Western Reserve University School
    of Medicine
Director of Behavioral Medicine in Obstet-
    rics and Gynecology
University MacDonald Women's
    Hospital
Cleveland, Ohio

Mary Elizabeth Roth, M.D., M.S.A
Chairman, Departments of Family
    Medicine
Providence Hospital and Medical Centers
Southfield, Michigan
McPherson Hospital
Howell, Michigan
Saline Community Hospital
St. Joseph's Mercy Hospital
Ann Arbor, Michigan

Ellen L. Sakornbut, M.D.
Associate Professor of Family Medicine
University of Tennessee, Memphis, College of Medicine
Memphis, Tennessee

Leslie A. Shimp, Pharm.D., M.S.
Assistant Professor of Pharmacy in Family Practice
University of Michigan Medical School
Associate Professor of Pharmacy
University of Michigan, College of Pharmacy
Ann Arbor, Michigan

Katherine Wilson Smith, M.D., F.A.A.P., F.S.A.M.
Associate Professor of Pediatrics
Section of Adolescent Medicine
Children's Mercy Hospital
Assistant Dean, Emeritus
Consultant to Dean for Special Programs
University of Missouri, Kansas City School of Medicine
Kansas City, Missouri

Mindy Smith, M.D., M.S.
Associate Professor of Family Practice
Michigan State University, College of Human Medicine
East Lansing, Michigan

Elizabeth Stifel, M.D.
Forbes Family Practice Residency Program
Forbes Health System
Pittsburgh, Pennsylvania

Marla Tobin, M.D.
Practicing Family Physician
Family Practice Associates of West Central Missouri
Higginsville, Missouri

Valerie K. Ulstad, M.D., F.A.C.C.
Assistant Professor of Medicine
Cardiovascular Division
University of Minnesota Medical School
Minneapolis, Minnesota
Director, Coronary Care Unit
Department of Cardiology
St. Paul Ramsey Medical Center
St. Paul, Minnesota

Mary E. Verdon, M.D.
Assistant Clinical Professor of Family and Community Medicine
University of California, San Francisco, School of Medicine
San Francisco, California

Table of Contents

Section III   Adulthood   73

INTRODUCTION

I

Cultural Values Affecting Women's Place in Medical Care

Hilde Lindemann Nelson

Introduction

Physicians are taught to note physiological differences between men and women. However, like everyone else, physicians do not always fully appreciate the degree to which the differences between women and men are not constructions of nature but constructions of society. Because our society is persistently focused on men, it seems normal and natural to us that man should be the measuring stick—the unstated point of reference—for what is paradigmatic of human beings. Woman is then defined in terms of her departure from that standard. In bodily terms, woman's difference from man is most evident in her reproductive organs, so these have become associated with her identity in a way that a man's

have not. Thus in the mid-1800s, the German physician Rudolph Virchow wrote, "Woman is a pair of ovaries with a human being attached, whereas man is a human being furnished with a pair of testicles." Another physician writing at the same time explained, "It is as if the Almighty in creating the female sex had taken a uterus and built up a woman around it" (1).

Woman's reproductive difference from man has been taken as a *defining* characteristic, but it has also marked her as abnormal. Whereas man is the norm, woman is not merely different, but *deviant*. The history of this idea goes back at least as far as Aristotle who defines woman as "a deformed man." Where Aristotle speaks of form, medicine has commonly used the language of disease. For example, in medical circles in the 19th and early 20th century, the thought that female functions were inherently pathological was advanced as a physiological fact. As the president of the American Gynecology Society stated in 1900:

> Many a young life is battered and forever crippled on the breakers of puberty; if it crosses these unharmed and is not dashed to pieces on the rock of childbirth, it may still ground on the ever-recurring shallows of menstruation, and lastly upon the final bar of the menopause ere protection is found in the unruffled waters of the harbor beyond reach of sexual storms (2).

Nor was the idea of woman's abnormality confined to her reproductive system. The Victorian *Encyclopedia of Anatomy and Physiology* treats woman as an underdeveloped man, noting that a boy at puberty "evidently passes into a higher degree of development than the female when he gets his beard, for the beard is a mark of our humanness" (1).

The acceptance by the medical profession of Darwinian evolutionary theory opened a large debate concerning woman's place in the natural order. A variety of scientific theories was put forward to explain woman's supposed lack of rationality—this being another crucial way in which women have been thought to deviate from the male norm. One such theory was that because men's brains weighed 10% more than women's brains on average, feminine irrationality could be chalked up to the "missing five ounces" of brain. This theory, however, ran afoul of "the elephant problem"—namely, that elephants, whose brains weigh more than men's, ought to be considerably smarter than humans of either gender. The conundrum this posed prompted a shift to the idea that the ratio of brain to body size is what determines intellect, but unfortunately for the scientists, it was discovered that the ra-

tio is higher in women than in men. The theory was abandoned.

However, this did not end the debate over the intellectual capacity of women's brains. In 1873, Dr. Edward Clarke, a professor of medicine at Harvard, published *Sex in Education; or, A Fair Chance for the Girls*, which went through seventeen editions over the next few years. In it, Clarke surveyed the best medical thinking regarding women, and after scholarly reflection he concluded that the mental exertion required for higher education sapped a woman's body of its vital forces to such an extent that her uterus would atrophy. Putting a woman's brain to masculine use would thus make her an asexual monster.

Woman in Need of Surveillance

Although the rhetoric has changed, the theme of woman's difference from man as pathological, and hence in need of medical treatment, can still be found in present-day medicine. What is new is that medicine tends to medicalize men's and children's bodies as well. Much of the current preoccupation with health, regardless of gender, takes the form of worrying: How high is my blood pressure? What are my cholesterol levels? Would it benefit me to take an aspirin every other day for my heart? Am I getting enough exercise? Have I fastened my seatbelt? What are those french fries doing to my arteries?

Indeed, the contemporary practice of medicine has so strongly impressed on us the need to discipline our bodies and maintain a daily vigilance over them that many of us do it without a physician's prompting. However, if this is true of the population generally, it is also true that women have been subjected and have subjected themselves to particularly close medical scrutiny. Women can now require medical management from puberty to old age without ever once being ill. Contraceptives that work on women's bodies (as opposed to condoms) require a doctor's prescription. A healthy cervix requires a Pap smear every year. Healthy breasts require mammograms. Uneventful pregnancies require amniocentesis, ultrasound, fetal monitoring, and cesarean sections. Menopause requires hormone replacement therapy.

All these interventions are designed to ward off possible pathologies, and many in fact do so (although they also induce them). Yet, add to these interventions the large signs in bars warning women who might be pregnant not to drink; add the ancient disciplinary pressures forcing women's bodies to conform to whatever shape and degree of thinness fashion happens to dictate; add the abortion debate, which makes women's bodies public to a far greater degree than men's; add recent calls for mandatory screening of all pregnant women for HIV; add the March of Dimes "Think Ahead" campaign to get women (but not men) to prepare for pregnancy by taking better care of themselves even before they conceive; and add the extent to which women are singled out specially for medical scrutiny. The message this scrutiny sends is that women are not competent to look after their bodies without a great deal of expert help. The fact that women have absorbed the message may explain why they use the health care system to a considerably greater extent than men do.

Physical Harms from Social Constructions

The fact that women's difference from men is regarded as deviant is in itself responsible for a number of ailments that bring women to their physicians' offices (3). Three spring readily to mind: (1) eating disorders, (2) depression, and (3) gender-related violence.

The social pressure to be thin is not the only force that triggers bulimia, anorexia, and compulsive overeating; these disorders are multidimensional, with familial, perceptual, biological, and cognitive factors interacting in varying combinations to produce life-threatening illness. However, the fact that 90% of all anorectics are women, as are 80% of the 5000 people annually who have part of their intestines removed to lose weight, suggests that eating disorders are closely related to the pathology of a society that increasingly imposes a tyranny of slenderness on its women (4). A medical response can be helpful (indeed), lifesaving (but sensitive), and sympathetic treatment will require physicians to understand the political and social components of the problem.

Women suffer from clinical depression twice as much as men do (5). In the 19th century, women who could afford to often responded to their severely constricted social roles by succumbing to "hysteria," and in extreme cases "brain fever." The liberation of women proceeds unevenly, and although certain gains have been made (e.g., we can vote and enter professions), many women are still marginalized and silenced by a sex-gender system that disvalues and abuses them (i.e., our concerns are dismissed and we are raped). A woman who responds to her situation by suffering from depression is pathologized: her treatment will rest on the premise that there is something the matter with her, not with her society. A relative lack of awareness in medicine of the social and political forces that create the conditions of women's oppression may explain why, despite the fact that primary care physicians are notoriously bad at diagnosing depression, women are given psychotherapeutic drugs by prescription at much higher rates than men (5).

Women who have been raped are also all too often treated by emergency room physicians as if the pathology were theirs, rather than that of a society that is indifferent or hostile to them (6). The profession is becoming aware of this and has attempted to cultivate less abusive and more humane responses.

However, there is reason to think that rape is still vastly underreported, and a primary care physician may be the very person to whom the rape victim might turn for help if the physician is receptive and kind. Physicians have only recently begun to ask the kinds of questions that elicit information about other kinds of violence against women, particularly domestic violence (7). A battered wife may explain away bruises, burns, or broken bones, but here again the physician can and should be her ally. Although this area of medicine is not yet well developed, a physician who is knowledgeable (e.g., who does not ask the conversation-stopping question, "Why don't you leave him?") will be able to refer the woman to the groups and social services she (and perhaps her children) may require.

Women as Maternal Background

In the area of reproduction it is particularly easy to see how public, visible, and socially problematic women's bodies are. Their instrumental use in the service of (possible) children becomes the topic of public policy in a way that no man's body ever does. The woman herself fades into the background, with the spotlight resting on her potential child. For example, in the vast number of reports discussing women as vectors of transmission for pediatric AIDS, only a few discuss the effects of the disease in women themselves. Similarly, women have been barred from certain (well-paying) jobs on the grounds that the work environment might pose a danger to fetal health, but their own health is not considered. This instrumental use of women is seen most dramatically, perhaps, in the increasingly successful attempts to keep first- and second-trimester pregnancies going in women who have died: here the woman's body has literally become mere maternal background (8).

Because pregnancy is socially linked to childrearing to a far greater degree than impregnating is, many social and medical practices rest on the assumption that the child's primary (or sole) caregiver is and should be its mother. This carries on the theme of woman as a means to the ends of others rather than as an end in herself. A more equitable distribution of responsibility for children would be achieved by loosening the link between pregnancy and rearing, and tightening the link between impregnating and rearing. Physicians can help with this, but they often unthinkingly reinforce the idea that men are not expected to care for the children they father. So, for example, responsible physicians oppose teenage pregnancy on the grounds that children should not be rearing children, yet when their teenage patients come into the office for a physical exam, it is the girls who are singled out for sex education and contraception. Having similar conversations with adolescent male patients might be a way of beginning to right the balance.

Women as Analogs: Research

Research on human subjects plays its own variations on the theme of man's body as the norm and woman's body as abnormal. The Women's Health Initiative, although methodologically flawed, is a welcome attempt to remedy what has appeared to be a persistent pattern of excluding women from clinical trials. The Physicians' Health Study, investigating whether aspirin could decrease the risk of heart disease, enrolled 22,000 men but no women. The Baltimore Longitudinal Study, begun on men in 1958 to investigate the physiology of aging, by 1984 still had no data on women. The possible impact of caffeine on heart disease was studied in 45,589 male research subjects; no female subjects were included. Also, a now-infamous pilot study at Rockefeller University, investigating how obesity affects breast and uterine cancer, enrolled only men (9).

Because many protocols do not specify the gender ratios of their research populations, a careful Institute of Medicine study was unable to demonstrate conclusively that women have systematically been barred from research (10), but that same absence of data on women means that we cannot know for certain what difference, if any, gender might make in the areas under investigation. Thus physicians are forced to treat women as male analogs, but they may not be. If as the General Accounting Office reported in 1992, only half of new drugs are analyzed by gender for safety and under half are analyzed for efficacy, then we do not know, for example, whether the cyclical nature of women's hormones affects how a great many drugs work. Ironically, it is precisely this hormonal fluctuation that has been invoked as a reason for excluding women from controlled trials.

Women as Other

Clinical decision-making can be much complicated by the conflict between the ethics of standard Western medicine and the ethics of a patient who is a member of an ethnic minority, as practices such as female genital mutilation remind us. Although cross-cultural sensitivity is crucial, it poses problems when the norms invoked belong not to the women in the culture but to the culture's dominant male interpreters (11). Sorting out what is owed to whom and the degree to which physicians ought to cleave to their own moral understandings is deeply difficult.

For US physicians the social pathologies that form the background for many native Americans create a further problem, as the physician participates in the very culture that has oppressed these tribes and created their social dysfunction. Native American women have many of the same socioeconomic troubles as other minority women, but they grapple with two additional and perhaps interre-

lated difficulties. First, a larger proportion of Native American women than any other group report that they have been raped and otherwise sexually assaulted. Second, alcohol and other drug use is high in this population. These factors combine to produce a death rate from alcoholism for Native American women that is 10 times that of other women in the 25- to 45-year age bracket, and a suicide rate for all ages that is twice that of other women (5).

Clinical decision-making is also frustrating and likely to misfire if physicians bring a heterosexist bias to their patients. Not all women are sexually active with men, and proceeding as if they are will result in inappropriate treatments. Lesbian women may not feel free, without encouragement and acceptance, to divulge their orientation to their physician, who may unthinkingly perform Pap smears or do pregnancy tests where these are not warranted.

Older Women

The inverted demographic pyramid presents our society for the first time with many old people (> age 65 years) and fewer young people (< age 65 years) to care for them. Because young and middle-aged adult women have increasingly joined the labor force, whereas men have largely failed to assume the domestic tasks that must nevertheless be done, women in these age cohorts can find it a real struggle to look after their aged parents (12). Older women tend to provide much of the care for their husbands, even when they are no longer healthy enough to do it.

Women still outlive men by an average of 7 years, but they spend their later years in worse health: older women are more likely than men to have three or more serious illnesses at once (5). Their own care can thus be problematic. Overmedication can be a serious concern, as can access to health care not covered by Medicare. Add ageism to sexism and a social problem of significant proportions looms ahead—one in which primary care providers will more often find themselves enmeshed.

Conclusion

All the considerations just surveyed may be taken as reasons for supposing that women's health care needs are in many respects quite different from men's. This raises the question whether women's health should be a formal medical subspecialty. There is much to be said on both sides of the debate. The concern that a separate clinical specialty reinforces the idea of man as the norm for human beings and woman as deviant cannot be lightly dismissed. On the other hand, there is evidence that primary care physicians who are women treat their women patients in ways that are more gender-sensitive than their male colleagues (13). It may be possible for both men and women to increase their gender sensitivity through formal training from a disciplinary base in which research and scholarship go on and in which services can be provided to other professionals who are not specialists in women's health.

No matter how the disciplinary boundaries are ultimately drawn, two tasks emerge for women's health policy. One is to learn much more about the ways in which women's bodies function differently from men's, taking careful account of social forces that interact with this functioning. The second task, arguably far more difficult, is to increase women's access to the health care system (14). In a country in which one fifth of women have no insurance at all and 27% have annual family incomes of less than $15,000 (as compared to 19% of men) (5), receiving necessary care can be a serious problem. For this reason, it may well be that the most crucial arena for promoting women's health lies not in physicians' offices and hospitals but in legislatures and corporate board rooms.

Nevertheless, primary care physicians have their work cut out for them. The field of medicine is changing rapidly, and one of those changes is a growing awareness of the need to acknowledge people's differences. Noting the significance of such particulars as age, economic status, ethnicity, education, religious beliefs, and *gender* is not only respectful of persons but is also good medicine.

References

1. Little MO. Feminist theory and bioethics. Kennedy Inst of Ethics J March 1996.
2. Ehrenreich B, English D. For Her Own Good: 150 Years of the Experts' Advice to Women. Garden City, NY: Anchor/Doubleday, 1978:99.
3. Sherwin S. No Longer Patient: Feminist Ethics & Health Care. Philadelphia: Temple University Press, 1992.
4. Bordo S. Unbearable Weight: Feminism, Western Culture, and the Body. Berkeley: University of California Press, 1993.
5. Horton JA, ed. The Women's Health Data Book: A Profile of Women's Health in the United States. 2nd ed. Washington, DC: Jacobs Institute of Women's Health, 1995.
6. Brownmuller S. Against Our Will: Men, Women, & Rape. New York: Fawcett, 1993.
7. Council on Ethical & Judicial Affairs. Physicians and domestic violence. JAMA 1992;267:3190–3193.
8. Nelson H. The architect and the bee. Bioethics 1994;8:247–267.
9. Dresser R. Wanted: single, white male for medical research. Hast Cent Rep 1992;22:24–29.
10. Mastroianni A, Faden R, Federman D, eds. Women and Health Research: Ethical and Legal Issues of Including Women in Clinical Studies. Vols. 1 & 2. Washington, DC: National Academy Press, 1994.
11. Nelson H, Nelson J. Feminism, social policy, and long-acting contraception. Hast Cent Rep 1995; 25(suppl):S30–S32.
12. Brody E. Women in the Middle: Their Parent-care Years. New York: Springer, 1990.
13. Franks P, Clancy CM. Physician gender bias in clinical decisionmaking: screening for cancer in primary care. Medical Care 1993;31:213–218.
14. Commonwealth Fund. The Health of American Women. New York: Louis Harris & Associates, 1993.

Women in the United States Health Care System

Louise S. Acheson

Introduction

This chapter provides an overview of the roles of women as formal and informal providers of health care in the United States health care system, as researchers and subjects for medical research, and as consumers of professional medical care. Some information pertaining to the place of women in US medicine has been summarized in the 1995 report of the Council on Graduate Medical Education, "Women & Medicine." (1)

The Popular Sector: Women as Lay Experts on Health

Medical anthropologists often describe three sectors of the health care system: the popular, folk, and professional sectors (2). The popular sector is where ill-health is first recognized and defined, and where most health care activities are initiated and carried out. Health-related activities in the popular sector can be characterized as informal, close-to-home, unspecialized, and mostly conducted by unpaid lay women. For every 100 self-identified symptomatic episodes, 5 come to professional medical attention and the other 95 are managed entirely in the popular sector, either without consulting others, or with advice from family, friends, or social contacts—usually women (2).

Members of one's own social network share a set of beliefs about health maintenance: there are "healthy" and "unhealthy" ways to eat, drink, sleep, dress, exercise, think, and live (2). These beliefs are shaped by the media, often targeting women directly, as in "women's magazines." Most health-maintenance activities of the family are considered a woman's responsibility. In traditional US culture, among others, women are the experts on nutrition, cooking and feeding, beauty, hygiene, household sanitation and esthetics, nurturing children, and maintaining social networks (but not such experts, until recently, on physical fitness). Women are the backbone of many mutual self-help groups. Women often have responsibility for evaluating family members' symptoms, applying home remedies, and deciding when and what outsiders to involve in a health problem. After professional consultation, lay women often are the ones to carry out and monitor the prescribed treatment.

The Folk Sector: Women as Healers

The age-old tradition of women as informal caregivers within the family led to a tradition of women as healers for those outside their families, e.g., shamans, herbalists, midwives (2, 3). Knowledge of poisonous and medicinal herbs probably came to women during garnering and preparing food. Midwifery evolved from experience with childbirth. In medieval Europe, nursing nuns were among the primary healers. The image of nurse as nun has been a powerful aspect of European health care until modern times (3). However, in recent European and North American history, the activities of women as nurses, folk healers, and midwives have fallen under the control of professional medicine, from which women were largely excluded (3–5).

Informal Caregiving

Unpaid women in our society perform most of the home care of children, sick people, the disabled, and the dependent elderly. This care is so much a part of cultural norms that it can seem invisible; Batseon (6) wrote, "Invisible care routinely given has meant that no need is ever apparent." Yet, increased longevity and fewer offspring have rather suddenly increased the likelihood that a woman will provide long-term care to elderly parents and parents-in law, and women's entry into the workforce has further increased the potential for role overload and strain. Currently one-fourth of the people in the US labor force, 80% of them women, provide unpaid care for a disabled elderly person (7). Eighty percent of women aged 25 to 54 years work outside the home, as do 44% of daughters providing personal care to their parents and over half of women with preschool children (7). Most women who do not work outside the home also have responsibility to care for children and/or other family members. Eighty-five percent of all "helperdays" of care for the elderly outside of nursing homes comes from family members (7). The average unpaid caregiver for an elderly family member spends 26 hours per week at this "job." When children, the sick, or elderly people require paid caretakers, most of these are also women.

Women as Paid Workers in the Health Care Industry

Seventy-five percent of US health workers are women: 97% of the 2 million registered nurses and 96% of practical nurses, 76% of 1.6 million allied health workers (e.g., therapists, technicians, dieticians, medical and dental assistants) (8, 9), and 88% of nurse's aides and home health aides (10). Currently 19% of the 670,000 US physicians are women (1). Approximately half of health care administrators and nearly all medical secretaries are women. It is estimated that approximately 20% of health care workers work part-time (9), and thus may not be eligible for full employment benefits. Many also work overtime.

The health labor force is hierarchical. As Butter and colleagues pointed out in their groundbreaking 1985 publication (10), there is a large gap between the autonomy, status, and pay of those at the top and bottom of this hierarchy, comparatively few jobs in the middle, and a credentialing system that makes mobility between hierarchical levels unlikely. Women are segregated in those health occupations of lower status and pay, especially occupations such as practical nursing that require the "psychosocial healing" rather than the "somatic-diagnostic-curing" skills (9, 10).

More women have been entering traditionally male-dominated health professions, especially since the 1970s. Although the representation of men among nursing students (11%) and graduates (9.9%) had doubled in 1992 compared with a decade before (8), men have not been entering traditionally "female" allied health occupations such as nurse's aide, laboratory technician, dietician, or therapist. The bulk of lower status jobs of the health workforce remains female.

When women do work in the elite, higher-paying health care jobs (e.g., physician, chiropractor, dentist, pharmacist), they have the largest discrepancy between their pay and that of men in the same field (10). The fe-male/male earnings ratio for registered nurses and dieticians is 1.00, for clinical lab technicians 0.89, and for physicians 0.63 (1, 9, 10). When the income of physicians is stratified according to specialty, years in practice, and age, or computed on a per visit or per hour basis, female physicians still earn 20 to 34% less than male physicians in the same category (1, 11). Thus the male/female discrepancy in earnings for physicians is not completely accounted for by the clustering of female physicians in less lucrative specialties, by female physicians seeing fewer patients or working fewer "hours," or by their more recent entry into practice. The gender gap in pay for academic physicians of equivalent rank (11.5% less for female full professors, 6.7% less for instructors in 1991) is smaller than that for practicing physicians, but it has widened since the 1970s (1, 12).

Women as Physicians: Gender Differences

After a 70-year period during which women comprised 4 to 8% of US medical students, the number of women in medical school began to increase in the 1970s and reached 40% of the entering students in 1993 (1). The number of women physicians is expected to nearly quadruple between 1970 and 2010. Whether by choice or by constraint, women physicians differ from men in several ways.

Specialty Clustering

Approximately 60% of women physicians, but only 40% of men physicians, are in family practice, pediatrics, psychiatry, internal medicine, or obstetrics and gynecology. Women were most of the pediatric, obstetric, and dermatology residents in 1993 (1). Women are especially underrepresented in surgical specialties, comprising only 20% of residents in 1990 (1). As the COGME report points out, "Under the current medical value system, the primary care specialties where women cluster are both less lucrative and less prestigious than many of the medical subspecialties dominated by male physicians" (1). Grueling and long training schedules and biased advising may be barriers to those women considering surgical or subspecialty training.

Practice Arrangements

Women, on the average, receive less family financial support for their education, and they graduate from medical school with approximately 10% more debt than men (1). Fifty-two percent of women and 60% of men physicians were in office practice in 1992. Ten percent of women were in hospital-based practice, 5% were in teaching/administration/research, and 22% were in residency. Women physicians are much less likely than men physicians to be self-employed in private group or solo practice and are more likely to be salaried (1, 13).

Hours Worked

Women physicians work 5 fewer hours per week and 1 year less in their lifetimes than men physicians, but the difference in hours worked has been diminishing in recent years (1, 13). In 1991, the mean number of hours worked per week by practicing physicians was 54.3 for women and 59.8 for men.

Practice Style/Communication Patterns

Women physicians have a different practice style than men. They schedule fewer patients per hour and spend a longer amount of time with each patient (1), although some comparisons have not controlled for case mix. A recent study using videotapes of primary care practitioners at the Davis Medical Center showed no difference in the amount of time spent by men and women physicians evaluating new patients. However, women physicians spent more time doing preventive services,

building an alliance with the patient, and giving information, whereas men physicians spent more time taking a medical history (14).

Other investigators have found that women physicians are more likely than men physicians to provide preventive screening for women (15). Women general practitioners listen longer to their patients before interrupting, are more attentive and nondirective, and less "presumptuous" (16). Women physicians are less frequently sued by their patients (13).

Family Responsibilities/Arrangements

Nowadays, approximately three-fourths of women physicians (and 90% of men) marry, although historically it was much less common for a woman physician to be married. Approximately half of women physicians marry other physicians (13). Fifty-five percent of men physicians but only 7% of women physicians have a spouse who does not work outside the home. Eighty-five percent of women physicians and 93% of men physicians have children (1). Ninety percent of men physicians with children say that their wife is the children's primary caretaker, but it is rare for a women physician to have a husband who does most of the child care. Women who are physicians rely heavily on paid child care and household help but also shoulder more domestic responsibilities themselves while not necessarily decreasing their professional responsibilities (1, 13).

Underrepresentation in Powerful Leadership Positions

Women in medicine experience gender bias at every stage of their careers (1), with the result that women are underrepresented in positions of leadership in organized medicine. In 1994, 8 of 55 national medical societies had women as elected officials. In academic medicine, women are overrepresented among assistant professors and non–tenure-track faculty, but comprise only 10% of full professors, 4% of department chairs, and 3% of deans (1, 17). Cohort studies suggest that men in academic medicine are promoted twice as quickly as women.

Gender Inequities in Medical Research

Women as Researchers

In 1989, only 14% of principal investigators on NIH-funded research grants were women, although women experienced an equal likelihood of funding per grant application compared with men applicants (1, 18). A study of women in academic internal medicine showed that they were less involved in research than men: 29% of women as compared with 16% of men had no research training. Fifty-five percent of women as compared with 44% of men had not been the first author of a report, whereas 16% of women versus 30% of men researchers aged 40 to 59 years were awarded NIH grants. Faculty women had less lab space than men with the same degree (17); the same held true in departments of psychiatry (1).

Women as Subjects for Research

Most of the scientific information currently used to make decisions about the medical care of women has been obtained from studies of men (19, 20). Some common problems affecting only women, such as uterine leiomyomata or contraceptive satisfaction, have rarely been studied, especially in the United States. Until recently, a small minority of human subjects for NIH-funded research has been women (21). Women of reproductive age have been excluded from testing of new drugs because of worries about fetal toxicity should they become pregnant, especially after the public became aware in the 1970s of the fetal effects of thalidomide and diethylstilbestrol (22). Testing of drugs and treatments in women is important to define the impact of hormonal sta-

tus (varying during the menstrual cycle and after menopause) and of women's differing body size and composition on drug metabolism and treatment effects. However, these factors have been seen as deterrents to including women in clinical trials (22).

The National Institutes of Health have issued a mandate for all research proposals to include women and minority subjects and have established the Office for Research on Women's Health, which funded the Women's Health Initiative. The Food and Drug Administration has changed its guidelines to allow inclusion of women as subjects for the clinical testing of new drugs (22).

Women as Medical Patients

Use of Professional Medical Services

Office Visits

At least 60% of office visits to physicians are made by women (1). Table 2.1 shows the most common problems for which women in different age groups contacted their physician, as recorded in the National Ambulatory Medical Care Survey (NAMCS) of 1989 to 1991 (1, 23). The most common reasons for women to visit a provider are for prenatal care (5% of visits by women patients), general examinations, respiratory infections, and high blood pressure. Other common office diagnoses are diabetes mellitus, glaucoma and cataracts, acne, allergic disorders, backache, joint pain, depression, and anxiety. Only 18% of women's contacts with physicians focused on reproductive health. The range of women's health problems in this national study is closely comparable with the range of women's health problems seen by family physicians in practice nationwide (24).

However, some essential aspects of care for women do not appear in surveys of office practice. A notable example is abortion. Ninety-five percent of first-trimester abortions take place at separate abortion facilities. It is

Table 2.1. Most Common Problems for Which Women Visited Physicians' Offices: NAMCS 1989 to 1991

Adolescent	Adult	Elderly
Sore throat	Prenatal care	Hypertension
Cough	General medical exam	General medical exam
General medical exam	Cough	
Earache	Depression, anxiety	Back pain
Headache	Sprains, strains	"Follow-up"
Nasal congestion	Vaginitis, vulvitis	Dizziness, vertigo
Abdominal pain	Urinary tract infection	Arthritis, leg sx.
Fever	Menstrual disorders	Diabetes mellitus
Skin rash, acne	Acne	Abdominal pain
Prenatal care	Sinusitis	Neuropsychiatric problems

Data from Rosenblatt RA, Hart LG, Gamliel S, Goldstein B, McClendon BJ. Identifying primary care disciplines by analyzing the diagnostic content of ambulatory care. J Am Board Fam Pract 1995; 8:34–45; and Mary Robeson, Jefferson Medical College, Personal Communication, April 1994.
NAMCS = National Ambulatory Medical Care Survey. URI = upper respiratory infection.

also recognized that psychological concerns are underrecorded when reasons for seeking help are tabulated. In a survey such as NAMCS, some common problems such as substance abuse and violence suffered by women are not recognized as causes of the women's presenting complaints (25).

Hospital Use

Excluding hospitalization for delivering a child, women in 1989 spent 14% more days in hospital than men. However, when expressed as days per 1000 population, the difference was only 5% (26). Table 2.2 shows the most common reasons for hospital use in 1989 (days of care per thousand population) and contrasts women and men in different age groups (26). Younger women are hospitalized most for obstetric, gynecologic, and psychiatric problems, whereas younger men have more trauma, alcoholism, and cardiovascular disease. Heart disease, cancer, and fractures become more common as women age.

The most common major surgeries in the United States are done only on women. The National Center for Health Statistics reported that in 1989 the most numerous operations on women were 938,000 cesarean sections, 541,000 hysterectomies, 389,000 tubal liga-

tions, and 213,000 cholecystectomies, whereas men received 376,000 prostatectomies, 288,000 fracture reductions, 271,000 coronary bypass operations, and 192,000 inguinal hernia repairs (27). Overall, women underwent 40% more major inpatient surgeries than men (operative vaginal deliveries and repairs, and cardiac catheterization not included).

Health Status of Women

Women's use of professional medical services is partly determined by their propensity to seek care and partly by the system's handling of their presenting problems. Gender bias may result in different intensities of evaluation and treatment between women and men (1). Use is not necessarily related simply to health status. Preventive services might keep some people healthy, whereas diagnosis and treatment sometimes may make people feel less healthy. Many individuals who are ill will not present for medical care. Often, adverse life experiences will result in somatic distress that brings women to consult clinicians (26). Because women live longer than men, they have a greater cumulative burden of chronic health problems. Women are more likely to reach very

Table 2.2. Days in Acute Care Hospitals per 1000 Women and Men, 1989 to 1991

Age group	Principal Diagnosis	Women	Men
All ages	Total	746.6	720.8
(age-adjusted)	Delivery	80.2	—
	Heart disease	70.8	104.6
	Malignant neoplasms	50.2	57.7
	Fracture	30.5	29.3
	Pneumonia	27.0	34.6
15–44 years	Total	588.2	371.5
	Delivery	196.2	—
	Psychoses	48.4	51.3
	Benign neoplasms	11.5	N/A
	Cholelithiasis	11.4	N/A
	Pelvic inflammatory dz.	10.3	—
	Pregnancy, aborted	9.0	—
	Fracture	N/A	25.8
	Alcohol dependence	N/A	21.2
	Heart disease	N/A	13.9
	Intervertebral disc dz.	N/A	9.4
	Lacerations & wounds	N/A	8.1
45–64 years	Total	850.0	962.1
	Heart disease	95.4	195.4
	Malignant neoplasms	92.2	96.8
	Psychoses	64.0	N/A
	Cholelithiasis	23.7	N/A
	Diabetes	22.3	N/A
	Cerebrovascular diseases	N/A	34.2
	Fracture	N/A	32.2
	Alcohol dependence	N/A	16.9
65+ years	Total	2850	3047
	Heart disease	497.8	603.6
	Malignant neoplasms	247.7	335.6
	Fracture	206.0	N/A
	Cerebrovascular diseases	205.1	207.7
	Pneumonia	139.6	200.8
	Hyperplasia of prostate	—	84.2

Data from National Center for Health Statistics. Most common principal diagnoses in non-federal, acute care hospitals, 1989. *Health, United States, 1990.* Hyattsville, MD: Public Health Service, 1991, 144–145.
N/A indicates that this diagnosis was not among the top six selected diagnoses for a particular age and sex group.

old age and become frail or demented. Overall, health status is worse for women than for men.

Fewer women sampled in the National Health Interview Survey (NHIS) described their health as excellent: 36% compared with 41% of men (1). The age-adjusted annual incidence of acute illness was 20% higher for women, and the numbers of restricted activity days and days lost from work as a result of illness per person per year were 30% higher for women than for men (1). Many chronic conditions that cause disability are more common in women, including obesity, diabetes, arthritis, thyroid disease, migraine, gastritis, colitis, and urinary problems (1, 21). Women of low education or income are more likely than poor, less educated men to have chronic health conditions that limit their activities or ability to work.

Population-based studies and an assessment of psychiatric care to women in the United States would suggest that either women bear a higher burden of psychological distress than men or that women's distress is more likely to come to medical attention and be interpreted as mental illness (29). Anxiety disorders and depression are more common among women than among men (28). Psychotropic drugs are prescribed twice as often for women as for men. Advertisements for psychotropic drugs picture women patients 15 times more often than men patients (2). The women are shown in stressful situations (e.g., cluttered house, crying children) and as emotional (e.g., tearful, anxious, depressed). The implication is that women's life situations generate undesirable emotional states that can best be alleviated by medication, rather than by social change. Women are twice as likely as men to receive electroshock therapy.

Women's Access to Medical Care

Employment-based financing of health insurance means that women are twice as likely as men to be underinsured (29). Women are more likely to forego employment to care for dependent family members, more likely to work part-time in nonunionized service jobs with poor benefits, and likely to be insured through their spouse, and so may lose their insurance if divorced (29, 30). Fourteen million young women have no health insurance, and 5 million more have coverage that excludes maternity care. Middle-aged women pay higher insurance

premiums than middle-aged men, and are twice as likely to have no insurance (29). For those insured through managed care organizations, it is still uncertain what effects this way of paying for care will have on women's health.

Women make up the vast majority of Medicaid recipients. Two-thirds of poor adults in the United States are women, but only 42% of poor women are eligible for Medicaid (29). Federal law since 1991 mandates expanded Medicaid coverage for pregnancy, but expanded eligibility terminates 60 days after delivery and excludes conditions not related to pregnancy.

The structure of Medicare benefits leads older women to incur substantially greater out-of-pocket expenses than men for their health care (30). Medicare does not cover prescription drugs or long-term care, both of which are more needed by women than by men because of women's greater longevity and greater burden of chronic illness. Medicare coverage is best for acute illnesses (more common in men) that result in hospitalization and death, whereas ambulatory care coverage under Medicaid Part B (more needed by women) requires premiums and copayments.

Financial barriers are certainly not the only impediments to women obtaining appropriate health care. They may visit clinicians for illness and may not receive preventive care or attention to their psychosocial issues. Some studies show that even during a "well-woman" visit, women are more likely to receive preventive screening from a woman practitioner than from a man (15). Many women are dissatisfied with their physician because they felt disrespected, "talked down" to, treated like a child, or sexually harassed (1). The pervasive model of having both an internist and a gynecologist may fragment care and result in omission or duplication of services. State restrictions on advanced practice nurses and federal restrictions on reimbursement may limit women's access to care by a midwife or nurse practitioner (29).

Redefining Women's Health

The ongoing task of developing core competencies and curricula in women's health for clinicians will address some current problems with medical care for women. Changes in the financing of medical research may make more of its fruits applicable to women. However, women's health refers to much more than re-productive health; it depends on more than state-of-the-art knowledge about a collection of diseases that frequently affect women. The challenge is to educate clinicians who will not be satisfied unless they join with women to promote health and healing as the women themselves envision it, even if this means many changes in the care of men, children, women, families, and communities.

Special Considerations for Nurse Practitioners and Physician Assistants

At the present time, there are approximately 48,000 nurse practitioners (NPs) in the United States, most of them women and most working in settings in which they care for women. Nurse practitioners help meet care needs in rural areas and the inner city, as well as deliver primary care to other underserved populations such as the elderly. Most nurse practitioner education programs are master's degree programs, with a few programs offering a certificate after additional clinical training beyond the master's degree in nursing. Although the vast majority of programs prepare family nurse practitioners, specialty tracts including gerontology, adult, oncology, and ob-gyn/women's health tracts also prepare advanced practice nurses to meet the care needs of women (31). Other advanced practice nurses including certified nurse midwives, certified nurse anesthetists, and clinical nurse specialists make up approximately 100,000 nurses in advanced practice roles (32).

In 1993, there were more than 23,000 physician assistants (PAs) practicing in the United States, 42% of whom were women. Although PAs work in a variety of settings, the largest concentration are in family practice settings, including physician group practices and outpatient clinics. Programs for educating PAs are located in academic settings, with most being 24 months long. Most students have extensive experience in the health field before entering their educational program (33).

Drastic changes in the health care system will continue to have an impact on all providers of women's care. Hospital beds (and hospitals) are projected to continue to close with massive expansion of primary care. Potential surpluses of specialist physicians and nurses who have been hospital-based mean that all providers and educators of those providers will have to change how clinicians are prepared for practice so that health care can be delivered in a cost-effective, yet comprehensive and holistic, manner (34). Perceptions of threats, turf battles, misunderstandings, lack of knowledge, or legal, autonomy, and reimbursement issues may keep providers from working together (32, 35). Those who are dedicated to meeting the primary care needs of women will overcome these or any other obstacles to closing the gaps in health care.

References

1. Council on Graduate Medical Education. Fifth Report: Women & Medicine. Washington, DC: US Department of Health and Human Services, Public Health Service. July 1995.

2. Helman CG. Culture, Health and Illness. 2nd ed. 1990. London: Wright.
3. Friedman E. Women and health care: The bramble and the rose. In: Friedman E, ed. An Unfinished Revolution: Women and Health Care in America. New York: United Hospital Fund of New York, 1994:1–12.
4. Shorter E. Women's Bodies: A Social History of Women's Encounter with Health, Ill-health, and Medicine. New Brunswick, NJ: Transaction, 1991.
5. Mitford J. The American Way of Birth. New York: Dutton, 1992.
6. Bateson MC. Composing a Life. New York: Penguin Books, 1992. Cited by Stein REK, Bauman LJ, Jessop DJ. Women as formal and informal caregivers of children. In: Friedman E, ed. An Unfinished Revolution: Women and Health Care in America. New York: United Hospital Fund of New York, 1994: 103–119.
7. Brody EM. Women as unpaid caregivers: the price they pay. In: Friedman E, ed. An Unfinished Revolution: Women and Health Care in America. New York: United Hospital Fund of New York, 1994: 67–86.
8. Fagin C. Women and nursing, today and tomorrow. In: Friedman E, ed. An Unfinished Revolution: Women and Health Care in America. New York: United Hospital Fund of New York, 1994:160–176.
9. Muller C. Women in allied health professions. In: Friedman E, ed. An Unfinished Revolution: Women and Health Care in America. New York: United Hospital Fund of New York, 1994:177–203.
10. Butter I, Carpenter E, Kay B, Simmons R. Sex and Status: Hierarchies in the Health Workforce. Washington, DC: American Public Health Association, 1985.
11. Crane M. Is doctors' hard work paying off? Med Economics 1993;70:100–111.
12. Donoghue GD. Eliminating salary inequities for women and minorities in medical academia. JAMWA 1988;43:1.
13. Bowman MA, Allen DI. Stress and Women Physicians. 2nd ed. New York: Springer-Verlag, 1990.
14. Bertakis KD, Helms LJ, Callahan EJ, et al. The influence of gender on physician practice style. Med Care 1995;33:407–416.
15. Lurie N, Slater J, McGovern P, et al. Preventive care for women: Does the sex of the physician matter? N Engl J Med 1993;329:478–482.
16. Meeuwesen L, Schaap C, Van der Staak C. Verbal analysis of doctor-patient communication. Soc Sci Med 1991;32:1143–1150.
17. Bickel J. Women in medical education: A status report. N Engl J Med 1988;319:1579–1584.
18. National Institutes of Health, Office of Research on Women's Health. Public hearing on recruitment, retention, re-entry and advancement of women in biomedical careers. Bethesda, MD. March 2–3, 1992.
19. Healy B. The Yentl syndrome. N Engl J Med 1991; 325:274–276.
20. Healy B. Women's health, public welfare. JAMA 1991;266:566–568.
21. Women's Health. Report of the Public Health Service Task Force on Women's Health Issues: Volume II. Washington, DC: Public Health Service, 1985. DHHS Publication PHS 85-50206.
22. Institute of Medicine. Report of a Workshop: Women and Drug Development. Washington, DC: National Academy Press, 1993.
23. Rosenblatt RA, Hart LG, Gamliel S, Goldstein B, McClendon BJ. Identifying primary care disciplines by analyzing the diagnostic content of ambulatory care. J Am Board Fam Pract 1995;8:34–45.
24. Unpublished data, American Board of Family Practice, 1994.
25. Koss MP, Koss PG, Woodruff WJ. Deleterious effects of criminal victimization on women's health and medical utilization. Arch Intern Med 1991;151: 342–347.
26. National Center for Health Statistics. Health, United States, 1990. Hyattsville, MD: Public Health Service, 1991.
27. Acheson LS. Depression or oppression? Arch Family Med 1993; 2:473–477.
28. Kassler RC, McGonagle KA, Zhao S, et al. Lifetime and 12-month prevalence of DSM-III-R psychiatric disorders in the United States. Arch Gen Psychiatr 1994;51:8–19.
29. Massion CT, Clancy CM, Maxell ME. Women's access to health care. In: Lemcke DP, Pattison J, Marshall LA, Cowley DS, eds. Primary Care of Women. Norwalk, CT: Appleton & Lange, 1995, 1–6.
30. Clancy CM, Massion CT. American women's health care: A patchwork quilt with gaps. JAMA 1992;268:1918–1919.
31. American Association of Colleges of Nursing. Fact Sheet Nurse Practitioners: roles and education. Washington, DC: December 1995.
32. Fitzgerald MA, Jones PE, Lazar B, McHugh M, Wang C. The midlevel provider: colleague or competitor? Patient Care 1995;15:20–37.
33. Salsberg ES, Kovner C. The health care workforce. In: Kovner AR, ed. Health care Delivery in the United States. New York: Springer, 1995:55–100.
34. Pew Health Professions Commission. Critical challenges: revitalizing the health professions for the twenty-first century. November 1995.
35. Havens DM, Evans EC. A future for nurse practitioners in managed care. J Pediatr Health Care 1995;9:88–91.

ADOLESCENCE

II

3

Psychosocial Development of Girls and Women

Valerie J. Gilchrist

Introduction

There have been considerable challenges and exciting new understandings and theoretical formations about women's psychosocial development over the past two decades. This chapter will review these newer perspectives, contrast them with the traditional understanding of psychosocial development, and discuss briefly the implications for the delivery of health care as clinicians.

First, a few disclaimers. What follows is one white middle class heterosexual interpretation—it is one lens. The theoretical perspectives described do not apply to all girls and women, but do apply to most girls and women in a primary practice. Secondly, because the chapter cannot do justice to all the theories and extensive writings, key writers in the area of development of girls and women are emphasized, but this discussion is not comprehensive. Hopefully, the reader will be intrigued and refer to the original texts and other authors. Thirdly, the focus will be on girls as they develop into women. This chapter will not discuss the development of adult or aging women.

Traditional and Recent Developmental Theories

Traditional developmental theorists such as Freud, Erikson, Piaget, Kohlberg, and Perry, although dealing with different aspects of human development, share several common perspectives. First, their theories are based on a hierarchical model in which development is understood as staged in an invariant sequence from simple to more complex. Secondly, there are similar attributes marking the highest levels of development. At the highest level, a person is independent and generative, using abstract and universal principles to guide his actions. Third, the models were fashioned by men and based largely on observations and studies of men. Women's development was either not reviewed nor was seen as deficient.

Beginning in the 1970s, several woman theorists began to explore women's development, such as Jean Baker-Miller and others at the Stone Center, Nancy Chodorow, Carol Gilligan, and Belenkey. These women agreed with traditional theories that women's development progressed differently from men's development, but they also challenged the basic assumptions. First, rather than viewing development as a sequence of stages, they suggested that many issues faced in human development such as issues of competence, identity, nurturance, stagnation, autonomy, and connection are circular, recurring, or oscillating (1, 2). Second, they suggested that the attributes of mature development in traditional developmental theories reflect the values of a patriarchal, Western, industrialized culture rather than the highest levels of human development. Third, these recent theorists rejected the conclusions that women's development was defective or that women did not reach the same level of mature development as men. "Inflexible application to development of a concept derived from development, without sufficient attention to the quality and nature of women's experiences, leads to a significant misunderstanding of women" (1). The women theorists conclude that the key to women's development is the value women place on the maintenance of connection and continuity of relationships.

These recent theories are not without their critics. They are often based on small studies of largely middle class white women (1). Much of what the relational theories propose as characteristic of women may be characteristic of any minority group with less access to power (i.e., not "women's intuition" but "subordinate's intuition"). Also men may develop as women do but manifest characteristics differently because of cultural mandates. Finally, examining "difference" always runs the risk of attributing to one group, in this case gender, specific characteristics that can be seen as "natural." Because women are socialized to attend to relationships, the risk is that all the relational tasks will be assigned to women and men will be relieved of that responsibility.

The following section will contrast the traditional theories and the recent theories in the following areas: relational and identity theories, moral development, and cognitive development. The second section will deal with adolescence and finish with a section on implications for clinical care.

Developmental Theories

Relational and identity theories

All of the major developmental theories recognize the initial attachment of infants to the primary caretaker, usually the mother. Freud (using the concept of the oral phase) and Erikson (referring to his theory of trust vs. mistrust) theorized that if basic needs were initially met, the infant could then begin in the later stages to separate from the mother. Infants of both genders initially identify with the caretaking women. This is subsequently encouraged in women, but discouraged in men. Nancy Chodorow argues that identity may be rooted in sameness for women, but men may need to differentiate themselves because of the role women play as primary caretakers.

Freud, theorizing that the basic underlying human drives were sexual and aggressive, described progressive stages of libidinal focus: (1) oral, (2) anal, (3) phallic, (4) repression in the latency stage, and (5) finally a mature genital focus. Boys and girls first differ at the phallic or oedipal stage as identity centers on the presence or absence of a penis. However, research shows that although women envy penises, men envy breasts. Both children assume that they have the characteristics of both sexes and have a sense of loss when they discover certain attributes do not belong to them. Also, neither boys nor girls move fully out of relationship with their mothers. Freud theorized that because there was no rejection of the primary caretaker, women have less developed superegos. Research shows women have highly developed superegos with more socially conforming, less aggressive behavior, and better self-control then men in middle childhood.

Erikson differed from Freud by giving more attention to developmental tasks than biological drives. He described a series of essential conflicts in eight successive stages throughout life span, each defined by an increasing sense of independent self. Erikson described the goal of the second stage of childhood as autonomy. However, this does not mean separation. Maintaining the relationships between the main people in her or his life is still the most important thing to the child. Rather than a separate sense of self, the child develops a more complex sense of self. During latency, the goal, according to Erikson, is industry. In school, girls form groups and talk, whereas boys engage in organized sports with rules that are goal oriented and competitive (2, 3). Rulebound competitive achievement situations, which for women threaten the web of connection, for men provide a mode of connection that establishes clear boundaries and limits aggression, and thus appears comparatively safe (3).

Finally, Erikson suggests that girls, because their identity is more relational, put the primary adolescent task of identity formation to one side and leave the individuation issues unresolved until they meet someone (i.e., a prospective husband) whose identity will help them make sense and shape of their own identity. Therefore, girls do not achieve true individuality but a borrowed one (4).

According to Baker-Miller and others at the Stone Center for Developmental Services and Studies of Wellesley College, "The development of a positive sense of knowing how to perceive, respond, and relate to the needs and feelings of the person is an important aspect of woman's self-development" (2). Rather than a close relationship with parents being described as "enmeshment or overdependency" in a relational model, it would be seen as healthy individuation. Relational issues have been phrased in regressive terms such as merged, symbiotic, or undifferentiated, rather than appreciating the development of more complex differentiated patterns of connection and intimacy. A girl's sense of self-esteem is enhanced, not threatened, by being in a relationship. This may not be true for boys. Within traditional theories of development, intimacy, empathy, and relatedness can be experienced as threats to autonomy, agency, and self-determination (2). Freud and Erikson describe adult dependency as pathological.

Surrey defines relationships as "an experience of emotional and cognitive intersubjectivity: the ongoing, intrinsic inner awareness and responsiveness to the continuous existence of the other or others and the expectations of mutuality in this regard (2). Self-development in women occurs in important relationships. The relationship-differentiation theory of self-development includes a focus on: (1) critical relationships evolving through the life cycle, (2) the ability to maintain relationships with tolerance, consideration, and mutual adaptation, (3) the ability to move closer to and further away from people at different times and within different contexts, and (4) the capacity to develop additional relationships (2).

Moral Development

Carol Gilligan began her research focusing on how people defined moral conflicts and problems. Kohlberg's stages of moral development trace a progression from egocentric understanding of fairness based on individual need, through a conception of fairness anchored in shared conventions of societal agreement, to a principled understanding of fairness that rests on a free-standing logic of equality and reciprocity. Using Kohlberg's hypothetical situations, she found that men and women viewed moral problems differently. In the classic dilemma of whether Heinz should steal drugs he cannot afford to save the life of his dying wife, boys see a conflict between life and property that can be resolved by logical deduction. For girls the issue becomes not whether Heinz should act in this situation, i.e., should he steal the drug, but rather how he should act in response to his awareness of his wife's needs. According to Kohlberg, the girls' reframing of the Heinz dilemma is interpreted as a lack of ability to understand the universal principles of rights and responsibilities, and is thus viewed as a less well-developed moral understanding.

Gilligan traces the development of women's sense of morality differently from men. Initially, both women and men focus on caring for the self. However, this is subsequently seen as selfish and self-centered, as girls discover the concept of responsibility, whereas boys discover the concept of fairness. For girls, good is equated with caring for others. However, the focus on others to the exclusion of oneself underlies the second transition, one that leads to understanding of the interconnections of oneself and others and an understanding of what constitutes care (3). The need to care for self is deliberately uncovered. In late adolescence and early adulthood, both sexes move away from their prior absolutes. For women, the absolute of care is modified by the recognition of their need to be there for themselves. For men, the absolutes of

truth and fairness are modified by knowing and acknowledging differences between self and others, and the existence of multiple truths (3).

Women impose a distinctive construction on moral problems, seeing moral dilemmas in terms of conflicting responsibilities. "Thus in all of the women's descriptions, identity is defined in a context relationship and judged by a standard of responsibility and care" (3). Separation is justified by an ethic of rights, whereas attachment is supported by an ethic of care. Thus, the ethical perspectives of women and men evolve out of their different experiences and development. "The moral imperative that emerges repeatedly in interviews with women is an injunction of care, a responsibility to discern and alleviate the 'real and recognizable trouble' of this world. For men, the moral imperative appears rather as an injunction to respect the rights of others, and thus to protect from interference the rights to life and self-fulfillment" (3).

Cognitive Development

William Perry theorized that young adults come to acquire knowledge by progressing through stages of (1) basic dualism, characterized by a dependence on authorities, (2) multiplicity as students question authorities, (3) relativism subordinate in which students developed an appreciation of evidence, (4) and finally to full relativism in which the student comprehends that "truth is relative, that the meaning of an event depends on the context in which the event occurs and on the framework that the knower uses to understand that event, and that relativism pervades all aspects of life, not just the academic world" (5).

Belenkey et al., in a 5-year study about how women view reality and draw conclusions about truth, knowledge, and authority found that women acquired knowledge differently. In the initial stage, silence, women described themselves as separate from knowledge, i.e., mindless, voiceless, and subject to external authority. The next stage, received knowledge, is similar to Perry's basic dualism. Women use listening as a way of knowing and are intolerant of ambiguity. As women start to appreciate their knowledge, however, they feel it as personal and private or subjective knowledge. This differs from Perry's multiplicity as women experienced their knowledge not just as another equally valid opinion but as opinion based on who they were and not knowable by another. Women in this stage were polite listeners. They distrusted logical analysis and abstraction and separated truth that comes from feelings within and ideas from without.

As the subjective knower's knowledge was questioned, however, she had to develop strategies to defend her knowledge or retreat to silence. Women then acquired procedural knowledge. They learned how to speak in measured tones, think before speaking, and form predominated over content. However, the women separated procedural knowledge into separate and connected knowing. Searching for a perspective to argue from was seen as separate. However, searching for a perspective to understand was seen as connected. Separate knowing was characterized by doubting, listening to reason, and self-extraction. Connected knowing involved empathy, conversing, sharing small truths, refusing to judge, and searching for collaboration.

The integration of both connected and separate knowledge moved women into constructed knowledge. This is a position from which women viewed knowledge as contextual and understood themselves as creators of knowledge. They valued both subjective and objective strategies for knowing. It is similar to Perry's full relativism. These women wanted to avoid what they saw as the shortcoming of separating personal and professional thought and feeling, self and other. "Constructivists seek to stretch the outer boundaries of their consciousness—by making the unconscious conscious, by consulting and listening to the self,

by voicing the unsaid, by listening to others and staying alert to the currents and undercurrents of life about them, by imagining themselves inside the new poem or person or idea that they want to come to know and understand" (5).

Adolescence—What Happens to Girls

The adolescent has increasing capacities—sexual, agentic, or the ability to act out, and cognitive. However, this is a time of contraction rather than expansion for women. The American Association of University Women's (6) study of 3000 boys and girls between the ages of 9 and 15 years found that adolescence for girls is marked by a loss of confidence and abilities, especially in math and science, an increasingly critical attitude toward her body, and a "blossoming sense of personal inadequacy" (7). Girls' loss of confidence preceded their drop in achievement. The AAUW study provided "factual evidence of years of research documenting systemic gender bias in American education" (7).

Classroom studies have found that boys overwhelmingly dominate. They ask more complex questions, are responded to more frequently by teachers, and are commended for their academic acumen. Girls are commended for social skills and docility (7). Antics of white boys are often considered inevitable and rewarded with attention, but the assertiveness of girls, especially black girls, is reprimanded (7). Orenstein, in a further study of both an inner city and a suburban school, observed that "By adolescence girls have learned to get along, while boys have learned to get ahead" (7). Not only are girls not encouraged academically, smart girls are singled out by their peers for stigmatization (7). Orenstein attributes this gender bias in education and the girls' response to it to their socialization. "The task is daunting: how can they [girls], after all, be both selfless and selfish, silent and outspoken, cooperative and competitive?" (7). The results of this conflict was that academically girls "opt out rather than act out" (7).

The AAUW study found that girls' adolescent development varied by ethnicity. Orenstein notes however that although "The pressures of poverty, discrimination, and the inadequacy of education . . . often overshadowed the gender differences. . . . Nonetheless, the strategies children pursued to maintain self-esteem in such an atmosphere were frequently dictated by gender" (7). African-American girls retained their self-esteem better than white or Latino girls. Between the ages of 9 and 15 years, the number of Latino girls who were "happy with the way I am" decreased by 38% compared to a 33% drop for white girls, and a 7% drop for African American girls (7). Latino girls reported the greatest plunge in self-esteem of any girls in adolescence. They had a more negative body image, were at greater risk of attempting suicide, reported higher levels of emotional stress, and were vulnerable to gang membership. They are twice as likely than white girls to become teenage mothers. In school, they were less likely than other girls to be called on to speak out in class, and least likely to be recognized as gifted (7). Urban Latino girls left school at a greater rate than any other group.

African-American girls' higher self-esteem through adolescence, however, was not related to academic performance, and they reported lower academic self-confidence than their white counterparts. To explain this discrepancy, some researchers have posited a vision of a dual self-esteem with a "private" component that encompasses a child's image of herself in her community and a "public" component that involves her interaction with larger society, in this situation, school (7).

Adolescence has been felt to be the time when an individual separates from her parents and thus achieves adult identity. However, Apter et al. concluded that neither boys nor girls developed along clear lines of individuation and separation but continued to develop through their parents as they continue to care deeply about their parents. They proposed a "model of adolescent development that involves 'connectedness' and 'individuation' as opposed to the more traditional notions of 'separation' and 'individuation'" (2, 4). Rather than try to separate from their parents, adolescents try to negotiate new relationships with their parents. Apter also rejects the traditional interpretations of conflicts and quarrels with parents, the role of peer groups, risk-taking behaviors, and the need for discipline as evidence of adolescents' separation from their families.

Apter sees quarrels between mothers and daughters not as evidence of separation but as evidence of people trying to correct one another's behavior, perception, or world view (4). " . . . most girls said that the person they felt closest to, the person they felt most loved by, the person who offered them the greatest support, was their mother. She was likely to be closer to her mother than to her friends, and closer to her mother than to any other member of the family" (4). The adolescent's greatest fear was the fear of abandonment (4). Pain and conflict between mother and daughter resulted from the mother feeling like her love was being rejected and the daughter feeling like her new personality was being devalued (4).

In order to facilitate the ability to look critically at oneself, the adolescent needs to question, revise, and criticize (4). This means conflict with parents and exploring new presentations of herself in other settings. During adolescence, a girl is sensitive to the way in which being with different people brings out different aspects of herself. She learns how to present herself to get support, establish a relationship, and thus learns who she is or can be. "Friends can mirror not only in acknowledgment and confirmation, but also to register the success of her self-presentation" (4). Friendships are not so much necessary to separate from the family but to establish another context in which to become individuated.

Apter found that adolescents did not want to be treated as equal. The adolescent is not searching for the parent to agree with her, but rather for recognition and validation—responding to feelings and thoughts the person is trying to put forward—whether directly or indirectly (4). In mid-adolescence, the girls were close to their mothers and enjoyed being with their mothers but did not seek a reciprocal type of conversation characteristic of friendship (4).

During adolescence, there is a split between the ability to reason and the ability to predict the outcome of an action. This results in a split between the sophistication of thought and action, resulting in risk-taking behaviors (4). Apter sees risk taking behavior not as rebellious but reflecting a cognitive immaturity. Apter recommends that discipline be authoritative, rather than authoritarian, egalitarian, democratic, or coerced. Even through discipline, a child must feel acknowledged.

Clinical Implications

Context is vital in understanding health and disease. Understanding differences in women's development, environments, and health fosters an appreciation in "both/and" and the "either/or" in comparison to men and traditional medicine (8). A sophisticated understanding of differences in development, rather than a simplistic interpretation that relegates expressive capacities to women and instrumental abilities to men allow appropriate interpretations of individual women's concerns and recommendations for change.

Women and men may vary in their sensitivity to changes. Women may attune to shifts in feelings, whereas men may be more alert to behavior or ideational changes. Women often want men's presence to support and witness.

Men seem propelled to act and effect change. This socialization is exemplified by the difference in speech and communication described by Deborah Tannen. Women tend to define power as having the strength to care for and give to others. Men have described power as power over rather than power with (1). Understanding these issues allows providers to understand what might be interpreted as either empowering or threatening in women and men.

A "relational" interpretation of women's development explains gender differences noted in projective testing. Women perceive danger in impersonal achievement situations and construe danger to result from competitive success. The danger women portray in their tales of achievement is the danger of isolation; the fear that in standing out or being set apart by success they will be left alone (3). This is not what has been interpreted as women's "fear of success" (3). In contrast, men more commonly see danger in close personal affiliation than in achievement and construe danger to a rise from intimacy. The danger men describe in their stories of intimacy is the danger of entrapment or betrayal, being caught in a smothering relationship, or humiliated by rejection and defeat.

Resilience has been described as the ability to survive stress. A relational view of resilience suggested by Jordan includes a move from control to supported vulnerability (i.e., the ability to ask for support), and from self-esteem to relational confidence (i.e., feeling confidence in a relationship), not just feeling good about oneself, but also one's ability to contribute to the other, from power over to empowerment and mutuality, and from a separate self to involvement (9).

The social expectations for men adolescents to experience increasing independence through separation and aggression results in their high risk for death to motor vehicle accidents and homicide. Gilligan concludes that " . . . the secrets of man adolescence revolve around the harboring of continuing attachments . . . " (3). The expectations for women to acquiesce to others result in restricting her potential, increasing her risk for abusive relationships, depression, suicide, and eating disorders. She experiences a " . . . silencing of her own voice, a silencing enforced by the wish not to hurt others, but also by the fear that, in speaking, her voice will not be heard" (3). Gilligan and Brown's longitudinal study of women suggests that the way to teach young women to grow within relationships is to model that behavior. "Women's ability to ask new questions about voice and relationship and girls' development depend on experiencing ourselves as able to speak and also to stay in relationship with women—to feel sadness and anger without experiencing these feelings as overwhelming or as endangering relationships" (10). Although young women search for growth within relationships, a concern is for those women who appear to confuse their identity with intimacy and define themselves through relationships with others. Appropriate counseling for all women honors their need for relationships, respects their sense that disconnections do violence to their sense of self, and yet encourages self-expression and voice.

Conclusion

Gender influences development almost from the moment of conception. During pregnancies in which parents know the infant's sex, comments differentiating kicks as either "future football kicks" referring to a man infant or a "dancing lesson" referring to a woman infant illustrate how the gendered images are projected on the children. When these social expectations augment or enhance abilities it is to be encouraged, but too often for either gender it limits potential. This chapter has summarized some recent challenges to traditional theories of human development. These theories are constantly under revision. Our understanding as providers, however, should recognize the multiplicity of social and biological influences on human development and the tremendous individual variation that we should seek to enhance.

Acknowledgments

I would like to thank Pat Anthony for her help preparing this chapter and both Arlene Brewster and Bill Scott for their insightful editing suggestions.

References

1. Tavris C. The Mismeasure of Women. New York: Simon & Schuster, 1992.
2. Jordan JV, Kaplan AG, Miller JB, Stiver IP, Surrey JL. Women's Growth in Connection: Writings from the Stone Center. New York: Guilford Press, 1991.
3. Gilligan C. In a Different Voice: Psychological Theory and Women's Development. Cambridge, MA: Harvard University Press, 1982.
4. Apter T. Altered Loves: Mothers and Daughters During Adolescence. New York: Ballantine Books, 1990.
5. Belenky BF, Clinchy BM, Goldberger NR, Tarule JM. Women's Ways of Knowing: The Development of Self, Voice and Mind. New York: Basic Books, 1986.
6. AAUW Survey. Shortchanging Girls, Shortchanging America. Washington, DC: American Association of University Women, 1991.
7. Orenstein P. Schoolgirls: Young Women, Self-esteem, and the Confidence Gap. New York: Doubleday, 1994.
8. Dan AJ, ed. Reframing Women's Health: Multidisciplinary Research and Practice. Thousand Oaks, CA: Sage Publications, 1994.
9. Jordan JV. Relational Resilience. The Stone Center, Work in Progress #57. Wellesley, MA: Wellesley College, 1992.
10. Brown LM, Gilligan C. Meeting at the Crossroads: Women's Psychological and Girl's Development. Cambridge, MA: Harvard University Press, 1992.
11. Baker-Miller J. Toward a New Psychology of Women. Boston, MA: Beacon Press, 1976.
12. Chodorow N. The Reproduction of Mothering: Psychoanalysis and the Sociology of Gender. Berkeley, CA: University of California Press, 1978.
13. Coll CG. Cultural Diversity and Implications for Theory and Practice. The Stone Center, Working Progress #59. Wellesley, MA: Wellesley College, 1992.

Rewards of Caring for and the Health Promotion of the Woman Adolescent

Katherine Smith and Laurie Hornberger

Introduction

Adolescence is a time that bridges childhood and adulthood. Its onset occurs with the beginning biological changes of puberty. The end of adolescence is more indefinite and encompasses biological, psychosocial, and cognitive maturity. For practical purposes, the adolescent age range is generally defined as the second decade of life.

During this second decade, rapid biological changes occur, resulting in adult stature and reproductive capability. Psychosocial maturation includes identity formation, autonomy, and independence from the family. The biological and psychosocial progressions are interrelated and complex. The importance of considering the psychosocial aspects of any biological disease makes it mandatory for providers to have an understanding of these relationships and to deal with the adolescent patient as a whole person.

Although adolescence is a relatively healthy age period as measured by traditional biomedical illness, violence and social problems related to high-risk behavior cause significant morbidity and mortality. Health behaviors established during youth contribute to adult morbidities such as cancer, heart disease, and stroke. Use of alcohol, drugs, and tobacco, and sexually transmitted diseases (STDs), unhealthy diet, and lack of physical exercise are all related to future health problems. Providers of adolescent health care should offer anticipatory guidance and preventive counseling for these biopsychosocial morbidities.

In this chapter, a review of physical development, common health problems, the health care visit, and special challenges in caring for adolescent girls and young women are described.

Pubertal Growth and Development

Puberty refers to the process of sexual maturation. Biologically, this includes the acquisition of reproductive capabilities and the development of secondary sexual characteristics. Although physical maturation may be complete early in adolescence, cognitive and social development is less advanced (Fig. 4.1). A constant challenge in working with adolescents is maintaining an awareness of this discrepancy. Interactions with teens should be guided by their level of cognitive and social maturity rather than their physical appearance. The biological changes of puberty will be reviewed here.

Normal Growth and Development

Endocrinology of Puberty

Puberty in girls progresses under the hormonal direction of the hypothalamic-pituitary-ovarian (HPO) axis (1). The hypothalamus produces gonadotropin-releasing hormone (GnRH) that is transported through the portal circulation to the anterior pituitary. There, GnRH stimulates the production of luteinizing hormone (LH) and follicle-stimulating hormone (FSH), and their release into the general circulation. In the ovary, FSH and LH trigger the production of sex steroids, including estrogens (predominately estradiol), progesterone, and small amounts of androgens. The sex steroids are responsible for the maturation of the genital tract and breast development

During childhood, the HPO axis operates under a sensitive negative feedback system. Small amounts of circulating sex steroids inhibit the release of GnRH, suppressing the axis and keeping their production at a low level. For poorly understood reasons, as puberty approaches the negative feedback loop becomes less sensitive. Increased amounts of sex steroids are needed to inhibit the release of GnRH, permitting increased production of gonadotropins and sex steroids. By midpuberty, the HPO axis also operates under a positive feedback system. Rising levels of estrogen stimulate production of LH, which is released as a surge midway in the menstrual cycle causing ovulation.

Average age relationships of pubertal, cognitive, and psychosocial maturation in adolescence.

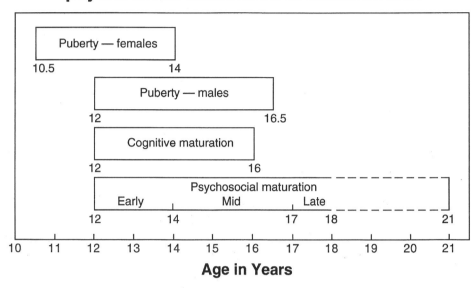

Figure 4.1. Average age relationship of pubertal, cognitive, and psychosocial maturation in adolescence. (Reprinted with permission from Johnston RL. Adolescent growth and development. In: Hoffman AH, Gerydanus D, eds. Adolescent Medicine. 2nd ed. Norwalk: Appleton & Lange. 1989:9.)

Other hormones also facilitate pubertal changes. Approximately 2 years before the activation of the HPO axis, the adrenal glands increase their secretion of the androgens dihydroepiandrosterone (DHEA), dihydroepiandrosterone sulfate (DHEAS), and androstenedione. Androstenedione is also produced by the ovaries and is converted in peripheral tissues to testosterone. The increase in adrenal androgens and their resulting physical effects—the development of pubic and axillary hair, acne, and adult body odor—are known as adrenarche. Although present before the visible onset of puberty, the adrenal androgens usually do not exert their effects until pubertal levels of gonadal sex steroids are present.

Growth hormone and somatomedin are responsible for linear growth. Growth hormone is secreted in greater amounts by the pituitary during puberty because of increased levels of sex steroids. Somatomedin is produced by various body tissues in response to the increase in growth hormone. Both act on bony growth plates to cause the pubertal growth spurt. Adequate thyroid hormone must be present for this growth to occur.

Physical Changes in Puberty
The onset of puberty in American girls is normally between age 8 and 13 years, whereas in boys it occurs between age 9 and 14 years. The complete course of female maturation takes an average of 4 years, but ranges from 1.5 to 6 years. The age at which puberty occurs in industrialized countries has declined by as much as 2 to 4 years over the last 150 years, presumably as a result of better nutrition and public health. In the United States, this downward trend has leveled off over the last 40 years and is not expected to continue.

The first noted pubertal change in girls is usually the development of breast buds (thelarche) (2). The emergence of fine pubic hair (adrenarche) soon follows, but occasionally it will precede breast budding. Breast and pubic hair growth have been well described by Tanner and Marshall, using a five-stage classification system; Tanner stage 1 indicates a prepubertal state, whereas Tanner stage 5 indicates a fully developed, adult appearance (3). Typically, the progression of breast and pubic hair growth through the Tanner stages is synchronous.

During puberty, the appearance of the genitals changes with estrogen stimulation. The labia majora and minora protrude and thicken. Hymenal tissue thickens and becomes redundant. As menarche approaches, the vagina decreases from a neutral pH to a more acidic pH of 4.5 to 5.0. Vaginal secretions increase with the production of a clear or milky discharge (physiologic leukorrhea). Internally, the uterus becomes more bulbous in shape, and both the ovaries and uterus enlarge.

Menarche, the onset of menstruation, is a mid-to late event in puberty (Fig. 4.2). Most girls begin menstruation during Tanner stage 4, approximately 2 years after thelarche, but some may begin as late as 5 years after thelarche. In the United States, the average age at menarche is 12.8 years. During the first 2 years of menses, as many as 55 to 90% of cycles may be anovulatory. This contributes to the menstrual irregularities and dysfunctional bleeding that young teens often experience. By 5 years postmenarche, only 20% of cycles are anovulatory.

The growth spurt in adolescent girls is usually underway at the time of thelarche and peak height velocity is reached before menarche. On average, the growth spurt occurs 2

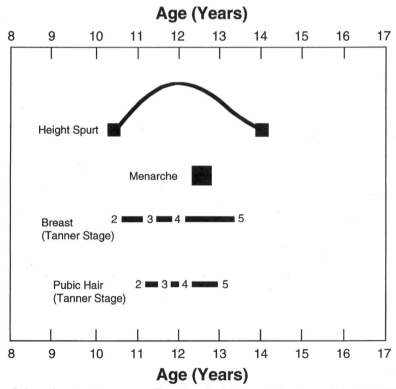

Figure 4.2. Pubertal events in women. (Reprinted with permission from Copeland KC, Brookman RR, Rauh JL. Assessment of Pubertal Development. Ross Laboratories PREP Series. Columbus, OH, Ross Laboratories, August 1986.)

years earlier in girls than in boys. Because they are younger and therefore shorter than boys at the onset of their growth spurt, and because the amount of growth during the puberty is slightly less, girls reach an adult height that is an average of 13 cm shorter than that reached by boys. Bone age, as determined by radiographs of the wrists, is a more accurate measure of pubertal progression than chronological age. Following menarche, girls will usually grow no more than an average of 5 cm and no longer than 2 years because of closure of the epiphyses.

Precocious Pubertal Development

Etiology

Any sign of pubertal development in girls before age 8 years is precocious (4). The causes of precocious puberty are classified into three broad categories based on whether the HPO axis has been activated at the hypothalamic level and whether sexual development is complete or partial.

Central, complete, or true precocious puberty is the result of premature production and secretion of GnRH, activating the HPO axis. The normal sequence of puberty may result, and menarche and fertility can be achieved. In most cases, complete precocious puberty is idiopathic. Other etiologies include anatomic defects of the central nervous system (CNS), brain tumors, postinfectious processes of the CNS, head trauma, and CNS irradiation.

Peripheral, or pseudoprecocious, puberty is the result of increased levels of circulating sex steroids without activation of the HPO axis. The physical features vary according to etiology and may or may not follow the normal pubertal sequence. The source of sex hormones may be exogenous, from certain medications, or endogenous. Endogenous estrogens may be produced by ovarian or adrenal tumors, or more commonly by ovarian follicular cysts. Primary hypothyroidism may also present with pseudoprecocious puberty.

Incomplete precocity refers to the premature appearance of isolated sexual characteristics in the absence of elevated gonadotropin levels and accelerated growth. Premature thelarche is most commonly seen during the first 2 years of life and is thought to be due to slightly increased levels of ovarian estrogens as the HPO axis is suppressed during infancy.

Premature, isolated menarche can occur but is uncommon. In these instances, other causes of vaginal bleeding including abuse, trauma, foreign bodies, tumors, and infection should first be explored. Premature adrenarche is generally idiopathic, but adrenal abnormalities must be considered, especially when other signs of virilization such as clitoromegaly, acne, and adult body odor are present.

Evaluation

In the evaluation of precocious pubertal development, previous and current heights must be plotted on a growth curve to determine if the child has entered a growth spurt. The initial laboratory evaluation of precocious puberty includes a bone age, estradiol levels, and thyroxine and thyroid stimulating hormone levels. Referral to a pediatric endocrinologist is recommended for further evaluation and management of patients with precocious puberty. Treatment involves management of the underlying problem and suppression of further pubertal development until an appropriate age.

Delayed Pubertal Development

Etiology

Delayed puberty in girls is the absence of physical signs of sexual maturation by the age of 13 years or lack of menses within 5 years of thelarche (5, 6). The causes of delayed puberty fall into three categories: hypogonadotropic hypogonadism, hypergonadotropic hypogonadism, and constitutional delay.

Hypogonadotropic hypogonadism refers to a failure of the HPO axis to secrete adequate amounts of GnRH and the gonadotropins. Without stimulation by these hormones, puberty does not progress. This problem may be an isolated one or part of a larger picture of hormone deficiency. Etiologies include CNS lesions and developmental defects, certain genetic syndromes and endocrinologic disorders, chronic illness and malnutrition (including anorexia nervosa), strenuous physical activity, and psychological stress.

Hypergonadotropic hypogonadism refers to a failure of the ovaries to produce sex steroids despite high levels of gonadotropins. Causes of this type of delayed puberty include gonadal dysgenesis, enzyme defects in the steroid synthesis pathways, chemotherapy and pelvic irradiation, ovarian failure, and destructive processes of the ovary.

Constitutional or idiopathic delay, the most common cause of pubertal delay, is a variant of normal growth but should remain a diagnosis of exclusion. Patients with constitutional delay usually have followed a normally shaped growth curve and have a bone age that corresponds to their height age. Often there is a family history of delayed growth and puberty.

Evaluation

Evaluation of the girl with delayed puberty begins with a search for chronic illness and plotting of a growth curve. A pelvic exam or ultrasound is necessary to rule out anatomic abnormalities. Laboratory testing includes a bone age and FSH and LH levels. A karyotype is indicated in cases of short stature, anatomic abnormalities, or extremely elevated gonadotropin levels. Consultation with a pediatric endocrinologist can be helpful. Treatment of pathologic delays involves hormone therapy.

Mortality, Morbidity, and Risk-Taking Behaviors

Because adolescents are basically healthy, preventive health care for adolescents consists primarily of counseling for risk-taking behaviors (Table 4.1).

Adolescent Mortality

Motor vehicle crashes, other unintentional injuries, homicide, and suicide are the leading causes of mortality in school-aged children and youth up to age 24 years. These causes account for nearly three fourths of all deaths (7).

Injuries

Motor vehicle accidents continue to be the leading cause of death for youth. Impairment with alcohol is an important behavioral factor for teen drivers. Many adolescents killed as drivers are positive for alcohol at the time of the accident. Fatal crashes occur more often for male adolescents than female. For nonfatal injuries, there is less gender discrepancy (8). Adolescent drinking and driving behaviors are shown in Figure 4.3.

Violence

Adolescents in today's society are not only involved with violence as victims and even perpetrators, but also as witnesses, resulting in both physical and psychological trauma. Firearm homicide is the second leading cause of death for all teenagers aged 15 to 19 years (9). Gun carrying, fighting, and school-related violence are generally less frequent in high school girls than boys (Fig. 4.4). However, school absenteeism caused by feeling unsafe is generally more common among the girls (10).

Suicide

Suicide is the third leading cause of death in the second decade. The upward trend in adolescent suicides is alarming, with the rate tripling between 1952 and 1992 (11). Availability of lethal methods, especially guns, is a possible contributor to this increase. Suicidal ideation and attempts are far more common in girls than in boys, particularly in younger ado-

Table 4.1. American Academy of Family Physicians Age Charts for Periodic Health Examination—November 1995*
Ages: 13–18 Years
Schedule: *At least one visit for preventive services should occur (See Preamble in Appendix C)*

Screening		
History	Physical Examination[2]	Laboratory/ Diagnostic Procedures
Interval medical and family history[1]	Height and weight	High-Risk Groups
Dietary intake	Blood pressure	Rubella antibodies (HR3)
Physical activity	*Tanner staging*[2]	VDRL/RPR (HR4)
Tobacco/alcohol/drug use	High-Risk Groups	Chlamydial testing (HR5)
Sexual practices	Complete skin exam (HR1)	Gonorrhea culture (HR6)
	Clinical testicular exam (HR2)	Counseling and testing for HIV (HR7)
		Tuberculin skin test (PPD) (HR8)
		Hearing (HR9)
		Papanicolaou smear[3]
		Total cholesterol[4,5]
		Lipoprotein analysis[5]

Counseling		
Diet and Exercise	Substance Use	Sexual Practices
Fat (especially saturated fat), cholesterol, sodium, iron[6], calcium[6]	Tobacco: cessation/primary prevention	Sexual development and be-havior[7]
Nutritional assessment	Alcohol and other drugs: cessation/primary preven-tion	Sexually transmitted diseases: partner selection, condoms
Selection of exercise program	Driving/other dangerous activities while under the influence	Unintended pregnancy and con-traceptive options
	Treatment for abuse	
	High Risk Groups	
	Sharing/using unsterilized needles & syringes (HR11)	

Injury Prevention	Dental Health	Other Primary Preventive Measures
Safety belts	Regular tooth brushing, flossing, dental visits	Breast self-examination[10]
Safety helmets		Testicular self-examination[11]
Violent behavior[8]		High-Risk Groups
Firearms[8]		Discussion of hemoglobin testing (HR12)
Smoke detector		Skin protection from ultraviolet light (HR13)
Noise induced hearing loss[9]		

Immunizations and Chemoprophylaxis
Tetanus-diphtheria (Td) booster[12]
High-Risk Groups
Measles-mumps-rubella (MMR) vaccine[13]
Fluoride supplements (HR14)
Influenza vaccine (HR15)
Pneumococcal vaccine (HR16)
Hepatitis B vaccine (HR17)

High-Risk Categories

HR1   Recent divorce, separation, unemployment, depression, alcohol or other drug abuse, serious medical illness, living alone, or recent bereavement.

HR2   Persons with increased recreational or occupational exposure to sunlight, a family or personal history of skin cancer, or clinical evidence of precursor lesions (e.g., dysplastic nevi, certain congenital nevi.)

HR3   Males with a history of cryptorchidism, orchiopexy, or testicular atrophy.

HR4   Females of childbearing age lacking evidence of immunity.

HR5   Persons who engage in sex with multiple partners in areas in which syphilis is prevalent, prostitutes, or contacts of person with active syphilis.

HR6   Persons who attend clinics for sexually transmitted diseases; attend other high-risk health care facilities (e.g., adolescent and family planning clinics); or have other risk factors for chlamydial infection (e.g., multiple sexual partners or a sexual partner with multiple sexual contacts).

HR7   Persons with multiple sexual partners or a sexual partner with multiple contacts, sexual contacts of persons with culture-proven gonorrhea or persons with a history of repeated episodes of gonorrhea.

HR8   Persons seeking treatment for sexually transmitted diseases; homosexual and bisexual men; past or present intravenous (IV) drug users; persons with a history of prostitution or multiple sexual partners; women whose past or present sexual partners were HIV-infected, bisexual or IV drug users; persons with long-term residence or birth in an area with high prevalence of HIV infection; or persons with a history of transfusion between 1978 and 1985.

HR9   Household members of persons with tuberculosis or others at risk for close contact with the disease; recent immigrants or refugees from countries in which tuberculosis is common (e.g., Asia, Africa, Central and South America, Pacific Islands); migrant workers; residents of correctional institutions or homeless shelters; or persons with certain underlying medical disorders.

HR10   Persons exposed regularly to excessive noise in recreational or other settings.

HR11   Intravenous drug users.

HR12   Persons of Caribbean, Latin America, Asian, Mediterranean or African descent.

HR13   Persons with increased exposure to sunlight.

HR14   Persons living in areas with inadequate water fluoridation (less than 0.7 parts per million).

HR15   Children with chronic pulmonary or cardiovascular problems including asthma; or who required medical followup or hospitalization during the past year for chronic metabolic disease (including diabetes mellitus), renal dysfunction, hemoglobinopathies, or immunosuppression (including immunosuppression caused by medications).

HR16   Children aged two and over with chronic illnesses specifically associated with pneumococcal disease or its complications, anatomic or functional asplenia, sickle cell disease, nephrotic syndrome or chronic renal failure, cerebrospinal fluid leaks, or conditions associated with immunosuppression (including HIV).

HR17   Homosexually and bisexually active men, intravenous drug users, recipients of some blood products, persons in health-related jobs with frequent exposure to blood or blood products, household and sexual contacts of HBV carriers, sexually active heterosexual persons with multiple sexual partners diagnosed as having recently acquired sexually transmitted disease, prostitutes, and persons who have a history of sexual activity with multiple partners in the previous six months.

[1]An updating of the previously obtained medical and family history is recommended by the subcommittee.

[2]A physical examination including Tanner stage is recommended at least once in this age group by the subcommittee.

[3]All women 18 years of age should have an annual Pap test and pelvic examination. All women between 13 and 18 who are or who have been sexually active, should also have an annual Pap test and pelvic examination. After a woman has had three or more consecutive satisfactory normal annual examinations, the Pap test may be performed at the discretion of the physician based on the assessment of patient risk but not less frequently than every three years.

[4]Child of a parent with a blood cholesterol of 240 mg/dL or higher

[5]Child of a parent or grandparent with a documented history of premature (age less than 55 years) cardiovascular disease

[6]For females

[7]Often best performed early in adolescence and with the involvement of parents

[8]Especially for males

[9]Education regarding hearing loss from recreational and personal listening devices is recommended by the subcommittee.

[10]The teaching of self-breast examination is recommended by the subcommittee at the time of initiation of pelvic examinations.

[11]The teaching of self-testicular examination is recommended by the subcommittee for male patients.

[12]Once between ages 14 and 16

[13]A second measles immunization, preferably as MMR (Measles, Mumps, and Rubella Vaccine, Live), is recommended by the subcommittee for all patients unable to show proof of immunity who are entering post secondary school education and for those becoming employed in medical occupations with direct patient care.

*These recommendations are provided only as an assistance for physicians making clinical decisions regarding the care of their patients. As such, they cannot substitute for the individual judgment brought to each clinical situation by the patient's family physician. As with all clinical reference resources, they reflect the best understanding of the science of medicine at the time of publication, but they should be used with the clear understanding that continued research may result in new knowledge and recommendations.

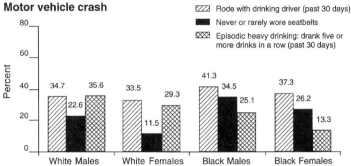

Figure 4.3. Drinking and driving: ages 10 to 24 years. (Data from 1993 National Youth Risk Behavior Survey.)

Violence Related Risk Behaviors
Age 10-24

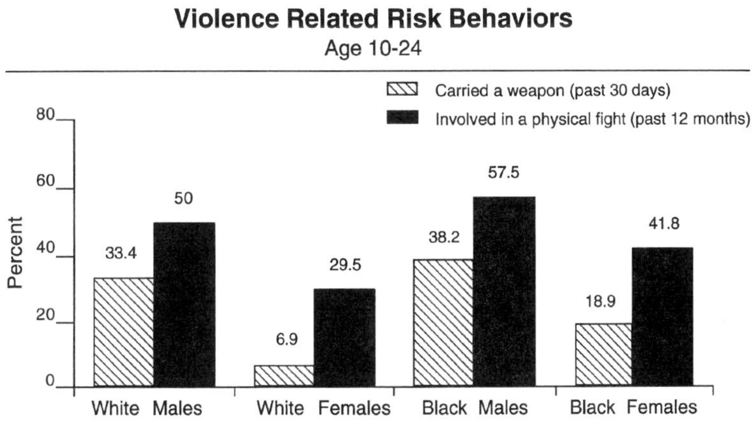

Figure 4.4. Violence-related risk behaviors: ages 10 to 24 years. (Data from 1993 National Youth Risk Behavior Survey.)

lescent girls. Complete suicides are more common in adolescent males. The death rate for suicide among girls is approximately one fifth that of boys (12).

Risk Taking and Predominant Morbidities

Risk taking can be defined as behavior by youth involved with potentially destructive activity, in spite of or without understanding of the consequences (13). During adolescence, two of the major risk behaviors are early sexual activity and substance abuse. Risk behaviors tend to cluster, and the presence of one indicates a need to assess for others.

The behaviors with extreme high-risk and negative consequences must be distinguished from normal risk taking behaviors of adolescents (14, 15). Experimentation during adolescence is important to normal development. Engaging in some lesser degree of risk behaviors serves the adolescent in achieving a sense of independence and mastery. However, the lag in cognitive and moral development compared with biologic growth, coupled with social expectations, predisposes the young adolescent to poor decision making.

Developmentally, adolescents have a sense of invulnerability, leading many girls to deny the dangers of their risk-taking behaviors. For example, sexually active girls may minimize their own risk of pregnancy. Disinhibition associated with substance use can compound other risk factors. Family and peer groups have a crucial influence on adolescent conduct.

Special attention should be given to girls with early physical maturation because of their asynchronous biopsychosocial development. These girls may seek greater independence and engage in premature sexual behavior (16).

Teenage Pregnancy and Sexually Transmitted Diseases

Nearly 70% of US high school students surveyed in 1993 reported ever having had sexual intercourse (10). Morbidities related to sexual behavior include teenage pregnancy and sexually transmitted disease (see Chapter 11.1).

The approximately 1 million teenage pregnancies each year in the United States continue to be the highest rate for nearly all developed countries. In 1992, rates of both gonorrhea and chlamydia were higher among adolescent girls than boys (17).

Substance Abuse

The use of psychoactive substances in the United States is higher than in any other industrial country (18). Substance abuse among adolescents is a problem of serious proportion. Initiation of drug experimentation peaks in adolescence, and the introduction of alcohol, tobacco, and marijuana, the so-called "gateway drugs," is commonplace. Their use gradually increases between 9th and 12th grades (10) (Fig. 4.5). Alcohol and drug use is implicated in early sexual activity, school drop-out, and adolescent mortality (19).

Adolescent alcohol and drug use has been tracked since 1975 (20). Survey data, how-

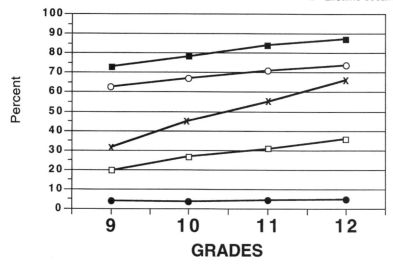

Figure 4.5. Female adolescent risk behaviors. (Data from 1993 National Youth Risk Behavior Survey.)

ever, can underestimate the extent of adolescent substance use, because school drop-outs are not included and are believed to be a high-risk group. Illicit drug use was on the decline, but since 1992 an alarming increase has been seen. More than one fourth of adolescent girls used an illicit drug in 1993 (10). Twenty-two percent of high school senior girls and 29% of senior boys used marijuana, although daily use was much lower in girls. The use of other illicit drugs including LSD, inhalants, stimulants, barbiturates, cocaine, and crack has been rising more gradually, but smaller proportions of girls than boys are involved in such use. Among 8th grade students surveyed, girls had higher rates of use of inhalants, stimulants, and tranquilizers, but by 12th grade boys were more likely to use these drugs.

Increasing drug use is believed to reflect a softening of belief about the dangers involved. The likelihood of drug use is affected by perceived dangers of use. A steady decline in the perceived danger of marijuana has been noted since 1991. Both perceived risk and peer disapproval have also been noted for LSD, cocaine, and crack. These attitudinal factors seem critical in predicting the future and can be influenced during the health visit.

Adolescent use of alcohol, always the number one drug of abuse, declined slightly in the early 1990s, but 1994 reports indicate a slight increase in the prevalence (21). Alcohol use may begin at an early age. Nearly one fourth of 10th grade students engage in binge drinking. Almost 9 of 10 senior students have tried alcohol. However, overall current use of alcohol by girls is less than that of boys. Both girls and boys are at high risk for alcohol abuse.

Tobacco use is currently a major public health concern. Initiation of daily smoking usually starts in grades six through nine and seldom occurs after high school (20). Eighty-seven percent of women who are daily smokers started smoking at or below 18 years of age (22). Younger adolescents are especially likely to underestimate smoking risks, and most adolescents overrate their ability to quit smoking. By 12th grade, 53% of adolescents who smoke 10 cigarettes a day are unable to quit (20).

Because a high percentage of adolescents participate in at least some experimental substance use, it cannot be viewed as unusual. Even occasional use of substances, however, may result in serious injury, especially from alcohol-related motor vehicle accidents. For a few girls, alcohol and drug use may be a component of problem behavior. Adolescent drinking has a significant correlation with antisocial behavior, precocious sexual activity, poor school performance, and family problems.

Most young people who use alcohol and other drugs do not develop chemical dependency. It is therefore more appropriate to use the terms "abuse" or "problem use" when referring to adolescents and to avoid use of the words "addict" or "alcoholic" because physical dependence with the development of withdrawal and tolerance is infrequent. In one study, continuation of youthful problem drinking into adulthood occurs less for women than men (23). Only 20 to 30% of women problem drinkers in high school and college continue to be problem drinkers as adults, although approximately 50% of the men continue to become adult problem drinkers.

Stress and Psychosomatic Conditions

The biopsychosocial development during the second decade of life is accompanied by considerable internal stressors. Always the underlying question "Am I normal?" occurs. A changing body image and the emphasis in today's society to be thin compound concerns with self-perception. A young adolescent girl, especially one with early puberty, is faced with expectations for mature behavior that are beyond her ability. She may need to cope with sexual advances and decisions for which she is unprepared. The middle-stage adolescent girl who is striving for freedom and independence may feel overwhelmed with choices related to both sexual activity and substance use. Parents may feel overly protective of their daughters and respond with restrictions that exacerbate the parent-child tension. Peer relationships during midadolescence can be fraught with loss and conflict. These are usual, everyday stressful events for teens. All this comes at a time when coping methods and experience are inadequate to deal with major problems.

Many young women also suffer dramatic stress from life events related to family and school. Adolescents can be faced with parental conflict and divorce. Approximately 40% of American children have experienced the divorce of their parents (24). Millions of children live with a substance-abusing parent. Financial and mental health problems are common family concerns.

Today, academic accomplishment has become the major task for youth. Schools become a major source of psychological risk and stress (25). Adolescents ranked in the bottom one third of any class can perceive shame and a sense of failure. School failure is a correlate to almost any health risk marker, such as early onset of sexual activity, teen pregnancy, and juvenile delinquency (26). Young adolescent women may perceive birth and motherhood as alternative ways to demonstrate their abilities.

Psychosomatic complaints are common among adolescent girls. They are more likely than boys to internalize stress and become depressed. This feature can be ascribed to sex role socialization but also may have an endocrine basis (26). Providers need to be aware of the impact of stress in the young woman's life and should include such information in history taking.

Psychosomatic complaints are physical symptoms accompanied by psychosocial dysfunction (27). Among adolescents, these complaints commonly include recurrent abdominal pain, dizziness, fatigue, headaches, and chest pain. Typically, the location of psychosomatic abdominal pain is vague and generalized, and no specific organ system is involved. Anxious adolescent girls often present with

dizziness and fatigue. The dizziness may be related to unrecognized periods of hyperventilation. A history of paresthesias is useful in making this diagnosis.

Fatigue is often a reflection of depression. Tension headaches are frequent in adolescents and are seen more commonly in girls than boys (28). Although underlying physical etiologies must be ruled out, a concomitant, detailed social history is important because psychosocial factors predominate. Family history is often positive in patients with migraine headaches. Chest pain in adolescent girls is seldom linked to cardiac disease. Anxiety and hyperventilation are common accompaniments.

Mental Health Issues

Two mental health problems that have significant morbidity for adolescent girls and young women are depression and eating disorders.

Depression

Depression occurs in 20% of female and 10% of male adolescents in the general population (29). Symptoms of depression are much more common than serious clinical depressive illness (see Chapter 8.1). Depressive syndromes include unipolar and bipolar disorders, organic affective disorders, dysthymia, adjustment reactions with depressed mood, and grief or bereavement reactions. Adolescents with serious or chronic physical illness can be reactively depressed.

Adult women have approximately twice the incidence of depression as adult men. This gender difference does not exist in prepubertal children but emerges during the early adolescent period. Exploration of variables that might predict severity of depression show that being a woman is significantly associated with greater severity of adolescent depression. Girls may bring more risk factors to the adolescent period perhaps because of their seemingly greater challenges for biological and social change (30). Girls who reach menarche earlier than their peers may be especially unhappy with their bodies. Puberty in girls is often concurrent with entrance into middle school, a combination that is associated with increased risk of depression in girls (31).

Victims of sexual abuse often suffer with depression. Twenty to 30% of adult women report that they were victims of sexual abuse either as children or adolescents (32). It is essential to inquire about sexual abuse when evaluating the depressed adolescent.

Risk factors that give early clues to the diagnosis of depression include a family history of depression, disruption, discord, abuse, or alcoholism. Weak attachments to both parents and peers are correlated with higher levels of depression (33). Adolescent girls are often affected by their social relationships with their same sex peers. Loss of a romantic relationship may also precipitate depression.

The symptoms of depression in adolescent girls include dysphoria, irritability, poor self-esteem, guilt, and loss of interest, which are often described by them as boredom. It is not always easy to distinguish the irritability and negativism of depression from the moodiness of normal adolescence. Withdrawal from the family can be a component of adolescent search for autonomy but is often more extreme in the young woman who is depressed. Inability to concentrate may lead to declining school performance. Physical symptoms of depression include change in appetite (either increase or decrease), low levels of energy, fatigue, and altered sleep patterns (either hyper- or hyposomnolence).

Suicide can be related to depression but it is more commonly associated with impulsivity and anger. Substance abuse is a common comorbidity to suicidal attempts. A history of loss or hopelessness in a depressed or troubled adolescent mandates screening for suicide intent. Other suicidal risk factors include a history of family disruption, depression or suicide, a recent loss, and previous suicidal behavior. Loss may be realized in many ways such as a

death, breaking up with a boyfriend, moving, or even changing schools. Loss can be assessed by asking if anything has made the girl feel sad, even so sad as to harm herself. Straightforward questions about suicidal ideation or plans do not encourage the behavior and is a requirement for prevention and intervention.

Eating Disorders

Eating disorders have significant prevalence in young women. Concern over body image and weight is common among high school girls (see Chapter 8.2). More than half high school girls attempt weight loss and approximately 45% of girls believe they are overweight (29). The perception that there is a weight problem often accompanies the normal shift to increased body fat during female puberty. Puberty is a risk factor for development of eating disorders, and the problem is more prevalent in those with an early pubescence (34). Eating disorders have a bimodal peak onset at the beginning and ending of adolescence. The second peak occurs at the end of high school and time of leaving home. The prevalence of eating disorders is reported to be 0.5 to 4% (35). Women outnumber men nine to one in anorexia nervosa and five to one in bulimia nervosa (36).

There are special features of eating disorders in adolescents that differ from those in adults. Many teens do not meet the full set of diagnostic criteria but suffer psychologically even before they lose 15% of their body weight. Growth retardation and short stature are severe problems especially when the eating disorders begin before the growth spurt. Weight evaluation must consider the pubertal growth phase. Failure to achieve expected weight gain is an appropriate measure. Amenorrhea can be a difficult criteria to meet because menstrual irregularity is common in the young adolescent. Delayed sexual development affects the premenarchal patient with anorexia nervosa and negates the menstrual criteria.

The peak growth spurt greatly increases nutritional needs. The malnutrition that accompanies eating disorders comes at a crucial time in the developing adolescent girl, resulting in the potential for serious osteopenia. Bone mineral density increases 10 to 15% during Tanner stage 4 to 5 and overall increases 45 to 60% during adolescence. Nutritional deficits prevent this deposition of bone minerals. Lifelong consequences may result from the food restriction of this disorder.

Early identification and intervention of young girls with eating disorders are essential. Family evaluation and therapy are extremely important in their management because the patients are still dependent and tied to their families.

The Adolescent Health Care Visit

Goals of the Visit

In 1992, the American Medical Association published its *Guidelines for Adolescent Preventive Services* (GAPS), a comprehensive list of recommendations for the routine health care of adolescents (37). GAPS uses a biopsychosocial approach to preventive health maintenance, placing an emphasis on risk factor assessment and anticipatory guidance. The American Academy of Family Physicians has similarly given recommendations for periodic health visits, also emphasizing psychosocial approach and counseling. Although annual visits are recommended, comprehensive physical exams may be indicated only once during each stage (early, middle, and late) of adolescence.

Creating the Right Environment

Adolescent girls are often reluctant to seek medical services because they feel uncomfortable in the health care setting. Attention to details in the care provider's office will put teens more at ease. All office staff must be accepting of adolescents and aware of their needs. A waiting area in which teens sit with other teens and young adults, that offers age-appropriate entertainment, such as youth-oriented magazines and videos, makes them feel welcome. Rights to privacy and confidentiality must be protected by all personnel. After establishing a relationship with the provider, adolescents should be allowed to schedule their own appointments and come to the office alone without a parent. At the time care is initiated, this policy should be presented to both patient and parent.

Interviewing the Teen and Her Parent

Organizing the Interview

With a new patient, it is wise to begin the interview with both the girl and her parent together. After hearing their concerns and obtaining a pertinent history, the care provider should then meet with both individually. Each may have agendas of her own. Confidentiality is defined or reviewed before sensitive areas of the psychosocial history are discussed. At the conclusion of the visit, recommendations and anticipatory guidance are discussed with both the adolescent and her parent.

Interview Style

An empathetic interview provides assessment of the patient's health problems and risks, and initiates a therapeutic alliance. Building rapport establishes a foundation for good clinical medicine. Nowhere is this more important than with adolescent girls. Adolescent health care providers must be sensitive to the subtle ways that their manner may influence this rapport.

Although her parent may be present, attention should be focused on the teen. Most questions should be directed toward her, and she should be encouraged to speak for herself. Positive behaviors by both the girl and her parent ought to be acknowledged and reinforced.

Simple layman's terminology may need to be used with teens because medical terminology can be misunderstood (38).

Questions, especially regarding sensitive issues, must be raised using a nonjudgmental, matter-of-fact style. Biased questions or statements, such as "You don't drink, do you?," tell the teen how the provider feels about a subject and may influence her answers. Assumptions must also be avoided. For instance, if the initial question about sexual activity is "Do you have a boyfriend?," the provider has assumed, perhaps mistakenly, that the girl is heterosexual.

Medical History

As part of the routine medical history, note previous medical and mental health problems. A neonatal and developmental history may be pertinent. Immunization records are reviewed. The family history includes the ages and health of immediate family members. Besides common familial illnesses, the clinician should ask specifically about substance abuse, alcoholism, and psychiatric illness.

The menstrual history is an important part of the review of systems because menstrual concerns are common in this age group. The history includes age at menarche, menstrual patterns, hygiene practices, and the presence and severity of dysmenorrhea. A nutritional screen, looking for adequacy of the diet, food faddism, and possible eating disorders is also incorporated into the review of systems. Questions should cover the patient's perceptions about her weight, eating patterns, and dieting habits.

Psychosocial History

Without a psychosocial screening, the health care provider may miss significant health risk factors and an opportunity to educate or intervene. Because the lives of adolescents and their families are constantly changing, reviewing the social history at each annual visit is essential. The psychosocial history includes questions that may touch on sensitive areas for the teen

and her parent. A few introductory words about why these questions are being asked will help them understand their importance.

A helpful mnemonic for remembering major topics in an adolescent psychosocial assessment is HEADDS: Home, Education, Activities, Drugs, Depression and Sex (Table 4.2) (39). The assessment is made with both the parent and the teen. The latter three areas (drugs, depression, and sex) are best covered with the teen alone. Even if a parent says that she is aware of her daughter's activities, the girl may feel more at ease in answering personal questions honestly without a parent in the room.

When screening for risk behaviors, proceed from general issues to more specific questions. Inquire first about risk behaviors in the family and peer group, and then about the teen's personal experiences. In the case of substance use, it may be less threatening to inquire about tobacco first, then alcohol and by illicit substances. Screening for chemical use should be more detailed if a patient has risk markers or behaviors; a positive family history of alcohol or drug problems is the most important risk marker. (Table 4.3) The provider must be alert to whether certain behaviors are interfering with adolescent development or causing functional impairment.

Physical Examination

Teens should be given a choice about whom they would prefer to be present during the physical examination. It is advisable for the examiner, especially if a man, to have a woman assistant present when performing breast, genital, and pelvic exams. The girl's mother, relative, or friend is not usually an appropriate chaperon. Girls need to be undressed and in a gown for all complete physical exams. Proper draping should be observed. Accurate measurements of height and weight must be plotted on age-adjusted curves. Tanner staging is recorded to document pubertal development.

Table 4.2. The HEADDS Interview: Psychosocial Assessment of the Teen

Home:

Who do you live with?

Where is the parent that doesn't live with you? Do you have contact with him/her?

Have there been changes at home recently, such as a move or someone new in the house?

Are the adults in your house employed? What kind of work do they do?

How does everyone get along at home?

Are you worried about anyone in your family?

Education:

Where do you go to school? What grade level are you in?

What sort of grades do you receive? Has this been a change?

Are you enrolled in special services, such as a learning disabilities class?

How many days of school have you missed this year? Why?

Do you plan to graduate from high school? What are your plans after high school?

Activities:

What do you like to do in your spare time? Do you have any hobbies?

Are you involved in any sports teams, clubs or groups?

Do you have friends? A close friend? What do you do with your friends?

Have you gotten in any trouble at school or with the law?

Drugs:

Do you smoke cigarettes? How much?

Many teens have used alcohol. Do your friends use alcohol or drugs? Describe their use.

When is the last time you used alcohol? How often do you drink? What do you like to drink? Have you ever been drunk?

Some teens have tried drugs other than alcohol, such as marijuana. Have you tried any of these drugs? Which ones? How often do you use them?

Depression:

Sometimes, people feel down, sad or depressed. Do you ever feel this way? When was the last time you felt this way? How long did the feeling last?

Do you ever have problems sleeping or concentrating because of worries or sadness?

Do you ever cry, or feel irritable and moody for no apparent reason?

Sometimes people think about hurting themselves or others when they are sad or angry. Have you ever thought about this? Do you feel this way right now?

Sex:

Most teens are thinking and talking about sex, and some have even had sexual experiences. Do you have any questions about sex?

Have you ever had sex before? Are you attracted to guys, girls or both? Have you had sex with guys, girls or both? How old were you when you first had sex? Was that by your choice? How many people have you ever had sex with?

When you do have sex, do you use any kind of protection against pregnancy? What?

Do you use condoms all the time, some of the time or never? If not always, why not?

Have you ever been pregnant? Have you ever had a sexually transmitted disease?

Who is aware of your sexual activity?

Has anyone ever forced you to have sex before, or touched you in places that you didn't want to be touched?

Table 4.3. Screening for Alcohol and Drug Abuse

Risk Markers for Alcohol and Drug Abuse
* Family history of alcohol or drug use problems
* Association with a drug-using peer group
* Early first use of cigarettes, alcohol, or drugs
* Long-standing problems at school
* Antisocial behavior
* Dysfunctional family history of alcohol or drug use problems
* Low value placed on social institutions or authority
* Tolerance of deviant or antisocial behavior
* Other problem behaviors (e.g., early sexual activity or eating disorders)

Behaviors that May Indicate Alcohol and Drug Abuse
* Worsening school performance
* Absenteeism from school or work
* Symptoms of acute/chronic depression or sadness
* Unexplained or recurrent accidents or fights
* Repeated overt intoxications
* Preoccupation with social activities in which drugs/alcohol might be present
* Decreased interaction with other family members and peers
* Drunk and disorderly conduct; driving while intoxicated

Adapted from The Project ADEPT Curriculum for Primary Care Physician Training, Brown University, 1989.

A teen must never be forced to undergo an exam. If she refuses a part of the exam that is essential to the evaluation of her complaints, the care provider will need to negotiate with her how and when this will be done.

A complete physical examination includes breast and external genital exams. Some view the breast exam as an excellent opportunity to teach self-exam skills. Whereas serious breast disease is uncommon in teens, debate exists whether girls should be actively encouraged to perform monthly self-exams. Care must be taken not to engender anxiety in the young adolescent.

A pelvic examination is suggested if a girl reports having had vaginal intercourse, has genital or lower abdominal complaints that necessitate an exam, requests contraception, or if she has reached 18 years and has never had an exam. To relieve her apprehension, it is helpful to explain to the girl how the exam is performed and to empathize with her that the exam can be embarrassing. She should be advised that she can tell the examiner to stop any time. The drape is arranged so that the examiner can see the girl's reaction. Simple muscle relaxation techniques may help a tense patient.

Laboratory Evaluation

Only a few laboratory tests are necessary in the routine health care of well adolescents. A hemoglobin level is suggested once after menarche. Screening for hemoglobinopathies in minority patients whose perinatal screening in uncertain may be indicated. Cholesterol testing is recommended only for those teens who have a positive or uncertain family history of cardiovascular disease or hypercholesterolemia. Serum chemistries and routine urinalyses are not recommended. A tuberculin skin test is suggested once during adolescence and annually in those at risk. Sexually active girls should receive annual Pap smears. Cervical cultures (or other sensitive diagnostic tests) for gonorrhea and Chlamydia, serologic testing for syphilis, and HIV testing may be indicated.

Immunizations

Because most public schools in the United States require the completion of the diphtheria-pertussis-tetanus (DPT) series, a single measles-mumps-rubella (MMR) vaccine and the oral polio vaccine (OPV) series prior to starting kindergarten, one can usually assume that teens have had these immunizations. However, parents and schools may not be aware of the need for immunizations beyond those given in early childhood.

In January 1995, a new childhood immunization schedule was approved (40). All children should have a tetanus booster between the ages of 11 to 16 years. This is usually given as diphtheria-tetanus (DT) vaccine; pertussis vaccine is contraindicated in teens and adults. A second MMR is now recommended between age 4 and 6 years or at age 11 to 12 years, if not previously given. The hepatitis B vaccine series, if not received earlier in childhood, should be administered to all adolescents.

There are few contraindications to these immunizations. The MMR is contraindicated during pregnancy. It may be wise to obtain a urine pregnancy test on all postmenarchal girls before administering an MMR injection. Mild illness, with or without fever, should not preclude immunization.

Live attenuated varicella vaccine became available in 1995 and recommendations for its use have been established (41). For school-aged children up to age 13 years without a reliable history of varicella infection, a single dose is given. For healthy teens and young adults who have no history of varicella infection, two doses are administered 4 to 8 weeks apart. Varicella immunization is also contraindicated during pregnancy.

Challenges

Meeting the Needs of the Adolescent Girl

Young women are interested in their health. In a survey of girls' and women's concerns in metropolitan Kansas City, health was number one. Access to health care, substance abuse, pregnancy, and pregnancy prevention were the top priority health issues (42). In a Canadian study of high school girls, the four health areas of greatest interest were those relating to risk taking, appearance, psychological issues, and health promotion or future orientation (43).

Health Promotion and the Care Provider

In the clinical setting, providers play a critical role in advancing the general knowledge received at school and in the media, and personalize the information to fit the adolescent's development stage and needs. Relating the patient's own social, sexual, and substance use behaviors to specific risks and potentials increases the impact of the educational effort. Didactic health education alone does little to change behavior. Concrete, personal, and confidential discussion may reinforce health promotion and enhance motivation.

A few specific health behaviors have been recommended as prevention priorities because of their great benefit and achievability. These include using seat belts, not drinking or using drugs and driving, condom use for those who are sexually active, not smoking, eating a low fat diet, and regular exercise (44).

Counseling and Compliance

Clinical skills helpful in facilitating communications include consideration of adolescent developmental stage, self-awareness, a nonjudgmental approach and active listening. These skills are particularly useful in caring for young women who may lack the ability or willingness to express themselves. Cognitive immaturity may limit both the patient's understanding and verbal expression. Guilt, shame, or fear that they will be lectured to may cause reluctance to talk.

Identifying the adolescent by psychosocial stage of development helps determine the level of communication and the need for parental involvement. Directions for the young immature girl should usually include parents. Conversely, involving the parents in directions to a middle-stage, rebellious adolescent girl may destroy the therapeutic intervention. Monitoring one's own reaction and feelings about adolescent behaviors enhances the ability to react nonjudgmentally. A conversational style and reflective listening facilitates the patient's expression and feeling of personal acceptance.

Adolescent compliance is complex and dependent on many factors such as self-concept, locus of control, and ability to think futuristically. Compliance is enhanced by a confidential, trusting relationship between provider and patient. Treatment options must be explained in a clear, concise manner.

A counseling plan evolves from the evaluation of the psychological health and risk behaviors of each patient. If problems are extreme, referral to a mental health specialist may be necessary. If problems and risks are not an issue, anticipatory guidance is the management of choice. Offering assistance in avoiding or delaying certain behaviors, such as sexual activity, is in order.

Counseling for intervention, e.g., condom use, has the goal of reducing the consequences involved in risk behavior. Guidance begins with educating about the facts, defining the problems, reviewing alternatives and options, and promoting a decision by the young woman that will modify her behavior. Guided decision making assists teens when they have inadequate information or are unable to process information for themselves (45). Shaking hands or signing a contract for behavioral change is sometimes a good strategy. Follow-up appointments are useful for reinforcement.

Working with Parents

The health provider has an obligation to parents as well as to the adolescent patient. The adolescent girl cannot be understood outside the context of her family. Although maturation involves the gaining of independence, family involvement is still important throughout the second decade of life. Insight into a young woman's behavior and concerns can be gained from a family history and a discussion of their lifestyle.

Offering anticipatory guidance to families is one of the most productive aspects of adolescent health care. If family dysfunction is perceived, counseling with both the teen and her parents is in order.

Legal Issues in Adolescent Health Care

Consent

Traditionally, parents have been thought to be the individuals best able to make medical decisions for their minor children. Parents are expected to have their children's best interests in mind and to have the maturity and experience to make appropriate decisions. In addition, parental decision-making has been thought to promote the cohesiveness of the family. However, parental consent requirements can create barriers to adolescent health care (46–48). Many teens have health concerns for which they would not seek help if parental involvement was necessary. Some live in homes with parents who are unresponsive to their needs or abusive. Others may live independently of their parents. The legal system recognizes these circumstances and allows adolescents to provide consent for their own health care in some situations. Laws regarding this are made on a state-by-state basis. Although most are similar, the individual health care provider needs to be aware of the laws in his or her state.

All states allow teens to consent for themselves to certain specific services. Typically these include pregnancy-related care, contraception, treatment of STDs including HIV, substance abuse treatment, and mental health care. Emergency medical services to preserve the health and life of a minor may also be provided without parental consent. Abortion services for minors in most states requires parental consent or notification. When this is the case, confidential and expedient "judicial bypass" must be available. Through judicial bypass, a teen may go to court to demonstrate her understanding of the abortion procedure and show that it would be in her best interests to terminate the pregnancy. With the court's approval, she may then consent for the abortion herself without parental notification.

Some adolescents have the ability to give consent for other health care services. "Emancipated minors" are those teens under the age of majority (established by the state) who by common law or state statutes are able to consent for all medical services. These individuals are generally those who live independently of their parents and are self-supporting, who are married or parenting, who serve in the military, or who have graduated from high school. "Mature minors" are older adolescents who are capable of understanding the risks and benefits of their own medical treatment and able to give informed consent. Although specific state laws may not define the mature minor, health care providers have not been held liable when the medical treatment has been for the minor's benefit, non-negligent, low risk, and within mainstream medical practice (49).

Confidentiality

Patient confidentiality in the adolescent health care setting is essential. Many teens are unaware of their rights to medical confidentiality and are unwilling to see their physician for a private health concern. The definition of confidentiality and its boundaries ought to be presented to each adolescent patient. All health services to which an adolescent can consent for herself are protected under her right to confidentiality. However, no guarantee of confidentiality can be made if it is discovered that a teen is being abused or her life, or someone else's, is in jeopardy. For example, if a girl reveals that she is being molested or considering suicide, the health care provider is obligated to involve her parents and possibly other professionals.

Payment

Millions of American adolescents have no health insurance, public or private (50). Even when insured, teenagers are often limited in the health care services they can obtain, or may not want to use insurance for fear of parental notification. Routine "check-ups," immunizations, and other preventive services may not be covered by insurance. Access to physicians and hospitals may be restricted. Mental health services and substance abuse treatment may be limited to a certain number of visits or annual expenditure. Nonphysician service providers may not be covered. Insurance billing may impede the adolescent's ability to obtain confidential care.

Conclusions

A major challenge factor in caring for adolescents is to empower and help them take charge of their own health. Serving as a respectful, nonjudgmental, extra-parental adult or mentor is a satisfying experience. Providers who feel comfortable with youth, and who have reviewed and resolved their own adolescent issues, will find working with adolescents fun and rewarding.

References

1. Lee PA, Reiter EO, Kulin HE. Neuroendocrinology of puberty. In: Sanfilippo JS, ed. Pediatric and Adolescent Gynecology. Philadelphia: WB Saunders, 1994:44–52.

2. Styne D. Normal growth and pubertal development. In: Sanfilippo JS, ed. Pediatric and Adolescent Gynecology. Philadelphia: WB Saunders, 1994:20–33.

3. Marshall WA, Tanner JM. Variations in the pattern of pubertal changes in girls. Arch Dis Child 1969; 44:291–303.

4. Schwartz ID. Puberty in girls: early, incomplete or precocious? Contemp Adolesc Gynecol 1995; 1:18–23.

5. O'Dea LS, Siegel SF, Lee PA. Pubertal disorders: precocious and delayed puberty. In: Sanfilippo JS, ed. Pediatric and Adolescent Gynecology. Philadelphia: WB Saunders, 1994:53–76.

6. Schwartz ID. Puberty in girls: normal or delayed? Contemp Adolesc Gynecol 1995;1:4–14.

7. Centers for Disease Control and Prevention. Mortality trends, causes of death, and related risk behaviors among U.S. adolescents. Atlanta: Centers for Disease Control and Prevention, 1993. Adolescent health: State of the Nation monograph series, No. 1. CDC Publication No. 099-4112.

8. Li G, Baker SP, Frattaroli S. Epidemiology and prevention of traffic-related injuries among adolescents. Adolesc Med State Art Rev 1995;6:135–151.

9. Singer MI, Anglin TM, Song LY, Lunghofer L. Adolescents' exposure to violence and associated symptoms of psychological trauma. JAMA 1995;273: 477–482.

10. Centers for Disease Control and Prevention. Youth risk behavior surveillance-United States, 1993. MMWR 1995;44:1–56.

11. Centers for Disease Control and Prevention. Suicide among children, adolescents and young adults—United States, 1980–1992. MMWR 1995;44: 289–291.

12. Rosen DS, Siangdong M, Blum RW. Adolescent health: current trends and critical issues. Adolesc Med State Art Rev 1990;1:15–31.

13. Irwin CE, Ryan SA. Problem behavior of adolescents. Pediatr Rev 1989;10:235–246.

14. Hofmann AE. Clinical assessment and management of health risk behaviors in adolescents. Adolesc Med State Art Rev 1990;1:33–44.

15. Jessor R. Risk behavior in adolescence: a psychosocial framework for understanding and action. J Adolesc Health 1991;12:597–605.

16. Irwin CE, Millstein SG. Biopsychosocial correlates of risk-taking behaviors during adolescence. J Adolesc Health Care 1986;7:82S–96S.

17. Centers for Disease Control and Prevention. Pregnancy, sexually transmitted diseases and related risk behaviors among US adolescents. Atlanta: Centers for Disease Control and Prevention, 1994. Adolescent Health: State of the Nation monograph series, No. 2. CDC Publication No. 099-4630.

18. Botvin GJ, Botvin EM. Adolescent tobacco, alcohol, and drug abuse: prevention strategies, empirical findings, and assessment issues. Dev Behav Pediatr 1992;13:290–301.

19. Gomberg ESL. Risk factors for drinking over a woman's life span. Alcohol Health Res World 1994; 18:220–227.

20. Johnston LD, O'Malley PM, Bachman JG. National survey results on drug use from the monitoring the future study, 1975–1993, volume 1-secondary school students. NIH Publication No.94-3809. Washington, DC: US Government Printing Office, 1994.

21. Press Release, University of Michigan News and Information Services, Ann Arbor, MI, Monday, December 12, 1994.

22. Centers for Disease Control and Prevention. Indicators of nicotine addiction among women—United States, 1991–1992. MMWR 1995;44:102–105.

23. Donovan JE, Jessor R, Jessor L. Problem drinking in adolescence and young adulthood. J Stud Alcohol 1983;44:109–137.

24. Greene JW, Werner MJ, Walker LS. Stress and the modern adolescent. Adolesc Med State Art Rev 1992;3:13–28.

25. Kagan J. Etiologies of adolescents at risk. J Adolesc Health Care 1991;12:591–596.

26. Blum, R. Adolescent medicine. JAMA 1990;263: 2621–2623.

27. Brown RT. Psychosomatic problems in adolescents. Adolesc Med: State Art Rev 1992;3:87–96.

28. Smith MS. Psychosomatic symptoms in adolescence. Med Clin North Am 1990;74:1121–1134.

29. Hogdman CH. Depression, suicide, out-of-control reactions, and psychoses. In: Hofmann AD, Greydanus DE, eds. Adolescent Medicine. 2nd ed. Norwalk CT: Appleton & Lange, 1989:581–591.

30. Nolen-Hoeksema S, Girgus JS. The emergence of gender differences in depression during adolescence. Psychol Bull 1994;115:424–443.

31. Petersen AC, Leffert N, Graham B, Ding S, Overbey T. Depression and body image disorders in adolescence. Womens Health Issues 1994;4:98–108.

32. Hibbard RA. Sexual abuse. In: McAnarney ER, Kriepe RE, Orr DP, Comerci GD, eds. Textbook of adolescent medicine. Philadelphia: WB Saunders, 1992:1123–1127.

33. Kandel DB, Davies M. Epidemiology of depressive mood in adolescents: an empirical study. Arch Gen Psychiatry 1982;39:1205–1212.

34. Killen JD, Hayward C, Litt I, et al. Is puberty a risk factor for eating disorders? Am J Dis Child 1992; 146:323–325.

35. Comerci GD, Kilbourne KA, Harrison GG. Eating disorders: obesity, anorexia nervosa, and bulimia. In: Hoffman A, Greydanus D, eds. Adolescent Medicine. Norwalk CT: Appleton & Lange, 1989:441–461.

36. Harper G. Eating disorders in adolescence. Pediatr Rev 1994;15:72–77.

37. Guidelines for Adolescent Preventive Services, Department of Adolescent Health, American Medical Association, 1992.

38. Ammerman AD, Perelli A, Adler N, Irwin CE. Do adolescents understand what physicians say about sexuality and health? Clin Pediatr 1992;31:590–595.

39. Goldenring JM, Cohen E. Getting into adolescent heads. Contemp Pediatr 1988;5:75–90.

40. Recommended childhood immunization schedule—United States, January 1995. JAMA 1995;273:693.

41. Committee on Infectious Diseases, American Academy of Pediatrics. Recommendations for the use of live attenuated varicella vaccine. Pediatrics 1995; 95:791–796.

42. Talbott LH, Noble E, Klein L. Women in the heart of America: concerns, needs, priority issues for the 1990's. Unpublished data from The Women's Foundation of Greater Kansas City, 1992.

43. McKay L, Diem E. Health concerns of adolescent girls. J Pediatr Nurs 1995;10:19–27.

44. Beach RK. Priority health behaviors in adolescents. Adolescent Health Update 1991;3:2.

45. Hofmann AE. Clinical assessment and management of health risk behaviors in adolescents. Adolesc Med: State Art Rev 1990;1:33–44.

46. US Congress, Office of Technology Assessment. Consent and confidentiality in adolescent health care decision making. In: Adolescent health-volume III: crosscutting issues in the delivery of health and related services, OTA-H-467. Washington, DC: US Government Printing Office 1991:123–154.

47. English A. Overcoming obstacles to adolescent care: legal issues. Adolesc Med: State Art Rev 1991; 2:429–436.

48. English A. Treating adolescents: legal and ethical considerations. Med Clin North Am 1990;74:1097–1111.

49. National Center for Youth Law. State minor consent statutes: a summary. Cincinnati: Center for Continuing Education in Adolescent Health 1995:3–7.

50. US Congress, Office of Technology Assessment. Financial access to health services. In: Adolescent health-volume III: crosscutting issues in the delivery of health and related services, OTA-H-467. Washington, DC: US Government Printing Office 1991: 77–118.

Suggested Readings

Friedman, AB, Fisher M, Schonberg SK, eds. Comprehensive Adolescent Health Care. St. Louis: Quality Medical Publishing, 1992.

McAnarney E, Kreipe RE, Orr DP, Comerci GD, eds. Textbook of Adolescent Medicine. Philadelphia: WB Saunders, 1992.

5

Adolescent Sexuality, Contraception, and Pregnancy

Reid B. Blackwelder

Introduction

Adolescent women require special consideration. This chapter provides practical insights
into special aspects of caring for adolescents,

increases the provider's awareness of the scope
of sexual activity of adolescents, and briefly
outlines contraceptive options with an emphasis on "realistic" choices for adolescents.
The issue of teenage pregnancy is complex,

but the problems facing the pregnant adolescent relate more to issues in prenatal care than to the age of the mother.

Adolescent contraception and pregnancy are perfect areas to practice the ideals of "Hygeia," an appreciation of the natural order of things, supporting the natural laws, and seeking balance in all things. Helping teenagers find balance in the reality of sexuality can be a goal. Striving to prevent pregnancy, instead of battling its consequences, can impact the epidemiologic data outlined below.

Epidemiology

Sexual Activity

Although there is a great deal of information about the epidemiology of adolescent sexual activity, use or lack of contraceptive methods, frequency of abortions, frequency of adolescent pregnancy, morbidity and mortality of adolescent mothers and their infants, and multiple comparisons between industrialized and less developed parts of the world, there is a great heterogeneity in the published numbers. Although the sexual activity of adolescents is roughly the same in industrialized countries, the United States has always demonstrated higher rates of adolescent pregnancy (1–3). In all these developed countries, such as the United Kingdom, Canada, France, the Netherlands, and Sweden, a teenage girl age 15 years or less is four times less likely to become pregnant than in the United States, although the rates of teenage sexual activity are similar in all the countries. Teenagers in the United States must use contraception less often or less efficiently (4).

Various studies have shown that between 7 and 30% of girls less than 15 years of age are sexually active (3). Fifty percent of all young women are sexually active by the age of 18 years (5, 6). CDC data from 1990 revealed that over two thirds of all young women are sexu-

ally active before the 12th grade. By age 20 years, up to 77% of young women and 86% of young men are sexually active (7, 8). These facts suggest the wide age range for onset of sexual activity. This dynamic reality makes the provider's approach to sexuality and sexual history-taking a critical part of dealing with the problem.

Contraception

Despite youthful sexual activity, contraception is not consistently used. A 1990 study found that between the ages of 15 and 19 years, 41% of all sexually active teenage women did not use any form of contraception during their first encounter (9). Medical research about rates of sexual activity, contraception, and pregnancy is one area in which most of the studies involve young women; little information exists about these issues in young men. What little data are available suggests that the rate of sexual activity is similar. Sixty percent of young men age 15 to 19 years were sexually active and 38% did not use any form of contraception in their first sexual encounter (4). At the other end of the continuum, the CDC 1990 US Youth Risk Behavior Survey showed that during their last sexual encounter, 25% of adolescents did not use any form of contraception (7, 10). Between their first and last encounter, up to 30% of unmarried young women age 15 to 19 years are not practicing active contraception during their encounters (11).

Despite these concerning habits, some encouraging changes have occurred. In 1982, young women age 15 to 19 years used condoms during their first intercourse only 23% of the time. In 1988 a survey documented an increase to 47% use of condoms during first sexual encounter (8).

Pregnancy

One serious consequence of adolescent sexual activity is subsequent adolescent pregnancy.

In this country, 1 million young women less than age 20 become pregnant each year, and of these pregnancies, 75% of them are unplanned (3). In 1990, 10% of all teenage women age 15 to 19 years became pregnant. Eighty-two to 95% of these pregnancies were unintended (12, 13). Forty percent of US adolescent pregnancies occur before the young women is age 17 years (13). However, a recent survey of pregnancy trends in women age 15 to 19 years demonstrated at least a leveling off of pregnancy rates, if not an actual decrease in pregnancy rate in 1992 (13).

Once pregnant, the teenage girl must make an important decision—whether to carry the pregnancy or seek an abortion. This decision is an extremely individual one that requires evaluating personal issues and is often quite stressful intellectually, emotionally, spiritually, and physically. This decision carries even more stress for teenagers. In teenage women over half of all unintended pregnancies end in voluntary interruption of pregnancy (8, 12). These numbers carry significant consequences for the young woman involved and the healthcare system. Of those pregnancies carried to term, 5% of the resultant births are put up for adoption (3) (Table 5.1).

The United States does a poor job of preventing teenage pregnancy. Providers must discuss contraception and work to make choices acceptable and available to young patients. Even with such discussions, teenage women get pregnant (14). Whether a teenage mother chooses to carry the pregnancy or end it, she needs information and support before, during, and after her decision. Primary care providers are uniquely situated to discuss this with teenagers.

Access to Care

Great variety in health care systems exists in the United States. Individual access to care is quite critical and is also changing. Adolescent patients have some special difficulties with access to health care (Table 5.2).

Teenagers may have difficulty finding providers either willing or comfortable in providing their care. Many pediatricians feel uncomfortable caring for teenagers, and many adult physicians may feel uncomfortable dealing with such young patients.

Interestingly and encouraging, teenagers want to discuss sexuality and related topics. In some studies, up to 66% of teenagers want to discuss these topics but the provider actually explored the issue only 22% of the time. Physicians are prone to directing the interview whatever the woman's age or medical issue. Even when teenagers have access to a primary caregiver, it is not uncommon for them to state

Table 5.1. Epidemiology of US Adolescent Sexuality

7–30% of women under age 15 years are sexually active.

50% of women under age 18 years are sexually active.

77% of women under age 20 years are sexually active.

86% of men under age 20 years are sexually active.

41% of women between 15 and 19 years did not use contraception at first encounter.

30% of women between 15 and 19 years are not using contraception now.

70% of adolescent pregnancies were unplanned.

40% of adolescent pregnancies occur in women less than age 17 years.

50% of adolescent pregnancies end in abortion.

2.5% of adolescent pregnancies end in adoption.

Table 5.2. Special Barriers to Access of Health Care Adolescents Have

Provider Problems
  Provider doesn't ask
  Provider controls interview
  Provider feels uncomfortable with adolescents
  Provider may have beliefs that make discussing adolescent sexuality difficult
  Provider may not have information or skill for working with adolescents
  Provider not able or willing to provide services adolescent needs
Adolescent Problems
  Lack of insurance or money
  Fear of disclosure or exposure
  Coming to provider with one problem while having another agenda
  No transportation
  Negative connotations of certain clinics or offices (e.g., Family Planning)
  Difficulty with authority figures
  Having adults at visits
  Difficulty expressing needs, especially to adults

one problem as entry into the health care system but to have another unvoiced problem possibly unrelated, such as complaining about irregular menstrual periods when they want contraception or complaining about nausea when they want pregnancy confirmation. Being open to the patient's own agenda is critical in ensuring an encounter meets the needs of the woman. If providers do not ask, the patient's beliefs, concerns, and needs may not be directly addressed (4). The provider may be uncomfortable with adolescents. Finally, provider's may have beliefs that make it difficult for them to be nonjudgmental to the needs of the adolescent.

Even when the heart is willing, the mind may not be able to cooperate. One of the reasons that providers may not discuss the topic is discomfort or feelings of inadequacy in their own training in providing such information (4). Providers in family practice, pediatrics, and OB/GYN have different experiences with the issues of adolescent women and different approaches to those problems in their formal training. Much of the individual practitioner's experience in training may come from anecdotal sources and other non-formal sources of information. A 1987 survey on sex education discovered that with respect to oral contraceptive pills (OCPs), many teachers and counselors were misinformed with regard to risks and benefits of the pill (12). It is the responsibility of the practitioner to be informed, to ask what information her/his patients have, and to distribute information appropriately.

Other issues concerning adolescents' access to information on sexuality and contraception involve more practical aspects of the location of such information, whether it is a physician's office, a family planning clinic, a school counselor's office, or elsewhere. Adolescents may not have the finances to pay a provider; if her family has insurance, she may be loathe to "charge it to her mother's bill," fearing breach of confidentiality or even her parents' inquiry into her visit to the physician. Family physicians and providers may have long been the "family" doctor. Fear of disclosure, whether founded or not, may keep the adolescent away.

In different communities, some sources may be associated with negative connotations. For instance, an adolescent woman at a family planning clinic might be seen as being there for "only one reason." Even having transportation to her provider's office may be difficult, particularly if the teenager is younger than the legal age for driving. Adolescents are often accompanied to appointments. Obviously, additional people change the dynamics of the interview. Difficulties with authority figures such as parents, teachers, nurses, or physicians will also limit teenagers in feeling comfortable asking questions or pursuing potentially terrifying physical examinations such as a first pelvic exam. Finally, it is not inconceivable that an interested and motivated young woman may manage to get to a practitioner's office, take control of the interview, ask specific questions about contraceptive choices, and discover that the particular practitioner she is working with does not provide the services that she needs. Again, the provider must decide what services to provide, clearly advertise them, and be comfortable in all aspects of any services rendered including education and information dispersal (4, 6).

The Adolescent Interview

Special Aspects

Adolescence is a tumultuous time. Dramatic and sometimes traumatic biologic, physical, emotional, and intellectual changes are occurring. These changes do not occur in a smooth continuum for all teenagers, nor do they always occur in a predictable way in a particular teenager. Instead, the changes are quite individual and vary from adolescent to adolescent. Moreover, the reaction of the teenager to these changes is also quite individual and is affected by that person's own support system such as family and friends.

Generally, adolescents are usually physically quite healthy; therefore, most issues of the major causes of adolescent morbidity and mortality such as trauma, violence, suicide, drug use, and pregnancy are preventive ones (5).

Adolescent Thinking

One of the more difficult aspects of the adolescent interview involves recognizing cognitive changes. Early in adolescence, teenagers have concrete modes of thinking, and thus have difficulty dealing with abstractions or recognizing that consequences result from their actions and must be dealt with. This mindset can lead adolescents to consider themselves invulnerable. Particularly concerning contraception and pregnancy, a teenager often feels it will happen to someone else and not to her. This sense can be reinforced if she has already experienced some unprotected sexual activity and has not yet dealt with the consequences of sexually transmitted diseases (STD) or pregnancy (4, 6).

In the typical medical interview, the provider may become quite frustrated when discussing the difference between the teenager's view of the issues and the adult's view, which the provider will probably share with the parents. As in any difficult interview setting, providers' abilities to temper their own responses and listen to patients as they discuss their feelings and concerns are essential skills (15).

Communication

Communication in the adolescent interview is the keystone to a successful encounter. Hard work must be done to develop trust and rapport with the adolescent. Practically, this realization means that the time must be made during the adolescent visit to allow this rapport to be developed (3, 5). Allowing additional time in this setting is even more important if the family is present during the visit. Family involvement should be encouraged because this support system is important to the adolescent, but it may discourage rapport.

Often, the first visit will involve both teenager and one or both parents. This allows the provider a chance to observe the interactions of all parties and to give each person a chance to set some agenda items. The practitioner may also use this time to explore the parents' needs or concerns, prepare them for the provider's need for private time with the adolescent, and stress the need for confidentiality of that encounter (5, 6).

The setting of the interview is important. All providers must consider their style of dress as important in their interactions with patients of all types. Some studies have suggested that adult patients prefer their health care providers to wear white coats; anecdotally, many pediatricians and other providers who work with teenagers often adopt a more informal style to help in developing rapport.

Interview Style

Perhaps the most valuable tool in working with adolescents in the health care setting is awareness of interviewing styles. Adopting a patient-centered approach that uses specific facilitative tools and skills allows the provider to develop a clear picture of the adolescent's perspective. Research supports improved satisfaction and health outcomes with this technique and suggests that the patient-centered interview more quickly sets the agenda for negotiation between provider and patient. Given the time constraints providers face and the additional requirements caring for teenagers creates, any skills that improve time utilization should be acquired. Moreover, the skilled use of nonverbal and verbal feedback and facilitation help establish good rapport (16–18).

Part of using the patient's perspective approach to interviewing involves recognizing cues and clues of the woman that might hint at a "hidden agenda." Such cues may include subjects that are easily tied into adolescent issues of appearance, sexuality, and contraception (e.g., as a young woman complaining of menorrhagia, irregular menses, acne, dysmenorrhea). Complaints of dysuria or abdominal pain may reflect a more serious concern about STDs. Sometimes the ticket to the physician's office may be something apparently totally unrelated to sexuality or contraceptive issues such as headache, chest pain, or other somatic complaint. Avoiding the trap of pursuing close-ended checklist-style questioning in response to each sign or symptom, and encouraging the adolescent to define her agenda can

prove clearly to her the concern and cooperation of the provider (7, 18).

Confidentiality

Finally, it is critical to reassure the adolescent that the issues raised during the interview and examination will be treated with the same respect and confidentiality as given any patient. This point should be made to the parents as well. Most states recognize the age of majority as age 18 years, although it is 19 years in Nebraska and Wyoming and 21 years in Missouri. Adolescents may be viewed as emancipated if they are married, pregnant, or otherwise independent from their parents. Moreover, many states have waivers for certain medical conditions. Providers should review the laws in the state in which they practice to avoid potential conflicts. The limits of this confidentiality are also critical and include suicidal ideation or plan, homicidal thought or impending harm to another person, sexual or physical abuse that mandates reporting, and dealing with life-threatening illness (5).

Sexuality

Sexuality is a fact of being human. The process of sexual identity and sexuality begins in childhood and is a natural part of life and a natural part of development. Moreover, these changes flow along a continuum that is variable depending on the individual. From the provider's perspective, all teenagers are sexual beings even if they are not currently or have not initiated sexual activity (15).

The timing of onset of puberty and the subsequent physiologic changes are different for each individual teenager. Moreover, the psychosocial development does not parallel the physical and physiologic changes that are occurring. This discontinuity creates a challenge for the provider. The issues and concerns will vary not only with each teenager but with each visit for a particular adolescent. In addition, although it is possible to follow physical development in a well-documented fashion along the lines of Tanner staging, a similar continuum is not as readily available for the psychosocial changes (19).

Certain broad categories of adolescence are regularly identified and include separation into early, middle, and late adolescence, corresponding to ages 10 to 13 years, 14 to 16 years, and older than age 17 years respectively. Early adolescence is often characterized by dramatic physical changes and a subsequent concern with distorted self-images caused by this body disproportion. The peer group at this time usually involves friends of the same sex. Middle adolescence is characterized by the transition from concrete to abstract thinking, with a changing relationship from parents and group friends to single partners, including opposite sex companions.

Traditionally, teenagers in the late adolescent period are less self-centered and more interested in other people, including forming closer relationships. Their thinking is more abstract and idealistic, but still carries that sense of invulnerability (5, 19, 20). Throughout this continuum, teenage women are more likely to pay close attention to one friend's input on sexual decisions, whereas teenage boys often relate more to their peer groups' input. Despite this attempt at categorizing the psychosocial and physiologic changes, each teenager is an individual whose own psyche and body will identify the particular issues for the visit.

Another important issue is avoiding one's own individual or cultural biases and expectations. An adolescent dealing with her or his sexuality is already embroiled within the turmoil of the psychosocial and physiologic changes. Adolescence is a common time for experimentation in many aspects of sexuality including same versus opposite sex partners. Many adolescents are dealing with questions about heterosexuality and homosexuality.

Gender identification is usually accomplished by age 2 years. Adolescence is a common time for same sex experimentation that often includes mutual masturbation or fondling without subsequent more intimate activities. Given the intense social and cultural pressures about one's sexual orientation, this aspect of sexuality must be explored in a patient-centered and nonjudgmental fashion (19).

Sexual History

Taking a sexual history from a woman is often an uncomfortable topic regardless of age. For adolescents, it can be particularly difficult. The provider should not joke about any issue relating to sexuality or the adolescent's sexual activity and must always respect the privacy of this information. It is always appropriate to admit one's own emotions, which might include personal discomfort, for breaking the ice in this phase of the interview. Moreover, this topic must be explored with adolescents of both genders.

The sexual history should include exploration of whether the teenager is sexually active and why or why not; this can identify her personal views, drives, and social influences. The number and types of partners, her particular experiences and emotional responses, and her use of contraception should all be addressed.

If the adolescent is sexually active, having her partner present at some phase should also be considered. Adolescents who acknowledge their sexuality and let others know that they are using contraception are better contraceptive users, although their rates of sexual activity are no different from other adolescents (4).

The provider must not make any assumptions regarding sexual activity, including that it is only defined by intercourse. Thirty-three percent of all young women have demonstrated some autoeroticism by age 10 years, whereas 36% of boys age 13 years have (5, 15).

By age 19 years, 91% of teenage women have had their breasts touched, and by age 16 years 34% have performed fellatio and 37% have experienced cunnilingus.

No assumption should be made about the emotional reactions of adolescents to their sexual activity. One study examining reactions of adolescents to their first sexual encounter noted that teenage women were excited 26% of the time compared with 46% of boys, happy 26% of the time compared with 42% of boys, afraid 63% of the time compared with 17% of boys, and curious 30% of the time compared with 23% of boys (15). Remaining nonjudgmental and patient-centered allows the provider to more appropriately address the individual's needs and concerns.

Identifying the reasons why a teenager is not using contraception is an important aspect of education and preventive care. Understanding these reasons can help in the discussion between the provider and the teenager about health services and needs, and can help identify the approach that would improve contraception. For example, the adolescent may feel that sex feels better without contraception and therefore chooses not to use it. Adolescents describe fear or ignorance as an impediment to use or may state they do not have enough time for contraception. They may also be concerned about discovery of sexual activity (4).

Finally, an even more troubling aspect of the sexual history involves identifying sexual abuse. Becoming a victim of sexual abuse is four times more common for teenage girls than teenage boys. In 1988, 100,000 cases of incest were reported, suggesting a much higher number that were not reported. Of that number, 12 to 24% resulted in pregnancy. Sexual abuse and incest increase the rate of attempted suicide and the use of tobacco, alcohol, and drugs in adolescent women (5, 21). This emotionally explosive issue may not be identified in the first encounter with an adolescent patient. The relatively common occurrence of abuse underscores the great importance of asking about these topics at each adolescent interview and doing so in a patient-centered, comfortable, and safe environment.

The Role of Education

Patient education is an important aspect of any medical encounter, but particularly so when dealing with adolescent sexuality and contraception. Although a recent survey shows that four of five states at least "encourage" sexual education, only 17 states and Washington, DC require sex education in the classes. Only seven along with the District of Columbia require instruction on pregnancy prevention (22). Access to information about sex and contraception is less available in the Unites States and may help explain why the United States has the highest adolescent pregnancy rate in the industrialized world.

The issue of sexual education is one that is often hotly debated in individual communities. Studies are also controversial. Some have indicated that more knowledge does not necessarily lead to any effect, whereas other studies suggest the effect may not be any change in the role of sexual activity, but rather an increase in contraceptive use (23–25).

Moreover, the effects of education may also be influenced by gender. One study suggests that teenage boys are less knowledgeable about contraceptives in general, and another notes that even after sex education classes teenage boys are less aware of the physiologic changes and issues regarding sex and contraception than teenage girls (26, 27).

A comprehensive review sponsored by the CDC and the Public Health Service in 1994 evaluated 23 studies of school-based sex education programs. The most effective studies focused on narrow goals, such as increasing condom use or decreasing risk for catching HIV, emphasized the role of social and peer groups in the learning process, or provided basic information along with an emphasis on teaching communication and negotiation skills. Specific results included a delay in initiating sex, and decreased rates of unprotected intercourse, frequency of sex, and number of partners (29). These suggestions can easily be translated into an office-based education program. The extent of such a program can be one-on-one brief, focused discussions between the provider and the teenager, or may be more extensive and involve other staff and resources. An even broader approach could be taken by expanding office-based techniques into the provider's community through school and family planning programs. Improving communication and education are the areas with the most potential for impacting consequences of adolescent sexuality.

The involvement and concerns of the parents with respect to sex education are also important. Some systems involve the parents directly in this process. Respecting the relationships of the family's systems and being available for education and assistance is imperative, although it may be time consuming. This practical need to provide time particularly during the adolescent visit for education can directly impact on the structure of the adolescent visit. This issue needs to be addressed when setting up an office and clinic schedule.

Often education involves evaluating anecdotal and peer-inspired ideas about contraception. Specifically, it is common to hear an adolescent woman feel that if sex is performed in certain positions she either can or cannot get pregnant, that the first time she has intercourse she can't get pregnant, that she can't get pregnant having sex during her menses, or that if she wishes or hopes strongly enough it will impact the possibility of her pregnancy (6). Even if the adolescent has tried to obtain information on sex and contraception from a source such as a school counselor, many of these sources are misinformed and

therefore may provide inaccurate information to teenagers. Remember also that adolescent thinking is different from that of adults. Subsequently, any education geared toward adolescents must be more concrete. For these reasons merely reciting a list of epidemiologic data may not mean much to even an interested teenage girl. Consider how this information can be presented to make it more realistic. Saying that 8 of 10 teenage girls who only have sex occasionally without birth control will be pregnant within 1 year may be more meaningful than stating 80% of adolescent pregnancies occur with sporadic unprotected intercourse within the first year.

Education provided in written brochures or other materials may be useful but also carries certain problems. Many education brochures are not necessarily marketed toward teenagers nor are they necessarily written at a literacy rate appropriate for teenage patients (28). Furthermore, written information can be lost, either accidentally or intentionally, for fear of being discovered by parents. Strongly consider going over education materials with teenagers and giving them the opportunity to discuss it and ask questions. The offer to go over this information with parents or sexual partners may be made, but the teenager must be allowed to give or deny permission to do so.

The Physical Examination

Except in the most extreme circumstances, the physical examination should come after rapport building and talking with the sexually active teenager. As difficult and uncomfortable as discussing these biopsychosocial topics may be for the provider and the teenager, the physical examination may be even more so. This potential discomfort must be realized and dealt with prior to the actual examination itself. Certainly the initial interview should be conducted with the teenager being clothed, rather than the circumstance that can exist in the adult gynecologic examination in which the interview and exam are done with a woman already gowned and on the examination table.

Approaching the examination in the same patient-centered manner as the history is crucial in making this a positive experience, especially in the setting of a first pelvic exam. Providing prior education about and discussing the examination, showing some positions or instruments involved, insuring the young woman has control over all aspects of the examination including the ability to stop it if it causes discomfort, and explaining different aspects of the procedure are essential parts of the adolescent pelvic examination (4, 5). It may be entirely appropriate to defer the actual examination until a later visit, and instead provide contraceptive education and discuss and demonstrate the pelvic examination at the first encounter. This deferment is particularly appropriate when the teenager is not sexually active. Even common gynecologic complaints such as dysmenorrhea and irregular menses may be dealt with without a full pelvic examination.

Even in the sexually active adolescent woman, the need to perform a pelvic examination may be outweighed by the need to provide access to contraception. A 1992 study documented no negative medical consequences to delaying the pelvic examination for up to 6 months along with concomitant oral contraceptive use (4). In a teenager who is not sexually active, the examination may be deferred until she is active or contemplating becoming active, although again emphasis on the need for contraception at first intercourse is imperative.

The actual examination of the adolescent woman should be no different from that provided to any woman during her gynecologic exam. Emphasis must be placed on comfort, control, involvement, and education. She should be offered the opportunity to observe the examination using a hand mirror. This technique is particularly useful in discussing the genital self-examination, an important part of preventive care for all ages of patients, but especially for teenagers. The need for a speculum examination over merely an external or digital examination should be decided ahead of time and discussed with the teenager. Particularly in teenagers who are not yet sexually active, a regular speculum exam or bimanual examination may be painful and scary, and may not provide any more information than might be obtained in a less uncomfortable manner. If appropriate, cultures and test for STDs and a Pap smear may also be done and can be planned for ahead of time.

Appropriate labs may also include a urine or serum pregnancy test. Urine pregnancy tests are now as sensitive as serum and can give results within minutes as soon as 10 days after conception, even before a missed period. Preventive care guidelines are outlined by the American Academy of Family Practice (see Table 4.1).

Contraception

Epidemiology

The lack of use of contraception is a key issue in the sexuality and sexual activity of adolescents. Some studies report active use of contraceptive methods. In one study of teenage girls age 15 to 19 years who were sexually active, up to 85% had used some form of contraception at one time or another. Unfortunately, similar studies also describe inconsistent use of whatever form of contraception is chosen. Moreover, adolescents are at a greater risk for failure from both contraceptive nonuse and inconsistent use, resulting in exceedingly high rates of conception (4, 6, 12). Half of the unintended pregnancies occur within the first 6 months of sexual activity, with 20% within the first month alone. Girls less than age 15 years are twice as likely to become pregnant as older adolescents (4).

Contraceptive use is influenced by many things including the individual's own view, the family support system, the peer group attitude, race, cultural background, sexual orientation, geographic location, education level, religion, and socioeconomic level (8). These influences can affect both the type of contraception chosen and the manner it is used. For example, younger white adolescent girls are less likely to use any contraception compared with older African-American adolescent girls, and are three times more likely to use withdrawal as their primary method of contraception when they do choose to use contraception (4). Girls age 12 to 15 years more commonly use condoms compared with older adolescent women. Older adolescent women are more likely to prefer OCs or the withdrawal method, although increasing use of condoms in these older adolescents has recently been documented (13). Interestingly, condoms and withdrawal method of contraception are much more common contraceptive choices of teenage boys (12). Few studies have been done concerning teenage boys and their contraceptive choices, and efforts to involve, educate, and support the contraceptive choices of teenage boys are needed (29).

Not all the available data are discouraging. When OCs are used, unmarried adolescent women have a lower contraceptive failure rate than never married adult women (12). Some more common problems sexually active adolescents may encounter may be helped by particular contraceptive methods (Table 5.3). Moreover, adolescents should be told that the risks of contraception are much less compared to those of pregnancy (see Chapter 10.2) (30).

Abstinence

The only contraceptive choice 100% effective in avoiding pregnancy and STD is abstinence. Twenty to 25% of age 19 years adolescent women have never had intercourse (15). Abstinence should be supported as a normal and healthy choice. Being given permission by an authority figure such as a physician or other health care provider that it is permissible not to have sex may be all that the girl needs to stand by her decision. In discussions of contraception with teenagers, abstinence should be discussed first, because it is certainly the most effective, safest, most readily available, and cheapest method available.

Abstinence may not mean the same thing to teenagers as to adults. Nonpenetrative sex may be considered "safe" or "not-really" sex, and the provider should discuss this with the woman. Occasionally an adolescent may choose to go only "part way." Such activity puts her at high risk for "unplanned" intercourse with all its risks. Moreover, unless such activities as oral sex are accompanied by the use of some barrier method such as a condom, she and her partner are still at risk for exchanging STDs.

Periodic Abstinence

Several natural methods of contraception have been evaluated for many years. These methods are only variably effective for prevention of pregnancy and offer no protection from

Table 5.3 Contraception Choices for Adolescents

Good Choices	Fair Choices	Poor Choices
Abstinence	Condoms	Periodic Abstinence
Oral contraceptives	Diaphragm	Coitus interruptus
Norplant	Cervical cap	IUD
Depo-provera	Spermicides	Sterilization
Morning after pill		

STDs. Given the frequency of irregular menses, the high frequency of anovulatory cycles, and the disassociation between the biologic and psychologic maturity in adolescent women, these methods are probably not practical for most teenagers. Moreover, the need for following records and limiting time of intercourse is not likely consistent with the lifestyle of most teenage girls (31, 32).

Coitus Interruptus

This method is used quite frequently by adolescents with pregnancy and STDs as the result. Although often acceptable as a contraceptive method in a continuing relationship in which the partners know each other's signals and usual sexual responses, coitus interruptus is unlikely to be an effective contraceptive in teenagers. Besides the insecurity and unpredictability of teenager's sexual relations, the commitment this method requires of both partners is doubtful in teenagers.

Barrier Methods

Condoms
Condoms are the most commonly used contraceptive method among adolescents and may be used with any other method. Of all the methods, they are most ideal for protection from STDs. Latex condoms with nonoxynyl-9 kill STDs, HIV, and sperm. When a spermicide is included in their use, their rate of protection from contraception is almost as good as OCs. Moreover, condoms do not require a prescription, are relatively easy to obtain, and are of low cost. Except for a rare case of sensitivity to latex, they are also free of adverse effects (4).

Diaphragm
Although diaphragms are an effective method in adult women, they are less so in adolescents. They are more likely to be successful in motivated mature adolescents who are comfortable in touching their genitalia. To be most effective, they should be combined with a spermi-

cide that makes their use messy. With a spermicide, they do provide some protection from STDs but are much less safe than abstinence or condoms in this regard. Some increased frequency of urinary tract infections has been noticed. Moreover, teenage girls are in a phase of rapid physical change; as weight changes, diaphragms need to be regularly reassessed and changed to insure proper fit. This creates a further barrier to effective use in adolescents.

Sponge/Cervical Cap
These methods are similar to the diaphragm and carry similar problems with compliance and protection. The 24-hour sponge has also been associated with an increased risk of toxic shock syndrome. The cervical cap is more difficult to insert than a diaphragm and can result in more odor and discharge, which may be unpleasant or frightening to the girl. Moreover, this method is contraindicated in anyone with an abnormal Pap smear. As sexually active adolescent women may not have had a baseline Pap smear and are less likely to get other examinations, this method is probably not practical for adolescents.

Spermicides
Spermicides are available in foam, cream, jelly, a tablet that turns into foam, and a film that becomes a gel. All spermicides increase the "mess" and disrupt the spontaneity of intercourse, and are therefore less likely to be used. Of the different spermicide forms, foam is probably more appropriate in adolescents because no waiting period is required for activation or the spermicidal activity. Any adolescent woman choosing a barrier method, including condoms, should be encouraged to also use spermicide in one form or another. This use increases the effectiveness of contraception and assists in protection from STD (6).

Oral Contraceptives (OCs)

Other than abstinence, under ideal conditions OCs provide the best protection against pregnancy. Even with usual use as compared to ideal use, OCPs are effective. Many options exist in selecting an OCP for an adolescent patient (see Chapter 10.2). A combination OCP is most commonly prescribed. Monophasic, biphasic, triphasic, and progestin-only pills exist. With triphasic OCPs, although irregular menses usually improve and lower hormonal effects are encountered, increased breakthrough bleeding is a frequent complaint by adolescent women. Moreover, adolescents often are troubled or confused by the multiple colors in a pack and are more at ease with the single colors of some mono or biphasic pills. The progestin-only pills are used only in selected cases as they tend to cause more bleeding and are somewhat less effective than other OCPs. It is important to pay attention to the pill's androgenic effects. The development of acne in a teenager can be devastating (12).

OCPs may be particularly effective in young women with gynecologic problems such as irregular menses and dysmenorrhea. Besides helping to minimize these problems, OCPs will give protection against pregnancy (7).

Clear discussion and education with respect to use and possible side effects of OCPs are critical in improving compliance. Particularly when dealing with adolescents who want immediate results, the time needed to evaluate the effectiveness of OCPs for treatment of gynecologic abnormalities should be discussed. She must realize it may take a couple of cycles (i.e., a few months) to see effects or to see adverse reactions minimize. Rapid shifting between different types of pills should be avoided as this might increase her sense of problems with all pills and decrease her compliance with them. As OCPs do not protect against STDs, their use should be encouraged in combination with condoms and preferably a spermicide (7). Be aware that most educational material and instructions for OCPs are written in the 10th to 12th grade level. Even if a young woman is in the 10th to 12th grade, she may not have the literacy level that would allow her to understand the written instructions. To reinforce a recurring point, personally discussing instructions and adverse reactions is more valuable than providing similar instructions in written form.

Injectable/Implantable/Insertable

Depo-Provera

Depo-Provera is an injectable form of Depot-medroxyprogesterone acetate. This hormone suppresses midcycle LH and results in anovulation. It may be given as an intramuscular injection every 3 months and is immediately effective in preventing conception. Its main side effects include weight gain, eventual amenorrhea, and uncertain time course and return of fertility. It requires a visit to a health care provider every 3 months and does not protect against STDs. Because of the lack of need to remember daily medication, compliance is improved and unintended pregnancy rate is lower.

Norplant

Norplant contains levonorgestrel and is the only approved progestin implant in the United States. It has the advantage of being effective for up to 5 years without need for regular injections or clinic visits. Because regular visits to a family planning clinic or physician's office, monthly prescriptions, or an OC/diaphragm container are not needed, adolescents who wish not to advertise their contraceptive use have less risk of discovery. Because it does require implantation, the surgical fee can present a significant cost barrier for an adolescent woman. Its effects are similar to those of Depo-Provera including irregular bleeding, weight gain, and eventual amenorrhea. As it is a long term means of contraception, the need for additional compliance is limited, although it is important to stress that the Norplant does not protect against STDs, and again its use with another form of contraception is strongly recommended. The effects of this medication tend to be easily reversible with removal of the device (4).

IUD

Currently only two IUDs are available in this country: the progestasert that requires placement every 12 months and the copper T380A that may be placed every 4 years. IUDs are not recommended for adolescents because of an increased risk of infection, an increased rate of expulsion, and an increased risk of long-term infertility. In fact, contraindications for the use of IUDs include age under 25 years, any woman who is nulliparous, or has a history of PID or multiple partners.

Morning After Pill

A method of contraception often not discussed is the so-called "morning after pill." One method involves the use of commonly prescribed OCP, Oval, which contains $50\mu g$ of ethinyl estradiol. Within 72 hours of exposure, and preferably within 12 to 48 hours, two pills should be taken, and this dose is repeated in 12 hours. Although not FDA approved, this use of ethinyl estradiol is quite effective in preventing conception and is most often mentioned in circumstances involving rape or in failure of a barrier method. It should also be considered in any woman who has had intercourse without any method of contraception being used. It should not be considered a standard form of birth control in adolescents, but may be considered under certain circumstances. This method also does not protect against STDs (6).

Sterilization

Sterilization is not considered an appropriate means of birth control in adolescents.

Adolescent Pregnancy

Epidemiology

The adolescent pregnancy rate is higher in the United States than in all other industrialized countries (1). The Allen Guttmacher Institute estimated that in 1987 one eighth of all births were to teenage women; moreover, 4 of 10 pregnancies occurred in women under the age of 20 years (15).

Prior to the 1970s, adolescent pregnancy was considered a moral issue with the pregnant teenager seen as a societal deviant. These deviants were excluded from society and were therefore invisible. It wasn't until the early 1970s when pregnant girls made it to the cover of such national magazines as *Life* that teenage pregnancy changed from a moral issue to a medical and technical one. This intellectual paradigm shift allowed for changes in how health care providers in this country could deal with what was now a more open and pressing issue.

Some issues affecting this increased risk of pregnancy include teenagers' cognitive immaturity and sense of invulnerability, the perceived need for spontaneity, low socioeconomic status, low self-esteem, the fear of contraceptive methods, and the fear of discovery. No clear correlation between adolescent drug use and adolescent pregnancy has been established (3, 16, 30).

Interestingly, from a purely biophysiologic standpoint, adolescent mothers age 15 years and older seemingly can cope quite well with the changes of pregnancy. Some increased risk of maternal morbidity and mortality is noted in adolescent mothers younger than 15 years. An increased risk of toxemia and anemia is fairly well established (13, 15). The psychosocial risks from adolescent pregnancy are much more important. Teenage girls who get pregnant are much less likely to finish high school. In one study up to two thirds never complete their high school education. A similar effect is noted in teenage boys who become fathers (15). A teenager's educational status is a direct predictor of employment and lack of education will delay career opportunities leading to increased poverty, previously identified as a risk factor for teenage pregnancy. This is self-perpetuating and leads to an increased need for public assistance and support for teenage mothers and their children (33). Moreover, for those teenage mothers who are married, the divorce rate is three times as high in this age group compared with other women (15).

Infants born to teenage mothers are also at higher risk for certain problems. The most consistent problem is an increased likelihood of a low birth weight. If the mother is less than age 15 years, there is twice the normal risk of having a low birth weight baby and even mothers age 18 to 19 years have a 1.3 times risk of a low birth weight infant (15).

Although other increased risks have been suggested such as prematurity, congenital anomalies, intrauterine growth retardation, and fetal/neonatal death, studies have been inconsistent on these associations. Most of the negative consequences associated with adolescent pregnancy are related to socioeconomic issues and antenatal health care rather than to physiologic age (13, 15, 28). Early detection of sexual activity is the most crucial element of affecting teenage pregnancy rates. This detection is accomplished by practicing the techniques and skills of patient-centered interviewing described earlier in this chapter.

Management of Adolescent Pregnancy

It is important to address the possibility of pregnancy prior to making the actual diagnosis. Again, conducting a woman-centered interview to identify the adolescent patient's own feelings, expectations, and desires about a potential pregnancy is much more important than the provider's own feelings and suggestions. Identifying her agenda can allow appropriate steps to be taken depending on the results of the pregnancy test. Particularly if the test is negative, knowing her feelings about a possible pregnancy can help the provider to negotiate contraception for the woman and her partner. It can also further reinforce the re-

lationship between the provider and the young woman and improve health maintenance.

If after this preliminary discussion the pregnancy test is positive, further explanation of the options available must be held. These options are to carry the pregnancy and keep the baby, carry the pregnancy and give the infant up for adoption, or terminate the pregnancy. Although these choices are extremely emotional for everyone, the young woman's views and needs must take priority. To ensure this priority, providers must completely clarify their own feelings about providing for adolescent patients in the realm of sexuality, contraception, and pregnancy. It is also important to know what resources are available depending on the choice the young woman makes. Given these options, it is imperative that an early decision be made and that the provider keep close follow-up with respect to whatever choice is made. This follow-up is critical no matter whether the mother chooses continuation of the pregnancy or termination.

If her choice is continuation of the pregnancy, the most important step to ensure a healthy mother and infant is early and complete prenatal assessment. The actual management of adolescent pregnancy should not differ from management of pregnancy in any woman and is more completely discussed elsewhere. Even so, the pregnant adolescent woman needs a thorough evaluation of her prenatal health status and assessment of such high-risk behavior as drug use, alcohol use, HIV risk, and assessment of her support system. The impact of her pregnancy on her school career and her rapidly changing psychosocial needs must be addressed. Given the high rate of failure to complete high school, every effort should be made to encourage the pregnant adolescent to continue her schooling either in the public system or with a home tutor.

The physical examination and prenatal laboratory evaluation are no different from that in any other pregnancy; however, do not assume an adolescent is comfortable with the aspects of an exam just because she is pregnant. It may still be her first pelvic exam. Approach it in the same patient-centered and respectful manner as for any teenager. General health maintenance may impact on immunizations normally prescribed to an adolescent woman, as it is not uncommon for high school or college age girls to require a second dose of MMR that would not be given if she is pregnant.

The one area of management that warrants particular emphasis in the pregnant adolescent is nutrition given the usually less than ideal diet of a teenager. Diet and nutrition are particularly critical in that many adolescent women are dealing with body image issues even without the complication of pregnancy. Specific instructions should include that weight gain is normal and expected and can be on average 28 to 30 pounds. She needs increased caloric intake of 200 to 300 calories per day, including 1.5 grams of protein per kilogram of body weight. Supplements of folic acid of 400 to 800 μg is required to prevent neural tube defects. Additional iron and calcium are also required as adolescent girls are at high risk for iron deficiency even in the absence of pregnancy, and need calcium for their own growth as well (15). Such instructions and calculations can be confusing, and merely supplying them or even providing a diet sheet probably guarantees "non-compliance." Concrete recommendations must be made such as an all-inclusive prenatal vitamin with minerals and specific meal suggestions.

The other issue in management of adolescent pregnancy is to work for more rather than less frequent prenatal visits. It might be preferable to see a pregnant adolescent as often as every 2 to 3 weeks rather than monthly. Realize that such suggestions may be difficult depending on the availability of psychosocial support, transportation, and providers. Similar issues require providing increased support for the teenage mother once her infant is born. The role of the family is particularly important at this stage.

Summary

Teenage girls are sexually active. Whether a specific young woman is active or not, she is still a sexual being and is dealing with a multitude of psychologic, psychosocial, biophysiologic, and emotional issues that are rapidly changing over a relatively narrow span of time.

A primary provider who chooses to care for an adolescent woman must incorporate her attitudes and needs in a practical fashion. Trying to make an adolescent's world "practical" can be frustrating as the thought process and communication skills differ widely not only between teenager and provider but also between teenagers. Such an approach allows for identification of the adolescent woman's issues and provides the caregiver with the opportunity to discuss her or his own issues as well. A patient-centered approach allows for negotiation between these two points of view and the best use of the time spent in the encounter.

Although a multitude of contraceptive options exist for women and men, many of these options are not practical nor necessarily safe for adolescents. The most appropriate and practical methods of contraception to discuss with a young woman are abstinence, OCPs, and condoms. Even though OCPs and condoms individually are appropriate methods for adolescents, given the higher failure rate of condoms in preventing conception and the failure of OCPs to prevent STDs, both methods should be recommended together. Such a "combination therapy" also helps minimize the real risk of inconsistent use of any one method or birth control by adolescent girls and boys.

Although some biomedical problems do seem closely associated with adolescent pregnancy, the most commonly associated morbidity of low birth weight infants can be ameliorated by early and close prenatal care. A thorough prenatal health assessment, combined with a woman-centered approach that is individualized for the particular adolescent woman, also helps to minimize the real psychosocial impacts such as failure to complete high school and social isolation.

References

1. Fielding JE, Williams CA. Adolescent pregnancy in the U.S.: a review and recommendation for clinicians and research needs. Am J Prev Med 1991; 7:47–52.

2. Alexander CS, Guyer B. Adolescent pregnancy: occurrence and consequences. Pediatric Ann 1993; 22:85–88

3. Cromer BA, Brown RT. Update on pregnancy, condom use, and prevalence of selected sexually transmitted diseases in adolescents. Curr Opin Obstet Gynecol 1992;4:855–859.

4. Braverman PK, Strasburger VC. Adolescent sexuality: Part 2 Contraception. Clin Pediatr 1993; 32:725–734.

5. Grant LM. Adolescent issues. In: Carr PL, Freund KM, Somani S, eds. The Medical Care of Women. Philadelphia: WB Saunders, 1995:32–43.

6. Woods ER. Contraceptive choices for adolescents. Pediatric Ann 1991;20:313–321.

7. Sulak PJ, Haney AF. Unwanted pregnancies: understanding contraceptive use and benefits in adolescents and older women. Am J Obstet Gynecol 1993; 168:2042–2048.

8. Schenker JK, Elchalal U. Behavioral and social issues in contraception. Curr Opin Obstetr Gynecol 1994;6:543–546.

9. Center for Population Options. Adolescent Sexuality, Pregnancy, and Parenthood. Washington, DC: May 1990.

10. Centers for Disease Control. Sexual Behavior Among High School Students: U.S., 1990. MMWR 1992;40:885–888.

11. Bachrach CA. Contraceptive practice among American women, 1973–1982. FAM Plann Perspect 1984;16:253–259.

12. Forrest JD. Epidemiology of unintended pregnancy and contraceptive use. Am J Obstet Gynecol 1994; 170:1485–1489.

13. Centers for Disease Control. State-Specific Pregnancy and Birth Rates Among Teenagers—U.S., 1991–1992. MMWR 1995;44:677–684.

14. Creatsas GK. Sexuality: Sexual activity and contraception during adolescence. Curr Opin Obstet Gynecol 1993;5:774–783.

15. Weil A. Spontaneous Healing. New York: Alfred A. Knopf, 1995:3–8.

16. Neinstein LS. Adolescent Health Care: A Practical Guide. 2nd ed. Baltimore: Urban & Schwarzenberg 1995:537–583.

17. Engel GL. Clinical application of the biopsychosocial model. In: Reiser DE, Rosen DH, eds. Medicine as a Human Experience. 1st ed. Baltimore: University Park Press, 1984:43–60.

18. Mishler EG, Clark JA, Ingelfinger J, Simon MP. The language of attentive womancare: a comparison of two medical interviews. J Intern Med 1989;4:325–335.

19. Stewart MA, Brown JB, Weston WW, McWhinney IR, McWilliam CL, Freeman, TR. Patient Centered Medicine: Transforming the Clinical Method. 1st ed. Thousand Oaks, CA: Sage, 1995

20. Hay Jr WW, Hayward AR, Groothuis JR, Levin MJ, Eds. Current Pediatric Diagnosis and Treatment. 12th ed. Norwalk, CT: Appleton & Lange, 1995:94–126.

21. Sanford W, Hauley NP, McGee E. Sexuality In: The Boston Homan's Health Book Collective. The New Our Bodies Ourselves: Updated and Expanded for the 90's. New York: Touchstone, 1992:204–232.

22. Raines TG. Family focused primary prevention of adolescent pregnancy. Birth Defects: Original Article Series 1991;27:87–103.

23. Kenny AM, Guardados S, Brown L. Sex education and AIDS education in the schools: what states in large school districts are doing. Fam Plann Perspect 1989;21:56–64.

24. Orr MT. Sex education in contraceptive education in U.S. public high schools. Fam Plann Perspect 1982;14:304–313.

25. Furstenberg FF, Moore KA, Peterson JO. Sex education and sexual experience among adolescents. Am J Pub Health 1985;75:1331–1332.

26. Zelnik M, Kim YJ. Sex education and its association with teenage sexual activity, pregnancy, and contraceptive use. Fam Plann Perspect 1982;14:117–126.

27. Polit DF, Kahn JR, Enman GM. Contraceptive Decision Making in Adolescent Couples. Final Report to the National Institute of Child Health and Human Development. American Institute for Research, 1981.

28. Elster AB, Panzarines. The adolescent father. SEM Perinat 1981;5:39–51.

29. Kirby D, Short L, Collins J, et al. School-based programs to reduce sexual risk behaviors: a review of effectiveness. Public Health Rep 1994;109:339–359.

30. Hankey T, Fleming M, Ning L. American Academy of Family Physicians. Committee on Health Education: Kansas City Annual Report 1995.

31. Hanson SL, Morrison DR, Gingsburg AL. The antecedents of teenage fatherhood. Demography 1989; 26:579–596.

32. Grimes DA. The morbidity and mortality of pregnancy: still risky business. Am J Obstet Gyn 1994; 170:1489–1494.

33. Bruni V, Perini R, Cirri R, Degl'Innocenti E, Michelozzi C, Verni A. Natural contraceptive methods. ACTA Europaea Fertilitatis 1991;22:47–50.

34. Spangler T. Natural birth control. Natural Health 1995:42–48.

35. Stanford JL, Weiss NS, Voight LF, Daling JR, Mabel LA, Rossing MN. Combined estrogen and progestin hormone replacement therapy in relation to risk of breast cancer in middle-aged women. JAMA 1995; 274:137–142.

36. Colditz GA, Hankinson SE, Hunter DJ, et al. The use of estrogens and progestins and the risk of breast cancer in post-menopausal women. NEJM 1995; 332:1589–1593.

37. Northrup C. Women's Bodies, Women's Wisdom. New York: Bantam Books, 1994.

38. Furstenberg FF, Brooks-Gunn J, Chase-Lansdale L. Teenaged pregnancy and child bearing. Am Psychol 1989;44:313–320.

39. Johnson JH. US differentials in infant mortality: why do they persist? Fam Plann Perspect 1987; 19:227–232.

Adolescence: Special Considerations for Nurse Practitioners and Physician Assistants

Nancy Alley

Adolescent Care

To promote adolescent health, specific areas must be addressed during the psychosocial assessment. Teenagers should be asked about stressful events they are experiencing, including stress resulting from the family, school, and peers. Providers might simply ask each adolescent what it is like for them at home and at school. Health care practitioners must also observe how the adolescent is coping with the stress and determine if the coping behaviors themselves are placing the woman adolescent at risk. Providers should determine, too, if the adolescent is aware of and using resources, such as school nurses, guidance counselors, or teachers (1).

At-risk adolescents must be identified and referred to appropriate mental health specialists. However, specialists who can meet the adolescent's complex needs may not be as accessible in some rural and other areas (2). The manifestations of adolescent depression may be different from those of the adult because adolescents tend to mask their depression by exhibiting behavioral and other problems, including anger, moodiness, self-destructive behavior, and a range of psychosomatic illnesses. The first indicator of despondency may be poor hygiene and appearance changes, for example, inappropriateness of dress for the season (3).

Providers must be aware of their own views of the period of adolescence. If they hold a negative view (as does society in general), then they may have a tendency to "blame adolescents for their own problems, as if they are caused by an intrinsic, emotional, or biologic state" (4).

Adolescents can have varied health-related concerns, including the future, their appearance, and STDs. However, their concerns about pregnancy, drug and alcohol use, and birth control may not be as critical to them as they are to the health care provider (5). While not negating the latter influences on health, practitioners must listen for and respond to the adolescent's reasons for health care visits.

Health teaching and other interventions should be presented within the framework of the adolescent's developmental level. During the early adolescent period, an emphasis might be made on the immediate consequences of a behavior, for example stained teeth and stale breath from smoking. Later in adolescence, clients can focus more on increased decision-making and future consequences of current actions. During any interactions, health care providers must be aware of the influence of their direct modeling of health-damaging behaviors on an adolescent's behavior choices (6).

Educational programs must move beyond the provision of technical information. For example, teaching about hygiene is useful in preparing young girls for menarche. However, these young girls will also want to know about the experiential aspects of menstruation, how menstruation feels, and what variations of the experience is normal (7). Young adolescents, especially, may be uneasy with their bodies and have difficulty with verbal expression of their concerns; they might not know medical terminology and hesitate to use slang to communicate with providers (8).

Time constraints and the provider's lack of communication skills can prohibit interactions that allow adolescents to discuss their concerns. Similarly, the girl can sense if the provider is uncomfortable or unwilling to discuss certain issues. To set the stage for a sexual history, providers might begin the encounter by warmly recognizing that the adolescent made and kept an appointment and assuring the confidentiality of the visit. To allow the adolescent to express concerns, providers can resist talking for more than 1 minute without giving the client a chance to respond and avoid the use of "should," a word that may be perceived as judgmental (8).

All adolescents must be asked about their sexual activity and use of contraception. Whatever the contraceptive option (except for abstinence), sexually active adolescents need an annual gynecologic examination, including Pap smears. Although many forms of contraception are safe and effective, adolescents have special contraceptive needs. For the adolescent who chooses Norplant, care providers have an ethical responsibility to consider possible parental coercion on the part of parents, guardians, or even other health care providers. Norplants may appeal to adolescents because of the privacy factor, but menstrual cycle changes can cause undue worry for an adolescent who does not know what to expect. Low-dose oral contraceptives, although generally a good method for most adolescents, require that the adolescent have a plan for taking the pills at the same time each day, often difficult for the young women who do not have a regular daily routine. Condom use requires an ability to negotiate with the sexual partner, a communication skill that the adolescent may need to be taught (8).

Pregnant teens have described themselves as scared, nervous, and needing help (9). The pregnant adolescent may delay seeking prenatal care for many reasons, including a denial of the signs and symptoms of pregnancy, embarrassment about becoming pregnant, and fear of telling parents and others. Once health care is sought, these young parents-to-be may need help clarifying the father's role, making use of family support systems, and setting realistic goals. They should be encouraged to maintain peer interactions and continue to meet educational needs.

Primary health care providers who encounter pregnant teens are also likely to have contact with adolescent parents. By observing and listening to these mothers, providers can assess their parenting skills and determine their needs. Providers should ask themselves: Does the mother express positive feelings? Can she recognize the child's needs? Does the young mother respond appropriately to the child's cues? Does she consider the child's needs before her own? Specific help can be given to the mother to enhance positive parenting behaviors (10).

Providers who are aware of the risk that an adolescent has been abused may be more attuned to possible signs and symptoms of abuse. The adolescent may not divulge the abuse but instead may have repeated somatic complaints, experience an unintended pregnancy, have STDs or UTIs, and/or manifest suicide gestures (11). The risk of sexual abuse in the young pregnant adolescent is high, and providers must investigate the possibility. The adolescent, not the provider, must decide when and who is a trustworthy adult who can be told about the pregnancy (12). Teenagers may be even more trapped than adult victims in relationships because they lack experience in decision-making and other resources for leaving the relationship. Shelters may be reluctant to admit adolescents, and adolescents may be uncomfortable in an environment of older residents. Parents may or may not support a pregnant adolescent's plans to leave an abusive boyfriend (13).

Adolescents may consult health care professionals about organic health problems, but they seldom seek help for social and behavioral problems responsible for most of their morbidity and mortality. Ideal intervention sites for these problems are not in clinics and offices, but schools and other community sites where contact with adolescents can be made (6). Although programs in these sites can address specific concerns such as nutrition or abuse, they must move beyond the provision of information. A number of protective factors, e.g., social skills, reflective tendencies, problem-solving abilities, strong self-identity, lead to resiliency in youth and an ability to succeed despite overwhelming barriers. This resiliency can be fostered within the family, school, and community (14).

References

1. Puskar KR, Lamb JM, Bartolovic M. Examining the common stressors and coping methods of rural adolescents. Nurse Practitioner 1993;18:50–53.
2. Roye CF. Breaking through to the adolescent patient. AJN 1995;95:19–24.
3. Morgan IS. Recognizing depression in the adolescent. MCN 1994;9:148–155.
4. Peterson AC. Psychological and social issues during adolescence. 1994;4:63–65.
5. McKay L, Diem E. Health concerns of adolescent girls. J Pediatr Nurs 1995;10:19–27.
6. Curtis S. Promoting health through a developmental analysis of adolescent risk behavior. School Health 1992;62:417–420.
7. Woods NF. Young women's health. In: Fogel CI, Woods NF, eds. Women's Health Care. 1995. Thousand Oaks, CA: Sage, 1995:60–75.
8. Harbin RE. Female adolescent contraception. Pediatr Nurs 1995:21.
9. May KM. Social networks and help-seeking experiences of pregnant teens. JOGNN 1992;21:497–502.
10. Fleming BW, Munton MT, Clark BA, Strauss SS. Assessing and promoting positive parenting in adolescent mothers. MCN 1993;18:32–27.
11. Pope C, Brucker MC. Adolescents as victims: an overview of the special impact of sexual abuse. NAACOG's clinical issues in perinatal and women's health nursing 1991;2:263–269.
12. Reedy NJ. The very young pregnant adolescent. NAACOG's clinical issues in perinatal and women's health nursing 1991;2:209–227.
13. Parker B. Abuse of adolescents: what can we learn from pregnant teenagers? NAACOG's clinical issues in perinatal and women's health nursing 1993;4:363–370.
14. Stotland NL, Romans MC. Executive summary: adolescent girls' health and self-esteem. Women's Health Issues 1994;4:57–59.

ADULTHOOD III

6.1

Preventive Health Care

Diane J. Madlon-Kay

Introduction

Principles of Preventive Health Care and Screening

The leading causes of death in women in the United States are diseases that are to a large extent preventable (1, 2). All five of the leading causes have risk factors that are modifiable (Table 6.1.1) (3). The incidence and mortality rates from cancer, the second leading cause

of death in women, are shown by cancer site in Table 6.1.2 (3). Primary care providers can intervene with screening, immunizations, and counseling, and can dramatically reduce morbidity and premature mortality in women.

As with other clinical practices, providers should carefully evaluate individual preventive services before incorporating them into routine practice. A condition can be justified for screening if it meets the following six criteria (4):

Table 6.1.1. The Five Leading Causes of Death in Women in the United States and Associated Modifiable Risk Factors, 1991

Cause of Death	Modifiable Risk Factor
1. Heart diseases	Tobacco use
	Elevated serum choles- terol
	High blood pressure
	Obesity
	Sedentary lifestyle
2. Cancer	Tobacco use
	Improper diet
	Alcohol
	Occupational exposures
3. Cerebrovascular diseases	High blood pressure
	Tobacco use
	Elevated serum choles- terol
4. Pneumonia, influenza	Tobacco use
	Lack of immunization
5. Chronic lung disease	Tobacco use
	Occupational exposure
	Environmental exposure

Data from Wingo PA, Tong T, Bolden S. Cancer statistics, 1995. CA Cancer J Clin 1995; 45:8–30.

Table 6.1.2. 1995 Estimated New Cancer Cases and Deaths in Women in the United States

Site	New cases (%)	Deaths (%)
Melanoma of skin	3	1
Oral	2	1
Breast	32	18
Lung	13	24
Pancreas	2	5
Colon and rectum	12	11
Ovary	5	6
Uterus	8	4
Urinary	4	3
Leukemia and lymphomas	6	8
All others	13	19

Data from Wingo PA, Tong T, Bolden S. Cancer Statistics, 1995. CA Cancer J Clin 1995; 45:8–30.

1. The condition must greatly affect the quality and quantity of life
2. Acceptable methods of treatment must be available
3. The condition must have an asympto- matic period during which detection and treatment significantly reduce morbidity and mortality
4. Treatment in the asymptomatic phase must yield a therapeutic result superior to that obtained by delaying treatment until symptoms appear
5. Tests that are acceptable to patients must be available at reasonable cost to detect the condition in the asymptomatic period
6. The incidence of the condition must be sufficient to justify the cost of the screening

In general, preventive interventions should not be used unless they have been shown to be effective in well-designed studies. Clinicians are unlikely to be able to assess the quality of scientific evidence for each preven- tive service individually. Therefore, many authorities including professional societies, government agencies, ad hoc committees, vol- untary associations, academic experts, and consensus panels have made recommenda- tions for the prevention of disease. Well- known examples include the Centers for Dis- ease Control and Prevention, US Preventive Services Task Force (USPSTF), and the American Cancer Society (ACS) (2, 5). Some organizations' policy statements do not de- scribe the methods used to generate their rec- ommendations. Others, notably the USPSTF, provide a detailed description of the method- ology used. Therefore, the clinician must be a discerning consumer of recommendations made by preventive care authorities.

It is not surprising, given the large number of authorities, that preventive care recom- mendations differ. However, major authorities do agree about many preventive services; these will be the focus of this chapter. Similarly, several preventive services are not recommended by any major US authority. An example is the yearly physical examination, a relatively ineffective ritual, which is no longer recommended by most authorities and has been replaced by a variety of screening tests, immunizations, and counseling interventions (6). Other services not routinely recommended for asymptomatic normal risk women include the chest radiograph, electrocardiogram, exercise stress test, multiple blood chemistry screens, sputum cytology testing, and multivitamin prophylaxis.

Preventive Care in Practice

The best health maintenance protocol is worthless unless it is used daily by clinicians on most of their patients. The delivery of preventive care, even for services on which all authorities agree, is far from satisfactory. Reasons include lack of clinician time, inadequate reimbursement, lack of clinician interest and knowledge, lack of patient involvement and knowledge, and lack of office or clinic systems to promote preventive care. Some of these factors are beyond the control of the practicing clinician, but many are not.

The first step in implementation is for every clinician or practice to create a clear, written protocol of preventive services to be delivered to patients. The protocol must be realistic and achievable. To ensure that the protocol is carried out efficiently and consistently, the participation of the office staff and clinicians is necessary (7).

Patient involvement can be promoted by educational materials and patient held records (8). Well-trained office staff can effectively provide counseling on many topics. Staff can also prompt clinicians and patients about preventive care.

A variety of office tools can improve preventive care. Most important is some form of tracking system, either paper-based (e.g., flowsheets or checklists) or computerized (9). Patient risk-factor assessment can be helped by using questionnaires or history forms completed by the patient or provider. Mailed postcards or letters can be used to prompt patients to come in for needed preventive care. Prevention prescription pads, chart stickers, and examination room posters are other effective office tools.

Every patient encounter should be used as an opportunity for preventive care. Many young adults visit their provider for acute care but rarely come in specifically for preventive care. Older patients with chronic medical problems visit regularly but often don't schedule preventive care appointments. An effective tracking and prompting system will allow the clinician to determine quickly a patient's needs for preventive care. The patient may at least be accurately informed of what is needed and a plan established to obtain it.

Finally, it is useful to have periodic or ongoing objective feedback on actual compliance with the preventive care protocol. Clinicians substantially overestimate the amount of preventive care they deliver to their patients.

Screening

The most recent recommendations from the American Academy of Family Physicians for periodic health exam are included in Table 6.1.3.

Physical Examination

The annual physical examination of healthy persons was first proposed as effective preventive medicine by the American Medical Association in 1922 (1, 2, 6). However, although routine visits with the primary care clinician are important, performing the same interventions on all patients as frequently as every year is not the most clinically effective approach to disease prevention. Rather, both the frequency and the content of the periodic health

Table 6.1.3. American Academy of Family Physicians
Age Chart for Periodic Health Examination—November 1995*
Ages: 19–39 Years
Schedule: Every 1–3 Years (See Preamble in Appendix C)

Screening		
History	Physical Examination[2]	Laboratory/ Diagnostic Procedures
Interval medical and family history[1]	Blood pressure[2]	Papanicolaou smear[5]
Dietary intake	Pelvic examination (for women)	High-Risk Groups
Physical activity	Clinical breast exam (for women)[3]	Fasting plasma glucose (HR6)
Tobacco/alcohol/drug use	Clinical testicular exam (for men)	Rubella antibodies (HR7)
Sexual practices	(HR4)	VDRL/RPR (HR8)
Height and weight	High-Risk Groups	Urinalysis for bacteriuria[6] (HR9)
	Complete oral cavity exam	Chlamydial testing (HR10)
	(HR1)	Gonorrhea culture (HR11)
	Palpation for thyroid nodules	Counseling and testing for HIV
	(HR2)	(HR12)
	Complete skin exam (HR5)	Hearing (HR13)
	Nonfasting or fasting total blood	Tuberculin skin test (PPD) (HR14)
	cholesterol[4]	Electrocardiogram (HR3)
		Colonoscopy (HR16)

Counseling		
Diet and Exercise	Substance Use	Sexual Practices
Fat (especially saturated fat), cholesterol, complex carbo- hydrates, fiber, sodium, iron[7], calcium[7]	Tobacco: cessation/primary prevention	Sexually transmitted diseases: partner selection, condoms, anal intercourse
Nutritional assessment	Alcohol and other drugs:	Unintended pregnancy and con-
Selection of exercise program	Limiting alcohol consumption	traceptive options for men
	Driving/other dangerous	and women
	activities while under the	
	influence	
	Treatment for abuse	
	High-Risk Groups	
	Sharing/using unsterilized	
	needles & syringes (HR18)	

Injury Prevention	Dental Health	Other Primary Preventive Measures
Safety belts	Regular tooth brushing,	Breast self-examination[9]
Safety helmets	flossing, dental visits	Testicular self-examination[10]
Violent behavior[8]		High-Risk Groups
Firearms[8]		Discussion of hemoglobin
Smoke detector		testing (HR22)
Smoking near bedding or upholstery		Skin Protection from ultraviolet
High-Risk Groups		light (HR23)
Back-conditioning exercises (HR19)		
Prevention of childhood injuries (HR20)		
Falls in the elderly (HR21)		

Immunizations and Chemoprophylaxis
Tetanus-diphtheria (Td) booster[11]
High-Risk Groups
Hepatitis B vaccine (HR24)
Pneumococcal vaccine (HR25)
Influenza vaccine[12] (HR26)
Measles-mumps-rubella vaccine (MMR) (HR27)

High-Risk Categories

HR1	Recent divorce, separation, unemployment, depression, alcohol or other drug abuse, serious medical illnesses, living alone, or recent bereavement.
HR2	Men with a history of cryptorchidism, orchiopexy, or testicular atrophy.
HR3	Persons with exposure to tobacco or excessive amounts of alcohol, or those with suspicious symptoms or lesions detected through self-examination.
HR4	Persons with a history of upper-body irradiation.
HR5	Persons with a family or personal history of skin cancer, increased occupational or recreational exposure to sunlight, or clinical evidence of percursor lesions (e.g., dysplastic nevi, certain congenital nevi).
HR6	The markedly obese, persons with a family history of diabetes, or women with a history of gestational diabetes.
HR7	Women lacking evidence of immunity.
HR8	Prostitutes, persons who engage in sex with multiple partners in areas in which syphilis is prevalent, or contacts of persons with active syphilis.
HR9	Persons with diabetes.
HR10	Persons who attend clinics for sexually transmitted diseases; attend other high-risk health care facilities (e.g., adolescent and family planning clinics); or have other risk factors for chlamydial infection (e.g., multiple sexual partners or a sexual partner with multiple sexual contacts, age less than 20).
HR11	Prostitutes, persons with multiple sexual partners or a sexual partner with multiple contacts, sexual contacts of persons with culture-proven gonorrhea, or persons with a history of repeated episodes of gonorrhea.
HR12	Persons seeking treatment for sexually transmitted diseases; homosexual and bisexual men; past or present intravenous (IV) drug users; persons with a history of prostitution or multiple sexual partners; women whose past or present sexual partners were HIV infected, bisexual, or IV drug users; persons with long-term residence or birth in an area with high prevalence of HIV infection; or persons with a history of transfusion between 1978 and 1985.
HR13	Persons exposed regularly to excessive noise.
HR14	Household members of persons with tuberculosis or others at risk for close contact with the disease (e.g., staff of tuberculosis clinics, shelters for the homeless, nursing homes, substance abuse treatment facilities, dialysis units, correctional institutions); recent immigrants or refugees from countries in which tuberculosis is common; migrant workers; residents of nursing homes, correctional institutions, or homeless shelters; or persons with certain underlying medical disorders (e.g., HIV infection).
HR15	Men who would endanger public safety were they to experience sudden cardiac events (e.g., commercial airline pilots).
HR16	Women aged 35 and older with a family history of premenopausally diagnosed breast cancer in a first-degree relative.
HR17	Persons with a family history of familial polyposis coli or cancer family syndrome.
HR18	Intravenous drug users.
HR19	Persons at increased risk for low back injury because of past history, body configuration, or type of activities.
HR20	Persons with children in the home or automobile.
HR21	Persons with older adults in the home.
HR22	Young adults of Caribbean, Latin America, Asian, Mediterranean, or African descent.
HR23	Persons with increased exposure to sunlight.
HR24	Homosexually and bisexually active men, intravenous drug users, recipients of some blood products; persons in health-related jobs with frequent exposure to blood or blood products, household and sexual contacts of HBV carriers, sexually active heterosexual persons with multiple sexual partners diagnosed as having recently acquired sexually transmitted disease, prostitutes, and persons who have a history of sexual activity with multiple partners in the previous six months.
HR25	Persons with medical conditions that increase the risk of pneumococcal infection (e.g., chronic cardiac or pulmonary disease, sickle cell disease, nephrotic syndrome, Hodgkin's disease, asplenia, diabetes mellitus, alcoholism, cirrhosis, multiple myeloma, renal disease or conditions associated with immunosuppression).
HR26	Residents of chronic care facilities or persons suffering from chronic cardiopulmonary disorders, metabolic diseases (including diabetes mellitus), hemoglobinopathies, immunosuppression, or renal dysfunction.
HR27	Persons born after 1956 who lack evidence of immunity to measles (receipt of live vaccine on or after first birthday, laboratory evidence of immunity, or a history of physician-diagnosed measles).

[1]An updating of the previously obtained medical and family history is recommended by the subcommittee.

[2]At every physician visit, with a minimum of every two years

[3]Every 1–3 years, starting at age 30 until age 40

[4]At least every five years

[5]All women 18 years of age and over should have an annual Pap test and pelvic examination. After a woman has had three or more consecutive satisfactory normal annual examinations, the Pap test may be performed at the discretion of the physician based on the assessment of patient risk but not less frequently than every three years.

[6]The optimal frequency for urine testing has not been determined. In general, dipsticks combining the leukocyte esterase and nitrite tests should be used to detect asymptomatic bacteriuria.

[7]For women

[8]Especially for young males

[9]The teaching of self-breast examination is recommended by the subcommittee at the time of initiation of pelvic examinations.

[10]The teaching of self-testicular examination is recommended by the subcommittee for male patients.

[11]Every 10 years

[12]Annually

*These recommendations are provided only as an assistance for physicians making clinical decisions regarding the care of their patients. As such, they cannot substitute for the individual judgment brought to each clinical situation by the patient's family physician. As with all clinical reference resources, they reflect the best understanding of the science of medicine at the time of publication, but they should be used with the clear understanding that continued research may result in new knowledge and recommendations.

examination must be tailored to the unique health risks of the individual patient and should consider the quality of the evidence to determine which specific preventive services are clinically effective. The portions of the physical examination that many authorities feel are effective in the preventive care of adult women are reviewed.

Breast Examination

Breast cancer is the most common type of cancer in women and the second leading cause of cancer death in American women (10, 11). The average lifetime risk for a woman in the United States of developing breast cancer is approximately one in nine (12, 13).

The sensitivity and specificity of clinical examination of the breast for breast cancer screening vary with the skill and experience of the examiner and with the characteristics of the individual breast being examined. The estimated sensitivity of clinical examination alone is approximately 45%. Data from studies using manufactured breast models show that for lumps 1-cm in diameter the mean sensitivity of examinations performed by registered nurses was 65% and by physicians was 87%.

The results of several large studies have convincingly proved the effectiveness of clinical breast examination with mammographic screening for prevention of breast cancer in women age 50 years and older. The effectiveness of clinical breast examination in isolation has not been well studied.

Most major authorities recommend clinical breast examinations, beginning at a variety of ages and at varying frequencies. For example, the ACS recommends that women have clinical breast examinations every 3 years from age 20 to 39 years. Annual clinical breast examinations should be performed on women age 40 years and older (12).

The breast examination involves bilateral inspection and palpation of the breasts and the axillary and supraclavicular areas. Examination should be performed in both the upright and supine positions. It is important that palpation be systematic. One of the best predictors of examination accuracy is the length of time spent by the examiner.

Pelvic Organ Examination

The pelvic examination is used in the detection of cancers of the female genital tract, namely, the ovaries, cervix, and endometrium (6). The pelvic examination is usually performed with the Papanicolaou (Pap) smear testing for cervical neoplasms.

Ovarian cancer is the fourth leading cause of cancer death in American women. The pelvic examination is of unknown sensitivity and specificity in detecting ovarian cancer. Small, early-stage ovarian tumors are often not detected by palpation, because of the deep anatomic location of the ovary. Thus, ovarian cancers detected by pelvic examination are generally advanced and associated with poor survival. The pelvic examination may also produce false positives when benign adnexal masses are found.

Approximately 15,800 cases of invasive cervical cancer will be diagnosed and 4800 women will die of cervical cancer in the United States in 1995. The pelvic examination is much less sensitive than Papanicolaou testing for cervical neoplasms (6).

Endometrial cancer is not a leading cause of death among North American women, although its incidence is relatively high (14, 15). Survival rates are relatively good, with 72% of all women with endometrial cancer alive after 5 years and 69% after 10 years. The techniques available for diagnosing endometrial cancer in the asymptomatic woman, unfortunately, are not ideal. The pelvic examination has never been effective in diagnosing endometrial cancer.

The pelvic examination is considered by several, but not all, major authorities to be a necessary component of the periodic health examination. The ACS recommends pelvic examination should be performed every 1 to 3 years for women age 18 to 39 years and annually for women over age 40 years (5). The USPSTF states that routine screening for ovarian cancer by pelvic examination is not recommended (2).

The woman should empty her bladder prior to the pelvic examination. A general inspection of the external genitalia should be performed with the woman in the lithotomy position. A speculum should be used to inspect the vagina and cervix. The lubricated index and middle fingers of one hand are placed into the vaginal vault, with the other hand on top of the abdomen for bimanual palpation of the pelvic organs. The hand is partially withdrawn from the vagina and inserted in the rectum to allow for palpation of the rectovaginal septum.

Digital Rectum Examination

Colorectal cancer is the third leading cause of cancer deaths in American women (16). Less than 10% of colorectal cancers can be palpated by digital rectal examination. Therefore, the examination is of limited value as a screening for colorectal cancer. However, because of its feasibility and low cost, several major authorities recommend its use. For example, ACS recommends annual digital rectal examination for all patients starting at age 40 years (5).

Patients may be examined by the left lateral decubitus position or standing bent over the examination table. Women may also be examined in the lithotomy position after a pelvic examination. The anal opening should be visually inspected. A lubricated, gloved index finger is inserted into the anal opening. All sides of the rectum should be palpated.

Skin Examination

Skin cancer is the most common type of cancer in the United States (17, 18). An estimated 7200 deaths from malignant melanoma and approximately 2100 deaths from other types of skin cancer will occur in 1995. Virtually 100% of skin cancers are curable if diagnosed and excised early. The principal screening test for skin cancer is clinical examination of the skin. Detection of a suspicious lesion is a positive screening test, and a suspicious lesion should be examined by skin biopsy. There are few studies evaluating the accuracy of the skin examination, however, and most suffer from important design flaws. Estimates of the sensitivity and specificity vary widely and with the type of skin cancer being sought. Factors affecting the yield of screening for skin cancer are the proportion of the body surface examined and the frequency of the examination.

Authorities vary on their recommendations for skin cancer screening. The ACS recommends that patients should undergo a cancer checkup that includes examination of the skin every 3 years for those age 20 to 39 years, and yearly after age 40 years (5). The USPSTF states that, although there is sufficient evidence to recommend for or against routine screening for skin cancer by primary care providers using the total-body skin examination, clinicians should be alert to skin lesions with malignant features when examining patients for other reasons (2).

The skin examination should be performed in a room that is comfortably warm with the lighting adjusted for optimal illumination. The patient should first be seated, then examined supine, then lying on the left side to ensure access to all areas of skin.

Thyroid Examination

Thyroid malignancy occurs twice as frequently in women as in men. Approximately 10,700 cases of thyroid cancer will be diagnosed in women in 1995 in the United States, with approximately 680 deaths in women attributed to the disease (6).

There is little information on the accuracy of neck palpation in detecting thyroid disease. Accuracy varies with the technique of the examiner and the size of the mass. Moreover, the benefits of early detection of thyroid cancer are not well defined.

Authorities vary on their recommendations for the screening thyroid examination. The ACS recommends that a cancer checkup, including palpation of the thyroid, should be performed every 3 years on individuals age 20 to 39 years and yearly for individuals age 40 years and older (5). The USPSTF states that screening asymptomatic adults for thyroid cancer using neck palpatation is not recommended (2).

When the provider examines the patient's thyroid gland, the patient should be seated with her neck flexed slightly for inspection. The provider should observe the patient's neck as she takes a sip of water; thyroid masses move up and down with swallowing. Standing behind the patient, the examiner palpates the thyroid gland. A malignancy may be palpated as a discrete area of firmness or hardness. Thyroid gland tenderness may also suggest malignancy.

Oral Cavity Examination

The oral cavity examination has two purposes: (1) to identify the presence of lesions that are precancerous or may predispose to cancer and (2) to identify dental disease (19, 20). The incidence of oral cancer is twice as high in men as in women. In 1995, an estimated 9300 women will develop oral cancer and 2900 women will die of it. Most Americans are affected by dental and oral health problems at some point in their lives. The most common diseases are dental caries and periodontal disease, both of which are largely preventable.

There is little information of the sensitivity of the oral examination in detecting oral cancer or on the frequency of false-positive results once a lesion is found.

Recommendations regarding the oral cavity examination vary. The USPSTF recommendation states that when examining the mouth, clinicians should be alert for obvious signs of oral disease such as untreated tooth decay, inflamed or cyanotic gingiva, loose teeth, and severe halitosis. There is sufficient evidence to recommend for or against routine screening of asymptomatic persons for oral cancer by primary care clinicians (2). The ACS recommends that individuals age 20 to 40 years should have a cancer checkup including examination of the oral region every 3 years. Those over age 40 years should have one yearly.

The recommended examination technique for oral cancer involves a careful exploration of the oral cavity with a gloved hand and a gauze pad, retraction of the tongue to expose the ventral and posterolateral surfaces and the floor of the mouth, and bidigital palpation for masses.

Tests

Blood Pressure

The prevalence of hypertension rises steadily as women age (21–24). Hypertension is a leading risk factor for coronary artery disease, congestive heart failure, stroke, renal disease, and retinopathy.

Office sphygmomanometry is the most appropriate screening test for hypertension in the asymptomatic population. Although this test is highly accurate when performed correctly, false-positive and false-negative results do occur. Therefore, it is commonly recommended that hypertension be diagnosed only after more than one elevated reading is obtained on each of three separate visits.

Treatment of hypertension is effective. Antihypertensive treatment has contributed to a 57% reduction in stroke mortality and a 50% reduction in mortality from coronary artery disease since 1972. The benefits of antihypertensive treatment are greatest in those with the most significant elevations in blood pressure. However, even patients with mild hypertension benefit from treatment.

All major authorities recommend periodic blood pressure readings. The USPSTF recommends that blood pressure should be measured regularly in all children and adults (2). The National High Blood Pressure Education Program of the National Heart, Lung, and Blood Institute recommends that blood pressure measurements should be performed on adults at least every 2 years, and at each patient visit if possible (23).

For the measurement of her blood pressure, the woman should be seated in a quiet environment for at least 5 minutes before the measurement is performed. The measurement should be performed with a mercury sphygmomanometer, if available. An appropriate-sized cuff should be used. The woman's arm should be bare. The arm should be supported horizontally so the cuff is positioned at heart level. The systolic and diastolic blood pressure readings should be identified by pressures corresponding to the first of two consecutive sounds and disappearance of the sound (not muffling), respectively.

Height and Weight

Obesity has been defined as 20% or more above desirable body weight (25). Twenty-five percent of white and 44% of African-American women are considered obese. Obesity is associated with multiple health risks, including hypertension, diabetes, hypercholesterolemia, and coronary artery disease. Obesity increases the risk of several cancers including cancer of the colon, rectum, gallbladder, biliary tract, breast, cervix, endometrium, and ovary.

Extremely overweight individuals can be identified easily in the clinical setting by their physical appearance. More precise methods are necessary to evaluate persons who are mildly or moderately overweight. The most common clinical method for detecting obesity, the evaluation of body weight and height based on tables of average weights, only approximates the extent of overweight. The criteria for desirable body weight are a matter of controversy among experts and vary considerably as presented in different weight for height tables.

Weight loss, through changes in diet, increased physical activity, and other interventions can decrease the risk of most forms of morbidity associated with obesity. Weight loss must be sustained to be beneficial.

Most major authorities, including the USPSTF, recommend periodic weight and height measurements (2). The American Heart Association recommends a body weight measurement every 5 years.

Height is most accurately measured with the woman barefoot or in socks or stockings only. Care should be taken to make sure that the woman is standing as erect as possible with feet flat on the floor. Weight is most accurately measured with the woman wearing minimal or no clothing.

Cholesterol

High blood cholesterol levels are a major modifiable risk factor for coronary heart disease, the leading cause of death for women in the United States (26, 27). Approximately 50% of adult women have serum cholesterol levels of 200 mg/dL or greater. Cholesterol levels rise steadily with age. On average, women's cholesterol levels are higher than men's from age 20 to 29 years and after age 50 years (24).

Several studies provide compelling evidence that the incidence of nonfatal myocardial infarction and fatal cardiac disease can be reduced by lowering serum cholesterol. These trials, however, used primarily white men age 35 to 59 years with serum cholesterol values above 255 to 265 mg/dL. A current focus of interest is the extent to which this evidence is generalizable to other populations, including women. Some studies suggest that diet, weight control, and exercise are not as effective in modifying lipoprotein levels in women as in men. Therefore, the importance of detecting high blood cholesterol may be reduced in women.

Most major authorities recommend periodic cholesterol measurements. The USPSTF recommends periodic measurement of total serum cholesterol for women ages 45 to 65 years (2). The National Cholesterol Education

Program of the National Heart, Lung, and Blood Institute recommends that adults should have a measurement of total blood cholesterol at least once every 5 years. HDL cholesterol should be performed simultaneously if accurate results are available (26).

Women who are pregnant or nursing should not be screened because their cholesterol levels may not be representative. Women need not vary their usual eating habits before undergoing screening for total blood cholesterol or HDL cholesterol. If possible, cholesterol tests should be performed on venous blood samples. Venipuncture should be carried out only after the patient has been in the sitting position for at least 5 minutes and the tourniquet should be applied for as brief a period as possible.

Papanicolaou Smear

The effectiveness of early detection of cervical cancer through Pap smear testing and early treatment has been impressive, resulting in a significant decrease in mortality from cervical cancer (28, 29). The incidence of invasive cervical cancer has decreased 70% because of screening. However, many women, particularly middle-aged poorer women, have not had regular Pap smears.

Depending on the technique used, Pap testing has a sensitivity of 50 to 90% and a specificity of 90 to 99%. Most of the false-negative Pap smears are thought to be caused by poor technique in performance and inadequate laboratory interpretation. Because of the long lead time from development of precancerous changes to invasive carcinoma (8 to 9 years by some estimates), almost all precancerous or early stage malignancies initially missed can still be detected by regular repeat testing.

All major authorities recommend periodic Pap testing. The USPSTF says that regular Pap testing is recommended for all women who are or have been sexually active. Pap tests should begin with the onset of sexual activity and should be repeated every 1 to 3 years at the

physician's discretion (2). The ACS recommends that all women should begin having annual Pap tests at the onset of sexual activity or at age 18 years, whichever occurs first. After a woman has had three or more consecutive satisfactory normal annual exams, the Pap test may be performed less frequently at the discretion of the patient and clinician (5).

Women should be instructed not to douche on the day of the exam. A Pap smear should not be performed if the patient has significant menstrual flow or obvious inflammation. The Pap smear should be performed before the bimanual exam and before obtaining culture specimens. The speculum should not be lubricated with anything but water. The cervix should be completely visualized. Excess cervical mucus should be gently removed with a swab. A wooden or plastic spatula, preferably Ayer's type, should be used first. The spatula should be firmly yet gently rotated circumferentially around the os at least one turn to obtain a 360° sample. This specimen should be promptly transferred to a slide. An endocervical brush should then be inserted into the os no deeper than the length of the bristled section. It should be rotated 360° and then the specimen transferred by rolling on the slide. Specimens should be uniformly applied to the slides without clumping. Fixation should be performed promptly to minimize air drying of the specimen.

Mammography

Breast cancer is the most common type of cancer in women and the second leading cause of cancer death in American women after lung cancer (10, 12, 30). The average lifetime risk for a woman in the United States of developing breast cancer is approximately one in nine.

The risk of dying from breast cancer increases with age; first deaths occur as young as age 30 years. Mortality from breast cancer does not plateau even in extreme old age. Mortality from breast cancer is strongly influenced by the stage at detection. The 5-year survival rate is

93% for women who have localized disease. The 5-year survival rate for women with distant metastases is only 18%.

Mammography is the most effective means of early detection of breast cancer, with sensitivity estimates of 70 to 90% and specificity estimates of 90 to 95%. The results of several large studies have convincingly proved that breast cancer screening by mammography reduces mortality from breast cancer by approximately 30% in women age 50 years and older. Most studies have not shown a clear benefit from mammography in women age 40 to 49 years.

Despite recommendations that women receive regular screening for breast cancer, too few women use this service. In 1990, 6% of women over age 40 years did not have a screening mammogram in the previous year, and 38% had never had a mammogram (24). Women without a primary provider or health insurance are much less likely to have screening mammography.

All major authorities recommend mammography, but at varying patient ages. The USPSTF recommends mammography every 1 to 2 years for women aged 50 to 69 years. The ACS states that women age 40 to 49 years should receive screening mammograms every 1 to 2 years (12).

The woman should wear pants or a skirt for her mammogram because she will have to undress from the waist up. She should be instructed not to use deodorants, powders, or other topical applications on the breasts or in underarm areas because they may cause artifacts on the mammogram. Because of potential premenstrual breast tenderness, it is preferable to schedule mammography at other times in the woman's menstrual cycle.

Tests for High-Risk Groups

Many screening tests are recommended only for members of high-risk groups and are not considered appropriate in the routine examination of all persons in the age group. The USPSTF recommends the tests shown in Table 6.1.4 for high-risk women (2).

Immunizations

Many vaccine preventable diseases occur among adults, particularly those who have missed both natural infection and past immunization (31, 32). Because some conditions are more serious, such as measles, or may have devastating secondary consequences, such as congenital rubella, physicians must ensure that their adult patients are protected.

A careful history of immunizations should be obtained from each new patient and reviewed periodically. This process should become as routine in the practice of clinicians who treat adults as it is among those who treat children. A patient's immunization history is determined most reliably by obtaining the information from records kept by the patient or the patient's previous clinician. Unfortunately, most adults do not have their own immunization records, and they may have received immunizations from several different providers in the past. Therefore, an accurate history is often difficult to obtain. Age, military service, and occupation may help determine immunization history.

Tetanus-Diphtheria (Td)

Tetanus and diphtheria occur almost entirely in unimmunized or incompletely immunized persons. Approximately 45 to 65 cases of tetanus occur in the United States each year. Although uncommon, tetanus remains a serious infection, with death occurring in approximately 30% of cases.

Diphtheria immunization of children has reduced its incidence in the United States to less than five cases yearly, primarily among adults. The case fatality rate is 5 to 10%, although no deaths have been reported in the last decade. Td toxoid is highly effective in producing protective antibody titers, but it requires a primary series of three doses followed by booster doses.

The traditional recommendation by the Advisory Committee on Immunization Practices (ACIP) and other authorities is that adults should receive a Td booster vaccination every 10 years. The American College of Physicians Task Force on Adult Immunizations (ACP) recently recommended an equivalent alternative strategy. They recommend a single Td booster given at age 50 years for persons who have completed the full pediatric series, including the teenage booster (31, 32).

Immunizations for High-Risk Groups

Many immunizations are recommended only for members of high-risk groups and are not considered appropriate in the routine examination of all persons in the age group. The USPSTF recommends the immunizations shown in Table 6.1.4 for high-risk women.

Counseling

The USPSTF has described the following 12 principles of patient education and counseling (2).

1. Frame the teaching to match the patient's perceptions.
2. Fully inform patients of the purposes and expected effects of interventions and when to expect these effects.
3. Suggest small changes rather than large ones.
4. Be specific.
5. It is sometimes easier to add new behaviors than to eliminate established behaviors.
6. Link new behaviors to old behaviors.

Table 6.1.4. US Preventive Services Task Force Recommendations for Selected High-Risk Women Ages 19 to 45 Years

Population	Potential Interventions
High-risk sexual behavior	RPR/VDRL; screen for gonorrhea, HIV, chlamydia, hepatitis B vaccine; hepatitis A vaccine
Injection or street drug use	RPR/VDRL; HIV screen; hepatitis B vaccine; hepatitis A vaccine; PPD; advice to reduce infection risk
Low income; TB contacts; immigrants; alcholics	PPD
Native Americans/Alaska Natives	Hepatitis A vaccine; PPD; pneumococcal vaccine
Travelers to developing countries	Hepatitis B vaccine; hepatitis A vaccine
Certain chronic medical conditions	PPD; pneumococcal vaccine; influenza vaccine
Blood product recipients	HIV screen; hepatitis B vaccine
Susceptible to measles, mumps, or varicella	MMR; varicella vaccine
Institutionalized persons	Hepatitis A vaccine; PPD; pneumococcal vaccine; influenza vaccine
Health care/lab workers	Hepatitis B vaccine; hepatitis A vaccine; PPD; influenza vaccine
Family history of skin cancer; fair skin, eyes, hair	Avoid excess/midday sun, use protective clothing
Previous pregnancy with neural tube defect	Folic acid 4.0 mg

Data from Report of U.S. Preventive Services Task Force. Guide to Clinical Preventive Services. 2nd ed. Baltimore: Williams & Wilkins, 1996.

7. Use the power of the profession.
8. Get explicit commitments from the patient.
9. Use a combination of strategies.
10. Involve office staff.
11. Refer.
12. Monitor progress through follow-up contact.

Patient behavior changes, although difficult to achieve, may be more valuable for health than many screening tests and immunizations that patients receive. Patients value the advice of clinicians. Studies show that even brief interventions may have a beneficial effect.

In the past, counseling and patient education were considered outside the traditional role of the clinician. The following counseling recommendations suggest a changing role both for clinicians and patients. The increasing evidence of the importance of personal health behaviors and primary prevention means that patients must assume greater responsibility for their own health. Clinicians may need to develop new skills in helping to empower patients and in counseling them to change certain health-related behaviors.

Exercise

Physical inactivity is associated with many leading causes of death and disability in the United States, including coronary artery disease, hypertension, diabetes, obesity, osteoporosis, and falls (33, 34). Regular exercise reduces cardiovascular disease risk, promotes weight loss and control, improves musculoskeletal functioning, and helps prevent diabetes. Even light exercise is beneficial for health.

The USPSTF states that counseling to promote regular physical activity is recommended for all children and adults (2).

To counsel about exercise, providers should ask women about their physical activity habits. An assessment should be made whether the patient's activities are sufficient to confer health benefits. Every patient should accumulate 30 minutes or more of moderate intensity physical activity on most days of the week. Patients lacking sufficient activity for health benefits and those wishing to improve physical activity habits should be helped in planning a program of physical activity. Such a program should be medically safe, enjoyable, inexpensive, convenient, realistic, and structured. Women may need help planning exercise admist the demands of home and work. However, there has been some realization of this; some health clubs have begun to provide child care for the woman who wants to exercise. Even patients who are unable or unwilling to participate in a regular exercise program should be encouraged to increase the amount of physical activity in their daily lives.

Alcohol and Other Drug Abuse

Substance abuse, the harmful or hazardous use of alcohol or other legal and illegal drugs, is a leading cause of premature and preventable illness, disability, and death in the United States (35–37). The abuse of alcohol costs society nearly twice as much as all other drugs combined.

Because women who drink alcohol consume less alcohol on average than men who drink, they have fewer alcohol-related problems and dependence symptoms than men (see Chapter 11.4) (24). However, there is evidence that when they drink comparable amounts, women are likely to be more impaired than men, both immediately and over longer periods of time. Smaller quantities of alcohol are required to produce intoxification in women than in men. There is some evidence that women are more likely than men to develop advanced liver disease, even with similar drinking histories.

Women use nearly all illicit drugs, but use them less frequently than men (24). Illicit drug use by women is highest among women during their child-bearing years. There has been a steady decline in the percentage of women reporting marijuana and cocaine use.

Women abuse medically prescribed psychotherapeutic drugs, such as sedatives, tranquilizers, and stimulants much more often than men (24). Women are more likely than men to become addicted to prescription drugs and to use them, often with alcohol to medicate themselves to cope with anxiety and depression.

The USPSTF recommends screening to detect problem drinking for all adult and adolescent patients (2). All persons who use alcohol should be counseled about the dangers of operating a motor vehicle or performing other potentially dangerous activities after drinking alcohol. The USPSTF also states there is sufficient evidence to recommend for or against routine screening for drug abuse.

To counsel, providers should ask women to describe the quantity, frequency, and other characteristics of their use of alcohol and other drugs. Such questions are of limited use in detecting substance abuse because of the tendency of patients to under report use. The use of brief screening questionnaires can help identify patients in need of more detailed evaluation. The four-item CAGE questionnaire has a relatively good sensitivity (85%) and specificity (89%). One "yes" response should raise suspicions of alcohol abuse. More than one "yes" response should be considered a strong indication that alcohol abuse exists. The questions are as follows:

1. Have you ever felt you ought to cut down on drinking?
2. Have people annoyed you by criticizing your drinking?
3. Have you ever felt bad or guilty about your drinking?
4. Have you ever had a drink first thing in the morning to steady your nerves or get rid of a hangover (eye-opener)? Persons in whom drug abuse or dependence is suspected should receive further evaluation to confirm the diagnosis (see Chapter 8.3).

Unintended Pregnancy

In 1988, US women age 15 to 44 years reported that 35% of their births in the preceding 5 years were unintended (38). In some populations up to 60% of births are unplanned (39). Most of the unintended births were mistimed, occurring sooner than wanted. However, nationally, up to half may be unwanted at the time of conception. Unwanted pregnancies lead to most of the 1.5 million induced abortions performed each year in the United States.

Modern contraceptives are safe and effective. Primary care clinicians are the main source of authoritative information and advice on responsible family planning practices for patients.

The USPSTF recommends periodic counseling about effective contraceptive methods for all women at risk for unintended pregnancy (2).

To counsel, providers should assess the sexual practices and need for contraceptive counseling for every patient. Patients should be educated about the important characteristics of different contraceptive methods. It is also important to discuss the ability of different contraceptive methods to protect against STDs and HIV infection.

Injury and Violence Prevention

Unintentional injuries are the sixth leading cause of death in women in the United States and the leading cause of death for those age 1 to 34 years (40–43). Motor vehicle crashes cause half the unintentional injury deaths. Most motor vehicle trauma is related to alcohol use and/or failure to use safety belts.

Injury to women because of violence is one of America's most widespread health problems, yet one of the least reported. Abuse occurs in up to 25% of all familial relationships. More than 1 million women seek medical assistance each year for injuries caused by battering.

The USPSTF recommends counseling to prevent household or recreational injuries. All patients should be urged to use occupant restraints for themselves and others, and to wear safety helmets when riding motorcycles.

To counsel about injury prevention, providers should advise women to use safety belts when operating or riding in a motor vehicle. All patients should be counseled on the importance of avoiding alcohol when driving, boating, swimming, and using motorized tools and firearms. All patients should be counseled to wear safety helmets while operating or riding motorcycles or bicycles, and to wear mouth guards when playing contact sports. All patients should be counseled to install and maintain smoke detectors in their residences. Patients should be advised about the dangers of keeping guns in the home. Patients should be counseled to be aware of the hazards and safety rules at the work site.

The American Medical Association recommends that all women patients should be screened for domestic violence (see Chapter 9.1) (42). To detect and counsel women who are victims of violence, providers should ask women directly whether they have ever been physically, verbally, or emotionally abused. The clinician must acknowledge the problem and affirm that battering is unacceptable. Information about (1) available community, social, and legal resources, (2) legal rights, and (3) a plan for dealing with the abusive partner should be made available to these women.

Dental and Oral Health

Most Americans are affected by dental and oral health problems at some point in their lives (44). The most common diseases are dental caries and periodontal disease, both of which are largely preventable. Oral-pharyngeal cancers are also a concern. They represent 2% of all cancers in women. The use of tobacco in all forms and the heavy abuse of alcohol are major causal factors.

The USPSTF recommends counseling patients to visit a dental care provider regularly, floss daily, brush their teeth daily with fluoride-containing toothpaste, and appropriately use fluoride for cavity prevention and chemotherapeutic mouth rinses for plaque prevention (2). The ACS recommends that patients be counseled about oral health during cancer-related checkups, which should occur every 3 years for those age 20 to 40 years, then yearly for those over age 40 years (5).

To counsel, providers should encourage women to see an oral health professional regularly (in general at least yearly). All patients should be encouraged to brush their teeth daily with a fluoride-containing toothpaste and to use dental floss each day. Patients should be counseled to avoid or cease the use of tobacco in any form and to limit alcohol consumption.

Breast Self-Examination (BSE)

Self examination is a less sensitive form of screening for breast cancer than clinical examination. Its specificity is uncertain. Among participants in a breast cancer registry, BSE was reported to detect 34% of cancers. Although training sessions increase detection rates, they also increase false-positive rates.

Major authorities disagree on their recommendation regarding BSE. The USPSTF states there is insufficient evidence to recommend for or against teaching BSE in periodic health examination (2). The ACS recommends monthly BSE for all women older than age 20 years (12).

Pamphlets, videotapes, and breast models are available from several sources, including the ACS, to assist in the instruction of women in BSE by clinicians.

Counseling for High-Risk Groups

Many counseling topics are recommended for members of high-risk groups and are not considered appropriate for all persons in the age group. The USPSTF recommends the counseling shown in Table 6.1.4 for high-risk women (2).

Special Considerations for Nurse Practitioners and Physician Assistants

To effectively implement preventive health care for women, nurse providers and physician assistants must recognize the multidimensionality of health—the interaction of physiological, psychological, sociocultural, spiritual, and developmental domains. As an active participant in her care, a woman must be given as much control as possible and as she desires. However, the care provider must guard against blaming the woman whose individual behaviors have resulted in an unhealthy state; not only do women have unequal opportunities for achieving health, but health may be related to factors beyond the woman's control (45).

Assessment of the woman must be done within the context of her home, community, and workplace. Household and garden chemicals, lead paint, vermin infestation, dust, pollutants, and heating systems are all potential hazards in the home; additionally, the woman may report stressful living conditions related to domestic or urban violence or other situations that she feels powerless to change. The community's history, climate, population mix, income base, housing, air and water quality, disease patterns, and support services are factors that providers within the community must recognize as influences on health (46).

A few basic screening questions about occupational exposures can guide the provider in determining if a more thorough occupational history is needed: What is your current job/career? How many hours per day or week do you work? Are there rotating shifts? What are your longest held jobs? What kinds of toxic chemicals, heavy lifting, prolonged sitting or standing are required? (46, 47). A woman's job as homemaker or wager earner can be a source of stress or satisfaction.

Cultural diversity is a reality today and health care providers must recognize the role that culture plays in a woman's health care practices. Women will vary in the degree to which their lifestyle and health practices reflect their traditional heritage. Providers should note beliefs about health and illness and culturally based health-promoting practices such as particular items of clothing, diet, or protective objects (48). Women may also use alternative forms of healing because of traditional cultural beliefs. Providers must ask women what they do to keep healthy including the use of medications, home remedies, and natural agents.

Counseling for preventive health care has been previously discussed. The relationships that women have and the demands of those relationships can be barriers to exercise and other health promotion strategies. Women may concentrate on their responsibilities and commitments to others and thus feel selfish and in conflict if they give attention to their own needs. Mothers of young children, in particular, have many roles that are high in demand, leaving little time and energy for self-care activities (49). Many women will have to learn to nurture and value themselves rather than nurturing only others (50).

Health care providers must recognize that health promotion is not apolitical. Rules, regulations, and economics will define what services are available and which groups of women access the services and how often. All providers concerned about women and their health must be active in articulating women's needs, validating screening, and care strategies through research and lobbying for changes.

References

1. Clinician's Handbook of Preventive Services. U.S. Department of Health and Human Services, 1994.
2. Report of the U.S. Preventive Services Task Force. Guide to Clinical Preventive Services. 2nd ed. Baltimore: Williams & Wilkins, 1996.
3. Wingo PA, Tong T, Bolden S. Cancer statistics, 1995. CA Cancer J Clin 1995;45:8–30.
4. Frame PS. A critical review of adult health care maintenance. Part 1: prevention of atherosclerotic diseases. J Fam Pract 1986;22:341–346.
5. Mettlin C, Dodd GD. The American Cancer Society guidelines for the cancer-related checkup: an update. CA Cancer J Clin 1991;41:279–282.
6. Oboler SK, LaForce FM. The periodic physical examination in asymptomatic adults. Ann Intern Med 1989;110:214–226.
7. Davis JE, McBride PE, Bobula JA. Improving prevention in primary care: physicians, patients, and process. J Fam Pract 1992;35:385–394.
8. Dickey LL, Petitti D. A patient-held minirecord to promote adult preventive care. J Fam Pract 1992; 34:457–463.
9. Carney PA, Dietrich AJ, Keller A, Landgraf J, O'Connor GT. Tool, teamwork, and tenacity: an office system for cancer prevention. J Fam Pract 1992; 35:388–394.
10. Harris JR, Lippman ME, Veronesi U, Willett W. Breast cancer. (First of three parts). N Engl J Med 1992;327:319–328.
11. Eddy DM. Screening for breast cancer. Ann Intern Med 1989;111:389–399.
12. Dodd GD. American Cancer Society guidelines on screening for breast cancer: an overview. CA Cancer J Clin 1992;42:177–180.
13. Richert-Boe KE, Humphrey LL. Screening for cancers of the cervix and breast. Arch Intern Med 1992; 152:2405–2411.
14. Mettlin C, Jones G, Averette H, Gusberg SB, Murphy GP. Defining and updating the American Cancer Society guidelines for the cancer-related checkup: prostate and endometrial cancers. CA Cancer J Clin 1993;43:42–46.
15. Pritchard KI. Screening for endometrial cancer: is it effective? Ann Intern Med 1989;110:177–179.
16. Richert-Boe KE, Humphrey LL. Screening for cancers of the lung and colon. Arch Intern Med 1992; 152:2398–2404.
17. Friedman RJ, Rigel DS, Silverman MK, Kopf AW, Vossaert KA. Malignant melanoma in the 1990s: the continued importance of early detection and the role of physician examination and self-examination of the skin. CA Cancer J Clin 1991;41:201– 226.
18. Koh HK, Lew RA, Prout MN. Screening for melanoma/skin cancer: theoretic and practical considerations. J Am Acad Dermatol 1989;20:159–172.
19. Mashberg A, Samit AM. Early detection, diagnosis,

20. Goodman HS, Yellowitz JA, Horowitz AM. Oral cancer prevention. The role of family practitioners. Arch Fam Med 1995;4:628–636.
21. Littenberg B, Garber AM, Sox HC. Screening for hypertension. Ann Intern Med 1990;112:192–202.
22. Littenberg B. A practice guideline revisited: screening for hypertension. Ann Intern Med 1995;122: 937–939.
23. National High Blood Pressure Education Program, National Heart, Lung, and Blood Institute. The fifth report of the Joint National Committee on the detection, evaluation, and treatment of high blood pressure (JNC V). Arch Intern Med 1993;153:154–183.
24. Horton JA, ed. The Women's Health Data Book. 2nd ed. Washington, DC: Elsevier, 1995.
25. Bray GA, Gray DS. Obesity. Part 1-Pathogenesis. West J Med 1988;149:429–441.
26. Expert Panel on Detection, Evaluation, and Treatment of High Blood Cholesterol in Adults. Summary of the second report of the National Cholesterol Education Program (NCEP) Expert Panel on Detection, Evaluation, and Treatment of High Blood Cholesterol in Adults (Adult Treatment Panel II). JAMA 1993;269:3015–3023.
27. Havel RJ, Rapaport E. Management of primary hyperlipidemia. N Engl J Med 1995;332:1491–1498.
28. Eddy DM. Screening for cervical cancer. Ann Intern Med 1990;113:214–226.
29. Koss LG. The papanicolaou test for cervical cancer detection. A triumph and a tragedy. JAMA 1989; 261:737–743.
30. Davis DL. Mammographic screening. JAMA 1994; 271:152–153.
31. ACP Task Force on Adult Immunization and Infectious Diseases Society of America. Guide for Adult Immunization. 3rd ed. Philadelphia: American College of Physicians, 1994.
32. LaForce FM. Immunizations, immunoprophylaxis, and chemoprophylaxis to prevent selected infections. JAMA 1987;257:2464–2470.
33. Pate RR, Pratt M, Blair SN, et al. Physical activity and public health. A recommendation from the Centers for Disease Control and Prevention and the American College of Sports Medicine. JAMA 1995; 273:402–407.
34. Harris SS, Caspersen CJ, DeFriese GH, Estes EH. Physical activity counseling for healthy adults as a primary preventive intervention in the clinical setting. Report for the US Preventive Services Task Force. JAMA 1989;261:3590–3598.
35. Bradley KA, Donovan DM, Larson EB. How much is too much? Advising patients about safe levels of alcohol consumption. Arch Intern Med 1993;153: 2734–2740.
36. Kitchens JM. Does this patient have an alcohol problem? JAMA 1994;272:1782–1787.

and management of oropharyngeal cancer. CA Cancer J Clin 1989;39:67–88.

37. Milhorn HT. The diagnosis of alcoholism. Am Fam Physician 1988;37:175–183.
38. Forrest JD. The delivery of family planning services in the United States. Fam Plann Perspect 1988; 20:88, 90–95, 98.
39. Rosenfeld JA, Zahorik PM, Batson J. Unplanned pregnancy: are family practice residents taking all opportunities to make a difference? JABFP 1994; 7:77–79.
40. Waller JR. The physician's role in preventing alcohol-related injuries. JAMA 1988;260:2561–2562.
41. Rosenberg ML, O'Carroll PW, Powell KE. Let's be clear. Violence is a public health problem. JAMA 1992;267:3071–3072.
42. American Medical Association diagnostic and treatment guidelines on domestic violence. Arch Fam Med 1992;1:39–47.
43. Council on Scientific Affairs, American Medical Association. Violence against women. Relevance for medical practitioners. JAMA 1992;267:3184–3189.
44. Greene JC, Louie R, Wycoff SJ. Preventive dentistry. I. Dental caris. JAMA 1989;262:3459–3463.
45. King PM. Health promotion: the emerging frontier in nursing. J Advanced Nurs 1994;20:209–218.
46. Keleher KC. Primary care for women: environmental assessment of the home, community, and workplace. J Nurse Midwifery 1995;40:88–96.
47. Wheeler L. Well-woman assessment. In: Fogel CI, Woods NF, eds. Women's Healthcare. Thousand Oaks, CA: Sage, 1995:141–187.
48. Spector RE. Cultural concepts of women's health and health-promoting behaviors. JOGNN 1995;24: 241–245.
49. Verhoef MJ, Love EJ, Rose MS. Women's social roles and their exercise participation. Women & Health 1992;19:15–29.
50. Davis MS, Youngkin EQ. Health and development through the life cycle. In: Youngkin EQ, Davis MS, eds., Women's Health. Norwalk: Appleton & Lange, 1994:17–32.

Suggested Reading

Horton JA ed. The Women's Health Data Book. 2nd ed. Washington, DC: Elsevier, 1995.

6.2

Smoking Effects and Cessation

Jean L. Kristeller and Thomas J. Johnson

Epidemiology

Since the first Surgeon General's Report on the health risks of smoking in 1964, the proportion of smokers in the US population has declined significantly (1). There are as many ex-smokers among living adults as there are current smokers. However, smoking continues to be the largest cause of preventable health problems in the United States (1). Between 26 and 28% of American men and 22 to 23% of American women were regular smokers in 1993 (2, 3).

Among older individuals, the percentage of women smokers is lower; among women over 85 years of age, more than 90% have never smoked.

Many more men who smoked have quit than women. Comparison of changes in the smoking rates for men and women suggest an ironic and sinister meaning to the advertising phrase, "You've come a long way baby." The rate of decline in cigarette smoking has been much sharper for men than for women. The primary reason for the shrinking gap has been that initiation of smoking increased in women, whereas it declined in men (1). Over the years, more women have started smoking, particularly young undereducated women.

Other trends in the demographics of smokers are also of concern. The proportion of smokers who come from lower income levels have increased over time, although the age of initiation has fallen, particularly among women (1). Most smokers begin smoking between the sixth and ninth grades, and few, if any, start after their 20s (4, 5). Smoking prevalences are higher among individuals with lower levels of education (1). Individuals with a high school education or less are three times more likely to smoke than those with a college education (1, 4, 5).

Differences in prevalence occur between racial and ethnic groups (1, 2); African-American men smoke substantially more (35.5%) than do white or Hispanic men. Hispanic women smoke at a lower level (15.5%) than either African-American or non-Hispanic white women, equal percentages of whom smoke (6). Much of the antismoking message has been directed toward the better-educated consumer, and educational level may account for much of the observed differences (7).

There are also regional differences in prevalence for some age groups. For example, 80% of all women age 65 to 74 years have never smoked, but this drops to 60% or less in urban New England and the South (8).

Risk from Smoking

Prior to the early 1980s, it was thought that smoking did not present as great a health risk for women as it did for men. Because rates of smoking in women did not begin a sharp rise until World War II, it was not until the late 1960s that adverse health effects of smoking began to be observed in women in rates comparable with those observed in men (9). In 1985, more than twice as many women died of smoking as in 1965, leading Solomon and Flynn to observe that "women who smoke like men die like men" (10).

According to the 1989 Surgeon General's Report, one of six deaths in the United States is attributable to smoking. In 1985, there were 390,000 deaths attributable to either smoking-related illness, effects of environmental tobacco smoke, cigarette-caused fires, or effects of maternal smoking (1). This implies that tobacco companies need to recruit 10,000 new smokers daily to replace those who have died.

Smokers die 12 to 15 years prematurely. Across several studies, mortality ratios for smokers ranged from 1.29 to 2.34 for men and from 1.20 to 1.90 for women (11). The cost of smokers' ill health, in terms of lost work time, decreased productivity, and excess health care costs, was estimated at over $100 billion for the year 1994 alone (12).

Cigarette smoke contains over 4000 compounds. The components of cigarette smoke most responsible for the health consequences of smoking are tar, nicotine, and carbon monoxide, besides many other toxic and mutagenic compounds (1). Cigarette, pipe, and cigar smoking all have an adverse impact on health, as do use of smokeless tobacco and exposure to environmental tobacco smoke. However, cigarette smoking carries the greatest risk by far.

Smoking and Women's Health

Fertility and Pregnancy Issues

Smoking has been consistently shown to decrease fertility in women of childbearing age, to lower the age of menopause, and to increase incidences of secondary amenorrhea and vaginal bleeding. These effects may be related to nicotine acting directly on the hypothalamus or pituitary, producing alterations in hormonal regulatory mechanisms (9).

Between 20 and 45% of pregnant women smoke during pregnancy (13). Smoking during pregnancy contributes to lower birth weights, increased prenatal and postnatal mortality, increased risk of spontaneous abortion, long-term deficiencies in physical and mental development, and, perhaps, Sudden Infant Death Syndrome (9, 13, 14). Nicotine crosses the placental barrier, resulting in increased fetal heart rate during the second trimester and in decreased fetal heart rate and breathing movements during the third trimester. The vasoconstrictive effects of nicotine, in combination with placental abnormalities associated with smoking and the presence of carbon monoxide in fetal hemoglobin, further contribute to reduced oxygen supply to the fetus (14). In addition, various toxic compounds, including cyanide, cadmium, and polycyclic aromatic hydrocarbons, may be deposited in the fetus or placenta (9, 14).

In the United States, women who continue to smoke during pregnancy are younger, less educated, more likely to be living with another smoker, less likely to have social support and encouragement for quitting, separated or never married, of lower income, and more likely to be depressed and/or consider their pregnancy unwanted compared with nonsmokers (2, 13, 15–17). Factors predictive of successful smoking cessation during pregnancy include previous success at quitting for at least 1 week, higher self-efficacy, stronger beliefs in the dangers of maternal smoking, greater use of prenatal health care services, and, among African-American women only, an intent to breast feed (15, 18, 19).

Over half the women who quit smoking during pregnancy start smoking again from 1 to 3 months postpartum, with 70% or more relapsing within 1 year (13). Factors found predictive of postpartum relapse include living with other smokers, lack of social support for maintenance of smoking cessation, concerns about weight gain, low self-efficacy, and formula feeding. Believing that children of smokers are more likely to develop infections is predictive of successful abstinence (13, 18–20).

Cardiovascular Disease

Heart diseases are the leading cause of death in the United States for both men and women, and for all major racial and ethnic groups (2). In both men and women, cigarette smoking is the major preventable cause of coronary heart disease, accounting for 40% of the attributable risk (21). For both African-American and white women, cerebrovascular diseases are the third leading cause of death (2). Smoking has been implicated as a risk factor for cerebrovascular disease, particularly among younger age groups (21). Smoking also is the leading risk factor for the development of atherosclerotic peripheral vascular disease and a strong contributor to the development of arteriosclerosis and aortic aneurysms.

Smoking interacts synergistically with many other independent risk factors for cardiovascular diseases, including hypertension and elevated blood cholesterol (9). For example, although an acute effect of cigarette smoking is to increase blood pressure, there is no evidence that smoking contributes to the development of hypertension (21). However, individuals with hypertension who also smoke cigarettes have a much greater risk for cardiovascular disease than would be the case from either risk factor acting alone.

Of additional concern to women is the synergistic effect of smoking and oral contraceptive use. Women who smoke and use oral contraceptives have 10 times the risk of a myocardial infarction (MI) compared with women who neither smoke nor use oral contraceptives (21).

A variety of causal factors are involved in the relationship between cigarette smoking and cardiovascular and cerebrovascular diseases. Carbon monoxide in cigarette smoke replaces oxygen in up to 10% of blood hemoglobin, increasing stress on the heart by depriving it of oxygen (22). Nicotine increases heart rate and oxygen consumption, contributes to rhythm irregularities, and produces vasoconstriction in the periphery (21). These effects are produced by nicotine's direct stimulation of the sympathetic nervous system, stimulation of the release of epinephrine and norepinephrine from the adrenal gland and peripheral nervous system, and stimulation of chemoreceptors in the aortic arch and carotid artery (23). Nicotine also contributes to damage of arterial walls, increases platelet aggregation, and increases the development of thrombi, causing myocardial or cerebral infarctions (21, 24). The synergistic effects of smoking and oral contraceptive use may be caused in part by exaggerated physiological responses to stress, including increased cholesterol and free fatty acids (25).

Of particular relevance to women is the role of smoking in developing high levels of triglycerides and low levels of high-density lipoproteins (HDLs). The association between low HDLs and heart disease is clearer for women than for men (26). Several recent studies support the possibility that smoking is a greater risk factor for cardiovascular disease in women than in men (27). Wister and Gee found that heavy smoking increased the risk of early death from ischemic heart disease fivefold for women, compared with threefold for men (27).

Quitting smoking does lower the risk of cardiovascular problems, both for healthy individuals and those who have developed cardiovascular diseases (24, 28). Individuals who quit smoking after their first heart attack reduced the risk of a second MI by up to 50%. Unfortunately, 50 to 70% of patients resume smoking after an MI (24). Although evidence is limited, relapse rates among women cardiac patients may be higher than among men (24).

Diabetes

Although smoking does not play a causal role in diabetes, it increases the risk of cardiac complications from diabetes approximately 10-fold and may be overlooked as a significant risk factor in management of diabetes. Smoking is a major factor in peripheral vascular disease and subsequent amputations. The rate of smoking among diabetics is as high or higher than in the general population. In particular, diabetic smokers may overvalue the benefits of smoking for weight and stress management (29).

Lung Disease

Chronic obstructive pulmonary disease (COPD), including chronic bronchitis, emphysema, chronic asthma, and chronic bronchiolitis, occurs only rarely in nonsmokers (see Chapter 14) (24). The 1984 Surgeon General's Report concluded that cigarette smoking is the major cause of COPD for both men and women (30). Although most Americans are aware of the effects of smoking on respiratory problems, as of 1986 substantial numbers of smokers still did not believe that smoking causes emphysema and bronchitis (1).

The death rate for COPD has remained relatively stable for white men during the past 10 years (between 28 and 29 deaths per 100,000), but the death rate for white women has been rising steadily since 1980, from 9.2 deaths per 100,000 at that time to just over 16 deaths per 100,000 in 1992 (2). Death rates for African-American women remain lower than for other groups, but they have also increased slightly, from 6.3 deaths per 100,000 in 1980 to approximately 11 deaths per 100,000 annually between 1988 and 1992 (31).

Besides COPD, functional impairments in respiration and significant respiratory symptoms such as cough, phlegm production, and shortness of breath are observable even in young smokers after as little as 1 year of smoking (31). The 1993 report of the Environmental Protection Agency on the dangers of environmental tobacco smoke (ETS) concluded that ETS causes increased risk of lower respiratory infections in infants and children up to 18 months, causes exacerbation of symptoms in children with asthma (including increase in asthmatic episodes), and is a risk factor for the development of asthma in healthy children and onset of asthma later in life (31). Rates of hospitalization for respiratory problems among children are approximately double if the mother or other primary caretaker is a smoker (9).

The exact causal mechanisms responsible for COPD remain incompletely understood (1). Cigarette smoke inhibits the action of cilia in the lungs and tracheae; this allows build up of foreign matter in the lungs and reduces ability to clear mucus from air passages (32). Cigarette smoke damages small airway passages in the lungs, producing chronic inflammation and bronchial obstruction (1, 30, 31). It also produces uninhibited proteolytic activity, consistently associated with emphysema. Other changes include increased mucus production as a result of hypertrophy and hyperplasia of upper airway mucous glands, destruction of the alveolar walls and decrease in lung elasticity, and perhaps increased mucosal permeability to allergens (31). Quitting smoking will lead to fewer symptoms, and with sustained abstinence, up to 50% reduction in mortality rates. However, mortality rates and pulmonary function in former smokers with emphysema will never entirely return to the levels for nonsmokers (28).

Cancer

Cancer is the second leading cause of death in the United States for both women and men across most ethnic groups (2). Tobacco use contributes to 25 to 30% of all cancer deaths, and heavy smokers have three to four times greater risk of cancer mortality than nonsmokers (31, 33). Cigarette smoking alone accounts for 85% or more of all deaths from lung cancer (31). The major cause of laryngeal cancer, cancers of the oral cavity, and esophageal cancer is cigarette smoking. Cigar and pipe smokers have a risk of laryngeal, oral, and esophageal cancer equal to that of cigarette smokers. Environmental tobacco smoke causes an estimated 3000 additional lung cancer deaths annually in nonsmoking adults. Cigarette smoking also contributes to the development of cancers of the bladder, kidneys, pancreas, and probably the stomach (33). Recent evidence has also supported a causal association between cigarette smoking and both cervical cancer (1) and cervical dysplasia (34).

A disturbing illustration of the effect of smoking on women's health may be the historical change in the prevalence of lung cancer among women. As the generations of women who started smoking in the 1940s and 1950s have grown older, the incidence of lung cancer in women has risen. The death rate per 100,000 from lung cancer in 1950 was 4.6 for white women and 4.1 for African-American women. By 1992 it had risen to over 27 per 100,000 for both groups (2). Lung cancer is now the leading cause of cancer death among women in the United States, and is second only to breast cancer in incidence (35, 36). Miller et al. found that women who smoke were 9 times more likely to die of lung cancer than nonsmoking women exposed to environmental tobacco smoke (ETS) and 42 times as likely as nonsmoking women who were not exposed to ETS (37). Women smokers develop lung cancer as severe as do men who smoke, but do so at a younger age and despite having smoked for fewer years (36). Among women diagnosed with breast cancer, smoking appears to increase the likelihood of cancer spreading to the lungs (38).

Smoking produces histologic changes and damage at a variety of sites, including changes and lesions of cells in the bronchial epithelium, lesions in the larynx, thickening and keratinization of oral mucosa, and cell abnormalities in the esophagus. Smoking and alcohol use appears to produce synergistic effects in some cancers, particularly laryngeal, oral, and esophageal cancers (33).

Individuals who quit smoking after cancer diagnosis may benefit by longer survival, development of fewer secondary cancers, fewer associated pathologies, and fewer medical complications and lower morbidity from cancer treatment, including chemotherapy, radiation, surgery, reduced unpleasant side effects from radiation therapy, increased rate of wound healing, less immunosuppression from radiation or chemotherapy, possible increased efficacy of chemotherapy, and better appetite and nutrition. Despite the once popular assumption that smoking cessation could do little for cancer patients (the "after all, they are going to die, so you might as well let them enjoy their cigarettes" mentality), quitting smoking is clearly a major step cancer patients can take toward both better survival and increased quality of life (32). Even in individuals with types of cancers not clearly linked to smoking (e.g., breast cancer, prostate cancer), quitting smoking will likely improve the prognosis through one or more of these effects.

Other Medical Issues

Smoking contributes to many other conditions of varying severity. Women who smoke are twice as likely to develop peptic ulcer disease, and continued smoking decreases the likelihood of ulcer healing (9). Women smokers are also more likely than nonsmokers to develop osteoporosis; this can contribute to disabling and potentially fatal fractures (1). Smoking affects the connective tissue of the skin, resulting in the wrinkled visage often associated with the older woman smoker. Although this may not be a significant health problem, it may be a negative effect of smoking that could serve as an important motivator for some individuals.

Smoking-related fires are the number one cause of civilian fire deaths in the United States (12), whether set by the smoker or by a child playing with readily available matches.

Such fires killed more than 2300 adults and children in 1983 and burned more than 5000 others.

Why Do Women Smoke? The Biopsychosocial Model

If there were one simple answer to the question of why women smoke, there would be no need for chapters such as this one. All serious thinkers in the addictions field must acknowledge that any addiction, nicotine dependence included, is "determined by an interplay of causes, no one sufficient, no one necessary" (39).

The biopsychosocial model presumes such a multiplicity of forces (40). This model recognizes that biological factors such as biochemistry, genetics, pathophysiology, psychological factors (e.g., learning experiences, motivation, self-image), and social factors (e.g., family dynamics), "peer pressure," and political and economic forces, all contribute. Table 6.2.1 outlines the major components of the biopsychosocial model as related to smoking and relates them to relevant intervention components. In comparison with men, women may be particularly sensitive to three factors: (1) dealing with stress or negative affect, (2) concern about weight gain, and (3) a greater need for social support.

Biological Factors

The biological basis of smoking addiction is attributable to the pharmacology of nicotine (41), and cigarettes are a highly effective drug-delivery device. Nicotine enters the bloodstream both through the lungs and the buccal mucosa and is rapidly distributed throughout the body, affecting the central nervous system in less than 1 minute (22, 23).

At the doses found in cigarette smoke, nicotine is a cholinergic agonist, attaching directly to acetylcholinesterase (ACh) receptors.

Table 6.2.1. The Biopsychosocial Model

Source	Factors Contributing to the Development, Maintenance, and/or Relapse of a Smoking Habit	Interventions Based on Each Factor
Biological or physiological factors	Pharmacology of nicotine, e.g., euphoriant effects, value as a positive reinforcer, anorexic effects	Nicotine replacement therapy, e.g., nicotine gum, nicotine patch
	Repeated exposure to nicotine—development of tolerance and withdrawal	Switching to lower nicotine brands; tapering (i.e., gradually reducing number smoked per day)
Psychological factors	Conditioned associations between situations, behaviors, and emotional states	Behavioral interventions, e.g., self-monitoring, stimulus control, aversive conditioning
	Lack of knowledge or misperceptions about the effects of smoking	Providing information about smoking
	Psychological stress or emotional dependence on smoking	Relaxation, meditation, or stress management training
	Lack of alternative coping skills	Functional response substitution
	Sensation-seeking personality style	Exploring motives and assessing alternatives
Social or cultural factors	Modeling of smoking behavior	Encourage individuals to identify with non-smokers and take more initiative; assertiveness training
	Social and cultural pressure to smoke	Culturally sensitive intervention; support local antismoking campaigns

Nicotine also stimulates the release of ACh in the cerebral cortex and the release of a host of pituitary (e.g., prolactin, ACTH, β-endorphin, β-lipotropin, growth hormone, vasopressin, neurophysin) and adrenal hormones (e.g., epinephrine, norepinephrine) (23). Recent evidence suggests that nicotine is a potent enhancer of synaptic transmission (42). This complexity of responses leads nicotine to have both stimulant and relaxant effects.

Nicotine is an addictive drug. According to the 1988 Surgeon General's Report it is to be considered in the same class as heroin or cocaine (41). According to the Diagnostic and Statistical Manual of Mental Disorders (DSM-IV) (43), nicotine dependence fits the following criteria: (1) users frequently and compul-

sively ingest the drug, (2) the drug produces a euphoria or high, and (3) the drug functions as a reinforcer (e.g., both humans and laboratory animals learn to perform various responses to self-administer the drug). As in other addictive substances, smokers also show both acute and chronic tolerance and a characteristic withdrawal syndrome when they cease to use the drug.

Unlike most other drugs of abuse, nicotine is not an intoxicant; however, most regular users become dependent and addicted. Progressing from initial use, through a period of "experimentation," to regular use to dependency may take several years (44). After more than approximately a half pack (10 cigarettes) per day, the smoker may be smoking to titrate blood nicotine levels at a regular level. A heavy smoker (40 to 80 cigarettes per day) averages a cigarette less than every 15 to 30 minutes during waking hours, maintains high levels of blood nicotine, and may start to experience disturbed sleep because of withdrawal during the night. As amount of cigarettes smoked increases, cutting back is increasingly likely to produce withdrawal symptoms and craving.

As with any drug, ingestion of nicotine occurs because the smoker is both seeking out the positive effects of the drug and avoiding the negative seeking effects of withdrawal. Positive effects reported by smokers are numerous. Smoking a cigarette also produces short-term increases in concentration and alertness, and leads to peripheral nervous system activation. It may, therefore, be used as a mild stimulant or to fight drowsiness. Paradoxically, in ways that are not yet clearly understood, smoking appears to decrease the experience of stress. However, withdrawal produces many opposite experiences, including agitation, irritability, disturbed sleep, and decreases in ability to concentrate. Most of the withdrawal symptoms peak after 3 to 4 days of abstinence and are greatly reduced by 1 week. Ability to concentrate gradually returns to normal in 3 to 6 weeks after quitting.

Particularly relevant to women are the documented effects on weight regulation. Nicotine, particularly when inhaled in tobacco smoke, acts as an effective anorexic by affecting taste bud sensitivity, appetite, and metabolism. Evidence suggests that smoking leads to an acute increase in resting metabolic rate (45). A biologically driven decrease in preference for sweet foods may occur (46). These factors, along with behavioral factors, may account for the 7- to 10-lb weight difference between smokers and nonsmokers; when someone stops smoking, this is also the average amount of weight gained. In one survey of ex-smokers, less than 15% of women reported gaining as much as 25 lbs (47).

Psychological Factors

Several types of conditioning (learning) processes are active in the development and maintenance of smoking behavior (48). The pharmacological effects of nicotine become associated with behaviors (e.g., opening a pack and lighting up) and situations (e.g., experiencing stress, drinking coffee) so that in time the situations become powerful triggers for smoking behavior. As with other drugs, those behaviors or situations alone can then come to trigger physiological changes experienced as a craving for the drug (49). In only 1 year, a one-pack-per-day smoker would engage in the behavior of smoking over 7000 times, each time strengthening the associations between smoking and a variety of situations and behaviors.

Early work on smoking motivation identified six dimensions: (1) reduction of negative affect, (2) stimulation, (3) habit, (4) pleasure, (5) addiction, and (6) physical manipulation, which have been replicated many times (50) and led to the development of the "Why Do You Smoke?" Scale (see Reference Materials and Other Resources). Women may be more likely to smoke both to reduce negative affect and to increase pleasure (51). Recent work identified three dimensions in young adults: (1) expectations for positive effects, such as stimulation and social facilitation, (2) reduction of negative emotions including anxiety, depression and irritability, and (3) desire for weight and appetite control, a dimension primarily important to women (52). This study also found that after smokers quit, the appeal of smoking for reducing negative affect dropped for men but remained elevated for female ex-smokers, suggesting that women in particular continue to miss the mood-elevating effects.

A variety of other psychological and social factors have been implicated in the development and maintenance of nicotine addiction. Although the idea of an addictive personality has little or no empirical support, both depression and antisocial personality disorder have been found to correlate positively with use of various psychoactive substances, including nicotine (53, 54).

Smoking may serve as a relatively easy way to rebel, to assert passage into adulthood. One study found that people who began smoking were more rebellious, impulsive, and extraverted (55). Those who were still smokers 20 years later were more hostile and sensation seeking. There were no differences, however, between men and women.

Stress

Stress is one of the three most common triggers, in addition to social pressures and drinking, given by smokers as a reason for relapse (56). It is also one of the most commonly cited reasons offered by women smokers for continuing to smoke (57). A large study of African-Americans found that those reporting higher levels of stress were more likely to be smokers; women in particular were more likely to smoke if they had weak social networks (58). Consistent with nicotine's effects on the endogenous opiates, some smokers may be "self-medicating" an anxiety disorder by smoking. However, all individuals experience stress because of normal life events, and and it may be quite common to develop a degree of dependency on nicotine as a way to handle effects of everyday stressors.

The relaxing effects of smoking may also be independent of the anxiolytic drug effects. Taking a smoking "break" to get away momentarily from daily hassles may become an important part of a smoker's routine. The act of inhaling deeply and regularly while attending to smoking rather than to a stressor may trigger some of the same "relaxation" effects that accompany certain meditation practices.

Depression and Other Psychiatric Disorders

Depression substantially decreases the likelihood of quitting smoking. Why this is the case is not completely clear. It may be because of

biochemical effects of nicotine, both on the central nervous system and through increased activation of the autonomic nervous system. Smokers are more likely to have a history of depression, and depressed individuals have lower quit rates (59). A recent study found that women who felt depressed were 1.5 times more likely to smoke (48). However, a prospective study of 3960 adults over 65 years of age found that whereas smokers were more likely to be clinically depressed, 3 years later this group was almost four times as likely to have quit smoking (60).

Other types of major mental illness, particularly chronic schizophrenia, also carry a particularly high comorbidity with smoking; up to 80% of individuals with major mental illness are smokers (61). The rate of smoking among alcoholics is also greater than 80% (62). Smokers also generally have higher levels of alcohol intake (63), even in relatively healthy high-functioning individuals (64).

Social Factors

Smoking habits develop early in life. A variety of sociocultural factors affect adolescent women and promote adoption of regular smoking. These include greater acceptability of smoking in lower socioeconomic groups, modeling of smoking behavior by parents or family members, the adolescent's fear of rejection by friends who smoke, desire to live up to the glamorous image of women portrayed in cigarette advertisements, and concerns about body weight and body image that may become paramount during adolescence. These factors are recognized and exploited by tobacco manufacturers to appeal to identified groups, with such cigarettes as Virginia Slims promoted with ads featuring extremely thin young women.

Many influences on adolescent boys and girls appear be similar, with social influence from both parents and peers playing a major role (65). However, weight management is much more salient for adolescent girls (66).

There is also typically a clustering of problems, with smoking particularly associated with poor school attendance (67). Adolescents acknowledge the health impact of smoking and the reality of addiction (68), but they are less likely to see these factors as personally relevant. Although the price of cigarettes is often raised as a barrier to initiation, compared with other drugs, cigarettes are inexpensive (even at $2.50 a pack, this is only 12 cents a "hit") and readily available from vending machines, if not from local stores that ignore age purchase rules.

Rates of both smoking and quitting vary considerably by ethnic group and by socioeconomic level (69). For example, a study of African-American women age 18 to 40 years living in public housing found that compared with other African-American women they started smoking earlier, were heavier smokers, and had less motivation to quit (70). However, in this study white women tended to be even heavier smokers and did not differ from more affluent African-American women in their interest in quitting or level of health concern. Contrary to stereotype, less-educated women of both races were more concerned about weight gain, and less educated African-American women among the non-public housing comparison group were the most concerned about negative health effects. Such complex relationships as this suggest the importance of understanding the issues as they are meaningful to each individual smoker.

Approaches to Quitting

Patterns of Cessation and Maintenance in Women

Women have lower quit rates than do men (9). This has been found within the general population and also within medical populations. For example, among the 4000 smokers with mild lung disease in the major NIH-funded Lung Health Study, 40.8% of men quit for at least 1 month after a 12-week group smoking cessation program with free access to Nicorette gum compared with 35.8% of the women (71). Women also were more likely to make use of the nicotine gum both initially and 2 years later. However, there were no differences in relapse rates after 1 year. There is limited evidence that women may also experience more distressing withdrawal symptoms, particularly within the first 24 hours of an attempt at quitting. They also have more increased symptoms in the second half of their menstrual cycle compared with the first half (72), and may be more susceptible to relapse-related to withdrawal symptoms (73).

However, when other variables are considered, gender may not have as clear an effect. For example, higher sustained abstinence rates among men in a group of cardiac patients disappeared when severity of disease, an independent predictor of abstinence, was considered (74). Women with more severe cardiovascular disease tended to be as likely to quit successfully, as were men with similar levels of disease. Depression may also play a similar role. Women are more likely to have higher levels of depression than men; this may account for the difference in sustained abstinence rates among some groups of individuals.

Many factors affect the ability to quit smoking and remain abstinent. Biological, psychological, and social factors affect most smokers, but to differing degrees and in different ways. Although there are common issues for most smokers, the following discussion of treatment issues will assume a high degree of individual difference among smokers, and will assume the need to assist every smoker in identifying and addressing those issues most important to herself.

Stages of Change

Individuals rarely quit using an addictive substance suddenly and without preparation. Change in any behavior, especially addictive behavior, may best be viewed as a process occurring over time. Prochaska and DiClemente described this process as involving a set of relatively distinct stages (75).

Smokers who are not actively considering stopping are at the "precontemplation" stage and are a minority of current smokers. Those individuals seriously considering quitting are in the "contemplation stage." Such individuals are more likely to take the time to attend to and think about information on the adverse effects of smoking or techniques of quitting.

Provider interventions and advice help the patient move from the precontemplation to contemplation stage. Various health issues, such as pregnancy, may also increase the frequency with which the patient reminds herself, "I really ought to quit." Although the contemplation stage includes smokers "seriously intending to quit within the next three months," the average length of time people remain contemplators is 3 years. Consequently, there may be many ways to help a smoker move more quickly toward quitting.

At the "prepared for action stage" an individual actively begins to prepare to quit smoking. She may switch to a lower tar/nicotine brand, cut down on number of cigarettes, and begin to think more negatively about smoking. The "action" stage is defined by actually quitting for at least 24 hours. Quitting or cutting down requires engaging in many behaviors, from getting rid of extra cigarettes to removing lighters and cleaning or throwing out ashtrays. Someone abstaining from smoking must resist many future temptations in order to remain an ex-smoker. Temptations include passing a display of cigarettes at the convenience store, being around active smokers, or being under stress. If abstinence is unsuccessful, full relapse most commonly results and the smoker returns to one of the previous stages. However, a smoker in the relapse stage (a smoker who quit for at least 24 hours in the last year) is more likely to quit permanently in the following year than someone who did not try. The typical smoker quits three times before reaching the "maintenance stage," defined as sustaining abstinence for 1 year.

According to the "stages of change" model, resistance or denial are not personality characteristics of an addict, but normal steps in the process of change. Consequently different interventions may be useful at different stages. Telling a precontemplator how to quit may be met with hostility or indifference, whereas more information on the dangers of smoking would be wasted on someone in the action stage. Finally, someone who has recently relapsed may benefit from reinforcement for the attempt, from being asked to consider what was learned from the previous quit and from encouragement to try again. Keeping the stages in mind when discussing a patient's smoking habit will allow more effective interventions by the primary care physician and reduce the natural frustration the physician may experience when a smoker does not quit despite advice to do so.

Treating Nicotine Addiction

Most individuals who have chronically used tobacco products will develop withdrawal symptoms when they quit using such products. The primary withdrawal symptoms, including irritability, restlessness, and anxiety, peak after about 3 to 4 days of abstinence and are substantially diminished after 7 days. However, certain other changes, such as craving cigarettes, change in appetite and decrements in concentration, may remain for several weeks to months.

The purpose of nicotine replacement therapy (NRT), including both nicotine gum and the recently approved nicotine nasal spray, is to reduce withdrawal symptoms; it is effective in that regard. The effectiveness of the nasal spray in long-term abstinence may be even higher than that of gum or the patch (Silagy et al., 1994). However, nicotine replacement does not diminish a smoker's report of cravings or desire to smoke (48), because it doesn't affect the strong habit components of smoking. Furthermore, nicotine absorbed through a patch or with gum does not offer the same positive central nervous system "hit" that occurs with smoking, although the nicotine spray, with a faster delivery time, may be better in this regard. The use of NRT can contribute substantially to an individual's ability to quit and remain abstinent over at least several months, but is easily overridden by other factors that can lead to relapse (76). However, most individuals use neither enough gum nor continue to use patches long enough to gain the full benefit. It is imperative that smokers view the use of NRT only as a way to limit the desire for nicotine—not as a magic cure while they are learning how to "be a non-smoker." Relapse prevention may also be served by encouraging the ex-smoker to keep either gum or the patch available on a per-need basis for several years to use whenever cravings are triggered by stress or other events.

Brand switching and tapering the number of cigarettes are two other approaches that can be helpful in reducing nicotine dependence. When switching to brands with lower levels of nicotine, smokers must guard against compensating for the decreased levels by inhaling more deeply or smoking more cigarettes. Tapering the number of cigarettes can be even more useful, as this decreases both the pharmacological dependence and the behavioral dependence. A recommended approach to tapering is to cut out "low need" cigarettes first and then progress toward cutting out more desired cigarettes. A typical protocol would be to reduce intake by a half pack per week, down to between 10 to 15 cigarettes, and then go "cold turkey." Tapering down further than this may be counterproductive as each cigarette becomes even more desirable.

Treating Psychological Dependency

Cognitive-behavioral smoking intervention techniques assist the smoker first in identifying their own patterns of psychological dependency and then in overcoming them (77). Self-monitoring involves having the smoker systematically record the time, place, situation, and level of desirability ("need") for each cigarette. This increases awareness of stimuli and situations that have become triggers for smoking. Usually 1 or 2 weeks of self-monitoring is adequate to identify basic patterns and to identify high and low "need" cigarettes.

Once triggers have been identified, two steps need to occur: breaking the associations between the situations and smoking, and helping the smoker find functional substitutes for cigarette. Some techniques are designed specifically to decrease the appeal of smoking. Aversion therapy, although not widely used, pairs noxious stimuli with the act of smoking by use of mental imaging, rapid smoking, or smoke holding (78). Some smokers use "butt" jars, carrying the ends of cigarettes in small jars of water and occasionally smelling the jar to remind them of the unpleasant side of smoking. Others may remind themselves of other negative consequences of smoking, form personal health problems to higher cleaning bills. Breaking habits may involve changing a daily routine, such as getting out of bed and going in to the bathroom immediately instead of reaching for the pack of cigarettes on the nightstand. Other stimulus control procedures include smoking by the clock (at regular time intervals rather than when a craving hits or whenever one feels like it), removing smoking-related paraphernalia (such as ashtrays or lighters) that trigger a desire to smoke from the home, office, and limiting all smoking to a designated smoking area.

Functional response substitution may be harder and take longer, but is even more important. Smoking serves many needs for most individuals, from relaxation to stimulation to a way to open a social conversation by offering a cigarette. Heavy smokers who began in high school may have developed few adult alternatives to smoking as a way to function in many parts of their daily life. How to relax without smoking, how to keep from being bored, or how to finish a meal without a cigarette may require not only some ingenuity and effort but also an extended trial-and-error learning process. Other types of response substitution may also be useful, such as engaging in a behavior difficult to do while smoking, such as chewing on a toothpick, gum, hard candy, or keeping one's hands busy fiddling with a pencil, rubber band, or other small object. Handling stress or other negative emotions may be particularly difficult if the primary way of coping with negative affect has been smoking. Learning deep breathing techniques, which mimic inhaling on a cigarette, may be particularly useful for some smokers.

Relapse prevention in relation to psychological factors often involves anticipating low-frequency events (e.g., a personal crisis, attending a party, celebrating a success) that had previously been associated with smoking and mentally preparing how to handle the situation without smoking. Another important element of relapse prevention is simply educating the smoker that urges or cravings may occur for a long time, even for many years; such urges do not mean that the ex-smoker is weak or destined to smoke again. An ex-smoker who slips and has a single cigarette is particularly vulnerable to the Abstinence Violation Effect (AVE). This is a common but dangerous reaction in which the person feels guilty for breaking her "vow of abstinence," blames herself for being "weak-willed," and then thinks that she might as well keep on going because she was destined for failure anyway. This pattern was first identified as characteristic of alcoholics attempting to abstain (79), but is familiar to most of us in regard to dieting and other types of self-control efforts.

Other Psychological Factors

Alcoholism
It is important to be sensitive to the increased difficulty that heavy drinkers may have in quitting smoking. At the same time, a heavy smoker may be more immediately vulnerable to lung or cardiac disease than to alcohol-related disease. The health care provider should not presume that an alcoholic is disinterested in stopping smoking nor refuse assistance until alcohol intake has ceased (62). For example, a high proportion of men who referred themselves to a hospital-based smoking program run by the first author were found to meet the criteria for alcohol dependency. Stopping smoking may provide a successful experience with changing an addictive behavior that could increase a sense of self-efficacy in changing drinking patterns. Many Alcoholics Anonymous groups are now smoke-free, further supporting such efforts.

Concern with Weight
For women, one of the most frequently cited concerns with stopping smoking is anticipated weight gain. One study found that over 20% of male smokers surveyed cited weight gain as the reason they returned to smoking (28). Although many more women than men perceive appetite and weight control as one of the desirable effects of smoking (52) and desire assistance with weight control when quitting (80). Women who continue to smoke in order to manage their weight may be masking mildly disordered eating patterns and may eat more when they stop smoking (81). In patients with bulimia, stopping smoking may lead to increased appetite and food intake (82). Among older smokers, both men and women often express concern about weight gain. Recent evidence also suggests that the initial weight gain after stopping smoking may reverse itself somewhat after approximately 2 years (83). Such a pattern might be particularly likely for women who initially substitute food for smoking and then gradually find other ways to manage their behavior. However, there is also substantial evidence that weight may be gained after smoking cessation with no increase in caloric intake (84).

Under no circumstances should the physician accept concern about weight as a legitimate reason to continue to smoke. One message that should be communicated is that smoking is an unhealthy way to control weight, particularly to any woman for whom both smoking and weight are current risk factors, such as diabetics, cardiac patients, or pulmonary patients. For example, a cardiac patient would have to gain up to 80 lbs to have weight reach the same level of risk as from one pack of cigarettes. At the same time, concern about weight should be treated as a legitimate and realistic concern. Inquiring into how much weight gain might be tolerated and offering assistance with compulsive eating patterns, if indicated, is appropriate. If craving for sweets is predominant, satisfying such cravings with low-calorie sweets or hard candy, rather than sweet foods also high in fats, such as cake or ice cream, may be helpful in the short term. Women who perceive extreme pressure to remain as thin as possible may need guidance in exploring these concerns. Smoking and eating may also serve similar psychological functions for women, in particular, relief of negative affect (85). Assisting a woman to look elsewhere to handle stress in her life, such as stress management or other brief therapy, may be important.

Unfortunately, efforts to reduce the amount of weight gained after stopping smoking by providing weight management programs have been discouraging in four well-controlled studies (10). Increased exercise also does not appear to counteract the changes that occur. The value of nicotine replacement therapy as a means to limit weight loss is not clear and results have been mixed (86). NRT may allow some women to limit weight gain while making other changes in eating habits, perhaps easing the degree of adjustment needed.

Social Factors

Social influence on smoking is important not only in initiation of smoking, but also in stopping smoking, and may be more important for women than for men (10). Someone with many friends and family members who still smoke may need help in seeing how she could set an example for others and in identifying possible allies among her social group. Such a smoker is also more likely to be presented with social situations that present temptations to smoke. Helping her plan ahead how to handle being offered a cigarette, being teased or even ridiculed about not smoking, or being the only non-smoker in a group, will decrease the likelihood of relapse. Receiving "negative" social support from a spouse, such as being nagged or having one's motivation questioned, is particularly threatening (87). It may be valuable for the physician to speak with the spouse or other close family members regarding how to best provide support for the smoker's decision to quit.

Provider Approaches to Intervention

Provider-Delivered Intervention

Introduction

Providers have contact with at least two thirds of smokers annually, providing an important opportunity for impact on smoking rates in general and on the health of smoking patients directly. A number of clinical trials have demonstrated clear effectiveness of even brief provider intervention (24). For example, providing simple advice to stop smoking has been shown to increase abstinence at 1 year from 1 to 2% up to approximately 5%. Augmenting such advice with 5 to 10 minutes of physician counseling and the prescribing of NRT produced quit rates of over 30% in a primary care population in the week after physician contact and increased long-term abstinence to 18% (88).

Despite such evidence, physicians often express little confidence in their ability to intervene with smokers. This lack of confidence may be caused by both a lack of training in how to provide interventions and to unrealistic expectations for success. Given that intense, multi-week stop smoking programs with preselected and highly motivated smokers usually produce abstinence rates of only 35 to 50%, a 10 to 20% rate of quitting following brief physician intervention is impressive and may be highly cost effective. Furthermore, even if a smoker does not attain extended abstinence, such counseling may help a smoker move forward through the "stages of change," preparing her to stop smoking in the future (Fig. 6.2.1).

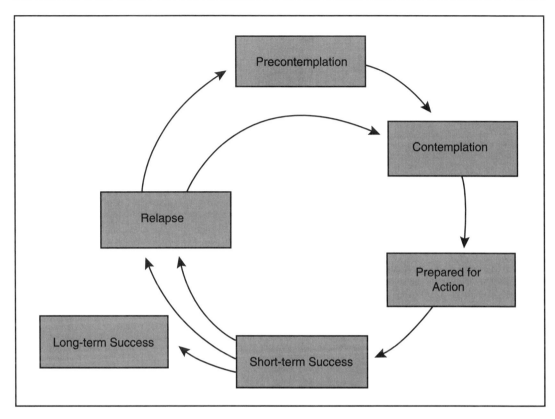

Figure 6.2.1. The stages of change model. (Adapted with permission from Prochaska JO, Di-Clemente CC. NIH Pub No. 92–3316, 1986.)

A Model of Provider-Delivered
Smoking Intervention

The National Cancer Institute (89) has recommended a basic model for physicians to use including the following elements: (1) *ask* smokers at every contact about their smoking; (2) *advise* all smokers to stop; (3) *assist* the patient in stopping smoking; and (4) *arrange* for follow-up. A variety of models exist for the content of each of these steps. Recommendations associated with this model appear below and in Table 6.2.2, but they are not the only approaches possible (90).

Ask. The question of current smoking status should be raised at every visit if an individual is known or suspected to be a smoker. Not inquiring may relay the message that smoking is relatively unimportant to the provider or even as indicating tacit approval. In addition to asking whether the person smokes, questions should address amount smoked, interest in quitting (to ascertain stage of change), history of most recent and longest quit attempt, and an assessment of nicotine dependency. This basic information can also be gathered in the waiting room by using a questionnaire. If a standard form is used and then placed in the chart, it will facilitate returning to the issue of smoking on subsequent visits.

Advise. This step can be as brief as saying: "As your provider, I advise you to stop smoking now." Such advice can then be extended to the patient's personal situation, " . . . because it will help with these colds you've been having," or " . . . I know you're under a lot of stress now, but I still think it is important for you to stop smoking. Perhaps I can help you with that."

Assist. How you assist the patient in be-

Table 6.2.2. A Model for Provider Counseling

Motivation to quit / to smoke

How do you feel about trying to stop smoking?
Why would you like to stop smoking?
What do you like about smoking?

Past experience

Have you ever stopped smoking in the past?
For how long?
What methods did you use?
Why did you start smoking again?

Exploring anticipated problems

What problems do you think you might have if you quit?
Which cigarettes will be the hardest to give up?

Exploring resources

How do you think you can handle that problem?
Is there someone who will support you?

Developing a plan

What do you think you could do now to stop smoking?
Shall we set a quit date?

Questions for follow-up

How did you do with your plan?
What helped you not to smoke?
What problems did you have?

Questions following relapse

What led to your first cigarette?
How did you feel after that?
What else could you have done to keep you from taking a cigarette?
What would you like to do now?

Adapted from Kristeller JL, Merriam PA, Ockene JK, Ockene IS, Goldberg RJ. Smoking intervention for cardiac patients: in search of more effective strategies. Cardiology 1993;82:317–324.

coming a non-smoker covers a wide range of possibilities. What is appropriate will depend on the stage of change of the smoker, the provider's ongoing relationship to the patient, whether she is appropriate for NRT, her knowledge of medical risks, her interest in a referral to a smoking intervention program, and the types of concerns she has about stopping.

The provider-centered counseling proto-col developed by Ockene et al. (91) can be adapted to virtually all smokers, regardless of stage. There are only five basic areas of questioning: (1) motivation: "How do you feel about stopping smoking?"; (2) past experience: "Have you ever stopped before?"; (3) problems: "What do you see as problems in stopping smoking?"; (4) resources: "What could you do to help with [those problems]?"; and (5) plan for action: "What kind of plan would you like to set up?" See Table 6.2.2 for sample questions in each of these areas and questions for use during a follow-up visit. The primary purpose of these questions is to empower the smoker to consider these issues, and second to provide information for the provider.

For the precontemplator, a question concerning stopping smoking may elicit a defensive insistence on planning to continue smoking; however, if this question is followed by an inquiry such as, "I understand . . . tell me what you like about smoking," defensiveness is likely to decrease, leading to a continued discussion. This individual may then be more responsive to further input such as self-help material and perhaps may move toward the contemplation stage.

For the contemplator, these questions may elicit considerable ambivalence, perhaps defensiveness and some expression of interest in quitting, but not in the immediate future. All five areas of inquiry are relevant, but the person is likely to place strong value on continuing to smoke and to perceive considerable difficulties in stopping. Advice can be focused on these difficulties; intermediate goals might be set, such as learning stress management techniques or reducing the number of places in which smoking occurs, in order to decrease nicotine dependency and increase self-confidence in quitting in the future.

For the smoker at the prepared-for-action stage who is interested in quitting, after exploring the five areas, it is important then to set a quit date; doing so invites a firm commitment from the patient and also makes clear the physician's commitment to the process. Ockene and her colleagues found that smokers often reported that setting a quit date was the most helpful component of the provider counseling. For this type of smoker, the appropriateness of NRT and her interest in using either nicotine gum or a patch should be considered. A high score on the Fagerstrom Dependence scale (92), smoking more than one pack per day, or concern about withdrawal symptoms, are all indicators of the possible value of an NRT. Although there appears to be higher acceptability of the patch by most patients, gum may be useful if an oral substitute for smoking is desirable. However, instruction in proper use of the gum is particularly important. This includes: (1) using enough (approximately half as many pieces per day as the number of cigarettes smoked), (2) using it for long enough (3 months), (3) chewing only to soften the gum and then "parking" it in the side of the mouth where it is absorbed through the buccal mucosa, and (4) avoiding acidic beverages (e.g., coffee, soda, juice) while chewing, as these block adsorption and increase swallowing of nicotine. Neither the patch nor gum should be used if the patient continues to smoke.

After quitting, the ex-smoker is extremely vulnerable to relapse for at least 3 months. Setting a follow-up visit or providing telephone follow-up, as a physician would for other indicated conditions, decreases relapse. Should a slip or relapse occur, however, the patient should be informed that this is not unusual, be asked to identify the "trigger" for the lapse and to explore how such a situation might be handled in the future (without smoking), and be encouraged to set a new quit date, if she is prepared to do so.

Special Issues for the Provider

Using Medical Problems to Motivate Quitting
To the provider, the most important reason to quit smoking are the medical risks associated with it. This is also true for many smokers. When the first Surgeon General's Report on Smoking came out in 1964, several million Americans reportedly stopped smoking. Even for adolescents, concern about health risks may play a role (68). Inquiring into what the patient believes about her own personal risk from smoking is very important. Personal risk may be minimized despite knowledge of increased risk of lung cancer or heart disease, for example, a smoker may overidentify with a friend or relative who lived to an old age as a heavy smoker, not understanding that some-

how that person was protected genetically or by the absence of cofactors from developing smoking-related disease.

Ironically, lung disease, other than cancer, does not seem to produce a high level of concern. The Lung Health Study (71) found that a history of asthma and current symptoms of breathlessness actually decreased by approximately 50% the likelihood that women (but not men) would stop smoking as a result of intervention. The risks associated with smoking are also usually greatly underestimated by diabetics. Hospitalized cardiac patients with limited disease (i.e., single vessel compared with triple vessel disease) have also been shown to be less likely to quit smoking than patients with more serious disease, perhaps because of a false sense of reassurance (93). Other problems, such as healing of ulcers or from surgery, often require the provider to clarify, in language that the patient can understand, the pathophysiological processes involved and the reasons that smoking presents a problem.

A preventive approach is also important. Although patients with diagnosed cardiac and pulmonary disease are likely to receive advice to stop smoking, patients with cardiac or pulmonary symptoms—but without diagnosed disease—have been shown to be no more likely to receive intervention from providers than patients with no such symptoms (94).

The provider must also look beyond obvious health concerns in motivating a smoker to stop. Although health issues are appropriately the provider's primary concern, they may not be the smokers. Asking, "Are there any other reasons why you would want to stop smoking?" may reveal both to you—and to the patient—more important motivators than health reasons. Asking this question is also likely to reduce patient defensiveness and can serve a motivating purpose in itself. Because changing any behavior, certainly one as complex as smoking, requires sustained motivation and focus, the point of counseling is not simply to educate but to empower future change. Leading the smoker to consider her own motivations,

not the provider's, is therefore an important step in the process of change.

Addressing Smoking with the Medical Inpatient
Suffering an MI may be the single most likely event to trigger a decision to quit smoking. However, without some type of intervention delivered in the hospital, most MI patients relapse after discharge. The JCAHO requirement that all hospitals be smoke free as of 1993 essentially requires a forced "quit" for all medical inpatients who smoke. However, as important, the hospital environment provides an opportunity for brief counseling and use of NRT that is often overlooked. Smoking intervention can be directly linked to medical management in a wide range of patients, including those on cardiac, oncology, pulmonary, endocrinology, gastrointestinal, maternity, and surgical services. However, only a small percentage of hospitalized smokers are prescribed NRT, and even fewer are provided with any counseling or follow-up (95). The provider or other staff should consider providing the same brief counseling described above, and should consider the appropriateness of NRT for all smokers, at least during hospitalization. Motivated patients can be assisted to make a plan for remaining abstinent, provided with a way to continue use of NRT, and with an opportunity for follow-up. Follow-up by a health counselor by telephone over a 3-month period has been shown to be as effective as face-to-face follow-up.

Paradoxically, referral of a medical inpatient to an outpatient smoking cessation group is often not effective. In our experience with cardiac patients, those who had already quit did not see the need for it, whereas those who did not quit in the hospital were inadequately motivated to participate. Furthermore, a group is rarely available soon enough after discharge to prevent relapse.

Making Referrals

For smokers for whom referral is appropriate, several options are commonly available. The most common is to a formal smoking cessation program, such as the Freedom from Smoking groups run by the American Cancer Society or hospital-based groups. The typical program is psychoeducational in orientation, provides six to eight meetings during which the smoker quits, while receiving substantial assistance with making behavioral changes and learning about relapse prevention. Specialized components may include aversive conditioning, hypnosis, or relaxation training. Hypnosis as a sole intervention has mixed support; although initially experienced as effective by many smokers, it may also be seen as a "magical" cure, thereby undermining efforts to make necessary long-term behavioral changes.

Absolute success rates of groups, as measured by 1 year of abstinence, are difficult to evaluate because of patient self-selection factors. Often, smokers who have failed many other efforts, yet are highly motivated, self-refer to such groups. Success rates vary from 20 to 40% when carefully scrutinized in clinical trials. An issue often overlooked is the reluctance of most smokers, even those who strongly desire to quit, to participate in such a group. Several studies have found that as few as 10% of referred smokers enroll in groups (96). Formal groups may be somewhat more appealing to and effective for women because of the availability of social support (10), but assessing individual interest in such an intervention is the most important factor.

However, as a sole treatment approach, referral to such groups is limited. Face-to-face intervention in the provider's office, even if brief, may have as much or more effectiveness overall. Another option to consider is referral to a psychotherapist or psychologist with experience with smoking cessation, particularly if there is evidence that the patient is using smoking to self-medicate or manage a psychiatric problem such as depression, anxiety, or an eating disorder.

Addressing Practice and Policy Issues

Although the provider wields considerable influence in encouraging individual smokers to quit, additional effectiveness may occur by influencing the health care setting and local insurance structure (97). Currently, relatively few insurers reimburse for smoking cessation programs or prescriptions for nicotine replacement therapy. Some forward-looking managed care groups have been more supportive of smoking intervention as a part of general care, particularly if they become aware of short-term benefits from quitting smoking, such as reduced respiratory problems, rehospitalization rates, and improved surgical recovery. Working with the local hospital or service provider structure to provide counseling to smokers, to support provision of NRT to motivated quitters, and to establish and maintain supplies of educational materials for smokers may make the physician's job easier. Requesting continuing medical education programs for providers and other medical staff on smoking cessation, initiating and/or supporting antismoking activities by the local medical associations, and promoting changes in state legislation related to education and regulation are all valuable efforts.

Special Considerations for Nurse Practitioners and Physician Assistants

Helping each woman identify factors in her life related to her smoking will help her plan strategies to stop smoking. Asking her about her work role may be helpful. Women's occupational status and control over work were significant predictors of smoking cessation in one long-term study. Women who perceived they had more control over their work were more likely to quit than women who believed they had less control (98). Qualitative research with a small group of women that explored the experience of smoking cessation provided themes that might give providers and women clues about readiness to quit smoking. Those women who quit smoking reported feeling stigmatized because of their smoking and consciously developing a negative attitude about their smoking. In addition, women who were becoming more committed to health and personal growth saw smoking as incongruent with their more health-focused lifestyle. Thus, providers who frequently discourage smoking and who encourage other positive health behaviors might affect women's success with smoking cessation at a later time (99).

Certain times in a woman's life may be more conducive to smoking cessation. For example, during pregnancy women are often more motivated to quit smoking and have more contact with health care providers. Greater success with interventions has been gained when providers intervene during early antenatal visits instead of referring pregnant clients to classes offered at other times. Women reported that trying to arrange additional time for smoking cessation classes was inconvenient and burdensome, making it apparent that providers must intervene during any "teachable moment" (100).

Pregnant women may not be aware of the risks of smoking during pregnancy or think that known risks do not apply to them. Even women motivated to quit are not always successful, perhaps needing more intensive strategies, including longer follow-up and monitoring of symptoms. Pregnant women have commented that they would like to have spousal support through their husbands' participation with them in a smoking cessation program (100).

Providers must ask not only about smoking, but also about the use of any tobacco prod-

ucts. Use of smokeless tobacco is more likely to occur in certain groups. In a review of the literature on smokeless tobacco, Goolsby (101) points out several high-risk groups, including youths and young adults, American Indians, and people who live in the Southeast. Although the highest prevalence of use is among men, the potential exists for use among women. Smokeless tobacco may be a gateway drug for other substance abuse and is a habit that is not easily broken (101).

References

1. United States Department of Health and Human Services. Reducing the health consequences of smoking: 25 years of progress. Rockville, MD: US Public Health Service, 1989.
2. National Center for Health Statistics. Health, United States, 1994 Hyattsville, MD: Public Health Service, 1995.
3. United States Department of Health and Human Services. National household survey on drug abuse: population estimates 1993. Rockville, MD: US Public Health Service, 1994.
4. Johnston LD, O'Malley PM, Bachman JG. National survey results on drug use from monitoring the future study, 1975–1992. Volume I: Secondary school students. Rockville, MD: National Institute on Drug Abuse, 1993.
5. Chen K, Kandel DB. The natural history of drug use from adolescence to the mid-thirties in a general population sample. Am J Public Health 1995;85: 41–47.
6. Ramirez AG, Gallion KJ. Nicotine dependence among African-Americans and Hispanics. In: Orleans CT, Slade J, eds. Nicotine Addiction: Principles and Management. New York: Oxford University Press, 1993:350–365.
7. Berman BA, Gritz ER. Women and smoking: current trends and issues for the 1990s. J Subst Abuse 1991;3:221–238.
8. Closher PL, Wallace RB, Pomrehn PR, LaCroix AZ, et al. Demographic and health characteristics of elderly smokers: results from established populations for epidemiologic studies of the elderly. Am J Prev Med 1990;6:61–70.
9. United States Department of Health and Human Services. The health consequences of smoking for women. A report of the surgeon general. Rockville, MD: US Public Health Service, 1980.
10. Solomon LJ, Flynn BS. Women who smoke. In: Orleans CT, Slade J, eds. Nicotine Addiction: Principles and Management. New York: Oxford University Press, 1993:339.

11. Shopland DR, Burns DM. Medical and public health implications of tobacco addiction. In: Orleans CT, Slade J, eds. Nicotine Addiction: Principles and Management. New York: Oxford University Press, 1993:339–349.

12. MacKenzie TD, Bartecchi CE, Schrier RW. The human costs of tobacco use. N Engl J Med 1995; 330:975–980.

13. Albrecht SA, Rosella JD, Patrick T. Smoking among low-income, pregnant women: prevalence rates, cessation interventions, and clinical implications. Birth 1994;21:155–162.

14. Walsh RA. Effects of maternal smoking on adverse pregnancy outcomes: examination of the criteria of causation. Hum Biol 1994;66:1059–1092.

15. Hanna EZ, Faden VB, Dufor MC. The motivational correlates of drinking, smoking, and illicit drug use during pregnancy. J Subst Abuse 1994;6:155–167.

16. Quinn VP, Mullen PD, Ershoff DH. Women who stop smoking spontaneously prior to prenatal care and predictors of relapse before delivery. Addict Behav 1991;16:29–40.

17. Tollestrup K, Frost FJ, Starzyk P. Smoking prevalence of pregnant women compared to women in the general population of Washington state. Am J Prev Med 1992;8:215–220.

18. O'Campo P, Faden RR, Brown H, Gielen AC. The impact of pregnancy on women's prenatal and postpartum smoking behavior. Am J Prev Med 1992;8: 8–13.

19. Wakefield M, Gillies P, Graham H, Madeley R, Symonds M. Characteristics associated with smoking cessation during pregnancy among working class women. Addiction 1993;88:1423–1430.

20. McBride CM, Piric PL, Currey SJ. Postpartum relapse to smoking: a prospective study. Health Ed Res Theory Pract 1992;7:381–390.

21. United States Department of Health and Human Services. The health consequences of smoking: cardiovascular disease. A report of the surgeon general. Rockville, MD: US Public Health Service, 1983.

22. Palfai T, Jankiewicz H. Drugs and human behavior. Dubuque: William C. Brown, 1991.

23. Henningfield JE, Cohen C, Pickworth WR. Psychopharmacology of nicotine. In: Orleans CT, Slade J, eds. Nicotine Addiction: Principles and Management. New York: Oxford University Press, 1993: 24–45.

24. Gritz ER, Kristeller JL, Burns DM. Treating nicotine addiction in high-risk groups and patients with medical co-morbidity. In: Orleans CT, Slade J, eds. Nicotine Addiction: Principles and Management. New York: Oxford University Press, 1993:279–309.

25. Davis MC, Matthews KA. Cigarette smoking and oral contraceptive use influence women's lipid, lipoprotein, and cardiovascular responses during stress. Health Psychol 1990;9:717–736.

26. Bruckert E, Turpin G. Estrogens and progestins in postmenopausal women: influence on lipid parameters and cardiovascular risk. Horm Res 1995;43: 100–103.

27. Wister AV, Gee EM. Ischemic heart disease: gender differences. Soc Biol 1994;41:110–126.

28. United States Department of Health and Human Services. The health benefits of smoking cessation. A report of the surgeon general. Rockville, MD: US Public Health Service, 1983.

29. Haire-Joshu D. Smoking, cessation, and the diabetes health care team: a review. Diabetes Educator 1991;17:54–67.

30. United States Department of Health and Human Services. The health consequences of smoking: Chronic obstructive lung disease. A report of the surgeon general. Rockville, MD: US Public Health Service, 1984.

31. United States Department of Health and Human Services. Smoking and tobacco control. Monograph 4. Respiratory health effects of passive smoking: Lung cancer and other disorders. The report of the U.S. environmental protection agency. Rockville, MD: US Public Health Service, 1993.

32. Wilson EO, Eisner T, Briggs WR, Dickerson RE, Metzenberg RL, O'Brien RD, et al. Life on Earth. Sunderland: Sinauer Associates, 1978.

33. United States Department of Health and Human Services. The health consequences of smoking: cancer. A report of the surgeon general. Rockville, MD: US Public Health Service, 1983.

34. deVet HCW, Sturmans F, Knipschild PG. The role of cigarette smoking in the etiology of cervical dysplasia. Epidemiology 1994;5:631–633.

35. Devesa SS, Blot WJ, Stone BJ, Miller BA, Tarone RE, Fraumeni JF Jr. Recent cancer trends in the United States. J Natl Cancer Inst 1995;87:175– 182.

36. Sarna L. Lung cancer: the overlooked women's health priority. Cancer Pract 1995;3:13–18.

37. Miller GH, Golish JA, Cox CE, Chacko DC. Women and lung cancer: a comparison of active and passive smokers with nonexposed smokers. Cancer Detect Prev 1994;18:421–430.

38. Scanlon EF, Suh O, Murthy SM, Mettlin C, Reid SE, Cummings KM. Influence of smoking on the development of lung metastases from breast cancer. Cancer 1995;75:2693–2699.

39. Fisher EB, Lichtenstein E, Haire-Joshu D. Multiple determinants of tobacco use and cessation. In: Orleans CT, Slade J, eds. Nicotine Addiction: Principles and Management. New York: Oxford University Press, 1993:60

40. Engel GL. The need for a new medical model: a challenge for biomedicine. Science 1977;196:129–136.

41. USDHHS. The health consequences of smoking—nicotine addiction: a report of the surgeon general. DHHS Pub. No. CDC 88–8406). Washington, DC: US Government Printing Office, 1988.

42. McGehee DS, Heath MJS, Gelber S, Devay P, Role LW. Nicotine enhancement of fast excitatory synap-

tic transmission in CNS by presynaptic receptors. Science 1995;269:1692–1696.

43. American Psychiatric Association. Diagnostic and Statistical Manual of Mental Disorders. 4th ed. Washington, DC: American Psychiatric Association, 1994.

44. Flay BR. Youth tobacco use: Risks, patterns, and control. In: Orleans CT, Slade J, eds. Nicotine Addiction: Principles and Management. New York: Oxford University Press, 1993:365–385.

45. Klesges RC, DePue K, Audrain J, Klesges LM, et al. Metabolic effects of nicotine gum and cigarette smoking: potential implications for postcessation weight gain? J Consult Clin Psychol 1991;59:749–752.

46. Grunberg NE. Nicotine, cigarette smoking, and body weight. Br J Addict 1985;80:369–377.

47. Williamson DF, Madans J, Anda RF, Kleinman JC, Giovino GA, Byers T. Smoking cessation and severity of weight gain in a national cohort. N Engl J Med 1991;324:739–745.

48. Fisher EB, Lichtenstein E, Haire-Joshu D. Multiple determinants of tobacco use and cessation. In: Orleans CT, Slade J, eds. Nicotine Addiction: Principles and Management. New York: Oxford University Press, 1993:59–89.

49. Niaura RS, Rosenhow DJ, Binkoff JA, Monti PM, Pedraza M, Abrams DB. Relevance of cue reactivity to understanding alcohol and smoking relapse. J Abnorm Psychol 1988;97:133–152.

50. Shiffman S. Assessing smoking patterns and motives. J Cons Clin Psych 1993;61:732–742.

51. Livson N, Leino EV. Cigarette smoking motives: factorial structure and gender differences in a longitudinal study. Int J Addict 1988;23:535–544.

52. Brandon TH, Baker TB. The Smoking Consequences Questionnaire: The subjective expected utility of smoking in college students. Psychol Assessment 1991;3:484–491.

53. Nathan PE. The addictive personality is the behavior of the addict. J Cons Clin Psych 1988;56:183–188.

54. USDHHS. The health consequences of smoking—nicotine addiction: a report of the surgeon general (DHHS Pub. No. CDC 88-8406). Washington, DC: US Government Printing Office, 1988.

55. Lipkus IM, Barefoot JC, Williams RB, Siegler IC. Personality measures as predictors of smoking initiation and cessation in the UNC Alumni Heart Study. Health Psychol 1994;13:149–155.

56. Shiffman S. Relapse following smoking cessation: a situational analysis. J Consult Clin Psychol 1982; 50:71–86.

57. Wheatley D. Stress in women. Stress Med 1991; 7:73–74.

58. Romano PS, Bloom J, Syme SL. Smoking, social support, and hassles in an urban African-American community. Am J Public Health 1991; 81:1415–1422.

59. Glassman AH, Cotler JE, Covey LS, Cotler LB, et al.

Smoking, smoking cessation, and major depression. JAMA 1990;264:1546–1549.

60. Salive ME, Blazer DG. Depression and smoking cessation in older adults: a longitudinal study. J Am Geriatr Soc 1993;41:1313–1316.

61. Resnick MP. Treating nicotine addiction in patients with psychiatric co-morbidity. In: Orleans CT, Slade J, eds. Nicotine Addiction: Principles and Management. New York: Oxford University Press, 1993:327–336.

62. Hurt RD, Eberman KM, Slade J, Karan L. Treating nicotine addiction in patients with other addictive disorders. In: Orleans CT, Slade J, eds. Nicotine Addiction: Principles and Management. New York: Oxford University Press, 1993:310–326.

63. Friedman GD, Tekawa I, Klatsky AL, Sidney S, et al. Alcohol drinking and cigarette smoking: an exploration of association in middle-aged men and women. Drug Alcohol Depend 1991;27:283–290.

64. Kronenfeld JJ, Goodyear N, Pate R, Blair A, et al. The interrelationship among preventive health habits. Health Educ Res 1988;3:317–323.

65. Ary DV, Biglan A. Longitudinal change in adolescent cigarette smoking behavior: onset and cessation. J Behav Med 1988;11:361–362.

66. Klesges RC, Klesges LM. Cigarette smoking as a dieting strategy in a university population. Int J Eat Disord 1988;7:413–419.

67. Daly KA, Lund EM, Harty KC, Ersted SA. Factors associated with late smoking initiation in Minnesota women. Am J Public Health 1993;83:1333–1335.

68. Stone SL, Kristeller J. Attitudes of adolescents towards smoking cessation. Am J Prev Med 1992;8: 221–225.

69. Fiore MJ, Novotny TE, Pierce JP, Hatziandreau EJ, Patel KM, Davis RM. Trends in cigarette smoking in the United States: the changing influence of gender and race. JAMA 1989;261:49–55.

70. Manfredi C, Lacey L, Warnecke R, Buis M. Smoking-related behavior, beliefs, and social environment of young black women in subsidized public housing in Chicago. Am J Public Health 1992; 82:267–272.

71. Nides MA, Rakos RF, Gonzales D, Murray RP, Tashkin DP, Bjornson-Benson WM, et al. (For the Lung Health Study Research Group) Predictors of initial smoking cessation and relapse through the first 2 years of the Lung Health Study. J Consult Clin Psychol 1995;63:60–69.

72. O'Hara P, Portser SA, Anderson BP. The influence of menstrual cycle changes on the tobacco withdrawal syndrome in women. Addict Behav 1989; 14:595–600.

73. Gunn RC. Reactions to withdrawal symptoms and success in smoking cessation clinics. Addict Behav 1986;11:49–53.

74. Ockene JK, Kristeller J, Goldberg R, et al. Smoking cessation and severity of disease: the Coronary Artery Smoking Intervention Study. Health Psych 1992;11:119–126.

75. Prochaska JO, DiClemente CC. Stages and processes of self-change of smoking: toward an integrative model of change. J Consult Clin Psychol 1983;51:390–395.

76. Hughes JR. Pharmacotherapy for smoking cessation: unvalidated assumptions, anomalies, and suggestions for future research. J Consult Clin Psychol 1993;61:751–761.

77. Lando HA. Formal quit smoking treatments. In: Orleans CT, Slade J, eds. Nicotine Addiction: Principles and Management. New York: Oxford University Press, 1993:221–245.

78. Lichtenstein E, Harris DE, Birchler GR, Wahl JM, Schmahl DP. Comparison of rapid smoking, warm, smoky air, and attention placebo in the modification of smoking behavior. J Consult Clin Psychol 1973;40:92–98.

79. Marlatt GA, Gordon JR, eds. Relapse Prevention. Maintenance Strategies in the Treatment of Addictive Behaviors. New York: Guilford Press, 1985.

80. Lando HA, Pirie PL, Hellerstadt WL, McGovern PG. Survey of smoking patterns, attitudes, and interest in quitting. Am J Prev Med 1991;7:18–23.

81. Pomerleau C, Ehrlich E, Tate JC, Marks J, et al. The female weight-control smoker: a profile. J Subst Abuse 1993;54:391–400.

82. Bulik CM, Dahl RE, Epstein LH, Kaye WH. The effects of smoking deprivation on caloric intake in women with bulimia nervosa. Int J Eat Disord 1991;10:451–459.

83. Chen Y, Horne SL, Dosman JA. The influence of smoking cessation on body weight may be temporary. Am J Public Health 1993;83:1330–1332.

84. Streater JA, Sargent RG, Ward DS. A study of factors associated with weight change in women who attempt smoking cessation. Addict Behav 1989; 14:523–530.

85. Beckwith JB. Psychological functions of eating, drinking, and smoking in adult women. Social Behavior Personality 1987;15:185–206.

86. Pirie PL, McBride CM, Hellerstedt WL, Jeffrey RW, et al. Smoking cessation in women concerned about weight. Am J Public Health 1992;82:1238–1243.

87. Cohen S, Lichtenstein E. Partner behaviors that support quitting smoking. J Consult Clin Psychol 1990;58:304–309.

88. Ockene JK, Kristeller J, Goldberg R, Amick T, et al. Increasing the efficacy of physician-delivered smoking interventions. J Gen Int Med 1991;6:1–8.

89. Glynn T, Manley M. How to Help Your Patients Stop Smoking. A National Cancer Institute Manual for Physicians. US Department of Health and Human Services, Public Health Service, NIH, National Cancer Institute. NIH Publication No. 93–3064, 1990, revised 1993

90. Orleans CT, Glynn TJ, Manley MW, Slade J. Minimal-contact quit smoking strategies for medical settings. In: Orleans CT, Slade J, eds. Nicotine Addiction: Principles and Management. New York: Oxford University Press, 1993:181–221.

91. Ockene JK, Quirk ME, Goldberg RJ, Kristeller JL, et al. A residents' training program for the development of smoking intervention skills. Arch Intern Med 1988;148:1039–1045.

92. Fagerstrom KO, Heatherton TF, Kozlowski LT. Nicotine addiction and its assessment. Ear Nose Throat J 1992;69:763–767.

93. Ockene JK, Kristeller JL, Goldberg R, Ockene I, et al. Smoking cessation and severity of disease: the coronary artery smoking intervention study. Health Psychol 1992;11:119–126.

94. Ockene JK, Hosmer DW, Williams J, et al. The relationship of patient characteristics to physician delivery of advice to stop smoking. J Gen Int Med 1987;2:337–340.

95. Kristeller JK. Use of the nicotine patch with hospitalized smokers: a lost opportunity. Paper presented at the Midwest Psychological Association. Chicago. May 1995.

96. Windsor RA, Cutter G, Morris J, Reese Y, Manzella B, et al. The effectiveness of smoking cessation methods for smokers in public health maternity clinics: a randomized trial. Am J Public Health 1985;75:1389–1392.

97. American Psychiatric Association. Position statement on nicotine dependence. Am J Psychiatry 1995;152:481–482.

98. Hibbard JH. Social roles as predictors of cessation in a cohort of women smokers. Women Health 1993;20:71–80.

99. Stegbauer CC. Smoking cessation in women. Nurse Practitioner 1995;20:80, 83–86, 89.

100. O'Conner AM, Davies BL, Dulberg CS, Buhler PL, Nadon C, McBride BH, et al. Effectiveness of a pregnancy smoking cessation program. JOGNN 1992;21:385–392.

101. Goolsby MJ. Smokeless tobacco: the health consequences of snuff and chewing tobacco. Nurse Practitioner 1992;17: 24, 28, 31, 35–36, 38.

Reference Materials and Other Resources

In addition to the following materials, many other resources are available from the American Cancer Society, American Lung Association, American Heart Association, and the Office of Cancer Communications, National Cancer Institute.

Orleans CT, Slade J, eds. Nicotine Addiction: Principles and Management. In: Comprehensive overview of current knowledge and approaches to treatment. New York: Oxford University Press, 1993:435.

Glynn T, Manley M. How to Help Your Patients Stop Smoking. A National Cancer Institute Manual for providers. Available from: The Office of Cancer Communications, National Cancer Institute, Building 31, Room 10A24, Bethesda, MD 20892.

"Why Do You Smoke?" National Cancer Institute, 1985. Same source as above. A brief patient questionnaire which allows self-evaluation of the six factors of smoking motivation based on the Horn-Waingrow Smoking Survey. Also contains related suggestions for quitting.

Tobacco and the Clinician: Interventions for Medical and Dental Practice. Monograph 5. Smoking and Tobacco Control. NIH Publication 94-3693. January 1994. 389 pages. The most up-to-date and comprehensive review of smoking and smoking intervention from the perspective of the medical practitioner.

Women and Tobacco. Published in 1992 by the World Health Organization, addresses tobacco use by women throughout the world. It is available from WHO Publications Centre, 49 Sheridan Ave, Albany, NY 12210.

Stop Smoking and Take Charge. A program for low-income, pregnant women, designed to coordinate with prenatal and postpartum physician visits, is available from the American Lung Association of Los Angeles County, PO Box 36926, Los Angeles, CA 90036, (800) 797-5864. It also includes provider training components.

Nico-Notes. Published quarterly by the HealthONE Center for Health Sciences Education. 1719 E. 19th Ave, Denver CO. 80218; Fax: 303–832–5137. A four page newsletter for health care professionals summarizing recent research on smoking and publications relevant to treatment of smoking. Very readable. Sources of material are always included.

6.3

Occupational Health

Linda M. Frazier

What is Occupational and Environmental Health?

Occupational health is a preventive medicine discipline devoted to promoting the health of workers. Primary care providers may become involved in occupational health by providing treatment for a worker with an occupational injury such as a back strain, by writing work restrictions for a patient with a personal health problem such as hearing impairment that requires job accommodation, or by working with safety professionals to reduce injury and illness risks in their own health care workplace.

Environmental health pertains to medical problems that may result from toxic environmental exposures, usually chemical or physical hazards. Lead toxicity from paint dust exposures during home renovation is an example. Concerns about cancer risk from small amounts of organic solvents in a contaminated water supply is another. Regardless of whether the exposure occurs outside of work or during paid employment, exposures, questions

Table 6.3.1. Professionals Who May Assist in the Care of a Patient with an Occupational or Environmental Health Problem*

Type of Professional	Certifying Organization	Areas of Expertise
Occupational medicine physician	American Board of Preventive Medicine	• Examines patients with complex occupational or environmental health problems or concerns • Provides corporate medical services on-site for employers • Takes detailed occupational and environmental histories during patient care to assess the likelihood or extent of exposure to chemical or other agents • Uses computerized toxicologic databases and other resources to assess work-relatedness of illnesses and to participate in exposure reduction initiatives at the workplace • Cares for occupational injuries and illnesses, including writing work restrictions, assessing impairment, negotiating with management for limited duty accommodation and managing referrals to other health care providers • Conducts worker and work site assessments for hazard identification and surveillance • Advises management as to which occupational medical legal issues may be important for a given patient or situation, such as the Americans With Disabilities Act, Workers' Compensation, OSHA Standards, Pregnancy Discrimination Act and others
Occupational health nurse	Occupational Health Nursing Association	• Manages occupational health services • Works with corporate leadership to improve safety • Provides first aid services to workers on site • Tracks and performs case management activities in complex workers' compensation injuries/illnesses • Administers screening examinations such as pulmonary function tests and audiograms used in medical surveillance of workers • Conducts worker and work site assessments for hazard identification and surveillance • Implements work site health promotion programs which may include helping employees monitor non-occupational health problems such as hypertension • Provides information to the treating physician about a patient's work tasks, availability of limited duty work
Industrial hygienist	American Board of Industrial Hygiene	• Evaluates work processes for potential exposures to workers or environmental emissions • Conducts environmental monitoring to quantitate levels of airborne chemicals, ambient noise, radiation, and other potential exposures • Makes recommendations to improve safety through engineering controls, administrative controls, work practices, personal protective equipment and worker training

Table 6.3.1.—*continued*

Type of Professional	Certifying Organization	Areas of Expertise
		• Recommends the most appropriate personal protective equipment for a given work task, including gloves, respirators, eye protection, hearing protection, and others • Fit tests respirators and trains workers in their use. Also trains workers in use of other personal protective equipment and in other safety procedures
Ergonomist	Board of Certification of Professional Ergonomics	• Assesses work station design • Conducts epidemiologic surveillance of work places for frequency of ergonomically related injuries and illnesses and of ergonomic exposures which may be causally linked to these • Makes recommendations to re-engineer the workplace to reduce ergonomic stressors • Trains workers to adjust work stations appropriately and to use neutral postures • Assists management to purchase ergonomically desirable equipment
Safety professional	Board of Certified Safety Professionals	• Facilitates workplace design changes to promote safe work practices including plant layout, safety devices on machines, use of safe clothing and personal protective equipment • Develops incentives for safe behaviors among workers • Conducts safety training for workers • Investigates occupational injury and illness incidents • Leads work site safety committee • Uses results of environmental monitoring conducted by industrial hygienists • Uses experience in safety technology and human behavior to enhance product safety

*Roles may overlap. Different professionals may perform a task in a work setting where other types of professionals are not available.

about toxicologic risk and medical management approaches are similar.

When reviewing studies of women's occupational health problems, it is important to determine how the investigators defined "occupational." Unpaid employment, self-employment, and second jobs may be difficult to categorize. For instance, when attempting to count occupational fatalities, one state may code death as a result of tractor rollover as nonoccupational if the primary occupation is not listed as farmer. In families that run small businesses in which' neither spouse has a formal salary line, the man may be given an occupational designation and the woman may be categorized as a wife.

The many types of professionals working in the occupational health field can assist the primary care provider to manage patients with occupational health problems or concerns (Table 6.3.1). Professionals who work for the patient's employer will usually have conducted multiple worksite walk-throughs, and thus will have detailed knowledge of work procedures and potential exposures. They may provide information over the telephone about specific job tasks and exposures. Under right-to-know legislation, corporations must provide the treating provider with Material Safety Data Sheets on products the patient has used if there is a concern about an occupational illness. These sheets can help identify the chemical constituents of products used. If environmental monitoring has been conducted, the corporate health and safety contact person may provide data that can help the primary care provider assess whether an illness is caused by work or formulate a treatment plan that may include work restrictions.

Occupational health and safety professionals may help to make changes in the workplace that will help the patient recover, such as reducing chemical exposures, developing a temporary limited duty job, or making ergonomic improvements in work station design. Only the largest companies will employ multiple types of occupational health and safety professionals. Because any of the professionals listed in Table 6.3.1 may work alone at a given facility, one professional may perform tasks listed for a different type of professional on the table (e.g., an industrial hygienist may direct the safety committee).

Historical Perspectives

Toxic disorders and illnesses caused by occupational exposures have been recognized periodically throughout history. Ramazzini (1633–1714) described many diseases of tradesmen and admonished providers to add one question to those that Hippocrates recommended for the patient's history, "What is your occupation?" (1). Occupational medicine did not develop as a discipline until the 20th century.

When Dr. Alice Hamilton began working on occupational health problems in 1910, injuries were often viewed fatalistically as accidents that could not be prevented. Even worse, several legal traditions made it nearly impossible for workers to obtain compensation for injuries that were clearly sustained on the job. The "as-

sumption of risk" doctrine held that an individual who took a job in a dangerous trade knew of its inherent risks and willingly accepted them, and therefore the employer was not liable. The "fellow servant rule" held that if the injury was caused by the negligence of a coworker, then the employer was not responsible. The "contributory negligence" doctrine held that the employer was not liable if the employee was injured because of his own negligence (1).

Even if a machine had dangerous unguarded moving parts, a lawsuit for a severe injury or death could be dismissed by demonstrating that the worker was not "careful." An unsophisticated worker had little chance of prevailing in court against these doctrines, often ending up disabled and impoverished.

Although the situation was difficult for a worker with an acute traumatic occupational injury, it was even more difficult for occupational illnesses that arose insidiously. In the early part of this century, the United States lagged behind Europe in recognizing industrial illnesses, in remediating exposures at the workplace, and in developing workers' compensation legislation. Through her work at Hull House in the industrial section of Chicago, Alice Hamilton became the foremost authority in the United States on lead poisoning and other toxic occupational illnesses (2–5).

Using shoe leather epidemiology, she visited plants, identified sources of exposure, and documented the extent of chemical poisoning by examining medical records. This type of data helped to stimulate the passage of workers' compensation legislation. These laws led to improvement in worker safety as employers became more knowledgeable about occupational risks and as they became financially responsible for occupational injuries and illnesses. Alice Hamilton became the first woman faculty member at Harvard University; her department later became the Harvard School of Public Health. She wrote the first textbook on occupational illnesses in the United States (6).

Today, most occupational illness and injury care is provided by primary care practitioners. Even though occupational medicine training is now required in all family medicine and internal medicine residencies in the United States, many graduates have little experience in this field. When caring for a patient with a workers' compensation claim for a back injury, it is still common to hear complaints that the patient contributed to the problem by being overweight, or that any patient with a history of back problems should know better than to take a job requiring lifting. These sentiments echo the legal traditions that preceded the establishment of no-fault workers' compensation legislation.

Medical records of patients cared for by providers frequently lack occupational and environmental histories, even for sentinel conditions in which an exposure could play a role in causing or exacerbating the illness or injury (7).

One hopes that tomorrow's providers will take better occupational histories than what Alice Hamilton found in 1910:

> It was not an easy task I faced, tracking down actual, proved cases of lead poisoning. . . . It meant digging up hospital records, for I had to be sure of the diagnosis, then a search for the home, and finally an interview with the wife to discover where the man had been working, for of course no hospital interne ever noted where the victim of plumbism had acquired the lead. Hospital history sheets noted carefully all the facts about tobacco, alcohol, and even coffee consumed by the leaded man, though obviously he was not suffering from these poisons; but curiosity as to how he became poisoned with lead was not in the interne's mental make-up (8).

Physiological Differences between Women and Men Workers

Historically, much emphasis has been placed on female physiology as a justification for various policies toward women. In Western culture, education and exercise were denied to upper class women because the general public, supported by the medical establishment, believed that these pursuits would diminish childbearing capacity. These concerns were not applied to lower class women who had to work for a living nor to black slaves (9, 10).

Sojourner Truth was an ex-slave who supported women's rights in the 19th century. At a time when women were held to be highly delicate creatures, her physical labors as a slave were the same as any black man. She said, "But ain't I a woman?" (11).

There are, of course, real physical differences between men and women. Which of these are relevant to occupational health? Women are on average smaller than men and have less muscle mass. Ironically, scant concern may be raised when a petite woman nurse is required to transfer a 180-lb adult patient from bed to a chair, whereas managers of some industrial jobs sometimes wish to exclude women from jobs that require lifts of lesser amounts. Women's maximum lifting capacity is reportedly 65% men's in early adulthood and 55% of men's at age 55 years (12).

These strength estimates are only population averages and there is much variability among individuals. An assessment of work capacity for an individual needs to consider specific characteristics of the applicant. A functional capacity examination can be performed by a physical therapist, e.g., assess an individual woman's strength. This type of examination may not measure endurance well, and performance may be influenced by the fact that the patient knows this is a test of work capacity. Most clinicians use an office history and physical examination instead. What is the prospective employee's level of fitness? What physical activities does she normally engage in (e.g., lifting children, other lifting as in an exercise program)? What, if any, orthopedic or other pertinent medical problems does she have?

Equally important is to assess the specific physical demands of the job in detail. What are the maximum and average lifts required on the job? What is the frequency with that lifts are undertaken? What body position is required for the lift? Is the object easy or difficult to grasp? What lifting assist devices are available? Are other workers present to allow team lifts?

From the ergonomic perspective, a well-designed job is one in which excessively forceful and awkward movements are not required of any worker, regardless of sex. The National Institute for Occupational Safety and Health (NIOSH) has recommended universal weight limits for various types of lifts (Table 6.3.2) (13).

Under the General Duty Clause (14), the Occupational Safety and Health Administration (OSHA) can cite employers who require workers to perform lifts in excess of the NIOSH Lifting Guides. For jobs with poorly designed lifting, it may be prudent for the company to improve task ergonomics rather than to attempt to reduce injuries only by worker selection.

There are other physiological differences between men and women in addition to lifting capacity. Because of women's smaller body size, some work stations and equipment designed for men may be too large. This can lead to ergonomic problems and sometimes to safety concerns, such as when a face-to-respirator seal is poor. An important ergonomic principle, however, is adjusting the work station to fit the worker rather than requiring the worker to use excessively awkward postures because of poor work station design. Again, under the General Duty Clause, employers can be considered responsible for following accepted ergonomic principles. The proposed OSHA ergonomic standard (15) further reinforces this concept. In OSHA's respiratory protection standard (16), employers are required to provide multiple sizes of respirators and to document that face-to-respirator fit is satisfactory.

Other physiological differences between men and women, such as body composition, surface area, blood tissue volume, and respiratory minute volume, may affect target tissue doses of chemical exposures and have been incorporated into quantitative toxicokinetic risk assessment models (17). The significance of these differences in the day-to-day work of women is unclear, and is probably of little importance compared to other factors such as person-to-person variation and environmental controls in the workplace (13).

Women's higher percentage of body fat provides a greater reservoir for fat-soluble compounds. There is great variation between individuals, with some obese men having a greater percentage of body fat than some thin women. Percentage of body fat has not been found to be clinically important in occupational toxic diseases, and again, all workers should be protected from excess exposure to hazardous chemicals.

A greater proportion of body fat also serves as an insulator, placing such individuals at risk for somewhat lower heat tolerance but improved cold tolerance. Heat stress can be a particularly important issue for both men and women when occlusive personal protective garments are required. Heat tolerance is highly variable among individuals of both sexes.

Table 6.3.2. Recommended Weight Limits Derived from the 1991 NIOSH Lifting Equation*

Lift Type	Maximum Weight (kg)
Floor-to-knuckle	10
Knuckle-to-shoulder	13
Shoulder reach	6
Floor-to-shoulder	4

*These lifts have been found to be rated as acceptable by 90% of the total working population, or 75% of women workers. The reference lift is a box 34 cm in width. It uses two hands, is in the sagittal plane (no trunk rotation), with a lifting frequency of 4 lifts per minute and a task duration of 4 hours. The shoulder reach begins with the box at shoulder height with elbows fully flexed, then moves the box to arm's length in front of the chest.
Data from Waters TR, Putz-Anderson V, Garg A, Fine LJ. Revised NIOSH equation for the design and evaluation of manual lifting tasks. Ergonomics 1993;36:749–776.

When environmental control is not possible, acclimatization, maintenance of adequate fluid intake, and use of an appropriate break schedule are the preferred methods for reducing heat stress.

Productivity has not been shown to be significantly affected by hormonal or other changes related to the menstrual cycle in the general population of women (13). If there are uncontrolled toxic exposures at the workplace, enhanced safety measures may be prudent during the preconception period, and during pregnancy and lactation. Because men are also subject to reproductive hazards, exclusion of women from exposure-prone work is not the preferred method of control. During normal pregnancy, lifting capacity may be limited in the third trimester, and in a complicated pregnancy additional restrictions may be required.

Occupational Health Problems in Jobs Commonly Held by Women

Attitudes about women's work may be colored by cultural expectations of women's role in society. The historical record is relatively silent on the nontraditional occupations of women until comparatively recently (10). The clinician could assume that it is men who work in dangerous jobs and that women's work is without significant occupational hazard.

These influences should not induce the primary care provider to take less complete occupational histories for women than for men. The most common jobs held by women in the United States today are shown in Table 6.3.3 (18). What may be surprising is the length of the list of reported occupational

Table 6.3.3. Potential Occupational Health Problems in the 20 Most Common Occupations of Employed Women in 1991

Occupation	Number of Women (% of workers who are women)	Reported Occupational Health Problems
Total US employment	53,284 (45.6)	
Office workers		
Secretaries*	3755 (99.0)	• Upper limb, shoulder and neck soft tissue pain syndromes, "cumulative trauma disorders" (keying more than 4–6 hours per shift with few interruptions, prolonged static awkward postures)
Managers and administrators	2660 (33.6)	• Back pain
Bookkeepers, accounting and auditing clerks*	1750 (91.5)	• Eye discomfort
Receptionists*	850 (97.1)	• Sick building syndrome
Administrative support occupations	841 (79.4)	• Environmental tobacco smoke exposure
Accountants and auditors	745 (51.5)	
General office clerks*	619 (80.9)	
Sales-Related Occupations		
Cashiers*	2023 (80.9)	• Cumulative trauma disorders (price scanners, lifting tasks)
Sales supervisors and proprietors*	1284 (34.3)	• Homicide (related to robberies)

Table 6.3.3.—continued

Occupation	Number of Women (% of workers who are women)	Reported Occupational Health Problems
Sales workers, other commodities*	1034 (71.1)	
Nursing Professions		
Registered nurses	1623 (94.8)	• Strain/sprains and other injuries of the back (patient lifting and transfers, prolonged standing) • Other musculoskeletal strain/sprains and injuries • Punctures and lacerations from sharps • Violent injuries (assaults by patients or others) • Infections (Hepatitis viruses, human immuno-deficiency virus, cytomegalovirus, herpes simplex, measles, mumps, rubella, parvovirus B19, varicella, tuberculosis, neisseria meningitides, scabies, and others)
Nursing aides, orderlies, and attendants*	1344 (89.2)	• Asthma from inhaled latex antigens (gloves), glutaraldehyde (disinfection of instruments), methyl methacrylate (orthopedic surgery adhesive) or powdered biological products (e.g., psyllium) • Dyshydrotic eczema of the hands, latex-related contact dermatitis or other hand dermatitis related to glove use • Circadian rhythm disturbance (frequent shift rotations) • Exacerbation of substance abuse (availability of addictive drugs) • Adverse reproductive outcomes such as miscarriage, reduced fertility (anesthetic agents, chemotherapeutic agents) • Mercury poisoning (broken sphygmomanometers, dental suite contamination) • Exposure to ionizing radiation and radio-pharmaceuticals
Child Care and Teaching		
Child care workers*	933 (96.0)	• Laryngeal overuse syndromes • Infections (parvovirus B19, hepatitis viruses, cytomegalovirus, head lice, and others)
Elementary school teachers	1309 (85.9)	• Musculoskeletal disorders (lifting children, prolonged standing) • Violent injuries (assaults by students)
Secondary school teachers	668 (54.7)	• Chemical exposures (art and craft materials, chemistry experiments)
Food Service Workers		
Waitresses*	1105 (81.6)	• Musculoskeletal disorders (lifting heavy food

Table 6.3.3.—continued

Occupation	Number of Women (% of workers who are women)	Reported Occupational Health Problems
		items, repetitive forceful hand use during cutting or stirring, prolonged standing and walking) • Burns (especially from grease) • Dyshydrotic eczema of the hands, latex-related contact dermatitis or other hand dermatitis related to glove use
Cooks, except short order*	834 (46.9)	• Punctures and lacerations from sharps • Asthma [(wheat flour dust and baking additives ("baker's asthma"), other food allergens (crab), smoke from mesquite broiling)] • Environmental tobacco smoke exposure

Other Occupations

Occupation	Number of Women (% of workers who are women)	Reported Occupational Health Problems
Machine operators, assorted materials*	865 (33.1)	• Cumulative trauma disorders of the upper limb, shoulder, and neck (prolonged repetitive forceful upper extremity activities, machine pacing, awkward wrist postures combined with repetition and force) • Back pain (lifting) • Circadian rhythm disturbance (frequent shift rotations) • May have chemical hazards and other exposures depending on work setting
Hair dressers and cosmetologists*	672 (90.2)	• Adverse reproductive outcomes such as miscarriage, reduced fertility (formaldehyde-based disinfectants, nail sculpturing) • Asthma (hair bleaching agents ["hairdresser's asthma"], latex [gloves]) • Hand dermatitis (gloves)
Janitors and cleaners*	657 (30.9)	• Musculoskeletal disorders (lifting, pushing, pulling, bending, prolonged standing and walking) • Punctures and lacerations from sharps • Dyshydrotic eczema of the hands, latex-related contact dermatitis or other hand dermatitis related to glove use, contact dermatitis from detergents • Acute reactive airways episodes (mixing bleach and ammonia which produces chloramine gas)

*Number of workers is listed in thousands. The 15 occupations marked with an asterisk have a 1991 median weekly earnings below the total for all women, which was $368.
Data from Women's Bureau, US Department of Labor. 1993 Handbook on Women Workers: Trends and Issues. Washington, DC: US Government Printing Office, 1993:17–25.

health problems in these careers. Many of women's injuries and illnesses are serious, such as homicide, asthma, and disabling back disorders. The occurrence of these occupational health problems is at odds with any assumption that women's work is without significant risk.

Women in Men-Dominated Jobs

Women today often work in the most common occupations of employed men (Table 6.3.4). In the United States, there are approximately 16,000 women carpenters. In an investigation of unionized carpenters in the state of Washington (19), women experienced an excess of nerve disorders of the wrist compared with men. Is this another example of the woman preponderance of carpal tunnel syndrome that may be hormonally mediated, or could this be because women have less upper body strength than men, making heavy carpentry tools more ergonomically stressful for women? In some work settings, it may be difficult for women to find well-fitting work gear and personal protective equipment, or

work stations that best fit their body size and configuration. Because few data exist on the work-related injuries and illnesses among women employed in nontraditional occupations, there is ample opportunity for study in this field.

Selected Occupational Illnesses and Injuries among Women

There are two ways in which the primary care provider should approach occupational health problems when taking care of a specific patient. First, when the patient indicates her job title, the provider should ascertain that potential job hazards may exist. Second, when her health problems are identified, the provider should determine whether these may be sentinel health conditions that could point to an occupational or environmental exposure that needs to be remediated (Tables 6.3.5 and 6.3.6).

In order to facilitate the latter task, some of the more difficult occupational health problems that women develop are described below. A woman may of course sustain any occupational injury or illness that a man may sustain

Table 6.3.4. Women Working in the 10 Most Common Occupations of Employed Men in 1991*

Occupation	Number of Men	Number of Women	Percent Women
Managers and administrators	5247	2660	33.6
Sales supervisors and proprietors	2445	1284	34.3
Truck drivers, heavy	1926	49	2.5
Engineers	1694	151	8.2
Janitors and cleaners	1469	657	30.9
Carpenters	1261	16	1.3
Sales representatives, commodities	1242	359	22.4
Laborers, except construction	1017	240	19.1
Supervisors, production occupations	1017	210	17.1
Cooks, except short order	944	834	46.9

*Number of workers is listed in thousands.
Data from Women's Bureau, US Department of Labor. 1993 Handbook on Women Workers: Trends and Issues. Washington, DC: US Government Printing Office, 1993:17–25.

Table 6.3.5. Causes of Occupational Asthma

Type of Agent	Examples	Occupations
High Molecular Weight Compounds (Allergic mechanism)		
Laboratory animals	Rats, mice, rabbits, guinea pigs	Laboratory workers, veterinarians, animal handlers
Birds	Pigeons, budgerigars, chickens	Bird fanciers, poultry workers
Insects	Cockroaches, grain, dust, and paper mites, crickets, moths, and others	Home contact, grain workers, research laboratory, fish bait breeders, entomologists
Plants	Grain dust, wheat or rye flour, coffee beans, castor bean, tea tobacco, hops	Grain handlers, bakers, millers, food processors, tea or tobacco worker, brewery worker
Biological enzymes	B. subtilis, trypsin, pancreatin, papain, pepsin, and others	Detergent industry, plastics and pharmaceutical industries
Others	Gums, crabs, prawns, hoya, silkworm larvae	Printers, gum manufacturers, crab and prawn processors, oyster farmers, sericulturists
Low Molecular Weight Compounds (Allergic or possible allergic mechanism)		
Diisocyanates	Toluene diisocyanate (TDI), Diphenylmethane diisocyanate, hexamethylene diisocyanate	Polyurethane industries, plastics, varnish, foundries, automobile spray painting
Anhydrides	Pthalic anhydrides, trimellitic anhydride	Epoxy resins, plastics
Wood dust	Western red cedar, california redwood, oak, and others	Carpenter, construction worker, cabinet maker, sawmill worker
Metals	Platinum, nickel, chromium, cobalt, vanadium, tungsten carbide	Refineries, metal plating, tanning, hard metal industry, arc welding
Fluxes	Aminoethyl ethanolamine, colophony	Aluminum soldering, electronics
Drugs	Penicillins, cephalosporins, phenylglycine acid chloride, piperazine hydrochloride, psyllium, methyl dopa, spiramycin, salbutamol intermediate, amprolium HCl, tetracycline, sulphone chloramides	Pharmaceutical worker, chemist, poultry feed mixer, brewery workers
Other chemicals	Dimethyl ethanolamine, persulphate salts and henna, ethylene diamine, azodicarbonamide, diazonium salt, hexachlorophene, formalin, urea formaldehyde, freon, parphenylene diamine, furan-based resins	Spray painters, hair dressers, photograph developers, plastics and rubber workers, dye workers, hospital staff, insulation and refrigeration installers, resin workers, foundry workers

Data from La Dou J, ed. Occupational Medicine. Englewood Cliffs, NJ: Appleton & Lange, 1990.

Table 6.3.6. Examples of Sentinel Pathophysiological Conditions That Require Occupational and Environmental Histories

Organ, Health Condition	Agent
Skin	
Acute irritant contact dermatitis	Severe cutaneous irritant such as an acid, alkali or solvent under occlusion; phototoxic chemicals
Chronic irritant contact dermatitis	Prolonged exposure to mild irritant such as detergent, soap, cutting oil, solvent
Allergic contact dermatitis	Epoxy resins, formaldehyde, dyes, acrylic monomers, rubber accelerators, metals, plants, pharmaceuticals
Contact urticaria	Animal allergens, food, ammonium persulfate (hair dressers), platinum, antibiotics, sodium benzoate
Vitiligo	Hydroquinones, p-cresol, phenols, 4-tert-butyl catechol
Chloracne	Chlorinated hydrocarbons such as dioxin, PCBs, dibenzofurans, azobenzenes, chlorinated napthalenes
Sun-related	Actinic skin damage, malignancies
Cutaneous infections	Bacteria (anthrax, brucella, erysipelothrix, tularemia, mycobacteria), fungi (candida, trichophyton, sporothrix, blastomyces, coccidioides, actinomyces, nocardia), viruses (orf, paravaccinia, herpes simplex), protozoa, metazoa, helminths, arthropods
Lung	
Asthma	See Table 6.3.4
Pneumonia	Agents which cause hypersensitivity pneumonitis (animal allergens, bacterial antigens, fungal antigens, inorganic haptens)
Acute or chronic bronchitis	Irritant dusts and fumes
Liver	
Acute hepatocellular injury (hepatitis, transaminitis)	Solvents (carbon tetrachloride, dimethylformamide, 2-nitro propane, tetrachloroethane, trichloroethylene, chloroform and others), halothane, phosphorus
Nervous System	
Depression, irritability, encephalopathy; peripheral neuropathy	Metals (arsenic, lead, mercury, tin, thallium), solvents (hexane, carbon disulfide, methyl n-butyl ketone, perchloroethylene, toleune, trichloroethylene, methyl ethyl ketone, styrene, xylene, ethylene dichloride, methylene chloride, methyl bromide, vinyl chloride, and others), carbon monoxide, nitrous oxide, organophosphate pesticides, acrylamide monomer
Carpal tunnel syndrome	Lead, some other agents associated with neuropathy
Headaches	Solvents, lead, carbon monoxide
Parkinson's disease	Manganese
Kidney	
Acute renal dysfunction	Metals (lead, chromium, cadmium, mercury, vanadium), solvents (carbon tetrachloride, ethylene dichloride, chloroform, trichloroethylene, tetrachloroethane, dioxane, toluene, eth-

Organ, Health Condition	Agent
	ylene glycols, phenols, and others), pesticides (organophosphates, carbaryl, organic mercurials), arsine, phosphorus
Chronic renal dysfunction	Metals (lead, cadmium, mercury, beryllium, uranium), silica, organic solvents, carbon disulfide
Blood	
Shortened red blood cell survival, hemolysis, or methemoglobinemia	Anilines, toluidines, napthalene, paradichlorobenzene, nitrates, trinitrotoluene, arsine, lead, copper
Porphyrias	Hexachlorobenzene, phenols, dioxin, vinyl chloride, lead, aluminum
Aplastic anemia	Benzene, trinitrotoluene, pesticides (lindane, pentachlorophenol, DDT), arsenic, ethylene glycol monomethyl or monobutyl ether, ionizing radiation
Thrombocytopenia	Toluene diisocyanate (TDI), pesticides (2,2-dichlorovinyl dimethylphosphate, dieldrin, pyrethrin, lethane, lindane, DDT), turpentine, vinyl chloride
Reproductive	
Miscarriage, delayed conception, birth defects and others; normal pregnancy (review history to prevent exposure)	Metals (lead, mercury, arsenic, manganese, cadmium and others), solvents (benzene, carbon tetrachloride, chloro form, methylene chloride, tetrachloroethylene, formaldehyde, xylene, carbon disulfide, styrene, toluene, chloropene, mixed organic solvents and others), anesthetic gases, drugs (chemotherapeutic agents and others), PCBs, 2,4-D, vinyl chloride, benzo(a)pyrene, glycol ethers, phthalates, diethylstilbestrol, ionizing radiation, certain infections, and others
Cardiovascular	
Arrhythmia	Organic solvents (1,1,1-trichloroethane, trichloroethylene), organophosphate and carbamate insecticides, arsenic, chlorofluorocarbon propellants
Coronary artery disease	Carbon disulfide (causes atherosclerosis), carbon monoxide (exacerbates ischemia)
Hypertension	Cadmium, carbon disulfide, lead

Data from Kipen HM, Craner J. Sentinel pathophysiologic conditions: an adjunct to teaching occupational and environmental disease recognition and history taking. Environ Res 1992;59:93–100; Larsen ME, Schumann SH, Hainer BL. Workplace observation: key to a meaningful office history. J Fam Pract 1983;16:1170–1184.

(e.g., noise-induced hearing loss). For more exhaustive treatment of occupational injuries and illnesses, several books are available (19, 20).

Cumulative Trauma Disorders

Cumulative trauma disorders are painful musculoskeletal conditions usually involving the hand, wrist, elbow, and arm (21). Some shoulder, neck, back, and lower extremity conditions have also been considered cumulative trauma disorders. The most common specific diagnoses are tenosynovitis, carpal tunnel syndrome, other nerve entrapments, and ganglion cysts. These disorders are not always caused by work. Occupational tendinitis is more frequently seen than carpal tunnel syndrome. Some patients have nonspecific pain or a fibromyalgia picture that can be more difficult to attribute to occupational activities.

Cumulative trauma disorders were initially described in industrial workers and meat cutters (22). There were 865,000 machine operators in the United States in 1991, one-third of whom were women. These jobs can convey a risk for musculoskeletal disorders of the upper extremity because they entail highly repetitive, forceful use of the hands. Often this is performed with extreme pronation, supination, or horizontal deviation of the wrist. Extreme tool vibration, direct blows to the carpal tunnel, and refrigerated temperatures are also risk factors (23, 24).

A combination of these risk factors (e.g., repetition plus force) is a stronger predictor of musculoskeletal problems than is a single risk factor. To prevent cumulative trauma disorders, ergonomic interventions can be accomplished. Tools and work stations can be redesigned to reduce wrist angles and to decrease the need for forceful exertions. Job rotation can reduce the number of hours per day that a tendon group is used.

Seven of the top 20 occupations of women involve office work. A growing literature has noted a high level of musculoskeletal symptoms among selected groups of office workers. Some investigators believe that normal discomfort or pain from nonoccupational causes has been mistakenly labeled as an occupational illness to the great detriment of patients (25), and prolonged splinting or poorly indicated surgical procedures make matters worse. Myofascial pain and carpal tunnel syndrome can occur spontaneously, or in the case of carpal tunnel syndrome, in response to nonoccupational risk factors such as diabetes.

Although it is not clear that occasional intermittent computer use is hazardous, extensive computer use has been associated with the development of musculoskeletal symptoms. Bernard et al. surveyed 973 newspaper employees and found a 1-year period prevalence of 41% for musculoskeletal symptoms of the upper extremities (26).

There was a dose-response relationship between symptoms and time worked at a video display station, with the most impressive association found in the group performing 6 or more hours per day of relatively continuous keying (27).

Factors related to workload demands, such as deadlines or perceived job stress, were also associated with symptom development. The provider can advise the patient to check her work station and adjust it as much as possible to achieve neutral body postures (Fig. 6.3.1).

In another study, inefficient keyboard styles were identified as an additional risk factor for musculoskeletal discomfort, suggesting that work station adjustment may not be the only remedial intervention needed. Training in less forceful and awkward keying techniques may be important (28).

Technique retraining may also help musicians and sign language interpreters who develop cumulative trauma disorders.

Occupational Asthma

Classic dust-related occupational lung diseases are diseases such as asbestosis and silicosis. Acute pulmonary edema may occur from inhalation of large amounts of toxic gasses, smoke, or fumes. Occupational asthma can be difficult to diagnose because it presents exactly like nonoccupational asthma. Symptoms may not develop until the evening when the patient has returned home after a day in which an occupational exposure occurred. Frequently, however, occupational asthma improves during weekends and vacations. Occupational asthma has a favorable prognosis when exposure to the precipitating agent is stopped within the first several months of symptoms (29).

Providers therefore need to maintain a high index of suspicion in order to determine

Adjust the seat height so upper arms hang vertically, elbows bent at about 90 degrees, shoulders relaxed, and wrists fairly straight.

Position the monitor about an arm's length away, directly in front of you. The top of the screen level with the eyes.

Use a document holder next to the screen rather than laying papers flat.

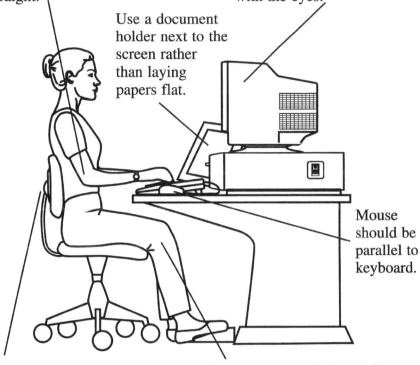

Mouse should be parallel to keyboard.

Adjust the backrest to support the small of the back and provide firm support.

Knees comfortably bent with feet resting on floor or on a footrest if the chair must be raised to adjust for height.

Figure 6.3.1. Ideal work station design for a computer user; the goal is to maintain neutral body postures. Shorter women may need to elevate the chair in order to attain a relatively horizontal wrist angle. This maneuver may necessitate a foot rest. Alternatively, remove the pencil drawer from the desk and attach a keyboard tray. Place the monitor away from windows or other sources of glare. Even the most "perfect" position is not good for a long period of time. Alternate placement of hard copy from the right to the left. Intermittently move about and stretch. Stay physically fit in an exercise program. An eye examination will detect correctable acuity problems that can lead to eye discomfort.

if there is a connection between asthma and an occupational or environmental exposure. A patient who smokes or who has had a viral upper respiratory infection can also have occupational asthma. The key is to determine if the patient works with an agent known to precipitate asthma (30).

Many women work in occupations where asthmagens may be present. If such a substance is present in the workplace, then one must determine the likelihood that the patient's respiratory tree was exposed to it. Handling small amounts of glutaraldehyde in a chemical fume hood would not be worrisome, but use of large quantities in an unventilated work area would be of concern. Exposure level measurements may be available from health and safety professionals at the workplace.

Toxic Effects of Chemicals

Like occupational asthma, other toxic effects of chemicals may mimic nonoccupational medical problems (31, 32).

The problem will not be cured or improved unless the true exposure is discovered. When mild transaminase elevations are found, for example, the provider should take an occupational and environmental history to determine if the patient has had significant exposure to any agents that could cause this. Further investigation should not stop after determining that the patient occasionally drinks alcohol. Even if she uses a computer at work, quickly ask the patient with carpal tunnel syndrome a few questions to determine if she could have significant exposure to lead. When the patient presents with depressed mood and irritability, don't attribute it only to social problems, premenstrual syndrome, or occupational stress without excluding exposure to neurotoxins.

Whether the patient's symptoms are caused by a chemical exposure hinges on an assessment of whether the individual is likely to have absorbed a significant internal body dose. It may be helpful to, like Alice Hamilton, visit the patient's workplace (33).

The busy clinician will not be able to visit every workplace, nor will this be needed. However, visiting workplaces periodically, will help the provider learn what questions to ask of the patient (and the employer contact) to better assess whether significant exposures are occurring.

The presence of an agent in a workplace is not the same as being exposed to it. Chemicals can be absorbed through the skin, gastrointestinal tract, or lungs. Skin absorption can be prevented by wearing gloves and protective clothing. For most solvents, a few drops touching the skin conveys a low risk of significant internal exposure, whereas prolonged contact with skin over a large surface area is of concern. Ingestion can occur through facial contamination or indirect exposure can occur when hands or consumables are contaminated. Using gloves, washing hands, and refraining from eating, drinking, smoking, or storing food or smoking materials in the workplace will reduce gastrointestinal exposure.

To prevent inhalational exposure, toxic agents that are volatile, such as organic solvents, should be handled with appropriate ventilation. Containers should be covered to reduce evaporation. Agitation of an agent may generate an aerosol. Finely powdered agents can produce airborne dusts. When engineering controls are insufficient, a respirator may be worn. Because the face-to-respirator seal may sometimes fail and because some respirators are uncomfortable to wear for long periods, engineering controls are preferred. The respirator must also be the correct kind for the type of chemical exposure, it must be maintained properly, and the worker must be trained in its operation and medically cleared to use it.

Homicide

Since Alice Hamilton's day, our society has made progress in recognizing that injuries are not just unpreventable accidents. However, for the most severe injury, homicide, much work remains to be done to put prevention into practice. During 1980 to 1989, 7600 United States workers were victims of homicide in the workplace (34).

Workplaces with the highest rates of occupational homicide were taxicab establishments, liquor stores, gas stations, detective/protective services, justice/public order establishments, grocery stores, jewelry stores, hotels/motels, and eating/drinking places. Although 80% of the victims were men, homicide was the leading cause of death from occupational injury among women. Death from occupational injury was caused by homicide in 41% of women who died while "on the job" (35).

Some homicides are caused by disgruntled workers, but robbery is a more common motive. For women, domestic violence may spill over into the workplace. A battered woman may be able to change her phone number and residence, but she may not be able to give up her job, the location of which is known to her assailant. Preventive measures can be used to reduce the risk of occupational homicide. These include (a) making high-risk work areas visible to more people, (b) improving lighting, (c) minimizing accessible cash on hand and posting signs to this effect, (d) installing silent alarms and surveillance cameras, (e) increasing the number of staff on duty, (f) providing training in conflict resolution and nonviolent response, (g) providing bulletproof enclosures, and (h) closing establishments during high-risk hours.

"Sick Building Syndrome"

Building-related health concerns most often occur among office workers. Reported symptoms include rhinitis, nasal congestion, pharyngitis, cough, dyspnea, conjunctival irritation, headache, dizziness, lethargy, fatigue, malaise, difficulty thinking, and rashes. Asthma may occur if an asthma precipitant is present.

Sick building concerns need to be addressed as a population issue, rather than as an isolated assessment of a single individual. This usually requires that the provider work with others to investigate the problem and develop solutions. Questions to answer are, "How many employees are affected? Are the affected employees experiencing similar symptoms or greatly different symptoms? Is the rate affected employees greater than

would be expected for common symptoms like upper respiratory irritation, fatigue, or headache? Are the similarly affected employees linked by location in the building? When did different workers' symptoms begin—at about the same time or not in a close temporal relationship? Were latencies consistent with known incubation periods for infectious diseases (e.g., Legionella)? What happened in the work area just before any outbreak seemed to occur, including renovations, ventilation changes, and application of pesticides or cleaning products?" and "Are symptoms consistent with the known effects of exposure to these agents?" Was the outbreak preceded by the appearance of a smell in the workplace and associated with a great deal of emotional distress among the affected individuals? If so, this suggests mass psychogenic illness. The initial medical and epidemiologic investigations should be carried out before or at least in conjunction with launching a search for toxic agents in the air (36, 37).

If there appears to be a plausible outbreak of symptoms, then any environmental investigation needs to be carried out by a qualified individual, such as a certified industrial hygienist. Beware of environmental "experts" without recognized credentials. A frequent source of discomfort is an abnormality in humidity or a low percentage of fresh air added during ventilation. Humidity can be measured. High carbon dioxide levels in the air are a marker for need of additional fresh air. A poorly functioning heating system can result in increased carbon monoxide levels.

Biological contamination may occur from animal dander, molds, dust mites, and other agents. Mold is a prominent concern if the building has flooded. An inspection of the ventilation system can reveal biological overgrowth. Be aware, however, that biologicals are normally present in ducts, in cooling system reservoirs, and in the air outside the building. These agents may not cause any health problems. To avoid being misled by air analyses, quantitative assessment of spores can be conducted, comparing indoor levels to outdoor levels. Air analyses are of uncertain value when it has not been established that a true outbreak of medically related symptoms has actually occurred.

Volatile organic compounds can contaminate indoor air, including formaldehyde, pesticides, solvents, and cleaning agents. Volatile organics present in building materials and carpet off-gas rapidly in the weeks following installation. In an outbreak occurring a year after a renovation, volatile organics should be less suspected than other agents such as biologicals or a high percentage of recirculated air. Lead contamination would be suspected in an older facility during a renovation that creates clouds of paint dust. Undisturbed lead paint is not a strong exposure risk for adults. Asbestos and radon can contaminate building atmospheres, but they are not associated with acute symptoms.

Multiple Chemical Sensitivity

Multiple chemical sensitivity is an acquired disorder characterized by recurrent symptoms, referable to multiple organ systems, occurring in response to demonstrable exposures to many chemically unrelated compounds at doses far below those established in the general population to cause harmful effects (38).

A synonym is "environmental illness." Patients may report symptoms such as fatigue, difficulty concentrating, difficulty breathing, and chest tightness. The patient may have a strong belief that the symptoms are caused by specific exposures, often to agents with olfactory cues. There is frequently a precipitating event, such as a chemical spill.

A variety of causes and treatments for this condition have been proposed. Clinical ecologists have advanced immunologic mechanisms, but scientific investigations using established approaches have failed to substantiate these (39). Some patients have been noted to have obsessive/paranoid characters and may be searching for a medical explanation for their physical symptoms (40). Others have noted denial by the patient of depression and anxiety. In a study of 41 women with the disorder, 12 had a history of early childhood sexual and physical abuse (41).

A survey analyzing diagnostic and treatment approaches for multiple chemical sensitivity was conducted among members of the Association of Occupational and Environmental Clinics (42). Member providers infrequently used allergy tests, immune tests, or brain scans for patient evaluation. Neuropsychological tests were conducted more than half the time by 38% of respondents and always by 24% of respondents. Psychological referrals were frequently made. The providers reluctantly recommended that the patient avoid the suspected agents on a trial basis, and sometimes restricted work activities, but they did not usually feel that industrial hygiene monitoring at the workplace was warranted. Behavioral techniques, including psychologic desensitization and biofeedback, were the most common therapeutic interventions.

Cancer

A common research technique to study associations between occupation and cancer is to investigate death certificates. This technique can be invaluable in delineating possible causal relationships, but women's risks may not be well characterized for several reasons. Some studies of occupational cancer exclude women because of the small numbers of women who work in occupations traditionally held by men. For many women, housewife is listed as the usual occupation on the death certificate, even if she has worked outside the home in the past. Job title is a relatively crude measure of exposure. Only one occupation can be listed on the death certificate, even if an individual has worked in several trades. Smoking history and information on other confounders are often not available. Death certificates do not list parity or age of first birth, both of which influence risk for breast cancer.

Research suggests increased risk among of esophageal, bladder, intestinal, and pancreatic cancer among women dry cleaning workers (43). Lung cancer rates may be elevated among women in the fur hat industry and motor vehicle assembly. Pancreatic cancer may be increased among women workers in paint, plastic, and trim departments. Brain cancer may be elevated among women rubber workers. Invasive cervical cancer appears to be increased among maids and cleaners, thyroid cancer among women dentists and dental assistants, esophageal cancer among women restaurant employees, salivary gland cancer among women hairdressers, and bladder cancer among women computer manufacturing workers (43). Further research is needed to confirm these findings.

Because the breast is a fatty tissue, breast cancer could potentially be increased by occupational exposure to fat-soluble toxins. Epidemiologic studies of breast cancer have not to date used precise estimates of chemical exposures, e.g., industrial hygiene monitoring. When occupation is used as a surrogate for exposure, women in occupations, both with and without presumed chemical exposures, have elevated rates. In one study, these occupations included housewives, nurses, laboratory technicians, teachers, social workers, secretaries, and meat wrappers (44).

In another study, elevated breast cancer rates were found in textile and apparel workers, receptionists, cosmetologists, artists, nurses, and teachers (45). In a third study, usual occupation listed on death certificates was linked to the NIOSH job exposure matrix to derive probable chemical exposures (46).

Elevated risk for breast cancer was found for presumed exposure to styrene, methylene chloride, carbon tetrachloride, formaldehyde, metals (e.g., chromium, arsenic, beryllium,

nickel, cadmium, lead, lead oxide), and acid mists. Further research is needed in this area, but the provider can use occupational history-taking skills to assess the likelihood of a patient's exposure to these and other agents. If it is likely that the patient is receiving a significant internal body dose of a potentially carcinogenic compound, then exposure prevention interventions are warranted.

Reproductive Issues

Reproductive health issues in the workplace do not apply only to women. Research on male reproductive effects, although still somewhat scanty, has revealed toxic effects of dibromochloropropane, lead, ionizing radiation, and other agents (47–49).

Substantial exposure to chemical agents that pose a nonreproductive health risk may also pose a concern for a woman in the preconception period and during pregnancy and lactation. General principles of industrial hygiene should be followed. When this cannot be achieved, the provider needs to decide with the patient if a work restriction is warranted. Determining the likely exposure level is crucial for this task.

Preconception is not a highly protected status from the legal perspective. Pregnancy is excluded from coverage under the Americans with Disabilities Act, and because the fetus is not an employee, workers' compensation does not apply. The Pregnancy Discrimination Act mandates that pregnancy be afforded the same medical leave as nonreproductive medical issues. Under the Family and Medical Leave Act, pregnancy-related leaves for up to 90 days per 12-month period must be granted.

If the patient needs to be removed for 9 months from a work environment that conveys high exposure to a reproductive toxin, she may not be able to argue legally that her job must be held for her. The provider can help her negotiate for voluntary accommodation, or she may need to leave her job to protect the pregnancy. The clinician should focus on writing only the work restrictions that are absolutely necessary, especially with respect to ergonomic issues that may not convey a risk to the general population. Because most chemical hazards with reproductive toxicity also are toxic to another organ system, the preferred approach is to remediate these exposures for all employees. For further information, consult an occupational reproductive health reference (47–49).

Stress

Both women and men are susceptible to life stressors, including stressors on the job. Do women have more occupational stress than men? Are certain occupations more stressful than others (e.g., traditional office jobs in which there is little autonomy, nontraditional jobs in which there are few women peers)? A MEDLINE search from 1984 to present reveals no study of occupational stress that was identified as a case-control, cohort, or cross-sectional study. Using more general search terms, no research was found to answer these questions. Occupational mental stress is a rising source of workers' compensation claims in the United States (50).

The minimum criteria for establishment of a claim vary greatly from state to state. Criteria for claim establishment can be written into the state's workers' compensation statute. If not, criteria must be determined from case law. The latter may lead to more variability in claims denial by insurance adjustors.

Claims can be categorized into three types that describe the proposed cause of the injury and the nature of its sequelae: physical-mental, mental-physical, and mental-mental. In each case, the mental health problem must be characterized fully, a process that may require psychological testing and evaluation of prior mental health problems. Diagnoses such as posttraumatic stress disorder should meet accepted diagnostic criteria.

In a physical-mental claim, an occupational injury such as a lumbar disc rupture is proposed as the cause of a mental health problem such as depression. Establishment of causality is complicated by predisposing factors in the patient's nonwork life such as prior history of depression and home stressors. In states in which it is difficult to establish a physical-mental workers' compensation claim, providers treating injured workers with psychological symptoms may find that their goal of caring for the whole patient compromised by insurance denials for mental health care. Psychological support can be provided by the provider for illness-coping issues. One may need to take care not to give the patient false expectations that provider testimony is guaranteed to force the workers' compensation carrier to pay for visits to a psychiatrist.

In a mental-physical claim, occupational stress is proposed as the cause of a physical problem. In some locales, myocardial infarctions suffered by police and fire fighters are automatically covered under workers' compensation. The proposed mechanism of injury is occupational stress over time leading to ischemic heart disease.

In a mental-mental claim, stress is proposed as the cause of a mental health problem. The easiest claims to establish are those in which a severe, life-threatening stressful event occurred. For example, a bank teller may develop posttraumatic stress disorder after being robbed at gunpoint on the job. More difficult to establish are claims in which the stressor proposed to have caused the mental health problem is not one that would cause the average person to be devastated, such as being exposed to asbestos without having contracted an asbestos-related disorder (51).

Other circumstances for which a claim might be filed may include criticism of job performance or disciplinary action by a supervisor, work that requires involuntary overtime, or continuous workload beyond what can reasonably be accomplished with the time and resources allotted (52). The success of these claims varies from state to state.

Individuals with personality disorders and a need to be vindicated for unfair treatment may be found among patients filing occupational stress claims for non–life-threatening events. The provider may insist that significant changes in the work be made or the patient's symptoms will not improve. A perhaps unintended consequence of this action may be dependency on the clinician. Although financial incentives (claim settlement) have been suspected as an important factor in some stress claims, a follow-up study showed that claimants did not appear to improve magically once settlement was accomplished: among 106 workers' compensation claimants who had psychiatric impairment, settlement was not generally associated with improved psychological well-being (53).

There is a need for population-based research to characterize occupational stress-related morbidity and to better define preventive interventions. Scholarly work that delineates proposed mechanisms of psychological stress points to high-demand, low-control jobs as an important source of occupational stress. Extremes in the following work-design factors are also stressing: (*a*) mental underload or overload, (*b*) responsibility for safety, (*c*) responsibility for other people, (*d*) responsibility for costly items or equipment, (*e*) solitary work, (*f*) burdensome interpersonal contacts, (*g*) repetitiveness, (*h*) forced work pace, (*i*) lack of input into how a task is accomplished, (*j*) precision demands, (*k*) haste, and (*l*) complex decision–making. Advocates in the mental health field and in business promote work organization that reduces these potential stressors (54–56).

Managing an Occupational Injury or Illness

Occupational injuries or illnesses should be managed as one would care for nonoccupational health problems, although there are some special features. The need for patient education and support is greater because the patient may have concerns about the impact on her job of filing a claim or about whether her job is safe. Workers' compensation has several administrative requirements. Effective communication with employers, especially by means of work restrictions, can help the patient recover as quickly as possible. Preventing injuries is preferable to treating them, and the provider can make an impact in this area.

Prevention

The difference between the occupational medicine mindset and the traditional medical approach is the sense of empowerment to prevent injuries and illnesses. The provider may reinforce basic safety principles with well patients whose job histories show injury or illness risk factors. Encouragement from the esteemed clinician may help the patient better comply with wearing safety glasses and hearing protection, to incorporate stretches and minipauses into typing routines, to engage in a strength and posture-maintaining exercise program, or to take the initiative to recruit coworkers for team lifts. This is primary prevention, and it differs little from encouraging weight loss and dietary fat reduction to prevent cardiovascular disease.

Primary prevention also encompasses efforts, after one injury has been sustained, to prevent the next worker from being injured. Sadly, the "accident investigation" at the workplace may only conclude that the employee should "be more careful." A provider who has a relationship with the safety program at the work site can help broaden the focus from the injured individual to remediable risks in process or tool design.

Secondary prevention aims to keep a preclinical condition from advancing to an outright injury or illness. The proposed OSHA ergonomic standard recommends that employers conduct symptom reviews among employees at risk for cumulative trauma disorders. Ergonomic improvements can be made in the job if discomfort levels increase, even if workers have not yet developed frank tendinitis or carpal tunnel syndrome. In many musculoskeletal pain syndromes, the physical examination and test results are unremarkable, so some clinicians and patients find it difficult to distinguish between discomfort and an injury or illness. If the patient is in the office, the clinician may treat the problem as an injury even if the discomfort is relatively minor, could be managed by self-help techniques, and has a good prognosis. It is important to explain the diagnosis and prognosis to the patient and to support self-care techniques whenever appropriate. Employers are wary of conducting symptom surveys among employees because they are concerned that everyone with a symptom will initiate a long workers' compensation claim.

A provider working with the company can help design the survey so that employees understand the difference between discomfort and severe injury. Survey results can be communicated realistically to workers. Comprehensive, rehabilitation-oriented medical care can be provided to any injured employees. The provider can advocate that the company be ready to implement ergonomic improvements if the survey reveals problem work areas.

Tertiary prevention aims to keep an occupational injury or illness from becoming disabling. This is the arena in which most workers' compensation dollars are spent. The occupational medicine clinician also views each injured patient as a potential index case who may reveal a remedial risk factor to a population. Rather than just writing a prescription and a work restriction for the patient in the office, a call (with the patient's permission) to the company safety officer may be warranted. Engineering controls and work practice changes may reduce ergonomic or chemical exposures. Personal protective equipment can be reviewed or a less toxic chemical can be substituted for a more toxic one. Safety officers approached in a nonconfrontational way may be highly responsive.

Workers' Compensation

Workers' compensation is a no-fault system that provides injured employees with medical care for the injury and reimbursement for lost wages during the recovery period. Each state and the federal government have different systems. Wage replacement may not begin with the first lost workday; the employee may need to use sick time for up to 7 days. State statutes typically place a cap on the amount of wage replacement given. For example, workers may receive two-thirds of their average weekly wage up to a certain ceiling. The economic hardship of receiving workers' compensation is therefore greater for higher-paid employees such as nurses.

To be eligible for workers' compensation, the injury or illness must "arise out of and in the course of employment." This means that the job should have contributed substantially to causing or exacerbating the condition. Onset of sciatica while walking to the restroom, although clearly occurring on the job, in some locales may not be considered to be caused by the job because walking short distances is part of everyday life and not specific to the job.

In some states, the insurance carrier may designate the provider, typically allowing the worker one independent medical examination of her own choosing. The provider is not asked to manage the workers' compensation patient as a whole person nor for as long as symptoms persist. Instead the focus is on providing care just for the injured part, and just until the patient obtains "maximum medical improvement." This means that all reasonable tests and treatment have been offered and the patient has reached a stable point. It does not mean that the patient is pain-free or completely well. The insurance carrier may assign a medical case manager who may attend clinic visits, call, or write to the provider. These individuals typically attempt to ascertain how far toward maximum medical improvement the patient has progressed and may suggest tests, treatment, or referrals to speed progress toward release of the patient from care. He or she may ask the clinician to clarify work restrictions. The carrier may provide vocational assistance if the patient cannot return to the full duties of the previous job.

If full recovery has not occurred, the clinician is asked to perform an impairment rating. The worker can then use this number to negotiate a monetary settlement of the claim. The clinician is required to use the criteria of the state's workers' compensation statute to determine the impairment rating. A rating is not something that the doctor "gives" to the patient. Rather, a rating is a technical task in which physical examination and test results are compared with a published table to determine a percentage impairment of the body part (57).

These tables almost never have an axis for pain level, and this is hard for patients to understand. In addition, the impairment percentages can be perceived as low compared with the impact the problem has had on the worker's life. It is important to communicate to the patient how the impairment rating is conducted so that she does not feel that an assignment of a 5% rating for the back means that the clinician only believes 5% of her symptoms are real.

Writing Work Restrictions

Work restrictions are a type of therapy, a safety rule, or both. They are most likely to achieve their desired result if they are clear and detailed. Avoid writing restrictions such as "light duty." Instead, indicate how many pounds should be lifted and how often. If a worker has an injured left hand, one can restrict her from using the left hand, rather than indicating she must be out of work. It is, then, up to the company to determine if a left hand restriction can be accommodated. The employee who stays at work on limited duty makes more money, is better able to continue deductions for personal health insurance, and is less likely to become estranged from the workplace.

Beware of writing vague work restrictions whose goal is only to attempt to maintain comfort. It may be better to teach the patient pain management techniques that do not require the intervention of a doctor. Therapeutic work restrictions are a form of prescribing rest for an affected body part. Rest is indicated in the initial phases of an injury, but it can be counterproductive if prolonged. Safety-based work restrictions are given to prevent the worker from further injuring herself (58).

Medical records generated during a workers' compensation claim must be released to the insurance carrier. If the clinician is also caring for other health problems in this patient, some thought should be given to whether unrelated but potentially prejudicial information should be recorded. Although the medical records must be released to the insurance carrier, the work restriction form that goes to the supervisor should not contain diagnoses or other clinical details.

Special Considerations for Nurse Practitioners and Physician Assistants

A woman's workplace is a significant part of her surroundings. Toxins from the workplace can pollute her larger environment and also be carried into the home. Additionally, work-related stress can affect not only her health, but the health of other family members (59). Even when women are not exposed to specific chemical, biological or other hazards, their work is often repetitive and fast paced, involving long periods of standing or sitting. In the service sector, women are expected to have a happy smile, even though the job may be temporary, low paying, and low prestige. In addition, little is known about the effects of job loss on a woman's health, perhaps because a woman who loses her job is suddenly considered to be a housewife (60). The complexity and skills of women's work, e.g., in computer service jobs, is often not recognized (61).

Occupational diseases can be difficult to diagnose. Many are not distinct from chronic illnesses, signs and symptoms are vague and nonspecific, there is a long latency period between exposure and disease, and/or the woman is fearful of reporting her work-related concerns. Unless the provider pays close attention to a woman's complaint in relation to her sequence of possible work exposure, occupation-related illnesses can be missed. Variables, including economic class, infections, stress, smoking, drugs, alcohol, and nutrition, can exacerbate symptoms and risks (59).

The possibility of sexual harassment at work leading to stress-related physical and psychological symptoms also must be considered. Referrals to legal experts, state agencies that deal with employment practices, or the Equal Employment Opportunity Commission can be suggested. Employee assistance programs for counseling may be available (62).

Preconception counseling includes a discussion of possible work-related risks, with encouragement to report pregnancies early to employers, especially if the workplace is hazardous. Women who fear job loss and thus want to conceal an early pregnancy must realize that the first trimester is the most dangerous time for fetal exposure to environmental hazards (63). Sparsity of knowledge about specific reproductive hazards, conflicting reports, and disagreement among experts about possible outcomes make it difficult to counsel for reproductive risks. The pregnant woman deserves as much information as is available, including the uncertainties, in order for her to make a well-informed decision (64).

An exhaustive occupational history is time-consuming and not needed unless an occupational disorder is suspected. For a routine screening health history, all women should be asked about their current and past jobs, exposures to possibly harmful substances, and any symptoms they think may be related to their jobs (59). Finding out why a woman works and if she thinks she has a choice in deciding how much to work will assist providers in understanding any concerns the woman has about her job.

References

1. National Safety Council. Accident Prevention Manual for Industrial Operations: Administration and Programs, Ninth Edition. Chicago: National Safety Council, 1988:1–16.
2. Rom WN. The discipline of environmental and occupational medicine. In: Rom WN, ed. Environmental and Occupational Medicine. 2nd ed. Rom WN, ed. Boston: Little, Brown & Co, 1992:3.
3. Hamilton A. Exploring the dangerous trades: the autobiography of Alice Hamilton. Boston: Little, Brown & Co, 1943.
4. Grant MP. Alice Hamilton: pioneer doctor in industrial medicine. London: Abelard-Schumann, 1967.
5. Sicherman B. Alice Hamilton: a life in letters. Cambridge, MA: Harvard University Press, 1984.
6. Hamilton A. Industrial Poisons in the United States. New York: Macmillan Company, 1925.
7. Frazier LM, Berberich JN, Evanoff BC. Residents medical records show poor generalist skills in occupational and environmental medicine. J Gen Intern Med 1995;10(suppl):88.
8. Hamilton A. Exploring the dangerous trades: the autobiography of Alice Hamilton. Boston: Little, Brown & Co, 1943:10.
9. Covey A. Work and family. In: A Century of Women. Atlanta: TBS Books, 1994:5–65.
10. Greenspan K. The Timetable of Women's History: A Chronology of the Most Important People and Events in Women's History. New York: Simon & Schuster, 1994.
11. Truth S. Narrative of Sojourner Truth. In: Washington M, ed. New York: Vintage Books, 1993:117–118.
12. Greenspan K. The Timetable of Women's History: A Chronology of the Most Important People and Events in Women's History. New York: Simon & Schuster, 1994.
13. Waters TR, Putz-Anderson V, Garg A, Fine LJ. Re-

vised NIOSH equation for the design and evaluation of manual lifting tasks. Ergonomics 1993;36:749–776.

14. National Safety Council. Accident Prevention Manual for Industrial Operations: Administration and Programs. 9th ed. Chicago: National Safety Council, 1988:20–21.

15. Occupational Safety and Health Administration. Ergonomic Protection Standard (proposed), Springfield, VA: National Technical Information Service, 1995.

16. Occupational Safety and Health Administration. Respiratory Protection. Code of Federal Regulations 29CFR 1910:134.

17. Silvaggio T, Mattison DR. Setting occupational health standards: toxicokinetic differences among and between men and women. J Occup Med 1994;36:849–854.

18. Women's Bureau, US Department of Labor. 1993 Handbook on Women Workers: Trends and Issues. Washington, DC: US Government Printing Office, 1993:17–25.

19. Herington TN, Morse LH, eds. Occupational Injuries: Evaluation, Management and Prevention. St. Louis: Mosby, 1995.

20. Agency for Health Care Policy and Research. Acute Low Back Problems in Adults (Clinical Practice Guideline Number 14). Washington, DC: US Government Printing Office. AHCPR Publication No. 95–0642. December 1994.

21. Rempel DM, Harrison RJ, Barnhart S. Work-related cumulative trauma disorders of the upper extremity. JAMA 1992;267:838–842.

22. Rempel DM, Harrison RJ, Barnhart S. Work-related cumulative trauma disorders of the upper extremity. JAMA 1992;267:838–842.

23. National Safety Council. Accident Prevention Manual for Industrial Operations: Administration and Programs. 9th ed. Chicago: National Safety Council, 1988:207–222.

24. Keyserling WM, Stetson DS, Silverstein BA, Brouwer ML. A checklist for evaluating ergonomic risk factors associated with upper extremity cumulative trauma disorders. Ergonomics 1993;36:807–831.

25. Hadler NM. Cumulative trauma disorders: an iatrogenic concept. J Occup Med 1990;32:38–41.

26. Bernard B, Sauter S, Fine L, Petersen M, Hales T. Job task and psychosocial risk factors for work-related musculoskeletal disorders among newspaper employees. Scand J Work Environ Health 1994;20:417–426.

27. National Institute for Occupational Safety and Health. Health Hazard Evaluation Report: Los Angeles Times, Los Angeles, CA HETA 90–113–227, January 1993.

28. Pascarelli EF, Kella JJ. Soft-tissue injuries related to use of the computer keyboard: a clinical study of 53 severely injured persons. J Occup Med 1993;35:522–532.

29. Cullen M. Clinical surveillance and management of occupational asthma: Tertiary prevention by the primary practitioner. Chest 1990;98(suppl 5):196S–201S.

30. Chan-Yeung M. Occupational asthma. Chest 1990;98(suppl 5): 148S–161S.

31. LaDou J, ed. Occupational Medicine. Englewood Cliffs, NJ: Appleton & Lange, 1990.

32. Kipen HM, Craner J. Sentinel pathophysiologic conditions: an adjunct to teaching occupational and environmental disease recognition and history taking. Environ Res 1992;59:93–100.

33. Larsen ME, Schumann SH, Hainer BL. Workplace observation: key to a meaningful office history. J Fam Pract 1983;16:1170–1184.

34. National Institutes for Occupational Safety and Health. Preventing Homicide in the Workplace. Washington DC, US Government Printing Office, DHHS (NIOSH) Publication No. 93–109, 1993.

35. Bell CA. Female homicides in United States workplaces, 1980–1985. Am J Public Health 1991;81:729–732.

36. American Lung Association, the American Medical Association, the US Consumer Product Safety Commission and the US Environmental Protection Agency. Indoor Air Pollution: An Introduction for Health Professionals. Washington, DC: US Government Printing Office, 1994:523–217/81322.

37. Fischman ML. Building-associated illness. In: LaDou, ed. Occupational Medicine. Englewood Cliffs, NJ: Appleton & Lange, 1990:453–458.

38. Simon GE, Daniell W, Stockbridge H, Claypoole K, Rosenstock L. Immunologic, psychological, neuropsychological factors in multiple chemical sensitivity. Ann Intern Med 1993;119:97–103.

39. American College of Providers. Clinical Ecology. Ann Intern Med 1989;111:168–178.

40. Rosenberg SJ, Freedman MR, Schmaling KB, Rose C. Personality styles of patients asserting environmental illness. J Occup Med 1990;32:678–681.

41. Selner JC, Staudenmayer H. Neuropsychophysiologic observations in patients presenting with environmental illness. In: Rest KM, ed. Proceeding of the Association of Occupational and Environmental Clinics (AOEC) workshop on multiple chemical sensitivity. Toxicology and Industrial Health Special Issue. 1992;8:145–155.

42. Rest KM. A survey of AOEC provider practices and attitudes regarding multiple chemical sensitivity. In: Proceeding of the Association of Occupational and Environmental Clinics (AOEC) workshop on multiple chemical sensitivity. Toxicology and Industrial Health Special Issue. 1992;8:51–65.

43. Pottern LM, Zahm SH, Sieber SS, Schneider IJ, LaRosa JH, Brown DP, et al. Occupational cancer among women: a conference overview. J Occup Med 1994;36:809–813.

44. Morton WE. Major differences in breast cancer risks among occupations. J Occup Med 1995;37:328–335.

45. Habel LA. Occupation and breast cancer risk in

middle-aged women. J Occup Med 1995;37: 349–356.

46. Cantor KP, Steward PA, Brinton LA, Dosemeci M. Occupational exposures and female breast cancer mortality in the United States. J Occup Med 1995;37:336–348.

47. Rudolph L, Forest CS. Female reproductive toxicology In: LaDou J, ed. Occupational Medicine. Englewood Cliffs, NJ: Appleton & Lange, 1990: 275–287.

48. Letz G. Male reproductive toxicology. In: LaDou J, ed. Occupational Medicine. Englewood Cliffs, NJ: Appleton & Lange, 1990:288–296.

49. Paul M, ed. Occupational and Environmental Reproductive Hazards. Baltimore: Williams & Wilkins, 1993.

50. Decarteret JC. Occupational stress claims: effects on workers' compensation. AAOHN J 1994;42: 494–8.

51. Perr IN. Asbestos exposure and posttraumatic stress disorder. Bull Am Academy Psychiatry Law 1993;21:331–44.

52. Eliashof BA, Streltzer J. The role of "stress" in workers' compensation stress claims. J Occup Med 1992;34:297–303.

53. Sprehe DJ. Workers' compensation: a psychiatric follow-up study. Int J Law Psychiatry 1984;7:165–178.

54. Elo A. Assessment of mental stress factors at work. In: Zenz C, Dickerson OB, Horvath EP, eds. Occupational Medicine, 3rd ed. St. Louis: Mosby, 1994:945–959.

55. Evanoff BA, Rosenstock L. Psychophysiologic stressors and work organization. In: Rosenstock L, Cullen Mr, eds. Textbook of Clinical Occupational and Environmental Medicine. Philadelphia: WB Saunders, 1994:717–728.

56. Kohn A. Punished by Rewards: The Trouble with Gold Stars, Incentive Plans, A's, Praise and Other Bribes. Boston: Houghton, Mifflin, 1993:181–197.

57. American Medical Association. Guides to the Evaluation of Permanent Impairment. Chicago: American Medical Association, 1993.

58. Wiesel SW, Feffer HL, Rothman RH. Industrial Low Back Pain: A Comprehensive Approach. Charlottesville, VA: Michie Company, 1985:662–666.

59. Keleher KC. Environmental assessment of the home, community, and workplace. J Nurse Midwifery 1995;40:88–96.

60. Messing K. Research directed to improving women's occupational health. Women Health 1992;18:1–9.

61. Teiger C, Bernier C. Ergonomic analysis of work activity of data entry clerks in the computerized service sector can reveal unrecognized skills. Women Health 1992;18:67–77.

62. Rogers B. Women in the workplace. In: Fogel CI, Woods NF, eds. Women's Health Care. Thousand Oak, CA: Sage, 1995:363–383.

63. Keleher KC. Occupational health: how work environments can affect reproductive capacity and outcomes. Nurse Pract 1991;16:23–24, 26–28, 33–34, 37.

64. Bernhardt JH. Potential workplace hazards to reproductive health. JOGNN 1990;19:53–61.

6.4

Sports Medicine

Lisa Nadler

Historical Perspective

Historically, sports medicine concerns are relatively new for women. This can only be put in perspective by examining the historical role of women in sports, or in any type of leisure activity that involves exercise (1). In the early 1800s, there were two major classes of women, those who worked who were primarily immigrants, poor, or enslaved, and those who stayed at home and were members of the middle or upper classes. For those who worked, the primary issue was survival and there was no

"leisure time" to speak of. Those who stayed at home were part of a society that encouraged physical weakness and frailty as a marker of "full womanhood." The "true" women of this era were frail, delicate, ethereal, and soft. Because the female reproductive system was considered inherently pathological and menstruation was considered a serious threat throughout life, women had little opportunity and minimal incentive to engage in any activities beyond archery, croquet, tennis, and golf. Women were allowed to swim, but only in full-length clothing because of the modesty of the era.

In the late 1800s, the suffrage movement began to organize and the inconsistencies between the health needs of working class women, who were required to and could tolerate long hours of physical labor, and the upper class who were felt to need constant rest and protection from any type of physical stress, were being recognized. During this era women also began to make gains in education, although there was still much fear and misinformation. One physician of the era wrote that he feared that "blood would be diverted to the woman's brain and away from her vital organs, resulting in tragic consequences!" To help educated women deal with these stresses, schools started to incorporate programs of "physical culture" emphasizing fresh air, cooperation, hygiene, and posture. Women physical educators were hired to encourage these activities, although the emphasis was still on preserving femininity and avoiding overexertion. Competition was considered evil, and girls were encouraged to avoid the development of muscles and scowling faces that might result from competitive sports.

During World War I, drastic changes occurred as women of all classes began working in factories to support the war effort. Companies began to support sports and recreation activities to help their workers deal with long hours and poor working conditions. Opportunities to participate in sporting activities continued to increase through the Roaring 20s but were set back during the Great Depression in which fewer women were employed and more stayed home in wife and mother roles. Despite this setback, the doors had been opened and World War II changed society's attitudes about women permanently. Women began driving and fixing trucks, riveting steel, and shattering previously held assumptions about women's physical capabilities. For the first time, the image of strong and able-bodied women was viewed as a positive. This is the time when the Professional Women's Baseball League formed. It thrived for many years, until the men returned from the war and public opinion again forced women back into the home.

Women have come a long way since those times, but the process has been slow and difficult. Only because there have been women brave enough to take risks and stand up to public opinion has progress occurred as rapidly as it has. For instance, it was not until 1967 that "K" Switzer entered the Boston Marathon. When officials discovered she was a woman, they attempted to physically remove her. She managed to elude them and, despite their efforts, finished the race. Because of her efforts, women began to compete in marathons. Yet, it was not until 1984 that the women's marathon was made an official Olympic sport. It was not until 1972 that Title IX was enacted, prohibiting discrimination based on sex in educational institutions receiving federal funding. Despite being enacted more than 20 years ago, it is only recently that this law has been enforced. It wasn't until 1973 that Billie Jean King took on Bobby Riggs. Her win resulted in a change in women's sports forever and allowed women to start bringing home the lucrative purses men had been receiving for years at the professional level.

Despite these gains, inequities still exist today. One 1990 study of four major newspapers revealed that men's sports stories outnumbered women's at a ratio of 23:1. The front page of sports sections were dedicated exclusively to women's sports only 3.2% of the time. Photographs of male athletes outnumbered those of female athletes at a ratio of 13:1 (2). A 1987 study showed that 57% of women still felt that they had to choose between their femininity and their athleticism, especially in those sports where strength and size were important to success (3). Obviously, this is still the case. The "sweethearts" of the Olympic Games are almost universally from the "feminine" sports like gymnastics and figure skating. Bonnie Blair only recently began to break down these stereotypes with her success in speed skating.

Girls and women will not choose to become involved in sports at any level until and unless the barriers to their participation are understood and dealt with. The historical perspective helps to identify their origins and allows women to begin to deal with the issues openly. Current barriers that girls and women must face include dealing with fears about the loss of femininity, being less attractive to men, developing muscles, and being labeled a lesbian. These, along with the lack of role modeling in the media and inequities in funding, equipment, and coaching, have resulted in girls and women participating in organized sports activities far less frequently than boys and men.

The benefits of physical activity and participation in athletic teams are far too valuable psychologically, physically, and sociologically to allow these barriers to hold women back. Health care providers must know what the barriers are to address them openly. Only then will they be able to successfully encourage women patients to engage in sports activities that will benefit them in all of these dimensions.

Benefits of Sports Participation

Evidence of the benefits of exercise is extensive and mounting. Much of the original work was done for men, but there is now significant literature available on the benefits of physical activity for women, too. Exercise benefits are documented both for prevention and for management of the diseases of coronary artery disease, hypertension, non–insulin-dependent diabetes mellitus, osteoporosis, obesity, depression, and anxiety. It has also been associated with lower rates of colon and breast cancers, stroke, and may be linked to lower incidence of back injuries.

Girls who are involved in high school sports have lower numbers of teen pregnancies, are less likely to become involved in substance abuse, are less likely to smoke cigarettes, and are three times more likely to graduate

from high school (4). Sports allow girls to learn about teamwork, goal setting, and the pursuit of excellence in performance. These along with other organizational- and achievement-related skills may provide a learning environment that is crucial in today's workplace. Women have had less opportunity to take advantage of these lessons in the past than their male peers. This may have resulted in a competitive disadvantage for achievement, not only in sports but outside sports.

Other health benefits for active women have been well documented. These include a decreased risk of breast cancer, reductions in the risk of osteoporosis (5), higher levels of self-esteem, and lower levels of depression (6). Women who participate in sports have more positive body images and higher states of psychological well-being than those who are less active and have a more sedentary lifestyle (7).

Who Is Involved? Participation through the Life Cycle

Athletes come in all shapes and sizes and with all levels of ability. It is helpful for providers to examine their own biases so that participation is not inadvertently discouraged. Two-hundred-pound women can run marathons, 4 foot, 11-inch basketball players can excel, and 80-year-old women can play volleyball. No matter the age or physical condition of the patient, it is important for the provider to inquire about the woman's activity level and to encourage any type of regular activity or sports participation available.

Early Involvement

Beginning sports involvement at a young age may lay the groundwork for continued participation through time. Activities such as swimming classes and basic gymnastics are offered in most areas for young girls. Providers should routinely ask about a child's participation in this type of activity as part of every well-child check. It may be important to emphasize the positive aspects of involvement to parents who have not had these opportunities themselves.

Equally important is addressing their fears about their child's safety. Discussions with parents explaining that their daughter will learn more quickly and feel more comfortable in the water if she begins when she is young or that she may be more coordinated if she participates in a stunts and tumbling class, are often well received. Besides the benefits of exercise alone, educating parents about the secondary benefits such as developing self-confidence, comfort with her body, and laying the groundwork for the development of self-esteem may provide good motivation for parents to seek out opportunities for their girls.

School Athletics

Grade school and prepubescent girls are less likely to come in for routine health maintenance than younger children; health care providers must be more creative about inquiring into sports involvement. Because of the importance of establishing an active lifestyle early, the topic of activity level, athletic involvement, and the benefits of staying physically fit should be addressed at every possible contact including acute care visits, school or camp physicals, or even a visit attended with their parent. This constant reinforcement from a respected person may provide the encouragement the girl or her family needs to stay involved as she ages and begins to respond to some barriers discussed above. At this age, the girl's perception of athletics is at least important to her parent's perception. Concerns about muscles and the opinions of their peers are beginning to be important and must be addressed.

Grade school athletes most commonly engage in T-ball, Little League baseball, soccer, track, figure skating, gymnastics, and swimming. These activities are often coed, especially in the younger age groups, although this is variable depending on the sport and the level of competition. Because children grow and develop physical skills at such different rates, there can be significant discrepancies in skill levels during these years. In many situations, girls have a significant advantage because they grow earlier and develop physical skills sooner than boys. Sports participation in this age group should focus on development of skills, cooperation and teamwork, and having fun. Providers will want to talk with parents about the importance of these goals and their role as a parent in their child's athletic development. This is the time for the parent to begin to consider what their own goals and needs are for their child's involvement in sports. Parents should be involved, providing support, encouragement, and skills training if they are qualified, and coaching and referee services.

Some children become discouraged about sports participation early because they cannot live up to their parent's expectations and competitive desires. They may be younger or physically less developed than the group they are playing with and have no sense of competition themselves. An office visit is an important time to not only encourage participation but to address these issues as well.

Adolescents

Adolescents, including pre- and postpubescent girls, encompass a wider variety of skill levels. At this age, girls may be involved in just about any sport, may be playing at a recreational, school, or elite level, or may be involved in a completely independent athletic program. Many barriers discussed above begin to have a more major influence in discouraging sports participation in this age group. Issues related to boys, muscles, sexual preference, and attractiveness become significant issues. In addition, the differences in ability, access to teams and coaching, cost of participation, and a family's ability to support a young athlete's involvement all become more significant issues.

This is an age in which the involvement of the provider is important. Unfortunately, it is an age in which girls do not commonly come into the health care setting. In addition, peer pressure can be so intense and so important at this age, addressing the barriers to continued sports participation may fall on deaf ears. The provider may only have a limited chance to address issues of continued participation with athletes of this age, but again advantage should be taken of every opportunity. Each encounter, whether at the school or the office, can be used to discuss these issues, serve as a role model, and encourage continued involvement in sports. Girls of this age are making major choices about their friends, their priorities, and are beginning to define their own lifestyle. It can also be a time to address parental issues from the child's perspective.

This is the age in which girls begin to experience overuse and more chronic injuries. Acute, traumatic injuries occur at any age, but younger children generally have more common sense about pain and tend to stop their activity when they have too much pain to continue. Older children and adolescents often have a coach or parent who may put pressure on them to continue despite pain. Here they begin to develop mental skills that allow them to ignore pain. These skills, which require great focus and control, may benefit the athlete in terms of their performance but may lead to injuries. The provider must understand what level the athlete is functioning at and what performance pressure they are under. Like any adolescent issue, looking at the athlete's life, beyond just the injury or the sport will be key in deciding which athletes need support, which need to be pushed, and which need to be held back and directed more carefully through a healing and rehabilitation process. This is an appropriate age to start addressing issues related to prevention of injuries, and helping the athlete to understand the role of pain and the need for common sense! In addition, the role of the parents and siblings from the girl's per-spective can provide important information about the motivation and support system behind any young athlete.

College Athletes

College age and young adult athletes will have more clear divisions between athletes who participate at the intramural or recreational level, independent athletes who are trying to maintain their fitness, and those involved at the varsity level. Each of these groups will have different concerns and different sports medicine needs. Generally, women who compete at the varsity level will have access to a team physician, someone who should have knowledge and expertise in sports-related injuries and medical conditions as well as the special medical, psychological, and nutritional needs of women athletes.

However, in terms of numbers, the recreational and independent athletes will far out number the varsity level athletes and will generally have more difficulty accessing health care providers who have knowledge and comfort in these areas. This older adolescent and young adult population still deals with the barriers discussed above but are generally able to address them more independently and more maturely than the younger adolescents. Proportionally, there are more chronic injuries in this age group than with the younger athletes, both in the varsity athletes because of more intense training and in the recreational and independent athletes because of less access to coaching and medical care.

Adult Athletes

Finally, there are the adult athletes. The transition time beyond college is difficult for many women, because families, outside commitments, and careers often take large amounts of the time previously devoted to exercise. Because this is a time when many women stop exercising regularly or participating in sports, the provider can be an important source of encouragement and support, helping to problem solve about how and when to find time for these activities. Although the percentage of women who remain involved in sports and athletic activities decreases significantly compared with the younger age groups, there are still large numbers of adult women athletes participating at all levels. These range from walking programs aimed at weight loss, to regular exercise for general health and fitness, to women who continue to compete in Master's swimming, Master's track, road races, local recreational and competitive leagues in a variety of sports, and tournament teams who travel for competition. Only a handful of women remain involved at an elite level once they get beyond college age.

The goals of adult athletes are often significantly different from those of younger athletes, but the health care needs are often greater because of decreased access to coaching and medical care and longer healing times from injuries, resulting in slower recoveries. Long-term participation is the primary goal in this age group; this requires a significant philosophical shift. This may require changes in training programs, rotating between several different activities, following slower, more carefully organized rehabilitation, or more careful selection of equipment. The importance of support and encouragement and education from a health care provider to help with this transition cannot be overemphasized. Exercising as an adult also requires more self-motivation and a change in performance expectations. Understanding that any activity and exercise is better than none, and being comfortable with missing days because of other life commitments, can be a difficult adjustment. In addition, a more common sense approach and being more carefully in tune with signals from the body that might be indicators of early injury are crucial skills that can take years to develop.

Older Women

The final group that needs consideration is the older adult. The physiological changes that oc-cur with aging are now understood to be more often from a lack of exercise than from pure physiological decline. Regular exercise by older patients has been shown to slow the decline in functional abilities while stimulating mental abilities. Helping motivate an older adult to start an exercise program can be difficult, but the benefits are well worth the effort. This group will need careful pre-exercise screening, thoughtful development of a slowly progressive exercise program that takes their safety into consideration, careful choice of exercise activities with guidance from the patient, and monitoring of progress over time. Supervised exercise programs may be ideal for screening, monitoring, and peer support when they are financially feasible and transportation is not an issue. However, any older adult can benefit from even a gentle home program (8).

Basic Sports Medicine Principles

Most girls and women who become involved in athletic activities will never participate at a level in which they will have access to a team physician. Providers must have knowledge about common sports-related injuries and problems that they will encounter in everyday practice. No longer is it acceptable to treat the patient with anti-inflammatories and RICE (Rest, Ice, Compression, and Elevation) alone. It is not appropriate to tell someone to stop an activity because of an injury without working through a rehabilitation program expecting reentry into that sport or problem-solving about an alternative exercise plan. The benefits of prevention and rehabilitation have not been taught well to providers during their training but are essential for the appropriate treatment of sports-related injuries.

In addition, the many health problems that are not related to specific injuries, such as exercise-induced asthma, need to be managed effectively so that they do not become a deterrent to continuing participation for the athlete.

Almost any injury can be improved by immobilization, rest, anti-inflammatory medication, ice, and elevation. However, this treatment alone results in a number of problems. There will always be a few acute traumatic injuries that cannot be prevented, but many injuries are because of preventable causes such as improper protective equipment, inadequate warm-up, too rapid an increase in pace or mileage, or improper rehabilitation of a previous injury. Chronic and recurrent injuries may also be the result of improper shoe choice or biomechanical asymmetries such as a mild scoliosis or a leg length discrepancy. Unless the provider is willing to search for the specific cause in addition to treating the injury itself, the success of the recovery process in the long run will be limited.

Reassessing traditional injury management techniques is an important part of caring for athletic injuries. RICE, as an initial treatment has an important role in early pain management and in limiting inflammation and swelling. However, beyond the first couple of days after an injury, its use should be limited. "**R**est" may be important for an acute injury but probably "relative rest" is a more appropriate term. Immobilization should only be used in the setting of a bony fracture or for extremely short times. Immobilization may help with pain management but rapidly results in significant atrophy of muscles in the area and allows the injury to begin to heal without the benefits of stretching the muscles and tendons involved. Both of these may contribute to prolonged rehabilitation and increased risk of re-injury. Most sports medicine physicians now advocate early mobilization and early strengthening programs for muscles in the area of the injury. In addition, alternative exercise programs should be encouraged from the time of the injury until the athlete has completed the rehabilitation process and is ready to return to their sport.

Ice is important initially for decreasing blood flow to the injured area and may be helpful for pain control. Care should be used not to put the ice directly on the skin because dermal damage may occur. In addition, ice should not be used for longer than 15 to 20 minutes at a time because of the risk of freezing damage to the underlying tissues. Athletes should be educated never to use heat for an acute injury, although it may be used safely and may be helpful for chronic injuries or during rehabilitation. Compression and **E**levation are both helpful for limiting swelling. Fluid and the inflammatory response may slow the healing process. Neither is helpful for the more chronic injury.

Preventative education about shoe choice, warm-up and warm-down time, changes in training routines, use of protective equipment (e.g., mouth guards for rugby and basketball players), stretching, nutritional needs, and benefits of cross-training may all be helpful in decreasing the number and severity of injuries.

Preparticipation Exams

Preparticipation exams are traditionally used in organized sports settings to determine the general health of the potential athlete, detect any conditions that might limit the athlete's participation or disqualify her completely, and assess her physical maturity. They also provide an opportunity for health education and counseling, and they meet the legal and liability concerns of the organization sponsoring the team. These exams are usually associated with school-based sports and there is considerable controversy about the specific strategies that should be used to conduct these exams. The controversies have included how often the exams should be required, whether they should be performed in a medical office setting or at a school, and whether they should be station-type (in which one person does just a small portion of an exam) or an entire exam performed by the same person.

Office setting exams clearly provide the best opportunity for screening and education but may result in exclusion of participants solely because of cost. School setting exams are usually performed on a large number of participants in a short amount of time and therefore require rapid exams, usually performed by health care providers who have never met the participants before and are often done in conditions such as locker rooms that limit privacy, ability to hear well, or immediate access to parents for clarification of historical issues. However, they are inexpensive and guarantee that screening will be performed prior to the start of practice. Station-type exams allow for maximal efficiency because each provider can focus on a particular aspect of the exam, but may not allow any confidential or potentially difficult issues such as eating disorders to be addressed because minimal rapport is developed. Complete history and physicals by one individual get around this issue, but again may be limited by cost and time constraints (9, 10).

At best, preparticipation exams may achieve the goals outlined above. At worst, they are a protection tool for the school against liability and do little to improve the health or safety of the athletes. It is the responsibility of each provider involved in preparticipation exams to work with the school or team officials involved to weigh the risks and benefits of each type of exam to maximize the yield for the participants. All providers involved must also assess their own comfort with the situation and decide whether to participate in the screening process as it is arranged. Provider should not put themselves in a situation in which they feel they cannot adequately perform the screening and therefore are potentially doing an inadequate job or exposing themselves to liability.

A preparticipation exam should include a general screening examination with the primary goal being to ensure safe participation for the athlete. Inquiries about past medical history, past surgical history, allergies, and medications provide the background as they would for any screening exam. In addition, athletes should be asked specifically about risk factors for cardiac disease, symptoms of exercise-related asthma, and whether they have a history of head or orthopedic injuries.

Additional medical history must be included in order to provide complete screening for girls and women. These include menstrual cycle issues including onset, frequency, flow rate, pain, and tampon use. Sexual activity, birth control, last gynecologic exam, and sexually transmitted disease risk should also be assessed, and specific questions about breast pain or support, anemia, and urinary tract infections should be asked. Nutrition issues including eating patterns, weight perception, stability of weight, diuretic use, laxative use, and vitamin intake are all important. Psychological issues should include whether the athlete wants to continue in their sport, concerns about competition and pressure, amount of time allocated to sports activities versus school, work, or other commitments, femininity, risk-taking behaviors, and sexual preference. It is also crucial to ask about substance use including steroids, traditional drugs, tobacco, and alcohol. Questions about exercise addiction should be included in this category, assessing whether there have been negative effects from excessive exercise, and assessing the role that exercise plays in the girl's mental health.

For the physical exam, it is important to consider whether the individual's perception of their weight matches the clinical picture. A graph of height and weight, if under age 18 years, should be included with routine pulse and blood pressure recording. The level of body fat and an assessment of physical maturity are more recent additions to the routine evaluation. Look for clinical signs or symptoms that might suggest anorexia, bulimia, and steroid or other substance use. In addition, this is the time to assess any musculoskeletal complaints the woman describes and assess strength and flexibility. It may be possible to prevent some orthopedic problems that are more common in women such as patellofemoral syndrome by noting patellar tracking problems early and beginning a preventative quadriceps strengthening program (11).

Few laboratory tests have proven to be cost-effective or have high enough yield to warrant routine performance during preparticipation exams (12). Other than those that are appropriate based on specific medical problems or symptoms, the only routine laboratory that might be warranted is testing for anemia in long distance runners. In this group, ferritin levels are a better screening test for iron deficiency in its early phases than hemoglobin or hematocrit.

From the information gathered above, the provider should derive an assessment and plan. The importance of identifying and treating potentially participation-limiting medical problems early cannot be emphasized enough. In addition, addressing old injuries or risk factors for future injuries and matching these with specific rehabilitation or training plans may help an athlete remain involved in their sport for many years. This is also a time to address prevention issues, changes in training methods, and psychological issues related to sports performance and participation. For the older athlete, continued encouragement of participation in any type of athletic activity and education about the importance of exercise over time in the prevention of osteoporosis, breast cancer, and weight-related problems are key.

Physiological Considerations for Women in Sports

Gender differences do not become a significant issue in sports performance until early puberty (13). Physiologically, adult women and men differ in skeletal makeup and arrangement, body composition, body fat amount and distribution, and volume and distribution of muscle tissues. Each of these differences, or the additive effect of them, explain the divergence in skills between men and women from the time of puberty on. They also explain why men and women may be predisposed to different types of injuries.

Women achieve skeletal maturity significantly earlier than men, reaching maximum height with epiphyseal closure by age 17 to 19 years. In addition, women generally have a wider, shallower pelvis resulting in a greater Q angle at the knee (the angle between the long shaft of the femur and the long shaft of the tibia). This may predispose women to more knee problems in sports in which running is involved. Women are also at significantly higher risk of osteoporosis because of lighter, thinner bones initially, followed by rapid bone loss with decreasing estrogen levels at menopause. This risk of osteoporosis may be decreased by maximizing peak bone mass in young women through adequate calcium intake and avoidance of hypoestrogenic states such as that seen in amenorrheic conditions. In addition, continuing weight-bearing exercise and considering postmenopausal estrogen replacement will help to decrease bone loss in older age.

Total body fat has been misused as a measure to determine optimal weight. Adult women have 8 to 10% more body fat than adult men. Women marathon runners may have body fat as low as 6 to 8 %, whereas women in team sports such as tennis, volleyball, and swimming may have body fat of 18 to 24%. There is no "correct" amount of body fat, and avoidance of excessively low body fat is important to avoid possible complications such as amenorrhea or disordered eating. The distribution of body fat is also important. The majority of women have a "gynoidal" fat distribution in which their fat is concentrated in the buttocks and thigh areas. This fat distribution is less commonly associated with health risks such as diabetes, lipid abnormalities, hypertension, and cardiovascular disease than is "android" fat distribution, in which fat is centered around the waist area. Android fat distribution is most common in men and postmenopausal women, but it may also be seen in a significant percentage of the general premenopausal population. The waist size to hip size ratio (WHR) is becoming a more common screening test for assessing health risk based on fat distribution. Low risk is less than 0.75 and high risk is greater than 0.80.

The disparity between the strength of men and women first becomes apparent at puberty. Between trained men and women this can be explained almost completely by differences in muscle mass. The total muscle cross-sectional area in women generally is 60 to 85% of men. Additional differences seen, mostly in upper body strength, can be explained by girls and women doing less upper body weight training. Women and men have the similar responses to weight training in terms of strength gain and muscle hypertrophy.

The resting metabolic rate (RMR) is dependent on the amount of muscle mass. Because women have less muscle mass, RMR is 5 to 10% lower, although trained women will have a higher RMR than untrained women. Because energy cost during activity is related to weight, women will burn fewer calories for a given duration and intensity exercise than men. This makes weight loss more difficult for women.

Psychological Considerations for Women in Sports

A girl who chooses to be involved in sports must come to terms with societal expectations about weight, muscles, femininity, aggressiveness, competitiveness, and sexuality that her male peers will not have to deal with (14, 15). For boys, sports involvement with excellence is an expectation and a source of great glory and pride, whereas for girls athletic involvement is met with second guessing and stereotyping about their motivation and goals. Girls may receive encouragement and support from their family or coaches but they must cope with these issues and accept far less reward than their male peers for athletic success. Family attitudes and support are key to a girl's sense of athletic accomplishment, but even this may not be enough in an environment in which there are few role models and little media coverage at the local or national level. Health care providers of either sex can be an important source of positive reinforcement and role modeling but must understand and feel comfortable addressing these issues openly.

As women get older and are no longer participating in school-based sports, role conflicts continue to exist. Although it is more acceptable to exercise as an adult athlete now than it was in the past, much of this is still done under the guise of "weight management" rather than for fun, for decreasing cardiovascular risk, improving mental health, or for decreasing the risk of breast cancer. Women who are involved in organized sports as adults or who participate in athletic activities must still battle stereotypes and misguided perceptions about their motivations. In addition, they will also have to deal with the conflicts of balancing exercise time with work and family. These remain a larger issue for women than men because of the inequities in societal expectations about how this balance is achieved.

Women who participate in sports often develop skills that help them cope with other aspects of their lives. In some instances, however, the very qualities that have allowed them to become successful athletes may cause them to have psychological or behavioral problems, many of which are not unique to women but are issues with sports involvement generally. When a woman develops her athletic identity at the expense of the other parts of her life, she is at risk psychologically. This single-minded focus may cause sacrifice in other areas to the point where the woman may not develop appropriate social skills or social life and may have no balance either socially or academically. If this athlete then loses her sport because of injury, skill loss, or because she has reached the limits of availability (graduation from college), this may be a devastating loss.

All athletes must deal with the stresses of competition. Although some athletes will thrive under pressure, at least an equal number will suffer adverse effects such as disabling anxiety, gastrointestinal distress, or an overwhelming concern about the impressions of others. Unless the athlete learns to cope with these high-stress situations and the symptoms they elicit, their performance may suffer and they may ultimately leave their sport because the symptoms are too aversive.

Drug use is no less a problem among women athletes than in the general population. Drugs may be used to enhance performance, or to cope with personal problems or competition stresses. They may be started because the athlete feels invulnerable and is looking for a new experience. There are also external drives such as peer pressure, financial incentives, and external pressures to succeed from parents or coaches that may lead to drug use or abuse (16).

Injury can be one of the most devastating issues psychologically for women involved in sports at any age. Changes in routine, inability to train or compete, pain, and changes in self-image may be devastating and result in significant depression. Providers who are caring for injured athletes must assess psychological issues carefully (17). Burnout is another consequence of sports involvement. Excessive training and repetitive workouts result in high physical and psychological stress. An athlete may experience depression, withdrawal, boredom, or a sense of physical fatigue. Athletes who are particularly driven or perfectionistic may be at higher risk for burnout symptoms. If not addressed either in terms of variety in training, cutting back on hours or mileage, or finding a better balance in their lives, an athlete is at risk for developing unhealthy coping styles or leaving their sport entirely (18).

Finally, women athletes are especially prone to eating disorders. An estimated 15 to 62% of women athletes have disordered eating patterns. This is more common in sports in which thinness is considered important such as gymnastics, figure skating, long distance running, and diving, but can be present in any athlete (19). Eating disorders may be initiated by pressures about weight maintenance from parents or coaches, but often the underlying personality structure of the athlete is a major contributor. Women who tend to be driven and performance-oriented may be more sensitive to societal and sports-related demands about their weight and may use their food intake as a method of gaining control over their bodies and their lives (Chapter 11.2).

Nutrition and Sport

Good nutrition is necessary for good performance (see Table 6.4.1). An athlete who is well nourished eats both the proper amount and a good balance of food; she will be better able to cope with the rigors of training or just the necessity of combining a day filled with exercise, work, and many other activities. Other than at the elite level, little emphasis has been placed on nutrition issues in athletes or the special needs of women. The specific nutritional needs of any sports participant will depend on their exercise goals and their training regimen. Recommendations can be separated into caloric needs, the balance of protein, carbohydrate, and fat in the diet, and special needs such as vitamins and minerals.

Table 6.4.1. Dietary Needs of the Female Athlete

Protein	15–18% of the total caloric intake
Carbohydrate	50–60% of the daily caloric intake
	Endurance athletes may require up to 60–70%
Fat	25–30% of the total caloric intake
Calcium	Adolescents and post-menopausal women: 1500 mg/day
	All other women: 1000–1200 mg/day
Water	One pint of water for each pound lost during exercise

Total Caloric Needs

Total caloric need will depend on exercise level of training. If the goal is high-level performance, caloric needs will be higher but will need adjustment based on the number of hours exercising per day, the demands of the specific sport, and the training season. If the goal for exercising is weight loss, the number of calories must be low enough to allow for a 1- to 2-lb weight loss per week, but high enough to avoid ketotic states in that the athlete is breaking down protein for energy requirements. Because of the high incidence of eating disorders in women athletes, regularly observing caloric intake, body weight, and percent body fat is important for all athletes.

One common misconception is that athletes have higher protein needs than the general population. The need for protein may be slightly higher for athletes during the weight training phases, but in general, protein should be limited to approximately 15 to 18% of the total caloric intake. This is usually not difficult to achieve in the average American diet, except in vegetarians in which special attention may need to be paid to ensure adequate intake. Carbohydrate is the primary energy source for physical activity and should make up 50 to 60% of the daily caloric intake. Carbohydrates are used primarily for anaerobic metabolism of glucose and for aerobic metabolism of glycogen. Endurance athletes may require up to 60 to 70% intake to meet their total caloric needs. Fat is a stored energy source used to supplement carbohydrates during aerobic activity. It is a less efficient energy source and should be limited to 25 to 30% of the total caloric intake. During exercise, short-lasting, high-output exercise uses anaerobic metabolism primarily of glucose and lactic acid. These come almost exclusively from carbohydrate sources. For longer exercise periods, the proportion of energy from fat use is higher.

Vitamins and Minerals

A well-balanced, adequate calorie diet should provide an athlete with adequate amounts of vitamins and minerals. Although there is little harm in a supplemental multiple vitamin, all sports participants should be cautioned against megadose vitamins or products billed as weight loss supplements. Calcium and iron are the two nutritional components that should be specifically considered for women. Low levels of calcium increase the risk of osteoporosis. Women who exercise do not have higher calcium needs than the general population, but the majority of American women do not get an adequate supply. Adolescent and postmenopausal women should get 1500 mg per day and all other women should get 1000 to 1200 mg per day. Calcium becomes even more of an issue in exercising women who become amenorrheic. It has recently been shown that this hypoestrogenic state causes rapid resorption of calcium from the bones and produces irreversible osteoporosis, predisposing the athlete to stress fractures and complete fractures and more severe osteoporosis with age. Calcium is best obtained from natural sources, primarily dairy, but supplements such as calcium containing antacids should be used if the dietary intake is insufficient to meet the goals listed above.

Iron requirements are higher for women than men because of the monthly blood loss with menstruation. In addition, "sports anemia" may compound this loss. This may occur through mechanical breakage of the blood cells or dilutional effects of increased blood volume in athletes. Ferritin is a more sensitive test for screening than hemoglobin. Again, dietary intake is the most efficient method of iron replacement, but iron supplements should be considered if dietary intake is inadequate.

Water and Electrolyte Requirements

Water is essential during exercise because of its importance in thermal regulation. Inadequate replacement can reduce performance and cause severe illness. Because sweat is hyposmolar, water is lost faster than sodium during exercise. For this reason, the ideal replacement for exercise of short duration is water alone; however, for exertion of greater than 1 hour, electrolyte replacement is important as well. One pint of water should be ingested for each pound lost during exercise. Cool fluids with 6 to 8% carbohydrate and a small amount of sodium are the ideal solution to maximize gastric emptying and absorption. Salt tablets are not appropriate because of their erosive effect on the gastric lining.

Disordered Eating

Eating disorders are common in women involved with sports (20) (see Chapter 8.2). The pressures to excel are often linked to minimizing body weight and reducing body fat in hopes of maximizing performance. Women do this through binging, purging, caloric restriction, use of laxatives, diet pills, diuretics, or excessive exercising. Although all forms of eating disorders are on a spectrum, the most severe can have profound physical and psychological effects and are almost always detrimental to athletic performance. The incidence in women athletes is probably considerably higher than in the general population, with estimates as high as 60% depending on how "disordered eating" is defined. Sports in which women are at the highest risk include those in which there is judging involved such as gymnastics or figure skating, sports in which leanness is linked to performance such as long distance running or swimming, and sports that use weight classifications such as rowing, weight lifting, and martial arts.

Many societal factors contribute to the development of disordered eating patterns, but there are several additional factors that make women athletes at greater risk. The competitive forces that are present in sports are not experienced by women in the general population. These forces may lead an athlete to lose weight at an inappropriate rate or in an inappropriate manner. In addition, athletes are often given weight goals by their coaches that are unrealistic or unobtainable and are provided with little supervision during weight loss. Athletes often have a heightened awareness of their body, but at the same time may be able to block out signals such as pain and hunger because of their athletic training. In addition, personality traits such as perfectionism and compulsiveness, which attract women to sports and make them successful, may be risk factors for disordered eating patterns and ultimately eating disorders. Finally, athletes may use food intake as a way to gain control over their lives and their bodies. Food can become the primary focus and can be used as a diversion from other important issues. The stakes are high in the more elite forums of sports, and women may be willing to take risks with their bodies and their health that they would not otherwise take (21).

The first step is prevention of disordered eating patterns. This can be done through education of the athletes, and the parents and coaches. Unrealistic expectations for performance and weight must be identified. When weight loss is important for performance, or if weight loss is the primary goal of the person participating in the activity, it should be done with careful guidance and supervision. These efforts alone will not be enough. There will still be athletes and sports participants who developed disordered eating patterns and then potentially severe eating disorders, no matter how much education is done. The second step therefore is identification of signs and symptoms when they occur. This requires education of coaches, parents, providers, and team physicians. Rapid weight loss, declining performance, attitudinal changes, frequent bathroom breaks, and avoidance of community eating situations may be early signs. Physical and laboratory abnormalities are not usually present until there is severe disease. Like substance abuse disorders, this is often a secretive illness with large amounts of denial and avoidance. Identification may be difficult even for experienced providers.

Disordered eating patterns and eating disorders should be screened for at every preparticipation exam and in any woman who has signs or symptoms suggestive of a problem. The earliest clues may be as nonspecific as slight weight changes or body image misperceptions. When a pattern of disordered eating or an eating disorder is suspected, a more complete evaluation including weight and nutritional history, weight perception history, athletic performance review, and physical and laboratory testing as indicated must be done. The support of a coach or parent is invaluable in helping evaluate the athlete and providing treatment if indicated. Treatment usually follows the models used in substance abuse. Education is important across the entire spectrum of disordered eating patterns. However, because this is often a disease of denial and involves such secrecy, this is rarely sufficient.

Because eating disorders can be progressive and ultimately fatal, an aggressive team approach to treatment is imperative. The involvement of a coach, parent, or significant other is vital along with the health care team including nutritionist, provider, mental health provider, and support network. Careful monitoring is crucial. One advantage of treating the more elite or varsity level athlete may be the control that can be exerted over their practice and competition involvement. Many health care teams will require an athlete to maintain a certain weight in order to participate.

Exercise-Associated Menstrual Abnormalities

Amenorrhea is less than two menses per year and oligomenorrhea, defined as three to nine menses per year, are common in athletic women (22) (see Chapter 12.1). The etiology of exercise-associated changes in reproductive endocrinology leading to oligomenorrhea and amenorrhea are complex and involve hypothalamic dysfunction, probably alterations in the secretion of GnRH. Menstrual dysfunction in athletes is most commonly associated with weight loss, lowered body fat, emotional stress, and intensive training, but what combination of factors or whether there is a genetic predisposition

in some women is unclear. There are women who have all of these risk factors who have normal menses and women who have only one of these issues who have amenorrhea. In addition, some women will have return of menses with only rest and no change in their body fat.

Women who have these menstrual irregularities have low levels of estrogen and progesterone, similar to postmenopausal women. In women athletes who have amenorrhea or oligomenorrhea, there is significantly less bone mass than in their athletic peers or in nonathletic women with regular menses. This low estrogen, low progesterone state most likely inhibits women's ability to develop normal skeletal mass, attain peak bone mass, and maintain normal amounts of bone. This leads to osteopenia and potentially osteoporosis, placing the athlete at risk for stress fractures and premature osteoporotic fractures (23). This bone loss is not entirely reversible even with estrogen replacement or normalization of menses through training and nutritional modification. This has tremendous implications for the long-term health of women, especially as the population continues to age (24).

Key to evaluating an athlete for oligomenorrhea or amenorrhea is to perform a complete evaluation. The diagnosis of exercise-associated amenorrhea is a diagnosis of exclusion, no matter how clear-cut the etiology seems to be. A complete history, physical, and appropriate laboratory evaluation is essential before concluding that there is not another etiology. The treatment decisions involve whether conception is desired and how willing the athlete is to change potential risk factors.

Assuming that conception is not desired, treatment should start with evaluating and optimizing the athlete's nutrition, decreasing the training intensity, increasing the body weight by a small percentage, and ensuring that the athlete is getting adequate amounts of calcium in their diet. Not all athletes are willing to alter their training and nutrition routines in this way. If they are receptive, this approach should be attempted first because it treats the underlying etiology. If the athlete is not willing to endorse these changes, estrogen replacement is a reasonable alternative approach. This can be done through birth control pills or through cyclic estrogen and progestin therapy similar to what would be used postmenopausally (25).

There will be athletes who are not willing to take exogenous estrogen because of side effects or their approach to life and medications. For women who are not willing to either modify their training and lifestyle or take exogenous estrogen, education is key. The woman must understand that she is estrogen deficient and as a result is at significant risk for osteoporosis no matter what her calcium intake is. In addition, it is important that she understand that this osteoporosis will put her at risk for stress fractures and is potentially irreversible that could cause her significant disability in her later years. If the patient understands this, her bone mineral density should be followed yearly along with continued monitoring for stress fractures and further education.

Adolescents may have either delayed menarche, secondary amenorrhea after only one or two periods, or more typically secondary amenorrhea years after onset on menses. Because the long-term effects of delayed menses and secondary amenorrhea in this age group is not known, the approach is often somewhat different. Many physicians are more aggressive about insisting on alterations in training routine, body weight, and nutrition. Because there is often a coach or a parent involved, this approach may be more successful than for an older woman. In addition, many physicians do not start estrogen supplementation until age 16 or 18 years unless there are birth control needs.

The combination of disordered eating, amenorrhea, and osteoporosis are so often found together they are known as "the female athlete triad" (26) (Table 6.4.2). The emphasis in women's health should be on prevention through education and early identification and

Table 6.4.2. Definition of the "Female Athlete Triad"

Disordered Eating	Binging, purging, caloric restriction, use of laxatives, diet pills, diuretics, or excessive exercising
Amenorrhea	Less than two menses per year
Osteoporosis	Lower bone mass than in their athletic peers or in nonathletic women with regular menses. Low skeletal mass, inability to attain peak bone mass and maintain normal amounts of bone. Osteopenia and potentially osteoporosis, stress fractures and premature osteoporotic fractures

treatment of these disorders. Additional research and then education about the health consequences of these disorders must be undertaken, and providers must know how to screen for and treat them effectively.

Summary

The importance of participation in sports for girls and women cannot be overemphasized. In spite of the many barriers that still exist, women have come a long way. Participation in athletics among women has reached record proportions, and many of the barriers are slowly coming down. Health professionals can encourage the continuation of these trends, first by participating in sports or at least living an active lifestyle themselves, thus providing a role model to patients. Second, providers can encourage an active lifestyle and participation in sports for *all* of their patients both women and men, and encouraging parents with young children to provide this role modeling from home. Finally, by understanding the physiological, psychological, nutritional, and medical issues unique to women athletes, providers are in a position to screen and monitor athletes more successfully and to treat their injuries or medical problems in such a way as to *encourage* their continued athletic participation.

References

1. Lutter JM. History of women in sports. In: Agostini R, ed. Clinics in Sports Medicine. Philadelphia: WB Saunders, 1994;13:263–279.
2. Duncan ML, Messner M, Williams L. Coverage of women's sports in four daily newspapers. Amateur Athletic Foundation of Los Angeles, 1992.
3. Miller Brewing Company: The Miller Lite Report on American Attitudes Toward Sports. Milwaukee, Miller Brewing, 1985.
4. Miami Herald, May 25, 1991. From: Institute for Athletics and Education, 1990:40.
5. National Osteoporosis Foundation: Fact Sheet, 1993.
6. Colton and Gore: Risk, Resiliency and Resistance: Current Research on Adolescent Girls, Ms. Foundation, 1991.
7. Chalip L, Villige J, Duignan P. Sex-role identity in a select sample of women field hockey players. Int J Sports Psych 1980;11:240–248.
8. Lefor N, Rousseau P. An exercise prescription for older patients. Geriatric Consultant 1991;Nov/Dec: 13–15.
9. Lombardo JA. Pre-participation physical evaluation. Prim Care 1984;11:3–21.
10. McKeag DB. Preseason physical examination for the prevention of sports injuries. Sports Med 1985;2: 413–431.
11. Johnson MD. Tailoring the preparticipation exam to female athletes. Phys Sportsmed 1992;20:61–72.
12. Committee on Sports Medicine and Fitness, American Academy of Pediatrics: Sports Medicine: Health Care for Young Adults. 2nd ed. Elk Grove Village, IL, American Academy of Pediatrics, 1991
13. Sanborn CF, Jankowski CM. Physiologic considerations for women in sports. In: Agostini R, ed. Clinics in Sports Medicine. Philadelphia: WB Saunders 1994;13:315–325.
14. Barnett NP, Wright P. Psychological considerations for women in sports. In: Agostini R, ed. Clinics in Sports Medicine. Philadelphia: WB Saunders, 1994; 13:297–313.
15. Cann A. Gender expectations and sports participa-
tion. In: Diamant L, ed. Psychology of Sports, Exercise and Fitness. New York: Hemisphere, 1991:187.
16. Cohen GL. Drug abuse in sport: an overview. in: Cohen GL, ed. Drug Abuse in Sport: A Monograph. Institute for International Sport 1988;1:2–5.
17. Smith AM, Scott SG, O'Fallon WM, et al. Emotional responses of athletes to injury. Mayo Clin Proc 1990;65:38–50
18. Feigley DA. Psychological burnout in high-level athletes. Phys Sportsmed 1984;12:109–119.
19. Brownell KD, Rodin J. Prevalence of eating disorders in athletes. In: Brownell KD, Rodin J, Wilmore JH, eds. Eating, Body Weight and Performance in Athletes. Philadelphia: Lea & Febiger, 1992:128.
20. Rosen LW, McKeag DB, Hough D, et al. Pathogenic weight control behavior in female athletes. Phys Sportsmed 1986;14:79.
21. Johnson MD. Disordered eating in active and athletic women. In: Agositini R, ed. Clinics in Sports Medicine. Philadelphia: WB Saunders, 1994;13: 355–369.
22. Shangold MM, Rebar RW, Wentz AC, et al. Evaluation and management of menstrual dysfunction in athletes. JAMA 1990 263:1665.
23. Barrow GW, Saha S. Menstrual irregularity and stress fractures in collegiate female distance runners. Am J Sports Med 1988;16:209–216.
24. Rigotti NA, Neer RM, Skates SJ, Herzog DB, Nussbaum SR. The clinical course of osteoporosis in anorexia nervosa: a longitudinal study of cortical bone mass. JAMA 1991;265:1133–1138.
25. Shangold M, Rebar RW, Wentz AC, Schiff I. Evaluation and management of menstrual dysfunction in athletes. JAMA 1990;263:1665–1669.
26. Nattiv A, Agostini R, Drinkwater B, Yaeger KK. The female athlete triad: the inter-relatedness of disordered eating, amenorrhea, and osteoporosis. In: Agostini R, ed. Clinics in Sports Medicine. Philadelphia: WB Saunders, 1994;13: 405–418.

Suggested Reading

Agostini R, ed. Clinics in Sports Medicine: The Athletic Woman. Philadelphia: WB Saunders, 1994;13:263–508.
Agostini R, ed. Medical and Orthopedic Issues of Active and Athletic Women. Philadelphia: Hanley & Belfus, 1994.
McKeag DB, Hough DO. Primary Care Sports Medicine. Dubuque, IA: Brown and Benchmark, 1993.

6.5

Nutrition Considerations

Jo Ann Rosenfeld

Introduction

Good nutrition is essential for healthy living and a good quality of life. It is also the primary method of treatment for a variety of medical problems from heart disease to irritable bowel syndrome. Obesity, eating disorders (Chapter 8.2), and poor eating habits are also contributing factors to many discomforts and illnesses. Nutritional assessment is important in preventive health care and an important evaluation for therapy for diseases from burns and trauma to COPD and cancer.

Many authorities including the American Academy of Family Physicians, the American College of Physicians, the American Heart Association and the US Preventive Services Task Force have all provided recommendations for a healthy diet. Basic guidelines are included in Table 6.5.1. Throughout this book, there are specific guidelines for athletes (Chapter 6.4), diabetic women (Chapter 15), perimenopausal women (Chapter 21), older women (Chapter 22), and women with pregnancy (Chapter 10.4), lactation (Chapter 17.1), obesity, anorexia (Chapter 8.2), and other times in the life cycle.

Table 6.5.1. Basic Guidelines for a Healthy Diet

Maintain a healthy weight

Eat a variety of foods

Eat a diet low in total fat, saturated fat, and cholesterol

Moderate use of sugars, salt and sodium, and alcoholic beverages

Eat a diet with 5 or more servings of vegetables, fruits, and grain products

Considerations for Providers

Because nutritional counseling spans preventive health care and a wide variety of medical conditions, it should be considered frequently. There are several considerations when discussing nutrition with a woman. Her level of desire for changing her diet and her prior knowledge will structure the conversation. The level of comfort of the provider is another. The provider can begin the discussion, consider any particular conditions that may need a special diet and provide the counseling himself or provide a referral to a nurse or nutritionist who can follow the woman over time. Nutritional changes are not sudden, but working with the woman over time is rewarding.

There are several medical conditions that require specialized nutritional support and counseling. Over- or underweight women will need various calorie and protein alterations to a general diet. Women with anorexia or bulimia will need intensive psychological assistance along with nutritional counseling. Women with diabetes, both type I and II, need a strict exchange diet with a reduction in fat content and a continuing relationship with someone to discuss diet over time. Women with COPD or infections will need increased calories. Vegetarians can adequately maintain a healthy diet; some experts believe it a more healthy diet than that of nonvegetarians. Fads, low calorie diets, and lack of variety should be avoided.

Certain situations may involve a worsening of diet. Living alone may lead to lack of preparation of regular meals, while significant demands of caregiving, work, and children may make taking time for a complete meal difficult. Poverty does not preclude a good diet, but may make it more difficult to provide variety and balance. Difficulty with vision in preparing the food, inability to drive to go shopping, arthritis that makes moving and picking groceries painful, or dementia may make preparing a good diet difficult.

General Recommendations

Recommended calories for women are less than that for men—usually 1200 to 1500 calories per day, but this can be increased for increasing levels of exercise and metabolic need, such as COPD or infections, or be decreased for losing weight. A consistent reduction of 250 to 300 calories per day should result in a 1- to 2-lb weight loss per week.

Figure 6.5.1 shows the Food Guide Pyramid that helps to illustrate the proper number of servings of each food group daily. The diet should be low in total fat. Fat should be less than 30% of the diet. Saturated fats should be 10% or less of the total diet calories. Cholesterol intake should be approximately 300 mg per day. Complex carbohydrates should make up 45 to 60% of the diet, and include grains, breads, fruits, and vegetables. Women with irritable bowel syndrome should increase their intake of bulk and dietary fiber. Sugars should be used in moderation. Protein should be 12 to 15% of the diet.

Salt intake, if possible, should be approximately 3 g per day, approximately one-half to one-fifth of the normal US diet. It may need to be lower for women with hypertension, congestive heart failure, or kidney failure.

The nutritional pyramid has been developed as a way to explain a healthy diet (Table 6.5.2). Explanation and discussion will not only interpret the information but show the woman how important the provider feels this is.

A well-balanced diet should provide most of the vitamins and minerals needed. However, an extra 1000 mg of calcium should be taken by premenopausal women, and 1500 mg should be taken by adolescents and postmenopausal women. Menstruating women who do not eat a great deal of red meat or other foods high in iron should probably supplement their diet with iron. A multivitamin with iron can be taken daily, but is not essential if the diet is well balanced.

A Guide to Daily Food Choices

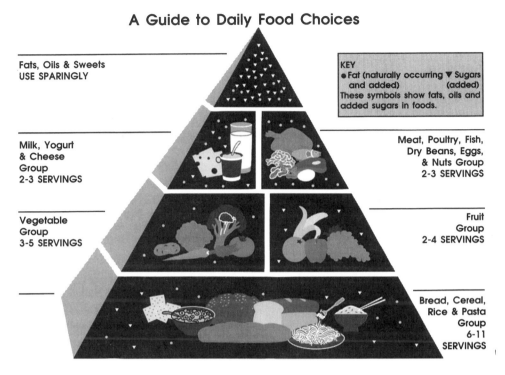

Figure 6.5.1.   Food guide pyramid.

Table 6.5.2. Recommendations for Daily Good Diet for Adult Woman*

Calories	1200–1500 per day
Fat	<30%
Saturated fats	<10%
Cholesterol	300 mg per day
Complex carbohydrates	45–60%
Protein	12–15%
Salt intake	3 g per day
Calcium	1000 mg calcium premenopausal women
	1500 mg by post-menopausal women and adolescents

*Not pregnant, breast-feeding, or trying to lose or gain weight

Special Situations

Chapters on pregnancy, lactation, preventive health care, and chapters on diabetes and coronary heart disease all explain particular considerations for nutrition.

Adolescents

It will be no surprise to learn that adolescents, although they need greater calories and protein, have an overall poorer diet. African-American adolescent women are at higher risk of a poor diet than other ethnic groups. Some of the factors that cause all adolescents to be at risk for a poorer diet are peer pressure, fad diets, pressure to be "thin," chaotic lifestyle in which regular meal times and sitting down to eat is unlikely, poverty, lack of opinion that nutrition is important, and easy availability of fast foods.

Adolescents need more calories than older women and more calcium, at least 1500 mg of calcium per day. Providers should discuss nutrition with adolescent patients. Sensitivity for fad dieting, anorexia, bulimia, and factors leading to lack of normality of mealtimes may aid in discovering teenage women who need more intense counseling and education.

Elderly

Nowhere is the social situation more likely to impact diet than in the elderly population. Living alone is a great deterrent to regular meals, as is a fixed low income. Getting a check once a month may make poor nutrition at the end of the month very likely without good planning. Inability to drive or to walk long distances around a huge grocery store comfortably, problems in vision or dentition, or dementia can all impact ability to plan a healthy diet.

Lack of electricity, fear of lighting stoves or burning themselves, and poor vision decreasing the likelihood of reading instructions or cooking appropriately, will decrease preparation of complete meals. Asking questions like "How do you get your groceries?" or "How often do you cook yourself dinner?" may help screen for problems. There are too many "tea and toast" elderly women who end up with nutritional anemias and unexplained malnutrition.

Some ways to overcome these problems are lunches at senior centers, helping women create social networks for eating and living together, services such as Meals-on-Wheels, and using local senior agencies for transportation and help obtaining groceries. A microwave may be easier to use than gas or electric stoves. A home visit by the provider or nurse may reveal lack of electricity, water, refrigeration, or heating for meal preparation. The provider may be able to help the woman use local social service agencies, families, or friends to overcome the obstacles.

Summary

Nutrition is an area of continuing concern that needs a place in many encounters. Women are unlikely to change quickly, but a continuing relationship over time can make nutrition an important part of the health prescription.

Special Considerations for Nurse Practitioners and Physician Assistants

Nutrition becomes a primary concerns at certain times in a woman's life, e.g., pregnancy or when there is a disease process related to nutrition. Providers who not only know about the importance of good nutrition, but also value it, will make nutritional assessment and counseling part of all periodic health care. Diet histories must become a routine component of clinical practice and can be informative for both the provider and the woman client. Not necessarily time-consuming, a history can elicit information about a woman's attitude about food and health, her cultural beliefs about food, economic or other factors that affect nutrition, and special practices, food allergies, and supplements. A 24-hour diet recall can be used to gather more specific data (1). Asking specifically about the indiscriminate use of supplements as substitutes for a well-balanced diet points out areas for teaching (2).

Providers also have to be aware that treatments they prescribe can have a negative effect on nutrition, a problem that may be of special concern for elderly women. Some drugs, including digoxin, fluoxedine hydrochloride, and hydralazine hydrochloride may cause anorexia; antibiotics and aspirin may lead to nausea. Laxative abuse by the woman may be contributing to malabsorption. Low-salt and low-fat diets are often perceived as less palatable, leading the woman to either cheat on her diet or eat less (2).

Multiple factors affect food consumption patterns in women, including the environment, personal and cultural preferences, economic resources, level of education, and personal goals and social roles. Providers have to be aware of the potential impact of new products on the market that are targeted to specific populations or address preferences for calorie, sodium, fat, or cholesterol reduction. These "designer" foods do not usually have an impact on the overall quality of a woman's diet, and in fact, may lessen the incentive of the woman to know about the nutritional quality of her diet. Eating away from home is also increasing, especially as a woman's income increases, often leading to the consumption of more fat and less calcium, fiber, vitamin A, and folate. Lack of time because of working may also lead to increased of consumption of timesaving foods in the home (3).

Awareness and evaluation of nutritional information in newspapers, magazines, and books and on television allow the provider to help the woman evaluate the accuracy of the media presentations and its meaning related to her own nutritional needs. Providers need to ask a woman what she's heard or read lately, especially related to her specific nutritional concerns. Most women understand that there is no single "wonder" food that will solve their problem. A no-fat potato chip is not necessarily a good food choice (3).

References

1. Worthington-Roberts B. Nutrition. In: Fogel CI, Woods NF, eds. Women's Health Care. Thousand Oaks, CA: Sage, 1995:221–260.
2. Johnson RM, Kaiser FE, Kerstetter JE, Reuben DB. Maintaining good nutrition in the elderly. Patient Care 1995;15:46–60.
3. Haines PS. Food consumption patterns in women. In: Krummel DA, Krisetherton PM, eds. Nutrition in Women's Health. Gaithersburg, MD: Aspen, 1996: 103–140.

Psychosocial Issues of Adult Women

Tina M. Kenyon

Introduction

There are as many variations in women's circumstances as there are individual women. Thus, although highlighting core issues that affect many women, this chapter cannot comprehensively address all the issues for all women throughout the world. The best approach for providers offering care to women is to know them individually, to learn how they view what they are experiencing, and to understand what contributions a provider can make to a woman's quality of life.

Where We Came from Often Influences Where We Are Going

The lessons a woman learns as she moves through childhood and adolescence into adulthood, whether positive or negative, have an impact on how she views herself in relationship to the world. Each woman has her own unique path to follow, and the era in which she was born may modify her approach to life (Table 7.1). Gail Sheehy outlines that "five different generations now occupy contemporary adulthood, spanning birth dates from 1914–1980." She identifies these genera-

Table 7.1. Some Possible Psychological Tasks for the Woman Age 18 to 45 Years

- Establishing self-identity independent from and yet coexistent with original family.
- Creating and maintaining independence either as a single person or in a relationship.
- Participating as member of a partnership or marriage.
- Taking responsibility for one's own health and life circumstances.
- Establishing a means of financial self-support and creating a satisfying work environment.
- Determining readiness for parenting or deciding not to become a parent.
- Establishing and maintaining a nurturing and secure family structure for raising children.
- Participating as a responsible member of extended family, e.g., caregiving.
- Balancing role demands, e.g., family, work, society.
- Attending her own physical, psychological, social, spiritual, and developmental needs.

tions as: (*a*) the World War II Generation, 1914–1929; (*b*) the Silent Generation, 1930–1945; (*c*) the Vietnam Generation, 1946–1955; (*d*) the Me Generation, 1956–1965; and (*e*) the Endangered Generation, 1966–1980." Ms. Sheehy describes events characteristic of each period and their potential influence on people's views (1).

The significant adults (e.g., parents, other relatives, teacher, coach, group leader) in her early life and their teaching/role modeling often have a significant impact on a woman's development. Because half of all mothers of American infants return to work and two-thirds of American children under age 4 are in day care, these care providers are often key. The peer group with whom a woman identifies and their norms can shape her behavior as well. Factors of race, economic circumstances, living conditions, geographic location, quality

of or lack of social support, level of education, cultural heritage, religious or spiritual beliefs, and family situation influence how each woman meets the developmental challenges she faces as she grows toward her later years. For the primary provider, learning about a woman's particular history, through events she sees as significant, will often shed light on her strengths and current difficulties.

Issues of Self-Esteem

A variety of sources provide a woman with information she uses to formulate her self-concept, and the coping mechanisms she chooses are most often closely related to her level of self-esteem. A woman's view of herself is rooted in the combination of messages she receives from early childhood forward. Encouraging as well as critical comments from those around her, in all spheres of life, contribute to the picture she believes others have of her. The opinions of others blended with her own self-assessment shape her overall sense of self. Add in the societal norms and media representations of concepts such as beauty, youth, attractiveness, success, and health, and the resulting pressure experienced by some women is enormous. Depending on how a woman fares in her comparison of herself to these "standards," an internal source of stress to become an "ideal woman" that cannot exist in reality can emerge.

Some women have successfully disregarded, and even rejected, these media portrayals. Instead, their goal is to feel comfortable with their own individuality. Cultural norms may also contribute to how a woman's behavior is influenced by outside factors. For example, a woman from a given culture is socialized to believe that being heavier is more attractive. However, when she comes to the United States, many in this society favor more slender women. Thus, she may receive negative messages about her body that conflict with her internal positive self-concept, causing distress.

Age-defying makeup, restrictive clothing

and shoes, hair coloring, cosmetic surgery, athletic equipment, weight loss products, and a myriad of other products and services are intensively marketed to women. They are meant to increase attractiveness, stop or delay the aging process, and promise health and long life. Many are expensive, and thus only available to a select group with financial resources. Young women striving for the ideal "Barbie doll" body can endanger their physical and mental health significantly. Women who are offered as "ideal" by the media are speaking out about the harmful practices and potentially fatal eating disorders that have overshadowed their lives. Clearly, norms of health and beauty that are attainable and more realistic are needed.

Another dimension of self-concept that must be discussed is competence. Achieving a sense of mastery, overcoming adversity, growing beyond painful experiences, and taking responsibility for one's own life can all contribute to increased self-esteem. In 1957, Simone de Beauvior said "It is not nature that defines woman: it is she who defines herself by dealing with nature on her own account in her emotional life" (2). Self-esteem and level of belief in one's own abilities are critical issues. They are often at the center of matters like adherence to treatment plans and how a woman progresses through life.

Health care providers can assist women in defining what success means to them and in setting reasonable goals. In the absence of encouragement from family, women can be well served by support from others, including their provider. When self-confidence improves, behaviors directed at self-care and health will likely become more frequent.

Life Events

Singlehood

Being single (without a significant long-term relationship) in this society has many implications. The meaning of being single should be explored with each individual woman. According to Tuula Gordon, "No one specific type of woman is likely to be single. Singlehood is a result of a complex interaction between structural, cultural and biographical aspects" (3). Unlike marriage, being single is not necessarily reinforced or supported in society. Women are single through a variety of circumstances including family constraints, widowhood, divorce, or a conscious choice to be single for religious or other reasons. Gordon also notes that some single women would be interested in a relationship "only if any required compromises are balanced by positive gains" (4).

People may make assumptions about a woman who is single, such as there must be something "wrong" with her or she must be a lesbian. She may be left out of certain social situations or fail to participate in others because she is single in a coupled society, further isolating her. Others may envy her freedom, or have pity for her circumstances (5). Carol Anderson and Susan Stewart observe that singleness encourages women in midlife to evaluate assumptions, expectations, and attitudes that have guided their lives thus far. The traditional assumption that having a mate and being a mother is the only route to happiness is questioned. The ability to be alone and comfortable may require a change in attitude and perspective (6).

Single women often find sources of support through hobbies, social groups, family, and friends. A sense of belonging and positive quality of life can result. Thus, they may not be reliant on any single relationship to address all of their needs.

There are also challenges facing women who either choose or are thrust into being single. Some encounter loneliness, isolation, economic difficulties, and depression. Each individual can explore a variety of ways of coping with these challenges such as developing new interests, seeking greater career satisfaction, financial reward, and physical exercise. Support from other single women or a therapist may help her learn to enjoy being alone. Practitioners should be sensitive to how each woman views her singleness, and assist her to either accept or change her circumstances.

Coming Together: Women as Partners

Both partners bring their backgrounds and experiences to their new relationship, creating a new entity with its own characteristics. Increasingly, the circumstances and parameters of relationships are evolving. Women are marrying at any time from adolescence to advanced age, with the trend moving toward "delaying" marriage past age in the 20s. Some women have a series of intimate relationships for varying lengths of time, and others marry for life. Divorce is more widely accepted as an alternative to an unhappy marriage. In some areas of the country, gay, lesbian, and bisexual couples are comfortable being open about their relationships. Legislation to allow same sex couples to become legally married is being considered in some states. For some couples, the commitment of marriage (whether religiously and/or legally recognized) is important. For others, cohabitating without formal marriage, or maintaining an intimate relationship with separate living quarters is preferable.

Half of all marriages in America end in divorce, although many of these women and men remarry. There are many issues that can create varying degrees of difficulty in relationships. Communication is frequently a prominent source of stress. Dr. Deborah Tannen asserts that women and men are socialized in different cultures, and thus have different styles of communication. "Pretending that women and men are the same hurts women, because the ways they are treated are based on norms for men (7). Acknowledging the gender differences in ways of speaking is an important concept. Couples may disagree on how money is brought in, dispersed, and spent. Decisions about whether to have children, and if so, how

many and when can be very complex. Styles of discipline and limit setting for parents are potentially different. How to interact (or not) with extended family and where to live can create conflict. Questions about pets, employment, and religious matters can all be sources of discord at one time or another in many relationships.

Couples are placed in the position of having to cope with the issues in the relationship, as well as outside influences. The level of satisfaction experienced by both partners depends on how conflict is dealt with, and how the goals and needs of each partner are addressed. Judy Mann offers an explanation. "All too often, the seething hostilities that explode into violence and divorce can be traced to gender roles learned in childhood, and to the misunderstandings and failed communications that occur years later when one party seeks to change the other" (8). The definitions of commitment, intimacy, and of the future of the relationship can be similar or different for each partner and must be discussed.

The provider must listen and keep an open mind when discussing the patient's intimate relationships, being careful not to assume the gender or age of the partner. Within a provider-patient relationship that is based on trust and mutual respect, a woman can more easily disclose sensitive information.

The provider should consider the cultural norms that guide a woman's choices regarding her relationships. For example, who is an unacceptable partner and when is the appropriate age for marriage may be factors. Interpretations or norms and traditions vary greatly among families. Consequently, gathering culture-specific information from the individual is indicated.

The provider should encourage communication while providing sympathetic listening. Providing supportive listening and a chance for ventilation, while validating normality and common experiences, may be sufficient in solving or easing the woman's concerns and needs. Encouraging and suggesting methods for enhancing communication between the partners may give the provider a means of helping the woman. Follow-up visits continue the support. Offering a forum in which both partners could discuss problems might give a short-term solution and start the process of communication. Providing further consultation to marriage counselors or therapists for longer-term therapy may be needed.

The provider should listen to indications that there may be violence in the relationship. The prevalence of violence in relationships is significant and greatly underreported. Domestic violence crosses all economic, social, cultural, age, and gender boundaries. It is impossible to ask the woman about violence to determine whether or not a woman is at risk in her relationships and to offer useful suggestions for further help (see Chapter 12.3).

Decisions Around the Inclusion of Children in a Woman's Life

Depending on a variety of factors, women make decisions about children. These choices may be limited by religious, geographic, economic, or familial factors. For example, technology available to more affluent women to address infertility is not accessible to economically disadvantaged women. Because engaging in the role of parent dramatically alters a woman's life, it is a decision that has long-term effects and bears thorough consideration.

Pregnancy
Access to birth control, abortion, prenatal care, and assistance with child care can all impact on the timing of pregnancy. Many pregnancies are unplanned, and half of these are unwanted and end in abortion (9). On the other hand, with increasing infertility many pregnancies are especially "valued" and important to the woman and her family.

Pregnancies can occur in a number of situations from the unwanted to the welcomed.

In cases of rape and incest, women have become pregnant under traumatic circumstances. Some women may have an unwanted pregnancy, but their beliefs may preclude them from either terminating the pregnancy or investigating adoption. Despite a child being initially unplanned and even unwanted, the woman may bond and desire the child by the time of delivery. When a woman wants to be pregnant yet cannot conceive, she may accept this situation or seek outside help. Technology now allows those with sufficient financial means to intervene in an effort to overcome infertility.

Pregnancy is a time of immense psychological change. Issues long hidden or forgotten become obvious and have to be considered urgently. Families examine their financial resources including medical insurance, and sufficient or not, stress can occur. Pregnancy or subsequent early motherhood often decreases or curtails the woman's salaried employment, causing more personal and financial stress, in turn causing personal isolation from typical patterns of coping such as work and contact with friends at work. Families often decide to relocate either with or away from extended family. Either case potentially causes new strains on the marriage. Women who smoke, abuse alcohol or other substances, or eat poorly may feel guilty and decide to change their lifestyles, causing strain and distress. Others may continue these behaviors despite the provider's cautions. Conflicts or issues with in-laws come to the forefront and must be considered. The woman will have concerns about the health of the growing child. Questioning her own ability to mother will also surface during pregnancy. She may feel sick for the first time in her life. In pregnancy she is facing something that can't be changed, taken away, stopped, or made to feel better. Alternatively and simultaneously, it can be a time of elation, expectation, fulfillment, fear, frustration, and joy.

The provider should supply time for the woman to express her concerns, questions, and uneasiness. Listening compassionately, validating the pertinence of her concerns, and expressing the universality of such experiences may relieve anxiety and support many women. Creating a therapeutic relationship with the woman will give her a foundation of support on which she can rely over time. The provider can give what medical information the woman desires, or contribute consultations or suggestions for further information. Support groups, such as prenatal or parenting classes, and talking with other women in similar circumstances are of considerable value.

Development and Birth

One great concern of the mother is the health of the growing child. Although medicine can provide information throughout the pregnancy, with prenatal tests available to detect genetic abnormalities and ultrasound to detect anatomical abnormalities, the apprehension often remains. If the woman can discuss her fears and concerns with her provider, it may help reassure her.

A normal birth in itself causes a complete alternation in the focus of the woman and her family. Overnight the woman becomes a 24-hour-a-day attendant and the infant becomes the central focus of the family's attention. Besides providing the baby's physical necessities, the mother often is, literally, the provider of sustenance, particularly if she is breast-feeding. Especially with a first baby, she may have concerns about her ability to care for the infant and produce sufficient milk. In addition, fatigue and changing health and sleep patterns decrease a woman's ability to cope. Remaining at home, often alone with a newborn, especially if she has worked out of the house may make her socially and emotionally isolated, further adding stress. An early home or office visit at 4 to 7 days of age in which the focus is divided between the child *and* the mother, including offering support from a nursing mother organization, friends, or support group, can help.

If there are real or suspected malforma-

tions, the provider will need to spend extra and continuing time with the woman and her family. Information must be given and repeated, along with offering support and counseling. The parents may need to decide whether to continue the pregnancy, and if so, they may be more adequately prepared to care for the special needs child. Infants born prematurely and/or with medical conditions that inhibit normal growth and development will place special stresses on the woman and her family. Grief for the "normal" child she has lost, fears for the pain and suffering of the child, and the stresses illness place on any family may intensify. Support from family and friends, support groups, and strong relationships with providers are invaluable. The woman will need continuing visits to the provider for help in grieving and coping. Referral to psychological counseling may be necessary.

The Lifelong Task of Parenting

It has been said that the role of parent is perhaps the most important in society. Current trends present new challenges to those who are responsible for any aspect of caring for children. How prepared are parents to guide children? Women are affected by their own childhood experiences. If their childhood was secure and structured, they are likely to raise children who are assured and self-confident. However, if they suffered as children, learning painful lessons through abuse or neglect, they will be influenced by these experiences. If their home situation lacked nurturing (or even basic supervision), these traumatic processes will likely impact on parenting ability, whether positively or negatively. It is important to consider a woman's heritage (i.e., culture, childhood experiences, and what lessons she uses to guide her behavior), and what it brings to her parenting style. Those who grew up in an environment with a substance-abusing parent may have learned responsibility and coping at an early age, but may have lost the opportunity to be a child. Others may have been loved, nurtured, and cared for despite extreme economic deprivation. Issues such as substance abuse, promiscuity, social and economic deprivation, and a language barrier can interfere with a woman's ability to parent effectively. As children grow, their developmental progress may trigger unresolved issues in the parent that may not be obvious to the patient or the practitioner. What a woman learned during her own childhood, emotions sparked by events in her child's life, and struggles that she faces all set the stage for her ability to assume the role of parent.

The age at which a woman becomes a parent is also a factor. Adolescents, often having insufficient emotional maturity and financial resources, can encounter unique difficulties, such as parenting while continuing to attend high school and dealing with their own problems of independence and identity while raising children. There appears to be a trend toward delaying age at pregnancy into the later 20s or 30s, or even early 40s for various reasons. A woman may wait until she has greater career stability or has found a partner to share the responsibilities. Others simply feel more emotionally prepared, or they may have finally overcome infertility. Later parenting has other stresses such as possibly less flexibility or having health problems of her own or her parents with which to cope.

A proportion of families are nontraditional, lacking the father and mother and children structure. Blended families with half- and step-siblings, single-parent families, and multigenerational families have been formed because of emotional, cultural, legal, and financial reasons. The woman's mother or her partner's mother may be a significant figure in the decision-making process. The grandparent may even assume the primary responsibility for raising her grandchildren when her child is unable to parent or opts out of the role.

When the legal system becomes involved, this becomes more complex. There is controversy if same sex parents or single individuals become adoptive parents, or if children from one race of culture are adopted by parents of another. Settlements regarding custody and support of children after divorce can be difficult.

Increasing numbers of households are headed by a single parent, most often a woman. Single motherhood is another significant stress. It can be the result of social situations, the absence of one parent, divorce, widowhood, or by choice. Simple everyday problems like sick children or getting the car inspected, or complex problems like getting sick herself, can become immense for a single mother. Many mothers feel the need to be "super-mothers," doing everything themselves; this eventually takes its toll on her own defenses and coping mechanisms. The provider should sensitively inquire into support systems (e.g., family, friends, church, other single mothers) who can provide comfort, aid, time, and even babysitting. Most important, the single mother is often amazingly isolated in daily struggles at work and home, and needs contacts with others. The provider should urge the single mother, just like any mother, to take time for herself and adult friends, and initiate and pursue social contacts, even if it requires more time. Single parents may need greater outside support and resources. However, in many instances, women continue to demonstrate their strength, resilience, and ingenuity. Even in homes in which two adults live, one may have most or all of the day-to-day responsibility for child rearing, making that individual virtually a single parent.

Given the best circumstances (i.e., adequate resources, stable family) the dangers facing children today can create a complex and arduous path toward adulthood. Peer pressure to drop out of school, to use substances, commit crimes, become sexually active in early adolescence, join gangs, engage in high-risk behaviors, and defy parental limits competes with family influences. Incidents of abduction from formerly safe areas such as playgrounds and victimization of children by group leaders and other trusted adults are causing concern for parents. Homicide and suicide, violence in schools and neighborhoods, children accidentally or intentionally harming each other with weapons, and other threats to children's safety and well-being are being reported with greater frequency. As children age, the concerns of parents change, but most parents remain concerned about their children well into adulthood. Education is an important tool in helping parents to be as constructive in their teachings as possible, avoiding instilling a sense of fear that can inhibit a child's functioning.

Providers can educate parents and children, both verbally and through the various age-specific written materials available, helping guide them through the lifelong tasks of parenting.

Life in the Sandwich Generation: Caregiving

Women have always cared for ill family members, especially elderly relatives, e.g., their mothers and fathers, and often their parents' parents, and even extended family members, such as aunts or uncles who never had children. However, the elderly are living longer than ever before and are likely to be well longer, although they may need some care. Again the task descends on the woman in the family. Women are "sandwiched" in a position of providing care for at least two generations simultaneously. Because families are having fewer children and having them later in life, women find themselves parenting children of ages ranging from infant to young adult in addition to caring for older relatives.

Decisions often arise regarding where the person in need will live. The quality of the relationships between the caregiver and the relative often strongly influence care arrangements. Some families welcome their elders to live with them, assist with the care of the chil-

dren, and enrich each other's lives. In other families, intolerable tension is created by trying to combine strong personalities or by sharing living quarters that may have inadequate space. Unfortunately, many families wait until arrangements need to be made emergently, rather than planning far in advance. Many emotions are associated with decisions about care for the senior members of the family, including guilt, satisfaction, joy, stress, uncertainty, sadness, and closeness.

In many families in the United States, the responsibility may either fall to or be specifically taken on by the female child, usually the oldest in age. If the elder needing care is insufficiently prepared financially for later life, the financial burden may also fall on the caregiver. Often the woman must quit her job or take a leave of absence, frequently without pay; caring for the elderly may impoverish the family. If travel is required in order to provide care, this can further tax the caregiver. As care needs may increase with the progression of age or illness, the situation may require more time and the elder may need to have care in a more supervised setting. Women must make difficult choices about how to spend their time, given home, family, job, friends, and other responsibilities in addition to the care of the elder. Usually, the woman sacrifices care of herself first.

The woman's partner and family may be of great help financially, physically, and emotionally in helping her care for the elderly relative. Alternatively, the financial strain and the change in physical and emotional living situations may create great stress. The husband or partner may help or may resent the financial burden, the lack of attention given to him, or the invasion of privacy, even if it is his relative. He may be at a point in his career when he has little time to contribute to caregiving. Children can see an elderly grandparent in the house as a chance to continue relationships or resent the intrusion of their mother's attention and time, or both. Women who work outside the home may be at a point in their careers when the intrusion of time and caring is exhausting and stressful, if not harmful. Women who work outside the home spend as much time with older parents as homemakers, but can spend more money on outside help as well.

Providers have traditionally been "patient-oriented," caring for either the elderly relative or the woman. At a time of caregiving, the provider may need to become "family-oriented," helping the whole family come to a diagnosis and treatment plan. Caring for the relative at home may or may not be the best solution for all the members of the family, the elder included.

If providers can encourage families to formulate a care plan far in advance of a crisis, this may help alleviate time pressure that can complicate decisions. Family involvement will also hopefully prevent all of the responsibility from being given to one person, and thus forestalling caregiver burnout. Providers can assist women by talking with the elderly parents whom she anticipates will need care and exploring the options available. She can investigate the Family and Medical Leave Act of 1993 that allows her to take up to 12 weeks of leave annually to care for an ill relative. Providers can help women find respite programs, if available, home health services, and support groups, such as those associated with families of Alzheimer patients. By assuming the caregiver needs care as well as the elder and helping her care for herself as well, the provider will give support and sanction for discussing concerns and needs. This may help burnout by helping those in the complex, demanding, and stressed group known as the "sandwich generation" to ensure care for themselves as well as for those around them.

Work and Education

The place of women in the workforce has taken place over time. Women do not always choose to work outside the home; many women are forced to by economic constraints.

Definitions of what a "job" is and a "career" is may differ by individual. A woman may be employed in a position that provides income, but limited satisfaction. In some areas of the country, and for some cultural groups, high rates of unemployment, competition for a few positions, and other limiting factors have made it difficult for women to explore new options. Access to vocational programs is growing, thereby offering options outside the traditional 4-year degree program. Certainly women with children, particularly single parents, have to be resourceful in finding child care so they can attend classes.

In many states, public welfare programs are providing day care and job training to help people achieve independence and self-reliance. Often, the only routes to a better paying and/or more satisfactory position are longevity in a company or further education. Many colleges and universities, in an effort to attract the "nontraditional" students such as working mothers, are offering courses during the evening or weekend hours. Some educational institutions are also shortening the length of time needed to earn the certificate or degree through creative means, such as offering credit for life experience. However, the decision to better one's career is often not a simple one. First, a woman must have some belief that she can achieve her goal, or at least that it is worth making the attempt. Also, support from family, friends, and coworkers and financial considerations must be weighed. Those with a great deal of family and work responsibilities may be reluctant to attempt to add more to an already full week. In most cases, a higher level of education can offer a woman more options.

As a result of increasing numbers of women working outside the home, the role of "homemaker" is often devalued. Women are asked if they work, and some make the comment, "No, I'm just a homemaker." Although the quality of the actual tasks may be different, many women who work inside the home would argue that they work just as hard as a women in the workplace. Some find it more fulfilling if they establish connections with peers working at home.

The world of work outside the home presents many challenges. Do couples compare their earning capacity with one another, and does that create stress? For some couples, it is not an issue. A woman returning to the workforce after a period of being at home to raise children may find it difficult to regain her previous level in the company hierarchy. Consequently, as author Felice Schwartz explains, "Knowing that to preserve their career momentum they must disassociate themselves from maternity as swiftly as they can, women often go back to their jobs before they are ready physically, mentally, or emotionally" (10). Women continue to face discrimination and sexual harassment, although more women appear to be pursuing action either within the place of employment or in the courts. Equal pay for equal or comparable work is still not a reality.

Whether a woman works inside or outside the home, she is likely to be the person responsible for making sure the daily activities (e.g., cooking, laundry) are completed. Thus, even if partner and children "help," it is still up to the woman to organize, facilitate, and delegate what needs to be done. The old cliché that "a father works from sun to sun, but a mother's work is never done" is still creating exhaustion.

Women's careers may be on a different timetable than the traditional men's careers. Often, time is taken out for bearing and rearing children. The "mommy-track" may seem, at first, a necessity and a favor for women, but the problems with promotion, tenure, seniority, and advancement by being considered different and less serious may generate stress. Alternatively, returning to work immediately after delivery for career or financial reason brings its own stress. The woman physician who returns to her patients and the woman

salesclerk who must return immediately or she will lose her job and her insurance are both under stress. The multiple roles the woman carries necessitates choices between (a) after-hours work and longer workdays that may be needed for continued employment and advancement and (b) caring for the home and children. Caregiving of elders can further complicate her time management. Providers should recognize these multiple demands and support women in many ways such as not undermining or denigrating daycare (such as offering children medicine which is given twice daily so medicine need not be given by daycare workers), offering evening and weekend hours, not assuming the woman is or can be the caregiver, or that she is at home, ever available.

Work in itself has not been shown to damage the health of the woman or her family. Numerous studies, from the Framingham study to long-term follow-up of children in daycare, have shown that if the mother finds satisfaction in her job, both she and her children benefit (11). Women who work outside the home have better health problems, and fewer psychological and somatic problems. Children of working mothers may suffer certain viral diseases earlier, but psychologically and educationally, if the mother is satisfied, do as well or better than children of at-home mothers, and they tend to be more independent and socially oriented.

The provider needs to discover what "work" a woman does, the setting in which she does it, and what it means to her. Positive reinforcement and ego support can be a great service.

Role Definitions

The responsibilities associated with the multiplicity of roles that a woman fulfills often compete, and the combination can at times be overwhelming. According to Maggie Mulqueen, "The woman attempts to fulfill a valued role associated with competence (therefore masculinity) according to societal norms, as well as fulfill the feminine role according to sex-role norms in her personal life. . . . what has been reported by and about these women . . . is burnout, divorce, depression, and latch-key children" (12).

Women have a multiplicity of roles that compete for time, energy, and attention. For example, one list might include the following: woman, daughter, partner, parent (which includes teacher, nurse, social worker, accountant, chauffeur, housekeeper, cook, mediator, judge, jury, nutritionist, spiritual leader, entertainer), sibling, aunt, niece, granddaughter, godparent, employer, employee, colleague, friend, neighbor, and lover. A woman must separate her own expectations of herself from the expectations she perceives from others, and the actual expectations of others. It is challenging at best to devise a system of time management that accomplishes the tasks at hand with enough flexibility to incorporate those unexpected events that inevitably occur. Unfortunately, for many women, caring for themselves is usually the last priority. Time for self-reflection, self-nurturing, and personal growth is often limited or absent unless a woman can make sure time is reserved for such activities. It may be helpful for a woman to list all of her roles and the corresponding responsibilities, and then estimate the amount of time each role requires in a typical week. It will often highlight how little time she reserves for those activities that would "recharge" her such as relaxing, socializing with friends, or doing activities she finds enjoyable. These activities need not be costly (so as not to create further financial concerns). Some roles may be more enjoyable despite their time demands, and others will likely be stressful as well as time-consuming.

Providers can assess how a woman is coping with multiple roles, and educate her about taking time for herself. Assisting the woman to assess her roles and responsibilities, and to ex-plore other resources that may further her ability to add her own needs to the list, can be helpful.

The Effects of the Mobile Society

Unlike any other period in history, people have the capability of being more mobile than ever before. The development of better transportation systems, improved highway networks, more means of communication through computers, cellular telephones, facsimile machines, and video technology have created a wide range of options for where we live and how we live.

An outgrowth of these changes is the scattering of some families over a much wider geographic area. With distance comes more communication and travel expenses, and that may limit the amount of face-to-face contact family members and friends have with each other. Distance may also complicate arrangements for the care of someone far away. However, it can also create needed space between family members who have stressful relationships.

Despite these advances, in some regions of the country extended families either share living quarters or relatives live in separate residences in close proximity to one another. When family members live close to one another, they can provide support and assistance, or there can be close observation, scrutiny of behavior, and an unwanted level of intimacy, or they may coexist. The quality of the relationships certainly offers a framework for how satisfactory the arrangement is for all concerned.

The setting in which a family lives also shapes the issues they face. Inner cities may be crowded, noisy, polluted, and dangerous. They may also offer more social, economic, cultural, and health care resources. Public transportation can make a greater variety of job possibilities accessible and allow more choices of where to live. Suburban living may still be crowded and polluted, but likely less noisy and less dangerous. Because suburbs are still close to urban areas, one can still access the resources of the city in a less urban setting. In rural areas, transportation can be less available and resources can be more sparse or absent. Health care needs may be more difficult to address because of limited availability. This setting is often quieter, safer, and environmentally cleaner than other areas. Any of these areas can suffer from high unemployment and economic depression. Families may live in a given area because of family tradition, inability to relocate for economic reasons, desirability, or quality of education systems, but the setting can have a range of influences socially and psychologically on how the family functions. As families move from one place to another for reasons related to employment, climate, desire for new experiences, or extended family, this can impact on continuity of experiences, particularly for children.

How women are "expected" to behave can vary by region as well. For example, a woman raised in an urban area on the east coast may have been socialized to behave differently than a woman in a rural Midwestern town. Regional differences in language, food, customs, and degree of openness to newcomers are elements of what the woman will experience living in this new area. Becoming comfortable with an unfamiliar state, city or town, neighborhood, and home often requires a period of adjustment. Learning where to procure needed goods, what the norms are, where essential services are, and exploring how one fits in are challenges that come with relocation.

Health care providers can offer understanding, information about key services in the area, and help support families as they adjust to new surroundings. School transitions may be particularly challenging for children. Providers can help normalize experiences and reduce anxiety as families cope with change.

Losses Experienced by Women

Loss, an expected though painful element of life, has taken on new dimensions because of such issues as AIDS, domestic violence, and increased street crime. The number of losses a woman faces during her lifetime, some of which are predictable and others not expected, often have lasting effects on how she copes. Although painful, loss can provide opportunities for further growth and learning.

In childhood through adolescence, a woman can lose relationships through death, abandonment, relocation, separation, and substance abuse. She can lose less tangible things like the dream of a happy childhood and her innocence. Loss at an early age can make dealing with losses later in life more complex, depending on what level of acceptance is achieved.

In adulthood, sources of loss diversify. Related to pregnancy, a woman can experience infertility and lose the dream of carrying and delivering a child. She can have a miscarriage at various stages of pregnancy or deliver a stillborn child. A woman can deliver a child that has a congenital anomaly or chronic illness and can lose the ideal of having a "healthy" child. At any stage of development from infancy to adulthood, it is said that the death of a child is the most stressful event a woman can experience. Some women lose their children through war, accident, disease, violence, accidental or intentional substance overdose, or suicide. Others "lose" children when they separate from the family, either as part of expected maturation or through stressful relationships. For many parents, the process of letting go can be quite difficult. Relationships with friends, neighbors, coworkers, and lovers begin and end.

Everyone at some point in the life cycle will die. Even the anticipated loss of an aging parent, spouse, or other family member is likely to be painful for a woman. The degree to which a woman is affected by these losses is a function of her relationship with the person who has died. For example, in the case of a person who was abusive and inflicted injury, a woman may be relieved at the person's death. When the woman and her significant other shared a close relationship over many years, she is likely to be profoundly affected by the death.

Unfortunately, with the advent of the HIV epidemic, losses of mind-boggling proportions have become part of the current reality. People of all ages are affected by this deadly disease. Some segments of the population, particularly the gay community, have felt the loss dramatically. The rate of HIV infection among heterosexuals is increasing. It is likely that in the years ahead everyone's lives will be touched by this disease, whether directly or indirectly. Many investigators, particularly Elizabeth Kubler Ross, have written a great deal on the subject of coping with loss and the emotional stages commonly experienced by those who are grieving (13).

Another disturbing trend that leads to several types of loss is the prevalence of violence in our society. Homicide is one of the leading causes of death for some segments of the population. Violence among adolescent women appears to be increasing as well. If apprehended, the offender can serve prison time, thus causing separation from the family.

Some women have cause to be fearful in their homes, in their neighborhoods, and in the workplace. There are disturbing reports of workers under stress or those seeking revenge returning to places of employment and killing and wounding coworkers. Children are bringing weapons to school and intentionally and/or accidentally injuring or killing each other with their parent's weapons at home. People are forced from their vehicles at gunpoint in carjackings. Drive-by shootings aimed at rival gang members are killing innocent people caught in the cross fire. Although people internalize the risks of living in our society

to varying degrees, the loss of an overall sense of safety is a significant one.

Losses not often considered as significant but possibly still painful are such things as loss of a home and one's possessions through war, natural disaster, theft, economic hardship, or relocation to an institution such as a nursing home. A woman often loses a sense of personal safety after being attacked. Loss of dignity can occur when an accident or illness renders a woman dependent on others. Losing a body part such as a breast or reproductive organs because of illness or injury has physical as well as psychological implications. The loss of hopes, dreams, and goals for various reasons can be devastating for some women. The significance of losing a pet, particularly when the woman received companionship from the pet, can sometimes be underestimated. Some women consider retirement as a loss of status in society. Through the desire to be accepted, or for other reasons, some women experience a loss of their cultural identity. In abusive relationships, women often lose their autonomy and self-determination. On a more philosophical level, some women experience a sense of despair and the loss of hope associated with current global problems such as environmental concerns and the threat of nuclear war. Judith Viorst, in her work *Necessary Losses*, describes a different kind of loss. She writes, "We will mourn the loss of others. But we are also going to mourn the loss of our selves—of earlier definitions that our images of self depend upon. For the changes in our body redefine us. The events in our personal history redefine us" (14). If women can become comfortable with their evolution as people, then it may be easier to accommodate the physical and emotional changes that accompany the process of growing older.

Practitioners may receive more information about the losses a woman has experienced by inquiry based on a broader definition of loss. Perhaps a woman has not identified the impact of losses that do not involve the death of someone, and with the provider's assistance she may be able to more clearly identify issues contributing to her current distress.

How Women Cope

The variety of coping strategies employed by women is both remarkable and important to examine. Some strategies are less functional than others and can create more difficulties. However, survival may be the only focus possible, regardless of its quality, given the conditions under which some women live.

From groups of Puritan women assisting each other with childbirth and newborn care, to "sewing circles" for wives of civil war soldiers to support each other, to the modern day groups that come together for a range of purposes, women have a long time tradition of group support. Common interests that bring women of all ages together include sports, investing, crafts, business interests, life situation similarities, and social causes. The group setting is a forum that can be used to facilitate coping.

The spectrum of experiences a woman is called upon to cope with evokes a range of responses. There are many positive ways of coping. Many women cope with their own adversity by helping others, at times to the detriment of their own quality of life. Women are testing traditional boundaries and limits, by participating in male-dominated professions, sports activities, and leisure pursuits, and demonstrating their abilities. Humor, and self-expression through art, music, dance, and writing may be therapeutic. Survivors of various forms of cancer are helping promote prevention and empowerment for others. On political, social, economic, and psychological fronts women are working to change the way they are treated and viewed in this society. Younger women are being encouraged to celebrate their femaleness, and their individuality. Emma Goldman, an early feminist and human-rights activist, said, "True emancipation begins nei-

ther at the polls, nor in the courts. It begins in a woman's soul" (15). Hopefully, the outstanding role modeling contributed by the millions of talented, capable, self-confident, assertive women is being internalized by the young women just beginning to formulate their approach to the world.

Conversely, some coping mechanisms are a detriment to the woman. First, substance abuse, as a response to stress, may be hidden by the woman and overlooked by the provider. Shame, guilt, and denial can be associated with substance abuse. In addition to alcohol, the woman may be self-medicating an anxiety or depressive disorder with prescription or over-the-counter drugs. These underlying problems are not always recognized and thus are not treated appropriately.

The provider should screen for a history of sexual assault, sexual abuse, domestic violence, and other traumatic events. These violent events often lead the woman toward certain coping styles such as dependence, acceptance, and continuation of violence. Prostitution and promiscuity, certainly grave risks to a woman's physical and emotional health and safety, may be traced back to earlier sexual trauma the woman has experienced. These patterns can also result from other situations such as homelessness or substance abuse.

Somatization is also usually connected with mental and emotional stress that has long passed the point of tolerance, and has thus become physical. Women can attempt to meet unfulfilled needs in dysfunctional ways, such as drug-seeking behavior. At the root of those dysfunctional requests there is often an unmet need.

For the provider, women who demonstrate manipulative or destructive behavior can be challenging to treat. Often, the team approach is most effective in those situations. Through screening for issues such as substance abuse, a history of physical or sexual abuse, anxiety, depression, and other significant events, the provider may develop a greater understanding of how to intervene. Likewise, the creative solutions that women generate to some complicated problems can offer the provider invaluable learning experiences. Each woman has a multidimensional story to tell, and it will often reveal clues that help the provider to help the patient.

Conclusion and Implications for the Primary Care Provider

Women's lives are intricate combinations of historical events, all their experiences, the world in which they live, influences of those around them, and how they see themselves. Providers are given the privilege of participating in the lives of women with whom they interact. Owing to the uniqueness of the individual, every provider does not form a positive relationship with every patient. Nevertheless, if an atmosphere of trust and respect can be fostered between a woman and her health care provider, the relationship can be mutually rewarding. Over a period of time, it is hoped that a woman would develop a level of comfort with the provider that allows her to be honest and to share sensitive information. Similarly, it is hoped that by assuring confidentiality, a nonjudgmental approach, and a willingness to help within sensible boundaries, the provider can assist the patient to reach this level of comfort. Primary providers enjoy the advantage of longitudinal relationships not found in episodic care. Therefore, they are in the optimal position to provide care that supports women through all the developmental stages of life. By remaining aware of how their own values, experience, and beliefs about women are woven into the style of practice, the provider can more effectively respond to women as individuals.

Special Considerations for Nurse Practitioners and Physician Assistants

An evaluation of a woman's psychosocial situation should be obtained early in the interview. Wheeler suggests some excellent interview questions, starting with a general question, "Can you tell me a little more about yourself?" Depending on the woman's response, the provider can ask her to "Tell me about your living situation" to gain information about who she lives with, the quality of her relationships and her community. Asking a woman what she would like to change about her living situation will give insight into the woman's perception about her living environment. Women should be asked about stressors they are currently experiencing and recent losses, including people, jobs, possessions, and dreams. Asking the woman who is the most important person in her life and who she can call on for help will give information about her support system (16).

In recent years, women have experienced greater freedom in decisions about education, marriage, childbearing, and careers. Although these opportunities are welcomed, women may experience stress because expectations are less defined and they combine life options that were not available to women in the past. Although women may welcome more egalitarian life patterns, they may experience conflict when confronted by others who expect more traditional behaviors (17).

Women who identify many life stressors or who present with recognized stress-related disorders need specific education related to coping with stress. In addition to major life events, women should realize that daily hassles and irritations add to their discomfort. Clinicians might help women group their stressors into categories (e.g., interpersonal problems, time demands, internal conflicts) so that specific strategies can be identified such as cognitive coping skills, relaxation techniques, meditation, time management, and assertive skills. Some problems areas might be more appropriately addressed by specialists in psychotherapy or marital counseling. Community education programs that teach relaxation strategies or time management strategies may be available (18). Women who join groups with other women can find strength in their shared experiences, thus becoming more self-sufficient, assertive, and knowledgeable (17).

Anger in women is an issue that is receiving increased attention. If excessive or managed inappropriately, it can contribute to physical or psychological illnesses. Women will often report anger when they feel out of control or powerless, especially when they are unable or do not wish to do all that is expected of them. As practitioners ask women about stressors in their lives, they can also ascertain how the women react to stressors. Women who admit that they have a "hot temper" or "fly off the handle easily" need to learn more healthy ways to manage their feelings, whether by confronting antagonists, talking with a friend, or using calming behaviors (19). Providers who wish more information on anger and health should see the article by Droppleman et al. (19).

Health problems of women may also result from internal and external pressures to change their bodies. Specific body parts are scrutinized at different times in our society, a practice that is dehumanizing and damaging to a woman's sense of wholeness. Although a woman may be within the normal range of variations, especially weight, she may feel pressured to conform to what she perceives to be the ideal figure and engage in practices such as chronic dieting, cosmetic surgery, and sunbathing, all of which may actually place her at health risk.

Providers can encourage women to (1) value characteristics such as creativity and intelligence instead of physical appearance alone; (2) define exercise as an enjoyable means to improve well-being instead of a punishment; and (3) focus on internal sensations of pleasure rather than viewing the body as an object. In addition, providers must guard against their own actions that might devalue a woman. Negative comments about a woman's weight or avoidance of eye contact during an examination can project a lack of acceptance to the woman (20).

References

1. Sheehy G. New Passages—Mapping Your Life across Time. New York: Random House, 1995:23–25.
2. Mann J. The Difference—Growing Up Female in America. New York: Warner Books, 1994:53–54.
3. Gordon T. Single Women. New York: University Press, 1994:24.
4. Gordon T. Single Women. New York: University Press, 1994:26.
5. Simon B. Never Married Women. Philadelphia: Temple University Press, 1987:81.
6. Anderson, Carol M, Stewart S. Flying Solo—Single Women in Midlife. New York: W. W. Norton and Co, 1994:136.
7. Tannen, Deborah. You Just Don't Understand—Women and Men in Conversation. New York: William Morrow and Co, 1990:16.
8. Mann J. The Difference—Growing Up Female in America. New York: Warner Books, 1994:58.
9. Rosenfeld, JA, Zahorik PM, Batson J. Unplanned pregnancy: are family practice residents taking all opportunities to make a difference? JABFP 1994;7:77–79.
10. Schwartz, Felice N, Zimmerman J. Breaking with Tradition—Women and Work, the New Facts of Life. New York: Warner Books, 1992:46.
11. Rosenfeld JA. Impact of Maternal Employment on health of the Family. Curr Prob Pediatr 1995; 25:1–10.
12. Mulqueen, M. On Our Own Terms—Redefining Competence and Femininity. Albany, NY: SUNY Press, 1992:14.
13. Kubler-Ross E. On Death and Dying. New York: MacMillan and Co, 1969.
14. Viorst J. Necessary Losses. New York: Simon and Schuster, 1986:265.
15. Kopp CB, Kirkpatrick M, eds. Becoming Female—Perspectives on Development. New York: Plenum Press, 1979:212.
16. Wheeler L. Well-woman assessment. In: Fogel CI, Woods NF, eds. Women's Health Care. Thousand Oak, CA: Sage, 1995:141–187.

17. Davis MS, Youngkin EQ. Health and development through the life cycle. In: Youngkin EQ, Davis MS, eds. Women's Health. Norwalk: Appleton & Lange, 1994:17–32.

18. Manderino MA, Brown MC. A practical, step-by-step approach to stress management for women. Nurse Pract 1992; 17:18–28.

19. Droppleman PG, Thomas SP, Wilt D. Anger in women as an emerging issue in MCH. MCN 1995; 20:85–94.

20. Low MB. Women's body image: the nurse's role in promotion of self-acceptance. AWHONN's clinical issues in perinatal and women's health nursing 1993; 4:213–219.

8.1

Depression
and Anxiety

Karen L. Hall

Introduction

Depressive and anxiety symptoms are complaints that present everyday. The etiology of these symptoms is diverse, and the differential for both crosses the boundaries from medical and psychiatric illness to the psychosocial stressors of life. Both depression and anxiety fall in the domain of universal human emotions, but when present in excess or interfering with everyday functioning can benefit from treatment and support.

Depression

Gender Differences in Depression

For some time physicians have anecdotally reported that depression was more common in women than men, but it was not until large scale surveys were accomplished that data supported this observation. In the early 1980s, the National Institute of Mental Health sponsored the Epidemiologic Catchment Area Survey (ECA) sampling people in five US cities. Nearly a decade later the Congressionally mandated National Comorbidity survey (NCS) broadened the picture by examining a population across the United States (1, 2). Both surveys were designed with several goals, one of which was to quantify the prevalence of psychiatric syndromes across the population. In both surveys depression was found to be common. The NCS, the more recent survey, reported a lifetime prevalence of depression of 21.3% for women and 12.7% for men, a ratio of approximately 2:1.

Most experts agree that depression incidence is equally divided between boys and girls, yet by adolescence, the 2:1 female preponderance is clearly established. It is not clear why this is so. Theories include biologic, sociologic, and neuroendocrine etiologies.

There are gender differences in function of neurotransmitters and neurostructural differences (such as in the corpus callosum, amygdala and hypothalamus) that may be involved in maintenance of mood (3). These differences may increase the vulnerability of depression in women.

The hormonal changes of adolescence may be suspect, because the observed increase in prevalence of depression is clearly noted then.

Studies do not support puberty in a pure cause and effect relationship, however. The timing of puberty, if early or if coincidental with major life changes (such as transition to junior high or high school), can contribute to depression (4).

A great deal of attention has been given to the consideration of sociological factors that may have an impact on women's vulnerability to depression. Researchers evaluating infant/adult interaction found that mothers appear more "in tune" with their sons than their daughters, and adults interact more socially with infants identified as male. There are observations that the richness of child's environment impacts on brain development; it is a fundamental concept behind Head Start. Interesting studies have illustrated the differences in treatment of girls compared with boys in the classroom, where boys are called on more, encouraged more, spoken to, and praised more often than girls. Other studies have shown that adults step in to rescue girls sooner than boys in achievement situations and that boys are encouraged to be more active and independent than girls. Girls on the other hand are often under adult supervision and encouraged in nurturing roles that may lead to greater self-evaluative concerns. These overly introspective behaviors may worsen or intensify depressive tendencies. Even today, the stereotypical female role is dependent, helpless, and passive. Boys are more likely to be imbued with an active, take charge attitude toward problems and daily life that may help to protect them from developing depression. Activity can set up a cascade of events such as endorphin stimulation that may also be of benefit in preventing depression. Another environmental stressor more common in girls is childhood sexual abuse, which may play a role in development of depression (Chapter 9.3) (5).

Additionally, the stressors faced by women in balancing family and career demands, pregnancy, the events of pregnancy loss, infertility, or single parenthood coupled with the trend toward greater social isolation may result in increased vulnerability to depression (6). Depression is increasing among young women during a time when greater opportunities for self-fulfillment and achievement are being realized (7). Despite the gradual opening of doors that have been traditionally closed to women, the frustration and stressors inherent in attaining these goals may have an impact on the development of depression. This may be especially problematic because of the societal pressures toward stereotypical roles and the make-up of the woman's psyche as she is raised in the current environment.

All these issues may impact on how women perceive themselves, their vulnerability, and their ability to affect the direction of their lives. It is likely that the cause of the higher prevalence of depression in women will prove to be multifactorial in nature, caused by a combination of these factors and others yet unknown.

Birth Cohort Effect

Another interesting trend is in the age of onset of depression in those born after World War II. In each successive decade since World War II depression has occurred in younger and younger age groups. This trend is independent of such factors as the increasing acceptance of depression as a diagnosis, the increasing acceptance of psychiatry as a branch of medicine, the development of biological psychiatry, and the changing definitions of depression. Providers need to be aware of this trend and its implications. Depression, once thought to be more common in the aged, is becoming a condition of youth. Because of this trend, practitioners should be alert for depression in their younger patients (8).

Definition of Depression

Although classically described as a condition of affect or mood causing a picture of pervasive gloom and loss of self-esteem, depression affects other brain functions as well. These include circadian rhythms, sleep, appetite, libido, arousal, and drive. The woman often first seeks the provider to obtain relief from these physiologic symptoms. Compared with the psychologic complaint, the patient may feel that the somatic symptoms are the only ones worthy of the provider's attention, or the patient may believe that the psychological symptoms are either not amenable to treatment or should be expected as an offshoot of the somatic problems.

The diagnostic evaluation of the patient with depressed mood begins with a careful history looking for symptoms that fulfill the criteria for major depression as designated by the Diagnostic and Statistical Manual of Mental Disorders, fourth edition (DSM IV) (see Table 8.1.1). The accepted criteria rest on the presence of a constellation of symptoms from a group of nine. Five or more of the nine symptoms must be present for at least 2 weeks, for most of the day. The symptoms must represent a change from previous functioning and significantly interfere with daily life. The first two,

Table 8.1.1 Criteria for Diagnosis of Depression

At least 5 of the 9 symptoms listed must be present for 2 weeks and #1 and/or #2 must be present

1. Sad or depressed mood most of the day, every day
2. Loss of interest in usual activities (anhedonia)
3. Fatigue
4. Weight gain/loss (without trying)
5. Sleep disturbance, hypersomnia or insomnia
6. Difficulty concentrating
7. Feelings of worthlessness, guilt
8. Psychomotor retardation/agitation
9. Suicidal ideation

Symptoms must represent a change in prior functioning and must interfere with daily living
Symptoms are not secondary to bereavement
Symptoms are not caused by a substance abuse disorder

depressed mood and anhedonia (loss of interest in all or most all usual interests), are essential criteria; one or both must be present. The remaining symptoms, to complete the total of at least five that must be present, include (*a*) insomnia or hypersomnia, (*b*) weight gain or loss (without trying), (*c*) feelings of worthlessness and guilt, (*d*) ongoing thoughts of death or plans of suicide, (*e*) psychomotor agitation or retardation, (*f*) fatigue, and (*g*) difficulty concentration.

Postpartum depression is not considered a distinct clinical entity. It is felt that depression occurring during this time represents an event that coincides with the postpartum period in a population already at risk for depression. DSM-IV lists a modifier code to acknowledge the timing of the depression. Risk factors for developing postpartum depression include prior incident and family history of depression, prior postpartum "blues," and history of PMS. Depression with a seasonal pattern, or seasonal affective disorder, is coded using a modifier to denote the onset of depression coinciding with seasonal changes. Also excluded is depressive symptoms associated with substance disorder, a condition that can alone precipitate depressive symptoms and is treatable by abstinence.

Risk Factors and Screening

Depression often goes unrecognized and untreated. The overlap of depressive symptoms with those of other conditions often masks the depression and delays treatment. Risk factors identified during history include (1) prior incident of depression, (2) family history of depression and BPAD, (3) chronic illness or severe medical illness, (4) chronic pain, and (5) sexual dysfunction or complaints. A history of prior depression is the strongest predictor of subsequent depressive event (see Table 8.1.2). Approximately 50% of patients with single event will have a recurrence. That percentage

Table 8.1.2. Risk Factors for Depression

History
    Prior incident of depression
    Family history of depression
    Chronic illness or severe medical illness
    Chronic pain
    Sexual dysfunction
    History of prior depression
Psychosocial factors
    Family problems
    Unhappy or abusive marriage
    Single parenthood
    Presence of young children in the home

increases to 70% after a second episode and 90% after a third (9).

Psychosocial risk factors include family problems, unhappy or abusive marriage, single parenthood, and presence of young children in the home. The more young children in the home, the higher is the incidence of depression. Interestingly, mothers who stay home with their young children report more depressive feelings than those who work (10). When these events are uncovered by history, the provider should be alert for the possibility of depression.

Differential Diagnosis

In considering the patient with depressed mood, the physician must rule out other medical, psychiatric, and psychosocial conditions before diagnosing major depression.

Psychiatric Syndromes

Depressed mood can accompany schizophrenia and other psychiatric syndromes. Adjustment disorder occurs following a stressor event such as divorce, loss of a job, onset of illness, or geographical move. The stressor precipitates the symptoms within 3 months of the event; in turn symptoms interfere with daily functioning. The mood changes of adjustment disorder clear within 6 months of the event. Adjustment disorder is one of the more common psychiatric diagnoses made in inpatients on medical and surgical wards.

Bereavement or grief reaction may fulfill many criteria for depression. However, grief usually does not demonstrate the overall negativity, sense of worthlessness, or self-doubt of major depression, except perhaps in cases of loss caused by spontaneous abortion, fetal demise, or child death. By criteria, it is excluded from the diagnosis of major depression. Should the symptoms persist for 2 months beyond the loss and meet the criteria, however, the diagnosis of depression may be appropriate and treatment indicated.

Patients with dysthymia, a chronic low-grade depression or "unhappiness" may present with some depressive symptoms, but because there is no change from previous functioning, major depression is not diagnosed. Dysthymic patients can, however, develop a depression on top of their dysthymia, a so-called "double depression" that can be difficult to treat.

In the initial history, careful questioning about prior manic episodes is important. A patient with bipolar affective disorder (BPAD), or manic-depressive disorder, may present in a depressed state and be treated with antidepressants precipitating a manic period or rapid cycling of their BPAD. Rapid cycling BPAD occurs more commonly in women and can also be difficult to treat. Approximately 5 to 19% of patients who present with single depressive event go on to develop BPAD. A positive family history of BPAD may help identify these patients. Other possible predictors of BPAD may be severe depression, psychotic features, or presentation of severe depression at a young age in a previously healthy patient. Symptoms that help uncover past manic episodes include (a) presence of periods of expansive or euphoric mood or irritability, (b) periods of pressure of speech or uncontrollable talkative episodes,

(c) flight of ideas, (d) grandiosity, (e) spending sprees (not associated with lottery winnings), and (f) increased goal directed activity either socially, sexually, or professionally. These symptoms may be elicited only from a family member or significant other.

To determine evaluation and treatment, complicated patients including those with comorbid conditions such as personality disorders, psychiatric illness, and substance abuse may need a referral. An ongoing relationship with a psychiatric referral source facilitates good quality and continuity of care.

Medical Disorders

Many patients with complicated or chronic medical conditions will develop depressed mood. If they meet the criteria for major depression, they may require treatment. Identification and treatment of other medical disorders may improve feelings of depression (see Table 8.1.3). These include thyroid disorders, vitamin deficiencies (notably vitamin B12), Cushing's syndrome, systematic lupus (SLE), diabetes, acute intermittent porphyria, heart disease, hypoxic conditions such as emphysema and certain degenerative neurologic disorders such as Parkinson's disease, multiple sclerosis (MS), and Alzheimer's disease. In the early stages, dementia of other causes may present with depressed mood.

Because the symptoms of depression are vague and overlap with symptoms of other illnesses, historical information is essential in eliminating the presence of other conditions. Thyroid disorders may present with fatigue but may also show cold intolerance, constipation, muscle cramping, stiffness and carpal tunnel syndromes, skin dryness, hoarseness or deepening voice, and hair loss. Cushing's syndrome may show the central weight gain pattern, diabetes, diastolic hypertension, hirsutism, or amenorrhea. Patients with sleep apnea (more common in men) complain of hypersomnolence and fatigue, but the physical

Table 8.1.3. Medical Differential Diagnosis of Symptoms of Depression

Thyroid disorders
Cushing's syndrome
Sleep apnea
Certain stroke syndromes (left anterior hemisphere)
Systemic lupus erythrematosis
Degenerative neurological conditions
   Parkinson's disease
   Alzheimer's disease
   Multiple sclerosis
Infections
   Tuberculosis
   Mononucleosis
   Hepatitis
Drug use
   Corticosteroids
   Anabolic steroids in abuse
   Digoxin
   Beta-blocker
   Oral contraceptives (with high estrogen levels, not in today's lower dose)
Alcohol or substance abuse

profile provides a clue to this diagnosis. Certain stroke syndromes, especially those involving the left anterior hemisphere, are commonly associated with the subsequent development of depressed mood and overt depression. SLE can present with depression, delirium, or psychosis. Approximately 50% of these patients also have a rash, either discoid or the characteristic malar or butterfly distribution, but urticarial, bullous, and maculopapular rashes have been described as well. Other degenerative neurological conditions such as Parkinson's disease and Alzheimer's disease can be complicated by depressed mood or can present with full-blown depression. Signs of Parkinson's disease include a "pill rolling" tremor that is more significant at rest, cogwheel rigidity, Parkinson's gait (small steps with lack of spontaneous movements such as arm swing, sometimes with speeding up as walking progresses called festination), "masked" or blank facies, and difficulty in initiating movement. Depressed mood or major depression may accompany MS. Other early findings of MS include (a) optic neuritis, partial or complete loss of vision with pain on eye movement, and (b) internuclear ophthalmoplegia (INO), inability to adduct one eye while the other is fully abducted. Bilateral INO in a young patient is considered MS until proved otherwise. Occasionally, mononucleosis, tuberculosis, and hepatitis can present with fatigue, anhedonia, and other symptoms of depression. Adherence to the DSM-IV criteria for depression in patients who present with more complicated medical symptoms can provide guidance for appropriate treatment.

Pharmacologic History

Substance use, especially cocaine and alcohol abuse, may precipitate depressive symptoms. Abstinence from substances can clear the depressive symptoms.

A history of concurrent drug use of both over-the-counter and prescription drugs, may point to drug reactions. Despite the conventional wisdom that there exists a causal relationship between certain medications such as reserpine or beta-blockers and depression, there are few prospective studies to prove this association. Most connections are made in anecdotal reports or case studies. There is some evidence that several agents do have a causal relationship: (a) corticosteroids; (b) anabolic steroids, in abuse not therapeutic uses; (c) digoxin, although delirium and cognitive changes are more common; (d) beta-blockers, although the constellation of symptoms reported includes the somatic group of depressive symptoms such as lethargy, fatigue, and decreased alertness and drive but not usually depressed mood or self-doubt; and (e) oral contraceptives, only those with high estrogen levels, not in today's lower dose pills. There is not good evidence for cause and effect for H_2 blockers, calcium channel blockers, metoclopramide, or clonidine (11, 12).

It is difficult to separate out the complex interactions of physiologic abnormalities that accompany medical illness with their concomitant stressors from the pharmacologic agents used to treat them. Only by using good scientific method can the contributions of each of these agents in causing depression be completely understood. Nevertheless, there may be a temporal relationship between observed depressive symptoms and the initiation of specific medications for individual patients. In each individual, the provider must weigh the evidence and alter the patient's drug regimen as it makes sense (11, 12).

Depression can be comorbid with virtually any other condition. If despite identification and proper treatment for comorbid condition the patient meets the criteria for major depression, treatment of the depression is warranted.

Laboratory Evaluation

Laboratory evaluation of the patient suspected of depression is aimed at exclusion of other diagnostic possibilities. There is no battery of screening tests that is universally accepted in evaluating the patient with depression.

Screening Tests
Despite a negative history and physical, helpful tests used to detect occult disease include the following: complete blood cell count (CBC), electrolytes, creatinine, glucose, calcium, phosphorus, albumin, protein, gammaguatamyl transferase (GGT), venereal disease laboratories research (VDRL) or radio plasma reagin (RPR), thyrotropin (TSH), urinalysis, electrocardiogram (ECG) and human chorionic gonadotropin (hCG). Routinely, the CBC can exclude anemia as the cause of fatigue and can help unmask an underlying vitamin deficiency or occult malignancy. A low

white blood count raises the question of undetected HIV. Electrolytes and blood glucose can screen for undiagnosed diabetes, renal insufficiency and hyponatremia which accompanies Addison's disease, psychogenic polydipsia often seen with antipsychotic medications, and syndrome of inappropriate secretion of antidiuretic hormone (SIADH) caused by a myriad of processes as well as medications. Hypokalemia can be caused by bulimia and laxative abuse in patients with eating disorders and in patients who use and abuse diuretics. Calcium and phosphorus abnormalities occur in hyperparathyroid and hypoparathyroid states, and both can present with changes in mood.

Albumin and protein provide information about the nutritional state of the patient; this is especially important in the elderly person. Most antidepressants are highly protein bound, and low albumin levels may impact on the adverse reactions of these drugs. A VDRL or RPR is useful for screening for syphilis, "the great imitator," that is making a comeback. Reactive VDRL or RPR tests should be followed by direct treponema tests to confirm syphilis. The indirect tests may be reactive in pregnancy and in certain immunological and rheumatological states such as lupus.

The recent advances in sensitive TSH tests make this test more reliable as a screen for thyroid disease (Chapter 15.2). The TSH test should be the more sensitive immunoradiometric assay technique. In the face of a negative history and physical exam, this test reliably distinguishes between high, normal, and suppressed TSH.

The urinalysis can provide clues to renal and urologic tract disease, and the HCG is vital in determining the appropriate treatment regimen. The ECG provides important information needed if the TCAs are going to be used and information about prior myocardial infarction, chamber enlargement, arrhythmias, and ST changes consistent with strain, infarction, and ischemia.

Additional Tests

In addition to the tests listed above, other tests may be indicated on the basis of historical clues or physical exam and will vary from patient to patient. These include (but are not limited to) ANA and other immunologic tests, erythrocyte sedimentation rate, lumbar puncture, electroencephalogram, neuropsychiatric testing, and imaging studies including computed tomography (CT) and magnetic resonance imaging (MRI). MRI is the most sensitive for identifying changes of MS and is superior to CT for identifying demyelinating processes. MRI also shows more detail for CNS structures and is unencumbered by interference from bone density unlike CT. CT, on the other hand, is more widely available and less expensive.

Depression Tests

There are no specific laboratory tests for depression. The dexamethasone suppression test (DST), which looks for the suppression of morning cortisol levels after an 11 PM dose of 1 mg of dexamethasone, is not abnormal in all patients with depression. The thyrotropin-releasing hormone stimulation test (TRH-stim), which looks for a blunted TSH response after the IV infusion of thyrotropin-releasing hormone (TRH), is also not diagnostic in the majority for patients. Both tests are cumbersome and expensive. The diagnosis of depression remains a clinical one, based on history and the constellation of findings defined in DSM-IV.

Treatment Issues

The initial stage of designing a treatment regimen is proper diagnosis using the DSM-IV criteria and eliminating or identifying other complicating conditions that may confound the diagnosis or interfere with treatment response.

The choice of treatment must also consider the patient's condition. Presence of comorbid conditions may preclude psychotherapy or pharmacotherapy alone. Sometimes, early referral to a psychiatrist may be wise. When the

Table 8.1.4. Risk Factors for Suicide

Prior attempt
Family history of suicide attempt
Male gender
Family history of substance abuse
Living alone
Substance abuse
Hopelessness
Psychosis
Caucasian
Medical illnesses
Advanced age

diagnosis is unclear, complicated by a second psychiatric illness, accompanied by a past history of manic episodes, psychosis, dysthymia, or personality disorder, a psychiatric consultation will provide guidance to appropriate treatment.

Especially important is the determination of suicidal intent. The incidence of suicide in the depressed population is nearly 20 times greater than that of the population at large and is the leading cause of death in this group. Every patient who has been diagnosed with depression should have suicidal ideation explored at each visit. Suicidal ideation mandates psychiatric referral and often inpatient hospitalization. Risk factors for suicide include male gender, living alone, feelings of hopelessness, prior attempt, family history of suicide, concomitant medical illness, advanced age, and substance abuse (see Table 8.1.4).

Psychotherapy

Studies have shown that psychotherapy alone is a good option for certain patients. As a primary care provider, one should have a working relationship with a local therapist who is trained and skilled in psychotherapy (e.g., psychiatrist, psychologist, psychiatric social worker) and can provide this service. Alternatively, the primary care physician, if motivated, can train to provide this care. Patients who may be amenable to this mode of therapy include those who are less severely depressed or who have no complicating features to their depression. Additionally, some patients may be averse to the use of pharmacologic agents or may have responded well to psychotherapy previously. In women, psychotherapy may be of particular benefit, alone or with other strategies. Helping women cope with stress, develop problem-solving skills, communicate effectively, and avoid ruminative cognitive styles are all goals of therapy. Group and individual therapy are options.

Pharmacologic Therapy

Pharmacologic options have expanded tremendously in recent years (see Table 8.1.5). Originally serendipitous findings led to the development of monoamine oxidase inhibitors (MAOIs) and tricyclic antidepressants (TCAs). These were the mainstays of treatment until the introduction of the new classes of antidepressants—the selective serotonin reuptake inhibitors (SSRIs), aminoketone (e.g., buproprion), and most recently the cyclohexanol venlafaxine.

The principles of pharmacologic treatment are (*a*) proper selection of drug, (*b*) close follow-up, (*c*) reassessment of dose if incomplete or no response, (*d*) increase in dose as appropriate, and (*e*) patience to allow an adequate length of time for response. All antidepressants take time to work. A typical "triphasic" response is to be expected: (*a*) sleep improves, which alone will improve a patient's feeling of well-being, (*b*) energy returns, and (*c*) mood lifts. In the second phase, a patient may recover the energy to do harm to herself while her mood is still bleak, so at this point she will need careful follow-up.

Initially, the patient should be seen weekly or biweekly, until the provider feels it is safe for her to be seen less often. Treatment needs to be tailored individually. If 6 to 8 weeks of an adequate dose of an antidepressant fails to elicit a response, an alternative agent may be selected. Failure of two adequate treatment trials may require referral to a psychiatrist. Strategies at this point include augmentation with thyroid hormone or the addition of a mood stabilizing drug such as carbemazepine or lithium. As the patient is followed during treatment, additional information discovered may alter the treatment plan, such as the uncovering of a substance abuse disorder or the appearance of symptoms or physical signs leading to the diagnosis of an untreated medical or psychiatric disorder (13).

Physicians who decide to care for patients with depression should choose several medications and become familiar with their side-effect profiles and contraindications, dosing, and other pharmacologic parameters.

Tricyclic Antidepressants (TCAs)

> amitriptyline (Elavil)
> amoxapine (Asendin)
> clomipramine (Anafranil)
> desipramine (Norpramin)
> doxepin (Sinequan)
> imipramine (Tofranil)
> nortriptyline (Pamelor)
> protriptyline (Vivactil)
> trimipramine (Surmontil)

Compared to other antidepressants, the tricyclics have the advantage of years of experience; this means that their actions, interaction, limitations, contraindications, and side effects are well known. Their greatest disadvantage and the reason for their fall from grace is their lethality in overdose. Imipramine, desipramine, and nortriptyline have established serum levels that help guide and monitor treatment; this offers an advantage to the other drugs in this group. Imipramine, a tertiary amine, is the most anticholinergic; nortriptyline and desipramine, both secondary amines are less so and cause less dry mouth, sedation, constipation, blurred vision, and tachycardia. The CNS anticholinergic syndrome of delirium, confusion, apathy, and the interference with encoding new memory is also a problem with this class. Because amitriptyline is the most anticholinergic of the group, its use in the elderly should be minimal if at all.

Table 8.1.5. Antidepressant Drugs: Dosing/Side Effects

Class	Agent	Neuro-transmitter	Half-Life (Hr)	Active Metabolite	Initial Dose (mg)	Maintenance Dose (mg)
TCA	Desipramine (Norpramin)	NE++++ S++	12–28	—	25QHS–25TID	50–300
	Imipramine (Tofranil)	NE++ S++++	6–28	Y	25QHS–25TID	50–300
	Nortriptyline (Pamelor)	NE++ S+++	18–48	Y	25QHS–25TID	50–200
SSRI	Fluoxetine (Prozac)	NE+/0 S+++++	4–6 days	Y	10QAM	10–60
	Paroxetine (Paxil)	NE+/0 S+++++	21	—	10QAM	10–20
	Sertraline (Zoloft)	NE+/0 S+++++	26	Y	50QAM	50–200
MISC	Buproprion (Wellbutrin)	NE+/0 S+/0	10–21	Y	50–75 BID/TID	300–450
	Venlafaxine (Effexor)	NE++++ S++++	5	Y	37.5 BID	75–250
	Nefazodone (Serzone)	NE+++ S+++	2–4	Y	75–100 BID	150–200
	Trazodone (Desyrel)	NE 0 S+++	6–13	Y	50–100	150–600
MAOI	Isocarboxazid (Marplan)	MAOI	UNK	—	30	30–50*
	Phenelzine (Nardil)	MAOI	1.5–4	—	15 TID	45–90*
	Tranyl-cypromine (Parnate)	MAOI	1.5–3	—	30	20–60*

NE=norepinephrine; S=serotonin; ANTICh=anticholinergic side effects; agitation, includes insomnia; ARRHY=arrhythmia; OH=orthostatic hypotension, nausea includes GI upset.
*after clinical response, maintenance dose may be able to be lowered.

Alpha-receptor blockade, more pronounced in the tertiary amines (e.g., imipramine, amitriptyline, doxepin) is responsible for orthostatic hypotension. In the elderly, this can lead to increased morbidity because of falls and interference with activities of daily living. All these agents lower the seizure threshold, have proarrhythmic effects in overdose and slow AV conduction. They should not be used with the class IA antiarrhythmics such a quinidine, procainamide (Pronestyl), or disopyramide (Norpace). Contraindications to the TCA class are myocardial infarction within the previous 6 months, second-degree/Mobitz II heart

| Side Effects | | | | | | | |
| CNS | | | Cardiovascular | | GI | | |
Anti Ch	Drowsy	Agita-tion	OH	ARRHY	Weight Gain	Nausea	Other Contra-indications, Cautions
+	+	+	++	++	+	0	MI past 6 mo Mobitz II & 3
+++	+++	+	+++++	+++	+++	+	degree heart block; urin. re-
+	+	0	++	++	+	0	tent not with MAOI
0	0	++	0	0	0	+++	Prozac: 5 wk washout be-
0	0	++	0	0	0	+++	fore MAOI, others 2 week,
0	0	++	0	0	0	+++	HA, sexual dysfunction SZ disorder
0	0	++	0	+	0	+	Bulimia, Anorexia
0	+	+	0	0	0	+++++	Sexual dysfunc-tion
0	++	+	+/0	+	0	0	Priapism
0	++++	0	+	+	+	+	Priapism
+	+	++	++	0	++	+	Not with TCA, SSRI, need
+	+	++	++	0	++	+	Washout time not w/SSRI
+	+	++	++	0	++	+	Cirrhosis, CHR, pheo, liver disease Low tyramine

block, third degree heart block, and closed angle glaucoma.

Despite the problems with this class of drugs, TCAs are efficacious and inexpensive. Generics are available for imipramine, desipramine, amitriptyline, and trazodone. There have been no data to show any of the newer agents are more efficacious in treatment of depression than the TCA class (14).

Selective Serotonin Reuptake Inhibitors (SSRIs)

fluoxetine (Prozac)
fluvoxamine (Luvox)

paroxetine (Paxil)
sertraline (Zoloft)

Introduced in 1988, fluoxetine is the first of a group of antidepressants called SSRIs. Fluoxetine has been followed by paroxetine, sertraline and fluvoxamine. Currently, fluvoxamine, is FDA approved only for obsessive-compulsive disorder (OCD). Fluoxetine is approved for use in depression, eating disorders, and OCD and has been shown effective in PMS. As a class, the SSRIs are safer in overdose situations than the TCAs. Unlike TCAs, the starting dose is generally the treatment dose, and titration of the drug is unnecessary. There are no accepted therapeutic serum levels, so drug levels cannot be used to help plan therapy. Additionally, the SSRIs take time to work as do the TCAs and show the same pattern of response in which energy improves before mood. An adequate trial of an SSRI is the same for other agents; treatment should not be abandoned before 8 weeks.

Important issues in the use of this class are interactions with other drugs and half-life of the compound and its active metabolites. Problematic in the use of fluoxetine is its long half-life of 4 to 6 days and the significant contribution of its active metabolite (norfluoxetine with a half-life of 4 to 16 days) to its pharmacologic activity. Four to five half-lives are required for a drug to reach steady state. In a drug with a significantly active metabolite such as fluoxetine, the half-life of the metabolite must be considered. So the time to steady state and washout on discontinuation for fluoxetine takes weeks. Paroxetine, with a half-life of 21 hours allows once daily dosing and has the additional benefit of having no active metabolites. Sertraline has a half-life of 26 hours and has one active metabolite, desmethylsertraline, which has a half-life of 2 to 4 days. This metabolite is 5 to 10 times less potent than the parent compound and is not thought to contribute to the action of the drug in clinical use.

All of the SSRIs are highly protein bound and can have interactions with other drugs. The SSRIs can cause movement disorders and agitation, treated by discontinuation of the drug. Additionally, all the SSRIs have the potential to produce the "sertonergic syndrome"—a hypermetabolic state thought to be caused by an overabundance of serotonin. Like the neuroleptic malignant syndrome of the antipsychotic medications, this is a potentially lethal condition requiring immediate medical intervention.

Recent research has focused on the metabolism of the SSRIs by the isoenzymes of the P450 liver enzyme system (see Table 8.1.6). This information helps to explain many of the drug to drug interactions with the use of the SSRIs (15).

Monamine Oxidase Inhibitors (MAOIs)

Isocarboxazid (Marplan)
Phenelzine (Nardil)
Tranylcypromine (Parnate)

MAOIs increase the body levels of epinephrine, norepinephrine, dopamine, and serotonin by inhibiting their degradation. Adverse effects include hypertensive crises when tyramine-containing foods are eaten, orthostasis, sexual dysfunction, weight gain, and sleep disturbance.

Many providers are reluctant to prescribe this class of drugs because of the dietary restrictions necessary for their use. They are more often used in treatment failures and are commonly prescribed by psychiatrists who are more familiar with their use.

Miscellaneous Classes

Aminoketones: Buproprion
Cyclohexanol: Venlafaxine
Triazolopyridine: Nefazodone, Trazodone

Trazodone and the newer nefazodone belong to a separate class of antidepressants. Trazodone acts via serotonin, whereas nefazodone

Table 8.1.6. Potential Interactions of the P450 System

CYP 1A2	CYP 2C	CYP 2D6	CYP 3A3,4
Acetaminophen	Diazepam	Clozapine	Alprazolam
Caffeine	Fluoxetine	Codeine	Astemizole
Fluvoxamine	Fluvoxamine	Desipramine	Carbemazepine
Imipramine	Hexobarbital	Encainide	Corticosteroid
Phenacetin	Imipramine	Flecanide	Cyclosporine
Phenothiazines	Phenytoin	Fluoxetine	Erythromycin
Phenytoin	Propranolol	Fluvoxamine	Fluoxetine
Theophylline	Tertiary TCAs	Haloperidol	Fluvoxamine
Warfarin	Tolbutamide	Metoprolol	Ketoconazole
	Warfarin	Norfluoxetine	Lidocaine
		Paroxetine	Midazolam
		Phenothiazines	Nefazodone
		Quinidine	Quinidine
		Risperidone	Sertraline
		Sertraline	Terfenadine
		Thioridazine	Triazolam
		Timolol	
		Venlafaxine	
		Verapamil	

Groups represent drugs with potential interactions that may differ from patient to patient.

affects norepinephrine and serotonin. Trazodone is the more sedating of the two. Both can cause the rare case of priapism, although it is more common with trazodone.

Buproprion is the single agent in its class. Its short half-life requires more than one daily dose. The total dosage should not exceed 450 mg because of the increased risk of seizures above that level. However, it is free of any anticholinergic and cardiovascular side effects and has no known drug to drug interactions.

Venlafaxine is also the single agent of its class and has effects on serotonin and norepinephrine. It has minimal effects on dopaminergic, muscarinic, histaminergic, or α_1 adrenergic receptors, resulting in fewer side effects. Its most common side effect is gastrointestinal distress, and its short half-life necessitates multiple doses daily. The newer agents have been used for shorter time period and there has been less clinical experience with their use.

Electroconvulsive Treatment

Electroconvulsive treatment (ECT) is an effective treatment for severe depression. It can be life-saving in the patient who cannot tolerate drug treatment or in whom a rapid response is urgent. For depression with psychosis or prominent vegetative signs, underlying complicated medical condition or severe depression in pregnancy, ECT may be suggested.

Length of Treatment

Once pharmacologic treatment has been chosen and appropriate dose has been reached, treatment response should be expected within 6 to 8 weeks. After the patient has recovered her mood, medication should be continued for approximately 6 months. At the end of that time, if the patient remains in full remission, tapering of the medication can be attempted over a month or several weeks. Should the patient relapse during the taper, the medication should be reinstituted at the last effective dose and continued until the woman is symptom-free for another 6 months or so. A medication taper can be attempted again if the patient is in full remission. Should the patient fail a second taper, the dose should again be reinstituted at the last effective dose and continued for at least 1 year. If a third taper attempt fails, then medication may be indicated indefinitely. Other factors that may require lifetime antidepressant therapy include (a) three or more episodes of major depression, (b) two episodes of severe depression accompanied by suicidal intent or attempt, and (c) two episodes of severe depression and a positive family history.

Conclusion on Depression

Only approximately one fourth of those women with depression are ever identified and adequately treated. Because depression is approximately twice as common in women as men, this has a great impact on women's health. The difficulties with diagnosing depression are failure to recognize the syndrome that presents with a constellation of somatic symptoms, which may overshadow the psychologic features, and lack of provider experience and knowledge about depression. Provider obstacles in treatment include failure to adequately treat because of insufficient dose or length of time. Patient obstacles to treatment continue to be social stigma, misunderstanding of the condition, and reluctance to seek help because of preconceived ideas about treatment, psychiatry in general, and the possible social ramifications of being labeled mentally ill.

Anxiety Disorders

Like depression, anxiety disorders as a group occur more commonly in women than men. NCS data show the lifetime prevalence of any anxiety disorder in women is 30.5%, and in men the prevalence is 19.25% (16).

Definitions from DSM IV

The psychiatric syndromes of which anxiety is a primary component include (a) generalized anxiety disorder, (b) panic disorder, (c) agoraphobia, (d) specific (formerly called simple) phobia, (e) social phobia, (f) post-traumatic stress disorder (PTSD), (g) acute stress disorder (ASD), which is similar to PTSD but more immediate and it has a shorter duration, (h) obsessive-compulsive disorder (OCD), and (i) adjustment disorder with anxious mood. Additionally, anxiety may accompany medical disorders and drug and alcohol abuse. To diagnose any anxiety as a psychiatric syndrome, interference with everyday functioning must be present.

Evaluation and History

A useful process to distinguish between syndromes is to first look for the presence of panic attacks. Panic is an overwhelming feeling of dread, fear of impending doom, or death or depersonalization that is accompanied by somatic symptoms such as palpations, sweating, chest pain, shortness of breath, nausea, and tremor. It is found in several anxiety disorders. DSM IV lists the criteria for panic attacks as the sudden onset of fear or dread accompanied by at least 4 of a set of 13 somatic symptoms (see Table 8.1.7). With fewer than four somatic symptoms, the attack is called a limited symptom panic attack. The presence of panic that occurs without precipitating event or trigger points toward panic disorder. Panic following a discrete stressor such as exposure to heights, dogs, or insects indicates a specific phobia, and if associated with social situations indicates social phobia.

The anxiety of PTSD and ASD follows an event that places a great stress on the psyche such as rape, near death experience, natural disaster, or war. The panic associated with PTSD and ASD is triggered by reminders of the traumatic event. PTSD and ASD are understandably common in women who have a

Table 8.1.7. Panic Attack Symptoms

Chest pain
Sweating
Trembling
Choking feeling
Fear of dying
Chills/hot flushes
Paresthesias
Palpitations/heart racing
Dizziness/lightheadedness
Fear of losing control
Nausea/GI distress
Feeling detached/unreal
Shortness of breath/smothering

history of rape (see Chapter 9.2) or assault, although PTSD is more commonly identified with Vietnam War veterans.

Panic is not generally a component of OCD or generalized anxiety disorder (GAD). However, panic can coexist with OCD.

Agoraphobia, a fear of enclosed spaces or places from which escape may be difficult, usually accompanies panic disorder and often develops as a consequence of a panic disorder. For complete discussions of the anxiety disorders, the DSM IV provides a detailed and readable overview.

Evaluation and Treatment

The evaluation of the patient with anxiety is similar to that of depression. Medical disorders may coexist with anxiety syndromes and can cause a general anxiety. Thyroid disorders can present with an anxious appearance as can other endocrine disorders. In general, a good history and physical aimed at uncovering other conditions is as important in anxiety as it is in depression. Routine laboratory studies previously discussed are also pertinent in the anxious patient. Substance abuse may coexist with or masquerade as an anxiety disorder.

Panic Disorder

Women make up about 60 to 75% percent of panic patients; NCS data reports a lifetime prevalence of 5% for women compared with 2% for men. Initially, many of these patients go unrecognized because their somatic symptoms crowd the presentation, and this leads to extensive medical work-ups, especially of the endocrine and cardiac systems. Panic patients are at risk for other comorbid conditions, especially depression, substance use, and agoraphobia.

Treatment must consider this multifaceted aspect of panic disorder and it requires both psychotherapeutic and pharmacologic interventions. Avoidance of substances that exacerbate anxiety such as caffeine, alcohol, nicotine, sympathomimetics, and illicit drugs is also important.

Pharmacotherapy has become more sophisticated and includes the TCAs, MAOIs, and benzodiazepines. There are convincing data for the efficacy of imipramine in the treatment of panic disorder. The dose begins at 10 mg per day and is titrated upward at 10 mg increments to 50 mg and then increased in 25 mg steps until a dose of 100 to 250 mg per day is reached. This slow start helps avoid any activation or adverse effects of the drug in these patients who tend to have greater sensitivity to medications. As with depression, a delayed response of 6 to 12 weeks can be expected in panic disorder, so treatment should not be abandoned prior to that time.

Other TCAs that have been used are nortriptyline, desipramine, and most recently clomipramine. In the benzodiazepine class, alprazolam (Xanax) is the only one FDA approved in the treatment of panic disorder. It decreases anticipatory anxiety and phobic reactions. The starting dose is 0.25 to 0.5 mg tid titrated to 2 to 6 mg per day. Some patients may require up to 6 to 10 mg per day. Initially, ataxia and sedation interfering with performance of complex motor tasks are noted, but tolerance to these effects develops over time, usually by

10 days. Disadvantages are the abuse potential and withdrawal syndrome. This syndrome includes seizures that can be avoided by gradually tapering the medication over 2 to 3 months; tapering also helps avoid rebound of panic. Others in the benzodiazepine class used in treating panic disorder include clonazepam (Klonopin) that can be dosed twice daily because of its longer half-life and lorazepam (Ativan).

Of the MAOIs, phenelzine has been shown the most effective in panic disorder. Like the TCAs, it takes 6 to 12 weeks to work and requires the same cautions (tyramine-free diet) as when used for depression. The initial dose is 15 mg per day; this is increased every 3 to 4 days to 60 to 90 mg per day divided twice daily. Besides these three classes, SSRIs are being evaluated in treatment as well.

Generalized Anxiety Disorder (GAD)

Prevalence data from NCS show a lifetime prevalence for GAD of 6.6% for women, 3.6% for men. GAD is characterized by excessive, incapacitating worry over life events such as health, job, children, and finances that are out of proportion to the likelihood of untoward events. The symptoms last longer than 6 months and are accompanied by somatic complaints such as restlessness, irritability, fatigue, and problems with concentration. GAD usually first presents in a patient aged in their 20s but can occur any time. Complications include substance use; comorbid conditions include depression, panic disorder, and social phobia.

Treatment includes supportive psychotherapy, cognitive and behavioral techniques with the goal of improving coping skills, and stress management. Pharmacotherapy includes the benzodiazepine class of anxiolytics. Alcohol should not be used with this class of agents. Buspirone (BuSpar), a nonbenzodiazepine anxiolytic has neither a withdrawal syndrome nor any of the adverse effects of the benzodiazepine class. Patients who have previously taken benzodiazepines are less likely to accept buspirone: it does not provide immediate relief. The initial

dose of buspirone is 5 mg tid titrated to 30 to 60 mg per day divided tid and continued for 4 to 6 weeks to reach maximum efficacy. Besides the "anxiolytics," the sedating TCAs and trazodone have been used with some success.

Social Phobia

Social phobia is characterized by fear of social and performance situations. The fear is excessive and incapacitates individuals in these situations leading to avoidance behaviors. Social phobias can be extremely disruptive especially in professional life in which patients may be required to interact with clients or other business people or speak in large or small groups. Those with severe social phobia may have difficulty in one-on-one situations, e.g., interacting with a supervisor. NCS data show a lifetime prevalence of 15.5% for women and 11.1% for men. Age at onset can be childhood or during teen years and is uncommon after the mid-20s.

Therapy includes psychotherapy and pharmacology. Behavioral therapy is based on progressive, incremental exposure to the phobic situation. There are no specific FDA approved medications for social phobia. In limited situations, such as performance anxiety, a small dose of benzodiazepine (e.g., as alprazolam 0.5 to 1.0 mg, clonazepam 0.25 to 0.5 mg) or beta-blocker (e.g., atenolol 25 to 100 mg, propranolol 20 to 80 mg) taken 1 to 2 hours prior to a performance or presentation may calm the anxiety and reduce the autonomic symptoms of tremor, tachycardia, and sweating. It is important to test the medication before a performance to titrate its effective dose and to avoid any untoward effects of the medication. Trials of other medications including SSRIs and MAOIs are ongoing.

Specific Phobia

Specific phobia is fear or anxiety elicited by a discrete stimulus such as heights, animals, or closed-in spaces. It is probably the most common of all anxiety disorders, with a lifetime prevalence of 15.7% in women and 6.7% in men. Many phobias begin in childhood, but others may appear in adulthood. Most patients never present with complaints to their physician because the feared object can be avoided (e.g., snakes). The patient clearly perceives the etiology of the anxiety, and many feel the phobia is not unreasonable (e.g., fear of large dogs). On the other hand, some patients may have difficulty with day-to-day functioning, such as if they have fear of flying and their job requires air travel, or they fear enclosed spaces and work on the 50th floor of a high-rise office building. Therapy for specific phobia is largely in vivo exposure in which the patient is taken by increments closer to the feared situation until the anxiety diminishes over time. Fear of flying presents a difficult situation, because it is difficult to recreate the stimulus without actually flying. In some larger cities there are programs designed for exposure therapy. For instance the patient will (1) stand in the air terminal, (2) enter the plane and sit, (3) enter and sit while the plane taxies but does not take off, and (4) finally board and take off. For those who do not have in vivo exposure treatments available to them or who have failed exposure treatment, a small dose of benzodiazepine such as alprazolam 0.5 mg taken 1 to 2 hours prior to the flight may be effective. Avoidance of other stimulants such as alcohol and caffeine and sympathomimetics during the flight is also important.

Adjustment Disorder with Anxious Mood

Adjustment disorder occurs within 3 months of an event and remits within 6 months. It may follow a move, divorce, loss of job, or another stressful life event. The primary treatment is supportive psychotherapy.

Post-Traumatic Stress Disorder (PTSD)/Acute Stress Disorder (ASD)

PTSD and ASD follow an extraordinarily stressful event and are characterized by recurrent reexperiencing of the event, agitation, hypervigilance, extreme arousal, and exaggerated startle responses. Reliving the event can be triggered by everyday stimuli. For example, earthquake victims may have a "flash-back" when they feel the ground vibrate as a heavy truck rolls by or combat veterans may reexperience battle when they hear a helicopter. Man-made events such as rape or torture are more likely to precipitate PTSD and ASD than are natural disasters or "acts of God." Both disorders can occur at any age; women, children, and the elderly are more vulnerable.

The primary difference between the two disorders is chronicity. Comorbidity with other anxiety disorders including OCD, panic disorder and GAD, and depression and substance use complicated treatment.

Therapy includes psychotherapy; there are no FDA approved drugs for pharmacology. Phenelzine (an MAOI), imipramine and amitriptyline (TCA antidepressants), and fluoxetine (a SSRI) have all had some success. Referral for these patients to providers who have had experience in treating them is often necessary.

Obsessive-Compulsive Disorder (OCD)

OCD is more common than once believed; it has a lifetime prevalence of 2.5%. It presents as early as the teenage years with a second peak in the mid-20s. Most of the patients are women and most are comorbid for other diagnoses including substance abuse, panic disorder, social and specific phobia, and major depression. The condition is characterized by recurrent obtrusive thoughts, commonly of contamination, doubt, and aggression that lead to compulsions or actions that are designed to alleviate anxiety. For example, a patient with thoughts of contamination may develop intricate hand washing rituals, or the patient with doubt may check and recheck to see that the stove, iron, and other appliance is turned off. The rituals consume more than a few hours each day and significantly interfere with daily functioning. Excessive orderliness and slowness can also be a form of OCD. It is not to be confused with obsessive-compulsive *personality* disorder that is a set of personality traits characterized by stubbornness, perfectionist behaviors, and rigidity.

Treatment of OCD entails a combination of pharmacotherapy and psychotherapy. Psychotherapy is designed around in vivo response prevention, similar to that of specific phobia. Pharmacologic therapy includes several agents. Clomipramine, a TCA, is prescribed in doses of 150 to 250 mg per day, beginning at 25 mg and titrating upward. Doses above 250 mg are not recommended as seizures are more likely in excess of that dose. Fluvoxamine, an SSRI, is also used. Fluoxetine has been found effective at doses of 20 to 80 mg per day. Trials of the other SSRIs are ongoing.

Anxiety Associated with a Medical Condition or Substance Abuse

Anxiety can be a prominent symptom of medical illness. In a patient with recently diagnosed medical problems, e.g., cancer or chronic disease such as diabetes, anxiety can be a component of adjustment disorder similar to depressed mood. Often supportive psychotherapy is the treatment of choice in this circumstance. Should the anxiety continue beyond a 6-month period, it may meet the criteria for GAD and be treated the same (17).

Substance abuse is commonly associated with anxiety. The treatment of choice is withdrawal and substance abuse treatment. Anxiety symptoms beyond the withdrawal period are especially problematic in this population, because long-term benzodiazepine use is relatively contraindicated. These patients are best referred to substance abuse centers in which providers are trained in treatment.

Conclusion on Anxiety

Anxiety presents commonly in women in primary care. Because not all anxiety is the same and treatment differs for individual anxiety disorders, a careful history and physical with pertinent laboratory evaluations helps diagnose the cause of the anxiety, enabling the provider to design the proper treatment regimen.

Treatment of Depression and Anxiety in the Elderly

Evaluation and treatment of specific disorders are similar to elderly and younger women. As patients age, they are more likely to have concomitant medical problems that complicate their care. Because they often have atypical presentations of illnesses such as silent myocardial infarction of silent ischemia, screening tests may be more important in this group.

One common atypical presentation in the elderly is depression that masquerades as dementia. The elderly woman may seem to be disoriented and have decreased higher cognitive function. Because depression is usually treatable, the differential is important. Yet, the presentations may be so similar that psychometric testing and/or a therapeutic trial of antidepressants may be needed to separate the two diagnoses.

Additionally, physiologic changes of aging may interfere with or complicate pharmacotherapy. Issues such as absorption, volume of distribution, lean body mass, and hepatic and renal insufficiencies are more common and more likely to cause problems with dosing medications in this age group. A "brown bag" consult, rounding up every medication, both prescription and over-the-counter, often helps treatment decisions and can help "clean up" pharmacotherapy, decreasing the chances for untoward medication interactions. For all psychotropic medications in the elderly, it is wise to start at a low dose and titrate upward slowly to avoid potentially devastating effects. This enables the provider to be alert for drug-to-drug interactions and to lower morbidity.

Conclusion

The extent of depression and anxiety symptoms and diagnoses in women are as complex and varied as women are as a group themselves. Providers must be cognizant of the many distinct presentations and knowledgeable of the treatments possible to serve women in these diseases.

Special Considerations for Nurse Practitioners and Physician Assistants

Determining a woman's mental status should be a part of every evaluation. Women who are depressed may seek help for symptoms such as fatigue, frequent headaches, constipation, difficulty sleeping, appetite changes, or decreased sex drive. Symptoms may be attributed to stress both by the woman and the provider (18). The depressed woman is not pleasant to be around and may cause the practitioner to feel sad. Yet, these women need time to describe their feelings; a thorough assessment and intervention require time and attention. To help in identifying depression, providers might use self-report questionnaires as case-finding tools to identify potentially depressed women (19).

Rarely, will providers work with depressed or anxious women who do not also have physical health problems. The number of physical and mental concerns can be overwhelming. Assuming that life-threatening problems are considered first, the provider can ask the woman what is bothering her most and develop a plan with her to address that problem first. Providers must avoid widely held beliefs that women can will themselves out of depression by keeping active, trying a change of scenery, or concentrating on happy thoughts (20).

Significant others must be involved in care. Their concern can improve self-esteem and decrease social isolation; they can assist depressed women in taking medications, making and keeping appointments, and improving their physical health through exercise and good nutrition (21).

Knowing when to refer a depressed woman to a mental health specialist is critical. Severe depression may be recognized by the "vegetative signs," such as unexplained weight loss, inability to handle ADLs, and insomnia or hypersomnia. In addition, suicidal ideation or plans and delusional thinking may be present (22). Suicidal clues can be overlooked or ignored especially by the provider who is uncomfortable when women express psychological distress. Some providers may attempt to cheer the woman; this only discounts her distress and increases the concealment of suicide. Providers must inquire about feelings of hopelessness and other signs of severe depression. Jokes about suicide must be investigated. Family members, teachers, and others may detect clues through essays, art, diaries, or other behaviors (21).

To help assess suicide risk, providers should have a standard set of questions so that adequate data can be gathered for decision-making about referral and immediacy of interventions. Information can be gathered by asking questions such as: Have you thought of hurting yourself? Have you felt that way recently or now? Have you done anything in the past to hurt yourself? What are you thinking of doing? Do you have the means of carrying out your plan? Clinicians should not fear asking about suicide because of worries that the woman might be insulted or might consider suicide because of the questions (20).

If the woman is determined not to be at immediate risk, a no-suicide contract might be developed in which the woman promises not to do anything self-destructive before calling for help. This agreement does not guarantee safety and may be ineffective with manipulative or angry women who do not have a relationship with the provider. Women should have numbers of a telephone hotline and significant others who are available (21).

Moderate or high-risk suicidal women, as well as those women the provider is unsure of, need referral to suicide prevention experts. Consultation or referral is often needed for those women with past suicide attempts, psychotic symptoms, substance abuse, unresolved PTSD, and other problems, or complications caused by medication side effects (21). Whether a woman is referred at once or treatment is initiated in the primary care setting will depend on the care provider's skills, available resources for care, and protocols for practice.

Prevention of mental health problems is a role that providers may not give sufficient thought. Policy changes to address factors that increase the stressors women face may act to improve the mental health of women. Providers who care for women have a responsibility to advocate the elimination of sex role stereotypes, provision of adequate child care, assurance of safe work environments, and elimination of the feminization of poverty. The organization of self-help groups in the community can also provide women with a setting in which coping measures can be shared and feelings of isolation prevented (22). Strategies for healthy diet, adequate rest, and exercise improve physical health; whether these strategies can enhance mental well-being and prevent depression is an area in which research is needed (23).

Women in poverty, homeless women, rural women, older women, and women from minority ethnic groups need special attention. Social and economic stressors, lack of social and educational opportunities, transportation difficulties, as well as lack of provider knowledge and understanding can contribute to the development of mental health problems. Mental health services may not take into consideration community barriers to health. To address such concerns, screenings for depression could take place in churches, recreational centers, and other community sites. Community-based self-help groups can be particularly helpful to some women, such as those experiencing grief reactions (22).

References

1. Reiger DA, Myers JK, Kramer M, et al. The NIMH Epidemiologic Catchment Area Program: historical context, major objectives and study population characteristics. Arch Gen Psychiatry 1984;41:934–41.
2. Blazer DG, Kessler RC, McGonagle KA, Swartz MS. The prevalence and distribution of major depression in a national community sample: the national comorbidity survey. Am J Psychiatry 1994;151:979–986.
3. Halbreich U, Lumley LA. The multiple interactional biological processes that might lead to depression and gender differences in its appearance. J Affect Disord 1993;29:159–173.
4. Ruble DN, Greulich F, Pomerantz EM, Gochberg B. The role of gender-related processes in the development of sex differences in self-evaluation and depression. J Affect Disord 1993;29:97–128.
5. Heller W. Gender differences in depression: perspectives from neuropsychology. J Affect Disord 1993;29:129–143.
6. ACOG Technical Bulletin Number 182, Depression in Women. Int J Gynecol Obstet 1993;43:203–211.
7. Silverstein B, Perlick D. Gender differences in depression: historical changes. Acta Psychiatr Scand 1991;84:327–331.
8. Klerman GL, Weissman MM. Increasing rates of depression. JAMA 1989;261:2229–2235.
9. Mood Disorders. In: Diagnostic and Statistical Manual of Mental Disorders. 4th ed. Washington, DC: American Psychiatric Association, 1994:317–391.
10. ACOG Technical Bulletin Number 182, depression in women. Int J Gynecol Obstet 1993;43:203–211.
11. Patten SB, Love EJ. Can drugs cause depression? A review of evidence. J Psychiatr Neurosci 1993;18:92–102.
12. Patten SB, Love EJ. Drug induced depression. Drug Safety, 1994;10:203–219.
13. AHCPR. Depression in Primary Care; Detection, Diagnosis and Treatment. 1993 AHCPR publication No. 93-0552.
14. Gelenberg AJ, Schoonover SC. Depression. In: Gelenberg AJ, Bassuk EL, Schoonover SC, eds. The Practitioner's Guide to Psychoactive Drugs. 3rd ed. New York: Plenum, 1991:23–89.
15. DeVane CL. Pharmacokinetics of the newer antidepressants: clinical relevance. Am J Med 1994;97 (suppl 6A):13S–23S.

16. Blazer DG, Kessler RC, McGonagle KA, Swartz MS. The prevalence and distribution of major depression in a national community sample: the national comorbidity survey. Am J Psychiatry 1994;151:979–986.
17. Ware MR, Ballenger JC. Anxiety disorders. In: Conn's Current Therapy 1996. Philadelphia: W. B. Saunders, in press.
18. Perry MV, Anderson GL. Assessment and treatment strategies for depressive disorders commonly encountered in primary care settings. Nurse Provider 1992;17:25–36.
19. U. S. Department of Health and Human Services. Depression in primary care: vol. 1. Detection and diagnosis. Clinical Practice Guidelines Number 5. AHCPR Publication No. 93-0550. April 1993.
20. Stotland NL. Depression: recognition, diagnosis, and management in the primary care setting. Primary Care Update OB/GYN 1994;1:2–8.
21. Valente SM. Evaluating suicide risk in the medically ill patient. Nurse Practitioner 1993;18:41–50.
22. Fishel AH. Mental health. In Fogel CI, Woods NF, eds. Women's Health Care. Thousand Oaks, CA: Sage, 1995:323–362.
23. Lee KA, Lentz MJ, Taylor DL, Mitchell ES, Woods NF. Fatigue as a response to environmental demands in women's lives. IMAGE: J Nurs Scholarship 1994;26: 149– 154.

Suggested Readings

Depression Guideline Panel. Depression in Primary Care: Detection Diagnosis and Treatment. Quick Reference Guide for Clinicians, Number 5, Rockville, MD. U.S. Department of Health and Human Services, Public Health Service, Agency for Health Care Policy and Research. AHCPR Publication No. 93-0552. April 1993.

Diagnostic and Statistical Manual of Mental Disorders, 4th ed. Washington, DC: American Psychiatric Association, 1994.

Ereshefsky L, Overman GP, Karp JK. Current psychotropic dosing and monitoring guidelines. Primary Psychiatry 1995:42–53.

Sapira JD. The Art and Science of Bedside Diagnosis. Baltimore: Urban & Schwarzenberg, 1990.

Wallach J. Interpretation of Diagnostic Tests. 5th ed. Boston: Little, Brown, and Co., 1992.

8.2

Eating Disorders

Kathryn M. Andolsek

Introduction

The United States is experiencing an epidemic of eating disorders (1). Thirty billion dollars annually is spent on the diet industry. Three quarters of women whose weights are in the normal range feel too fat and desire to lose weight, although on average their ideal weights are only slightly heavier than the weights of women with anorexia nervosa (2). At any time, 80% of American women report they are dieting or manipulating food intake and weight (3).

These statistics are not unexpected, because thinness is regarded as a virtue in US culture. Magazines and television feature exceedingly thin models, and beauty is defined by competitive pageants that are won by women with increasingly smaller waist and hip sizes. Cigarettes are named "Slims" and Hershey chocolate bars are described as "thin," and although most people gain a few pounds with age, Aunt Jemima has gotten thinner. A popular comic strip, "Cathy," even features a woman character who diets constantly.

Perhaps because of this societal pressure to be slim, eating disorders, which once were recognized primarily as problems of white middle class or upper middle class adolescent women, are increasingly found among women of every age, as well as among minorities and men. Older adult women, like their younger counterparts, can experience eating as both a measure of physical health and a potentially powerful means of controlling their environment (4).

In women, eating disorders may adversely impact fertility and pregnancy during the reproductive years, and their overall health and nutritional status during later life. Older women, for example, have a poorer nutritional status than men and are more apt to be at either end of the weight continuum—overweight or underweight (5). Sixteen percent of white and 18% of African-American women over 60 years of age eat fewer than 1000 kcal daily. For those below the poverty level, these percentages are 27 and 36, respectively (6).

This chapter will discuss how to diagnose and treat disorders of eating and feeding in women, including obesity, bulimia nervosa, binge-eating disorder, anorexia nervosa, atypical eating disorders, and weight cycling. In addition, a list of national organizations that offer support and information to people with eating disorders is provided in the Appendix. Not considered but still important to our practices are the women and children who suffer adverse health consequences because of grossly inadequate nutrition because of poverty and homelessness.

Obesity

The average American adult weighed 3.6 kg more in 1991 than in 1980 (7, 8). During that period, average caloric consumption increased by 100 to 300 kcal/day, although measured activity levels of at least one segment of the population, high school students, declined.

Obesity is the excess accumulation of fat. Various methods have been developed to measure or estimate a person's fat content including anthropometric measurements based on height, weight, or skinfold thickness, "ideal body weights" derived from actuarial data, such as the Metropolitan Life Insurance Company tables, hydrostatic weighing, or techniques utilizing bioelectrical impedance. The best clinical and epidemiologic measure of adiposity is the body mass index (BMI). The BMI equals one's weight divided by the square of one's height, or BMI $= kg/m^2$. Using this measure, obesity is defined as a body weight that is 20% above the ideal body weight for height, or weight at the 85th percentile. A BMI indicative of being overweight would be 28 for men and 27 for women (9). Ideal body weight for a woman can be approximated as 100 lbs plus 5 lbs for every inch over 5 feet in height. For men, it is approximated as 135 lbs plus an additional 5 lbs for each inch over 5 feet in height. By this standard, one third to one fourth of the population of the United States is obese (10–12). Obesity, therefore, is one of the most common conditions encountered in primary care.

Obesity increases with age and is inversely related to socioeconomic class. One fourth of non-Hispanic white women are obese, and obesity is even more prevalent among women of other ethnic groups (Table 8.2.1) (7). Over 40% of African-American, Mexican-American, Puerto Rican, and native American Indian women are obese. Over 60% of native Hawaiian women are obese. Among women in the same ethnic group, poorer women have a greater risk of obesity (13, 14). Much less difference has been found among African-American, Hispanic, and non-Hispanic white men.

People are becoming obese at younger ages. Three quarters of obese adolescents become obese adults. Obese adults are frequently heavier than individuals who become obese at older ages (15). The prevalence of obesity is disproportionately high among women. More than twice as many women as men attempt to lose weight

Table 8.2.1 Prevalence of Overweight (Body Mass Index > 27.3 kg/m² among Adult Women in U.S. Minority Populations

Minority Population	(%)
Non-Hispanic whites	24
Cuban Americans	32
Puerto Ricans	40
American Indians/Alaskan natives	40
Mexican Americans	42
Non-Hispanic blacks	44
Western Samoans	46
Native Hawaiians	63
Samoans in Manu'a	77
Samoans in Tutuila	79
Samoans in Hawaii	80

Data from Kumanyika SK: Special issues regarding obesity in minority populations. Ann Intern Med 1993;119:650–654.

(16). In addition, women spend more time on weight loss regimens and make more attempts to lose weight than men (17). Among adolescents, 44% of women and 15% of men attempt to lose weight, and 26% of women and 15% of men attempt to keep from gaining weight (18).

Obesity increases the risk of several disease conditions. Persons more than 20% heavier than their ideal body weight risk hypertension, diabetes mellitus type II, hyperlipidemia, coronary heart disease, and cancer. Obesity is also associated with congestive heart failure, gall bladder disease, gout, sleep apnea, other pulmonary dysfunction, and osteoarthritis (19, 20). Extreme obesity shortens life.

Although more common, obesity may not have the same adverse consequences in minority women as in non-Hispanic white women, assuming no associated health conditions exist that could be treated with weight loss, such as diabetes or hypertension. The risk/benefit ratio of interventions to treat obesity remain to be evaluated on a population-specific basis, including important variables such as gender and race (21). However, within the range of nor-

mal weights, if the individual's body mass indices remains less than (27), there is no advantage to being thinner compared to heavier.

Causes of Obesity

Obesity is a mismatch of consumed nutrients and energy expenditure. The underlying reasons for this imbalance are not clear but appear to be multifactorial, reflecting inherited, environmental, cultural, socioeconomic, and psychological conditions. Genetic contributions are being recognized and may lead to improved treatment in the future (22).

Surplus nutrients are converted to triglycerides and stored in adipocytes, a process regulated by the enzyme lipoprotein lipase. The activity of this enzyme varies among body regions. Lipoprotein lipase is metabolically extremely active in abdominal fat, but far less active in fat stored in the body regions around the hips. Excess fat deposits that accumulate in metabolically active sites increase an individual's risk of hyperlipidemia and coronary heart disease. Stress and cigarette smoking can further increase abdominal fat distribution.

A waist-to-hip ratio greater than 1 in women and 0.8 in men indicates an increased risk for coronary heart disease, stroke, and death. Significant ethnic differences among women are revealed by this measure; African-American and Mexican-American women have higher average waist-to-hip measurements than white women.

Energy is expended in three ways. Most individuals expend 60% of their energy via the resting metabolic rate (RMR) and another 20% in the thermic effect of activity—an effect that can be increased by exercise. The remaining energy is expended in dietary-induced thermogenesis, or rather the energy expended in digestion, absorption, and storage of nutrients.

Approximately 3500 excess calories produce 1 lb of adipose tissue. A 500-kcal deficit per day produces a 1-lb loss of weight over 1 week. Total calories ingested compared with energy expenditure is critical in weight balance. However, not all calories are metabolically equivalent. Ingested fat is more calorie dense, does not regulate appetite or satiety well, and is more efficiently stored in adipocytes than either protein or complex carbohydrates. Although consumption of total calories and protein has remained fairly constant, the percent of fat in the average diet has increased since 1900. In 1910, the average diet consisted of 27% fat, but by 1984 the percentage of dietary fat had risen to 44%.

Although some secondary causes of obesity exist such as hypothyroidism, Cushing's syndrome, chromosomal and congenital abnormalities, and some central nervous system lesions, patients with primary obesity are by far the most common. Nonetheless, obesity is still commonly misunderstood as a disorder of willpower. Many obese people are stigmatized and suffer social and occupational discrimination. The psychologic dysfunction of obese individuals is generally the effect of rather than the cause of their obesity. Stereotypes are common and frequently inaccurate. Most obese individuals do not consume more calories than nonobese individuals. They do, however, consume calories in excess of their energy expenditure. In fact, obese individuals may be more metabolically efficient. They compensate metabolically to a greater extent than the nonobese by adjusting their RMR during periods of dietary restriction, and they exhibit fewer thermic effects in response to food or exercise consumption. These characteristics were no doubt an evolutionary advantage when food was in short or sporadic supply.

The Concept of Obesity as a Chronic Disease

Although obesity is a chronic disease much like diabetes mellitus or hypertension, the health care model frequently treats it as more of an acute or subacute illness. This leads to unrealistic expectations and frustration for both patients and health care providers. After initial treatment, the average patient regains at least one third of the weight lost within 1 year, and most regain the remaining weight lost within 5 years of treatment cessation. Short-term approaches to weight loss rarely succeed. Successful treatment should be viewed as "palliative and not curative" (23). Management of obesity requires a lifelong commitment to changes in lifestyle, behavior, and diet. As Yanovski points out, diabetic patients who are treated for 6 months are not expected to remain euglycemic for the remainder of their lives (24). According to Yanovski, both patients and providers should conceptualize obesity as a chronic medical disorder, because such a conceptualization is:

- Consistent with current research demonstrating genetic and biologic components
- Decreases some of the stigma associated with the condition, recognizing that it is not a failure of willpower or a moral weakness
- Recognizes the heterogenous nature of the development of and maintenance of obesity
- Supports individualizing treatment approaches
- Emphasizes the long-term nature of the disorder, allowing both patients and physicians to set realistic expectations, including relapses

Evaluation of the Obese Patient

Health care offices should be accessible to large individuals. Armless chairs in the waiting areas, a variety of appropriately sized blood pressure cuffs, large-sized examining gowns, and useful scales should all be available. Suggestions for adapting a standard scale for patients weighing more than 159 kg are given in Table 8.2.2. In addition, attitudes of providers and staff may need to be addressed. For more information on this subject, contact the National Association to Advance Fat Acceptance (see Appendix).

Table 8.2.2 Steps for Adapting a Standard Scale for Use with Patients Weighing More Than 159 kg (350 lb)

1. Weigh an average-size person on the scale.
2. Record the weight.
3. Attach an elastic band to the earpieces of a stethoscope and attach the stethoscope to the outer edge of the balance bar. Make sure the stethoscope is not touching the side of the scale—it must hang freely.
4. Weigh the average-size person again.
5. Record this weight. Subtract the second weight from the first and note the difference.
6. Weigh the stethoscope still attached to the balance. Weigh the overweight patient and record the weight—it will now be measurable at less than 159 kg.
7. Add the difference obtained in Step 5 to the weight recorded in Step 6. The sum is the patient's accurate weight.

Data from Yanovski SZ: A practical approach to treatment of the obese patient. Arch Fam Med 1993;2:310.

Some patients may present specifically with concerns regarding their weight. Others may present with a related complaint, such as an orthopedic problem, or a seemingly unrelated problem, such as sinusitis. The health care encounter should focus on the primary concern of the patient. After this is addressed, the provider should inquire whether the patient's obesity has ever presented or caused any problems. If so, the readiness of the patient to pursue an evaluation should be assessed. If the patient is open to pursuing the evaluation, a full history and evaluation can be scheduled.

Components of this evaluation include (1) age at onset of obesity, (2) family history and previous dieting history (including methods tried, successes, and failures), (3) current diet, (4) exercise habits, (5) binge-eating, (6) purging, (7) fasting, (8) social support, (9) motivation for weight loss, (10) goals and expectations, and (10) determination of the time, motivation, and money the patient is able to commit to a weight loss program.

A drug history should be taken (Table 8.2.3). Tricyclic antidepressants cause weight gain in at least one third of patients. Other drugs that can cause weight gain include the phenothiazines, especially chlorpromazine and thioridazine (less weight gain with haloperidol), valproic acid, carbamazepine, and steroids.

A medical review of systems should be taken. Rapid weight gain is suspicious for causes other than primary obesity. Specifically, the patient should be questioned regarding symptoms suggestive of hypothyroidism, pituitary and adrenal disease, hypothalamic processes, and polycystic ovary condition. Rare inherited causes, such as Prader-Willi syndrome, are usually suggested by the history and physical examination.

A family history of obesity and other associated medical conditions should be obtained. A positive family history is common. Obesity will develop in 80% of children of two obese parents but in only 14% of children of two nonobese parents. This finding can sometimes

Table 8.2.3 Drugs that Can Cause Weight Gain

Tricyclic antidepressants
Phenothiazines
Haloperidol
Valproic acid
Carbamazepine
Steroids
Oral contraceptives

motivate obese parents to change the family's diet and exercise routines to try to prevent it in their children. The patient's weight, height, BMI, and blood pressure should be recorded.

Because of the increased risk of central obesity, an accurate waste-to-hip ratio should be obtained. The waist should be measured at the smallest horizontal circumference between the twelfth rib and the iliac crest. The skin should not be compressed, and a flexible, non-stretchable tape measure should be used.

Laboratory evaluation should include a lipid profile and measurement of fasting or postprandial blood glucose levels. If other medical conditions are suspected based on the patient's history or physical examination, additional laboratory testing may be considered.

Treatment

Realistic goals for weight reduction should be set. Patients may never achieve ideal body weight. Weight loss of 10% of initial body weight, however, can favorably affect hypertension, hyperlipidemia, glycemic control, and joint discomfort. It can also improve functional status, reduce work absenteeism, promote social interaction, decrease sleep apnea, and enhance mood. Patients may prefer to focus on these outcome measures rather than a specified amount of weight lost. They can be optimistic regarding positive benefits they themselves can perceive even if they never achieve ideal body weight.

At this stage of the evaluation, an assessment of the patient's motivation and ability to change behaviors and commit to a treatment plan should be ascertained. In general, women are more motivated by appearance rather than fitness; the reverse is true for men (18). Some patients will be unable or unwilling to commit to a weight loss regimen at the time of the evaluation. Health care providers can negotiate what, if any, changes in diet and activity the patient is willing to consider. They should reassure patients of continuing compassionate care regardless of weight and offer further management options in the future when the patient is ready to pursue weight loss.

Weight Loss Modalities

Patients who are motivated can be managed in a stepped-care approach that incorporates one or more of the following modalities: caloric restriction and composition, behavioral therapy, drug treatment, and surgery. Patients with greater degrees of obesity or medical complications related to their weight should be offered more intensive treatment. One treatment algorithm is presented in Figure 8.2.1.

The NIH Technology Assessment Conference Panel (16) concluded that few scientific studies have evaluated the effectiveness and safety of most weight loss methods; fewer still have evaluated success over long periods of follow-up. Characteristics of the most successful programs are realistic goals, promotion of slow, steady weight loss, a reasonable diet, and education about new dietary practices compatible with a lifetime of weight control. Successful programs prepare patients to deal with high-risk emotional and social situations, self-monitor progress, use problem-solving in difficult situations, and reduce stress. They accept relapse and help patients plan for it.

Barriers to successful weight loss include a patient's lack of feelings of self-efficacy, failing to lose weight early on, lack of social and professional support, serious social or psychologic problems (e.g., depression), and terminating the program. The panel recommended that, when evaluating available programs, patients inquire regarding the percentage of all participants who begin the program and complete it, the percentage of those who complete the program who achieve various degrees of weight loss, the proportion of weight loss maintained at 1, 3, and 5 years, and the percentage of participants who experience adverse medical or psychologic effects (16).

Classification → Stepped Care → Matching
Decision   Decision   Decision

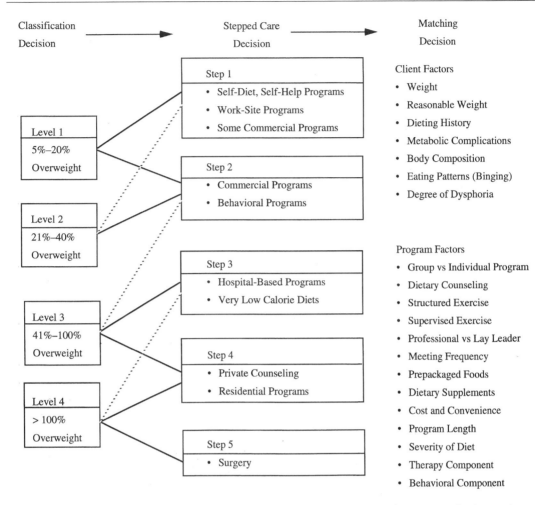

Figure 8.2.1. A stepped care approach to selecting obesity treatment. A conceptual scheme showing the three-stage process used to select a treatment for an individual. The first step, the "classification decision," classifies individuals into four levels by percentage overweight. These levels dictate which of the five steps would be reasonable in the second stage, the "stepped care decision." This indicates the least intensive, costly, and risky approach that will be used from among alternative treatments. The third stage, the "matching decision," is used to make the final selection of a program and is based on a combination of client and program variables. The dashed lines between the classification and stepped care stages show the lowest level of treatment that may be beneficial, but more intensive treatment (solid lines) is usually necessary for people at the specified weight level. (Reprinted with permission from Yanovski SZ: A practical approach to the obese patient. Arch Fam Med 1993:2:309–316.)

Treatment during Pregnancy

Weight loss during pregnancy and lactation can adversely affect fetal weight and milk characteristics. Specific management plans for pregnant and nursing women should be developed with a knowledgeable provider and often a nutritionist. Obese or overweight women should not attempt to reduce their weight during a pregnancy. Healthy birth weights of infants can usually be achieved with less weight gain. Generally, a 15-lb weight gain is recommended during pregnancy for the obese woman.

Lactation will usually promote modest weight loss. Too rapid weight loss, however, can compromise milk supply and composition. Obese or overweight women should avoid losing more than 1 to 2 lbs weekly while nursing. Both mother and baby should be medically evaluated. The recommendations for weight loss management that follow are for nonpregnant, nonlactating women.

Caloric Restriction and Composition

Nutritional therapy is aimed at restricting calories and reducing the percentage of calories obtained from fat to less than 30% of total calories. Reduction of dietary fat alone will produce little weight loss because many foods low in fat are still high in calories. Low-fat foods that increase the ratio of saturated fat to polyunsaturated fat may produce adverse effects on lipids even when total fat consumption is decreased. Low-fat diets (less than 30%) will help to maintain the new body weight after a weight reduction diet and prevent the development of obesity.

Almost all fad and commercially available diets are variations on this principle. Most diets decrease calories by limiting food choices. Low-calorie balanced diets, usually in the range of 1000 to 1400 kcal daily, produce predictable patterns of weight loss as long as the patient adheres to the regimen.

Very low-calorie diets (approximately 400 to 800 calories daily) have been promoted for more than 20 years. They produce more rapid weight loss because of the significant caloric restriction. The typical program lasts 12 weeks, and many are combined with behavioral modification techniques. Patients can expect to lose 20 to 25 kg during the active treatment period and can lose more if they use the behavioral modification techniques and a low-calorie diet plan in the weeks and months afterwards. Only a small percentage of patients achieve their ideal body weight through these programs, but those who do are more likely to maintain their weight loss over time.

Early diet formulations used collagen as the protein source. The occurrence of sudden death, arrhythmias, and disability led to newer formulations that employed casein, egg, and soy as protein sources and enriched the mineral and electrolyte content. Weight is regained rapidly if the very low-calorie diet is not combined with other treatment and aggressive maintenance strategies.

Contraindications to very low-calorie diets include myocardial infarction, angina, major arrhythmia, stroke, bleeding ulcer, significant liver or kidney disease, or cancer. Patients should also be excluded if they require therapeutic doses of aspirin.

Side effects of very low-calorie diets include hair loss, thinned skin, dizziness, fatigue, and temperature instability. These tend to be transient. Occasional patients are allergic to the protein source. More significant medical side effects include an increased risk for gallstones and acute gallbladder disease. Some authorities recommend prophylactic ursodeoxycholic acid to decrease the incidence of these complications. Because of the frequency and potential severity of complications, diets of less than 800 kcal/day should not be undertaken without medical supervision. Most patients regain their previous weight after such severely restricted diets (25).

Increased Physical Activity

Increased physical activity should be prescribed even though it may or may not augment weight loss. In general, exercise by itself will contribute a weight loss of 4 to 7 lbs over several weeks to months. However, exercise has beneficial effects independent of weight change. These include improved cardiovascular fitness, increased high-density lipoprotein, reduced waist-to-hip ratio, enhanced well-being, and increased lean body mass. Exercise also decreases the tendency to regain weight after cessation of a weight loss program. Even if weight loss is not achieved, overweight men and women who are active and fit have lower rates of morbidity and mortality than overweight persons who are sedentary. Individuals should begin exercising slowly to avoid injury and to incorporate this new behavior into a daily routine. Activities should be compatible with the individual's lifestyle and interests (26).

Behavioral Therapy

Behavioral modification is the single most important component of any management plan for patients with obesity. It involves changing habits and, frequently, modifying attitudes. It works best when patients are encouraged to take active roles in developing the management strategy. Patients identify eating or lifestyle behaviors that require modification, set specific behavioral goals, modify the behavior, and reinforce desired behavior. Common techniques include self-monitoring, stimulus control, design of a system of rewards, and attention to the social environment.

Self-monitoring, in general, involves the keeping of a diary by the patient of foods eaten correlated with the emotional and physical settings surrounding their consumption. This strategy, coupled with simple recommendations to decrease usual food portions by half, proved successful in a family practice with scheduled regular follow-up (27). Willingness and adherence to keeping the food diary predicted the group of patients most successful with weight loss (27). Stimulus control techniques dissociate events that trigger eating from the eating itself.

Rewards are best designed by an individual to praise appropriate behavior and discourage inappropriate ones. The home, family, or occupational environment may require modification or restructuring to facilitate patient success.

Behavioral modification can be implemented by lay individuals or professionals. It can be used alone or in conjunction with other programs. It should aim for gradual, sustainable changes and provide some form of ongoing support for these changes when the formal program has ended. Behavioral modification extends the interval before weight is regained.

It has not proven as effective with African-American women as with white women.

Drug Treatment

Patients with significant obesity, or who have significant symptoms from their obesity (e.g., hypertension), should be considered candidates for pharmacologic therapy. Medication should be viewed as part of a total management strategy and not the sole component. Appetite suppressants are the major class of drugs currently available. These consist of drugs that act either on the noradrenergic or serotonergic nervous systems. Noradrenergic medications include the over-the-counter medication phenylpropanolamine (25 mg tid). This compound's long-term benefits are not well documented, and there is a potential for its misuse. Other drugs in this class are available by prescription only.

Fenfluramine (10, 20, or 40 mg bid before meals) and fluoxetine (40 to 60 mg/day) are inhibitors of serotonin reuptake. They have few central stimulatory effects. Fenfluramine is not addictive. Its major side effects are drowsiness, diarrhea, and sleep disturbances. Depression can occur if the drug is withdrawn abruptly, however. Fluoxetine shows a dose-response effect on weight loss. Most patients will lose weight for the first 8 weeks of treatment, but many treated for more than 16 to 20 weeks begin to regain weight.

Phenteramine 15 mg after breakfast and fenfluramine 20 mg to 40 mg 1 hour before the evening meal has also been used in combination. If more drug is necessary, 20 mg fenfluramine has also been added to the morning dose of phenteramine. Weight loss continues or is maintained in most patients until the medications are stopped. In addition to the side effects of fenfluramine, other common complaints include dry mouth. Dexfenfluramine will likely be available in late 1997. Thermogenic drugs, including sympathomimetic compounds and endogenous hormones, such as thyroid, insulin, and growth hormones, are no longer used. Sympathomimetic compounds such as ephedrine in combination with caffeine have shown promise.

Gut peptides, cholecystokinin, pancreatic glucagon, and bombesin are mediators of satiety. Clinically, their use is limited by poor bioavailability when given orally. A lipase inhibitor is currently under study as are agents to block carbohydrate digestion, block lipid digestion, stimulate lipid oxidation, and provide a source of nonabsorbable fat (28).

Surgery

Surgery is reserved for those individuals who are morbidly obese, or 100 lbs or more above ideal body weight. Early surgical modalities such as jejunoileal bypass and complete gastric bypass procedures are no longer used because they had significant long-term complications (i.e., electrolyte imbalance, chronic diarrhea, osteoporosis, liver failure). Vertical gastric banding is most commonly used at the present time. No difference in weight loss at 3 months has been found in patients treated with very low-calorie diets or surgery; however, 30% of patients treated with gastric banding maintained a weight loss of greater than 10 kg at 5

years compared with 17% of patients treated with very low-calorie diets.

Surgical mortality is approximately 1%. Complications include rupture of the suture line, ventral hernia, gastric ulcer, nausea, and heartburn. For unexplained reasons, most patients experience a decrease in appetite. Experimental surgical methods are under development.

Bulimia Nervosa

Bulimia nervosa, a syndrome characterized by intense preoccupation with food, is manifested as secretive binge-eating episodes alternating with rigorous fasting, severe dietary restrictions, self-induced vomiting, rigorous exercise, or the use of laxatives or diuretics. Binge-eating is defined as eating, while feeling unable to control food intake. During a binge episode, an average of 1200 kcal is consumed, generally consisting of "junk food" or food high in carbohydrates. An average of at least two binge episodes a week is necessary to fulfill the criteria for the DSM-III-R diagnosis of bulimia nervosa (Table 8.2.4) (29).

Table 8.2.4 DSM-IV Criteria for Bulimia Nervosa

- Recurrent episodes of binge-eating; an episode of binge-eating is characterized by eating in a discrete period of time (e.g., within any 2-hour period) an amount of food that is definitely larger than most people would eat during a similar period of time and under similar circumstances, and a sense of lack of control over eating behavior during the episode (e.g., a feeling that one cannot stop eating or control how much one is eating)
- Recurrent inappropriate compulsory behavior in order to prevent weight gain, such as self-induced vomiting, misuse of laxatives, diuretics or enemas, strict dieting or fasting, or excessive exercise.
- The binge eating and inappropriate compensatory behaviors both occur on average, at least twice a week for at least 3 months
- Self-evaluation is unduly influenced by body shape and weight
- The disturbance does not occur exclusively during episodes of bulimia nervosa

    Purging type: during the current episode of bulimia nervosa the person has regularly engaged in self-induced vomiting or the misuse of laxatives, diuretics, or enemas

    Non-purging type: during the current episode of bulimia nervosa, the person has used other inappropriate compensatory behaviors such as fasting or excessive exercise

Data from Diagnostic and Statistical Manual of Mental Disorders. 4th ed. Washington, D.C: American Psychiatric Association, 1994.

Symptoms characteristically begin when the patient is between 17 and 25 years of age. However, because of the secretive nature of the episodes and the patient's reluctance to discuss them even with family and friends, the condition may not be recognized for many years. It is not uncommon for women to first present aged in their 30s and 40s. At least nine screening questionnaires have been developed to identify patients with eating disorders. None have proven useful to a primary care practice, primarily because they are lengthy and lack adequate validation. Two questions—"Do you ever eat in secret?" and "Are you satisfied with your eating patterns?"—have been proposed for inclusion in the more traditional medical review of systems. These two questions are highly sensitive and specific in identifying known patients with bulimia (30).

Little is known about the pathogenesis of bulimia. Its prevalence, or at least its recognition, seems to have increased during a time when patients are significantly preoccupied with their body shape and have increased information regarding dieting. Bulimic women seem to respond differently to satiety cues. After major dietary restraint, they will react to caloric "preload" by eating more of a subsequent snack than will women with normal eating patterns. Prevalence rates for bulimia vary widely. At least 1.5% of women have bulimia (31), whereas some high school and college studies have reported rates as high as 18%.

The typical patient is a somewhat underweight woman who binge eats and purges 14 times each week. Bulimic episodes may be triggered by an attempt to diet, and dietary restriction aggravates the symptoms. The condition is rare in men.

Binge-eating leads to weight gain, which in turn leads to purging, fasting, and dietary restriction. Fasting and dietary restriction result in relative starvation, which decreases the woman's resting metabolic rate. The woman's weight will then increase even at her low caloric intake. A vicious cycle is created of more binge/purge/fasting episodes, all in an attempt to control weight.

Binge episodes may also affect moods. The increased intake of "sweets" increases brain serotonin levels, which may explain why women report less stress after a binge episode. For many, however, these positive feelings fade quickly and are replaced by guilt and self-recrimination.

History and Evaluation

Bulimia nervosa should be suspected in women who are slightly underweight, women with aggressive exercise programs, a positive family history, frequent dieting, weight fluctuations of more than 10 lbs, or women whose nutritional histories reveal they eat little or no food for breakfast or lunch. Runners, gymnasts, fashion models, and dancers are particularly at risk. Among men, wrestlers are most prone to bulimic behaviors. At physical examination, characteristic clues include dental erosion (which is irreversible) or periodontal disease from vomiting, enlarged salivary glands (this effect is generally bilateral and the parotid gland particularly may be affected), or Russell's sign, skin lesions on the dorsum of the hand, particularly over the metacarpophalangeal joints from self-induced vomiting. The skin lesions may be superficial ulcerations, hyperpigmented calluses, or hypertrophied scarring (32).

Laboratory abnormalities include hypokalemia and an increased serum amylase of parotid origin. Routine outpatient electrolyte evaluation is a poor screening method for detecting occult or denied bulimia, however, and the serum potassium level does not help determine the overall severity of an eating disorder or whether inpatient care is warranted (33).

Emotional function should be assessed as other psychiatric conditions may coexist, such as depression, impulsive behaviors (i.e., kleptomania, self-mutilation, promiscuity, overspending), obsessive-compulsive disorder, and alcohol and drug abuse. One third of bulimic patients had positive responses to the CAGE alcohol screening tool in one study (30). Sexual abuse has been reported in as many as 50% of bulimic patients, a prevalence similar to that found in patients with other psychiatric symptoms (34).

Complications

Medical complications are rare in this disorder but include ruptured esophageal varices from vomiting and acute gastric dilation. Other complications include (1) electrolyte disturbances (characteristically hypokalemia or hypochloremic alkalosis from vomiting), (2) mineral and fluid imbalances, (3) hypomagnesemia, (4) gastric and esophageal irritation and bleeding, (5) large bowel abnormalities from laxative abuse, (6) dental enamel erosion, (7) parotid enlargement, (8) hyperamylasemia, and

(9) rarely, Mallory-Weiss tears. Ipecac abuse may cause a cardiomyopathy that can result in sudden death. One 30-mL bottle of ipecac contains 21 mg of emetine base. An accumulated dose of 1.25 g can cause peripheral muscle weakness or result in the death of an adult.

Treatment Options

Treatment options include nutritional rehabilitation, family interventions, and psychosocial and pharmacologic modalities. Hospitalization treatment for uncomplicated bulimia nervosa is rarely necessary. Outpatient or day hospital programs are preferred unless patients are suicidal, have severe concurrent alcohol or drug abuse, or have life-endangering medical problems that cannot be managed on an outpatient basis. Guidelines for the treatment of patients with bulimia nervosa are given in Table 8.2.5 (35).

Table 8.2.5 Suggested Guidelines for the Treatment of Bulimia Nervosa

1. Establish relationship of trust with the patient
2. Collaborate with the woman in her own care and participation in her own treatment and facilitate her control over her own treatment
3. Assess woman and her story comprehensively, including need for inpatient treatment (should be needed rarely) and triggers to binging
4. Interrupt binge-purge behavior as first priority within 2 to 3 months of treatment, encourage regular eating, and discourage periods of fasting
5. Restore nutritional and physiologic status
6. Involve the patient's family
7. Develop, when possible, support from other women with eating disorders
8. Validate patient self-reports (e.g., use of calendars to record symptom-free days)
9. Utilize team approach to combine behavioral, cognitive-behavioral, interpersonal, educational nutritional, self-help, and psychodynamic methods to individualize treatment. Behavioral learning principles are most critical.
10. Collaboratively plan a 1-year maintenance program
11. Consider antidepressant medications along with psychological therapies
12. Attend to concurrent substance abuse disorders because successful treatment for bulimia nervosa is unlikely in the presence of an active substance abuse disorder
13. Construct problem-solving strategies for addressing relapses

Data from Yager J. Psychosocial treatments for eating disorders. Psychiatry 1994;57:162 and Gallager-Allred C, Gabel LL. Managing common adolescent nutritional problems. Fam Pract Recert 1995;17:27–29.

Psychotherapy

A variety of psychosocial approaches have been used. Cognitive-behavioral therapy, interpersonal psychotherapy, and behavioral therapy have been compared in multiple studies. All have been effective in reducing binge-eating. Cognitive-behavioral therapy has more successfully changed patient perceptions of body image and controlled vomiting. Cognitive-behavioral therapy has also proved superior to antidepressant medication by itself or in combination with cognitive-behavioral therapy for bulimic patients who are not depressed.

Cognitive-behavioral therapy involves the institution of three regular meals daily, reintroducing previously avoided food to the diet, correcting body image distortions, addressing food issues, and providing specific skills to cope with lapses. The patient is involved in self-monitoring of dietary binge-eating and purging. Four to 6 months of treatment is required (36).

Interpersonal therapy ignores eating and eating behaviors, focusing instead upon self-esteem, family, and interpersonal issues. There is extreme variability in treatment response. Some patients respond well to interpersonal therapy and family therapy. In others, eating symptoms improve but other psychiatric symptoms develop or intensify. Group psychotherapy, particularly when combined with dietary counseling, demonstrates moderate efficacy. Twelve-step programs, such as Overeaters Anonymous, have been helpful to some patients, especially as an adjunct to other treatment and for long-term prevention of relapse. Chapters of these organizations vary significantly, and clinicians should collaborate with patients to assess their experiences with these programs. Twelve-step or other programs that focus on abstinence but have no nutritional or behavioral components are not recommended as sole therapy (37, 38).

Some traditional treatment programs have been criticized for being based on masculine beliefs about illness, treatment, and recovery. Recovery in these programs is conceived of as independent of symptoms and focuses on development of the patient's self-reliance and independence. Women may heal better in settings that emphasize relational development, mutually interactive treatment, and collaboration among patients and providers (39).

Recognizing that loss of control is a central feature among patients with bulimia nervosa, certain programs give patients control of their own treatment program (40). Some self-help programs provide manuals that help the patient incorporate the program's principles with her own suggestions for normalizing her diet as well as with suggestions derived from individual or group counseling.

Pharmacological Therapy

Among pharmacologic strategies for the treatment of bulimia, the drugs of choice are antidepressants. Bulimics responded to antidepressants more favorably than to placebo in controlled trials. Bulimia, however, is not a type of depression; bulimic patients do not consistently demonstrate depression or depressive symptoms. Even when they are depressed, the degree of depression in bulimic patients is unrelated to the severity of their bulimic symptoms and the degree of improvement with antidepressant treatment.

Nondepressed and depressed patients with bulimia respond equally well to antidepressants that increase dietary restraint and decrease hunger. Tricyclic antidepressants have been considered the first-line treatment for bulimia. Imipramine 200 mg h.s. has demonstrated benefit. In one study, 50% of treated patients stopped binge-eating and purging; others, although not completely cured, decreased the frequency of their episodes (41). The monoamine oxidase inhibitors have also been used to treat bulimia, especially phenelzine and isocarboxazid. They are viewed as problematic, however, because of the necessary dietary restrictions required with their use. Phenytoin, naloxone, fenfluramine, naltrexone, tryptophan, carbamazepine, and lithium have been less effective (42). Other drugs with proven efficacy in this disorder include desipramine and trazodone. Serotoninergic reuptake inhibitors also have been used. Patients typically require higher doses of fluoxetine (60 mg/day rather than 20 or 40 mg) to control symptoms.

Long-term pharmacologic treatment is necessary to prevent relapse. If medications are not achieving the desired effect, patient adherence should be assessed. Patients fail to comply with drug treatment regimens for any number of reasons. In addition, the possibility of recurrent vomiting decreasing the amount of drug absorbed should be considered. If truly a drug failure, a different medication should be selected. It is not uncommon to try two or three agents before one demonstrates benefit. Most treatment programs allow individualization of management, including timing and selection of medication. Seventy percent of those who complete treatment programs substantially reduce their symptoms for as long as 6 years. Little is known about the natural history of untreated bulimic patents, although over time reduction in symptoms has been suggested (43, 44).

Binge-Eating Disorder

Like bulimic patients, individuals who have binge-eating disorder consume large quantities of food and feel lack of control over these episodes. They do not purge or fast, however. Patients are frequently obese or at least moderately overweight. Approximately 2% of adults have binge-eating disorder. The prevalence may be much higher, especially among participants in weight control groups. As many as 30% of obese enrollees in weight control programs have this disorder. It is the only eating disorder that afflicts a large number of men, although women are still overrepresented with a 3:2 female-to-male ratio.

Typical patients are over 40 years of age and seek treatment for weight control; they do not complain of binge-eating. Patients alternate diet restriction with binge-eating, experiencing wide weight fluctuations of more than 5 kg. Because of the weight fluctuations, these obese patents may be at greater coronary heart disease risk than obese patients who do not binge. Dietary restriction and emotional disturbances commonly trigger episodes of binge-eating.

Depression, anxiety, and personality disorders are more common in the obese who binge than those who do not. The inclusion of this large subset of obese patients in previous research probably was responsible for erroneous conclusions regarding excess mental health conditions among all obese individuals. Because treatment and prognosis differ depending on whether the obese patent binges, this diagnosis is important. Common weight fluctuations of more than 10 lbs should suggest binge-eating disorder. Treatment modalities include the tricyclic antidepressant desipramine, the serotonin reuptake inhibitor fluoxetine, and cognitive-behavioral and interpersonal therapy. With treatment, 50% of patients will cease to binge.

Anorexia Nervosa

Anorexia nervosa, the rarest of the eating disorders, is characterized by significant dietary restriction, massive weight loss, and, in women, amenorrhea. The prevalence is 0.2 to 1.0% among women, and 0.015 % in men (32). Its incidence is inversely related to socioeconomic status. There is a family component. It is eight times more common in women with relatives who also had anorexia nervosa (32). Depression also runs in these families. Symptoms characteristically begin when the patient is mildly overweight. The patient feels fat and desires to be thin. Her concept of thinness is significantly unrealistic (45). The significant dietary restriction is accompanied by higher levels of endogenous opiates. The endocrine abnormalities of these women are almost always secondary to starvation and most normalize with refeeding. Criteria for diagnosis are presented in Table 8.2.6. There are two subtypes of patients with anorexia nervosa: restricting and bulimic. Approximately half of patients are in each subtype. Patients with the restricting subtype achieve weight loss through dietary restriction. They limit energy intake to as few as several hundred kcal daily, limit food selection, and demonstrate obsessive-compulsive symptoms. Patients with the bulimic subtype suffer from frequent eating binges and purges and are self-destructive. Some of the "binges" may not be objectively a binge; patients may purge after only minimal quantities of food. Up to half of patients develop bulimic symptoms. Restricting and bulimic subtype behavior may alternate in the same patient. Patients from both subtypes may exercise excessively, demonstrate bizarre food preferences, isolate themselves socially, display diminished sexual interest, and be depressed.

History and Evaluation

The typical patient is an adolescent woman who gradually loses weight over several months. She has amenorrhea and disturbed eating patterns, is significantly concerned with any weight increase, and feels fat. She may exercise excessively and present with related orthopedic problems. Prepubertal patients are also encountered with arrested sexual development. This disorder may also present in early adult life; frank anorexia nervosa may appear for the first time in the older woman (46).

On physical examination, the patient characteristically will display some or all of the following signs or symptoms: (a) extreme emaciation, (b) dry skin, (c) fine body hair (lanugo), (d) cold, discolored extremities, (e) muscle wasting, (f) peripheral edema, (g) bradycardia, (h) low blood pressure, (i) decreased bone

Table 8.2.6 DSM IV Criteria for Anorexia Nervosa

- Refusal to maintain body weight at or above a minimal normal weight for age and height (e.g., weight loss leading to maintenance of body weight less than 85% of that expected; or failure to make expected weight gain during period of growth, leading to body weight less than 85% of that expected)
- Intense fear of gaining weight or becoming fat even though underweight
- Disturbance in the way in which one's body weight, size, or shape is experienced; undue inflation of body weight or shape in self-evaluation or denial of the seriousness of the current low body weight
- In postmenarcheal women, amenorrhea in the absence of at least three consecutive menstrual cycles when otherwise expected to occur (primary or secondary amenorrhea); a woman is considered to have amenorrhea if her periods occur only following hormone, e.g., estrogen administration
- Restricting type; during the current episode of anorexia nervosa the person has not regularly engaged in binge-eating or purging behavior (i.e., self-induced vomiting or the misuse of laxatives, diuretics, or enemas)
- Binge-eating/purging type; during the current episode of anorexia nervosa the person has regularly engaged in binge-eating or purging behavior (i.e., self-induced vomiting or the misuse of laxatives, diuretics, or enemas)

Data from Diagnostic and Statistical Manual of Mental Disorders. 4th ed. Washington, DC: American Psychiatric Association, 1994.

density, and (10) difficulties with concentration, memory, and judgment. Pubic and axially hair is preserved. Patients may display dehydration, electrolyte disturbances, gastrointestinal motility disturbances, infertility, hypothermia, and psychologic impairment from starvation. Behavioral signs include restricted food intake, odd food rituals, intense fear of becoming fat, avoiding situations in which food may be present, and excess weighing.

Results of laboratory studies are usually normal despite profound inanition. Potassium levels may be decreased and results of liver function test may be abnormal because of fatty infiltration of the liver. Endocrine evidence points to hypothalamic dysfunction: gonadotropin levels are extremely depressed, and follicle stimulating hormone (FSH) and estrogen levels are low. Levels of total serum thyroxine and T3 are decreased, whereas those of free T4 and prolactin are usually normal. Resting plasma cortisol levels are generally elevated. These laboratory values do not generally require treatment. They will normalize with refeeding.

Significant medical complications of anorexia include arrhythmias, cardiomyopathy, and congestive heart failure, especially during refeeding. Anorexia nervosa must be differentiated from other mental health conditions, notably depression and schizophrenia. Although anorexia nervosa may coexist with depression, it is usually simple to attribute the profound weight loss to anorexia nervosa. The weight loss is far greater than that characteristically seen in depressed patients. The delusions of schizophrenic patients may center on food, but generally their body images are not distorted.

Anorexia in a pregnant women can be a significant problem. Nausea only adds to the problems of vomiting. Hyperemesis gravidarum is hard to differentiate from anorexia exacerbation. Treatment is supportive and may require frequent hospitalizations for intravenous hydration and intensive counseling.

Differential Diagnosis

Diabetes mellitus, certain brain tumors, and various gastrointestinal disorders need to be excluded to arrive at the diagnosis of anorexia nervosa. Gastrointestinal conditions that can present similarly include gastroesophageal reflux disease, peptic ulcer disease, intestinal motility disorders, malabsorptive states, pancreatic disease, hepatitis, gallbladder disease, irritable bowel syndrome, and Crohn's disease. Crohn's disease presents as weight loss, anorexia, nausea, vomiting, and diarrhea in patients between 15 and 35 years of age. Gastroparesis can occur in patients with eating disorders and responds to prokinetic agents as well as weight gain (47). Depression may cause loss of appetite accompanied by weight loss, but generally not of the same magnitude that occurs with anorexia nervosa. Schizophrenic patients may present with abnormal or delusional eating, but these symptoms tend to be extremely significant.

Treatment Options

The most successful treatments focus on weight restoration in conjunction with individual behavioral and family therapy. Restoration of body weight is the primary early treatment goal. Outpatient treatment is possible in approximately half of the patients (48). Behavioral therapy links rewards to weight gain. Family therapy in particular has improved long-term outcome (49). Inpatient units may be necessary for patients with more severe disease. They decrease opportunities for exercise and motivate weight gain through reinforcement and provision of large meals. Whether a strict milieu is more beneficial than a lenient milieu is controversial. Lenient programs enlist the patient's cooperation, participation, and sense of control. They increase staff satisfaction by reducing policing functions and decrease opportunities for conflict. Nasogastric tube feedings and total parenteral nutrition are now only rarely used.

Table 8.2.7 Guidelines for Treating Patients With Anorexia Nervosa

1. Assess physical status, eating disorder history, associated psychiatric disturbances, substance use, developmental history, and family history
2. Interview the family
3. Restore weight to begin normal menses
4. Provide positive reinforcement and reward system and return control of eating back to the patient
5. Avoid tube feedings and parenteral nutrition unless life-threatening medical complications arise
6. Consider individual psychotherapy for motivated patient who is able to participate
7. Consider family therapy for all patients, focusing on reduction in blaming, improving communications regarding family conflicts, and preparing the family to deal with patient and common issues. Avoid family therapy if one or more family members are rigidly destructive
8. Individualize modalities to the cognitive and defensive styles, psychologic, and belief systems of the participants.

Data from Yager J. Psychosocial treatments for eating disorders. Psychiatry 1994;57;157.

Patients undergoing refeeding should be prepared for the unpleasant side effects that may sabotage their commitment to new behaviors. Refeeding symptoms that should be anticipated and discussed include sudden weight gain as a result of fluid retention, dramatic daily weight fluctuations, constipation, gas, cramping, early satiety, postprandial sweating, and edema.

Medication alone is not an effective therapy for anorexia. Malnourished patients develop more side effects and are less responsive to antidepressant medication than other patients. Tricyclics in particular may increase the risk of hypotension and arrhythmia. Some symptoms of depression improve with refeeding.

Antidepressants are helpful if the patient has true coexisting depression. Estrogen and calcium should be considered to reduce calcium loss and the risk of osteoporosis. Yager's summary of guidelines for treating patients with anorexia nervosa are presented in Table 8.2.7 (35).

After 10 years of treatment, 25 to 40% of anorexics are fully recovered, 20 to 30% have a poor treatment outcome, 2% are obese, and the remainder have intermediate levels of recovery. Poorer prognosis is associated with lower initial weights, vomiting, failure in previous treatment, and disturbed family relationships. Mortality is 20% at 20 years, primarily from sudden death or suicide. Even patients who do well need to participate in maintenance programs to prevent relapse.

Weight Cycling

Although not a specific eating disorder, weight cycling is common and may have adverse health effects. Weight cycling is the wide fluctuation in weight seen as a result of dieting and regaining of weight, or a binge-eating disorder. Patients experiencing weight cycles have higher dietary fat intakes, their abdominal fat distribution is increased, and they have increased rates of death from coronary heart disease and cancer (50, 51).

Atypical Eating Disorders

Many patients do not fulfill strict criteria for one of the eating disorders yet have a preoccupation with body weight, food, and eating. These disorders in many ways represent a continuum. They are common. Health care providers should incorporate questions regarding weight fluctuations in their patient evaluation and assess dietary adequacy in their patients. Weight cycling or dietary restrictions should prompt further inquiry into the patient's reasons. Providers should also be careful not to contribute to these behaviors iatrogenically by recommending weight loss to groups particularly at risk, such as adolescent women, without plans for management and follow up.

Weight Changes in the Elderly

In older patients, changes in body weight are an important vital sign. Evaluation and intervention should be prompt. If poverty, lack of mobility or social support influence the patient's eating behavior, other social support systems should be put in place, such as Meals On Wheels, assistance from chore workers, or senior day care. Poverty, widowhood, isolation, impaired mobility or other physical disability, poor dental and oral health, and coexisting conditions such as dementia may adversely affect taste or saliva production and contribute to the unpalatability of food, thus decreasing food intake in this age group.

Institutionalized women in particular are at risk for protein calorie malnutrition. Food is frequently unattractive in these settings and interactions around mealtime may be unpleasant. The institutionalized resident may seek attention or assert through food behaviors (5). Long-term care staff and families who provide care to older relatives should understand the symbolic importance of food to avoid vicious cycles of food refusal and the response of frustration, anger, and even neglect.

Conclusion

Weight problems and eating disorders should be suspected in a variety of women patients a provider sees. Compassion, continuity of care, and long-term goals and follow-up can provide significant improvement.

Special Considerations for Nurse Practitioners and Physician Assistants

Women face many pressures because of the disparity between how they look and how they think they should look. Even though a woman's body is in the range of normal variations, she may perceive it as unacceptable. Providers may have their own body biases and then have to work with the woman to determine how the woman sees herself (52).

Primary care providers who have experienced the frustration of working with overweight women, and perhaps been offended by problems related to hygiene and skin integrity, must guard against communicating negative feelings to their overweight patients (53). Women who are obese need help finding a long-term solution for their problem and need to be matched with a treatment program that provides weight loss (if that is the mutual goal) with minimum health risks. Undesirable consequences, such as gall stones, cardiac arrhythmias, and nutritional deficiencies, can result from various weight loss programs (54).

A woman who wants to lose weight can be asked about her past tactics to maintain or lose weight. She may need help identifying unsuccessful or dangerous weight loss methods, setting realistic goals, recognizing poor eating habits and stressors that affect eating patterns, identifying safe and enjoyable activities, eliciting the support of family and others, and evaluating the various weight-loss programs available to her (53). Myths about exercise, e.g., that it must be strenuous to burn calories or that it increases appetite, must be addressed

(55). Counseling and support must be individualized to the woman's culture, resources, environment, and schedule (56).

Eating disorders such as bulimia and anorexia exist on a continuum from mild discontent to extreme dysfunction. Primary care providers should still be concerned even when all criteria for diagnosis are not met. Assessment is often difficult because of secrecy or the woman's lack of concern about the problem. In addition to the warning signs and diagnostic criteria discussed earlier, clinicians can ask all women if they are satisfied with their body weight and shape. Many women will express some discontent, but particularly negative or intense answers are indications for further assessment (57). Asking about fad diets or weight loss programs, claiming not to have time to eat, or compulsion about exercising are also clues to possible eating disorders. Women who have parents or siblings or siblings preoccupied with weight or food, who live in situations characterized by chaos, or who are experiencing a crisis can be at increased risk. Questioning the woman about craving or eating large amounts of high-calorie food, hiding food, chronic dieting, eating until interrupted, and depression, guilt or hating herself because of eating can provide additional data (58).

Providers who work with adolescents should follow their weights closely, noting significant decreases that might indicate anorexia. Weight fluctuations, complaints of bloating or stress, and facial swelling might indicate bulimia (59). In addition, women with eating disorders may have a great deal of fear associated with being weighed, and use overhydration, dehydration, heavy clothing, or other means to alter their weight (60).

There are several treatment issues to consider when evaluating anorexia nervosa, bulimia nervosa, and binge-eating disorder. Women with anorexia may be resistant to treatment that involves gaining weight; those with bulimia may avoid discussing the problem because of embarrassment. Interventions can

be costly and long-term, and insurance may not be available or cover all costs. The type of treatment preferred by the woman is considered as well as the expertise of the specialist. In some cases, the woman may prefer a woman therapist (69). Legal issues also have to be considered if there are life-threatening disorders and the client resists hospitalization (71).

The specific role of the practitioner will depend on work setting, level of education, and expertise. Referral to a physician for physiologic complications and collaboration with therapists are principles of care for eating disorders (69). An interdisciplinary team of physicians, practitioners, nutritionists, and mental health professionals is often indicated (67).

Prevention of eating disorders are emphases in primary care settings and the community. The dangers of dieting can be addressed in school and other community group settings. Some organizations are active in opposing media advertising that promotes thinness or attaining an ideal body (69).

References

1. Haller E. Eating disorders: a review and update. West J Med 1992;157:658–662.
2. Kurtzman FD, Yager J, Landsverk J, Wiesmeier E, Bodurka DC. Eating disorders among selected female student populations at UCLA. J Am Diet Assoc 1989;89:45–53.
3. Davis WN. Psychology of Women and Residential Treatment for Eating Disorders: the Renfrew Perspective. Philadelphia: Renfrew Foundation, 1992.
4. Field HC, Domangue BB, eds. Eating Disorders Throughout the Life Span: Geriatric Eating Disorders. New York: Praeger, 1987.
5. Vergrugge LM. Women and men: mortality and health of older people. In: Riley MW, Hess BB, Bond K, eds. Aging in Society: Selected Reviews of Recent Research. Hillsdale, NJ: Lawrence Erhbaum, 1983:139–185
6. Roughan PA. Mental health and psychiatric disorders in care of the older woman. Clin Geriatr Med 1993;9:173–190
7. Kuczmarski RJ, Flegal KM, Campbell SM, Johnson CL. Increasing prevalence of overweight among US adults. The National Health and Nutrition Examination Surveys, 1960 to 1991. JAMA 1994;272:205–211.

8. Pi-Sunyer FX. The fattening of America. JAMA 1994;272:272–238.
9. Williamson DF. Descriptive epidemiology of body weight and weight change in adults. Ann Intern Med 1993;119:646–649.
10. Garrow JS. Should obesity be treated? Treatment is necessary. BMJ 1994;309:654–655.
11. Stamler J. Epidemic obesity in the United States. Arch Intern Med 1993;153:1040–1044.
12. Williamson DF. Descriptive epidemiology of body weight and weight change in U.S. adults. Ann Intern Med 1993;119:646–649.
13. Kumanyika SK. Special issues regarding obesity in minority populations. Ann Intern Med 1993;119: 650–654.
14. Rodin J. Cultural and psychosocial determinants of weight concerns. Ann Intern Med 1993;119:643–645.
15. Gallagher-Allred C, Gabel LL. Managing common adolescent nutritional problems. Fam Pract Recertification 1995;17:21–34.
16. Anonymous. Methods for voluntary weight loss and control. NIH Technology Assessment Conference Panel. Consensus Development Conference, 30 March to 1 April 1992 [review]. Ann Intern Med 1993;119:764–770
17. Byers T. Body weight and mortality. NEJM 1995; 333:723–724.
18. Manson JE, Willett WC. Stampfer MJ, Colditz MB, et al. Body weight and mortality among women. NEJM 1995;333:677–685.
19. Launer LJ, Harris T, Rumpel C, Madans J. Body mass index, weight changes, and risk of mobility disability in middle-aged and older women. JAMA 1994;271:1093–1098.
20. National Institutes of Health. Health implications of obesity: National Institutes of Health Consensus Development Conference statement. Ann Intern Med 1985;103:1073–1077.
21. Iribarren C, Sharp DS, Burcheifl CM, Petrovich H. Association of weight loss and weight fluctuations with mortality among men. Japanese American 1995;333:686–692.
22. Arner P. The beta 3-adrenergic receptor—a cause and cure of obesity [editorial]? N Engl J Med 1995; 333:352–354.
23. Edwards KI. Obesity, anorexia, and bulimia [review]. Med Clin North Am 1993;77:899–909.
24. Yanovski SZ. A practical approach to treatment of the obese patient. Arch Fam Med 1993;2:309–316.
25. Bray GA, Gray DS. Obesity, part I: pathogenesis. West J Med 1988;149:429–441.
26. Blair SN. Evidence for success of exercise in weight loss and control. Ann Intern Med 1993;119:702–706.
27. Miller DC. Treatment of obesity in family practice. J Fam Pract 1978;6:761–767.
28. Bray GA. Use and abuse of appetite-suppressant drugs in the treatment of obesity. Ann Intern Med 1993;119:707–714.
29. Anonymous. Practice guideline for eating disorders. Am J Psychiatry 1993;150:212–228.
30. Freund KM, Graham SM, Lesky LG, Moskowitz MA. Detection of bulimia in a primary care setting. J Gen Intern Med 1993;8:236–242.
31. Bulimia prevalence rates. Sci Am Med CD ROM.
32. Mitchell JE, Seim HC, Colon E, Pomeroy C. Medical complications and medical management of bulimia. Ann Intern Med 1987;107:71–77.
33. Greenfeld D, Mickley D, Quinlan DM, Roloff P. Hypokalemia in outpatients with eating disorders. Am J Psychiatry 1995;152:60–63.
34. Pope HG, Hudson JI. Is childhood sexual abuse a risk factor for bulimia nervosa? Am J Psychiatry 1992; 149:455–463.
35. Yager J. Psychosocial treatments for eating disorders [review]. Psychiatry 1994;57:153–164.
36. Garner DM. Psychotherapy outcome research with bulimia nervosa [review]. Psychother Psychosom 1987;48:129–140.
37. Fairburn CG, Jones R, Peveler RC, et al. Three psychological treatments for bulimia nervosa: a comparative trial. Arch Gen Psychiatry 1991;48:463–469.
38. Wilfley DE, Agras WS, Telch CF, et al. Group cognitive-behavioral therapy and group interpersonal psychotherapy for the nonpurging bulimic individual: a controlled comparison. J Consult Clin Pychol 1993;61:296–305.
39. Bloom C, Gitter A, Gutwill S, Kogel K, Zaphiropoulos L. Eating Problems: A Feminist Psychoanalytic Treatment Model. New York: Basic Books, 1994.
40. Eating disorders review. Nutrition and the M.D. 1995;6:4–5.
41. Rossiter EM, Agras WS, Losch M, Telch CF. Dietary restraint of bulimic subjects following cognitive-behavioral or pharmacological treatment. Behav Res Ther 1988;26:495–498.
42. Crow SJ, Mitchell JE. Rational therapy of eating disorders. Drugs 1994;48:372–379.
43. Yager J, LandsverK J, Edelstein CK. A 20 month follow-up study of 628 women with eating disorders: course and severity. Am J Psychiatry 1987;144:1172–1177.
44. Hsu LKG. The outcome of eating disorders, part II: bulimia nervosa eating disorders review. Nutrition and the M.D. 1994;5.
45. Crisp AH, Palmer RL, Kalucy RS. How common is anorexia nervosa? A prevalence study. Br J Psychiatry 1976;128:549–554.
46. Morley JE. Anorexia in older patients: its meaning and management [review]. Geriatrics 1990;45:59–62, 65–66.
47. McClain CJ, Humphries LL, Hill KK, Nickl NJ. Gastrointestinal nutrition: aspects of eating disorders [review]. J Am Coll Nutr 1993;12:466–474.
48. Crisp AH, Norton K, Gowers S, et al. A controlled study of the effect of therapies aimed at adolescent and family psychopathology in anorexia nervosa. Br J Psychiatry 1991;159:325–333.

49. Russell GF, Szmukler GI, Dare C, Eisler L. An evaluation of family therapy in anorexia nervosa and bulimia nervosa. Arch Gen Psychiatry 1987;44:1047–1056.
50. Hamm P, Shekelle RB, Stamler J. Large fluctuations in body weight during young adulthood and 25-year risk of coronary death in men. Am J Epidemiol 1989; 129:312–318.
51. National Task Force on the Prevention and Treatment of Obesity: Weight Cycling. Task Force Statement. JAMA 1994;272:1196–1202.
52. Low MB. Women's body image: the nurse's role in promotion of self-acceptance. NAACOG's clinical issues in perinatal and women's health nursing 1993;4:213–219.
53. Vickers MJ. Understanding obesity in women. JOGNN 1993;22:17–23.
54. Olson A. Women, obesity, and the results of medical management. NAACOG's clinical issues in perinatal and women's health nursing. 1993;4:220–226.
55. Grubbs L. The critical role of exercise in weight control. Nurse Pract 1993;18:20, 22, 25–26.
56. Fisher AC, Murtaugh MA. The evaluation and treatment of obesity. Primary Care Update for OB/GYNs 1994;1:68–71.
57. Wilfley DE, Grilo CM. Eating disorders: a women's health problem in primary care. Nurse Pract Forum 1994;5:34–45.
58. Kiszka SA. Dieting to death. Adv Nurse Pract 1994; 2:9–10, 12, 15.
59. White JH. Women and eating disorders. NAACOG's clinical issues in perinatal and women's health nursing. 1993;4:227–235.
60. McDuffie JR, Kirkley BG. Eating disorders. In: Krummel DA, Kris-Etherton PM. Nutrition in Women's Health. Gaithersburg, MD: Aspen, 1996: 58–102.
61. Jacobsen J. How thin is too thin: diagnosis and treatment of anorexia nervosa. Primary Care Update for OB/GYNs. 1995;2:191–194.

Appendix

The following organizations can provide patients with support and helpful information about eating disorders:

Take Off Pounds Sensibly
800–932-8677

American Heart Association
800-AHA-USA1

American Anorexia/Bulimia Association Inc.
293 Central Park West
New York, NY 10021
(212)501–8351

National Association of American Anorexia
  Nervosa
PO Box 7
Highland Park, IL 60035
(708)831–3438

American College Health Association
1300 Piccard Drive, Suite 200
Rockville, MD 20850

Anorexia Nervosa and Related Eating Disorders, Inc.
PO Box 5102
Eugene, OR 97405
(503)344–1144

National Anorexic Aid Society
Box 29461
1925 East Dublin/Granville Road
Columbus, OH 43229
(614)436–1112

National Association of Anorexia Nervosa
  and Associated Disorders
Box 7
Highland Park, IL 60035
(312)831–3438

National Association to Advance Fat Acceptance
Health Kit for Health Professionals
NAAFA PO Box 188620
Sacramento, CA 95818

Overeaters Anonymous
Box 92870
Los Angeles, CA 90009
(213)542–8363

8.3

Addictive Behaviors

Diane Beebe

Introduction

Addiction is the compulsive use of a substance despite physical, psychological, or social harm to the user (1). Drug abuse is the second most common psychiatric disorder among women age 18 to 24 years (2). Approximately 6% of adult women have serious problems with alcohol (3), and approximately 30% of women age 15 to 35 years smoke cigarettes. Most prescriptions for antianxiety and antidepressant medication are written for women (4). Of pregnant women, 20% continue to smoke cigarettes, 19% use alcohol, and 6% use illicit drugs, mostly marijuana and cocaine (5). Most abusers, including women, concomitantly use more than one substance (3). Women are much more likely than men to use prescription medications along with alcohol or other drugs, creating potentially dangerous combinations. Substance abuse is a continuing and expanding problem and it begins at an early age. Individuals who have not used "gateway" drugs, such as alcohol, tobacco, and marijuana, by age 20 are less likely to develop substance abuse problems (3). Every provider will be faced daily with women who have problems with addictive behaviors that profoundly affect health.

The Addictive Personality

Illicit drug use is the use of illegal drugs or the use of prescription-type psychotherapeutic drugs for nonmedical purposes (1). People use mood-altering substances for a variety of reasons. Some find excitement. Others use them as a way to feel better or escape psychologically or physiologically painful conditions. The drugs may stimulate or sedate and may temporarily enhance mental or physical performance.

Theories

Although no studies have proven that an addictive personality exists, many believe that some people are more prone than others for developing addictive behaviors. Certain personality traits may predispose to addiction. Addiction itself may create secondary pathology often viewed as an addictive personality (6).

There are several reasons individuals give for using alcohol and other drugs. These include depression, lack of self-esteem, peer-pressure, self-reinforcing thoughts, self-medicational use to reduce physical or emotional stress, and social influences (7).

Three components to addiction have been identified: the genetic or biochemical, the behavioral, and the psychological component (6). Addictive behavior may be genetic or cultural. Men are at higher risk than women to inherit the tendency for alcoholism (8). However, there is also often a strong family history of alcoholism in women, especially combined with depression (9). Alcoholic women are much more likely than alcoholic men to marry an alcoholic (8). Alcohol and any drug use is a contributing factor to domestic violence, particularly men against women violence (1).

Much of addiction may be biochemical. The abused substance causes biochemical changes of varying power. The "high" that is produced with addiction results in physical dependence, reinforcement of the behavior, and habitual use of the substance. The reinforcing phenomenon may be stronger as with the use of certain chemicals such as cocaine or weaker in the more behavioral addictions like shopping or gambling (6).

Physical dependence is marked by developing tolerance to the effects of the drug and a period of withdrawal with discontinuance of use (1). The behavioral component of addiction consists of the positive and negative reinforcement of the addiction. Addiction occurs when the use of the drug or mode of action becomes the sole means for dealing with a feeling or circumstance. The initial reinforcement is positive, but as use continues, the reinforcement is to avoid the negative feelings of withdrawal (6).

Psychologically, the addict uses the particular addiction to gain control of a situation. This use may relieve a physically uncomfortable feeling such as anxiety, or serve as a solution to a problem. The addiction of course does not solve the problem but only creates others. The addict develops an increased reliance on the behavior and fails to develop the normal skills needed to react to the precipitating situation. Certain characteristics of addictive disorders exist. Denial, secrecy, and conscious dishonesty become more prevalent. Users develop powerful conditioned responses and self-reliance on the abused substance (6).

Alcohol

Epidemiology

Alcohol use is a major problem among women. Of an estimated 15.1 million alcoholics, 4.6 million of them are women (10). Additionally, 6 million women drink excessively. Approximately 6% of adult women have serious problems with alcohol. This accounts for one third of all problem drinkers in the United States (9). Sixty-four percent of women age 18 years and older drink alcohol (5). Two to 9% of pregnant women are estimated to be heavy drinkers (2).

The number of elderly who are alcoholic is generally considered to be lower than in other age groups: 15 to 58% of the elderly are treated for alcoholism in clinics, hospitals, and nursing homes (3). In US and Canadian surveys from 1964 to 1990, in all age and ethnic groups, women were less likely to abuse alcohol than men, and if they did use alcohol, they were less likely to drink heavily. Three to five times more men are considered heavy drinkers. Meta-analyses of world data show that women drinkers drink less frequently and consume smaller amounts per occasion than men drinkers. In the United States, women's lower consumption of alcohol is mostly caused by decreased intake per occasion rather than to less frequent indulgence (10).

Age

Between 1964 and 1984, more women age 50 to 64 years began drinking than ever before. Light drinking, consumption of less than 0.22 ounces of ethanol a day, increased in women age 18 to 20 years. Heavy drinking, 60 or more drinks a month, increased in women age 21 to 34 years, as it did similarly for men in this age group (11).

Pregnancy

With the great increase in advertisements explaining the hazards of drinking during pregnancy, there has been a decline in consumption. The incidence of drinking decreases throughout pregnancy. Even so, approximately 25% of pregnant women continue to use alcohol, and 3% report binge drinking (3). Two to 9% of pregnant women are estimated to be heavy drinkers. Drinking rates are highest among low socioeconomic pregnant women (2).

Employment

A few studies found that women who are employed outside the home are more likely to be drinkers than homemakers. Amount and rates of drinking varies with the type of employment. Women employed in occupations in which over 50% of the employees are men have higher alcohol consumption. Some reasons may include peer influence, increased stress in a men-dominated work environment, and more opportunities for job-related alcohol consumption. Women employed part-time have higher rates of heavy drinking and drinking problems than those who are employed full-time or are homemakers (10).

Homeless Women

Alcohol and other drug abuse may be the cause and/or result of homelessness and may prevent women from finding and keeping employment. Alcohol and drug abuse is a significant problem in the homeless population, more so than in the general population. Homeless women without dependent children have lower rates of substance abuse rates than homeless women with dependent children or homeless men. However, the prevalence of alcohol and drug use among homeless women with children is still higher than for other poor women with children. Alcohol and drug use in this highly vulnerable population may lead to sexual promiscuity, prostitution, or criminal behaviors, all of which lead to more personal health risks (12).

Consequences of homelessness for the children are significant. Neglect, abandonment, or abuse may occur from the inability of the mother to meet the physical, psychological, or financial needs of the children. Substance-abusing homeless women seek less health care, including prenatal care. Lack of prenatal care may have serious consequences for the woman and her child. Substance abuse may put a woman, particularly a homeless woman, at risk of losing custody of her children (12).

Marital Status

Single, divorced, or separated women show higher rates of heavy drinking than married women, although widows show the lowest rates. Levels of alcohol consumption among women with partners correlated with their partner's drinking behaviors. Cohabitation with a partner outside of marriage carried the highest rate of drinking, heavy drinking, and alcohol-related problems of any living situation. These situations may afford the greatest lifestyle stress with the least amount of support. The effect of divorce on drinking patterns and of drinking on divorce is uncertain. In nonproblem drinkers, divorce may increase the risk of problem drinking, although in problem-drinkers faced with the stress of an unsatisfying marriage, divorce may serve as a remedy to the problem (11).

Ethnicity

Nearly half of African-American women abstain from alcohol, although only one third of white women abstain. In African-Americans, heaviest alcohol consumption occurs in middle-age. Drinking problems peak in white women aged in their 20s, and after age 40 years in African-American women. Hispanic women have low rates of drinking problems. This is in great contrast to the much higher rates of alcoholism in Hispanic men compared with both African-American and white men. Mexican-American women and those Hispanic women who are more climatized into American society have increased risks for drinking problems.

The highest rates of alcohol abuse among all groups are found in Mexican-Americans. Statistics for Asian-Americans are not available. Native Americans have higher rates of alcohol abuse and morbidity than the general population, although variations among tribes certainly exist (4).

Older Individuals and Alcohol Use

In the elderly population, there are three patterns of alcohol use: (1) early onset lifelong drinkers, (2) intermittent episodic drinkers, and (3) late onset drinkers who start usually as a response to changes or stressors (4). Alcoholism in the elderly may be underdiagnosed because of inappropriate screening measures and poor recognition. Most older alcoholics seek health care for diagnoses other than alcoholism. In elderly patients treated in health care facilities, alcoholism rates range from 15 to 58%. Prevalence among elderly in the community is estimated to be 1.5% in women compared to 14% in men (4).

Higher blood levels of alcohol occur in elderly women and men who consume the same amount of alcohol as younger individuals. This is caused by a decrease in total body water with aging. All women, especially older women, have lower total body water, so older women are likely to have higher blood alcohol levels and subsequent complications with less alcohol consumed than men. The elderly are also at higher risk for alcohol-drug interactions (4).

Risk Factors

Childhood sexual abuse increases the likelihood of alcohol abuse in later life. Other factors which may be associated with problem drinking include low self-esteem, prior use of drugs, and nontraditional sexual behavior (11).

Diagnosis

Alcoholism is a chronic, progressive disease that affects the physical, psychological, and social aspects of the user's life as a result of repeated and excessive use of the alcohol. Many questionnaires are available for screening. The CAGE questionnaire addresses the need to Cut down on the drinking, the Annoyance of others asking about the drinking, the Guilt associated with drinking, and the use of alcohol as an early morning Eye opener (Table 8.3.1). Special questions for women may address carrying alcohol in their purse, the relationship of drinking to and the effect on their menstrual cycle, and effects on their children and in their domestic relationships, especially related to any physical violence (13). Less than half as many women than men meet diagnostic criteria for alcoholism (11). Women tend to drink more at home and alone. This may be related to the greater stigma of alcohol use in women

Table 8.3.1. Screening Questions for Women for Alcohol Abuse—The CAGE with Added Questions for Women

C – Have you ever felt the need to CUT down on your drinking?

A – Have people ever ANNOYED you by criticizing your drinking?

G – Have you ever felt bad or GUILTY about drinking?

E – Have you ever taken a morning EYE-opener to steady your nerves?*

Other Questions for Women:

1 – Do you carry alcohol in your Purse or put it in a secret place?

2 – Does your drinking ever affect your Relationship with your children or husband?

3 – Do you do most of your drinking Alone?

4 – Do you think your Appearance has changed, or you have neglected it?

5 – Do you drink more at different points of your Menstrual cycle?

6 – Do you use any other Medications for your nerves?

*Modified from Ewing JA. Detecting Alcoholism The CAGE questionnaire. JAMA 1984;252:1906.

than in men. They are less likely to be identified as alcoholic by others, including their provider. In one study, less than half of the women sought help from their physician or other community professional. Nearly half of these women had been prescribed medications for nervous disorders. Within the workplace, fewer women are referred for alcohol treatment than men (14).

Complications

Most surveys were designed to assess men drinking patterns and problems. Questions have been raised as to the accuracy of recording problems among women drinkers because surveys may not include indicators particular to women such as fatigue, neglect of personal appearance, and frequent illness. In surveys, women were less likely than men to report problems related to alcohol. Of these problems, however, women were more likely to report those of a psychological nature such as depression and loss of interest in things, whereas men more often reported problems with social functioning (e.g., job-related, school problems, police/driving under the influence problems). Women tend to internalize stress; men tend to exhibit stress outwardly. In women who are heavy drinkers, initiating fights with spouses, others, and children is the problem most often reported (11).

Women experience alcohol-related drinking and medical problems earlier than men and often with consumption of less alcohol. Women have less total body water and half the amount of the enzyme gastric alcohol dehydrogenase. The lower body water content in women leads to a smaller volume of distribution and higher blood alcohol concentration in the blood given the same amount of ingested alcohol regardless of body habitus (4).

Liver Complications

Women experience a higher level of liver pathology than men. Cirrhosis can develop with half the alcohol consumption of men. Once liver disease develops, it progresses at a faster rate in women than in men. Women have a lower survival rate associated with alcoholic cirrhosis. Mortality rates for cirrhosis are twice as high for nonwhite women as for whites. Native American women develop cirrhosis 36 times more often than white women and are six times as likely to die from it (8).

Gynecologic Complications

Multiple gynecologic problems including sexual dysfunction and infertility may accompany alcohol abuse in women. Heavy alcohol consumption is commonly associated with menstrual irregularities, amenorrhea, and worsened premenstrual symptoms (8). The relationship of alcohol to the endocrine system is not well defined. Stimulation of prolactin, corticotropin-releasing factor (CRF), adrenocorticotropic hormone (ACTH), and adrenal hormones may occur. Alcohol may suppress follicle-stimulating hormone (FSH) and alter estradiol levels, contributing to menstrual and reproductive problems (13).

The reduction in inhibitions while drinking may be a potentially dangerous situation for women who may more readily succumb to sexual advances or be targets for assault. Forty-five to 70% of women admitted to alcohol treatment programs report a history of rape, incest, or both (8). Any increase in sexual activity with multiple partners increases a woman's risk of contracting sexually transmitted diseases, including human immunodeficiency virus. Pregnancy may also be a consequence. Some reports link the use of alcohol to an increased incidence of breast cancer (15). Alcohol may also increase the risk of osteoporosis.

Obstetrical Complications

Many obstetrical complications occur with the use of alcohol during pregnancy. Most commonly, intrauterine growth retardation is seen. Combined use of alcohol and tobacco increases this risk (2). Two or more drinks a day are associated with triple the risk of preterm labor. With maternal alcohol use, there are longer hospital stays for the infant, often in ICU (12).

Fetal abnormalities depend on the trimester in which drinking occurs; first trimester drinking is associated with anatomical abnormalities and probably central nervous system damage (8). Use of alcohol during pregnancy may result in a variety of birth defects, most notably Fetal Alcohol Syndrome (FAS) and fetal alcohol effects (FAE). FAS may be the leading cause of mental retardation in the Western world (8). It occurs in 1.9 per 1000 live births worldwide. There is a slightly higher incidence of FAS in North America of 2.2 per 1000 live births. In the alcohol-abusing pregnant population, this incidence may rise to 25 per 1000 live births. There are nearly 7000 infants born annually in the United States with FAS. The rate is higher in areas of predominantly African-American and low socioeconomic women than in white middle-class mothers. The highest rates are seen in Native American women in the southwestern United States (2). Lesser teratogenic effects of alcohol are termed FAEs. Alcohol in any amount is felt to be unsafe during pregnancy and may produce FAE or FAS (8). There is no clear relationship between the quantity of alcohol and severity of FAS (2). However, cessation of alcohol during pregnancy may decrease the risk of FAS and intrauterine growth retardation (IUGR).

There are three characteristics of FAS. These include (1) prenatal and postnatal growth retardation, (2) craniofacial anomalies (e.g., small head circumference, flattening of facial features), and (3) central nervous system dysfunction and mental retardation. Major organ system malformation may occur (4). No screening tests are available to identify FAS or FAE early in pregnancy (2). Pregnant women need to be questioned on each prenatal visit about alcohol use and counseled on its fetal effects.

Psychological Effects

More women than men alcoholics, as well as women cocaine-abusers, receive a concomitant diagnosis of depression (4). Additionally, there is a strong correlation between a family history of depression and alcoholism in women. Alcoholic women suffer particularly from low self-esteem, low self-image, and a sense of hopelessness and powerlessness. Up to 40% of women alcoholics attempt suicide, compared with 8.8% of nonalcoholic women (9). Depressive symptoms resolved more slowly with abstinence in women than in men (4).

Treatment

Treatment issues particular to women include underrecognition and underdiagnosis of alcohol and drug abuse, stereotyped views of women and substance abusers, child care issues while in treatment, and the threat of losing children (5). The social stigma of alcohol use appears to be greater for women. This may result in hesitancy in seeking treatment (8)

Women are, however, often quicker than men to recognize a problem with alcohol (9). Women report a noticeable decline in self-esteem, a change in their aggressiveness, and a preoccupation with alcohol (16). Alcoholic women make up the same proportion of the treatment center population as they do in society (8). Women tend to seek help earlier than men and view treatment as more effective (14).

Payment for alcohol treatment for women may be more difficult, if women are covered under spousal policies that exclude such treatment or are employed in jobs without health benefits. Many traditional alcohol treatment facilities may not attend to the needs of women (12, 14) (Table 8.3.2). Women are left more often by their partners than are men substance

Table 8.3.2. Special Needs of Women in Alcohol Treatment Centers

Insurance	Does she have insurance? Has she been employed? Does her spouse or partner have insurance to cover it? If her husband leaves or divorces her, will she still be covered?
Marital counseling	Women are often left by husband. How is her marriage/partnership? Does she or both of them need counseling? Does she need counseling to deal with separation or divorce?
Coexistent addictions and detoxification	Women are more likely to be using and abusing other medications and illegal street drugs.
Health Care	Does she need prenatal or other health care?
Child Care	Is there any available in the treatment center? Can children be taken back to their own school from the treatment center? Will she lose her children? Does she have a place or family for them to go?
Social service	Will she lose her children? Must she go to court? Does she need legal counseling? Will she need public assistance, housing, AFDC, WIC, and/or welfare until she finds a job?
Vocational training	If she has lost her job or is divorced and must now work, will she need vocational counseling, including assertiveness training and employment skills?
Coexistent psychiatric disorders	Women frequently need group and personal therapy including gender-specific therapy groups and self-esteem building. Is she a survivor of child abuse or spousal abuse?

abusers. Women in treatment need traditional services such as detoxification, but more attention must also be paid to child care concerns, psychiatric and comorbid conditions, education of friends and family, and vocational training (3). Women need parenting education, assertiveness training, and employment skills (8). Women tend to benefit more from supportive and skill-building therapy rather than from confrontation. Issues to address in gender-specific therapy groups include shame and poor self-esteem, both found more commonly in women abusers (4).

Treatment facilities for women also need to attend to special needs such as comprehensive counseling services for incest, childhood sexual abuse, and spousal abuse. Concomitant prescription drug abuse is common and needs to be addressed in the treatment facility (14). Many are not equipped to care for the pregnant woman. Many are not able to treat the dual diagnosis of drug abuse and psychiatric problems, a situation more common in homeless women than in other abusing women (12).

Other barriers to treatment exist, particularly for the pregnant woman using illegal street drugs. Presentation for prenatal care may result in criminal prosecution. Depending on state law, newborns of addicted mothers may be placed in state custody (12).

Once in a treatment program, age is not a deterrent to a good response. Older patients respond equally well to treatment as do their younger counterparts. Some may require longer stays and more intense treatment because of the association of more medical problems. Withdrawal from alcohol can be worse in the older age group, perhaps because of a decline in the ability of the nervous system to respond to stimuli (4). Women are equally successful in treatment programs as men. Self-esteem improves after treatment as do many psychiatric symptoms. Thirty percent of Alcoholics Anonymous members are women (8).

Nicotine—Cigarette Smoking

Both pharmacological and nonpharmacological factors serve as stimuli for smoking. Altered bioavailability of several neuroregulators provides temporary increases in performance and affect. Smoking to cope includes use to relax, relieve boredom, and decrease negative affect. Women tend to smoke for pleasure more than men (see Chapter 6.2) (17).

Prevalence

The incidence of smoking has increased in American culture. More than 22% of all adult American women smoke. By the year 2000, women will smoke at the same rate as men (18). The image of the woman smoker has changed considerably over the years. Traditionally, smoking by women had a more negative connotation than that by men. Women smokers were often viewed as unladylike, common, or cheap (19). Newer advertising campaigns portray women who smoke as popular, glamorous, sexy, and independent. This may partly explain why smoking among teenagers is more common in women than men (15). The use of smokeless tobacco products in young men may also be a factor. The rate of smoking cessation peaks for women at age 40 years, whereas men continue to quit throughout older age (20). Between 25 and 40% of pregnant women smoke. Teenagers, single mothers, low socioeconomic level, and low education level women have greater tendency to smoke during pregnancy (21).

Complications

The complications of smoking are well-covered in Chapter 6.2. Women who smoke are at increased risk for coronary artery disease, especially if using oral contraceptives (15). Current or past smoking in middle-aged women is associated with greater alcohol intake (20). Concomitant use of alcohol with cigarette smoking in any age group increases the risk for oral, laryngeal, and esophageal cancer in women and men (15). Smoking is related to other cancers in both sexes including stomach, kidney, bladder, and pancreas. In women smokers, there is an increased risk of cancer of the uterine cervix. Lung cancer deaths among smokers have increased at a faster rate in women than in men. It is the leading cause of cancer death among American women (15). Women smokers age 35 years and older are 12 times more likely to die from lung cancer and 10.5 times more likely to die from emphysema and chronic bronchitis than nonsmoking women (18). Prenatal use of nicotine increases the risk of spontaneous abortion, fetal and neonatal death, and Sudden Infant Death Syndrome (SIDS). Infants born to smoking mothers weigh less than average, probably caused by decreased uteroplacental circulation (15). Nicotine prevents as much as 25% of oxygen from reaching the placenta (18). Nicotine is also passed to infants through breast milk.

Treatment (see Chapter 6.2)

The use of medications such as nicotine patches and gum may help to reduce the craving for nicotine. Women join support groups and smoking cessation clinics more often than men. These groups lend the needed support for many women to quit. However, women are slightly less successful than men in quitting. Women relapse for different reasons than men, primarily because of stress, weight control, and negative emotions (18).

Other Drugs

Cocaine

Prevalence
Cocaine use in the United States is increasing. More than four million Americans use cocaine regularly, and over 20 million persons have tried it (22). There is a high prevalence of cocaine use in the low-income, inner-city areas

(2). Lifetime use is predominantly in poor, minority, adolescent mothers (4). Many drug-addicted inner-city women have small children who are vulnerable to abuse, neglect, and lost opportunities. The number of mothers who have lost children to foster homes and state welfare agencies is rising and is a major consequence of drug use (23).

General Effects
The medical complications of cocaine on the body do not vary between the sexes. Cocaine is absorbed from all mucous membranes, including the vagina, which could add significant risk to women who engage in "body-packing" for transport of drugs. Cocaine is metabolized by hepatic and serum cholinesterases to substances that are excreted in the urine. Fetuses, infants, and pregnant women, as well as elderly men and patients with liver disease, have lower plasmacholinesterase activity. This may account for greater susceptibility to cocaine's effects and toxicity in these groups (24).

Users of cocaine experience the stimulant effects of excitement, tremors, and nervousness. Visual and tactile hallucinations are common (25). Cardiovascular complications are the most common and serious adverse effects of cocaine use (22). Cocaine possesses direct cardiotoxic effects that can result in myocardial infarction, dilated cardiomyopathy, myocarditis, pulmonary edema, left ventricular failure, and sudden death. All types of cardiac dysrhythmias may occur. Cocaine stimulates the sympathetic system causing increased heart rate, increased blood pressure and force of myocardial contraction, and increased oxygen demand with decreased myocardial blood supply (24).

Experience with the use of thrombolytic therapy for acute myocardial infarction in young menstruating women is limited. With the increased incidence of myocardial infarction in young cocaine-abusing women, this issue must be addressed. Limited observation has shown only an increase in menstrual flow with no significant complications. Uterine bleeding, other than normal menstrual flow, is a contraindication to thrombolytic use, thus limiting its use in this high-risk population (24).

Acute cocaine toxicity may also result in malignant hyperthermia, seizures, and respiratory arrest. Sudden blood pressure surges may cause cerebrovascular accidents, bleeds, or aneurysmal rupture (25). Inhaled crack cocaine may produce direct pulmonary effects.

Prenatal Effects

Between 10 and 45% of women cared for at urban teaching centers use cocaine during pregnancy. The use of cocaine prenatally, especially in the form of crack, has continued to increase to as much as 20-fold in 8 years in New York City alone. Concomitantly, infant mortality and low birth weight infants have also increased. In utero cocaine exposure increases the risk nearly fourfold of an infant dying before 1 year of age. Cocaine readily crosses the placenta and the fetal blood-brain barrier. Premature separation of the placenta (abruptio placenta) and spontaneous abortions, at a rate of 38%, over twice that of heroin, are the most common complications. Women who abuse cocaine have 10 times the rate of stillbirths as women who are drug-free during pregnancy (2).

Impairment of placental blood flow by cocaine contributes to IUGR. Cocaine may also have some direct teratogenicity, e.g., bilateral cryptochordism, hydronephrosis, bone defects, ossification delay, eye defects, anencephaly. Of these, microcephaly is the most common brain abnormality reported in cocaine-exposed infants. Ischemic and hemorrhagic brain lesions may occur. Neurologic and motor impairment, abnormal sleep patterns, irritability, tremors, and seizures are not uncommon. Cocaine is excreted in breast milk. Exposed infants can develop signs of acute cocaine intoxication (2).

Over 6 billion dollars a year in additional health care costs are incurred to take care of women and children addicted to cocaine. Much of this cost is attributed to neonatal hospitalization (22). The anorexia caused by cocaine may affect a user's general nutritional state (26).

Treatment

Cocaine intoxication is generally self-limited. Immediate therapy is supportive and involves management of resultant hyperthermia, hypertension, seizures, and cardiac dysrhythmias. Craving for the drug may be reduced by use of dopamine agonists (25).

Long-term treatment focuses on community and social support of the women and their children. A common goal for women in recovery is to reestablish relationships and assume care of their children, perhaps having them returned from other care situations. As with alcohol or other drug addictions, treatment facilities must facilitate child care, employment, and education (23).

Other Stimulants

Other stimulant drugs such as amphetamines and methamphetamines create an excitatory state and physiologic effects much like cocaine. Also like cocaine and opiates, amphetamines and methamphetamines have direct effects on fetal development (26). Transplacental exposure may cause intrauterine growth retardation, placental hemorrhage, fetal distress secondary to bradycardia or meconium aspiration, decreased fetal head circumference, abnormal development of the fetal brain, and neonatal anemia. Infants may exhibit poor feeding habits, lethargy, and minor neurological abnormalities. Subsequent growth and development is generally normal in these children (25).

Opiate Narcotics (Morphine and Heroin)

Prevalence

More than 57% of all heroin users in the United States are women (1). Although any woman may abuse any drug, opiates are most commonly used by minority women of low socioeconomic status (26).

General Effects

Opiates bind to central nervous system, gastrointestinal, and genitourinary receptors (22). They produce analgesia, drowsiness, euphoria, and respiratory depression. Pupillary constriction, slurred speech, and impairment of attention or memory occurs acutely. Long-term use may deplete the body's natural stores of dopamine and endorphins and lead to chronic depression (25). Heroin crosses the blood-brain barrier quicker than morphine because of its lipid solubility. Altered hypothalamic functioning may increase prolactin levels (22).

In heroin addicts, low birth weight infants caused by small gestational age, prematurity, or both, are common. Separation of direct drug effect from lack of prenatal care, general malnutrition, and other societal factors is difficult in all drug dependent populations. Most studies fail to show a significant increase in birth defects in infants exposed in utero to narcotics (22). Short-term withdrawal symptoms are common in infants (26). Naloxone (Narcan) is a specific antagonist for opioid intoxication. This should be used in conjunction with supportive measures.

Phencyclidine (PCP)

Phencyclidine (PCP) is most commonly known as angel dust. A hallucinogen, it produces sympathetic stimulation, confusion, euphoria, and a feeling of depersonalization. The acute toxic state consists of hypertension, tachycardia, hyperthermia, and hyperreflexia. Pupils are normal in size, and eyes generally remain open with horizontal and/or vertical nystagmus commonly present. Psychosis or a schizophreniform state with auditory hallucinations are common (25).

Phencyclidine crosses the placenta, and fetal levels may exceed maternal levels by 10-fold. Despite this, no significant teratogenic risk has been confirmed. Most neonatal manifestations include irritability, hypertonicity, and jitteriness (25).

Treatment of acute toxicity is mainly supportive with control of the hypertension and agitation. Patients should receive minimal stimulation.

Cannabis (Marijuana)

Marijuana is the most commonly used illicit drug in the United States (1). According to the 1990 National Household Survey on Drug Abuse, approximately half of all women age 18 to 34 years have used marijuana (27). Over 36% of all marijuana users are women (1). Marijuana, when smoked, produces euphoria, motor retardation, and depersonalization. Psychosis and paranoia may occur (28). Generally, women decrease their marijuana use after determination of pregnancy. Young, single women of low socioeconomic status and low educational level are most likely to continue to use marijuana during pregnancy. This group is also more likely to use other drugs including alcohol during pregnancy (27). Prenatal marijuana exposure may cause decreased fetal growth, severe IUGR, prematurity, small head circumference, and low birth weight (26). Multiple drug use is common, and abnormalities may not be isolated to use of one particular drug. Generally, morphologic abnormalities and developmental problems are not seen in marijuana-exposed infants (27).

Prescription Drugs

The majority of users of mood-altering prescription drugs are women. Women receive more prescriptions than men for psychoactive substances, especially for depression and anxiety symptoms (3) (see Chapter 8.1). Benzodiazepines and barbiturates, commonly used for sleep and anxiety states, produce sedation, slurred speech, dilated pupils, and nystagmus.

Ataxia and respiratory depression may occur in higher doses (28).

The elderly are at particular risk for alcohol-drug interactions because one fourth to one third of prescription drugs are consumed by the elderly. Use of over-the-counter medications is high in the elderly population, many of which can interact adversely with alcohol (4).

Other Addictions

People may experience addictive behavior to other activities including pathologic gambling, eating disorders, and sexual behavior. Any addiction involves the potential for either producing pleasure or relieving pain. Individuals who engage in one addiction are at risk for another. Eating disorders (see Chapter 8.2) have been associated in women with compulsive gambling (29). Women with eating disorders also have a higher incidence of alcohol abuse than other women (30).

Chemically, increased levels of norepinephrine metabolites have been found in pathological gamblers. In some eating disorder states, increased levels of opioids have been measured (29).

Conclusions

Women with addiction problems and their complications will be seeking help from providers daily. Cigarette abuse, alcoholism, or marijuana smoking touches many parts of the woman's and her family's life. The addiction may be hidden, so the provider must be suspicious when consequences occur, but supportive and vigorous in offering treatment and follow-up. Because regular treatment programs are not usually receptive or conducive to women's special problems, the provider may need to work with the woman, service, and community to create innovative answers to the woman's continuing problem.

Special Considerations for Nurse Practitioners and Physician Assistants

Primary care providers will encounter large numbers of women who suffer from substance abuse, a disease ignored or underdiagnosed with treatment focusing on complications rather than the disease itself. Presenting problems such as weight loss may be treated without trying to deal with the possible underlying problem of addiction, and women may be referred for help without the intensity of assessment that is given to other chronic illnesses (31). Providers may be especially reluctant to identify ADD problems among well-educated and otherwise successful women (32).

Avoiding diagnosis of substance abuse is aided by the addict's, and perhaps the family's denial, that there is a problem. Health care providers themselves may feel threatened and

minimize the problem if the woman's history and symptoms mirror their own habits. In order to obtain an in-depth history, providers must be aware of their own biases, misconceptions, stereotypes, and fears about substance abuse (31).

Early recognition of alcohol abuse is essential if low-cost, simplified interventions are to be implemented and serious health problems minimized. A complete drinking history should be obtained on any woman who says she uses alcohol, and at each visit the woman should be questioned about frequency and amount of drinking and physical problems that might result from continued use. If a woman states she is abstinent, or if she quit because of health reasons, the provider should determine if she has never used alcohol, family conflict, health problems, or previous treatment (33). Clues to alcohol use include the illnesses associated with chronic alcohol consumption, impaired social or occupational functioning, and personality changes. Laboratory testing may reveal elevated liver function tests and uric acid, and below normal magnesium, phosphate, and potassium levels, hypoglycemia, elevated HDL, reduced serum B12 and folate, reduced hemoglobin and hematocrit, and elevated mean corpuscular volume (MCV) (34).

Helping women to understand the possible consequences related to drug abuse can provide motivation for change. A positive approach is to emphasize the improved quality of her life without reliance on drugs. As partners, the woman and provider might identify some achievable goals as directions for care. In addition, with the woman's permission, family or other support systems can be used to help with goal achievement. Use of support groups such as Alcoholics and Narcotics Anonymous, hospital treatment, nonhospital residential programs, and halfway houses can help. No primary provider is in a position to deal with all the potential issues, making use of multidiscipline teams essential (31).

Women who are attempting to stop substance abuse will often relapse. Qualitative research has shown that reasons for relapses of alcoholics may depend on the stage of recovery. Patients who continue to deny that alcohol is a problem lack internal motivation to stop drinking and need help admitting their problem. Others who admit they have a problem, but stop drinking only as a means to obtain or maintain something such as a job or relationship, need assistance in becoming internally focused. Even alcoholics with internally focused recovery goals need to learn to cope with unexpected, stressful events without the use of alcohol (35).

Primary care providers are also in a position to help identify factors that prevent drug abuse in the populations they serve. Young Hispanic women who refrained from drug use, despite pressures to use them, reported influencing factors such as family values, personal competence (e.g, self-esteem, assertiveness), adult developmental roles (e.g., parenting), personal goals, enduring emotional relationships, and economic participation/community resources. Further study is needed to determine if enhancing these factors in other young women can deter drug use (36).

References

1. Bureau of Justice Statistics. Drugs, crime, and the justice system. Washington, DC: Department of Justice, Bureau of Justice Statistics. December 1992.
2. Moroney JT, Allen MH. Cocaine and alcohol use in pregnancy. Adv Neurol 1994;18:231–242.
3. Day NL, Cottreau CM, Richardson GA. The epidemiology of alcohol, marijuana, and cocaine use among women of childbearing age and pregnant women. Clin Obstet Gynecol 1993;36:232–245.
4. Closser MH, Blow FC. Recent advances in addictive disorders. Special populations. Women, ethnic minorities, and the elderly. Psychiatr Clin North Am 1993;16:199–209.
5. Substance abuse likely to continue during pregnancy. Family Pract News 1995;25:2
6. Keller LE. Addiction as a form of perversion. Bull Menninger Clin 1992;56:221–231.
7. Allen JP, Faden V, Rawling R. Relationship of diagnostic, demographic, and personality variables to self-reported stimuli for chemical use. Addict Beh 1992;17:359–366.
8. Quinby PM, Graham AV. Substance abuse among women. Primary Care 1993;20:131–141.
9. Hennessey MB. Identifying the woman with alcohol problems. Women's Health 1992;27:917–925.
10. Wilsnack SC, Wilsnack RW. Epidemiology of women's drinking. Subst Abuse 1991;3:133–157.
11. Wilsnack RW, Wilsnack SC. Women, work, and alcohol: failures of simple theories. Alcohol: Clin Exp Res 1992; 16:172–179.
12. Robertson MJ. Homeless women with children: the role of alcohol and other drug abuse. Am Psychol 1991;46:1198–1204.
13. Gearhart JG, Beebe DK, Milhorn HT, Meeks GR. Alcoholism in women. Am Fam Phys 1991;44a: 907–913.
14. Smith L. Help seeking in alcohol-dependent females. Alcohol 1992;27:3–9.
15. Alcoholism and drug dependency. Harrison's Principles of Internal Medicine. 12th ed. New York: McGraw-Hill, 1991:2146–2161.

16. Klee L, Schmidt C, Ames G. Indicators of women's alcohol problems: what women themselves report. Intern J Addic 1991;26:879–895.

17. Ahijevych K, Wewers ME. Factors associated with nicotine dependence among African American women cigarette smokers. Res Nurs Health 1993;16:283–292.

18. American Lung Association Fact Sheet. Women and Smoking. March 1995.

19. Jenks RJ. Attitudes, perceptions, and risk-taking behaviors of smokers, ex-smokers, and nonsmokers. J Soc Psychol 1992; 132:569–575.

20. Perkins KA, Rohay J, Meilahn EN, Wing RR, Matthews KA, Kuller LH. Diet, alcohol, and physical activity as a function of smoking status in middle-age women. Health Psychol 1993;12:410–415.

21. Behnke M, Eyler FD. The consequences of prenatal substance use for the developing fetus, newborn, and young child. Int J Addict 1993;28:1341–1391.

22. Glantz, JC, Woods, JR. Cocaine, heroin, and phencyclidine: obstetric perspectives. Clin Obstet Gynecol 1993;36:279 –301.

23. Dumas L. Addicted women: profiles from the inner city. Nurs Clin North Am 1992;27:901–915.

24. Das G. Cardiovascular effects of cocaine abuse. Int J Clin Pharmacol Ther Toxicol 1993;31:521–528.

25. Beebe DK, Walley E. Smokable methamphetamine ("Ice"): an old drug in a different form. Am Fam Phys 1995;51: 449–453.

26. Brooks-Gunn J, McCarton C, Hawley T. Effects of in utero drug exposure on children's development. Arch Pediatr Med 1994;148:33–39.

27. Richardson GA, Day NL, McGauhey PJ. The impact of prenatal marijuana and cocaine use on the infant and child. Clin Obstet Gynecol 1993;36: 302–318.

28. Gagne RJ. Care of the patient who misuses drugs. Taylor RB, ed. Family Medicine Principles and Practice. 4th ed. New York: Springer-Verlag, 1994: 462–470.

29. Lesieur HR, Blume SB. Pathological gambling, eating disorders, and psychoactive substance use disorders. J Addict Dis 1993;12:89–102.

30. Goldbloom DS. Alcohol misuse and eating disorders: aspects of an association. Alcohol Alcohol 1993;28:375–381.

31. Caulker-Burnett I. Primary care screening for substance abuse. Nurse Pract 1994;19:42–48.

32. Hughes TL, Fox MI. Patterns of alcohol and drug use among women: focus on special populations. NAACOG's clinical issues in prinatal and women's health nursing 1993;4: 203–212.

33. Kappas-Larson P, Lathrop L. Early detection and intervention for hazardous ethanol use. Nurse Pract 1993;18:50, 53–55.

34. Antai-Otong D. Helping the alcoholic patient recover. AJN 1995;95:22–29.

35. Wing DM. Understanding alcoholism relapse. Nurse Pract 1994;19:67–69.

36. Lindenberg CS, Gendrop SC, Nencioli M, Adames Z. Substance abuse among inner-city Hispanic women: exploring resiliency. JOGNN 1993;23:609–616.

9.1

Partner Violence

Sandra K. Burge

Introduction

Family violence has been recognized as a serious American public health problem, reaching "epidemic proportions" according to the American Medical Association (1). Family violence is widely prevalent, causes serious psychological and physical damage, and daily brings individuals to the attention of the health care system. Primary care providers are in an ideal position to recognize and intervene with violence because they provide ongoing, whole-person care and have contact with people of all ages. Through screening, patient education, counseling, support, and referral, providers can contribute to violence prevention and intervention efforts and help to reduce the violence in their patients' lives.

In this chapter, "partner violence" refers to the infliction of harm by one intimate partner to the other, with the intention of causing pain or controlling the other's behavior. This phenomenon has been called woman battering, spouse abuse, wife abuse, or domestic violence. The frequency and severity of partner violence varies widely, and can be inflicted by women or men, homosexuals or heterosexuals, and people of all ethnic groups and income levels.

However, violence perpetuated by men against women is particularly dangerous. Women account for 70% of all murdered spouses in the United States, and are 10 times more likely than men to be assaulted by an intimate other, as defined by the National Crime Victimization Survey (2). Among these women—approximately 572,000 assaulted by intimates per year—27% receive medical care and 15% require hospitalization (2). Stets and Straus found that women who were punched, choked, kicked, stabbed, or shot by a husband were 7.3 times more likely to seek medical treatment than men who were similarly assaulted by a wife (3). Heterosexual partner abuse causes serious consequences for women; for that reason, this chapter will focus on man-to-woman violence.

Prevalence

The incidence of partner violence in the United States is about 11 to 12% every year (Table 9.1.1) (4). In 1975 and 1985, Straus and Gelles conducted large national surveys on family violence using the Conflict Tactic Scale, a series of questions about aggressive behaviors. An individual was considered "moderately" violent if he or she grabbed, pushed, slapped, or threw things at a spouse. "Severe" violence included punching, kicking, choking, or threatening or using a knife or gun on one's spouse. The lifetime prevalence of moderate spousal violence among these American couples was approximately 21% (5).

Studies using similar methods have been conducted in medical clinical settings, where investigators found similar or higher rates of partner violence (Table 9.1.2) (6–15). Two prenatal studies found low "current" rates of violence, 4 and 8%. However, these interview questions were limited to the current pregnancy, whereas other studies anchored current rates to the past year. In most clinical studies, lifetime prevalence is remarkably high, ranging from 10 to 54%. These data indicate that violence is prominent in the lives and histories of many women who visit their doctors.

The Nature of Violent Relationships

Why do people hit their partners? Many theories exist (16). From a strictly psychological standpoint, some believe that men who hurt their partners have some psychopathology that explains why they act in violent ways. From a strictly sociological standpoint, scholars point out that our society implicitly condones husband-to-wife violence and creates structures that support men who hit, but suppress women who try to escape violent relationships. In the middle are social psychological theories such as Social Learning theory, stating that children model behaviors seen in adult family members and test them in their relationships with others. Social Exchange theory posits that violence occurs when the rewards of violence outweigh the consequences. When violence "works," i.e., it stops an argument or

Table 9.1.1 Straus & Gelles National Prevalence Studies

Husband-to-wife violence within the past year	1975 (%)	1985 (%)
Any violence	12.1	11.3
Severe violence	3.8	3.0

Data from Straus MA, Gelles RJ. Societal change and change in family violence from 1975 to 1985 as revealed by two national surveys. J Marriage Fam 1986; 48:465–479.

Table 9.1.2. Reports from Women in Ambulatory Health Care Setting about Current and Past Man-to-Woman Assaults

Authors	Settings	N	Current (%) Prevalence	Lifetime (%) Prevalence
Rath et al., 1989 (6)	Family medicine	218	na	46
Hamberger et al., 1992 (7)	Family medicine	394	23	39
Elliott and Johnson, 1995 (8)	Family medicine	42	12	36
Gin et al., 1991 (9)	Internal medicine	139	17	34
		319		
Stark et al., 1979 (10)	Emergency department	481	3–19	10–25
Abbott et al., 1995 (11)	Emergency department	648	17	54
Goldberg and Tomlanovich, 1984 (12)	Emergency department	274	na	24
Hillard, 1985 (13)	Prenatal clinic	742	4	11
Helton et al., 1987 (14)	Prenatal clinic	290	8	23
McFarlane et al., 1992 (15)	Prenatal clinic	691	17	na

brings about another reward, that outcome reinforces the violent behavior, beginning a cycle of interactions that is difficult to break.

Those who work with men who batter their partners understand that violent behavior is only part of the picture.

> *"When we talk about battering. . . , we are not talking about an isolated instance of aggression. We are talking about an atmosphere that is created by many forms of abuse and a cycle that seems to increase over time in frequency and intensity. . . Physical violence does not have to occur frequently to create a climate of fear. . . Violent relationships are characterized by fear, oppression, and control. (emphasis is theirs; p. xx–xxi) (17).*

Men who batter tend to use several strategies that function to control their partners' behaviors and to keep them in the relationship. Pence and Paymar identified a series of controlling behaviors that characterize these relationships (see Fig. 9.1.1) (18). The Power and Control Wheel acknowledges that violence is part of a pattern of behaviors that are a constant force in women's lives, rather than isolated incidents of aggression. Besides physical harm, men who batter may use intimidation, threats, insults and guilt, economic control, male privilege, isolation, denial, or may manipulate their partners through their children. In some relationships, physical assaults may be infrequent, but they reinforce the power of other tactics on the wheel.

Who are the Victims?

Few traits characterize the woman who enters into a relationship with a violent man. There is no "Typical Victim Profile." Two studies (12, 19) examined predictors of lifetime abuse among family practice and emergency department patients and found "neither demographic nor health factors could accurately predict who had been victimized. . ." (p. 537) (19). Others found that younger women and unmarried women are at higher risk for abuse (20, 21). Many have proposed that pregnant women are at particularly high risk; however, the data in Table 9.1.2 do not necessarily support this belief. Furthermore, an analysis by Gelles found no differences caused by pregnancy (21). Women under age 25 years (who were more

Power and Control Wheel

Figure 9.1. Power and control strategies in violent relationships.

likely than older women to be pregnant) were more likely to experience abuse within the past year than older women (27% versus 11%). In an extensive, systematic review of partner abuse research, Hotaling and Sugarman noted only one consistent predictor of being an abused woman: across several studies, women who were abused by their husbands were likely to have witnessed parental violence during their childhood (20).

Who are the Perpetrators?

According to Hotaling and Sugarman's review, men who are physically abusive toward their partners are generally violent. They are also likely to be sexually violent and to be aggressive toward their children (20). Other predictors of battering behavior include low income, education, and socioeconomic resources, high alcohol use, and low levels of assertiveness (20).

Men who batter differ from nonviolent men in intimacy, impulsivity, and problem-solving skills (22). They score higher on anxiety, depression, and negativity scales (23). In addition, like women who are battered, men who batter are likely to have witnessed parental violence during their childhoods (20).

Consequences of Violence

Psychological Consequences

Victimization can cause serious psychological consequences. Victims of violence, compared with nonvictims, have more difficulty coping with anger or aggression, have lower self esteem, and are less able to trust important others (24). Two studies tested abused women using the Minnesota Multiphasic Personality Inventory and found elevations on depression, anger, confusion, fearfulness, paranoia, and social introversion scales (25, 26). In Rosewater's study, more than half of abused women had significant elevation on a chemical abuse index (26). Women who have been abused by their partners are also at high risk for suicide (27, 28).

Several investigators have diagnosed high rates of post-traumatic stress disorder among samples of battered women, including elements of depression, anxiety, intrusion, and avoidance. In these studies, the severity of the symptoms was positively related to severity and the recency of the violence (29–31). Life threats within the relationship were a key risk factor (30). Women in violent marriages with few personal resources such as education or employment and with low levels of social support also demonstrated greater psychological problems (31, 32). To summarize, women at highest risk for psychological problems appeared to be stuck in dangerous, controlling relationships, and were isolated from outside sources of support that would help them to assess and escape the violence.

Acute Medical Consequences

To a health care professional the most obvious consequence of partner violence is physical trauma. Physical damage resulting from violence can range from minor bruises to death. In 1992, more than 2000 people in the United States were known to be murdered by intimate others—spouses, ex-spouses, boyfriends, or girlfriends (27). Stark et al. estimated that battering accounts for half of all serious injuries women bring to the emergency room (10) and data from the National Crime Victimization Survey cited above underscored the frequency and severity of those injuries (2). However, because medical records inconsistently address violence, and because most women do not bring their injuries to providers, the actual medical impact is unknown.

The injuries of battered women look different than those of accident victims. Battered women are more likely than accident victims to have facial injuries, and 13 times more likely to have injuries in the chest, breasts, or abdomen (10). They are more likely to have multiple injuries than accident victims and to have injuries in various stages of healing. Furthermore, because abuse tends to be repetitive with escalating severity, victims' visits to providers are repeated with increasingly severe injuries.

Long-Term Medical Consequences

Besides acute injuries, battered women have a higher prevalence of chronic health problems. They often see their providers for relief from vague, unremitting symptoms (33). They have higher health care use than other women, visiting their providers twice as often, and they incur health care costs that are 2.5 times higher (34). Common complaints of battered women include somatic symptoms such as insomnia, fatigue, gastrointestinal symptoms, premenstrual symptoms, chronic pain, and anemia (33, 35, 36). Battered women experience more negative pregnancy outcomes, including miscarriages, stillbirths, and low birthweight newborns (14). Finally, victimization may be associated with negative health behaviors such as eating disorders, substance abuse, and risk for sexually transmitted diseases and HIV (33).

Effects on Children

The impact of violence in intimate relationships extends beyond the battered woman; children are also at risk. Hotaling and Sugarman found that men who batter their wives are also likely to be violent with their children (20). Children of battered women have poorer adjustment than children in nonviolent families (37). Infants who witness violence are often characterized by poor health, poor sleeping habits, and excessive screaming. Preschoolers show signs of terror exhibited as yelling, irritable behavior, hiding, shaking, and stuttering. School-age children experience more somatic complaints and regress to earlier stages of functioning. Adolescents may use aggression as a predominant form of problem solving, may project blame onto others, and may exhibit a high degree of anxiety (e.g., bite nails, pull hair, somatize feelings).

As adults, children of battered women are likely to have violent relationships. The single most consistent predictor of becoming a batterer or a battered wife is witnessing parental violence as a child (20). Thus, the impact of partner violence is widely felt—by the victim, by her children, and perhaps by succeeding generations who learn about intimacy in a violent context.

Screening for Violence

Many providers feel awkward asking patients about emotionally painful experiences. However, patients are accepting of this practice and, in fact, often expect it. In a brief survey about family conflict, 261 family practice patients from six private practices were asked,

"Do you think doctors should ask patients about family stress or conflict?" Only 3% said, "no, never," while the remainder—97%—responded, "yes, sometimes," or "yes, often" (38). Other research agrees with this position: *the single most important thing a provider can do for a battered woman is to ask about violence* (39).

When Should I Ask about Violence?

Questions about violence and victimization can be considered preventive medicine questions, and can be included in any prevention-related visit, such as annual or general exams, pre-employment physicals, prenatal visits, well-baby visits, premarital exams, and adolescent general exams and sports physicals. Providers can ask about violence during an initial getting-to-know-you visit in the context of a trauma, hospitalization, social, or sexual history. Even if this new woman does not yet trust the provider enough to reveal abuse, asking the question sends several positive messages: "This is legitimate medical business; I am concerned about your safety and the stress in your life; I am willing to hear about violence—it is not too shameful, deviant, or insignificant for us to discuss; furthermore, the situation is not hopeless, but can be changed."

Additionally, providers should ask about violence when they hear patients dropping a clue. For example:

A 55-year old woman presented to our residents' clinic for routine followup of her hypertension. After a brief discussion about symptoms, medications, and side effects, the resident stood to retest her blood pressure. As he placed the cuff around her arm, she sighed and said, "I know its going to be high today. I didn't get much sleep last night." She paused, "We had a misunderstanding." The resident asked, "What do you mean by 'a misunderstanding'?" and he learned that the woman's husband had a pattern of ter-

rorizing his wife, several times a year, usually after an evening of heavy drinking. The night before this visit, the husband had "merely" destroyed property, but last Christmas, he threatened her with a shotgun. Recently, her adult son had joined the father in drinking and abusing her.

How Should I Ask about Violence?

First a caution: Do not use the words, "violence," "abuse," "assault," or "rape" unless the woman uses them first. These abstract terms are subject to a variety of interpretations, but most individuals understand them to mean immoral, illegal, or abnormal behavior. Why would women with violent partners not apply the term "abuse" to their relationships? First, for women who were raised by aggressive, controlling men, violent behavior may appear to be a normal life pattern. Second, many women may be hesitant to apply immoral terms to their husbands. Third, the nature and progression of many abusive relationships can delay this cognitive connection.

A violent pattern generally begins with a minor aggressive event that is distressing but does not cause the couple to split. A violent husband's impulse is to apologize deeply, then to justify his behavior so that he and his wife maintain the belief that he is a moral man. Over time, an abused wife will learn to tolerate and forgive more severe aggression (40). If she is isolated from those who might question this pattern, she is likely to tolerate more violence. However, most abused women have a limit: if the children witness violence, if injuries occur, if her life is threatened, or if the children are hit, then she will recognize the behavior as dangerous or unreasonable and seek help. Thus, many women will not apply the term "abuse" to their situation until the violence has advanced a great degree. To discover aggressive patterns early, a provider must use other terms.

The rules for asking about violence are (1)

to avoid abstract concepts and (2) to focus on behaviors. Ambuel and colleagues from the Family Peace Project in Milwaukee recommend this question to screen for current victimization (41):

> *"In my practice I am concerned about prevention and safety, especially in the family. Are you in a relationship now where you are afraid for your personal safety, or where someone is threatening you, hurting you, forcing you to have sex, or trying to control your life?"*

To screen for past victimization experiences, Ambuel et al. recommend the following:

1. "As an adult, has anyone ever forced you to have sex when you didn't want to?"
2. "Have you ever been in a relationship where your partner hurt you, or threatened you, or forced you to have sex, or tried to control your life?"
3. "When you were young—a child or a teenager—did anyone ever hurt or hit you, or force you to have sex?"

Note these questions set a context for asking about violence ("I am concerned about safety"), they are brief and simple, and they focus on a variety of behaviors that characterize abusive relationships: harm, force, threats, and control.

Clinical Interventions for Battered Women

The impact of violence on a woman's health and family life demands a comprehensive response from providers. Treating acute injuries, while important, is not enough. In fact, some claim that ignoring violence works to enable men to keep hitting (10). Effective interventions require a safe, collaborative, accepting patient-provider relationship, and a longitudinal approach.

The Clinical Environment

Safety

Safety is primarily addressed through confidentiality. With all patients, providers should arrange to talk in private and to assure confidentiality of their discussions. Partners who are extremely controlling may try to stay in the room during an office visit. The provider can respectfully address the partner's concerns about the woman's medical problems, then invite the partner to wait outside during the physical exam. At that time, confidential discussions may occur. No information should be shared with the woman's partner without her permission.

> A 25-year-old woman came to our urgent care clinic for treatment of a vaginal discharge. Her husband was with her. They had recently reunited after a marital separation of 3 months. When the lab results were returned, the provider presented the diagnosis of gonorrhea to the couple. After a brief discussion about treatment, the provider left the room for his prescription pad. When he returned, the woman was nursing a bloody nose, the result of a physical attack by her husband.

Collaboration

When working with battered women, a collaborative position, not a directive one, provides the best benefit to the woman. Being directive replicates the dynamic between an abused woman and her controlling partner, and does not encourage her to act independently of powerful others. The provider must recognize that the responsibility for change belongs to the woman, and that she knows best when a particular strategy will be safe and

helpful. The provider's role should be that of consultant and supporter, presenting intervention options to the woman and encouraging all steps toward safety.

Acceptance

A nonjudgmental approach is necessary, but not always easy. Kurz and Stark found that health care workers were most sympathetic with battered women who were taking action to change their life situation, but irritated with others whom they described as "passive," "evasive," "uncooperative," or had "AOB" (alcohol-on-breath) (27). These professionals included more pejorative terms in battered women's medical records than in other records, and were more likely to make inappropriate referrals and discharge plans for battered women.

What they confronted in these patients were behaviors that were adaptive in a violent environment, e.g., passivity, evasiveness, mistrust, "self-medication," but frustrating in a health care environment in which self-motivation and cooperation were expected. Understanding the source of troublesome behaviors will help the provider maintain the objectivity and the acceptance needed to avoid mismanagement of battered women.

The Intervention Process

Assess Readiness for Change

Women who suffer clear consequences of partner abuse but who will not change their situations can be frustrating to providers and other caregivers. Before dispensing advice, the provider should assess the woman's readiness for change. Prochaska and colleagues have developed a model that describes an individual's progression through several steps of behavior change (see Table 9.1.3.) (42). When working with battered women, consider one of five stages:

1. *Precontemplation* is characterized by the statement, "My relationship is not a prob-

Table 9.1.3. "Stages of Change" for Battered Women

Stages of Change	Patient's Belief	Physician "Nudging" Strategies
Precontemplation	"My relationship is not a problem"	"What would it take for his anger to be a problem for you?
Contemplation	"The violence is a problem, but I'm not ready to change things"	"When would you know it was time to make changes in your life?
Preparation	"The violence is a problem, and I'm planning some changes"	Support Clarify plans Community resources Anticipatory guidance
Action	"I am making changes to end the violence"	Support Community resources Anticipatory guidance Coping strategies
Maintenance	"I am adapting to the changes I have made"	Support Community resources Coping strategies

Data from Prochaska JO, Velicer WF, Rossi JS, Goldstein MG, Marcus BH, Rakowski W, et al. Stage of change and decisional balance for 12 problem behaviors. Health Psychol 1994; 13:39–46.

lem." In these relationships, the frequency and severity of violence may be low, and/or the women may believe their partners' aggression is normal or justified.

2. *Contemplation* is characterized by, "I know the violence is a problem, but I'm not ready to do anything about it." Some women believe that the benefits of staying with their partners outweigh the costs of enduring the abuse. For others, low self-esteem, depression, or lack of access to assistance may render them incapable of making any change in the situation.

3. *Preparation* is characterized by, "I know the violence is a problem, and I'm planning changes." Women who change or leave violent relationships need preparation time. Some have to save money to move; some need to find employment; some must think through how they will explain the separation to family, friends, children, and spouse; and some must plan a careful escape.

4. *Action* is characterized by "I am making changes to end the violence," and gener-

ally describes the early phase of the new lifestyle. This is an unstable period, when women discover the costs of change. Women who leave their partners will discover loneliness, uncertainty, poorer finances, and the entire burden of child-rearing. Many partners will work hard to get the woman back into the relationship using seduction, threats, or both. This phase is the most dangerous for women; partners who are extremely controlling will exaggerate their measures of coercion when challenged by separation. Most women will find the change too difficult and go back into the relationship. However, when violence reemerges, most women will try to leave again.

5. *Maintenance* is characterized by "I am adapting to the changes I have made."

Providers can best enable women to change violent relationships when they begin "where the woman is," help patients assess their relationships, and nudge them along this continuum of readiness to change. Nudging strategies are outlined in Table 9.1.3. A continuity-of-care practice in which providers see patients several times over long periods of time is an ideal setting to encourage the next step. In each of these discussions, the provider should express concern for the woman's safety and health, and willingness to discuss relationship issues at any time. Even if the woman is reluctant to change her relationship now, she should know that the provider is a source of support and information when she is ready. For example:

> A 32-year-old woman came to clinic for her annual pelvic exam. Her husband had driven her and their two young children to the clinic, and was expected to return after he finished some errands. Instead of undressing for the exam, she engaged her provider—with whom she had a long-standing and trusting relationship—in a decision-making discussion about leaving her violent marriage. The woman had prepared for escape: her children were with her; she had one entire paycheck in her pocket; she knew the battered women's shelter was available to her; she was prepared to file for divorce. However, she risked losing everything she owned. Her husband was a violent, unpredictable man, and she believed he would burn down the house rather than allow her to return for clothing and furniture. She couldn't decide. The provider dialed the shelter number, and put her in touch with a counselor who helped her weigh her choices. She went to the shelter that night, and two days later returned to her house with a police escort and safely removed her possessions.

Assess Danger

Providers should help patients assess the danger that the violent partner presents. Prior to discharging a woman from care, the provider can ask, "Do you feel safe going home?" If the answer is negative, providers can present and discuss other options. Other indices of lethality include availability of weapons, severity of past violence, a pattern of change in severity over time, life transitions such as pregnancy, separation or divorce, drug and alcohol abuse, and history of violence/suicide attempts in partner. Finally, providers should inquire about the safety of the children. If child abuse has occurred, the provider is obligated to report the situation to Child Protective Services.

Develop an Emergency 'Safe-Plan'

If the provider determines that a woman is in danger of serious harm from her partner, but she is not yet ready to leave the relationship, the provider should encourage her to develop a "safe-plan" that can be implemented in an emergency. The provider can begin with a statement of concern, then assess the woman's preparedness to escape: "I am concerned that your husband will hurt you badly next time he gets angry. Can you recognize how dangerous he could be before he actually hurts you? Do you have a plan to get away from him quickly?" Discussion should address predicting the next episode of violence, whether to leave the house, when to leave, where to go, how to arrange transportation, how long to stay away, what to take (e.g., clothes, money, important papers), and whether to get legal protection. Most women have resources that allow them some respite and protection, such as a relative who will temporarily shelter them, but others will need public assistance. For this reason, the provider needs to be acquainted with local agencies who can provide shelter and services to abused women.

Describe Community Resources

Another important service a provider can offer to a battered woman is a description of community resources that may help her to change the violent relationship. Table 9.1.4 lists a variety of such resources. In a study of women who "beat" wife-beating, subjects claimed that the

Table 9.1.4. Referrals and Community Resources for Partner Violence

Battered women's shelters
Treatment programs for men who batter women
Women's centers
Mental health centers
Private psychotherapist or psychiatrist
Clergy
Support groups for battered women
Family counseling clinics
Alcoholics anonymous, if appropriate
Narcotics anonymous, if appropriate
Al-anon groups
Legal advocacy
Police
911

best help was available from social service agencies, women's self-help groups, and women's shelters (43). Such agencies guide women to basic resources such as food, shelter, jobs, and legal assistance, and offer emotional support. Other important resources are treatment programs for men who batter women. Most batterers' programs involve several weeks of group therapy, followed by individual therapy. The Duluth program addresses each of the issues portrayed in the Power and Control Wheel in Figure 9.1.1 (18). Most men who attend batterers' programs are mandated into treatment by the courts; however, therapists generally welcome self-referrals and provider-referrals as well. Providers should be familiar with a wide variety of referral sources that can address violence in families.

Documentation

Well-documented medical records are important for any health problem, but are especially useful when following chronic conditions. For battered women, the medical record also represents legal evidence about the violence. The AMA recommends inclusion of the following,

especially for women seen soon after a violent event (Table 9.1.5) (1).

Document the chief complaint and an objective description of the violent event, using the woman's own words whenever possible. The provider's interpretations (e.g., "woman was abused") should not be included. The record should contain a complete medical history and a relevant social history. The provider should provide a detailed description of injuries, including type, number, size, location, resolution, and possible causes. Use of a body-map is recommended. The woman's explanations of the injuries and the provider's opinion about the adequacy of those explanations should be recorded.

Color photographs can be useful if they clearly portray an injury. Photographs with subtle or unidentifiable findings can be used against a woman in court as evidence that the injuries were not serious. Guidelines for photographs include the following: (1) take photos before medical treatment (if possible); (2) use color film with a color standard; (3) photograph from different angles, full body and close-up; (4) hold up a coin, ruler, or other object to illustrate the size of an injury; (5) include the woman's face in at least one picture;

Table 9.1.5. Documenting Partner Violence

Chief complaint
Objective description of event
Complete medical history
Relevant social history
Description of injuries
Diagnostic tests
Photographs
Police
    Name of officer
    Actions taken
    Case number
Assessment

Data from American Medical Association. Diagnostic and Treatment Guidelines on Domestic Violence. Chicago: American Medical Association, 1992.

(6) take two pictures of each major trauma area; (7) mark photographs precisely, including the woman's name, location of injury, names of the photographer, and others present.

The documentation must include results from all pertinent laboratory tests and diagnostic procedures. Imaging studies can be particularly useful as legal evidence.

If the police are called, record the name of the officer, the actions taken, and the case number.

Follow-Up

Finally, follow-up is necessary. Options discussed in the provider's office require contemplation, planning, and time on the part of the woman. Providers should use regular appointments or phone conversations to monitor safety and the decision-making process. One discussion does not "cure" violence in a family, but continuing communication, support, and exploration of options will empower women to make changes that eliminate violence from their lives.

A Few Words about Prevention

What can primary care providers do to prevent family violence? Prevention can be conceptualized at three levels: (1) primary prevention guides a woman to avoid the problem altogether; (2) secondary prevention identifies a problem in early stages, and prevents damage; and (3) tertiary prevention identifies a problem in later stages, treats the current damage, and seeks to prevent further damage. Primary care providers can use all three levels of prevention when working with families in their clinical practices.

Primary Prevention

Good parent education may prevent violence before it happens. Teach parents what to expect from their children at every level of development, reviewing cognitive as well as physical and motor expectations. Offer parents nonviolent options for disciplining their children. Allow them to ventilate about the frustrations of parenting and to discuss the impact of parenthood on their intimate relationship. If partner/spousal conflict becomes serious, remind them that they are the models for their children's future relationships, and guide them to appropriate therapy. Avoiding violence in this generation should also influence relationships in the next generation.

Secondary Prevention

Especially with young men and women, ask about the quality of their relationships. If they describe "fights" or "problems with temper," ask them about hitting or hurting each other and ask about their parents' relationships. People in early stages of aggressive relationships may not identify violent behaviors as an ongoing problem. Men who hit are remorseful, and women who are hurt are convinced that these events are rare. Both believe the violence will never happen again. Express concern about physical fights. Describe negative consequences for couples in which deliberate harm is inflicted: injuries, divorce, arrest, emotional distress in their children, and adult children who become batterers or victims. Even if they do not believe their conflicts are serious, if hitting has occurred, gently encourage them to seek counseling for a relationship "tune-up" that will help them learn to relate to each other in the best possible ways.

Tertiary Prevention

Currently, tertiary prevention is our country's most common violence prevention strategy. Action is taken when professionals identify a chronic and dangerous pattern of behaviors. At this late stage, it is difficult to save the marriage, and the "treatment of choice" for many professionals is to get the woman out of the relationship before further harm is done. When speaking to the battered woman, acknowledge the stress she endures in her daily life. Assess current levels of danger and her readiness to change. Label the violence as a problem, and inform her that there are options she can consider. In a collaborative fashion, list those options with her input. Ask her to devise an escape plan in the event that the batterer becomes dangerous again. Document any injuries. Follow up frequently in order to assess ongoing levels of danger and to provide her a place of safety and support.

Special Considerations for Nurse Practitioners and Physician Assistants

Violence will be a part of the lives of many women who seek health care. Because it is not possible to predict which client will be affected, health care providers must be careful about assuming that a certain population of women in their practice is at risk. For example, providers may not think of violence, especially sexual violence, as an issue for older women. Yet, these women may have experienced violence in younger years or for many years, and they may still be in a violent situation.

All nurse practitioners' or physicians' encounters with women should be assessed for violence. It is not sufficient to screen only during the initial visit. Providers can tell women that the issue is significant enough to be raised again, thus encouraging women to reveal abuse they have denied in the past or to disclose abuse that has occurred recently (44). Abuse can be insidious, starting with minor psychological abuse and increasing to more severe abuse over years so that women may not recognize and verbalize the actions as abuse (45).

Victims of abuse may be at risk of more than physical harm and must be assessed for such consequences as increased suicide risk, substance abuse, and mental health problems including depression, panic, anxiety, insomnia, and other disorders. Screening should also include other risks to health such as the presence of a gun in the household (46). Women who view firearms as protection against violence should realize the associated risks of having guns in the home (47).

Even after a woman leaves a violent situation, providers must continue to be available, if at all possible. The woman will likely continue to face barriers related to societal tolerance to woman abuse, sex role stereotyping, legal system ineffectiveness, and assumptions about her role in the abusive situation (44). Many women will leave and go back to a relationship several times.

Woman abuse is a unique health problem that presents a challenge to providers because the etiology lies outside the client and the solution involves more nonmedical components than medical ones (46). Violence against women is also a global problem because of the comparative physical strength of men over women, the inferior social status of women that places them in jeopardy, and various cultural belief systems that condone or allow such behavior (48). Providers must become aware of unique risks that might be faced by women of various cultures and develop culturally sensitive approaches when planning care with women (48–51).

Providers must join with other concerned individuals and groups to institute prevention efforts at the professional, community, and political level if violence is to be eliminated. Posters and literature about violence should be available in primary care facilities in highly visible places and discreet places such as bathrooms and examining rooms. Myths about violence can be confronted in community educational programs and violence can be included as a topic of health fairs. Concerned providers can advocate for a decrease in media violence and seek adequate funding for women's shelters, quality housing, education, and job opportunities (44).

References

1. American Medical Association. Diagnostic and Treatment Guidelines on Domestic Violence. Chicago: American Medical Association, 1992.

2. United States Department of Justice. Violence between intimates. Bureau of Justice Statistics: Selected Findings. November 1994; Washington, DC: NCJ-149259.

3. Stets JE, Straus MA. Gender differences in reporting marital violence and its medical and psychological consequences. In: Straus, MA, Gelles RJ, eds. Physical Violence in American Families: Risk Factors and Adaptations to Violence in 8,145 Families. New Brunswick, NJ: Transaction, 1995: 151–165.

4. Straus MA, Gelles RJ. Societal change and change in family violence from 1975 to 1985 as revealed by two national surveys. Marriage Fam 1986;48:465–479.

5. Straus MA, Gelles RJ, Steinmetz SK. Behind Closed Doors: Violence in the American Family. Garden City, NY: Anchor Press/Doubleday, 1980.

6. Rath GD, Jarratt LG, Leonardson G. Rates of domestic violence against adult women by men partners. Board Fam Pract 1989;2:227–233.

7. Hamberger LK, Saunders DG, Hovey M. Prevalence of domestic violence in community practice and rate of physician inquiry. Fam Med 1992;24:283–287.

8. Elliott BA, Johnson MMP. Domestic violence in a primary care setting: patterns and prevalence. Arch Fam Med 1995;4:113–119.

9. Gin NE, Rucker L, Frayne S, Cygan R, Hubbell FA. Prevalence of domestic violence among patients in three ambulatory care internal medicine clinics. J Gen Intern Med 1991;6:317–322.

10. Stark E, Flitcraft A, Frazier W. Medicine and patriarchal violence: the social construction of a "private" event. Int J Health Services 1979;9:461–493.

11. Abbott J, Johnston R, Koziol-McLain J, Lowenstein SR. Domestic violence against women: incidence and prevalence in an emergency department population. JAMA 1995;273:1763–1767.

12. Goldberg WG, Tomlanovich MC. Domestic violence victims in the emergency department. JAMA 1984;251:3259–3264.

13. Hillard PJA. Physical abuse in pregnancy. Obstet Gynecol 1985;66:185–190.

14. Helton AS, McFarlane J, Anderson ET. Battered and pregnant: a prevalence study. Am J Pub Health 1987;77:1337–1339.

15. McFarlane J, Parker B, Soeken K, Bullock L. Assessing for abuse during pregnancy: severity and frequency of injuries and associated entry into prenatal care. JAMA 1992;267:3176–3178.

16. Gelles RJ, Straus MA. Determinants of violence in the family: toward a theoretical integration. In: Burr WR, Hill R, Nye I, Reiss I, eds., Contemporary Theories about the Family. New York: Free Press, 1979.

17. Barnet OW, LaViolette AD. It Could Happen to Anyone: Why Battered Women Stay. Thousand Oaks, CA: Sage, 1993.

18. Pence E, Paymar M. Education Groups for Men Who Batter: The Duluth Model. New York: Springer, 1993.

19. Saunders DG, Hamberger LK, Hovey M. Indicators of woman abuse based on a chart review at a family practice center. Arch Fam Med 1993; 2:537–543.

20. Hotaling GR, Sugarman DB. An analysis of risk markers in husband to wife violence: the current state of knowledge. Violence Victims 1986;1:101–124.

21. Gelles RJ. Violence and pregnancy: are pregnant women at greater risk of abuse? In: Straus MA, Gelles RJ, eds., Physical Violence in American Families: Risk Factors and Adaptations to Violence in 8,145 Families. New Brunswick, NJ: Transaction, 1995:279–286.

22. Barnett OW, Hamberger LK. The assessment of maritally violent men on the California Psychological Inventory. Violence Victimization 1992;7:15–28.

23. Hastings JE, Hamberger LK. Psychosocial modifiers of psychopathology for domestically violent and nonviolent men. Psych Rep 1994;74:112–114.

24. Carmen EH, Rieker PP, Mills T. Victims of violence and psychiatric illness. Am J Psychiatry 1984;141: 378–383.

25. Gellen MI, Hoffman RA, Jones M, Stone M. Abused and nonabused women: MMPI profile differences. Personnel Guidance J 1984;62:601–604.

26. Rosewater LB. Battered or schizophrenic? Psychological tests can't tell. In: Yllo K, Bograd M, eds. Feminist Perspectives on Wife Abuse. Newbury Park, CA: Sage, 1988:200–216.

27. Kurz D, Stark E. Not-so-benign neglect: the medical response to battering. In Yllo K, Bograd M, eds. Feminist Perspectives on Wife Abuse. Newbury Park, CA: Sage, 1988:249–266.

28. Bergman B, Brismar B. A 5-year followup study of 117 battered women. Am J Pub Health 1991;81: 1486–1489.

29. Kemp A, Rawlings EI, Green BL. Posttraumatic Stress Disorder (PTSD) in battered women: a shelter sample. J Traumatic Stress 1991;4:137–148.

30. Houskamp BM, Foy DW. The assessment of post-

traumatic stress disorder in battered women. J Interpersonal Violence 1991;6:367–375.

31. Astin MC, Lawrence KJ, Foy DW. Posttraumatic stress disorder among battered women: risk and resiliency factors. Violence Victims 1993;8:17–28.

32. Mitchell RE, Hodson CA. Coping with domestic violence: social support and psychological health among battered women. Am J Community Psychol 1983; 11:629–654.

33. Koss MP, Heslet L. Somatic consequences of violence against women. Arch Fam Med 1992;1:53–59.

34. Koss MP, Woodruff WJ, Koss PG. Relation of criminal victimization to health perceptions among women medical patients. J Consulting Clin Psychol 1990;58:147–152.

35. Haber JD, Roos C. Effects of spouse abuse and/or sexual abuse in the development and maintenance of chronic pain in women. Adv Pain Res Therapy 1985;251:3259–3264.

36. Kerouac S, Taggart ME, Lescop J, Fortin MF. Dimensions of health in violent families. Health Care Women Int 1986;7:413–426.

37. Jaffe PG, Wolfe DA, Wilson SK. Children of Battered Women. Thousand Oaks, CA: Sage, 1990.

38. Burge SK. Stop the abuse: teaching providers to intervene with family violence. Presented at the American Psychological Association Annual Convention, Presidential Miniconvention, "To Your Health: Psychology Through the Life Span." New York: August 1995.

39. Finkelhor D, Yllo K. License to Rape: Sexual Abuse of Wives. New York: Free Press, 1985.

40. Browne A. When Battered Women Kill. New York: Free Press, 1987.

41. Ambuel B, Brownell EE, Hamberger LK. Implementing a community model for training medical students and physicians to diagnose, treat, and prevent family violence. Presented at the Society of Teachers of Family Medicine "Violence Education Conference," Albuquerque, NM, November 1994.

42. Prochaska JO, Velicer WF, Rossi JS, Goldstein MG, Marcus BH, Rakowski W, et al. Stages of change and decisional balance for 12 problem behaviors. Health Psychol 1994;13:39–46.

43. Bowker LH. Beating Wife-Beating. Lexington MA: Lexington Books, 1983.

44. King MC. Changing women's lives: the primary prevention of violence against women. AWHONN's Clinical Issues in Perinatal and Women's Health Nursing 1993;4:449–457.

45. Campbell JC, Landenburger K. Violence against women. In: Fogel CI, Woods NF, eds. Women's Health Care. Thousand Oaks, CA: Sage, 1995:407–426.

46. Plichta S. The effects of woman abuse on health care utilization and health status: a literature review. Women's Health Issues 1992;2:154–163.

47. Bonderman J. Armed by fear: self-defense handguns and women's health. Women's Health Issues 1995;5:3–7.

48. Stern PN. Woman abuse and practice implications within an international context. In: Sampselle CM, ed. Violence Against Women: Nursing Research, Education, and Practice Issues. NY: Hemisphere, 1992:143–152.

49. Barbee EL. Ethnicity and woman abuse in the United States. In: Sampselle CM ed. Violence Against Women: Nursing Research, Education, and Practice Issues. NY: Hemisphere Publishing, 1992:153–166.

50. Bohm DK. Nursing care of Native American battered women. AWHONN's Clinical Issues in Perinatal and Women's Health Nursing 1993;4:425–436.

51. Rodriquez R. Violence in transcience: nursing care of battered migrant women. AWHONN's Clinical Issues in Perinatal and Women's Health Nursing 1993;4:437–440.

9.2

Rape

Zelda L. Powers and JoAnn Rosenfeld

Incidence and Prevalence

Violence against women is a significant public health problem that is reaching epidemic proportions. Sexual assault may be the fastest growing, most frequently committed, and most under reported violent crime (1–3). Women constitute more than 90% of the rape victims identified by the National Crime Victimization Survey (NCVS) (4). Nationally, one out of every eight adult women in America, or at least 12.1 million women, has been the victim of forcible rape sometime in her lifetime (4). Other studies estimate that one in five women has experienced rape (5, 6). Thirty-nine percent, or an estimated 4.7 million women, were raped more than once, and 5% were unsure about how many times they had been raped (4).

Because over 80% of the rapes on adult women were executed by men with whom the women were acquainted or romantically involved, rape is one of the most under reported of the violent crimes in the United States today (7). The NCVS estimates that 46% of completed rapes are never reported to the criminal justice system (4), whereas other studies estimate that as many as 90% go unreported (2, 3).

Myths about Rape

There are still many misconceptions about rape throughout our society (Table 9.2.1). Despite the fact that society's attitudes are slowly changing and new laws are being passed, people still believe that victims invite rape by mis-

Table 9.2.1. Myths about Rape

Myth	Reality
Most women are raped by strangers	80% of women are raped by acqaintances, husbands, or lovers
Most rapes are reported	46–90% go unreported
Victims invite rape by their conduct	No behavior in a woman is associated with rape
Rape victims are always assaulted; there should be bruises	Most rapes victims have no signs of physical abuse
If the rape isn't resisted, the woman must have wanted it	Over half the victims are scared and submissive, afraid of physical danger and injury
If the woman gets pregnant from a rape, she must have wanted or enjoyed it	Pregnancy from a rape is an unfortunate catastrophe, not a sign of enjoyment
Rape victims should be hysterical	Many rape victims are calm or controlled or quiet
Rape occurs on dark streets, where the woman should have known not to be or go	Most rapes occur in the home

conduct or provocation. In fact, there is no type of behavior on a woman's part that is associated with incidents of rape (2). Rape is also stereotyped as a physically violent assault; therefore, bruises and wounds are expected and should be evident to prove that the woman resisted the assault (2). Although it is violent, often the violence is psychological rather than physical (3). Between half and two thirds of rape victims have no evidence of physical trauma (8). More than half of victims are submissive (2). The victim is placed in the position of having to decide whether she is in more danger from the rape itself or the potential for physical injury if she resists. Although the social climate is changing, still many women who have been raped choose not to become involved in the criminal justice system because of these misconceptions.

Involvement with Providers

Because of the high prevalence of sexual violence, providers are seeing an increasing number of women who have experienced rape. Rape victims are more likely to visit a physician or provider than they are to visit a mental health professional (9); medical treatment is more socially sanctioned than psychological

treatment, and physical symptoms are perceived as more conspicuous than psychological distress (8, 10). Understandably, women strongly resist the stigma of being labeled a "psychiatric patient." Therefore, it is the role of primary care providers to identify, treat, and serve as a frontline resource for women who have experienced sexual violation.

The provider's role transcends the traditional focus on emergency and forensic intervention. Essential to treatment is an awareness of short- and long-term sequelae for women who have been raped and how both their physical and psychological well-being have been affected.

Immediate Care of the Rape Victim

Only a small minority of victims seek help acutely. Of those who do, most often they present to hospital emergency rooms. However, some may occur in primary care offices.

Acute Psychological Care

In addition to the protocol established for forensic and medical examinations of victims of sexual assault, every provider should have clear step-by-step guidelines for acute care that include prevention or alleviation of psychological distress. These guidelines should take into account the victim's relationship to the attacker, the age of the victim, if the attacker is currently present in the emergency room or office with the victim or resides in the same home, and safety precautions, if appropriate. If the victim is a minor, state laws mandating reporting to designated legal authorities must be followed. Providers should have telephone numbers and name of contact individuals for rape crisis volunteers, victim assistance programs, abuse shelters, human service agencies, as well as legal and law enforcement authorities easily accessible. They should be aware of the procedures for linking victims to resources (Table 9.2.2).

Immediately following the assault, the victim is thrust into a state of crisis. Her initial reactions might include shock, numbness, withdrawal, and denial. She may present an unnaturally calm and detached affect from shock, or she may be crying or angry (11). She should be allowed to articulate her feelings of anger, fear, or disbelief. It is not appropriate at this time to ask probing questions or make verbal observations about her behavior. It is important to assume the victim is telling the truth.

The woman should be encouraged, although not coerced, to report the assault to the proper legal authorities. Even if she does not wish to make a formal report, she should speak with a legal representative immediately because her feelings or plans may change.

If available, rape crisis volunteers should be used to provide support and stay with the victim. The victim should be encouraged to call a friend or relative. Counseling should be encouraged immediately and the provider should offer to make the referral to an appropriate mental health professional.

It is important that the provider prepare the victim for the psychological and physical reactions to rape. Typical symptoms immediately following the assault include feelings of humiliation, degradation, guilt, shame, embarrassment, self-blame, anger, and fear of another assault as well as those symptoms consistent with rape trauma syndrome (12). Often the initial symptoms lessen after the first 2 weeks and the victim may appear to have adjusted. However, from 2 to 3 weeks to several months post-assault, symptoms often recur and may intensify. Some victims may experience a peak in the severity of symptoms by 3 weeks post-assault and continue at a high level for the next month (8). For these reasons, follow-up should be scheduled weekly during the first month following the rape.

The psychological effects for many will continue up 2 years and more (13). As well, she must deal with the effect of the rape on her family, friends, and "significant other." During this long-term phase of reorganization she may experience numerous lifestyle changes; she might move, change jobs, interrupt intimate relationships, and withdraw from previously supportive environments. Suicidal ideations might occur during this time (14). Regular follow-up care and psychological support are critical throughout the first year.

Table 9.2.2. Necessary Referral Organizations Contacts and Numbers

Emergency room
Child protective services
Adult protective services
Sheriff or state police
Rape crisis volunteer
Abuse crisis hotline
Victim assistance programs
Abuse shelter
Legal aid society

Rape Trauma Syndrome (RTS)

A significant proportion of rape victims are likely to suffer long-term psychological aftereffects related to rape trauma syndrome (RTS). RTS is classified as a post-traumatic stress disorder in the Diagnostic and Statistical Manual of Mental Disorders.

RTS is a set of behavioral, somatic, and psychological reactions to the attack. It is described as a two-phase reaction: an acute phase lasting from a few days to several months after the assault and a long-term phase that may last from several months to years (2, 12). The severity of the symptoms and the recovery period may be affected by overlapping psychosocial variables such as the degree of physical threat, severity, injuries, duration of the violence, age of the victim when it occurred, the number of assailants, relationship between the victim and the perpetrator, a prior history of sexual abuse, and other life stressors (15, 16). The victim's psychological and coping ability prior to the violence and her supportive resources will influence her post-traumatic response and adaptation (5, 12).

During the acute phase the classic symptoms include (1) haunting, intrusive recollections, (2) re-experiencing the event through dreams or flashbacks, (3) numbing of feelings, (4) hypersensitivity to the environment, (5) feelings of shock, denial, or disbelief, (6) sleep disturbances, and (7) distress when exposed to certain stimuli (17). The victim often experiences feelings of embarrassment, self-blame, and powerlessness (2).

Later, she may experience mood swings, nervousness, irritability, and have difficulty concentrating. As time passes, anger often emerges toward the assailant, men in general, the legal system, physicians, providers, and often the family. Underlying the anger are feelings of despair, hopelessness, and shame (3). Internalization of these feelings may result in clinical depression. Fifty percent of victims experience clinical depression following rape (3). Suicidal ideation can persist for years following the violation (14). Substance abuse is one of the most common maladaptive coping strategies used by rape victims (14).

The long-term phase can last from 2 to 3 months to several years (2). Given the nature of rape, the immediate resulting distress is understandable. The longevity of the effects is surprising. Approximately 25% of victims experience severe and long-term symptoms. When evaluated many years post-assault, women who have experienced rape are more likely to receive diagnoses of major depression, alcohol abuse and dependence, drug abuse and dependence, generalized anxiety, and obsessive-compulsive disorder than women who have not suffered from rape (8). Fifty-eight percent are likely to experience sexual dysfunctions including fear of sex, arousal dysfunction, and decreased sexual interest (see Chapter 12.7) (18). They may continue to experience anxiety, nightmares, vulnerability, loss of control, mistrust of others, phobias, and somatic symptoms. Women who have been sexually violated experience significant restrictions in their lifestyle and activities, often becoming socially withdrawn and isolated. Almost half had lost their jobs in the year following the rape because of the severity of their reactions to the trauma (14). Fifty to 80% suffer a loss of boyfriends or husbands after the assault (3). Interpersonal problems also include a proneness to revictimization and transgenerational transmission of violence (18). Acquaintance rapes are as devastating to the victim as a rape by a stranger (8).

Sexual assault victims perceive themselves as having poorer physical health than nonvictims do, experience more symptoms across body systems, and engage in more injurious health behaviors such as smoking and failure to use seat belts (19). Therefore, they tend to be high users of medical resources.

Acute Medical Evaluation

Although the primary concerns of the rape victim are psychological and social, there are necessary and immediate medical concerns, examinations, and treatments (Table 9.2.3). Most often these occur in the emergency room, but often it may occur in primary care offices. The woman's primary provider can do the obligatory medical examination and treatment and provide and coordinate psychological and social follow-up. There are three main medical concerns: trauma, infection, and pregnancy.

Medical History

After a rape, following emergent medical and emotional care, a complete history is needed, including detailed description of the assault. The interview should always be handled in a direct and sensitive manner. Often a team approach may be necessary, especially if the victim is a child or the assailant is a family member. Specific discussion of possible sites of trauma and penetration is necessary. Penetration and ejaculation increase the likelihood of infection and pregnancy. The woman should be asked whether oral or anal sex was involved; in 20 to

Table 9.2.3. Medical Evaluation of a Victim of Recent Sexual Assault

	Adult	Child
Immediately		
History	History of assault from patient	History of assault from child and
	Inquiry into safety	other adults (may need social
	Menstrual history	workers, psychologists, etc.)
	Medical history	Inquiry into safety
	Emotional status	Emotional status
	Other accompanying symptoms: GI, GU	Other accompanying symptoms: GI, GU
Physical	General appearance	General appearance
	Status of injuries	Status of injuries
	Photography	Photography
	Genito-urinary exam	GU exam—perhaps under anesthesia
Laboratory	Pubic hair scrapings	
	Vaginal vault content sampling	
	Genital and anal discharge sampling and microscopic evaluation including wet prep for trichomonas, yeast, and Gardenerella, semen	
	Culture for Gonorrhea, Chlamydia in cervix, anus, pharynx, possibly for herpes simplex virus	
	Blood for syphilis, HIV, hepatitis B, and serum frozen for future testing	
	Pregnancy test	
Treatment		
For infection	Ceftriaxone 250 mg IM then doxycycline 100 mg bid x10d unless pregnant or intolerant-Erythromycin 400 mg qid or EES 800 mg tid for 10 d	Amoxicillin 50 mg/kg with probenecid 25 mg/kg (up to 1 g) or ceftriaxone 125 mg IM, then doxycycline or EES alternative for 7–10 days
For pregnancy	Ovral two tablets within 72 hours of rape and two tablets 12 hours later (or four Lo-Ovral twice)	None if prepubertal
At 2–3 weeks	Pregnancy test	None of prepubertal
At 6 weeks	Syphilis, HIV, hepatitis B tests, and others, if indicated	
At 3–6 months	HIV test, others if indicated	

35% of rapes, oral or anal penetration occurs (20).

Physical Examination

First, the woman needs to be examined completely over her whole body, looking carefully for signs of trauma even if she is asymptomatic. The neck, face, and genitals are the most common sites of trauma. The woman should be examined for contusions, bruises, abrasions, lacerations, bite marks, swelling, and scratches. Photographs should be taken of all the injuries.

If the rape victim is a child, examination may need to be postponed, either until a sympathetic supportive (to the child) adult is available or until it can be performed under anesthesia. Extreme sensitivity to emotional trauma and response of a female exam is necessary. If the external exam is normal, no further examination may be necessary. Vaginal contents can be aspirated with a sterile eye dropper; a complete pelvic exam with speculum is not necessary. However, if the external genital exam shows recent trauma or vaginal penetration, a more complete exam is indicated, even if anesthesia is necessary.

For a woman, after a complete physical, a speculum and bimanual exam is necessary to look for signs of trauma, prior pregnancy, or infection. The hymen, anal, and oral mucosa should be inspected for trauma, seminal fluid, or infection. A digital rectal exam may be indicated to examine for a relaxed external sphincter, signs of trauma, anal fissures, or bleeding (21).

Laboratory Examination

The laboratory examination has three purposes: (1) to discover previous pregnancy or infection, (2) to document rape legally and medically, and (3) to find signs of acquired infection or pregnancy (Table 9.2.3).

First, swabs of vaginal, cervical, and anal areas are cultured and stained and examined microscopically. Any seminal fluid or vaginal pool fluid is carefully collected, put in sterile containers, and sent for examination for semen and acid phosphatase, by forensic personnel. Pubic and any other hair samples are taken and placed in a sterile container for future legal and medical examination.

Cultures should be obtained from the cervix and vagina, urethra, anus, and pharynx for gonorrhea and chlamydia. A wet prep to test for trichomonas and clue cells for Gardenerella is also necessary. Determination of genital pH may help diagnose these. The normal genital pH is 3.5 to 4.5; a higher pH may signal a trichomonas or Gardenerella infection. A cervical mucous swab can be cultured for herpes simplex virus (HSV) (22).

Serum test for syphilis and human immunodeficiency virus (HIV) should be done and additional serum saved for future testing especially for hepatitis B. A baseline pregnancy test is indicated.

Examination of the woman's genitalia with a colposcope may find vaginal and cervical lacerations otherwise undetected. Photography of these lesions if found is necessary.

Follow-up cultures and serology are important. Repeat cultures for GC and chlamydia, wet preps for trichomonas or Gardenerella, and culture for HSV (especially if there are symptoms) are mandatory. Repeat serological testing for syphilis, HIV hepatitis B, and pregnancy at 6 weeks and HIV at 3–6 months should be done.

Treatment

Trauma

Trauma with rape in not uncommon, either in the genitalia or other parts of the body. Any suspicious lesions should be radiographed and photographed. More significant lesions may require suturing or even surgery under anesthesia for repair. Four percent of women require surgery for genital trauma including perineal or vagina lacerations, contusion, or abrasions (23). Treatment may require suturing or observation with analgesia, heating pads, local anaesthetic, and/or antibiotic ointments. Sitz baths may help swelling and abrasions in the genital area.

Infection

Prophylactic treatment for possible infection may be indicated. In children, because the assailant is usually a family member and available for examination, it is suggested that prophylactic treatment only be used if (1) there is confirmation that the assailant is infected, (2) the child is unlikely to return for follow-up, (3) she has signs of infection, or (4) she was assaulted by a stranger. The child should be treated orally for gonorrhea, sparing her the IM medication, with 125 mg ceftriaxone, amoxicillin 50 mg/kg/d with probenecid 25 mg/kg (to a maximum of 1 g), doxycycline (50 mg bid), or erythromycin 50 mg/kg/d for 7 days.

In adults, prophylaxis is more commonly given. Ceftriaxone 250 mg IM, 3.0 g amoxicillin with 1.0 g probenecid or erythromycin (EES) 800 g qid for 7 days, are possible treatments for gonorrhea. Then, doxycycline 100 mg bid for 7 days should be added for treatment of chlamydia.

Psychological Medication

The need for psychotherapeutic agent, is disputed. If given, they should be short-acting and few in number. The woman should be accompanied by a friend or relative while taking the medication.

Pregnancy Prophylaxis

If the woman is post-pubertal post-coital contraception should be offered and encouraged. The overall risk of conception following a rape is 2 to 4% (22). Post-coital contraception is effective if taken within 72 hours of rape. It is more effective if taken within 12 to 24 hours. Two Ovral or 4 Lo-Ovral tablets taken as soon as possible, and then two or four more tablets taken after 12 hours will prevent 96 to 98% of pregnancies. A follow-up pregnancy test at 2 to 6 weeks is indicated.

Later Psychological Care

Many victims present much later after a rape to private providers with complaints based on symptoms without disclosing that an assault has occurred (9). Some do not present until months after the incident, and then do so repeatedly. Complaints might include gastrointestinal symptoms, headaches, sleep disturbances, eating disorders (24), genitourinary disturbances, PMS, chronic pelvic pain, and skeletal muscle tension (8, 12). Depression and anxiety are also common complaints of rape victims.

The highest priority is identifying victims of sexual violence at the health care entry point. The American Medical Association has adopted a policy urging all providers to use standardized screening techniques to assess for current or past sexual assault as part of the medical interview with all women patients. Because many patients will not spontaneously disclose this information, the physician must ask specific questions. During the initial interview and after asking about menses and pregnancy, the provider might simply ask the patient if she has had any adverse sexual experiences, or "Have you ever been pressured or forced to have sex against your will?" Providers should avoid using words such as rape, incest, and child molestation, and should focus instead on describing behaviors involved. This screening should take place under circumstances that provide privacy and safety. By asking direct questions, providers imply that they discuss this issue with all women, the problem is appropriate for discussion, they are willing to listen, and they do not view sexual violence as the result of the victim's behavior. Many patients require time to develop a trusting relationship with their provider before disclosing this information.

When women disclose a history of sexual violence either immediately following the attack or several weeks or months post-assault, their reactions may vary. Some may exhibit crying or other behavioral manifestations of fear and trauma. Others remain quiet and withdrawn in an attempt to maintain control. Some seem to act inappropriately, smiling and laughing because they are "happy to be alive." It is not the provider's role to judge reactions, but to provide support regardless of the reaction. Care must be offered in a concerned, nonjudgmental manner. The provider should give due validation by explaining that many women share similar sexually violent experiences from both strangers and intimates and that often they are afraid to tell anyone about it. The provider should also stress to the patient that their symptoms "make sense" given the history of sexual abuse. This acknowledgment of itself may help the patient feel less isolated and overwhelmed by her experience.

The medical documentation should include indications of a trauma history from the screening, a description of symptomatology, and any referrals made. This will provide for future continuity of care.

A treatment plan based primarily on the treatment of symptoms will only initiate a cycle of patient contacts with service providers. After first determining that the presenting complaints are not the result of a physical illness, the provider should encourage the patient to consider psychotherapy. Long-term counseling is often beyond the expertise of primary care providers and they should not be required to carry the full burden of intervention. Medical providers should develop linkages and maintain reciprocal relations with various community resources that may be used in providing care for their patients. Referral should be made as quickly as possible. Whenever possible, these resources should be "trauma-specific." Rape victims should be referred to those with expertise in rape crisis. Group therapy has been found to be an effective treatment model in enabling victims to validate feelings and share grief. Victims with underlying psychopathology, such as a history of psychiatric difficulties, or who has evinced problems in addition to those related to the rape, may need more specialized treatment. Rape victims who do not recover from the trauma within 3 months are not likely to do so without mental health therapy (15).

Identification of rape victims and addressing the underlying etiology is the highest priority of health care providers. Then physical and psychological interventions can be coordinated in developing a treatment plan. Whether encountering a rape victim either in the acute phase or the long-term reorganization phase, the provider can play a significant role in her healing process. A sensitive, thorough medical evaluation, long-term follow-up care, referral to appropriate community resources, and psychological support are critical for her recovery. Unless primary care providers take the initiative in screening for trauma specific sexual histories on a routine basis, many victims of sexual assault will not be identified.

Special Considerations for Nurse Practitioners and Physician Assistants

Rape can occur in all ages and all socioeconomic groups. Nurse practitioners, clinicians, and physician assistants in various settings may be the first point of contact for women who have been raped. In some emergency departments, registered nurses are being trained to provide comprehensive care (including forensic evidence collection, prevention of STDs and pregnancy, crisis intervention, accurate documentation, and referral) so that rape victims can be treated quickly and competently (26). All health care providers who work with women must have specific protocols for care such as those previously discussed. Use of a sexual assault examination form helps assure complete examination and documentation (27).

During an examination for rape, the provider must demonstrate respect, let the woman know that she is safe, and give her privacy without leaving her alone. Document if the woman douched, bathed or showered, gargled, changed clothes, or took other actions to cleanse herself (28). Explaining aspects of the examination, tell her to inform the examiner if there is discomfort or pain, thus giving her back some sense of control in the situation.

Asking about abuse and rape should be a routine part of every woman's history. If the woman denies that there is a problem, the provider might say that many women do have such experiences and invite the woman to return if she ever has a problem in the future. Such statements let the woman know that the practitioner is open to further discussion. It may be necessary to ask any adults who are present to leave during the interview because they could be the abuser (29). Whether a rape was recent or in the past, women need to know that they are not to blame for someone else's behavior. A victim should be told she did not cause the rape to happen and given reassurance that whatever she did (resisting or submitting in fear) was the best decision she could make at that time (26).

Practitioners may find themselves angry with the person who committed the rape or the system that allowed it to happen. Criminal justice systems and social service agencies may be reluctant to intervene when sexual abuse involves two adults who have a relationship. A primary barrier confronting women in marital rape is the attitude of society in general (30). Providers of care may also find themselves angry toward the victim herself when she will not leave an abusive situation or if she explains away bruises as a result of a fall or her own clumsiness. A victim's culture will determine how she defines the problem, her attitudes about sharing it with health care providers, and her expectations of intervention (31). Women may not perceive that forced sexual

relations by their husbands are criminal acts that should be punished. Sadly, even health care providers may hold on to beliefs that what goes on between a man and his wife is no one's business, or that a woman must enjoy being abused, otherwise she would leave the situation (32). In addition, providers may hesitate to explore clues of past sexual violence because of problems in their own past that they have not confronted.

When rape has occurred, providers can offer to call the police, rape crisis advocates, or a safe house. However, the woman herself will have to make the final decision, and it may be a decision that the provider does not understand. If the woman will not leave a potentially dangerous situation at the present time, she should develop a plan to prepare for the possibility of having to leave suddenly in the future, e.g., by having a bag packed with clothes, money, credit cards, and familiar toys for any children (33). Specific information about shelters and legal resources should be given to women at risk.

Providers should help the victim identify support systems and offer to call family or friends for support. People who are emotionally close to a victim will be impacted by the rape. They may be supportive or may believe and act on some of the myths about rape, perhaps blaming the woman or doubting her story. Family members and friends may patronize or overprotect the victim, thus reinforcing her feelings of helplessness. Practitioners may have opportunities to help these "indirect" victims discuss their feelings, dispute myths, and prepare for predictable psychological and physical problems (28).

Rape prevention is a community problem. Various professionals in the community have contact with rape victims, including school personnel, social workers, and law enforcement officers. All must be aware of the potential for rape. All women must realize that they are at risk and avoid alcohol and drug use, dating situations, unfamiliar partners, and environments that place them at higher risk. Local communities must make it clear that violence against women is not tolerated. Safe places and counseling must be available. Women must feel free to disclose rape without feeling they have failed in the role society has given them to maintain harmony in the home and family (31). Total attitudinal changes must occur to prevent rape. Teaching boys and girls about respect, empathy, and nonviolent conflict resolution can help break the cycle of violence (29).

References

1. Sexual assault: an overview. Washington, DC: US Victims Resource Center, Dept. of Justice, 1987.
2. Gibe LH, Paddison P. Rape, sexual assault, and its victims. Psychiatry Clin North Am 1988;11:629–648.
3. Dunn SF, Gilchrist VJ. Sexual assault. Primary Care 1993;20:359–373.
4. National Victim Center, Rape in America: A Report to the Nation, Arlington, VA. 1993.
5. Goodman LA, Koss MP, Russo NF. Violence against women: physical and mental health effects. Part I research findings. Appl Preventive Psych 1993;2: 79–89.
6. Koss MP, Heslet L. Somatic consequences of violence against women. Arch Fam Med 1992;1:53–58.
7. Russell DEH. The prevalence and incidence of forcible rape and attempted rape of females: Victimology: An International J 1983;7:81–93.
8. Koss MP. Rape, scope, impact, intervention, and public policy responses. Am Psychologist 1993;49:1062–1069.
9. Koss MP, Koss PG, Woodruff WJ. Relation of criminal victimization to health perceptions among women medical patients. J Consult Clin Psych 1990; 58:147–152.
10. Kimmerling R, Calhoun KS. Somatic symptoms, social support, and treatment seeking among sexual assault victims. J Consult Clin Psych 1994;62:333–340.
11. Council on Scientific Affairs, American Medical Association. Violence against women: relevance for medical practitioners. JAMA 1992;267:3184–3189.
12. Block AP. Rape trauma syndrome as scientific expert testimony. Arch Sexual Behavior 1990;19:309–323.
13. Hanson RK. The psychological impact of sexual assault on women and children: a review. Ann Sex Res 1990;3:187–232.
14. Ellis E, Atkeson B, Calhoun K. An assessment of long-term reaction to rape. J Abnormal Psychol 1981;90:263–266.
15. Kilpatrick DG, Saunders BE, Veronen LJ, Best CL, Von JM. Criminal victimization: lifetime prevalence, reporting to police, and psychological impact. Crime Delinq 1987;33:478–489.
16. Sales E, Baum M, Shore B. Victim readjustment following assault. J Soc Issues 1984;37:5–27.
17. Moscarello R. Psychological management of victims of sexual assault. Can J Psychiatry 1990;35:25–30.
18. McCann IL, Sakheim DK, and Abrahamson DJ. Trauma and victimization: a model of psychological adaptation. The Counseling Psychologist 1988;16: 531–594.
19. Koss MP, Koss PG, Woodruff WJ. Deleterious effect of criminal victimization on women health and medical utilization. Arch Intern Med 1991;151:342–347.
20. Glaser JB, Hammerschlag MR, McCormack WM. Current concepts: sexually transmitted diseases in victims of sexual assault. N Engl J Med 1986;315: 625–627.
21. Council on Scientific Affairs, American Medical Association. Council Reports: Violence Against Women: Relevance for Medical Practitioners.
22. Committee on Adolescence. American Academy of Pediatrics: sexual assault and the adolescent. Pediatrics 1994;94:761–765.
23. Ruckman LM. Victims of rape: the physician's role in treatment. Curr Opin Obstet Gynecol 1993; 5:721–725.
24. Kirland K, Mason R. Victims of crime: the internists' role in treatment. Sci Med J 1992;85:965–968.
25. Kilpatrick D, Best C, Veronen L. Mental health correlates of criminal victimization: a random community survey. J Consult Clin Psych 1985;53:866–873.
26. Ledray LE, Arndt S. Sexual assault victim: a new model for nursing care. J Psychosocial Nurs 1994;32: 7–12.
27. Richards J. Sexual assault. In: Star WL, Lommel LL, Shannon MT, eds. Women's Primary Health Care. Washington, DC: American Nurses Association, 1995:14-45–14-54.
28. Heinrich LB. Care of the female rape victim. Nurse Pract 1987;12:9–27.
29. Campbell JC, Landenburger K. Violence against women. In: Fogel CI, Woods NF, eds. Women's Health Care. Thousand Oaks, CA: Sage, 1995:407–425.
30. Smith M, Martin F. Domestic violence: recognition, intervention, and prevention. MEDSBURG Nurs 1995;4:21–25.
31. King MC, Torres S, Campbell D, et al. Violence and abuse of women: a perinatal health care issue. AWHONN's Clin Issues Perinatal Women's Health Nursing 1993;4:163–172.
32. Henderson AD, Ericksen JR. Enhancing nurses' effectiveness with abused women. J Psychosocial Nurs 1994;32:11–15.
33. Wardell D, Campbell J. Abuse often increases during pregnancy. NAACOG newsletter 1992;19:1, 6–7.

9.3

Long-Term Consequences of Childhood Sexual Abuse

Marybeth Hendricks-Matthews

Introduction

Adult survivors of childhood sexual abuse must come to terms with the horrific childhood experiences that threatened their physical, psychological, and spiritual integrity. For some survivors, there is a minimal amount of compromise to their adult functioning. For many others, the legacy of abuse includes persistent psychological and somatic symptoms. Providers, whether they realize it or not, see patients who have a wide array of symptoms rooted in their past abuse. Unfortunately, these abuse survivors cannot be treated effectively without an understanding and appreciation of the symptoms' contextual links to the women's abuse histories (1).

This chapter will discuss the devastating impact that childhood sexual abuse has on later functioning and will discuss how to identify and treat adult survivors of child-hood sexual abuse. Strategies for avoiding or lessening the potential for survivor retrauma-tization during health care procedures are given.

Definitions

Childhood sexual abuse is "a sexual act im-posed on a child who lacks emotional, motiva-tional, and cognitive development. The abil-ity to lure a child into a sexual relationship is based on the all-powerful and dominant posi-tion of the adult or older perpetrator, which is in sharp contrast to the child's age, depen-dence, or subordinate position. Authority and power enable the perpetrator, implicitly or di-rectly, to coerce the child into sexual compli-ance" (2).

There is disagreement in the literature re-garding the incidence of incest, primarily at-tributable to differences among researcher's definitions (3). Within the past few years, however, there has been recognition that child sexual abuse and incest are far more common than once thought; there are high incidence and high prevalence rates. One study of child-hood sexual abuse histories in a primary care setting found that approximately 40% of their sample of 162 women had experienced some form of childhood sexual contact and one in six had been raped as a child (4). In a recent survey of 665 patients age 18 to 35 years (90% of whom were women) at a university-based family practice clinic, incest was reported by 20% (3).

Using a conservative measure of rape, a re-cent study of American women found that more than three fifths (61%) of all forcible rapes of women occurred before the age of 18 years (29% occurred before age 11 years, and 32% between age 11 and 17 years). Seventy-eight percent of all completed child and ado-lescent rapes were perpetrated by family mem-bers or acquaintances (5).

Traumatic Effects of Sexual Abuse

To appropriately treat and manage survivors of childhood sexual abuse, providers must ap-preciate that presenting symptoms represent coping mechanisms used to protect the indi-vidual during the abuse or later to ward off feelings of overwhelming helplessness and ter-ror. If symptoms are decontextualized from the abuse, survivors often appear "crazy," when in reality their symptoms are attempts to master their trauma. Some most common symptoms and clinical presentations are listed in Table 9.3.1.

Although there is no single syndrome that is uniformly present in adult survivors of sex-ual abuse, there is great consistency in mental health symptoms, particularly depression and anxiety. These sequelae can be found alone or in combination with physical and behavioral symptoms. Even without the benefit of thera-peutic intervention, some survivors can main-tain the outward appearance of being unaf-fected by their abuse. Most, however, are suffering and experience pervasive and delete-rious consequences (6).

Table 9.3.1. Common Symptoms in Adult Survivors of Childhood Sexual Abuse

- Depression
- Anxiety, panic attacks
- Chronic headaches, migraines
- Gastrointestinal problems
- Pelvic pain
- Dissociative symptoms
- Alcohol, drug abuse
- Repeated self-injury
- Sexual dysfunction
- Suicide attempts
- Eating disorders
- PTSD symptoms
- Expectation of premature death
- Intolerance of, or constant search for, intimacy

Childhood Sexual Abuse Accommodation Syndrome

Summit has described the childhood sexual abuse accommodation syndrome, linking the trauma experienced by a child during sexual abuse to the adult survivor's presenting symptoms (7). The five phases of the syndrome are:

1. Secrecy and silence
2. Helplessness and vulnerability
3. Entrapment and accommodation
4. Delayed, conflicted, and unconvincing disclosure and
5. Retraction

Secrecy and Silence

Abuse of the trusted relationship is characterized by secrecy. The child's silence is guaranteed by threats of physical harm, bribery, or sending confusing messages that distort a child's perceptions. Guilt and shame are also a part of children's experiences, further silencing them. Additionally, secrecy isolates children and they depend on the abuser even more to "explain" the reality and meaning of the abuse.

Helplessness and Vulnerability

Especially when young, children are dependent on their caretakers for all their physical needs and for love. They are also extremely invested in believing that their parents are only concerned with their best interests and cannot tolerate the idea that a parent could be abusive. Consequently, children alter their view of the abuse to match the views of the perpetrating parent(s).

Entrapment and Accommodation

Summit describes the entrapment of the child as the abuse predictably continues and frequently escalates in severity (7). Because children are so invested in viewing the abusive parent as loving, they develop a framework for justifying the abuse as related to their own badness. In adult survivors of childhood abuse, this belief may be expressed as low self-esteem, depression, or self-injurious behaviors. The accommodation also leads to the most enduring legacy from the abuse, a disordered and fragmented identity.

Delayed, Conflicted, and Unconvincing Disclosure

Early attempts by most children in dysfunctional homes to break the silence of abuse are often met with disbelief, and when believed with victim blaming. The child must adjust to a world in which abusive behavior is accepted and her truth, unaccepted.

Retraction

Retraction is often a part of this syndrome because the child is overwhelmed by the events that are set in motion if she reveals the abuse. Social services may become involved and the perpetrator may have to leave the family; a retraction is made to restore the family's equilibrium.

Providers who do not understand the child sexual abuse accommodation syndrome will not likely recognize the adult abuse survivors for whom they provide care (7, 8). Those who do appreciate and understand the experiences of sexually abused children (and their coping strategies) will more readily recognize the symptoms of adult survivors as rooted in their abuse.

The Consequences of Child Sexual Abuse

Courtois has conceptualized the primary aftereffects of childhood sexual abuse into seven distinct but overlapping categories:

1. Symptoms of PTSD
2. Emotional reactions
3. Self-perceptions

4. Physical and biomedical effects
5. Sexual effects
6. Interpersonal effects
7. Social functioning (9).

Abuse response is greatly variable and idiosyncratic within the seven categories. Further, at times survivors may be symptomatic and at other times relatively symptom-free. Such variability of symptom constellation is the norm. Providers must appreciate this to work effectively with survivors.

Symptoms of Post-Traumatic Stress

Adult survivors of childhood abuse frequently have symptoms of post-traumatic stress disorder (PTSD). Especially prominent are PTSD-related flashbacks—"sudden, intrusive, sensory experiences, often involving visual, auditory, olfactory, and/or tactile sensations reminiscent of the original assault, experienced as though they were occurring in the present rather than as a memory of a past event." Triggers of flashbacks include sexual stimuli or interactions, abusive behavior by other adults, disclosure of one's abuse experiences to others, and reading or seeing sexual or violent media depictions (10).

Courtois notes that dissociative disorders (e.g., psychogenic fugue, psychogenic amnesia, derealization, multiple personality disorder) have been linked to sexual abuse and are conceptualized as complex post-traumatic conditions (9). Atypical dissociative symptomatology and related features are also typically seen in sexual abuse survivors (11).

Emotional Reactions

Emotional sequelae are the most frequently reported (12). Although depression, anxiety, and anger are most prevalent, fear, shame, humiliation, guilt, self-blame, grief, and urges to self-harm are often mentioned. These emotions may have behavioral, somatic, and/or relational manifestations (9).

Self-Perceptions

If children are mistreated by important family members, the child's sense of self is badly damaged and the world comes to be viewed as unsafe. Without basic trust, individuals lack the ability to self-soothe, causing them to overreact to stress or painful events.

This inability to comfort oneself can also cause problems in defining oneself as separate from others. "Adults molested early in life have more problems in understanding or relating to others independent of their experiences or needs, and they may not be able to perceive or experience their own internal states independent of the reactions or demands of others" (13).

Courtois notes that "To defend themselves against the full implications of the abuse experience (especially when the abuser is a parent or is otherwise highly valued by the child or from whom the child should expect safety and nurturance), children often incorporate the blame for the abuse and develop a negative identity as a result." Most, if not all, sexually abused children make sense of the abuse by developing the belief that something about them caused the abuse to happen or that they somehow deserved to be abused. They maintain the image of the abuser as "good" while they make themselves "bad," thereby deserving of the abuse and not deserving of assistance and rescue (9).

Physical and Biomedical Effects

Wahlen, summarizing the biomedical sequelae of child sexual abuse, described the following groups of symptoms: (*a*) chronic and/or diffuse pain, either the result of trauma or conversion symptoms representative of the abuse, (*b*) symptoms of anxiety and/or depression, (*c*) eating and substance abuse disorders, (*d*) the results of self-neglect, and (*e*) others (3).

Wahlen (3) described diffuse pain syndromes that included various forms of headaches, and gastrointestinal (GI) and genitourinary pain syndromes. The site of the GI complaints may suggest the site of abuse. Upper GI complaints of nausea, gagging, and vomiting may be signs of oral sexual abuse, whereas rectal pain, cramps, diarrhea, and constipation (often associated with functional bowel disease or IBS) (see Chapter 16) may be signs of anal abuse, including excessive enemas. Conversion symptoms, especially neurological ones such as fainting and seizures, and respiratory complaints including hyperventilation may also occur.

Sexual abuse may produce somatization disorders (3). Signs of depression and anxiety, including fatigue, can also suggest childhood sexual abuse. Addictive behaviors including eating disorders may be associated with sexual abuse. Finally, "self-neglect, including neglect of basic needs such as sleep, rest, and food, can result in exacerbation of medical problems, and predisposing to medical problems. The survivor can have dental problems, made worse by dental phobia, and will often avoid preventive health examinations out of fear of providers" (3).

Sexual Effects

Disturbances in sexual identity and sexual functioning are prominent in studies of incest survivors (14). Briere and Elliott refer to the pronounced sexual dysfunction in adult survivors of incest as "the most obvious example of conditioned, abuse-related fear" (10). They report that because of the association between sexual stimuli and invasion or pain, many adults abused as children report fear or anxiety-related difficulties during sexual contact.

In adults abused as children, the most frequent chronic sexual problems include fear of intimate relationships, feelings of repulsion or lack of enjoyment, flashbacks during sexual activity, dysfunctions of desire and arousal, and primary or secondary anorgasmia. Compulsive promiscuity and prostitution may also be present as the result of learning "all you're good for

is sex" (12). Childhood sexual abuse survivors frequently confuse sexuality with nurturing behavior.

Interpersonal Effects

For incest survivors the ability to have emotionally healthy relationships with others may be profoundly damaged. Courtois relates that the relationships of many survivors are "unstable and include patterns of excessive self-sufficiency, the caretaking of others, extreme dependence, and overcompliance, learned helplessness and nonassertion, withdrawal, and hostility" (9).

The impairment with separating self from others may manifest as problems with defining one's own boundaries and individual rights when faced with the needs and demands of others. Such problems are frequently associated with great difficulties in interpersonal relationships, including gullibility, inadequate self-protectiveness, and great likelihood in being victimized or abused by others (10).

Perhaps one of the most disturbing sequelae to childhood abuse is the apparent vulnerability of such women to be revictimized, often later in life by individuals who may or may not be known to them. Such revictimization proneness may be the result of a general vulnerability in dangerous situations and to exploitation by untrustworthy people. Childhood abuse seems to have the effect of making adult women less skilled at self-protection and more apt to accept victimization from others (12).

Social Functioning

The social functioning ability of incest survivors is variable. It can range from exceptional and overfunctioning to greatly impoverished and deviant, such as delinquency, prostitution, dangerous sexual practices (including sadomasochism, indiscriminate sexual activity, and sexual abuse of others), and substance abuse. Overfunctioning is often an attempt to palliate the profound low self-esteem that survivors have and to channel their anxiety. Conversely, it is thought that the most marginally functional and disenfranchised members of society also have histories of sexual abuse at the core of their dysfunctions (9).

Adult survivors of childhood sexual abuse comprise a significant percentage of mental health clinical populations (15, 16). Various studies indicate that over 50% of women hospitalized for psychiatric reasons have experienced childhood sexual abuse. One expert explained that "the victim's survival is dependent on adjusting to a psychotic world where abusive behavior is acceptable, but telling the truth about it is sinful . . . Victims accommodate to the judgment others make about the abuse . . . The most enduring legacy of (the accommodation) is a disordered and fragmented identity" (17).

Moderating and Mediating Variables

Briere and Elliott, in discussing factors that intensify the effects of childhood sexual abuse, found that increased distress often results from the following situations: extended and frequent abuse, molestation at an early age, use of force, abuse by a biological parent, and more than one abuser. "More extreme psychological problems are also predicted by the presence of other concomitant forms of childhood maltreatment, including physical and psychological abuse or neglect, and/or subsequent revictimization in adulthood" (10).

Screening

Because sexual abuse histories often hold the key to unlocking the origins of the patients' symptoms, and because most survivors welcome this discussion with health care providers, providers must become skilled in and comfortable with screening for childhood sexual abuse.

Only recently, when organized medicine finally recognized the extent of family violence, have recommendations been made to screen all patients (especially women) for histories of abuse (6, 18). With adult survivors of childhood sexual abuse, there are generally several "red flags" that are present during the initial encounter that should lead the physician to suspect abuse. Many of these "red flags" are symptoms presented in Table 9.3.1 and also include the presence of inappropriate affect and "thick chart syndrome," i.e., excessive office visits. Another opportunity to screen for a history of childhood sexual abuse is during a standard psychosocial, gynecologic, or sexual history taking.

Wahlen (3) provides excellent, detailed suggestions for the taking of a sexual abuse history. She has noted that components of a successful inquiry about a history of sexual abuse include the following:

1. Empathy: "This may be a difficult question to hear, but the answer may help me to help you better . . . "
2. Give patient control over disclosure (when, what, how): "You may want to just think about this before you answer this question, and I will support your decision either to answer or not . . . "
3. Link symptoms to abuse: "In my experience, some people who have symptoms similar to yours have had experiences in childhood of being abused or hurt in some way . . . "
4. Avoid asking the patient to make judgments about authority figures being abusive. Many survivors have difficulty saying they were abused because of one or more of the following reasons: (1) they know they were abused but fear retribution from the perpetrator; (2) they are still in denial about the severity of the effects of the abuse so don't see themselves as having experienced abuse; and/or (3) they perceive the perpetrator as "good" and themselves as "bad" and deserving of the abuse so they don't define the behavior as abuse. An example of a question to ask is:

"As a child, did someone who was important to you ever touch you in a way which made you uncomfortable?"

5. Make the question "natural": Become as comfortable asking patients about incest as you are asking them about coughs.

6. Normalize the experience: "About one in five adults were sexually abused as a child. I ask all my adult patients if they have ever been touched by someone important in their life in a way that made them uncomfortable . . . "

Sometimes, even when questions are carefully phrased and the assessment has "been done correctly," some patients with abuse histories will not admit to the experiences. Often, survivors need to test providers to make sure they are trustworthy of such information. In other instances, repression does not allow the survivor access to such memories at the time of the provider's questioning. Despite the possibility that adult survivors cannot respond positively to the provider's questions, they will be made aware that the provider is someone who considers such information essential to comprehensive health care (1). Not asking about abuse gives tacit support to the belief the survivor may already hold—abuse doesn't matter, should have no long-term effects, and isn't worth mentioning (19).

Physical examination of the patient can also lend itself to an assessment for childhood sexual abuse history. Generally, however, before an exam is initiated, the skilled and knowledgeable practitioner already has a high index of suspicion.

Besides the routine physical, extra attention should be paid to skin, thyroid, breasts, pelvic exam, and the patient's ability to relax. Scars from self-mutilation may be indications of a history of sexual abuse.

Women who were sexually abused may react in various ways to pelvic exams. Not every survivor of sexual abuse has problems tolerating a pelvic exam. Women survivors, especially those most severely traumatized, may not object to pelvic exams because they feel that their body can and should be used by others and they cannot control it. "They also might have learned to dissociate, a defense mechanism that results in a split between mind and body, a "numbing out," or the ability to be off in the distance watching what was happening to their body but not to feel it" (19).

Intervention

Once a survivor of childhood sexual abuse history is known, there are many ways that the provider can offer support.

Empowering Messages

Some positive and healing responses to the disclosure of her abuse include the following (1, 3, 8, 19):

1. You were the victim of the abuse. You are in no way to blame. The perpetrator is always at fault.
2. It took a great deal of courage to disclose the abuse.
3. Indicate that she has been heard and believed.
4. Let her know that her symptoms "make sense" given what she experienced and that she is not "crazy."
5. Let her know that she has the right to say "No" and that she can and should set limits for herself. She has the right to control who touches her body and when and how.

Counseling Referral

Because of the complexity of response to trauma and the profound mental health sequelae that usually accompany it, traumatized patients will generally benefit from referral to mental health specialists. Primary care providers can be a powerful ally in the patient's healing if they are prepared to make referrals to therapists who specialize in treating trauma. Unfortunately, because of the recent media attention to PTSD, some therapists and programs have simply "jumped on the bandwagon," presenting themselves as trauma specialists when this is not true.

Matsakis provides suggestions for the minimum set of criteria for effective PTSD therapy (20). Effective therapists will do the following:

- See the trauma as real and important in itself, apart from any preexisting psychological problems and any current social, family, or personal pressures.
- View survivors as capable of being healed—not as willing participants in the trauma or as hopeless psychiatric cases.
- Educate survivors about the nature of trauma, PTSD, and secondary wounding experiences, about the specific factors in their particular category of trauma that may affect them, and about the nature of the healing process itself.
- Either teach survivors coping skills such as assertiveness, stress management, relaxation techniques, and anger management, or make appropriate referrals for survivors to receive such help.
- Use medication and behavior-management techniques when appropriate, but not to the exclusion of examining their present and past with the goal of understanding what occurred and their feelings about those events.
- Be aware of the effects of sex-role stereotyping, racism, and blame-the-victim attitudes on the healing process.

Providers may begin compiling a list of such experts in a number of different ways. Often, contacting state boards of medicine or psychology can be beneficial in locating therapists who are skilled in treating victims of trauma. Veterans centers, battered women's shelters, and rape crisis centers are often familiar with therapists and programs that treat various types of trauma. Because of the relationship between trauma histories and alcohol and drug abuse, therapists should be skilled in working with individuals who have dual diagnoses (1).

The patient should not feel abandoned or rejected when a counseling referral is made. If it is appropriate, the provider should emphasize his/her ongoing involvement in the patient's case. If the therapist or agency that the woman is being referred to is known personally by the provider, the woman will feel more trusting about the referral. The provider should also reassure the survivor that they are not "crazy," but are reacting in normal, predictable ways for someone who has survived such abuse (1).

Avoiding Retraumatization

Providers must be sensitive to the risk of retraumatizing adult survivors of childhood sexual abuse during health care procedures. The risk of retraumatization is present during such care as many procedures involve touch, are invasive, and are performed by authority figures in positions of control or power. All procedures need to be thoroughly explained in advance, and whenever possible the patient should be allowed to suggest ways that the procedure can be done to lessen her fear. This may mean allowing friends or family members to be present (9).

Pelvic, rectal, oropharyngeal, and breast exams may be particularly traumatic for sexual abuse survivors. Techniques suggested to increase the woman's comfort include talking her through the steps, maintaining eye contact, allowing her to control the pace, allowing her to see more (e.g., use of a mirror in pelvic exams), or having her help during her exam (i.e., putting her hand over the provider's to guide the exam) (6).

Conclusion

Long-term effects of childhood sexual abuse are varied, complex, and often devastating for survivors. The abuse frequently results in the formation of psychological, physical, and behavioral symptoms. Such symptoms, although once adaptive survival strategies, may produce deleterious long-term consequences, especially with regard to mental health sequelae. An understanding of and appreciation for the long-term effects of abuse are essential in differential diagnosis, treatment strategies, and patient care. Health care providers who do not educate themselves about the link between childhood sexual abuse and adult survivors' presentations may inadvertently victimize the individual again by providing inadequate medical care.

Special Considerations for Nurse Practitioners and Physician Assistants

Providers must recognize the life-span continuum of violence against women. Damage caused in childhood can be carried into adulthood, affected by factors such as the nature of the traumatic event itself, the woman's age when the trauma occurred, and contextual or environmental factors including the family system, poverty, education, and culture (21).

A woman who is a survivor of childhood abuse may not know who she can trust. Therefore, it is imperative that health care providers show her they are trustworthy, such as by following through on promises and maintaining confidentiality. The woman is vulnerable to revictimization and providers must not (even unknowingly) be participants in this process. Never should a practitioner make disparaging comments about the woman; nor should the woman feel that her symptoms are not being taken seriously. Providers who approach the woman in a patriarchal, insensitive manner, who trivialize symptoms, and prescribe unnecessary or inappropriate treatment may leave the woman feeling betrayed. Especially in a man-dominated system that does not value or understand women's experiences, the woman may be at increased risk of continued abuse (22). Being exposed and/or having unwelcome people present during care may reenact the woman's vulnerability and inability to protect herself (23).

Dyehouse (22) summarized the sources of abuse within the health care system as follows: (1) sexual abuse in the therapeutic relationship, (2) pathologizing of feminine characteristics such as nurturing and supporting behaviors by labeling them as codependency behaviors or devaluing them, (3) family therapy that may not address gender-based power imbalances in the family, (4) diagnostic criteria that may lead females to be more commonly labeled as depressed because they more readily express emotional pain and discomfort, (5) surgical abuse including overuse of hysterectomy, cesarean section, and mastectomies, and (6) chemical abuse evidenced by overprescription of tranquilizers and sedatives and indiscriminate use of insufficiently tested drugs.

The gynecologic examination, in particular, places women in positions of vulnerability because of the lithotomy position, unseen manipulation by someone who may be a relative stranger, and the insertion of objects into body openings. Feelings of powerlessness, violation, and betrayal may be evoked. Whether or not a woman has revealed past abuse, the provider can assist her to have a sense of control during the examination. Information about the purpose of procedures should be shared and the woman asked how she feels about them. If a pelvic examination is difficult, the examiner should stop, acknowledge the difficulty, and ask the woman whether to continue. Offering the woman an option of rescheduling gives her control in the situation (24).

Providers can increase a woman's comfort and sense of control by asking her how they can adapt their practice to meet her needs. However, providers who have not screened for childhood sexual abuse may not understand the woman's responses during care. Avoidance of screening can be caused by a fear of provoking emotions that the provider cannot manage or a fear of bringing the provider's own past abuse into the present situation (21, 23). In addition, abuse can provoke deep emotions in providers who may not have access to structured support for processing their feelings. If they do not recognize and take their own feelings seriously, they may react with impatience, irritation, and anger toward clients. Caregiving cannot be a detached process; the relationship between provider and client is a part of the healing process (24).

References

1. Hendricks-Matthews MK. Recognition of sexual abuse. J Am Board Fam Pract 1993;6:511–513.
2. Sgroi S. Handbook of Clinical Intervention in Child Sexual Abuse. Cambridge, MA: Lexington Books, 1982.
3. Wahlen SD. Adult survivors of childhood sexual abuse. In: Hendricks-Matthews MK, ed. Violence Education: Toward a Solution. Kansas City, MO: Society of Teachers of Family Medicine, 1992: 89–102.
4. Walker EA, Torkelson N, Katon WJ, Koss MP. The prevalence rate of sexual trauma in a primary care clinic. J Am Board Fam Pract 1993;6:465–471.
5. National Victims Center. Rape in America: A Report to the Nation. Washington, DC: National Victims Center, 1992.
6. Goldman L, Hendricks-Matthews MK, Horan D, Kaplan S, Warshaw C. Mental Health Sequelae of Family Violence. Chicago: American Medical Association, in press (1995).
7. Summit R. The child sexual abuse accommodation syndrome. Child Abuse Negl 1983; 7:177–193.
8. Bala M. Caring for adult survivors of child sexual abuse: issues for family physicians. Can Fam Phys 1994;40:925–931.
9. Courtois CA. Adult survivors of sexual abuse. In: Elliott BA, Halverson KC, Hendricks-Matthews MK, eds. Family Violence and Abusive Relationships. Philadelphia: WB Saunders, 1993:433–446.
10. Briere JN, Elliott DM. Immediate and long-term impacts of child sexual abuse. The Future of Children 1994;4:54–69.
11. Anderson G, Yasenik L, Ross C. Dissociative experiences and disorders among women who identify themselves as sexual abuse survivors. Child Abuse Neglect 1993;17:677–686.
12. Hendricks-Matthews MK. Survivors of abuse: health care issues. In: Elliott BA, Halverson KC, Hendricks-Matthews MK, eds. Family Violence and Abusive Relationships. Philadelphia: WB Saunders, 1993:391–406.
13. Cole PM, Putnam FW. Effect of incest on self and social functioning: a developmental psychopathology perspective. J Consult Clin Psychol 1992;60:174–183.
14. Putnam FW. Disturbances of "self" in victims of childhood sexual abuse. In: Kluft RP, ed. Incest-Related Syndromes of Adult Psychopathology, Washington, DC: American Psychiatric Press, 1990:113–131.
15. Moscarello R. Victims of violence: aspects of the 'victim-to-patient' process in women. Can J Psychiatry 1992;37:497–502.
16. Rieker PP, Carmen EH. The victim-to-patient process: the disconfirmation and transformation of abuse. Am J Orthopsychiatry 1986;56:360–370.
17. Randal J. The legacy of abuse: how it contributes to illness. SAMHSA News 1994;2:8–9.
18. Council on Scientific Affairs. Violence against women: relevance for medical practitioners. JAMA 1992;267:3184–3189.
19. Holz KA. A practical approach to clients who are survivors of childhood sexual abuse. J Nurse Midwifery 1994;39:13–18.
20. Matsakis A. I Can't Get Over It: A Handbook For Trauma Survivors. Oakland, CA: New Harbinger, 1992.
21. Mackey TF. A psychological model for analysis of outcomes related to trauma. In: Sampselle CM, ed. Violence Against Women. New York: Hemisphere, 1992:45–68.
22. Dyehouse JM. Abuse of women in the health care system. In: Sampselle CM, ed. Violence Against Women. New York: Hemisphere, 1992:219–234.
23. Seng JS, Petersen BA. Incorporating routine screening for history of childhood sexual abuse into well-woman and maternity care. J Nurse Mid wifery 1995; 40:26–30.
24. Chalfen ME. Obstetric-gynecologic care and survivors of childhood sexual abuse. AWHONN's Clin Issues Perinatal Women's Health Nurs 1993; 4:191–195.

10.1

Women's Sexuality: A Paradigm Shift

Beth A. Alexander

Introduction

Classically, men's bodies have been viewed as "the perfect model" and women's bodies were "a weaker reflection," (1) inferior in many respects, including sexual functioning. Freud reinforced this view in his discussions of "immature clitoral and mature vaginal" orgasms, a view accepted by both professionals and lay people for many years. Although Masters and Johnson, in their classic research in the 50s and 60s, documented the embryologic and functional similarities between men and women, the opinion that women are sexually inferior or less important is still pervasive in the culture.

Recent research and writing in the past 20 to 30 years have clarified many issues about female sexuality, opening the doors to improved discussions with women about their goals and expectations for their sexual expression. The following ideas are now included in the understanding of women's sexuality:

- Sexuality includes more than heterosexual intercourse, and involves a wide range of behaviors including fantasy, self-stimulation, noncoital pleasuring, erotic stimuli other than touch, communication about needs and desires, and the ability to define what is wanted and pleasurable in relationships.

- Women generally place emphasis on emotional and physical aspects of a sexual relationship, in addition to orgasmic components.

- Women and men form their ideas of what are sexually appropriate and desirable from many years of "cultural scripting." These scripts are often different for men and women, and form the basis of many of the challenges that women have in sexual relationships. Examples of this scripting include the view that sexually aggressive men are "studs," whereas sexually aggressive women are "whores" (2).

- Women are as complex as men in terms of sexual anatomy, and are capable unlike most men, of multiple and frequent orgasms during a single sexual encounter (1, 3).

- Women who masturbate and can show partners what stimulation they prefer, and those who can initiate sexual activity, are more likely to be satisfied with their sexual relationships.

- Women have the right to physical and sexual relationships that are voluntary, wanted, pleasurable, and never coercive.

As women are freed from previously restrictive views of sexuality, they become better able to define what they would like in terms of their own sexual expression (with or without a partner), better able to learn and explore their own capability for sexual enjoyment, and better able to negotiate with partners what is wanted in a relationship. This way of thinking about sexuality does not propose *one* preferred way of viewing sexual relationships, but a range of possibilities for sexual expression from which women can learn and make choices.

Physiology of Sexual Response in Women

There are several models describing the physiology of sexual functioning. Masters and Johnson described the four-phase model that includes excitement, plateau, orgasm, and resolution (4). Kaplan modified this model by describing a desire phase, arousal phase (excitement and plateau), and orgasm phase in her triphasic model (5). Loulan, in her work on lesbian sexuality, describes a six-phase model including (*a*) willingness, (*b*) desire, (*c*) excitement, (*d*) engorgement, (*e*) orgasm, and (*f*) pleasure (6). Whatever the terms and categorization used to discuss sexual response, the bodily changes that occur with sexual interaction are well described and similar across the various models. Table 10.1.1 summarizes the physiologic changes that occur with sexual arousal, along with the symptoms a woman may present with when each phase of the sexual response cycle is adversely affected.

Sexual Concerns through the Life Cycle

During the Time of Fertility

A woman may spend a considerable portion of her life trying to or trying not to get pregnant. Either situation may influence her sexual needs and responsiveness.

For the woman desiring contraception, different methods of contraception definitely may affect sexual arousal. A woman who does not want to get pregnant and who does not use a contraception method, or is too insecure to discuss it with her partner, may have significant problems enjoying and responding to sexual stimuli. Hormonal contraception, OCPs, or injectable contraception have been reported to affect libido positively and negatively, although most women find no effect on desire or performance. Some women find im-

Table 10.1.1. Sexual Response Phases in Women

Phase of the Response Cycle	Physiologic/Psychologic Changes	Presenting Symptoms when Affected
Willingness (described by Loulan)	An openness or receptivity to sexual stimulation	Woman may describe actively avoiding the possibility of sexual arousal
Desire (Kaplan)	Active awareness that sexual stimulation is wanted, affected by a variety of stimuli (mediated in the brain)	Lack of desire when appropriate stimuli are available; disinterest in sexually erotic triggers
Arousal (Masters and Johnson, Kaplan)	Vascular engorgement of genital tissues, resulting in vaginal lubrication, swelling of tissues, skin flush over chest, and increased muscular tension (mediated by parasympathetic nervous system)	Lack of lubrication, failure to become aroused, even though sexual interaction is desired
Orgasm	0.8 sec contractions of the pubococcygeal muscles, resulting in intensely pleasurable sexual release (mediated by the sympathetic nervous system)	Failure to reach orgasm with the kind of stimulation given

provement in their sexual life knowing pregnancy is unlikely. Similarly, women who have had tubal ligation or other forms of sterilization report an improvement in sexual relations once the fear of pregnancy is removed. Women who use barrier contraception and fear failure, STDs, and/or pregnancy can find that the fears intrude on sexual desire and enjoyment. Some forms of contraception such as creams and gels may add to the sensual pleasure of the woman, or decrease it because of lack of spontaneity and messiness. The couple can use the application of condoms, diaphragms, and vaginal suppositories in foreplay and in increasing sensual communication.

For women who are desiring pregnancy, especially those with infertility problems, the pressure and need to time intercourse may intrude or interfere with pleasure and communication. Sexual relationships may become a chore or a job. Providers should urge the woman and the couple to discuss their feelings with each other.

During Pregnancy

Relationships between the woman and her partner during pregnancy are often altered. The woman can have increased intimacy or ambivalence about sexual contact. The commonest change in sexual interest among pregnant women is decreased desire in the first and third trimesters, caused by nausea and more discomfort from size. In the second trimester, there is usually increased desire when women feel good. Orgasm may be triggered more easily during pregnancy because of increased vascular flow to genital tissue, particularly clitoral erectile tissues.

Women can safely have intercourse and enjoy sexual stimulation during pregnancy. As the pregnant woman gets larger, or if she gets short of breath lying flat, she may find different positions more comfortable, particularly side-to-side or woman superior. Nonpenetrative sexual contact may be more comfortable. Vaginal penetration is only contraindicated in pregnancy if the woman is at risk for premature labor, has had premature labor in this pregnancy, or has a placenta previa.

Motherhood

Being a mother allows little privacy and little rest, both necessary for sexual enjoyment. Fear of another pregnancy may also impinge on desire and response. When surveyed, most mothers of small children said they fantasized more about sleeping than sex.

The provider should encourage the couple to find private time to continue their sexual relationship. Adequate contraception and time to sleep will help.

Gynecological Disease or Illness

Acquiring a STD or developing vaginal, cervical, or endometrial disease influences a woman's sexuality. If she acquires a STD, the woman usually expresses anger toward her partner and resists sexual relations in general. Women who had cervical intraepithelial neoplasia requiring laser therapy expressed a significant decrease in sexual desire, responsiveness, and interest in sexual relations, and increased anger toward their partner.

Single Women

Whether single because of choice or loss of a partner, the single heterosexual woman faces different challenges in sexual relationships today with the threat of STDs and AIDS. The provider can review STD prevention and contraceptive options (7). The provider should not take it for granted that the woman is sexually active, that she is celibate, or that she is sexually active with men, but should actively listen and give information as needed.

Older Women

As women age, the most notable changes in sexual response are those that reflect decreased androgen production, affecting libido, and decreased estrogen production, affecting vaginal lubrication. Additionally, the vascular changes that occur in arousal and the intensity of the muscular contractions with orgasm are diminished moderately after the age 55 to 60 years. However, most women can fully express their sexuality well into old age. Older women's needs and desire for sexual expressions are as varied as the number of older women (see Chapters 22 and 23).

Sexual History Screening

During screening exams, it is important to ask routinely about a woman's sexual functioning. Many women still believe that it is "normal" for men to enjoy sex more than women do and to have more need for sexual contact. Few women have had the opportunity to discuss what they need and want in terms of sexual satisfaction, nor do they often know how to go about changing sexual relationships so that they are more satisfying. Thus, taking the opportunity to ask a few screening questions about sexual functioning is important, if only to send a message that the subject is important and is a legitimate topic of concern in the health care setting.

When asked "Do you have any concerns about sexual functioning?", most women will respond negatively. This question can then be followed up with a comment such as, "I assume this means you are satisfied with the frequency of sexual contact, your ability to have orgasms, and your ability to communicate with your partner about sexual issues." This statement often clarifies what many women might hope to expect from a good sexual relationship, and often opens the door for more conversation. If the screening questions do not elicit concerns, then the topic can be nicely closed by a statement such as, "This is a common concern for many women at some time in their adult lives, and one that I hope you will feel free to raise if you have questions." In this way, the permission for sexuality to be an appropriate health concern is established. The yield for this brief screening conversation may occur many visits later, when an issue arises for the women.

Special Screening Concerns

STD Risk Assessment

Taking a sexual history includes inquiries about STD risk (see Chapter 11.1). Often missing in these risk assessment protocols is an exploration of whether a woman knows how to raise the subject of STD risk with a potential partner, and whether she is comfortable obtaining specific information about risk to her health and insisting on testing for STDs and appropriate condom use. This conversation may be particularly important for those women who are likely to encounter the greatest risks—those who are young, those who have had many sexual partners, and those who do not believe their lives are worth protecting. As Harriet Lerner notes, women historically have serviced others at the expense of self (8). This pattern is particularly persistent in sexual relationships in which the exposure to STDs is possible or likely. This may be partially the reason the rates of HIV infection for women are increasing faster than for any other population subgroup. Thus, a conversation with women patients about how they would go about protecting themselves is as critical as the assessment of STD risk.

Populations that Are Ignored/Presumed to be Nonsexual

In discussions about sexuality, providers often presume that older women, women with disfiguring body changes, and women with cognitive or emotional disability are not sexual. Most often, it is discomfort on the part of the provider or lack of knowledge about how to raise sexual issues with populations with spe-

cial needs that limits the conversation. Thus, in screening exams with these women, it is important to ask directly whether there are any concerns related to sexuality or sexual functioning and then follow the patient's lead. Ideally, with women who face body-altering surgery, particularly mastectomy and gynecological surgery, this conversation should arise both before and after the surgery, with the woman and with the couple together. Similarly, when talking to women who are aging, it is important to preemptively discuss the changes that may occur in sexual functioning with age, rather than presume knowledge or lack of interest.

Issues Related to Sexual Orientation

Providers also should not presume heterosexual orientation, but simply should ask whether a woman's partner or partners, is a man, woman, or both. Women who claim a lesbian identity may be hesitant to let a provider know this until they are sure of acceptance, respect, and continuing good health care. It is also appropriate and sometimes important to lesbian patients to discuss what will be recorded in the chart about their sexual orientation before data are entered, because this information has sometimes been used in discriminatory ways against this population. Sexual issues with lesbian patients are similar to those encountered by heterosexual patients. However, decisions about whether to have children or decisions related to openness about sexual orientation often can be stressful and may affect health. It is also important to know whether the woman wishes to have another individual, such as a partner, involved in health care discussions and decisions, including advance directives.

Sexual History

Women who have concerns about sexual functioning often prefer initially to discuss these issues with their primary care provider. The diagnostic interview for sexual concerns should help the provider and woman understand the specific nature of the problem, identify the woman's goals for improved sexual functioning, and outline options that meet the needs of the woman and consider her view of the problem. Common causes of difficulties in sexual functioning in relationships include the following:

- Informational: lack of adequate information or misinformation about sexuality of self or partner.
- Communication: inability to communicate with a partner about one's needs and desires in sexual interaction.
- Relationship: difficulties in a relationship that make sexual interaction unwanted, unhealthy, or not pleasurable.
- Physical: illness or medication that impairs a person's normal physiologic sexual response.
- Psychiatric: psychiatric illness that impairs a woman's ability to enter into a mutually enjoyable sexual relationship.
- Life stress: conditions in one's environment, including poverty, fatigue, and overwork, that make sexual interaction and pleasure a low priority (often appropriately) at the time; however, the lack of sexual interaction is problematic by either the woman or a partner.

Table 10.1.2 lists some issues that a provider should consider when taking a history of a specific sexual concern, along with their diagnostic significance.

Common Sexual Concerns of Women

Lack of Desire

This is probably the most common sexual concern that women bring to primary care providers. Libido is controlled by a complex set of neurohormonal triggers in the brain, but is mediated primarily by androgens in both men and women. Androgens are produced in the adrenal glands and the ovaries in women. Following either surgical or natural menopause, women often experience a decline in libido. It is appropriate in either situation to consider a small amount of testosterone, besides estrogen, to help symptoms of decreased libido not obviously caused by other factors.

With this concern, often the presenting request is for a "check on hormones" during a routine gynecologic exam. This query should prompt the provider to ask about sexual functioning. When this issue is raised, it is important to learn whether it is a concern of the woman, or whether it is primarily a concern of her partner. There can be normal variability and difference in libido, both over time and between two people. Defining libido as "deficient" is relative and needs to be clarified specifically.

The most important diagnostic issues are the assessment of the total health of the relationship, a diagnostic screen for depression, and a screen for chronic stress. Most cases of decreased or absent libido are not caused by an absence of libido but by a suppression of erotic input. This suppression may be a logical adaptation to an unhealthy relationship, chronic unresolved anger, fatigue, stress, or overwhelming life circumstances. When depressed libido is an adaptation to factors such as these, the primary approach should be dealing with the causative agent, rather than labeling the woman with a diagnosis of a sexual problem.

Decreased drive can also be caused by drug and alcohol abuse, severe anxiety disorders, and long-standing psychiatric problems that prevent a woman from allowing herself intimacy on any level. Phobic avoidance of sexual contact usually has its etiology in previous, perhaps repressed, sexual or emotional traumatic experiences. When these causative agents are discovered, it is important not to attempt solutions through sexual therapy but to address the underlying causes.

Generally, decreased desire develops over a period and is one of the more difficult sexual complaints to treat. It requires a skilled thera-

Table 10.1.2. Issues and Their Relevance to Consider in Sexual History

Issue or Question	Relevance for Diagnosis or Treatment
What does the woman or couple see as the problem?	Important to have the patient's definition of the problem guide plans for therapy, rather than fixed definition of normal or abnormal functioning
What happens in a typical sexual encounter? (in detail)	Allows clinician to make the best diagnosis based on patient's description
What phase of the sexual response cycle is affected?	May help in pointing to relationship, organic, or emotional cause
Is the problem primarily organic or primarily psychogenic?	Directs how much lab and physical evaluation should be done
Is the onset gradual or sudden?	Gradual onset more likely to have organic etiology; sudden onset more likely to have life cause or relationship etiology
Has the problem always been present?	Consider developmental factors, "sexual scripting" or abuse
Are there concerns about sexual orientation?	Needs to be clarified before sexual therapy initiated
Is the problem global or person specific?	Global is usually organic, or deep seated psychogenic, while person specific symptoms are generally non-organic, and relational in etiology
Are there drugs, alcohol or medication causes that might affect the phase of sexual response affected?	Alcohol is the most commonly missed issue
What is the general health of the relationship? (communication, conflict resolution)	If the relationship is troubled, sexual difficulties are expected, and the focus of treatment should be on the relationship
Is the woman comfortable with masturbation?	This is often a cornerstone of treatment for arousal and orgasmic concerns, and it is important to know if this is possible
What would the woman consider to be helpful?	Important to know what "successful" resolution entails to make treatment plans

pist, often one with marital/relationship training as a primary focus. Only in the case in which decreased libido can be historically directly traced to surgical or natural menopause can hormonal therapy be curative (Table 10.1.3).

Helping Couples Communicate

Good communication within a relationship is essential for satisfaction with sexual relationship. Sexual relationships are a form of communication. Yet many women and many couples have difficulty discussing sex and communicating their needs, desires, and dislikes. A provider

should discuss with the woman how she and her partner communicate about sexual issues. If skills need to be developed, either the provider can offer bibliotherapy, work with the couple in a primary care setting, or refer them to a skilled therapist or couples' workshops.

Problems with Arousal and Orgasmic Dysfunction

The definition of orgasmic dysfunction should be provided by the patient. It is dependent on whether the woman is satisfied with her ability to reach orgasm with the stimulation she re-

Table 10.1.3. Common Causes of Sexual Dysfunction by Phase

Phase	Common Illness	Common Medications that Cause Dysfunction	Common Psychological/ Life Stressors
Willingness	Chronic serious illness	Probably none	Previous sexual trauma, chronic anger in relationship
Desire phase	Conditions that impair testosterone production, oophorectomy being the most common; pituitary or adrenal disease; CNS disease	Antipsychotic drugs; antianxiety drugs; progestins; cimetidine; narcotics; tricyclic antidepressants; betablockers	Depression; anger or conflict in relationship; chronic stress; fatigue; traumatic stress involving sexual abuse; negative body self-image
Arousal phase	Vascular disease; inadequate estrogen levels; diabetes; alcoholism	Beta blockers, thiazides; centrally acting antihypertensives; ACE inhibitors; anticholinergic drugs, esp. antihistamines	Inability to abandon self to physical pleasuring, and maintain focus on erotic sensations; inadequate stimulation; lack of knowledge about body
Orgasm phase	Advanced diabetes; advanced vascular disease; chronic debilitating illness	Narcotics; antianxiety drugs; sedatives; alcohol; tricyclic antidepressants; trazadone	Inadequate stimulation; lack of knowledge about stimulation needed; fear of loss of control; self-observation inhibiting erotic focus

Data from Kaplan HS. The New Sex Therapy. New York: Bruner/Mazel, 1974; Kaplan HS. Disorders of Sexual Desire. New York: Bruner/Mazel 1979; Kaplan HS. Evaluation of Sexual Disorders. New York: Bruner/Mazel 1979; Alexander EA, Allison AL. Sexuality in older adults. In: Reichel W. ed. Care of Elderly: Clinical Aspects of Aging, 4th ed. Baltimore: Williams & Wilkins, 1995;540–46; Halvorsen JG, Metz ME. Sexual dysfunction, part 1: classification, etiology, and pathogenesis. J Am Board Fam Pract 1992;5:51–61.

ceives. One cultural "script" that many women accept is that they should be orgasmic with the thrusting of intercourse alone. Usually, women need more clitoral stimulation than is provided with penetration only, and it is the minority of women who reach orgasm without additional clitoral stimulation.

Sometimes when women are concerned about orgasmic ability, simply providing information and education is the appropriate intervention. However, women may wish to expand their ability to have orgasms under different conditions, and may wish to explore the possibility of becoming multiply orgasmic. Other women may still need to learn the conditions

necessary for them to have orgasms at all, and will need to start at a different point.

The principles of treatment for women who wish to expand their orgasmic capacity are straightforward, and are as follows:

- Clear definition of what the woman would like to achieve.
- Education, if needed, about one's body, specifically genital anatomy.
- Self-pleasuring to explore the kinds of stimulation that are most arousing and pleasurable, including the use of vibrators, use of sexual fantasy, and visual erotic material.

- Awareness of how one's erotic focus gets interrupted in arousal and can be maintained, e.g., fantasy.
- Transfer of learned skills and information to partner, with development of communication skills, if necessary.
- Use of sensate focus exercises to expand couple's awareness of what is erotic and pleasurable (see Table 10.1.4).
- Reinforcement of permission to be selfish in sexual pleasuring, and the principle of taking turns in giving and receiving pleasure.

When women have concerns about orgasmic functioning, it is important to make sure that the dysfunction is not secondary to another sexual problem, particularly inhibited desire or difficulty in arousal secondary to lack of erotic focus. Careful history can separate these, although arousal problems are generally accompanied by problems in orgasm, and in some sense are part of a continuum. Asking the question, "What goes on in your head while you are making love?" generally can uncover problems with erotic focus that interfere with orgastic reflex.

Table 10.1.4. Bibliotherapy Resources for Women with Concerns about Sexuality

Barbach L. For Yourself: The Fulfillment of Female Sexuality. New York: New American Library, 1975.

Butler R. Love and Sex after Sixty. New York: Harper and Row, 1988.

Covington S. Awakening Your Sexuality. New York: HarperCollins. 1991.

Lopiccolo L, Lopiccolo J, Heiman J. Becoming Orgasmic: A Sexual Growth Program for Women. New York: Prentice-Hall, 1986.

Zilbergeld B. The New Male Sexuality. New York: Bantam, 1993.

Disorders of Sexual Pain

The most common problems involving sexual pain for women involve inadequate lubrication, infection, or vaginismus. When a woman reports discomfort during sexual activity, the provider should assess the location of the discomfort, the timing of its occurrence during sexual interaction, and whether the woman is currently, or has ever been, orgasmic. Pain with sexual activity is the one sexual complaint that mandates a careful physical examination. Dyspareunia can be caused by infections, inadequate estrogen support, inadequate stimulation causing inadequate lubrication, tissue alteration from surgery or childbirth, and by involuntary spasm of the pubococcygeal muscle (vaginismus).

Pelvic inflammatory disease typically causes pain with intercourse that is described by the woman as being "deep" in her pelvis. Candida infections, inadequate estrogen support, inadequate lubrication from insufficient stimulation, and vaginismus are experienced as pain near the introitus.

Vaginal pain caused by inadequate lubrication during intercourse can be secondary either to inadequate estrogen support from surgical or natural menopause, or to inadequate stimulation during sexual arousal. A maturation index, history, and examination of the vaginal mucosa can easily separate these two causative factors. When women have pain secondary to inadequate stimulation, they are rarely orgasmic. However, this is not true when vaginal irritation is caused by estrogen deficiency.

Vaginismus is the involuntary spasm or contraction of the pubococcygeal muscle when a women either anticipates or experiences attempted entry of the vagina by either a speculum or penis. This diagnosis should be suspected when pelvic exam is impossible on young women, or when they report the inability to consummate a marriage. Precursors of this condition are often traumatic sexual experiences, or occasionally painful gynecologic examinations. Sometimes there is no known history of trauma; the trauma may be repressed or dissociated. A history of repressive and negative messages about sexuality, causing a phobic reaction to any anticipated sexual contact, may be coincident with this diagnosis.

Although therapy generally helps adult women understand the impact of previous traumatic sexual experiences, this psychotherapy is not usually necessary for treatment of vaginismus. When there is a partner involved, it is critical for that person to understand that the muscle spasm of vaginismus is not under conscious control and is not a reflection on the relationship or on the woman's feelings about her partner. It also is important that continued attempts at intercourse be stopped, as this reinforces the reflexive response.

Treatment of vaginismus can be done readily and involves teaching the woman how to relax her pubococcygeal muscles, allowing entry of a single finger, with progressive entry of two to three fingers. The control is assumed by the patient and then transferred to a partner. Once she easily allows entry of her own fingers, then she can allow her partner's fingers into the vagina. It may be helpful to have the woman attempt a mild valsalva when entry of finger is initiated, as it is impossible to "bear down" and contract the pubococcygeal muscle simultaneously. Decisions about psychotherapy should be supported, if there is a history of sexual trauma, but should remain with the woman and should not be tied to treatment of this disorder. Generally, four to five sessions with progressive homework exercises produces a cure. If no progress is made, one should suspect deeper psychological issues or relationship problems as an underlying cause.

Bibliotherapy is often helpful and effective for women who want to explore and expand orgasmic responsiveness, for those women who cannot afford therapy, or for women trying to understand the impact of cultural messages on their sexual development. Helpful resources are listed in Table 10.1.4.

Conclusion

The most important message is that each woman is an individual and her needs and expectations of her sexual relationship are particular to her situations. The provider must be willing to ask, listen, and offer concern and interest, without judgements. Many problems can be improved by education, counseling, and simple and effective treatment.

Special Considerations for Nurse Practitioners and Physician Assistants

Most women view sexuality as a total body experience that cannot be separated from other parts of their life. However, no two women will experience sexuality alike, nor will any one woman experience it the same way throughout her life (9). Yet, despite the importance of sexuality to a woman, health care providers may avoid sexual health assessment, thus fostering beliefs that the subject is taboo. They may avoid discussing sexuality because of their own discomfort, presumptions that the woman will find questions intrusive or insulting, beliefs that sexuality is not relevant to the woman's current health problem, and fears that the woman may raise concerns that the clinician cannot deal with (10).

All women must be given opportunities to express concerns and ask questions about their sexuality. Practitioners must never assume that certain women, such as nuns and disabled or obese women, have no sexual feelings or needs (9). Similarly, older women who do not have a partner or whose partner is disabled still have needs for touch, closeness, and support that they may want to discuss (11, 12). Assumptions about heterosexuality must be avoided. Because of providers' negative attitudes about lesbians, discomfort about treating them, and lesbians' fears about disclosure, providers often miss clues about a woman's lifestyles and sexuality. In addition, providers may lack knowledge regarding lesbian women and their potential risks (or lack of risks) related to STDs, vaginitis, cervical dysplasia, or breast problems (13). Setting aside these personal biases must be a conscious act and requires practice (10).

Body image is an important aspect of sexuality, and providers should ascertain how a woman feels about her body. If a disability has caused a body alteration or requires the use of an assistive device, a woman may view her body as a problem and source of anxiety. Changes in physical appearance caused by surgery, arthritis, and other problems can also alter body image. Illnesses, both chronic and acute, as well as their medical and surgical treatments, can affect a woman's sexuality because of problems such as pain, fatigue, stress, and fear (9). Practitioners should be aware that a woman's complaints about a medical problem may mask sexual concerns.

In order to obtain a sexual history, providers must choose a private, comfortable location and assure the woman of confidentiality. Obtaining the history while the women is fully clothed will help increase her comfort level. A thorough history will require time and might be completed over several meetings. Generally, initial questions are less threatening (e.g., obstetric or menstrual history), with more sensitive topics and current sexual practices asked about later. If terminology used by either the provider or the woman is not clearly understood, they should feel comfortable asking for clarification. "Why" questions should be avoided because

they can connote disapproval or moralizing (10).

Use of an organized history format can provide structure and increase the provider's comfort. However, flexibility is essential and the interview must be adjusted according to the woman's needs. If the woman appears uncomfortable during the assessment, the provider can acknowledge the feelings and reflect them back to the woman (10).

Often, after a brief screening history (as discussed earlier), a sexual problem history is obtained to collect information on a woman's specific concern. In-depth histories to elicit extensive information about emotions, sexual practices, and self-concept take several hours and should be conducted by professionals with specific training in sexual counseling or therapy. Providers should not feel inadequate if they cannot address all sexual issues that are raised. They may have to search for answers, consult with other professionals, or make appropriate referrals to help women. What is most important is that the issue of sexuality is not ignored (10).

Providers who care for women must be comfortable with their own sexuality if they are to be comfortable discussing it with women. They must be willing to introduce the topic of sexuality and not assume that the woman will bring up the subject if there is a problem. In addition, providers should have current knowledge about the effects of illnesses and treatments on sexuality and frankly discuss the possible effects of illnesses or treatments on sexual behavior (9, 12).

References

1. Chalker R. Updating the model of female sexuality. SIECUS 1994 June/July;22:1–6.
2. McCormick N. Sexual Salvation: Affirming Women's Sexual Rights and Pleasures. Westport, CN: Praeger, 1994:15–29.
3. Darling CA, Davidson JK, Jennings DA. The female sexual response revisited: understanding the multi-

orgasmic experiences in women. Arch Sex Behav 1991;20:535.

4. Masters WH, Johnson VE. Human Sexual Response. Boston: Little, Brown and Co, 1966.

5. Kaplan HS. The New Sex Therapy. New York: Bruner/Mazel, 1981.

6. Loulan J. Lesbian Sex. San Francisco: Spinsters Ink, 1984:43–45.

7. Smith T. Adult sexual behavior in 1989: number of partners, frequency, and risk. Paper presented at the annual meeting of the American Association for the Advancement of Science, New Orleans, LA: February 1990.

8. Lerner H. Dance of Intimacy. New York: Harper and Row, 1989.

9. Bernhard LA. Sexuality in women's lives. In: Fogel CI, Woods NF, eds. Women's Health Care. Thousand Oaks, CA: Sage, 1995:475–495.

10. MacLauren A. Primary care for women: comprehensive sexual health assessment. J Nurse Mid Wifery 1995;40:104–119.

11. Fogel CI. Women and sexuality. In: Youngkin EQ, Davis MS, eds. Women's Health, Norwalk, Appleton & Lange, 1994:61–74.

12. Morrison-Beedy D, Robbins L. Sexual assessment and the aging female. Nurse Pract 1989;14: 35–45.

13. Roberts SJ, Sorensen L. Lesbian health care: a review and recommendations for health promotion in primary care settings. Nurse Pract 1995;20:42–47.

10.2

Contraception

Elizabeth N. Stifel and Janice Anderson

Introduction

Contraception, or birth control, affects life decisions individuals make about sexual intimacy, reproduction, and family circumstances; these are among the most basic human concerns. Contraception can allow a woman the freedom to determine when and if she will have children, and it has major implications on how she will live her life. Contraceptive choices are inextricably intertwined with how a woman feels about herself, her sexuality, and her relationships. Its failure always results in significant consequences for the woman and often for her partner.

Making decisions about contraception is a complex process. In an era of safer and more efficacious contraception, 50 to 60% of all pregnancies in this country are unplanned (1, 2). The challenge to a provider is to understand the woman's needs and desires regarding birth control, and to discuss them with her in a way that enables her to choose a method she can use with confidence, with regularity, and with as little ambivalence as possible. By doing this, the provider empowers the woman to make decisions about birth control. This allows her to have rewarding relationships and to be in final control of her life choices.

This chapter discusses the interaction between women and providers as they consider the issue of contraception; their discussion may or may not include actual family planning. In addition, the chapter includes discussions of women issues, provider issues, the decision-making process, and information about available methods of birth control. It recognizes that there is no perfect birth control method—one that is 100% effective with no risks. This chapter provides a way to think about pregnancy prevention, but it is not an exhaustive discussion of methods of contraception. There are excellent, frequently updated references available to provide that information. Two commonly used reference materials are *Contraceptive Technology*, by Hatcher and his colleagues (3), and *Managing Contraceptive Pill Patients*, by Dickey (4).

Over half of all pregnancies in the United States are unplanned. Many factors probably contribute to this, but many women are poorly informed about the efficacy and health risks of contraception, or are dissatisfied or uncomfortable with available methods (5, 6). For a woman to appropriately decide to use a method of birth control requires the health care provider's commitment to a well-defined process. This process includes a careful history, a physical, and a discussion with the woman to consider which kind of birth control will be most acceptable to her. The discussion must attend to both the woman's expressed needs and the complex issue of patient education,

given the inaccurate knowledge many women apparently have.

Woman-Centered Issues

History

The patient history needed for a discussion of contraception should be many-faceted. The provider should obtain the history with unconditional positive regard, openly and nonjudgmentally, by listening actively to the woman. The history should include the following:

1. Medical history: a careful history of past and current medical problems is necessary if good recommendations are to be made.
2. History of contraceptive use: this includes identifying any methods used in the past and their success or failure and what contributed to either. Did the woman ever become pregnant on any contraceptive method? Did she stop one, and if so, why?
3. The woman's attitude toward contraception: how does the woman feel about preventing pregnancy? It is important to include issues such as ambivalence about preventing pregnancy, anger about the responsibility she must take, and deeply held religious beliefs.
4. Sexual behavior: if the woman has more than one partner or if her partner is not now or has not in the past been monoga—mous, because the method of contraception should also take sexually transmitted disease (STD) prevention into consideration. Women with regular frequent sexual behaviors may require or do better with some forms of contraception, whereas women with irregular or infrequent sexual relations can use other forms of contraception. For example, a monogamous long-married couple will do better with natural family planning than a single teenager with multiple sexual partners.

5. Woman's understanding of her own sexuality and feelings about her body: many diverse factors can be included in this category. For example, there is the woman who may find sexual response less satisfying if contraception is used, or the woman who has difficulty with and will not tolerate the irregular bleeding progestin-only methods may produce. There is also some reason to believe that women who are unhappy with sexual intimacy are less effective contraceptors (7). A woman's understanding of contraceptive use, its effect on her and on sexual functioning is important to her choice of method.

6. Ability to make choices: can the woman evaluate available choices? Barriers to understanding may include language, mental challenge, reading difficulty, and major psychiatric illnesses.

7. Beliefs about contraception: to provide useful information, it is critical to know what the woman believes about contraception, whether the information is accurate or not. It is useful to place contraceptive use in context with other life events, including pregnancy, to appreciate the relative risks associated with each of them (see Table 10.2.1). No form of contraception carries greater risk than pregnancy. A recent study suggests that many women feel contraceptives are far less effective and have more risks than is actually shown (Table 10.2.2) (8).

8. A woman's partner: her partner's feelings about pregnancy prevention will make some alternatives more desirable than others. These feelings may include (a) whether he agrees with the decision to prevent conception, (b) his reactions to various methods of contraception, and (c) last, but certainly not least, his willingness to participate in the contraceptive process.

9. Cost and accessibility: no matter how desirable a method is, if it is cost-prohibitive, it is not available to the woman.

Physical Examination

As with any woman-provider encounter, a careful physical examination with special attention to factors influencing the use of any particular method of birth control is essential. The extent of the exam will obviously be influenced by factors such as the most recent ap-

Table 10.2.1. Relative Voluntary Behaviors Mortality Risk

Activity	Chance of Death in 1 Year
Contraception	
Birth control pills—nonsmoker	1/63,000
Birth control pills—smoker	1/16,000
IUDs	1/100,000
Tubal ligations	1/67,000
Pregnancy	1/11,000
Legal abortion before 9 weeks	1/260,000
Driving a car	1/6000
Power boating	1/6000
Canoeing	1/100,000
Using tampons	1/350,000

Table 10.2.2. Percentage of Women Believing the Failure Rate of Different Forms of Contraception Is Greater than 10%—1993 Data

Form of Contraception	%
Oral contraceptives	41
IUDs	46
Condom	65
Diaphragm	59
Gels/spermicides	68
Implant	24
Injection	27

Data from Murphy P, Kirkman A, Hale RW. A national survey of women's attitudes toward oral contraception and other forms of birth control. Women's Health Issues 1995;5:94–99.

pointment prior to this visit and the goal of that previous appointment. If the woman has not been engaged in regular health maintenance, this is an appropriate time to consider issues such as Pap smears, cultures, immunizations, and other indicated screening measures. It is critical during the actual physical to be alert for clues to problems the woman has not discussed in the history. These may involve matters as diverse as evidence of heart disease, abuse, STDs, or uterine abnormalities.

Provider Issues

One reason women do not seek health care is dissatisfaction with the way that communication with the health care provider is handled (9). Many women report feeling that the provider either does not hear them or talks down to them (10). There are several ways to improve communication and collaboration.

1. Collaboration: in any interaction, the discussion must be centered on the woman. Moving too quickly to a decision about what is the best method of contraception for a given woman runs the risk of providing an objectively good method that the woman will not use and/or will not tell the provider is unacceptable. A slightly less efficacious method, used regularly, is probably more desirable than a never-used, highly efficacious method (11). The process between woman and provider should be one of collaboration and support.

   Women most successfully use health care systems that are collaborative and that tolerate a fair amount of patient autonomy (12). Many women are less likely to use a traditional system and less likely to interact well with it, because it is in such an environment that power struggles occur. Power struggles can lead to such behaviors as denying a woman a prescription for oral contraceptives because she missed

her yearly Pap smear, which is a behavior that can easily result in an unwanted pregnancy.

2. Being informed: providers should know what methods of contraception are available, their benefits, risks, and accessibility, and to be willing to refer if they do not provide a particular choice.

3. Providing a safe environment: women need to feel that they are taken seriously and that the practitioner is respectful of their expressed wishes and comfort (13, 14).

4. Information transfer: people learn in many different ways. It is important to be prepared to meet the needs of the learner, which may mean providing oral explanations, video presentations, hands-on exposure to various methods using models and written information. If written material is used, it should correspond to the reading level of the woman.

5. Symptoms: the provider must hear what symptoms the woman has had with previous choices and accurately understand the effect they may have had on her.

6. Cost: the woman and the clinician need to know the ultimate financial cost of contraception, including the cost of the office visit. The woman should feel free to reject a method because it is prohibitively expensive.

Decision Making

For many (but not all) women, deciding to use contraception requires a basic change in behavior. Prochaska and DiClemente showed that changes in behavior proceed through predictable stages. The first stage is *precontemplation*, in which the need for change is apparent to persons other than the woman; the woman may say she does not want to be pregnant but makes no move to prevent conception. The second stage, *contemplation*, involves considering contraception. It is followed by *preparation*, a move to decide to make the change and to carry out the steps necessary to do so (e.g., making an appointment or gathering information). *Action* refers to actually making the change, such as keeping the appointment and initiating use of a particular method. It may be complicated by *relapse*, a reversion to the unwanted behavior, which may occur at any stage of the process. *Reversion* might mean not taking pills or using condoms. The last stage is *maintenance*, a period that lasts at least 6 months. After that there is a lower risk of stopping the use of the contraceptive method unless there is an active decision to do so (15). The provider's role is one of active listening, clarifying, and providing information and support. Decision making requires tolerance for different values and for behaviors that seem self-defeating. This process and the actual choice of method will vary greatly among individuals and among identified groups of individuals, such as teens, older women, and differently enabled persons.

Whatever the model of decision making, when the choice to use contraception is finally made, an actual assessment of contraceptive options and their appropriateness in the woman's life should have been considered (Table 10.2.3) First, consider those options that are biomedically

Table 10.2.3. Steps in Choosing Contraceptive Method

One	Consider those options that are biomedically available Identify risk factors from the history and physical and eliminating methods that are absolutely contraindicated
Two	Identify factors relating to life style, beliefs, and partners What is acceptable to woman and her partner?
Three	What side effects are tolerable and intolerable?
Four	Of these choices which are more efficacious?
Five	Consider STD protection

available to the woman. This includes identifying risk factors from the history and physical and eliminating methods that are absolutely contraindicated. When this has been accomplished, the factors that were identified in the history relating to lifestyle, beliefs, and partners become the next determinants. An important goal is to identify a method that has the highest acceptability and efficacy for the particular woman. Although the clinician's goal may be to provide the most efficacious method biomedically available, the woman may do much better with a method that is a little less effective, but one that she will use consistently. Finally and importantly, there should be a way for the woman to give feedback about success or problems—via office visit, phone contact, or mail.

Contraceptive Choices Available

Every woman should know the range of contraceptive choices available. This information gives her the ability to make other decisions, gives her backup methods, and allows her to protect herself from STDs. It is equally important for each woman to make an informed choice and sometimes (e.g., Norplant) to sign a consent form (Fig. 10.2.1). Table 10.2.4 provides the relative efficacies of the methods discussed below.

There are two types of error possible with contraception—method and human error. All forms of contraception, except abstinence, have some inherent method error, or failures. Some male condoms break (approximately 3%); there are 1 to 3 pregnancies per 1000 women using oral contraceptives per year even if they are taken perfectly. However, human error is often unavoidable and adds to this rate. Failure to properly use the condom increases its pregnancy rate to 10 to 15 per 100 women per year; missing a pill increases the failure rate to 2 to 3 per 100 women per year. Collaboration, education, and satisfaction will decrease the human error rate.

NATIONAL WOMEN'S HEALTH NETWORK MODEL CONSENT FORM
DEPO-PROVERA

1. I, _____ request injection of Depo-Provera from Dr. _____ and/or
_____ RN/PA.

2. I have been given information on all methods of birth control (including birth control pills, IUDs, Norplant, condoms, diaphragm, caps, spermicides, and sterilization) and have decided that Depo-Provera is the best choice for me at this time. I realize that I may change my mind about what type of birth control I want to use at any time.

3. I am making this decision free of coercion or pressure. Payment for my health care services and/or eligibility for health care services will not be affected if I choose another method or choose not to use any method of birth control.

4. I understand that Depo-Provera is a shot. I understand that the shot cannot be reversed if I change my mind or do not like its effects and that I will have to wait for the drug to wear off, which takes about ten months.

5. I understand that I may have an allergic reaction to Depo-Provera. Allergic reactions are rare, but as with any drug, they may occur.

6. I have been told that Depo-Provera is a highly effective birth control method, and that less than one woman out of every 100 who use Depo-Provera for one year will get pregnant. I understand that if I want to continue using Depo-Provera to prevent pregnancy, I have to return every three months for another shot.

7. I understand that Depo-Provera cannot prevent diseases such as AIDS, syphilis, gonorrhea, herpes, or genital warts. I realize that I need to use a barrier method such as a condom unless I am sexually active with someone who is not engaging in high risk behavior which includes: having sex with other people, using intravenous drugs, or receiving a blood transfusion before 1986.

8. I understand that Depo-Provera has some side effects and that most women gain weight and have irregular bleeding. Some women also experience depression, decreased sex drive, headaches, acne, hair loss and nervousness.

9. I understand that Depo-Provera has been associated with breast cancer in women under 35 years old in some studies, and that Depo-Provera is currently being studied to determine if a report of bone loss is accurate. These possible complications have not been proven to be caused by Depo-Provera.

10. I have been told that some rare, but serious, complications can be caused by Depo-Provera. I will call the office if I have heavy bleeding, severe headaches, depression, frequent urination, or sudden or severe weight gain.

11. I understand that I should not use Depo-Provera if there is any chance that I might be pregnant because of the risk of birth defects and interfering with the growth of the fetus.

12. I understand that no studies have yet shown any harm in children who have been breast fed by women using Depo-Provera. I also realize that Depo-Provera is present in breast milk and is absorbed by babies who breast feed.

13. I have been given an information sheet on Depo-Provera. I have read and discussed it and all my questions have been answered to my satisfaction. If I am unable to read this consent form or information sheet, it has been explained to me fully and my questions have been answered.

14. If I have any questions, I can call _____ at the following phone number: _____ .

Signature: _____ Date: _____

Health Care Provider: _____ Date: _____

If client cannot read this form, name of person who has read it to her and witness:

Translator: _____

Witness: _____

Figure I0.2.I.   Sample consent form for Depo-Provera from the National Women's Health Network.

Table 10.2.4. Efficacy of Different Forms of Contraception

Method	Failure Rate*	
	Ideal Use	Usual Use
No method	85	85
Withdrawal	4	19
Spermicides	6	21
Natural family planning	3	20
Diaphragm	6	18
Condom—male	3	12
Oral contraceptive	0.1–0.5	1–2
Depo-Provera	0.3	0.3
Norplant (6)	0.09	0.09
Female sterilization	0.4	0.4
Male sterilization	0.15	0.15

*Number of pregnancies in 100 women using this method over 1 year (100 woman–years).
Data from Hatcher RA, Trussell J, Stewart F, Stewart GK, Kowal D, Guest F, Cates W, Policar MS. The essentials of contraception: effectiveness, safety, & personal considerations. In: Contraceptive Technology. 16th ed. New York: Irvington, 1994:107–137.

Abstinence

Abstinence is the most effective and safest method of contraception and is a choice that may be respected and supported. It has no method error but has a high human error risk.

Natural Family Planning

This method is a highly effective form of contraception when used by adequately trained and motivated couples, with a failure rate of only 3 to 6%. It was developed in response to a need for birth control that did not depend on any artificial means but on the woman's natural cycle. The first attempt to control fertility in this way was the so-called "rhythm method," based on a woman's past menstrual cycles. Because of the variability in most women's cycles, however, it was almost impossible to accurately predict fertility this way and the method was notoriously ineffective. The fertility awareness methods used now are far more sophisticated and depend on daily observation of cervical mucus and basal body temperature—the symptothermal method of natural family planning.

The method is dependent on the commitment of both partners and can lead to an enhanced relationship with heightened awareness of their mutual sexuality. Other advantages are that it is nonhormonal, that it is an acceptable choice for members of some religious denominations that reject artificial forms of birth control, and it is a way for people who prefer natural approaches to control their fertility. Its major disadvantages include a need for compulsive daily attention to one's biological state. It can add further stress to an already busy couple, because there is a need for partner cooperation, and because it has a failure rate that may not be acceptable (16).

A couple desiring to use this method must train with a "thoroughly trained natural family planning counselor." It is a method that requires support and education (17).

The provider should (1) guide the couple in exploring their motivation to use this method, (2) refer the couple to a natural family planning counselor, (3) teach that this method does not protect against STDs, counseling is, therefore, necessary, and (4) provide information about postcoital contraception (see Chapter 10.3).

Coitus Interruptus

Coitus interruptus is an ancient and commonly used method to control fertility. It has virtually no side effects, is universally available, and has no cost. The man must withdraw his penis from his partner's vagina prior to ejaculation. Therefore, coitus interruptus requires mutual trust and commitment and is, thus, relationship-building. It works best for couples who know and can appreciate each other's sexual responses, and thus this method may not be a good method for teenagers. Fear of failure may, on the other hand, inhibit relaxation and satisfaction. Typical use failure rate is 19%; perfect use failure rate is 4%. Disadvantages include its ineffectiveness when compared to other methods and the fact that it does not protect either partner from STDs.

Patient education is imperative. Although many couples find themselves periodically relying on this method, perhaps for lack of an immediately available alternative, providers seldom recommend it and seldom teach its use well.

The provider should explain the following:

1. Ejaculate must be deposited away from both vagina and labia.
2. Pre-ejaculate may contain sperm, decreasing the effectiveness of the method. The man should urinate and wash the tip of the penis before intercourse. The man should avoid multiple orgasms.
3. Withdrawal may be emotionally difficult as either or both partners may worry about the timing of withdrawal.
4. The man is primarily responsible for this method.
5. This method does not protect against STDs; therefore, counseling is necessary.
6. Postcoital contraception may be necessary (see Chapter 10.3).

Barrier Methods

Male Condom

The male condom is one of the oldest known forms of contraception. It became popular in the 18th century primarily as a prophylactic against STDs and has continued its popularity as people recognize its effectiveness as protection against HIV and other STDs. It is primarily the man's responsibility, but that responsibility may be shared between partners. The male condom prevents conception by trapping ejaculate in a sheath that covers the penis. The condom is most commonly made of latex; it is also manufactured from animal sources, and most recently from a new polymer. The latex version is effective both in preventing pregnancy and STDs, including HIV. Condoms made from animal sources are effective in preventing pregnancy but not in preventing STDs. The new polymer condom has recently been developed for people who have latex allergies. It has the same characteristics as the latex version but may be more fragile (18).

The ideal condom failure rate is approximately 2%, but a more typical rate is 12%. The condom is easily available and requires no provider visit; it is moderately priced and easy to use. Its biggest disadvantage is breakage. In addition, it may be objectionable to either partner because it may lessen sensation and spontaneity because it must be used before intromission, and it requires attention during withdrawal.

The couple should be aware of the following:

1. Efficacy is related to consistency of use.
2. There should be no contact between penis and labia or vagina before the condom is in place.
3. The condom should be put on in such a way that there is approximately a ½-inch space between the end of the penis and the end of the condom. Care should be taken

not to trap air in the dead space because it increases pressure and may cause breakage.

4. The condom may be used with contraceptive foam or jelly, or with a diaphragm or cervical cap, increasing its effectiveness to over 99% and adding extra protection if there is breakage.
5. After intercourse, the ring at the base of the penis should be kept tight to prevent leakage. The penis should be withdrawn while it is still erect.
6. The couple should have information about postcoital contraception (see Chapter 10.3).

Female Condom

With the spread of HIV, women need a method of disease protection and contraception that is easily available and that they control. In response, the female condom was developed in the 1980s. The model available in the United States is a long polyurethane sheath with a ring at each end; one ring fits in the vagina around the cervix and the other is placed at the introitus. It prevents conception by trapping the ejaculate in the sheath.

The female condom is easily available, although at somewhat higher cost than the male version. It has the advantage of being the woman's responsibility. Placement may occur up to 8 hours before use, allowing greater spontaneity; it does not require a provider visit. People have found it both a positive addition to lovemaking and a barrier. It decreases genital contact, which may be a positive feature if STD prevention is needed, but it may decrease pleasure in lovemaking.

The woman should know the following:

1. Her vaginal anatomy so that she can identify her cervix.
2. The condom must be in place before any genital contact occurs.
3. Techniques to prevent spills; the lower end of the condom should be tightly closed before removal.

4. Information about postcoital contraception (see Chapter 10.3).

Diaphragm

The diaphragm was introduced in the early 20th century and was the first form of contraception that gave women the ability to control conception themselves. The diaphragm is a shallow, cup-shaped device made of latex; it has a firm exterior ring. It is used with spermicide and covers the cervix, impeding the passage of sperm into the cervical os, allowing the spermicide maximal interaction with the sperm and preventing fertilization.

The diaphragm is an effective method of contraception. The best failure rate is 6%. In typical use, it is approximately 82% effective. It has a lower failure rate, the longer and more often the woman uses it. It may be inserted up to 6 hours prior to use, thus allowing some degree of spontaneity. It is relatively easy to use, requires little upkeep, does not require frequent office visits, and is particularly acceptable to women who do not want to take medication, who cannot use hormonal methods for medical reasons, or who have infrequent sexual relations.

It requires motivation to use the diaphragm during all sexual activity. It may be disturbing to women who do not feel comfortable touching their bodies and cannot be used in some situations in which the woman's anatomy is not conducive to a good fit. These situations include extreme retroversion of the uterus, prolapse, significant cystocele, and rectocele. Improper fit can lead to pregnancy, vaginal erosion, and UTIs. Because of its failure rate, the diaphragm is not the best method if pregnancy is absolutely unacceptable for either medical or life-situation reasons.

Diaphragms require prescriptions. They come in various sizes. The provider can learn fitting best by practicing under competent supervision. Once the diaphragm is fitted, the woman is asked to practice inserting it while in the office and is then checked by the practitioner. She may be asked to use it for 1 or 2 weeks with a backup method and return to the office for a check of placement.

The woman should know the following:

1. Efficacy is directly related to use.
2. The diaphragm may be inserted up to 6 hours before intercourse and is left in place 6 hours afterwards.
3. If more than one encounter occurs, more jelly is used. The diaphragm is not removed.
4. Placement must be checked with each use.
5. The diaphragm should be washed with mild soap and air dried after each use.
6. Before each use, the diaphragm should be checked for pinholes or other defects.
7. The diaphragm should be replaced every 2 to 3 years. The fit must be checked if there is weight gain or loss of more than 10 lbs.
8. This method does not protect against STDs; therefore, counseling is necessary.
9. She should have information about postcoital contraception (see Chapter 10.3).

Cervical Cap

The cervical cap is similar to the diaphragm in both efficacy and function. It is a latex cap that fits over the cervix and is also used with spermicidal jelly. Its major advantage is that it may be left in place for 48 hours and may not require any additional spermicide if there is more than one encounter.

A concern with its use has been expressed, based on a small group of women who have had abnormal Pap smears within 3 months of initiating use. The numbers are small enough that they are not statistically significant but have led to recommendations that users get more frequent Pap smears (19). This has the disadvantages of both increased cost and investment of time. Other disadvantages include decreased efficacy in parous women, some difficulty inserting, and more anatomical barriers to a good fit.

Cervical caps are fitted by the practitioner. Training should be done by a practitioner expert in the skill. Providers must attend a special course before they can order or prescribe cervical caps.

The woman should know the following:

1. General education for use of the cap is similar to that of the diaphragm.
2. Ideally, the cap should be in place 30 minutes before intercourse to provide good suction.
3. It may be left in place for 48 hours.
4. It should be left in place for 6 hours after intercourse.
5. It may not be necessary to add extra spermicide for each sexual encounter.
6. She may need more frequent Pap smears.
7. This method does not protect against STDs; therefore, counseling is necessary.
8. She needs information about postcoital contraception (see Chapter 10.3).

Foams, Jellies, Film, and Suppositories

Foams, jellies, film, and suppositories are collectively called intravaginal spermicides. They inactivate sperm by destroying its cell membrane. Efficacy is approximately 82% in typical use and approximately 90% in perfect use among nulliparous women. Their efficacy drops in parous women to 74% in typical use and 84% in perfect use.

These spermicides have the advantages of being easily available, easy to use, and reasonable in cost. They do not require provider visits. They are the woman's responsibility but their insertion may be used as part of foreplay.

They have the disadvantage of being needed at the time of, or about 15 to 30 minutes before intercourse, thus decreasing spontaneity. Local irritation or allergic reactions may occur in either partner. Certain anatomical differences such as a septate vagina or significant prolapse obviate their use.

The woman should know the following:

1. They must be used with each encounter.
2. They should be renewed after 1 hour if there are further encounters.
3. She needs to find out how long before intercourse a particular choice needs to be inserted.
4. She needs information about postcoital contraception (see Chapter 10.3).
5. These methods do not protect against STDs; therefore, counseling is necessary.

Intrauterine Device

The intrauterine device was introduced in the United States in the late 1960s. After a period of popularity, it has almost disappeared as a method of birth control because of concerns about infection rates and infertility caused particularly by one kind of IUD. More recently, interest in the IUD has been renewed. Current studies suggest that the newer IUDs, especially the medicated ones, do not have rates of pelvic inflammatory disease (PID), ectopic pregnancy, or resultant infertility as high as previously suspected (20).

The IUD works by interfering with sperm transport to the fallopian tubes and by increasing ovum transport through the tubes. There is no evidence that it is an abortifacient. It has the advantages of being a one-decision method; it is functional for 1 to 8 years, depending on type, and does not require partner participation. It has significant initial cost that may make it unavailable for some women; however, its complete cost is actually quite small when averaged over 8 years.

Its disadvantages include the fact that use is discouraged in women who are not monogamous or who have a history of recurrent STDs. It is probably not a good choice for nulliparous women because of the slightly increased risk of infertility following use, and

should be used with caution in women with valvular heart disease or with uterine abnormalities. Other problems include increase in menstrual bleeding, dysmenorrhea, and risk of expulsion.

The device is inserted and removed by the provider who should be specifically trained to do the procedure.

The woman should know the following:

1. There are risks and benefits of the device.
2. There is an increased incidence of dysmenorrhea and of increased bleeding with menses.
3. The strings should be checked each month after the menstrual cycle to insure that the device is in place.
4. The clinician should be called if there is onset of severe lower abdominal pain, fever, new or unusual discharge, or a general feeling of illness.
5. The clinician should be notified of any missed menstrual periods.
6. This method does not protect against STDs; therefore, counseling is necessary.

Oral Contraceptives

Birth control pills were first introduced in the 1960s and provided a highly efficacious method of contraception never before available, allowing women a significant degree of sexual freedom. The early birth control pills were high-dose hormones with significant side effects as opposed to the low-dose pills (estrogen less than 50 μg) available today. It was in response to their introduction that Barbara Seaman wrote her book about the dangers of "the pill" (21), and the National Women's Health Network lobbied for better information for women; this eventually led to lower-dose pills, better studies, and package inserts.

Hormonal contraception works via several mechanisms. Any given pill may have one or several of the following mechanisms: (1) LH/FSH suppression that inhibits ovulation,

(2) changes in the fallopian tube and in the endometrium that inhibit zygote transport and implantation, and (3) changes in cervical mucus that inhibit sperm transport and incapacitation of sperm.

There are two types of pills currently available. One is the combination type containing both estrogen and progesterone and the other kind is the progestin-only pill, or "minipill," that contains progesterone only (Fig. 10.2.2).

When women are interviewed about the pill, clearly there is significant misinformation.

Most commonly, the efficacy is underestimated, and the association with cancer is overrated (8).

Combination Pills

Combination pills contain both estrogen and progesterone. Different brands have varying types and amounts of hormones. They are almost all low-dose and may be mono-, bi-, or triphasic; the latter two vary progesterone, and rarely estrogen, throughout the cycle. The "low dose" are the pills that are the most frequently used and safest pills; they are prepara-

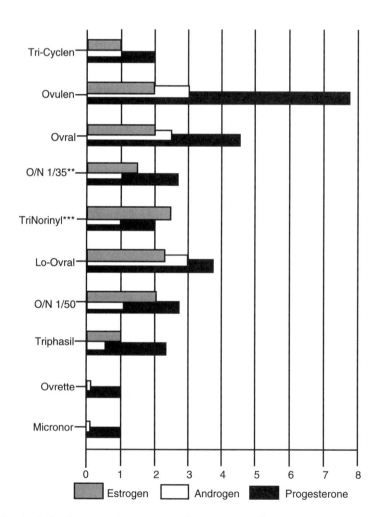

Figure 10.2.2.   Relative hormonal potencies of common oral contraceptive preparations: ** Ortho Novum 1/35 and Norinyl 1/35 are chemically the same, as are Ortho Novum 1/50 and Norinyl 1/50; *** Trinorinyl and Ortho/Novum 7/7/7 are similar.

tions that have less than 50 μg of estrogen. There is a new group of combination pills with different progestational agents that may offer some advantage.

The pill is an extremely effective form of birth control, approaching 100% when used as prescribed, with typical effectiveness approximately 97%. It has the advantages of continual protection; it is easy to use and does not require partner participation. Other benefits include regular and lighter menstrual periods with decreased dysmenorrhea. It may improve acne, treat endometriosis, decrease hirsutism, and is associated with decreased risk of both endometrial and ovarian cancer. Women using this method have fewer and less severe cases of pelvic inflammatory disease but actually have a higher incidence of chlamydia.

The pill does have annoying side effects such as intermittent bleeding (Table 10.2.5), weight gain, and irritability; these may cause a woman to stop using this method. These side effects are listed in more detail in Table 10.2.6 in which they are categorized by hormone effect. Pill type can be adjusted to lessen side effects; Table 10.2.6 describes hormone effects

and Table 10.2.7 explains estrogen and progesterone potencies.

There are factors that decrease efficacy, requiring use of a backup method. These include commonly used medications, such as antibiotics and anticonvulsants. However, any drug interaction should be considered before adding any new medication. The other common problem affecting efficacy is any combination of vomiting and diarrhea. In both cases, the woman should use another method.

More importantly, the pill has significant, absolute contraindications that include any thromboembolic disease, liver disease or tumor, breast cancer or undiagnosed breast mass, uterine or ovarian cancer, undiagnosed uterine bleeding, pregnancy, and sustained uncontrolled hypertension. It is also contraindicated in any woman over 35 years of age who smokes (Table 10.2.8). However, diabetes, controlled hypertension, obesity, age over 35 years, and family history of medical problems are not absolute contraindications; pregnancy still has a higher associated morbidity and mortality than any form of contraception.

A group of pills with newly developed progestins have recently become available. A recent

Table 10.2.5. Breakthrough Bleeding and Relative Androgen Effects with Some Oral Contraceptive Preparations

Preparation	Percent of Women Who Experience Spotting during Third Month of Use	Relative Androgen Effects*
Ovrette	34.9	1.0
Micronor	42.3	1.0
Triphasil/Trilevlen	15.1	2.3
Norinyl 1/50/Ortho 1/50	10.6	2.7
Lo/Ovral	9.6	3.7
Trinorinyl/Ortho Novum 7/7/7	12.2–14.7	2.0
Norinyl 1/35/Ortho 1/35	14.7	2.7
Ovral	4.5	6.2
Ovulen	7.7	1.7
Ortho Tricyclen/Cyclen	7–9	2.0

*Androgen effects, e.g., acne, hair gain/loss.
Data from Dickey RP. *Managing Contraceptive Pill Patients.* 5th ed. Durant, OK: Creative Infomatics, 1987.

Table 10.2.6. Estrogen, Progesterone, and Androgen Effects of Oral Contraceptives

Estrogen excess
Nausea and vomiting
Dizziness
Edema
Irritability
Bloating/cyclic weight gain
Increased fat deposit (female distribution)
Leukorrhea (clear vaginal discharge)
Uterine enlargement
Leiomyomata growth
Cervical ectropian
Cystic breast changes
Increased breast size (ductal and fatty tissue)
Visual changes
Chloasma, hyperpigmentation
Telangectasia
Vascular headache
Hypertension
Hypermenorrhea, menorrhagia, dysmenorrhea

Estrogen deficiency
Early spotting (D 1–14)
Hypomenorrhea
Amenorrhea
Small uterus
Pelvic relaxation cystocoele, rectocoele
Nervousness
Vasomotor symptoms
Atrophic vaginitis

Progesterone excess
Noncyclic weight gain
Increased appetite
Tiredness
Fatiguability
Depression
Breast tenderness
Increased breast size (alveolar tissue)
Change in libido
Dilated leg veins
Pelvic congestion
Decreased days of flow
Moniliasis
Oily skin and scalp
Acne
Hirsutism
Rash
Pruritis
Cholestatic jaundice
Post-pill amenorrhea
Headache
Hypertension

Progesterone deficiency
Late spotting and breakthrough (day 15–21)
Hypermenorrhea
Dysmenorhea
Delayed withdraw bleed
Decreased breast size
Weight loss

Table 10.2.6.—*continued*

Androgenic symptoms/associated with the progestin used

Increased appetite	Cholestatic jaundice
Weight gain	Pruritis
Hirsutism	Depression, fatigue
Acne	Adverse change in lipid profile (incr LDL,
Oily skin	decr HDL)
Rash	Increased breast size (alveolar tissue)
Increased libido	

Table 10.2.7. Relative Potency of Estrogen and Progestins in Some Oral Contraceptive Preparations

Name of Pill	Amount and Type of Estrogen	Relative Potency	Amount and Type of Progestin	Relative Potency**
Micronor	None	None	0.35 mg NE	.12–.35
Ovrette	None	None	0.075 mg NG	.15–.75
Triphasil } Tri-levlen }	EE 30/40 μg EE 30 μg	1.0	Levonorgestrel— 0.05/0.075/0.125 mg	.375–7.0
Norinyl 1/50 } Ortho 1/50 }	M 50 μg	1.0	NE 1.0 mg	1.0
Lo/Ovral	EE 30 μg	1.0–1.2	NG 0.3 mg	.3–9.0
Trinorinyl	EE 30 μg	1.2–1.4	NE 0.5/1.0/0.5 mg	0.5–1.0
Ortho Novum 7/7/7	EE 30 μg		NE 0.5/0.75/1.0 mg	0.5–1.0
Norinyl 1/35 } Ortho Novum 1/35 }	EE 35 μg	1.2–1.4	NE 1.0 mg	1.0
Ovral	EE 50 μg	1.7–2.0	NG 0.5 mg	2.5–15
Ovulen	M 100 μg	2.0	Ethynodiol Diacetate 1.0 mg	1.0–15

*NE = Norethindrone; NG = Norgestrel; EE = Ethinyl estradiol; M = Mestranol.
**There is much disagreement about the relative strengths of progestins.
Data from Hatcher RA. *Contraceptive Technology*, 16th ed. New York: Irvington, 1994:107–137; and Dickey RP. *Managing Contraceptive Pill Patients*, 5th ed. Durant, OK: Creative Infomatics, 1987.

Table 10.2.8. Absolute Contraindications to Use of Contraceptives

History of any thromboembolic disease, e.g., PE, DVT, stroke

Liver disease or tumor

Breast cancer or undiagnosed breast mass

Uterine or ovarian cancer

Undiagnosed uterine bleeding, pregnancy

Sustained hypertension

Woman aged over 35 years who smokes

review finds them equivalent in efficacy to those already available with fewer side effects, less breakthrough bleeding, less androgenicity and less adverse effect on lipid and carbohydrate metabolism. It is not clear yet what advantages or disadvantages will result from their use. Further study and larger populations are needed (22).

The woman should know the following:

1. All women need adequate instruction to give informed consent to use the pill.
2. There are warning signs that require imme-

diate provider notification. These include chest pain, dyspnea, migraine headaches, visual problems, leg swelling or tenderness, severe abdominal pain, jaundice, weakness or speech defect, breast mass, or any symptom that concerns the woman and is present longer than 3 months.

3. Smoking is contraindicated in women over 35 years of age and strongly discouraged in anyone using this method.
4. She should suspect any drug used as causing an interaction that may decrease efficacy.
5. She should have a general list of common side effects and remedies.
6. She should be given specific instructions regarding how the pills should be taken, including when to start her particular brand of medication, the meaning of the different colors, the time of day, and what to do if a pill is missed (see Table 10.2.9).
7. If there are problematic side effects, but not the warning signs, call the provider: do not stop the pill.
8. She should have a backup method in the event she decides to stop the pill without notifying provider.
9. This method does not protect against STDs; therefore, counseling is necessary.
10. She should have information about post-coital contraception (see Chapter 10.3).

Progestin-Only Pills

The progestin-only pill, or minipill, was developed in response to the need for an alternative when estrogen is contraindicated. Its contraceptive effect comes from changes in cervical mucus and changes in the endometrium. It is most advantageous for women who prefer oral contraception and cannot use an estrogen-containing one. It is the pill of choice for lactating women because it does not affect milk supply (23).

It has several disadvantages when compared to the combination pill. These include increased risk of pregnancy, decreased efficacy (approximately 97%), particularly in the first 6 months, irregular bleeding, and other complaints associated with progesterone use.

The woman should know the following:

1. Use a backup method during the first 7 to 28 days unless lactating full time.
2. Take the pill at the same time each day.
3. Know that if pills are taken more than 3 hours late, use a backup method for 48 hours.
4. Check with the clinician if she has no period for 45 days.
5. Call the provider immediately if she experiences severe lower abdominal pain.
6. This method does not protect against STDs; therefore, counseling is necessary.

Table 10.2.9. Instructions if Oral Contraceptive Pills Are Missed

One missed pill	Take two pills as soon as possible and use an alternate method for 1 week
Two missed pills	Take two pills as soon as possible, and take two pills the next day; abstain or use backup for 7 days
Three or more missed pills	Will probably have some bleeding; begin new pack the following Sunday or that day if not Sunday start; use a backup for the first seven days of the new pack
Missed one pill and missed a period	Check pregnancy test; discontinue pills if test is positive
Missed a period, no missed pills	Check pregnancy test or basal body temperature for three days; if temperature is 98°, probably not pregnant, but get pregnancy test
Missed two periods	Get pregnancy test; stop taking pills, and see a provider

7. She should have information about post-coital contraception (see Chapter 10.3)

Long-acting Progestational Agents

Long-acting progestational agents provide contraception for periods of 3 months or 5 years. They work as do other progestational agents by causing change in the cervical mucus that make it hostile to sperm, suppressing LH, preventing ovulation (this may not happen in every woman in every cycle), and interfering with cyclic maturation of the endometrium. They both have high degrees of efficacy and few serious side effects.

Norplant

Norplant or levonorgesterol implants became available in 1991. The system has six silastic capsules about the size of match sticks that are surgically placed under the skin, usually of the upper inner arm. Each capsule has 35 mg of levonorgesterol that is released over a 5-year period. The progestin released the first year is approximately 85 mg; it decreases to approximately 30 mg in the fifth year. Norplant has a failure rate of 1.5% in women weighing 153 lbs or less; its failure rate is 2.4% in women weighing 154 lbs or more. Its highest rate of efficacy is 0.09% in the first year (24).

Norplant has the advantages of being effective, long term, and requiring no partner participation. It has better continuity than either oral contraceptives or Depo-Provera. In addition, it is quickly reversible once removed and is associated with decreased menstrual flow and pain, lower risk of PID (perhaps because of changes in cervical mucus), and fewer cases of ovarian and endometrial malignancies.

One of Norplant's major disadvantages is cost. It is significant at onset but averages less than oral contraceptives over 5 years. Other disadvantages include lack of protection against STDs and side effects. These are common reasons for women to discontinue use. These side effects include all the progestational effects listed in Table 10.2.5. The most problematic ones are menstrual irregularities (with the most annoying being frequent bleeding or spotting), weight gain, headaches, depression, and pelvic pain. One further disadvantage includes difficulties with removal. Absolute contraindications include active thromboembolic disease, unexplained vaginal bleeding, pregnancy, acute liver disease and tumors, and breast cancer. Significant risks include stroke, thrombocytopenia, and pseudotumor cerebri (25). Other risks are keloid formation, local infection, ovarian cysts, and, rarely, peripheral neuropathies (26). Drug interactions, most often seen with rifampin and antiseizure medications, may decrease efficacy and make this method a poor choice. Removal can also be difficult because of the unavailability of a trained clinician and technical problems.

It is important to provide careful education before using this method. Many women have been told the side effects, have the Norplant inserted, and then choose to stop use because of those effects. It is important to educate in an interactive way so that a woman can consider what a given side effect might mean to her.

Norplant is inserted and removed by the health care provider. The provider needs to be trained to do these procedures.

The woman should know the following:

1. Adequate information so she can give informed consent.
2. An understanding of the side effects.
3. Call the provider if there is arm pain, any sign of infection at the insertion site, or expulsion of a rod.
4. No period after a long time of regular periods, heavy bleeding, or severe lower abdominal pain requires immediate attention.
5. Any severe headaches, migraines, or blurred vision are cause for concern.
6. All women must have removal available if they desire it and should have information about the process.
7. This method does not protect against STDs; therefore, counseling is necessary.

Depo-Provera

Depo-Provera is medroxyprogesterone acetate in an oil base. It is available in injectable form and is given every 3 months. It has a failure rate of 0.3% and continuation rates that are approximately 15% lower than Norplant over 5 years.

Advantages are similar to Norplant. Depo-Provera is particularly useful when short-term effective contraception is needed, such as while awaiting sterilization or when using a medication that is a teratogen. Making the decision to discontinue this method of contraception is easier than making one to discontinue Norplant. However, reversibility may take up to 10 months. There are no drug interactions with commonly prescribed medications that influence effectiveness. Its cost over a 5-year period is between that of Norplant and the pill.

Disadvantages are similar to those involved with Norplant. In addition, Depo-Provera may be associated with a decrease in bone density in longer-term users; this is also a concern in younger users. There is also a question of an association with breast and cervical cancers (27). High-density lipoprotein levels fall significantly. Although first-year users have a higher rate of menstrual irregularities, long-term users are more likely to experience amenorrhea than Norplant users. Contraindications are the same as for Norplant.

The woman should know the following:

1. Adequate information so she can give informed consent.
2. Side effects must be detailed and stressed.
3. Depo-Provera is ideally given in the first 5 days of the cycle. If it is given later, she should use a backup method for 14 days.
4. Weight gain may be a problem. Calories should be watched.
5. Call the provider if there is heavy bleeding, headache, depression, or frequent urination.
6. Return for injections every 3 months; use reminder card and calendar.

7. This method does not protect against STDs; therefore, counseling is necessary.

Sterilization

There may come a time in a woman's life when she decides that she has finished childbearing and wants to consider the permanent protection of sterilization. In women, this entails surgery to ligate, clip, or destroy part of the fallopian tubes, thus preventing fertilization.

Advantages include permanence, no maintenance, no partner cooperation, and spontaneity in lovemaking. Disadvantages may include the woman's emotional response (e.g., grieving), permanence, no STD protection, risks of ectopic pregnancy if it fails, and unclear effects on pelvic pain, menstrual pattern, and perhaps hormones. No good pre- or post-sterilization studies have been conducted to date.

Sterilization involves a serious decision, and it needs to be treated as such. For most of human history, society has determined that a woman's value is determined by her ability to bear children. The decision she makes when she chooses tubal ligation is not only to give up childbearing but also to give up the potential to do so. It is worth bringing that into the woman's consciousness and discussing it before a final decision is made. Women may respond in many ways, perhaps marking the event as a kind of passage from one potency to another, and even marking it with some kind of ritual.

The woman should know the following:

1. Adequate information to give informed consent about the procedure and its short- and long-term complications.
2. Be able to focus attention on the meaning of the procedure for each herself.
3. Know that this method does not protect against STDs; therefore, counseling is necessary.

Male Sterilization

In a continuous relationship, contraception may be possible by the sterilization of the man by vasectomy. Advantages include permanence, no maintenance, and spontaneity in lovemaking. Disadvantages may include difficulty getting partner cooperation, break-up of the relationship with subsequent need for different contraception, permanence, and the lack of STD protection.

Special Considerations

Women Aged over 35 Years

Because the average age of menopause in this country is approximately 50 years of age, contraception is needed by sexually active women over the age of 35 years. With one or two exceptions, all forms of contraception are available to this age group. Some women will want to continue to use low-dose (i.e., less than 35 μg estrogen) combination oral contraceptives until menopause. Then they may want to consider hormone replacement therapy.

The absolute contraindication to continuing oral contraceptives in this age group is smoking. There is clearly documented, increased risk of myocardial infarction, stroke, and thromboembolic events with continued use of combination pills in a smoker. Progestin-only methods may be more acceptable possibilities. The effect of hormonal methods on lipid profiles and on breast cancer are not well-defined yet. Barrier methods (with the understanding that the cervical cap may not be as effective in parous women) are good choices, as is the IUD. Some women may choose sterilization. This must be a well-considered decision, considering not only giving up the possibility of having more children.

Disabled Women

Women may have disabilities that make the use of certain contraceptive methods unac-

ceptable. Table 10.2.10 details those disabilities and the methods that are good choices for use in each circumstance. More information is available from the US DHSS publication, "Family Planning Services for Disabled People" (28).

Teenagers

The high rate of teen pregnancy in this country is a cause for concern for all health care providers. Most studies show that many teen pregnancies result from "a quick, often unsatisfying try at sex." (29) Prevention may be partially dependent on the clinician's acceptance of the teen's choices. The provider can and should support the young woman's decision to choose abstinence or to be sexually active in response to her own need and decision-making process, not her partner's. Simultaneously, all teen women should be given information about contraception and specifically told that an effective (better than 99% efficacy) contraceptive, foam or condoms, is as close as the nearest drugstore or supermarket. This method additionally provides STD protection. Teens should also be informed about the "morning-after pill" (see Chapter 10.3).

Teens can use most of the methods of contraception discussed in this chapter; however, IUDs and sterilization are not good choices. Combination pills are effective but depend on the woman remembering to take them every day and to use a backup method when indicated. Providers may want to consider risk/benefit issues in recommending hormonal methods in the first years post-menarche, realizing that pregnancy is a greater risk than oral contraception. Oral contraceptives may put some women at risk for early onset of breast cancer (age less than 35 years). At this time there are no identifying factors for people who may be at risk (30). Depo-Provera has a similar risk associated with its use; however, both long-acting progesterone methods (Depo-Provera and Norplant) are viable possibilities.

Table 10.2.10. Reproductive and Contraceptive Considerations for Women with Physical Disabilities

Condition	Female Reproductive Implications	Female Contraceptive Implications		
		Diaphragm	IUD	Pills
Amputations	Menstruation, fertility unaffected except in hemicorporectomy	Assistance needed if upper extremities involved	Client unable to check strings if upper extremities involved	Contraindicated if vascular or circulatory problems occur
Blindness/visual	Menstruation unaffected Pregnancy unaffected unless diabetes involved Genetic counseling may be indicated			May be contraindicated if impairment due to diabetes, glaucoma, or vascular disease
Cancer—breast or reproductive system	Fertility, menstruation may be affected depending on organs involved, related hormonal function, and therapeutic measures used Pregnancy may represent increased risk		May be contraindicated if malignancy is uterine	Contraindicated if estrogen based
Cardiovascular accident (CVA, stroke)	Menstruation, fertility unaffected			Absolutely contraindicated; other options depend on dexterity
Cerebral palsy	Menstruation, fertility unaffected	May be difficult for client to place	May be difficult to insert	May be contraindicated
Epilepsy, migraine	Fertility, menstruation unaffected Pregnancy probably unaffected			May either cause conditions to become less manageable or improve them
Multiple sclerosis (MS)	Menstruation, fertility unaffected Pregnancy possible, may or may not exacerbate MS symptoms (no conclusive study)		May be contraindicated because pelvic inflammatory disease (PID) and other problems could remain undetected due to lack of sensation	May be contraindicated
Muscular diseases	Menstruation, fertility, pregnancy unaffected Genetic counseling essential for women who have dystrophies of genetic origin	May be difficult to insert if upper extremities involved	May be difficult to check strings if upper extremities involved	May increase the risk of thromboembolism

Table 10.2.10.—*continued*

Condition	Female Reproductive Implications	Female Contraceptive Implications		
		Diaphragm	IUD	Pills
Polio	Fertility, menstruation unaffected. Pregnancy and delivery may be difficult for women with back deformity		May be contraindicated due to increased anemia	
Rheumatoid arthritis	Fertility, menstruation, pregnancy unaffected Pregnancy often responsible for remission of symptoms; symptoms (pain and swelling) often recur about six weeks postpartum	May be difficult to insert due to hand deformities	May be contraindicated	May be contraindicated
Scoliosis	Fertility, pregnancy unaffected. Genetic counseling indicated	May be difficult to insert or fit	May be difficult to insert or fit	
Short	Fertility usually unaffected; Turner's syndrome includes infertility Pregnancy rarely carried to full term; Cesarean delivery usually indicated	May be difficult for a woman with extremely short arms	May be difficult to place properly	May be contraindicated
Spinal cord injury	Menstruation, fertility unaffected Menstruation may be delayed up to one year following trauma Pregnancy carries increased risks (i.e., urinary infection, decubiti, autonomic hyperreflexia during labor and delivery)		May be contraindicated because PID and other problems could remain undetected due to lack of sensation	May be contraindicated when circulatory problems are present; thrombophlebitis could go undetected due to lack of sensation in extremities

Data from United States Department of Health and Human Services. *Family Planning Services for Disabled People—a manual for service providers.* 1981.

Barrier methods are all potential choices but depend on both availability, which for teens may depend on having adequate financial resources, and on use. They can also become a source of disagreement between partners.

Lactating Women

Breast-feeding often confers some contraception, as most breast-feeding women do not ovulate for several months after giving birth. However, it is not possible to predict for any given woman when she will again ovulate and be fertile. Therefore, if pregnancy is not desired, it is wise to use some form of contraception. Lactating women can use most methods of contraception with some cautions. All barrier methods are available to them and are the preferred choice. They should be aware that nonoxynoyl-9 is secreted in small amounts in breast milk. The IUD, particularly the copper-containing varieties, is a good choice in a monogamous relationship. Progestin-only contraceptives are acceptable and do not have the side effect of reducing milk supply (31). They are generally started approximately 6 weeks postpartum. The minipill is highly effective until ovulation occurs. However, then, it is wise to consider other forms of contraception. Depo-Provera and Norplant are longer-acting methods that secrete small amounts of progesterone into breast milk; they are also good choices.

In the Future

Society as a whole, health care providers, and women will need to cooperate if the problem of mistimed and unwanted pregnancies is to be addressed and alleviated. A three-pronged approach, including better education and support of young women, easier accessibility to contraceptive methods, and more research for better methods, is desirable.

Many women have significant misinformation about contraception. Others are dissatisfied with methods they have used. Further, young people receive varying amounts of (and frequently poor-quality) information, both about their own sexuality and about issues related to contraception and STD transmission. A commitment of public health personnel and other health care providers to provide easily available quality information would be a first step toward resolving these issues. It is also necessary to foster an environment for young women that strengthens their own self-esteem. By so doing, they may feel able to reject requests for intimacy that come from their partner's needs and not their own.

Contraceptives need to be accessible, affordable, and available. If obtaining oral contraceptives means a medical appointment weeks in the future, the motivation may be gone by the day of the visit. Allowing this method of birth control to be an over-the-counter may be an answer. It is also important for women to know where and how to obtain other methods.

There is ongoing research to develop new methods of contraception and to improve old ones. Unfortunately, there is also disincentive to do this because of the controversy surrounding certain methods, the long period needed for approval, and liability issues. In the future, there will be newer versions of progesterone implants, a combination injectable contraceptive, and perhaps hormone-impregnated vaginal rings. More distant are new methods for men that will be hormone- or vaccine-based. There are also vaccine methods being developed for women. In 30 years or so, there may be "reversible sterilization based on the molecular interception of events involved in sperm-oocyte recognition and fusion" (32).

The first two of these approaches, education and accessibility, are available to us as health care providers today. The last, research, can be simplified by lessening those factors that slow progress in developing new ways to prevent pregnancy.

Special Considerations for Nurse Practitioners and Physician Assistants

Health care providers must evaluate their own thoughts and beliefs about contraception, sexuality, and abortion to determine whether or not they can interact with patients within the context of the patient's own value system (33). A woman's values, which may not reflect the provider's values, must direct her decision making as long as her choice is safe. Some clinicians may need to become more aware of their own personal values about sexuality and contraception so that they can avoid unduly influencing the woman's decisions. The values clarification tool is designed to facilitate in providers open discussion of their values (34).

Providers should be aware, too, of the power they hold when presenting information about various contraceptives. Unintentional variations in terminology or inflection can lead the woman to believe that the provider thinks a particular choice is best. Even accurate information can be given in such a way to influence the woman's decision (34).

The perceptions that a woman has about various birth control methods are shaped by many factors, including the media, that can influence the information she receives. Especially in the case of oral contraceptives, the information received is rarely positive, leaving the health care provider to explain the beneficial aspects and to help the woman understand the possible negative effects in the context of her total contraceptive decision-making process. Older women especially may have a negative impression of oral contraceptives or IUDs because of their past experiences or media publicity (35). Thus, even if a woman comes to the clinical setting asking for a specific method of birth control, the provider needs to be sure she is aware of all her options.

When discussing a potential contraceptive, providers should ask the woman what she has heard about that method. Many women still believe that there are substantial risks, especially cancer, with oral contraceptives; 4 in 10 women believe that the health risks from taking oral contraceptives are greater that the risks from childbearing (36). Providers should also ask women to tell them about their previous negative experiences with contraceptive methods, because such experiences may indicate knowledge deficits that the provider can correct (37).

A woman who does not understand how to use a method of contraception is more likely to experience method failure. Some methods, such as the diaphragm and cap, require practice if they are to be used correctly. Women need opportunity to insert and remove these devices with the provider's guidance and certainly before they are needed for pregnancy protection (33). This means that sufficient time, at least 30 minutes, must be allowed for the initial fit and patient practice. Providers can determine if the woman is comfortable touching her genitals by asking the woman if she is comfortable using tampons (38).

To help a woman maintain compliance with her chosen method of contraception, the following strategies can be used: (1) show the method to the woman and let her handle devices and products, (2) use visual aids to reinforce instructions, (3) have the woman repeat instructions or return the demonstration of how she will use the method, (4) have the woman sign a "compliance contract" that states she will not stop using the method until she talks to her provider about her questions and concerns, (5) be concrete about follow-up and ask the woman to schedule an appointment before she leaves the office, and (6) provide instructions for an over-the-counter method also when the woman's method of choice requires a prescription (33).

The occurrence of side effects affects compliance. Although "nuisance side effects" do not cause the practitioner to worry about serious health consequences, they are annoying and inconvenient to the patient (33). Providers must take seriously a woman's complaints about irregular bleeding, weight gain, nausea, or other problems. Education about these possible side effects should occur before the contraceptive method is chosen and again if problems actually occur. If the side effects do not resolve spontaneously or the woman continues to be worried, the practitioner must either help the woman manage the bothersome side effects or assist her in finding another method. Specific resources on contraceptive methods, such as the book by Hatcher, give excellent suggestions for handling patient concerns (39).

Additional counseling attention should be given to the woman who is less likely to be successful in her contraceptive use. Women who have a history of an unintended pregnancy, who have no specific plans for the future, who feel that an unplanned pregnancy is acceptable, or who lack family or other support can benefit from special attention (40). When a parent and an adolescent come together for care they may have different agendas, the adolescent desiring birth control and the parent wanting the provider to stop the adolescent's sexual activity. Health care providers facing this dilemma will have to clarify the adolescent's needs and expectations related to the visit (41).

Acknowledgment

This chapter is supported in part by DHHS Training Grant No. ID15PE101880J. The authors gratefully acknowledge the assistance provided by Kathleen Chrisman, PhD, Joan R. Price, RNC, PNP, and Robert J. Grealish, MD.

References

1. Horton JA, ed. Reproductive health. In: The Women's Health Data Book. 2nd ed. A profile of women's health in the United States. Washington, DC: The Jacobs Institute of Women's Health, 1995:1–30.
2. Rosenfeld JA, Zahorik PM, Batson J. Unplanned pregnancy: are family practice residents taking all opportunities to make a difference? J ABFP 1994; 7:77–79.
3. Hatcher RA, Trussell J, Stewart F, Stewart GK, Kowal D, Guest F, et al., eds. Contraceptive Technology. 16th ed. New York: Irvington, 1994.
4. Dickey RP. Managing contraceptive pill patients. 5th ed. Durant, OK: Creative Infomatics, 1987.
5. Murphy P, Kirkman A, Hale RW. A national survey of women's attitudes toward oral contraception and other forms of birth control. Women's Health Issues 1995;5:94–99.
6. Rosenfeld JA, Zahorik PM, Saint W, Murphy G. Women's satisfaction with birth control. J Fam Pract 1993;36:169–173.
7. Goldfarb L, Gerrard M, Gibbons FX, Plante T. Attitudes toward sex, arousal, and the retention of contraceptive information. J Pers Soc Psychol 1988;55:634–641.
8. Murphy P, Kirkman A, Hale RW. A national survey of women's attitudes toward oral contraception and other forms of birth control. Women's Health Issues 1995;5:94–99.
9. Northrup C. Getting the most out of your medical care. In: Women's bodies, women's wisdom: creating physical and emotional health and healing. New York: Bantam, 1994:544–565.
10. The Commonwealth Fund. The Commonwealth Fund Survey of Women's Health. New York: CS Farr, Chairman, 1993.
11. Nickerson CAE, McClelland GH, Petersen DM. Measuring contraceptive values: an alternative approach. J Behav Med 1991;14:241–266.
12. Woods NF. New models of women's health care. Health Care Women Intl 1985;6:193–208.
13. Northrup C. Getting the most out of your medical care. In: Women's Bodies, Women's Wisdom: Creating Physical and Emotional Health and Healing. New York: Bantam,1994:544–565.
14. Nickerson CAE, McClelland GH, Petersen DM. Measuring contraceptive values: an alternative approach. J Behav Med 1991;14:241–266.
15. Prochaska JD, DiClemente CC, Norcross JC. In search of how people change: applications to addictive behaviors. Am Psychol 1992;47:1102–1114.
16. Northrup C, ed. Our fertility. In: Women's Bodies, Women's Wisdom: Creating Physical and Emotional Health and Healing. New York: Bantam, 1994:324–373.
17. Northrup C, ed. Resources. In: Women's Bodies, Women's Wisdom: Creating Physical and Emotional Health and Healing. New York: Bantam, 1994:674–689.
18. Pearson C. Condom alert: Avanti plastic condom breaks four times as often as latex. Network News 1995;July/August:3.
19. Anonymous. The cervical cap. Med Lett 1988; 30:93.
20. Chi I-C. What we have learned from recent IUD studies: a researcher's perspective. Contraception 1993;48:81–108.
21. Bell S. Birth control. In: The new our bodies, ourselves. NY: Touchstone, 1992:259–307.
22. Speroff L, DeCherney A. The Advisory Board for the New Progestins. Evaluation of a new generation of oral contraceptives. Obstet Gynecol 1993;81:1034–1047.
23. Diaz S, Croxatto H. Contraception in lactating women. Curr Opin Obstet Gynecol 1993;5:815–822.
24. Hatcher RA, Trussell J, Stewart F, Stewart GK, Kowal D, Guest F, et al. Norplant, Depo-Provera, and progestin-only pills (minipills). In: Contraceptive Technology. 16th ed. New York: Irvington, 1994:285–326.
25. Wysowski DK, Green L. Serious adverse events in Norplant users reported to the Food and Drug Administration's MedWatch Spontaneous Reporting System. Obstet Gynecol 1995;85:538–542.

26. Hueston WJ, Locke KT. Norplant neuropathy: peripheral neurologic symptoms associated with subdermal contraceptive implants. J Fam Pract 1995;40:184– 186.
27. Staffa JA, Newschaffer CJ, Jones JK, Miller V. Progestins and breast cancer: an epidemiologic review. Fertil Steril 1992:57;5473–5491.
28. United States Department of Health and Human Services. Family planning services for disabled people—a manual for service providers. 1981.
29. Lott B. Adolescence: mixed messages and real options. In: Women's Lives: Themes and Variations in Gender Learning. 2nd ed. Pacific Grove, CA: Brooks/Cole, 1994:68–91.
30. Pearson C. You saw it here first: oral contraceptives increase the risk of breast cancer in young women. Network News 1995;July/August:2.
31. Hatcher RA, Trussell J, Stewart F, Stewart GK, Kowal D, Guest F, et al. Postpartum contraception and lactation. In: Contraceptive Technology. 16th ed. New York: Irvington, 1994:433–452.
32. Lincoln DW. Contraception for the year 2020. Br Med Bull 1993;49:222–236.
33. Moore R. Contraception issues & options for young women. Wyeth-Ayerst Laboratories and Association of Women's Health, Obstetric, and Neonatal Nurses. Fair Lawn, NJ: MPE Communications, 1994.
34. Low MB. Personal values and contraceptive choices. NAACOG's Clin Issues Perinatal Women's Health Nurs 1992;3:193–198.
35. Hillard PA. Contraceptive use and attitudes among US women. Women's Health Issues 1994;4:138–143.
36. Murphy P, Kirkman A, Hale RW. A national survey of women's attitudes toward oral contraception and other forms of birth control. Women's Health Issues 1995;5:94–99.
37. Norris AE, Ford K. Urban, low-income African-American and Hispanic youth's negative experiences with condoms. Nurse Pract 1993;18: 40–48.
38. Tagg PI. The diaphragm: barrier contraception has a new social role. Nurse Pract 1995;20:36–42.
39. Hatcher RA, Trussell J, Stewart F, Stewart GK, et al., eds. Contraceptive Technology. 16th ed. New York: Irvington, 1994.
40. Still JM, ed. Issues in Contraceptive Method Selection. Wyeth-Ayerst Laboratories and Association of Women's Health, Obstetrics, and Neonatal Nurses. Fair Lawn, NJ: MPE Communications, 1994.
41. Hawkins J, Matteson PS, Tabeek ES. Fertility control. In: Fogel CI, Woods NF, eds. Women's Health Care. Thousand Oaks, CA: Sage, 1995: 281–322.

10.3

Postcoital Contraception and Abortion

Jo Ann Rosenfeld

Postcoital Contraception

Introduction

Postcoital contraception (PCC) is often overlooked as a form of contraception in the United States. More widely used in Europe, it can be used as a "morning-after" pill for unprotected intercourse, rape, or intercourse with a "failed" contraceptive method, or a continuing method of contraception for women in special circumstances, such as women who have isolated or infrequent intercourse. Most women use PCC only once, followed by conventional contraceptive methods.

PCC can relieve the psychologic stress of a woman who has had an episode of unprotected intercourse and who anticipates an un-

315

intended pregnancy. It may lead to a decrease in the abortion rate. For adolescents, who often do not use any or any effective contraception with their first sexual encounters, PCC, if widely known and available, might be an excellent alternative. One expert believes that the wide availability and knowledge of PCC in the Netherlands have contributed to lower teenage pregnancy and abortion rates than in the United States or United Kingdom (1).

A major impediment to its use in the United States, United Kingdom, and Australia is patients' and providers' lack of information. There is difficulty obtaining PCC in the United States, and little research on its use (2). An Australian study of health care providers found that only 11% of women who wanted PCC could obtain it (3). Only 44% of general practitioners spontaneously provided information about PCC; most of the physicians would only give information if specifically asked. Only 60% said they would prescribe, to women using condoms or diaphragm for regular contraception, a pack of Nordials (approximately equivalent to Ovrals available in the United States) as a back-up PCC method for failed barrier contraception. Women providers were more likely to prescribe PCC than men providers. Many physicians' information about PCC was incomplete; only 58% knew the correct prescription for the Yuzpe regimen (3).

Who Uses Postcoital Contraception

PCC is used primarily in four circumstances: (1) women who have had unprotected intercourse, (2) those whose method "failed" (e.g., condom breakage or slippage, diaphragm breakage), (3) women after rape, and (4) occasionally by women who have intermittent isolated intercourse.

PCC may be a good method for teenagers. Sixty percent of teenagers do not use contraceptives at the first sexual experience (1). PCC might be an opportunity to prevent an unintended and possibly unwanted pregnancy and present an opportunity for counseling and prescribing of a more effective and continuing contraceptive agent. One study of women undergoing abortion found that 25% became pregnant at first intercourse (1). In a review of a family planning association in New Zealand, most of the women using PCC were under age 25 years and 10% were under 15 years. The most frequent reason for use was "no contraception used" (4).

However, most women who use PCC have had a method failure (5). In one Australian study, almost half of the 400 women who used PCC stated they had intercourse using a condom that broke or slipped; another one-fourth had "forgotten a condom" at a fertile time in their cycle. Sixty-four percent were in a regular relationship (3). In a college health service in which PCC was readily available, it was not the teenagers on their first intercourse who were using it. PCC was used primarily by older (over age 20 years) women who had been in a relationship an average of 2.7 years. Two-thirds had been using some form of contraception (one-third condoms and one-third prescribed methods) (2). Of those women who requested PCC and had been using condoms, two-thirds reported breakage, leaking or slippage, whereas of those who used diaphragms and requested PCC, most had failed to use it (2).

Medical Therapies

Copied after the veterinary practice, medical PCC was begun in 1960s, in the United States with diethylstilbestrol (DES) and in Europe with ethinyl estradiol (EE). Now, there are a variety of medication protocols (e.g., EE alone, estrogen-progesterone combination (Yuzpe), danazol) with slightly different efficacies and side effects (Table 10.3.1).

Ethinyl Estradiol
The morning-after pill (MAP) in Europe is estrogen, usually EE. First used in the Netherlands in 1964, by 1975 it was used 55,000 times per year (1).

Table 10.3.1. Postcoital Contraceptive Agents

	Trade Names	Failure Rates	Dosage	Side Effects
Ethinyl Estradiol (EE)	(Not available in US as single preparation	0.15–0.6%	5 mg EE PO for 5 days	54% nausea, 24% vomiting, 23% tender breasts, 11% menorrhagia.
Combined Estrogen- Progestin (Yuzpe)	Ovral (0.5 mg norgestrel/0.05 mg EE) Levlen 0.15 levo-norgestrel/0.03 mg EE	1.8–2.3%: 1.22% if taken within 12 hours 4.9% >48 hours after un-protected intercourse; rs	50 μg EE - 250 μg LE (or com-parable norgestrel) combined tablet - two pills q 12 h for a total of 2 doses	57% no side effects; 28–74% some nausea, 9.6–22% vomiting; 22% breast tenderness
Danazol	Danocrine	2%	800 mg PO	19.3% breast ten-derness, 31.6% nausea, 3.6% vomiting, allergic reactions
IUD	Copper-T	0.1%		Long-term contra-ception, infections/infertility risks
Mifepristone RU-486	Not available in the United States	0.5%	600 mg single dose	Nausea 36.4%, vomiting 3.6%, breast tender-ness 23.6%, pro-longation of cycle

EE works by interfering with pregnancy, if taken within 72 hours of coitus, possibly by shortening the transport time of fertilized ovum and by retarding the maturation of en-dometrium. It does not work once the ovum is implanted. In a large series, the pregnancy rate with a dosage of EE 5 mg a day for 5 days was 0.15% (1).

There were significant side effects; 54% of women reported nausea, 24% vomiting, 23% tender breasts, and 11% menorrhagia. If the woman vomited the EE, a second dose was given 30 minutes after an antiemetic. The length of menstrual cycle changed in 24% of women: 11% had shorter periods, 13% longer (1).

In the United States DES was used. How-ever, now, DES has a specific warning that it should not be used as a PCC.

Combined Estrogen-Progesterone

This combination is the most commonly used PCC. Called the Yuzpe method after the physi-cian who proposed it, four tablets, each one containing 50 μg of EE and 250 μg of levo-norgestrel (LN) are given as two tablets immediately within 72 hours of coitus and two tablets 12 hours later.

This method allows excellent efficacy with a lower hormonal dose, although the side effects were as frequent as with EE alone. In one study, 46% of women reported nausea and 13% vomiting (1). The pregnancy rate was 1.2% if taken within 12 hours of unprotected coitus, 2.3% if within 48 hours, and 4.9% within 48 to 72 hours (4, 6).

There are no oral contraceptive pills (OCP) in the United States that contain the exact amounts of EE and LN used in the Yuzpe method. Ovral has been used most often (2 tablets q 12 h twice) as equivalent; it has norgestrel 500 μg and EE 50 μg. Only two US OCPs, Levlen and Nordette, contain LN, although the dose in each pill is only 150 μg with 30 μg EE. Three pills would have to be taken of these (q 12 h twice) to approximate the Yuzpe regimen's dosage, and there would still be too little EE. Ovral has been the OCP most often used and studied in the United States.

Progesterone Alone

In attempts to decrease hormone dosage, levonorgestrel alone has been studied. One study compared LN (0.75 μg for two doses 12 hours apart) with the Yuzpe regimen. Pregnancy rates were comparable, and side effects were much less with LN (1).

Danazol

Danazol (Danocrine) has also been investigated for use as a PCC. Taken as one dose of 800 mg, it has a pregnancy rate of 2% but significant side effects. Women complained of breast tenderness, nausea, vomiting, and occasional allergic reactions.

Antiprogestins during Luteal Phase

Antiprogestins (AP) bind competitively to progesterone receptors to oppose the effect of endogenous progesterone. Administration of the AP mifepristone (MFP or RU486) during luteal phase produces a dramatic drop in pro-

gesterone and estradiol levels. This had been called contragestion. When given from day 21 to 28 of the menstrual cycle after an unprotected intercourse, implantation is inhibited and pregnancy is prevented. The result is that uterine bleeding resembling menstruation occurs approximately 2 days after ingestion, irrespective of the presence of early conceptus and whether it was implanted (1).

Prescribed as three 200 mg tables given at approximately day 21 of the menstrual cycle, it had a pregnancy rate of 1.6% (1, 5). The next menstrual period was considered heavy or was longer than 4 days in only one out of four women. MFP worked best as a one-time PCC. If used repeatedly, in subsequent months, the pregnancy rate increased.

Comparisons

Whether PCC prevents pregnancy is dependent on the time of the woman's menstrual cycle. In studies that compared one method to another, it is difficult to compare the efficacies of different methods unless the time the coitus occurred in the woman's menstrual cycle and the likelihood of pregnancies for that time are considered. The rate of pregnancy from any one coital episode is 4 to 10% on average, but can be much higher depending on time in the woman's cycle.

Webb compared the Yuzpe regimen with danazol (600 mg q 12 h twice) and with MFP (600 mg PO once) (7). Pregnancy rates were 2.62% for the Yuzpe method, 4.66% for danazol, and 0% for MFP. The Yuzpe regimen produced early bleeding and MFP prolonged the cycle. The number of pregnancies in women on danazol was close to the number predicted so it was decided danazol had little effect. All three had significant side effects. Seventy-five percent of the women on Yuzpe method had nausea and 22% experienced vomiting, whereas women on danazol complained of breast tenderness and nausea, and women on MFP complained of nausea, vomiting, breast tenderness, and menstrual cycle prolongation (5).

Glasier studied 800 women, half on Yuzpe method and half on MFP. None of the women on MFP became pregnant, although four on the Yuzpe regimen did, but the difference was not statistically significant (8).

Pooled studies showed a pregnancy rate of 0.6% for EE in over 3100 women in four studies, 1.8% for combined estro-progestin combinations, 2.0% for danazol, and 0.1% for the IUD.

Instrumentation

Lippes proposed the use of IUD, placed postcoitally, to prevent pregnancy. It can be an alternative to hormonal PCC, if the woman presented more than 72 hours but less than 7 days postcoitus and if she wants to use an IUD or is someone in whom estrogens were contraindicated. An IUD placed within 7 days of conception prevents implantation as effectively as an IUD already in place.

The major contraindication to postcoital IUDs has been the risk of infection, especially if the woman already has or may have just acquired a sexually transmitted disease, such as in a rape. IUD insertion can produce serious complications of cervicitis, salpingitis, and PID. Use of IUD is not suggested in nulliparous women because of increased risk of sterility.

The IUD has good efficacy. The Copper-7 and the Copper-T IUDs were used in over 5000 women for PCC and there were no pregnancies. Overall the pregnancy rate is 0.1% (1).

Summary

There are effective medical therapies of PCC. The Yuzpe regimen of combined estrogen-progesterone preparation is effective and well-tested, although nausea and vomiting may limit its use. IUDs placed postcoitally are also extremely effective. In the future, MFP may be used as PCC. Lack of physician and patient knowledge and familiarity are the most important problems in the use of PCC. Physicians should consider prescribing a pack of Ovrals to their women who use condoms, diaphragms, or other barrier methods for use as a PCC for times when there may be a method or human failure.

Abortion

Abortion is and has been a fact for generations. Hippocrates and early Greek materia medica texts mention it as does early Christian literature.

Incidence

There are approximately 1.5 million legal abortion per year in the United States and 30 to 40 million worldwide (9, 10). Ten percent of American women have had an abortion, and 23% of these have had multiple abortions (11). Ninety percent of the legal abortions in the United States are first trimester abortions (10).

Legal abortions have not adversely affected the pregnancy mortality rate and the mortality of pregnancy is still higher than that of abortion. There are 9 maternal deaths for every 100,000 live births, mostly from hemorrhage, preeclampsia/hypertension, and pulmonary embolism. The legal abortion mortality rate is less than 1 per 100,000 live births (12). Any form of contraception including legal abortions carries less morbidity and mortality than pregnancy (12).

Some experts feel that the availability of legal abortions actually reduces pregnancy maternal morbidity. Since 1973, the year of legalization of abortion in the United States, maternal mortality rates have decreased. In the United Kingdom since the legalization of abortion, there were no deaths from abortion, whereas there were 75 to 80 in the 3 years prior to legalization (13).

Although not generalizable to the US experience, when abortion was made illegal in Romania, the maternal mortality rate went from what it was in most of eastern Europe to ten times that of other eastern European countries. Approximately 500 women per year (or

10,000 or more deaths in 23 years) died of complications of illegal abortions including hemorrhage, sepsis abdominal trauma, and poisoning. After abortion was legalized in 1989, maternal mortality fell by 50% in 1 year (13).

Who Gets an Abortion?

The reasons for a therapeutic abortion (TAB) are usually complex and multifactorial. The woman may be single, financially insecure, have too many children, have significant college or work plans, have problems with her marriage, or lack emotional or social supports (14). Occasionally, it is performed for reasons of infidelity or unwilling intercourse. Contraceptive failure is not usually the primary reason.

Single parenthood was the single greatest reason given for choosing an abortion. In married women, the abortion risk increases with parity but not with age alone. Cohabiting women had abortion rates close to but greater than married women. However, in the last few years (1988 to 1990 as compared to 1979 to 1981) there has been a decreasing rate of abortion in unmarried women over age 20 years and in married women with two or more children (15). The rates of abortion for all other groups of women have remained stable, except married women age 20 to 24 years whose rate increased.

Effects

Psychological

Usual reactions. The choice of an abortion is not easy or effortless. The woman may have pressure from family, husband, and friends to have or not have an abortion. Expectations about finishing school, continuing work, and family and religious principles may affect the decision (16).

The quality of the studies about the effects of induced abortions is variable. Some were done before abortion became legal and viewed only skewed or unusual populations of women or those who were trying to get abortions on "psychiatric" grounds. Many did not examine the women before the abortion or more than a few weeks after, several had no control groups, and several had stated biases. The results listed below were based on studies done after legalization of abortion (in the United States or United Kingdom) and those that either used a control group or used the women as their own controls over time.

Many women at the time of the abortion are ambivalent about having an abortion, but less than 10% of women had long-term emotional or major psychological sequelae from therapeutic abortions (14, 17–22). The incidence of psychiatric morbidity following TAB is low. In one prospective 15-month study, the hospital admission rate caused by post abortion psychiatric problems was only 0.3 per 1000 women, much less than 1.7 admission per 1000 women occurring after normal deliveries (23). Common short-term reactions include guilt, a sense of loss, grief, sadness, self-reproach, regret, and reduced self-esteem; these reactions tend to be mild and short-lived. A short period of mourning is normal (24).

Several studies found that there may be positive psychological and emotional effects for the women who obtain a legal abortion of an unwanted pregnancy in the first trimester (14, 17). One study of teenagers who chose TAB showed that 2 years later their lives may have been improved; they were more likely to have graduated high school or still be attending school (25).

Table 10.3.2. Women More Likely to Have Serious Emotional Consequences of Abortion

Abortion in the second trimester
Abortion for medical or genetic reasons
Women with repeat abortions
Women with preexisting psychiatric problems
Teenagers who insist on secrecy
Women with ambivalence or poor psychosocial adaption

Unusual reactions. There are some women at greater risk of developing a negative long-term responses to abortion (Table 10.3.2). Women may have more emotional and psychological consequences if they had difficulty making the decision or if they had a second trimester abortion that was not performed for medical or surgical reasons. Perhaps because women who have second trimester abortions are more likely to have delayed seeking help and to have greater ambivalence, they may have more emotional and psychological sequelae (14, 17, 22). Women who delayed their abortion were more likely to be adolescents or older (14, 26). Teenagers who insisted on secrecy had an increased incidence of guilt feelings (27). Women who had abortions for medical or genetic indications, those who had severe preexisting psychiatric illness, and those with poor psychosocial adjustment were much more likely to have emotional and psychiatric problems after abortion (14). Catholic and more religious women were at greater risk for negative emotional effects (18, 28).

Women who had had multiple abortions were more likely to have psychological problems (16). These women were more likely to have unstable personal relationships and social situations, psychological problems, persistent ambivalence, and motivational problems (14, 16).

Second trimester abortions are definitely harder medically and emotionally. Medically, second trimester abortions are more difficult and have greater morbidity and mortality. Either they are performed for women who have decided late or delayed seeking help or for women for medical and genetic reasons. In the former group of women, there is an increased incidence of preexisting psychological and social problems, and as stated above, increased likelihood of long-term emotional problems. A more complex, more painful procedure in which fetal parts may be seen can create greater stress and disturbances.

Abortions for medical and genetic reasons. Women who have second trimester abortions for medical and genetic reasons are usually older, married, and desired the pregnancy. Their grief response is similar to those who have lost a newborn (29). They often have a mental or even ultrasound picture of the child, making it much more substantive.

There is an increased incidence of depression in women and their spouses who choose abortion because of genetic or medical reasons (14, 30, 31). They are at higher risk for prolonged psychiatric treatment in the subsequent year (32). One study showed that 77% had an acute grief reaction immediately post-abortion, and 46% remained symptomatic 6 months later and required continuing medical support (33). Yet, most of the families said that they would consider abortion again for the same diagnosis.

The woman's and husband's reactions may include guilt at having done something wrong to cause the abnormal fetus, guilt at being a defective parent or having defective genes, anxiety that they cannot have another baby, guilt for a perceived or real stigma of terminating the pregnancy, and doubts whether they had made the right decision. The guilt may be expressed as anger at everyone, including the physician and health care team. Usually the grief expresses itself as acute and episodic periods of psychological anxiety and pain. The couple may feel unable to face friends and social circumstances related to babies or face others who are insensitive to the gravity of their loss, so they become increasingly isolated socially.

These families need intense support in the hospital and afterwards. The family must not have to tell their situation repeatedly, continually rejustifying their decision to everyone. The woman must have support for pain relief. The hospital staff must provide respectful treatment for the woman, her fetus, and her family.

Grief counseling is necessary. Post-abortion visits for counseling, information, and contraceptive advice are necessary (16). The woman and her family must be allowed to discuss the choices and their emotional response. For some, a ritual of self-forgiveness and absolution may be necessary, especially for those who have profound regrets (16). The family should not be encouraged to start childbearing again until they are ready. Counseling should consist of helping the couple overcome feelings of guilt, decreased self-worth, and feeling of defectiveness. Information should be given so that the family can make future informed decisions. Support groups to discuss and express feelings may be of help (16, 34).

Denied and postponed abortions. Denied abortions and mandatory waiting periods have induced some emotional consequences. One British study of over 300 women denied abortion found that continuation of the pregnancy led to serious psychiatric problems. One third of the mothers who kept their children showed signs of resenting them (35). Another study found that 35 to 50% of women denied abortion reported continued negative feelings toward the child and ongoing adjustment problems several years after the procedure was denied (23).

Mandatory waiting periods create anguish. A survey of 426 women who had to wait more than 24 hours for an abortion found that 59% had problems because of the delay such as mental anguish, incurred added transportation expenses, additional nausea, and additional missed work or school (23).

Medical Effect

Morbidity and mortality. The morbidity and mortality of legal abortions are low. The mortality rate is 0.4 to 1 woman per 100,000 abortions (10, 23, 36). Twenty-three percent of the deaths are caused by infection, 23% from embolism, 20% from hemorrhage, and 16% from anesthetic complications (10). The mortality rate was higher in minorities, women over age 35 years, and women who had older gestational-aged fetus. Yet, this was much lower than the mortality from live births (9.1 maternal deaths per 100,000 live births) (23).

The complication rate of legal abortions was also low, approximately 1%, with a failure rate of 0.5%. The risk of both increases with the gestational age of the fetus. At 8 weeks gestational age or earlier, women who had no preexisting complications or conditions had a complication rate of 0.2%. This rose to 0.6% at 13 to 14 weeks gestational age and 1.5% at 14 to 20 weeks (23). Vacuum aspiration procedures had a complication rate of only 0.2%, whereas dilation and evacuation (D&E) procedures had a complication rate of 0.7%.

The rate of complications is decreasing. The most common complication is the need for a repeat procedure that occurs in approximately 0.23%; most often the initial procedure missed the fetus usually because it was so small (23).

The complication rate of illegal abortions is high; in one study 22% had post-abortion sepsis and 11% required subsequent hysterectomy (23).

Long-term effects. Most women who have an abortion desire future children, and so any long-term effects on fertility would be important. One first-trimester induced abortion does not increase the woman's subsequent risk of spontaneous abortion, ectopic pregnancy, stillbirth, infant mortality, congenital anomalies, low-birth weight infants, or subsequent major complications during pregnancy and delivery (23, 37). Women who have had more than one abortion are not at increased long-term risk of spontaneous abortion (23).

Vacuum aspirations, comprising 90% of all abortions, do not increase the risk to future childbearing. However, second trimester D&E abortions do increase the risk of subsequent spontaneous abortion, premature deliveries, and low-birth weight babies (23).

Procedures

Medical Abortions

In the last few years there have been two paths of investigations of medications for medical abortions. The first, started in France, have investigated using antiprogestins, specifically MFP, with different prostaglandin analogues (PGA) at differing doses. The second, in the United States, has evaluated the use of anti-metabolites such as methotrexate and PGA analogs, such as misoprostol (Cytotec).

Antiprogestins. MFP with PGA is effective in producing a medical abortion in the first trimester. MFP is given as a single 600 mg dose to a woman wanting an abortion of a fetus of less than 56 days gestational age, and then it is followed 48 hours later by either gemeprost or misoprostol, both PGAs.

Both gemeprost and misoprostol are prostaglandin E_1 analogs that are used with MFP to complete a medical abortion. Misoprostol is oral, whereas gemeprost is a 1 mg vaginal suppository and is not available in the United States. Use of MFP with either is effective, with a success rate of 93 to 99%, and both regimens are a safe alternative for terminating a pregnancy in the first trimester (38).

Use of MFP (200 mg) with misoprostol (600 mg) 48 hours later had a 93% complete abortion rate. There were typical PGA side-effects of diarrhea in 7%. Sixty-two percent of women required analgesia (39).

Other regimens have been investigated to decrease the failure rate and speed the expulsion time. A regimen of MFP and then 1 mg gemeprost had a shorter time to expulsion of fetus (average 3.6 hours) than MFP and misoprostol (400 µg) (40), but success rates with both were comparable. In one study, 88% of women who used gemeprost completed the abortion within 4 hours of its administration, although with misoprostol expulsion often took much longer and one woman needed a subsequent vacuum extraction. Many fewer women in the group who used gemeprost needed any opioid analgesia (38).

One study compared gemeprost alone (1 mg q 6 h vaginally, for up to three doses) with MFP (200 to 600 mg) and gemeprost for women requesting an abortion of less than 56 days gestation. Complete abortion occurred in 87% of patients with gemeprost alone and 98% with both (41).

There has been some investigation into medical abortions in the second trimester. One study examined 100 women who were given 200 mg MFP and then 36 hours later gemeprost repeated every 6 hours for up to 24 hours until abortion occurred; 96% of women aborted with 12 hours of the first dose of gemeprost, and 99% with 24 hours. Abortion occurred more quickly in multiparous patients. The median number of doses of gemeprost needed was two. Side effects included vomiting in 31% of women and diarrhea in 5%. Eighty-four percent of women required opioid analgesia. Thirty-three percent required evacuation of the uterus following abortion (42). This regimen could be used for second trimester medical abortions in a day-ambulatory care center since most occurred within 12 hours of administration of medication.

Other studies have shown that gemeprost, given for second trimester abortions, is as effective as intravenous (IV) oxytocin and amniotomy in achieving a vaginal delivery. There are the advantages; amniotomy and IV oxytocin are not necessary and it is less invasive, but it is slower. Labor was milder with gemeprost and did not start for an average of 7 hours (43).

In the United States, prostaglandin F2a vaginal suppositories have been used to induce abortions in the second trimester for fetal death in utero and occasionally for other reasons. Inserted vaginally every 3 to 6 hours until passage of the fetus and placenta, the suppositories have the side effects of nausea, vomiting, and hypotension. Hospitalization for IV fluid hydration and sedation has been necessary. Mean time of fetal expulsion in one study was 13.4 hours with 90% of women aborting within 24 hours (36).

Antimetabolites. There have been US investigations of antimetabolites and PGA, alone and in combination, which show effective rates of abortion, although the failure rates are higher than those with MFP or gemeprost.

One US trial used methotrexate for women

requesting an abortion of a fetus of less than 56-days gestational age (44). Vaginal misoprostol alone was compared with 50 mg methotrexate/m$_2$ IM with misoprostol. Administration of misoprostol was repeated 24 hours later if abortion had not happened. The combination was much more effective than misoprostol alone; 90% had a complete abortion in the group using methotrexate and misoprostol (61% within 24 hours), whereas only 47% did with misoprostol alone. Side effects included diarrhea in 18% and vomiting in 5%.

Surgical Procedures

There are two major types of surgical abortions. For first and early second trimester abortions, up to 12 to 15 weeks gestational age, suction curettage (vacuum aspiration) has been used most often. For second trimester abortions, the procedures available are amniotomy with infusion of saline (urea was used in the past) with subsequent IV oxytocin or D&E.

Suction curettage is used in 90% of first trimester abortions in the United States. The uterine size and position are determined. The procedure starts with dilation of the cervix by cervical dilators 10 to 12 mm. Some operators insert laminaria into the woman's cervix 6 to 18 hours before surgery to ease the mechanical dilation needed. Then a suction curette 1 mm smaller than largest dilator is passed, in rotary and to and fro motions until the uterus is emptied of its contents. Products of conception are sent for pathological analysis. This can be done without pharmacological anesthesia, or with oral or IV anxiolytics and analgesics, or most usually under paracervical anesthesia.

Complications include hemorrhage, uterine perforation, infection, and incomplete abortion or failure. The later the abortion is done, the higher the risk of blood loss and uterine perforation. Prophylactic antibiotics are often given.

Second trimester abortions are performed by intramniotic injection or D&Es. Intramniotic injection of saline initiates labor, and IV oxytocin continues it. The woman experiences labor, lasting 12 to 24 hours, with passage of the fetus and placenta, with accompanying pain and need for opioid analgesia. Incomplete passage of the fetus and placenta may require a subsequent D&C. Complications include hemorrhage, infection, and the added complications of a D&C including uterine perforation.

In D&E, after 15 weeks gestation, fetal parts are removed with a suction curette 12 to 16 mm in diameter. Usually the cervix is dilated before with laminaria or prostaglandin E$_2$ suppository placed q 3 to 6 hours up to two times. Anesthesia needed can be paracervical block with or without IV analgesia and anxiolytics.

One study suggested the use of IV metoclopramide for women undergoing second trimester abortions. Women given metoclopramide had lower opioid analgesic requirement, lower pain scores, quicker passage of the fetus and placenta, and earlier discharge from the hospital (45).

Post-Abortion Care

The most important part of the care of the woman who has had an abortion is counseling. The woman must have conscientious guidance and suggestions about future contraception needs. Counseling about acute feelings of grief and guilt, and providing the opportunity for further visits are important.

Women who are Rh-negative must have Rhogam for Anti-D prophylaxis whether they had a medical or surgical abortion. If the pregnancy is less than 12 weeks gestational age, 50 µg Rhogam should be given within 72 hours; 300 µg should be given for an abortion of an older gestational age fetus (46).

Most providers prescribe prophylactic antibiotics. Either doxycycline 100 mg bid or erythromycin 250 mg qid for 7 to 10 days will decrease the incidence of post-abortion infections (48).

The beta HCG pregnancy test will remain positive in significant amounts for weeks after an abortion. A positive test does not mean that the pregnancy is continuing or that there was a twin pregnancy. It is often still positive at 2 weeks post-abortion, but usually negative by 3 weeks.

Early Complications

Complications of suction curettage that appear with 24 hours include hemorrhage, pain, uterine perforation, cervical lacerations, uterine atony, and hemorrhage (Table 10.3.3).

Mild bleeding is common after suction curettage. Moderate bleeding and cramps 1 to 3 days after the procedure may be caused by endometritis. If examination shows a normal or slightly boggy uterus, a trial of antibiotics with the addition of methylergonovine 0.2 mg tid by mouth for 3 days is often adequate. Uterine atony with a boggy uterus usually responds to methylergonovine 0.2 mg tid for 3 days. Cervical lacerations or trauma can cause moderate or severe bleeding, will be obvious on re-examination, and will require suturing.

Severe bleeding is usually indicative of incomplete emptying of the uterus and will usually require reusing the curette and completing the procedure. If there is sudden pain during the procedure, especially abdominal, or later abdominal pain, findings suggesting peritonitis, or sudden passage of suction curettage, suspect uterine perforation. Immediate laparotomy is suggested. High fevers, shock, or deterioration is rare but demands admission to the hospital.

Cramping is normal after abortion. It should be treated with tylenol or nonsteroidal anti-inflammatory agents, rest, heating pad, and uterine massage. A few patients may require stronger medicine.

Occasionally pain is caused by uterine atony. The uterus will be larger than before the abortion and hard. The woman is usually tachy-cardic and may have a fever. Usually, this must be treated by a D&C.

Later (Greater than 48 hours) Complications

The most common late complication is hemorrhage. From 24 hours to 2 weeks post-abortion, hemorrhage (defined as more than two maxipads per hour) is most likely caused by failure to rest. After an evaluation in the office or emergency room to rule out cervical laceration, trauma, or retained products of conception, the woman needs rest and instruction to refrain from physical activity including jogging, taking long walks, swimming, and heavy lifting for 2 weeks. Oral methylergo-novine 0.2 mg tid for three days may help. Uterine atony that presents with bleeding and a boggy uterus will also respond to methylergonovine (48).

Another cause of hemorrhage is subinvolution of uterus 3 to 6 days after termination. The cause is unknown. The woman will complain of light bleeding at first, then heavy several days later. Treatment is rest and a uterine contractile agent like methylergonovine. This will stop bleeding if there are no infections or retained products.

After 2 weeks, the most common cause of hemorrhage is retained products of conception, but trauma or blood coagulopathies are possible causes. If the cause is retained products, a D&C is often necessary. Uterine massage and administration of uterotonic drugs may be used in addition. Blood and fluid replacement may be necessary and monitoring blood pressures and fluid status in the hospital is suggested.

Infection can occur later than 48 hours after abortion. Women can complain of fever and chills, foul smelling vaginal or cervical discharge, pain in abdomen or pelvis, and prolonged bleeding or spotting. On exam, the uterus and adnexae may be tender with open os, sometimes with tissue. There may be a fever with a temperature greater than 102° and occasionally signs of sepsis. The most common

Table 10.3.3. Post-Abortion Suction Curettage Complications

Time After Abortion	Symptom	Causes	Findings	Treatment
Early (within 24 hours)	Hemorrhage—mild	Usual	Normal firm uterus	Reassurance
	Hemorrhage—moderate	Endometritis	Normal or boggy uterus, cramps, no or low fever	Antibiotics; methylergonovine 0.2 mg tid for 3 days
		Cervical laceration	Laceration	Suturing
	Hemorrhage-severe	Incomplete abortion	Large uterus, cramps	Repeat procedure; D&C
	Pain	Cramping	Normal	Tylenol or NSAIDS, rest, heating pad, uterine massage
		Uterine atony	Large hard uterus, tachycardia and fever	D&C
Late (1–14 days)	Hemorrhage—moderate	Women's failure to rest	Normal exam	Rest and methylergonovine
		Uterine atony	Boggy uterus	Methylergonovine
		Subinvolution	Light bleeding at first, then heavy several days later	Rest and methylergonovine.
Late	Hemorrhage	Retained products of conception	Boggy large uterus, cramps, fever	Repeat procedure
		Trauma	Laceration or abrasions on exam	Suturing
		Blood coagulopathy		Correction of abnormality
Late	Infection	Retained products of conception, PID and abscesses	Fever and chills, foul smelling vaginal or cervical discharge, pain in abdomen or pelvis, and prolonged bleeding or spotting. Tender uterus and adnexae	Antibiotics, often IV, including coverage of anaerobes; evacuation of uterine contents may be necessary
		Endometritis—chlamydia; the diagnosis is uncomplicated endometritis	Tender and firm uterus, closed os with no tissue; temperature of less than 102°	200 mg doxycycline immediately then 100 mg bid for 10–14 days with rest and acetaminophen

cause is infected retained products of conception, although pelvic inflammatory disease and abscesses can occur. Antibiotics, often IV, are needed; they should include coverage of anaerobes. Evacuation of uterine contents may be necessary (36).

However, most postabortion infections are caused by untreated infections, including chlamydia, present at the time of surgery. The woman has a tender firm uterus and a closed os with no tissue. She has usually a fever with a temperature of less than 102°. The diagnosis is uncomplicated endometritis. Treatment is 200 mg doxycycline immediately then 100 mg bid for 10 to 14 days with rest and acetaminophen.

Prophylactic antibiotics can reduce the incidence of postabortion infection by 66% (48). One dose of oral doxycycline 500 mg may give effective prophylaxis but most providers prescribe doxycycline 100 mg bid for 7 days routinely. Women should be instructed to take their medications even if they feel well. Alternatively erythromycin 250 mg qid for 7 days can be used (48).

Role of the Primary Care Provider

Abortion is never an easy answer. Each individual provider must come to his or her own decision as to the place of counseling about abortion in his or her practice. The woman makes any final decision, but knowledge of all the possibilities and nonjudgmental guidance, although this may be difficult if not impossible for some, can only aid a woman in her choice. The best way may be to provide easy and effective counseling about contraceptive choices.

Special Considerations for Nurse Practitioners and Physician Assistants

A nurse practitioner or physician assistant may be the first to discover a pregnancy. Providers must allow the woman to express her feelings about the pregnancy by asking, if necessary, "how do you feel about this pregnancy?" or "what are your plans?" Making a comment such as "congratulations, you're pregnant" may keep a woman from expressing her ambivalence or negative reactions to the situation.

Women making decisions involving PCC or abortion are often in a crisis situation, which is not the ideal time to make an important decision; yet time is limited for the decision to be made. These women deserve compassionate, well-informed caregivers who can facilitate the decision-making process by listening, providing accurate information, and making appropriate referrals to specialists or clinics that will in turn offer a safe, caring atmosphere.

Providers who may encounter women in these circumstances should evaluate whether they wish to provide PCC and abortion counseling, and, in turn, decide whether their beliefs or feelings will prohibit them from providing supportive and nonjudgmental care. If the practitioner cannot provide holistic care to these women, then a person who can offer such care must be available. Decisions about handling these situations must be made before they arise. Practitioners must guard against pressuring a woman to make a decision either to terminate a pregnancy or let the pregnancy progress. Biological, social, moral, and emotional factors toward and against abortion, bearing a child, or keeping or relinquishing a child must be weighed if the woman is to make a well-thought-out choice (49).

If PCC is prescribed, practitioners must be sure that specific directions are given about how many and what kind of pills to take and when to take them. The woman should be told to take pills with food to help prevent nausea and what to do if she vomits; use a barrier method of contraception until her next period; and see her provider if her period does not occur. Women need to choose a contraceptive method for the future and understand its use (50, 51).

Care provided to women should be continuing and long-term, preferably by a consistent provider, especially when there is increased likelihood of negative long-term effects (see Table 10.3.2). Referral resources for more serious emotional responses must be available. Because PCC and abortion are not usually first-choice methods of contraception, discussion of sexual activity and preventions of future pregnancies (and STDs) should occur.

References

1. Haspels AA. Emergency contraception: a review. Contraception 1994;50:101–108.
2. Percival-Smith RK, Abercrombie B. Postcoital contraception: some characteristics of women who use this method. Contraception 1988;37:425–429.
3. Weisberg E. Practical problems which women encounter with available contraception in Australia. Aust NZ Obstet Gynaecol 1994;34:312–315.
4. Bagshaw SN, Edward D, Tucker AK. Ethinyl oestradiol and d-norgestrel is an effective emergency contraceptive: a report of its use in 1200 patients in a family planning clinic. Aust NZ Obstet Gynaecol 1988;28:137–140.
5. Webb AM. Alternative treatments in oral postcoital contraception: interim results. Adv Contracept 1991;7:271–279.
6. Kane LA, Sparrow MJ. Postcoital contraception: a family planning study. NZ Med J 1989;102:151–153.
7. Webb AMC, Russell J, Elstein M. Comparison of Yuzpe regimen, Danazol and Mifepristone (RU-486) in oral postcoital contraception. Br Med J 1992; 305:927–931.
8. Glasier A, Thong KJ, Dewar M, Mackie M, Baird DT. Mifepristone (RU-486) compared with high dose estrogen and progestogen for emergency postcoital contraception. N Engl J Med 1992;327:1041–1044.
9. Westfall JM, Kallail KJ, Walling AD. Abortion attitudes and practices of family and general practice physicians. J Fam Pract 1991;33:47–51.
10. Avrech OM, Golan A, Weinraub Z, Bukovzky I, Caspi E. Mifepristone (RU486) alone or in combination for termination of early pregnancy: a review. Fertil Steril 1991;56:385–391.
11. Carnes JW. Psychosocial disturbances during and after pregnancy. Postgrad Med 73:135–145.
12. Grimes DA. The morbidity and mortality of pregnancy: still a risky business. Am J Obstet Gynecol 1994;170:1489–1494.
13. Stephenson P, Wagner M, Badea M, Serbvanescu F. Commentary: the public health consequences of restricted induced abortion—lessons from Romania. Am J Pub Health 1992;82:1328–1330.
14. Lazarus A, Stern R. Psychiatric aspects of pregnancy termination. Clin Obstet Gynecol 1986;13: 125–134.
15. Skjeldestad FE, Borgan JK, Daltveit AK, Nymoen EH. Induced abortion: effects of marital status, age and parity on choice of pregnancy termination. Acta Obstet Gynecol 1994;73:255–260.
16. Rosenfeld JA. Emotional response to therapeutic abortion. Am Fam Phys 1992;45:137–141.
17. Adler NE, David HP, Major BN, Roth SH, Russo NJ, Wyatt GE. Psychological responses after abortion. Science 1990;248:41–44.
18. Osofsky JD, Osofsky HJ. The psychological reaction of patients to legalized abortion. Am J Orthopsychiatry 1972;42:48–60.
19. Dagg PK. The psychological sequelae of therapeutic abortion—denied and completed. Am J Psychiatry 1991;148:578–586.
20. Lazarus A. Psychiatric sequelae of legalized elective first trimester abortion. J Psychosom Obstet Gynaecol 1985;4:141–150.
21. Niswander KR, Singer J, Singer M. Psychological reaction to therapeutic abortion. Am J Obstet Gynecol 1972;114:29–33.
22. Belsey EM, Greer HS, Lal S, Lewis SC, Beard RW. Predictive factors in emotional response to abortion: King's termination study—IV. Soc Sci Med 1977; 11:71–82.
23. Council on Scientific Affairs, American Medical Association. Council Report: Induced termination of pregnancy before and after Roe v. Wade: trends in mortality and morbidity of women. JAMA 1992; 268:3231–3239.
24. Urquhart DR, Templeton AA. Psychiatric morbidity and acceptability following medical and surgical methods of induced abortion. Br J Obstet Gynaecol 1991;98:396–399.
25. Sabin LS, Hirsch MB, Emerson MR. When urban adolescents choose abortion: effects on education, psychological status and subsequent pregnancy. Fam Plann Perspect 1989;21:248–255.
26. Bracken MB, Hachamovitch M, Grossman G. The decision to abort and psychological sequelae. J Nerv Ment Dis; 1974;158:154–162.
27. Wallerstein JS, Kurtz P, Var-Din M. Psychosocial sequelae of therapeutic abortion in young unmarried women. Arch Gen Psychol 1972;27:828–832.

28. Lemkau JP. Emotional sequelae of abortion. Psychol Women Q 1988;12:461–472.

29. Rosenfeld JA. Bereavement and grieving after spontaneous abortion. Am Fam Phys 1991;43:1679–1684.

30. Blumberg BD, Golbus MS, Hanson KH. The psychological sequelae of abortion performed for a genetic indication. Am J Obstet Gynecol 1975;122:799–808.

31. Kirk EP. Psychological effects and management of perinatal loss. Am J Obstet Gynecol 1984;149:46–54.

32. Rayburn WF, Laferla JJ. Midgestational abortion for medical or genetic indications. Clin Obstet Gynecol 1986;13:71–82.

33. Van Putte AW. Perinatal bereavement crisis: coping with negative outcomes from prenatal diagnosis. J Perinatol Neonatal Nurs 1988;2:12–22.

34. Seller MJ, Barnes CH, Ross S, Barby T, Cowmeadow P. Grief and mid-trimester fetal loss. Prenat Diag 1993;13:341–348.

35. Pare CMB, Raven H. Follow up of patients referred for termination of pregnancy. Lancet 1970:635–638.

36. Complications of Abortion. World Health Organization Publications. England, 1995.

37. Frank PI, McNamee R, Hannaford PC, Kay CR, Hirsch S. The effect of induced abortion on subsequent pregnancy outcome. Br J Obstet Gynaecol 1991;98:1015–1024.

38. Somell C, Olund A. Induction of abortion in early pregnancy with mifepristone in conjunction with gemeprost. Acta Obstet Gynaecol Scand 1993;72:39–42.

39. Thong KJ, Baird DT. Induction of abortion with mifepristone and misoprostol in early pregnancy. Br J Obstet Gynaecol 1992;99:1004–1007.

40. Somell C, Olund A. Induction of abortion in early pregnancy with mifepristone in conjunction with gemeprost. Acta Obstet Gynaecol Scand 1993;72:39–42.

41. Norma JE, Thong KJ, Rodger MW, Baird DT. Medical abortion in women of less than or equal to 56 days amenorrhea: a comparison between gemeprost (a PGE1 analogue) alone and mifepristone and gemeprost. Br J Obstet Gynaecol 1992;99:601–606.

42. Thong KJ, Baird DT. Induction of second trimester abortion with mifepristone and gemeprost. Br J Obstet Gynaecol 1993;100:758–761.

43. Mac Lennan A. Genital persuasion: prostaglandins for induction of labour. Med J Aust 1991;155:5–6.

44. Creinin MD, Vittinghoff E. Methotrexate and misoprostol vs. misoprostol alone for early abortion. A randomized controlled trial. JAMA 1994;272:1190–1195.

45. Rosenblatt WH, Cioffic AM, Sinatra R, Silverman DG. Metoclopramide-enhanced analgesia for prostaglandin induced termination of pregnancy. Anest Analg 1992;75:760–763.

46. Thong KJ, Norma JE, Baird DT. Changes in the concentration of alpha-fetoprotein and placental hormones following two methods of medical abortion in early pregnancy. Br J Obstet Gynaecol 1993;100:1111–1114.

47. Nichols KA, Rasmussen SJ. Postabortion medical care: management of delayed complication. JAMWA 1994;49:165–167.

48. Barnes AB, Cohen E, Stoeckle JD, McGuire MT. Therapeutic abortion: medical and social sequels. Ann Intern Med 1971;75:881–886.

49. Lethbridge DJ. Unwanted pregnancy. In: Fogel CI, Woods NF, eds. Women's Health Care. Thousand Oaks, CA: Sage, 1995:455–473.

50. Narrigan D. Postcoital contraception. Nurse Midwifery 1994;39:363–369.

51. Hatcher RA, Trussell J, Stewart F, et al. Contraceptive Technology. New York: Irvington, 1994:415–432.

Caring for the Pregnant Woman and Planning for the Delivery

Louise S. Acheson

Introduction

In historical perspective, it is a recent development for women to possess the current degree of control over reproduction. Over the last 50 years, the experience of childbearing for women who have access to contraception and modern medical care has been transformed. Until this century a married European or American woman gave birth to an average of six children, five of whom survived, and she had a 1 in 12 lifetime chance of dying in childbirth (1). Now pregnancies are fewer and safer. The mean number of pregnancies per woman is 2.7 and there is an average of 2.2 live births per married woman age 18 to 34 years in the United States (2). Most women now do not fear death because of pregnancy; maternal mortality in developed countries has decreased 100-fold in the past half-century to less than 1 per 10,000 births (7.8 per 100,000 in 1992 in the United States) (3).

Expectations for childbirth have arisen including "control" over the natural birth process (by women themselves, by society, and especially by the medical care system) and for a nearly perfect outcome for each birth (4, 5). The accepted place and attendants for birth have changed dramatically (6, 7). Through ultrasonography and other technology, a woman's womb has become more "transparent" (even occasionally bypassed, as in surrogate motherhood), with an increasing focus of attention on the fetus and away from the woman (5). According to historian Edward Shorter, it is "the 'discovery of the fetus' that has caused the massive increase in obstetric intervention of the last forty years" (1). Frequently in recent times, childbearing women's needs and prerogatives have tended to be discounted in honor of the purported "safety" of the fetus, as if this were attainable apart from the mother's well-being (8–10). Legally, the fetus is gaining ground over the woman. Even when terms are needed to describe the inseparable interdependence of woman and fetus, we often refer mechanistically to "the maternal-fetal unit" when "unity" might have more positive connotations. Paradoxically, in the United States relatively little societal support has been extended to optimize the health of mothers with infants after or apart from childbirth (11, 12).

Childbirth must be viewed from a woman's health perspective. In many societies unlike the United States, "childbearing is seen as an expression of health rather than illness" (4). Childbirth care must recognize and celebrate the birth experience as an active and formative one that may affect the woman's self-concept for the rest of her life (13). Many routine obstetrical practices are not supported by strong scientific evidence, so it is possible to give women choices. As women vary greatly in their needs, so they will vary in their choices of childbirth experience. Evidence about the outcomes of different forms of care needs continual development.

The Cochrane Pregnancy and Childbirth Database (CCPC), stemming from the work of the Oxford Perinatal Group (14, 15), has analyzed the data on childbirth outcomes from randomized, controlled trials. The CCPC is limited by not including data from uncontrolled trials and observational studies. This chapter will summarize evidence about the effects of selected aspects of perinatal care on the health of childbearing women, but obviously cannot serve as a complete guide to pregnancy care.

Society and Pregnancy

Disparities in Birth Outcome Based on Class and Race

In the United States, significant disparities in birth outcomes based on socioeconomic class and race have persisted for decades, although vital statistics have most often been compiled by race without regard for socioeconomic status. The rates of low birth weight, prematurity, perinatal and infant death, and maternal mortality are at least doubled in disadvantaged populations (2). Epidural anesthesia, cesarean delivery, and breast-feeding are more common among the higher income women.

There are many complex reasons for this disparity. Perinatal morbidity and mortality for each birth weight are influenced by the woman's (and infant's) access to tertiary care technology, whereas the incidence of low birth weight is determined more by local access to primary prenatal caregivers (16). The disparity between rich and poor in birth-weight-specific mortality has lessened since regional perinatal care referral systems have been established, but access to primary prenatal care is still problematic for many disadvantaged women. Their higher relative risk of prematurity and low birth weight has not changed in decades (17).

Access to Prenatal Care

Nationwide, approximately 70% of obstetricians and 29% of family physicians deliver babies (18). Approximately 21,600 obstetricians each attending approximately 160 births per year and 16,500 family and general practitioners each attending an average of 35 births a year (18). There are 4000 nurse-midwives each attending 45 births annually (19), accounting for a total capacity, if perfectly distributed, only 20% higher than the actual number of births in the United States (approximately 4 million annually). However, the United States currently has a relative shortage and maldistribution of prenatal care and obstetric providers (16).

Realistically, this problem may not be remedied without continued and increased provision of primary obstetric care by family physicians and certified midwives. Evidence from epidemiologic studies shows that in rural areas unavailability of local perinatal care causes women to travel to receive care and increases perinatal morbidity and mortality (16). Two thirds of obstetrical care in rural areas of the United States is provided by family physicians; in many places, they are the only providers.

Poor women still have difficulty accessing prenatal care even with expanded Medicaid coverage. Family physicians care for a higher proportion of lower income pregnant women than do obstetricians in both rural and urban areas (16). Further, some evidence suggests that women with few prenatal risk factors may have better birth outcomes when cared for by family practitioners or midwives in smaller, local clinics and delivery units (20).

Preconception Care

In 1989 the US Public Health Service recommended expanding the scope of prenatal care to begin prior to contraception and to emphasize screening and intervention for psychosocial determinants of health (21). "Preconception care" in its narrow sense refers to screening before pregnancy for medical, obstetrical, psychosocial, and genetic risk factors that might affect perinatal health, and risk-reducing interventions, many of which are best accomplished before conceiving a child (22, 23). Common examples include (a) testing women from higher-prevalence ethnic groups for diseases like the Tay-Sach's disease carrier state (more complex once the woman is pregnant), (b) immunizing susceptible nonpregnant women against rubella or varicella (live virus vaccines are contraindicated during pregnancy), (c) diagnosing and tightly controlling women with diabetes mellitus to reduce its teratogenic effect, (d) advising the daily use of folate by all women to prevent neural tube defects, (e) HIV counseling and testing, (f) identifying and treating substance abuse, (g) advising all women to avoid teratogenic exposures, and (h) planning to refer women with indications such as incompetent cervix for early maternal-fetal medicine consultation. All these presuppose an intention to become pregnant and are extensions of the risk assessment traditionally carried out at the first prenatal visit. However, the most basic aspect of preconception care is to ascertain whether the woman desires or intends to have a child soon given her resources health and life situation, and to provide acceptable contraception if she does not (23). There are many opportunities for preconception care in a variety of medical situations—at well-child visits, when women present with a negative pregnancy test (24), or at follow-up visits for chronic illness.

Activities, Diet, and Medications during Pregnancy

Exercise

Recent guidelines from ACOG about exercise in pregnancy acknowledge the limitations of scientific evidence on this topic and liberalize previous recommendations (25). Mild-to-moderate exercise at least three times per week is encouraged for healthy women, except those with "incompetent" cervix, pregnancy-induced hypertension, vaginal bleeding, intrauterine growth retardation, or a history of preterm labor. It is important to avoid overheating by drinking extra fluids and wearing appropriate clothing. Hypoglycemia is more likely during pregnancy and should be counteracted by liberal intake of carbohydrates. Pregnant women have diminished aerobic capacity; they should stop exercising when fatigued and not exercise to exhaustion. Nonweight-bearing exercise such as swimming or cycling reduce the risk of injury compared to weight-bearing exercise. Exercise with the potential for abdominal trauma is contraindicated.

Nutrition and Weight Gain

Few subjects are more emotionally laden to women in US culture than eating and body weight. Weight gain must be closely watched during pregnancy, because suboptimal weight gain can be associated with intrauterine growth retardation, whereas obesity and excessive weight gain may be associated with gestational dia-

betes, large infants, and potentially more difficult deliveries, or of preeclampsia. Women with "normal" body mass indices of 19.8 to 26 are advised to aim for a weight gain of 3 lbs per month, totaling 25 to 35 lbs during the pregnancy (26). Underweight women should gain more weight and overweight women should gain less (as little as 15 lbs for obese women).

The amount of extra weight retained 6 months after childbirth (an average of 3 lbs) is directly related to the amount gained in pregnancy: in one study, women who gained more than 35 lbs retained 11 lbs, whereas women who gained less than 25 lbs lost 2 lbs (11). A healthy diet during pregnancy is like a healthy diet for any young women, except that the requirement for calories, folate, and iron is increased. Vitamin and mineral supplements are commonly recommended; if iron-deficiency anemia is present in early pregnancy, supplemental iron should be prescribed in addition to the 65 mg per day contained in most prenatal vitamins. Practical information for clinicians about nutrition in pregnancy is contained in publications of the Institute of Medicine (26).

Work

Despite an enormous recent increase in the proportion of pregnant women employed, evidence about the effects of work during pregnancy is scant and inconsistent. Some investigators have found adverse effects, such as premature contractions or low birth weight, caused by strenuous work or extreme hours of work (> 80 hours per week) during pregnancy. Heavy lifting and prolonged motionless standing are contraindicated in pregnancy. Carpal tunnel syndrome caused by repetitive motion is often exacerbated by pregnancy. Approximately 15% of employed women of childbearing age are estimated to be exposed to workplace chemicals or physical conditions that might be hazardous during pregnancy (22, 23). Preventing exposure without denying women job opportunities has proven to be a political issue.

Medications

Any medication taken by the mother during pregnancy may reach the fetus. The effect of that medication on the fetus depends on the time in gestation the medication was taken, how it is eliminated by the mother and by the fetus, whether it accumulates in the fetus, how sensitive a growing fetus is to the drug, the molecular size of the drug, and its lipophilic nature (27). Some drugs, such as acetaminophen, are well tolerated by mother and fetus. Some, such as hydantoin or thalidomide, are toxic to the infant, although therapeutic to the mother. Drugs, such as alcohol or cancer chemotherapeutic agents, are toxic to mother but more harmful to the growing fetus. There are few studies proving the safety of any drug in pregnancy. Most drug studies concerning pregnancy are performed on rats or rabbits using levels of drugs hundreds to thousands of times stronger than the dosage for humans; whether these are generalizable to humans is unknown. Drug studies done in humans are either retrospective, with recall bias (women whose children are not perfect are more likely than other women to remember taking a drug, or if prospective, need huge numbers of women.

Nonetheless, caution should be used when prescribing any medications for pregnant women. Because many women do not realize they are pregnant until past the second month, providers should consider any woman who is sexually active and not using a reliable form of contraception to be potentially pregnant. Each prescription written should be evaluated in this light: does the need for this drug balance its teratogenic potential?

Several drugs are contraindicated in pregnancy, considered Class X (Table 10.4.1). Many drugs are relatively contraindicated. The provider should have a strong reason for using them; the benefits to the mother should outweigh the risks to the fetus (Table 10.4.2) For example, hydantoin causes a "Dilantin syndrome" in 25% of fetuses, consisting of prena-

Table 10.4.1. Medications Contraindicated in Pregnancy—Class X*

Thalidomide

Warfarin

Many cancer chemotherapeutic agents, e.g., aminopterin, vincristine, vinblastin, methotrexate

Diethylstilbesterol

Isotretinoin (Accutane)

Chloroamphenicol

Alcohol

*FDA Category X—Fetal abnormalities have been demonstrated in animal and human studies and the risks of drugs clearly outweigh the benefits.

Table 10.4.2. Medications that Are Relatively Contraindicated in Pregnancy: Benefit to the Mother Should Outweigh Risks to Child—Category C or D*

Amphetamines

Anaesthetics, general

ACE inhibitors

Antiseizure medications, e.g., hydantoin, valproic acid

Antibiotics, e.g., trimethoprim, tetracycline, ciprofloxin, gentamycin, streptomycin

Antidepressants (varies)

Antipsychotic medications

Anxiolytics, e.g., benzodiazepines

Nonsteroidal anti-inflammatory drugs

Sulfony ureas

*FDA Category C—drug has caused fetal harm in animals, but human data are not available; Category D—human experience associated birth defects with these drugs, but the benefit of these drugs may be acceptable despite their known risks, in life-threatening situations.

tal growth retardation, neurodevelopmental retardation, and facial dysmorphology, but it may be the only medication that controls the mother's seizures. On the other hand, a woman with deep venous thrombosis cannot use warfarin; it is teratogenic and causes bleeding in mother and fetus. Heparin can safely be used

Table 10.4.3. Some Common Medications Often Used in Pregnant Women

Antibiotics
  Penicillins
  Cephalosporins
  Macrolides, e.g., erythromycin,
    clarithromycin
  Nitrofurantoin
  Isoniazide (INH)
Antihypertensives
  alphamethyl dopa
  vasodilators, e.g., hydralazine
Antiasthma medications
  Theophylline
  Alupent, Proventil, terbutaline
  Inhaled corticosteroids
Acetaminophen
Insulin
Heparin
Thyroid medications
Antacids

instead. Some drugs that are often used during pregnancy are presented in Table 10.4.3.

Sexual Relations

Except for women with a history of premature labor in the current pregnancy, sexual intercourse has not been documented to have any deleterious effect on pregnancy outcome (28). Abstention from intercourse and orgasm is often advised when the woman is at high risk for premature delivery. Experience suggests that intercourse and nipple stimulation at term can initiate labor.

Women's sexual feelings vary throughout pregnancy, although diminished desire for sex is common during the initial postpartum weeks or months. Sexual intercourse may become uncomfortable late in pregnancy. The couple may want to try different positions, with the woman on top, hands-and-knees, or side-to-side. For some people, giving birth is a powerfully erotic experience. In addition, breastfeeding and the exercises often recommended for the circumvaginal muscles after childbirth are connected to sexual sensations.

Prenatal Diagnosis and Screening for Birth Defects

Screening and prenatal diagnosis of congenital anomalies currently has as its main purpose the recognition of serious defects during the first half of pregnancy so that selective abortion may be offered. Despite experimental techniques, few antenatally diagnosed fetal problems are successfully treated in utero.

Genetic counseling may be indicated if the family history of either parent includes consanguinity, recurrent spontaneous abortion, stillbirth or infant deaths, mental retardation, congenital anomalies including cardiac and neural tube defects, chromosome abnormalities, heritable conditions including hemoglobinopathies, cystic fibrosis, muscular dystrophy, Huntington's chorea, or Tay-Sach's disease, or if the mother will be age 35 years or more at the time of the birth (29).

Screening for open neural tube defects and for Down syndrome (Trisomy 21) has recently been performed using measurement of maternal serum AFP, estriol, and HCG ("Triple Check"). Abnormal values lead to ultrasonography for dating and anatomy, followed, if indicated, by examination of fetal cells from amniotic fluid.

If cells are needed for chromosomal or metabolic analysis for genetic disease, chorionic villus sampling or amniocentesis can be performed. Chorionic villus sampling can diagnose chromosomal abnormalities at 9 to 11 weeks gestation. The transabdominal route is safer and less operator-dependent than the transcervical route and may still be associated with a higher risk of fetal damage or pregnancy loss than amniocentesis (30). Amniocentesis with culture of fetal skin fibroblasts can be undertaken from 14 weeks on. The fluid can also be tested for alpha-fetoprotein (AFP). Current guidelines suggest offering prenatal diagnosis to all pregnant women over age 34 years, because their risk of chromosome abnormalities (approximately 1:160 at age 35 years) is greater than the risk of pregnancy loss from amniocentesis (29). It is controversial whether maternal serum screening (the Triple Check) followed by sonography can achieve comparable sensitivity in detecting Down syndrome.

Routine Sonography

Routine screening of all pregnancies with ultrasound examinations at 18 weeks gestation leads to earlier detection of multiple gestation, more accurate dating, and possibly increased detection of fetal anomalies (31). However, the large RADIUS trial conducted in primary care practices in the United States revealed no benefit in terms of perinatal morbidity and mortality from screening ultrasound examinations in pregnancies with no other specific indication for testing (32, 33). Only 17% of major fetal malformations were detected prior to 24 weeks gestation. In contrast, the Helsinki trial showed a higher rate of detection and abortion of anomalous fetuses with routine ultrasounds (34). Potential benefits such as parental satisfaction or practitioner reassurance were not measured but are likely to be important determinants of the use of this technology. Currently, ACOG recommends sonography during pregnancy in cases with one of the specific indications listed by an NIH consensus panel in 1983 (35), but not for routine screening. Screening sonography in all US pregnancies would increase the cost of care by an estimated $512 million (33).

Problems in Early Pregnancy

Discomforts of Early Pregnancy

Typical discomforts of early pregnancy include breast soreness or itching, sleepiness, constipa-

tion, and especially nausea and vomiting. All of these discomforts tend to resolve spontaneously after the first trimester. Pregnancies with nausea and vomiting are less likely to end in spontaneous abortion than pregnancies without.

If simple measures such as a bland diet, dry food before arising, liquids mainly between meals, and avoiding cooking odors do not control nausea and vomiting, antihistamines are effective and probably safe. Pyridoxine, 10 mg, a constituent of the now unavailable antinausea drug Bendectin, provided short-term relief of nausea and vomiting in the only controlled trial of its use.

Constipation responds to the same measures that are effective in nonpregnant people: stool bulk agents, increased fiber and fluid intake, and mild laxatives (e.g., senna). Migraines intensified in early pregnancy tend to resolve after 20 weeks of gestation; acetaminophen, narcotic analgesics, and possibly metoclopramide are acceptable treatments.

Effects of Current and Past Abuse on Pregnancy

Domestic violence is more common in pregnancy than gestational diabetes. Screening of all pregnant women, recommended by the US Surgeon General, reveals a prevalence of 4 to 37% (36, 37). Screening can be accomplished with simple questions such as, "In the past year, have you been hit, slapped, kicked, or otherwise physically hurt by someone? Has anyone forced you to have sexual activities?" (37). Battered women are more likely to be abused during pregnancy and experience more adverse pregnancy outcomes, including injuries, spontaneous abortions, placental abruption, stillbirths, and low birth weight infants (38). When assault by a partner is identified, it is important to consider associated problems of sexually transmitted infections, substance abuse, and child abuse in the family. It is also imperative to assess the degree of danger to the woman (of which she may have the most accurate knowledge) and to work with her to develop a plan for her safety.

When a pregnant woman presents with a history or signs of trauma (especially to the abdomen, breasts, or perineum), the possibility of assault should be explored. A woman in the latter half of pregnancy with acute, blunt trauma to the abdomen from any cause should be monitored for 24 hours for bleeding, fetal heart rate abnormalities, and contractions indicating abruption, and evaluated for rupture of membranes (e.g., pooling of fluid, alkaline pH, ferning of vaginal secretions) and for fetal-maternal transfusion (Kleihauer-Betke test) if she is Rh-negative (39).

The experience of past abuse, especially sexual abuse during childhood, may have lasting effects on a woman's bodily symptoms, health practices, and responses to medical care (38). The effects of past abuse in pregnancy, labor and delivery, and postpartum are only beginning to be studied (40). Childhood sexual abuse is associated with increased rates of teen pregnancy and late prenatal care. Domestic violence may interfere with the establishment of lactation (41).

Substance Abuse in Pregnancy

Cigarette Smoking
Smoking causes increases in perinatal morbidity and mortality, increased incidence of low birth weight babies and prematurity, and has been linked with sudden infant death syndrome (SIDS). Smoking cessation is beneficial at any time in pregnancy (42). Thirty-nine percent of smokers quit smoking during pregnancy but 70% resume smoking after delivery. Continued avoidance of smoking cessation postpartum benefits not only the mother but the child, by reducing the child's exposure to carcinogens and nicotine, and reducing the incidence of otitis media, asthma, respiratory infections, and SIDS (11). Nicotine replacement with patches or gum is not recommended in pregnancy.

Alcohol Abuse
Alcohol is the most frequent teratogen and toxic exposure during pregnancy (43). Fetal alcohol syndrome (FAS), consisting of a triad—prenatal and postnatal growth retardation, abnormal morphology, especially in the face, and neurodevelopmental abnormalities—occurs to the children of chronic and binge drinkers. Fetal alcohol effects (growth and mental retardation or dysfunction without facial morphology differences) occur in greater numbers, and often with less exposure. No safe level of alcohol use in pregnancy has been determined (see Chapter 8.3). All pregnant women and women at risk for pregnancy should avoid alcohol use and should be screened for problem drinking (e.g., with TACE questions). Women who continue to drink or use illegal drugs during pregnancy may need referral to multidisciplinary substance abuse treatment programs. Specific treatment programs for pregnant women are rare.

Cocaine Use
Perinatal problems from cocaine use are caused by ischemia and hypertension from intense vasoconstriction, maternal malnutrition from appetite suppression, social disorganization, and cocaine's direct effects on the developing nervous system (43). Cocaine use in pregnancy is associated with intrauterine growth retardation, prematurity, abruption, preeclampsia, stillbirths, and a variety of congenital malformations. Cocaine-exposed neonates have abnormal behavior years after birth, including hyporesponsiveness, irritability, feeding problems, and developmental delays. These women are difficult to treat and often have many other problems, including substance abuse, multiple addictions, poor social situations, poverty, lack of social supports, and sometimes homelessness, IV drug abuse, prostitution, and increased exposure to HIV. Few centers exist for detoxification of the cocaine or multiply addicted pregnant women, and those that do exist are often overwhelmed. A multidisciplinary approach will be needed.

Unfortunately, just when these women need help, the legal system is now sometimes prosecuting them for child abuse in utero or for "supplying" drugs to their fetuses. Pregnancy care in prison may be rudimentary and erratic. Prosecution may result not only in their imprisonment, but in loss of their children. These punitive policies often drive women away from prenatal and postpartum care or make them hide their addictions from their providers.

Early Pregnancy Bleeding and Loss

Evaluation of Bleeding in First Trimester

It is common for a woman to present with vaginal bleeding early in pregnancy before she registers for prenatal care, sometimes knowing, sometimes suspecting, and sometimes not knowing that she is pregnant. One third of normal pregnancies have some bleeding in the first trimester, and only one third of recognized pregnancies with bleeding go on to spontaneous abortion. Vaginal bleeding, thus, does not necessarily signal fetal demise.

The causes of vaginal bleeding are many. First the provider should establish that the bleeding is vaginal. Anorectal or urinary tract problems cause bleeding that may, at first, be considered vaginal (Table 10.4.4). Second, it should be established that the blood is coming from the cervical os. Vaginal and cervical sources of bleeding are much more common than spontaneous abortion. Vaginitis, condylomata, cervicitis, cervical polyps, and less commonly cancer can all cause vaginal bleeding.

However, if the bleeding is coming from the cervical os, the standard diagnostic tests are the quantitative beta-HCG levels and ultrasound (44). In a healthy early pregnancy, the HCG level should approximately double within 48 hours. Transvaginal sonography should show an intrauterine gestational sac that has a beta-HCG level of 2000 mIU/mL or more and can also detect retained products. A fetal pole and fetal heart motion are visible by 5 weeks from the LMP. If only transabdominal ultrasound is available, an intrauterine gestation should be identifiable above a beta-HCG level of 6000 mIU/mL, but an adnexal pregnancy will be missed in up to half of cases. Other tests sometimes useful in diagnosis include serum progesterone levels (less than 25 ng/mL in 99% of nonviable pregnancies), uterine curettage with examination for chorionic villi, culdocentesis for hemoperitoneum, and laparoscopy.

Spontaneous Abortions

Spontaneous abortion occurs in approximately 9% of clinically recognized pregnancies, but in 31% of all pregnancies. It is usually caused by fetal chromosomal anomalies or an anembryonic gestation. Threatened and inevitable spontaneous abortion in the first trimester may be managed expectantly (no known treatment prevents SAB), whereas incomplete spontaneous abortion with severe pain or heavy bleeding or second trimester missed abortion may require suction curettage. Of unselected first trimester abortions presenting to family physicians, almost half were completed spontaneously and half required suction curettage because of pain and/or hemorrhage (45).

Women with spontaneous abortions may not have a prenatal care provider. Often they need medical treatment suddenly, receive care at emergency facilities, and may be sent home without a follow-up contact. Women who have

Table 10.4.4. Causes of First Trimester Bleeding

Nonvaginal

Rectal, e.g., hemorrhoids, infectious or inflammatory diarrheas

Urinary, e.g., cystitis, urethral varicosities, bladder tumors, nephrolithiasis, nephritis

Vaginal, e.g., vaginitis, trauma, condylomata

Cervical, e.g., cervicitis, cervical polyps, cancer

Uterine, e.g., spontaneous abortion, implantation bleed, subchoronic hemorrhage had spontaneous abortions are often ambivalent or can grieve as intensely as women who have had a child who died as a newborn. They have had no time to prepare for grief and are both the victim and the survivor. They often feel guilty that they may have caused the miscarriage by particular actions or by having "defective" gynecological organs or genes. They may feel they have failed their function as women. Society has no recognition of death in a miscarriage; there is no funeral or customary ritual. Family and friends may not have known the woman was pregnant or may not understand the depths of feeling involved. "You can have another," or "It's lucky—it would have been malformed," are possible comforts others may give inappropriately. The woman and her family need time to grieve and need acceptance that such feelings are important. Follow-up visits with a primary care provider are essential. Dissemination of any information that is known, offers for genetic counseling, reassurance, grief counseling, and discussion of birth control options in order to give her time to recover are all parts of this visit. Some women may need more visits, others may need just one or two (46). All nonviable pregnancies should be followed until the pregnancy test is negative, to detect persistent trophoblastic tissue manifested by persistently elevated HCG levels.

Ectopic Pregnancy

Ectopic gestations occur in 1.4% of pregnancies, but are more common in women with previous tubal infections or scarring (as from pelvic inflammatory disease, ruptured appendix or previous salpingostomy), infertility treatment, smoking (possibly related to tubal hypomotility), DES exposure, and with abnormal embryos (47). Classic symptoms of ectopic pregnancy with bleeding or rupture include vaginal bleeding, abdominal pain, and syncope, usually at 9 to 12 weeks gestation. However, with early ultrasound diagnosis it is increasingly recognized that some ectopic pregnan-

cies resorb spontaneously without medical intervention. Hemodynamically stable patients with ectopic pregnancy may be observed, treated medically with methotrexate, or by laparoscopic salpingostomy, salpingotomy, or salpingectomy. Laparotomy may be needed in women actively hemorrhaging.

Infections during Pregnancy

Sexually Transmitted Diseases

Prenatal care involves preventing, screening for, and treating sexually transmitted diseases (STD). Many pregnant women feel liberated from the need for contraception during gestation, but counseling to use condoms and safer sexual practices to prevent STDs may be an important aspect of care.

Syphilis

Syphilis infects the fetus transplacentally. In 10 to 50% of cases, it causes fetal death. If it is untreated, it causes a congenital infection sometimes manifested by skin rash, deafness, keratitis, osteochondritis, and snuffles, but more often asymptomatic with intramuscular penicillin (48). Congenital infection may be averted if syphilis is treated early in pregnancy. A serologic test for reagin (RPR, VDRL) is a sensitive screening test, but it is nonspecific. If the VDRL is positive, syphillis should be confirmed by a positive test for treponemal antibodies (FTA) (Chapter 11.1).

Chlamydia and Gonorrhea

Chlamydia trachomatis and gonorrhea acquired by the neonate during birth cause ophthalmic infections; chlamydia is a common cause of neonatal pneumonia. These infections are carried asymptomatically by the majority of infected women but may cause urethritis, purulent cervicitis, or chorioamnionitis. Both can be detected during pregnancy by culture or DNA probe.

Gonorrhea is treated with ceftriaxone 250 mg intramuscularly. The standard treatment for chlamydia during pregnancy is erythromycin 500 mg by mouth four times a day for 1 week. Azithromycin, 1 g, by mouth as a single dose is effective and much less likely to lead to vomiting, but has not been extensively tested for use in pregnancy (49). If these are not tolerated or are contraindicated because of allergy, an 85 to 95% cure rate has been reported for pregnant women using amoxicillin 500 mg by mouth three times a day for 1 week. Doxycycline is contraindicated because of staining of fetal bones and teeth.

Human Papilloma Virus and Cervical Dysplasia
Condylomata acuminata caused by human papilloma virus (HPV) can proliferate dramatically and are difficult to eradicate during pregnancy, presumably because of physiologically decreased cell-mediated immunity. Many clinicians defer treatment until postpartum, unless the lesions are likely to interfere with delivery. Podophyllin is contraindicated during pregnancy, as is cryotherapy of the cervix. It is not known whether the natural history (progression or regression) of cervical dysplasia with HPV is different during pregnancy.

If a Pap smear during pregnancy shows HPV, dysplasia, or carcinoma in situ, colposcopy without endocervical curettage is indicated and the frequency of follow-up is based on the results. If invasive cervical cancer is found, a cesarean hysterectomy may be necessary. Because of the high prevalence of HPV in adults and the seemingly low attack rate for exposed neonates, cesarean delivery is not indicated to prevent neonatal HPV infection (e.g., laryngeal papillomatosis).

Herpes Simplex
In contrast, herpes simplex genital lesions in a woman at the onset of labor constitute an indication for cesarean delivery to prevent neonatal exposure (50). Up to half of women with positive cervical cultures for herpes are asymptomatic and without visible lesions. Newborns may be partially protected by maternal antibody in cases of recurrent herpes, reducing the attack rate. There is a high attack rate (30 to 50%) for neonates exposed to primary herpes simplex infection. One half of infected infants die and another 40% have severe neurological damage.

Women should be screened for a history of genital herpes in themselves or a partner and asked to report genital blisters or ulcers during pregnancy. Herpes cultures at term take too long (several days) to be clinically useful, and if performed only in women with a history for herpes, will miss half of those women shedding the virus; therefore, they are not recommended for screening. Acyclovir has not been tested for safety during pregnancy; it is currently recommended only for life-threatening maternal infections. If a suspicious lesion is seen on a woman in labor, an urgent Tzanck smear of the ulcer or blister fluid can be performed to look for multinucleated giant cells. However, if there is any question, a cesarean section is indicated.

After the birth, mothers with lesions should use good handwashing and avoid direct exposure of the infant to herpes lesions, but need not be separated from their babies. Potentially infected infants need to be isolated from other babies in the nursery.

Hepatitis B
The Centers for Disease Control and Prevention recommends universal screening for hepatitis B surface antigen in pregnant women (51). Selective screening based on a history of risk factors was found to miss half of antigen-positive women. Exposed infants can be protected from perinatal infection by administering hepatitis B immunoglobulin (0.5 mL intramuscularly) along with the first dose of hepatitis B vaccine within 72 hours after birth (48).

Human Immunodeficiency Virus (HIV)
Since the publication of results from the Pediatric AIDS Clinical Trials Group Protocol 076 (52), a stronger argument can be made for rou-

tine, universal screening (subject to the woman's refusal) for HIV antibody during pregnancy. This randomized trial showed a 68% reduction in transmission of HIV to the newborn (mostly assumed to occur during the birth process) from 25.5 to 8.3% with the use of zidovudine (AZT) 100 mg orally five times a day from after 14 weeks gestation until delivery and 2 mg/kg intravenously followed by 1 mg/kg/hr during labor for HIV positive women, plus zidovudine for the newborn (2 mg/kg orally every 6 hours) for 6 weeks. The study excluded women previously treated with AZT, but included those with normal CD4 lymphocyte counts. Severe adverse effects in the women were unusual, although the long-term effects on HIV disease progression have not yet been evaluated; many infants had transient anemia. This protocol is currently recommended for pregnant women known to be HIV positive and meeting the inclusion criteria of the trial.

Screening all newborns for HIV after delivery would seem to have little benefit, and mandatory HIV testing during pregnancy would be ethically questionable because the main benefit of screening is for the fetus. In countries with sanitary water supplies and infant formula available, women with HIV infection should be counseled not to breast-feed because breast milk contains infected cells that can transmit infection to the newborn (53). In addition, invasive procedures such as amniocentesis, fetal scalp electrodes, and fetal blood sampling should be avoided if possible.

Group B Streptococcal Cervical Infections
Group B streptococcal infection (GBS), initially an ascending infection of the amniotic fluid and membranes during labor, is the leading cause of early neonatal sepsis and plays an important part in causing postpartum endometritis after vaginal delivery. Intestinal and vaginal colonization with GBS is common (15 to 40% of pregnant women) and can be detected antenatally with vaginal and anal cultures (54). However, treatment before labor is not likely to eradicate GBS and is not recom-

mended unless GBS bacteriuria is found. Protocols for treatment with ampicillin during labor have demonstrated efficacy in reducing neonatal sepsis and death from GBS.

Two cost-effective strategies are feasible: (*a*) prenatal screening and intrapartum treatment of only those women shown to be colonized with GBS who develop risk factors for chorioamnionitis (e.g., premature labor, prolonged rupture of membranes, fever, maternal or fetal tachycardia), using 2 g of ampicillin intravenously every 6 hours during labor; or (*b*) treating all women with risk factors for infection during labor without screening (54). How best to deal with pretreated newborns is still controversial. Research continues on development of a rapid and sensitive intrapartum test for GBS and on development of a vaccine.

Discomforts of Late Pregnancy

Backache is exceedingly common, occurring in 75% of pregnancies. The change in back mechanics related to carrying a load in the abdomen with stretched abdominal muscles is exacerbated by loosening of the pubic and sacroiliac joints. Women carry their newborn infants, so it is not surprising that most women with antepartum back pain also have postpartum backache. Osteopathic manipulation, simple exercises for back stretching and pelvic tilts, and mechanical modalities including a pelvic support belt have been tried with varying success, but relatively little is known scientifically about the best approaches to this common problem.

Other common discomforts of late pregnancy include gastroesophageal reflux, edema and varicose veins, carpal tunnel syndrome, and disturbed sleep. Varicose veins and relaxation of the lower esophageal sphincter with slower gastric emptying become worse because of the pregnancy hormones progesterone and relaxin. Standard antireflux measures including positioning, frequent small meals, antacids (e.g., Gaviscon), and possibly metoclopramide (Reglan) are appropriate. Support stockings or graduated compression stockings and lying on the left side can ameliorate edema and varicosities. Temporizing measures such as splinting the wrist in a neutral position are used for carpal tunnel syndrome until the swelling associated with pregnancy subsides postpartum. Sleep is disturbed by nocturia, heartburn, fetal movements, and various musculoskeletal discomforts during late pregnancy, and by the infant's demands postpartum; compensatory daytime napping or reductions in demands are often needed, but this need is often not legitimized by the woman or those around her.

Giving Birth

Childbirth Preparation

In the last 20 years, childbirth preparation, parenting, and breast-feeding classes have become popular. Initially, childbirth education was part of the consumer-driven natural childbirth movement, but more recently such classes are offered by hospitals and providers to prepare expectant couples for the hospitals' routines. Women are generally encouraged to attend with their support person or "labor coach," and to practice forms of concentration, relaxation, and visualization that may help with pain management during labor. Women and their partners also learn what to expect and what behavior is "appropriate" during the different stages of labor. Classes usually discuss comfort measures and self-care during pregnancy, labor, and postpartum, infant care and feeding, possible medical interventions during childbirth, concerns of the group members, and exercises to prepare for birth (typically pelvic tilts, positions such as squatting for second stage labor, pelvic floor tightening and relaxing exercises, and stretching of the vaginal opening by massage) (55). The time devoted (typically 12 hours) is more than could be provided in the context of office

prenatal visits and has the advantages of couple and group process and a self-help orientation. Prenatal preparation has rarely been subjected to rigorous scientific evaluation but has become part of American culture.

Labor Support

Strong scientific evidence demonstrates the benefit of a supportive female companion, sometimes called a "doula," who remains by the woman's side to comfort and encourage her throughout labor. Doula support (compared to laboring alone) shortens labor, decreases the use of epidural anesthesia, oxytocin, operative vaginal and Cesarean deliveries and the incidence of maternal fever, sepsis workups and prolonged hospital stay for the newborn (56). A randomized trial of providing doula support for middle-income women accompanied in labor by their male partner also showed a reduced cesarean section (CS) rate (57).

Surroundings and Attendants for Birth

Most labors proceed to a healthy birth with no need for specific medical intervention. The root of the word "obstetrics" is "to stand by." A "midwife" is "with the woman," suggesting the traditional birth attendant's role of watchful waiting and support of the laboring woman. The experience of labor a woman undergoes depends on a variety of factors including her wishes, knowledge, and understanding, her medical and obstetrical history, and circumstances of her and her infant's health during labor, and as well the philosophy and practice patterns of her provider, her health insurance, her hospital, and even her obstetrical nurses. Generally, laboring women attended by family physicians and midwives come to the hospital later in labor, are less likely to have augmentation or induction of labor, episiotomies, continuous electronic fetal monitoring, or operative vaginal or CS deliveries than comparable "low-risk" women attended by obstetricians, without any difference in outcome for the infants (58–60). However, observational and epidemiologic evidence suggests that the setting for childbirth also has a substantial influence on birth outcomes, with interventions such as CS more common in high-volume private hospitals and less common in public hospitals, teaching hospitals, and level 1 facilities (61, 62). When the same practitioners attend births in diverse settings, their practice style varies with the milieu (63).

Much interest surrounds the problem of "triageing" women to appropriate birth settings and attendants so as to avoid unnecessary interventions in labor for those likely to have uncomplicated births while making secondary and tertiary care available to those who require it. Prelabor screening can identify two thirds of mother-infant pairs who will have birth complications or require obstetrical intervention with a specificity on the order of 50% (64, 65). On the other hand, the negative predictive value of such screening tools for problems other than failure to progress in labor is high, making it possible to predict with 90 to 99% success those women who will not have adverse outcomes (64).

These women should choose a childbirth setting in which they feel safe and comfortable. The available evidence suggests that intentional home births or births in a freestanding birth center with trained attendants can be as safe as hospital births for low-risk pregnancies, and are considerably less expensive (66). Women and providers who have chosen out-of-hospital births have been highly motivated. Approximately 20% of women who desire an out-of-hospital birth develop an indication for referral to a level II or III facility prior to labor, and 2.5 to 16% require intrapartum or postpartum transfer. Emergency transfers occur in approximately 2.5% of carefully screened cases (66).

Avoidance of Unnecessary CS

The current (1992) CS rate in the United States is 22.6%, nearly double what many experts feel is the optimal rate. Efforts to reduce cesarean births have focussed on payer and tort systems, hospitals, practitioners, obstetrical conditions, and characteristics of women (67). The most common reasons for CS are previous cesarean birth, "cephalopelvic disproportion" (diagnosed when there is arrest of progress in labor), breech presentation, "fetal distress," multiple gestation, and various emergencies such as placenta previa, abruption, or cord prolapse. CS is more common when the woman is well educated, older, or has private insurance coverage. CS rates can be reduced when all cases are peer-reviewed and when influential practitioners take leadership in reducing them. Eliminating differences in practitioner reimbursement between vaginal and CS deliveries is being tried by third-party payers. The routine use of continuous electronic fetal heart rate monitoring has been shown to increase the CS rate for "fetal distress"; the availability of fetal capillary pH measurements attenuates the increase. External cephalic version to reduce the incidence of breech presentation at term and selective vaginal breech delivery can reduce CS for malpresentation (68).

A large impact on overall CS rate would result from an increase in the proportion of women with previous low transverse uterine incisions who subsequently have vaginal births (VBAC). Currently only 25% of candidates for VBAC deliver vaginally. There is some evidence that labor management by family practitioners or midwives results in fewer CS and more VBACs than for comparable groups of patients managed by obstetricians, but the mediating factors are unclear. Medical interventions that may slow labor progress or result in minor malposition of the fetus can contribute to the CS rate by leading to an assessment of "cephalopelvic disproportion." Immobilizing women in labor and early epidural anesthesia may be two such avoidable interventions. Continuous labor support lowers the proportion of CS births. Finally, pregnant women and medical professionals need to share more realistic expectations of the costs and benefits of CS, especially realizing that this operation, compared with vaginal delivery, entails greater risks and costs to the mother that should be balanced against fetal indications and factors of convenience, fear, uncertainty, and fatigue, which often lend impetus to a decision to operate.

Electronic Fetal Heart Rate Monitoring

Routine electronic fetal heart rate monitoring (EFM), like routine sonography, was studied in randomized, controlled trials only after its widespread adoption. Controlled trials from North America and Europe comparing EFM to intermittent auscultation of the fetal heart rate for uncomplicated labor demonstrate a doubling of the CS rate, which is less significantly increased if fetal capillary pH is used to confirm the impression of fetal distress, and no effect on infant morbidity or mortality except in two studies (69). In one large study, EFM was associated with fewer neonatal seizures, but no difference was found in long-term CNS morbidity of the children (70). ACOG guidelines consider auscultation of the fetal heart rate following a contraction at regular intervals (15 to 30 minutes during active labor and 5 minutes during second stage labor) equivalent to continuous EFM. Intermittent auscultation may be more comfortable for the woman in preserving her mobility and may result in fewer CS, but some women prefer the monitor because it is reassuring to them. Techniques for ambulatory monitoring by telemetry, although universal for cardiac patients, have not been developed or adopted for women in labor. EFM is the standard of care for complicated labors in the United States.

Epidural Analgesia

Epidural analgesia provides excellent relief from the pain of contractions with minimal systemic absorption and varying degrees of muscle paralysis. Women with epidural analgesia are usually confined to bed and continuous electronic monitoring is used. Hypotension from vasodilation caused by the anesthetic can usually be prevented by preloading with an intravenous fluid bolus. A study of ambulation with low-dose epidural analgesia showed that one third of women were unable to ambulate, one-third tried and fell, and one-third could safely walk (71). The degree to which a continuous epidural infusion of anesthetic slows the progress of labor is controversial. Usually, the second stage of labor is lengthened (72). A case-control study of elective epidural analgesia suggested a ninefold increased relative risk of cesarean delivery for lack of progress in labor (73). A randomized controlled trial comparing epidurals with systemic narcotics gave similar results; epidural analgesia before 5-cm cervical dilation was associated with a 10-fold increased risk of CS, but CS was not more likely if the epidural was deferred until the active phase of labor (74). However, another randomized trial showed no difference in CS. Some investigators have reported a linear increase in maternal temperature with the duration of epidural anesthetic infusion, resulting in a higher incidence of maternal fever when epidurals are used (75). These fevers are unlikely to be caused by chorioamnionitis and are more likely to reflect disturbed thermoregulation caused by the anesthetic; yet there is no clinically reliable way to distinguish which mothers and newborns to investigate and treat for sepsis. Based on current evidence, physicians and nurses should advise women that epidural analgesia for labor pain has drawbacks as well as benefits, and that if it is to be used it should usually begin in the active phase of labor.

Labor and Delivery

Care of the woman during labor and of the family immediately after delivery is beyond the scope of this chapter. A woman-centered approach to the birth itself and evidence bearing on the issues and practices of childbirth can be found in a variety of sources including those referenced in Table 10.4.5.

Table 10.4.5. Sources for Labor and Delivery Care

- Smith MA, Acheson LS, Byrd JE, et al. A critical review of labor and birth care. J Fam Pract 1991;33:281–292.
- Smith MA, Ruffin MT, Green LA. The rational management of labor. Am Fam Physician 1993;47:1471–1481.
- Kitzinger S, Simkin P, eds. Episiotomy and the Second Stage of Labor. 2nd ed. Seattle: Penny-press, 1990.
- Chalmers I, Enkin M, Keirse M, eds. Effective Care in Pregnancy and Childbirth. New York: Oxford University Press, 1989.
- Ratcliffe S, Byrd J, Sakornbut E, eds. Pregnancy and Perinatal Care in Family Practice. New York: Hanley and Belfus, 1996.
- Enkin MW, Kierse MJNC, Renfrew MJ, Neilson JP, eds. Pregnancy and Childbirth Module of the Cochrane Databases of Systemic Reviews. London: BMJ publishing group, 1996. (updated biannually) {P.O. Box 295, London WCI H9 TE, #0171-383-6185.}
- Simkin P. The Birth Partner: Everything You Need to Know to Help a Woman through Childbirth. Boston: Harvard Common Press, 1989.
- Klaus P, Klaus M, Kennell J. Mothering the Mother. Addison Wesley, 1993.

Postpartum Health

After giving birth, women need time for themselves for rest and a lot of time to interact with their newborns. However, hospital routines appropriate for sick individuals are inappropriate for normal postpartum women and infants. Rooming-in, liberal family visitation, self-administration of medication, and early discharge may improve their postpartum well-being. Although early discharge is apparently safe for most women, few women have chosen it, despite attempts by hospitals and payers.

Emotional support from others, including the father of the baby, and exemption from usual roles and responsibilities are crucial for the woman during postpartum recovery. Both medical care and social policy need to change to address these needs. ACOG recommends a maternity leave for healthy mothers of 2 weeks before and 6 weeks after delivery. In most western European and affluent countries, leaves of 14 to 18 weeks are customary. Recovery past 6 weeks may be necessary for women who have had a CS, have less support, have more children at home, or breast-feed round-the-clock. There are few accommodations to facilitate breast-feeding in the workplace, although it is desirable for breast-feeding to continue (see Chapter 17.1).

Most methods of contraception are suitable postpartum, except for breast-feeding mothers who should avoid combination oral contraceptives, especially in the first 6 weeks. Lactational and postpartum amenorrhea of 6 or more months is not unusual. Pregnancy rates for lactating women who continue amenorrhea are less than 2% in the first 6 months and approximately 7% in the first year after childbirth (11).

Summary

Maternity and childbirth encompass only 5% of women's lives, and yet often become the focus of much provider-woman interaction. As with other parts of a woman's life, evaluation, consideration of problems and concerns, and delivery of services, including labor and delivery, should be individualized after discussion with the woman and her family. Offering alternatives in this area in which there are so few documented certainties is reasonable and considerate.

Special Considerations for Nurse Practitioners and Physician Assistants

On a daily basis, women are confronted with a barrage of advice, data, and opinions about reproductive health. The possibilities and choices for care can seem overwhelming, leading to anxiety, uncertainty, and insecurity (77). The many different providers involved in pregnancy care must not add to the confusion, but instead provide holistic, coordinated care that keeps the woman's interests in the forefront.

Providing accurate, timely information to the woman is essential. As an example, danger signs for each trimester are discussed and provided in writing. However, this and other information is given in the context of empowering the woman and decreasing anxieties about the pregnancy. Providing a specific plan of action if a danger sign occurs will help the woman feel more in control and less fearful of the situation.

Ideally, assessment and care related to pregnancy will start before pregnancy. Asking a reproductive-aged woman during regular and periodic primary care if she is planning to become pregnant or if she has thought about starting a family can lead to further discussion about preconception needs. Better definition of family planning goals, maintenance of health and protection of fertility, and reduction of risks to future pregnancies are topics to be addressed. Special attention can be given to medications that the woman is currently taking or that the clinician might prescribe on this or future visits (78). Because many teratogens can cause harm before the woman realizes she is pregnant, education about potential risks could be included in school health programs (79). To be effective, preconception care needs to be universally applied and not limited to certain groups that the provider believes to be high-risk (80).

Barriers to receiving prenatal care need to be determined on an individualized basis. Some barriers can be removed by providing evening care, child care services at clinics, and staff with positive attitudes (81). More commonly than structural barriers such as child care, money, and transportation, women have reported many motivational or attitudinal barriers to adequate care. Being undecided about having a baby, feeling that she knows what to do because of a previous pregnancy, being unaware of the pregnancy, expressing denial and ambivalence, are reasons women have given for not getting early or more frequent prenatal care. Multiple barriers to adequate care are often present (82, 83).

Pregnant teenagers have reported needs for emotional and financial support, yet their perceived support and network size may diminish as pregnancy advances. Practitioners who work with pregnant women can help identify sources of support, and especially for teenagers, may help form peer groups (84).

As health care providers work together to provide comprehensive skilled care to pregnant women and their families, they must become more aware of their use of pejorative terminology about pregnancy and childbirth. Some terms, such as "incompetent cervix," "failed induction," or "failure to progress" suggest that women's bodies are ineffectual or faulty. Other terms refer to imprisonment, such as "confinement," "term," "trial of labor," and "arrest of labor progress" (85). Providers should make a conscious effort to avoid this common terminology.

Providers will have to work diligently to provide culturally competent care to minority populations (83). There are no known cultures in which childbearing is viewed with indifference. To gain a better appreciation for the cultural meaning of childbirth, providers can find out what childbearing means to the woman, if childbirth is viewed as a wellness or illness experience, if there are nutritional or activity practices or restrictions, and expectations about support and pain management (86).

Providers are also likely to encounter more women with disabilities, both acquired and congenital, who are experiencing childbearing. The woman with a disability is the best source of information about her own disability. Time and effort should be devoted to determining her sources of support and the services she needs. Depending on the exact disability and the woman's needs, referral to support groups and to care specialists may be appropriate (87).

References

1. Shorter E. Women's Bodies: A social history of women's encounter with health, ill-health, and medicine. New Brunswick: Transaction Publishers, 1991.
2. National Center for Health Statistics. Health, United States, 1990. Hyattsville, MD: Public Health Service, 1991, 54–55, 62.
3. Kochaneck KD, Hudson BL. Advance report of final mortality statistics, 1992. Monthly Vital Statistics Report, 1994:43.
4. Kitzinger S. Childbirth and society. In: Chalmers I, Enkin M, Keirse M, eds. Effective Care in Pregnancy and Childbirth. Oxford: Oxford University Press, 1989:99–109.
5. Acheson LS, Mitchell LM. The Routine Antenatal Diagnostic Imaging with Ultrasound Study: the challenge to practice evidence-based obstetrics. Arch Family Med 1993;2:1229–1231.
6. Mitford J. The American Way of Birth. New York: Dutton, 1992.
7. Jordan B. Birth in four cultures. 4th ed. Waveland Press, 1993.
8. American College of Obstetricians and Gynecologists. Patient Choice: Maternal-fetal conflict. Washington, DC: The American College of Obstetricians and Gynecologists, 1989.
9. Kolder VE, Gallagher J, Parsons MT. Court-ordered obstetrical interventions. N Engl J Med 1987;316:1192–1196.
10. Nelson LJ, Milliken M. Compelled medical treatment of pregnant women: Life, liberty and law in conflict. JAMA 1988;259:1060–1066.
11. Acheson LS, Danner SC. Postpartum care and breastfeeding. Primary Care 1993;20:729–747.
12. Hughes DC, Runyan SJ. Prenatal care and public policy: lessons for promoting women's health. JAMWA 1995;50:156–159.
13. Simkin P. Just another day in a woman's life? Women's long-term perceptions of their first birth experience. Part 1. Birth 1991;18:203–210.
14. Enkin MW, Kierse MJNC, Renfrew MJ, Neilson JP, eds. Pregnancy and Childbirth Module of the Cochrane Database of Systematic Reviews, London: BMJ Publishing Group, 1995 (updated biannually).
15. Chalmers I, Enkin M, Keirse M, eds. Effective Care in Pregnancy and Childbirth. Oxford: Oxford University Press, 1989.
16. Nesbitt TS, Baldwin LM. Access to obstetric care. Primary Care 1993;20:509–522.
17. Culpepper L, Jack B. Psychosocial issues in pregnancy. Primary Care 1993;20:599–619.
18. American Academy of Family Practitioners. OB Key Contact Newsletter. October 1994.
19. Wolfe SM, ed. Delivering a better childbirth experience: nurse-midwives provide an important alternative in obstetric care. Public Citizen Health Research Group Health Letter 1995;11:1–7.
20. Klein M. The effectiveness of family practice maternity care: a cross-cultural and environmental view. Primary Care 1993;20:523–536.
21. Public Health Service Expert Panel on the Content of Prenatal Care. Caring for our future: The content of Prenatal Care. Washington, DC: Public Health Service, 1989.
22. Jack BW, Culpepper L. Preconception care. Risk reduction and health promotion in preparation for pregnancy. JAMA 1990;264:1147–1149.
23. Levitt C. Preconception health promotion. Primary Care 1993;20:537–549.
24. Jack BW, Campanile C, McQuade W, Kogan MD. The negative pregnancy test: an opportunity for preconception care. Arch Fam Med 1995;4:340–345.
25. American College of Obstetricians and Gynecologists. Exercise during pregnancy and the postpartum period. Technical Bulletin 189. Am Fam Physician 1994;49:1258–1259.
26. Institute of Medicine Committee on Nutritional Status during pregnancy and lactation. Nutrition during pregnancy and lactation: an implementation guide. Washington, DC: National Academy Press, 1992.
27. Briggs GF, Freeman RK, Yaffe SJ. Drugs in Pregnancy and Lactation. 3rd ed. Baltimore: Williams & Wilkins, 1990.
28. Kitzinger S. Sex during pregnancy: the sexuality of birth after childbirth & breastfeeding. In: Women's Experience of Sex. New York: Penguin Books, 1983:198–230.
29. American College of Obstetricians and Gynecologists. Antenatal diagnosis of genetic disorders. (ACOG Technical Bulletin 108) Washington, DC: ACOG, 1987.
30. Neilson JP, Alfirevic Z, Gosden C. Chorion villus sampling compared with amniocentesis for prenatal diagnosis. In: Enkin MW, Kierse MJNC, Renfrew MJ, Neilson JP, eds. Pregnancy and Childbirth Module of the Cochrane Database of Systematic Reviews, London: BMJ Publishing Group, 1995:244–257.

31. Neilson JP. Routine ultrasound in early pregnancy. In: Enkin MW, Kierse MJNC, Renfrew MJ, Neilson JP, eds. Pregnancy and Childbirth Module of the Cochrane Database of Systematic Reviews, London: BMJ Publishing Group, 1995:83

32. Ewigman BG, Crane JP, Frigoletto FD, LeFevre ML, Bain RP, McNellis D. A randomized trial of prenatal ultrasound screening: impact on perinatal outcome. N Engl J Med 1993;329:821–827.

33. LeFevre ML, Bain RP, Ewigman BG, Frigoletto FD, Crane JP, McNellis D, and the RADIUS Study Group. A randomized trial of prenatal ultrasonographic screening: impact on maternal management and outcome. Am J Obstet Gynecol 1993;169:483–489.

34. Saari-Kemppainen A, Karjalainen O, Ylostalo P, Heinonen OP. Ultrasound screening and perinatal mortality: controlled trial of systematic one-stage screening in pregnancy. Lancet 1990;336:387–391.

35. US Department of Health and Human Services, Public Health Service, National Institutes of Health. Diagnostic ultrasound imaging in pregnancy. Washington, DC: US Government Printing Office, 1984. NIH Publication No. 84-667.

36. US Department of Health and Human Services. US Department of Justice. Surgeon General's Workshop on Violence and Public Health: Report. Washington, DC: US Department of Health and Human Services, 1986.

37. McFarlane J, Parker B, Soeken K, Bullock L. Assessing for abuse during pregnancy. JAMA 1992;267:3176–3178.

38. Koss MP, Heslet L. Somatic consequences of violence against women. Arch Fam Med 1992;1:53–59.

39. Pearlman MD, Tintinalli JE, Lorenz RP. Blunt trauma during pregnancy. N Engl J Med 1990;323:1609–1613.

40. Rose A. Effects of childhood sexual abuse on childbirth: one woman's story. Birth 1992;19:214–218.

41. Acheson LS. Family violence and breastfeeding. Arch Fam Med 1995;4:650–652.

42. Windsor RA. The Handbook to Plan, Implement and Evaluate Smoking Cessation Programs for Pregnant Women. White Plains, NY: March of Dimes Birth Defects Foundation, 1990.

43. Chazotte C, Youchah JR, Haris-Allen M, Geller A, Kandall S, Fleischman AR, et al. The March of Dimes Substance Abuse Curriculum for Obstetricians and Gynecologists. White Plains, NY: March of Dimes Birth Defects Foundation, 1995.

44. Apgar BS, Churgay CA. Spontaneous abortion. Primary Care 1993;20:621–627.

45. Ambulatory Sentinel Practice Network. Spontaneous abortion in primary care. J Am Board Fam Pract 1988;1:15–23.

46. Rosenfeld JA. Grief and bereavement after spontaneous abortion. Am Fam Phys 1991;43:1679–1684.

47. Carson SA, Buster JE. Ectopic pregnancy. N Engl J Med 1993;329:1174–1180.

48. Schutze GE, Landers S. Management of infants born to women with sexually transmitted diseases. Am Fam Physician 1994;50:1479–1486.

49. Majeroni BA. Chlamydial cervicitis: complications and new treatment options. Am Fam Physician 1994;49:1825–1829.

50. American College of Obstetricians and Gynecologists. Perinatal herpes simplex virus infections. Washington, DC: ACOG Technical Bulliten No.122, 1988.

51. Prevention of perinatal transmission of hepatitis B virus: prenatal screening of all pregnant women for hepatitis B surface antigen. MMWR 1988;37:341–351.

52. Connor EM, Sperling RS, Gelber R, et al. Reduction of maternal-infant transmission of human immunodeficiency virus type 1 with zidovudine treatment. N Engl J Med 1994;331:1173–1180.

53. Peckham C, Gibb D. Mother-to-child transmission of the human immunodeficiency virus. N Engl J Med 1995;333:298–302.

54. Mohle-Boetani JC, Schuchat A, Plikaytis BD, Smith JD, Broome CV. Comparison of prevention strategies for neonatal group B streptococcal infection: a population-based economic analysis. JAMA 1993;270:1442–1448.

55. Scherger JE, Levitt C, Acheson LS, et al. Teaching family-centered perinatal care in family medicine, Part 1. Fam Med 1992;24:288–298.

56. Kennell J, Klaus M, McGrath S, Robertson S, Hinckley C. Continuous emotional support during labor in a U.S. hospital. JAMA 1991;265:2197–2201.

57. Kennell J, McGrath S. Labor support by a doula for middle-income couples: the effect on Cesarean rates. Pediatr Res 1993;33:12A.

58. Hueston WJ, Applegate JA, Mansfield CJ, et al. Practice variations between family physicians and obstetricians in the management of low-risk pregnancies. J Fam Pract 1995;40:345–351.

59. Hundley VA, et al. Midwife managed delivery unit: a randomised controlled comparison with consultant led care. BMJ 1994;309:1400–1404.

60. Deutchmann ME, Sills D, Connor PD. Perinatal outcomes: a comparison between family physicians and obstetricians. J Am Board Fam Pract 1995;8: 440–447.

61. Stafford RS. Alternative strategies for controlling rising Ceasrean section rates. JAMA 1990;263: 683–687.

62. Tussing AD, Wojtowycz MA. The Cesarean decision in New York State, 1986: economic and noneconomic aspects. Med Care 1992;30:529–540.

63. Chaska BW, Mellstrom MS, Grambsch PM, Nesse RE. Influence of site of obstetric care and delivery on pregnancy management and outcome. J Am Board Fam Pract 1988;1:152–163.

64. Kelly RB, Acheson LS, Zyzanski SJ. Comparison of three prenatal risk scores in a series of low-risk pregnancies. Fam Med 1988;20:122–127.

65. Wall EW. Assessing obstetric risk: a review of obstetric risk-scoring systems. J Fam Pract 1988;27:153–163.

66. Rooks JP, Weatherby NL, Ernst EKM et al. Outcomes of care in birth centers: The National Birth Center Study. N Engl J Med 1989;321:1804–1811.

67. VanTuinen I, Wolfe SM. Unnecessary Cesarean sections: halting a national epidemic. Washington, DC: Public Citizen's Health Research Group, 1992.

68. Acheson LS. Management of breech presentation. Clinical Consult Obstet Gynecol 1993;5:267–275.

69. Nelson JP. EFM + scalp sampling vs. intermittent auscultation in labour. In: Enkin MW, Kierse MJNC, Renfrew MJ, Neilson JP, eds. Pregnancy and Childbirth Module of the Cochrane Database of Systemic Reviews. London: BMJ Publishing Group, 1995.

70. MacDonald D, Grant A, Sheridan-Periera M, Boylan P, Chalmers I. The Dublin randomized controlled trial of intrapartum fetal heart rate monitoring. Am J Obstet Gynecol 1985;152:524–539.

71. Oriol N. Report of a study on walking epidural. Presented at the 10th BIRTH conference, Boston, MA, 1992.

72. Johnson S, Rosenfeld JA. Effect of epidural anesthesia on length of second stage of labor. J Fam Pract 1995;40:244–247.

73. Niehaus LS, Chaska BW, Nesse RE. The effects of epidural anesthesia on type of delivery. J Am Board Fam Pract 1988;1:238–244.

74. Thorp JA, Hu DH, Albin RM, et al. The effect of intrapartum epidural analgesia on nulliparous labor: a randomized controlled prospective trial. Am J Obstet Gynecol 1993;169: 851–858.

75. Churgay CA, Smith MA, Blok B. Maternal fever during labor—what does it mean? JABFP 1994;7: 14–24.

76. Gjerdingen DK, Froberg DG, Kochevar L. Changes in women's mental and physical health from pregnancy through six months postpartum. J Fam Pract 1991;32:161–166.

77. Stotland NL. Social change and women's reproductive health care. Women's Health Issues 1990;2:4–11.

78. Bauer WS, Ludka DA. Getting pregnancy off to a good start—before it starts. Contemp Nurse Pract 1995;1:16, 19–26.

79. Conover E. Hazardous exposures during pregnancy. JOGNN 1994;23:524–532.

80. Cefalo RC, Moos M. Preconception care: a focus on primary prevention. Primary Care Update OB/Gyn 1994;1:188–193.

81. McClanahan P. Improving access to and use of prenatal care. JOGNN 1992;21:280–284.

82. Passannante MR, Espenshade J, Weiss G. Prenatal care use at an inner-city university hospital: why so low? Women's Health Issues 1994;4:209–218.

83. Burks JA. Factors in the utilization of prenatal services by low-income black women. Nurse Pract 1992;17:34, 46, 49–50.

84. May KM. Social networks and help-seeking experiences of pregnant teens. JOGNN 1992;21:497–502.

85. Freda MC. Childbearing, reproductive control, aging women, and health care: the projected ethical debates. JOGNN 1994;23:144–152.

86. Callister LC. Cultural meanings of childbirth. JOGNN 1995;24:327–331.

87. Wasser AM, Killoran, CL, Bansen, SS. Pregnancy and disability. NAACOG's Clin Issues Perinatal Women's Health Nurs 1993;4:328–337.

10.5

Infertility

Miriam B. Rosenthal

Introduction

The ability to bear children when and if one wishes is considered a part of normal adult development for both women and men. Fertility has been highly valued and viewed as the link between generations. However, approximately 10 to 15% of couples of reproductive age in the United States are having difficulty with conception and/or with the ability to bear a child. Approximately 4.9 million women aged 15 to 44 years have impaired fertility, 2.2 million have no children (primary infertility), and 2.7 million have one child or more but are having difficulty having as many as desired (secondary infertility). Since 1988, there has been an increase in the problem of infertility caused by delaying childbearing and an increase in women aged 35 to 44 desiring offspring. Increasing numbers of women and men are seeking treatment. Approximately 43% of women with infertility problems seek help and approximately 24% of these women receive high-tech treatments such as tubal surgery, intrauterine inseminations, ovulation inductions, or in-vitro fertilization (1, 2).

However, even without treatment, approximately half of the infertile women eventually conceive. Some variables affecting who conceives are duration of the infertility problem, age of the woman, and medical problems (2). The emotional pain caused by infertility is considerable, and there has been increasing attention paid to the psychological effects and how these might be optimally helped (3, 4).

The primary care clinician is often the first medical person whom the individual or couple may consult regarding their concerns about having children. The clinician may do the early diagnostic work and counseling during much of the couple's attempts at pregnancy. Most important, these clinicians will care for the family with or without children. This chapter gives an overview of some problems of infertility, some treatment issues including the incredible advances in technology, and addresses the psychological aspects.

Motivations for Childbearing

The ability to reproduce is considered central to one's core gender identity, self-concept, and body image. A new baby may bring considerable joy to a family. This does not mean that everyone wants children, but for many individuals the desire to experience a pregnancy, or to impregnate a partner, and to have and raise a child is compelling. The wish for a pregnancy is not always the same as the wish for a child. Part of a person's adult development is related to identifying with one's parents and having offspring. A woman may long to have a pregnancy to assure herself that her body is working properly, particularly her reproductive organs. For a man, the ability to impregnate a partner assures him of his virility. The wish for a biological child may represent a response to parental, societal, or cultural pressures, a need to carry on one's genetic heritage, a way of achieving immortality, or a way of preserving or enriching a relationship. It may be a way of responding to a loss such as the death or departure of a parent or a close person. There is controversy over whether the longing for a child is instinctual or societally conditioned (5, 6).

Definitions

A couple is defined as infertile if they have a year of unprotected regular intercourse and do not conceive. The term "fecundability" refers to the probability of achieving a pregnancy within one menstrual cycle (approximately 25% normally). Birth rates in the United States have declined from 55 per 1000 population in 1790 to 15.5 per 1000 population in 1990. The most popular explanations for this decrease are (*a*) changing roles for women, (*b*) later marriages, (*c*) delayed age of childbearing, (*d*) knowledge that almost all children survive to adulthood, (*e*) an increase in effective use of birth control, (*f*) liberalization of abortion, (*g*) environmental concerns, and (*h*) a worrisome economy.

Etiology

Infertility was often considered a woman's problem. Yet, in approximately 40% of couples, male factors are involved wholly or in part. Infertility increases with age especially for women aged over 35 years (7). The most common physical problems that have been clearly identified in the United States as causes of infertility are ovulatory problems, fallopian tubal disease, semen factor problems, and endometriosis (1).

Ovulation problems are found in approximately 40% of cases. Causes of anovulatory cycles are multiple and include physiological causes, such as after pregnancy or hormonal contraception, hypothalamic-pituitary dysfunction, medications, thyroid or other hormone dysfunction, or ovarian failure (see Chapter 12.2). Fallopian tube pathology may be caused by pelvic infections, often from sexually transmitted diseases, intrauterine devices used for contraception, or occasionally peritoneal infection caused by a ruptured appendix (2). Some less well-demonstrated causes, some of which are still controversial, relate to cervical factors, luteal phase deficiencies, and sexual problems that interfere with performance such as erectile dysfunction, vaginismus, and lack of desire. In approximately 10 to 30% of couples, there are multiple factors. Unexplained infertility occurs in approximately 17 to 20% of couples (1, 2).

Male infertility has been studied less well than infertility in women. Of the 40 to 50% of male subfertility, approximately half have potentially treatable conditions such as varicoceles, medication use, ductal obstruction, (e.g., epididymal, vasal, ejaculatory), an endocrinopathy, or infections (8, 9).

Evaluation

The woman usually initiates the infertility workup by expressing her concerns to a primary care clinician. A careful history and physical exam are suggested, and if a male partner is involved, he should be included early in the investigation.

The evaluation and early stages of treatment often proceed at the same time. Much of the evaluation and treatment can be performed by the primary care provider. Some providers, with interest and expertise, may feel more comfortable going further. At the point when assisted reproductive technology is contemplated, consultation with a fertility-specialist/gynecologist and his team is usually needed. However, the provider is likely to continue to be involved with the family as the infertility workup and treatment continues.

The first step (Table 10.5.1) is counseling and education. Explanations about reasonable expectations, such as how long after stopping oral contraceptives it can take to reestablish regular ovulatory cycles, how long it may take for the average couple to become pregnant, and the fertile times of the menstrual cycle, may reassure the woman and eventually solve the infertility problem. Generally, 80% of women under age 35 years using no contraception who are having regular sexual inter-course become pregnant within 1 year. Of the remaining 20%, two-thirds will conceive within 2 years. Only 1 of 6 to 8 sexual intercourses at the time of ovulation produce a pregnancy that survives 2 weeks. Waiting 3 to 6 months with assurance, education, and learning the time of ovulation may be reasonable. However, for women over 35 years of age, the clinician may wish to move ahead more rapidly in looking into causes for infertility (2).

Dispelling some myths such as those stating that nervousness causes infertility, that adoption increases the couple's chances for becoming pregnant, and that taking a vacation will solve the problems is helpful. The clinician must point out that unexplained infertility is not synonymous with psychogenic infertility, although there are certain psychological causes.

Secondly, a complete history of the couple should be obtained. History of sexually transmitted diseases, abdominal or genitourinary surgery, previous pregnancies with other partners, abnormal Pap smears, pelvic inflammatory disease, medication use of both partners, menstrual history, and general medical history including comorbid conditions is essential. Medication use by both partners should be evaluated for its necessity.

Table 10.5.1. First Steps in Evaluation of a Couples' Fertility

- Counseling and education
- Complete medical, sexual and genito-urinary history of both partners
- Complete physical examination of both partners
- Cultures for STDs
- Endocrine assessment
- Ovulation assessment (3–6 months)
- Postcoital test for sperm viability
- Assessment of fallopian term patency by hysterosalpingogram
- Semen evaluation
- Psychological evaluation
- High-risk obstetrical and genetic consultation

A sexual history is important. Frequency, use of contraceptives, methods of sexual intercourse, frequency of ejaculation in vagina, satisfaction, and presence of other partners should all be questioned. Having sexual intercourse regularly, but failing to ejaculate into vagina because of anal or oral sex or because of premature or retarded ejaculation will decrease the likelihood of pregnancy.

A complete physical examination of both partners—a complete medical and gynecological exam for the woman and a complete examination including genitourinary examination of the man—is essential. In both individuals, the provider should watch for signs of STDs, malformation, and surgery. Cultures should be done for STDs including Chlamydia trachomatis, Ureaplasma, urealyticum, and Mycoplasma hominis (1). If any abnormalities are found, they should be treated while the fertility workup continues. Infections should be treated. If the woman is noted to have signs of endometriosis or PID, a pelvic ultrasound, a hysterosalpingogram, and a consultation for laparoscopy may be the next step.

Laboratory evaluation is essential. An endocrine evaluation should be done including studies of thyroid and adrenal. Prolactin levels should be obtained if the woman has galactorrhea.

Then, and while the above is continuing, the woman and provider can assess the presence of ovulation by a careful menstrual history, monitoring of basal body temperature (BBT), and/or endometrial biopsy. A minimum of 3 months of record keeping of BBT charts is necessary to detect if the woman is ovulating by this method. However, it takes a great deal of thoroughness and constancy to accomplish this. Over-the-counter LH surge predictors are now available and, although expensive ($35 to $55 per month), can be used to both determine ovulation and allow the couple to act immediately. Follicle stimulating hormone levels may be helpful also in assessing ovarian function (2).

For women who have had repeated miscarriages and/or fetal loss, consultation with a high-risk obstetrical consultant may be considered. Genetic counseling, chromosomal studies, and evaluation for syndromes such as the lupus anticoagulant that can cause recurrent miscarriage, may be needed.

If the woman is ovulating and all other tests have been normal, the next step may be either a postcoital test or a semen analysis. A postcoital test provides information about the survival of sperm in the vagina after exposure to cervical mucus and information about the sperm. Sperm analysis can be done 2 to 5 days after avoiding sexual activity; two to three specimens should be assessed. The specimens should be collected in clean containers, not condoms that may have spermicidal properties. It should be delivered to a laboratory within 1 hour of collection and protected from the cold. The World Health Organization guidelines for normal values are in Table 10.5.2. Fallopian tube patency can be assessed by hysterosalpingogram or observations at laparoscopy.

Concurrently a psychological evaluation is best done comprehensively at the start of any infertility workup. This would include history of depressive syndromes, eating disorders, premenstrual dysphoric disorders, any other major psychiatric disorders, and family history

Table 10.5.2. Normal Semen Analysis

Volume	2 mL or more
Sperm concentration	20 million/mL or more
Motility	50% or more with forward progression or 25% or more with rapid progression within 60 minutes of ejaculation
Morphology	30% or more normal forms
White blood cells	Fewer than 2 million per mL

of mental illness. Behaviors such as alcohol abuse, illegal drug use, or smoking should be identified. It is helpful to know about the individuals' coping mechanisms and their relationship strengths for both heterosexual and homosexual individuals (10–12).

Treatments

Often the woman becomes pregnant during the evaluation phase of an infertility workup that can take 3 to 6 months. Increased sexual intercourse at the appropriate time of month may succeed. Treatment may include correction of thyroid abnormalities, treatment of infections, cessation of medications, and treatment of endometriosis with medications and/or laparoscopic ablation. Surgery for tubal disease is still controversial in the treatment of infertility (1). Psychological support is helpful throughout these procedures and can be provided by the provider, staff member, or a mental health person.

Ovulation Induction

After the evaluation and correction of any obvious problems, the evaluation may have shown a paucity or complete lack of ovulation. The next step may be ovulation induction. The provider may not feel comfortable and referral may be suggested at this time.

A simplistic first-step approach to ovulation induction in a woman less than age 35 years who has time to try different methods is the use of an oral contraceptive agent for 3 months. Sometimes, afterwards, ovulation may occur. This method may be no better than placebo (waiting another 6 months), but certainly has less expense, side effects, and less chance of multiple births.

Ovulation induction medications include clomiphene citrate, an antiestrogen preparation, gonadotropin preparations, and pulsatile gonadotropin-releasing hormone administra-

tion (1). Ovulation induction by clomiphene citrate is often tried first because it is the least expensive, can be given orally, and has a lower rate of multiple pregnancies. Use of clomiphene and other ovulation-induction medications require careful observation and repeated serum estradiol levels and pelvic ultrasounds. Ovarian hyperstimulation syndrome must be recognized if abdominal pain and distention becomes prominent.

These medications often cause considerable emotional lability. Infertility patients may not complain about medication side effects because their wish to have a child is so great. They may minimize their discomfort. Knowing about the psychological side effects of the medications often provides great reassurance.

Intrauterine Placement of Semen

If ovulation is occurring, and if the postcoital test is abnormal, the next step may be placement of semen directly into the uterus with a catheter at the time of ovulation. This is an attempt to bypass the cervical factors.

Assisted Reproductive Technology (ART)

The first in vitro fertilization baby, Louise Brown, was born in England in 1978. Since then, there has been a tremendous growth in knowledge about ART. ART includes those treatments for infertility in which ova are retrieved from the ovary, subsequently fertilized with sperm, and transferred back to the woman's uterus. The most common procedures are in vitro fertilization (IVF) with transfer of the preembryo into the uterus, gamete intrafallopian transfer (GIFT) with the placement of ova and sperm in the fallopian tube, and zygote intrafallopian transfer (ZIFT) in which the fertilized oocytes are placed in the uterus or tubes. Ovulation induction with Clomid or Pergonal or other regimens usually precedes the above procedures, although natural cycles also are used at times. Excess preembryos are sometime cryopreserved to be used later. They may be transferred to the patient's uterus, donated to another couple, stored for a certain length of time, or destroyed (2).

The success rates, namely the delivery of a live baby, after ART procedures have been steadily increasing, and in some programs they are as high as 20% or more. However, this means that many patients are not able to become pregnant or have miscarriages. Women may feel a great sense of loss and despair, or more hopefully can consider adopting or restructuring their lives without children. A major goal of counseling and support is to help decide how many cycles women should go through and when to stop treatments (13–16).

Another advance in reproductive technology has been the ability to provide ova and sperm from another person for those individuals whose own gametes may not be usable. At this time, sperm can be cryopreserved while ova cannot be (2).

Ovum Donation

In this procedure, another woman (outside the couple) who has viable ova and agrees to donate ova is usually given ovulation-inducing medication. Then her ovaries are monitored with pelvic ultrasound and ova are recovered with ultrasound guided transvaginal follicular aspiration. These ova are fertilized with the male partner's sperm and combined with IVF or GIFT. The medical indications for ovum donation are (a) premature ovarian failure, (b) ovarian dysfunction due to chemotherapy or radiation, (c) presence of genetic abnormalities especially the X chromosomes such as Turner's syndrome, or (d) poor response to ART because of "poor" quality of ova and/or embryos. The use of donor eggs has enabled some "older" women to have babies, the oldest at this time is a woman in Italy aged 63 years (17–19).

The recipients and the donors in such programs require counseling and support during these procedures. Donors need to give fully informed consent. To do this, they need to know

and understand the procedures. They need to decide whether they want to be anonymous or known to the recipient. Above all, if they do not have any children, they need to ask about the risk to their own future fertility. In some programs, egg donors are recruited from the community, are paid, and are tested extensively including not only physical and genetic attributes but psychologically. In some programs, other women going through ART procedures give some of their excess ova in exchange for reduced fees.

The recipients in egg donor programs need to discuss secrecy and disclosure to family, friends, and subsequent children, the risks of multiple births, the use of multifetal pregnancy reduction if there are multiple fetuses, and how they feel about the use of another woman's genetic material. For both donor and recipient, there are issues about self-esteem, body image, and femininity. Again, the ovarian stimulating drugs may cause emotional swings. For the primary care clinician, knowledge of these issues may help with medical care and counseling often done outside the fertility clinic. If the woman is successful and delivers a live child, the clinician may be asked to discuss with the parents the issues of disclosure, how much information should be given to a child about the mode of conception, who the donor was, and with whom this information should be shared. The family doctor above all may need genetic information later for treating medical conditions.

Sperm Donation

Sperm donation may be either from a husband or "donor." Approximately 30,000 babies are born each year with donor sperm, although this figure is probably low. "Donor" sperm is usually obtained from men whose identities are not revealed to the recipient, although many of their characteristics and physical features are. There are sperm banks in many parts of the country. The donor sperm is placed in the uterus or combined with ART procedures.

In some localities, women inseminate themselves. Donor insemination, often called therapeutic donor insemination (TDI) is indicated for male infertility, noncorrectable male ejaculatory dysfunction, blood RH problems, male hereditary or genetic disorders, unexplained female infertility, or for women without a male partner. Donors are selected based on good health and absence of genetic disorders, alcohol, or drug abuse. The American Society for Reproductive Medicine (ASRM) publishes guidelines for sperm donation.

Donors are screened for disease especially for hepatitis, sexually transmitted diseases, and human immunodeficiency virus. Donors are tested initially for HIV antibodies, the semen is frozen, and the donor is retested in 180 days. Donors are compensated financially in differing amounts, but ASRM recommends that the amounts not be such that "monetary incentive is the primary factor in donating sperm." Consent forms must be signed. Record keeping has not been guided by any legal guidelines. It is recommended that records be complete especially regarding HIV status, be confidential, and be available if recipients, offspring (after reaching a certain age), and donor all agree. Although frozen sperm produces lower pregnancy rates, it is safer to use frozen sperm and its use is recommended (20).

Disclosure to offspring is still debated, and individuals and partners must make their own choices often with sensitive counseling. There is no evidence for increased psychological problems for couples or offspring (21–25).

Complications of Assisted Reproductive Pregnancies

Pregnancies following ART involve no increase in spontaneous abortions and no increase in congenital malformations. If there are increases in ectopic pregnancies or heterotopic pregnancies, these may be associated with tubal diseases, tubal surgery, prior ectopics, pelvic adhesions, endometriosis, and history of sexually transmitted diseases.

Special Issues in Infertility

Use of Surrogates in Infertility

The term "surrogate mother," when used in infertility treatments, refers to the use of a woman to carry a fetus for a woman who is unable to do so. The surrogate carries a baby who will be relinquished to the "commissioning couple" at birth. Here IVF and embryo transfer are combined with the use of another woman as the carrier. There are considerable ethical and legal issues about surrogacy, but it is being carried out in several states in the United States. Surrogates are usually paid an agreed fee, and contracts are written about behaviors during the pregnancy. Surrogates and commissioning couples require considerable counseling for the best outcome. Because many couples travel far to infertility clinics and the surrogates may come from other geographic areas, the primary care clinician may be caring for the couple during and after the birth of their child. There are considerable ethical, legal, and psychological issues beyond the scope of this chapter (26).

Multiple Births and Multifetal Pregnancy Reduction

ART has led to an increase in the number of multiple gestations. Although these have brought the much-sought-after pregnancy to many, multiple gestations have some risks to the health of the mother and the resulting children. There is increased risk of prematurity, preeclampsia, placenta previa, abruptio placentae, and cord accidents. There is an increase in perinatal mortality. Therefore, in some of these pregnancies, the number of fetuses is reduced (27, 28).

The association of any abortion procedure with infertility, although it is done to increase the survival of the remaining fetuses, has political and theological overtones in the highly emotional arena today. The current procedures use a transvaginal or transabdominal approach to a fetal sac, using ultrasound and intracardiac injection of potassium chloride. This is done best during the 7th to 13th week of gestation. The most common complications include further pregnancy loss, bleeding, and infection. There are only a few centers now doing these procedures.

Pretreatment information and education counseling can be of great value to these women and their partners. It is recommended that this include an understanding of the risk that multifetal pregnancy carries to mother and infants and that fetal reduction may be advised. Couples may have to travel some distance for the procedure. They need to receive ongoing support from their original treatment team (29).

Psychological Effects of Infertility and ART

Most couples believe that when they want to have children they can do so. Many have planned their lives carefully, postponing marriage and childbearing while accomplishing other goals. There is considerable frustration, sadness, and a feeling of loss of control to learn that their plans may not be fulfilled.

The psychological effects of infertility are shaped by many factors: (a) one's age when the infertility problems are diagnosed, (b) stage of development, (c) basic personality structure, (d) coping styles and defense mechanisms, (e) preexisting psychopathology, culture, and religion, (f) partner support and attitudes of family and friends, (g) medical causes of the infertility, (h) motivations for pregnancy, and (i) importantly, the skill of the providers who care for the individual, present the information and options, do the procedures and treatments, and help with decisions about stopping treatments if unsuccessful. There is no evidence from many studies to suggest that infertility patients experience psychopathology more often than the population in general or have any special personality style or disorder. Most infertility patients cope well with difficult treat-

ments and are in fact more compliant and agreeable than might be expected, considering the costs, and time they demand.

The psychological effects and reactions are many and variable. They may include depressive symptoms, guilt, shame, a sense of loss, and a sense of sadness with the appearance of each menstrual period. There may be marital, partner, and sexual problems. Some individuals become totally obsessed with getting pregnant so that they may give up job or friends, try each new treatment, avoid family functions where there are children, and avoid relatives at holiday times (30).

The kind of diagnostic procedure that couples goes through may be experienced as intrusive with evaluation of private aspects of one's life and reproductive function. The procedures need not be dehumanizing if done in a sensitive and caring manner. Criticisms of procedures often have to do with how the staff delivers them rather than the procedures themselves.

Infertility also includes women who have experienced repeated fetal loss, and for them this represents personal and difficult situation often not understood by others.

ART offers to infertile individuals and couples the possibility of a biological child, restoration of defective body image, and fulfillment of dreams. However, the success rates are low. Some become depressed clinically after such failures, but many cope and adjust well and consider other options such as adoption or being without children.

Psychological Counseling in Infertility and ART

Depending on the interests, familiarity of the woman and her family, knowledge of the procedures, and expertise in counseling, the provider may wish to counsel the woman and couple herself or use other resources in the community.

Counselors should be familiar with the subject of infertility and its treatments. They must also consider the conflicting perspectives that they may have: the welfare of resulting children, the needs of infertile couples, needs of prospective donors or surrogates, societal standards, and demands of the clinic and medical personnel with whom she or he works. Patients need to be informed about confidentiality.

Counseling may include information giving and education and discussing "implications"—exploring personal and family aspects of the infertility workup and treatments. Psychological support would include discussing the stress of procedures, hormone treatments, cycles of hope and despair, failure to achieve pregnancy, dealing with family and friends, baby showers, holidays, miscarriages, and multiple pregnancy. This may be individual or group. Self-help groups such as RESOLVE have been especially useful to individuals (31). Therapy includes a focus on healing, adjustment of expectations, resolving the anger that may be present if pregnancy does not occur, and restoring an intact body image and self-esteem. Behavioral and cognitive treatments include relaxation and imaging methods and can be very helpful. Some questions that counselors must ask include: What is true informed consent? Can participants withstand the rigors of the procedures? Are there pros and cons to disclosure to family, friends, and the child? Are their psychological sequelae to the procedures? Who should be ruled out from participation in certain procedures?

Some helpful interventions include (*a*) normalizing powerful emotions, (*b*) assessing and reassuring individual regarding psychological reactions, (*c*) giving permission to avoid painful situations and temporary withdrawal from social events, (*d*) teaching coping strategies, (*e*) encouraging self-care, nutrition, rest, exercise, and work, (*f*) helping with pain, secrecy, uncertainty, and shame, (*g*) discussing the impact on marriage and sex, and (*h*) helping partners to know that they may not deal in the same way with stress. Counselors also need to consider their legal and ethical responsibilities and it will be increasingly important to do so.

Bioethical and Legal Issues

There has been considerable thought given to the bioethical and legal aspects of reproductive technology. The United States Constitution protects the rights of persons to procreate by the "right to privacy" provisions (32, 33). There is concern, however, about how much this extends to medical assistance to infertile persons. Most insurance companies do not cover much of the infertility treatments, especially those requiring considerable technology. Therefore, much of this is available only to those with considerable economic resources. Questions arise about who should have access to these treatments and how individuals seeking such treatments should be screened psychosocially, if at all. There has been concern about the marital status of couples coming for treatments; some clinics refuse treatments to single or lesbian women, whereas others do not have such limits. Controversies have risen about the use of reproductive technology by some religious groups, and the use of donor gametes and surrogates has been especially questioned. Some of the other areas which have been discussed concern:

1. The ethics of denying information about their origins to children born of reproductive technologies especially when donor gametes are used
2. Age limits for women undergoing treatments
3. Using ART for nonmedical but social reasons
4. The disposal of excess embryos
5. Multifetal pregnancy reduction

A major concern has been how much these technologies should be monitored and what sorts of legal regulations are appropriate. In many countries there are already laws being enacted that regulate ART. Some states in the United States have regulation already, but there are no federal laws at this time or even guidelines.

Legal issues at this time mainly concern issues of informed consent and quality assurance (2, 3). Some courts have held infertility practitioners responsible for giving information about the nature of the infertility problems, risks of the treatments, alternative treatments, and potential success rates in numbers of live births per cycle of treatment in their clinic. Other matters relate to potential outcomes of excess embryos in ART, written directives about the disposition of the embryos in cases of divorce or death of a partner, side effects of the treatments such as ovarian hyperstimulation syndromes with the use of ovulation induction, and, generally, the kinds of side effects that may result from any of the treatments (32–35).

Quality assurance statutes relate to standards for procedures for patients, for donors, for surrogates. They have written requirements for personnel working in infertility clinics, screening of patients and donors, and record keeping. There are no laws that keep clinics from treating single women with ART proce-dures, yet many women who choose to become pregnant by donor insemination have trouble finding practitioners who will treat them. It is important that primary care practitioners think about the bioethical and legal matters, and have some participation into legislation as it begins to evolve.

Conclusions

Infertility causes significant psychological and medical disturbances in the life of a woman and her partner. The primary provider will often be approached to start evaluation and treatment, and often will be successful in helping the couple conceive. ART therapies are developing at a tremendous rate. Although they are becoming more and more available and successful, legal and moral controversies, expense, and limited access are continuing difficulties. Counseling the woman and her family in this changing area will be a challenge for the provider.

Special Considerations for Nurse Practitioners and Physician Assistants

There are many variations in a couple's understanding and management of infertility. Some will view it as a condition that has been cured by treatment or parenthood and no longer relevant to them. Others see infertility as a permanent condition, feeling "emotionally infertile" even after delivering a baby. Providers must give attention to the patient's experiencing of infertility and avoid focusing only on medical diagnosis and treatment (36). Couples may need assistance separating treatment success and failure from personal success and failure. Health care providers may also feel a sense of failure when a woman does not achieve a pregnancy (37).

Couples have different choices about pur-suing infertility assessments and treatment. Some will not have the economic means to pursue specialist help. Others will feel pressure to try every technological option, in essence "making a career out of the pursuit of pregnancy" (36). They may need assistance making a decision to stop treatments and pursue other aspects of their lives (37).

In general, providers should work with the couple as patients when evaluating infertility problems. However, recognition must be given to the different responses and needs of each individual (36). Women have been shown to undergo more tests and treatment and exhibit more stress than men (38). Women undergoing donor artificial insemination rate the experience more stressful than their husbands, citing factors such as feeling a sense of failure, being unable to discuss the matter with friends or family, timing clinic visits, and being concerned about the donor (39).

Many tests and interventions for infertility are common. Any diagnostic test for infertility can be highly stressful to a woman, not only because of the test procedure itself, but also because the test results may threaten her sexual identity (38). Whether testing is done through the primary care setting or after referral to specialists, women need continuing support and acknowledgment of their feelings.

The achievement of a pregnancy will not necessarily solve all the couple's emotional problems, and they may continue to need counseling related to unresolved marital issues, conflicts with health care providers, self-image problems, or unrealistic expectations about pregnancy. Couples will need education about adaptations to pregnancy, nutrition, preparation for labor, and other routine prenatal care (40).

Helping couples identify sources of support (such as RESOLVE) during evaluation and treatment can help them cope. Additionally, couples who have decided to pursue adoption need the assistance of a social worker, attorney, or others who have expertise with the adoption process. Providers who care for women and their adopted children can help parents understand reactions such as disappointment in the physical characteristics of the child, a response that occurs also when biological children do not fulfill a parent's fantasies. Couples will continue working through other issues, including when to tell the child, whether or not to maintain contact with the biological parent or parents, and how to handle possible negative responses of family and friends. Providers should initiate discussions related to parenting issues and be knowledgeable of available support groups for adoptive parents (41).

Fertility preservation must be addressed in the primary care setting. Providers working with women will have many opportunities to counsel about prevention of STDs and PID, choices in contraception, workplace hazards, and the use of tobacco, alcohol, and drugs (42). Minor causes of infertility can often be addressed by the practitioner, including coital technique, intercourse timing, and stopping the use of lubricants and douches (43).

How much evaluation and treatment is done in the primary care setting will depend on the practitioner's practice setting, credentials of the practitioner and staff, and resources for treatment. Physician consultation is needed for abnormal findings and discussion of treatment modalities (44). Evaluation by reproductive specialists is recommended if the woman has not conceived in 1 year, or sooner if findings indicate the need or the couple is anxious (45). When a referral is made to a reproductive specialist, the provider should tell the woman what to expect in terms of testing, options, time, and costs that may not be covered by insurance (43).

References

1. Jones H. The infertile couple. N Engl J Med 1993; 329:1710–1715.
2. Speroff L, Glass RH, Kase NG. Clinical Gynecologic Endocrinology and Infertility. Baltimore: Williams & Wilkins, 1994
3. Mahlstedt P. The psychological component of infertility. Fertil Steril 1985;43:335–338.
4. Morse CA, Van Hall EV. Psychosocial aspects of infertility: A review of current concepts. J Psychosom Obstet Gynecol 1987;6:157–164.
5. Hoffman LW, Hoffman M. The value of children to parents. In: Fawcett JT, ed. Psychological Perspectives on Population. New York: Basic Books, 1973: 19–73).
6. Rosenthal M. Psychiatric aspects of infertility and assisted reproductive technologies in infertility and reproductive medicine. In: Diamond MP, DeCherney A, eds. Psychol Issues Infertil 1993;4:471–482.
7. Nachtigall RD. Age Related Infertility: Guideline for practice: American Society for Reproductive Medicine, 1995.
8. Sandlow Jl, Donovan JF. Letter to ed. N Engl J Med 1994;330:1154.
9. Dubin L, Amelar RD. Etiologic factors in 1294 consecutive cases of male infertility. Fertil Steril 1971; 22:469–474.

10. Burns LH. An overview of the psychology of infertility In: Greenfield D, ed. Infertility and Reproductive Medicine Clinics of North America. Philadelphia: WB Saunders, 1993:433–454.
11. Freeman EW, et al. Psychological evaluation and support in a program of in vitro fertilization and embryo transfer. Fertil Steril 1985;43:48–53.
12. Klock SC, Maier D. Guidelines for the provision of psychological evaluation for infertile patients at the University of Connecticut Health Center. Fertil Steril 1991;56:680–685.
13. Covington S. Preparing the patient for in vitro fertilization: psychological considerations. Clin Counsult Obstet Gynecol 1994;6: 131–137.
14. Daniluk J, Patinson T, Zouvez C, Mitchel J. Factors related to couples' decisions to attempt in vitro fertilization. J Asst Reprod Genetics 1993;10:310–316.
15. Dennerstein L, Morse C. A review of psychology and social aspects of in vitro fertilization. J Psychosom Obstet Gynecol 1988;9:159–170.
16. Greenfeld D. Assisted reproductive technology: a complex counseling challenge. Clin Counsult Obstet Gynecol 1994;6a:138–142.
17. Braverman AM. Oocyte donation: psychological and counseling issues. Clin Consult Obstet Gynecol 1994; 6:143–149.
18. Braverman A, Corson S. Factors related to preferences in gamete donor sources. Fertil Steril 1995;63:543–549.
19. Healey B. Egg donors for hire: a medical dilemma in search of solutions, not college students. J Women's Health 1995;4:107–109.
20. Guidelines for Gamete Donation: 1993. American Fertility Society Supplement 15–95.
21. Braverman A, Corson S. Factors related to preferences in gamete donor sources. Fertil Steril 1995;63:543–549.
22. Klock SC, Jacob MC, Maier D. A prospective study of donor insemination recipients: secrecy privacy and disclosure. Fertil Steril 1994;62:477 –484.
23. Mahlstedt P, Probasco K. Sperm donors: their attitudes toward providing medical and psychosocial information for recipient couples and donor offspring. Fertil Steril 1991;56:747–753.
24. Mahlstedt P, et al. Emotional factors and the in vitro fertilization and embryo transfer process. J In Vitro Fertil Embryo Transf 1987;4: 232–236.
25. Schover, LR, Collins, RL, Richards, S. Psychological aspects of donor insemination: evaluation and follow up of recipient couples. Fertil Steril 1992;57:583–590.
26. Franks DD. Psychiatric evaluation of women in a surrogate mother program. Am J Psychiatry 1981; 138:1378–1379.
27. Ormont MA, Shapiro PA. Multifetal pregnancy reduction. A review of evolving technology and its psychosocial implications. Psychosomatics 1995;36: 523–530.
28. McKinney M, Dawney J, Timor-Tritsch L. The psychological effects of multifetal pregnancy reduction. Fertil Steril 1995;64:51–61.
29. Greenfeld DA, Walther, VN. Psychological considerations in multifetal pregnancy reduction. Infertil Reprod Med Clin North Am 1993;4: 533–543.
30. Downey J. Mood disorders, psychiatric symptoms and distress in women presenting for infertility evaluation. Fertil Steril 1989;52:425–432.
31. Menning B. The emotional needs of infertile couples. Fertil Steril 1980;34:31–33
32. Andrews L. Legal issues in reproductive technologies. Syllabus Legal and Bioethical Challenge to Effective Counseling. American Fertility Society. San Antonio, TX, November 1994.
33. Williams RS. Taking the legislative initiative: the Florida Assisted Reproductive Technology Act of 1993. Fertil Steril 1994;61:815–816.
34. Jones H. The status of regulation of assisted reproductive technology in the United States. J Asst Reprod Genetics 1993;10:331–335.
35. Robertson JA. Ethical and legal issues in human egg donation. Fertil Steril 1989;52:353–363.
36. Sandelowski M. On infertility. JOGNN 1994;23: 749–752.
37. Olshansky EF. Redefining the concepts of success and failure in infertility treatment. NAACOG's Clin Issues Perinatal Women's Health Nurs 1992;3: 343–346.
38. Halman LJ, Andrews FM, Abbey A. Gender differences and perceptions about childbearing among infertile couples. JOGNN 1994;23:593–600.
39. Pratte TW, Gass-Sternas KA. Appraisal, coping, and emotional health of infertile couples undergoing donor artificial insemination. JOGNN 1993;22: 516–527.
40. Garner C. Infertility. In: Fogel CI, Woods NF, eds. Women's Health Care. Thousand Oaks: Sage, 1995: 611–628.
41. Sherrod RA. Helping infertile couples explore the option of adoption. JOGNN 1992;21:465–470.
42. Keating CE. The role of the expanded function nurse in fertility preservation. NAACOG's Clin Issues Perinatal Women's Health Nurs 1992;3: 293–300.
43. Samuels JI. Facing infertility. ADVANCE Nurse Practitioners 1995;3:12–16.
44. Weseman LM. Infertility. In: Star WL, Lommell LL, Shannon MT, eds. Women's primary health care. Washington DC: American Nurses' Association, 1995:12-59–12-71.
45. Wood SC. Infertility. In: Youngkin EQ, Davis MS, eds. Women's Health. Norwalk: Appleton & Lange, 1994:161–202.

10.6

Caring for Adoptive Mother

Jo Ann Rosenfeld

Introduction

With more women putting off childbearing into later years, and with the increase in infertility, adoption has become a choice for more women and families. Approximately 35,000 children in the United States are adopted yearly, half of these through private adoption (1). There are approximately 8000 to 10,000 children adopted from foreign countries into the United States yearly (2). Adoption has also become a more visible choice, with greater media and legal attention, perhaps because of the increased numbers and perhaps because of the fact that "baby boomers" and middle-class women are adopting babies. Nonetheless, despite media attention, adoption is an absolutely private decision between the woman and her partner, and at times her family. Het-erosexual and homosexual couples are using adoption as a means of continuing their family. The primary care provider may be asked to care for the birthmother and the adoptive mother in this process.

Caring for the Birthmother

Historically, until recently, many adolescents and unmarried women who became pregnant put their child up for adoption, with little or no control of the process or the decision. After the 1970s when social standards changed, adoption became one of several choices. In the 1990s, only 5% of children born to unmarried mothers are placed in adoption (1).

The decision to place a newborn for adoption is difficult and emotionally exhausting.

The provider may be involved at the time pregnancy is discovered or during prenatal care. Counseling about options and adoption will take time and involvement; providers may want to attempt themselves or may want to refer the woman to a responsible nonjudgmental social work or agency. The decision for the woman is seldom simple, and may change several times over the course of the pregnancy and early childhood. The decision involves many considerations (e.g., financial, educational, religious, social, marital status, and family status or number of children) and many other people including the teenager's mother and father (3), the baby's father, other family members, religious leaders, and friends (4). Certainly the provider cannot act as judge, but only as supporter. Making sure the woman knows that care will continue no matter what her decision is important.

During prenatal care, a complete history including social and family history is essential. The woman may not know or be hesitant about giving information about the birthfather; reluctance may be associated with an incestuous relationship. The woman may be at higher risk for sexually transmitted diseases. The family and social situation of a woman who contemplates adoption is likely to be disturbed, and careful history taking of the family and its relationships are important.

The care the woman receives during pregnancy, labor, and delivery should be identical to anyone else's. However, delivery may not be as joyful a time, and a sense of grieving may be present. Encouraging the woman to take an interest in the child and see and hold it often helps the grieving process. If the woman wants to go home early or wants to be hospitalized away from the obstetrical floor, these wishes should be honored.

The adoption may be through an agency or private. An agency and its personnel should be a support for the woman legally and emotionally. Often there is structured counseling involved. With different agencies, many mothers have some input into the family or situation for their child. In a private adoption, the mother can choose who, where, and how the child is adopted, but there are fewer supports and the birthmother will need her own lawyer. The mother may want to know the prospective parents, and may want different amounts of interaction with them. The provider should discuss specifically the wishes and plans of the birthmother, especially for the delivery and hospital care, and make the hospital aware of these plans. The provider should urge the woman to have the legal work done in advance.

No matter how prepared the woman is, giving up the child will be difficult. The provider or counselor and woman should discuss what she is likely to feel and what the normal grieving reaction will be. It will take her time to recover, and she will need support from her provider and others during this period and later (1).

Caring for the Adoptive Mother

The provider is often asked to perform an "adoption" physical in the course of the home study adoption process. At this time, the provider can discuss with the woman and/or couple their thoughts and plans for the adoption and the concerns and problems it may involve, without being judgmental. Helping the woman voice her thought-processes may help her crystallize her plans and goals. Later, during the adoption process, the provider may be called on to (a) help the woman deal with the stress of the process, (b) give advice as to the health or disease state of the proposed adopted child, (c) treat the child once adopted, (d) help the woman deal with new problems fitting the child into the family, or (e) later helping the woman and her child deal with adoption. Adoption creates different stresses to which the provider should be sensitive. Working with the woman and family will create a stronger family structure and provider-woman relationship.

The Decision

The decision to adopt is seldom made suddenly or hastily. Many factors may weigh in the balance, such as infertility, failure of infertility evaluations and treatment, desire for children of same genetic composition, desire to help needy children, genetic diseases, desire for more children without increasing birth rate, and single parenting or homosexual partners. The woman and her partner may have experienced a period of intense pressure to "have a baby," and then failing or deciding to stop infertility treatments, they turn their whole passionate attention to adopting. The provider needs to discover how the woman and her partner have come to the decision. Urging them to get the most information possible is always helpful as they start this process.

The decision also entails how the couple intend to adopt and what considerations are important. Adopting from a cousin or an unknown "friend of a friend" has a whole different group of concerns and obstacles than adopting through an established organization; adopting in the United States is different from adopting from foreign countries, and adopting across racial or ethnic lines causes another group of considerations and problems forward.

The woman may be under intense personal pressure to have a child "no matter what," because of personal, family, or biological urgency. She may feel she is a "failure" for not producing a child or not being physically able to have a child. She may have had powerful insistence to have "only her own child." Adoption may be a first or last step. It may come to her with forceful compulsion to succeed at last.

The provider should help the woman verbalize and deal with some of these forces by asking how she came to the decision to adopt. If she has long-term feelings of failure and inadequacy, she and her partner may need some counseling. Without acting as an authority, the provider should inquire into the woman's plans, just as she would ask about childbirth

plans. Has she contacted an agency or a lawyer? Does she know what is involved? Has she discussed the cost, i.e., does she have the means to pay for the adoption and raise a child? The woman must also determine whether the child will be covered for preexisting conditions under her insurance. Insurance companies do not always cover adopted children from the date of adoption for preexisting conditions the way they do a child who is born with a birth defect. If the child has any medical condition, such as is common with foreign adoptions or medically needy children, this can create huge uncovered medical bills. There may be ways around this, if it is thought of in advance.

Other plans concerning her and the family should be discussed. Has she investigated whether she will get "maternity leave?" Many jobs give maternity leave as "sick leave" and adopted parents can only take vacation time for adoption maternity. Now she can take time off unpaid under the Family and Medical Leave Act. If she is compelled to take 3 to 6 months by the agency or government, this may be a significant financial burden. Some adoptive agencies or countries want one parent at home with the child.

If she is adopting a medically disabled or foreign child, has she thought of what disabilities she can handle? Discussing medical problems with her provider may be a sensible way to deal with this. A woman living alone in an apartment on the third floor without elevators cannot adopt a child in a wheelchair without adaptations. A woman who has had little work with deaf children and individuals will need help adopting a child who is deaf. Adopting across racial or ethnic lines may entail discussion with the whole family group. Language may be a significant problem. Child care plans should have been discussed. Adopting older children should involve some discussion with possible school systems, arranging alternate ways of mainstreaming children who may be behind or do not speak English. Adopting children with disabilities should entail examining the community's resources for disabled children.

Preadoption Physical

The provider is often asked to complete a preadoption physical attesting to the health of the woman and/or couple. Unlike a sports or driver physical, the provider is examining the woman for conditions that would prevent her from successfully raising a child to adulthood. Although the provider can express an opinion as to the wisdom of an adopting woman who has a certain medical condition, often it is the woman, the court system, the social service or adoption agency, or even country of the child that makes a decision. The decision is often out of the provider's hands. For example, many agencies and countries will not let a child go into a house with parents more than 40 years older than the

child. Some countries will not let obese parents adopt. It also depends on the situation of the child and family. If the only one able and willing to care for a child is her grandmother with COPD, the grandmother's degree of disability may be allowed by the court judge to be higher than if she was adopting strangers.

Any condition in the woman that requires that she be taken care of by others (e.g., uncontrolled seizure disorder), any progressively worsening condition (e.g., myasthenia gravis, liver failure, AIDS, or cancer), or any disease in which sudden death is possible should indicate hesitation about adoption (Table 10.6.1). Some conditions that would suggest hesitation or reconsideration about adoption include age greater than 50 years, metastatic or "noncured" cancer or AIDS. Known substance abuse of alcohol or illegal drugs, or a history of spousal or child abuse, must be indicated. Type I diabetes mellitus with disabling complications, unre-

Table 10.6.1. Conditions that May Make a Woman Hesitate to Adopt

Age > 50 years	
Social history	Family member with progressive disability requiring caretaking by woman
	History of alcohol or drug abuse
	History of abusing or neglecting a child
Medical history	
Neurological disease	Progressive diability: multiple sclerosis, myasthenia gravis, uncontrolled seizure disorder
Lung disease	COPD requiring homebound oxygen, alpha-1-antitrypsinase deficiency, cystic fibrosis
Heart disease	Severe and worsening CHD, severe and worsening valvular disease or myopathy, uncontrolled ventricular arrhythmias
Endocrine	Type I diabetes (worsening disability)
	Morbid obesity*
HEENT	Blindness (*), deafness*
Cancer	Metastatic or spreading cancer or cancer with poor prognosis
Psychological	Severe disability, recurrent hospitalizations or suicide attempts; severe depression,* anorexia/bulimia*
Infections	AIDS
Liver	Failure or worsening disease
Renal	Failure or worsening disease

*Depends on degree of disability and adoptive agency and country.

pairable cardiac valvular disease, severe coronary heart disease, uncontrolled ventricular arrhythmias, and renal or liver failure should cause some hesitation. Women who have had severe psychological problems requiring repeated psychiatric hospitalizations or suicide attempts should not adopt. However, any history of other diseases depends on the degree of disability. A woman with severe COPD on oxygen would be unlikely to care for an infant successfully, but a woman with well-controlled asthma could. Cancer of the lung, recently diagnosed, would cause hesitation; a history of cancer of the breast, stage I, treated successfully without recurrence for 5 or more years may not.

The provider should help the woman accurately assess her health and the health of her family. A spouse with severe disabling condition that will require over years more care may impede the woman's ability to raise a child. Without being judgmental, the provider should help the woman see her situation reasonably.

The Wait

There is an intense and painful period between the decision to adopt and the final acceptance of the child, and a longer time before the child is legally adopted. This period can cause a significant amount of strain and anticipation for which the provider may be consulted.

If this is a private adoption, without an agency, illegal in some states, the woman and/or couple will have to make arrangements on their own. There will be a significant wait for the biological mother to decide, to arrange the adoption, and finally to deliver the child. At any point, there can be serious difficulties from finding out prenatally something may be wrong with the child, from a birthmother deciding not to put the child up for adoption, or wanting it back later. A waiting adoptive mother is likely to suffer several significant reverses, all emotionally shocking, if not disabling.

If the adoption is occurring through an agency, the woman and family are likely to have as many emotional trials, but they will be buffered sometimes by the agency. There is often no referral for adoption (calls that there may be a child ready) until the child is legally "free" to be adopted. The legal inconveniences are often handled by the agency. However, there may be several referrals before the final matching is made, and again the child can become sick or other problems occur. As well, the nuisances of dealing with social service agencies, opening one's home and life to a home study and postadoption placement, although necessary and well-meant, are other problems. The anxiety about dealing with the legal system, going to court, and getting everything "legalized" may be profound.

In either case, the woman is likely to need ventilation and counseling. She may come to the provider with stress-related illness or exacerbations of disease such as gastroesophageal reflux disease, headaches, or irritable bowel disease. Providing a sympathetic listening may be the primary treatment needed.

Fitting the Child into the Family

Once the child comes, there will be three main types of problems—illness of the child, the adaptation of the family to the child and the child to the family, and later handling the child-parent discussions of adoption.

Adopted children with medical problems will need evaluation and referral. The change of situation may often make assessment of problems difficult for a time, and problems, especially psychological or developmental, may have to be reassessed several times. Adopted children from foreign countries may have a variety of medical and definitely psychological problems. They need to be seen immediately by a provider, and often tested for several diseases including tuberculosis, hepatitis, intestinal parasites, and malnutrition. Several visits may be needed. Unless a small infant, the child will also have to adapt to a new confusing culture and often a new language. Urging the family to take time off, to use counselors and translators, and to expect this to take time will help. The woman and her family may get frustrated, as the child often will, making these adaptations.

Any new child or family member will necessitate change in the already complex family structure. Single women becoming parents with the inherent inability of society to understand the demands and stresses this brings will undergo significant changes. The provider will need to encourage single parents of adopted children, just like any single parents, to make sure to get help, to ask family and friends to assist with care and companionship, and to take time for themselves.

Any couple with a new child will have changes to make. The fact that they go from an adult couple (which they often have been for years) to parents literally overnight, as they may have to fly out the next night to pick up their new child, adds stress that may manifest in anxiety, worried-parent phone calls, and visits to provider and stress-related illnesses. Most parents have 9 months to plan and prepare, emotionally and physically; adopted parents may or may not.

Adopting older children or adding an adopted child to a family with children brings special problems. Family counseling with the children before and after the adoption may be needed. Older children often have psychological needs and problems, from either foreign adoption or domestic foster homes, that will need continuing counseling for child and family. Language may be a problem.

Finally, sooner or later the woman and family will need to discuss with the child the process of adoption. There are several books (only a few of which are listed in Table 10.6.2) that can help the child and the parents discuss adoption. The provider may be asked to help suggest "the right words" or help the family deal with the pressures this produces. Referral to agencies and useful texts about this are indicated. Bibliotherapy is helpful in this area; there are books for all ages of children and adults.

Table 10.6.2. Some Books about Adoption for Children

Fowler, Susi Greg. *When Joel Comes Home.* Greenwillow Books

Lifton, Betty Jean. *Tell Me a Real Adoption Story.* Knopf

Turner, Anne. *Through Moon, and Stars and Night Sky.* HarperCollins and Harper Trophy books

Conclusion

The provider may interact with the woman and/or family who adopts a child at several times and in many ways before, during, and after the adoption. Counseling nonjudgmentally, providing medical advice and judgment, and offering support and referral to other sources when needed, the provider can profoundly interact positively in adoption.

References

1. Melina CM, Melina L. The physician's responsibility in adoption, part I: caring for the birthmother. JABFP 1988;1:50–54.
2. American Academy of Pediatrics. Committee on early childhood, adoption and dependent care. Pediatrics 1994;93:339–341.
3. Rosen RH. Adolescent pregnancy decision-making: are parents important? Adolescence 1980;15:43–54.
4. Grow LJ. Today's unmarried mothers: the choices have changed. Child Welfare 1979;58:363–371.

10.7

Lesbian Health Issues

Bickley Craven

Introduction

Lesbian health care is not synonymous with women's health care. Besides the issues specific to all women, lesbians have several unique concerns in the medical, social, and psychological areas (1). Lesbians are estimated to comprise between 2 and 10% of the population of US women, and providers see lesbians daily in their practices (2, 3).

A dictionary might define lesbian as a "female homosexual" or a woman who is sexually attracted to or has sex with other women (4). In reality, many consider that lesbianism is not defined by the gender of a woman's sexual partner but is a multifaceted identity. Emo-tional, affectational, political, cultural, intellectual issues, and sexual behavior are all determinants of a lesbian identity. The term lesbian is preferred by most lesbians over "gay" or "homosexual" because it suggests the whole identity rather than just sexual behavior. Not all women who have sex with other women consider themselves lesbians. Lesbians are included in all groups defined by race, ethnicity, religion, economics, geography, and age. The lesbian population is as diverse as society. Lesbian relationships range from celibacy, partnering with one other woman for life, or being sexually involved with men and/or women.

The universal experience of lesbians and other sexual minorities is one of marginalization and stigma that often leads to poor medical care (4–6). This chapter provides information to help primary care providers improve their care of lesbian patients.

Patient-Provider Relationship

Lesbian Health Care Experiences

Homophobia has been described as the irrational fear, hatred, and intolerance of homosexuals (1). Homophobia is widespread in Western society and can have many negative effects on lesbians living in an intolerant society (1, 5–8). Heterosexism assumes that heterosexuality is the norm, that it is superior to any other expression of sexuality and that every person is heterosexual no matter how much evidence there is to the contrary (6, 7, 9, 10).

"Coming out" is a phrase used to describe the process a lesbian woman experiences as she becomes aware of her own homosexuality and reveals it to others. "Coming out," a shortened term for "coming out of the closet," refers to a hiding place in which one does not have to disclose her true identity. By coming out the lesbian risks "stepping out of a place believed to be safe, physically and emotionally" (6, 8, 11).

Many lesbians fear encounters with health care providers and for good reason (Table 10.7.1). In a review of articles concerning lesbian health care from 1970 to 1990, Stevens outlines several recurrent themes lesbians report during health care experiences. Heterosexist assumptions by health care providers are a major hindrance to effective patient-provider communication. A patient's positive response to the question, "Are you sexually active?" may result in the provider asking, "What do you use for birth control?" This and similar assumptions of heterosexuality make it difficult for the lesbian patient to reveal her identity to a health care provider. An assumption of heterosexuality can lead to incorrect diagnoses, inappropriate prescribing, and unneeded health education. One lesbian describes going through a fitting for a diaphragm rather than coming out to her health care provider (4, 5, 9, 11).

A second theme is that most lesbians want to reveal their sexual orientation to their health care providers. In general, lesbians feel that their health care will be positively influenced if they can come out. The actual percentage of lesbians who report disclosing their sexual orientation to providers in various studies ranged from 18 to 91%. However, when lesbians risk coming out to providers, many negative reactions are encountered. These reactions include anxiety or hostility on the part of the health care provider, less likelihood of physical touch, unwanted mental health referrals, demeaning jokes, invasions of privacy, and breaches of confidentiality (4, 5, 9, 12).

Access to quality primary care is limited

Table 10.7.1. Special Concerns in Lesbian Woman—Provider Relationship

Concern that revealing status or "coming out" will result in substandard care
    Anxiety or hostility on the part of the provider
    Less likelihood of touch
    Unwanted mental health referrals
    Invasions of privacy and breaches of confidentiality
Concern that not revealing status will result in substandard care
    Contraceptives prescribed or insisted on without need
    No valid recognition of health needs
Desire to reveal lesbian status
Concerns about allowing involvement of partner in health decisions

for lesbians. Finding providers and systems free of homophobia/heterosexism is a difficult task. Lesbians, like many women, may be paid lower wages and receive fewer health benefits. Lesbians generally cannot claim their partners or extended family members as dependents when they do have health insurance (9).

Provider Issues

In 1986, Matthews et al. reported a 1982 survey of all members of the San Diego County Medical Society regarding their attitudes toward homosexuality. Approximately 23% of all respondents were rated as homophobic. More recent graduates were more accepting of homosexuality than their older colleagues. Thirty percent of respondents would not favor admitting a highly qualified homosexual applicant to medical school, and more than 40% would cease to refer patients to a known homosexual colleague practicing pediatrics. In spite of these negative attitudes toward colleagues, three fifths of the physicians reported no negative feelings in treating homosexual patients (13). In 1988, Prichard and colleagues surveyed family medicine residents and fellows and compared the results to the physicians in southern California described above. Physicians in training appear less uncomfortable with homosexuals. However, 10% still feel qualified homosexual candidates should not be admitted to medical school, and 30% would not refer patients to a gay pediatrician (14).

Lesbian phobia among BSN nursing educators was surveyed by Randall in 1989. Fifty-two percent of respondents felt lesbianism is not a "natural expression of human sexuality." Fifty percent were misinformed about lesbian sexuality and 20% erroneously felt lesbians are a common source for transmitting AIDS. More than one-fourth reported they would have difficulty conversing with someone they knew to be lesbian. Unlike the physicians mentioned above, only 8% felt lesbians should not be nurses (15). Similarly, a group of women nurs-

ing students in the Midwest was also found to be homophobic. Only 24% said they would be willing to invite a lesbian to their home (16).

The American Association of Physicians for Human Rights (AAPHR) that is now known as the Gay and Lesbian Medical Association (GLMA) surveyed its members concerning antigay discrimination in medicine and published the results in May 1994. Surveys mailed to 1311 AAPHR members had a 54% return rate. The responses represent a broad range of common experience of lesbian and gay physicians and medical students. Sixty-seven percent of those responding reported knowing of patients who received substandard care because of their sexual orientation. Actual observation of colleagues providing reduced or denying care to gay, lesbian, or bisexual (LGB) patients was reported by 52%. Eighty-eight percent of respondents heard colleagues make disparaging remarks about LGB patients. Ninety-eight percent of respondents felt LGB patients have medical concerns that might be overlooked if they do not disclose their sexual orientation to providers. However, 64% of respondents felt patients risk substandard care if they do reveal their sexual orientation and only 14% disagreed with this statement (17).

Heterosexism by the provider leads to invisibility of the lesbian patient. If a group of people "do not exist," then their health concerns are ignored, they are excluded from research, and their concerns are omitted from medical education curricula. This neglect means the lesbian population receives woefully poor care (1, 4, 5, 7).

Providers receive little education about lesbian patients. Some medical school curricula ignore lesbian concerns altogether. A 1991 study revealed homosexuality was taught in medical schools a mean of only 3 hours and 26 minutes (7). Health surveys and tumor registries do not identify lesbians. It is currently impossible to prove the supposition of Suzanne Haynes, PhD, Chief of Health Education in the National Cancer Institute, that lesbians are at increased risk of breast cancer. The large Nurse's Health Study of Harvard Medical School (Boston, MA) enrolled 116,000 women and has yielded much information about women's health. However, the study neglected to ask about sexual orientation. At this time, there are little data to help guide the clinician's care of lesbian patients. A positive sign is the fact that the National Institutes of Health's Women's Health Initiative will stratify data by sexual orientation. This will provide clinicians with the first large study of health information about lesbians (18).

Patient-Provider Interaction

Providers can do many things to improve their interactions with lesbian patients. First is an honest evaluation of the provider's own bias. Providers should critically examine their attitudes toward lesbians in society and as patients. If bias is identified, it should be addressed. The provider who wishes to provide sensitive and quality care for lesbian patients will probably have to create their own education. Discussing issues with lesbian or gay colleagues may help. If some provider's patients are "out," asking the patients for feedback concerning patient provider interactions may be helpful. Providers should read, study, and seek out information about lesbians and lesbian organizations. Providers should become familiar with the language of lesbian patients including "out of the closet," "out," "lesbian," "gay," "homophobia," and "heterosexism." Education is necessary for the provider to gain the knowledge to appropriately counsel patients regarding specific health concerns.

The primary care office should be made more lesbian friendly. Statements regarding antidiscrimination may be worded to include sexual orientation. All information gathering should help the lesbian woman reveal her orientation. Registration forms can be altered to include such statements as "living with a partner" or "in a relationship" in addition to mar-

ried, divorced, or single. "Name of spouse" or "partner" may be substituted for wife or husband. Encourage staff to consider patients' living situations and put patients at ease. Pamphlets in the waiting rooms can address lesbian issues such as safer sex for lesbians. Periodicals or brochures from local or national lesbian and gay organizations may also be placed in the waiting room (4, 5, 7).

History taking allows the provider to "connect" with a lesbian patient. Providers should examine their history-taking critically for vestiges of heterosexism and should maintain an open, nonjudgmental attitude. While taking a social history, the provider may ask, "Are you presently living with a partner?" or "Are you in a relationship?" or "Is there a person or persons you want to be included in our discussions?" These types of questions signal the patient that the provider is open to her lesbianism and to including her partner, friend, or other support person. The provider can further improve rapport by inquiring about important persons or events in the lesbian's life. After a lesbian patient comes out, it is recommended by some psychologists that the provider be "lesbian affirmative in their interactions" with the patient. Active validation of the patient's sexual orientation may help the patient develop a more positive self-image and overcome some of the negative effects of homophobia and heterosexism (11).

When taking the sexual history, patients may prefer a statement of ubiquity such as, "For me to give appropriate care, it is important for me to ask all my patients about their sexual history." Asking questions such as, "Are you sexually active with men, women, or both?" or "Do you have an intimate relationship with a man or a woman?" may allow any patient to self disclose the nature of their intimate relationships. A patient's specific behaviors are the key to health issues. A patient who identifies herself as lesbian may need to be asked, "Have you ever had sex with a man?" when evaluating her individual health risks.

Lesbian patients may have concerns about confidentiality and about what appears in their chart. The provider should initiate a discussion of these issues with the patient. If the patient is uncomfortable with charting that she is lesbian, use a coded entry in the chart that will signal to the provider the confidential information discussed (4, 5, 7).

Mental Health

Coming Out

Lesbians do not have more psychologic illnesses than heterosexual women. However, lesbians do have unique psychologic stressors (4, 5). "Coming out" is often a central part of a lesbian's stress. A common misconception is that coming out is a one time event. In reality, coming out is a process consisting of several stages. Mattison and McWhirter describe these stages as (*a*) self-recognition, (*b*) disclosure to others, (*c*) socialization with other gay people, (*d*) positive self-identification and integration, and (*e*) acceptance. A person's progression through these stages is rarely linear and may be affected positively or negatively by the lesbian's own psyche, her family's and friends' reactions, and by societal attitudes (8).

"Internalized homophobia" refers to the lesbian's internal struggle with self-doubt or negative attitudes toward being lesbian. These doubts may persist even as a lesbian recognizes her identity and discloses it to her family or society. Internalized homophobia may impair her ability to have healthy relationships or hinder her from reaching her full potential. Working through the last vestiges of her own homophobia is necessary for a lesbian to reach the final stage of integration and acceptance.

Depression, Incest, and Suicide

The National Lesbian Health Care Survey (NLHCS) surveyed 1925 lesbians from across the United States in 1984 to 1985, and a sig-

nificant portion of the survey pertained to mental health issues (19). The survey uncovered a high prevalence of depression, incest, and attempted suicide. One third of the respondents reported depression. A history of attempted suicide was reported in 18% of lesbians, and 19% had a history of incest. These rates of depression and incest are commensurate with levels reported in heterosexual women. However, the rate of attempted suicide is higher than the general US population of women. Suicide rates for professional women, however, are higher than in the general population, and this group of lesbians included many professional women. Seventy-five percent of the lesbians surveyed used professional mental health services, compared to approximately 30% of heterosexual women. Suggested reasons for this increased use of mental health services include stress caused by societal oppression and acceptance of therapy, and personal growth in the lesbian community. Lesbians who were more out were more likely to seek counseling for issues pertaining to being lesbian such as difficulty with family or lovers (19).

Substance Abuse

For years researchers have described alcohol use as a problem in the lesbian community, and previous estimates of alcoholism or heavy drinking in the lesbian community were approximately 30%. The studies on which these estimates were based were often flawed and included such biases as recruiting participants in gay bars (20, 21). More recent studies show that levels of alcohol use in lesbians may be lower than previously reported and similar to rates of use in heterosexual women. In the NLHCS, only 6% of lesbians said they drank daily, 25% drank alcohol more than once a week, and 14% worried about their alcohol use (19).

In the only survey in which participants were identified by random selection, Bloomfield reports on alcohol use in a sample of women living in San Francisco. Comparisons are made between lesbian/bisexual and heterosexual women. Across the spectrum from abstinence through ingestion of greater than 60 drinks per month, lesbian and heterosexual women reported similar rates of alcohol use (21). These results are confirmed by McKirnan and Peterson who surveyed lesbian alcohol use in Chicago in 1989 (22). Both large studies were done in urban settings, and no significant differences between rates of alcohol use in lesbians and heterosexual women were found. By comparison, rates of heavy use (greater than 60 drinks in 30 days) for lesbians and heterosexual women in these urban centers were double the rate found in population data in 1984. Whatever the actual rate of alcoholism and heavy alcohol use in the lesbian community, it is probably lower than that reported from earlier "clinical" samples of lesbian women (21, 22).

Use of tobacco by lesbians has also been studied. The NLHCS found that 30% of lesbians smoke cigarettes daily (19). A study of lesbians in southern states revealed that more than 40% of lesbians surveyed used tobacco. By comparison nationally, 22% of women over age 35 years revealed using tobacco in the past month in 1990 (23). Screening all women for often used "licit" drugs and "illicit" drugs is an important component of quality primary care.

Lesbian Adolescents

Lesbian youth are particularly at risk. Homelessness in a large metropolitan city, suicide and attempted suicide, and substance abuse are all conditions for which the lesbian adolescent is at increased risk. An important developmental task for the lesbian adolescent is to develop a lesbian identity or fusion of one's emotions and sexuality into a meaningful whole. The stigmatization of lesbians and societal heterosexism or homophobia make the process of establishing this identity difficult (24).

Lesbian adolescents experiencing confusion concerning sexual orientation may pre-sent with depression, decreased school performance, substance abuse, acting out, or suicidal ideation. Lesbian youth are two to three times more likely to attempt suicide than other youth and may comprise 30% of all completed youth suicides (25).

Lesbian youth who have the benefit of acceptance, support, and validation have no more serious mental health problems than the general adolescent population. Maternal acceptance may be a significant contribution to a lesbian's development of healthy self-esteem. Presenting a nonheterosexist attitude and assuring confidentiality may allow the lesbian adolescent to feel safe and come out to the provider. Also, an educated, sensitized primary care provider can be an excellent source for information and referral to supportive lesbian resources (24–26).

Violence in Lives of Lesbians

Violence is an everyday occurrence in the lives of women and thus in lesbians. In the National Lesbian Health Care Survey, 16% of women reported being physically abused as adults. More than 50% of these women reported being abused by their lovers and 27% by their husbands. The gender of "the lovers" was not specified. However, this survey was specifically titled and distributed to self-identified lesbians; most "lovers," if not all, would likely be women (19).

Research on battering within lesbian relationships is less comprehensive than that pertaining to domestic violence. Renzetti proposes the major determinants of violence in lesbian couples relate to dependency/autonomy issues and the balance of power in the relationship. The batterer is more dependent and uses violence to try to curb her partner's independence. Although the victim of battering has more financial and education resources, the batterer is the decision maker for the couple (27). Substance use, especially alcohol, was reported in 64% of battering incidents in lesbian relationships in 1989 (28).

Victims report the response to lesbian battering from providers including physicians is often "not helpful at all." Responses are often perceived as homophobic and sexist. Friends, counselors, and relatives are rated as more helpful, but are not overwhelmingly supportive of the victim or challenging to the batterer. This lack of support worsens a victim's low self-esteem, undermines her efforts to improve her situation, and allows the batterer to escape the consequences of her actions (11, 29).

Hate crimes, also known as bias crimes, are acts of violence directed at an individual who is identified as a member of a minority. Violence against lesbians and gay men has escalated in recent years. The US Department of Justice reports that lesbians and gay men may be the most victimized minority in the nation. Lesbians may be the victims of verbal abuse, physical violence, threats of violence, property damage, or murder. Family members or community authorities may commit these crimes. Many lesbian adolescents who leave home may do so because of violence (1, 4, 5). Fourteen percent, or one in seven, of the LGB medical professionals surveyed have been subjected to violence because of their own sexual orientation (17). Providers should be vigilant for signs of abuse and ask about violence in the lives of lesbian patients. Sensitivity to these additional stresses and appropriate management are suggested.

Medical Issues

The most serious health risk to lesbians is the avoidance of regular primary care. Because of negative experiences in medical settings or fear of such experiences, many lesbians delay seeking health care (1, 4, 9, 11). One researcher, in 1981, found the average time between Pap smears for lesbians was 21 months, compared to 8 months for heterosexual women (30). A pattern of seeking medical care only at times of health crisis leads to inadequate screen-ing for preventable or modifiable illnesses and may be a significant detriment to a lesbian's health.

General health screening and preventive care for women throughout the life cycle are an integral part of quality primary care. Screening lesbian patients for coronary artery disease, hypertension, anemia, or any variety of disorders should follow the same standards of care as for all patients (31). Appropriate screening or education of patients in primary care is dependent on the patients' individual circumstance.

Gynecological Care

Most lesbians are currently exclusively sexual with women or celibate. However, 75 to 80% of women who self-identify as lesbian have had heterosexual experiences (32). A woman's gynecologic health is affected by her sexual history. The provider is encouraged to become familiar with the range of human sexual behavior and develop skill in obtaining the sexual history. Lesbian sexual activities may include kissing, breast stimulation, masturbation, manual and/or oral stimulation of the genitals and/or anus, use of sex toys or devices, penetration of the vagina or anus with the fingers or devices, and/or rubbing the clitoris against the partner's body. Some lesbians participate in sadomasochistic activities (4, 5). After an appropriate history provides the needed information for an individual patient, her primary care should be based on her specific life situation instead of on assumptions made because of her sexual orientation.

Screening for cervical cancer is recommended for all women. Risk factors for cervical cancer include early age at first intercourse, history of more than one male sexual partner, human papilloma virus infection, other sexually transmitted diseases (STDs), and smoking. Few women, including lesbians, encountered in the usual primary care practice are low risk. If a lesbian woman's history defines her at risk for cervical cancer, she is still at risk though she may currently be sexual only with women. The American Cancer Society (ACS) and other preventive health guidelines do not address the situation of women who have only been sexual with other women or celibate when making recommendations regarding cervical cancer screening (31).

In 1990, Edwards and Thin described a series of 27 unselected lesbian patients cared for in one clinic in London, England. The investigators found that 10 of 27 patients had abnormal Pap smears. These findings suggest that some lesbians are at high risk for cervical dysplasia and cancer (33). Many lesbians delay seeking health care. Delay increases the risk for women to develop more advanced cervical dysplasia before it is detected. Education of an individual lesbian regarding her personal risk and encouragement of regular exams at an interval appropriate for her situation is recommended. If a woman has no risk factors and has only been sexual with women, then less frequent cervical screening, such as every 3 years, may be indicated (4).

Studies of STDs in lesbians were published in the early 1980s. Gonorrhea, chlamydia, and syphilis infections are quite rare in lesbians who are sexually active with women only. Testing for these infections is only indicated in those lesbians who have recently been heterosexually active (33–35). Genital infections with human papilloma virus (HPV) and herpes simplex virus (HSV) were found in greater frequency in lesbian women in 1990 than in earlier studies (32–34). Both viruses can be transmitted in sexual intercourse without penetration. HSV may be spread by orogenital and/or by genital-genital contact. Avoiding contact with active HSV lesions is appropriate. HPV infection is likely contracted by most lesbians during heterosexual activity. However, vulvar warts in a woman without heterosexual activity have been described (33) and HPV may be spread by fomite transmission (36). This suggests transmission of the HPV virus between women during sexual activities is not just a theoretical risk. Sexual

partners of women with HPV infection should be evaluated. Counseling regarding the association of HPV with cervical dysplasia and recommended cervical cytology is also suggested. Unlike gay men, enteric infections are generally infrequent in lesbians. Testing for hepatitis B virus is not routinely suggested in lesbians unless other risk factors exist (4).

Vaginitis is relatively common in lesbian patients. Trichomonas can be spread by fomite transmission and has been found in women who are sexually active only with other women. Lesbians with documented trichomoniasis and their sexual partners should be treated. Vaginal candidiasis has been transmitted between women and treatment of sexual partners, especially if they are symptomatic, is recommended. Bacterial vaginosis is a third common vaginitis seen in lesbians. The pathogenesis of this infection is less well understood. Women with symptomatic bacterial vaginosis should be treated. Evaluation of her sexual partner is indicated if the partner is symptomatic, or if the index patient has recurrent bacterial vaginosis (4, 33).

HIV/AIDS

The Center for Disease Control's definition of lesbian, for HIV epidemiologic purposes, is a woman who has only had sexual relations with other women since 1977 (37). This limited definition ignores most of the women who identify themselves as lesbian (5, 35). Of the lesbians identified with AIDS by the CDC through June 1991, 93% are documented to be injection drug users and the remaining 7% received blood transfusions (37). In December 1993, Rich and associates reviewed five cases of presumed "female to female" transmission of HIV infection. It is concluded that this is an inefficient mode of HIV transmission. However, the evidence of these cases and the known risk of "female to male" transmission suggest there is risk of transmission during lesbian sexual activity, although it is much less than for heterosexual activity (38).

The lesbian community and individual lesbian patients need appropriate information and counseling regarding safer sex practices (39). For sex with partners whose serostatus is unknown, lesbians should avoid contact with cervical or vaginal secretions and blood, whether from menstruation or from trauma. Also, avoidance of contact with any genital ulcerative lesions, such as HSV, and with breast milk is recommended.

There are techniques that may result in safer sex. Even in a monogamous couple safer techniques may be indicated. During oral-genital sex, a barrier between the genitalia and mouth and tongue is advised. Plastic food wrap can be laid flat against the genitalia to provide protection. Condoms or latex gloves may be cut and laid out flat as another alternative. Finger cots or latex gloves can protect the hands during vaginal penetration or caressing. If sex toys are shared, they should be washed in appropriate bleach solutions or covered with a fresh condom between each woman's use. Genital-genital stimulation may transmit virus if genital lesions or sores exist. Use of plastic wrap can also be used in this situation to prevent sharing of vaginal secretions. Please note the efficacy of these barrier methods in preventing woman-to-woman transmission has not been studied. Any woman engaging in heterosexual activity should use a condom with spermicide for penile intercourse (1, 4, 5, 6).

HIV infection is also potentially transmitted by semen used for artificial insemination (40). Sperm banks routinely test for HIV antibody at the time of donation and test the donor again 6 months later before releasing the sperm. Fresh sperm given from a seronegative donor may not be safe because of the delay in seroconversion or window period. Women should avoid fresh semen for artificial insemination. If fresh semen is used, frank discussion concerning the donor's HIV risk status and testing the donor for HIV antibody twice, 3 to 6 months apart, is recommended.

Cancer

Information about cancer specific to lesbians is generally unavailable. This lack of information may be remedied in the near future as large studies of women's health begin to stratify women based on sexual activity or sexual orientation. Breast cancer risks that may affect lesbians disproportionately include nulliparity, age greater than 30 years at first childbirth, never having breast fed, "never married" status, high body fat percentage, and high dietary fat intake (41, 42).

Increased risk of ovarian and endometrial cancer is associated with nulliparity, and use of oral contraceptives lowers a woman's risk of both cancers (43, 44). Those lesbians who have always partnered with women and have had no children, therefore, may fall into a high-risk category for both. Recommendations concerning screening activities are best made for the individual based on current guidelines for cancer screening.

Lesbian Families and Parenting

Lesbian families are as diverse as lesbians themselves. Asking the lesbian from whom she receives primary emotional support may help define the woman's family as she perceives it. She may have an extended family of friends who serve as an emotional support network, and she may or may not be close to her biological family.

Members of lesbian families have few rights protected under existing laws. To ensure partners and/or friends are included in decision making for health care, a lesbian may want to use a durable power of attorney for medical care. Through this mechanism, she can designate her partner or other loved ones to make medical decisions in case she is unable to do so. This protects the patient's designated decision maker in cases in which the biological family may disagree. Unless specified in her will, a lesbian's assets and belongings will not automatically go to her partner. When the practitioner learns of a patient's lesbianism, clarifying these issues and encouraging her to seek legal protection is in order (1, 4–6).

Currently there are estimated to be between 1 and 5 million lesbian mothers in the United States, although 4 to 6 million people have one or more lesbian and/or gay parents. Lesbians become parents in many ways including previous heterosexual relationships, artificial insemination (AI), heterosexual intercourse, adoption, or by becoming foster parents. Studies have shown that children of lesbian and gay parents do not differ from children of heterosexual parents in terms of psychological and social relationships. Children growing up in gay or lesbian families are more tolerant of diversity and more open to the discussion of issues of sexuality and interpersonal relationships. Open communication with children about their parents' lesbianism improves healthy functioning of the family (45, 46). Providers should encourage lesbian parents or prospective lesbian parents to seek legal aid and protect their parental rights. It is important for couples to solidify in writing their agreements concerning child custody and support and consent for treatment early while planning to raise a child together.

As recently as 1990, it was estimated that between 5,000 and 10,000 lesbians had borne children after "coming out." This number is likely underestimated because of the hidden nature of lesbian parents. Many lesbians have used AI as the mode of achieving pregnancy. With AI or heterosexual intercourse, issues of safety regarding HIV/AIDS need to be considered. The primary care provider may be called upon to provide information, referral, or to perform insemination. Investigators have supported the ethical justification for insemination of lesbians. If an individual practitioner has moral objections, the lesbian patient should appropriately be referred. Legal statues regarding artificial insemination vary by state. Sensi-

tivity to the complexities of the lesbian family is imperative if the practitioner is to provide maximal care and support to the family (1, 4–6).

Issues of Older Lesbians

Aging in America's youth oriented society is not pleasant for many individuals. The aged are often without adequate resources and face isolation. Older lesbians may be "triply invisible" as they are women, aged, and lesbian (47). The women who are now age 65 or older lived most of their lives during a repressive period of US history. The increased exposure to lesbian culture and activism of the 1970s and 1980s may not impact their lives as greatly as for younger lesbians. Lesbian concerns regarding loneliness, failing health, and limited income are similar to all aging persons. In addition, lesbians worry about discrimination as a result of sexual orientation, gender, or age. Older lesbians may have "come out" in their youth or in later stages of life. Many older lesbians have been married to men and have children. Some of these older women have significant fears of rejection from their adult children and even grandchildren (48). Kehoe reports that, on average, the lesbians studied were well adjusted and aging positively (47, 49). Quam and Whitford suggest that lesbians have less fears aging when they have support from other lesbian women (48). In the few studies regarding older lesbians the respondents tend to be white, self-identified lesbians, with above average education and income. The findings may not be generalizable to the almost 2 million US lesbian women over age 60. Women of ethnic minorities, from rural areas, and with less economic advantages may have more difficulty in their later years (47–49).

Providers can be sensitive to the needs of older lesbians. It is important not to assume an older woman who is living alone is a widow of a heterosexual relationship. Asking an older person "Who is most important to you?" or asking about a patient's "support system" may allow the older lesbian patient to feel less invisible to the practitioner. The health professional may be a great source of support for women who are "triply invisible" (47, 50).

Conclusion

Lesbians are a minority who face obstacles in obtaining quality primary health care. Difficulties for lesbians in mental health and social arenas often result from living in an intolerant world. The major health risk for lesbians is de-

lay in seeking health care secondary to negative experiences and expectations of their care. Information about medical care of lesbians is limited by incomplete research and education programs. Preventive services can be tailored to the individual woman, based on her personal history. Lesbian parents, families, adolescents, and elders are some members of the diverse lesbian community who have been discussed. Primary care providers can, and are implored, to improve their care of lesbian patients by eliminating their personal bias, becoming educated about health care for lesbians, and being open to the lesbians in their practices.

Special Considerations for Nurse Practitioners and Physician Assistants

Many health care providers are uncomfortable asking about a woman's sexuality, or assume that a woman has no concerns in this area unless she initiates the subject. Providers who are uncomfortable with the whole area of a woman's sexuality will have great discomfort recognizing other than heterosexual lifestyles. They may miss clues about a woman's lifestyle and sexuality, important information may not be shared, and needed health care interventions may not implemented (51). If assumptions about heterosexuality are evident early in the patient-provider encounter, the lesbian's disclosure and openness becomes even more complex (52). In addition, providers have to be sensitive to the woman's designation of "family" and avoid the assumption of traditional family support (53). The woman's preference in the use of the words "gay" or "lesbian" or neither should be determined (54).

Those providers who are most sensitive and open to caring for lesbians may need to help lesbian clients find out about them as a source of health care. Advertisements in the gay and lesbian press and the presence of les-

bian-sensitive publications and educational materials in the office can help women identify providers who are comfortable with lesbian clients. Those providers who are uncomfortable with lesbian clients might be helped by taking part in educational training, reading, or talking openly with lesbian women (51).

Finding support services to help lesbians cope with partner violence and bereavement after the loss of a partner also may be difficult in some areas (53). Lesbian clients who experience sexual problems related to postabuse or postrape syndrome or vaginismus need referral to therapists skilled in working with sexual dysfunction and with lesbian women (54). (See the references by Deevey and Rankow for lists of support groups and services.)

When a provider uses questions about birth control to initiate the sexual history, lesbian women may perceive less openness to her lifestyle. They may also feel badgered by providers who cannot separate the idea of sexual activity from pregnancy risk. However, providers must recognize that some lesbian women, for various reasons, have sexual relationships with men, making it necessary to consider the possibility of pregnancy when establishing a diagnosis or prescribing drugs (54).

As previously discussed, providers must assure the lesbian of confidentiality in the medical record. Recognizing that people other than the provider will have access to the record, providers can increase confidentiality by using gender-neutral terms for partners, by not writing "gay" or "lesbian" in the record, and by respecting the woman's preferences (54). On the other hand, keeping information off the written record means that the lesbian will have to come out over and over to various providers (55). Determining the woman's preferences is essential. Providers need to assess closely those women who are anxious about maintaining a high degree of secrecy to determine the level of support they have available and the disruption in their lives that this secrecy is causing. These women may benefit from referral to a support group or a supportive counselor if their isolation is an issue (51).

A lesbian who has not disclosed her sexual orientation may discuss her choice with her health care provider. She should be assisted to explore possible risks of disclosure (e.g., loss of employment, avoidance by family of origin, loss of support from religious community, possible legal sanctions in some areas) and possible benefits of disclosure, including improved self-esteem, freedom from living a lie, and improved communication with heterosexuals (53).

Lesbian women are as diverse as the population at large and their behaviors and needs will change over time. They face the same barriers to health care as all women, plus additional obstacles. Fear of painful, unknown, or embarrassing procedures can be compounded if there is lack of openness and trust between client and provider. Even sympathetic or supportive providers may not have adequate information about the health needs of lesbians (56). The client, too, may not feel trust in the

provider's recommendations for care if she has not been truthful or complete in her sharing of information (52).

All clients deserve to be treated with dignity and kindness and with care based on current knowledge and skills. All providers must develop an approach that is sensitive to the specific differences and needs of each woman. At the macrolevel, preventive health care for women must be available in settings that are not devoted almost exclusively to birth control or reproductive care. No woman should feel that she is out of place or unwanted (57).

Suggested Readings

Gold MA, Perrin EC, Futterman D, Friedman SB. Children of gay or lesbian parents. Pediatr Rev 1994;15:354–358.

Mattison AM, McWhirter DP. Lesbians, gay men, and their families. Psychiatr Clin North Am 1995;18:123–137.

Rankow EJ. Lesbian health issues for the primary care provider. J Fam Pract 1995;40:486–493.

White J, Levinson W. Primary care of lesbian patients. J Gen Intern Med 1993;8:41–47.

References

1. Simkin RJ. Unique health care concerns of lesbians. Can J Obstet Gynecol 1993;5:516–522.
2. Diamond M. Homosexuality and bisexuality in different populations. Arch Sex Behav 1993;22:291–310.
3. Kinsey AC, Pomeroy W, Martin CE, Gebhard PE. Sexual Behavior in the Human Female. Philadelphia: WB Saunders, 1953.
4. White J, Levinson W. Primary care of lesbian patients. J Gen Intern Med 1993;8:41–47.
5. Rankow EJ. Lesbian health issues for the primary care provider. J Fam Pract 1995;40:486–493.
6. Zeidenstein L. Gynecological and childbearing needs of lesbians. J Nurse-Midwifery 1990;35:10–18.
7. Simkin RJ. Creating openness and receptiveness with your patients: overcoming heterosexual assumptions. Can J Obstet Gynecol 1993;5:485–489.
8. Mattison AM, McWhirter DP. Lesbians, gay men, and their families. Psychiatr Clin North Am 1995;18:123–137.
9. Stevens PE. Lesbian health care research: a review of

the literature from 1970 to 1990. Health Care for Women International 1992;13:91–120.

10. Peteros K, Miller F. Lesbian health in a straight world. In: Worcester N, Whatley MH, eds. Women's Health—Readings on Social, Economic, and Political Issues. Dubuque, IO: Kendall Hunt Publishing, 1988.

11. Gentry SE. Caring for lesbians in a homophobic society. Health Care for Women International 1992; 13:173–180.

12. Johnson SR, Palermo JL. Gynecologic care for the lesbian. Clin Obstet Gynecol 1984;27:724–731.

13. Matthews WC, Booth MW, Turner JD, Kessler L. Physicians' attitudes toward homosexuality—survey of a California county medical society. West J Med 1986;144:106–109.

14. Prichard JG, Dial LK, Holloway RL, Mosley M, Bale RM, Kaplowitz HJ. Attitudes of family medicine residents toward homosexuality. J Fam Pract 1988; 27:637–639.

15. Randall CE. Lesbian phobia among BSN educators:a survey. J Nurs Educ 1989;28:302–306.

16. Eliason MJ, Randall CE. Lesbian phobia in nursing students. West J Nurs Res 1991;13:363–374.

17. Schatz B, O'Hanlan K. Anti-gay Discrimination in Medicine: Results of a National Survey of Lesbian, Gay and Bisexual Physicians. San Francisco: American Association of Physicians for Human Rights, 1994.

18. Cotton P. Gay, lesbian physicians meet, march, tell Shalala bigotry is health hazard. J Am Med Assoc 1993;269:2611–2612.

19. Bradford J, Ryan C, Rothblum ED. National lesbian health care survey: implications for mental health care. J Consult Clin Psych 1994;62:228–242.

20. Mosbacher D. Lesbian alcohol and substance abuse. Psychiatric Ann 1988;18:47–50.

21. Bloomfield K. A comparison of alcohol consumption between lesbians and heterosexual women in an urban population. Drug Alcohol Depend 1993;33: 257–269.

22. McKirnan DJ, Peterson PL. Alcohol and drug use among homosexual men and women: epidemiology and population characteristics. Addict Behav 1989; 14:545–553.

23. Skinner WF. The prevalence and demographic predictors of illicit and licit drug use among lesbians and gay men. Am J Public Health 1994;84:1307–1310.

24. Sanford ND. Providing sensitive health care to gay and lesbian youth. Nurs Pract 1989;14:30–47.

25. Gibson P. Gay male and lesbian youth suicide. In: Rockville, MD: Alcohol, Drug Abuse, and Mental Health Administration 1989, DHHS Pub No 89–1621:3–110–3–1424.

26. Smith S, McClaugherty LO. Adolescent homosexuality: a primary care perspective. Am Fam Physician 1993;48:33–36.

27. Renzetti CM. Violence in lesbian relationships. J Interpersonal Violence 1988;3:381–399.

28. Schilit R, Lie GY, Montagne M. Substance use as a correlate of violence in intimate lesbian relationships. J Homosex 1990;19:51–65.

29. Renzetti CM. Building a second closet: third party responses to victims of lesbian partner abuse. Family Relations 1989;38:157–163.

30. Simkin RJ. Lesbians face unique health care problems. Can Med Assoc J 1991;145:1620–1623.

31. Hayward RSA, Steinberg EP, Ford DE, Roizen MF, Roach KW. Preventive care guidelines. Ann Intern Med 1991;114:758–783.

32. Johnson SR, Smith EM, Guenther SM. Comparison of gynecologic health care problems between lesbians and bisexual women. J Reprod Med 1987;32: 805–811.

33. Edwards A, Thin RN. Sexually transmitted diseases in lesbians. Int J STD AIDS 1990;1:178–181.

34. Robertson P, Schachter J. Failure to identify venereal disease in a lesbian population. Sex Transm Dis 1981;8:75–76.

35. Johnson SR, Guenther SM, Laube DW, Keettel WC. Factors influencing lesbian gynecologic care: a preliminary study. Am J Obstet Gynecol 1981; 140:20–28.

36. Ferenczy A, Bergeron C, Richart RM. Human papillomavirus DNA in fomites on objects used for the management of patients with genital human papillomavirus infections. Obstet Gynecol 1989;74: 950–954.

37. Chu SY, Hammett TA, Buehler JW. Update: epidemiology of reported cases of AIDS in women who report sex only with other women, United States, 1980–1991. AIDS 1992;6:518–519.

38. Rich JD, Buck A, Tuomala RE, Kazanjian PH. Transmission of human immunodeficiency virus infection presumed to have occurred via female homosexual contact. Clin Infect Dis 1993;17:1003–1005.

39. Stevens PE. Lesbians and HIV: clinical, research, and policy issues. Am J Orthopsychiatry 1993;63: 289–294.

40. Chiasson MA, Stoneburner RL, Joseph SC. Human immunodeficiency virus transmission through artificial insemination. J Acquir Immune Defic Syndr 1990;3:69–72.

41. Kelsey JL. A review of the epidemiology of human breast cancer. Epidemiol Rev 1979;1:74–109.

42. Byers T, Graham S, Rzepka T, Marshall J. Lactation and breast cancer. Am J Epidemiol 1985:121: 664–674.

43. The Cancer and Steroid Hormone Study of the Centers for Disease Control and the National Institute of Child Health and Human Development. The reduction in risk of ovarian cancer associated with oral contraceptive use. N Engl J Med 1987; 316:650–655.

44. Dickey RP. Managing Contraceptive Pill Patients. 7th ed. Durant, OK: Essential Medical Information Systems, 1993:14–17.

45. Gold MA, Perrin EC, Futterman D, Friedman SB.

Children of gay or lesbian parents. Pediatr Rev 1994;15:354–358.

46. Patterson CJ. Children of lesbian and gay parents. Child Dev 1992;63:1025–1042.

47. Kehoe M. Lesbians over 65: a triply invisible minority. J Homosex 1986;12:139–152.

48. Quam JK, Whitford GS. Adaptation and age-related expectations of older gay and lesbian adults. Gerontologist 1992;32:367–374.

49. Kehoe M. Lesbians Over 60 Speak for Themselves. New York: Harrington Park Press, 1988.

50. Deevey S. Older lesbian women an invisible minority. J Gerontol Nurs 1990;16:35–39.

51. Roberts SJ, Lorensen L. Lesbian health care: a review and recommendations for health promotion in primary care settings. Nurse Pract 1995;20:42–47.

52. Denenberg R. Report on lesbian health. Women's health issues 1995;5:81–91.

53. Deevey S. Lesbian health care. In: Fogel CI, Woods NF, eds. Women's Health Care. Thousand Oaks: SAGE, 1995:189–206.

54. Lynch MA. When the patient is also a lesbian. NAACOG's clinical issues in perinatal and women's health nursing 1993;4:196–202.

55. Stevens PE. Structural and interpersonal impact of heterosexual assumptions on lesbian health care clients. Nurs Res 1995;44:25–30.

56. Rankow EJ. Breast and cervical cancer among lesbians. Women's Health Issues 1995;5:123–129.

57. Stevens PE. Lesbians' health-related experiences of care and noncare. Western J Nurs Res 1994;16:639–659.

11.1

Sexually Transmitted Diseases

Marla Tobin

Introduction

In the last 20 years, there has been a great expansion of knowledge about sexually transmitted diseases (STDs), because there have been more diseases identified, the pathogens' courses are better understood, and newer treatments have been developed. Today, exposure to STDs is common. There will be 12 million new cases of STDs this year in the United

States (1). Often the woman may not be aware of the disease or be asymptomatic. STDs are associated with more serious long-term complications in women than in men. These complications include the following:

1. An increased risk for genital cancer (human papilloma virus [HPV]).
2. Infertility secondary to tubal damage (gonorrhea, chlamydia, pelvic inflammatory disease [PID]).
3. Pregnancy complications such as tubal pregnancy, miscarriage, and premature delivery.
4. Transmission of serious or fatal infections to the fetus or at delivery (herpes, chlamydia, hepatitis B, syphilis, HPV).
5. Increased risk of acquiring or transmitting HIV via ulcers (syphilis, chancroid, herpes) or cervical discharge (gonorrhea, chlamydia, trichomonas, mucopurulent cervicitis).
6. Higher transmission rate from infected man to noninfected woman than from infected woman to infected man (2).

Primary care providers see women with STDs regularly and have a tremendous opportunity to impact the epidemic of STDs by education and prevention programs. Through screening, the severity of complications and the spread of disease can be decreased.

Epidemiology

Because one in four Americans will contract a STD at some point, most individuals are at risk (3). However, 66% of all STDs occur in those under age 25 years and 25% of STDs occur in adolescents (3). This has significant consequences for the woman, her children, and the family, with the high rate of teenage pregnancy, the infertility risk of STDs, and the potentially deadly results of hepatitis B and HIV transmission. STDs are truly an epidemic (see Table 11.1.1.).

Table 11.1.1. Incidence of STDs in the United States in 1993

STD	Incidence (cases per year)
Chlamydia	4 million
Trichomoniasis	3 million
Gonorrhea	1.8 million
HPV	1 million
Mucopurulent cervicitis	1 million
PID	1 million
Genital herpes	200,000–500,000
Hepatitis B	100,000–200,000
Syphilis	120,000
HIV	40,000
Chancroid	5000
LGV	1000

Infections

Chlamydia

Epidemiology

Chlamydial venereal disease, caused by *Chlamydia trachomatis*, has become widespread. With a known yearly incidence of over four million cases a year, it is the most common STD. However, because of the difficulty of identifying the organism, the problems of inadequate screening, the paucity of symptoms, the lack of a "typical" presentation, and the misdiagnosis of many cases of chlamydia as nonspecific PID, urethritis, or cervicitis, the absolute magnitude of this disease is unclear.

Women under 20 years of age have a two to three times higher risk of infection. Women with multiple sexual partners have a five times greater risk of infection. Chlamydia is commonly found in women that have had or are currently carrying other STDs. It is closely associated with gonorrhea.

However, its sequelae are significant. This disease is responsible for 250,000 cases of PID, 30,000 cases of infertility, and 10,000 cases of ectopic pregnancy each year. The estimated annual costs for these sequela for 1990 were estimated to be 781 million dollars in the United States besides pain and emotional costs (3).

Clinical Course

The difficult thing about diagnosing chlamydia is that up to 75% of all infected women and 25% of all infected men are completely asymptomatic. Patients must be screened before they present with symptoms.

Typical symptoms can include lower abdominal pain, pelvic pain, dysuria, dyspareunia, and vaginal discharge. The woman may report spotting after intercourse and that her partner has an infection or dysuria. Chlamydia may often be the cause of persistent or recurrent vaginal infections or dysfunctional bleeding problems. It is a major cause of pelvic pain. The classical presentation of PID with peritoneal signs, fever, discharge, and abdominal and pelvic pain seldom occurs.

On examination, the woman may have anything from a normal abdominal exam to mild bilateral lower quadrant pain to a surgical abdomen with peritoneal signs. On pelvic exam, there may be an inflamed cervix, called mucopurulent cervicitis. The cervix may be eroded, bleeding, irritated, and there may be an abnormal cervical or vaginal discharge.

Chlamydia represents the cause for approximately 25% of urethral syndromes and from 10 to 40% of all acute PID. In addition to ectopic pregnancy and infertility in women, chlamydia can cause conjunctivitis and pneumonia in newborns. It may also be a cause of premature rupture of membranes and preterm labor. During pregnancy, gonorrhea with chlamydia poses a special risk for infecting the infant during labor, causing ophthalmia neonatorum. However, routine application of topical ophthalmic erythromycin or silver nitrate in newborns, required by most states, will prevent this.

Diagnosis

Chlamydiae are obligatory intracellular parasites often occurring in small numbers and eas-

ily killed in culture and transport. Recent development of a polymerase chain reaction (PCR) test for chlamydia may significantly boost the screening for this disease with a more accurate, simple, and reliable test. The PCR technology multiplies specific DNA sequences of chlamydia 100,000-fold or greater. It has a sensitivity of 97% and a specificity of 99% for endocervical specimens compared to culture sensitivity of 85% and specificity of 100%.

The former gold standard for diagnosis was culture. Cultures, of course, require up to 72 hours and are often fragile to transport. Culture is closely rivaled by DNA probe testing for chlamydia. With good sensitivity, specificity, and predictive values, DNA probes have the advantage of ease of transport, shorter turn-around time, and there is a probe that simultaneously tests for gonorrhea.

Rapid chlamydia tests are less expensive and readily available. There are two types of a rapid antigen detection methods: (1) using direct fluorescent monoclonal antibodies and (2) using enzyme-linked immunosorbent assay technology. These methods have good sensitivities and specificities in high prevalence populations, but the positive predictive values drop as the prevalence gets lower.

Screening and Prevention

Ideally, chlamydia screening should be done on all sexually active women age 20 years or younger and in any women who recently have acquired another STD. Women age 21 to 35 years should be screened if they have a new partner, a high-risk partner, or more than two partners in the last 2 months. Prevention of chlamydia centers on aggressive screening, concomitant treatment of chlamydia and gonorrhea, and prenatal screening.

Treatment

The drugs of choice for chlamydia are either doxycycline 100 mg orally twice a day for 7 days or azithromycin 1 g orally in a single dose (see Table 11.1.2). Alternate regimens include such

Table 11.1.2. CDC Recommendations for Treatment of STDs—1993

Chlamydia infections	Doxycycline 100 mg orally bid x 7 days[*] or azithromycin 1 g orally once
	Alternate regimens
	Ofloxacin 300 mg orally bid × 7 days[*,**] or erythromycin base 500 mg orally qid × 7 days
	or erythromycin ethylsuccinate 800 mg orally 4 times a day × 7 days
In pregnancy	Erythromycin 500 mg qid × 7 days or
	amoxicillin 500 mg PO tid × 10 days
Gonococcal infections	Cetriaxone 125 mg IM in a single dose
	or cefixime 400 mg orally in a single dose
	or ciprofloxacin 500 mg orally in a single dose[*]
	or ofloxacin 400 mg orally in a single dose[*,**]
	plus
	A regimen effective against possible coinfection with *C. trachomatis*, such as doxycycline 100 mg orally bid × 7 days[*]
External HPV treatment	Cryotherapy or podofilox 0.5%[*]
	or podophyllin 10–25%[*]
	or trichloroacetic acid (TCA) 80–90%
	or electrodesiccation or electrocautery
	or laser
Herpes simplex virus	First clinical episode genital herpes
	Acyclovir 200 mg orally 5 times a day × 7–10 days or until clinical resolution is attained
	First clinical episode of herpes proctitis
	Acyclovir 400 mg orally 5 times a day × 10 days or until clinical resolution is attained
	Recurrent episodes
	Acyclovir 200 mg orally 5 times a day × 5 days
	or acyclovir 400 mg orally tid × 5 days
	or acyclovir 800 mg orally bid × 5 days
	Suppressive dose
	Acyclovir 400 mg orally bid
	or acyclovir 200 mg orally 3–5 times a day
Severe disease (disseminated)	
	Acyclovir 5–10 mg/kg body weight IV every 8 hours × 5–7 days or until clinical resolution is attained
Syphilis—early	Benzathine penicillin G, 2.4 million units IM in a single dose
	Penicillin allergy
	Doxycycline 100 mg orally bid × 2 weeks[*]
	Erythromycin 500 mg qid × 14 days
late	Benzathine penicillin G, 7.2 million units total, administered as 3 doses of 2.4 million units IM each, at 1-week intervals
	Penicillin allergy
	Doxycycline 100 mg orally bid × 2–4 weeks
Chancroid	Azithromycin 1 g orally in a single dose
	or ciprofloxacin 500 mg bid × 3 days[*,**]

Table 11.1.2.—*Continued*

	or ceftriaxone 250 mg IM in a single dose
	or erythromycin base 500 mg orally qid × 7 days
Lymphogranuloma venereum	Doxycycline 100 mg orally bid × 21 days*
	or erythromycin 500 mg orally qid × 21 days
	or sulfisoxazole 500 mg orally qid × 21 days
	or equivalent sulfonamide course

*Contraindicated in pregnancy.
**Contraindicated in women age <17 years.

drugs as ofloxacin, erythromycin base, erythromycin ethylsuccinate, and sulfisoxazole (2).

Erythromycin and azithromycin are reasonable choices during pregnancy. Use of azithromycin may increase compliance because it has once daily dosing and less nausea. It has displayed excellent cure rates. Both are class B drugs in pregnancy.

Gonorrhea

Epidemiology

Gonorrhea is caused by *Neisseria gonorrhea*, a gram-negative diplococcus. Although the total incidence of gonorrhea has decreased slightly recently, it is probably under reported. Prevalence is going up in adolescents and inner city areas, especially with the association of drug abuse. Teenage women are the highest risk group for contracting gonorrhea. In 1991, the rate of gonorrhea in African-Americans was 40 times higher than whites, whereas in Hispanic-Americans there was a rate twice that of whites (3).

Women are twice as likely to contract gonorrhea from an infected man partner as men are from an infected woman (4). Adolescents are a higher risk because they are more likely not to use contraception and because their cervical columnar epithelium cells grow rapidly, making them easily infected by *N. gonorrhea*. Because gonorrhea infects columnar epithelium, sites of infection can include the cervix, urethra, rectum, and oropharynx.

Clinical Course

Gonorrhea may present as cervicitis, a vaginal discharge, dysfunctional bleeding, dysmenor-rhea, dyspareunia, or dysuria. Symptoms begin 1 to 3 weeks after exposure. As many as 50% of women who have gonococcal cervicitis also have gonococcal urethritis. In women, 50% with gonococcal cervicitis may be asymptomatic making early detection and treatment impossible. Anorectal gonorrhea occurs in 30% of women with cervical disease, is usually asymptomatic, and is not necessarily related to anal intercourse. Gonococcal pharyngitis occurs because of oral sex with an infected partner. It may present like any other bacterial pharyngitis or be asymptomatic in as many as 60% of cases. This presentation of gonorrhea in multiple areas emphasizes the need for culturing the cervix, urethra, rectum, and oropharynx.

Gonorrhea PID usually presents classically with vaginal discharge, abdominal and pelvic pain, and can progress to peritonitis and tubo-ovarian abscesses. Treatment may require hospitalization and parental antibiotics. The major sequela of gonorrhea is infertility. Gonorrhea can have a systemic bacteremia-arthritis syndrome with gonorrhea that can present with single large joint septic arthritis, fever, pustular lesions, and a high white blood count (WBC). Gonorrhea is one of the two most common causes of septic arthritis in young adults. The organism can often be seen by gram stain and be cultured from the pustular lesions or joint fluid. The treatment is high-dose parenteral antibiotics.

In pregnancy, gonorrhea can infect the infant during labor, causing gonococcal ophthalmia. It can also cause premature ruptured membranes, chorioamnionitis, and preterm labor.

Diagnosis

The hallmark of gonorrhea on gram stain is gram-negative intracellular diplococci. However, unlike diagnosis in men in which gram stain of the penile discharge is diagnostic, sensitive, and specific, in women gram stain of cervical or vaginal discharge detects it in only approximately 60% of all cases. For a sensitive culture, Thayer-Martin medium must be immediately inoculated and then incubated in 5% carbon dioxide; this will detect 80 to 90% of uncomplicated anal or genital gonorrhea.

DNA probe and polymerase chain reaction tests, now in common use, are sensitive, specific, and easier to transport than cultures. The DNA probe is commercially packaged in combination with chlamydia DNA probe; this simplifies the diagnosis of concomitant chlamydia that occurs with gonorrhea 30 to 50% of the time in women.

Treatment

Since 1976, gonorrhea strains resistant to penicillin have been identified and are increasingly more common, making penicillin no longer the treatment of choice. One case of gonorrhea in five is now penicillin resistant. There is also growing resistance to tetracycline.

Treatment of uncomplicated gonorrhea of any site can be successful with a single dose of ceftriaxone 125 mg IM, cefiximine 400 mg orally, ciprofloxacin 500 mg orally, or ofloxacin 400 mg orally (Table 11.1.2). All are highly effective. However, recently a few cases of gonorrhea resistant to quinolones such as ciprofloxacin and ofloxacin have been reported. For disseminated gonorrhea the recommended treatment is ceftriaxone 1 g IV or IM every day until there is clinical improvement; then an oral regimen is completed. It is estimated that 15% of gonorrhea today is penicillinase producing *Neisseria gonorrhea*. In many urban areas resistant gonorrhea represents at least half of all cases. Proper treatment is therefore important.

CDC recommendations include treatment for chlamydia with any diagnosis of gonorrhea. Chlamydia presents in up to 30% of patients with gonorrhea. There are several alternative regimens. However, tetracycline and the quinoline antibiotics are not approved for pregnant or nursing women or for those under the age of 18 years.

Pelvic Inflammatory Disease

Pelvic inflammatory disease can be caused by gonorrhea, chlamydia, anaerobic bacteria, *Mycoplasma homicus*, and a variety of other microbial organisms. It afflicts more than 1 million women yearly and is estimated at costing 4.2 billion dollars yearly directly and indirectly (4). PID is a group of diagnosis including salpingitis, oophoritis, endometritis, parametritis, and peritonitis.

The consequences of PID are severe. When these bacteria invade the tubes, tubal damage causes infertility in 10 to 20% of the women with one episode of PID. Two episodes leave 35 to 50% of women infertile and 75% are infertile by the third episode of PID. PID increases the risk of ectopic pregnancy 6- to 10-fold, and chronic pelvic pain remains in 20%.

Risk Factors

Most women who get PID are young; most are younger than age 30 years. One third of the cases are in women younger than age 20 years, and two-thirds in women less than age 25 years. One of eight sexually active teenagers will acquire PID, as compared to 1 in 80 women over age 24 years (5). Women with multiple sexual partners have a fourfold greater incidence in PID. PID is more common in nulliparous women and in women with a previous history of PID.

Contraceptive choice affects the risk for PID. Use of an IUD increases a woman's risk of PID two to nine times; 6% of IUD users will have a febrile episode of PID. Oral contraceptives decrease the risk, although the cause is not known. Barrier methods provide some protection against all STDs, including PID; use of diaphragms or condoms decrease the risk of

PID at least 40% (6). Fifteen percent of women who have a gonorrhea infection will develop PID. Douching may also contribute to bacteria ascending into the uterus.

Symptoms

Classic symptoms are pain and tenderness in the lower abdomen possibly with fever, and chills, usually just after menses. Pain is the most common symptom; 90% of women with PID complain of back, flank, or pelvic pain. The pain has usually been present less than 15 days and it is exacerbated by movement and sexual intercourse. Forty percent of women with PID have fever, chills, nausea, and vomiting. Fifty-five percent have a vaginal discharge, and 35% have irregular vaginal bleeding.

The woman may have peritoneal signs of abdominal rigidity, guarding, rebound, and extreme tenderness. There may be increased cervical or vaginal discharge and tenderness of cervical motion. The pain should be bilateral. Although salpingitis can occur in greater severity on one side than another, pain in only one adnexa suggests ectopic pregnancy, or if on the right side suggests appendicitis. Sometimes there are minimal symptoms, but intense tubal damage can occur leaving the woman scarred, infertile, or with chronic pain from PID.

Diagnosis

The diagnosis is clinical. The woman must present with the following three symptoms:

1. Abdominal direct tenderness
2. Tenderness with motion of cervix and uterus
3. Adnexal tenderness

Besides this, she must have one of the following:

1. Gram stain of cervical or vaginal discharge showing gram-negative intracellular diplococci
2. Temperature > 38°C
3. Leukocytosis >10,000

4. Purulent material from peritoneal cavity by culdocentesis or laparoscopy
5. Pelvic abscess, induration, or mass completely on bimanual or ultrasound

Cultures should be taken from the cervix. If the gram stain of cervical mucus shows gram-negative intracellular diplococci, gonorrhea is the organism, but many infections are caused by chlamydia. An elevated WBC and an elevated erythrocyte sedimentation rate are common. A palpable tender mass or ultrasound evidence of pelvic inflammation may also be helpful. Occasionally laparoscopy, endometrial biopsy, or culdocentesis is used for diagnosis.

PID is diagnosed correctly only 60 to 65% of the time because of its variable presentation and many physicians' low index of suspicion. Maintaining a high level of awareness for PID risk factors improves diagnosis.

The differential diagnosis includes several emergency diagnoses: ectopic pregnancy, ruptured tubo-ovarian cyst, ruptured ovarian cyst, twisted ovarian cyst, acute diverticulitis, degenerating leiomyoma, endometritis, and acute appendicitis should all be considered. Pregnancy needs to be excluded.

Treatment

PID regimens must cover gonorrhea, chlamydia, gram-negative bacteria, anaerobes, and others. Aggressive management is necessary to reduce sequela. Hospitalization is advised if the woman has signs of peritonitis or a surgical abdomen, she is pregnant, dehydrated and/or unable to keep liquids and medicines down, or is an adolescent (Table 11.1.3). A pelvic abscess, nausea and vomiting, or a high fever, elevated WBC count or signs of sepsis would also require hospitalization. If a patient has HIV, is noncompliant, or does not respond to an outpatient regimen within 48 hours, she should be hospitalized. There is some evidence that inpatient parenteral treatment of any case of PID may cause less scarring and subsequently less chance of infertility.

Table 11.1.3. Indications for Hospitalization with PID

History
    Pregnant
    Dehydrated (e.g., unable to keep liquids down)
    Nausea and vomiting
    HIV
    Adolescents
    Does not respond to outpatient treatment
        within 48 hours
    Difficulty getting pregnant
    History of PID or chlamydia infection in past

Physical examination
    Signs of peritonitis or a surgical abdomen
    High fever
    Signs of sepsis (e.g., hypotension, pallor)

Laboratory
    High WBC count

Table 11.1.4. PID Inpatient Treatment

CDC regimen A-1993
    Cefoxitin 2 g IV every 6 hours
        or
    Cefotetan 2 g IV every 12 hours
        plus
    Doxycycline 100 mg IV or orally every 12
        hours[*]
CDC regimen B-1993
    Clindamycin 900 mg IV every 8 hours
        plus
    Gentamicin loading dose IV or IM (2 mg/kg
        of body weight) followed by a mainte-
        nance dose (1.5 mg/kg) every 8 hours

[*]Contraindicated in pregnant women.

Table 11.1.5. PID Outpatient Treatment

CDC regimen A-1993
    Cefoxitin 2 g IM plus probenecid, 1 g orally
        in a single dose concurrently, or
    Ceftriaxone 250 mg IM
        or
    other parenteral third generation
        cephalosporin (e.g., ceftizoxime or
        cefotaxime)
        Plus
    Doxycycline 100 mg orally bid × 14 days[*]
CDC regimen B-1993
    Ofloxacin 400 mg orally bid × 14 days[*]
        Plus
    either clindamycin 450 mg orally qid
        or
    metronidazole 500 mg orally bid × 14 days[**]

[*]Contraindicated in pregnant women.
[**]Contraindicated in first trimester of pregnancy.

The CDC outlines two inpatient regimens (see Table 11.1.4). One uses cefoxitin 2 g IV every 6 hours or cefotetan 2 g IV every 12 hours plus doxycycline 100 mg IV or PO every 12 hours. The second inpatient plan includes clindamycin 900 mg IV every 8 hours and gentamicin IV or IM. Several outpatient regimens are also outlined in Table 11.1.5.

Sequelae of PID

Acute episodes of PID are usually easily cured and the woman becomes asymptomatic. Some episodes may result in scarring with adhesions and chronic pelvic pain or tubo-ovarian abscesses. Fitz-Hugh-Curtis syndrome, an infectious perihepatitis, diagnosed clinically with PID and right upper quadrant abdominal pain, can occur. The most severe sequelae are tubal scarring and subsequent infertility. Silent or "quiet" PID, such as infections with chlamydia often are, can cause tubal stenosis and infertility and the woman may not even know she had infections.

Human Papilloma Virus (HPV)

There are over 40 types of human papilloma virus (HPV), small DNA tumor viruses that cause genital warts. The types 6 and 11 are commonly found in external and benign lesions, whereas other types such as 16, 18, 31, 33, and 35 have a higher potential for malignancy. HPV infections are serious because some of them lead to cervical cancer.

HPV infection is extensive. The incidence of HPV (over 1 million cases per year) is grossly underestimated. Pap smear and DNA testing show up to half of all adolescents and 20 to 30% of the general population have been infected with HPV. Only one in three cases is symptomatic by the presence of warts. Risk factors include age less than 25 years, multiple partners, intercourse at an early age, smoking, and immune suppression.

Symptoms

A rough spot on the genital or perianal region is often the presentation for HPV. However, many cases are discovered only through evaluation of an abnormal Pap smear. Often HPV is found as a co-infection in women with recurrent vaginal discharge.

Diagnosis

Although the appearance of vaginal warts is classic, many cases of HPV are subclinical and require Pap tests, colposcopy, and biopsies for diagnosis (see Chapter 12.3). Pap, cytology, and DNA testing are also used to confirm the diagnosis (7).

Treatment

Like many other DNA viral diseases, HPV often remains in a subclinical state after treatment. Debulking or eradicating visible lesions does not cure HPV or prevent spread or sequela. Treatment includes cryosurgery, podofilox 0.5% solution, 80 to 90% trichloroacetic acid, laser, electrosurgery, or other destruction such as LEEP (see Chapter 12.3). Podophyllin has been used in the past but is used less often now because of its toxicity and the inability to use it in pregnant women. For pregnant women treatment options include cryosurgery, TCA, electrocautery, or laser. Transmission of HPV to the infant with vaginal delivery is low, but can cause respiratory papillomatosis in young children. There is some recent evidence that 50% of HPV-infected women who use condoms for

at least 2 years will not have detectable infection and can be presumed to be cured (7).

The seriousness of HPV is that a few strains seem to lead to cervical cancer. With its increasing incidence, especially in younger women, there is a fear of increasing incidence of cervical cancer. Approximately 70 to 80% of cells taken from cervical cancer lesions contain HPV DNA (8).

Herpes Simplex Virus (HSV)

Because HSV is a DNA virus, it can recur and does not have a cure. It is estimated 30 billion Americans are infected with herpes, most of whom are asymptomatic. The infection is particularly serious for newborns and immunocompromised patients. Of the 400 to 1000 infants born each year with congenital HSV infection, 65% will die if not treated appropriately, and 50% of the survivors will have serious permanent neurological damage.

Symptoms

When symptomatic, herpes presents as small, multiple, painful blisters or ulcers around the genitalia. Usually the first episode is symptomatic with localized genital pain, flu-like symptoms, fever, malaise and a longer duration, averaging 12 days. Recurrences are usually milder, lack systemic symptoms, and last on average 4 to 5 days. Viral shedding can occur at any time, even when no lesion is present, making prevention of herpes spread difficult. Condom use does not prevent transmission. Any multiple ulcerated or blister lesions from the waist to the knees should be presumed to be herpes simplex genitalis infection until proved otherwise.

Diagnosis

Again the key to diagnosis is suspicion of any single or grouped blister or ulcer-like lesions, especially if there is more than one. Culturing the herpes virus is much easier on primary episodes, but is the best diagnostic tool. Culture of a primary lesion yields herpes in 95%, whereas a recurrent lesion cultures positive only 65% of the time. A smear of fluid from the lesion or ulcer placed on a slide and fixed just like a Pap test (Tzank smear) can be sent for pathological diagnosis. Finding multinucleated giant cells with intranuclear inclusions is diagnostic for herpes. Measuring HSV titers can help determine if the woman has been exposed and infected.

Treatment

There is no cure, but antiviral treatment can reduce or suppress symptoms and speed resolution of the lesions. Other symptomatic treatments such as sitz baths, local anesthesia, and local hygiene are helpful for comfort.

The current CDC recommendations suggest use of acyclovir 200 mg orally five times a day for 7 to 10 days for the first episode of genital herpes. Because recurrent cases are often milder, treatment remains on an individual basis. For women with six or more recurrences a year, suppressive therapy with acyclovir 400 mg orally twice a day for a year may diminish symptoms and the number of episodes.

For women with a history of herpes, screening in pregnancy and especially watchfulness at the time of delivery is key. Active lesions or documented viral shedding is an indication for Cesarean delivery to prevent exposure of the newborn at vaginal delivery to this potentially deadly virus.

Syphilis

Epidemiology

Syphilis, caused by infection by the spirochete *Treponema pallidum*, is acquired through sexual contact. Over the past decade, with the increasing incidence of illicit drug use, HIV, and high-risk sexual behavior, the incidence of syphilis has risen to a 40-year high (9). Sexual contact with an infected individual will transmit the disease approximately 60% of the time.

In 1991, the incidence of syphilis in African-Americans was 62 times higher than among whites, whereas for Hispanics the rate was six times higher than among whites. Although all genital ulcers deserve evaluation for syphilis, syphilis has been called "the great imitator,"

and any erythematous rash can be syphilis. Any genital ulcer, and any painless ulcer anywhere on the body, should be considered syphilis until proven otherwise.

Symptoms

The classic chancre of syphilis is a painless, indurated ulcer present 2 to 6 weeks after infection, often resolving spontaneously. It can occur anywhere, although it is more likely in the genital region. Unfortunately, for women, it can appear in the vagina or on the cervix and be totally unnoticed. Approximately half of the women with untreated primary syphilis will progress to the secondary phase, whereas the other half proceed directly to latent phase (10).

After the spirochete enters the body, approximately 9 weeks after inoculation, in half the patients, it produces a generalized maculopapular rash involving the palms and soles, mucous patches, condyloma lata, and generalized lymphadenopathy (secondary syphilis). Latent syphilis is the period between primary and secondary and tertiary syphilis in which there are no typical clinical signs or symptoms. Tertiary syphilis may include involvement of the cardiovascular, central nervous, or muscular system and gummas in internal organs. Although clinically syphilis is described as primary, secondary latent, or tertiary, for treatment purposes it is early (primary, secondary, or latent less than 1 year), late (latent more than one year, cardiovascular, gumma), or neurosyphilis.

Diagnosis

Definitive diagnosis of syphilis is made by demonstrating *T. pallidum* from a skin lesion by either dark field microscopic examination or direct fluorescent antibody testing. Screening for syphilis with bloodwork should be done with either Venereal Disease Research Lab (VDRL) or the rapid plasma reagin (RPR) tests. To confirm the diagnosis from a positive screening the fluorescent treponemal antibody absorption test (FTA-ABS) or the microhemagglutination assay tests (MHA-TP) are used.

All pregnant women should be screened

for syphilis to reduce congenital syphilis risks. Forty percent of newborns with congenital syphilis die. Any patient with a genital ulcer should always receive testing for syphilis.

Treatment

The drug of choice for treating syphilis at all stages is parenteral penicillin G. For patients not allergic to penicillin, the treatment for primary and secondary syphilis is benzathine penicillin G 2.4 million units IM once. For nonpregnant patients that have penicillin allergies, treating primary and secondary syphilis with doxycycline 100 mg orally twice a day for 2 weeks or tetracycline 500 mg orally four times a day for 2 weeks is recommended. The VDRL or RPR should be followed at 3 months and 6 months to ensure the titer drops at least fourfold. Failure of the VDRL or RPR to decrease marks a treatment failure and flags a patient who should have HIV screening.

If syphilis has been present for over 1 year ("late" syphilis), the recommendation is benzathine penicillin G 7.2 million units total in three weekly doses of 2.4 million units IM each. The doxycycline or tetracycline course for penicillin-allergic nonpregnant patients

with latent syphilis is extended to 4 weeks. All pregnant patients should receive the penicillin regimen with appropriate desensitization for those allergic to penicillin.

Other Ulcerative STDs

Ulcerative STDs have taken on new importance in the past decade because of their link with increased HIV transmission (Table 11.1.6). Although genital herpes is by far the most common, syphilis and in some areas chancroid need special consideration. Lymphogranuloma venereum (LGV) is rare but occasionally seen in the United States. The patient with genital ulcers must be tested for other STDs, because as many as 3 to 10% of patients with genital ulcers carry two ulcerative STDs.

Chancroid

Chancroid is linked with HIV transmission. As many as 1 in ten patients with chancroid also has HSV or syphilis. Chancroid outranks syphilis in cases worldwide, but is less common in the United States.

Chancroid, caused by *Hemophilus ducreyi*, presents as a purulent, painful inguinal lym-

Table 11.1.6. Characteristics of STDs with Genital Ulcers

	Herpes	Syphilis	Chancroid	LGV
Characteristic lesion	Multiple small-grouped vesicles that form shallow ulcers	Indurated painless papule, ulcer, clean chancre	Purulent, foul-smelling, irregular, erythematous ulcer with exudate	Small shallow ulcer that heals spontaneously
Incubation	2–7 days	>2 weeks	2–12 days	5–21 days
Pain	Yes	No	Yes	No
Lymph nodes	Tender bilateral lymphadenopathy	Rubbery, firm, nontender	Present in more than half, painful, forms buboes	Nodes matted in clusters unilateral or bilateral
Diagnosis	Tzanck smear or HSV culture	Dark field exam or serology	Gram stain or culture	Serology
Treatment	Acyclovir*	Penicillin G	Azithromycin Ceftriaxone Erythromycin	Doxycycline* Erythromycin Sulfisoxazole

*Not indicated in pregnancy.

phadenopathy. If untreated, it creates buboes. Women usually have several ulcers most often located on the labia, fourchette, or vestibule. Painful swollen lymph nodes develop in approximately half those infected a few days after the ulcer. They may be unilateral or bilateral, and if left untreated, they coalesce into a type of abscess called a bubo.

Chancroid is difficult to culture, but the organisms can be seen as gram-negative rods on gram smear in chains with a classic "school of fish" appearance. The CDC has noted that probable diagnosis is made when a woman has one or more painful genital ulcers, syphilis has been excluded by darkfield exam or serology, and herpes has been excluded by clinical or laboratory means. The combination of a painful ulcer and tender, inguinal lymphadenopathy, and supportive lymphadenopathy is almost pathognomonic for chancroid.

The treatment of choice for chancroid is either azithromycin, oral erythromycin base, or intramuscular ceftriaxone. When treated the ulcer should heal in 1 week and be undetectable in 30 days. The buboes and lymphadenopathy may take several weeks to resolve.

There is temptation to try to drain buboes, but this is contraindicated as fistulas and increased scarring result. If a bubo approaches 5 cm in size and appears likely to rupture, aspiration with a large needle may improve its healing and reduce scarring. The aspirated material, however, is not likely to culture the organism.

Lymphogranuloma Venereum

LGV patients usually present after the ulcer has healed and can present as a unilateral or bilateral lymphadenopathy or proctitis.

LGV is caused by L-serotypes of *Chlamydia trachomatis*. The initial stage after incubation of 3 to 21 days is a small papule or ulcer often resembling herpes. This lesion is usually small, painless, transient, and resolves spontaneously in 3 to 4 weeks. The second stage is characterized by painfully inflamed and enlarged lymph nodes. In women, because the cervix and vagina are primary sites, the deep iliac and retroperitoneal lymph nodes may form a pelvic mass and present with pelvic, abdominal, or low back pain. The tertiary stage is characterized by proctocolitis, rectovaginal fistula, swelling of the labia, and perianal ulcerations and scarring.

LGV is no longer diagnosed by the Frei test. It now requires either (*a*) a positive serologic test such as complement fixation or microimmunofluorescence, (*b*) isolation of chlamydial organisms, or (*c*) histology showing chlamydial elemental or inclusion bodies in tissue. After treatment, patients with LGV should be retested for syphilis and HIV at a 3-month follow-up visit because there are frequent concomitant infections.

LGV is most commonly treated with doxycycline 100 mg orally twice a day for 21 days. Alternate regimens may include erythromycin or sulfisoxazole. Treatment not only cures the infection but also prevents ongoing tissue damage. With any ulcerative STD, testing needs to be complete for all ulcerative STDs.

Hepatitis B Virus

Epidemiology

Sexual transmission accounts for one-third to two-thirds of the 200,000 to 300,000 new cases of hepatitis B virus in the United States each year. This reflects a 50 percent increase over the past decade. Six to 10% of adults infected will become chronic carriers, spreading the disease and risking fatal complications. Perinatal HBV transmission occurs in from 10 to 85% of infected hepatitis B mothers. Twenty-five percent of infected newborns will die, and of the rest 85 to 90% will be chronic carriers without treatment. It is essential to screen all pregnant women for this disease and to promote vaccination and infant treatment to reduce this disease.

Symptoms

Most HBV infections have minimal symptoms. Symptoms may include nausea, vomiting, fatigue, jaundice, fever, dark urine, abdominal pain, or arthralgias. HBV infections can have various but uncommon systemic symptoms from rashes to arthralgias, or depression to neurological changes.

Diagnosis

Diagnosis of HBV requires determination of the following tests:

- Hepatitis B surface antigen (HbsAg): to detect acute HBV or the chronic carrier state.
- Hepatitis Be core antigen: to document currently infectious
- Anti-HbsAg: to show past infection with present immunity.
- Anti-HBe core antigen: to show past or current infection.

In addition to these tests consideration to testing for hepatitis A or C should also be performed, especially because hepatitis C is becoming increasingly common.

Treatment

There is no treatment available. Fluids, rest, and general health maintenance for supportive care are recommended.

However, there is a vaccination against HBV. All newborns, children, health care workers, adolescents, individuals with multiple sexual partners, IV drug users, and others exposed to blood products should be vaccinated. Active management of babies born to hepatitis B positive mothers includes HBIG (hepatitis B immunoglobulin) and vaccination.

Prevention of STDs

Education of patients with STD prevention and screening is now an important part of wellness promotion. Because so many of these diseases have minimal or delayed symptoms and devastating sequela, the lives, health, and fertility of an entire generation may be at stake. The repeated message of safe sex and condom use applies to all STDs and must be emphasized. Condom use can prevent or decrease the spread or transmission of gonorrhea, chlamydia, HPV, LGV, chancroid, HBV, syphilis, and HIV.

Treatment of partners is essential in all STDs. This must be confidential and effective to prevent further spread. Testing for other STDs should be offered to anyone found to have a STD, or with a history of or risk factors for STDs. Promotion of the hepatitis B vaccine and screening at risk patients are key ways primary care providers will slow the epidemic of STDs.

Special Considerations for Nurse Practitioners and Physician Assistants

Nurse practitioners and physician assistants must never adopt a less vigilant attitude about STDs because of more effective treatment or a trend toward decreasing rates, as happened with syphilis in the mid-20th century. Even if the overall rates of a STD are decreasing, the problem can remain endemic in certain areas (11). Care has to be taken when designating certain populations (such as lower socioeconomic groups) as high risk and others as lower risk, because some differences in statistics could be due to more thorough reporting in public health clinics as compared to private physician offices (12). Certain groups of women are at higher risk, e.g., young women; but all currently or previously sexually active women must be assessed.

Many women are not aware of their personal risk for STDs. Telephone interviews with 1000 randomly selected women revealed that three out of four women age 18 to 24 years were not worried about getting a STD and two thirds knew almost nothing about STDs. Additionally, these women believed that being monogamous protected them, not realizing that their partners' sexual encounters increased their risk (13). Women may also believe they are safe from STDs because they have only one sexual partner at a time (serial monogamy). Providers must help all sexually active women understand the possible long-term consequences of their decision (12).

How often a woman is screened will depend on an assessment of her risk level. At the time of screening, an open discussion should include information on sexual modes of transmission and prevention of reinforcement and transmission to others (14). When treatment is prescribed, providers must be aware that medications may produce more side effects than the STD. These side effects should be discussed with the women, as well as any possible interactions with food or OTC preparations. The cost of medications (e.g., azithromycin versus doxycycline) must be considered (12, 15). The woman should feel free to call the provider if she has any questions.

Treatment may be long and involve changes in sexual behavior, thus involving the woman's sexual partner or partners. Optimally, the partner will understand the infection, testing, treatment modalities, responsibilities, and how the woman can be supported. Providers can offer to counsel the woman and her partner together (14). If present during a counseling session, the partner can be instructed to seek diagnosis and treatment if unusual rashes, sores, or dysuria develop and to inform their partner of symptoms (15). Women may also be counseled to examine their partners for lesions, rashes, discharge, and odor before sexual activities and to ask them about infections. Asking a partner about STDs assumes that the partner will know if he has been infected and that he will not lie.

In practice, discussion of STDs with a partner is often an unrealistic expectation that assumes equality in the relationship, comfort in discussing sex, and enough self-esteem to risk rejection. A woman may also resist notifying her partner because of her guilt about her STD or her anger at the partner who transmitted an infection (12). Role playing or giving the woman a script to use on the telephone may assist her in notifying her partner. Women should be told if an STD has to be reported and assured that the information is not made available to anyone else without her permission (16).

Because many STDs have no cure and devastating consequences, prevention must be the focus of care. The use of condoms should continue to receive emphasis, realizing, however, that condoms do not offer absolute protection from STDs. Men and women should be taught the correct use of latex condoms, and the female condom should be presented as an option. However, for many women, asking a male partner to use a condom goes against role expectations of couples that women follow the lead of men. In addition, the issue of condom use has to be readdressed with each sexual encounter and suggests that there have been other relationships than the current one (12). Women should address condom use with a partner at a time removed from the sexual act (16).

Teaching about safe sex practices for the prevention of STDs must be appropriate to the woman's skill, culture, language, and age. Written lists of safe sex options for physical intimacy can be given (17). Women should be reminded to avoid situations when safe sex is hard to practice, such as the use of alcohol and drugs that affect decision-making. Women should also become familiar with their bodies and recognize changes that might indicate STDs. Genital self-examination is a self-care technique that providers should teach their clients.

Prevention of STDs must also occur at the community level and beyond. Preventive practices must be integrated into prenatal care, mental health, and other practice areas. Putting more emphasis on the screening of men for STDs might increase their responsibility for behavior change (12). This means that all providers must be comfortable asking about STDs and knowledgeable about screening and treatment. Community-wide efforts to increase awareness of STD risk and prevention measures could include the use of media, lay community health workers to make contacts, and portable clinics or vans (18).

References

1. Guttmacher Institute. Facts in brief: STDs in the United States, 1994.
2. Donovan P. Testing Positive: Sexually Transmitted Disease and the Public Health Response. New York: Alan Guttmacher Institute, 1993.
3. Guttmacher Institute, Facts in Brief, Sexually Transmitted Disease (STDs) in the United States, September 1993.
4. Gibbs RS, Sweet RL. Evaluating and treating obstetric and gynecologic infections: a clinician's guide. Gardiner-Caldwell SynerMed, 1995:28.
5. Rosenfeld W. Sexually transmitted diseases in adolescents: update 1991. Pediatr Ann 1991;20:303–312.
6. Hatcher RA. Contraceptive Technology. 16th ed. New York: Irvington, 1994.
7. Moscicki CA, Palefsky J, Smith G, et al. Variability of human papilloma virus DNA testing in longitudinal chohor of young women. Obstet Gynecol 1993; 82:578–585.
8. McCance DJ. Human papilloma virus infections in the aetiology of cervical cancer. Cancer Surv 1988; 7:499–506.
9. Bolon, et al. Syphilis, Are you missing it? Patient Care 1993 (Oct 15):126– 155.
10. Goens JL, Janniger CK, DeWolf K. Dermatological and systemic manifestations of syphilis. Am Fam Physician 1994;50:1013–1020.
11. Tillman J. Syphilis: an old disease, a contemporary perinatal problem. JOGNN 1992;21:209–213.
12. Leonardo C, Chrisler JC. Women and sexually transmitted diseases. Women Health 1992;18:1–15.
13. Campaign for Women's Health & American Medical Women's Association. Women and sexually transmitted diseases: the dangers of denial. New York: EDK Associates, 1994.
14. Kelley KF, Galbraith MA, Vermund SH. Genital human papillomavirus infection in women. JOGNN 1992;21:503–515.
15. Erickson MJ. Chlamydia infections: combating the silent threat. J Nurs 1994;94:16B–16F.
16. Fogel CI. Sexually transmitted disease. In: Fogel CI, Woods NF, eds. Women's Health Care. Thousand Oaks, CA: Sage 1995:571–609.
17. Hatcher RA, Trussell J, Stewart F, et al. Contraceptive Technology. 16th ed. New York: Irvington, 1994:51–106.
18. Killian C. Pregnancy: a critical time to target STDs. MCN 1994;19:156–161.

Suggested Reading

Centers for Disease Control. 1993 Sexually Transmitted Diseases Treatment Guidelines. MMWR 1993;42: RR-14.

Youngkin EQ. Sexually transmitted diseases: current and emerging concerns. JOGNN 1995;8:743–758.

11.2

Women and AIDS

Kay A. Bauman

Introduction

As the numbers of AIDS cases and deaths continue to rise unremittingly throughout the world, the incidence continues to rise faster in women than in men. The importance of HIV disease lies in the fact that it is an infectious disease that is transmitted sexually, by blood or blood products, and from mother to newborn; yet it is a disease for which there is neither a ready cure nor one on the horizon. Thus, providers must remain competent to care for the manifestations of this disease indefinitely. This chapter will (a) discuss the epidemiology of the disease, (b) describe the disease as it pertains to women, including many social issues women must face, (c) characterize the clinical presentation, in particular gynecologic disease and the disease in pregnancy, (d) offer specific suggestions for improved care for women at risk of or with HIV, and (e) finally provide some specific recommendations for community and political activism regarding women in this epidemic.

Epidemiology

The numbers continue to grow, so much so that they are hardly noticed anymore. As of January 1, 1992, an estimated 4.7 million women worldwide were infected with HIV, approximately 40% of the total of over 11 million persons infected (1). By the next decade, 50% of all cases are expected to be women. In 1993 in the United States, AIDS was the fourth leading cause of death among all women age 25 to 44 years, and the first cause of death for women in New York City age 15 to 35 years. For African-American women, AIDS was the leading cause of death in that same age range, and for Hispanic women it was the third leading cause of death.

In no other disease except AIDS have cumulative numbers been measured since the recognition of the disease. In 1985, the cumulative percentage of women with AIDS was only 7% of the total, but at the end of 1994 it was nearly 14% (2). However, for specific states, this cumulative percentage has been even greater; for instance, in Florida, 19% of the cumulative percentage of persons with AIDS are women, and the rate in New York is 20%.

Another way to emphasize the increasing burden of the epidemic on women is the decreasing male-female ratio over the years of the epidemic and in those recently infected. Early in the epidemic the male-female ratio was as high as 15:1. The current US men to women ratio is 7:1. Of AIDS cases diagnosed first in 1994, the ratio is 4.7:1, and of HIV cases diagnosed in 1994, that ratio is 3.5:1 (3).

For younger adults, there is an even greater impact of the disease on women, and in certain populations the rate in women is close to that in men and occasionally may outnumber that in men. Internationally in those countries in which previously a male-dominated epidemic existed, an increase in rates in women is also occurring. For example, in France, the male-female ratio has decreased from 3.4:1 in 1985 to 2.7:1 in 1990 (4).

Minority women carry an overwhelming burden of this epidemic. Although only 21% of the US population are minorities, 76% of women AIDS patients are minority women. For the most part these are African-American (55%) and Hispanic (21%) women. Because infected women include infected mothers, it follows that for pediatric AIDS in which the vast majority is perinatally acquired, 81% are minority infants. The current rates for AIDS in the specific ethnic groups represented in the United States are: (5)

Asian Pacific Islanders	1.3 per 100,000
Caucasian	3.8 per 100,000
American Indian/ Alaska Native	5.8 per 100,000
Hispanic	26.0 per 100,000
Black	62.7 per 100,000

At the time of diagnosis of AIDS, women are 2 to 5 years younger than men on the average. Eighty-four percent in the United States are in the 15- to 44-year range. In adolescents diagnosed with AIDS, 34% are women.

Although in the United States the AIDS epidemic has primarily been an urban epidemic, the numbers are slowly growing to include increasingly rural populations, particularly in the South. For example, in the state of Georgia, the metropolitan Atlanta AIDS rate for 1992 was 14.4 per 100,000 population and 6.7 per 100,000 for the rest of the state. In the Northeast the epidemic has remained predominantly urban, such that only 1% of the infections are in rural populations. In the South approximately 10% of the HIV-positive individuals live in rural areas.

In the United States, the pattern of transmission for women has changed significantly over the last decade. Early in the epidemic, many women were infected by blood transfusions, and over half were infected by intravenous (IV) drug use. By 1994, this pattern had changed; 41% were infected by IV drug use, 38% were infected heterosexually, and only 2% were infected by blood or blood products. Thus, risky behavior by women is increasingly defined as having a heterosexual sex partner who carries the virus. Women with more sex partners, increased frequency of vaginal or anal intercourse, and a decreased use of condoms put themselves at greatest risk for HIV transmission. As providers understand that heterosexual sex is an increasing risk for women, they are more likely to understand the need for routine HIV counseling and testing for these same women, just as screening for chlamydia and gonorrhea has become routine today for a large population of women.

Table 11.2.1 shows prevalence rates of HIV in various international populations. The percentage of HIV positive varies widely from nearly zero in Canadian prenatal patients to 87% of Abidjan, Ivory Coast prostitutes.

Women who know themselves to be at risk do change their sexual behavior (6). French women decreased their sexual activity after learning of their HIV-positive status, increased their condom use significantly (from 33% pretest to 51% posttest), and increased their contraceptive coverage (64 to 76%), thus decreasing their risk of becoming pregnant. The woman partners of HIV-positive men with hemophilia have increased their use of condoms from 7% in 1985 to 69% in 1991. They have also decreased their incidence of anal and oral sex, although they did not change their use of other contraceptive practices. Although this is an impressive increase in self-protection for the at-risk woman partners of men with hemophilia and HIV, the remaining 31% of those same women were still putting themselves at risk (7).

Injection drug use, either by themselves or their partners, is the behavior that puts the greatest number of women at risk. Only when increased attention is given to the drug use epidemic will this mode of transmission for HIV disease decrease in incidence. Many AIDS prevention programs emphasize cleaning needles, or not sharing drug paraphernalia. These programs are slowly stabilizing or even decreasing the numbers of new HIV-infected drug users in many major cities in the United States (8). Nonetheless, the overwhelming evidence is that needle-sharing and inconsistent condom use in drug-using communities is exceedingly common (9). In New York City, for example, HIV-positive individuals did not change their drug use after learning of their HIV-positive status, but they did decrease but not eliminate their needle-sharing, and did not increase their condom use (10). In New York City in 1993, 52% of women injection drug users (IDUs) shared their needles at least once per month in the year prior to being interviewed (11). In Harlem, of a population of 215 sexually active, drug-using women, 26% had been in jail in the previous year, 22% were homeless, and 74% had traded sex for drugs, particularly those who used crack and had a history of STDs (sexually transmitted diseases). Internationally, in a population of 1570 women injectors in 12 different cities, 54% had never injected with used equipment. However, of the 46% who did use others' equipment, the majority generally cleaned it, although often ineffectively (12). Most of these IDUs were sexually active with a primary partner and the majority (70%) had unprotected sex with that partner.

In the United States, there have been reported six cases of HIV positivity from artificial insemination (13). Because women are transfused twice as often as men, they have twice as many transfusion-related AIDS cases in the United States. Careful screening of semen donors and donors of blood and blood products has drastically decreased the risk to both women and men of these modes of HIV transmission.

From the beginning of the epidemic, there have been many discussions on the efficiency of transmission from men to woman compared to from woman to men. In African countries it

Table 11.2.1. Prevalence Rates of HIV in Various International Populations

Group of Women Tested	Location	Year	N	% HIV +	Other Tests	Reference
General						
ER	Bronx, NY	1989	856	7.8	Compared to 14.6% males HIV positive, risk assessments done less frequently for females; usually only limited to injection drug use	47
Sexually active females (non-IDU)	Brooklyn	1990–1991	372	2.4	35% had at least 1 STD	24
Army reservists	United States	1985–1993	122195 96001	0.65 prevalence 0.12 incidence	No change in rate over time Increased in minorities	20
FP Clinics						
FP clinics	Kenya	Published 1994	4404	4.9	Risk factor was uncircumsised husband; only 5.2% had ever used condom! Most women were married and had only one sex partner in previous year	43
FP clinics	Tanzania	1991–1992 prevalence study 1992–1993 incidence	2285 754	11.5 3.6	HIV positive *increases* with education of female and partner! Increased with IUD use (OR 2.5) and GC (OR 2.0) No variation in incidence of HIV with contraceptive use	45 79
Prenatal						
Prenatal	Florida, rural	Published 1992	1084	5.1	Black women, 8.3% HIV positive; none of positive were IDUs; 33% of crack users were HIV positive (OR 3.3)	31
Prenatal drug users only	Harlem, NYC	Published 1994	1300	20	63% of HIV positive had cervical disease 33% of HIV negative had cervical disease	18
Prenatal	Louisiana	1988–1991	202178	0.15	Orleans Parish 0.53% HIV positive	52
Prenatal ages 15–24	Brazil, general Pub.		1044	0.2		69
Prenatal	Brazil, Rio de Janeiro	Published 1993	4536	0.8		57

Type	Location	Year	Number	%	Comments	Ref
Prenatal (deliveries)	Canada, Ontario	1989–1991	94119	0.03		90
Prenatal	France	1987–1992	16520	1.16	No change over years of study	84
Prenatal	France, Paris	1993	7072	0.6	HCV 1.3%; if HCV positive then 13% had HIV; if HCV negative then 0.4% had HIV	19
Prenatal	Haiti	Published 1994	664	8.4		6
Prenatal	India	1993–1994	13335	0.7	1.1% had positive VDRL but only a few had both diseases	37
Prenatal	Italy	1990–1992	25634	0.24	Noteworthy difference; HIV-positive women thus choosing abortion more	32
Abortion			9422	1.13		
Prenatal	Kenya	1989	4883	6.5	Syphilis increase from 2.9 to 5.3% over same time, syphilis OR 2.5 for HIV positive	86,36
		1991		13.0		
Prenatal	Malawi	Published 1992	4229	19.7	9.2% positive for HBV with 0.4% carriers; 1.9% positive HCV ab.	61
Prenatal	Puerto Rico	1989–1990	997	0.8		26
Prenatal	Rwanda	1989–1991	5288	9.8	OCs increased rate of HIV infection	16
Prenatal	Senegal	1991–1992	4698	0.7		65
Prenatal	Togo, rural	1992–1993	512	1.8		56
Prenatal	Uganda, rural	1990–1992	409	21.5	Comparisons are 32.1% HIV positive of general outpatients and 49.5% HIV positive of all inpatients; prenatals are 39.1% positive for syphilis.	76
Prenatal	Zaire	1989–1991	4205	3.1	Stable and remains low compared to East Africa neighbors	54
STD Clinics						
STD clinics	California	1989	17210	0.57	Increased in African-American 25–29 yrs, IDUs and San Francisco location	96
STD clinic	Brazil	Published 1993	400	2.0	VDRL positive 6.6%; HBV positive 19%; chlamydia 3%	9
STD clinic	London	1989–1990	850	0.35	Unchanged rate since 1986, decreasing GC rates; other STD rates unchanged	53
STD clinic	Uganda	1989–1991	1823	52		89
IDUs						
IDUs	International 12 cities	1989–1992	1570	20	Range: Glasgow less than 1% to Madrid 63%	85

Table 11.2.1.—Continued

Group of Women Tested	Location	Year	N	% HIV +	Other Tests	Reference
Prostitutes						
Prostitutes	9 European communities	1990–1991	866	5.3	31.8% in IDUs; 1.5% in non-IUDs; increased with STD hx (ulcerative)	2
Prostitutes	Ivory Coast, Abidjan	Published 1993	278	87	High rates STDs: trichomonas 28%, GC 31%, syphilis 20%, genital ulcer 21% HIV-2: 3.1% in HIV negatives 40.8% in HIV positives	87
Prostitutes	Argentina, Buenos Aires	1989–1991	178	11.6	81% condom use 9.3% IDUs 22.9% positive syphilis	64
	Dominican Republic	1990 1991 1992	2354 2754 >2800	unk. 2.9 1.9	Syphilis 13.7% positive; 4.4% GC positive Syphilis 8.6% positive; 2.2% GC positive Syphilis 7.4% positive; 1.9% GC positive	29
Prostitutes	Scotland, Glasgow	Published 1992	197	2.5	70% IDUs	59
Prostitutes	Thailand	1992	797	22.3	Regional differences between North (14%) and South (30.2%); Condom use 24–34%	51
Prison						
Prisoners	California (Orange County)	1985–1991	3051	2.7	Only change over time 2.5 to 2.7%	34
Prison intake	NYC	1989	546	25.8	Compared to 16.1% HIV positive in men (n=1690); rates in women increase with age; rates higher in white and Hispanic women than black. Age <20, 14.3% HIV positive Highest rates in IV heroin users	94
Prisoners	Quebec	Published 1991	394	6.9	13% positive in IDUs	39

has been apparent that transmission was essentially equal in both directions. However, in the United States and in many European countries, the transmission from men to women was significantly greater than the reverse. Several studies in the United States, Italy, and in a group of European cities have shown that the efficiency of HIV transmission indeed is greater from man to woman, the range being between 1.9 and 2.3 times more efficient than for woman to man (14, 15). In another study that examined the woman-to-man transmission, out of 224 couples in which the woman was HIV positive, only 6.4% of the men became HIV positive (16). A behavior associated with transmission was anal sex. A decreased CD_4 count or an AIDS diagnosis in the index case also was associated with transmission.

The Disease in Women

Natural History

Because most AIDS cases in the early years of the epidemic were in men and all of the natural cohort studies have been of men, it is not surprising that diagnostic categories for AIDS specific to women were missing until January 1993. Thus, the early AIDS data underrepresented women. Of AIDS diagnostic categories added in 1993, invasive cervical cancer pertains only to women, but recurrent bacterial pneumonias and possibly tuberculosis are also more common in women. The current staging system for AIDS is built on cohort studies done on predominantly populations of men. Lifson et al. have suggested a more appropriate staging system be devised for women (17). They propose a system that reflects HIV outcomes for women and for men, and that would be appropriate for both clinical and research use. Natural history studies on women began enrollment in April 1993. This is almost 10 years after the well-known MACS (Multi-center AIDS Cohorts Studies) began.

Early in the epidemic, it was thought that survival times for women were shorter than for men. More recent studies, such as one with IDUs in San Francisco in 1993, showed equal progression to AIDS when women and men IDUs were compared (18). The opportunistic infections were also similar in both groups. A second study supporting equal survival compared women who acquired HIV disease by transfusion to HIV-positive men with hemophilia (19). Survival time was equal from AIDS diagnosis to death for both groups. Studies that have carefully matched controls show nearly equal survival data.

Women tend to seek treatment later than men. Women present for testing, for example, when a child (13.5%) or partner (17.5%) is diagnosed with AIDS, or the women herself becomes symptomatic (26%) or has an opportunistic infection (10%) (20). This New York study also showed that only 10% of women discovered their HIV status by routine screening. At the time of determination of HIV positivity, the mean CD_4 count for these women was 367. Just as in older men, older women who present with HIV disease die more rapidly than younger women.

Clinical Trials

Women have not been studied in natural history studies and they were underrepresented or omitted entirely in early clinical trials. This exclusion of women in clinical trials is not peculiar to AIDS. A common reason for exclusion is that drugs being studied have not been proven safe to a developing fetus should the woman become pregnant. However, the exclusion of women who might become pregnant resulted in the exclusion of all women. Another reason for the exclusion of women in early drug trials was that many women infected with HIV were IDUs. The stereotype for the drug user presumed noncompliance, which is a particular disadvantage for investigational protocols. Studies showed that drug users and gay men had equal compliance with research. A recent study in 1994 showed that HIV-positive minority women were well motivated to participate in clinical trials and demonstrated good compliance with protocols (21). Compliance was not a major hindrance to participation, but rather participation was limited by the paucity of protocols available for pregnant HIV-positive women. Only 6.7% of 11,909 early ACTG (AIDS Clinical Trials Group) participants from 1987 to 1990 were women. Nearly half the participants were white and only 23% were IDUs. Cumulative AIDS cases then were 11.5% women, of which 27% were white and 51% were IDUs. Thus women were underrepresented in numbers in the trials, and the population distribution was not representative of HIV-positive women.

Clinical trials for asymptomatic persons with HIV now have increasing numbers of women. Because women are more represented in the newer wave of infected persons, more are available for these trials. If the principal investigator (PI) or co-principal investigator of a clinical trial is a woman, there are twice the percentage of women enrollees as when the PI is a man (10.8% versus 5.3%)

Prevention and Transmission Issues

Early in the epidemic, women received attention as vectors of infection to their "innocent" newborns rather than deserving of attention themselves. It is interesting that the major clinical trial involving women that has changed provider behavior is the zidovudine (ZDV) trial for interruption of HIV transmission to newborns (22). Prenatal HIV screening has become the standard of care; thus ZDV can be offered to infected mothers who meet the criteria.

Of critical importance is an ability for women to prevent the transmission of HIV to themselves. Although condom use has increased worldwide, dramatically so in some populations, there are still many locations in which condoms are not culturally acceptable. A woman's suggestion for their use may incur violence. The varied use of condoms for birth control in various countries prior to AIDS suggests their varied cultural acceptability for prevention of transmission of HIV. In the pre-AIDS era, condom use in Africa and most of the Middle East was 0%, in Asia 1 to 5%, in Latin America 1 to 9%, in the United States and Canada 7%, in the United Kingdom 22 to 31%, in Mexico 1%, and in Japan 50% (23). Although there is a new female condom on the market in a few locations, it has not been well studied for STD prevention and it is certainly not widely available, acceptable, or inexpensive.

Woman-to-woman transmission is generally overlooked in the literature, although there are a few case reports. Generally, woman-to-woman transmission is an inefficient mechanism for HIV transmission. This is supported by an interesting retrospective study in the United States of 960,000 women blood donors. Of the 144 who were HIV positive, none had sex exclusively with other women (24).

There continue to be many unknowns regarding transmission in women. For example, the transmission of AIDS by sex during menses has not been adequately studied. Early in the epidemic, it was considered that birth control pills, because they cause cervical ectopy, might enhance HIV transmission. However, a recent study in Italy showed a protective role for oral contraceptives (odds ratio [OR] = 0.4) (25). This study also looked at IUD use and its relationship to HIV transmission for heterosexual women. IUDs were associated with increased transmission (OR 2.1). There are no data on the association between injectable contraceptive use and HIV.

Psychosocial Issues

Because women with HIV disease in the United States are predominantly in racial and ethnic minorities, lower socioeconomic, and linked to the drug-using population, their epidemic has very special implications. For example, for many women the HIV disease is complicated by drug use. HIV-infected women may be women in poverty, have limited economic opportunity, are often unemployed, or may be homeless. Because a goal for women (as well as for men) must be interruption of transmission of HIV, the accompanying social issues that are related to empowerment of women must be addressed.

Internationally, cultural roles are equally challenging. For example, in Uganda, because men are permitted to have multiple sexual partners, the wife's ability to control the infection may be limited (26). Thus, prevention efforts cannot focus only on women.

There are high levels of both emotional and physical abuse in this population. Domestic violence is common and often increases in incidence with pregnancy. It also may increase at the time a woman reveals to her partner that she is HIV positive (27).

Access to health care is a consideration for HIV-infected women. Women may first pay attention to sick children or a sick partner before they address their own HIV disease management. A study of five major service locations in a January 1995 report to the Committee on Labor and Human Resources showed that women accessed Ryan White funded services equal to or greater than men. Substance abuse treatment and housing were particularly difficult to access (28). Fragmentation of care can affect accessibility. HIV-positive women may use infectious disease services for health care, but many of these providers may not provide competent gynecological care. Women frequently do not describe their gynecological symptoms unless asked, so many of these problems go undiagnosed and unmanaged.

HIV-infected women who are drug users also have high crime and incarceration rates (29). Women are more likely than men to be arrested for crimes related to drugs, although they do have shorter prison stays. This results in higher HIV positivity rates for women prisoners than men in New York City. A study of 10 prison facilities in 10 states also found a higher incidence of AIDS in women prisoners. In this study, the range of HIV positive for men was 2.1 to 7.6%, compared to 2.5 to 14.7% HIV positive for women (30). Younger women had significantly higher rates than men of the same age.

Although it is assumed that HIV causes high psychologic impact on women, studies have not supported this finding. Often studies have inadequate controls so that it is impossible to separate out the substance abuse related problems, the socioeconomic problems and problems related to homelessness from those psychological problems specifically related to HIV disease. In a study of the psychosocial impact of HIV on women, a comparable group of HIV-positive and HIV-negative women showed no difference in psychiatric history or current psychological functioning in anxiety, depression, social support, or locus of control (31).

Women who are HIV-infected, feeling the stigma of HIV disease, often feel isolated and full of shame. They are confused regarding sexual activity and fear transmission, appropriately for sexual activity but inappropriately for nonsexual activity. The primary adjustments are coping with a life-threatening disease and adaptation to death and dying. Other problems women note are coping with illness and being a mother simultaneously, the problem of how and when to disclose their disease to their uninfected children, and for many women a feeling of loss of reproductive choice. One study showed the most common psychiatric problem related to HIV disease in women was sexual dysfunction once seropositivity was known (32).

Prostitution has been widely studied internationally, because for many years it was assumed that prostitutes provided a nidus of infection for HIV-negative men. Prostitution is indeed common among drug-using women, either as a direct exchange of sex for drugs or as a way to earn money to pay for drugs. Current studies show a high use of condoms with customers when a woman is employed in the sex industry (33–35). As consistent a result, however, is the low use of condoms by the woman with her primary partner at home.

A study of injection drug-using women internationally showed that 29% reported prostitution but the range was wide, from 14% in London to 71% in Berlin. Table 11.2.1 shows rates of HIV seropositivity in prostitutes in various countries where that has been studied (12).

A final social impact of this epidemic is the high numbers of children of HIV-positive mothers worldwide that will be orphaned before the age of 15 years (1, 36). Often both mothers and fathers will die of AIDS before the children are grown. This is also reflected as an individual problem for many HIV-infected women—"who will care for my children?"

Clinical Presentations

General

Women infected with HIV present with the same range of diseases that men do, particularly if controlled for mode of transmission. There are, however, some important differences. This most important is that women more often present with death compared to men (27.5% compared with 12.2%) (37).

The primary presenting AIDS diagnosis (after a laboratory diagnosis of <200 CD_4 cells) varies from country to country. In some places, *pneumocystis carinii* pneumonia PCP is still a primary diagnosis for women; in others esophageal candidiasis has been a major presenting disease (38). HIV wasting disease, herpes simplex, tuberculosis, sepsis, and bacterial pneumonias are also common in women. Kaposi's sarcoma (KS) is rare in women. In the few studies that address this difference, it appears that the women who have KS have ac-

quired it sexually, often from men who also had sex with men. This incidence difference for KS in women supports the current research that identifies a gamma herpes virus as the long-sought cofactor for the transmission of Kaposi's sarcoma (39).

Although at this time lymphomas are decreased in women, this could be related to life expectancy. As the epidemic progresses more of this cancer in HIV-infected women may be found, just as its incidence has increased over time in men.

Because the range of diseases is generally similar for women as for men, it is believed that the treatments for these diseases should also be similar. There are changes that must be considered, however, if women are pregnant. For example, the tuberculosis medications streptomycin and pyrazinamide must be avoided.

Specific Stressors for Women

Women with HIV disease deserve attention for specific stressors their gender defines. There are six areas in which women with HIV disease face particularly high levels of stress.

Partner

Often women with AIDS are already caring for sick partners. Revealing HIV status to a new partner may be extremely difficult. If an infected woman is in a relationship with a new partner or a partner that is uninfected, there is significant tension with intercourse even if a condom is used. This results in discordant sexual relationships. Sometimes sex is avoided completely with a resultant stress on the primary relationship.

Reproductive Decisions

If a woman chooses not to conceive when she had previously wished to, it is a significant personal loss. For many women who become pregnant, it is a difficult decision whether to bring that child into the world. There can be extreme guilt for mothers who have already passed HIV on to a child.

Children

HIV-infected women have described disclosing their HIV status to their children as a highly stressful event. These women wish to be honest, yet protect their children from the social stigma of AIDS and help them face community ignorance. They know at times their children will be overwhelmed with worries of a future without a mother. Sometimes this results in child behavior problems (40). For a woman already pregnant, the fear of having an infected baby produces extreme anxiety. If the child does acquire AIDS, the mother also fears the huge care role required while her own health may be deteriorating. Determining guardianship for their uninfected children can be a major concern for mothers.

Disclosure to Family

Women suggest that disclosing their HIV status to parents, siblings, or others in an extended family is highly stressful.

Occupation/Economic

Women are often heads of households and thus the wage earners for the family. HIV/AIDS-related fatigue threatens job performance and job security, just as it does for men who are infected with HIV. As women spend less time or no time in their jobs, the family income is decreased, while there is an increase in expenditures for HIV care. When women are out of work permanently because of their disease, it may mean their insurance has been lost. This, along with declining health, adds to the economic stress.

Social/Loss

Women may be overwhelmed by the amount of grieving required when losing children, a partner, and/or friends to AIDS. If women are involved in a women's support group, this means that they can feel additional personal loss of new friends gained through this social unit. As one woman sees another from her support group dying, it creates apprehension for her own future.

Gynecologic

Because gynecologic care is often inadequately covered in clinical management texts on HIV disease, the following discussion will be more specific than for other diseases. Most women, at some time during their HIV infection, face gynecologic problems. Early in the course of HIV disease, when there may be little or no decrease in CD_4 count, recurrent vaginal candidiasis occurs and may become refractory to topical treatment. For women, recurrent or refractory vaginal candidiasis can occur even before oral thrush. Sometimes oral antifungal agents may be required to resolve this infection, such as oral ketoconozole or fluconazole. HIV-infected women also face candidal infection with species other than *albicans* (see Chapter 12.7).

Immune-suppressed women with HIV disease have increased evidence of HPV infections and an increased progression to CIN (cervical intraepithelial neoplasia) and cervical cancer compared to immune competent women (41). Not only are the well-known precancerous types of HPV (16/18, 31/33/35, 6/1) common in HIV-infected women but types not generally cancer-producing may also cause CIN in this group (42). Rates of CIN are significantly greater in HIV-positive women at all levels of immune suppression. A controversy exists, however, whether all HIV-infected women need routine colposcopy. Colposcopy discovers abnormalities not found by Pap screening in both HIV-positive and -negative women. The question yet to be answered is whether Paps continue to be an adequate screening device with colposcopy used only to follow-up abnormalities or whether routine colposcopy should be made available to all HIV-infected women.

Current recommendations support two Pap tests for HIV-infected women 6 months apart. If both of these and all previous Pap tests have been completely negative, annual Pap test screening is adequate. However, when an abnormality is detected, colposcopy should be performed. DelPriore et al. suggested that because the positive predictive value of an abnormal Pap test in a HIV-infected population is so high, it makes sense to treat at the time of colposcopy, not merely do selective biopsies (43). This would save both time for the women (one less visit) and the cost of that extra provider visit. This suggestion then could increase compliance for women in obtaining adequate medical care for themselves, and would allow them to have their cervical disease treated earlier.

An overlooked area for Pap test abnormalities is in anal cytology. In a 1994 study of 114 HIV-infected women, it was found that 14% of the population had abnormal anal cytology, whereas 11% had abnormal cervical cytology (44). Although it is impossible to know whether this single, small study represents the US population, providers must be aware of precancerous changes in the female anal canal.

Many HIV-positive women will simultaneously have a STD. For example, in a Baltimore study of 78 HIV-infected women, 70% had genital infections (45). HIV diseases have long been associated with genital ulcer disease, specifically, in the United States, with *Herpes simplex* virus and syphilis, and in other countries with chancroid. However, multiple studies support that HIV-infected women have considerable problems with nonulcerative STDs as well, as an increased percentage with chlamydia (18.3% in seropositive versus 8.1% in seronegative women) (46). Another study supported the role of STDs in HIV sero-conversion and found the odds ratio for having HIV in women with gonorrhea was 4.8, for chlamydia 3.6, and for trichomonas 1.9 (47). Syphilis is much more common in a group of HIV-infected women than HIV negative women, but biological false-positive tests for syphilis are also far more common (5.8% compared to 0.2%) (48). These biological false-positive tests are more common in injection drug users. Table 11.2.1 summarizes rates of many STDs including hepatitis B in HIV patients, noted in populations internationally.

Although the pathogens for pelvic inflammatory disease (PID) are no different in HIV-positive than in HIV-negative women, the disease does not seem to have a more complicated course. Women more frequently have severe pain, fever, cervical inflammation and discharge and more commonly need inpatient treatment. Nonetheless, they seem to respond equally to standard treatments for PID (49).

Menstrual disorders are not different in HIV-infected women than in the general population, although this topic has not been widely studied (50). A case controlled study showed no changes in oligomenorrhea, amenorrhea, menorrhagia, dysmenorrhea, and dyspareunia in a study of 55 HIV-positive women. There was also no change in menstrual complaints with changing CD_4 count or with AIDS symptoms.

Pregnancy

As more women are infected with HIV, more pregnant women will be infected. The US rates, which have been stable from 1989 to 1993, are 1.6 infected women per 1000 women giving birth. This amounts to approximately 7000 HIV-positive women giving birth per year. The rates are extremely variable geographically, urban versus rural, and by race or ethnicity. For example, the highest general rate is in New York State, where the rate is 8.4 per 1000, followed by New Jersey with 5.2 and Florida with 4.8. Ahead of all of the states, however, is the rate for Washington, DC, which is 15 per 1000 (2). In New York State, the rate for urban African-American women is 19.1 and for nonurban African-American women is 10.3. Comparison rates for Florida are urban African-American women 17.3 and nonurban African-American women 6.9. Table 11.2.1 shows that other countries have an even higher number of HIV-infected, childbearing women.

Infection does not seem to affect fertility. HIV disease does not appear to progress with pregnancy. Drug-using women are as likely to have children as non–drug-using women. Although early data seemed to suggest that HIV-positive women did not choose abortion more ften than HIV-negative women, there is now contradictory evidence. A recent study on attitudes of HIV-positive women toward childbearing shows a change from pre-HIV testing to posttesting. Fifty-nine percent wanted children prior to their being HIV tested; after the results were known to be positive, only 17% wanted to have children (51).

Women also increased their use of birth control from 39% prior to determining their HIV status to 70% afterward. Condom use increased from 4% prior to testing to 54% after testing. In another study (n = 200) that compared equal numbers of HIV-positive and HIV-negative women, approximately one third of each group learned of their HIV status early enough to obtain an abortion; 2.9% of HIV-negative women chose abortion, whereas 18.8% of HIV-positive women chose that procedure (52). Internationally, of Italian women seeking abortion, the HIV-positive rate rose from 0.8% in 1990 to 1.5% in 1991. Simultaneously, the positivity rates for women delivering babies have seemed to decrease slightly.

Nonetheless, most HIV-infected women who become pregnant do deliver. For many women, pregnancy increases status or self-esteem, or is a cultural or family responsibility. Fertility is usually the norm and life continues with HIV much as it did without it, at least for many years.

When large groups of women delivering babies are studied, 60% of HIV-positive women did not know they were infected until screened during their pregnancy. A study in London in 1992 showed that, of the mothers of 445 HIV newborns, only 20% knew that they were HIV-positive prior to the pregnancy (53).

Rates of transmission to newborns vary with different studies, year, and location, but generally are in the 13 to 30% range. Recent seroconversion or advanced disease in the mother (such as a positive viral antigen test or a rapidly decreasing CD_4 count) is consistent with increased transmissions to the neonates (54).

Transmission can occur at any time during pregnancy, delivery, or with breast-feeding. Half or more of the transmissions, however, occur at the time of delivery. Current zidovudine (ZDV) trials show a decrease in transmission during pregnancy from 25.5% with placebo to 8.3% treated with ZDV (22). These extremely promising results make it mandatory for providers to offer HIV testing to all prenatal patients so that HIV-positive women can be offered ZDV during their pregnancies. This drug appears safe when taken in the second and third trimesters. Birth defects on ZDV were equal to those of the general population (54) and there were no changes between the placebo and test groups in rates of preterm births, SGA or LGA babies, or rates of anemia in the mothers (22). In this clinical trial, ZDV was given after 14 weeks of gestation at a dose of 500 mg daily and during labor at 2 mg/kg loading dose and then 1 mg/kg per hour infusion. The baby was then given ZDV at a dose of 2 mg/kg every 6 hours for its first 6 weeks of life. A recent nonrandomized, small study gave prenatal patients the same doses of ZDV, but did not give the babies the antiretroviral drug and the same range of decrease of infected infants resulted, from 29% to 4% (55).

Although some aborted fetuses already show evidence of HIV infection, investigators are yet unable to identify infected fetuses early in pregnancy so selective abortion might take place. A twin study showed that the first twin was infected at a higher rate than the second twin (56).

There are highly variable rates of transmission to newborns by breast feeding. Mothers recently infected and thus carrying a high viral load or similarly those late in the disease have rates of transmission as varied at 16 to 87% (1). Because the risks of bottle feeding in developing countries can carry a 1.5- to 5-fold increased risk of infant mortality from diarrhea and malnutrition, the advice for HIV-positive mothers to bottle feed must be weighed against the risk of other health hazards. In many developing countries, if breast feeding was stopped, the fertility rates would increase and a com-

Table 11.2.2. Specific Guidelines for HIV-Positive Pregnant Women

- Proactive nutritional management.
- Routine use of ZDV after the first trimester for women whose CD_4 counts are less than 500; ZDV should be continued IV during labor and be given orally to the neonate for the first 6 weeks of life.
- For women who have a CD_4 count less than 200 or have previously been infected with *Pneumocystis carinii* pneumonia (PCP), trimethoprim/sulfamethoxazole, dapsone, or inhaled pentamidine should be offered. Although sulfas are generally avoided late in pregnancy for HIV-negative women, many providers consider the benefit for both PCP and toxoplasmosis prophylaxis to be greater than a questionable small risk of increased teratogenicity or interference with folic acid metabolism. HIV-positive sulfa allergic nonpregnant women may be offered a combination of dapsone and pyramethamine to prevent both PCP and toxoplasmic encephalitis, but pyramethamine is contraindicated in pregnancy.
- STD should be sought and aggressively treated during pregnancy, with particular attention to those associated with preterm delivery.
- Premature rupture of membranes should be aggressively treated.
- No fetal blood sampling or scalp electrodes should be used.
- With current information there is no recommendation to change the mode of delivery for a woman's HIV status.
- Particular attention should be paid to disinfecting the cord prior to cutting to avoid a source of contamination of the infant by the infected mother's blood.
- Babies should be washed immediately, especially prior to insertion of IV lines.
- No breast-feeding is recommended in the United States and Europe.
- Disposable equipment should be used whenever possible, with attention to appropriate biohazard disposal of contaminated materials. Appropriate worker protection should be used related to the degree of potential workplace exposure.
- Baby should be watched for drug withdrawal and treated when appropriate.
- Hepatitis B immunoglobulin is indicated for babies of hepatitis B surface antigen carrier mothers.
- No isolation is needed for the babies in the nursery. Routine universal precautions are adequate.
- A private toilet and shower should be available for women delivering and during their postpartum stay.
- HIV knowledgeable primary care should be available for follow-up for both mother and newborn. The primary care provider should include in eventual discussions with the mother, plans for future care of the child in the likely event the mother may become unable to care for it.

pensatory increase in available contraception would be necessary. There are no reported studies of the impact of breast feeding on the mother's immune status, nutritional health and related HIV progression.

A few studies show no apparent increased risk of ectopic pregnancy, low Apgars, early neonatal complications, or stillbirths in HIV-infected women. These results vary from country to country. There is some evidence of an increase in spontaneous abortions in HIV-infected women. One study shows an increase from 7% in HIV-negative to 15% in otherwise matched HIV-positive women (57). Preterm deliveries, however, are increased in HIV-positive women. For example, in Spain in a study of 344 women, 18.6% of HIV-positive women had premature infants, compared to 7.5% of the HIV-negative women (58). A confounding factor in this study and thus perhaps in other studies is that the rate of prematurity was primarily in HIV-infected women who were current drug addicts. This study found that 24.3% of current drug addicts had premature babies, whereas former drug users had only an 8.5% rate of prematurity.

For many women pregnancy may be an impetus for improved care. It is a time when drug-using women may request help in addressing their addictions. Providers should assess whether methadone maintenance by heroin using women might be safer than unsafe drug withdrawal during pregnancy for those who choose this time to become clean.

Specific Guidelines for Pregnancy Management (Table 11.2.2)

Suggestions for Improved Care for Women

Testing and Counseling

It has become the standard of care to offer HIV testing to all women who present for prenatal care. The next step is to offer counseling and testing to all women. If testing is suggested, at least 80% of women will comply. Providers currently offer HIV testing to women who present with sexually transmitted diseases, are diagnosed with tuberculosis, or have a history of injecting drugs. It is important to offer testing to these women and it is equally important to make counseling and testing more widely available to all women. In a supportive study of over 150 women current drug users, 95% had received gynecological care and 85% had had a Pap test within the previous 2 years (59). Nonetheless, two thirds of these women were not asked about drug use or offered HIV testing. Most women are accessing health care providers, but two-thirds are still not being adequately assessed, counseled, and screened for HIV disease.

The power of counseling and testing is twofold; it identifies HIV-positive women and it allows them to enter medical treatment at the earliest possible stage of their disease. A negative test result can be equally powerful. Women can be counseled regarding risks for HIV disease and can receive information that will help them protect against disease transmission.

There is often debate regarding consensual testing versus mandatory testing. In the United States, mandatory testing is required for Job Corp, federal prisons, immigration, and joining the military. The UK has required prenatal testing since 1989. Because there is now a therapy that can reduce the transmission from mother to newborn, it is suggested in the United States that mandatory prenatal testing may be both moral and economical. If unborn babies can have their risk of infection with HIV decreased to one-third by their mothers taking ZDV, it may be appropriate to identify all women whose babies might benefit from such therapy. A study by Sobo supported the routinization of HIV testing for women (60). In this study, women preferred that HIV testing be routine rather than discussing their own risk behaviors. If providers routinely offer testing, clarifying with patients that it is not automatic but rather consensual, more women will be identified earlier with HIV.

Although the occurrence of one sexually transmitted disease should alert the health care provider to look for others, HIV is often overlooked. For example, in many clinics, women who present with a vaginal discharge are routinely tested for chlamydia and gonorrhea, yet these same women rarely receive HIV testing. Women who present with herpes, trichomonas, or venereal warts have higher rates for HIV positivity, but are rarely offered routine HIV testing. Cervical dysplasia, because of its relationship to the human papilloma virus, can now be considered a STD and thus can qualify the women for testing for other STDs including HIV. Although recurrent or persistent vaginal candidiasis is not a sexually transmitted disease, any woman who presents with this disorder should be offered HIV testing.

The health care provider suggesting HIV testing needs to discuss with the patient the options of testing in the provider's office versus testing at an anonymous test site. Levels of confidentiality for both options can be addressed. When a woman agrees to be HIV tested, it is appropriate to discuss, prior to testing, to whom she wishes to disclose the results. It is a highly emotional time for a woman to consider the effect of a potential positive HIV test on previous or current sexual partners, children, parents, or workmates. "Before-testing" can be an important time to discuss protective behavior to avoid future HIV infection even if the test comes back negative.

Medical and Psychological Care

Although routine counseling and testing for all women would identify the greatest number HIV-infected, many health care providers will prefer to improve risk history taking to help select women for whom HIV testing can be strongly recommended. Thus, in a good general history for women, it is increasingly important to emphasize gynecological problems, including the STDs mentioned above, tuberculosis risks, history of IV drug use, history of transfusions, and a history of exchanging sex for money or drugs. A good history for HIV risk also includes the health or lifestyle behaviors of that woman's sex partner or partners. Once a woman is found HIV-positive, assessment of her disease will include staging the disease with a CBC and CD_4 count. Additional assessments will include tests for chlamydia, gonorrhea, syphilis, trichomonas, a PPD test, and evaluation for hepatitis B status.

The primary care provider needs to follow the gynecological status as well as the overall health status. Care for women in general does not differ from care for men except for screening for cervical cancer. As noted previously in this chapter, the current recommendation is two Pap tests, 6 months apart for HIV-infected women. If these tests are negative, then annual Pap testing is adequate. Some providers recommend Pap tests every 6 months once the CD_4 count drops below 500 or if there is a history of abnormal Pap tests. Some recommend Pap tests every 3 months once the CD_4 count drops extremely low. Currently, colposcopy is recommended for evaluation of any abnormal Pap test. Fertility counseling should be made available for HIV-infected women, and may include a hormonal method of contraceptive and condom use. Women choosing to get pregnant can decrease the risk to their babies by taking ZDV during pregnancy.

Immunizations to be provided for HIV-infected women include Pneumovax, to be given when HIV positivity is diagnosed, annual influenza vaccine, and hepatitis B vaccine when appropriate. It is the health care provider's responsibility to work with patients to enter drug treatment programs when indicated, knowing facilities available in one's own community and the admission requirements for each. Often women will choose to have their children with them during rehabilitation and specific programs that allow women to enter with children should be discovered.

Because HIV management is a partnership between the provider and the woman, this may require education on both sides. If the health care provider is of a different race or ethnicity than the patient, for example, the provider may need to be educated for culturally sensitive care to occur. Then trust can be built and compliance with recommendations may better be accomplished.

Counseling should be made available for the patient and her family. Specific points of stress are (a) the time of diagnosis and (b) the general adjustment to life with symptomatic HIV. Patient educational topics include the physical changes to expect with HIV disease, such as fatigue and weight loss; the emotional impact of the disease and the ways it can be similar to other chronic diseases but can differ with the additional AIDS stigma or the dual diagnosis with drug addiction, relationship stressors, and job and financial stresses.

A discussion of the change in priorities that often is required for HIV-infected women is appropriate: this change may mean medical care for oneself carrying a higher priority than maintaining one's job. A particular problem for many infected with HIV is achieving a balance in life so that HIV does not totally dominate. The primary care provider can help a patient achieve this balance.

Community/Political Activism

Besides being health care providers, physicians, nurse practitioners, physicians' assistants, and nurses have political clout. This clout can be used in many ways to improve the care for HIV-infected women in one's communities and countries. A specific area, for example, is to try to encourage that clinical trials include women. Current NIH guidelines generally now require the inclusion of women. This priority is still fuzzy, however, because phase I studies exclude women of childbearing potential, and in order for phase II studies to include women, the study outcome must meet the health needs of women specifically or there must be minimal risk or a specific benefit to a potential fetus. An example of a specific area of research related to women that needs attention includes creating a vaginal virucide that would enable a woman to get pregnant, but not become infected with HIV. A psychosocial area of research needed is the

relationship between partner notification of the woman's HIV positivity and domestic violence. Other research areas pertinent to women are the use of the "bloodless" Cesarean section to decrease the risk of transmitting HIV from an HIV-positive woman to her newborn, a means of viricidal cleansing of the birth canal prior to delivery, and a potential way to boost the maternal immune response such as vaccination with HIV hyperimmune globulin.

Community activism needs to make sure that community AIDS resources meet the needs for women and men. This means there must be women specific support groups, perhaps with provisions for child care. Another area for political activism is increased availability of drug treatment programs, and specifically, programs that allow women to keep their children with them. Yet another area requiring attention is support for the often controversial HIV educational and prevention programs in schools, churches, and communities.

Conclusion

HIV is a widespread infectious disease for which no curative antiviral medication or preventive vaccine is available or in sight. Providers and other health care workers must be cognizant to counsel and screen for HIV and competent to care for those who are infected including the increasing numbers of women. Providers also must work with patients in prevention skill development and with communities for more accessible prevention programs.

Special Considerations for Nurse Practitioners and Physician Assistants

Nurse providers and physician assistants who work with women in the primary setting will encounter women with risk of or infection with HIV. Using data gathered through an HIV

risk-assessment form completed by over 17,000 women seeking primary health care services, Lauver et al. found that 14% of the sample were at high risk for HIV. Prevalent risk factors included having sex with persons at high risk, having sex with more than 6 persons a year, and having more than two STDs. In addition, there were low rates of consistently using condoms and getting tested for HIV (61).

If screening is done only on women who acknowledge that they are at risk, many women who could benefit from testing and interventions will be overlook. According to a recent study, most American women (73%) do not perceive that they could be at risk, and many rely on monogamy to protect themselves even when their partners have sexual histories that may put them at risk (62). Some women also mistakenly think they have been tested for HIV in the past and are negative when actually only a blood chemistry or other test was done (63).

Disclosure counseling by providers to patients and patients to others "sets the tone and foundation for patients' acceptance, knowledge base, and attitudes about their own HIV infection" (64). Before testing, the woman should be told about reporting requirements and consent (written, if required) should be obtained. In addition, the provider should help the woman identify who she can call upon if results are positive. Women could be asked what changes they might make even if the test results are negative.

The waiting period between testing and results can be an anxious time and the woman should know how much time is required and that a second test may have to be done. If results are negative, the woman needs to know how to stay negative and that, if she has been exposed in the past 6 months, she needs retesting. Positive results must be shared in private with sufficient, uninterrupted time for her to discuss feelings, talk about how she thinks others will react, and obtain information on available services. Partner notification should be encouraged and health care providers should offer to assist if needed. A phone call to the woman should be made within a day or two of the disclosure session (64–66).

Providers must be comfortable discussing

sexuality and asking specific questions about sexual and other risk behaviors. Women can be told that the care provider asks the same questions of all women. Specific questions must be asked about sexuality, e.g., does she have sex with men, women, or both; how many persons has she had sex with in the past week, month, or year; has her male partner had sex with other men; has she used drugs, what kind, how often, and route; does she use clean needles? (67) If resistance is met to direct questions, the interviewer can rephrase or ask the woman what makes her uncomfortable about the subject. Understandable language must be used (66).

All women should be assessed for risk factors. Health care providers who are uncomfortable with the topic may contribute to the number of misdiagnosed or underdiagnosed cases because they can easily attribute the symptoms to other problems (68). During pregnancy, for example, many of the symptoms of HIV infection are similar to common complaints of pregnancy.

Providers must ask women about their support systems and relationships. Women with HIV may feel isolated and alone with an illness often described by the public as a gay male disease. They have also reported stigma and shame and felt they were presumed to be promiscuous. Families may still view them as caretakers for others, and women themselves may find that role easier than caring for themselves. They may have children to provide for, who may or may not be infected, and plans to be made for the children after their death (69).

Relationships with sexual partners and risk behaviors must be addressed. A woman's life situation of drug abuse or prostitution contributes to the spread of the disease as does the risk of abuse for some women who attempt to negotiate safe sex practices (70). Safe sex skills, not just facts, must be taught. If power imbalance in a sexual relationship contributes to high-risk practices, the provider can ask the woman to bring in her partner, arrange telephone counseling with a male counselor, or give printed material developed for male partners (71).

Much of the management of the disease will be done in outpatient settings so the woman will be responsible for identifying early symptoms and keeping herself and others as healthy as possible. Education must be individualized to the woman's needs, but might include (*a*) handwashing precautions; (*b*) use of protective equipment when needed; (*c*) common sense approaches to cleaning and laundering; (*d*) nutrition; (*e*) disease prevention through immunizations; and (*f*) avoiding toxoplasmosis by cooking meat and not being responsible for changing a litter box (70, 72).

No single profession can offer the total range of services needed for a woman with HIV. Health care providers must be familiar with local legal, social, nutritional, home care, hospice, and other resources. If not available, community-based organizations for women must be fostered. Physician consultation is needed to develop a plan of care when there is evidence of a major infection, if there is lack of response to interventions, or when serious side effects develop to therapy. If there is moderate or severe anxiety or depression, consultation or referral for psychological or psychiatric services must be available (72). Ultimately, the woman herself must determine what is most vital to her and what services she needs most. Primary care providers can then assist her to "fight the good fight" on her own terms (70).

References

1. Mann J, Tarantola D, Netter T. AIDS in the world, Harvard College, 1992:29–30, 210, 225, 617–629, 671–672.
2. CDC: Update: AIDS among women—United States, 1994. MMWR 1995;210:81–84.
3. CDC: Birth outcomes following zidovudine therapy in pregnant women. MMWR 1994;43:409, 415–416.
4. Morlat P, Parneix P, Douard D, et al. Woman & HIV infection: a cohort study of 483 HIV-infected women in Bordeaux, France, 1985–1991. The Groupe d' Epidemiologie Clinique de SIDA en Aquitaine. AIDS 1992;6:1187–1193.
5. CDC: HIV/AIDS Surveillance Report 1994;6:10–16, 30–34.
6. DeVincenzi I, Jadand C, Zagury P, Deveau C, Bucquet D. Pregnancies, contraception and condom use in a cohort of 414 HIV infected women. Int Conf AIDS 1994;10:66 (abstract no. 217C).
7. Dublin S, Rosenberg PS, Goedert JJ. Patterns and predictors of high-risk sexual behavior in female partners of HIV-infected men with hemophilia. AIDS 1992;6:475–482.
8. Watters J, Estilo M, Clark G, Lorvick J. Syringe and needle exchange as HIV/AIDS prevention for injection drug users. JAMA 1994;271:115–120.
9. Wallace M, Galanter M, Lifshutz H, Krasinski K, Sharp V. Women at high risk of HIV infection from drug use. Int Conf AIDS 1992;8:D473 (abstract no. PoD5519).
10. Abdul-Quader AS, Tross S, Silvert HM, Simons PS. Women who borrow: determinants of borrowing injection equipment in female injecting drug users (IDUs) in New York City. Int Conf AIDS 1993; 9:822 (abstract no. PO-D08-3629).
11. el-Bassel N, Schilling R, Gilbert L, Serrano Y, Farugue A, Edlin B, et al. Correlates of sex trading among female drug users in Harlem. Int Conf AIDS 1992; 8:C352 (abstract no. PoC 4658).
12. Taylor A, Green ST. Risk behaviors among female drug injectors in 12 cities. WHO Collaborative Study Group. Int Conf AIDS 1994;10:334 (abstract no PD0515).
13. Araneta M, Mascola L, Eller A, et al. HIV transmission through donor artificial insemination. JAMA 1995;273:854–858.
14. Comparison of female to male and male to female transmission of HIV in 563 stable couples. European Study Group on Heterosexual Transmission of HIV. 1992;304:809–813.
15. Nicolosi A, Correa Leite ML, et al. The efficiency of male-to-female and female-to-male sexual transmission of the human immunodeficiency virus: a study of 730 stable couples. Italian Study Group of HIV Heterosexual Transmission. Epidemiology 1994; 5:570–575.
16. Nicolosi A, Musicco M, Saracco A, Lazzarin A. Risk factors for woman-to-man sexual transmission of the human immunodeficiency virus. Italian Study Group on HIV Heterosexual Transmission. J Acquir Immune Defic Syndr 1994;7:296–300.
17. Lifson AR, Allen S, Wolf W, et al. Classification of HIV infection and disease in women from Rwanda. Evaluation of the World Health Organization HIV staging system and recommended modifications. Ann Intern Med 1995;122:262–270.
18. Moss AR, Vranizan K, Osmond D, Winslow K. Progression to AIDS and survival in HIV-infected female and male injection drug users. Int Conf AIDS. 1993;9:657 (abstract no. PO-C04-2638).
19. Holman RC, Chorba TL, Clarke MJ, Evatt BL. Epidemiology of AIDS in females with hemophilia and

other chronic bleeding disorders in the United States; comparisons with males with chronic bleeding disorders and AIDS and with nonhemophilic female blood-transfusion recipients with AIDS. Am J Hematol 1992;41:19–23.

20. LaTrenta L, Jacobs J, Goldstein M. Characteristics of women in a New York City HIV Clinic. Int Conf AIDS 1992;8:C364 (abstract no. PoC 4728).

21. Bardeguez A, Grandchamp J, Picardi J, McSherry G, Connor E. Two-years experience in enrollment and retention of pregnant women in AIDS clinical trials; new challenges, new perspectives. Int Conf AIDS 1994;10:35 (abstract no. 434B).

22. CDC: Zidovudine for the Prevention of HIV Transmission from mother to infant. MMWR 1994;43: 285–287.

23. Population Information Program. The Johns Hopkins University: Population Reports: Update on Condoms-Products, Protection, Promotion. Population Reports 1982;X:H131–132.

24. Petersen LR, Doll L, White C, Chu S. No evidence for female-to-female HIV transmission among 960,000 female blood donors. The HIV Blood Donor Study Group. J Acquir Immune Defic Syndr. 1992;5:853–855.

25. Gervasoni C, Lazzarin A, Musicco M, Saracco A, Nicolosi A. Contraceptive practices and man-to-woman HIV sexual transmission. The Italian Partner Study. Int Conf AIDS 1992;8:C351 (abstract no. PoC4651).

26. McGrath JW, Rwabukwali CB, Schumann DA, et al. Anthropology and AIDS: the cultural context of sexual risk behavior among urban Baganda women in Kampala, Uganda. Soc Sci Med 1993;36: 429–439.

27. North RL, Rothenberg KH. Sounding board: partner notification and the threat of domestic violence against women with HIV infection. N Engl J Med 1993;329:1194–1196.

28. GAO/HEHS. Ryan White Care Act: Access to Services by Minorities, Women, and Substance Abusers. January 1995.

29. Weisfuse IB, Greenberg B, Back A, et al. HIV-1 infection among New York City inmates. AIDS 1991; 5:1133–1138.

30. Vlahov D, Brewer TF, Castro KG, et al. Prevalence of antibody to HIV-1 among entrants to U.S. correctional facilities. JAMA 1991;265:1129– 1132.

31. Pergami A, Gala C, Burgess A, et al. The psychosocial impact of HIV infection in women. Psychosom Res 1993;37:687–696.

32. Brown GR, Rundell JR. A prospective study of psychiatric aspects of early HIV disease in women. Gen Hosp Psychiatry 1993;15:139–147.

33. Day S, Ward H, Perrotta L. Prostitution and risk of HIV: male partners of female prostitutes. Br Med J 1993;307:359–361.

34. Peeters M, Alary M, Laga M, Piot P. Determinants of condom use in European female sex workers. The European Working Group on HIV Infection in Female Prostitutes. Int Conf AIDS 1992;8:D497 (abstract no. PoD 5649).

35. Ward H, Day S, Mezzone J, et al. Prostitution and risk of HIV: female prostitutes in London. Br Med J 1993;7:356–358.

36. Michaels D, Levine C. Estimates of the number of motherless youth orphaned by AIDS in the United States. JAMA 1992;268:3456–3479.

37. Women and AIDS—unexplained higher risk of death. AIDS Treat News 1995;214:2–3.

38. Hay PE, Thomas BJ, Horner PJ, et al. Chlamydia trachomatis in women: the more you look, the more you find. Genitourin Med 1994;70:97–100.

39. Cesarman E, Change Y, Moore PS. Kaposi's sarcoma-associated herpes virus-like DNA sequences in AIDS-related body-cavity-based lymphomas [see comments]. N Engl J Med 1995;332:1227–1228.

40. Semple S, Patterson T, Temoshok L, et al. The HIV Neurobehavioral Research Center (HNRC) Group: Identification of psychological stressors among HIV-positive women. Women & Health. 1993;20: 15–36.

41. Sun XQ, Ellerbrock TV, Lungu O, et al. Human papillomavirus infection in human immunodeficiency virus-seropositive women. Obstet Gynecol 1995;85: 680–686.

42. Paavonen J, Lehtinen M. Human papillomaviruses and anogenital neoplasia. The AIDS Reader 1991: 116–122.

43. DelPriore G, Maag T, Bhattacharya M, et al. The value of cervical cytology in HIV-infected women. Gynecol Oncol 1995;56:395–398.

44. Williams AB, Darragh TM, Vranizan K, et al. Anal and cervical human papillomavirus infection and risk of anal and cervical epithelial abnormalitites in human immunodeficiency virus-infected women. Obstet Gynecol 1994;83:205–211.

45. Keller J, Anderson J, Abrams J, Stanton D, Chiasson RE. Cervical cytology and genital infections with HIV positive women. Int Conf AIDS 1992;8:TU32 (abstract no. TuB 0530).

46. Spinillo A, Gorini G, Regazzetti A, et al. Asymptomatic genitourinary chlamydia trachomatis infection in women seropositive for human immunodeficiency virus infection. Obstet Gynecol 1994;83: 1005–1010.

47. Laga M, Manoka A, Kivuvu M, et al. Non-ulcerative sexually transmitted diseases as risk factors for HIV-1 transmission in women: results from a cohort study. AIDS 1993;7:95–102.

48. Augenbraun MH, DeHovitz JA, Feldman J, et al. Biological false-positive syphilis test results for women infected with human immunodeficiency virus. Clin Infect Dis 1994;19:1040–1044.

49. Hanna L. Women & HIV/AIDS, reports from Berlin. BETA 1993:25–28.

50. Shah PN, Smith JR, Wells C, et al. Menstrual symptoms in women infected by human immunodeficiency virus. Obstet Gynecol 1993;83:397–400.

51. Lai KK. Attitudes toward childbearing and changes in sexual and contraceptive practices among HIV-infected women. Cleve Clin J Med 1994;61:132–136; quiz 161.

52. Sunderland A, Minkoff HL, Handte J, Moroso G, Landesman S. The impact of human immunodeficiency virus serostatus on reproductive decisions of women. Obstet Gynecol 1992;79:1027–1031.

53. Davison C. Surveillance of HIV & AIDS in pregnant women and their children in the British Isles. The RCOG and BPSU HIV/AIDS Reporting Schemes. Int Conf AIDS 1992;8:C281 (abstract no. PoG 4219).

54. Jackson JB, Kataaha P, Hom DL, et al. Beta 2-microglobulin HIV-1 p24 antibody and acid-dissociated HIV-1 p24 antigen levels: predictive markers for vertical transmission of HIV-1 in pregnant Ugandan women. AIDS 1993;7:1475–1479.

55. Boyer PJ, Dillon M, Navaie M, et al. Factors predictive of maternal-fetal transmission of HIV-1. Preliminary analysis of Zidovudine given during pregnancy and/or delivery. JAMA 1994;271:1925–1930.

56. Goedert JJ, Duliege AM, Amos CI, Felton S, Biggar RJ. High risk of infection with human immunodeficiency virus type 1 for first-born, vaginally delivered twins. Lancet 1991;338:1471–1475.

57. Miotti PG, Dallabetta GA, Chiphangwi JD, Liomba G, Saah AJ. A retrospective study of childhood mortality and spontaneous abortion in HIV-1 infected women in urban Malawi [see comments]. Int J Epidemiol 1992;21:792–799.

58. Carieras R, Torrent A, Rovira MT, et al. Obstetrics pathology in HIV positive pregnant women. Int Conf AIDS 1994;10:192 (abstract no. PB0783).

59. Queen P, Cagle H, Fisher D, Haverkos H. Female drug users: provider assessment of AIDS risk. Int Conf AIDS 1994;10:331 (abstract no. PD0505).

60. Sobo EJ. Attitudes toward HIV testing impoverished inner-city African-American women. Med Anthropol 1994;16:17–38.

61. Lauver D, Armstrong K, Marks S, Schwartz S. HIV risk status and preventive behaviors among 17,619 women. JOGNN 1995;24:33–39.

62. The Campaign for Women's Health, American Medical Women's Association. Women and sexually transmitted diseases: the dangers of denial. New York: EDK Associates, 1994.

63. Witt RC, Silvestre AJ, Rinaldo CR, Lyter DW. Guidelines for disclosing HIV-antibody test results to clients Nurse Provider 1992;17:55–63.

64. U.S. Department of Health and Human Services. Evaluation and management of early HIV infection. Clinical Practice Guidelines Number 7. AHCPR Publication No. 94-0572, Jan. 1994.

65. Fogel CI. Sexually transmitted diseases. In: Fogel CI, Woods NF, eds. Women's Health Care. Thousand Oaks, CA: Sage, 1995:571–609.

66. Nolte S, Sohn MA, Koons G. Prevention of HIV infection in women. JOGNN 1993;22:128–134.

67. ———.Clinical guidelines. Adult counseling for sexually transmitted diseases and HIV infection. Nurse Pract 1995;20:76–79.

68. Sipes C. Guidelines for assessing HIV in women. MCN 1995;20:29–37.

69. Chung JY, Magraw MM. A group approach to psychosocial issues faced by HIV-positive women. Hospital Community Psychiatry 1992;43:891–894.

70. Zelewsky MG, Birchfield M. Women living with immunodeficiency virus: home care needs. JOGNN 1995;24:165–172.

71. Hatcher RA, Trussell J, Stewart F, Stewart G, et al. Contraceptive Technology, 16th ed. NY: Irvington, 1994:51–75.

72. Shannon MT. Human immunodeficiency virus. In: Star WL, Lommel LL, Shannon MT, eds. Women's Primary Health Care. Washington, DC: American Nurses' Association, 1995:11–25, 11–38.

12.1

Menometrorrhagia and Causes of Abnormal Premenopausal Vaginal Bleeding

Robert E. Nesse

Introduction

Abnormal vaginal bleeding is a common reason for visits to primary care providers, and it imposes a significant physical, emotional, and financial burden on women. Fifteen percent of otherwise healthy women have menometrorrhagia during their lifetime, and in a primary care practice, abnormal vaginal bleeding has an annual incidence of 20/1000 women between the ages of 20 and 55 years (1). In a typical gynecology outpatient practice, 21% of patients are referred because of abnormal vaginal bleeding (2).

Abnormal vaginal bleeding is a major cause of surgery for young women. Two hundred women in England were followed between 1983 to 1989. Each had presented to physicians with irregular menstruation. Of the 145 patients with menorrhagia, 60% had received a hysterectomy (2).

Definition of Normal Menstrual Cycle and Abnormal Vaginal Bleeding

Chiazze and his colleagues studied the menstrual cycles of over 2000 women. Cycle lengths averaged 28.1 days, with a standard deviation of 3.95 days (3). The variation in cycle length is highest at the onset of menarche and in the perimenopausal period after age 40 years. (Fig. 12.1.1.). The length of normal menstrual flow is defined as less than or equal to 1 week.

A usual menstrual interval is 28 days in normal women, with a standard deviation of less than 4 days (Table 12.1.1). Greater than 90% of all women have a normal menstrual interval of 20 to 36 days. Intervals outside these boundaries are considered abnormal and labeled as polymenorrhea and oligomenorrhea, respectively. Blood loss greater than 80 mL is associated with a negative iron balance on a usual diet. Flow this brisk is also associated with other symptoms such as pain and clots or problems with hygiene or social function. Thus, menstrual flow of greater than 80 mL per cycle is menorrhagia. Although this term refers to menstrual flow blood loss of precise measurement, as a practical matter, most providers would define menorrhagia as a patient's perception of greatly increased flow, changed flow or flow

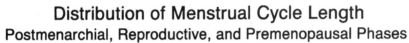

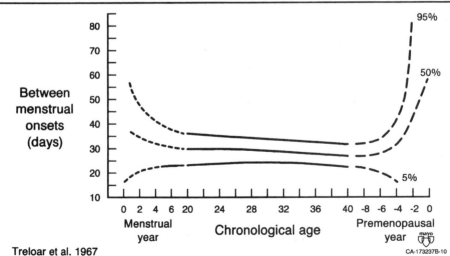

Figure 12.1.1. Distribution of menstrual cycle length. Postmenarchial, reproductive, and premenopausal phases.

Table 12.1.1. Terminology of Menstruation

Menarche	First menstrual period and reproductive life span
Menopause	Last menstrual period and life span thereafter
Perimenopause	Time prior to menopause with menopausal symptoms
Polymenorrhea	Menstrual interval <21 days
Oligomenorrhea	Menstrual interval >36 days
Menorrhagia	Menstrual blood loss >80 mL
Metrorrhagia	Irregular menstrual bleeding
Menometrorrhagia	Irregular, heavy menstrual bleeding

associated with anemia, significant clotting, or other symptoms.

Although commonly used, the term "spotting" is indefinite and associated with most types of abnormal bleeding. It is often most used by providers and women in the context of small amounts of menstrual bleeding associated with regular menstrual interval. The term "dysfunctional uterine bleeding" is reserved for those women with irregular menses who have had a secondary cause of this problem, such as systematic disease, medication use, or organic lesions, excluded by prior diagnostic work-up. The term "menopause" refers to the time after the women's last menstrual flow and the term "perimenopause" refers to changes in menstrual flow and other system changes in the years just prior to this event.

Physiology of Normal Menstruation

Regular and predictable menstrual flow depends on the coordination of many complex and neurochemical and hormonal actions with appropriate end-organ response from the uterus. The functional components of the menstrual cycle are the hypothalamic-pituitary axis, the ovary, and the uterus (Fig. 12.1.2).

Hypothalamic-Pituitary Axis

The hypothalamic-pituitary axis begins in the arcuate nuclei of the hypothalamus, which in response to feedback from gonadotropins and estrogen (and other unknown stimuli) secrete gonadotropin-releasing hormone (GnRH). GnRH has a short half-life, but its effect on the anterior lobe of the pituitary is ensured by rapid transport from the hypothalamus to the pituitary in the portal vein system of the gland. GnRH release is pulsatile, and appropriate pituitary response to GnRH stimulus depends on appropriate quantity and timing of GnRH release.

When GnRH reaches the anterior pituitary, the gonadotropic cells of the pituitary respond and produce the gonadotropins, follicle stimulating hormone (FSH), and luteinizing hormone (LH). FSH and LH are released into the general circulation and stimulate the ovary. Ovarian response may vary, depending on the quantity and quality of FSH and LH receptors within that target organ (4).

FSH stimulates the stratum granulosum cells of the ovary that produce estradiol and stimulate follicular growth. The follicle's production of estrogen and progesterone in the system provides feedback and (with other factors) stimulates changes in the production of FSH and LH from the anterior pituitary gland. When serum estrogen levels remain at or greater than 200 picograms/mL in the serum for over 24 hours, a significant increase in FSH and LH occurs called the FSH/LH surge (5).

This induces production of protein kinases that cause inflammation and rupture of the ovarian follicle. Follicle rupture is followed by remodeling of the follicular cells that form the columnar cells of the corpus luteum. The corpus luteum regresses after 10 to 12 days, forming the corpus albicans, and hormonal levels of estrogen and progesterone drop.

The normal uterus responds to the presence of estrogen and progesterone in a predictable way. The active layer of the uterus called the endometrial layer is composed of the stratum compactum, stratum spongiosum, and the stratum basalis. In the follicular phase of

Hypothalamic – Pituitary – Ovarian Axis
Hormone and Anatomic Relationships During a Menstrual Cycle

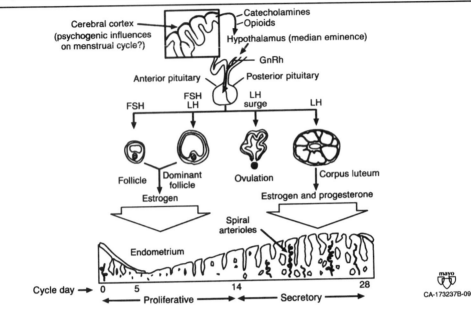

Figure 12.1.2. Hypothalamic-pituitary-ovarian axis. Hormone and anatomic relationships during the menstrual cycle.

the menstrual cycle, estrogen stimulates endometrial tissue proliferation in the stratum compactum with regeneration of endometrial glands and blood vessels. In the secretory phase of the menstrual cycle, progesterone stimulates endometrial glands that increase in volume and begin to secrete mucus. Blood vessels grow out from the stratum basalis and become coiled and increase in volume.

In the absence of pregnancy, decreasing levels of estrogen and progesterone occurring at the end of the cycle lead to significant changes in the endometrium. As estrogen and progesterone levels drop, prostaglandin effects emerge in the endometrium, causing ischemia and myometrial hyperactivity. Spiral arterioles constrict, and endometrial tissue becomes necrotic. Fragmentation of this tissue is then followed by a slough of the endometrial layer.

The prostaglandin milieu influences the volume of menstrual flow. Prostaglandins G_2

and H_2 cause production of thromboxane A_2 with resulting vasoconstriction and platelet aggregation. Prostaglandin I_2 is also formed and functions as a potent vasodilator. A balance between these prostaglandins is required for appropriate control of menstrual flow (6).

Although the description of menstruation sounds quite destructive, cells in the stratum basalis layer expel secretory products, debris is cleaned up, and through orderly regression a framework is maintained for the next cycle.

Pathophysiology of Abnormal Vaginal Bleeding

Introduction

It is remarkable, considering the complexity of the endocrine and target organ systems associated with menstruation, that menstrual flow ever occurs normally. However, abnormal bleeding has many discrete causes, and a thorough understanding of the pathophysiology of abnormal vaginal bleeding is necessary for appropriate diagnosis and management. There is a significant association between abnormal vaginal bleeding and systemic disease, changes in body metabolism (e.g., exercise, stress, diet), side effects of medication, and organic lesions. In addition, in the absence of these above factors, dysfunction anywhere along the axis can be associated with anovulation and abnormal vaginal bleeding (Table 12.1.2).

Abnormal Vaginal Bleeding in Systemic Disease

It is not surprising that abnormal vaginal bleeding is associated with several systemic diseases. Many diseases that affect overall constitution and metabolic rate will cause abnormal vaginal bleeding, but a small subgroup of diseases seem to be particularly associated with this problem.

Table 12.1.2. Causes of Irregular Menstrual Bleeding

Systemic diseases
  Thyroid disease
  Chronic liver disease
  Chronic renal disease
  Diabetes
  Cushing's disease
  Autoimmune diseases
Stress, exercise, and nutrition
  High-stress situations
  Excessive exercise
  Overweight
  Anorexia
Organic gynecologic pathology
  Leiomyomas
  Endometrial cancer
  Endometrial hyperplasia
  Cancer of cervix
Medications
Dysfunctional uterine bleeding

Thyroid Disease

Excessive menstruation is a complaint of 40% of women with myxedema and subclinical hypothyroidism present in up to 20% of women screened for thyroid function who had presented with abnormal vaginal bleeding (7). Hyperthyroidism is associated with increased peripheral conversion of androgen to estradiol and an increase in prolactin level. In addition, hyperthyroid women have a constant elevation of LH with decreased androgen clearing that can be associated with anovulation (8).

Chronic Liver and Renal Disease

Women with cirrhosis because of chronic alcoholism have high rates of amenorrhea and infertility. Valimaki et al. found decreased estradiol levels, progesterone levels, and testosterone levels in nine cirrhotic women when compared to a control population. Estrone levels were increased because of decreased hepatic clearance and/or increased peripheral conversion of fatty tissue (9).

Women with renal insufficiency are commonly noted to have absent or irregular menstruation. The menstrual abnormality emerges with serum creatinine levels greater than 5 and persists in over 90% of women, even after dialysis (10). After renal transplant, menstrual irregularities may improve.

Diabetes

Prior to the introduction of insulin, infertility rates in diabetic women approached 90%. In spite of better control with insulin, some form of menstrual dysfunction is still present in 30% of women with insulin-dependent diabetes and secondary amenorrhea or oligomenorrhea rates are double that of a control population (11).

The diabetic population does not have any evidence of impaired production of progesterone or estradiol from the ovary, yet significant rates of anovulation occur within the population. The pulse frequency of GnRH release is abnormal in diabetics (11). In addition, changes in neurotransmitter levels in the dopaminergic system are documented in diabetics and may be associated with this abnormality (12).

Cushing's Disease

The production of corticoids in women with Cushing's syndrome results in classic symptoms of central obesity, striae, hirsutism, and amenorrhea or abnormal menstruation. The presence of abnormal menstruation or amenorrhea may precede other somatic manifestations of the disease. Women with Cushing's disease have appropriate increases of FSH levels in response to GnRH stimulation, but LH levels do not increase to the physiologic level needed for ovulation to occur. Thus, normal ovulation is inhibited (13).

Autoimmune Disease

Autoimmune diseases, such as systemic lupus, rheumatoid arthritis, and thrombocytopenia purpura, are commonly linked with premature menopause and disruption of menstruation. Thirty-nine percent of women in one study who had premature menopause in the absence of other major systemic disease or chromosomal abnormalities were found to have an autoimmune disorder (14). Antibodies in the woman's system may react with the ovarian parenchyma or FSH and LH receptors.

Stress, Exercise, and Nutrition and Their Association with Abnormal Vaginal Bleeding

The body's response to any increase in metabolic demand or a decrease in nutrition should naturally be one of conservation. There is a decrease or absence of menstrual flow associated with increased demands imposed on the body by significant stress or exercise or decreased supply of energy substrate because of diet or starvation. However, studies attempting to expose the hormonal or neurochemical changes that lead to amenorrhea in these conditions have been frustrating and contradictory.

In a study of 150 first-year women medical students, stress scales showed a predictable and significant increase. There was no evidence to support that at a given level of perceived stress menstrual dysfunction occurred (15). However, many providers can relate numerous examples in which a significant stressor or emotional trauma was followed by cessation of menstrual flow.

Exercise has been noted to have an effect on menstruation. When runners with amenorrhea are compared to control runners with normal menstruation, Chin et al. found that norepinephrine levels showed a significantly higher rise from baseline in those subjects with menstrual disorder. The significant change in norepinephrine levels may interfere with GnRH pulse cycling (16).

Exercise is also significantly associated with production of endorphins (the runner's "high"), and these have been found to exert a tonic inhibition on GnRH release (17). In an investigation of the association between menstrual cycle irregularity and exercise, Bonen found that changes in menstrual cycle could not be accounted for purely by training time and effort. In addition, although body composition was obviously changed by exercise, there was no way to reliably provoke secondary amenorrhea by exercise effort or exercise-related change in body composition (18).

The association between anorexia, starvation, and amenorrhea has been well documented (19). Significant weight loss is associated with decreased gonadotropin production, and follicular development is slowed.

Similarly, morbid obesity can cause metorrhagia. Estrogen can be deposited in fat and irregularly released, causing irregular cycles and heavy bleeding.

Abnormal Vaginal Bleeding and Organic Pathology

Introduction

Tumors and inflammatory lesions of the uterus, cervix, or vagina can present initially as abnormal vaginal bleeding.

Leiomyomas are found in 20% of women over age 35 years, and 30% of these women have abnormal vaginal bleeding (20). Submucous leiomyomas are most often associated with the abnormal bleeding, given their location just underneath the endometrial layer. In this position, they can disrupt vascular supply to the endometrium, and bleeding results because of necrosis and ischemia. Tumors in the myometrium (intramural leiomyomas) may distort the uterus and cause pain, but are less commonly associated with abnormal bleeding (21).

Endometrial hyperplasia and endometrial cancer often present with abnormal vaginal bleeding. Seltzer et al. studied 500 perimenopausal women and found that 91 of the women (19%) had a presentation of menorrhagia or metrorrhagia. Endometrial biopsies from these women yielded 11 with hyperplasia, including two with atypical hyperplasia. Cervical cancer was found in two women, and endometrial and ovarian cancer was found in an additional two women (22).

Endometrial hyperplasia has a peak incidence in perimenopausal women at age 50 years. The uterine endometrial tissue will develop hyperplasia, most often in an environment of unopposed estrogen. Hyperplasia without atypia has not been shown to be a reliable precursor of endometrial carcinoma (23), but there is definitely an association between atypical hyperplasia and endometrial carcinoma. It is assumed that in many circumstances, endometrial carcinoma emerges from the hyperplastic endometrium.

Endometrial cancer has a peak incidence in the postmenopausal age group at approximately age 60 years (see Chapter 12.4). There is a definite association between chronic anovulation and endometrial neoplasms, supporting the etiologic role of unopposed estrogen. The endometrial cancer risk in women with chronic anovulation is three times that of control populations (24). Additional factors that impose a higher risk for the development of endometrial cancer include exposure to exogenous estrogen, obesity, and nulliparity.

Invasive squamous cell carcinoma of the cervix is the most common cervical cancer. The average age for development of carcinoma in situ is 38 years, and the average age of invasive cervical cancer is 48 years. Cervical cancer typically presents as spotting with regular menstrual flow, but if it occurs in the perimenopausal age group, it may be hidden within other menstrual abnormalities.

Vaginal and vulvar cancer are much less common cancers of the genital tract and are generally associated with bloody discharge rather than abnormal menstrual flow.

Drug Use and Abnormal Vaginal Bleeding

The use of licit and illicit drugs can affect normal menstrual function. Heroin and other central nervous system drugs are associated with abnormal menstrual flow. In a study of 81 heroin addicts, 90% had menstrual abnormalities while using the drug, and 48% of the abnormalities persisted after use was curtailed (25). The active ingredient in marijuana (THC) in experimental animals has been shown to inhibit the LH surge with resulting anovulation. It is not clear whether recreational use of this drug, even in heavy amounts, is associated with anovulation in a clinical setting (26).

There are many common medications that can inhibit or cause abnormal vaginal bleeding (Table 12.1.3). The most common medication in use associated with a change in menstruation is the oral contraceptive pill. Spotting occurs in up to 20% of all women in the first 3 months of oral contraceptive use. Menstrual cycle problems after the initial few months are associated with inadequate endometrial support by the predetermined doses of estrogen or progesterone, and with adjustment the abnormal bleeding can usually be resolved.

The use of the progesterone-only contraceptive pill and subdermal progesterone implants is also associated with abnormal menstrual flow. Persistent irregular flow, although not increasing the number of days of bleeding

12.1.3. Medications Associated with Abnormal Vaginal Bleeding

- Phentolamine
- Tricyclic antidepressants
- Corticosteroids
- Major tranquilizers
- Propranolol
- Digoxin
- Cyprohepatine

or the total blood loss, affects 20 to 30% of all users.

Dysfuntional Uterine Bleeding

In the absence of systemic disease, organic lesions, medication side effects, and significant changes in metabolism or nutrition, the diagnosis of dysfunctional uterine bleeding (DUB) is considered. Polycystic ovary disease can cause DUB in young women. Although often described as a triad of amenorrhea, hirsutism, and infertility, abnormal bleeding patterns are found in up to 30% of women rather than complete amenorrhea (27).

Any disruption to the cyclic release of GnRH, FSH, or LH can result in chronic anovulation. Dysfunctional uterine bleeding with anovulation is most common in the perimenopausal woman and is considered to be because of a decreased sensitivity of the ovary to gonadotropin stimulation. The most common presentation of DUB is breakthrough bleeding. In this situation, the ovary responds to FSH stimulation and estrogen is produced. However, the ovary does not fulfill the estrogen production necessary for the FSH/LH surge to occur. The follicle persists making estrogen, but the endometrium support is tenuous and small cyclical changes in estrogen supply are followed by irregular breakdown and slough of endometrium with resulting metrorrhagia.

Estrogen withdrawal bleeding occurs when follicle's production of estradiol in response to FSH stimulation leads to a significant build-up of endometrial tissue over time. Eventually, the estrogen feedback does trigger the LH surge. Ovulation results, and 2 weeks later, heavy sustained menstrual flow occurs.

Not all causes of DUB can be explained by the classic FSH/LH feedback loop. Additional classes of reproductive hormones including inhibin, oocyte maturation inhibitor, follicle regulatory protein, and gonadotropin surge-inhibiting factor have been described. In the future, a better understanding of these factors will undoubtedly improve the understanding of dysfunctional uterine bleeding.

Diagnosis and Management

Introduction

Because 14% of all women with DUB are later found to have other pathology, careful diagnosis of women with abnormal bleeding is important (28). The diagnosis of abnormal bleeding is complicated by the fact that it is often subjective in nature, and the woman may have no discrete somatic or laboratory evidence of the abnormality. A careful history and physical exam begins the diagnostic work-up.

Appropriate Historical Information

The provider should gather menstrual information first (Table 12.1.4), including an attempt to quantify menorrhagia. Menstrual pad counts are used as an approximation, but this method correlates poorly with actual measurements (29). A better understanding of most women's situations, is gained by inquiring about changes in flow from their expectation of normal and associated symptoms, such as clotting of menstrual flow or significant cramping and pain.

A medication history should be sought on

12.1.4. Historical Information for Abnormal Vaginal Bleeding

	Range of Normal
Menarche	Age 8–16 years
Frequency	21–35 day interval
Duration	2–8 days
Menstrual flow	Less than 80 mL (ask about change)
Other bleeding	Midcycle spotting only
Menopause	Age 35-55 years
Last menstrual period	

all women, and personal changes in diet, exercise, and significant life stressors should be noted.

Physical Exam

The physical examination should evaluate changes in overall physical condition, seek evidence of systemic disease, and specifically investigate for the presence of organic pathology in the genitourinary tract.

The woman's general nutritional status, skin turgor, and muscle tone should be noticed. Her skin should also be specifically inspected for unusual striae or petechiae. Systemic sequelae of thyroid disease should be sought, and the woman should be inspected for evidence of hirsutism or virilization. A careful pelvic examination with visual inspection of the cervix, vaginal wall, and introitus is mandatory, and bimanual evaluation of uterine size and ovarian size should be performed. The woman's breasts should be inspected for evidence of galactorrhea.

Laboratory Testing

The use of the laboratory in the evaluation of abnormal vaginal bleeding is directed by the history and physical, but generally includes both routine and endocrine tests (Table 12.1.5).

A complete blood count and reticulocyte count is helpful to evaluate for blood abnormalities and indirectly assess iron status. Because of the association between abnormal menstrual flow and subclinical hypothyroidism, determination of TSH and T4 levels are helpful. A pregnancy test should be obtained on any woman if indicated. A pap smear should always be performed in the presence of abnormal vaginal bleeding.

Other testing is not considered standard in all cases, although it can be helpful. Serum FSH and LH levels can be obtained. An LH to FSH ratio greater than 2:1 supports the diagnosis of either chronic anovulation or polycystic ovary disease, but some women with these problems may have normal values. An FSH greater than 40 μg is indicative of ovarian failure. Serum prolactin should be obtained in women with galactorrhea or secondary amenorrhea in the absence of other obvious causes. Women with hirsutism or virilism should have dehydroepiandrosterone and testosterone levels drawn to look for androgenic abnormalities. In those women with history or physical findings suggestive of systemic disease, appropriate screening tests are reasonable but extensive undirected testing is rarely fruitful.

12.1.5. Laboratory Evaluation for Dysfunctional Uterine Bleeding

Routine Laboratory Testing
- CBS
- TSH
- Pregnancy test
- Pap smear

Additional Laboratory Tests with Specific Indications
- FSH/LH
- Prolactin level
- Testosterone level
- Dehydroepiandrosterone (DHEA) level
- Liver and kidney function testing
- Cortisol level

Imaging Tests

Indirect imaging and direct inspection of the endometrium has added to the diagnostic precision and management of abnormal menstruation. Transvaginal ultrasound has been used in the investigation of postmenopausal abnormal vaginal bleeding. Postmenopausal bleeding may be associated with atrophic change of the endometrium, polyps, or pathology such as hyperplasia or carcinoma. Transvaginal ultrasound can accurately measure endometrial tissue thickness. Women with atrophic, and thus benign endometrium, have thin layers of tissue, whereas those with hyperplasia and/or carcinoma have greater thicknesses. Assessment of endometrial tissue by transvaginal ultrasound has sensitivity of between 80 to 97% in differentiating hyperplasia and carcinoma from benign conditions (30, 31). However, another study showed a negative predictive value of only 94%, leading to the suggestion that histologic examination of the endometrium remains the "gold standard" at the present time (32).

Hysteroscopy has been used to directly visualize the endometrium. Advances in equipment and technique have allowed this procedure to be done as an outpatient. Diagnostic hysteroscopy is generally well tolerated in the office setting without general anesthesia. When the diagnosis of abnormal vaginal bleeding is not otherwise defined (particularly in the postmenopausal woman), hysteroscopy can allow directed biopsy and compares favorably to dilatation and curettage. In a study of 110 women over 40 referred for postmenopausal bleeding, hysteroscopy confirmed a benign etiology for 95% of the women, thus directing a more conservative management strategy (33).

Other Diagnostic Tests

The evolution of magnetic resonance imaging and sophisticated ultrasound techniques have led to other diagnostic tests that hold promise for the future. Uterine artery flow velocity measurement and MRI are presently in experimental use for the evaluation of abnormal vaginal bleeding (34).

Invasive Procedures

Advances in noninvasive imaging and laboratory evaluation have decreased, but by no means eliminated, the role of invasive diagnostic testing. However, the evaluation of the uterus has evolved beyond the standard use of early dilatation and curettage for diagnosis.

Endometrial biopsy is a standard outpatient procedure. Although traditionally considered to be of use in histologic confirmation of ovulation through its ability to allow distinction between proliferative and secretory tissue, some studies have shown that women with classic history of anovulation do not always have pathologic results from endometrial biopsy that support this diagnosis (35). However, the use of endometrial biopsy with an outpatient sampling instrument can effectively rule out hyperplasia and endometrial carcinoma. Prospective studies of endometrial biopsy results have showed reliable differentiation of endometrial carcinoma from benign disease (36–38). The procedure is generally well tolerated and has a small rate of complication (39).

The procedure can be done with premedication using a nonsteroidal anti-inflammatory drug and, in the absence of obvious contraindication such as cervical stricture, pregnancy, and sepsis, can provide an adequate sample.

Dilatation and curettage (D&C) presently requires anesthesia and burdens the woman with significant expense and discomfort. These facts should make the provider's use of the D&C for purely diagnostic reasons a secondary option.

Treatment

Proper differential diagnosis provided by history, physical exam, and appropriate diagnostic tests directs management of the woman with abnormal bleeding and increases the rates of satisfactory outcome (Table 12.1.6).

Table 12.1.6. Treatment of Anovulatory Bleeding

	Medical options	Surgical options
Acute bleeding		
Severe, unstable (orthostatic hypotension, hematocrit <25)	Hospitalization, transfusion, CE* 25 mg IV q 4 h up to 6 doses	Uterine curettage Radiologic embolization Hysterectomy
Less severe	Oral contraceptives, 1 qid for 3–5 days or tid x 7d, then QD x 1–3 months Progestin: MPA** 10–20 mg/day or norethindrone 0.35–0.70 mg/day for 7 days	
Chronic bleeding	Oral contraceptives, 1/day Progestin: MPA** 10–20 mg/day on days 1–12 of each month Cyclic estrogen and progestin: CE* 0.626–2.5 mg/day on days 1–25, MPA** 5–20 mg/day on days 13–25 NSAIDs during period of bleeding GnRH agonist for refractory cases	Endometrial ablation Hysterectomy

*CE = conjugated estrogens.
**MPA = medroxyprogesterone acetate.

Medication Side Effects

The presence of a medication known to cause abnormal bleeding in a woman should naturally lead the clinician to modify or eliminate the medication. However, this is not always possible. A dialysis patient on anticoagulants can present a significant challenge, because dysfunctional uterine bleeding can present with significant hemorrhage. The use of appropriate low dose contraceptives may be indicated in this woman group with appropriate caution.

Women on central nervous system (CNS) drugs such as antidepressants or tranquilizers who are unable to discontinue these drugs should also be considered for management with oral contraceptives.

Management of Organic Pathology

Organic lesions within the genitourinary tract often require appropriate surgical intervention. However, the automatic use of hysterec-

tomy has been preempted by new techniques. Hysterectomy still has an appreciable mortality of 6 per 100,000 women, and morbidity and loss of productivity are significant.

Hysteroscopically directed endometrial surgery can effectively remove polyps and submucous leiomyomas with good results (40, 41). Ablation of the endometrium by the use of the Yag laser or electroresection is beginning to gain acceptance and has good patient satisfaction rates with reliable results of amenorrhea (42).

Dysfunctional Uterine Bleeding in the Absence of Systemic Disease or Organic Lesions

Therapy of the woman with abnormal bleeding using D&C is still indicated to gain control of emergency hemorrhage not responsive to medical management. It is immediately effective in many instances. However, in many women, the D&C provides only temporary control of bleeding, and women will have recurrent symptoms. The management of the woman with DUB should initially focus on appropriate use of medical therapy. Severe or emergency menorrhagia associated with anovulation may be managed with IV estrogen, oral use of progesterone agents, or a combination of progesterone and estrogen in commonly available oral contraceptive pills. In each instance, the therapy works to support the endometrium and appropriately stimulate change to secretory histology. As the external hormonal support is withdrawn, the woman should be cautioned that heavy flow will likely occur, but that this flow will be self-limited. Careful support and follow-up by the clinician is mandatory during this time.

If the woman presents with metrorrhagia or menometrorrhagia and is not experiencing any significant exacerbation of the problem, several medical options are available.

New low-dose oral contraceptive pills are not contraindicated in nonsmoking women before the usual perimenopausal period, and therefore they can be used to control symptoms of DUB. In addition, they may be protective for the anovulatory woman because they prevent the development of hyperplasia.

Women in the perimenopausal age group may benefit from cyclic use of progesterone. Ten mg of medroxyprogesterone for 10 to 12 days per month promotes normal menstrual flow and protects against endometrial hyperplasia. A 6-month cycle of medroxyprogesterone use can be followed by observation and may be repeated if needed. As the woman moves beyond menopause, the absence of estrogen in the system may cause atrophy with irregular bleeding once again. Once organic lesions are ruled out, it is appropriate to consider adding estrogen to the woman's progesterone regimen.

Management of Idiopathic Menorrhagia

Menorrhagia is an annoying problem for women of all ages and is associated with significant dis-

ability and loss of productivity because of limits on activity imposed by pain and heavy menstrual flow. An active search for organic lesions such as leiomyoma should precede medical therapy, especially in women who develop menorrhagia later in life.

The knowledge that prostaglandins are intimately involved in the regulation of menstrual flow supports the application of prostaglandin inhibiting agents such as nonsteroidal anti-inflammatory drugs (NSAIDs) in the management of this condition. Medications such as Naprosyn (500 mg bid) and mefenamic acid (500 mg bid) decrease flow by 20 to 40% (43, 44). Other NSAIDs are also effective.

Many women with idiopathic menorrhagia respond well to oral contraceptive drugs. For those women who do not wish to become pregnant and do not have contraindications, oral contraceptives are a reasonable first choice for complete management of menorrhagia.

Danazol is a synthetic steroid with androgenic properties that is known to induce endometrial atrophy. In the usual dose of 200 mg per day, menstrual flow is decreased by 60% (45). Women can experience significant side effects of the androgen action of this medication including weight gain, headache, acne, and muscle cramping. Its use is best reserved for specialty management of menorrhagia not responsive to other measures detailed above.

Conclusion

The management of abnormal vaginal bleeding requires all the skills and patience of the clinician and an open and sharing relationship with the woman burdened by this condition. Recent advances in the understanding of the disorder and advances in medical and surgical approach to its management promise a future with more satisfactory outcomes for the woman and provider.

Special Considerations for Nurse Practitioners and Physician Assistants

Because there is no male analogy to the process of menstruation, this female process came to be viewed in pathological terms in the late 19th and early 20th centuries. The negativity associated with the normal process of menstruation continues to the present. Providers who are explaining normal menstrual bleeding to women use terms that have a negative connotation, terms such as "sloughing," "wasting," "failed" production, "deprived" endometrium, "diminished" supply of oxygen, "shedding," "debris," and "necrosis." Seeing menstruation as failed production contributes to the negative view. Even though in men only one of every billion sperm fertilizes an egg, this male process is never pictured as a failure or waste. Providers should tell women that the purpose of the menstrual cycle is to produce menstrual flow, so that the process and product can be perceived as desirable unless a pregnancy is wanted (46).

Bleeding, whether normal menstrual flow or menorrhagia, must be assessed within the context of the woman's culture. Providers should ascertain what too little or too much bleeding means to the woman. Failure to menstruate may be seen as a sign of disease, whereas the loss of blood can be viewed as life-threatening (46, 47). Women will also use terms specific to their culture to describe bleeding. For example, in South Central Appalachia, some women described menstruation as the "curse," "falling off the roof," "granny cramps," the "plague," and "period"; heavy bleeding is often referred to as "flooding" (48). Women in the past and some seen in current practice feel dominated by their menstrual cycle. Menstruating women may still be viewed and perceive themselves as weak, suffering, unstable, and not able to carry out normal duties, and in some cultures even today they may not be touched by men while menstruating (49).

Menstruation is not always discussed openly, and some women may use words such as "period" or "time of month" to refer to the process. Providers should acknowledge that some women are uncomfortable talking about either cyclical or irregular bleeding. To help a woman define what is normal for her, she should be encouraged to keep a menstrual cycle chart, noting related factors during cycles such as dysmenorrhea or the use of medications. When the client brings charts with her on return visits, they can be used for teaching tools, e.g., to explain how the days of the cycle are numbered and when ovulation usually occurs. Thorough teaching in other areas may alleviate women's concerns about bleeding. If women know that irregular bleeding is common, especially during the first cycles of hormonal contraceptives, then their worries about bleeding can be lessened.

Quantifying flow is often difficult for the provider and the woman. In addition to asking about the number of pads used and their saturation, providers should ask about change in her personal pattern of protection and in daily activities because of heavy flow. To assess for ovulation during the history, providers can ascertain if the woman experiences Mittelschmerz, PMS symptoms, or dysmenorrhea, all indicators that ovulation is occurring. Noting associated symptoms such as (a) clotting, (b) foul odor, (c) vaginal discharge, (d) fever or chills, (e) gastrointestinal or urinary symptoms, and (f) type, location, and duration of pain can assist in diagnosis. It is important to inquire if the woman ever had bleeding problems before and to obtain a record of previous examinations and treatment (47).

When women present with complaints of postcoital bleeding, irregular spotting, or oral contraceptive breakthrough bleeding, the history related to STD risk is especially important. Other risk factors for reproductive tract infection include IUD use, recent vaginal birth or abortion, cervical or endometrial biopsy or other instrumentation of the uterus, and distant infections such as tuberculosis (50).

Examination of the bleeding woman can be difficult, but the exact source of bleeding must be identified. The woman can be given materials to cleanse her genitalia and perineal areas so that any bleeding from those sites can be observed. By locating and swabbing the cervix free of blood, the examiner can observe if bleeding recurs from the os. A sponge forceps and gauze may be needed to remove blood from the vagina so that the vaginal walls and cervix can be examined (51).

Consultation with a physician should be available for cases of abnormal bleeding, especially if there is a mass, abnormal Pap test, or high risk of cancer. Patients with acute, heavy bleeding should be managed by a physician. Consultation/referral to a specialist is indicated for women who have identified endocrine or systemic pathologies, coagulation disorders, or other underlying conditions (52).

References

1. Schneider LG. Causes of abnormal vaginal bleeding in a family practice center. J Fam Pract 1983;16:281–283.
2. Coulter A, Bradlow J, Agass M, Martin-Bates C, Tulloch A. Outcomes of referrals to gynecology outwoman clinics for menstrual problems: an audit of general practice records. Br J Obstet Gynaecol 1991;98:789–796.
3. Chiazze L, Brayer FT, Macisco J, Parker M, Duffy B. The length and variability of the menstrual cycle. JAMA 1968;203:89–92.
4. Espey L, Ben Halim I. Characteristics of control of the normal menstual cycle. Obstet Gynecol Clin North Am 1990;17:275–297.
5. Fritz M, Speroff L. Current concepts of the endocrine characteristics of normal menstrual function: the key to diagnosis and management of menstrual disorders. Clin Obstet Gynecol 1983;26:647–689.
6. Long C, Gast M. Menorrhagia. Obstet Gynecol Clin North Am 1990;17:343–359.
7. Wilansky D, Greisman B. Early hypothyroidism in patients with menorrhagia. Am J Obstet Gynecol 1989;160:673–677.
8. Southern AL, Olive J, Gorden JJ. The conversion of androgens to estrogen in hyperthyroidism. J Clin Endocrinol Metab 1974;38:207–214.
9. Valimaki M, Pelkanen R, Salasbora M. Sex hormones in amenorrheic women with alcoholic liver disease. J Clin Endocrinol Metabol 1984;59:133–143.
10. Steinkampf M. Systemic illness in menstrual dysfunction. Obstet Gynecol Clin North Am 1992;17:311–319.
11. Griffin M, South S, Yankov V, Booth R, Asplin C, Velhuis J, Evans W. Insulin-dependent diabetes mellitus and menstrual dysfunction. Ann Intern Med 1994;26:331–340.
12. Djursing H, Carstensen L, Hagen C, Nyboe-Anderson A. Possible altered dopaminergic modulation of pituitary function in normal menstruating women with insulin-dependent diabetes mellitus. Acta Endocrinol Metabol 1984;107:450–455.
13. Boccuzzi G, Angeli A, Bisborie D. The effect of synthetic LH-releasing hormone on release of gonadotropin in Cushing's disease. J Clin Endocrinol Metabol 1975;40:892–895.
14. Alper M, Gurner P. Premature ovarian failure: its relationship to auto-immune disease. Obstet Gynecol 1985;66:27–30.
15. Clarvit S. Stress and menstrual dysfunction in medical students. Psychosomatics 1988;29:404–409.
16. Chin N, Chang F, Dodds W, Kim M, Malarkey W. The acute effects of exercise on plasma catecholamines in sedentary and athletic women with normal and abnormal menses. Am J Obstet Gynecol 1987;157:938–944.
17. DeCree C. Endogenous opioid peptides in the control of the normal menstrual cycle and their possible role in athletic menstrual irregularities. Obstet Gynecol Surv 1989;44:720–732.
18. Bonen A. Exercise-induced menstrual cycle changes: a functional, temporary adaptation to metabolic stress. Sports Med 1994;17:373–392.
19. Knuth U, Hull M, Jacobs H. Amenorrhea and the loss of weight. Br J Obstet Gynaecol 1977;84:801–807.
20. Awwad J, Toth T, Schiff I. Abnormal uterine bleeding in the perimenopause. Int J Fertil 1993;38:261–269.
21. Jutras M, Cowan B. Abnormal bleeding in the climacteric. Obstet Gynecol Clin North Am 1990;17:409–425.
22. Seltzer V, Benjamin F, Deutsch S. Perimenopausal bleeding patterns and pathology findings. JAMWA 1990;45:132–134.
23. Ferency A, Gelfand M, Tzepus F. The cytodynamics of endometrial hyperplasia in carcinoma: a review. Ann Pathol 1983;3:189–202.

24. Coulam C, Annegers J, Kranz J. Chronic anovulation syndrome and associated neoplasia. Obstet Gynecol 1983;61:403–407.
25. Stoffer S. A gynecologic study of drug addicts. Am J Obstet Gynecol 1968;101:779–783.
26. Neinstein L. Menstrual dysfunction in pathophysiologic states. West J Med 1985;143:476–484.
27. Smith S. Dysfunctional uterine bleeding. Br J Hosp Med 1985;34:351–354.
28. Hodgen C. Neuroendocrinology of the normal menstrual cycle. J Reprod Med 1989;34:68–75.
29. Fraser I, McCarron G, Markham R. A preliminary study of factors influencing perception of menstrual blood loss. Am J Obstet Gynecol 1984;149:788–793.
30. Cacciatorre B, Ramsay T, Lehtovirta P, Ylostalo P. Transvaginal sonography and hysteroscopy in postmenopausal bleeding. Acta Obstet Gynecol Scand 1994;73:413–416.
31. Karlsson B, Granberg S, Wikland M, Ryd W, Norstrom A. Endovaginal scanning of the endometrium compared to cytology and histology in women with postmenopausal bleeding. Gynecol Oncol 1993;50:173–178.
32. Dorum A, Kristensen B, Langebrekke A, Sorens T, Skaar O. Evaluation of endometrial thickness measured by endovaginal ultrasound in women with postmenopausal bleeding. Acta Obstet Gynecol Scand 1993;72:116–119.
33. Townsend D, Fields G, McCauslend A, Kauffman K. Diagnostic and operative hysteroscopy in the management of persistent postmenopausal bleeding. Obstet Gynecol 1993;82:419–421.
34. Weiner Z, Beck D, Rottem S, Brandes J, Thaler I. Uterine artery flow velocity wave forms and color flow imaging in women with perimenopausal and postmenopausal bleeding. Acta Obstet Gynecol Scand 1993;62:162–166.
35. Nedoss B. Dysfunctional uterine bleeding: the relationship of endometrial histology. Am J Obstet Gynecol 1971;109:103–106.
36. Einerth Y. Vacuum curettage by the vabra method: a simple procedure for endometrial diagnosis. Acta Obstet Gynecol Scand 1982;61:373–376.
37. Batool T, Reginald P, Hughes J. Outpatient pipelle endometrial biopsy in the investigation of postmenopausal bleeding. Br J Obstet Gynaecol 1994;101:545–546.
38. Mackenzie I. Routine outpatient diagnostic uterine curettage using a flexible plastic aspiration curette. Br J Obstet Gynaecol 1985;91:1291–1296.
39. Rosenthal T, Perropato T, Doemlant M, et al. Endometrial sampling: an analysis of 310 procedures performed by family physicians. J Fam Pract 1989;29:249–251.
40. Townsend DE, Fields G, McCausland A, Kaufman K. Diagnostic and operative hysteroscopy in the management of persistant postmenopausal bleeding. Obstet Gynecol 1993;82:419–421.
41. Brooks P, Clouse J, Stockwell-Morris L. Hysterectomy vs. resectoscopic endometrial ablation for the control of abnormal uterine bleeding. J Reprod Med 1994;39:755–759.
42. Erin J. Endometrial ablation in the treatment of menorrhagia. Br J Obstet Gynecol 1994;101: 19–22.
43. VanEijkeren M, Godelieve C, Christians C, Geuze H, Haspels A, Sixma J. The effects of mefenamic acid on menstrual hemostasis and essential menorrhagia. Am J Obstet Gynecol 1992;166:1419–1428.
44. Ylikorkala O, Pekonan F. Naproxen reduces idiopathic but not fibromyoma-induced menorrhagia. Obstet Gynecol 1986;68:10–12.
45. Higham J, Shaw R. A comparative study of danazol, a regimen of decreasing doses of danazol and norethindrone in the treatment of objectively proven unexplained menorrhagia. Am J Obstet Gynecol 1993;169:1134–1139.
46. Martin E. Metaphors of bleeding in women. NAACOG's Clin Issues Perinatal Women's Health Nurs 1991;2:283–288.
47. Fogel CI. Common symptoms: bleeding, pain, and discharge. In: Fogel CI, Woods NF, eds. Women's health care. Thousand Oaks, CA: Sage, 1995:517–570.
48. Cavender A, ed. A Folk Medical Lexicon of South Central Appalachia, Johnson City, TN: History of Medicine Society of Appalachia, 1992.
49. Baker S. Menstruation and related problems and concerns. In: Youngkin EQ, Davis MD, eds. Women's Health. Norwalk, CT: Appleton & Lange, 1994:77–100.
50. French JI. Abnormal bleeding associated with reproductive tract infection. NAACOG's Clin Issues Perinatal Women's Health Nurs 1991;2:313–321.
51. Murata JM. Abnormal genital bleeding and secondary amenorrhea. JOGNN 1993;19:26–36.
52. Star WL. Abnormal uterine bleeding. In: Star WL, Lomomell LL, Shannon MT, eds. Women's Primary Health Care. Washington, DC: American Nurses' Association, 1995:12-3–12-12.

Suggested Readings

Fritz Ma, Speroff L. Current concepts of the endocrine characteristics of normal menstrual function: the key to diagnosis and management of menstrual disorders. Clin Obstet Gynecol 1983;6:647–689.
Leon S, Israel MD. Diagnosis and treatment of menstrual disorders and sterility. Br J Obstet Gynaecol 1994;101.

12.2

Ovulatory Disturbances and Amenorrhea: A Physiologic Approach to Diagnosis and Therapy

Jerilynn C. Prior

Introduction

Women have been experiencing menstrual cycles, ovulating, and producing offspring since the origins of *homo sapiens* as a species. Although anatomic drawings date to prehistory and some are in printed documents from the 1500s, it is only in the last 100 years that the complex, integrated physiology of the female reproductive system has begun to be understood (1, 2).

The purpose of this chapter is to describe

the variations within the normal menstrual cycle and their causes, creating a woman-centered understanding of the physiology of the menstrual cycle and reproduction. In one study, almost half of the women who experienced menstrual disturbances, from amenorrhea to ovulation problems, had spontaneous recovery of their problems (3); this suggests that many changes within menstrual cycles or in cycle interval are caused not by diseases but by imbalance of hypothalamic origin. Therefore this review will focus on the etiologies for and prevention of menstrual cycle changes.

Definitions

Secondary Amenorrhea

Amenorrhea is defined as no vaginal bleeding for 6 or more months ($>$ 180 days) in a woman who has had previous menstrual cycles. It may be physiological such as after pregnancy, during lactation, or on oral contraceptives. It may caused by ovarian failure or by endocrine causes such as pituitary diseases (i.e., prolactin-producing benign tumors). Many times it is caused by a minor adaptive disturbances in the hypothalamic stimulation of the reproductive system. This occurs in response to weight loss, illness, emotional stress, or excessive exercise in association with weight loss or stress.

Oligomenorrhea

Oligomenorrhea is vaginal bleeding that occurs at intervals of 37 to 180 days (i.e., intervals between the normal menstrual cycle and amenorrhea). It is also usually caused by hypothalamic imbalance.

Normality

A normal menstrual cycle has (*a*) a normal cycle interval between the start of flow until the day before the next flow (21 to 36 days), (*b*)

normal flow, and (*c*) normal ovulatory characteristics such as luteal phase length. Menstrual flow normally lasts 3 to 6 days and blood loss ranges from 10 to 40 mL (less than 80 mL). The usual soaked pad or tampon holds 5 mL (1 teaspoon) of blood, so there should be no more than 16 soaked pads or tampons per cycle.

Luteal phase length (the time from egg release until the start of the next flow) should be 10 to 17 days. Ovulation means the release of an egg and conversion of the dominant ovarian follicle to a corpus luteum with subsequent production of luteal phase progesterone levels.

A menstrual cycle can be documented as ovulatory by several direct and indirect methods (Table 12.2.1): a midcycle serum or urinary LH peak 12 or more days before the onset of flow followed by evidence of normal progesterone secretion (serum progesterone level over 16 pmol/L, and usually over 45 pmol/L at the midluteal phase), serial ovarian ultrasounds showing appropriate progression of a dominant follicle and its disappearance, or by a statistically significant basal temperature plateau of 3 or more days.

Luteal Phase Disturbance

Luteal phase disturbances encompass a variety of patterns of decreased corpus luteum proges-

Table 12.2.1. Methods for Documenting a Menstrual Cycle as Ovulatory

Midcycle serum or urinary LH levels 12 days before menses with normal serum progesterone ($>$ 16 pmol/L or over 45 pmol/L at midluteal phases)

Serial ovarian ultrasounds showing progression of dominant follicle and its disappearance

Statistically significant basal temperature plateau of 3 days or more

Endometrial biopsy with appropriate secretory maturation

terone secretion. These include short luteal phase cycles, in which a significant temperature plateau occurs but is less than 10 days in length, or those cycles in which the time from the midcycle LH peak to the onset of flow is less than 12 days, although the ovulatory progesterone threshold (16 pmol/L) was achieved.

Luteal phase insufficiency is another kind of luteal disturbance in which ovulation is diagnosed, but the progesterone levels are lower than normal despite a significant temperature plateau of normal length. Luteal phase disturbances can occur in menstrual cycles of any interval and commonly occur in cycles of normal length. These disturbances may also be diagnosed by an endometrial biopsy that shows poorly developed secretory changes for the number of days it is obtained before flow starts.

Anovulation

Anovulation means no egg was formed or released and there is no corpus luteum production of progesterone. This may be associated with normal, low, or high rates of estrogen production, with or without a midcycle estrogen peak. Anovulation can occur in cycles of any interval. Anovulation can occur in association with low, normal, or high levels of androgen production.

Androgen Excess

Androgen excess means that male hormone levels (e.g., testosterone, androstenedione, dehydroepiandrosterone sulfate) are produced in abnormally high levels by either the ovaries or adrenal glands. The most common cause is anovulation with increased pituitary stimulation of the ovary (high LH levels), usually developing at puberty, postpartum, and when discontinuing OCPs or after hypothalamic amenorrhea. The clinical signs are acne, oily skin, and increased hair in a male pattern or alopecia (male pattern baldness). The most extreme (and rare) androgen excess is called virilization in which the woman develops a male body shape, clitoromegaly, and breast atrophy.

Ovarian Cysts

Ovarian cysts arise when the developing follicle produces a quantity of fluid that would normally be dispersed into the peritoneum following ovulation. However, if follicle maturation is arrested before ovulation, the cyst will continue to be present for several weeks. Ovarian cysts may be an anatomic consequence of anovulation. The polycystic ovary commonly occurs before menarche, during puberty, during pregnancy, or during use of the oral contraceptive pill. If anovulatory androgen excess occurs, the ovary may be enlarged with a thickened outer layer (theca) besides having several or many cysts.

Climacteric Definitions

Perimenopause is the 2- to 6-year transition from the reproductive portion of the life cycle to menopause. It is a clinical diagnosis based on observed changes in menstrual flow and interval with or without the onset of vasomotor symptoms in a woman who is over 36 years of age.

Menopause is the completion of ovarian function diagnosed by 1 year of absent flow in a woman over 40 years of age. Premature menopause is abnormal and is defined as a 1-year absence of flow and a high FSH in a woman age less than 40 years old. In a woman who has had a hysterectomy, it is difficult to distinguish between perimenopause and menopause because both may have symptoms and show elevated FSH levels. However, a menopausal woman will no longer perceive cyclic or intermittent breast tenderness.

Vasomotor symptoms are episodic feelings of heat with or without perspiration, sometimes preceded by sensations of anxiety, palpitations or nausea, that usually resolve within 5 or 10 minutes and may occur during the day (hot flushes or flashes) or during sleep (night sweats).

Health Consequences of Ovulation Disturbances and Amenorrhea

Even if pregnancy is not wanted, amenorrhea and ovulation disturbances cause important health risks (Table 12.2.2). The most important prospectively documented health risk of hypothalamic amenorrhea is rapid bone loss and increased risk for osteoporosis (4). Vaginal dryness and uncomfortable intercourse, or even decreased size of the vagina, are associated with chronically low estrogen and progesterone levels.

When ovulation is disturbed, therefore, progesterone levels are abnormally low and not cyclic, but estrogen production is high or normal; the health consequences are much more widespread. Ovulation disturbances are associated with irregular and heavy uterine bleeding (5), anemia caused by excess menstrual blood loss, and sometimes disturbing premenstrual symptoms (6).

If anovulation is chronic, there is a high

Table 12.2.2. The Health Consequences of Disturbed Menstrual Cycles

Amenorrhea and oligomenorrhea
  Osteoporosis
  Infertility
  Accelerated bone loss
  Urogenital atrophy with dyspareunia
Ovulation disturbances
  Osteoporosis
  Subfertility
  Irregular, unpredictable flow, spotting
  Dysfunctional uterine bleeding
  Endometrial hyperplasia and cancer
  Anemia caused by excess uterine blood loss
  Distressing premenstrual symptoms (PMS)
  Acne, hirsutism, oily skin, androgenic alopecia
  Polycystic ovarian changes
  Mastalgia and fibrocystic breast disease
  Increased risk for breast cancer
  Accelerated bone loss

risk for endometrial hyperplasia (5) and endometrial cancer (7), and an increased risk of breast cancer (7, 8). In chronic anovulation, breast symptoms are increased, mastalgia sometimes develops, and breasts tend to be fibrocystic (9). Acne and hirsutism, often with accompanying polycystic ovarian changes, are also strongly and causally related to nonovulation (10). Finally, normal women with regular cycles who have one nonovulatory and several short luteal phase cycles during the year lose trabecular spinal bone at a rate of 4% per year (11). Epidemiologic data in a population-based large study confirmed this observation (12).

Therefore, knowing that health risks are associated with disturbances of the menstrual cycle, especially with absent or abnormal ovulation, providers need to understand how they develop and how to diagnose them.

Ovulatory Disturbances

Ovulatory disturbances may occur in cycles with perfectly normal intervals and flow and without any signs or symptoms of androgen excess, and yet may have important health implications. Except for congenital diseases, most changes in menstrual cycles during the reproductive years are caused by adaptations or maladaptions related to the life cycle, changes in weight, medications, psychosocial stresses, excessive exercise, and/or illness (13).

No matter what the cause, ovulation disturbances are subtle. Figure 12.2.1 shows, in a bar diagram form, the major types of cycles that may occur. The top three cycles are identical in length (28 days), vary little in the standard deviation of length ($\pm$ 3 to 6 days), but have major difference in their progesterone productions (from absent to normal). Therefore, progesterone production differences and most ovulation disturbances are subclinical and not easy to differentiate from normal.

Ovulation disturbances probably occur in over one third of all cycles in women who have regular cycles (11, 14, 15). Evidence that ovu-

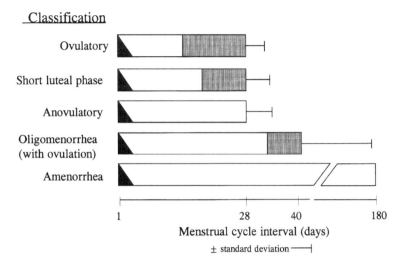

Figure 12.2.1. This bar graph shows in a stylized fashion that cycles of a mean 28 days in length may vary significantly in progesterone production and ovulatory characteristics. Likewise, oligomenorrheic cycles may end in ovulation or not. Amenorrhea is by definition absence of menstrual flow for 180 days (6 months) or longer: dark triangle is menses; shaded areas are periods of high-progesterone production.

lation disturbances are common comes primarily from a prospective 1-year study performed in 66 women that were carefully screened to have normal ovulation on two consecutive cycles before enrollment (11). A population-based study in young women with regular cycles has also recently found that those with bone density values in the lowest 10% have lower levels of excretion of both estrone and progesterone in overnight urine samples than those women with normal bone density values (12).

Laboratory Diagnosis of Ovulation Disturbances

Normal ovulation requires that three characteristics be met: (1) release of an egg (ovulation), (2) at least 10 days from egg release until the onset of the next flow, and (3) a progesterone level of 16 nmol/L or more. Egg release is usually necessary before the granulosa cells create a corpus luteum capable of making progesterone (the exception is the rare so called "unruptured corpus luteum"). It is not necessary to actually visualize the egg being released to know ovulation has occurred. An in-

direct, anatomic assessment of ovulation is possible if a woman has daily transvaginal or pelvic ultrasound examinations that show the development, growth, and eventual disappearance of a dominant cyst.

Practical assessments of ovulatory function are indirect, however, and evaluate the quantity and duration of progesterone secretion. Serum peak progesterone levels normally rise 1400% above the follicular phase baseline levels (16). Criteria based on urinary and salivary progesterone level changes are less clearly defined (17), and require a careful understanding of the specificity and sensitivity of the assays used.

In clinical practice, the diagnosis of ovulation is commonly made with a single serum sample for progesterone level. Ovulation can be said to have occurred if a serum progesterone taken 10 to 1 days before the next flow is above 16 nmol/L (5 ng/dL). However, the single-sample method cannot define the duration of the luteal phase and is subject to specificity problems because progesterone secretion is pulsatile (18). A minimum 10-day duration of the corpus luteum appears to be necessary to produce the secretory transformation of the endometrium that is required for implantation of a fertilized ovum (19) and to prevent bone loss (11). The need to define the duration of the time of high progesterone production makes multiple samples necessary (16, 20, 21). Progesterone can be documented in its free form in saliva (22) and in a complex metabolite form in urine. Therefore, daily or every other day saliva or urine samples can be used to document the onset and duration of the luteal phase. However, both methods are less sensitive than serum progesterone methods.

Nonlaboratory Documentation of Ovulation

An indirect way to define luteal phase duration is with documentation of the day on which an LH peak occurs before the start of the next flow. A serum LH peak (triple the follicular baseline and over 40 IU/L) is necessary before ovulation can be assumed to follow. Documentation of a serum or urine LH peak requires daily midcycle blood or urine testing. For aid in fertility, commercial urinary LH kits are available without a prescription. However, because (although rarely) an LH peak of apparently normal characteristics has been documented that is not followed by ovulation (23), this is not a specific assessment.

Another method for documentation of the presence and duration of luteal phase is using core temperature (Fig. 12.2.2). Because progesterone causes an average luteal phase basal temperature increase of 0.3°C (0.6°F) mediated

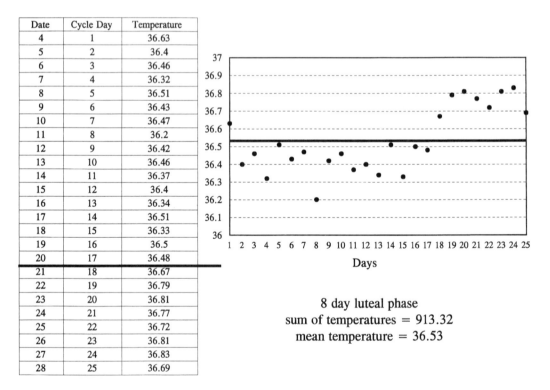

Date	Cycle Day	Temperature
4	1	36.63
5	2	36.4
6	3	36.46
7	4	36.32
8	5	36.51
9	6	36.43
10	7	36.47
11	8	36.2
12	9	36.42
13	10	36.46
14	11	36.37
15	12	36.4
16	13	36.34
17	14	36.51
18	15	36.33
19	16	36.5
20	17	36.48
21	18	36.67
22	19	36.79
23	20	36.81
24	21	36.77
25	22	36.72
26	23	36.81
27	24	36.83
28	25	36.69

8 day luteal phase
sum of temperatures = 913.32
mean temperature = 36.53

Figure 12.2.2. This shows a sample set of temperature data for a 25-day cycle that had a short luteal phase of 8 days. A portion of a calendar on which Celsius temperatures are written is shown on the left. In the bottom right all of the temperature values have been added to achieve a sum which is divided by the number of days in the cycle to obtain a mean temperature. This mean line is drawn across both the graphed temperatures (on the right) and the list temperatures (on the left) to show the onset of the luteal phase. This mean temperature method has been validated against the midcycle serum LH peak day.

through hypothalamic temperature-sensitive neurons, documentation of temperature is a reliable way to confirm the presence of ovulation and the duration of the luteal phase. Basal temperature methods have been faulted in the past, not because there is any doubt that progesterone influences temperature, but because other variables such as eating, illness, and change in time of day in which the temperature is taken also influence oral basal temperature readings (24). These difficulties can be overcome if the temperatures are taken with a digital thermometer (no problem of shaking down and reading a mercury thermometer) and recorded in a list to two decimal places (e.g., 36.78), (rather than being graphed by the woman, in which error is common), and if a quantitative rather than an "eyeball" method for analysis is used. The basal temperature method of ovulation documentation has been made into a quantitative, reliable test by blinded comparison with the serum LH peak in the same cycle and use of a statistical method (25). See Figure 12.2.2 for a practical example of a menstrual cycle temperature list and its analysis in graphic form to produce a luteal phase length.

Critique of Methods to Document Ovulation

The methods to document ovulation and luteal phase length that have been discussed above must be compared, not only for their reliability and accuracy but also for their cost, availability, and acceptability to women. Multiple serum samples are invasive, cause major disruptions in a woman's schedule, and are costly to analyze. Serial ultrasound measurements, besides being expensive (over $100 per test), are uncomfortable (because the transabdominal test requires a full bladder, or the vaginal requires a probe in the vagina), are not available in every community, and necessitate daily midcycle visits to a hospital or laboratory. Urine tests require not only the collection but also the transport of large volumes of fluid that many women find distasteful. Salivary tests

have the advantage of being less cumbersome and unpleasant but require immediate freezing of the sample and often take 5 or more minutes to collect (20). The midcycle urinary LH tests, which are available as spot urine test kits for fertility planning, are expensive and often require multiple days of testing before a positive test is reached. Furthermore, approximately 20% of cycles proven ovulatory by other ways do not have a detectable urinary LH peak (26). Basal temperature monitoring is limited by requirements for the woman to be disciplined about taking and recording the temperature, ability to do her own temperature data analysis, and for a predictable sleeping schedule (24, 25).

Of all the present methods for the diagnosis of ovulation and luteal phase length, basal temperature is least invasive, inexpensive, and is most likely to be able to give both an accurate diagnosis of ovulation and a reliable estimate of the duration of the luteal phase (25). However, none of the above methods are suitable for population-based epidemiological studies, especially because sampling for more than two cycles is needed to establish a reliable understanding of ovulatory characteristics in a given woman (11).

Self-Diagnosis of Ovulation Disturbances

There is a set of personal observations that a woman could use to accurately document ovulation. Many observant women assert that they can tell; by noticing certain indicators, that their period is coming. Because hormones cause changes in the breast, cervical secretions, fluid balance, and emotions, these changes, called molimina, can be a set of reliable indicators of ovulation.

Sixty-one women referred to an endocrinologist with clinical signs of androgen excess, all of whom reported regular menstrual flow were systematically asked, "Can you tell, by the way you feel, that your period is coming?" Most (n = 46) of these women with androgen excess had no signs that suggested the impending flow. If the woman, however, reported experiencing breast tenderness, with or without fluid, appetite, and emotional changes, they were likely to have ovulated in that cycle, based on a single serum progesterone level that was appropriately timed between day 11, and 1 day before the next flow.

What Causes Ovulatory Disturbances?

The precise mechanisms for ovulatory disturbances originate with an imbalance or incoordination in the signals from the hypothalamus and pituitary to the ovarian follicle. However, there has been little research prospectively on sequential menstrual cycles. Ovulatory disturbances are both variable from cycle to cycle and entirely reversible to normal. Ovulatory disturbances are prevalent immediately after puberty, following pregnancy, and in the transition into the menopause (5, 14, 27, 28). These changes occur during puberty because the entire hypothalamic-pituitary-ovarian axis is just developing into reproductive potential. It is less clear why the perimenopause should have disturbances of ovulation except that intraovarian and ovarian feedback to the pituitary and hypothalamus may be altered (28–30). It is hypothesized that inhibin (a small ovarian hormone made within the granulosa and corpus luteum cells that suppresses FSH) may be made in lower quantities and thus allow higher pituitary FSH secretion (31).

The pituitary and hypothalamic signals to the ovary are variable in response to many changes in the external and internal environments. Four categories of "stressors" have been shown to disturb ovulation: illness, weight loss, emotional stress, and exercise training (32).

Illness is associated with a decrease in serum FSH level in menopausal women; this is reversible, and the levels return to normal when the women recover (33). Weight loss is associated with anovulation (34, 35) or with an increased prevalence of luteal phase distur-

bances. Women who exercise and lose weight have more anovulatory cycles than similarly exercising women who did not lose weight (23). Exercise training in normal weight women has been shown to suppress ovulation temporarily and reversibly (36, 37). Subtle attitudes toward eating associated with fear of gaining weight, as documented by the Eating Restraint scale of the Three Factor Eating Questionnaire (38), have been shown to be associated with shortening of the luteal phase length in three different groups of normal weight, healthy, regularly cycling women (15, 39, 40).

Most women are not ill, losing weight, or exercising strenuously, and yet many are responding to stress. For example, ovulation disturbances are common during the school year in young women studying to become nurses. These ovulatory changes improve during the summer away from school (41). Unfortunately, stress is difficult to quantify; the hormones that mediate stress, such as cortisol, have such a wide reference interval that clinical differentiation of the stressed from the nonstressed individual is almost impossible. Studies of this phenomenon need to be individualized with prospective monitoring of the menstrual cycle (including ovulation and luteal phase length), the external environment (e.g., changes in weight, exercise), and the person's emotional responses over time. Only in this context would change in the stress hormones become useful for helping a given woman.

Despite these limitations, many studies (mostly in athletes) have shown higher urinary cortisol excretions in women with amenorrhea (42–45). Measurement of cortisol excretion could differentiate between those who did not recover their cycles (high-cortisol excretion) compared with women who did (lower cortisol excretion) (42). Studies of cortisol excretion in women with ovulation disturbances have not yet been shown to be diagnostic or predictive.

Particularly vulnerable times for ovulation disturbances include during recovery following a time of amenorrhea, in a strenuously training athlete who decreases her exercise, after stopping an OCP, following delivery, or discontinuing lactation. When the recovery occurs with increased weight and/or decreased stress, there is often an overshoot in estrogen production. This is often associated with increased feelings of frustration, depression, or anxiety, fluid retention, breast enlargement and soreness, and excessive appetite.

One mechanism that explains this is the production of a dominant follicle that matures to a midcycle estrogen peak but is not followed by ovulation (Fig. 12.3.3). Because the pituitary LH and FSH productions are normal, a new dominant follicle may be recruited and produce a second and perhaps higher estrogen peak. Commonly, endometrial stimulation is maximal so bleeding will start. This flow occurs at a time of increased cervical mucous, enlarged breasts with nipple tenderness, and adverse mood symptoms that are typical of PMS. A woman who has severe premenstrual symptoms will often report, if she can remember, that before this troublesome cycle she had experienced disturbed cycles, some significant changes in her social situation, weight, or ex-

ercise. Although PMS may occur in ovulatory or nonovulatory cycles, a common hormonal factor is the increased estrogen production (6).

The major exception to the adaptation model of ovulation disturbances presented above is a benign prolactin-producing adenoma. Therefore, if the anovulation is chronic, measuring a serum prolactin will screen for an adenoma. An abnormally high serum prolactin level (above 100 μg/L) suggests the presence of a prolactin-producing pituitary tumor that can usually be effectively treated with prolactin-lowering dopaminergic medications (bromoergocriptine) without pituitary surgery.

Prolactin levels higher than normal (2.7 to 26 μg/L) but less than 100 μg/L may be caused by many medications used for nausea or psychiatric illness (Table 12.2.3) or by unknown causes. Treatment of this moderately elevated prolactin level with bromoergocriptine in low doses (less than 5.0 mg/d), starting with half a 2.5 mg tablet with food at bedtime, will usually restore normal ovulation and fertility. Bromoergocriptine therapy is ideally combined with cyclic progesterone therapy (as described below) because of the common association of prolactinomas and low bone density. Because estradiol may directly stimulate the

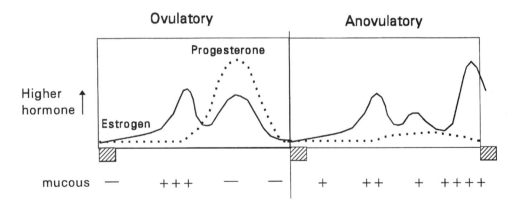

Figure 12.2.3. This diagram illustrates a normal ovulatory cycle on the left and a cycle of normal length and lack of ovulation on the right. Because luteal phase progesterone levels inhibit the stretchiness of cervical mucus, the promi-

nent stretchy mucus before flow becomes a way of documenting nonovulatory cycles. In this case, the high estrogen is associated with increased premenstrual breast, fluid, and mood symptoms.

Table 12.2.3. Some Medications That Can Interfere With Menstrual Cycle

Antiseizure medications

Barbituates

Haldol

Monoamine oxidase inhibitors

Phenothiazines (especially Mellaril, Navane)

Antinausea medications (meclopropamide)

Narcotics

pituitary lactotroph cells, caution should be used in treating these and patients with prolactinomas with oral contraceptive agents.

Therapy of Ovulation Disturbances

The goal of treating ovulation disturbances is restoring balance. The provider must make a supportive, respectful, noncontrolling relationship with the woman to help her to understand her own potential to be normal. Furthermore, it requires empowering her to observe changes within herself using tools such as a daily "menstrual cycle diary" (45) and the basal temperature record.

The next step is to determine whether there is any evidence of androgen excess. This is obtained both from her history and from examination looking for signs of androgen excess including acne, male-pattern facial and body hair, and temporal balding.

If androgen excess is present, the woman is likely to have normal to high levels of estrogen and low or very low progesterone levels. Therefore, she is at increased risk for endometrial cancer, possibly breast cancer, and prolactinomas (7, 8), and (because of high androgens) is usually not at risk for low bone density (46). If she is plucking facial or breast hair, having electrolysis, or needing acne treatment, it is necessary, besides treatment of the cycle, to block the actions of androgens. For this purpose, spironolactone, an androgen-receptor

blocking agent, is given in a dose of 100 mg once or twice a day. It is a safe and effective antiandrogen (47). However, spironolactone given alone in this population will cause irregular and sometimes heavy flow.

In the woman with anovulatory androgen excess, cyclic progesterone or medroxyprogesterone will control flow. In addition, these progestins will compete for the 5-alpha reductase that converts testosterone to dihydrotestosterone, the active skin androgen cyclic progesterone complements spironolactone therapy.

For the woman with hypothalamic disturbances of ovulation, besides promoting nutritional and emotional health, it is also necessary to restore a more normal menstrual cycle hormonal balance by replacing the missing or inadequate cyclic progesterone production. This is most easily and least expensively done with medroxyprogesterone acetate (MPA), a nonandrogenic synthetic progestin, given in a dose of 10 mg/d for 14 days each cycle. In practical terms for women with normal flow, this is given days 14 to 27 after the start of flow (Fig. 12.2.4).

If flow starts during the MPA, the full 14 days of therapy should still be completed. If flow starts before the ninth day of MPA therapy, for the next three cycles the dose should be increased to 15 mg/d (1½ tablets/day) for 14 days. If flow starts before cycle day 12 (which rarely occurs except in women with androgen excess, obesity, or in the perimenopause) the MPA should be begun earlier in the cycle (e.g., day 10) and continued for 14 days. If no flow occurs following any cycle of MPA (if pregnancy is possible, it must be excluded), the next dose should be begun 14 days after stopping the last 14-day cycle. Oral micronized progesterone in a dose of 300 mg/d given at bedtime (because it causes somnolence) can be substituted for cyclic MPA.

The purposes for cyclic progesterone therapy can be understood by looking again at the health risks of disturbed ovulation. In women

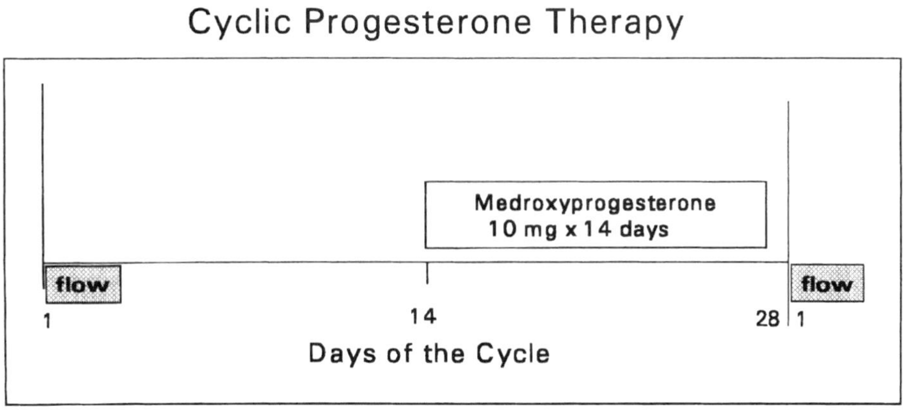

Cyclic Progesterone Therapy

Figure 12.2.4.   This diagram shows how to prescribe exogenous MPA acetate (10 mg/d for 14 days) so that it fits within a normal cycle.

with acne and male-pattern hair, along with spironolactone, cyclic MPA will decrease the androgen excess and restore normal ovulatory levels of progesterone (10). This therapy will control irregular or heavy flow, decrease anemia, prevent severe breast tenderness and cyst formation, help alleviate other premenstrual symptoms, and prevent endometrial cancer. There is currently no direct evidence this therapy will prevent breast cancer, but there is also no evidence it increases breast cancer risk. Importantly, based on the evidence that progesterone sits on an osteoblast receptor and increases its metabolism (48), cyclic progesterone therapy will increase bone density. This is an important benefit for the woman with amenorrhea, oligomenorrhea, and anovulation or short luteal phase cycles with normal cycle intervals because bone loss occurs in these women despite normal weight, good calcium intakes, and healthy exercise habits (3). Cyclic MPA for only 10 days per cycle has been shown in a randomized, placebo-controlled trial to cause a significant 2%, 1-year increase in spinal bone density measured by dual energy radiograph absorptiometry (3).

There are few contraindications to cyclic progesterone therapy. Allergy is rare to either

MPA or progesterone. There are no absolute or relative contraindications to MPA therapy, although those women with significant liver disease should probably avoid oral micronized progesterone. Although drug information sources continue to list thrombosis, migraine headaches, edema, hirsutism, and mood symptoms as side effects of MPA and progesterone, these have not been documented in randomized, placebo-controlled trials of physiological doses of MPA or progesterone alone (without estrogen). The side effects are listed because they have been reported to occur during therapy with oral contraceptive agents containing high doses of estrogens and androgenic progestins.

There are many uncontrolled studies in menopausal women in which cyclic MPA is reported to cause premenstrual symptoms. However, several double-blind placebo-controlled trials have not supported this, and no high prevalence (more than placebo) of adverse symptoms was found in one controlled study in reproductive-age women given cyclic MPA during assessment of bone density (3).

In summary, short luteal phase or anovulatory cycles are common in reproductive-age women and carry many significant health consequences. Although some women will present with severe breast swelling, will be incidentally found to have multiple ovarian cysts, or will have spotting or heavy flow, the diagnosis is commonly suspected only when a woman with regular periods has difficulty getting pregnant or is specifically asked. If androgen excess occurs with ovulatory disturbances, it is treated with the antiandrogen, spironolactone 100 to 200 mg/d, continuously along with cyclic MPA 10 mg/d on days 14 to 27 of the cycle. Therapy with cyclic MPA is indicated because it restores the normal cyclic estrogen/progesterone balance and increases bone density. Also it helps a woman know when her period is coming. It probably has other health benefits such as decreasing mastalgia and cystic breast problems, decreasing heavy flow and anemia, and preventing endometrial cancer.

Amenorrhea and Oligomenorrhea

The diagnosis of amenorrhea is simple—no period for 6 or more months by history. Primary amenorrhea is never having menstrual periods; the differential diagnosis includes chromosomal disorders, such as Turner's syndrome, testicular feminization, and abnormalities of the genital tract. Secondary amenorrhea is the cessation of flow after it has begun. The diagnosis of oligomenorrhea is also straightforward: over 36 days between episodes of flow, although the long cycle may be ovulatory or not.

Whenever the flow is seriously disturbed, pregnancy, premature menopause, medication use, thyroid dysfunction, and a prolactin-producing pituitary tumor must be excluded. Therefore the minimal evaluation should begin with a review of medications. Psychotropic medications, including phenothiazines, barbiturates, and anti-seizure medications can all affect menstrual cycles.

Laboratory evaluation (Table 12.2.4) should include screening for (1) pregnancy (with a urine or blood beta-HCG level), (2) a primary ovarian problem (such as Turner's syndrome by history, examination, or if suspected, by chromosome studies), (3) thyroid dysfunction (with thyroid function tests), (4) premature menopause (with a serum FSH level), and (5) a pituitary problem (with a serum prolactin level). The FSH will be twice the upper limit of normal if ovarian failure is causing the disturbed cycle interval. If prolactin excess causes the sparse flow, the value will usually be more than twice the upper limit of normal. If a benign prolactin-producing pituitary adenoma is the cause, the prolactin level will be over 100 μg/L. Intermediate elevations of prolactin may be caused by drugs used for nausea or severe anxiety and are often unclear. Although good population data are sparse, hypothalamic/pituitary changes cause most cases of amenorrhea and oligomenorrhea developing after a normal puberty. By definition, hypothalamic causes for loss of flow and ovulation are maladaptive and reversible. Often periods are far apart in the teenage years, after oral contra-

Table 12.2.4. Laboratory Evaluation of Amenorrhea/Oligomenorrhea

Primary Cause	Laboratory Evaluation	Abnormal Level Indicating Condition
Pregnancy	Beta-HCG	> 25 IU
Thyroid dysfunction	TSH	2 units above upper normal
Increased prolactin	Prolactin	2 times normal
Prolactin-secreting tumor	Prolactin	> 100 units
Premature menopause	Serum FSH level	Twice midcycle peak level

ceptives are stopped, following delivery of a baby, or if significant weight loss has occurred.

It is normal to have amenorrhea during full lactation. This is physiological and reversible amenorrhea and does not need to be medically treated with other than nutritional support unless low bone density is present. Then, once lactation is established, cyclic MPA may be given for 14 days on and 14 days off until flow begins to occur. When spotting starts, this is evidence suggesting the pituitary is again stimulating follicles to produce estrogen. The cyclic MPA can then be timed to correspond to the missing luteal phase.

Therapy of Premature Ovarian Failure

Ovarian causes for amenorrhea are diagnosed by repeatedly elevated levels of serum FSH. In practice, FSH should be measured monthly for 3 months before it is concluded that the amenorrhea is likely irreversible. Even after repeated high FSH levels, however, there is sometimes temporary recovery of ovarian function. Causes for hypergonadotrophic amenorrhea in women age less than age 40 years are premature ovarian failure caused by Turner's syndrome, a viral illness that causes autoimmune reactions and alters ovarian function, chemotherapy or radiation, or more commonly is unexplained.

The treatment varies, depending on whether a woman wishes menses or not. Either hormones can be given to match the normal cycle with menstruation or continuous dosing of progesterone can be given to avoid menstrual flow. To recreate normal menstruation, estrogen can be given days 1 to 25 of the calendar month and allowing a few days without a high level similar to low levels during the normal menstrual flow. Medroxyprogesterone or progesterone should be prescribed in physiological doses (MPA 10 mg/d or oral micronized progesterone 300 mg/d) for 14 days (days 12 to 25 of the calendar month). Continuous dosing of progesterone every day and cycle estrogen

described will cause, in 85% of women, amenorrhea without risk of osteoporosis.

The woman who desires pregnancy may find, for reasons that are unclear, she has an ovulatory cycle following a couple of replacement cycles of hormones. She may then, because most of the hormones for pregnancy are made in the placenta, carry the pregnancy to term but will often find she is again in premature ovarian failure following the delivery.

Although the woman with either hypothalamic (reversible) or hypergonadotrophic (irreversible) amenorrhea is often provided with OCP as a form of therapy, it is preferable for those with permanent amenorrhea who need estrogen and progesterone to be given physiological therapy with cyclic estrogen and progesterone. OCPs provide pharmacologic and much higher doses of estrogen and androgen-derived progestins. Even current formulations of OCPs have estrogen doses equivalent to five times the normal menstrual cycle level. OCPs contain androgen-derived progestins that may cause lipid abnormalities. Inadequate data are presently available about the long-term effects of these various therapy choices on bone density.

Based on the concept that approximately 35 to 40 years of cyclic high estrogen and progesterone levels are optimal for a woman's health, these therapies are continued until the woman reaches the age of 50 years (the mean age of menopause). When she is aged 50 years, she can begin first to lower the dose of estrogen while keeping cyclic progesterone the same. Tapering off the hormones over several cycles is necessary because rebound vasomotor symptoms (hot flush and night sweat problems) can be triggered by abrupt decreases in estrogen levels. If the bone density is normal and vasomotor symptoms are not a problem, both hormones can be stopped. Although current recommendations suggest estrogen therapy will decrease heart disease, randomized data are absent and lifestyle (e.g., diet, exercise, weight, habits) changes are more physiologic.

Therapy for Hypothalamic Amenorrhea and Oligomenorrhea

The woman who develops oligomenorrhea or amenorrhea because of grief, stress, travel, or weight loss needs support for her emotional distress, which consists of group or individual counseling while being treated with cyclic MPA acetate 10 mg/d (or oral micronized progesterone 300 mg/d) for 14 days on and 14 days off. This therapy should be continued while she continues to be amenorrheic. When she begins to have any flow (even spotting), the cyclic progesterone should be fitted into her cycle so that it is given starting the 14th day after the onset of flow and continued for 14 days.

It is difficult to know when to stop the therapy so that steps can be taken to determine hypothalamic-pituitary recovery. Cyclic progesterone therapy is helpful to increase bone density, provide a predictable period (when it begins again), and give a woman a sense that she is normal. The woman must first achieve a normal and stable weight, no longer be compulsively exercising, and be in a socially supportive situation. If she has not been keeping a diary, this is a useful time for her to start. When she is regularly observing changes in her own cycle, while on the therapy, she is likely to be recovering. Cyclic progesterone should not be stopped before the woman is aware she is experiencing cyclic stretchy midcycle mucous, has achieved Tanner 5 breast changes, and has a spinal bone density within one standard deviation of the peak young normal mean value. If MPA, rather than oral micronized progesterone therapy is being used, a serum progesterone level can be obtained in the week before expected flow because MPA does not cross-react with the serum progesterone assay. If the level is over 16 nmol/L (or 5 ng/dL), this is presumptive evidence of ovulation although it does not provide information about the luteal phase length.

The woman needs to know that amenorrhea develops as a protective response. It can and will reverse to normal and her fertility can be normal. Forty-four percent of the 61 women with initially abnormal cycles taking part in a randomized placebo-controlled trial of cyclic MPA with or without extra calcium developed normal ovulatory cycles. The women who recovered to normal ovulatory cycles had no increased weight, decreased exercise, or other obvious changes to explain this recovery; this was also not associated with either the cyclic MPA or calcium therapies. Recovery may have occurred because these women, who had been charting, keeping their basal temperatures, and interacting with research assistants and other women with similar cycle disturbances, had learned about themselves and (by inference) become less stressed about their own reproductive functions.

Special Considerations for Nurse Practitioners and Physician Assistants

Amenorrhea is a symptom that can result from many causes, making thorough assessment essential. The extent to which a practitioner will be involved will depend on the practice setting, educational preparation and skills, protocols, and consultation agreements. Ordering special radiographs, CAT scans, or MRIs may require consultation and/or referral (49). Women with primary amenorrhea and with secondary amenorrhea caused by central lesions, autoimmune diseases, psychiatric problems, or complex endocrine or metabolic diseases need specialist evaluation (50).

Sometimes the history will reveal that amenorrhea is not worrisome, and perhaps even an expected event, e.g., the woman has received Depo-Provera. However, if the woman expresses concern, she needs education and reassurance (51). The meaning of amenorrhea to the woman and her fears related to it must be determined (49).

The adolescent with amenorrhea presents special problems. Not only must developmental changes be thoroughly assessed, but providers must also determine the meaning of amenorrhea to the adolescent (and perhaps her parents). Although chronic systemic diseases are not usually a problem for this age group, they need to be ruled out. Information about the girl's school and home situation, diet, exercise patterns, substance use, sexual activity, and contraception is needed. Her fears related to amenorrhea need to be determined (49).

During the pelvic examination, the examiner should note the presence of pink, moist, and rugated vaginal mucosa and clear cervical mucus in the os, both indicators of estrogen. The presence of a cervix is a good indicator that a uterus is present. The bimanual examination can confirm the presence and size of the uterus (50, 52).

Women whose amenorrhea is related to strenuous exercise may have been told in the past not to worry about the condition and will need explanation of the practitioner's more recent concerns about bone loss (51). The woman will have decisions to make about her exercise program, whether to decrease its intensity or duration and try to gain some weight or to continue her current program. Other factors that can contribute to amenorrhea, such as lifestyle or increased stress, should also be investigated (49).

When hormones (e.g., progesterone) are given for evaluation or treatment of amenorrhea, women should be told if they should expect cyclic withdrawal bleeding and when. Although heavy bleeding can occur when progesterone therapy is initiated, abnormal bleeding should be reported (49). Keeping a chart of medications, bleeding, and related symptoms is helpful.

References

1. Hubbard RW. The Politics of Women's Biology. New Brunswick, NJ: Rutgers University Press, 1990.
2. O'Brien M. The Politics of Reproduction. London: Routledge & Kegan Paul, 1981.
3. Prior JC, Vigna YM, Barr SI, Rexworthy C, Lentle BC. Cyclic MPA treatment increases bone density: a controlled trial in active women with menstrual cycle disturbances. Am J Med 1994;96:521–530.
4. Biller BM, Coughlin JF, Saxe VC, Schoenfeld DA, Spratt DS, Klibanski A. Osteopenia in women with hypothalamic amenorrhea: a prospective study. Obstet Gynecol 1991;78:996–1001.
5. Fraser IS, Baird DT. Endometrial cystic glandular hyperplasia in adolescent girls. J Obstet Gynecol 1972;79:1009–1013.
6. Hammarback S, Damber J, Backstrom T. Relationship between symptom severity and hormone changes in women with premenstrual syndrome. J Clin Endocrinol Metab 1989;68:125–130.
7. Coulam CB, Annegers JF, Kranz JS. Chronic anovulation syndrome and associated neoplasia. Obstet Gynecol 1983;61:403–407.
8. Cowan LD, Gordis L, Tonascia JA, Jones GE. Breast cancer incidence in women with a history of progesterone deficiency. Am J Epidemiol 1981;114:209–214.
9. Sitruk-Ware LR, Stenkers N, Mowezowicz, Mauvais-Jarvis P. Inadequate corpus luteal function in women with benign breast cancer disease. J Clin Endocrinol Metab 1977;44:771.
10. Berga SL, Yen SSC. Opioidergic regulation of LH pulsatility in women with polycystic ovary syndrome. Clin Endocrinol 1989;30:177–184.
11. Prior JC, Vigna YM, Schechter MT, Burgess AE. Spinal bone loss and ovulatory disturbances. N Engl J Med 1990;323:1221–1227.
12. Sowers MF, Shapiro J, Zhang B. Urinary ovarian and gonadotrophin hormones in premenopausal women with low bone mass. J Bone Miner Res 1995;10: M377.
13. Prior JC, Vigna YM, McKay DW. Reproduction for the athletic women: new understandings of physiology and management. Sports Med 1992;14:190–199.
14. Vollman RF. The menstrual cycle. In: Friedman EA, ed. Major Problems in Obstetrics and Gynecology. Vol 7. Toronto: WB Saunders, 1977:11–193.
15. Barr SI, Janelle KC, Prior JC. Vegetarian versus nonvegetarian diets, dietary restraint, and subclinical ovulatory disturbances: prospective six month study. Am J Clin Nutr 1994;60:887–894.
16. Nielsen HK, Brixen K, Bouillon R, Mosekilde L. Changes in biochemical markers of osteoblastic activity during the menstrual cycle. J Clin Endocrinol Metab 1990;70:1431–1437.
17. Finn MM, Gosling JP, Tallon DF, Madden AT, Meehan FP, Fottrell PF. Normal salivary progesterone levels throughout the ovarian cycle as determined by a direct enzyme immunoassay. Fertil Steril 1988;50:882–887.
18. Baird DT. Prediction of ovulation: biophysical, physiological and biochemical coordinates. In: Jeffcoate SL, ed. Ovulation: Methods for its Prediction and Detection. London: John Wiley & Sons, 1983:1–17.
19. Davis OK, Berkeley AS, Naus GJ, Cholst IN, Freed-

man KS. The incidence of luteal phase defect in normal, fertile women, determined by serial endometrial biopsies. Fertil Steril 1989;51:582–586.

20. Finn MM, Gosling JP, Tallon DF, Bayne S, Meehan FP, Fottrell PF. The frequency of salivary progesterone sampling and the diagnosis of luteal phase insufficiency. Gynecol Endocrinol 1992;6:127–134.

21. Landgren BH, Unden AL, Diczfalusy E. Hormonal profile of the cycle in 68 normally menstruating women. Acta Endocrinol 1980;94:89–98.

22. Tallon DF, Gosling JP, Buckely PM, et al. Direct solid phase enzymeimmunoassay of progesterone in saliva. Clin Chem 1992;30:1507–1511.

23. Bullen BA, Skrinar GS, Beitins IZ, von Mering G, Turnbull BA, McArthur JW. Induction of menstrual disorders by strenuous exercise in untrained women. N Engl J Med 1985;312:1349–1353.

24. Lenton EA, Weston GA, Cooke ID. Problems in using basal body temperature recordings in an infertility clinic. Br Med J 1977;1:803–805.

25. Prior JC, Vigna YH, Schulzer M, Hall JE, Bonen A. Determination of luteal phase length by quantitative basal temperature; validate against the midcycle LH peak. Clin Invest Med 1990;13;123–131.

26. Elking-Hirsch K, Goldziecher JW, Gibbons WE, Besch PK. Evaluation of the ovustick urinary luteinizing hormone kit in normal and stimulated menstrual cycles. Obstet Gynecol 1986;67:450–453.

27. Metcalf MG. Incidence of ovulatory cycles in women approaching the menopause. J Biosoc Sci 1979;11:39–48.

28. Van Look PF, Lothian H, Hunter WM, Michie EA, Baird DT. Hypothalamic-pituitary-ovarian funtion in perimenopausal women. Clin Endocrinol 1977;7:13–31.

29. Metcalf MG, Donald RA, Livesey JH. Pituitary-ovarian function in normal women during the menopausal transition. Clin Endocrinol 1981;14:245–255.

30. Hee JP, MacNaughton J, Bangah M, Burger HG. Perimenopausal patterns of gonadotrophins, immunoreactive inhibin, oestradiol and progesterone. Maturitas 1993;18:9–20.

31. Prior JC. The perimenopause: pathophysiology, symptoms and therapy. In: Medifacts Healthcare Communications (tape) Ottawa: Medifacts Groups Limited, 1994.

32. Prior JC. Endocrine "conditioning" with endurance training: a preliminary review. Can J Appl Sport Sci 1982;7:149–157.

33. Warren MP, Siris ES, Petrovich C. The influence of severe illness on gonadotropin secretion in the postmenopausal female. J Clin Endocrinol Metab 1977;45:99–104.

34. Pirke KM, Schweiger U, Strowitzki T, et al. Dieting causes menstrual irregularities in normal weight women through impairment of luteinizing hormone. Fertil Steril 1989;51:263–268.

35. Schweiger U, Laessle RG, Pfisher H, et al. Diet-induced menstrual irregularities: effects of age and weight loss. Fertil Steril 1987;48:746.

36. Prior JC, Ho Yeun B, Clement P, Bowie L, Thomas J. Reversible luteal phase changes and infertility associated with marathon training. Lancet 1982;1:269–270.

37. Shangold MM, Freeman R, Thysen B, Gatz M. The relationship between long-distance running, plasma progesterone, and luteal phase length. Fertil Steril 1979;31:130–133.

38. Stunkard AJ, Messick S. The three-factor eating questionnaire to measure dietary restraint, disinhibition and hunger. J Psychosomatic Res 1985;29:71–83.

39. Tuschl RJ, Laessle RG, Kotthaus BC, Pirke KM. Behavioral and biological correlates of restrained eating. Ann N Y Acad Sci 1989;575:585–586.

40. Barr SI, Prior JC, Vigna YM. Restrained eating and ovulatory disturbances: possible implications for bone health. Am J Clin Nutr 1994;59:92–97.

41. Nagata I, Kato K, Seki K, Furuya K. Ovulatory disturbances. Causative factors among Japanese student nurses in a dormitory. J Adolesc Health Care 1986;7:1–5.

42. Ding JH, Sheckter CB, Drinkwater BL, Soules MR, Bremner WJ. High serum cortisol levels in exercise-associated amenorrhea. Ann Intern Med 1988;108:530–534.

43. Loucks AB, Mortola JF, Girton L, Yen SSC. Alterations in the hypothalamic-pituitary-ovarian and the hypothalamic-pituitary-adrenal axes in athletic women. J Clin Endocrinol Metab 1989;68:402–411.

44. Biller BM, Federoff HJ, Koenig JL, Klibanski A. Abnormal cortisol secretion and responses to corticotropin releasing hormone in women with hypothalamic amenorrhea. J Clin Endocrinol Metab 1990;70:311.

45. Prior JC. Exercise induced menstral disturbances. In: Adashi E, et al., eds. Reproductive Endocrinology, Surgery and Technology. Philadelphia: JB Lippincott, 1996:1077–1091.

46. Dixon JE, Rodin A, Murby B, Chapman MG, Iogelman I. Bone mass in hirsute women with androgen excess. Clin Endocrinol 1989;30:271–277.

47. Corrol P, Michaud A, Menard J, Freifeld M, Mahoudeau J. Anti-androgenic effect of spironolactone: mechanism of action. Endocrinology 1975;97:52–58.

48. Prior JC. Progesterone as a bone-trophic hormone. Endocrinol Rev 1990;11:386–398.

49. Fogel CI. Common symptoms: bleeding, pain, and discharge. In: Fogel CI, Woods NF, eds. Women's Health Care. Thousand Oaks, CA: Sage, 1995:517–570.

50. Baker S. Menstruation and related problems and concerns. In: Youngkin EQ, Davis MS, eds. Women's Health. Norwalk, CT: Appleton & Lange, 1994:77–100.

51. Webb TS. Evaluation and management of amenorrhea. ADVANCE Nurse Practitioners 1995;3:28–30.

52. Uphold CR, Graham MV. Clinical guidelines in family practice. Gainesville, FL: Barmarrae, 1993:616–619.

12.3

Cervical Cancer and Screening

Diane M. Harper

Introduction

Cervical cancer causes approximately 6000 deaths yearly in the United States and there are approximately 13,000 new cases per year. However, it is a preventable and curable disease; no woman should die of cervical cancer. With the use of Papanicolaou tests (Pap) and appropriate follow-up, the incidence of cervical cancer has declined since 1946, and there has been an 80% reduction in cervical cancer death rates since 1955 (1, 2). However, cervical cancer is increasing in younger populations. During 1950s, 9% of invasive cervical cancer was found in women aged under 35 years; by 1991, 22% of invasive cervical cancer was in this age group (3). Many women who develop cervical cancer have not had a Pap smear, or have not had one for more than 5 years. It is a challenge for the provider and the medical system to find ways to screen for and treat cervical cancer and its precursors, thereby preventing it.

Natural History of Cervical Cancer

Cervical cancer occurs from the malignant transformation of one cell in the transformation zone. In fetal life, the endocervical glandular cells of mullerian origin cover the ectocervix. The point at which the glandular cells meet the squamous cells is the original squamocolumnar junction. These glandular cells form villi that are covered with a single layer of columnar epithelium. Occasionally there are reserve cells in the basement membrane. The columnar epithelium has little neoplastic potential.

The squamous epithelium is mature, glycogenated, and stratified. The lowest layer of cells is a single layer of basal cells that progresses to several layers of parabasal cells, intermediate cells, and superficial cells. This stratified epithelium has virtually no neoplastic potential.

At puberty, the surge of estrogen causes an acidic shift in the vaginal pH. The reserve cells sitting below the columnar epithelium are stimulated to replicate. As they do, the parabasal-type reserve cells push the columnar epithelium upward. When there are five or six cell layers of parabasal-type cells, the columnar epithelium is shed completely. The parabasal-type cells mature into intermediate and superficial cells, transforming the columnar epithelium into stratified squamous epithelium. This process of changing cell types is called squamous metaplasia. Squamous metaplasia occurs with an inflammatory infiltrate, which if biopsied is read as chronic cervicitis. This is a normal finding in cervical epithelium undergoing transformation. The area of squamous metaplasia is the transformation zone. This area must be sampled at the time of the Pap smear.

A malignant transformation of one cell in this transformation zone is the cause of most squamous cervical cancers. Because it takes approximately 26 years from malignant transformation of one cell to death from cervical cancer, and because the transformation zone is readily visible and easy to sample and biopsy, precancerous changes can be identified and readily treated before invasive disease occurs (4).

Risk Factors

The greatest risk factor for developing cervical cancer is never, or seldom having a Pap smear. Women who have annual Pap smears have almost no chance of developing cervical cancer. The rate of cervical cancer in women who have not had a Pap smear is 50 to 60 per 100,000 (3), as compared to one to five per 100,000 women for women who had a Pap smear once in 3 years (5). In one study of women with cancer of the cervix, 39% had never had a Pap smear, and 10% had not had one for more than 5 years (6). Half of cervical cancers in the United States occur in women who have never been screened, and over 60%

occur in women who have not had a smear in the 5 years preceding their diagnosis of cancer.

Women who have sexually transmitted diseases, have multiple male partners, are sexually active at a younger age, and have had either herpes simplex (HSV) type 2 genital or human papilloma virus (HPV) infections are at higher risk for cervical cancer (7). Cigarette smoking and passive smoke exposure place the woman at higher risk for developing cervical cancer, with a relative risk of 3.43 for a current smoker (4, 8). This increased risk may be caused by altered cellular immunity.

Race, education, tobacco use, increased parity, and oral contraceptives do not increase a woman's chances of developing a high-grade lesion. Postmenopausal women on hormone replacement therapy are not at an increased risk for cervical cancer.

Human Papillomavirus (HPV)

Many epidemiologic and virologic studies have shown that HPV is a causative agent for cervical cancer. There are over 40 types of HPV. Twenty-one mucosotropic types of HPV colonize the cervical epithelium. Types 6, 11, and some 40s are unlikely to produce cancer, and infection with these is considered low-risk for cancer. These types are never associated with invasive squamous cell carcinoma of the cervix. The intermediate risk types are 31, 33, 35, 51, and 52. The high-risk types, especially prevalent in invasive cervical cancers, are 16, 18, 45 and 56. Unfortunately, in clinical practice serotyping HPV is not practical or easily available presently.

The low-risk types (i.e., benign HPV) remain extrachromosomal in the colonized cervical epithelium, manifesting themselves as koilocytotic atypia. The high-risk HPV types become incorporated into the host genome and lose the morphologic characteristics of koilocytes seen in cytology and pathology specimens. The high-risk types (e.g., 8, 16, 45, and 56) cause de novo development of CIN II/III

lesions within 24 months of infection bypassing an atypical or CIN 1 stage.

Screening

Recommendations

Different organizations (American Cancer Society, American Academy of Family Physicians, American College of Obstetricians and Gynecologists, US Preventive Health Services Task Force) have slightly differing recommendations for Pap smear intervals, although all agree on the necessity of testing. All women who are or who have been sexually active, or have reached age 18 years, should have an annual Pap smear and pelvic examination. After a woman has had three or more consecutive satisfactory normal annual examinations, the Pap smear may be performed less frequently, at 3- to 5-year intervals (9) in an average risk women. A high-risk woman should maintain annual Pap smear screening. A high-risk woman is any woman who has had a previously abnormal Pap smear, condylomatous warts, or any grade of intraepithelial neoplasia of the vulva, perineum, anus, vagina or cervix, has had early onset of coitus, or is immunocompromised from HIV disease, organ transplantation, or any other cause (10). A woman who is sexually active and has never had a Pap smear, or whose Pap smear greater than 5 years ago is also considered at high risk for cervical cancer until she has a Pap smear, then her risk category depends on the above listed conditions. Race, education, tobacco use, parity, oral contraceptives, and number of sexual partners do not increase a woman's chances of developing a high-grade lesion (11). Postmenopausal women on hormone replacement therapy are not at an increased risk for cervical cancer.

Efficacy and Use

Pap smears have never been proven in large prospective studies to prevent the incidence of invasive cancer or cancer death. Yet, by their widespread use in the United States the incidence of cancer and cancer death has decreased.

A test that is readily available and accurate should be widely used. Yet Pap smear screening is voluntary and not universal in the United States. Approximately one third of all eligible women present for screening in any given year. One quarter of women over the age of 18 years have not presented for Pap screening over a 3-year time frame and 15% of women over the age 65 years have never had a Pap smear (12). In Finland, all women get an invitation for a Pap smear every 5 years, yet 25% are still noncompliant. African-American and Latino women, women living in the inner city or in rural areas, women older than 65 years, and low-income women are the highest risk for episodic or no screening (13). Elderly, African-American, and poor women often do not have Pap smears until ill with another disease. Women who were seen by nurse practitioners were three times more likely to have had Pap smears than women seen by physicians (14). More intensive and widespread educational efforts for patients and physicians are needed to increase the likelihood of women obtaining regular Pap smears.

Pap Smear

Technique

The woman's comfort, privacy, and modesty should be considered. The examination should not be interrupted, and the room should be warm enough. The table should be covered with a pad to prevent secretion contamination. A chaperon or supportive person, besides the nurse, may be appropriate and reassuring, especially for younger women. Pap smears should be performed in nonmenstruating women.

An adequate Pap smear will have cells from both the transformation zone and the endocervix. The transformation zone will contain both metaplastic squamous cells and glandular cells. The endocervical canal must be sampled, because between 12 and 18% of the cervical cancers detected are adenocarcinomas. The Ayre's spatula is an effective method of retrieving exfoliated cells from the ectocervix. Other plastic variations on this tool are also acceptable. The endocervix must be sampled with a brush in all nonpregnant women. The use of the Ayre spatula with the endocervical nylon brush is the most effective in producing samples with endocervical components (15). Other studies have agreed that using the endocervical brush and spatula increased the number of smears that contain endocervical cells for both reproductive age and postmenopausal women. The order of sampling is inconsequential. Of the 50,000 to 300,000 cells transferred to the glass slide, only a dozen or less will be abnormal. Automated preparations to develop a monolayer of exfoliated endocervical and ectocervical cells will make the screening process more efficient for the cytologist and offer a method of computerized quality assurance.

Cytopathology Classifications and Further Evaluation

Pap Classification

Pap and Traut developed the first classification system for cervical cytology. The five classes were numerated I through V. Class I is a normal smear, class II is an atypical smear, class III indicates some type of dysplasia, class IV is carcinoma in situ (CIS), and class V is invasive squamous cell carcinoma. This system is inadequate in three respects: (*a*) it does not have a histologic counterpart, (*b*) it cannot diagnose noncancerous changes, and (*c*) it does not reflect the natural history of either cervical or vaginal neoplasia.

World Health Organization/Cervical Intraepithelial Neoplasia System

In the 1970s, Pap smear cytology was classified as a cervical intraepithelial neoplasia continuum. Normal smears had no abnormality. Atypical smears were commonly associated with condylomatous or koilocytotic atypia. CIN I or mild dysplasia was the disruption of the lower one third of epithelial maturation. CIN II or moderate dysplasia is the disruption of the lower two thirds of the epithelial maturation. CIN III-CIS is the disruption of the entire epithelial maturation. This system combined the CIN III and CIS classifications together as one entity. This system emphasized the natural history of cervical cancer, as it was known then. A lesion developed from CIN I and progressed to CIN II to CIN III to CIS and then to invasive cancer. Biopsy confirmation of the cytologic abnormality also emphasized treatment of all CIN lesions as early precursors to cervical cancer.

Bethesda System

The Bethesda System was refined in 1991 to report the Pap smear cytology reflecting the current knowledge of the development of cervical cancer. This cytopathology report requires three components. The first is a statement on the adequacy of the specimen, the second is a statement of general categorization, and the third is a descriptive diagnosis of the general categorization.

Statement of Adequacy of the Specimen

The specimen is judged satisfactorily adequate or not. Satisfactory indicates that the smear

had both endocervical and metaplastic ectocervical cells easily visible, and no more than 50% of the cells are obscured by inflammation, blood, or debris. If any abnormal cells are present, the smear is considered satisfactory, even if it is deficient in other ways.

"Satisfactory for evaluation but limited by . . ." is the next classification. A smear may be limited by one or more of four factors. The first is a lack of metaplastic or endocervical cells. This occurs when the transformation zone is not sampled. Excessive mucus, an atrophic cervix, a pregnant cervix, a nulliparous cervix, and a cervix after an ablative or excisional treatment procedure are the most common reasons for this limitation. In the perimenopausal or postmenopausal woman with an atrophic cervix, it is important to use a brush to evaluate the endocervical canal and to prepare the woman before taking the Pap smear. Preparations include the use of an intravaginal estrogen cream applied as a half applicator every night for 6 weeks, stopped the week before the smear. If the smear is limited solely by a lack of endocervical cells, especially in pregnancy, the smear does not have to be repeated before the next annual screening.

The second is a smear that is satisfactory but limited by partially obscuring inflammation, blood, or debris. This means that the inflammation or blood obscures more than 50%, but less than 75% of the cells on the smear. Any irritative effect can cause the inflammation. The woman must be reminded not to douche, have intercourse, or use tampons, cervical caps, sponges, pessaries, or any intravaginal medications for at least 48 hours before her exam. She must be cultured for gonorrhea and chlamydia, if this was not routinely done at the time of the Pap smear and treated if either is positive. Do not treat empirically with any intravaginal or oral medications without finding a causative organism. Inflammation, blood, and cellular debris are hallmarks of cervical cancer so the cytology should be repeated in 8 to 12 weeks.

The third is a smear limited by drying artifact. Air drying causes an increased nuclear-cytoplasmic ratio mimicking dysplastic cells. The fourth is a lack of patient information. It is important to include the patient's name, record number, last menstrual period, and any ablative or excisional therapy that the woman has undergone for laboratory quality assurance standards.

Unsatisfactory means that more than 75% of the cells on the slide were obscured by blood, inflammation, or debris (such as lubricant), or that the slide itself was broken in transit. An unsatisfactory smear must be repeated in 8 to 12 weeks.

General Categorization

The smear is either within normal limits or has benign cellular changes or epithelial cell abnormalities (Figure 12.3.1). If the smear is satisfactory and within normal limits, then the woman may have routine cytology screening.

Benign cellular changes are either reactive, reparative changes, or infection. The reactive changes include reparative changes from inflammation, postmenopausal atrophy, radiation effects, or changes from an intrauterine contraceptive device. Reactive and reparative changes are normal and do not need to be treated with any type of intravaginal cream nor the smear repeated before the routine screening interval.

If an infection is identified on Pap smear, the woman's chart must be audited for a symptomatic discharge at the time of screening, for wet mount examination results, if any antibiotic or antifungal medications were prescribed, and to check if gonorrhea and chlamydia cultures were taken.

Squamous Cell Abnormalities

Epithelial cell abnormalities are either of squamous or glandular origin, and the squamous cell abnormalities are classified into four categories. This reflects the natural history model of the HPV-infected cervical squamous epithelium

The first category, atypical squamous cells of undetermined significance (ASCUS), is not inflammatory nor koilocytotic atypia, but a limited and specific atypia of a squamous cell of uncertain significance. Approximately 5% of all Pap smears are read as ASCUS. ASCUS can be left unqualified or read as favoring a reactive/reparative or a malignant change.

The proportion of ASCUS smears reported is correlated to the percentage of the population that has high-risk sexual behaviors. At colposcopy between 5 and 13% of ASCUS smears are high-grade dysplasia, and between 13 and 25% of ASCUS smears are low-grade dysplasia. Others have documented that between 25 and 60% of ASCUS smears being abnormal at colposcopic biopsy. There are three management options. The first option is to repeat the cytology every 4 to 6 months until there are three consecutive satisfactory and "within normal limits" smears. This option is appropriate for women who promptly follow up for their medical care. If a second ASCUS smear develops during this frequent screening, a colposcopically directed biopsy of the cervix and endocervical curettage must be performed.

The second option is to have every woman with ASCUS undergo a colposcopically directed biopsy and endocervical curettage if an abnormal area is detected. This option may lead to overdiagnosis and subsequent overtreatment of minor low-grade lesions. The third option is to use an intermediate triage test to stratify women into low- and high-risk groups. HPV testing and cervicography can be possible triage tests. If the woman tested positive for intermediate and high-risk HPV types, then she could be triaged into colposcopy. There are no long-term studies that show how HPV testing or cervicography will be developed as triage testing.

ASCUS smears associated with severe inflammation must be evaluated. Severe, dense inflammation can be a hallmark of cervical cancer or of a cervical infection. The Pap smear that reads ASCUS with severe inflammation is the most common single Pap diagnosis preceding the detection of cervical cancer. The woman must be screened for *Chlamydia trachomatis*, *Neisseria gonorrhea*, herpes simplex virus, and *trichomonas vaginalis*. If the Pap smear, the wet mount, or the cultures are positive for these organisms, the woman must be treated. The woman must not be treated with nonspecific vaginal creams. An organism must be identified before treatment. The woman must be asked to return for a repeat Pap smear in 8 to 12 weeks from treatment or from the time of the initial smear if no organism was identified.

ASCUS in the postmenopausal woman reflects the exfoliation of parabasal cells that resemble dysplastic cells cytologically. Topical estrogen therapy may be used if the woman does not want to take oral hormone replacement therapy. Intravaginal estrogen is dosed as half applicator every night for a minimum of 3 weeks, preferably 6 weeks, with cessation of all intravaginal creams 1-week prior to the repeat smear. The repeat smear should be repeated no sooner than 6 weeks from the ASCUS smear because of atrophy.

If the ASCUS smear favors a malignant process, the woman should undergo a colposcopically directed biopsy and endocervical curettage. If the woman has ever had an abnormal Pap smear, or if she is unreliable for cytology follow-up, then she should undergo a colposcopic evaluation.

Women whose Pap smears are repeatedly ASCUS must have a colposcopic evaluation. If the colposcopy is satisfactory, biopsies are normal, and the endocervical curettage is normal, then Pap smear screening can revert to annual screening if the Pap smear remains ASCUS. Any change in Pap smear reading must have colposcopic evaluation. Most women with repeated ASCUS smears are HPV negative and do not develop any type of squamous intraepithelial lesion.

Low-Grade Squamous Intraepithelial Lesion (LSIL). Low-grade squamous intraepithelial lesions combine the HPV effects of koilocytosis with mild dysplasia/CIN I. This combination reflects the epidemiology of cervical cancer. Both mild dysplasia and HPV positivity can regress to normal in the natural course of time. Unless the cervix is infected with both low- and high-risk types of HPV, koilocytosis does not progress into cervical cancer.

The LSIL Pap smear must be viewed as a positive screening test, not a confirmed diagnosis. The Interim Guidelines recommend one of three management options. The first is to follow the woman with repeat cytology every 4 to 6 months until three consecutive Pap smears are satisfactory and within normal limits. If any of the Pap smears are abnormal, then the woman must have a colposcopic examination. LSIL smears regress to normal in 22 to 78% of the women. Many studies have reported that many (50.4 to 95%) women's Pap smears regressed to a normal within as little as 18 months (13–16). Less than 2% of lesions progressed from what was called mild dysplasia to cancer, and less than 16% progressed to CIN II/III or HSIL (16, 17, 19). The second is to have every woman with a LSIL smear undergo colposcopy.

On the other hand, LSIL smears may indicate a high-grade lesion at biopsy time in as many as 40% of the cases. The third option is to use a triage test to separate women into low- and high-risk groups. HPV DNA-typing and cervicography may be useful triage tests. If the woman was triaged into the low-risk group, then she could be followed with repeat cytology every 4 to 6 months. If she was

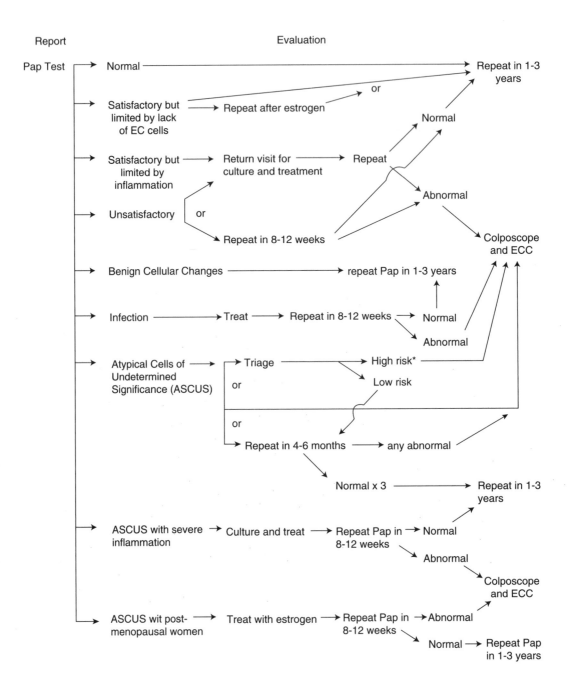

Figure 12.3.1. Algorithm for evaluation of Pap smear.

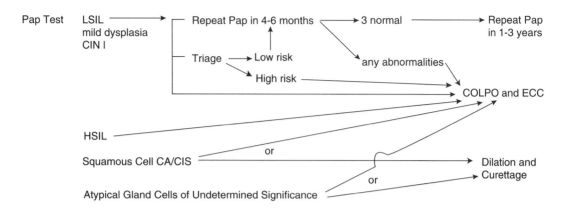

ECC- Endocervical curettage
LSIL- Low grade squamous intraepithelial lesion
HSIL- High grade squamous intraepithelial lesion

* High risk - any history of abnormal Pap, poor complier, unlikely to return, any HPV changes

Figure 12.3.1.—*Continued*

triaged into the high-risk group, she could undergo colposcopy with biopsy and endocervical curettage.

High-Grade Squamous Intraepithelial Lesion (HSIL). A high-grade squamous intraepithelial lesion combines a moderate and severe dysplasia with carcinoma in situ. Epidemiologically, these three precursors to cervical cancer behave similarly.

A woman with a high-grade smear must undergo a colposcopically directed biopsy with endocervical curettage. A Pap smear with HSIL is a positive screening test and the clinician must rule out microscopic or frank invasion. If the colposcopy is adequate, the biopsy results agree with the Pap smear findings, the endocervical curettage findings are negative and there is no invasion, then appropriate treatment—cryotherapy, LEEP, or other—can be done. If the colposcopic examination is unsat-

isfactory, then a conization procedure that does not have obscuring thermal artifact at the margins is mandatory.

Squamous Cell Carcinoma. A woman with squamous cell carcinoma on screening Pap smear must, at minimum, have a colposcopically directed biopsy and endocervical curettage to determine whether the carcinoma is microinvasive or frankly invasive. If the colposcopic examination is unsatisfactory or carcinoma identified, then a conization procedure is mandatory, and perhaps further surgery.

Glandular Cell Abnormalities
Benign endometrial cells seen in a postmenopausal woman on Pap smear is normal and the woman should be placed in the routine screening pool.

Atypical glandular cells of undetermined

significance (AGUS) encompass everything from reactive changes to adenocarcinoma. Adenocarcinoma of the cervix is approximately 12 to 18% of the cases of cervical cancer (20). Adenocarcinoma of the cervix is increasing in frequency in women under 35 years. Women with AGUS must undergo a colposcopic examination. Half of the women with an AGUS smear have an associated squamous abnormality that was not detected on Pap smear. Every woman with an AGUS smear must undergo an endocervical curettage and colposcopically directed biopsies if the squamous component is also abnormal. The same high-risk types of HPV are associated with adenocarcinoma.

If no abnormality is found, or if the atypical glandular cells are considered to be of endometrial origin, the woman must undergo an endometrial biopsy, a fractional dilation, and curettage or a hysteroscopy with biopsy. If no abnormality is found, the original Pap smear must be reviewed by the original pathologist and re-reviewed by a second pathologist. If both reviews are still atypical, then the woman must undergo an evaluation of her ovaries, tubes, gastrointestinal tract, and breasts to rule out a glandular primary carcinoma of these sites.

Adenocarcinoma of the cervix usually presents with abnormal bleeding. It is infrequently found by Pap smear or colposcopy and is usually already invasive when found (21).

Adenocarcinoma in situ (AIS) and Adenocarcinoma. A woman with AIS or adenocarcinoma on screening Pap smear must undergo a conization biopsy to determine the depth of invasion.

Epithelial Cell Abnormalities in Pregnancy

The purpose of Pap smear screening in pregnancy is to screen women who otherwise might not present for routine screening and to rule out invasive cancer (Figure 12.3.2). The incidence of invasive cervical cancer in pregnant women ranges from 1:250 to 1:5000. Pregnancy does not change the natural history of invasive cervical cancer even when stratified for stage at presentation.

For women who have a smear with ASCUS and/or LSIL, they should usually have two colposcopic examinations during pregnancy, depending on the gestational age at presentation for prenatal care. The cytology and colposcopy should be performed every 8 to 10 weeks or at 28 weeks gestation. Cytology is repeated at the postpartum examination. The abnormalities can resolve in the postpartum state because of tissue loss with the labor and delivery process, and because of the reestablishment of the maternal immunocompetence. Colposcopy during pregnancy is challenging because the changes associated with invasive cancer can be mimicked by the decidualization of the cervix.

A woman with a high-grade lesion during pregnancy must undergo a colposcopically directed biopsy. An endocervical curettage should never be performed in pregnancy. If the lesion is not cancerous, then she should be followed by sequential colposcopic and cytologic examinations every 8 to 10 weeks prior to delivery. Cytology is repeated at the postpartum examination. If the original biopsy indicates cancer, a wedge biopsy or a conization must be performed to determine whether the cancer is microinvasive or frankly invasive. The larger tissue sample allows assessment of the involvement of the lymph vascular space, the surface area of the tumor, and the extent of invasion, all prognostic indicators for survival.

If microinvasion is identified on wedge or cone biopsy and the woman is less than 28 weeks gestation, then the decision to abort the pregnancy and immediately treat the microinvasion must be made between the physician

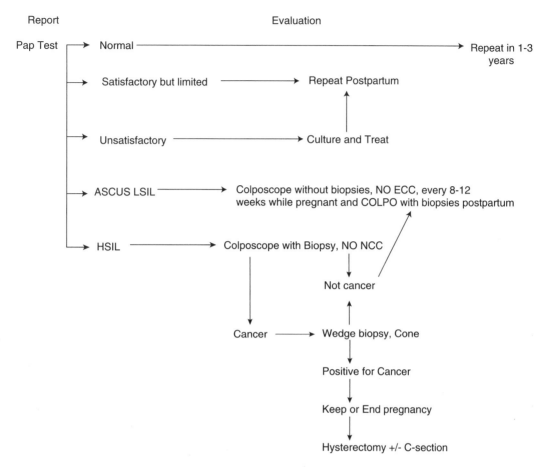

Figure 12.3.2.   Algorithm for evaluation of Pap smear findings in a pregnant woman.

and woman. If the woman is more than 28 weeks gestation and high-risk features are present in the tissue specimen. Then a Cesarean section with radical hysterectomy is recommended. If there are no high-risk features, then the choice of a vaginal delivery or a cesarean section must be made between the physician and the woman.

If the wedge or cone biopsy shows frankly invasive carcinoma and the gestational age is less than 28 weeks, a radical hysterectomy with sacrifice of the pregnancy is recommended. If the gestational age is more than 28 weeks, then a Cesarean section with radical hysterectomy is recommended.

Psychological Effect

An abnormality on the screening Pap smear immediately creates fear in the woman's mind ranging from biopsies and needles to disfigurement and death. Many women believe that any abnormality on a Pap smear means cancer. Further evaluation with time off from work or school, expense, uncertainty about the diagnosis or the consequences of the findings, fear of discomfort or pain, anticipation, fear and anxiety all can be logical consequences of the abnormal Pap. The woman may fear the possibility of cancer more than anything else, and desire that anything be done, just so the diagnosis is made or excluded, including "just taking it all out." Other women may fear disfigurement, loss of sexual identity, and changes in personal body image. Some women may be so glad it isn't cancer, they are willing to go through anything else. Other women's fear of discomfort, procedures, and pain will outweigh any other concerns. Women facing further procedures often show a great deal of anger toward husbands or partners, lack of sexual desire, decreased vaginal lubrication, and decreased arousal and incidence of orgasm (22).

The provider must be willing to spend time with patients, explaining what has been discovered, how the woman may have developed it, and what the next steps will be. Second, time must be spent finding out what the patient knows, understands, experiences, and believes about her present cytological diagnosis. The provider needs to be aware of the choice of words and the way the diagnosis is explained. The provider cannot expect close follow-up unless the woman agrees. No matter how simple and quick the procedure may seem to the provider, to the woman it may be potential death and disfigurement. Results should be obtained as quickly as possible and transmitted to the woman quickly, with time for discussion of future consequences if needed. This may need to be done in a scheduled office visit, rather than over the phone. Provider availability for answering questions that arise is important; the woman may be so anxious about the procedure, she cannot ask her questions or hear the answers.

Treatment

There are two general rules prior to treatment. The first is that a histologic diagnosis must be made. The Pap smear is a result of a screening test and must be confirmed or denied by a colposcopically directed biopsy with endocervical curettage. At this time there is not enough evidence to support the use of an endocervical brush to replace the endocervical curettage as a routine histologic sampling device. The second is that the treatment must destroy the entire transformation zone and the entire lesion. Women with invasive cancer present on biopsy and an abnormal endocervical curettage do not undergo a conization procedure; a radical hysterectomy or radiation therapy is the appropriate treatment.

Lesion Severity

A woman with a low-grade lesion (CIN I or HPV effect) confirmed by colposcopy should be informed that between 22 and 78% of these lesions can spontaneously regress to normal without any treatment (Fig. 12.3.3). If she chooses not to be treated she must be followed cytologically every 4 to 6 months until the lesion regresses to normal (indicated by three normal consecutive smears) or until the lesion progresses into a high-grade lesion at which time a colposcopically directed biopsy with endocervical curettage is the appropriate management. If she chooses to be treated, after treatment she must return for cytology follow-up every 4 to 6 months for the next 2 years. If all Pap smears remain normal, then she can return to the routine annual screening recommendations.

If the woman chooses to be treated, there is no one method that should be used routinely. Every treatment is tailored to the individual woman's needs.

A woman with a confirmed high-grade lesion (CIN II, CIN III, CIS) must be treated with an ablative or excisional method. This lesion will develop into invasive cancer in as little as 18 months.

Cryosurgery

There are requirements necessary for use of cryosurgery as treatment of LSIL or HPV

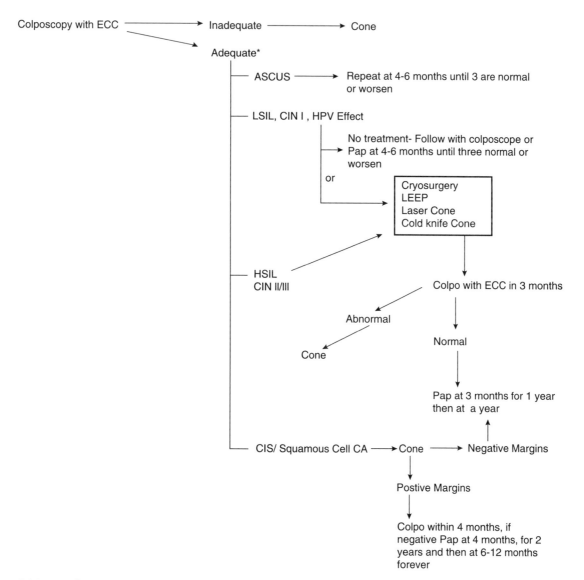

* Adequate Colposcopy includes that the whole Transformation Zone was seen, the whole lesion was seen and found to be totally on the ectocervix, and that the biopsy report agrees with the Pap test findings.

Figure 12.3.3. Algorithm for evaluation of colposcopy report.

effect reported in Table 12.3.1. All must be met for cryosurgery to be used.

Technique

Nitrous oxide (kept at $-90°C$) is the most commonly used agent to remove heat from the cervix. The size "D" tank must have a minimum of 40 kg/cm pressure to ensure adequate flow of nitrous oxide to the cryoprobe tip. The cryoprobe tips are either nippled or flat, 19 mm or 25 mm in diameter. The large, nippled 25-mm probe causes complete themoneclosis of CIN 3/CIS lesions when applied for a double 5-minute freeze. The cryoprobe is activated for 5 minutes, the cervix is allowed to thaw to pinkness (usually another 5 minutes), and the cervix is refrozen for another 5 minutes. All other methods have up to a 65% failure rate of destroying the 5-mm maximal depth of CIN 3/CIS invasion. Some women have a small-diameter cervical opening; for these women the 19-mm cryoprobe is the largest that will fit and should be used.

A thin layer of lubricant is placed on the cryoprobe for separation after the procedure. An anesthetic block is placed either paracervically or intramucosally. A 5-minute double freeze is performed. Lubricant is reapplied after the thaw if there is insufficient lubricant to cover the cryoprobe tip for the second freeze.

Documented adverse effects from this procedure include pain and cramping during the freezing phase and vaginal discharge for many weeks thereafter. A sloughing of the tissue eschar usually occurs on the fourth or fifth day posttreatment with a malodorous discharge. Up to 9% of sexually active adolescents treated with cryosurgery develop acute pelvic inflammatory disease within 1 month of the treatment. A small number of case reports document acute bilateral salpingitis, requiring intravenous antibiotics, local infection with mild endometritis and parametritis and heavy vaginal bleeding, mucometra, pyometra, and vasomotor syncope.

Long-term effects can include cervical stenosis in up to 3% of cases, and residual dysplasia if the appropriate cryosurgical method is not used. Hydrohematometra can occur when the cervical os is blocked by postcryosurgery cellular debris and the serosanguinous straw-colored fluid accumulates in the endocervical canal and into the uterus. This "plug syndrome" may cause uterine cramping and pain similar to labor contractions.

When the indications for cryosurgery are strictly followed, the success rate for treating CIN III/CIS lesions is equivalent to all other methods.

Table 12.3.1. Requirements for Use of Cryosurgery

- The entire transformation zone must be visualized by an experienced colposcopist
- The entire lesion must be visualized colposcopically
- The entire lesion cannot extend into the endocervical canal more than 5 mm
- There is no discrepancy between the cytology, colposcopy, and histology
- There must be no suspicion of invasive cancer cytologically, colposcopically, or histologically
- The endocervical curettage is sufficient and normal
- The transformation zone and lesion must be completely covered by the cryoprobe, or covered within 5 mm of the lateral edge of the probe's surface
- The lesion must not occupy more than two quadrants of the cervix
- The woman must not be pregnant

Loop Electrosurgical Excision Procedure (LEEP)

The minimum requirements for use of indications for LEEP are listed in Table 12.3.2, and contraindications are listed in Table 12.3.3.

The LEEP "see and treat" method has un-

Table 12.3.2. Requirements for Use of LEEP

- The entire transformation zone must be visualized by an experienced colposcopist
- The entire lesion must be visualized colposcopically
- There is no discrepancy between the cytology, colposcopy, and histology
- The lesion extends out onto the ectocervix, and/or the lesion extends into the canal where the suspicion of invasive cancer is low

Table 12.3.3. Contraindications for LEEP

- Pregnancy
- Implanted pacemaker
- Cardiac arrythmia
- Invasive squamous or glandular cancer
- Any lesion in which thermal artifact could obscure the diagnosis of invasion
- Any lesion that extends peripherally from the cervix onto the vaginal surface

dergone limited evaluations. It should be used only in those women at high risk for cervical cancer and noncompliance, and whose screening Pap smear correlates to the colposcopic evaluation indicating a high-grade lesion.

Technique

The procedure is usually well tolerated. The woman must be informed that other pelvic organs can be transected by LEEP inadvertently, i.e, vagina, bladder, rectum. She must be informed that surgery, i.e., the ligation of the uterine arteries, may be required if the cervical arteries are transected and do not respond to outpatient hemostatic procedures. Informed consent must be obtained.

A nonconducting speculum is used for the examination. A colposcopic evaluation is performed to delineate the entire transformation zone and visualize the extent of the lesion with 5% acetic acid. Half-strength Lugol's solution can be applied after the acetic acid examination to stain the epithelium for the procedure. A paracervical block or an intramucosal block provides equal anesthesia for the procedure.

LEEP removes the specimen in one piece, allowing cytological examination to examine the specimen for invasion. The procedure is performed under local anesthesia and can take less than 15 minutes (23).

The loop is placed a few millimeters above the cervix and lateral to lesion or edge of TZ. The current is applied before it touches the cervix or there will be a greater chance of thermal injury. The loop is pushed to a depth of 5 to 8 mm, then drawn slowly through tissue until loop is 5 mm past the edge of TZ then removed perpendicularly to avoid injury to vaginal tissue (24). The tissue specimen is hat- or button-shaped, approximately 1.5 cm in diameter and 0.8 cm in depth. The cervix is usually healed within 1 month (3).

The loop size is chosen to fit the woman's transformation zone. Rarely is there a need to use a loop deeper than 8 or 10 mm. A dispersing pad is placed as close as possible to the vagina on the inner thigh to create as short a pathway as possible for the electricity to return to the generator. The generator is set at a wattage that will allow tissue vaporization, but not carbonization. Usually the wattage is between 30 and 50 watts. The current is set on a blended current. A smoke evacuator is operational. The excision is performed as seen in Figure 12.3.1.

Hemostasis must be obtained prior to removing the speculum. If there is little bleeding, the lateral rim and the specific bleeders can be cauterized with silver nitrate sticks. If the bleeding is persistent, a ferric subsulfate solution thickened into Monsel's solution can be applied with pressure until hemostasis is obtained. Alternatively, a 5-mm rollerball can be used to seal the cut surface. The current is changed to a pure current and the wattage may need to be increased as thermal artifact is now desired. The rollerball is held a few millimeters from the surface of the cut surface, and the electricity is allowed to arc to the tissue creating the hemostasis. The rollerball will only arc to dry tissue, making this method inappropriate if there is much bleeding that cannot be blotted immediately prior to sealing the surface.

Complications from LEEP include cervical stenosis in up to 3% of the cases, toxic shock syndrome, other infections, and cervical incompetence.

The cervix is healed in approximately 1 month. During the healing process the woman is asked not to have intercourse, douche, or use tampons to reduce the risk of infection. The lesions are eradicated approximately 95% of the time.

Laser Surgery

Laser has the same cure rate as cryosurgery and LEEP. The indications for laser are similar to LEEP: the entire transformation zone must be visualized by an experienced colposcopist; the entire lesion must be visualized colposcopically; there is no discrepancy between the cytology, colposcopy, and histology; there must be no suspicion of invasive cancer systemically; and/or the lesion extends into the canal where the suspicion of invasive cancer is low. The advantage that laser has over cryosurgery and the LEEP is that a lesion that extends peripherally out on the ectocervix approaching the vaginal walls can be ablated without destroying excessive healthy tissue.

Contraindications for laser include pregnancy, invasive squamous or glandular cancer, and any lesion in which thermal artifact could obscure the diagnosis of invasion.

There are two distinct uses for laser. The first is an ablation in which the tissue is vaporized and the crater seared for hemostasis. This method is similar to cryosurgery because there is no tissue specimen for histologic confirmation that the lesion was entirely destroyed. The second is an excisional method in which the laser acts as a knife to cut a conization specimen. The most often cited problem with laser cones is the extremely charred specimen that does not allow the margins to be evaluated.

Laser surgery should be performed by those who have had training in the physics of laser surgery and have been proctored extensively in the technique. Complications of laser therapy are similar to LEEP.

Cold Knife Conization

Cold knife conization is the oldest and traditional method for treating a woman with dysplasia. The indications for cold knife conization are included in Table 12.3.4. There are no contraindications to a cold knife conization. Complications include hemorrhage especially if done during pregnancy to rule out invasion, cervical stenosis, cervical incompetence, and infection.

Positive Margins

With LEEP, laser, and cold knife conizations, a tissue specimen is evaluated to confirm the presence of disease found colposcopically at biopsy. Both LEEP and laser can have thermal artifact obscuring the cone margins, depending on the skill of the operator. The advantage

Table 12.3.4. Indications for Cold Knife Conization

- An abnormal endocervical curettage specimen
- Microinvasion on colposcopically directed biopsy
- Discrepancy between the cytology, the colposcopy, and the histology of the abnormality especially if the cytology was high grade or suggestive of cancer that was not confirmed at colposcopy
- The lesion extends far into the endocervical canal
- Cytologic or biopsy evidence of CIN II/III, HSIL, severe dysplasia

of a cold knife conization is that the margins are available to be clearly read.

If the cone margins are positive for residual disease after the loop electrosurgical excision procedure, laser excision, or cold knife conization, the woman must be followed with an endocervical curettage and cytology 4 months after the procedure, and if normal, with Pap smears every 4 months for the first 2 years and every 6 months to yearly thereafter. Between 50 and 78% of women with positive cone margins were found to have residual intraepithelial lesions or invasive cancer at the time of hysterectomy. More importantly, one study looked at the recurrence rate of CIS in women who had a conization procedure and found that up to 30% had a recurrence of the CIS if the margins were positive, but only a 3% recurrence if the margins were negative.

Other Surgeries

Hysterectomy is not indicated for an intraepithelial lesion alone. If there are other noncancerous abnormalities with the uterus that warrant a hysterectomy, treating the intraepithelial lesion with hysterectomy at the same time is appropriate. If the woman no longer desires fertility and she has positive cone margins, then a hysterectomy is appropriate.

A woman desiring a permanent method of sterilization, such as a bilateral tubal ligation, must have a current normal Pap smear. If her cytology is abnormal, she must undergo a colposcopic examination to ensure that her disease is not microinvasive or frankly invasive. Permanent sterilization can then be accomplished by the radical hysterectomy appropriate for treatment of her cancer.

Posthysterectomy Screening

If the woman had her hysterectomy for any cancerous reason, then yearly vaginal smears are recommended. The incidence of vaginal cancer is rare. When it does occur, more than half of the cancers are located in the upper third of the vagina, approximately 30% are in the lower vagina and a small number present in the middle-third. If the pathology report on the uterus from the woman's hysterectomy indicates no high grade or cancerous cervical disease, then increasing the vaginal screening interval to every 3 years is appropriate in low-risk women.

Older Women

Screening for cervical cancer in older women is controversial and its benefits uncertain. There have been few studies on cervical cytological abnormalities or cervical cancer's natural history that have included older women, and upper age limits for screening have not been universally suggested.

Between the ages of 45 and 65 years, screening for cervical cancer should probably follow the recommendations for younger women. Once a woman has two or three normal screening Pap smears, the screening can be done at longer intervals, perhaps every 3 years. If the woman has had a hysterectomy, the indications for vaginal Pap smears are vague. However, regular bimanual examinations, especially if the woman still has ovaries, continue to be important.

Special Considerations for Nurse Practitioners and Physician Assistants

Cervical cancer is related to several social and physical factors, including multiple interactions of viral products (particularly HPV) and circulating nicotine metabolites. Women can be educated about protecting themselves from the development of cervical carcinoma through specific protective actions, including using condoms, practicing abstinence, delaying first intercourse, screening partners, practicing monogamy, and stopping smoking (25, 26).

Frequent screenings might help reduce false-negative rates in high-risk women (27). However, access to adequate screening and follow-up is limited for many groups of women, especially women who do not seek health care unless they are experiencing an acute illness. Consideration should be given to screening women during acute care and other nongynecologic visits if they are not likely or able to return for health maintenance visits. Every visit can be viewed as an opportunity for education and encouragement for screenings (25). Community-wide education and screening programs to reach women who would otherwise not receive care must give attention to the cultural background of the women they hope to reach. Depending on their cultural environment, women may have differing beliefs about health, fate, pain, and touch. If community efforts are to be successful, then members of the group to be reached must be involved through consultation, focus groups, or other means (28).

All health care providers, including office and clinic staff, can help ensure optimal sampling for the Pap smear. Routine screenings should be scheduled, if possible, at midcycle and women told not to douche, use vaginal medications, or have intercourse for 24 to 48 hours before the screening. Screenings are not scheduled during the woman's menses or if she is experiencing bleeding. However, if the woman is unlikely to return at another time (or if the practitioner is concerned about abnormal bleeding), the smear can be collected (25, 26).

At the time of the Pap smear, the clinician should explain what the Pap smear is and the range of results that might be reported. Women also need to know the limitations of the Pap smear, for example, that it does not test for uterine cancer. Ideally, abnormal results are discussed with the woman by the clinician who performed the examination (23). A system of record-keeping must be instituted to ensure that there is follow-up and communication of results for all Pap smears.

A woman who has an abnormal Pap smear needs compassionate and continuing care. Although cervical cancer is linked to STDs, telling a woman with invasive cancer that her condition was caused by an STD may sound to her like an accusation of promiscuity and create an unnecessary burden of guilt at a time when she is dealing with her immediate fears related to cancer, treatment, and even death (25). However, avoidance of STDs will have to be discussed at some point in order for a woman to take actions to reduce her risk for recurrence. Providers need to emphasize the multifactoral etiology of the disease, including unknown factors.

Referrals, consultations, and follow-up will depend on site-specific policies. Depending on the site resources and the expertise of the practitioner, colposcopy, and curettage, if indicated, may be performed by the practitioner or the woman may be referred. Referral to a physician is mandatory if malignancy is indicated (30). When the woman needs referral for more definitive diagnosis and management, the primary care provider can explain possible treatment modalities and continue to be available for support and to meet other health care needs.

The woman with a negative Pap smear deserves the same teaching regarding protective actions. In addition, the clinician must view a negative Pap smear with skepticism if there are worrisome history or examination findings, e.g., abnormal cervical contours, lesions, unexplained postcoital bleeding. In these cases, further testing should be done (25).

References

1. Richart RM, Wright TC. Controversies in the management of low-grade cervical intraepithelial neoplasia. Cancer Suppl 1993;71:1413–1421.
2. Anderson GH, Benedet JL, Le Riche JC, Matisic JP, Thompson JE. Invasive cancer of the cervix in British

Columbia: a review of the demography and screening histories of 437 cases seen from 1985–1988. Obstet Gynecol 1992;80:1–4.

3. Loop electrosurgical excision procedures gaining acceptance for cervical intraepithelial neoplasia JAMA 1991;266:460–461.

4. Hollingworth T, Barton S. The natural history of early cervical neoplasia and cervical human papillomavirus infection. Cancer Surv 1988;7:519–527.

5. Stenkvist B, Bergstrom R, Eklund G, Fox CH. Papanicolaou smear screening and cervical cancer: what can you expect? JAMA 1984;252:1423–1428.

6. Anderson MC, Brown CL, et al. Current views on cervical intraepithelial neoplasia. J Clin Pathol 1991; 44:969–978.

7. Nelson JH, Averette HE, Richart RM. Cervical intraepithelial neoplasia (dysplasia and carcinoma in situ) and early invasive carcinoma. CA—A journal for clinicians 1989;39:157–178.

8. Slattery ML, Robison LM, et al. Cigarette smoking and exposure to passive smoke are risk factors for cervical cancer. JAMA 1989;261:1593–1603.

9. Fink DJ. Change in American Cancer Society checkup guidelines for detection of cervical cancer. CA Cancer J Clin 1988;38:127–128.

10. Kjaer SK, Dahl C, Engholm G, Bock JE, Lynge E, Jensen OM. Case-control study of risk factors for cervical neoplasia in Denmark. II: Role of sexual activity, reproductive factors, and veneral infections. Cancer Causes Control 1992;3:339–348.

11. Koutsky LA, Holmes KK, Critchlow CW, Stevens CE, Paavonen J, Beckmann AM. A cohort study of the risk of cervical intraepithelial neoplasia grade 2 or 3 in relation to papillomavirus infection. N Engl J Med 1992;327:1272–1278.

12. Koss LG. The Papanicolaou test for cervical cancer detection: a triumph and a tragedy. JAMA 1989; 261:737–743.

13. Bearman DM, MacMillan JP, Creasman WT. Papanicolaou smear history of patients developing cervical cancer: an assessment of screening protocols. Obstet Gynecol 1987;69:151–155.

14. Cox TJ, Schiffman MH, Winzelberg AJ, Patterson JM. An evaluation of human papillomavirus testing as part of referral to colposcopy clinics. Obstet Gynecol 1992;80:389–395.

15. Pretorius RG, Sadeghi M, Fotheringham N, Semrad N, Watring WG. A randomized trial of three methods of obtaining papanicolaou smears. Obstet Gynecol 1991;78:831–836.

16. Noda K. Cervical Intraepithelial neoplasia and microinvasive carcinoma of the cervix. Curr Top Pathol 1985:57–79.

17. Johnson LD, Nickerson RJ, Easterday CL, Stuart RS, Hertig AT. Epidemiological evidence for the spectrum of change from dysplasia through carcinoma in situ to invasive cancer. Cancer 1968;22:901–914.

18. Nasiell K, Nasiell M, Vaclavinkova V. Behavior of moderate cervical dysplasia during long-term followup. Obstet Gynecol 1983;61:609–614.

19. Nasiell K, Roger V, Nasiell M. Behavior of mild cervical dysplasia during long-term follow-up. Obstet Gynecol 1986;67:665–669.

20. Kudo R. Cervical adenocarcinoma. Curr Top Pathol 1985;85:81–111.

21. Hopkins MP, Roberts JA, Schmidt RW. Cervical adenocarcinoma in situ. Obstet Gynecol 1988;71:842–844.

22. Campion MH, Brown JR, et al. Psychosexual trauma of an abnormal cervical smear. Br J Obstet Gynaecol 1988;95:175–181.

23. Luesley D, Cullimore J. The treatment of cervical intraepithelial neoplasia. Cancer Surv 1988;7:529–545.

24. Clavert JF, Rosenfeld JA. Office gynecology. Monograph Edition No. 179. Home Study Self-Assessment program. Kansas City, MO: American Academy of Family Physicians, April 1994.

25. Cain JM. Etiology and screening of cervical cancer. Primary Care Update OB/Gyn 1994;1:235–240.

26. Griffin J. Abnormal pap test results: meaning and management. ADVANCE Nurse Pract 1995;3:16–21.

27. Schaffer SD, Philput CB. Predictors of abnormal cervical cytology: statistical analysis of human papillomavirus and cofactors. Nurse Pract 1992;17:46–50.

28. Varricchio CG. Issues to consider when planning cancer control interventions for women. Women's Health Issues 1995;4:64–72.

29. Rubin MM, Lauver D. Assessment and management of cervical intraepithelial neoplasia. Nurse Pract 1990;15:23–31.

30. Hanson LN. Abnormal cervical cytology. In: Star WL, Lommel LL, Shannon MT, eds. Women's Primary Health Care. Washington, DC: American Nurses Association, 1995:13–17.

12.4

Endometrial Cancer

Jo Ann Rosenfeld

Epidemiology

Endometrial carcinoma (EC), cancer of the body of the uterus, is the fourth most common cancer in women and the most common gynecological cancer (1). It occurs in over 31,000 women per year and it caused nearly 6000 deaths in 1994 (2). Luckily, most endometrial cancer is found early while it is at stage I; when found early, it has a survival rate of approximately 90% (1). Thus, appropriate evaluation and treatment by the primary provider is essential.

Risk Factors

Hormonal Risk Factors

The greatest risk factor for EC is postmenopausal unopposed estrogen use, which increases the risk of EC fivefold (3). The risk is higher with higher doses of estrogen replacement therapy, and persists even up to 5 years after discontinuation of use. Unopposed estrogen use causes endometrial hyperplasia that leads to EC. Women who develop endometrial hyperplasia, usually from ERT use (see Chapter 20), have a higher incidence of endometrial carcinoma. The histological diagnosis of endometrial adenomatous hyperplasia on a biopsy or endometrial currettage carries a 25% risk of developing EC; with the diagnosis of "atypia" on a biopsy, the risk rises to 50% (1). However, with concurrent use of progesterone, the rate of EC falls to nearly that of women not taking ERT.

Women with other high-estrogen states, such as those with polycystic ovary disease, have an increased incidence of EC, especially at younger ages. Early menarche, late menopause, nulliparity, and infertility have also been linked with an increased risk of developing EC (4). The relative risk for EC in a nulliparous woman is 2.8 and 2.4 for a woman with early menarche (4).

Surprisingly, however, use of oral contraceptives (OCPs) is protective, reducing the risk of both concurrent and subsequent EC (1, 5). The relative risk of EC in OCP users is 0.4, as compared to women who never used OCPs (6, 7). Use of IUDs may also be protective, with an odds ratio of developing EC 0.32 in IUD users (8). Whether injectable or implantable progestins affect EC risk is presently not known.

Other Risk Factors

Risk factors for EC include increasing age, post-menopausal state, and obesity, possibly because of chronic high levels of estrogen (1). Ninety-five percent of cases of EC occur in women over age 40 years and 75% in women over age 55 years (9). Weighing over 200 lbs has a relative risk of 7.2 for EC, as compared to a woman weighing less than 125 lbs (4). Lack of physical activity has also been linked to EC (10).

Other risk factors include diabetes mellitus (DM) and hypertension. There is a 2.8 times greater incidence of EC in women with DM (11). Over half the women with EC have hypertension, although the increased risk disappears when weight is controlled (4). Women with other cancers, especially those of the breast, colon, and thyroid, have a slight increase in endometrial cancer (Table 12.4.1).

Table 12.4.1. Risk Factors for Endometrial Carcinoma

High estrogen states
    Polycystic ovary disease
    Obesity
    Unopposed estrogen therapy
Menopausal state
Age over 55 years
Diabetes
Hypertension
Lack of physical activity
Cancer of colon, breast, or thyroid

Clinical Presentation

The most common presentation of endometrial carcinoma is postmenopausal bleeding (PMB); 90% of women with EC present with PMB. This presentation is usually early in the course of the cancer, and thus usually promises a good prognosis. Twenty-five percent of women with PMB have EC and its presence demands a complete evaluation. Ten to 20% have hyperplasia, endometrial polyps, or fibroids. In up to 60% percent of women with PMB, no cause is ever found. Other symptoms including bladder problems, urinary incontinence, and pelvic pain may occur.

Evaluation of Postmenopausal Bleeding

The physical examination of the woman with PMB should include a complete abdominal examination. A pelvic examination may discover other causes of bleeding such as fibroids, cervicitis, cervical polyps, trauma, and vaginal warts. Uterine size, tenderness, and adnexal masses or tenderness should be noted.

A hemoglobin level or hematocrit, erythrocyte sedimentation rate, and bleeding studies are often indicated to discover the degree of hemorrhage. A Papanicolaou test only picks up 20% of EC, but it is a good first step in the evaluation.

Surgical procedures, typically a dilation and curettage (D&C), are the conservative and traditional method of evaluating post-menopausal bleeding. A D&C is definitive, definitely ruling in or out cancer, but it is invasive, painful, and often requires a hospital stay, even if short. Although D&Cs can diagnose endometrial cancer, they can miss other causes such as fibroids.

Hysteroscopy, now occasionally an office procedure, can be used to identify lesions such as fibroids or polyps within the uterine cavity that may be causing PMB. Although it cannot rule out cancer, hysteroscopy would be a useful adjunct with a negative D&C or negative endometrial biopsy, although further studies are necessary. It is usually well tolerated.

However, recently, endometrial biopsies by a variety of instruments have been performed in the office with good specificity and sensitivity (up to 97%). These can be done quickly, at the first office visit, and may require only psychoanesthesia or a paracervical block. There are fewer complications and less pain.

There are several different tools for office endometrial sampling. The Novak or 14-inch Kervorkian metal curettes (12, 13), or the Pipelle plastic curettes all achieve good histologic specimens, although the Pipelle causes less pain (14). The Kervorkian is a 14-inch narrow (4-mm wide) metal instrument with a slightly curved sharpened curette-like end (2-mm wide). The Pipelle is a flexible polypropene suction aspirette (3.1-mm wide). All tools produced adquate speciments that correctly identified the tumor grade when compared to specimens from D&C (15).

However, endometrial sampling only avoids a D&C in women who prove to have cancer. Alone, sampling is only sufficient if the diagnosis is positive for carcinoma. Sampling may miss the carcinoma. A negative sample still requires a subsequent D&C to rule out carcinoma, with or without use of hysteroscope for diagnosis of fibroids or endometrial polyps.

Lately, the endometrial sampling by any of the curettes, combined with transvaginal ultrasound to determine endometrial lining thickness, may be adequate to rule out carcinoma,

making a D&C unnecessary in some women. A multicenter Nordic study of almost 1200 women with PMB found that if the endometrial lining measured less than or equal to 4 mm when measured by transvaginal ultrasound, the risk of cancer was only 5.5%. Women with endometrial carcinoma had an average endometrial lining thickness of 21.1 ± 11.8 mm. No malignancy was found in women with endometrial lining thicknesses of less than 5 mm. This study suggests that in a woman with a thin lining (≤ 4 mm) and negative endometrial biopsy a D&C may not be necessary (16).

Staging of Endometrial Carcinoma

The predictor of outcome and the determination of extent and type of radiation therapy necessary is the stage of the disease at diagnosis (see Table 12.4.2). A consensus by FIGO (International Federation of Gynecology and Obstetrics) created a surgical staging system in which poor histological differentiation, involvement of cervix, depth of invasion of myometrium, and spread beyond the uterus are poorer prognostic signs. EC spreads usually locally through the myometrium, and then into other gynecological organs before local metastases, and only finally to distant metastases.

Stage I is limited to the endometrium, with stage IB including invasion of less than half the myometrium, or IC over half the my-

Table 12.4.2. Classification and Prognosis of Endometrial Carcinoma

Stage	Definition	Five-year Survival (%)
Stage I	Disease limited to the endometrium	72
Stage IB	including invasion of less than half the myometrium	
Stage IC	over half the myometrium	
Stage IIA	Only endocervical involvement	56
Stage IIB	invasion of cervical stroma	
Stage III	Invasion in serosa, adnexa, or vagina	32
Stage IV	Bowel, bladder, or distant metastases	11

ometrium. Stage I has an overall 5-year survival of 72%, but this can approach 100% if the pathology appears well differentiated, or can decrease to only 50% with poorly differentiated carcinoma (1). However, 10% of women with stage I EC have occult ovarian metastases at the time of diagnosis.

Stage IIA includes endocervical involvement, whereas stage IIB indicates invasion of cervical stroma. Stage II has a 5-year survival of 56%. Stage III is tumor invasion in serosa, adnexa, or vagina, with a 5-year survival of 32%, whereas stage IV indicates bowel, bladder, or distant metastases, and has a 5-year survival of 11%. Survival prediction can be improved or worsened by degree of differentiation of the tumor (1).

Certain molecular biological markers and DNA analyses may have prognostic significance for endometrial cancers. Women with endometrial cancers negative for expression of p53 gene had a 90% 5-year survival, as compared to 12% in women who have an overexpression of p53 (17). Thirty percent of endometrial carcinomas were aneuploid and these had a poorer prognosis. However, these markers require further investigation.

Treatment

The treatment for EC is total abdominal hysterectomy with bilateral oophosalpingectomy. Often adjunctive pelvic radiation is suggested. Stage IA diseases requires no further therapy. However, two thirds of recurrences occur within 3 years, so women with EC should be followed closely.

However, in women with stage I disease and poor risk factors, radiation is suggested because 14% will have vaginal wall recurrences. This can reduce the recurrence rate to 2%. In patients with higher stage carcinoma including myometrial invasion, spread to the cervix, or poorly differentiated carcinoma, whole pelvic radiation is suggested. If found to have periaortic node metastases, wider field radiation may be necessary.

Progestins have been used to shrink the tumor, including DES. Recently, in the United Kingdom gonadotropin-releasing hormone analogs (leuprorelin 7.5 mg depot monthly) were used in women with recurrent EC who often had metastases beyond the pelvis. In a small study, 6 out of 17 women had a partial response (18). Chemotherapy, only used as palliation, has also been used, including 5-fluorouracil, doxorubicin, and cyclophosphamide.

Conclusion

Endometrial cancer is a serious cause of cancer in women that often presents as postmenopausal bleeding at early stages and has a good long-term prognosis. Evaluation with a D&C, or possibly endometrial biopsy and transvaginal ultrasound with close follow-up, are sufficient. Treatment is surgical, often with radiation, with chemotherapy used only for palliation of recurrent or metastatic disease. By vigorously evaluating PMB, providers may affect the woman's prognosis significantly.

Special Considerations for Nurse Practitioners and Physician Assistants

Treatment of endometrial cancer involves surgery that alters the genital anatomy, possibly leading to damaging psychosexual consequences for some women. In a review of the literature, Bachmann (19) discusses several possible consequences, including depression, worries about accelerated aging and loss of femininity, and concern about the loss of childbearing ability even in women who do not want more children. Negative changes may occur because of the surgery itself, preexisting depression, and fears and myths about surgery. In contrast, other studies have indicated that removal of the uterus involves no extra psychological risks, and in fact, an improvement in sexual functioning occurs in the majority of women (19). Primary care providers, along with the specialists to whom women are referred, must consider women's psychological makeup and educational needs preoperatively.

Women's concerns about cancer and reproductive surgery continue after the immediate postoperative period. Practitioners in the primary care setting should not neglect to ask women about their adjustment and elicit any continuing fallacies and misconceptions. How a woman describes her surgery (e.g., "they took everything out") may reflect the woman's body image. Providers should avoid such expressions such as these that can have negative connotations (20).

Women may not have incorporated or understood the preoperative and postoperative teaching done during the time surrounding surgery. Some may not realize that they will no longer menstruate or erroneously believe that the vagina was removed or sewn shut (20). Others may not know if their ovaries were removed or left in place. Symptoms such as vaginal dryness, hot flashes, and decreased sex drive may be caused by removal of the ovaries or impaired ovarian function and can be alleviated. Woman who have had surgery may need help understanding instructions about intercourse and other forms of sexual expression, even after they have been released by their surgeon. Provider-initiated sexual assessment and counseling should continue, with specific instructions, if needed, related to position changes, tenderness and other sensations, and lubrication (20, 21)

Primary providers might also give the woman information about community organizations and health professionals who deal with women's issues if this has not been previously done (19). In addition, for those women with more long-term needs, home care with a multidisciplinary approach is an option for infusion therapy, symptom palliation, nutrition, chemotherapy, and hospice care (22).

References

1. Von Gruenigen VE, Karlen JR. Carcinoma of the endometrium. Am Fam Phys 1995;51:1531–1536.
2. Boring CC, Squires TS, Tong T. Cancer statistics, 1994. CA Cancer Clin J 1994;44:7–26.
3. Persson I, Adami HO, Bergkvist L, et al. Risk of endometrial cancer after treatment with oestrogens alone of in conjunction with progesterone: results of a prospective study. Br Med J 1989;298:147–151.
4. Brinton LA, Berman ML, Morel R, et al. Reproductive, menstrual and medical risk factors for endometrial cancer: results from a case control study. Am J Obstet Gynecol 1992;167:1317–1325.
5. The Cancer and Steroid Hormone Study of the Centers for Disease Control and the National Institute of Child Health and Human Development. Combination oral contraceptive use and the risk of endometrial cancer. JAMA 1987;257:796–800.
6. Stanford JL, Brinton LA, Berman ML, et al. Oral contraceptives and endometrial cancer: do other risk factors modify the association? Int J Cancer 1993;54:243–248.
7. Schlesselman JJ. Net effect of oral contraceptive use on the risk of cancer in women in the United States. Obstet Gynecol 1995;85:793–801.
8. Catestllsague X, Thompson WD, Dubrow R. Intrauterine contraception and the risk of endometrial cancer. Int J Cancer 1993;54:911–916.
9. Pacheco JC, Kempers RD. Etiology of postmenopausal bleeding. Obstet Gynecol 1968;32:40–46.
10. Sturgeon SR, Brinton LA, Berman ML, et al. Past and present physical activity and endometrial cancer risk. Br J Cancer 1993;68:584–589.
11. MacMahon B. Risk factors for endometrial cancer. Gynecol Oncol 1974;2:122–129.
12. Ferenczy A, Shore M, Guralnick M, Gelfand MM. The Kevorkian curette. An appraisal of its effectiveness in endometrial evaluation. Obstet Gynecol 1979;54:262–267.
13. Oliveira MM, Farias-Eisner RP, Pitkin RM. Endocervical sampling by Kervorkian curette or pipelle aspiration device: a randomized comparison. Am J Obstet Gynecol 1995;172:1889–1894.
14. Stovall TG, Ling FW, Morgan PL. A prospective randomized comparison of the Pipelle endometrial sampling device with the Novak currette. Am J Obstet Gynecol 1991;165:1287–1290.
15. Larson DM, Johnson KK, Broste SK, Krawisz BR, Kresl JJ. Comparison of D&C and office endometrial

biopsy in predicting final histopathological grade in endometrial cancer. Obstet Gynecol 1995;86:38–42.

16. Karlsson B, Granberg S, Wikland M, et al. Transvaginal ultrasonography of the endometrium in women with postmenopausal bleeding—a Nordic multicenter study. Am J Obstet Gynecol 1995;172:1488–1494.

17. Pisani AL, Barbuto DA, Chen D, et al. HER-2/neu, p53, and DNA analyses as prognosticators for survival in endometrial carcinoma. Obstet Gynecol 1995;85:729–734.

18. Gallagher CJ, Oliver RTD, Oram DH, et al. A new treatment for endometrial cancer with gonadotrophin releasing hormone analogue. Br J Obstet Gynecol 1991;98:1037–1041.

19. Bachmann GA. Psychosexual aspects of hysterectomy. Women's Health Issues 1990;1:41–49.

20. Williamson ML. Sexual adjustment after hysterectomy. JOGNN 1992;21:42–47.

21. Bernhard LA. Sexual counseling of women having gynecologic surgical procedures. AWHONN's Clinical Issues Perinatal Women's Health Nurs 1993;4:250–257.

22. Lowdermilk DL. Home care of the patient with gynecologic cancer. JOGNN 1995;24:157–163.

12.5

Ovarian Cancer

Rick D. Kellerman

"Please, someone, protect me from this cancer."
—Gilda Radner,
It's Always Something, 1989 (1).

Introduction

Since the death of comedienne Gilda Radner from ovarian cancer, increased attention has been focused on the causes, risk factors, screening, and treatment of this lethal disease. In 1995, approximately 26,600 women in the United States were newly diagnosed with ovarian cancer and 13,200 American women died

of the disease (2). The overall 5-year survival for white American women is 42% and for black American women is 38% (2). This low survival rate is partly attributed to the fact that 80% of women with ovarian cancer are diagnosed at advanced stages of the disease (3). When diagnosed and treated at the earliest stages, 5-year survival rates approach 100% (4).

Primary care physicians who treat women will invariably be asked questions about ovarian cancer and its early diagnosis, and most will be involved in the treatment of women with ovarian cancer. Especially important is

479

the understanding of clinical signs and symptoms, risk factors, screening options, and prognosis.

Pathology and Staging

Ovarian cancer is not just one entity. The ovarian cancers can be categorized into three major groups: epithelial, germ cell, and stromal tumors. Epithelial tumors account for more than 80% of reported cases and may be further categorized by cell types. These include (*a*) papillary serous tumors (the most common ovarian cancer), (*b*) clear cell, which because of its relative insensitivity to chemotherapy has the worst total prognosis, (*c*) mucinous, which is often associated with normal or minimally elevated CA-125 levels, (*d*) endometrioid, which may be associated with endometriosis and endometrial cancer, and (*e*) ovarian tumor of low malignant potential, an intermediate form of epithelial ovarian cancer that is usually associated with a good prognosis, whatever the stage (5–7).

Germ cell tumors account for less than 5% of ovarian cancers and are most common in young women. Stromal tumors are rare with unpredictable biologic behavior (5).

Accurate staging is critical in developing a treatment plan and offering prognostic information. Appropriate surgical referral by the primary care physician is essential. One study has shown that improved survival outcomes are obtained when the primary surgery for ovarian cancer is performed by gynecologic oncologists or obstetrician-gynecologists, as compared to general surgeons (8). Adequate staging may be dependent on surgical specialty of the operator. McGowan et al. reported that 97% of women staged by gynecologic oncologists were adequately staged, compared to 52% by obstetrician-gynecologists and 35% by general surgeons (9). One multicenter group reported that only 25% of women evaluated by restaging laparotomy had an initial surgical incision judged adequate to allow complete examination of the abdomen and pelvis (10).

Ovarian cancer is divided into four stages (Table 12.5.1). Stage I defines disease limited to the ovaries. Stage II is disease extension limited to the true pelvis. Stage III has tumor implants in the abdomen, superficially on the liver, and/or positive retroperitoneal or inguinal nodes. Stage IV is distant metastatic disease, including pleural disease and parenchymal liver metastasis (11).

Tumor grade affects prognosis. Well-differentiated tumors have a better prognosis than intermediately differentiated or poorly differentiated tumors (12).

The 5-year survival, depending on the histologic type of carcinoma, grade, and substage, ranges from 70 to 100% for stage I, 60 to 70% for stage II, 20 to 30% for stage III, and about 10% for stage IV disease. For any given patient, however, the statistic for survival or cure is a dichotomy: 0 or 100% (4, 7, 13, 14).

Table 12.5.1–Staging of Ovarian Cancer and 5-Year Survival

Stage	Disease Extension	5-year Survival (%)
Stage I	Disease limited to the ovaries	70-100
Stage II	Disease extension limited to the true pelvis	60-70
Stage III	Tumor implants in the abdomen, superficially on the liver and/or positive retroperitoneal or inguinal nodes	20-30
Stage IV	Distant metastatic disease including pleural disease and parenchymal liver metastasis	10

Clinical Presentation

Many women with ovarian cancer have no symptoms. Others have only vague complaints of abdominal fullness, pelvic pressure, low backache, nausea, early satiety, constipation, and gas. Women with more advanced disease may present with weight loss, cachexia, intra-abdominal mass, ascites, pleural effusion, or intestinal obstruction. Rarely, women may present with a torsed ovary, a newly developed umbilical hernia or an umbilical lymph node known as Sister Mary Joseph's node, or brain metastasis. Unfortunately, the patient's complaints are more common and more severe when the tumor has already spread beyond the pelvis (5, 7, 14).

Various paraneoplastic conditions may be associated with ovarian cancer. Hypercalcemia may be humorally mediated and is more often associated with clear-cell ovarian cancer (15, 16). Cerebellar degeneration associated with symptoms of vertigo and imbalance, the new onset of seborrheic keratosis (Leser-Trelat sign), and chronic disseminated intravascular coagulation known as Trousseau's syndrome have all been associated with ovarian cancer (7, 17, 18).

Most women diagnosed with early ovarian cancer are asymptomatic. Their disease, when identified, is found during routine pelvic examination. The pelvic examination may reveal an ovarian mass in a premenopausal woman or a palpable ovary in a postmenopausal woman. Because the normal ovary of a postmenopausal women is less than 1 cm in its longest diameter, a palpable ovary in a postmenopausal woman is considered ovarian carcinoma until proven otherwise (6, 7, 14).

Evaluating a Pelvic Mass

In the premenopausal woman, most pelvic masses will not be ovarian carcinoma. A pelvic mass discovered in a postmenopausal woman is much more suspicious for ovarian cancer.

The differential diagnosis of a pelvic mass is lengthy and includes benign ovarian pathology including (a) functional cysts and endometriosis, (b) fallopian tube abnormalities such as tubo-ovarian abscesses and hydrosalpinx, (c) ectopic pregnancy, (d) uterine fibroids, (e) bowel pathology such as appendicitis, (f) diverticulitis, (g) inflammatory bowel disease, (h) colon cancer, and (i) other varied findings such as pelvic kidney, urachal cyst, distended bladder, retroperitoneal neoplasms, and abdominal wall masses. Palpation of the enlarged uterus of pregnancy may be mistaken for an adnexal mass (19).

One approach to evaluation of a pelvic mass is given in Figure 12.5.1. If ovarian cancer is high on the list of differential diagnosis, preoperative complete blood cell count multichemistry profile, and chest radiograph are suggested as part of the preoperative work-up (5). Preoperative bowel preparation is indicated because of the possible necessity for bowel resection (5).

The need for MRI, CT, IVP, and barium enema preoperatively must be assessed on a case-by-case basis (5). Extensive preoperative imaging adds little useful information, unless other organ involvement is specifically suspected. Although ultrasound helps differentiate benign from neoplastic ovarian tumors, there is overlap of sonographic diagnostic feature. Ultrasound has not been useful in assessing the extent of neoplastic disease in women with known ovarian cancer (20).

Treatment of Ovarian Cancer

The provider should manage the care of women with ovarian cancer in consultation with qualified gynecologic oncologists and gynecologic surgeons. Once cancer of the ovary is diagnosed, it is important to provide realistic treatment options, with special attention to quality of life concerns and appropriate psychological

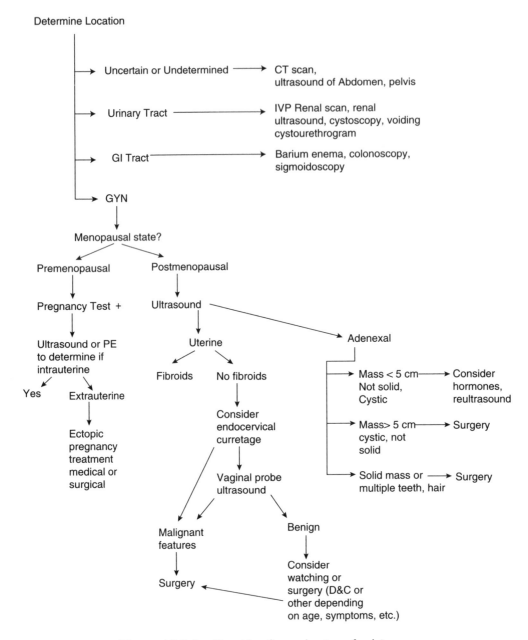

Figure 12.5.1   Algorithm for evaluation of pelvic mass.

support and counseling. Women will have individual preferences for vigorous versus limited treatment protocols (5).

Surgical Treatment

Mainstays of current medical treatment of epithelial ovarian cancer include aggressive cytoreductive surgery ("debulking") and chemotherapy. When epithelial ovarian cancer has been diagnosed, total abdominal hysterectomy, bilateral salpingo-oopherectomy, omentectomy, biopsy of any gross lesions, and collection of ascites or peritoneal washings are recommended. Biopsy of retroperitoneal lymph nodes may also be performed (5, 7). "Second-look" laparotomy is suggested only if the findings at surgery would contribute to management or are part of a research protocol (5, 7).

Chances for cure and prolonged survival are inversely proportional to the amount of diseased tissue left after aggressive "debulking" surgery. Women with stage III or IV ovarian cancer whose largest residual tumor implants were under 0.5 cm in diameter have a median survival of 40 months, whereas those with tumor implants of 0.5 to 1.5 cm in diameter have a median survival of 18 months. Those with implants over 1.5 cm have a median survival of 6 months (21, 22).

In highly select situations, young women with early-stage disease who wish to remain fertile may elect unilateral salpingo-oophorectomy (5, 23).

Chemotherapy

For many women, precise recommendations for postoperative adjuvant chemotherapy do not exist (5). When adjuvant chemotherapy is recommended, cisplatin plus cyclophosphamide, carboplatin plus cyclophosphamide, or cisplatin plus paclitaxel (Taxol) are combinations frequently prescribed (5, 7).

Future treatment protocols may involve instillation of intraperitoneal chemotherapy, high-dose chemotherapy, autologous bone marrow transplantation after myeloablative chemotherapy, tumor-directed antibodies conjugated with toxins or radioisotopes, and new chemotherapeutic agents (7).

Follow-Up and Postoperative Treatment

For asymptomatic women who have completed surgical and chemotherapeutic treatment protocols, follow-up is generally performed every 3 to 4 months for the first 2 years. An interval history, physical including rectovaginal pelvic examination, and CA-125 are performed at each visit. This combination has been shown to detect disease progression in 90% of women with recurrent epithelial ovarian cancer. After 2 years of stable findings, less frequent follow-up examinations can be scheduled. Of course, the personal needs of individual women for more frequent follow-up must be considered (5).

For women with an elevated CA-125 level prior to surgery, a rising CA-125 level during follow-up is a reliable predictor of relapse. However, a stable low CA-125 level does not exclude relapse (5). Interval routine follow-up with radiological imaging techniques has not been shown to improve the detection of recurrence (5).

Complications

Complications of surgery for ovarian cancer include bleeding, infection, pulmonary embolism, urologic, and bowel injury. Small bowel obstruction may occur from either the tumor itself or as a complication of surgery and/or radiation therapy, and may be a frustrating recurrent problem. Appropriate nutritional support, attention to electrolyte status, judicious use of medications that adversely affect bowel peristalsis, and decompression by gastrotomy or nasogastric or long intestinal tubes may be required. In selected women, repeat surgery for relief of bowel obstruction and for palliation may be indicated (5, 14).

Women with ovarian cancer may develop massive ascites and pleural effusions, both of which may require drainage for relief of symptoms. Lower extremity edema from venous and lymphatic obstruction may develop and may be poorly responsive to therapy. Pain may be controlled with oral, rectal, transdermal, or patient-controlled intravenous pump analgesia (14).

The primary care physician must help provide appropriate emotional support, accurate information, and realistic expectations to the woman and her family.

Prevention and Screening

For women with only one or no first degree relatives with ovarian cancer, there is currently no evidence to support routine screening. With current technologies, there is no evidence that deaths from ovarian cancer are decreased by screening. False-positive results from inappropriate screening with current radiologic imaging technologies and tumor markers, may put women at risk for invasive procedures (e.g., laparotomy), unnecessary expense, and anxiety (5, 6, 24, 25).

Currently, no major professional organization recommends screening for ovarian cancer. The US Preventive Services Task Force says that "screening of asymptomatic women for ovarian cancer is not recommended. It is clinically prudent to examine the uterine adnexa when performing gynecologic examination for other reasons (26). The American Academy of Family Physicians, the American College of Obstetricians and Gynecologists, and the American College of Physicians do not advocate routine screening, although periodic pelvic examination is recommended (27–29).

Asymptomatic women who request screening for ovarian cancer should receive a detailed personal and family history, be counseled about their individual risk, and be educated about the limitations of screening with currently available technologies. For women who give a history suspicious of a hereditary ovarian cancer syndrome, referral to a gynecologic oncologist should be considered (25, 29). Some centers recommend routine screening protocols for women from families with hereditary ovarian cancer syndromes (30, 31).

Pelvic Examination

The routine pelvic examination has limitations in its ability to detect early ovarian cancers (32). Van Nagell et al. screened 1300 asymptomatic postmenopausal women with transvaginal ultrasound. Pelvic examination failed to detect the two stage I tumors that van Nagell identified by transvaginal ultrasound (33). Pelvic examination failed to detect the sole ovarian cancer identified by abdominal ultrasound in a study by Andolf et al. (34). The combination of interobserver variability and inadequate examination caused by woman body habitus makes the routine pelvic examination an imperfect screening tool for the detection of early pelvic masses.

Transabdominal Ultrasound

Although ultrasound is the preferred method for imaging of the female pelvis, its lack of specificity and positive predictive value make it unacceptable as a modality to screen women for ovarian cancer (15, 20, 32, 35). The specificity of four screening studies using transabdominal sonography ranged from 75 to 97% (25, 34, 36–38). In the largest study, Campbell et al. screened 5479 asymptomatic women annually for 3 years and detected 5 stage I ovarian cancers, out of 338 total abnormal screens. The odds of detecting primary ovarian cancer at surgery after an abnormal transabdominal ultrasound on these asymptomatic women were 1 in 67 (36).

These odds, the total low incidence of ovarian cancer, the costs of screening, and controversy about how to manage nonmalignant abnormal findings all argue against using transabdominal sonography for screening (35).

Transvaginal Ultrasound

Transvaginal ultrasound has better quality and resolution than transabdominal ultrasound. It also eliminates the need for the woman to have a full bladder. Transvaginal ultrasound may also lend itself to the development of a scoring system based on morphologic characteristics of the ovary that allows differentiation between benign and malignant tumors (39). The two largest ovarian cancer screening studies using transvaginal ultrasound showed specificity of 98% and 97% (33, 40). The low incidence of ovarian cancer in the general population, the lack of data showing that screening for ovarian cancer leads to improved survival, the unnecessary costs, and inconvenience relegate transvaginal ultrasound to the category of unproven experimental technology (33, 40).

Transvaginal Color-Flow Doppler Ultrasound

Ovarian cancers are characterized by the formation of new and abnormal vascularization that shows low impedance to blood flow (6). This characteristic may help improve the specificity of transvaginal ultrasound when it is combined with color-flow Doppler evaluation of ovarian blood flow (40, 41). However, transvaginal color-flow Doppler ultrasound is time-consuming and expensive (14). Its usefulness for screening of the general population is investigational and unconfirmed (6, 25).

Computed Tomography Scan

The usefulness of computed tomography (CT) scanning for early detection of ovarian cancer is limited by cost and the potential hazards of ionizing radiation and contrast media (6). CT scanning is limited in its ability to differentiate small tumors from surrounding normal tissue (42).

Tumor Markers

There are several biologic tumor markers associated with cancer of the ovary, the best known and studied being CA-125. CA-125 is a cell-surface antigen that is used to clinically monitor women with known epithelial ovarian cancer (43). Unfortunately, because it is elevated in only 80% of women with epithelial ovarian cancers, it is not sensitive enough to serve as a screening test (6, 25, 44, 45). CA-125 is nonspecific for ovarian cancer and may also be elevated in women with other malignancies such as lung, breast, colon, cervical, endometrial, and pancreas cancer. It may also be elevated in women with endometriosis, pelvic inflammatory disease, pregnancy, benign ovarian cysts, leiomyoma uteri, cirrhosis, and pericarditis (6, 25, 44). CA-125 levels increase during menses (46).

Molecular Biomarkers

Chromosome analysis of molecular biomarkers such as the BRCA1 gene, p53 tumor suppressor gene, and oncogenes is investigational and has not been clinically studied as a screening tool (6).

Risk Factors

Although many risk factors for ovarian cancer have been identified, a clinically useful screening profile to detect the woman at high-risk to develop ovarian cancer is not available. Risk factors that have been associated with an increased risk of epithelial ovarian cancer include advancing age, nulliparity, a personal history of endometrial, breast, or colon cancer, and a family history of ovarian cancer (5, 7, 25, 30, 47).

Factors linked with a reduced risk of ovarian cancer include an obstetrical history of one or more full-term pregnancies, a history of breast feeding, and the previous use of oral contraceptives (25, 47, 48). Risk decreases with increased duration of oral contraceptive use and persists long after cessation of use (48). The risk of ovarian cancer decreases 11% with every year of use of oral contraceptives, with an approximate 50% reduction after 5 years of use that persists for at least 10 years. There is little additional protective effect after the fifth year (49).

Other proposed risk factors for ovarian cancer for which there are inconclusive findings include the effects of exogenous chemicals such as talc and asbestos, high consumption of animal fats, whole milk, protein, lactose, and total calories, history of infertility, use of fertility drugs, incomplete pregnancies (i.e., stillbirth, abortion, ectopic pregnancy), early menarche, increased age at menopause, and use of estrogen replacement therapy (25, 47).

Ingestion of green vegetables, carrots, grains, vitamin A, vitamin C, and dietary fiber, early age at first pregnancy, tubal ligation, and hysterectomy may be associated with a decreased risk, although the evidence is weak or inconclusive (47).

Of all the risk factors, a family history of ovarian cancer is the most important. There are two familial patterns for ovarian cancer—"hereditary ovarian cancer syndromes" and "a family history of ovarian cancer." The provider should be aware that the medical literature often confuses the two (31).

Hereditary Ovarian Cancer Syndromes

Less than 1% of women are considered at increased risk for ovarian cancer caused by three well-delineated hereditary ovarian cancer syndromes (5). These three syndromes include the following: (a) site-specific ovarian cancer, the most common familial syndrome, restricted to families with ovarian cancer only; (b) breast and ovarian cancer syndrome, a clustering of both breast and ovarian cancer in extended family pedigrees; and (c) Lynch II syndrome (Cancer Family Syndrome) which includes early onset-nonpolyposis colon cancer, endometrial cancer, upper gastrointestinal cancer (including biliary ducts, pancreas, and small bowel), renal pelvis and ureteral cancer, and ovarian cancer (5, 24).

Hereditary ovarian cancer syndromes are inherited in an autosomal dominant pattern with variable penetrance (30). Women in families with a hereditary ovarian cancer syndrome may have a lifetime risk of developing ovarian cancer that is as high as 50% (31). These women require special attention for screening and genetic counseling. Unfortunately, it is difficult to differentiate between women with these syndromes and women who have a "family history of ovarian cancer."

Women with hereditary ovarian cancer syndromes are characteristically diagnosed at a younger age than nonhereditary cancers. Furthermore, the average age at time of diagnosis is younger in successive generations in families with these syndromes. However, it is unclear whether diagnosis at younger ages is caused by self-selection for early screening or other factors such as tumor virulence (30). The provider should be alert for clues suggesting a hereditary syndrome. Such clues might be ovarian and related cancers in multiple members of two or more generations, premenopausal and perimenopausal age at diagnosis, a mother or paternal aunt and approximately half the sisters with ovarian cancer (25, 31, 50).

Family History of Ovarian Cancer

Approximately 7% of women with ovarian cancer have a positive family history, but less than 10% of these women are from families with a hereditary ovarian cancer syndrome (50, 51). A "family history of ovarian cancer" refers to those women who have isolated relatives with ovarian cancer but are not from families with a hereditary syndrome (25, 31). Ninety percent of women with a positive family history have only one affected relative (31).

The lifetime probability of a 35-year-old woman developing ovarian cancer in her lifetime is 1.6% if she does not have a positive family history of the disease. This increases to 5 to 7% if she has one or two family members with ovarian cancer, whether they are first- or second-degree relatives, and assuming she is not from a family with a hereditary ovarian cancer syndrome (31). This risk would decrease total life expectancy by 4 to 7 months (31).

Genetic Counseling

It is important to differentiate between women who have a family history of a hereditary ovarian cancer syndrome and those who have a relative with a sporadic case of ovarian cancer. Confirming the relative's pathologic diagnosis and developing a family cancer genogram that includes all cancers with special attention to ovarian and breast cancer from both paternal and maternal sides of the family may help distinguish those women who are at high risk (50).

The provider should consider referral of women at high risk for a hereditary ovarian cancer syndrome for genetic counseling. This referral should be to a multidisciplinary team with genetic, oncologic, and psychologic expertise. The team should have established, well-considered protocols that include precounseling education and assessment, state-of-the-art testing, and follow-up services for the management of risk and for emotional support of women and their families (52).

It has been recommended that women from families with a hereditary ovarian cancer syndrome who have not completed childbearing and are less than age 35 years, be screened twice-yearly with complete physical examination including pelvic examination, serum CA-125, and sonography of the ovaries (30). For women from families with a hereditary ovarian cancer syndrome over the age of 35 years who have completed childbearing, prophylactic oophorectomy is recommended, with the understanding that no prospective studies have been performed, that long-term estrogen replacement therapy may be suggested, and that rare cases of intra-abdominal carcinomatosis after prophylactic oophorectomy have been reported (30, 31, 50, 53). Oral contraceptives have been suggested as a means to decrease risk for women with a family history of ovarian cancer or a hereditary syndrome (31).

If all women over age 40 years undergoing a hysterectomy also had oophorectomy, 1000 cases of ovarian cancer could be prevented. This must be balanced against the risk of noncompliance with ERT and its risk (50).

Genetic research, pushed forward by the Human Genome Project, will create new opportunities, challenges, and dilemmas for providers and their women patients. In 1991, a single gene locus, BRCA1, responsible for the development of some familial breast-ovarian cancers was identified on chromosome 17q (52, 54). It has been predicted that screening for mutations of the BRCA1 gene "is likely to be the first widespread presymptomatic genetic test that finds its way into general medical practice (52)."

The implications for preventive health care are obvious. It has been estimated that 1 in 200 to 400 American women may be carriers of the BRCA1 mutation and may have a lifetime risk of developing ovarian cancer between 25 and 85% (52). Identification of these women would allow intense clinical monitoring, early intervention, individualized decision making for prophylactic oophorectomy, and childbearing options (52). Simultaneously there are profound psychological, social, and economic considerations.

Special Considerations for Nurse Practitioners and Physician Assistants

Nurse practitioners and physician assistants will encounter women for whom ovarian cancer is a concern. Some women will be healthy, but will have concerns or have made a self-diagnosis of ovarian cancer, perhaps because of recent publicity. Other women will be identified at risk because of family history. More commonly, the practitioner will interact with a woman who has vague, persistent physical complaints that may be ovarian cancer, yet for whom this differential diagnosis has not always been considered (55).

Women may give family histories of relatives with diagnoses of ovarian cancer or more generalized histories of women's cancer or stomach cancer. If the women can obtain medical documents or more specific diagnoses, they can make all health care providers aware of their history (55). A woman's own symptoms, often vague but persistent, must be taken seriously.

Many women have misconceptions about their need for pelvic examinations, especially when the need for childbearing or family planning care has passed. Women should understand that there is more to a pelvic examination than the Pap test and that the Pap test does not screen for all types of gynecologic cancer (55). Teaching a woman about her internal organs and the need for a bimanual examination may increase her compliance with recommended screenings. Similarly, health care providers who are performing "routine" Pap tests must take the opportunity to thoroughly assess the adnexae and perform a rectovaginal examination as a part of this routine care (56).

Providers must know and provide current information to women who are concerned about ovarian cancer and ask about screening tests. Although screening is not always recommended or needed for each of these women, providers can offer each woman information about actions that might lessen her risk. For example, although talcum powder is not definitely implicated as a causative factor, women can discontinue its use because it is not essential for good hygiene. Likewise, a woman can be advised to lower her intake of animal fat and increase fiber, not as definite measures to protect from ovarian cancer, but as general health-protecting measures. At appropriate times, providers can also discuss potentially protective measures such as beast-feeding and use of oral contraceptives (55).

Evaluation of an ovarian mass is often difficult. If a malignancy is suspected, referral to a physician should be made. As appropriate tests are arranged in consultation with the physician, practitioners must help the woman understand the importance of testing and referrals. Even when the woman is referred to a gynecological oncologist or other specialist for treatment, the primary care practitioner will often have continued contact for other aspects of health care and opportunities to offer support (57).

References

1. Radner G. It's Always Something. New York: Simon & Schuster, 1989.
2. Wingo PA, Tong T, Bolden S. Cancer Statistics, 1995. CA Cancer J Clin 1995;45:8–30.
3. Granai CO. Ovarian cancer—unrealistic expectations. N Engl J Med 1992;327:197–200.
4. Young RC, Walton LA, Ellenberg SS, Homesley HD, Wilbanks GD, Decker DG, et al. Adjuvant therapy in stage I and stage II epithelial ovarian cancer: results of two prospective randomized trials. N Engl J Med 1990;322:1021–1027.
5. NIH Consensus Development Panel on Ovarian Cancer: ovarian cancer screening, treatment and follow-up." JAMA 1995;273:491–497.
6. Teneriello MG, Park RC. Early detection of ovarian cancer. CA Cancer J Clin 1995;45:71–87.
7. Cannistra SA. Cancer of the ovary. N Engl J Med 1993; 329:1550–1559.
8. Nguyen NH, Averette HE, Hoskins W, Penalver M, Sevin BY, Steren A. National survey of ovarian carcinoma Part V. The impact of physician's specialty on patient's survival. Cancer 1993;72:3663–3670.
9. McGowan L, Lesher LP, Norris HJ, Barnett M. Mis-staging of ovarian cancer. Obstet Gynecol 1985;65: 568–572.
10. Young RC, Decker DG, Wharton JT, et al. Staging laparotomy in early ovarian cancer. JAMA 1983; 250:3072–3076.
11. Qazi F, McGuire WP. The treatment of epithelial ovarian cancer. CA Cancer J Clin 1995;45:88–101.
12. Ozols RF, Garvin AJ, Costa J, Simon RM, Young RC. Advanced ovarian cancer: correlation of histologic grade with response to therapy and survival. Cancer 1980;45:572–581.
13. Hand R, Fremgen A, Chmiel JS, Recant W, Berk R, Sylvester J, Sener S. Staging procedures, clinical management, and survival outcome for ovarian carcinoma. JAMA 1993;269:1119–1122.
14. Mann WJ. Diagnosis and management of epithelial cancer of the ovary. AFP 1994;49:613–618.
15. Nussbaum SR, Gaz RD, Arnold A. Hypercalcemia and ectopic secretion of parathyroid hormone by an ovarian carcinoma with rearrangement of the gene for parathyroid hormone. N Engl J Med 1990;323: 1324–1328.
16. Allan SG, Lockhart SP, Leonard RC, Smyth JF. Paraneoplastic hypercalcaemia in ovarian carcinoma. Br Med J 1984;288:1714–1715.
17. Case Records of the Massachusetts General Hospital (Case 34-1989). N Engl J Med 1989;321:525–535.
18. Holguin T, Padilla RS, Ampuero F. Ovarian adenocarcinoma presenting with the sign of leser-trelat. Gynecol Oncol 1986;25:128–132.
19. DiSaia PJ, Creasman WT. Clinical Gynecologic Oncology. St. Louis: Mosby 1993:301.
20. Council on Scientific Affairs, American Medical Association. Gynecologic sonography: report of the ultrasonography task force. JAMA 1991;265:2851–2855.
21. Hacker NF, Berek JS, Lagasse LD, Nieberg RK, Elashoff RM. Primary cytoreductive surgery of epithelial ovarian cancer. Obstet Gynecol 1983;61: 413–20.
22. Berek JS, Hacker NF, Lagasse LD, Poth T, Resnick B, Nieberg RK. Second-look laparotomy in stage III epithelial ovarian cancer: clinical variables associ-

ated with disease status. Obstet Gynecol 1984;64:207–212.

23. Miyazaki T, Tomoda Y, Ohta M, Kano T, Mizuno K, Sakakibara K. Preservation of ovarian function and reproductive ability in patients with malignant ovarian tumors. Gynecol Oncol 1988;30:329–341.

24. Runowicz CD. Advances in the screening and treatment of ovarian cancer. CA Cancer J Clin 1992;42:327–349.

25. Carlson KJ, Skates SJ, Singer DE. Screening for ovarian cancer. Ann Intern Med 1994;121:124–132.

26. Report of the United States Preventive Services Task Force. Guide to Clinical Preventive Services: An assessment of the effectiveness of 169 interventions. Baltimore: Williams & Wilkins, 1989:18–85.

27. American Academy of Family Physicians. Age Charts for Periodic Health Examination, 1994.

28. American College of Obstetricians and Gynecologists, Committee on Gynecologic Practice. ACOG Committee Opinion: Routine Cancer Screening. October 1993; No. 128.

29. American College of Physicians. Screening for ovarian cancer: recommendations and rationale. Ann Intern Med 1994;121:141–142.

30. Piver MS, Baker TR, Jishi MF, et al. Familial ovarian cancer: a report of 658 families from the Gilda Radner familial ovarian cancer registry 1981–1991. Cancer 1993;71:582–588.

31. Kerlikowske K, Brown JS, Grady DG. Should women with familial ovarian cancer undergo prophylactic oophorectomy? Obstet Gynecol 1992;80:700–707.

32. Jacobs I, Stabile I, Bridges J, et al. Multimodal approach to screening for ovarian cancer. Lancet 1988;1:268–271.

33. van Nagell JR, Depriest RD, Puls IE, Donaldson ES, Gallion HH, Pavlik EJ, et al. Ovarian cancer screening in asymptomatic postmenopausal women by transvaginal ultrasound. Cancer 1991;68:458–462.

34. Andolf E, Jorgensen C, Astedt B. Ultrasound examination for detection of ovarian carcinoma in risk groups. Obstet Gynecol 1990;75:106–109.

35. Andolf E. Ultrasound screening in women at risk for ovarian cancer. Clin Obstet Gynecol 1993;36:423–432.

36. Campbell S, Royston P, Bhan V, Whitehead MI, Collins WP. Novel screening strategies for early ovarian cancer by transabdominal ultrasonography. Br J Obstet Gynaecol 1990;97:304–311.

37. Andolf E, Svalenius E, Astedt B. Ultrasonography for early detection of ovarian carcinoma. Br J Obstet Gynaecol 1986;93:1286–1289.

38. Goswamy RK, Campbell S, Whitehead MI. Screening for ovarian cancer. Clin Obstet Gynecol 1983;10:621–643.

39. DePriest PD, Shenson D, Fried A, et al. A morphology index based on sonographic findings in ovarian cancer. Gynecol Oncol 1993;51:7–11.

40. Bourne TH, Campbell S, Reynolds KM, et al. Screening for early familial ovarian cancer with transvaginal ultrasonography and colour blood flow imaging. Br Med J 1993;306:1025–1029.

41. Kurjak A, Zalud I, Alfirevic Z. Evaluation of adnexal masses with transvaginal color ultrasound. J Ultrasound Med 1991;10:295–297.

42. Hricak H. Carcinoma of the female reproductive organs: value of cross-sectional imaging. Cancer 1991;67(4 suppl):1209–1218.

43. Bast RC, Klug TL, St. John E, et al. Radioimmunoassay using a monoclonal antibody to monitor the course of epithelial ovarian cancer. N Engl J Med 1983;309:883–887.

44. Helzlsouer KJ, Bush TL, Alberg AJ, et al. Prospective study of CA-125 levels as markers of ovarian cancer. JAMA 1993;269:1123–1126.

45. Helzlsouer KJ, Alberg AJ, Bush TL, Comstock GW. CA-125 as a screening test for ovarian cancer (letter). JAMA 1993;269:3106–3107.

46. Pittaway DE, Fayez JA. Serum CA-125 antigen levels increase with menses. Am J Obstet Gynecol 1987;156:75–76.

47. Tortolero-Luna G, Follen Mitchell M, Rhodes-Morris HE. Epidemiology and screening of ovarian cancer. Obstet Gynecol Clin North Am 1994;21:1–22.

48. The Centers for Disease Control Cancer and Steroid Hormone Study. Oral contraceptive use and the risk of ovarian cancer. JAMA 1983;249:1596–1599.

49. Hankinson SE, Colditz GA, Hunter DJ, et al. A quantitative assessment of oral contraceptive use and risk of ovarian cancer. Obstet Gynecol 1992;180:708–714.

50. Nguyen NH, Averette HE, Janicek M. Ovarian carcinoma: a review of the significance of familial risk factors and the role of prophylactic oopherectomy in cancer prevention. Cancer 1994;74:545–555.

51. Grover S, Quinn MA, Weideman P. Patterns of inheritance of ovarian cancer: an analysis from an ovarian cancer screening program. Cancer 1993;72:526–530.

52. Biesecker BB, Boehnke M, Calzone K, et al. Genetic counseling for families with inherited susceptibility to breast and ovarian cancer. JAMA 1993;269:1970–1974.

53. Tobacman JK, Tucker MA, Kase R, et al. Intra-abdominal carcinomatosis after prophylactic oophorectomy in ovarian-cancer-prone families. Lancet 1982;2:795–797.

54. Narod SA, Feunteun J, Lynch HT, et al. Familial breast-ovarian cancer locus on chromosome 17q12-q23. Lancet 1991;338:82–83.

55. Brucks JA. Ovarian cancer. Nurs Clin North Am 1992;27:835–845.

56. Seltzer V. Screening for ovarian cancer: an overview of the screening recommendations of the 1994 NIH consensus conference. Prim Care Update OB/GYNs; 2:132–134.

57. Star WL. Pelvic masses. In: Star WL, Lommel LL, Shannon MT, eds. Women's Primary Health Care. Washington, DC: American Nurses' Association, 1995:12-99–12-108.

Vaginitis

12.6

Deborah G. Haynes

Introduction

One of the more frequent reasons women consult physicians in the United States is for the evaluation and treatment of vaginal discharge (1). The most commonly occurring causes of vaginitis are infections, including bacterial vaginosis, candidiasis, and trichomoniasis. There are also noninfectious causes of vaginitis. Atrophic vaginitis, associated with aging, is increasing in incidence. Contact irritants, mechanical irritation, and allergic reactions, although less common, can cause sufficient vaginal symptoms to require treatment.

Characteristics of the Normal Vaginal Discharge

The normal vaginal discharge is formed by serum transudate from the vaginal capillary beds, Bartholin's glands, and the cervix. The normal vaginal discharge consists of water, electrolytes, epithelial cells, microorganisms, and organic compounds. There are usually only a few white blood cells present.

Estrogen levels and vaginal pH influence which organisms are found in the vaginal flora. Normally, the lactic acid content of vaginal secretions results in a pH less than 4.5. This pH favors the growth of lactobacilli and these, in turn, inhibit the growth of most other bacteria. Lactobacilli make up 95% of all bacteria usually recovered from the vagina, but corynebacteria, streptococci, and staphylococcus epidermidis may also be found.

There is a wide range that is "normal" in vaginal discharges. The discharge usually appears white or slate-colored with a curdy, moderately thick consistency. There is minimal or no odor present. The quantity of secretions varies from person to person and over time in the same person. A change in an individual patient could be caused by age, hormone status, excessive douching, other illnesses, pregnancy, or medications. A discharge with changes in color, consistency, odor, volume, and irritative symptoms is often the hallmark of vaginitis.

History and Physical Examination

Vaginitis is usually caused by an infection, and the three most common etiologies of vaginitis are candidiasis, bacterial vaginosis, and trichomoniasis. Other noninfectious causes may be discovered by history. A thorough history, physical exam, and appropriate laboratory tests can help make the correct diagnosis.

The history should include a description and duration of the symptoms, recent and usual sexual activity, contraceptive use, medication use, and history of similar infections including treatment and response. Some common complaints may include a change in discharge, soreness, irritation, pruritus, dysuria and/or dyspareunia. The discharge should be described by color, amount, consistency, and odor. The provider should consider sexual abuse and/or partner violence in a woman who complains of chronic or recurrent discharge, dyspareunia, pruritus, or vaginal pain without physical findings of obvious cause.

The pelvic exam includes a thorough inspection and palpation of the perineum, skin folds, mons pubis, and vulva, followed by a speculum exam. The color, consistency, odor and volume of vaginal secretions, the presence of any erythema, petechiae, ulceration, edema, atrophy of the vaginal walls, and discharge through the cervical os should be noted. It is important to obtain a swab from the middle third of the vagina for pH estimation.

Laboratory Evaluation

The minimum evaluation of the vaginal discharge consists of testing the vaginal washings for pH, and an additional swab obtained for microscopic evaluation using normal saline and 10% potassium hydroxide (KOH). If there is any concern about sexually transmitted diseases, swabs for culture or DNA probe for chlamydia and *Neisseria gonorrhea* and culture or Tzanck smear for herpes simplex virus (HSV) should be obtained from the cervix. Cultures should also be taken from any ulcerated lesion for HSV. Swabs from any single ulcerated lesions may be evaluated under dark field, if available, for syphilis. Cultures can also be obtained for candida species.

Infectious Vaginitis

Candidiasis

Causative Organisms and Risk Factors
Candida albicans causes 80 to 90% of the cases in the United States. However, other Candida

species such as *C. glabrata* and *C. tropicalis* are showing increasing incidence. These Candida species can be differentiated on microscopy. *C. albicans* has spores and mycelia, *C. glabrata* has clusters of spores but no germinal tubes or mycelia, and *C. tropicalis* has hyphae but no true chlamydospores or germinating tubes.

Predisposing factors for candidiasis include pregnancy, estrogen use, antibiotic usage, metabolic factors, and diet. Pregnancy is the most common predisposing factor. High-dose oral contraceptives were previously a significant cause of Candida vaginitis, but the new low-dose estrogen formulations do not predispose to vaginitis. Antibiotic use decreases the protective resident bacteria, especially lactobacilli, and this subsequently leads to an increased risk of Candida vaginitis. The most frequent antibiotics that cause this are tetracycline, ampicillin, and cephalosporins. Diabetes mellitus and other diseases that decrease the immune response increase the risk of Candida vaginitis.

Candida vaginitis has never been considered a sexually transmitted disease. However, one study revealed a high correlation of positive cultures with the same Candida species in samples obtained from sexual partners (2). The treatment of the woman's partner or partners should be considered in women with recurrent candidiasis.

Clinical Features and Physical Examination

Vulvar pruritus occurs in more than 90% of women with Candida vaginitis. Vaginal itching is actually probably vestibular pruritus and occurs particularly prior to menses and after intercourse. It may be sufficiently severe to interfere with normal activities, sexual relations, and rest. Women may also complain of burning, especially on urination. This is exacerbated if the woman has excoriations secondary to scratching. Increased frequency of urination and dyspareunia are often reported. The discharge is often described as "cottage cheese-like" but it may vary considerably in quantity and consistency.

The woman's perineum and surrounding skin may be red, swollen, and excoriated. There may be satellite lesions, similar to those with candida diaper dermatitis. The excoriations can be secondarily infected. In well-established or severe infections, erythema and swelling of the labia and vulva may be present. A speculum exam may reveal white plaque-like patches of discharge on the vaginal mucosa, usually with a normal cervix.

Diagnosis

The diagnosis of vulvovaginal candidiasis depends on the presence of clinical features and the demonstration of yeast on microscopic analysis. The vaginal pH will be less than 4.7. On wet prep, a predominance of lactobacilli and diagnostic spores, hyphae, or filaments are present. A 10% KOH solution is the most helpful laboratory test to identify these organisms because it causes the spores, hyphae, and filaments to stand out much more easily. Spores and conidia are strongly gram-positive if gram staining is performed. In uncertain cases, culture may be necessary.

Management

Treatment strategies for Candida vaginitis include topical and oral polyenes and imidazoles, boric acid, and gentian violet (Table 12.6.1).

Topical antibiotics are more common treatment. Nystatin, a polyene, was the primary treatment against Candida until the imidazoles were discovered. The imidazoles include clotrimazole, miconazole, butoconazole, and triaconazole. The agents prevent formation of normal yeast cell walls and are all equally effective against *C. albicans*. Most are all effective against *C. glabrata*, but in higher concentrations than that needed against the albican species. Clotrimazole may be more effective against *C. tropicalis*. New oral formulations of the imidazoles such as ketoconazole and fluconazole have come in to significant use. The advantage of fluconazole is the ease of treatment with a one-time dose of 150 mg.

Gentian violet has been used for years. It completely inhibits candidal growth, is not

Table 12.6.1   Treatments for Candida

Topical Vaginal Medications

Generic	Trade	Preparations	Dosage and Length of Treatment
Nystatin	Mycostatin	Cream, powder	bid x 7 days
Butoconazole	Femstat	2% cream	qhs (5 g) x 3 days
Clotrimazole	Gyne-Lotrimin	200 mg tab	bid x 3 days
		cream (60 g tube)	bid x 3 days
	Mycelex	100 mg tablet	qhs x 7 days
		1% Cream	qhs x 7 days
		500 mg vaginal tablet	qhs x 1 day
Miconazole	Monistat	200 mg suppository	qhs x 3 days
		100 mg suppository	qhs x 7 days
		2% vaginal cream	qhs x 7 days
	Dual Pak	cream and suppository	qhs x 3 days
Terconazole	Terazol*	80 mg suppository	qhs x 3 days
		0.4% cream	qhs x 7 days
	Terazol-3*	0.8% cream	qhs x 3 days
Tioconazole	Vagistat	6.5% ointment	qhs x 1 day
Oral Medications			
Fluconazole	Diflucan	150 mg PO	once
Ketoconazole	Nizoral	200 mg PO	bid x 5 days
Itraconazole	Sporanox	200 mg PO	qd x 3 days
		200 mg PO	bid x 1 day
Other			
Gentian Violet			
Vaginal Staining			once per week
Boric acid		600 mg bid	intravaginal x 14 days

*Should be avoided in at least the first trimester of pregnancy.

contraindicated in pregnancy, and is cost-effective. It is active against both C. *albicans* and C. *glabrata*, but a few strains of C. *tropicalis* may be resistant. The rate of irritant reactions is low. However, it may cause a temporary bright clothing stain and is not often aesthetically acceptable. A 1% aqueous solution can be painted on the affected mucus membranes or skin at weekly or monthly intervals. Boric acid can be used, although seldom recommended, as a 600-mg gelatin capsule in the vagina daily for 2 weeks. It has minimal side ef-

fects. A 72% cure rate at the end of 30 days has been reported (3). In pregnant women, the treatment for candida includes nystatin, miconazole, or clotrimazole. Terconazole should be avoided in the first trimester, and boric acid should not be used by pregnant women.

Recurrent Infection

Women with three or more culture proven episodes of Candida yearly may be classified as chronic, recurrent, or relapsing cases (Fig. 12.6.1). The primary reason for these infec-

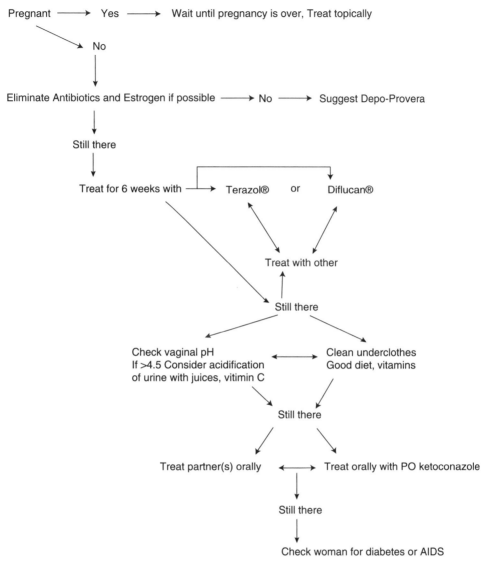

Figure 12.6.1   Suggested algorithm for treatments of recurrent candida vaginitis.

tions may be misdiagnosis resulting in treatment for C. *albicans* when the woman actually has glabrata or tropicalis species. Appropriate therapy using Terazol or fluconazole should be successful. Additionally, there are many phenotypic strains within the species C. *albicans* and great variety (4). This ability to have random or induced alterations in growth characteristics can lead to resistance.

C. *albicans* also can inhabit areas between the epithelial cells and, therefore, may persist after apparently successful treatment. Women with recurrent or relapsing infections should be treated for a minimum of 2 weeks to prevent recurrence. Candida can also inhabit locations including fomites that act as a reservoir for the fungus. Underclothing can be a contributing agent in recurrent infections. Routine laundering does not sterilize fabrics and boiling underwear between wearings may be needed. If fabrics cannot tolerate such high temperatures, these garments can be sterilized by microwave. Placing a freshly washed, wet article of underclothing into a microwave for 5 minutes is adequate to kill the Candida organism (5). Another more practical option for women is to wear and regularly change disposable panty liners.

The digestive tract may be the reservoir for Candida. Women with chronic vaginal candidiasis may benefit from a prolonged course of oral antifungal agents. Suggestions include Ketoconazole 400 mg every day for 2 weeks followed by 100 mg daily for 6 months or fluconazole 150 mg every week for 4 to 6 weeks. Oral nystatin can be used tid for 1 to 3 months. Nystatin is cost-effective but the frequent dosing makes compliance a problem. If there is any concern that the sexual partner is the reservoir, the partner should also be treated with oral agents.

Estrogen use has been associated with increased Candida colonization. Women with recurrent yeast infections should use low-dose oral contraceptives or estrogen replacement. One study achieved a decreased recurrence rate by using Depo-Provera in reproductive-aged women (6).

If women with recurrent, chronic, or relapsing disease have optimal nutrition, candida infection may improve. Women should be encouraged to eat a healthy, well-balanced diet and to use appropriate supplemental vitamins and minerals to ensure adequate host resistance. Women can reduce recurrence rate of candidiasis by changing their diet, including a decrease in the intake of milk, syrup, and sweeteners with lactose.

Women with recurrent, chronic, or relapsing disease may have an underlying systemic disease. Physicians should evaluate these women for diabetes mellitus and AIDS.

Bacterial Vaginosis

Causative Organisms
Bacterial vaginosis is the most common cause of bacterial infection in the sexually active adult woman. Bacterial vaginosis was once thought to

be caused exclusively by *Gardnerella vaginalis*, but is caused by the symbiotic interplay of many vaginal organisms, especially anaerobes (7). This syndrome is called "bacterial" because of the many types of bacteria involved and "vaginosis" because there is no increase in leukocytes and there is little true inflammatory response in this condition (see Table 12.6.2).

The frequency of bacterial vaginosis has remained constant or only slightly increased in the past 15 years. This syndrome accounts for approximately one third of the women with vaginal complaints. There has been no proof that this is a sexually transmitted disease.

Clinical Features and Physical Examination
Women present with significant complaint of a malodorous, profuse discharge that is thin, homogenous and gray/white or has yellow/green tints. Women often complain of increased discharge after intercourse or at the time of their menses. Women may describe the odor as "fishy."

The physical exam reveals a normal, pink vagina with gray/white, homogeneous discharge. The odor is often noted during the speculum exam.

Diagnosis
Three of the four properties listed below are sufficient to establish the diagnosis of bacterial vaginosis. These properties include clue cells on wet mount, pH >5, a malodorous profuse discharge, and thin, homogeneous, gray/white secretions.

Table 12.6.2 Common Bacteria Found in B. Vaginosis

Bacteroides
Mycoplasmas
Mobiluncus
Peptostreptococcus
Peptococcus
Porphyromonas (former *B. melaninogenicus*)

Microscopic exam of the secretions shows clue cells without obvious yeast or trichomoniasis. Many bacteria are present along with few white blood cells and a significant absence of lactobacilli. Clue cells are vaginal epithelial cells covered with attached bacteria or mixed types that obscure the edge of the cell. The single finding of clue cells predicts bacterial vaginosis with approximately 95% reliability (8).

The vaginal pH should be measured accurately. Colorfast strips, which have a recognizable color change at increments of 0.2 to 0.4, are recommended. These strips are not light sensitive and have a long shelf life. It is important that the speculum is not lubricated or moistened with tap water as these factors influence the pH findings. The pH is usually in the 5 to 6 range for bacterial vaginosis; yeast is unlikely at levels above 4.5; contamination of the strip with cervical mucus or Trichomonas may be suspected if pH is 6 or more.

The whiff or Amine test is performed by adding 10% KOH to a swab of vaginal secretions. A fishy odor predicts bacterial vaginosis with 95% reliability. The odor is the result of vaginal secretion amine oxides being converted to free amines. This reaction is enhanced by the presence of mobiluncus bacteria. This fishy odor can also be present after intercourse or menses because of the alkaline nature of semen and blood. It is important that the woman not douche or have intercourse before the test because this can also change the pH results.

Culture of *Gardnerella vaginalis* or anaerobes is not clinically useful, because they may be normal contaminants of the vagina. Increased numbers or growth on culture media does not reliably predict disease.

Management

All experts recommend treating symptomatic women, but treatment of asymptomatic women or their sexual partners remains controversial. New studies have shown serious morbidity can be associated with bacterial vaginosis under certain conditions (see Table 12.6.3). Many inves-

Table 12.6.3 Serious Morbidity and Associated Sequelae of Bacterial Vaginosis Vaginitis

Pelvic inflammatory disease
Endometriosis
Urinary tract infection
Premature labor
Premature rupture of membranes
Chorioamnionitis
Cervical dysplasia
Postpartum endometriosis
Postsurgical infections

tigators now advise treatment for asymptomatic bacterial vaginosis in women who are pregnant or who are about to undergo vaginal or abdominal surgery (9). Pregnant women should be treated to decrease the risk of premature rupture of membranes, premature labor, and postpartum endometriosis (10).

Some investigators recommend that male partners of women with recurrent bacterial vaginosis undergo treatment. However, studies comparing male partners who were treated with a control group found no difference in cure rates in the women at 21 days posttreatment.

The drug of choice for bacterial vaginosis is oral metronidazole and the most common dose is 500 mg bid for 7 days (11). A single 2-g dose has proven effective, but it is associated with a higher recurrence rate. Metronidazole should not be taken in the first trimester of pregnancy, and can cause significant stomach upset and should be taken with milk or food; women should be advised that it produces a significant antabuse-like reaction to alcohol. Table 12.6.4 shows additional treatments that have become available for treatment of bacterial vaginosis. The new vaginal preparations of metronidazole and clindamycin avoid many systemic side effects (12).

Treatment of pregnant women with bacterial vaginosis has been controversial because metronidazole was considered contraindicated

Table 12.6.4   Treatment regimens for Bacterial Vaginosis

Drug		Effective-ness (%)
Clindamycin	300 mg P.O. bid x 7 days	94
Metronidazole	500 mg P.O. bid x 7 days	96
Clindamycin vaginal cream 2%	5 g qd x 7 days	94
Metronidazole vaginal gel 0.75%	5 g bid x 5 days	
Metronidazole	2 g single dose	85

in the first trimester. Amoxicillin 500 mg bid for 7 days had been used, but it was shown to be ineffective in some studies. Clindamycin 300 mg bid for 7 days has been the therapy of choice. A meta-analysis of seven studies showed that metronidazole does not increase teratogenic risk (13).

Trichomoniasis

Causative Organism and Epidemiology
Trichomonas vaginalis is a motile, ovoid, anaerobic, flagellated protozoan. It is the third most common cause of vaginitis in the United States. Trichomonas vaginalis uses specific adhesions to attach to the mucus membranes of the cell. When this organism is present, there is a significant disappearance of lactobacilli.

Risk factors for trichomoniasis include multiple sexual partners, previous history of sexually transmitted disease, coexistent Neisseria gonorrhea, and nonuse of barrier or hormonal contraception. There is significant agreement that trichomoniasis is a sexually transmitted disease. The organism can survive on wet surfaces and clothing for periods of time and can live a long time in the vagina without causing infection. Nonsexual infections are believed to be extremely rare (14).

Clinical Presentation and Physical Examination
Trichomonas vaginitis exhibits a variety of symptoms compared to other causes of vagini-

tis. This organism can be asymptomatic in up to 50% of women for long periods of time. The most common symptoms are vaginal discharge and pruritus. Women may also complain of vulvovaginal irritation, dyspareunia, and dysuria.

On assessment, women may have copious vaginal discharge that is frothy and yellow/green in color. There is often significant vaginal erythema, an alkaline pH, and some investigators have described the "strawberry vagina" appearance in this condition. Trichimonas infection causes a specific cervical appearance on colposcopy of "double" capillaries.

Diagnosis
The most rapid diagnosis can be achieved with microscopic evaluation using a wet mount with normal saline. Motile parasite observation is diagnostic in 60 to 80% of the cases. A pH greater than 6 suggests trichomoniasis, atrophic vaginitis, normal nonestrogenized vagina or small bowel fistula. If the woman's symptoms are not diagnostic or the microscopic evaluation is negative, then Diamond's media culture can detect 95% of cases. This culture is especially helpful in recurrent, asymptomatic, or subclinical infection.

Pregnant women with vaginal trichomoniasis are at increased risk of premature rupture of membranes. One way to screen these women is to test pH in the third trimester. If the pH is greater than 5, then appropriate testing for bacterial vaginosis and trichomoniasis should be performed. More research is needed to define the exact correlation between Trichomonas and perinatal morbidity.

Management
All symptomatic women with trichomoniasis and their recent sexual contacts should be treated. Metronidazole 2 g orally once or 1 g bid for 1 day is the drug choice for treatment. Splitting the dose decreases the incidence of nausea. Cure is achieved in 82 to 88% of treated women. When both the woman and the sexual contact are treated, the cure rate rises to greater than 95%. Other treatment reg-

imens include metronidazole 250 mg tid for 7 days and 500 mg bid for 5 days. Because of GI upset and the need for abstinence of alcohol, these regimens have poor compliance. Side effects from oral metronidazole include a metallic taste, nausea, occasional vomiting and diarrhea. In higher dosages, distal numbness and neutropenia can occur.

True resistant cases are treated with increased dosages of metronidazole. Initial treatment is to repeat the 2-g dose and this will achieve an 85% cure rate. Some investigators recommend augmenting with topical metronidazole .075% gel twice daily to increase the vaginal concentrations. However, because Trichomonas vaginalis can be found in Bartholin's glands and Skene ducts, it is important that oral treatment always be part of the regimen. Phenobarbital and phenytoin have been reported to interfere with metronidazole and have caused therapeutic failures. Some experts recommend taking the women off these medications while treatment is performed with the 1-day dose.

Treatment in first trimester pregnancy continues to be controversial because of the concern over metronidazole's safety. As mentioned previously, some experts feel metronidazole is safe to use. Other experts recommend Chlortrimazole vaginal tabs, 100 mg daily, for 6 to 12 days to help with palliative treatment until the woman is in the second trimester and then to use metronidazole.

Other Infectious Causes

Any organism that can cause cervicitis can cause vaginitis also. This includes gonorrhea, chlamydia, and herpes simplex (see Chapter 11.1).

Noninfectious Vaginitis

Atrophic vaginitis

Etiology

The most common vaginal disorder in postmenopausal women not taking estrogen is atrophic vaginitis. Atrophic vaginitis is caused by a change of predominant bacterial species from the lactobacilli dominant flora to a dominant coliform type of bacteria flora, a change in the vaginal pH from approximately 4 to a level of 6.5 to 7, and a thinning of the vaginal mucosa increasing the risk of infections.

Clinical Features and Physical Examination

The most frequent symptoms of atrophic vaginitis include pruritus, pain, dysuria, dyspareunia, labial swelling, and a vaginal discharge that may be tinged with blood and may have a significant odor. The woman may complain of mild urinary incontinence. The clinical course for this type of vaginitis is usually progressive.

Physical findings reveal a thin, pale pink, vaginal mucosa with erythema and some petechiae. There are few or no vaginal folds and vulvar atrophy may also be apparent.

Diagnosis

Diagnosis is usually made by history. The woman is postmenopausal and has typical findings on physical examination. However, in a postmenopausal woman who presents with vaginal spotting or bleeding, malignancy is a consideration. A complete history and physical exam, including a Pap smear and a wet mount, should be performed. If the source of the bleeding cannot be easily visualized, an endometrial biopsy to rule out a uterine source of bleeding may be necessary. The wet mount in atrophic vaginitis shows red and white blood cells with immature epithelial cells. Many bacteria are present, but usually only one or two predominant species will be present on the culture.

Management

Estrogen is the specific drug of choice to treat and prevent atrophic vaginitis. The maintenance of sexual activity and use of lubricants and moisturizers are helpful in the prevention of recurrence.

Topical estrogen is needed, initially, to restore vaginal moisture. It can take 2 to 24 months to totally eliminate vaginal dryness with topical estrogens. Initial treatment with estrogen cream should be daily for 2 to 4 weeks. As the vaginal symptoms improve, therapy can be reduced to every other day and subsequently to once or twice a week. Initially, to avoid effects of estrogen such as breast tenderness, the dosage can be gradually increased starting with a one-fourth applicator over several days and working up to a half applicator and then a full applicator. Intravaginal medication can be systemically absorbed, so the same contraindications that apply to systemic estrogen therapy should be observed (15). The woman can also be offered oral medications, if she is a candidate for long-term estrogen replacement therapy.

Lubricants and moisturizers can be useful in relieving discomfort while waiting for estrogens to restore the vaginal mucosa. These are particularly necessary to allow pain-free intercourse. Water-based lubricants are limited in usage to immediately before intercourse because of their short action. Vaginal moisturizers last up to 72 hours and help stimulate natural secretions.

Contact, Irritant, and Allergic Reactions

Clinical Features
Contact vaginitis is an inflammatory response to an irritant or allergen. Primary irritants include vaginal sprays, bubble baths, spermicides, latex condoms, strong detergents, synthetic materials, and scented toilet tissue. Occasionally intravaginal medications used in the treatment of vaginitis can also cause a significant response.

Common responses to an irritant or allergic reaction include erythema, edema, vesicular lesions, and weeping lesions. Women with contact vulvovaginitis may present with varying degrees of tenderness, pain pruritus, and burning.

Management
Wet compresses with Burrow's solution may afford quick relief. Topical steroid creams, including fluocinolone acetonide, triamcinolone acetonide, and hydrocortisone acetate are also effective. Antihistamines for treatment of vulvar pruritus are not helpful. The most important management step is to remove the causative agent to prevent further recurrence.

Mechanical Irritation

Occasionally, mechanical irritation from new onset or other sexual relations can cause significant vaginitis with symptoms of pain, swelling, redness, and discharge. As with contact-irritant caused vaginitis, treatment would include warm soaks or compresses, topical steroid creams, and temporary avoidance of sexual relations.

Conclusion

Vaginitis, whether caused by infectious or noninfectious causes, is usually easily treatable.

Special Considerations for Nurse Practitioners and Physician Assistants

Although vaginal secretions are a normal experience for women during their childbearing years, many women will have concerns. Women who know the characteristics of normal discharge, how discharge may change during the menstrual cycle, and changes that may indicate infection can make better decisions about their care. If a woman determines she needs an examination for vaginal symptoms, she should come when symptoms are present and before using any medications or a douche (16).

While eliciting a history, health care providers should ask about lifestyle behaviors, including personal hygiene, that might influence the vaginal environment. Douching can irritate vaginal tissue, alter the vaginal environment, and predispose the woman to infection. The woman should be asked also about the use of sprays, deodorants, powders, perfumes, antiseptic soaps, or detergents (especially recent changes) that might cause irritation or allergic reactions. In addition, nylon panties or tight-fitting clothing that does not allow free air flow and absorption of moisture can cause irritation (16). The presence of any pruritus, rash, or discharge in the sexual partner should be noted (17).

A woman should be given information about possible treatments and involved in the choice of treatment. Some women may want to try more natural self-help regimens to restore the vaginal flora and promote healing, especially for localized, non-STD vaginal infections. (For more information, see the references by Fogel and the Boston Women's Health Collective.) Other women will ask about self-treatment using over-the-counter medications, which can be an acceptable alternative if the woman has had a previously confirmed yeast infection, knows the signs and symptoms of yeast, and seeks care for numerous recurrent or chronic infections (16).

A woman needs to know if her infection is sexually transmitted and if her partner should be treated. Practitioners should ask the woman if she has concerns about telling her partner and should help her practice what to say if needed. The providers should also offer to assist her in educating the partner about treatment, avoiding intercourse during treatment, or use of a condom. Informational handouts can be given to the woman to take to her partner.

Instruction should be given about correct use of any medications (e.g., insertion of creams or suppositories and then lying down), possible side effects, signs of allergic reactions, and the necessity of completing a course of treatment even though problems such as pruritus and discharge may be alleviated earlier. When vaginal medications are used, women

should be instructed to continue them during menses and avoid the use of tampons that can absorb the medication (17, 19). If a vaginal cream, e.g., Monistat, interferes with condom or diaphragm integrity, the woman at risk of pregnancy should be informed (20).

In addition to treating the specific infection, providers must give attention to comfort measures. Warm sitz baths several times a day may relieve some symptoms. Use of a hair dryer on low setting may help dry irritated external areas (19). The use of water-soluble lubricants, masturbation without penetration, and position changes may help the woman experiencing dyspareunia. The provider can enhance comfort during the speculum examination by helping the woman use relaxation and breathing techniques (16).

Self-care and prevention are keys to health care. In addition to education regarding hygienic practices that may cause irritation or alter the vaginal environment, providers should discuss good general health measures, including reduction of stress, adequate rest, good nutrition (possibly low in refined sugars), and personal hygiene as needed. Women who use diaphragms or cervical caps should know how to clean them correctly. Instruction about frequent changing of tampons and sanitary pads may be needed, as well as counseling not to wear tampons to bed or with scanty flow, because this practice may predispose to vaginal or cervical trauma (16).

Current understanding of the vaginal ecologic system and therapeutic and preventive modalities based on ecologic balance is sparse. Many common recommended behavioral and self-care activities, such as avoidance of tight clothing and use of yogurt, lack sufficient study to provide a reliable knowledge base for clinical practice. Some commercially available products may actually contain bacterial contamination (21). Practitioners must know which modalities are based on research and must also be willing participants in interdisciplinary research to find effective treatments.

A vaginal infection can impact a woman's lifestyle considerably. Practitioners who use a sensitive, individualized approach to care will not only treat the immediate problem, but educate and counsel the woman on prevention of future infections (and possible prevention of pelvic inflammatory disease or preterm births) and promotion of better general health (21, 22).

References

1. Soble J. Vulvovaginitis. Dermatol Clin 1992;10: 339–359.
2. Horowitz BJ, Edelstein SW, Lippman L. Sexual transmission of Candida. Obstet Gynecol 1987;69: 883–886.
3. Swate TE, Weed JC. Boric acid treatment of vulvovaginal candidiasis. Obstet Gynecol 1974;43:893–895.
4. Soll DR, Langtium CJ, McDowll J, Hicks J, Galask R. High frequency switching in Candida strains isolated from vaginitis patients. J Clin Microbiol 1987;25:1611–1622.
5. Friedrich EG Jr, Phillips L. Microwave sterilization of Candida on underwear fabric. J Reprod Med 1988;33:421–422.
6. Dennerstein GJ. Depo-Provera in the treatment of recurrent vulvovaginal candidiasis. J Reprod Med 1986;31:801–803.
7. Mead PB. Epidemiology of bacterial vaginosis. Am J Obstet Gynecol 1993;169:446–449.
8. Thomason JL, Gelbart SM, Anderson RJ, et al. Statistical evaluation of diagnostic criteria for bacterial vaginosis. Am J Obstet Gynecol 1990; 162:155–160.
9. Faro S, Phillips LE, Martens MG. Perspectives on the bacteriology of postoperative obstetric-gynecologic infections. Am J Obstet Gynecol 1988;158: 694–700.
10. Burtin P, Taddio A, Ariburnu O, et al. Safety of metronidazole in pregnancy: a meta-analysis. Am J Obstet Gynecol 1995;172:525–529.
11. Sweet RL. New approaches for the treatment of bacterial vaginosis. Am J Obstet Gynecol 1993;169: 479–482.
12. Neri A, Rabinerson D, Kaplan B. Bacterial vaginosis: drugs versus alternative treatment. Obstet Gynecol Surv 1994;49:809–813.
13. Burtin P, Taddio A, Ariburnu O, et al. Safety of Metronidazole in pregnancy: a meta-analysis. Am J Obstet Gynecol 1995;172:525-529.
14. Kaufman RH, Faro S, Friedrich EG, et al. Benign diseases of the vulva and vagina. 4th ed. St. Louis: Mosby-Year Book, 1994:338–351.
15. Handa VL, Bachus KE, Johnston WW, et al. Vaginal administrations of low-dose conjugated estrogens: systemic absorption and effects on the endometrium. Obstet Gynecol, 1994: 84:215–218.
16. Fogel CI. Common symptoms: bleeding, pain, and discharge. In: Fogel CI, Woods NF, eds. Women's Health Care. Thousand Oaks, CA: Sage: 1995:517–570.
17. Hawkins JW, Roberto-Nichols DM, Stanley-Haney JL. Protocols for Nurse Practitioners in Gynecologic Settings. 5th ed. New York: Tiresias Press, 1995:81–101.
18. The Boston Women's Health Collective. The New Ourbodies, Ourselves. New York: Simon & Schuster, 1992:604–608.
19. Bennett EC. Vaginitis and sexually transmitted diseases. In: Youngkin EQ, Davis MS, eds. Women's Health. Norwalk, CT: Appleton & Lange, 1994: 203–250.
20. Hatcher RA, Trussel J, Stewart F. Contraceptive Technology. 16th ed. New York: Irvington Publishers, 1994:145–178.
21. Overman BA. The vagina as an ecological system: current understanding and clinical applications. J Nurse Mid wifery 1993;38:146–150.
22. McGourty MK. Vaginal infections: keys to treatment. Contemp Nurse Pract 1995;1:18–23.

Suggested Readings

Glass R. ed. Office Gynecology. Baltimore: Williams & Wilkins, 1993.
Taylor B. Difficult Medical Management. Philadelphia: WB Saunders Company, 1991.
DeCherney AH, Pernoll ML, eds. Current Obstetric and Gynecologic Diagnosis and Treatment, 8th ed. Connecticut: Appleton & Lange, 1994.

12.7

Dyspareunia and Pelvic Pain

Patsy Parker and Jo Ann Rosenfeld

Introduction

Although dyspareunia and chronic pelvic pain are often difficult to diagnose and treat, the primary care provider can influence the woman's health and well-being and often provide treatment that helps the woman tremendously. By taking a positive attitude and creating a therapeutic relationship over time, the provider can often improve if not cure symptoms. With both dyspareunia and pelvic pain, women often have a long and complicated history that involves several different episodes and locations of the pain and usually several providers with differing treatments. Little research has been done on women with these problems, and what has been investigated has usually entailed only one perspective, either by surgeons with biomechanical models of pain or psychologists with completely psychological etiologies. Unless providers realize that a woman's pain is likely to be mixture of both, they will likely become frustrated along with their patients.

Pelvic pain and dyspareunia can both have their roots in childhood sexual abuse. Women who have been sexually abused as children have a higher incidence of both chronic pelvic pain and dyspareunia (1). Chronic pelvic pain can be related to early pelvic inflammatory disease, adhesions, or have an unknown physical cause that is buried in the sexual, physical, and psychological events of the abuse. Dyspareunia can develop because of painful and unpleasant sexual encounters as a child that bring back enough bad memories to make intercourse painful as an adult.

An Approach to Dyspareunia

It is difficult to determine the prevalence of dyspareunia. One study of 324 women surveyed at random found that 39% never had dyspareunia, 28% had short-term dyspareunia that resolved, and 16% complained of chronic dyspareunia their whole sexual lives (2).

In women with dyspareunia, providers should screen for and be open to the possibility of a history of childhood or adult sexual abuse or rape. Many women, if asked, will honestly be willing to discuss such episodes. Even if the woman is not ready to talk about it, asking shows that the provider considers such a history important and will be willing to listen and believe her. Questions like "Some women with painful intercourse have had a previous history of rape, sexual abuse, or being forced to have sex against their will; did this ever happen to you?" and "Pelvic pains sometimes come from difficulty or unpleasant episodes of sexual intercourse; has that ever been the case with you?" can open the door and give the woman permission to discuss her own situation. If the provider is the first health professional a patient tells that she has been sexually abused, it is important

that she be listened to and believed. Many providers may be uncomfortable dealing with these issues. However, discovery and discussion are important tools for all providers; counseling can be referred to a therapist trained and knowledgeable in these concerns.

The primary care provider can make a definite impact on this problem. The cause is usually multifactorial. There is often a medical component (e.g., vaginitis, lack of lubrication) and a psychological element (e.g., fear of pain and lack of constructive communication of that fear to partner) that both need work for improvement. Often even partial recovery creates a significant improvement in the woman's and her partner's lives. Almost all dyspareunia creates or is influenced by less than adequate communication that needs addressing for the partnership's well-being.

History

With dyspareunia, women often have a lengthy history. There was a first episode of pain, fear that intercourse would hurt again, and then delay in trying to have intercourse again. Perhaps an intervening vaginal infection or just enough time occurred, and intercourse did hurt, so the cycle continued. At some point, guilt and shame about not having intercourse make the problem even harder to resolve. Getting to the cause of the dyspareunia takes time, attention to detail, and sensitivity.

To begin helping a patient with dyspareunia, the first step is obtaining a good history. First are questions about the occurrences: When did the problem start? How often does it happen? What were the circumstances, where was the pain? Next should be a detailed discussion of when the pain occurs: (a) Were you well lubricated? (b) Have you ever had any pelvic inflammatory disease (PID)? and (c) A history of PID increase the risk of dyspareunia (odds ration = 3.87) (3).

After this, the provider should discover what the woman and her partner have done about the dyspareunia, if anything. Have they discussed it? Failure of communication of this problem is a symptom of a larger and more widespread communication problem.

A social and sexual history is last. Questions include (1) How is your relationship doing? (2) Does this bring back any memories or events that happened as a child? (3) Have you had problems with all lovers, or only recently? (4) Have you ever had sexual intercourse without pain?

Physical Examination

The physical examination for the woman with dyspareunia can be totally normal and uneventful or can be painful, difficult, and even impossible. The woman should be made as comfortable as possible in a well-heated room. If she chooses, a companion of her choice can be present. The provider should assure the woman that the examination can be stopped whenever she wishes or when she feels pain.

The external genitalia and introitus should be closely examined for lesions, lacerations, or infection. A finger should be introduced gently into the vaginal vault. If this is tolerated and no vaginismus occurs, a speculum should then be introduced. A smaller than usual speculum, a Peterson (long and narrow), virgin, or even a nasal speculum may be needed. Cultures should be obtained, if indicated. The bimanual exam, if tolerated, is important to look for deep tenderness or masses. A rectal exam is not needed, unless history or physical examination suggests endometriosis.

Etiology and Treatments

Usually this is a chronic or long-term problem. There are three major kinds of pain with intercourse: pain with entry, pain in some specific location of the vagina or labia, and pain with deep penetration (Table 12.7.1).

Pain with entry may be caused by a variety of causes. The most common is lack of lubrication. Women do not always have an accurate idea of how they function sexually and may

Table 12.7.1. Etiologies of Dyspareunia

Pain on entry
  Lack of lubrication
    Lack of knowledge of sexual response
    Lack of arousal
    Postmenopausal vaginal atrophy
  Labia minora tear
  Vaginitis
  Excessive douching with irritation
  Vaginismus
Pain in specific area of vagina
  Tight hymenal ring
  Old scars or lesions, abscesses, and gland enlargements
Pain with deep penetration
  Mass
  Endometriosis
  Adhesions
  Vaginismus
  Condyloma acuminata
  Psychological stress or problems

suppose that it only takes a short while to be well lubricated. If a woman is aroused mentally, then it may take only a short time to be well lubricated. If she is not, then it can take some time, even 30 to 40 minutes, to become lubricated with fairly direct stimulation. Fear or anxiety about pain with intercourse may make the whole process take even longer. Postmenopausal vaginal atrophy may also decrease lubrication significantly, and can be treated with topical or oral estrogen, if not contraindicated (see Chapters 20 and 21).

Treatment can start with education about the sexual arousal and response process. Discussion with the woman and her partner can improve the situation. Exercises over several weeks, like "sensate" exercises for sexual dysfunctions (see Chapter 10.1), attempts at better communication between partners before and during sexual intercourse, and use of lubricants may all improve the symptoms.

Another common cause of pain with entry is a small tear in the posterior part of the introitus that is recurrently injured. If a small tear occurs with intercourse, it needs to heal open. However, in repose, the labia minora and the sides of the vagina are next to each other, so rather than healing open, the tear can continue to heal closed. Then, each time intercourse is attempted, the tear is opened again, causing a new episode of pain. In this situation, sometimes a tear is found on pelvic exam, or the woman may know that this area is the location of her pain. Then the solution is either having frequent (several times a week for 1 or 2 weeks) intercourse or using her fingers in her vagina frequently (three times a day) to help the area heal open.

Another cause of pain with entry is a vaginal infection. Treating a vaginitis may improve symptoms significantly, especially a yeast vaginitis (see Chapter 12.6). If women have been douching, sometimes stopping will help. Vaginismus is involuntary tightening of the pubococcygeal muscles around the introitus at attempted penetration or vaginal examination, causing pain with entry. The pain then reinforces the spasm. This is often noticed on pelvic exam and can be treated successfully by the provider and woman over time. Women with dyspareunia often have had a history of painful examination, sexual trauma, or strict religious upbringing. Vaginismus can be treated while the woman discusses and deals with previous sexual trauma and its effects on her life, either with the provider or with another counselor. Unless the woman realizes the impact of her history on her problem, it is unlikely she can overcome it.

To treat vaginismus, the provider teaches the woman through gradual exercises to learn how to keep her pelvic muscles relaxed. Because the provider can work with the woman in the office over time, this can be successfully treated by the primary provider. The woman and/or her partner gradually work putting a finger nearer and nearer to the introitus and then into the vagina in separate sessions occurring over weeks. Gradually the woman gets used to either fingers or dilators in her vagina. She needs to start with a small diameter and work up to larger sizes. Often inserting the objects herself can give her a measure of control so that the treatment does not feel like a further violation.

Occasionally pain with entry is caused by a tight hymenal ring. On pelvic exam the vagina may be open anywhere from a cotton swab to a fingertip. The treatment is either surgery or stretching with graduated dilators or fingers.

Sometimes women have pain in a specific area of the vagina or labia. It is important to find the area in question. Often having the woman point to the area may be the most direct and easiest way to find the area. Inspection and palpation may reveal a reason for the pain. Sometimes an old delivery injury has left a scar that does not stretch, muscles that were not correctly repaired, or an inclusion cyst that is causing pain. If nothing is discovered on exam of an area with distinct pain, a referral to a gynecologist may be appropriate.

Pain with deep penetration can also be caused by a variety of causes. The vagina, although it has pressure sensation, has no light touch enervation. Although there are some treatable causes, many women with pain on deep penetration have a psychological component that will need treatment. Sometimes the cervix is struck with intercourse; using different positions in sexual intercourse may help. Large condyloma acuminata can cause bleeding, adhesions, and pain on deep penetration; it can be treated. Adhesions and endometriosis can also cause pain with deep penetration. They are both diagnosed and treated surgically.

A Couples' Approach

While the above medical causes are being investigated, treated, and cured, the provider should talk with the woman about her present and past relationships. The woman may need long-term counseling for other psychological problems. Failure of relationships and inadequacy of communication about sexual intercourse cause, contribute to, or will be the result of dyspareunia. The provider should discuss with the woman how she is communicating with her partner. The provider may want to provide counseling for both members of the couple, or refer them to a counselor and/or a sexual therapist for continued therapy.

An Approach to Chronic Pelvic Pain

Acute pelvic pain is consistent with a variety of medical conditions in the genitourinary and lower gastrointestinal tract, several of them relative emergencies. Urinary tract infections, nephrolithiasis, torsion of bowel (volvulus) or ovaries, diverticulitis, appendicitis, bowel rupture, intussusception, rectal problems, ectopic pregnancy, spontaneous abortion, and PID are all causes of acute pelvic pain, some of which require emergent diagnosis and treatment. These will not be discussed in this chapter.

Chronic pelvic pain (CPP) is defined in one of three ways: (*a*) pain lasting over 6 months, (*b*) pain that lacks apparent physical cause, or (*c*) pain accompanied by altered life behaviors including sexual life, work, recreation, and mood (1).

CPP can be difficult to diagnose and improve. The approach to the history and physical has no emergencies, and diagnosis may take several visits and treatment may take several more. It is often difficult to diagnose with any accuracy one specific reason for the chronic pain, and this creates significant frustration for the woman and her provider. Often the woman either "doctor-shops" until she is given a hysterectomy, another operation, or is dependent on narcotics, or she withdraws completely from health care providers in frustration and often uses alternate healers. However, the provider should not approach pelvic pain with the belief that either it is all "biomechanical," i.e., pain in a certain muscle group requiring lidocaine injections or all caused by uterine prolapse requiring surgery, or all "psychiatric." Studies performed on women in "chronic pain" or "chronic pelvic pain" clinics were usually performed either by surgeons or psychologists, and the problems of the women seen were unlikely to be generalizable to primary care practice. Each woman is different, and each woman with pain usually has components of both types of causes. A woman with endometriosis is likely to have "medical" pain that then causes emotional and psychological distress. Women under chronic stress are more likely to notice mild to moderate discomfort.

Women who have a history of spontaneous abortions, documented extrauterine pelvic inflammatory disease, or leiomyomata are at greater risk for CPP (3). There is no increased risk of CPP with increased gravidity, parity, or number of elective abortions (4).

Chronic Pain Syndromes

Many women with chronic pelvic pain belong to a group of women with chronic pain syndromes that include irritable bowel syndrome, chronic back pain, chronic headaches, chronic upper gastrointestinal distress, and often other pain syndromes (5). These women often have had a history of childhood abuse, sexual abuse, and partner violence (1, 6–8). They are women who tolerate pain poorly and develop a chronic self-cycling process.

Women with CPP, in one study, met the criteria for major depression and lifetime substance abuse more than controls (7). Another study found that 59% of women seeking evaluation in a pelvic pain clinic scored high on a depression scale (1). Many have a high incidence of marital distress and sexual dysfunction, including dyspareunia.

Treatment is difficult and requires a multidisciplinary approach of psychologist, counselor, primary care provider, physical therapist, and sometimes rehabilitation therapist.

History

When a woman presents with pelvic pain, history is the first step. Sometimes women who have had pelvic pain have had it for so many years or have so many different pains that the story is long and complex. What is relevant may be determined by the setting. For example, at 4 AM in the emergency room getting all the details of a 20-year history of pelvic pain is not possible or sensible. In that situation, concentrating on the current pain episode and how she was treated in the past will most quickly reach the goals of making some diagnosis and more importantly making the pain stop. However, as her primary care provider, understanding what happened with the first episode 20 years ago may help to understand what to do in the present.

The timing of the pain and its quality are important: (a) When did this episode start? (b) What made it start, what makes it stop, how long does it last? (c) Does it radiate anywhere, is it sharp, dull, crampy? and (d) Are there times when it goes away completely or is it there all of the time? Ask the woman to describe the pain herself, using her own words. Also ask her to rate the pain on a scale from one to 10, with 10 as the worst pain that she has ever had. This rating will quickly show the importance of the problem. If the woman has more than one pain, it often helps to characterize each pain separately, essentially getting a separate history about each pain. The history of the pain is important. Questions such as (a) "Have you had a similar pain before?" (b) "What happened then?" (c) "How did the doctor fix it?" and (d) "Have you had any surgery for the pain?" all are useful. The provider should question the function of the urinary and gastrointestinal systems. Bladder and bowel dysfunction may suggest nongynecological causes of chronic pelvic pain, although these often coexist.

Physical Examination and Radiological Evaluation

Anything in the lower genitourinary or gastrointestinal tract can cause chronic pelvic pain. A complete examination including abdominal examination is important, looking for tenderness, masses, and organomegaly. A genital examination, similarly, looks for enlargement of ovaries or uterus, masses, tenderness, signs of infection, PID, or endometriosis. A rectal and rectovaginal examination is important because endometriosis implants can occur in the rectovaginal septum. Radiological examination would include an ultrasound of the pelvis. Vaginal ultrasonography has become accurate in diagnosing causes of CPP and may help to avoid the need for laparoscopy (9). Further studies, such as abdominal ultrasound of kidneys, CT scan of the abdomen, IVP, or barium enema depend on discovering history or physical suggesting disease there.

A laparoscopy is often indicated if the diagnosis is unclear. A laparoscopy can diagnose endometriosis, adhesions, or masses, biopsy suspicious area, and even treat by lysing adhesions. In some series of referred patients, up to 88% of laparoscopies done for CPP showed pathology (up to 40% adhesions, and over 30% endometriosis) (1). Although, in controlled studies, more women with pain had positive pathological laparoscopic findings than women without pain, the amount of pathology could not always be correlated with amount of pain (10). If laparoscopy is positive for endometriosis, treatment can be started. If negative, the results can reassure the woman that she is normal.

If the pain is severe, long-standing, or the woman wants to know what is going on, a pelvioscopy may be indicated. It is important to talk about the risk and complications of the procedure so the woman understands that there is some risk involved in trying to be more definitive about her pain. Some women at that point will decide the pain is really not worth surgery;

others will be quite clear that they need to know what is going on with their bodies.

Relationship between Pain and Anxiety

In the discussion of pelvic pain, emotional, social, and psychological issues arise. The pain is in the pelvis, while the subjective response varies with the woman. The woman may not appreciate what stress can do. Helping the woman to talk about her fears, understand her stress, respect her body, and get reassurance are all important therapeutic modalities to try. Everyone hurts more when they are worried or anxious. Helping women to feel safe and secure in their bodies may help to relieve pain. A few women with chronic pelvic pain may be candidates for a chronic pain clinic. If all other methods of diagnosis and treatment have been tried, then a more chronic approach may be in order.

Causes of Pelvic Pain and Therapy

The etiology of CPP is complex, often overlapping, and often involves nongynecological symptoms (Table 12.7.2). Most often more than one of these causes pain. Then there is anxiety, stress, and spasm, which causes more pain. Psychological components are involved in most causes of CPP, but if the medical elements are treated and a therapeutic relationship is established with the provider by which counseling is provided, significant improvement is likely.

The most common cause of CPP is probably gastrointestinal (11). Irritable bowel syndrome (IBS) (see Chapter 16) and constipation can both cause CPP. IBS often is associated with gynecological symptoms, especially CPP. IBS symptoms worsen during menstruation, and women with IBS and CPP often have depression, somatization, substance abuse, and a history of childhood sexual abuse (12). Diverticulosis and diverticulitis, although usually intermittent and acute, can lead to chronic pain.

Urinary problems can also cause CPP, including urethral pain and urethritis, intersti-

Table 12.7.2. Some Causes of Chronic Pelvic Pain

Gastrointestinal
  Irritable bowel syndrome
  Constipation
  Diverticulitis/diverticulosis
Urological
  Urethritis/urethral syndrome
  Cystitis
  Bladder spasms
  Chronic or recurrent pyelonephritis
Musculoskeletal pain
  Lumbosacral pain
  Myofascial pain
Gynecological
  Pain with ovulation
  Ovarian cysts
  Dysmenorrhea
  Endometriosis
  Adhesions
  Chronic PID
  Cancers of ovary and uterus
Nerve entrapment syndromes of lower abdominal wall
  After cesarean section

tial cystitis, and bladder spasms (1). Chronic musculoskeletal pain either in the pelvic musculature or lower back can cause CPP. Nerve entrapment after surgery or cesarean section can also cause chronic pain.

Pain with Ovulation

Pain may occur in ovulating women between the ages of 12 to 55 years. Usually its onset is midcycle or a few days earlier. It can be quite sharp and may last for several days. It usually will resolve spontaneously.

Ovulation pain is caused when the ovary develops a follicle. At the time of ovulation, the egg is extruded into the peritoneal cavity along with some follicular fluid. The egg is then transported into the fallopian tube where it may be fertilized.

During the process of follicular development, the ovary may actually double in size. Because it is the serosal, peritoneal surface of the ovary that contains nerves, this process of stretching may be painful. Many women do not realize that their ovaries change size each month. Helping them to understand the process may be enough to alleviate some of their anxiety about the pain. When the egg is extruded into the peritoneal cavity, there can be a small amount of bleeding with the process. The irritation of the blood in the peritoneal cavity can also cause pain.

Ovulation pain is often a clinical diagnosis based on the time in the cycle that the pain occurs. An ultrasound can demonstrate a follicle.

Reassurance, time, heat, and nonsteroidal anti-inflammatory agents may help the pain to pass. Oral contraceptive agents with a high estrogen dose will prevent ovulation. Both Depo-Provera and Lupron/Synarel will also prevent ovulation, but each of these has more major side effects.

Ovarian Cysts

Functional ovarian cysts most frequently occur in ovulating women age 12 to 55 years. Usually the onset of the pain is midcycle or a few days earlier. It can be quite sharp and may last for several days or weeks, and it may be associated with bleeding or spotting. The pain usually will resolve spontaneously.

Each month with ovulation rather than just forming a small follicle the ovary may form a cyst. These are larger collections of fluid in the ovary that may be associated with either the follicle or the corpus luteum. When the serosal surface of the ovary stretches, there is pain. Cysts may vary in size from less than 1 cm to many centimeters.

There may be bleeding into the cyst causing hemorrhagic cysts and stretching. Other kinds of cysts may not cause any pain, but may be confused on an ultrasound with a functional cyst. Cysts can also form on the tube and within the broad ligament. These are present throughout life and are totally benign and ir-

relevant, except that they may be confused with a cyst that is causing pain.

An ultrasound will show a cyst in the ovary. It often appears as a simple anechoic round structure. The ultrasound cannot differentiate a simple functional cyst from any other kind of cyst. A hemorrhagic cyst may appear as a complex mass, part solid and part cystic. It may also appear as an anechoic mass with matter in the bottom.

Functional cysts and hemorrhagic cysts usually resolve with time or suppression of ovulation with an oral contraceptive agent. Often waiting 1 or 2 months will allow the cyst to resolve. If the cyst is still present on ultrasound after 1 or 2 months, laparoscopy should be considered. A laparoscopic evaluation and pathology may be the only way to categorize cysts. Any cyst that is larger than 5 to 8 cm should be evaluated with a diagnostic laparoscopy and probably oophorectomy.

Ovarian Torsion

Infrequently an ovary or an ovarian cyst will twist on its vascular pedicle causing swelling and extreme pain. This is usually a diagnosis that is made in the emergency room and is treated surgically on an emergent basis. This is usually acute pelvic pain and not chronic.

Endometriosis

Endometriosis is the development of endometrial glandular implants on areas that are not the endometrium. Responsive to hormonal cycles, these implants mimic the menstrual cycle, causing pain by enlarging and stretching. The area of pain is determined by location of the implants. Rupture or leakage of fluid into the peritoneum from these implants can also cause pain. With menses, there can be bleeding into the peritoneal cavity. Blood in the peritoneal cavity and the stretching of the peritoneal surfaces causes pain. The degree of the pain and the amount of the endometriosis may not be related. The implants can occur anywhere, even in pleural space and peritoneum, but they most often occur in the tubes, ovary, pouch of Douglas, and pelvic areas.

The pain is usually crampy or sharp lower abdominal pain that starts with the onset of menses. Over time, the pain may be prolonged so that it eventually is present all of the time.

The cause of endometriosis is unknown. It has been attributed to retrograde menses, congenital abnormalities of the peritoneal surface (because it can be present in men also), and problems with the local immune system. Rarely, it can be hematogenously spread. It can also be found in scar tissue from an incision that penetrated into the endometrial cavity (i.e., cesarean section) or at the distal end of the round ligament in the groin. Endometriosis often causes infertility.

Diagnosis. Endometriosis is suspected by history and diagnosed by laparoscopy or pelvioscopy. Up to 47%, with an average of 15%, of women who have laparoscopy for CPP have endometriosis (1). The amount of endometriosis found has no relation with the amount of pelvic pain.

Treatment. Endometriosis is estrogen-dependent. It may be treated with hormonal suppression, inducing the absence of menses for 6 to 9 months. Hormones that can be used to treat endometriosis include oral contraceptives, Provera, Depo-Provera, Lupron (a synthetic gonadotropin-releasing hormone analog in depot form), or danazol (Table 12.7.3). Studies comparing OCPs, danazol, and gonadotropin-releasing hormone have found similar significant improvement in pelvic pain, whereas OCPs are better tolerated and less expensive than the other two forms (13). Surgical ablation using laser or electrocautery is another approach. In persistent cases surgical removal of uterus, tubes, or ovaries may be indicated.

Adhesions

Adhesions cause a sharp or dull pulling sensation that is located anywhere in the abdomen and can be felt any time of the month. Adhesions are filmy or dense sheets of scar tissue that can form between any two abdominal organs, e.g., bowel and bowel, uterus and tubes, uterus and bowel. Adhesions form when the body is trying to heal itself; they can occur after intra-abdominal infections like PID or after surgery. Pain can occur when usually mobile structures (like the bowel) are held in place and cannot move. Pain can also occur if the ovary is unable to move when it usually expands and contracts with ovulation.

Diagnosis. Adhesions are most accurately diagnosed with laparoscopy or pelvioscopy. Sometimes they can be seen on ultrasound, but the information is often hard to interpret and may be interpreted as large loculated areas.

Treatment. Adhesions can be surgically removed, but new adhesions can form as the result of surgery. The number of adhesions present may not have a direct relationship to the amount of trauma. In women with adhesions, laparoscopic lysis of those adhesions improved CPP in 75% of women without a psychologi-

Table 12.7.3. Pharmacological Treatment of Endometriosis

Medication	Dosage	Side Effects/Disadvantages
Oral Contraceptives	Variable	Pregnancy prevention, weight gain/loss, nausea
Danazol (Danocrine)	800 mg every day	Nausea, vomiting, headache expensive, amenorrhea
Leuprolide (Lupron Depot)	3.75 mg once monthly	CV, GI, and gynecomastia, dizziness, headache, ECG changes, amenorrhea
Medroxyprogesterone (Provera)	10 mg every day 25 days a month	Bloating, nausea, vomiting
Depo-Provera	One every 3 months	Irregular periods

cal component to their CPP and in 40% of women of women with a chronic psychological pain syndrome (14).

Chronic Pelvic Inflammatory Disease

Chronic PID can cause crampy or sharp pelvic pain that may come or go; its onset may be either acute or slow. This may be caused by re-inflammation of an old episode of acute PID.

The diagnosis is based on a history of PID. Sometimes it can be confirmed by finding a complex mass on ultrasound that responds to antibiotic treatment. Usually the white count is not elevated. Treatment includes a short course of antibiotics. Persistent cases may be treated for as long as 2 months.

Cancers of the Female Reproductive Tract

Cancers of the female reproductive tract usually do not present with pain (see Chapters 12.3, 12.4, 12.5). Often women who present with pain or other symptoms are mostly concerned that they might have cancer. If the pain is caused by cancer, there is usually metastases to pelvic lymph nodes, rectosigmoid, and bone, with poor prognosis.

Urethritis

Urethral syndromes and urethritis can cause CPP, although the pain will be described as burning in the urethra and pain with urination. This is diagnosed by clinical suspicion, physical exam, and culture of urine and urethra. Visual inspection may show a herpetic lesion or erythema. Urine culture should be negative. Urine analysis may show trichomonads, candida species, or white or red blood cells.

Treatment includes antiviral or antibiotics based on the presumed etiology. Pyridium, a bladder anesthetic, will help relieve the pain.

Chronic or Recurrent Pyelonephritis

Pain from chronic pyelonephritis may be flank pain that feels like a burning or a constant ache. It may be associated with bladder or lower abdominal pain. Women may also have crampy abdominal pain from an accompanying ileus. The pain is caused by inflammation of the kidney and may be from swelling of the renal capsule.

Symptoms and signs include fever, chills, costovertebral angle tenderness on exam, pyuria, and leukocytosis. After obtaining a urine culture, antibiotics are started intravenously. Hospitalization is usually needed.

Irritable Bowel Syndrome

IBS presents as crampy abdominal pain associated with bloody or mucousy diarrhea (see Chapter 16). Women with IBS often have co-existent CPP and have similar histories of substance and childhood sexual abuse. IBS predisposes a woman to have a hysterectomy (12).

Therapeutic Approach to Chronic Pelvic Pain

CPP must be approached and treated medically and psychologically simultaneously. The provider and woman must make a contract and agree to investigate and treat likely biomedical causes, while investigating the woman's response to her pain, her possible previous history of abuse, and her present psychological state. This can be done with the provider and/or with a counselor or therapist. The history, physical, and minimal tests should eliminate most possible causes of CPP. If anything is discovered, such as urethritis or chronic constipation, this should be treated. If there is no improvement over a few visits, or no one cause is determined, a laparoscopy is indicated for diagnosis and often treatment. This may diagnose adhesions, endometriosis, or other pelvic pathology, or reassure the woman and provider. If endometriosis is discovered, treatment can be started, but will need to be evaluated over several months to determine response.

During this time, no narcotics should be given. Nonsteroidal anti-inflammatory agents are good analgesics, and tricyclic and the newer serotonin-specific uptake inhibitor antidepressants can be used in addition.

A multidisciplinary approach can reduce the frequency of hysterectomy for CPP (11). Hysterectomy should not be contemplated in the early evaluation, as it provides a cure for only a small percentage of women with CPP. Medical treatment for CPP produces significant improvement in pain and quality of life (15). Except for cancer, large fibroids, and severe endometriosis, hysterectomy is seldom indicated (see Chapter 21). In one study of women followed for over 1 year after hysterectomy for CPP who had large fibroids, over one-fourth still had significant persistent CPP (4). Removing the uterus, tubes, and ovaries is un-

likely to relieve pelvic pain that has a psychological component, and causes other medical and psychological problems. Continuing counseling and therapy, including sexual therapists and/or chronic pain specialists, may be needed.

Conclusions

With a combination of a moderate medical evaluation, an ongoing therapeutic relationship between the provider and woman, and counseling, definite improvements may be made in the symptoms of CPP.

Special Considerations for Nurse Practitioners and Physician Assistants

Some women will accept a level of pain during sexual activity and not bring the problem to the provider's attention unless they are specifically asked about pain or discomfort. In addition, women and their providers are sometimes unsure about what type of language to use when talking about sexuality. Highly technical medical terms or slang terms with pejorative connotations may not be appropriate. Using several synonyms or descriptive words can help ensure that the woman and provider understand each other's meanings. Providers must not hesitate to clarify the meaning of any terms the woman uses. If the provider periodically repeats back to the woman what she understands is being said, the woman then has a chance to correct or expand the information (16).

Once a woman has expressed a sexual problem and the provider has gathered additional data regarding onset and course, it may be helpful to ask the woman why she thinks she has the problem and what attempts she has made to solve or deal with the problem. Myths and misconceptions, fears, misinformation, significant life events, or sexual traumas might

come to light through this approach. The provider can also clarify with the woman what she would like from the primary care visit (16).

Women who experience vaginismus may be highly motivated to break the cycle of pain and muscle spasm. An extremely gentle, limited pelvic examination can help break the cycle (17). Whereas the woman needs reassurance that she can "unlearn" her response to the fear of pain, both she and her partner need to understand that she does not consciously cause the muscle contractions to occur (18).

A detailed history is the most important diagnostic tool for vulvodynia, a chronic vulvar discomfort with complaints of burning, irritation, stinging, or rawness. Many factors probably contribute to the problem, including infections such as chronic candidiasis or HPV, dermatoses, and iatrogenic factors such as surgery and topical steroids. While investigating the possible physical markers of vulvodynia, the provider must be aware of the daily problems some of these women have faced for years. Women may think they are the only ones with symptoms, fear cancer, and become frustrated with unsuccessful and often unsympathetic treatment. Providers can also become discouraged when symptom control, but not cure, becomes the objective of care (19).

Care of a woman with any chronic pelvic pain can be a frustrating, time-consuming, and challenging problem in primary care. A multidisciplinary approach, many patient visits, and early referrals may be indicated. Physician consultation is needed to ensure a coordinated approach to management, and referral to appropriate specialists is needed for specific somatic pathologies. If somatic pathology has been ruled out, specialist care may be helpful for pain management through relaxation techniques, hypnosis, biofeedback, guided imagery, and other modalities. Cost and coverage by health insurance should be explored with the woman (20).

References

1. Steege JF, Stout AL, Somkuti G. Chronic pelvic pain in women. Toward an integrative model. Obstet Gynecol Surv 1993;48:95–110.
2. Glatt AE, Zinner SH, McCormack WM. The prevalence of dyspareunia. Obstet Gynecol 1990;75:433–436.
3. Heisterberg L. Factors influencing spontaneous abortion, dyspareunia and pelvic pain. Obstet Gynecol 1993;81:594–597.
4. Reiter RC, Gambone JC. Demographic and historical variables in women with idiopathic chronic pelvic pain. Obstet Gynecol 1990;75:428–432.
5. Thompson WG, Creed F, Drossman DA, et al. Functional bowel disease and functional abdominal pain. Gastroenterol Int 1992;5:75–79.
6. Reiter RC, Shakerin LR, Gambone JC, et al. Correlation between sexual abuse and somatization in women with somatic and nonsomatic chronic pelvic pain. Am J Obstet Gynecol 1991;165:104–111.
7. Harrop-Griffiths J, Katon W, Walker E, et al. The association between chronic pelvic pain, psychiatric diagnoses and childhood sexual abuse. Obstet Gynecol 1988;71:589–594.
8. Walling MK, Reiter RC, O'Hara MW, et al. Abuse history and chronic pain in women: I. Prevalence of sexual abuse and physical abuse. Obstet Gynecol 1994;84:193–199.
9. Nolan TE, Elkins TE. Chronic pelvic pain. Differentiation anatomic from functional causes. Postgrad Med 1993;94:125–128.
10. Fukaya T, Hoshiaia H, Yajima A. Is pelvic endometriosis associated with chronic pain? A retrospective study of 618 cases diagnosed by laparoscopy. Am J Obstet Gynecol 1993;169:719–722.
11. Gambone JC, Reiter RC. Nonsurgical management of chronic pelvic pain: a multidisplinary approach. Clin Obstet Gynecol 1990;33:205–211.
12. Longstreth GF. Irritable bowel syndrome and chronic pelvic pain. Obstet Gynecol Surv 1994;49:505–507.
13. Vercellin P, Trespidi L, Colombo A, et al. A gonadotropin releasing hormone agonist versus a low dose oral contraceptive for pelvic pain associated with endometriosis. Fertil Steril 1993;60:75–79.
14. Steege JF, Stout AL. Resolution of chronic pelvic pain after laparscopic lysis of adhesions. Am J Obstet Gynecol 1991;165:278–281.
15. Carlson KJ, Miller BA, Fowler FJ Jr. The Maine women's Health Study: II. Outcomes of non-surgical management of leiomyomas, abnormal bleeding and chronic pelvic pain. Obstet Gynecol 1994;83:566–572.
16. Dunn ME. Sexual health. In: Lichtman R, Papera S, eds. Gynecology. Norwalk: Appleton & Lange, 1990:427–434.
17. Sarazin SK, Seymour SF. Causes and treatment options for women with dyspareunia. Nurse Pract 1991;16:30, 35–36, 38, 41.
18. Ayres T. Sexual dysfunction. In: Star WL, Lommell LL, Shannon MT, eds. Women's Primary Health Care. Washington, DC: American Nurses' Association, 1995:12-160–12-170.
19. Jones KD, Lehr ST. Vulvodynia: diagnostic techniques and treatment modalities. Nurse Pract 1994;19:34, 37–40, 42–45.
20. Star WL. Pelvic pain-chronic. In: Star WL, Lommell LL, Shannon MT, eds. Women's Primary Health Care. Washington, DC: American Nurses' Association, 1995:12-113–12-122.

13.1

Risks and Prevention of Arteriosclerotic Heart Disease

Valerie K. Ulstad

Introduction

Cardiovascular disease is the leading cause of death in women. Cardiovascular disease is a progressive process of atherosclerotic plaquing throughout the vasculature in the body. The predominant clinical manifestation of cardiovascular disease in women and men is coronary heart disease (CHD)(1). This is a process involving the progressive occlusion of the coronary arteries serving the ventricular myocardium. CHD may be clinically silent for decades and then eventually confront the clinician as a chronic problem (chronic stable exertional angina or congestive heart failure) or as an acute problem (unstable angina, acute myocardial infarction [AMI] or sudden cardiac death). Other important manifestations of cardiovascular disease include cerebrovascular disease and peripheral vascular disease that should be assumed to coexist with CHD.

The actual number of myocardial infarctions in men and women is similar, although women develop the disease when they are approximately 10 years older (2). Although CHD is the leading cause of death in American women, many women do not believe that they are at risk. A common misperception is that CHD is only a man's disease and that the most likely threat to a woman's life is breast cancer. Over a lifetime, a woman is 10 times more likely to develop CHD than she is breast cancer (3). An equal number of deaths from CHD occur in women as in men. After age 60 years, one in four women and men dies of CHD (4).

The Framingham Heart Study, a longitudinal cohort study of cardiovascular disease, started in 1948 and included women from the beginning. The initial rationale for inclusion of women in this study was to potentially understand why young women were protected from CHD compared to young men. The Framingham study found the following:

1. Women seem to develop CHD manifestations 10 years later than men
2. Women tend to present with angina as their initial manifestation of CHD,

whereas men tend to present with an AMI
3. Silent or clinically unrecognized MIs are more common in women than in men
4. That the case fatality rate for acute MI is higher in women than in men (5).

During the last 20 years, the annual mortality rate from acute MI has fallen. The decline in CHD, morbidity, and mortality has been less dramatic in women compared to men and less in African-Americans compared to whites (6). Risk factor reduction in the general population has probably resulted in reduced incidence of acute MI and sudden coronary death. Improvements in medical care have probably contributed by decreasing the case fatality rate from acute MI (3). Risk factor reduction in the population may be as important as recent technological advances to this decline in mortality.

The most common presenting symptom of CHD in women is chest discomfort. Many studies have suggested that evaluation of women with chest pain have been inadequate when compared to men (7, 8). Women with chest discomfort, particularly premenopausal women, are often given the label "anxious woman" without appropriate evaluation or education regarding risk factor modification. The chest discomfort is often a warning sign. Chest pain in women compatible with angina pectoris should lead to an evaluation for CHD, including diagnostic testing and risk factor modification. A major goal for women's health must be to prevent the development of CHD, to slow the progression and to promote the regression of CHD that has already developed in order to improve the quality and quantity of life, and to evaluate the woman with chest discomfort completely and compassionately.

The focus of this chapter will be on the three most important issues confronting the primary care provider: (1) the primary prevention of CHD in women including an emphasis on risk factor modification and patient education, (2) the secondary prevention of recurrent cardiac events in women with established cardiovascular disease, and (3) the outpatient evaluation of chest discomfort in women.

Pathophysiology

The atherosclerotic process involves many different specific cell types in the blood vessel wall and seems to depend on blood vessel wall injury for initiation. The role of traditional cardiovascular risk factors like hypertension and hypercholesterolemia in acute and chronic vascular injury is a subject of intense study. Chronic CHD develops over time as these lesions grow, resulting in the inability of the coronary artery to vasodilate in response to the increased metabolic needs of the tissue it supplies. Such a woman may have ischemic chest discomfort with exercise or emotional stress. Acute ischemic syndromes are the result of rupturing or fissuring of the atherosclerotic plaque with the development of superimposed platelet-rich thrombus adhering to the "crack in the plaque." Prevention of the clinical manifestations of CHD hinges on the prevention of plaque formation. The presence of plaque sets the stage for acute ischemic syndromes.

Although there is evidence that the stabilization and regression of atherosclerotic plaques may result in decreasing clinical events (9), the prevention of plaque formation is the way to prevent the clinical manifestations of cardiovascular disease. Recent evidence suggests that newly formed plaques are in fact the more dangerous types that may go on to acutely fissure, leading to superimposed thrombus and acute vessel closure (10). The atherosclerotic process may be highly modifiable.

Primary Prevention of CHD in Women

The risk factors for CHD in women are similar to those in men. In the Framingham Heart Study, risk factors for CHD included impaired glucose tolerance, cigarette smoking, elevated systolic or diastolic blood pressure, increased total serum cholesterol, increased low-density lipoprotein (LDL) levels, decreased high-density lipoprotein (HDL) levels, older age, and lack of serum estrogen after natural or surgical menopause.

Gender influences the significance of certain risk factors. Diabetes, hypertriglyceridemia, and low HDL levels are stronger risk factors in women than in men. Obesity and sedentary lifestyle are also risk factors in women. The Framingham study has been used to develop sex specific risk factor prediction charts that can help determine an individual's probability of developing CHD. The 5- and 10-year CHD risk can be roughly estimated by using a simple worksheet, the components of which are objective, independently predictive of CHD, and simple to measure (11). Clinicians may find such nomograms helpful. However, practically speaking, women should be given information about risk factor modification whenever risk factors are present, be offered nonpharmacologic methods to alter risk factors whenever possible, and be empowered to work with the health care provider to prevent CHD. Table 13.1.1 summarizes important aspects of primary prevention of CHD in women.

Increased Age

The incidence of CHD in women age 35 to 44 years is 1 per 1000, increasing to four per 1000 in women age 45 to 54 years. In the fifth decade, the incidence of CHD is half that in men. By the sixth decade, the incidence of CHD is equal in women and men. One in four women over the age of 65 years has CHD (12).

Family History of Premature Heart Disease

A family history of a first-degree male relative less than age 55 years or woman relative less than age 65 years who developed clinically manifest CHD or experienced sudden unexplained death is a definite risk factor (13). A

Table 13.1.1   Primary Prevention of Heart Disease in Women– A Partnership

Provider Actions To Promote Understanding

EMPOWER

- To control one's own health
- Risk factors can be modified
- Healthy heart habits in the home

EDUCATE

- Prevalence of heart disease in women
- Individual's risk factors
- Importance of plaque prevention

Patient Actions to Maintain Health

Modification of stress

Low-fat diet

No passive or active inhalation of cigarette smoke

Knowledge of own blood pressure and cholesterol (total and HDL)

Weight control

Control of diabetes

Regular exercise

Recognition of importance of prompt evaluation of chest discomfort

Discussion with health care provider about the risks and benefits of HRT (if menopausal)

family history of early heart disease is a strong predictor of CHD. Family-related variables such as cultural habits, socioeconomic status, education, and insurance coverage also play a role in the modification of atherosclerotic development and progression, the recognition of and adaptation to disease, and recovery from serious illness (14).

Race

CHD is a particularly important threat to African-American women, who have a higher incidence of CHD and an earlier mortality from CHD than both African-American men and white women and men (15). Data in other groups of women are lacking.

Diabetes Mellitus

Diabetes is a more potent risk factor for CHD in women than in men and negates the gender differential of the age of onset of CHD. Diabetics may have impaired estrogen binding that eliminates the protection against CHD that endogenous estrogen probably provides to premenopausal women (16). Mortality rates from CHD are 3 to 7 times higher among diabetic women than among nondiabetic women as compared with rates that are 2 to 4 times higher among diabetic men when compared to men without diabetes (17). Optimal control of diabetes is important for a variety of reasons, but the increased risk of subsequent cardiovascular events probably persists compared to the nondiabetic (18). Diabetics must vigorously modify other cardiovascular risk factors to avoid compounding the CHD risk.

Smoking

As many as 30% of US women are smokers. Smoking is the major cause of CHD in young and middle-aged women. Epidemiologic studies have shown a close association of smoking with stroke, sudden cardiac death, and peripheral vascular disease. The more cigarettes a woman smokes, the higher the risk. As compared to nonsmokers, a woman who smokes 1 to 4 cigarettes a day is at twice the risk of an acute MI, whereas a woman who smokes greater than 25 cigarettes per day has a fivefold increase in risk of a coronary event. A woman who smokes greater than 45 cigarettes a day has 11 times higher risk (19). Women who smoke have their first MI 19 years earlier than women who do not smoke (20).

Yet, quitting smoking is important. After smoking cessation, this risk is reduced to the level of a nonsmoking woman within 3 to 5 years. This is independent of the amount smoked, the age of quitting, or the duration of the smoking habit (21).

The effect of smoking is particularly potent among women with other risk factors for CHD: there is synergy of risk factors. Cigarette smoking leads to direct vascular injury, potentially triggering the progressive atherosclerotic process and potentially promoting plaque rupture and the development of acute ischemic syndromes. Nicotine, the active ingredient in tobacco smoke, can cause spasm in coronary arteries that have no significant angiographic stenosis (22). In habitual smokers, smoking 1 cigarette causes increases in arterial wall stiffness that may lead to plaque rupture (23). Other disadvantageous effects related to cigarette smoking include lower HDL levels, lower serum estrogen levels, increase in serum fibrinogen levels, earlier onset of menopause (24). Environmental tobacco smoke inhalation appears to increase the coronary death rate among nonsmokers by 20 to 70% (25).

Hypertension

Hypertension is a blood pressure of more than 140/90 mm Hg, or the need to use antihypertensive medication (26). Hypertension strongly and independently increases the risk of CHD in women (26). Systolic hypertension and diastolic hypertension are risk factors for CHD in women (27). After age 45 years, 60% of white women and 79% of African-American women in the United States have hypertension (12). Isolate systolic hypertension should be treated and affects approximately 30% of women over age 65 years (12). More women than men develop hypertension with increasing age (12).

Hypertension causes changes in the vascular system through increased shear force, especially at vessel branches, leading to damage of the blood vessel wall and promotion of the atherosclerotic process. The relative risk for

CHD is 3.5 for hypertensive women compared to nonhypertensive women. The relative risk of stroke is 2.6 for hypertensive women (27). A 10 mm Hg increase in systolic blood pressure produces a 20 to 30% increase in the risk of CHD and stroke in women (12). In women, a decrease of 6 mm Hg in diastolic pressure significantly reduced total mortality from vascular disease by 21%, fatal and nonfatal stroke by 42%, and fatal and nonfatal CHD by 14% (28).

Treatment of hypertension begins with nonpharmacologic therapies. Factors that promote the development of hypertension that may be modified include overweight, excessive alcohol consumption, high sodium intake, lack of potassium intake, cigarette smoking, and lack of physical activity (29). There have been no trials of nonpharmacologic treatment of hypertension in which the results were reported separately for women.

Hyperlipidemia

Most of the prospective observational studies have reported a positive association between total cholesterol levels and CHD in women. Clinical trial data or primary prevention of CHD by modification of the lipid profile in healthy women are limited because the predominant data obtained have been from men or from studies with relatively few women participants. None of these studies have adequate statistical power to estimate the effect of altered cholesterol profiles on the risk of CHD in healthy women (16).

The consistency of observational data suggest that interventions to lower LDL cholesterol levels and raise HDL cholesterol levels should benefit both women and men (16). These studies show that a total cholesterol above 260 mg/dL increases a woman's risk of mortality by 1.4. A decreased level of HDL cholesterol is a particularly strong predictor of an increased risk of CHD in women (30). HDL cholesterol level is second only to age as a predictor of death from cardiovascular causes among women. A 10 mg/dL change in HDL results in a 42% change in the risk for CHD in women (30). Women displayed an increased mortality with a relative risk of 1.7 with HDL less than 50 mg/dL, compared to women with an HDL over 50 mg/dL. Elevated triglyceride levels were an independent risk factor for CHD in women but not in men.

The new cholesterol guidelines include specific recommendations with respect to cholesterol management in women (13). For example, because of the advantageous effects on the lipid profile of postmenopausal women, hormone replacement therapy is currently recommended by the NCEP II as a first pharmacologic option for postmenopausal women with hypercholesterolemia (13).

Obesity

There is a direct positive association between obesity and the risk of CHD in women. Obesity is a well-established cause of diabetes mellitus, lipid abnormalities, and hypertension in women (31). In the Nurses Health Study, a prospective cohort study that involved over 120,000 middle-aged women, age 30 to 55 years, the risk of CHD was over three times higher among women with a body mass index of 29 or higher than among lean women. Even women who were mildly to moderately overweight (body mass index of 25 to 28.9) had nearly twice the risk of CHD as lean women. An independent effect of obesity persists even after adjustment for known cardiovascular risk factors (31).

Direct evidence that weight loss reduces the risk of CHD is lacking. These data are difficult to obtain because of the difficulties in maintaining weight loss. LDL levels and blood pressure can be reduced by weight loss (32). Prevention of obesity is important because treatment is so difficult. Excess abdominal and upper body adiposity is associated with a particularly high risk of CHD in women (33). The

risk of CHD rises steeply among women whose waist-to-hip ratio is higher than 0.8 (34). It is unclear whether the risk associated with body fat distribution can be modified.

Sedentary Lifestyle

Most of the epidemiologic studies that have been conducted to assess the relation of exercise to CHD included only men. The few studies that have included women suggest that physically active women have a 60 to 75% lower risk of CHD than sedentary women (16).

Aspirin

Prophylactic aspirin may be used in women over age 50 years with risk factors although benefit has not yet been shown in a prospective randomized clinical trial. Clinical trial data in men and cohort study data in women have been supportive of the prophylactic use of aspirin (35). Until results of a clinical trial in women are completed, clinicians should make individual decisions regarding potential benefit for their women. The Women's Health Study, a randomized trial of low-dose aspirin (100 mg on alternate days) in over 40,000 healthy women health professionals, age 45 years or older, is presently investigating the benefits in women (36).

Aspirin may reduce the risk of CHD, but it may increase the risk of hemorrhagic stroke in women. The ratio of the incidence of hemorrhagic stroke to that of MI is higher in women than in men, again pointing out the dangers of extrapolation of data derived only in men (16).

Antioxidants

Vitamin E, beta carotene, and vitamin C may reduce the risk of cardiovascular disease in women. In the Nurses' Health Study, the use of vitamin E supplements was associated with a small reduced risk of CHD. The study design did not prove cause and effect. Any potential benefit of antioxidant vitamins in the prevention of CHD is likely to be small so that reliable data can only come from large scale randomized trials in women.

Hormone Replacement Therapy (HRT)

Many observational studies have consistently shown a 40 to 50% reduction in the risk of CHD among postmenopausal women taking HRT (37). Because these are observational studies, selection bias and uncontrolled confounding variables cannot be excluded (38). The decision to treat a woman in these studies was made between the woman and her provider. Healthier, more compliant women who regularly have their prescriptions filled, and thus have better access to regular health care, may have been the ones to receive HRT. These characteristics may have been the explanation, or part of the explanation for the "beneficial" effects of HRT seen. Only a randomized double-blind clinical trial, in which the known and unknown confounding variables are equally distributed between the placebo and the treatment groups can answer the question about the protective effect of hormone replacement in CHD prevention in the healthy postmenopausal woman and the importance of that effect. The findings have been consistent and demonstrate a potentially large protective effect of unopposed estrogen in the mortality from CHD. It is widely believed that part of the benefit seen in these observational studies is real.

The decision to take HRT should be individualized for each woman with the help of her provider. The potential effect on the complete health of the woman is the important to consider (see Chapter 23.1) (39). Estrogen may significantly decrease the risk of CHD, the risk of fractures caused by osteoporosis and the frequency of disabling perimenopausal symptoms; however, it is a recognized cause of endometrial cancer and gallbladder disease. The possible influence of HRT on development of breast cancer is not yet clear, although the in-

creased risk is likely to be small. CHD is much more common than breast cancer. Until the results of randomized trials are available, the observational study evidence supporting the use of estrogen to prevent CHD has to be considered on its inferential merit.

A protective effect of estrogen is biologically plausible because estrogen has been shown to reduce LDL cholesterol levels and increase HDL cholesterol levels by 10 to 15% (40). The lipid benefits probably account for half the protective effect seen with estrogen (41). Estrogen has also been shown to have direct beneficial effects on the vasculature particularly through endothelial function (42). Estrogen has vasodilatory effects mediated by the formation and release of endothelium-derived relaxing factor (EDRF), reduction of endothelin levels, and the promotion of prostacyclin production (43).

The addition of a progestinal agent to HRT may decrease the risk of endometrial cancer and increase the compliance by decreasing bleeding, but whether the combined treatment will still provide protection against CHD is unclear. The best evidence comparing estrogen alone with combined regimens using estrogen and progestinal agents comes from the recently reported Postmenopausal Estrogen/Progestin Intervention trial (44). This randomized double-blind placebo controlled trial followed 875 healthy postmenopausal women for 3 years to test the effect of unopposed estrogen and three combined estrogen-progestin regimens on various cardiovascular risk factors. All hormone regimens increased HDL levels, decreased LDL levels, and lowered fibrinogen levels with little effect on insulin levels or blood pressure. Although estrogen alone raised HDL levels more than did estrogen-progestin regimens, the women taking unopposed estrogen had an increased rate of endometrial hyperplasia, a precursor of endometrial cancer. Each of the three estrogen-progestin regimens raised HDL levels significantly compared to placebo. Use of cyclic micronized progesterone had a more favorable effect on HDL levels than did medroxy-progesterone acetate. These findings strongly suggest a potential cardioprotective benefit from estrogen alone or in combined form with progestin by their advantageous effect on known cardiovascular risk factors. However, this study did not prove that hormones protect the heart. The PEPI study served to show which preparations should be used in randomized controlled trials.

Conclusive answers to many of these questions should be coming from the Women's Health Initiative, a large scale multicenter randomized trial evaluating a variety of potentially preventive therapies including HRT in healthy postmenopausal women. This study will examine the effects of HRT, low fat diet and vitamin D and calcium on the incidence of cardiovascular disease, certain cancers and fractures in women. The results of this trial will be reported in eight to 10 years. Until the results of this trial are available, health care providers will need to make individual decisions with women based on the available data. Women must understand that the likelihood of developing CHD is 10 times that of developing breast cancer.

Secondary Prevention of CHD in Women

Individuals with a history of cardiovascular disease are at the greatest risk of future premature cardiovascular morbidity and mortality. Such individuals have a relative risk of cardiac events of five to seven times that of individuals the same age without heart diseases (45). A history of CVD is the strongest predictor of future CVD events and such an individual deserves aggressive intervention to improve survival and maintain quality of life. Table 13.1.2 summarizes important aspects of the secondary prevention of recurrent cardiovascular events in women with CHD.

Smoking cessation, blood pressure control,

Table 13.1.2   Secondary Prevention of Cardiovascular Events in Women with Established Vascular Disease

Cardiovascular Events
Previous PTCA
CABG
Previous MI
Cerebrovascular disease
Peripheral vascular disease
Prevention
Smoking cessation
Hypertension control
Stress management
Measures to raise HDL
LDL <100 mg/dL
Aspirin
Hormone replacement therapy
Beta-blockers
ACE inhibitors with decreased LV function
Prompt response to symptoms

regular exercise and weight control continue to be extremely important in these women. There are several other issues that deserve particular attention to these high risk women.

Lipid-Lowering Therapy

Every woman with known CHD should have a complete lipid profile performed after an overnight fast. Desirable levels of serum lipids in women with CHD are LDL cholesterol <100 mg/dL, HDL >35 mg/dL and triglicerides <200 mg/dL (13).

Lipid-lowering therapy produces a decrease in lipid-rich plaques that are predisposed to plaque rupture (8). Elevated LDL cholesterol levels and low HDL levels may adversely affect the vasodilation properties of the diseased vessel (7). The Scandinavian simvastatin trial dramatically showed that cholesterol reduction results in a decrease in both cardiovascular and noncardiovascular mortality. This study included men and women with documented CHD, randomized to simvastatin or placebo with a 5- to 6-year follow-up. There was a 30% decrease in total mortality, a 42% decrease in CHD death, and a 27% decrease in coronary revascularization in the simvastatin group compared to placebo (7). This was the first trial to show that cholesterol-lowering reduces major CHD events in women with known CHD and the first to show improved survival in the elderly with known CHD. Decreases in clinical events with lipid lowering therapy may reflect changes in underlying lesion morphology.

Women with CHD or other evidence of vascular disease should have lipid levels assessed and modified as needed. Diet and exercise should be the cornerstones of therapy. Dietary therapy should be tailored to reduce saturated fats and replace them with monosaturated and polyunsaturated fats. Calorie restriction should be recommended, if weight loss is indicated. Frequent and consistent encouragement about dietary compliance and weight control by the clinician will maximize success. If diet, weight reduction, and exercise have not reduced LDL cholesterol to the desired levels in 3 to 6 months, drug therapy should be considered (13). Atherosclerosis is a diffuse disease with a natural course of relentless progression, systemic therapy such as lipid-lowering therapy should be used to a greater extent than limited lesion specific therapy like angioplasty (46).

Aspirin

Aspirin reduces the incidence of subsequent MI, stroke, and death from cardiovascular causes approximately 25% in women and men with established vascular disease (47). Aspirin has been shown to have a benefit in women and men with evolving MI (48). The recommended dose of aspirin for secondary prevention is 100 to 325 mg daily continued indefinitely.

Hormone Replacement Therapy

Consistent evidence from a small number of studies supports a beneficial effect of estrogen in postmenopausal women with existing CHD. This beneficial effect is probably greater than in healthy women without CHD. Estrogen may be more effective in reducing mortality in women with moderate or severe CHD than in women with mild CHD (49).

Atherosclerotic coronary arteries have impaired endothelial function. These impaired functions may contribute to the pathogenesis of coronary vasospasm, which may promote plaque rupture, thrombosis, and MI (42). In postmenopausal women with documented CHD, the vascular responses of atherosclerotic coronary arteries normalized within 20 minutes of exposure to 17-beta-estradiol (50). This was not seen in men of similar age with CHD. Sublingual estrogen administration reduces episodes of angina and improves treadmill times in women with CHD (51). The benefit of estrogen combined with progesterone in women with an intact uterus remains to be determined. A major intervention trial, the Heart and Estrogen-Progestin Replacement Study (HERS) sponsored by Wyeth-Ayerst is proceeding in women with established CHD to evaluate combined HRT against placebo for the prevention of recurrent events in postmenopausal women with known CHD.

Other Medications

Beta-blockers reduce the risk of all cause mortality and coronary mortality, including nonfatal MI and sudden cardiac death in women and men (52). ACE inhibitors reduce the risk of these same complications in the postinfarction woman or man with left ventricular dysfunction postinfarction (53).

Psychosocial Factors

Modification of psychosocial factors may reduce the risk of subsequent events in women with known CHD. The Lifestyle Heart Trial showed regression of atherosclerotic lesions in a small group of intensively treated women who received stress management training

(54). The weakness of the study was that subjects were mostly men. This is an important issue to consider in all women: stress may adversely affect the individual's ability to comply with overall secondary prevention regimen.

Evaluation of Chest Discomfort in Women

Angina Pectoris

Chest discomfort is the most common presenting symptom of CHD in women (5). A good history is essential to direct an appropriate evaluation of chest discomfort. Important aspects of the history include location, quality and duration of the discomfort, and precipitating and palliating factors. Angina pectoris is generally characterized by substernal discomfort that may radiate to the neck or left arm, but it can be perceived anywhere between the xiphoid process and the ears. Angina is a disagreeable pressure-like sensation, not stabbing or sharp in nature. Discomfort that is pleuritic or positional is not angina.

Angina is a clinical manifestation of myocardial ischemia caused by an imbalance between myocardial oxygen supply and demand. Any activity that increases the workload of the heart can precipitate angina in a person with a significant ($\geq 70\%$) stenosis in a coronary artery. Classic situations that provoke angina are exertion, emotional stress, cold, sexual activity, and after a meal. Angina is more common in the first hours after awakening. Anginal discomfort typically lasts from 2 to 5 minutes and the abnormal chest sensation completely disappears between episodes. Chest discomfort that has been constant for days to weeks is not angina. Classic ischemic pain is relieved by cessation of activity or nitroglycerin.

Clinical features that suggest angina are the same in women as in men (55). The woman's risk factors should be considered, but atherosclerosis can exist in women without recognized risk factors. The absence of risk factors does not rule out the clinical diagnosis of myocardial ischemia. Women delay seeking medical attention for evaluation of their chest discomfort compared to men (56). If symptoms of angina begin suddenly in a woman with no previous symptoms, if such symptoms occur at rest in a woman with previously known CHD, or if a low level of activity provokes chest discomfort that sounds ischemic, the woman should be promptly evaluated and hospitalization should be strongly considered. Such symptoms may represent unstable angina resulting from a ruptured cholesterol plaque with superimposed thrombus causing intermittent coronary artery occlusion.

Type of Chest Discomfort Predicts CHD Prevalence

In the Coronary Artery Surgery Study (CASS), 20,000 patients (19% women) were prospectively enrolled and underwent coronary angiography to determine CHD prevalence (57). The CASS study included patients from 15 medical centers in different parts of the United States, and the patients were classified by chest pain description. In this study, typical angina was characterized by substernal discomfort that was precipitated by exertion and relieved with rest or nitroglycerin in less than 10 minutes. Typical angina often radiated to the shoulders, jaw, or ulnar aspect of the left arm. Patients with atypical angina had most of the features of angina, but were unusual in some aspect, such as atypical radiation of the discomfort, nitroglycerin was not always effective, or the pain went away only after 15 to 20 minutes of rest. Nonspecific chest pain had none of the features of typical angina.

Significant CHD, defined as an epicardial coronary artery stenosis of $\geq 70\%$ or left main coronary stenosis of $\geq 50\%$, was found in 72% of women with typical angina, 36% of women with atypical chest pain, and 6% of women with nonspecific chest pain. The women in

CASS were age 30 to 70 years. These numbers have been duplicated in other angiographic studies and can serve as pretest probabilities for women with chest pain. These compare to prevalences of 93% for typical angina, 66% for atypical angina, and 14% for nonspecific chest pain in men. The clinical assessment of the likelihood of CHD is important because it dictates the next step in the clinical evaluation and affects the interpretation of the stress test results (Fig. 13.1.1). Diagnostic and prognostic information is available from the results of the exercise test in women.

Stress Testing in the Diagnosis of CHD in Women

The goal of the clinical evaluation (a history and stress test in appropriate women) is to determine which woman has a high likelihood of a significant coronary stenosis as the cause of the symptoms. The diagnostic benefits of exercise stress testing depend on the prevalence of CHD determined by the woman's symptoms and age (57, 58). Stress testing can then be used to augment the predictive value of the clinical history. The positive predictive value of a positive test is influenced by the prevalence of the disease and the sensitivity of the test. Women and men with typical angina and men with atypical angina are three subgroups with a relatively high prevalence of significant CHD. Women with atypical angina are at an intermediate prevalence. Women and men with nonspecific chest pain have a low prevalence of significant CHD (57).

In the postmenopausal woman with typical angina, if the baseline ECG is normal, a regular treadmill is probably the test of choice in the woman with typical angina. Since the pretest probability of an important coronary obstruction is already fairly high (72%), a positive test will simply further increase the likelihood that the woman has an important coro-

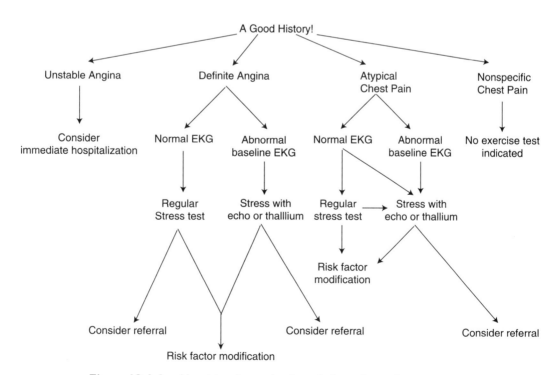

Figure 13.1.1   Algorithm for evaluation of chest discomfort in women.

nary lesion. In a premenopausal woman with typical angina, the approach should be more like that in women with atypical angina.

In the woman with atypical symptoms, with a normal baseline EKG, there is a 30% pretest probability of an important coronary lesion. A positive regular treadmill test enhances the post-test probability to only approximately 35 to 40%. Most of the positive stress test results will be false-positive tests. Before referring the woman with a positive stress test for coronary angiography, a repeat stress test using another imaging modality such as thallium or echo to enhance sensitivity and specificity should be done. This approach helps to avoid sending too many women for unnecessary angiograms. An alternative strategy in the woman with atypical angina would be to automatically use a stress test with an imaging modality in a woman with atypical chest discomfort because of the low pretest probability.

In women with a low pretest probability of CHD, a negative exercise test is powerful in excluding important coronary obstruction because the pretest probability is lowered further by the negative test. A young to middle-aged woman with atypical chest pain who can exercise to an adequate intensity with a negative exercise has a high specificity for the absence of significant coronary obstruction (59).

In a woman with nonspecific chest pain that has no features suggesting angina pectoris, exercise treadmill testing should not be done for the diagnosis of CHD. The rate of false-positive tests is high when the test is applied to a population with a low prevalence of disease.

A "non-diagnostic" stress test is different from a negative stress test. This usually means the test was inconclusive, usually because the target level of work was not achieved. This type of result can still give the clinician useful information but should not be interpreted as a negative test.

If a stress test is truly negative, the woman can be followed. The assumption should not be, however, that the woman does not have CHD, but rather that the woman has a low likelihood of an important coronary artery obstruction. Preventive recommendations to inhibit the formation of atherosclerotic plaque should be made in any woman with chest pain. Other causes of chest discomfort should be pursued according to the clinical characteristics of the discomfort.

Prognostic Information from the Stress Test

Prognostic information can also be obtained from stress testing. A stress test is not simply positive or negative. There are degrees of positivity that can guide clinical decision making. Predictors of subsequent cardiac events based on a routine Bruce exercise test are chest pain during maximal exercise, duration of exercise less than 6 minutes, failure to attain 90% of the age-predicted maximum heart rate, and ischemic ST depression, particularly if it lasts more than 4 minutes into recovery (59). For example, a woman with angina and a strongly positive exercise test, characterized by reproduction of her symptoms at a low level of exercise with significant ST depression, would have a high probability of having severe three-vessel CHD or significant left main disease and should probably be referred for cardiac catheterization to assess her revascularization options.

A woman with angina and excellent exercise tolerance with symptoms of angina at high levels of exercise and 1 mm of ST depression after 8 minutes of exercise probably does not have severe disease and probably does not need cardiac catheterization. She does require aggressive risk factor modification and antianginal therapy.

Contraindications to a Stress Test

Contraindications to stress testing include severe aortic stenosis, unstable angina, severe anemia, electrolyte disturbances, and decompensated congestive heart failure.

Stress Testing when the Baseline ECG is Abnormal

If the baseline ECG is abnormal, with testing ST segment abnormalities, an imaging modality should be used with exercise testing. Causes of such abnormalities include left ventricular hypertrophy, intraventricular conduction abnormalities (i.e., LBBB), or the use of digoxin. Even if the resting ECG is normal, the ST segment changes with exercise are not interpretable if the woman is on digoxin. Absence of ST-segment deviation, during an exercise test in a woman receiving cardiac glycosides, is considered a valid negative response (60). Digoxin therapy is a common indication for stress testing with an additional imaging modality.

What Type of Stress Test Should Be Used?

Regular stress testing is inexpensive, widely available, and duplicates the type of activity that provokes the symptom that the woman is experiencing. Regular stress testing is most useful in women with typical angina. Stress testing with an imaging modality like echocardiography or thallium should be used if the baseline ECG is abnormal. Stress testing with an imaging modality should also be used either as a first test or after a positive regular stress test in a woman with atypical chest pain. It is desirable to avoid performing two stress tests in women with atypical chest pain, and some investigators advocate for stress testing with echo imaging as the first stress test in women with atypical chest discomfort as the most cost-effective option (61).

Stress thallium increases the sensitivity of regular stress testing by 10%. At peak exercise, a small dose of thallium-201 is injected intravenously. Immediately after exercise, the woman's heart is imaged to look for areas of abnormal perfusion manifest as "cold spots" on the scan. Images are obtained again several hours later and are compared to the images obtained immediately post-exercise. If a cold spot

is filled in on the later scan, this suggests reversible myocardial ischemia. If a cold spot persists, it suggests either severe ischemia or infarcted tissue. Stress thallium has a 70 to 75% sensitivity and 90% specificity. The major drawback of thallium scintigraphy in women is the incidence of breast artifacts because of signal attenuation of myocardial activity by breast tissue (62).

Two-dimensional echocardiographic imaging performed during bicycle or treadmill exercise permits the detection of ischemically induced regional wall motion abnormalities. This method is typically cheaper than thallium. Stress echocardiography has a sensitivity of 76 to 88% and a specificity of 85% in women. In women with baseline ECG abnormalities, the accuracy of stress echo was 82% (62). Adequate echo images cannot be obtained in approximately 10% of women. Although stress echo and stress thallium have comparable sensitivities, stress echocardiography may have an advantage over thallium in the avoidance of breast artifact (62).

A woman with other medical problems who cannot exercise can undergo provocative testing with pharmacologic stress testing (63, 64). Myocardial oxygen demand can be increased with the use of dobutamine or myocardial oxygen supply can be altered with vasodilatory agents such as adenosine or dipyridamole. In general, pharmacologic stress testing is more commonly used in women because they are older at the time they develop their chest discomfort. Pharmacologic testing is done with an imaging modality and EKG monitoring.

After the Stress Test

The most important test in women with chest pain is a good history and follow-up visit, especially if the reason for the chest discomfort is unclear. There will always be some uncertainty with exercise stress testing and the responsible clinician must be willing to reevaluate the original hypothesis if it does not fit the woman's course. CHD is never "ruled out" with a stress test; rather a low probability evaluation suggests that the woman does not have a fixed, dynamic, or mixed lesion that obstructs flow to the myocardium with the augmentation in coronary blood flow needed to meet the metabolic demands of the working heart. Risk factors should still be modified in all women, particularly in women with chest discomfort. The woman should be told to return if bothersome symptoms recur. The clinician must consider the pathophysiology of acute ischemic syndromes and not be misled in a subsequent evaluation by a previously normal stress test or angiogram with mild CHD.

Gender Differences with Invasive Studies and Mortality

It has been reported in retrospective studies that women with the same degree of proven disease were less likely to receive invasive and surgical treatment for CHD and more likely to have medical therapy (65, 66). Other studies have found that women had a lower rate of referral for cardiac catheterization, even when controlled for age (67). A prospective study of 410 women with CHD found that women were referred for catheterization less often, but also had a lower probability of heart disease as determined by the cardiologists (68).

Some studies showed that women were more likely to have complications with thrombolytic therapy. Few large studies reported results by gender, and those that did often did not control for risk factors and medical status at time of MI and thrombolytic therapy. In these studies, fewer women than men were eligible for thrombolytic therapy, because they were older and had more comorbid conditions (69). Even among eligible patients, women were less likely to receive thrombolytic therapy than men.

Women have had higher in-hospital mortality with angioplasty than men. However,

studies have suggested that this was caused by poorer clinical characteristics at the time of their procedure. After successful angioplasty, the long-term prognosis for women was excellent (70).

Early studies suggested that once women develop an MI, they have higher rates of mortality in-hospital and during the first 30 days. Women who had an MI had higher incidence of risk factors, such as history of hypertension, congestive heart failure and diabetes, and a higher rate of complications such as cardiogenic shock and congestive heart failure. Women with MIs were more likely than men to have more unfavorable psychosocial factors such as social isolation, poor emotional support, depression, and poor socioeconomic resources, which are factors associated with poor prognosis after MI. Women are older and more likely to be widowed and live alone. They were less likely than men to have had a previous MI, smoke, or have arrhythmias (69). In a meta-analysis of studies from 1966 to 1994, although only a few of the studies reported data by gender, much of the women's excess and early mortality after MI is explained by more unfavorable risk factors and older age; when these variables were controlled for, the mortality risk for women after MI was similar to that in men (69).

Conclusions

CHD in women can be prevented. The woman and her primary care provider are in partnership in this endeavor. When CHD already exists prevention becomes even more urgent. Chest discomfort is the most common presenting symptom of CHD in women. A careful history and thoughtful application of diagnostic testing are important in the primary care setting to appropriately evaluate the woman with chest discomfort. The efforts of the primary care provider in these three areas will greatly enhance the cardiovascular health of women.

Special Considerations for Nurse Practitioners and Physician Assistants

Screening for modifiable risk factors and early management of problems can have a profound effect on a woman's future health and well-being. Outcomes can be optimized if risk reduction and education begin early in life. Although universal screening of children and adolescents for cholesterol is not recommended, selective screening is based on family history risk factors for CAD and risk factors in the children themselves, such as diabetes, hypertension, sedentary lifestyle, smoking, and obesity (72, 73). Early establishment of healthy habits can prevent CAD; however, even in old age, behavioral changes such as nonsmoking and increased activity may benefit health and quality of life (74).

Women at risk of coronary heart disease will often have multiple risk factors. They should understand that one drug (e.g., estrogen or a lipid-lowering agent) can have only a limited effect unless other lifestyle factors are considered (71). Plans for lifestyle modifications must be developed with the active participation of the woman.

Women may have different motivations to exercise, including physical appearance, weight management, self-esteem, and stress reduction. Likewise, women may face barriers to exercise that outweigh the benefits as they perceive them. Women should identify potential barriers, such as cost, time, or lack of support, so that they can plan strategies to overcome the obstacles to good health practices. Providers should also work with each woman to plan an individualized exercise program tailored to the woman's level of fitness, general health status, age, and motivation. Pre-exercise evaluation should be done; women over 50 years and those with more than one CAD

risk factor should be referred to specialists for graded exercise testing (75).

Diets for the prevention and treatment of high blood cholesterol can also help the woman to lose weight. Suggested food choices and serving sizes should be given to the woman. Modifications of the diets based on cultural preferences (e.g., Mexican-American, Asian-American) are available and referral to nutrition counselors is an option in many settings. Often women must learn skills in addition to knowledge if lifestyle changes are to be made. If the person who purchases and prepares food does not have the ability to modify calorie and fat intake, interventions related to diet are not likely to be successful (76). This same type of individualized plan developed with the client must be used for other lifestyle modifications such as smoking cessation.

Similarly, health care providers must work with women to help them continue recommended therapies such as estrogen, antihypertensives, and lipid-lowering agents. For example, women may express worries about estrogen related to weight gain, bleeding, breast changes, cancer, and PMS. Providers must address concerns when initiating therapy and invite clients to call them with any questions (77).

Making lifestyle behaviors to prevent or help managed CAD will be facilitated if there are community efforts to improve health. Health care providers must be active in educating community members of all ages about risk factors and developing community facilities to promote health. Providers as members of their communities can be involved in promoting health through walking and biking trails, fitness programs, health fairs, and other endeavors.

References

1. Wenger NK, Speroff L, Packard B. Cardiovascular health and disease in women. N Engl J Med 1993;329:247–256.
2. Castelli WP. Prevention and management of cardiovascular risk in women: cardiovascular disease in women. Am J Obstet Gynecol 1988;158:1553–1560.
3. Grady D, Rubin SM, Petitti DB, et al. Hormone therapy to prevent disease and prolong life in postmenopausal women. Ann Intern Med 1992;117: 1016–1037.
4. Rich-Edwards JW, Manson JE, Hennekens CH, Buring JE. The primary prevention of coronary heart disease in women. N Engl J Med 1995;332:1758–1766.
5. Lerner DJ, Kannel WB. Patterns of coronary heart disease morbidity and mortality in the sexes: a 26-year follow-up of the Framingham population. Am Heart J 1986;111(2):383–390.
6. Gillum RF. Trends in acute MI and coronary heart disease death in the United States. J Am Coll Cardiol 1993;23:1273–1277.
7. Ayanian JZ, Epstein AM. Differences in the use of procedures between women and men hospitalized for coronary heart disease. N Engl J Med 1991;325:221–225.
8. Steingart RM, Packer M, Hamm P, et al. Sex differences in the management of coronary artery disease. N Engl J Med 1991;325:226–230.
9. Scandinavian Simvastatin Survival Study Group. Randomised trial of cholesterol lowering in 4444 patients with coronary heart disease: the Scandinavian Simvastatin Survival Study (4S). Lancet 1994;344: 1383–1389.
10. Falk E, Shah KS, Fuster V. Coronary plaque disruption. Circulation 1995;92:657–671.
11. Anderson KM, Wilson PWF, Odell PM, Kannel WB. An updated coronary risk profile: a statement for health professionals. AHA Medical/Scientific Statement. Office of Scientific Affairs, Circulation 1991;83:356–362.
12. Bush TL. The epidemiology of cardiovascular disease in post-menopausal women. Ann NY Acad Sci 1990;592:263–271.
13. Summary of the Second Report of the National Cholesterol Education Program (NCEP) Expert Panel on Detection, Evaluation, and Treatment of High Blood Cholesterol in Adults (Adult Treatment Panel II). JAMA 1993;269:3015–3023.
14. Judelson DR. Coronary heart disease in women: risk factors and prevention. JAMWA 1994;49:186–197.
15. Keil JE, Loadholt CB, Weinrich MC, et al. Incidence of coronary heart disease in blacks in Charleston, South Carolina. Am Heart J 1984;108: 779–786.
16. Rich-Edwards JW, Manson JE, Hennekens CH, Buring JE. The primary prevention of coronary heart disease in women. N Eng J Med 1995;322:1758–1766.
17. Barrett-Connor E, Wingard DL. Sex differential in ischemic heart disease mortality in diabetics: a prospective population-based study. Am J Epidemiol 1983;118:489–496.
18. The Diabetes Control and Complications Trial Research Group. The effect of intensive treatment of diabetes on the development and progression of long-term complications in insulin-dependent diabetes mellitus. N Engl J Med 1993;329:977–986.
19. Willett WC, Green A, Stampfer MJ, et al. Relative and absolute excess risk of coronary heart disease among women who smoke cigarettes. N Engl J Med 1987;317:1303–1309.
20. Hansen EF, Andersen LT, Von Eyben FE, et al. Cigarette smoking and age at first acute MI, and influence of gender and extent of smoking. Am J Cardiol 1993;71:1439–1442.
21. Rosenberg L, Palmer JR, Shapiro S. Decline in the risk of MI among women who stop smoking. N Engl J Med 1990;322:213–217.
22. Sugiishi M, Takatsu F. Cigarette smoking is a major risk factor for coronary spasm. Circulation 1993;87:76–79.
23. Kool MJF, Hoeks APG, Struijker Boudier HAJ, Reneman RS. Short- and long-term effects of smoking on arterial wall properties in habitual smokers. J Am Coll Cardiol 1993;22:1881–1886.
24. Benowitz NL. Pharmacologic aspects of cigarette smoking and nicotine addiction. N Engl J Med 1988;319:1318–1330.
25. Wells AJ. Passive smoking as a cause of heart disease. J Am Coll Cardiol 1994;24:546–554.
26. Joint National Committee on the Detection, Evaluation, and Treatment of Blood Pressure: The Fifth Report of the Joint National Committee on Detection, Evaluation, and Treatment of High Blood Pressure (JNC-V). Arch Intern Med 1993;153:154–183.
27. Fiebach N, Herbert P, Stampfer M, et al. A prospective study of high blood pressure and cardiovascular disorders in women. Am J Epidemiol 1989;130:646–654.
28. Collins R, Peto R, McMahon S, et al. Blood pressure, stroke and coronary heart disease. Two short-term reductions in blood pressure; overview of randomized drug trials and their epidemiological context. Lancet 1990;335:827–838.
29. Stamler R, Grimm RH Jr., Dyer AR, et al. Cardiac status after four years in a trial on nutritional therapy for high blood pressure. Arch Intern Med 1989;149: 661–665.
30. Jacobs DR Jr, Meban IL, Bangdiwala SI, Criqui HA. High density lipoprotein cholesterol as a predictor of cardiovascular disease mortality in men and women: the follow-up study of the Lipid Research Clinics Prevalence Study. Am J Epidemiol 1990;131:32–47.
31. Manson JE, Colditz GA, Stampfer MJ, et al. A prospective study of obesity and the risk of coronary heart disease in women. N Engl J Med 1990;322: 882–889.
32. Wood PD, Stefanick ML, Williams PT, Haskell WL. The effects of plasma lipoproteins of a prudent weight reducing diet, with or without exercise, in over-

weight men and women. N Engl J Med 1991;325: 461–466.

33. Kaplan NM. The deadly quartet: upper-body obesity, glucose intolerance, hypertriglyceridemia, and hypertension. Arch Intern Med 1989;149:1514–1520.
34. Bjorntorp P. Regional patterns of fat distribution. Ann Intern Med 1985;103:994–995.
35. Manson JE, Stamper MJ, Colditz GA, et al. A prospective study of aspirin use and primary prevention of cardiovascular disease in women. JAMA 1991;266:521–527.
36. Women's Health Study Research Group. The Women's Health Study: rationale and background. J Myocardial Ischemia 1992;4:30–40.
37. Stampfer MJ, Colditz GA. ERT and coronary heart disease: a quantitative assessment of the epidemiologic evidence. Prev Med 1991;20:47–63.
38. Barrett-Conner E, Bush TL. Estrogen and coronary heart disease in women. JAMA 1991;265:1861–1867.
39. College of Physicians. Guidelines for counseling postmenopausal women about preventive hormone therapy. Ann Intern Med 1992;117:1038–1041.
40. Nabulsi AA, Folsom AR, White A, et al. Association of hormone replacement therapy with various cardiovascular risk factors in postmenopausal women. N Engl J Med 1993;328:1069–1075.
41. Bush TL, Barrett-Connor E, Cowan LD, et al. Cardiovascular mortality and noncontraceptive use of estrogen in women: results from the Lipid Research Clinics Program follow-up study. Circulation 1987; 75:1102–1109.
42. Williams JK, Adams MR, Herrington DM, Clarkson TB. Short-term administration of estrogen and vascular responses of atherosclerotic coronary arteries. J Am Coll Cardiol 1992;20:452–457.
43. Reis SE, Gloth ST, Blumenthal RS, et al. Ethinyl estradiol acutely attenuates abnormal coronary vasomotor responses to acetylcholine in postmenopausal women. Circulation 1994;89:52–60.
44. The Writing Group for the PEPI Trial. Effects of estrogen or estrogen/progestin regimens on heart disease risk factors in postmenopausal women. The postmenopausal estrogen/progestin interventions (PEPI) trial. JAMA 1995;273:199–208.
45. Kannel WB, Sorlie P, McNamara PM. Prognosis after initial MI: the Framingham Study. Am J Cardiol 1979;44:53–59.
46. Gotto AM. Lipid lowering, regression, and coronary events. A review of the Interdisciplinary Council on Lipids and Cardiovascular Risk Intervention, Seventh Council Meeting. Circulation 1995;92:646–656.
47. Antiplatelet Trialist' Collaboration. Collaborative overview of randomised trials of antiplatelet therapy. I: prevention of death, MI, and stroke by prolonged antiplatelet therapy in various categories of patients. Br Med J 1994;308:81–106.
48. ISIS-2 (Second International Study of Infarct Survival). Randomised trial of intravenous streptokinase, oral aspirin, both or neither among 17,187

cases of suspected acute MI: ISIS-2. Lancet 1988;2:349–360.
49. Sullivan JM, Vander Zwaag R, Lemp GF, et al. Postmenopausal estrogen use and coronary atherosclerosis. Ann Intern Med 1988;108:358–363.
50. Collins P, Rosano GMC, Sarrel PM, et al. 17(-estradiol attenuates acetylcholine-induced coronary arterial constriction in women but not men with coronary heart disease. Circulation 1995;92:24–30.
51. Rosano GMC, Sarrel PM, Poole-Wilson PA, Collins P. Beneficial effect of oestrogen on exercise-induced myocardial ischemia in women with coronary artery disease. Lancet 1993;342:133–136.
52. Yusuf, S, Peto R, Lewis J, et al. Beta blockade during and after MI: an overview of the randomized trials. Prog Cardiovasc Dis 1985;27:335–371.
53. Pfeffer MA, Braunwald E, Moye LA. Effect of captopril on mortality and morbidity in patients with left ventricular dysfunction after MI: results of the Survival and Ventricular Enlargement Trial. N Engl J Med 1992;327:669–677.
54. Ornish D, Brown SE, Scherwitz LW, et al. Can lifestyle changes reverse coronary heart disease? The Lifestyle Heart Trial. Lancet 1990;336:129–133.
55. Cunningham, MA, Lee TH, Cook EF, et al. The effect of gender on the probability of myocardial infarction among emergency department patients with acute chest pain: a report from the Multicenter Chest Pain Study Group. J Gen Intern Med 1989;4:392–398.
56. Moser DK, Dracup K. Gender differences in treatment-seeking delay in acute myocardial infarction. Prog Cardiovasc Nur 1993;8:6–12.
57. Chaitman BR, Bourassa MG, Davis K, et al. Angiographic prevalence of high-risk coronary artery disease in patient subsets (CASS). Circulation 1981;64:360–367.
58. Weiner DA, Ryan TJ, McCabe CH, et al. Exercise stress testing: correlations among history of angina, ST-segment response and prevalence of coronary artery disease in the Coronary Artery Surgery Study (CASS). N Engl J Med 1979;301:230–235.
59. Pratt CM, Francis MJ, Divine GW, Young JB. Exercise testing in women with chest pain. Are there additional exercise characteristics that predict true positive test results? Chest 1989;95:139–144.
60. Braunwald E, ed. Heart Disease. A Textbook of Cardiovascular Medicine. 4th ed. Philadelphia: WB Saunders, 1992.
61. Marwick TH, Anderson T, Williams MJ, et al. Exercise echocardiography is an accurate and cost-efficient technique for detection of coronary artery disease in women. J Am Coll Cardiol 1995;26:335–341.
62. Shaw LJ, Miller DD, Romeis JC, Kargl D, Younis LT, Chaitman BR. Gender differences in the noninvasive evaluation of patients with suspected coronary artery disease. Ann Intern Med 1994;120:559–566.
63. Lam JT, Chaitman BR, Glaenzer M, et al. Safety and diagnostic accuracy of dipyridamole-thallium imag-

ing in the elderly. J Am Coll Cardiol 1988;11:585–589.

64. Shaw L, Chaitman BR, Hilton TC, et al. Prognostic value of dipyridamole thallium-201 imaging in elderly patients. Am Heart J 1992;124:861–869.

65. Tobin JN, Wassertheil-Smoller S, Wexler JP, et al. Sex bias in considering coronary bypass surgery. Ann Intern Med 1987;107:19–25.

66. Maynard C, Litwin PE, Martin JS, Weaver WD. Gender differences in the treatment and outcome of acute myocardial infarction: results from the Myocardial Infarction Triage and intervention registry. Arch Intern Med 1992;152:972–976.

67. Steingart RM, Packer M, Hamme P, et al. Sex differences in the management of coronary heart disease. N Engl J Med 1991;325:226–230.

68. Mark DB, Shaw LK, DeLong ER, Califf RM, Pryor DB. Absence of sex bias in the referral of patients for cardiac catheterization. N Engl J Med 1994;330:1101–1104.

69. Vaccarino V, Krumholz H, Berkman LF, Horwitz RI. Sex differences in mortality after myocardial infarction: is there evidence for an increased risk for women? Circulation 1995;91:1861–1871.

70. Bell MR, Frill DE, Garratt KN, et al. Coronary artery disease interventions: long-term outcome of women compared with men after successful coronary angioplasty. Circulation 1995;91:2879–2881.

71. Philosophe R, Seibel MM. Menopause and cardiovascular disease. NAACOG's Clinical Issues Perinatal Women's Health Nurs 1991;2:441–451.

72. Reece SM. Toward the prevention of coronary heart disease: screening of children and adolescents for high blood cholesterol. Nurse Pract 1995;20:22–32.

73. Clinician's Handbook of Preventive Services. US Department of Health and Human Services. Washington, DC, 1994.

74. Guinn B. Modifying influences on serum lipids among postmenopausal women. Women's Health Issues 1994;4:156–161.

75. Ainsworth BE. Approaches to physical activity in women. NAACOG's Clinical Issues in Perinatal and Women's Health Nurs 1993;4:302–310.

76. Krummel DA. Cardiovascular disease. In: Krummel DA, Kris-Etherton PM. Nutrition in Women's Health. Gaithersburg, MD: Aspen, 1966:383–417.

77. Ravnikar VA. Compliance with hormone replacement therapy: are women receiving the full impact of hormone replacement therapy preventive health benefits? Women's Health Issues 1992;2:31–36.

13.2

Hypertension and Stroke

Jo Ann Rosenfeld and Joann Falkenburg

Hypertension

Hypertension and its complications cause significant morbidity and mortality for women. Hypertension contributes to renal disease and failure, coronary artery disease (CAD), ischemic cardiac disease, angina, myocardial infarctions, heart failure, retinopathy, and cerebrovascular disease. Although most individuals are asymptomatic, serious damage and even death can occur.

In few diseases, besides hypertension, there is definite evidence that early detection, treatment, and control will definitely reduce morbidity and/or mortality. Although much of the "proof" was obtained in studies that specifically excluded or neglected women, prevention and treatment is more important in hypertension than in other diseases. Because heart disease is the primary killer of women and hypertension contributes greatly to CAD, providers must aggressively detect and treat hypertension.

Definition

Hypertension is systolic blood pressure (SBP) readings of greater than 130 mm Hg and diasolic blood pressure readings (DBP) of greater than 90 mm Hg (Table 13.2.1) in a woman or

533

Table 13.2.1. Definition of Hypertension

	Systolic (mm Hg)	Diastolic (mm Hg)
Normal	<130	<85
High normal	130–139	85–90
Hypertension		
Stage 1 - mild	140–159	90–99
Stage 2 - moderate	160–179	100–109
Stage 3 - severe	180–209	110–119
Stage 4 - very severe	>210	>120

Adapted from Joint National Committee on the Detection, Evaluation, and Treatment of Blood Pressure: The Fifth Report of the Joint National Committee on Detection, Evaluation, and Treatment of High Blood Pressure (JNC-V). Arch Intern Med 1993;153:154–183.

man not on antihypertensive medications, who has not had a cigarette or taken caffeine, and is not acutely ill (1). It is recommended to document a hypertensive reading more than once, preferably at least three separate times. However, a person with a high blood pressure reading should not wait for confirmation before treatment.

Epidemiology

Over 50 million individuals have hypertension in the United States, and the incidence increases with age, especially for women (2). At age 45 years, 79% of African-American women and 60% of white women in the United States have hypertension. Only half of all individuals with hypertensive disease are diagnosed, and approximately only half of these are well controlled (1).

Risk Factors

There are several risk factors for hypertension that may be modified such as sodium intake, alcohol abuse, obesity, and lack of physical activity. Smoking cessation is important because of its primary pressor effect. Observational studies have supported a link between high sodium intake and hypertension. Women, in addition to the elderly and African Americans, seem to be more likely than white men to become hypertensive with similar high sodium loads. Even moderate reductions in sodium intake often reduces blood pressure readings (3).

Alcohol intake of greater than 60 mL per day has been associated with an increase in hypertension. Obesity has been linked to an increased risk of hypertension, and weight reduction reduces blood pressure in obese individuals. Regular physical activity reduces diastolic blood pressure as much as 20 mm Hg after 3 months of daily walking (4). Dietary fat and caffeine intake have not been linked to increased risk of hypertension.

Some risk factors are not modifiable. African-American women and men are at higher risk of developing hypertension than white women and men (5). Men are more likely to develop hypertension than women. A family history of essential hypertension is predictive of hypertension in men more often than women.

Complications

Hypertension causes damage in the vascular system, especially cerebrovascular system, causing cardiomyopathy and worsening coronary heart disease, and damaging the renal system and retinas (6).

Heart and Cardiovascular System

Heart disease is the most common cause of death in women, and hypertension worsens heart disease significantly. Hypertension strongly and independently increases the risk of CAD in women (1). Women with hypertension have 3.5 greater risk of developing CAD than nonhypertensive women. Treating hypertension by lowering SBP even 10 mm Hg reduces the increased risk of CHD.

Renal System

Approximately 15 to 20% of renal failure is attributable to hypertension (7). Elevated blood pressures cause damage to the glomeruli and renal parenchyma, causing loss of filtration units and ultimately failure. Diabetes may add to this damage. Elevated blood pressure affects the renin-angiotensin system, further affecting renal function and blood pressure control. Angiotensin converting enzyme inhibitors (ACEI) are protective of renal function in diabetics, and thus, may be a good choice in hypertensive diabetic women.

Treatment

Men and African-American women clearly benefit from aggressive hypertension control in reduced morbidity and mortality. White women have not been shown to benefit from therapy, although quality of life improved with treatment (5). Whether white women were intensively studied is debatable.

Nonpharmacological treatment should be considered first. Nonpharmacological treatment in women may be more effective and more important than in men. Weight reduction, salt intake reduction, increased physical activity, alcohol moderation, and smoking cessation are more effective in controlling hypertension without medication in women than men (8).

Recent recommendations for control of hypertension have discarded the stepped care approach to treatment. Any number of different classes of hypertensive medications can be used in women as they are in men. "Gender has not been found to determine drug responsiveness" (1). Diuretics (e.g., HCTZ, loop diuretics such as furosemide, potassium-sparing diuretics, combinations), adrenergic inhibitors including beta-blockers (i.e., propranolol or more selective timolol), alpha-beta-blockers (labetalol) and alpha-receptor blockers (e.g., prazosin, terazosin), ACEIs (e.g., captopril, enalopril), centrally acting agents (clonidine), and calcium channel blockers (e.g., diltiazem, verapamil, nifedipine) are all good first therapies. One medication should be started, and then the

woman should be reevaluated several times over the following weeks to months. Medication levels should be increased to maximum dose or until symptoms appear before starting a second medication. Choice of medication will depend on cost, availability, formularies, comorbid conditions, tolerance of side effects, and concerns of compliance. These must be individualized between the provider and the woman.

There are some differences to be considered in the antihypertensive treatment of women. First, use of thiazide and loop diuretics as first treatment may not be suggested in women, especially those on digoxin, because of development of hypokalemia; however, not all studies agree. In women, thiazide diuretics increase total cholesterol and lower HDL-cholesterol; HDL-cholesterol levels may be more important in the development of coronary disease in women (5). On the other hand, there is some evidence that thiazide diuretics in women may be somewhat protective of the development of postmenopausal osteoporosis (8).

There is some evidence that beta-blockers and diuretics may precipitate diabetes, especially in women, and thus, these antihypertensives should be avoided as first-line therapy in obese or diabetic women, those with family histories of diabetes, or a history of hyperinsulinemia (9). Women, especially smaller older women, on prasozin may be more likely to develop significant hypotensive effects. Also, women are more likely to develop a chronic irritating cough with ACEIs than men, often necessitating change of medication.

Effect of Hypertension on Women

Providers should be aware of the woman's understanding and beliefs about her hypertension and medication and its effects. The provider must know and work with the patient or this chronic disease cannot be controlled. Only working together over time can the woman and the provider hope to control her hypertension. One study showed that women who believed that they had "high-blood" did well with diet and weight control. However, women who believed that hypertension was "hypertension" felt that this was an emotional state and that medication had no effect. Instead they tried to improve their "nerves" and stress, and subsequently had poor control of blood pressure (10). More importantly, only 2 of 15 physicians caring for the women in this study recognized the differences in the women's perceptions of the diagnosis of hypertension.

Quality of life issues with treatment have not been as well investigated in women as in men. Sexual dysfunction, specifically anorgasmia, can occur with medications that cause impotence in men (5).

Special Situations

Hypertension in the Elderly

Hypertension increases with age, and because most elderly patients are women, hypertension occurs frequently in older women. Approximately half of women age 65 to 74 years are hypertensive, and two thirds of hypertensive patients over age 65 years are women (11). Control of hypertension in this group is important both for the prevention of CAD, stroke, renal failure, and complications, and the improvement of quality of life.

Older hypertensives have low blood volume and cardiac output, lower volumes of distribution, decreased responsiveness to some medications, and increased incidence of side effects, especially on neurological and mental status.

Unmedicated, uncontrolled hypertension makes women feel ill. Higher blood pressure levels correlate with poorer cognitive functions (12). In one study, higher blood pressure levels were associated with lower levels of social activity and less enjoyment from that activity in one study. Higher blood pressure levels also correlated with increased sleep disturbances and increased physical symptoms (12).

When treated, older women have improved quality of life. Although there have been many studies comparing antihypertensive medication and the quality of life, few have specifically examined their effect on women. One prospective study compared hypertensive older women's response to atenolol, enalapril, and isradipine over a 22-week period. There were no differences between the response to the three medications; all improved the women's quality of life, although side effects differed (11). In another prospective study, older women had more side effects, worsened quality of life, more cessation of use, and poorer blood pressure control with atenolol compared to enalapril or diltiazem (13). More studies are needed that specifically target women.

Hypertension and Pregnancy

Hypertension adds particular risks to pregnancy, both to the mother and the infant. First, it is difficult to diagnose hypertension during pregnancy. The systolic blood pressure, diastolic blood pressure, and mean arterial pressure decrease significantly to normal or below normal in the first half of pregnancy. Providers who do not have prepregnancy blood pressure measurements may be surprised by a rapid rise in blood pressures in the second half of pregnancy and may be unsure whether it is caused by preeclampsia (PE) or the natural rebound of chronic hypertension.

However, if the blood pressure is controlled and the woman has good renal function (> than 70 mL/min creatinine clearance and serum creatinine level < 1.5 mg/dL), the pregnancy should not have an increased risk of maternal or perinatal mortality.

Women with chronic hypertension who become pregnant or who are planning to conceive should avoid using beta-blockers, diuretics, and angiotensin-converting enzyme inhibitors. Conservatively and traditionally, either alphamethyldopa (Aldomet 500 to 1000 mg bid PO) or hydralazine (10 to 25 mg tid PO) have been prescribed for the pregnant hypertensive woman. Lately, calcium channel blockers, specifically nifedipine or verapamil, in sustained-release form have been used successfully to decrease blood pressure, and may even decrease the risk of developing PE.

Hypertension can affect the morbidity and mortality of pregnancy by causing increased risk of PE, eclampsia, abruptio placenta, disseminated intravascular coagulation, intraventricular bleeds and stroke, and renal failure. The risk of PE rises with the degree of diastolic blood pressure. Nonhypertensive healthy pregnant women have an 8% risk of developing PE; women with chronic DBP of 95 mm Hg have a 50% risk, whereas those with DBP of greater than 100 mm Hg have a 100% risk (14).

Finally, chronic hypertension and its vascular disease affects the infant. It increases the risk of perinatal mortality, primarily because of a premature delivery rate of 25 to 30%, and the incidence of intrauterine growth retardation (15). Lowering the woman's blood pressure to normal reduces the risk of fetal mortality.

Hypertension and Oral Contraceptives

Hypertensive women can take oral contraceptive pills (OCPs), if their hypertension is in good control and they are nonsmokers. The lower dose OCPs, those with less than 35 μg of ethinyl estradiol or its equivalent, pose little additional risk to a hypertensive woman under treatment (14). She should be evaluated more often than yearly for hypertensive control. Both low- and high-dose OCPs can affect blood pressure (16). If the addition of the OCPs threatens the control of hypertension, progestin-only preparations—either oral (Micronor or Ovrette), injectable (Depo-Provera), or implanted (Norplant)—are good alternatives.

Hypertension and Estrogen Use

The effect of estrogen replacement therapy (ERT) on hypertension is not clear. Many studies find a decrease in blood pressure with ERT use (8) (see Chapter 20).

Stroke

Epidemiology

The third leading cause of death in the United States is stroke (17). Women are less likely to die from embolic stroke (9% as compared to 23% for men) and are more likely to survive 5 years (60% as compared to 52%) (18). Women are at increased risk of subarachnoid hemorrhage as compared to men (19). There is some evidence that the incidence of stroke has increased in the last 20 years in women. In Sweden, incidence of stroke in women increased 38% from 1975 to 1986 (20).

Risk Factors

There are several risk factors for stroke that are modifiable and that, if changed, can reduce the woman's risk of stroke. Cigarette smoking is a significant one (21). Hypertension, alcohol abuse, oral contraceptives, and ERT have also been linked to increased incidence of stroke. Alcohol abuse has been linked with embolic stroke in men, but association in women has not been investigated (16). Atrial fibrillation, more common in men than women, can increase the likelihood of embolic stroke.

Hypertension is the most common risk factor for stroke. The relative risk of stroke is 2.6 for hypertensive women (22). Treating hypertension reduces the risk of stroke. Reducing DBP in a woman even by 6 mm Hg can reduce the risk of fatal and nonfatal stroke by 42% (23).

Whether oral contraceptive use has been linked to incidence of stroke is controversial. The Nurses' Health Study, a prospective study of over 110,000 women on the effects of OCPs, found that there was no increased risk of stroke in women using OCPs when controlled for age and cigarette use (24). Other studies disagree and link OCPs with increased risk of stroke and increased mortality with stroke (25).

Seventy-four percent of hemorrhagic strokes in two groups of premenopausal women occurred in the week prior to menses or during menses, a time of high progesterone and low estrogen (18). However, women who smoke and take OCPs have a six times greater risk for hemorrhagic stroke than women who take OCPs and do not smoke (16, 18). Many of the studies were done with OCPs with higher dosage of estrogen than occur in most OCPs now.

Effect of Stroke on Women

Women are the caretakers and the widows. First, they are much more likely to care for a family member (e.g., husband, parent, parent-in-law) who suffers a stroke. Loss of income, social supports, change of life-style, and great stress are all results of continuing long-term care of a family member who has had a stroke (see Chapter 22).

On the average, a married woman will live 8 years beyond the death of her spouse. A stroke, even one with little disability, is a catastrophe. Loss of income, freedom, privacy, ability to live in her own home, and increased likelihood of hospitalization and chronic nursing home care are often the sequelae for a single or older woman who has a stroke. Women are more likely to be disabled from a stroke than men and tend to live longer after a stroke. Family members will need to become involved (see Chapter 22). The provider will need to work closely with the family and with an interdisciplinary team, including occupational and physical therapists, rehabilitation workers, and home health workers and nurses.

Depression is common after a stroke. Providers should spend time talking with the woman on a regular basis to determine her status and should suggest counseling and therapy, if needed.

Prevention

Primary Prevention
Control of hypertension, cessation of smoking, weight reduction, increase of physical activity,

and moderation of alcohol and fat intake will all decrease the likelihood of strokes.

A meta-analysis of over 14 studies of cigarette smoking and stroke in women found that current smokers had more than a four times greater risk of subarachnoid stroke than nonsmokers, and women who smoked even 15 cigarettes a day had a doubling of their risk for embolic stroke (26). The Nurses' Health Study of over 117,000 nurses showed that smokers were more than two times more likely to have a stroke, the more cigarettes smoked increased the risk, and that cessation of smoking is important to decrease the risk in all age groups. In cigarette smokers, the risk of having a stroke decreases soon after cessation, and the benefits of smoking cessation are independent of the number of cigarettes the woman smoked per day and the age at starting (20). Because more women are smoking and more women have smoked longer (see Chapter 6.2), these effects will become more important in the number of women with strokes.

Secondary Prevention
Women have been purposely excluded from most large prospective studies on the effect of aspirin use in prevention of strokes, partially to avoid the confusion about hormonal state. In eight studies in which women were included, five found that men were protected from developing strokes by daily aspirin use whereas women were not. The remaining three studies showed that there was no prevention of stroke in men or women with the use of aspirin. However, few of these studies included more than one-third women patients (16). Aspirin has been linked in some studies to an increase in hemorrhagic stroke, especially in pregnant women.

Ticlopidine recently has been suggested for use in women unable or intolerant of aspirin to prevent stroke. It has been found to be as effective as aspirin in preventing strokes in women (16). However, it is very expensive and can cause neutropenia, requiring frequent complete blood counts with more cost and invasive blood-drawing. Diarrhea, skin rashes, and urticaria are other side effects.

Summary

Hypertension in women presents with the same risk factors and should be treated just as aggressively. Control of hypertension is important, starting with nonpharmacological therapy that may be more efficacious in women. Certain medications may need to be avoided in women, but each woman must be approached individually, taking into consideration her beliefs and understanding, if the provider can help the woman control her blood pressure.

Special Considerations for Nurse Practitioners and Physician Assistants

Measurement of blood pressure is essential in order to diagnose hypertension and to evaluate the success of interventions. Yet, errors in techniques and lack of standardization of this procedure are common among the various personnel who measure blood pressures in primary care settings. A proper-sized cuff will have a bladder that encircles at least 80% of the upper arm. If a large adult cuff needs to be used, it should be noted on the written record (27). Measurement is made after 5 minutes of rest with the woman seated and her arm bared, supported, and at heart level. Equipment must be in proper working order and calibrated if needed. All personnel must use the same point, i.e., disappearance of sound, for the diastolic reading (28).

Especially for the elderly or diabetic woman who may have orthostatic or autoimmune disease, both supine and standing readings should be measured at the initial visit. Notation should be made of any factors that might elevate blood pressure, including smoking, eating, anxiety, talking, exertion, cold weather, bladder distention, and drugs (27). Women should be informed of their blood pressure readings and encouraged to keep their own records of measurements.

Some women will attribute their hypertension to "nervousness" or "stress," or state that their blood pressure is normal at home ("white coat" hypertension). These women may already have increased peripheral resistance, and treatment, in general, is based on the office measurements. For some of these women, ambulatory blood pressure monitoring is recommended (28). Likewise, isolated systolic hypertension in the elderly is treated (29).

The recommended lifestyle changes may be overwhelming to the woman with newly diagnosed hypertension. She may need help setting realistic goals and deciding what changes she can make immediately and what goals are more long term. Discussing with the woman how she will integrate lifestyle changes into her normal routines is well worth the time and effort. Some women will need special assistance to initiate changes, e.g., nutrition counseling for weight loss. Women with known cardiac or other serious health problems will need supervised exercise testing and perhaps referral to a medically supervised rehabilitative program in order to meet their activity goals (29).

Drug compliance can be an issue especially when the woman is asymptomatic without treatment, and the drug itself causes adverse reactions that affect her quality of life. If a woman understands her potential risks from hypertension, she may be more compliant with drug and other management strategies. Her concerns about side effects must be addressed and drug therapy individualized to meet her needs (30).

Consultation is indicated for refractory or suspected secondary hypertension and severe hypertension, especially if associated with angina, CHF, encephalopathy, or nephropathy. Immediate consultation is sought for hypertensive crisis (31).

References

1. Joint National Committee on the Detection, Evaluation, and Treatment of Blood Pressure. The fifth report of the joint national committee on detection, evaluation, and treatment of high blood pressure (JNC-V). Arch Intern Med 1993;153:154–183.
2. Bush TL. The epidemiology of cardiovascular disease in post-menopausal women. Ann NY Acad Sci 1990;592;263–271.
3. Rose G, Stampler J. The Intersalt study: background, methods and main results. INTERSALT cooperative research group. J Hum Hypertens 1989;3:283–288.
4. Cade T, Mars D, Wagemaker H, et al. Effect of aerobic exercise training on patients with systemic arterial hypertension. Am J Med 1984;77:785–790.
5. Anastos K, Charney P, Charon RA, et al. Hypertension in women: what is really known? Ann Intern Med 1991;115:287–293.
6. Houston MC. New insights and approaches to reduce end-organ damage in the treatment of hypertension: subsets of hypertension approach. Am Heart J 1992;123:1337–1367.
7. Brunton SA. Hypertension. Monograph Edition No. 176. Home Study Self-Assesment program. Kansas City, MO: American Academy of Family Physicians, January 1994.
8. Kaplan NM. The treatment of hypertension in women. Arch Intern Med 1995;155:563–567.
9. Bengtsson C, Blohme G, Lapidus L, Lissner L, Lundgren H. Diabetes incidence in users and non-users of anti-hypertensive drugs in relation to serum insulin, glucose tolerance and degree of adiposity: a 12-year prospective population study of women in Gothenburg, Sweden. J Intern Med 1992;231:583–588.
10. Health Beliefs and Compliance with prescribed medication for hypertension among black women—New Orleans, 1985–1986. MMWR 1990;39:701–703.
11. Croog SH, Elias MF, Colton T, et al. Effects of antihypertensive medications on quality of life in elderly hypertensive women. Am J Hypertens 1994; 7: 329–339.
12. Robbins MA, Elias MF, Croog SH, Colton T. Unmedicated blood pressure levels and quality of life in elderly hypertension women. Psychosomatics 1994; 56:251–259.
13. Applegate WB, Phillis HL, Schnaper H, et al. A randomized controlled trial of three antihypertensive agents on blood pressure control and quality of life in older women. Arch Intern Med 1991;151:1817–1822.
14. Rosenfeld JA. Hypertensive disease in pregnancy. FP Recert 1988;10:75–85.
15. Sullivan JM, Lobo RA. Contraceptive choices for women with medical problems: considerations for contraception in women with cardiovascular disorders. Am J Obstet Gynecol 1993;168:2006–2011.
16. Woods JW. Oral contraceptives and hypertension. Hypertension 1988;11:11–15.
17. Hershey L. Stroke prevention in women: role of aspiring versus ticlopidine. Am J Med 1991;91:288–292.
18. Sacco R, Wolf P, Kannel W, McNamara PM. Survival and recurrence following stroke. The Framingham Study. Stroke 1982;13:290–295.
19. Longstreth WT, Nelson LM, Koepsell TD, van Belle G. Subarachnoid hemorrhage and hormonal factors in women: a population-based case-control study. Ann Intern Med 1994;121:168–173.
20. Terent A. Increasing incidence of stroke among Swedish women. Stroke 1988;19:598–603.
21. Kawachi I, Colditz GA, Stampfer MJ, et al. Smoking cessation and decreased risk of stroke in women. JAMA 1993;269:232–236.
22. Fiebach N, Herbert P, Stampfer M, et al. A prospective study of high blood pressure and cardiovascular disorders in women. Am J Epidemiol 1989;130:646–654.
23. Collins R, Peto R, McMahon S, et al. Blood pressure, stroke and coronary heart disease. Two short-term reductions in blood pressure; overview of randomized drug trials and their epidemiological context. Lancet 1990;335;827–838.
24. Colditz GA. Oral contraceptive use and mortality during 12 years of follow-up. The Nurses' Health Study. Ann Intern Med 1994;120:821–826.
25. Layde PM, Beral V, Kay CR. Royal College of General Practitioners' Oral Contraceptive Study. Lancet 1981;1:541–546.
26. Colditz GA, Bonita R, Stampfer MJ, et al. Cigarette smoking and risk of stroke in middle-aged women. N Engl J Med 1988;318:937–941.
27. Cacciabaudo JM, Pecker MS. Hypertension: managing the silent killer. Comtemp Nurse Pract 1995; 1:24,26–30.
28. Davis PJ. Hypertension evaluation and treatment revisited: joint national committee recommendations. Primary Care Update OB/Gyn 1994;1:26–32.
29. Uphold CR, Graham MV, eds. Clinical Guidelines in Family Practice. Gainesville, FL: Barmarrae, 1993.
30. Noel HC. Continuing education forum: essential hypertension; evaluation and treatment. J Natl Acad Nurse Pract 1994;2:421–435.
31. Scarr E. Hypertension. In: Star WL, Lommel LL, Shannon MT, eds. Women's Primary Health Care. Washington, DC: American Nurses' Association, 1995:6-15–6-21.

13.3

Venous Diseases

Mitchell S. King

Venous Diseases

Up to 50% of adults have signs and symptoms caused by lower extremity venous disease (1). Women experience these problems more often than men. This chapter will discuss the common causes of venous disease in women and the differential diagnosis of extremity swelling.

Varicose Veins and Chronic Venous Insufficiency

Varicose veins occur in up to 20% of adults, but 60 to 70% of these cases occur in women (1). Varicose veins and associated superficial venous insufficiency cause 10% of cases of chronic venous insufficiency (CVI) and subsequent venous ulcers (2). The remaining 90% of cases of CVI are caused by disease within the deep venous system. CVI occurs in 2 to 7% of the population and can lead to venous ulceration. Besides the frustration, pain, and suffering of the individual patient, CVI leads to considerable expense in health care dollars and time lost from work (1).

Anatomy and Physiology

Normal drainage of blood from the lower extremity veins into the central venous system depends on a series of venous valves that are aided by compression from surrounding skeletal muscles of the calf and thigh (the "muscle pump"). Blood exits the dermal venules and superficial veins into the tibial, popliteal, and femoral veins with subsequent drainage in the iliac and more proximal veins. Normal ambulatory venous pressures measured in the feet are 15 to 30 mm Hg (3).

The presence of functional venous valves is necessary to maintain these low pressures, to prevent reflux of blood into previously emptied veins, and to prevent formation of a column of blood with resultant higher venous pressures. When these valves malfunction and pressures rise, varicose veins, CVI, and venous ulcers occur. The risks of developing lipodermatosclerosis (stasis dermatitis) and venous ulcers rise proportionately to the rise in ambulatory venous pressures, with the risk being 50% or more with pressures greater than 60 mm Hg (4).

Varicose veins can be primary or secondary. Primary varicose veins are caused either by the absence or malformation of valves within the saphenous or perforating veins or by muscular defects/laxity within the vein walls. Secondary varicose veins can occur after a deep vein thrombosis (DVT) or as the result of other acquired or congenital causes of obstruction or malfunctioning of the deep venous valves.

When valvular incompetence occurs, the superficial veins are subjected to increased blood flow as blood that normally exits through the deep veins is recirculated into the superficial veins. The superficial veins are then exposed to increased venous pressures that can then be transmitted to the dermal venules and lead to edema formation. In more severe cases, this leads to CVI, lipodermatosclerosis, and venous ulcers. Similarly obstruction within the deep veins, which may occur with DVT, may lead to increased venous pressures with a similar result.

As the muscle pump mechanism fails and CVI occurs, leg edema results. Leakage of fibrinogen, formation of fibrin cuffs around dermal venules, and stagnation of white blood cells with increased local inflammatory response cause chronic skin changes of CVI called "lipodermatosclerosis" (5). Venous ulcers can occur and are associated with poorer venous emptying and higher ambulatory venous pressures.

Clinical Course

There is a genetic predisposition to acquiring varicose veins. They typically appear for the first time in adulthood. In women, the varicosities become more apparent after onset of menstrual function and pregnancy. During pregnancy, varicosities will become more prominent because of the increased progesterone levels, expanded blood volume, and the relative venous obstruction and resultant venous hypertension (6).

Clinical Evaluation

Women with CVI can present with complaints of lower extremity swelling, recurrent thrombophlebitis, aching, ulceration, or with concerns about the visual appearance of varicosities. These symptoms may vary with pregnancy or the different phases of the menstrual cycle. Physical examination may have findings of varicosities, telangiectasias, edema, or ulcerations.

Medical causes for lower extremity swelling, such as heart, liver, or renal failure, or anasarca caused by malnutrition, low albumin, or low colloid pressures should be considered. Then further evaluation of the extent of venous disease can occur. CVI is usually bilateral. Unilateral CVI can occur as the long-term result of DVTs, trauma, or congenital malformations of a leg. However, sudden, recent, or subacute swelling or redness of one limb is suspicious for other serious diseases such as a DVT, pelvic, gastrointestinal or genital masses, or arterial obstruction and requires complete and intensive evaluation.

Initial testing may include duplex scanning and air plethysmography. Duplex scanning can assess anatomy, presence of obstruction, and presence of valvular reflux. Air plethysmography looks at the functional aspects of the muscle pump and valvular mechanisms by measuring the venous refill time, ejection fraction, and residual volume fraction. If clinically suggested, more invasive testing such as ambulatory venous pressure measurement and ascending or descending venography can be performed. The invasive tests should generally be reserved for patients refractory to conservative medical management in whom surgery is a consideration.

Treatment

Initial treatment of varicose veins and CVI include lifestyle modification. Moderate exercise that may strengthen muscles and improve the "muscle pump" and weight reduction closer to ideal body weight may help. Modification of work regimens, including intermittent walking rather than sitting or standing only, may ease CVI also.

Further treatment may include use of support shoes or stockings and TED stockings. These are over-the-counter, inexpensive, come in a few sizes, and can be cosmetically acceptable. More effective, but more cumbersome and cosmetically less acceptable treatment is the use of gradient compression stockings, typically using 30 to 40 mm Hg stockings. These are prescribed, made to order for the individual patient, and are more expensive. In more severe cases of CVI, periodic use of intermittent pneumatic compression devices may be helpful. Pentoxifylline may help decrease the inflammatory skin changes of lipodermatosclerosis and venous ulcers through its effects on white blood cells (7).

Surgical Treatment

Prior to surgical treatment, testing to define the anatomical and functional defects in the venous system is important to the success of therapy. When there is reflux at the saphenofemoral junction, ligation and stripping the saphenous veins is successful. For localized varicosities in which the saphenofemoral junction is competent, stab evulsion or sclerotherapy may be appropriate. Sclerotherapy is useful in treating telangiectasias, and it achieves cosmetic success and symptomatic success in 85% of patients (8). For patients in whom superficial vein surgeries have failed and with evidence of deep venous valvular defects, valvuloplasty or valve replacement may be indicated (9).

Complications of venous ligation, stripping, and stab evulsion therapies for varicose veins may include hematoma formation, infection, nerve injury, and recurrence of varicosities. Nerve injury is more common with stripping procedures when the vein is stripped from the groin to ankle. Procedures involving stripping from groin to the knee, although somewhat less successful, have less nerve injury. Superficial thrombophlebitis can occur with the stab evulsion technique. Recurrence of varicosities can occur in 10 to 60% or more of patients (10). Sclerotherapy complications include hyperpigmentation, capillary dilation, and rarely, skin necrosis, significant thrombophlebitis, or sensitivity reactions.

Venous Stasis Ulcers

Venous stasis ulcers caused by CVI can usually be cured by time and rest with elevation of legs. The ulcers can be single or multiple, and although they usually begin as superficial ulcerations, they can progress to deep, serious wounds with infection. Treatment while small and superficial is important.

The woman should stay off her feet as much as possible, with the legs elevated above her pelvis, i.e., sitting or lying with legs raised.

The ulcers can be dressed with any of several homemade and/or commercial preparations. Normal saline on 2 x 2 sponges covered by dry dressings (wet-to-dry), betadine and sugar, and other homemade dressings, and/or Duoderm, Aquaflow, and other commercially available dressings are all available and effective. The ulcer needs to be kept clean, with dead tissue removed, and dry. Daily or twice daily bandage changes are necessary. If the ulcer is deep, whirlpool treatments may help removal of dead tissue. Infection is usually not a problem early with superficial ulcers, and antibiotics are not necessary. Unna boots are useful local treatment for venous ulcers. Healing may take 2 to 8 weeks. Because the ulcers are caused by a chronic condition, CVI, they often recur in the same or other sites.

Complications include an autosensitization process and deep infection. Chronic weeping, itching and scratching of ulcers, and the chronic skin changes can lead to redness, swelling, and even rashes distant from the ulcers. Infection is not the cause in this case, and steroids rather than antibiotics are needed.

Alternatively, local cellulitis, lymphadenitis, and systemic infection can occur from these ulcers, requiring local and parenteral antibiotics and hospitalization. Although in diabetics many kinds of bacteria and polymicrobial infections can occur, usually cellulitis is caused by Streptococcus or Staphylococcus. Surgical debridement may be necessary.

Venous ulcers refractory to medical care require further evaluation and consideration of the possibility of arterial disease as a contributing cause, because use of compression stockings with arterial disease has been reported to worsen extremity ischemia (11).

Deep Vein Thrombosis

Deep vein thrombosis and subsequent pulmonary embolism are responsible for significant morbidity and mortality. It is estimated that 50,000 to 100,000 hospitalized patients per year die because of pulmonary embolism, accounting for approximately 3.5% of all inpatient deaths (12). In addition, DVTs cause CVI in up to 75% of patients (4). DVTs are both underdiagnosed and undertreated.

Virchow, in the 1800s, realized the importance of deep vein thrombosis and recognized a triad of conditions under which DVTs are likely to develop. Venous stasis, venous endothelial damage, and a hypercoaguable state are the predisposing factors leading to DVT (13). Risk factors for developing DVT include (a) a personal prior or family history of DVT, (b) lower extremity orthopedic surgery, (c) surgical procedures lasting longer than 30 minutes, (d) age greater than 40 years, (e) malignancy, (f) cerebrovascular accident, (g) obesity, (h) congestive heart failure, (i) use of oral contraceptive pills (OCP), (j) pregnancy, (k), immobilization, (l) trauma, and (m) varicose veins.

The risk associated with use of OCPs is related to estrogen, with increasing risk associated with increasing doses of estrogens (14). Progesterone use does not increase the risk for DVTs. A history of DVT or pulmonary embolism is an absolute contraindication for OCP use. Hormone replacement therapy does not appear to pose a risk for developing DVT, perhaps because the dosage of estrogen is much lower (15).

Clinical Evaluation

In diagnosing DVT, a high index of clinical suspicion is required. Patients must present with minimal complaints such as lower extremity aching, swelling, sensation of warmth, or tenderness. In eliciting the history, a careful search for risk factors should be pursued. Physical examination may reveal edema, erythema, warmth, tenderness, and possibly palpable cords, but the physical can be normal. A positive Homan's sign (pain in calf on flexion of foot) often occurs with calf vein DVTs.

Diagnosis

Venography is the gold standard test for diagnosing DVT. However, this test is associated with a risk of causing DVT and IV contrast dye sensitivity. Venography can be employed when DVT is strongly suspected but results of noninvasive tests are negative. To diagnose DVT, duplex scanning has become the test of choice. Impedence plethysmography (IPG) is another noninvasive test often used to diagnose DVT, although less sensitive than duplex scanning. Both tests have limitations with regard to diagnosing calf vein thrombi. Fewer than half the clinically suspected cases of DVT are confirmed by radiological testing (16).

Calf vein thrombi are not significant unless they propagate proximally, which occurs in 20% of cases. If calf vein thrombi are a concern with negative duplex scans or IPG testing, serial scans can be performed over several days to assess for propagation (17). Laboratory testing for the patient with venous thrombosis includes a complete blood count, prothrombin time (PT), and partial thromboplastin time (PTT). In younger patients, patients with recurrent or family history of DVT, and those without risk factors for DVT, assessment of a hypercoagulable state may be indicated. This may include protein C, protein S, and antithrombin III levels, and the presence of lupus anticoagulants. Anticoagulant use, pregnancy, OCP use, and renal or liver disease need to be considered in interpreting these tests (18).

Treatment

DVTs are treated with anticoagulants, primarily to prevent pulmonary embolism (PE), because 90% of PEs come from DVTs (16). Thus, superficial venous thromboses and calf vein DVTS that are not propagating upward (80% of all calf DVTs) are not treated with anticoagulants, but with warm compresses three to four times a day and nonsteroidal anti-inflammatory drugs and close follow-up. Thigh vein DVTs and the 20% of calf vein DVTs that propagate to the thigh are initially treated with heparin, unless contraindications to its use exist such as increased risk of bleeding or heparin sensitivity. Many hospitals and services have a prewritten protocol for use.

Treatment is initiated with a bolus of 80 units per kilogram of heparin followed by infusion of 18 units per kilogram of heparin per hour. PTTs are followed every 6 hours initially, and the infusion is adjusted to maintain a PTT of 2.0 to 2.5 times control. Attainment of therapeutic PTT within 24 hours is important in preventing propagation of thrombus and pulmonary embolism (15). After 24 hours, when a therapeutic PTT has been attained, PTT can be followed every 12 to 24 hours and Coumadin can be initiated.

Coumadin is generally initiated with a dose of 10 mg oral daily. Subsequent doses of Coumadin are adjusted based on the prothrombin time international normalized ratio (INR) to attain an INR of 2.0 to 3.0. After a therapeutic PT has been attained, heparin can be stopped. Coumadin use is generally continued for 3 months, unless recurrent thromboses or factor deficiencies are found. Then, lifetime Coumadin use may be suggested.

The advantages of chronic Coumadin use must be weighed against its hazards. Individuals at risk for bleeding, such as those with a history of peptic ulcer disease, should not use Coumadin chronically. Individuals at risk for falls such as the elderly, the disabled, those with neurological diseases, gait disorders, seizure disorders, or substance or alcohol abuse that might involve episodes of uncontrolled falling or unconsciousness should also not chronically use Coumadin. In individuals who have recurrent thromboses and who cannot safely take long-term Coumadin use, Greenfield filter placement should be considered.

With short-term use, heparin can cause thrombocytopenia and complete blood count with platelet counts should be monitored. Hyperkalemia and elevated liver transaminases can also occur. With long-term therapy, as in pregnancy, osteoporosis can occur, and calcium supplements should be given. Risks associated with Coumadin use include risk of bleeding and, rarely, Coumadin-induced skin necrosis. Coumadin interacts with many medications and introduction of new medications may require modification of dosage and closer monitoring of PT values.

In patients who are unable to receive anticoagulants, consideration should be given to placement of a Greenfield filter. Use of low-molecular weight heparin for treatment of DVT is currently being investigated.

DVTS in Pregnancy

Because of hormonal effects on coagulation and decreased venous return caused by the enlarging uterus, DVTs are more common in pregnancy, particularly in women with a previous history or other risk factors for DVTs. Prevention of situations in which DVTs may occur may decrease the incidence. Pregnant women should refrain from long car drives, airplane trips, or any other activity with long periods of sitting or lying without adequate time to walk and move the "muscle pump." Use of support hose may help.

Presentation of DVTs in pregnancy may be typical (e.g., heat, redness, swelling, pain) or may be heralded only by aching in the calves or increased unilateral swelling. DVTs may be masked by the chronic swelling of venous insufficiency. Evaluation is similar to that in nonpregnant women, except venography with IV contrast dye should not be used. Nuclear scans, if needed, can be substituted.

During pregnancy, Coumadin is contraindicated because it can cause a teratogenic syndrome, and it crosses the placental barrier, causing maternal and fetal hemorrhage. After initially treating the patient with intravenous heparin, subcutaneous heparin is used in doses of approximately 17,500 units every 12 hours and adjustments made to attain a PTT 2.0 times control (19). Chronic heparinization at home may be necessary until delivery.

DVT Prophylaxis

Prophylaxis against DVT should be provided to most hospitalized patients. Patients without apparent risk factors can be fitted with gradient compression stockings and treated with subcutaneous heparin 5000 units every 12 hours from initial hospitalization until they are ambulatory or discharged. Moderate risk patients can be provided with pneumatic compression stockings and with heparin subcutaneously.

High-risk patients, such as those with two or more risk factors, prior history of DVT, or undergoing lower extremity orthopedic surgery should be given oral Coumadin dosed as above, or subcutaneous enoxaparin 30 mg, every 12 hours can be given. These latter two therapies can be continued until hospital discharge, or oral Coumadin can be continued for 6 to 12 weeks as empiric therapy unless a negative imaging study is obtained (20).

Superficial Thrombophlebitis

Superficial thrombophlebitis generally occurs in association with varicose veins, but can also occur with infection, trauma, or because of IV cannulation. Treatment involves heat, elevation, and nonsteroidal anti-inflammatory medications. Extension into the deep venous system can occur, and then diagnostic testing is indicated.

In the lower extremity, if the thrombosis is above the knee and approaching the saphenofemoral junction, consideration should be given to use of anticoagulant therapy and ligation of the vein. If there are no apparent inciting causes for the thrombophlebitis, then consideration should be given to assessing for malignancies or other hypercoaguable states.

Lymphedema

Lymphedema refers to impairment in lymphatic drainage, generally of an extremity, and results from congenital or acquired disruption of lymphatic flow. Primary or congenital lymphedema is a rare disease, occurring in 1 per 100,000 of the population with approximately 80% of cases occurring in women (21).

Secondary causes of lymphedema are more commonly encountered and may be caused by malignancy, trauma, surgery, infection, chronic inflammation, or radiation. Worldwide, the most common cause of lymphedema is infection, with filiariasis being the most common infection. In North America, the most common causes are malignancy and radiation therapy (22).

Clinical Course and Evaluation

Patients with primary lymphedema present with painless swelling of one or more extremities. There may be a positive family history for lymphedema. Patients with secondary lymphedema may present similarly, but have a history of prior infection, malignancy, radiation, surgery, or trauma. Physical findings early in the disease may include distal edema (which may be pitting), redness, and warmth, besides any findings associated with the underlying cause. Chronic changes may include nonpitting edema and skin thickening.

The differential diagnosis of a single swollen extremity includes (a) DVT, (b) CVI, (c) lympedema, (d) liver or renal disease, (e) congestive heart failure, (f) thyroid disease, (g) malignancies, (h) medication use, (i) trauma,

(j) hematoma formation, (k) aneurysm, (l) arteriovenous malformations or fistulae, (m) and Baker's cysts. The history, physical, urinalysis, BUN, creatinine, and thyroid function testing will identify medical causes. Duplex scanning has been recommended as the initial imaging test to evaluate for DVT and other anatomic causes of swollen extremity (23).

Further evaluation includes lymposcintigraphy to assess lymphatic function and possibly MRI and/or CT scanning to detail anatomy of the soft tissues for malignancies. MRI is also useful in differentiating lipedema, CVI, and lymphedema (24).

Treatment

Treatment of lymphedema includes exercise, massage, and compression of the extremity. Pneumatic compression can be used initially in more severe cases, followed by gradient compression stockings. Attention to skin care is important to prevent infectious complications. Benzopyrones are a group of medications that have been shown useful to help reduce lymphedema but are unavailable in the United States (25). Reconstructive surgery can be performed for extreme cases of lymphedema refractory to other measures.

Venous Diseases in the Elderly

Deep vein thrombosis, CVI, and varicose veins increase incidence with increasing age. Secondary lymphedema is more likely in the elderly. Evaluation of the swollen extremity in the elderly patient would be similar to the younger patient. However, DVT, CVI, malignancy, and underlying medical disease are more likely diagnoses.

Treatment guidelines for the elderly patient usually are the same as for younger patients. However, chronic use of Coumadin may be contraindicated if the patient is likely to be only intermittently compliant or is at risk for falls. In more frail patients, more conservative measures may be used and surgical procedures avoided if possible.

Special Considerations for Nurse Practitioners and Physician Assistants

Because chronic venous insufficiency and related problems are so common in women, providers must recognize women at risk, be alert to the often vague signs and symptoms of problems such as DVT, and make preventive care a part of their routines. A woman with impaired venous return may complain of her legs feeling heavy or tired, itching, leg cramps at night, or a dull ache in her legs, especially after prolonged standing—all symptoms that could be easily "explained away" or even ignored by the busy practitioner.

Ask the woman if she has a past history of thrombosis and determine the provoking factor (e.g., pregnancy or postpartum, oral contraceptives, immobilization, trauma). Determine if there are current risk factors such as cancer, obesity, oral contraceptive use, inflammatory bowel disease, or congestive heart failure. Ask women specifically about work that involves long hours of standing or sitting (26, 27). Inquire about recent immobilizations, e.g., because of long trips, illnesses, and recent surgeries or pregnancies. Because of early discharge, a woman may not experience problems such as DVT until she is home after gynecologic surgery or delivery. (DVT, although most likely immediately postpartum, can occur up to 8 weeks postpartum).

During the physical exam, providers should note the amount and location of edema. One predictor of DVT is a difference between leg circumference of 3 cm in the calves and 4 cm in the thighs (28). The presence of signs of inflammation (e.g., edema, pain, heat) especially if unilateral, increases the suspicion of DVT. With chronic venous insufficiency, the skin may be thickened, darkened, or brownish, dermatitis and varicosities may be present, and stasis leg ulcers may be present, especially on bony prominences such as the ankle.

Early signs and symptoms of DVT can be absent or nonspecific. Even when suspicion is high, DVT cannot be diagnosed and treated based on clinical judgement alone. Following established protocols, the provider must consult or refer for diagnostic studies and treatment. Interventions in the primary care setting for problems related to chronic venous insufficiency might include the following:

1. Use appropriate compression stockings, being sure that the woman knows how to apply them correctly, avoiding wrinkles or rolling down stockings that can create a tourniquet.

2. For stasis ulcers, use rest for 2 to 3 days with elevation of legs and wet to dry or other dressings (per protocol). Teach the woman or family member how to change dressings and recognize signs of infection. Unna boots may be used at times instead of dressings. Recheck ulcer in 2 to 7 days, depending on its status and ability of the woman to treat it and recognize problems. Consult for leg ulcers that do not improve after 3 to 4 days of therapy or for signs of cellulitis, extreme infection, large deep ulcers, and acute arterial occlusion (29).

3. Consult for diuretic orders if edema is significant.

4. Monitor women who are taking warfarin via established protocols. Check all other

drugs that are being prescribed for possible effect on warfarin, e.g., metronidazole and perhaps some sulfonamides that may enhance warfarin's anticoagulant effect (26).

The woman who is taking warfarin must understand the importance of taking the medication and getting laboratory work as scheduled. Written and oral teaching should be reinforced as needed about signs of bleeding, including less obvious signs such as new onset severe headaches, abdominal or flank pain, melena, or coffee-ground emesis. The woman must be aware of pharmacologic agents that are to be avoided (e.g., aspirin) and combination drugs that contain these products. The nonpregnant woman of childbearing age who is taking an anticoagulant must be counseled about prevention of pregnancy. Because nearly all women, especially as they age, will have some risk of venous stasis and DVT, all practitioners must act to prevent the pain, disability, and cost associated with such problems. The triad of early detection, prevention, and self-care can help protect the woman from complications that cause pain and disability and may even threaten her life.

References

1. Callam MJ. Epidemiology of varicose veins. Br J Surg 1994;81:167–173.
2. Sumner DS. Pathophysiology of chronic venous insufficiency. Sem Vasc Surg 1988;1:66–72.
3. Nicholaides AN, Zukowski AJ. The value of dynamic venous pressure measurements. World J Surg 1986;10:919–924.
4. Hopkins NFG, Wolfe JHN. Deep venous insufficiency and occlusion. Br Med J 1992;304:107–110.
5. Gourdin FW, Smith JG. Etiology of venous ulceration. South Med J 1993;86:1142–1145.
6. Bergen JJ. Varicose veins: chronic venous insufficiency. In: Moore WS, ed. Vascular Surgery. Philadelphia: WB Saunders 1993:783–791.
7. Oxpentifylline for venous leg ulcers. Drug Ther Bull 1991;29:59–60.
8. Weiss RA, Weiss MA, Goldman MP. Physicians' negative perception of sclerotherapy for venous disorders: review of a 7 year experience with modern sclerotherapy. South Med J 1992;85:1101–1106.
9. Bergan JJ. New developments in the surgical treatment of venous disease. Cardiovasc Surg 1993;1:6 24–631.
10. Sarin S, Scurr JH, Smith PD. Assessment of stripping the long saphenous vein in the treatment of primary varicose veins. Br J Surg 1992;79:889–893.
11. Callam MJ, Harper DR, Dalle JJ, Ruckley CV. Arterial disease in chronic leg ulceration: an underestimated hazard? Lothian and Forth Valley Leg Ulcer Study. Br Med J 1987;294:929–931.
12. Rubenstein I, Murray D, Hoffstein V. Fatal pulmonary emboli in hospitalized patients: an autopsy study. Arch Intern Med 1988;148:1425–1426.
13. Silver D. An overview of venous thromboembolism prophylaxis. Am J Surg 1991;161:537–540.
14. Gerstman BB, Piper JM, Tomita DK, Ferguson WJ, Stadel BV, Lundin FE. Oral contraceptive estrogen dose and the risk of deep venous thromboembolic disease. Am J Epidemiol 1991;133:32–36.
15. Devar M, Barrett-Conner E, Renvall M, Reigal D, Ramsdell J. Estrogen replacement therapy and the risk of venous thrombosis. Am J Med 1992;92:275–282.
16. Brunader RE. Diagnosis and evaluation of thromboembolic disorders. J Am Board Fam Pract 1989;2:106–118.
17. Hulsman MV, Buller HR, Ten Cate JW, et al. Management of clinically suspected acute venous thrombosis in out-patients with serial impedence plethysmography in a community hospital setting. Arch Intern Med 1989;149:511–513.
18. Bolan CD, Aiving BM. Recurrent venous thrombosis and hypercoaguable states. Am Fam Physician 1991;44:1741–1751.
19. Laros RK. Thromboembolic disease. In: Creasy RK, Resnik R, ed. Maternal-Fetal Medicine. Philadelphia: WB Saunders, 1994:792–803.
20. Paiement GD, Wessinger SJ, Harris WH. Cost-effectiveness of prophylaxis in total hip replacement. Am J Surg 1991;161:519–524.
21. Smeltzer DM, Stickler GB, Schirger A. Primary lymphedema in children and adolescents: a follow-up and review. Pediatrics 1985;76:206–216.
22. Gloviczki P, Wahner HW. Clinical diagnosis and evaluation of lymphedema. In: Rutherford RB, ed. Vascular Surgery. Vol. II. Philadelphia: WB Saunders, 1995:1899–1920.
23. Buchbinder D, McCullough GM, Melick CF. Patients evaluated for venous disease may have other pathologic conditions contributing to symptomatology. Am J Surg 1993;166:211–215.
24. Duewell S, Hagspiel KD, Zuber J, von Schulthess GK, Bollinger A, Fuchs WA. Swollen lower extremity: role of MR imaging. Radiology 1992;184:227–231.
25. Casley-Smith JR, Morgan RG, Piller NB. Treatment of lymphedema of the arms and legs with 5,6-benzo-alpha-pyrone. N Engl J Med 1993;329:1158–1163.
26. Kayser S. Thromboembolic disease. In: Herfindal

ET, Dick GR, Hart LL, eds. Clinical Pharmacology and Therapeutics. 5th ed. Baltimore: Williams & Wilkins, 1992:712–729.

27. Ligeti RA. Prevention of deep vein thrombosis. J Am Acad Physician Assist 1990;3:319–328.

28. Simmons S. Venous thromboembolism. In: Lemcke DP, Pattison J, Marshall LA, Cowley DS, eds. Primary Care of Women. Norwalk, CT: Appleton & Lange, 1995:311–330.

29. Uphold, CR, Graham MV. Clinical Guidelines in Family Practice. Gainesville, FL: Barmarrae, 1993:482–489.

13.4

Congestive Heart Failure and Valvular Disease

Carol M. Buchter and Kara J. Quan

Introduction

Congestive heart failure (CHF) is a clinical condition characterized by the heart's inability to pump sufficient blood to meet metabolic demands or to do so only at an abnormally elevated filling pressure. It is not a distinct syndrome but is the final common pathway for a variety of conditions.

Epidemiology

More than 2 million Americans have heart failure and more than 400,000 new cases are diagnosed annually. It is the only cardiac disease increasing in prevalence, because of both the aging of the US population and improved treatment of hypertension and acute myocardial infarction. Much of our information regarding the incidence, prevalence, and natural history of heart failure is derived from the Framingham study (1), a longitudinal study of more than 5000 residents of Framingham, MA begun in 1949 and continuing to today (2). The incidence of heart failure is less in women than in men in all age groups, but is more prevalent in women after age 80 years. The total incidence is known to increase sharply with increasing age.

Prognosis

The prognosis of symptomatic heart failure is poor with approximately 50% 5-year mortality in all patients with symptomatic heart failure because of left ventricular systolic dysfunction and 50% 1-year mortality in those patients with the most severe symptoms. The prognosis in heart failure is related to the extent of symptoms, the extent of myocardial dysfunction, the etiology of dysfunction (with coronary artery disease conferring increased mortality), and the degree of sympathetic nervous system activity as measured by plasma norepinephrine

concentration. Generally, women with symptomatic heart failure have a better prognosis than do men.

However, idiopathic cardiomyopathy occurs more often in men and has an improved survival. The Framingham study documented a 5-year survival of 57% in women compared with 38% in men with symptomatic heart failure (3).

Etiology

CHF may result from chronic ischemic heart disease, hypertensive heart disease, or valvular heart disease (Table 13.4.1). Additionally, CHF may be the result of cardiotropic viral infections (most typically echovirus or coxsackievirus), autoimmune disorders, thyroid dysfunction, or direct effects of alcohol, anthracycline antineoplastic agents, or other myocardial toxins. The most common pathophysiologic abnormality causing heart failure is systolic myocardial dysfunction, leading to ineffective pumping action. Diastolic dysfunction, characterized by abnormal relaxation or filling of the ventricle, may account for up to 30% of cases of heart failure. Heart failure may occur without either primary or secondary myocardial abnormalities.

Table 13.4.1. Causes of Congestive Heart Failure

- Chronic ischemic heart disease
- Hypertensive heart disease
- Valvular heart disease
- Cardiotropic viral infections (most typically echovirus or coxsackievirus)
- Autoimmune disorders
- Postpartum cardiomyopathy
- Thyroid dysfunction
- Direct effects of alcohol, anthracycline, antineoplastic agents, or other myocardial toxins

Postpartum Cardiomyopathy

Postpartum cardiomyopathy is a relatively uncommon problem, representing less than 1% of all cardiovascular problems associated with pregnancy. Postpartum cardiomyopathy criteria include (1) development of cardiac failure in the last month of pregnancy or within 5 months postpartum, (2) absence of a determinable etiology for cardiac failure, and (3) absence of demonstrable heart disease before the last month of pregnancy (4).

Postpartum cardiomyopathy occurs in approximately 1 in 4000 deliveries. In the United States, it is more common in older, multiparous African-American women. Toxemia and twin pregnancies have been identified as predisposing factors; the role of malnutrition is speculative. The exact etiology of this condition is unknown, but proposed mechanisms include viral infection, autoimmunity, and hormonal changes.

Clinical recovery occurs in over half of all women with postpartum cardiomyopathy (5). The rapidity with which heart size returns to normal affects the long-term prognosis with resolution of cardiomegaly within 6 months associated with improved survival, although the risk of recurrent cardiomyopathy with subsequent pregnancies remains.

Physiology

When left ventricular systolic function declines, a wide array of adaptive mechanisms occurs to maintain sufficient cardiac output and blood supply to vital organs. These adaptive mechanisms are modulated by activation of the sympathetic nervous system and the renin angiotensin aldosterone system, and they include compensatory tachycardia, vasoconstriction, and salt and water retention. These compensatory mechanisms, although adaptive in acute heart failure, are maladaptive in chronic heart failure. They lead to worsening conges-

tive symptoms because of salt and water retention and to further decreases in cardiac output because of the increased afterload caused by peripheral vasoconstriction. Because cardiac output is the product of both heart rate and stroke volume, tachycardia will acutely increase cardiac output, but a sustained increase in heart rate may further weaken an already compromised cardiac muscle. Indeed, precipitation of severe systolic dysfunction and clinical heart failure frequently occurs following a prolonged period of elevated heart rate. Manipulation of these excessive, and therefore maladaptive compensatory mechanisms, are the basis of many therapeutic options in the treatment of heart failure, including reducing preload to relieve congestive symptoms, reducing afterload to improve forward cardiac output, improving contractility, and reversing deleterious neurohormonal activation.

Following an acute myocardial infarction causing limited left ventricular systolic dysfunction, ventricular remodeling occurs (6). This progressive ventricular dilatation, without additional myocardial damage, is an important cause of clinical heart failure many years after acute myocardial infarction. Remodeling can be lessened or prevented with afterload reduction therapy began before the development of heart failure.

Risk Factors

Many risk factors for the development of heart failure are modifiable (Table 13.4.2). Inadequately controlled hypertension induces pressure overload on the left ventricle, leading to hypertrophy and ultimately to depressed contractility. Hypertension was identified as the etiology of heart failure in three fourths of all women and men with heart failure in the Framingham study (1) and has been identified as a commonly associated condition in all subsequent studies of heart failure. Diabetes mellitus, hypercholesterolemia, cigarette smoking,

Table 13.4.2. Risk Factors for Ischemic Cardiomyopathy

- Inadequately controlled hypertension
- Diabetes mellitus
- Hypercholesterolemia
- Cigarette smoking
- Obesity

and obesity all contribute to the development of atherosclerosis, a leading cause of systolic dysfunction. Diabetes is a stronger risk factor for the development of heart failure in women than in men, conferring a five-fold excess risk in women and a 2.4-fold excess risk for men. This excess risk is not solely because of accelerating atherosclerosis, as the risk persists after exclusion of patients with coronary heart disease.

Evaluation

The diagnostic evaluation of heart failure must include an explanation of the underlying pathophysiologic abnormality and a search for etiology. The symptoms of heart failure are nonspecific, and a woman should not be erroneously labeled with heart failure unless objective findings on physical examination or corroboration of clinical suspicion with diagnostic testing is present. A careful history and physical will provide important information concerning the presence of heart failure and its possible etiologies.

Physical Findings

The symptoms of heart failure are divided into those caused by pulmonary or systemic vascular congestion (backward failure) and those caused by inadequate cardiac output (forward failure). Examples of congestive symptoms include orthopnea, paroxysmal nocturnal dyspnea, exertional dyspnea, and cough because of pulmonary congestion seen in left heart failure

and abdominal or lower extremity discomfort because of systemic venous congestion of right heart failure. Inadequate cardiac output because of left heart failure causes depressed mentation, fatigue, and exercise intolerance (Table 13.4.3).

Radiologic Evaluation

Both systolic and diastolic dysfunction may lead to the identical clinical syndrome of heart failure, but treatment for these two conditions is different. Echocardiography or radionucleotide ventriculography will differentiate between systolic and diastolic dysfunction and, thus, guide therapeutic decisions. Although radionucleotide ventriculography provides a more accurate assessment of ventricular function, echocardiography provides additional potentially valuable information including valvular function and wall thickness. As recommended by the US Public Health Service's Agency for Health Care Policy and Research (7), all patients initially presenting with heart failure should have an objective measurement of ventricular function, preferably with echocar-

Table 13.4.3. Signs and Symptoms of Congestive Heart Failure

Pulmonary vascular congestion
    Orthopena
    Paroxysmal nocturnal dyspnea
    Exertional dyspnea
    Cough
    Shortness of breath
    Wheezing
Systemic vascular congestion
    Abdominal enlargement
    Ascites
    Hepatomegaly
    Peripheral edema
Inadequate cardiac output
    Depressed mentation
    Fatigue
    Exercise intolerance

diography. It is not necessary to reassess ventricular function regularly, but repeat testing may be suggested if there is a significant change in the woman's clinical condition.

Medical Therapy of CHF

Traditionally, diuretics are the first drugs used. Diuretics reduce congestive symptoms and are beneficial to patients with heart failure and fluid overload. However, diuretics do not improve cardiac output and have not been shown to improve survival in patients with heart failure. They have no role in the treatment of patients with asymptomatic ventricular dysfunction. When used as monotherapy, the sympathetic nervous system and renin angiotensin systems are activated, with potentially deleterious effects (8).

Digitalis is an orally active agent with modest inotropic activity and favorable neurohormonal actions, including lessening of sympathetic nervous system activation. Although in use for more than 200 years, digoxin has only recently been proven beneficial in the symptomatic treatment of patients with CHF, whatever the cardiac rhythm. In the RADIANCE trial (9) that studied 178 patients with mild to moderate CHF treated with digoxin, diuretics, and angiotensin converting enzyme inhibitors (ACEI), each patient was randomized to continue or to be withdrawn from digoxin. Over the 12 week study period, those patients withdrawn from digoxin had a significantly increased incidence of worsening heart failure requiring increased diuretics, emergency room evaluation, or hospital admission. The PROVED trial (10) found similar results in patients with CHF with stable symptoms on digoxin and diuretics; withdrawal of digoxin resulted in worsening clinical status. The effects of chronic digoxin therapy on survival in heart failure are unknown, but they are the subject of an ongoing large multicenter trial (11).

Afterload reduction therapy is the only treatment proven to improve survival in patients with heart failure. The first proof of survival benefit came in 1986 (12), when the V-HeFT trial compared hydralazine plus isosorbide dinitrate with prazosin and placebo in patients with Class II and III heart failure, despite treatment with digitalis and diuretics. The nonspecific vasodilating combination of hydralazine (a pure arteriolar dilator) and isosorbide dinitrate (primarily a venodilator), improved survival by 36% over 3 years when compared with either the alpha-receptor antagonist prazosin or with placebo. Shortly after this landmark study, multiple trials using ACEI confirmed survival benefit in patients with mild, moderate, and severe heart failure (13, 14). In 1991, V-HeFT II (15) compared the ACEI enalapril with hydralazine plus isosorbide dinitrate and found despite a more significant symptomatic and hemodynamic benefit in the hydralazine plus isosorbide dinitrate group, survival was improved to a greater degree with enalapril. More recently, several trials such as the Survival and Ventricular Enlargement (SAVE) trial (16) and the Studies of Left Ventricular Dysfunction (SOLVD) trial (17) have demonstrated the benefits of ACEI in patients with depressed left ventricular function, even in the absence of heart failure symptoms. The SAVE trial enrolled more than 2000 patients, 3 to 16 days following an acute myocardial infarction, with a left ventricular ejection fraction of less than 40% in the absence of symptomatic heart failure. A 19% reduction in mortality was seen at 42 months in patients treated with captopril. This survival benefit persisted whether patients received aspirin, beta-blockers, or thrombolytic therapy.

Because of these trials, afterload reduction therapy is recommended for all patients with left ventricular ejection fractions of less than 40%, whatever the presence or severity of heart failure symptoms. All patients postinfarction should be screened for reduced ejection fraction except for those patients with an initial small non–Q-wave inferior infarction (7). ACEI are the treatment of choice, with hydralazine plus isosorbide dinitrate given to those patients intolerant of ACEI. Contraindications to ACE inhibitors include a known previous hypersensitivity reaction including angioneurotic edema, hyperkalemia, or symptomatic hypotension.

Although digoxin is the only available orally active positive inotrope, several potent intravenous positive inotropic agents are available for the treatment of refractory heart failure. Beta-adrenergic receptor agonists (e.g., dobutamine) and phosphodiesterase inhibitors (e.g., amrinone, milrinone) increase cardiac contractility by increasing intracellular calcium concentration. Although these potent agents can produce significant improvements in cardiac output and an impressive reduction in symptoms because of either congestion or low cardiac output, their use is limited by their negative impact on survival (18). All presently available intravenous inotropes cause tachycardia, predispose to supraventricular and ventricular arrhythmias, and worsen rather than improve the neurohormonal activation of heart failure.

Vesnarinone is an orally active positive inotrope presently undergoing clinical trials for the treatment of severe heart failure. Preliminary studies (19) have shown significant improvement in survival with the use of this unique agent with phosphodiesterase inhibition, sodium channel antagonism, and Vaughn-Williams Class III antiarrhythmic properties (19).

First-generation calcium channel blockers, such as nifedipine, verapamil, and diltiazem, are inappropriate agents for the treatment of heart failure. These agents all possess negative inotropic action and increase activity of the sympathetic nervous system and renin angiotensin aldosterone system. Newer calcium channel blockers, including amlodipine and felodipine, produce systemic vasodilatation without negative inotropic effect and have

a favorable neurohormonal action. Ongoing trials such as PRAISE and V-HeFT III are studying the effects of these calcium channel blockers on symptoms and survival in patients with CHF.

Other therapeutic modalities of promising but unproven benefit in the treatment of heart failure include beta-adrenergic receptor blockade, anticoagulation, and antiarrhythmic therapy, particularly with amiodarone. Several studies of chronic beta-blocker therapy in heart failure patients have shown improvement in symptoms and a trend toward reduced mortality (20, 21).

Women in Major Trials of Heart Failure

Women have been represented to a variable degree in the major heart failure mortality trials. V-HeFT I and II, enrolling a total of 1146 men, included no women. The Cooperative North Scandinavian Enalapril Survival Study (CONSENSUS I) (13) and SOLVD (14, 17), with a combined enrollment of more than 7000 patients had between 11 and 30% women. Only two heart failure trials have specifically examined the effect of gender on the importance of beneficial treatment effects. CONSENSUS enrolled 253 women with severe heart failure, of whom 30% were women. Women treated with enalapril had a modest 6% mortality reduction, whereas the mortality in men was reduced by 51% at 6 months. The SOLVD prevention and treatment trials showed a trend toward increasing mortality, longer time to first heart failure hospitalization, and decreased onset of new or increasing heart failure in women compared with men treated with enalapril.

The SAVE trial (16) studied 2231 patients with asymptomatic left ventricular dysfunction after myocardial infarction; 18% were women. Captopril produced a 25% risk reduction for death in women versus 22% in men and a risk reduction of the combined endpoint of cardiovascular death and morbidity of 4% in women versus 28% in men. Unfortunately, the study did not have sufficient statistical power to adequately address this gender issue.

Surgical Therapy of CHF

Surgical treatment of heart failure includes coronary revascularization, with either angioplasty or coronary bypass surgery, in patients with ischemic cardiomyopathy. Transplantation is an option for patients with end-stage cardiac disease, a left ventricular ejection fraction generally less than 25%, and an expected survival without surgery of less than 1 year. From 1988 to 1992, women represented between 17 and 19% of patients undergoing transplantation. Women experience slightly more rejection episodes than do men after transplant and have a slightly reduced 1- and 3-year survival (22). Nonetheless, this surgery is an important option for some patients with severe heart failure.

Valvular Heart Disease

Valvular heart disease plays a significant role in the spectrum of cardiovascular disease. One major cause of valvular lesions is rheumatic fever, and statistics reveal a resurgence in this disease and an increased prevalence in women and in the aging population (23). The natural history of each valvular lesion is different. Some may involve irreversible myocardial damage, whereas others are benign. It is important to understand the natural course of the disease before beginning treatment (Table 13.4.4).

The approach to valvular heart disease has evolved as our knowledge has increased. A simple approach using noninvasive techniques has made the evaluation of valvular lesions more readily available, safe, and cost-effective. Echocardiography has decreased the need of cardiac catheterization in some lesions, but cardiac catheterization may still be used to quantitate lesion severity and assess associated abnormalities before surgery.

Similarly, the management of valvular disease has changed. Knowledge of the appropriate timing of surgical intervention and the optimal medical treatment requires insight into the woman's situation.

Mitral Stenosis

Etiology and Pathophysiology
Mitral stenosis is the most common valvular lesion; it is most often caused by rheumatic fever, and two thirds of those affected are women. After an acute episode of rheumatic fever, significant anatomical changes, including thickening and calcification of the valve leaflets and fusion and shortening of the chordae tendineae, develop slowly over many years. Mitral regurgitation may be present, because of the deformed mitral valve. Left atrial enlargement, elevated left atrial pressure, and pulmonary hypertension may occur. Atrial fibrillation often occurs because of atrial enlargement and inhomogeneous atrial depolarization.

Clinical Manifestations
Symptoms of mitral stenosis typically occur more than 10 years after an episode of acute rheumatic fever. Mild to moderate pulmonary congestive symptoms slowly progress to severe pulmonary compromise. Fatigue and cachexia are late findings because of decreased cardiac output. Intermittent atrial fibrillation may cause peripheral emboli. Hemoptysis may result from pulmonary vasculature rupture. Hepatomegaly, ascites, and peripheral edema also may be seen.

Physical findings include a decreased pulse pressure caused by a low stroke volume and a loud first heart sound caused by the rapid rise in left ventricular systolic pressure, causing mitral valve closure. An opening snap can be heard if the mitral valve is pliable. A low-pitched rumbling diastolic murmur follows the opening snap, loudest in early diastole during rapid ventricular filling and with atrial contraction. Late

Table 13.4.4. Characteristics of Valvular Disease

Valvular Lesion	Causes	Symptoms	Physical Findings	ECG-Chest Radiograph Findings	Treatment
Mitral stenosis	Rheumatic fever	Dyspnea, fatigue, cachexia, hemoptysis	Decreased pulse pressure A loud first heart sound An opening snap A low-pitched rumbling diastolic murmur A loud P_2 Hepatomegaly Ascites Peripheral edema	ECG-atrial fibrillation, left atrial abnormality and RVH XRAY-enlarged left atrium, straightening of the left heart border, double density at the right heart border, posterior displacement of the esophagus, elevation of the left main stem bronchus, pulmonary edema	Medical: if atrial fibrillation is present, anticoagulation, ventricular rate control, diuretics and salt restriction, endocarditis prophylaxis Surgical-presence of moderate to severe heart failure despite maximal medical therapy or systemic embolization in the face of therapeutic anticoagulation
Mitral regurgitation	Rheumatic fever: congenital anomalies and associations include ostium primum atrial septal defect and Marfan's syndrome Other etiologies include infective endocarditis, mitral valve prolapse, ruptured chordae tendineae, papillary muscle dysfunction, and hypertrophic or dilated cardiomyopathy	Prolonged asymptomatic period Later pulmonary congestion ensues, and pulmonary hypertension	Hyperdynamic left ventricular impulse Left parasternal lift A soft first heart sound A widely split second heart sound A third heart sound The holosystolic murmur of mitral regurgitation Right-sided heart failure	ECG-left atrial enlargement and left ventricular hypertrophy. Atrial fibrillation Radiograph-left atrial and left ventricular enlargement and pulmonary venous congestion	Afterload reduction, salt restriction, diuretics, and digoxin Surgical: moderate to severe heart failure, despite maximal medical therapy

Condition	Etiology	Symptoms	Physical signs	ECG / Radiograph	Management
Mitral valve prolapse	Marfan's syndrome, other connective tissue diseases, ostium secundum atrial septal defect, and hypertrophic cardiomyopathy	Chest pain; tachypalpitations orthostatic hypotension and syncope	Midsystolic click and late systolic murmur	ECG—usually normal, but nonspecific inferior ST depression and T wave abnormalities or premature ventricular and supraventricular complexes. Radiograph—normal	Endocarditis prophylaxis. Beta-blockade may provide symptomatic relief of chest pain
Aortic stenosis	Rheumatic fever. Bicuspid aortic valve	Asymptomatic for years. When CHF, angina, or syncope occurs, there is a rapid clinical decline. Sudden cardiac death	Pulsus parvus et tardus and a carotid thrill ("shudder"). A systolic ejection murmur in the aortic area. An aortic ejection click; the second heart sound may be paradoxically split. A fourth heart sound is often present, and a third heart sound may be heard	ECG—left ventricular hypertrophy, intraventricular conduction delays, and bundle branch blocks. Atrioventricular block. Radiographs: left ventricular prominence, calcification of the aortic valve, and possibly poststenotic aortic root dilatation	Limitation of activity. Surgical: onset of symptoms of CHF, angina, or syncope heralds a grave prognosis and is generally an indication for valve replacement
Aortic regurgitation	Rheumatic fever, subvalvular stenosis, ventricular septal defect, and aortic dilation because of ankylosing spondylitis, Marfan's syndrome, systemic hypertension, aortic dissection, or aortic trauma	Asymptomatic, for years	Head bobbing, titubation, and pistol shot pulses occur. To and fro murmurs are heard over the femoral arteries with light compression by a stethoscope (Duroziez's sign) and pulsatile blushing of the nail bed (Quincke's sign). Rapid upstroke of the pulse with a collapsing quality (water hammer pulse)	Cardiomegaly and pulmonary congestion. ECG—left ventricular hypertrophy. Radiograph: left ventricular and aortic dilation	Endocarditis prophylaxis, salt restriction, diuretics, digitalis, and afterload reduction. Surgical: timing of aortic valve replacement is controversial because there is a prolonged asymptomatic window. In asymptomatic women, evidence of progressive left ventricular systolic dysfunction may indicate the need for surgery

features include a loud P2 caused by pulmonary hypertension, a right ventricular impulse, and signs of right-sided heart failure.

Diagnosis

In mitral stenosis, electrocardiographic findings include atrial fibrillation, left atrial abnormality (if sinus rhythm is maintained), and right ventricular hypertrophy. Chest radiography reveals an enlarged left atrium, straightening of the left heart border, a double-density at the right heart border, posterior displacement of the esophagus, and elevation of the left main stem bronchus. Large pulmonary arteries and pulmonary venous congestion are common findings. Two-dimensional echocardiography can accurately estimate the mitral valve area. The normal valve area is 4 cm^2; severe mitral stenosis has a valve area of less than 1 cm^2. M-mode echocardiography reveals thickened mitral leaflets, anterior movement of the posterior leaflet during systole, and decreased mid-diastolic mitral closure (E-F slope). Doppler echocardiography reveals reduced diastolic slope, increased velocity across the mitral valve, and increased pressure half-time as blood is forcefully transported across the stenotic valve (24). Cardiac catheterization enables direct measurement of the valve gradient and estimate of mitral valve area.

Treatment

Women may be managed medically for many years. If atrial fibrillation is present, anticoagulation is mandatory and ventricular rate control is often required. Control of the ventricular rate of atrial fibrillation may decrease left atrial pressure, thus decreasing exertional dyspnea. Diuretics and salt restriction are useful for control of congestive symptoms. As with all significant valvular abnormalities, endocarditis prophylaxis should be given according to the American Heart Association guidelines (25).

The presence of moderate to severe heart failure, despite maximal medical therapy or systemic embolization in the face of therapeutic anticoagulation, is indication for surgery. Pulmonary hypertension increases the surgical risk but is not an absolute contraindication because the pulmonary vascular resistance and left atrial pressure will improve following surgery.

Open or closed mitral valve commissurotomy may provide many years of symptomatic improvement. Catheter balloon valvuloplasty is the treatment of choice for young women with stenotic valves that are not heavily calcified, and may be an option in elderly women who are high-risk surgical candidates. Valve repair or replacement is preferred in women with concomitant mitral regurgitation.

Mitral Regurgitation

Etiology and Pathophysiology

Rheumatic fever is the most common cause of mitral regurgitation, occurring less frequently in women than in men. Associated aortic valve disease suggests rheumatic heart disease as the etiology. Congenital anomalies and associations include ostium primum atrial septal defect and Marfan's syndrome. Other etiologies include infective endocarditis, mitral valve prolapse, ruptured chordae tendineae, papillary muscle dysfunction, and hypertrophic or dilated cardiomyopathy.

Clinical Manifestations

The clinical course of chronic mitral regurgitation is characterized by a prolonged asymptomatic period as the left ventricle ejects blood into a low-pressure left atrium, providing a state of reduced afterload. As mitral regurgitation progresses, left ventricular function declines, pulmonary congestion results, and pulmonary hypertension may develop.

Physical findings include a hyperdynamic left ventricular impulse and left parasternal lift. A soft first heart sound, a widely split second heart sound, and a third heart sound are often heard, along with the holosystolic murmur of mitral regurgitation. Late features include signs of pulmonary hypertension and right-sided heart failure. With acute mitral regurgitation, regurgitant blood flow enters a small or normal-sized noncompliant left atrium. As the left atrium has not had time to dilate, pulmonary edema develops quickly.

Diagnosis

In mitral regurgitation, electrocardiographic findings include left atrial enlargement and left ventricular hypertrophy. Atrial fibrillation is less common than in mitral stenosis. Chest radiography reveals left atrial and left ventricular enlargement and pulmonary venous congestion. Echocardiography provides a semiquantitative estimate of the severity of mitral regurgitation, and left atrial size, left ventricular function, and the presence of valvular vegetations. Cardiac catheterization measures the severity of regurgitation by quantifying the amount of contrast that fills the left atrium after injection into the left ventricle.

Treatment

Women with heart failure are managed with afterload reduction, salt restriction, diuretics, and digoxin. Women with moderate to severe heart failure, despite maximal medical therapy, should be considered for surgery. Those with lesser symptoms and evidence of myocardial dysfunction (e.g., decreasing ejection fraction, increasing systolic left ventricular diameter) are also surgical candidates. Mitral regurgitation occurs into a low-pressure left atrium that decreases afterload and may mask subtle degrees of left ventricular systolic dysfunction. Therefore, a low normal or mildly reduced ejection fraction in a woman with moderate or severe mitral regurgitation implies significant depression of contractility and suggests the need for surgical intervention. Lastly, acute severe mitral regurgitation is an indication for emergent valve repair or replacement.

The mitral valve is usually replaced with a bioprosthetic or metallic valve. Newer valvuloplasty repair techniques may avoid prosthetic valve complications. This may be especially useful in women of childbearing age or in elderly women at risk for falls who are not ideal candidates for anticoagulation (26).

Mitral Valve Prolapse

Etiology and Physiology

Mitral valve prolapse is a common congenital condition, consisting of myxomatous degeneration of the mitral valve leaflets. It is the most prevalent valvular abnormality in the Western hemisphere, occurring in 0.3 to 0.6% of the population, and is found in twice as many women as men (23, 27). The etiology is unknown, although it is associated with Marfan's syndrome, other connective tissue diseases, ostium secundum atrial septal defect, and hypertrophic cardiomyopathy. Significant mitral regurgitation, chordal rupture, infective endocarditis, and sudden cardiac death caused by mitral valve prolapse occur less frequently in women than in men.

Clinical Manifestations

Many symptoms comprise the "click-murmur" syndrome of mitral valve prolapse, and women are more symptomatic than men. Chest pain is the most frequent symptom, and its mechanism is uncertain. Tension on the papillary muscles or ischemia of the papillary muscles may be the cause. Although these women may develop exertional chest pain, their exercise capacity is normal.

Tachypalpitations caused by supraventricular or ventricular arrhythmias are infrequent and rarely represent a risk for sudden cardiac death. Other manifestations are orthostatic hypotension and syncope (28).

Physical findings include a midsystolic click and late systolic murmur. With ventricular contraction, the mitral valve leaflets prolapse into the left atrium and produce the "click." The subsequent mitral regurgitation produces the systolic murmur. Valsalva maneuvers or standing will decrease the preload of the left ventricle and will move the click and murmur earlier into systole. Because of its association with connective tissue diseases, there is a high incidence of bony chest abnormalities, pectus excavatum, and thoracic scoliosis.

Diagnosis

With mitral valve prolapse, the electrocardiogram is usually normal, but nonspecific inferior ST depression and T-wave abnormalities or premature ventricular and supraventricular complexes may be seen. Chest radiography is usually normal, unless significant mitral regurgitation is present. Associated thoracic spine abnormalities may be noted. Two-dimensional echocardiography reveals systolic bowing of the anterior or posterior mitral valve leaflets into the left atrium.

Treatment

The natural history of the syndrome is benign. Endocarditis prophylaxis is recommended for those women with mitral valve prolapse accompanied by mitral regurgitation. Beta-blockade may provide symptomatic relief of the chest pain and tachypalpitations. Premature ventricular contractions are not treated with antiarrhythmics unless ventricular tachycardia is demonstrated. If acute or severe mitral regurgitation occurs, mitral valve repair or replacement should be considered.

Aortic Stenosis

Etiology and Pathophysiology

Aortic stenosis is three times less frequent in women than in men. Congenital bicuspid aortic valve is the most common cause of aortic stenosis. The two aortic cusps thicken and become stenotic by the sixth decade of life. Similarly, a structurally normal tricuspid aortic valve may calcify from "wear and tear" associated with increased age. These women often present when aged in the seventh and eighth decades. If concomitant mitral stenosis is seen, rheumatic heart disease is the most likely etiology.

Obstruction of the aortic valve elevates left ventricular systolic pressure and results in left ventricular hypertrophy, maintaining stroke volume and cardiac output. Left ventricular hypertrophy and increased wall tension produce increased oxygen demand and decreased coronary artery flow, resulting in angina. Vigorous atrial contraction produces a fourth heart sound in association with elevated left ventricular end-diastolic pressure, which may lead to CHF. Effort syncope is caused by peripheral vasodilation and an inability to augment cardiac output with exertion.

Clinical Manifestations

Individuals with acquired severe aortic stenosis may be asymptomatic for years, although symptomatic congenital aortic stenosis may present in childhood or young adulthood. Once CHF, angina or syncope occurs, there is a rapid clinical decline. Sudden cardiac death occurs in 3% of patients.

Physical findings include pulsus parvus et tardus and a carotid thrill ("shudder"). A systolic ejection murmur in the aortic area is usually harsh in quality and radiates to the carotids. If severe aortic stenosis is present, the murmur peaks in late systole, and the left ventricular impulse is sustained and diffuse. An aortic ejection click is auscultated, if noncalcified congenital bicuspid aortic stenosis is present. The aortic component of the second heart sound is diminished, and the second heart sound may be paradoxically split. A fourth heart sound is often present, and a third heart sound may be heard with decompensated left ventricular failure.

Diagnosis

In aortic stenosis, electrocardiographic findings include left ventricular hypertrophy, intraventricular conduction delays, and bundle branch blocks. If calcific aortic stenosis is associated with calcification of the conduction system, atrioventricular block may occur. Chest radiographs show left ventricular prominence, calcification of the aortic valve, and possibly poststenotic aortic root dilatation. Cardiomegaly and pulmonary congestion are seen with left ventricular failure. Echocardiography reveals severe left ventricular hypertrophy and thickened aortic valve cusps with decreased excursion. Doppler velocities estimate the severity of the aortic stenosis by measuring the pressure gradient across the aortic valve.

If the aortic stenosis is severe, cardiac catheterization should be performed to evaluate the valvular gradient and to evaluate for concomitant coronary artery disease. During cardiac catheterization, the gradient between the aorta and left ventricle is measured simultaneously with the cardiac output to calculate valve area. The normal aortic valve area is 2.5 cm^2, and no gradient is present. Critical aortic stenosis is present when the valve area is less than or equal to 0.7 cm^2 and the mean gradient is 50 to 60 mm Hg in the presence of normal systolic function. Pressure gradients will lessen as systolic function declines. Right-sided pressures are normal unless decompensated left ventricular failure is present.

Treatment

In patients with hemodynamically significant aortic stenosis, strenuous physical exertion should be avoided. Limitation of activity has been associated with decreased incidence of sudden cardiac death and increased complete survival.

The onset of symptoms of CHF, angina, or syncope heralds a grave prognosis and is generally an indication for valve replacement. There is an operative mortality of 3 to 6% with an increased operative mortality (up to 15%) observed in association with poor left ventricular function. Systolic function may improve once the obstruction is relieved; therefore, severe left ventricular dysfunction is not an absolute contraindication for surgery. For elderly women who may be poor surgical candidates, catheter balloon valvuloplasty may be an option, although the hemodynamic improvement is typically of brief duration.

Aortic Insufficiency

Etiology and Pathophysiology

Rheumatic heart disease is the most common etiology of aortic regurgitation; it also may result from acute aortic valvulitis or from calcific aortic stenosis. Other conditions associated with aortic insufficiency are subvalvular stenosis, ventricular septal defect, and aortic dilation because of ankylosing spondylitis, Marfan's syndrome, systemic hypertension, aortic dissection, or aortic trauma.

Clinical Manifestations

Aortic regurgitation results in left ventricular volume overload. Via the Frank-Starling mechanism, the ventricle compensates by increasing its end-diastolic volume. Once the ventricular volume exceeds its capacity to dilate, left ventricular end-diastolic and left atrial pressures increase. With left ventricular dilation, secondary mitral regurgitation may occur. Systolic function remains normal until severe left ventricular dilation occurs. These compensatory mechanisms for chronic aortic insufficiency are efficient, and women may be asymptomatic for years. With acute aortic regurgitation, there is no opportunity for left ventricular dilation, resulting in high ventricular compliance and elevated left ventricular end-diastolic pressure. Mitral valve preclosure then occurs, protecting the left atrium and pulmonary vasculature. However, if mitral regurgitation is present, acute pulmonary edema will result.

Many physical findings of chronic aortic regurgitation are caused by increased pulse pressure secondary to the large stroke volume, causing increased systolic and decreased diastolic pressures. Head bobbing, titubation, and pistol-shot pulses occur. To and fro murmurs are heard over the femoral arteries with light compression by a stethoscope (Duroziez's sign), and pulsatile blushing of the nail bed (Quincke's sign) is seen. Rapid upstroke of the pulse with a collapsing quality (water-hammer pulse) and bifid carotid pulses are often present. The aortic component of the second heart sound may be decreased, and a third heart sound is present in decompensated heart failure. The classic diastolic decrescendo murmur of aortic regurgitation is heard best at end expiration with the woman leaning forward. Murmurs because of aortic dilation may be loudest at the second right intercostal space, whereas valvular aortic regurgitation is heard best at the second left intercostal space. Because of the large stroke volume, a systolic ejection murmur may be heard in the aortic area, even if aortic stenosis is not present. In chronic aortic regurgitation, a low-pitched diastolic rumble (Austin-Flint murmur) may be heard at the apex because of flow across the mitral valve, which closes early (29, 30).

Diagnosis

In aortic insufficiency, electrocardiographic findings include left ventricular hypertrophy. Chest radiograph and echocardiography reveal left ventricular and aortic dilation. Other echocardiographic findings include diastolic fluttering of the anterior mitral valve leaflet, caused by the regurgitant aortic jet striking the open mitral valve during diastole. Doppler velocities give a semiquantitative estimate of the severity of aortic regurgitation. Acute aortic regurgitation may show mitral valve preclosure. During cardiac catheterization, the amount of reflux of contrast into the left ventricle is quantitated after injection into the aortic root. Aortic root size, coronary anatomy, left ventricular ejection fraction, and the presence of mitral regurgitation are evaluated also. Left ventricular and aortic systolic pressures are often elevated, and aortic diastolic pressure is low. Left ventricular end-diastolic pressure is normal, unless severe aortic insufficiency or decompensated left ventricular failure is present.

Treatment

Endocarditis prophylaxis is necessary. Salt restriction, diuretics, digitalis, and afterload re-

duction are helpful with mild congestive symptoms. The timing of aortic valve replacement is controversial because there is a prolonged asymptomatic window. In asymptomatic women, evidence of progressive left ventricular systolic dysfunction may suggest the need for surgery. If valve repair or replacement is unduly delayed, irreversible left ventricular dysfunction may result. In women with aortic root disease, the ascending aorta may need to be repaired or replaced also. With acute aortic insufficiency, urgent valve repair or replacement is required. Use of vasodilators, such as nitroprusside, is recommended before surgery.

Right-Sided Valvular Disease

Rheumatic fever is the usual etiology for tricuspid valvular disease. As with mitral stenosis, tricuspid stenosis is seen more often in women than in men. Pulmonic valve disease usually results from congenital heart disease. All these right-sided valvular lesions are accurately diagnosed with echocardiography. The medical treatment includes endocarditis prophylaxis and depends on the presence of any associated valvular lesions. Indications for surgery are severe tricuspid stenosis or severe tricuspid regurgitation.

Pregnancy and Valvular Heart Disease

Although uncommon, heart disease is an important cause of maternal death during pregnancy, labor, or delivery. Optimal management of valvular disease requires correlation of the hemodynamic consequences of the valvular lesions to the normal cardiovascular adaptations of pregnancy. The expected rise in cardiac output in pregnancy is caused predominantly by an increase in stroke volume with less of an increase in heart rate. With conditions of slow left ventricular filling such as mitral stenosis, there is difficulty in tolerating an increased heart rate, and these women may develop pulmonary edema. On the other hand, women with aortic or mitral regurgitation should have no difficulty with an increment in heart rate and often have no cardiac symptoms during pregnancy.

In women with aortic stenosis, the vasodilation of pregnancy may lead to syncope. Additionally, an increase in stroke volume in pregnancy will cause an increase in left ventricular work. This may not be matched by an increase in blood flow, resulting in angina.

In conditions with right ventricular outflow tract obstruction or pulmonary hypertension in association with an intracardiac shunt, the fall in systemic vascular resistance associated with pregnancy will cause an inevitable increase in right-to-left shunting. This will decrease maternal oxygen tension and jeopardizes fetal growth. In addition, maternal and fetal mortality is increased.

Anticoagulation during Pregnancy and Postpartum

Indications for anticoagulation during pregnancy include rheumatic mitral valve disease with paroxysmal or chronic atrial arrhythmias, and mechanical valve prostheses. Warfarin crosses the placenta and is teratogenic; first trimester use of warfarin carries a 5 to 15% risk of fetal abnormalities. Second and third trimester administration of warfarin may result in maternal hemorrhage and fetal death. Postpartum hemorrhage is more likely in women taking warfarin in the first 2 weeks following delivery. For the newborn, the concentration of warfarin in breast milk is low, and breastfeeding should not affect the clotting mechanisms of the infant (31, 32).

The anticoagulant of choice during pregnancy is heparin, which does not cross the placental barrier and is not teratogenic. The risk of fetal hemorrhage and premature labor is small. Maternal complic ations include heparin-induced thrombocytopenia, bony demineralization, and bleeding. Similar to warfarin, the concentration of heparin in breast milk is quite low (30). Intermittent subcutaneous

heparin or continuous intravenous heparin has been used with the partial thromboplastin time, maintained at 1.5 to 2.0 times control (8). Occasionally heparin is given in the first trimester and warfarin is given in the middle trimester. The prothrombin time is maintained at 1.5 times control during warfarin administration. During the last 2 weeks of pregnancy, heparin therapy is substituted to decrease the risk of fetal hemorrhage postpartum. Full anticoagulation with warfarin may be resumed 1 day after delivery.

Special Considerations in the Elderly

The incidence of CHF increases sharply with advancing age and thus is encountered most commonly in the elderly. The major clinical manifestations of heart failure, dyspnea, and fatigue are nonspecific, and their presence in the elderly may not always signal true myocardial dysfunction. Elderly women with symptoms or signs suggesting heart failure should have an objective measurement of myocardial function with echocardiography or radionucleotide ventriculography. All therapeutic options for treatment of heart failure are applicable as well to the elderly.

Although many forms of valvular heart disease such as mitral stenosis or mitral valve prolapse more commonly present in relatively young women, aortic stenosis is frequently a disease of the elderly. Advanced age is not a contraindication to valve replacement surgery, although the operative risk is increased in the presence of concomitant artery disease.

Conclusion

Congestive heart failure and valvular heart disease affect women of all ages and should be rigorously investigated and treated.

Special Considerations for Nurse Practitioners and Physician Assistants

Symptoms of heart failure often develop slowly because compensatory mechanisms occur, making it imperative that the provider pay close attention to this possibility in the woman at risk. The most common symptom is shortness of breath, which may be noticed first by the woman with exertion, and then progressing to orthopnea, PND, and rest dyspnea. More subtle, and thus overlooked, symptoms include chronic cough, anorexia, insomnia, fatigue, and confusion (33).

Goals of management include recognizing correctable causes of CHF, protecting myocardial function, and relieving symptoms, thus maintaining optimal quality of life (33). Patient education is critical, because it is the woman (and caregiver) who need to be aware of subtle changes in physical and mental status that indicate worsening of her condition. In addition, the woman should note how she responds to changes in diet, activity, stress level, and medications. Providers can work with the woman to identify a regular home exercise/activity regimen that meets her need for rest and activity, perhaps through referral to a cardiac rehabilitation program (34).

Sexual difficulties are common because of reduced physical capacity and fears. Providers may have to initiate discussion about modification of sexual practices to accommodate limited activity tolerance. Planning sexual activity at times when she is more rested, using alternate positions for intercourse, and communicating affection in other ways can be suggested (34).

Specific help may be needed to comply with sodium restriction, including instructions about food labeling and hidden sources of sodium in over-the-counter medications. Referral to a dietician for counseling specific to the woman's medical needs and dietary customs is indicated. If anorexia is a concern, eating six small meals a day and vitamin or liquid dietary supplements may help. Women should monitor their weight daily at the same time and on the same scale, reporting gains greater than 3 lbs since the last clinical evaluation (34). Weight is also measured at each clinical visit.

Avoidance of infections, which may precipitate failure, is important, as women with CHF are more susceptible to infections. In addition to receiving flu vaccines, the woman should avoid people with infections and report fevers or other signs of infections early (33).

Information about medications is presented orally and in writing with encouragement of the woman (and caregivers) to understand the rationale for use. Problems with compliance can occur when the woman perceives that there is no improvement with the medication or adverse reactions occur. Other obstacles to compliance include lack of finances, family or social support, or transportation. Multiple providers may be prescribing medications, making collaboration essential (35).

The majority of deaths resulting from heart failure occur in the home. Women should discuss advance directives with their family and primary provider. If resuscitation is desired, family members need to learn CPR, but also need to discuss possible feelings of guilt or grief if resuscitation attempts are unsuccessful (34).

Women with CHF are seen every 1 to 2 weeks until symptom-free and dry weight is maintained. Visits every 3 to 6 months are then scheduled. Consultation with a physician is needed for emergency situations and for clients with newly diagnosed CHF, renal disease, liver failure, or newly diagnosed arrhythmias (36).

References

1. McKee PA, Castelli WP, McNamara PM, Kannel WB. The natural history of CHF: the Framingham study. N Engl J Med 1971;283:1441–1446.
2. Kannel WB. Epidemiological aspects of heart failure. Cardiol Clin 1989;7:1–9.
3. Ho KKL, Anderson KM, Kannel WB, Grossman W, Levy D. Survival after the onset of CHF in Framingham Heart study women. Circulation 1993;88:107–115.
4. Demakis JG, Rahimtoola SH, Sutton GC, et al. Natural course of peripartum cardiomyopathy. Circulation 1971;44:1053.
5. O'Connell JB, Costanzo-Nordin MR, Subramanian R, et al. Peripartum cardiomyopathy: clinical hemodynamic, histologic and prognostic characteristics. J Am Coll Cardiol 1986;8:52–56.
6. Pfeffer MA, Pfeffer JM, Lamas GA. Development and prevention of CHF following myocardial infarction. Circulation 1993;87 (suppl IV):120–125.
7. U.S. Department of Health and Human Services, Public Health Service, Agency for Health Care Policy and Research. Heart failure: evaluation and care of women with left-ventricular systolic dysfunction. Rockville: AHCPR Publications, 1994.
8. Captopril-Digoxin Multicenter Research Group. Comparative effects of therapy with captopril and digoxin in women with mild to moderate heart failure. JAMA 1988;259:539–544.
9. Packer M, Gheorghiade M, Young JB, Costantini PJ, Adams KF, Cody RJ, et al. for the RADIANCE Study Group. Withdrawal of digoxin from patients with chronic heart failure treated with angiotensin-converting-enzyme inhibitors. N Engl J Med 1993;329:1–7.
10. Uretsky BF, Young JB, Shahidi E, Yellen LG, Harrison MC, Jolly MK, on behalf of the PROVED Investigative Group. Randomized study assessing the effect of digoxin withdrawal in patients with mild to moderate chronic CHF: results of the PROVED trial. J Am Coll Cardiol 1993;22:955–962.
11. Yusuf S, Garg R, Held P, Gorlin R. Need for a large randomized trial to evaluate the effects of digitalis on morbidity and mortality in CHF. Am J Cardiol 1992;69: 64G–70G.
12. Cohn JN, Archibald DG, Ziesche S, et al. Effect of vasodilator therapy on mortality in chronic CHF: results of a Veterans Administration cooperative study. N Engl J Med 1986;314:1547–1552.
13. The CONSENSUS Trial Study Group. Effects of enalapril on mortality in severe CHF: results of the Cooperative North Scandinavian Enalapril Survival Study (CONSENSUS). N Engl J Med 1987;316: 1429–1435.
14. The SOLVD Investigators. Effect of enalapril on survival in patients with reduced left ventricular ejection fractions and CHF. N Engl J Med 1991;325: 293–302.
15. Cohn JN, Johnson DG, Ziesche S, et al. A comparison of enalapril with hydralazine-isosorbide dinitrate in the treatment of chronic CHF. N Engl J Med 1991;325:303–310.
16. Pfeffer MA, Braunwald E, Moye LA, et al. Effects of captopril on mortality and morbidity in patients with left ventricular dysfunction after myocardial infarction: results of the survival and ventricular enlargement trial. N Engl J Med 1992;327:669–677.
17. The SOLVD Investigators. Effect of enalapril on mortality and the development of heart failure in asymptomatic patients with reduced left ventricular ejection fractions. N Engl J Med 1992;327:685–691.
18. Packer M, Carver JR, Rodeheffer RJ, et al. for the PROMISE Study Research Group. Effect of oral milrinone on mortality in severe chronic heart failure. N Engl J Med 1991;325:1468–1475.
19. Feldman AM, Bristow MR, Parmley WW, et al. for the Vesnarinone Study Group. Effects of vesnarinone on morbidity and mortality in patients with heart failure. Vesnarinone Study Group. N Engl J Med 1993;329:149–155.
20. Waagstein F, Bristow MR, Swedberg K, et al. for the Metoprolol in Dilated Cardiomyopathy (MDC) Trial Study Group. Beneficial effects of metoprolol in idiopathic dilated cardiomyopathy. Lancet 1993;342: 1441–1446.
21. CIBIS Investigators and Committees. A randomized trial of β-blockade in heart failure: the Cardiac Insufficiency Bisoprolol Study (CIBIS). Circulation 1994;90:1765–1773.
22. Wechsler ME, Giardina EV, Sciacca RR, Rose EA, Burr ML. Increased mortality in patients undergoing cardiac transplantation. Circulation 1995;91:1029–1035.
23. Rackley CE, Wallace RB, Edwards JE, Katz NM. Valvular heart disease. In: Hurst JW, Schlant RC, eds. The Heart, Arteries, and Veins. 7th ed. New York: McGraw Hill, 1990:795–876.
24. Chiang CW, Kuo CT, Chen WJ, Lee CB, Hsu TS. Comparisons between female and male patients with mitral stenosis. Br Heart J 1994;72:567–570.
25. Durack DT. Prevention of infective endocarditis. N Engl J Med 1995;332:38–44.
26. Breall JA, Gersh BJ. Common manifestations of valvular heart disease in the elderly. Cardiol Rev 1995;150–158.
27. Kloner RA, Mamby SA. Valvular heart disease. In: Kloner RA, ed. Guide to Cardiology. 2nd ed. New York: Le Jacq Communications, 1990:261–280.
28. Cowley AW, Dzan V. Working group on noncoronary cardiovascular disease and exercise in patients. Med Sci Sports Exercise 1992;24(suppl):277–286.
29. Miles WM, Zipes DP. Acquired valvular heart disease. In: Andreoli TE, Carpenter CJ, Plum F, Smith LH, eds. Cecil Essentials of Medicine. Philadelphia: WB Saunders, 1986;47:51–61.
30. Braunwald E. Valvular heart disease. In: Braunwald E, ed. Heart Disease: A Textbook of Cardiovascular

Medicine. Philadelphia: WB Saunders, 1992:1007–1077.

31. Oakley CM. Pregnancy in heart disease: pre-existing heart disease. In: Douglas PS, ed. Heart Disease in Patients. Philadelphia: FA Davis, 1989:57–63.

32. Wenger NK, Speroff L, Packard B, eds. Cardiovascular health and disease in women: cardiovascular disease and pregnancy. Cardiovasc Rev Rep 1995;40–46.

33. Miller MM. Current trends in the primary care management of chronic congestive heart failure. Nurse Pract 1994;19:64–70.

34. Dracup K, Dunbar SB, Baker DW. Rethinking heart failure. Am J Nurs 1995;95:22–27.

35. Kegel LM. Advanced practice nurses can refine the management of heart failure. Clin Nurse Specialist 1995;9:76–81.

36. Uphold CR, Graham MV. Clinical guidelines in family practice. Gainesville, FL: Barmarrae, 1993:439–448.

14

Respiratory Disease

Mary E. Verdon

Introduction

Respiratory problems are common for both women and men. With cigarette abuse and occupational illness as common causes of respiratory disease, men's respiratory problems have dominated providers' attention. Unfortunately, with increasing incidence of smoking and occupational exposures, women are also developing those chronic respiratory conditions and cancer in increasing frequency. Lung cancer, with its poor cure rate, is the third most frequent cancer and the leading cause of cancer mortality in women. However, many respiratory diseases like asthma are more common in women, and some attack women and men equally. Providers of care to women must consider respiratory disorders frequently and in detail.

Common Problems

Cough

Cough is one of the more common reasons people seek medical treatment. In adults, it is the fifth most frequent symptom of patients seen by outpatient physicians and accounts for 30 million office visits annually. It is normal to cough once or twice an hour to maintain airway hygiene; coughing more often than this is abnormal. The leading cause of acute cough, in both smokers and nonsmokers, is infection with either the common cold or tracheobronchitis. Although these conditions are usually short-lived, cough may linger for 1 to 3 weeks because of simple epithelial damage or overt bronchial hyperactivity (1).

Evaluation of Chronic Cough

Chronic cough is a cough persisting over 3 weeks (Table 14.1). The most common cause of chronic cough is the postnasal drip syndrome (PDS); this can produce a cough even in the absence of the typical symptoms of throat clearing or sensation of postnasal drip. PDS accounted for 87% of patients in one study of chronic cough in selected nonsmokers (2). The causes of PDS include allergic and vasomotor rhinitis, acute nasopharyngitis, and sinusitis. The next most common causes of chronic cough are asthma and gastroesophageal reflux disease (GERD). Asthma can present with cough as the only symptom, but usually a careful history will reveal other symptoms of hyperreactive airways. Cough can be the only manifestation of GERD dis-

Table 14.1. Some Causes of Chronic Cough

Postnasal drip (allergic rhinitis and sinusitis)
Cough-variant asthma
Gastroesophageal reflux
Chronic bronchitis or COPD
Angiotensin-converting enzyme inhibitor
Restrictive lung disease
Postviral bronchial hyperresponsiveness
Psychogenic (rare, diagnosis of exclusion)
Pulmonary tumors
Tobacco smoke

ease. Prolonged esophageal pH monitoring may be required to make the diagnosis of GERD, especially in cases when barium swallow is normal (3). Chronic bronchitis frequently causes chronic cough in smokers and responds to smoking cessation. In one longitudinal study, chronic cough was reduced by 50% in ex-smokers compared with subjects who continued to smoke (4). With more women smoking and smoking longer, this is becoming a greater problem in women (see Chapter 9.2).

The cough of ACE inhibitors can develop in up to 15% of people on these medications. The cough has variable onset, occurring from 3 to 4 weeks to 1 year from the initiation of the drug. It may be worse at night and in the supine position, mimicking GERD. The cough from ACE inhibitors is more common in women and nonsmokers. Switching among the various inhibitors does not affect the cough, but reducing the dose of the drug may decrease the frequency. If necessary, the cure for the cough of ACE inhibitors is stopping the medication (5). Lung cancer can also present as a chronic cough, although this is rare in nonsmokers. Usually the cough will be associated with weight loss or hemoptysis, and patients will have a history of smoking or exposure to asbestos (6).

Treatment

The treatment of chronic cough depends on the suspected diagnosis. One approach to treatment is a series of easily initiated steps (Fig. 14.1). The first step is to start an antihistamine-decongestant for possible postnasal drip syndrome. Patients who do not respond to this in 1 week are evaluated for asthma with pulmonary function tests (PFTs) and, if necessary, bronchoprovocation challenge tests. Alternately, a therapeutic trial of a bronchodilator inhaler (Alupent, Ventolin, or Proventil) at bedtime can be tried.

If asthma is not the cause, sinus and chest

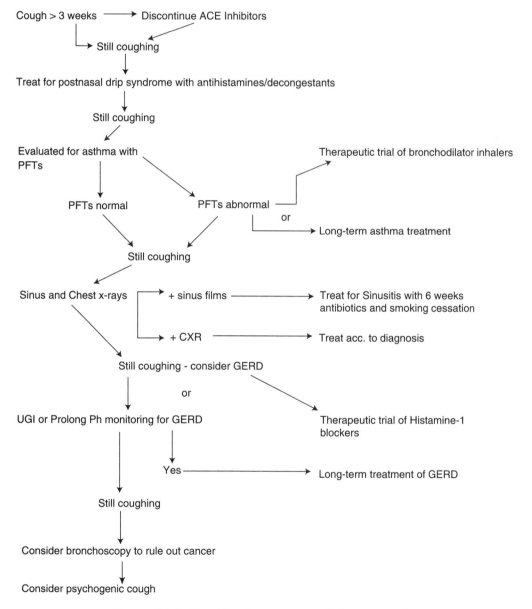

Figure 14.1. Algorithm for treatment of chronic cough.

radiographs can be done. If these are normal and the patient continues to cough, an upper GI or prolonged esophageal pH monitoring can be done to diagnose GERD, or a therapeutic trial of an antihistamine-1 blocker can be tried. If GERD is discovered, it should be treated with histamine-1 blockers, lifestyle changes, and other medications (Chapter 20). If a diagnosis of gastroesophageal reflux is excluded, then bronchoscopy can be considered. If bronchoscopy is normal, then uncommon conditions such as psychogenic cough are explored. Once a diagnosis is made, specific therapy is successful in most patients with cough (2).

Although nonspecific antitussive therapy accounts for millions of dollars in pharmaceutical sales in the United States, studies considering its efficacy have shown conflicting results (Table 14.2). Nonspecific antitussives are considered clinically useful only if they have been shown to significantly decrease cough frequency or intensity (or both) by objective measures in randomized, double-blind, placebo-controlled studies. Antitussive therapy includes demulcents, local anesthetics, narcotics, and centrally acting agents. A demulcent is a slippery, mucilaginous fluid that allays irritation and soothes inflammation, especially of the mucous membranes. The simplest demulcent is 1 to 2 L of water per day. Other common demulcents are hard candy, cough drops, honey, lemon, menthol, and camphor. The major ingredient in most over-the-counter cough preparations is sugar, which encourages saliva production and swallowing. The act of swallowing may interfere with the cough reflex and both the saliva and sugar act as a demulcent. The literature on the effectiveness of demulcents is contradictory (7).

Local anesthetics, like benzonatate, prevent sensory nerve traffic in both myelinated and nonmyelinated nerves, and are consistently effective antitussive agents (8).

Opiates, including codeine, are often considered the drug of choice for treating cough, although the literature regarding their efficacy is also conflicting. Dextromethorphan, a nonnarcotic diomer of the codeine analogue levorphanol, acts centrally, as do opiates, to suppress cough. A recent study showed that neither dextromethorphan nor codeine was significantly more effective than placebo (9). Although systemic morphine has proven to suppress cough in high doses, the efficacy of most opiate-containing cough mixtures probably lies in their sugar solution. For a cough

Table 14.2. Types of Antitussive Therapy

Type	Definition	Examples
Demulcent	A slippery, mucilaginous fluid that allays irritation and soothes inflammation, especially of the mucous membranes	One or 2 L of water per day, hard candy, cough drops, honey, lemon, menthol, and camphor Sugar Anything that promotes swallowing
Local anesthetics	Substances that prevent sensory nerve traffic in both myelinated and nonmyelinated nerves, and have been shown to be one of the most consistently effective antitussive agents.	Benzonatate
Opiates	Centrally-acting cough suppressant	Codeine, dextromethorpan
Expectorants	Used to enhance mucous production and clearance	Guaifenesin
Mucolytics	Used to thin sputum	Iodinated glycerol

caused by the common cold or acute bronchitis of viral etiology, the most cost-effective approach is telephone counseling to use liquids with honey or sugar.

Expectorants are used to enhance mucous production and clearance. Guaifenesin is the most commonly used expectorant, and several studies have demonstrated increased sputum volume resulting from its expectorant action at maximum doses of 2400 mg/day. Although patients reported a reduction in sputum thickness, it is ineffective in suppressing cough.

Mucolytics are used to thin sputum. With the common cold, guaifenesin is no more efficacious than placebo (10). Iodinated glycerol is a commonly used mucolytic that was recently shown to improve general condition in patients with chronic bronchitis. In a randomized, double-blind, placebo-controlled design, it increased the ease of bringing up sputum and decreased cough frequency, severity and chest discomfort (11).

Hemoptysis

Hemoptysis, or coughing-up blood, is a common complaint in primary care. Major hemoptysis (> 600 mL over 24 to 48 hours) is a life-threatening emergency that requires hospitalization. Less than 200 mL of hemoptysis over 24 hours, or minor hemoptysis, can be evaluated as an outpatient. First, it is necessary to confirm that the problem is true hemoptysis and is not caused by nosebleeds, oral pathology, or hematemesis. The possible causes of hemoptysis include a wide range of diagnoses (Table 14.3).

The main concern in evaluating hemoptysis is to rule out bronchogenic cancer. The initial evaluation, after a history and physical exam have excluded benign causes, usually includes a chest radiograph. Further work-up of women patients, including referral for bronchoscopy, is based on risk factors for lung cancer. Many investigators recommend limiting bronchoscopy to those with two or more of the following risk factors: male sex, age over 40 years, relevant chest radiographic abnormality, and greater than 40 packs per year of smok-

Table 14.3. Causes of Hemoptysis

Inflammatory
  Bronchitis
  Bronchiectasis
  Lung abscess
  Pneumonia
  Tuberculosis
Parasitic
  Amebiasis
  Ascariasis
  Paragonimiasis
Fungal
  Aspergilloma
  Actinomycosis
  Histoplasmosis
  Coccidioidomycosis
  Cryptococcosis
Neoplastic
  Bronchogenic carcinoma
  Bronchial adenoma
  Metastatic cancer
Vascular
  Left ventricular failure (CHF)
  Mitral stenosis
  Aneurysm
  Pulmonary embolism
  Primary pulmonary hypertension
  Arteriovenous malformations
  Eisenmenger's syndrome
  Pulmonary vasculitis: Wegener's granulomatosis, Goodpasture's syndrome
  Collagen vascular: SLE, Scleroderma
Traumatic and hemorrhagic
  Foreign body aspiration
  Lung contusion
  Hemorrhagic diathesis; anticoagulant therapy
  Bronchoscopy
Miscellaneous
  Cystic fibrosis
  Endometriosis
  Amyloid

ing history. Additional risk factors can include more than 30 mL blood expectorated daily and recurrent or persistent hemoptysis (lasting longer than a week). For women not meeting this criteria, the most reasonable initial approach is observation, moving to bronchoscopy only if hemoptysis persists.

The most common finding on bronchoscopy in unselected patients presenting with hemoptysis is normal or no abnormality (57%) and bronchitis (33%). In retrospective studies of bronchoscopies performed for hemoptysis, in patients with normal chest radiograph, only approximately 5% of the subjects, who were predominately men, had bronchogenic carcinoma (13). In patients with focally abnormal chest radiograph, there is a much higher yield from bronchoscopy (14).

Pulmonologists who see a different, nongeneral population have different indications for and results from bronchoscopy. In a recent study of pulmonologists, the majority said that they performed bronchoscopy, when consulted, on all patients with hemoptysis. Major reasons cited include fear of litigation and the belief that primary care providers expect bronchoscopy as part of the routine work-up for hemoptysis (15).

Dyspnea

Dyspnea, or shortness of breath, is a complex symptom that develops with information from the respiratory center to the brain. As with pain, the psychologic and intellectual characteristics of the individual influence this symptom. Dyspnea can be the result of malfunction in any organ system that causes interference with breathing, increased demand for breathing, or effective weakening of the respiratory pump. In most diseases with this symptom, dyspnea is caused by an imbalance between ventilatory demand and ventilatory capacity, and involves disruption of either oxygen delivery, carbon dioxide elimination, or both. A careful history can categorize dyspnea as acute, subacute, or chronic.

The differential diagnosis for acute dyspnea includes pneumonia, pulmonary embolism, congestive heart failure, myocardial infarction, shock, and acute lupus erythematosus (Table 14.4). The acute onset of dyspnea at rest is the dominant feature of pulmonary embolism; it is one pulmonary disease that can present abruptly. Intermittent dyspnea is likely caused by treatable diseases such as asthma, congestive heart failure (CHF), pleural effusion, or pulmonary emboli. Dyspnea is the most frequently reported symptom in patients with CHF.

Chronic shortness of breath, described as persistent or progressive in nature, is characteristic of chronic obstructive lung disease, interstitial lung disease, and dysfunction of the diaphragm or chest wall. Nocturnal dyspnea may be brought on by asthma, CHF, gastroesophageal reflux, or nasal obstruction. Exercise-induced asthma can present as dyspnea occurring after activity. Shortness of breath presenting without any clear relationship to

Table 14.4. Some Causes of Dyspnea

Cardiac:	acute pulmonary edema, arrhythmias, CHF, myocardial infarction, pericarditis, valvular heart disease
Pulmonary:	acute bronchitis, asthma, bronchiectasis, chronic bronchitis, emphysema, interstitial lung disease, lung cancer, pleural effusion, pneumonia, pneumothorax, pulmonary embolism, pulmonary hypertension, tracheal or laryngeal stenosis, pleural disease (e.g., effusion, thickening)
Other:	anemia (Hgb < 7), cerebral vascular accident, chest wall/neuromuscular disease (e.g., prior polio, Guillain-Barre syndrome, muscular dystrophy, systemic lupus erythematosus, hyperthyroidism) cirrhosis, metabolic acidosis, obesity, kyphoscoliosis, pregnancy or other abdominal mass, and psychogenic disorder (e.g., panic disorder, anxiety, depression)

physical activity suggests a mechanical or psychologic problem (16).

In one study, a relationship was shown between the patients' description of dyspnea and its underlying cause. "Shallow" breathing was associated with neuromuscular disorders, "tight" breathing with asthma, and the sensation of "suffocating" with CHF (17). The differential diagnosis of dyspnea can be difficult, especially differentiating heart failure from exacerbations of existing lung disease, asthma, or pulmonary embolism. One study of hospitalized patients found that history alone determined the correct diagnosis in 74% of cases (18). Another study demonstrated that lung disease can be differentiated from heart failure using a patient's systolic blood pressure response to a bedside Valsalva maneuver (19). In individuals without congestive heart failure, the systolic blood pressure rises with straining, falls below baseline as positive intrathoracic pressure is maintained, and rises above baseline (overshoots) with release of strain. Absence of the overshoot and, occasionally, almost flat or square wave pressure response to Valsalva is evidence of left ventricular dysfunction.

The initial work-up of dyspnea can include a chest radiograph, spirometry, and an electrocardiogram. The degree of abnormality in PFTs correlates only moderately with the severity of dyspnea. Treatment of dyspnea is directed at improvement of the underlying condition.

Chest Pain

Chest pain is commonly encountered by providers caring for women. Diagnosis requires a careful history that considers age, cardiac risk factors, past medical history, and characteristics of the pain. Time of onset, quality of the pain and any associated symptoms all help differentiate between causative disorders. When pain is aggravated by taking a deep breath, coughing, sneezing, or movements of the trunk, it is considered "pleuritic pain" and pleuropulmonary disorders are the major differential.

Musculoskeletal disorders often have dull, gnawing or aching pains, and there will be chest wall tenderness. Cardiovascular and gastrointestinal pain is often accompanied by historical risk factors or associated symptoms (20). For a more thorough discussion of these areas, see Chapter 16.

Infections

Upper Respiratory Infections

Common Cold
The common cold is an acute self-limited upper respiratory infection characterized by sore throat, nasal congestion, and rhinitis. Characteristically there is no temperature elevation and cough is not a prominent feature. The known etiologies of the common cold include over 100 types of viruses in six different families. The major types include rhinovirus, respiratory syncytial virus, parainfluenza and influenza virus, and adenovirus. In approximately 35% of cases, the cause is unknown. The average adult suffers from a cold 2 to 4 times yearly; children have 6 to 10 colds a year.

Common colds are not caused by exposure to damp, cold weather, but rather from exposure to infected individuals. In a recent study, psychological stress was associated with an increased risk of developing a cold (21). Persistent cold symptoms of longer than 10 days and a change in nasal discharge from clear to purulent suggest possible bacterial sinusitis. Sinusitis is also associated with headaches, constitutional symptoms, and risk factors such as a history of allergic rhinitis. Currently, treatment of the common cold is only palliative. There is no evidence that any of the common over-the-counter preparations shorten the duration of acute viral upper respiratory infections (22).

Bronchitis
Bronchitis accounts for approximately 12 million physician visits yearly and is one of the top 10 most commonly diagnosed illnesses in offices of general and family physicians (23). Acute

bronchitis is characterized by cough and sputum production with upper respiratory tract symptoms in the absence of fever. Acute bronchitis typically lasts 7 to 11 days, although one third of patients cough for more than 1 month. It is viral in etiology in 80% of cases, with *Mycoplasma pneumonia* and *Chlamydia pneumoniae* making up most of the nonviral causes (24). Bronchitis is caused by many of the same viruses as the common cold and probably represents a more severe host response to the same agent.

The physical exam in bronchitis may reveal rhonchi or wheezes but no evidence of pulmonary consolidation. Pneumonia can usually be excluded by the absence of abnormal auscultatory findings on lung examination. Fever is uncommon unless influenza virus is the causal agent. Antibiotic treatment of acute bronchitis is not recommended in healthy women who have no significant systemic symptoms. Bacteria like *Haemophilus influenzae, Streptococcus pneumoniae, Moraxella catarrhalis*, and *Bordetella pertussis* cause less than 10% of cases of acute bronchitis.

In patients with underlying chronic obstructive pulmonary disease (COPD), it is common practice to treat bronchitis with antibiotics. In these cases, trimethoprim-sulfisoxazole is the drug of choice. Non-smokers with persistent cough should be evaluated in the same way as patients with chronic cough. Atypical pneumonia can also present as "bronchitis."

Pneumonia

Pneumonia is a common problem; there are approximately 4 million cases each year in the United States, with approximately one in five of these requiring hospitalization. Yet, pneumonia accounts for less than 10% of acute respiratory tract illnesses (25). In a recent study, predictors of pneumonia included the following: (1) temperature over 37.8°, (2) pulse greater than 100 beats/minute, (3) rales, (4) decreased breath sounds, and (5) absence of asthma (26).

Historically, pneumonia has been classified into two clinical syndromes, "typical" or "atypical." "Typical" or classic pneumonia is the result of bacterial pathogens such as *S. pneumoniae, H. influenzae,* and *S. aureus,* and sometimes gram-negative enteric bacteria. It presents with rapid or sudden onset of fever and shaking chills, productive purulent cough, and pleuritic chest pain. There is evidence of rales and lung consolidation on chest examination, including dullness to percussion, increased fremitus, and egophony. Laboratory testing reveals leukocytosis, sputum gram stain can provide clues to the etiologic agent and sputum culture can be positive for one of the above agents. In typical or classic pneumonia, evidence of lobar consolidation on a chest radiogram is expected (27).

The "atypical" pneumonia syndrome has been associated with M. *pneumoniae,* influenzae viruses, C. *pneumoniae* and *Legionella* species. The clinical presentation has an insidious onset, and includes low-grade or no fever, a nonproductive cough, headache, sore throat, myalgia, and fatigue. Extrapulmonary symptoms of "atypical" pneumonia can also include diarrhea, abdominal pain, earache, or arthralgias (28). On physical exam, instead of pulmonary consolidation, scattered wheezing, rhonchi, or rales will be noted. Blood cultures are negative, and white cell counts are usually less than 10,000/mm³. Less common agents of this syndrome include Q fever and *Chlamydia psittaci.* The chest radiograph of atypical pneumonia can include subsegmental infiltrates in the lower lobes, diffuse patchy infiltrates, and diffuse interstitial changes (29).

Making the diagnosis by clinical presentation is unreliable because of the great degree of overlap among the symptoms of various etiologic pathogens in pneumonia (30). If pneumonia is suspected, a chest radiograph usually confirms the diagnosis. Radiographs also help to determine severity by identifying women with multilobar involvement. Certain features on chest radiographs may suggest a specific etiology. However, radiographic features are too inaccu-

rate to reliably provide a specific causative diagnosis (31). Many clinicians empirically treat low-risk women, reserving a chest radiograph for those who do not respond to treatment.

It is commonly recommended to obtain sputum gram stains and/or sputum cultures on all patients suspected of having pneumonia prior to initiating treatment (32). However, sensitivity and specificity for these tests vary widely. Both sputum gram stains and cultures are limited by factors such as inadequate specimen collection, contaminating microflora, or the absence of sputum production. In many studies, including a recent large review of community-acquired pneumonia, sputum cultures helped make an accurate microbiologic diagnosis in less than 50% of patients (33). Other than chest radiograph, no routine test is advocated prior to treating a woman for pneumonia as an outpatient. In women who are hospitalized, or are being considered for hospitalization, there may be a benefit from obtaining blood cultures, complete blood counts (CBC), electrolytes, and evaluation of blood oxygen levels.

Because of the limitations of diagnostic testing, treatment of pneumonia is often empiric. One recommended treatment approach includes risk stratification based on age, comorbidity, and severity of illness (Table 14.5). Comorbidity is coexisting illness with chronic obstructive lung disease, diabetes mellitus, renal insufficiency, congestive heart failure, chronic liver disease, and other similar medical conditions (34).

Hospitalization is indicated for patients with community-acquired pneumonia who are at risk of dying or having a complicated course (Table 14.6). All patients with any of the following should be hospitalized: (1) severe vital sign abnormality defined as pulse more than 140/minute, a systolic blood pressure less than 90 mm Hg, or a respiratory rate more than 30/minute, (2) altered mental status, (3) hypoxemia defined as PaO_2 less than 60 mm Hg on room air, (4) a suppurative pneumonia related infection, (5) an acute coexistent medical problem, or (6) a new severe laboratory abnormality such as WBC $< 4 \times 10^9/L$ or $>30 \times 10^9/L$, or absolute neutrophil count below $1 \times 10^9/L$, serum creatinine of >1.2 mg/dL, or BUN >20 mg/dL. Besides these indications for hospitalization, other factors have been identified that predict a complicated course in pneumonia. If two or more of these factors are present, hospitalization is advised. These factors include age over 65 years, presence of coexisting illnesses (e.g., diabetes mellitus, renal insufficiency, CHF), previous hospitalization within 1 year, fever of 38.3°C, hematocrit less than 30%, BUN over 15 mg/dL, and suspected high-risk etiology (e.g., suspicion of aspiration, staphylococcal, gram-negative rod) (35).

Tuberculosis

Epidemiology

Until the introduction of effective chemotherapy, tuberculosis was an important cause of disease and death, accounting for up to one out of every seven deaths in Europe in the 1800s. Anyone malnourished or sick for another reason, especially for example a postpartum or pregnant woman, was likely to acquire it. After effective therapy was introduced in the 1950s and 1960s, rates of new cases of tuberculosis decreased an average of 5% a year until 1984, when they hit a plateau. Between 1985 and 1990 the number of new cases of tuberculosis reported to the Centers for Disease Control rose for the first time.

Reasons cited for this increase include infection with the HIV, outbreaks among the homeless, and the continued influx of infected foreign-born persons. Tuberculosis incidence is highest and rising among certain risk groups including African-Americans, Latinos, Asian/ Pacific Islanders, and foreign-born women from countries with a high prevalence of the infection (36). Other high prevalence groups include medically underserved, low income or homeless women, Native Americans, migrant farm workers, AIDs patients, alcoholics, intra-

Table 14.5. Empiric Treatment of Pneumonia

Type Patient	Organisms	Antibiotics
Outpatient pneumonia without comorbidity and age <60 *	S. pneumoniae M. pneumoniae Respiratory viruses C. pneumoniae H. influenzae Miscellaneous: Legionella species S. aureus, M. tuberculosis, endemic fungi, aerobic gram-negative bacilli	Macrolide** or Tetracycline
Outpatient pneumonia with comorbidity and/ or > age 60	S. pneumoniae Respiratory viruses H. influenzae, S. aureus Aerobic gram-negative bacilli Miscellaneous: M. catarrhalis, Legionella species, M. tuberculosis, endemic fungi	2nd-generation cephalosporin or TMX/Sulfa or beta-lactamase inhibitor +/- a macrolide#
Hospitalized patients with community H.- acquired pneumonia	S. pneumoniae Influenzae Polymicrobial (including anaerobic bacteria) or beta-lactamase Aerobic gram-negative bacilli inhibitor Legionella sp.; S. aureus C. pneumoniae; Respiratory viruses Miscellaneous: M. pneumoniae,	2nd or 3rd-generation cephalosporin +/− macrolide#
Severe hospitalized community-acquired pneumonia*	S. pneumoniae Legionella species### Aerobic gram-negatives M. pneumoniae; Miscellaneous: H. influenzae, M. tuberculosis, endemic fungi Respiratory viruses	Macrolide** PLUS 3rd-generation cephalosporin with antipseudo-monas activity or other anti-pseudomonal agents such as imipenem/cilastatin, ciprofloxacin

* Excludes patients at risk for HIV

**Erythromycin. The newer macrolides, clarithromycin or azithromycin, should be considered in those intolerant of erythromycin, and in smokers (to treat H. influenzae.)

***Many isolates of S. pneumoniae are resistant to tetracycline, and it should be used only if the patient is allergic to or intolerant of macrolides.

#If infection with Legionella sp. is a concern.

##Rifampin may be added if Legionella sp. is documented.

###Although uncommon because of high mortality associated with P. aeruginosa pneumonia, an aminoglycoside should be added, at least for the first few days of treatment, whether one is using a third-generation cephalosporin, imipenem, or ciprofloxacin.

(Reprinted with permission from American Thoracic Society. Guidelines for the initial management of adults with community-acquired pneumonia: diagnosis, assessment of severity, and initial antimicrobial therapy. Am Rev Respir Dis 1993;148: 1418–1426.)

Table 14.6. Possible Indications for Admission to Hospital with Pneumonia

* Severe vital sign abnormality defined as pulse more than 140/minute, a systolic blood pressure less than 90 mm Hg, or a respiratory rate more than 30/minute
* Altered mental status
* Hypoxemia defined as PaO_2 less than 60 mm Hg on room air
* A suppurative pneumonia-related infection
* An acute coexistent medical problem
* A new severe laboratory abnormality such as WBC < 4×10^9/L or >30×10^9/L, or absolute neutrophil count below 1×10^9/L; serum creatinine of >1.2 mg/dL or BUN >20 mg/dL. OR, two or more of the following factors
    * presence of coexisting illnesses (e.g., diabetes mellitus, renal insufficiency, CHF)
    * previous hospitalization within 1 year
    * fever over 38.8°C
    * hematocrit less than 30%
    * BUN over 15 mg/dL, and
    * suspected high risk etiology (e.g., suspicion of aspiration, staphylococcal, gram-negative rod)

venous drug users, and residents of long-term residential facilities such as nursing homes, prisons, and psychiatric institutions (37). Asymptomatic tuberculosis infection is found in up to 50% of homeless persons, many of whom are women with children (38). There is an increased rate of tuberculosis infection in children under 5 years of age and in adults over 65 years of age. It is often the initial manifestation of HIV infection, and serologic testing for HIV infection is recommended in all patients with active tuberculosis. Multidrug-resistant tuberculosis, a relatively new development, occurs predominantly in HIV infected individuals (39).

Tuberculosis is caused by Mycobacterium tuberculosis and it is spread by airborne droplet nuclei through coughs or sneezes. It is not highly contagious; only about 30% of close contacts and 15% of other contacts of an active case contract the disease. Once the bacillus is inhaled, it reaches the alveoli and is engulfed by macrophages. Initially the tubercle bacilli multiply in the macrophages and spread via the lymphatics to the regional lymph nodes

and through the bloodstream to distant organs where they can remain quiescent but viable. Tissue damage is caused by the host's reaction to the tubercle bacillus, rather than by the organism itself.

Within 2 to 10 weeks of infection, the host develops an immune response. In approximately 90% of cases the host's immune system limits the growth of the bacilli, allows for healing of the initial lesions, and permanently prevents disease from occurring. The bacilli are dormant but viable within these individuals. In approximately 5% of cases, early progression to clinical disease occurs within a few years of exposure. Another 5% will develop active disease years or decades after initial infection. Thus, a distinction is made between infected individuals and latent tuberculosis (e.g., positive skin test, no clinical, radiologic or bacteriologic evidence of disease), and diseased individuals or active tuberculosis (confirmatory bacteriologic evidence, or both a significant skin reaction and clinical and/or radiologic evidence of current disease). Although most infected individuals are neither ill nor contagious, over 90% of cases of active tuberculosis arise from this pool, estimated to be 10 to 15 million people in the United States (40).

Medical conditions that can increase the risk of tuberculosis after infection include (a) silicosis, (b) gastrectomy, (c) jejunoileal bypass, (d) chronic renal failure, (e) weight 10% below ideal body weight, (f) diabetes mellitus, (g) prolonged use of high dose corticosteroid therapy, (h) use of other immunosuppressive therapy, (i) HIV infection, (j) leukemias, (k) lymphomas, and (l) other malignancies (41).

Clinical Presentation

Symptoms of active tuberculosis include cough, hemoptysis, weight loss, fatigue, fever, night sweats, hoarseness, or chest pain. Active tuberculosis can also be asymptomatic or extrapulmonary. Extrapulmonary tuberculosis can involve the lymphatic or hematopoietic systems or the genitourinary organs and can cause meningitis, pericarditis, osteomyelitis, and hepatobiliary disease.

Diagnosis

Tuberculins are culture extracts of M. tuberculosis containing antigens to which the infected individual has become sensitized. When injected intracutaneously, there is a delayed (cellular) hypersensitivity reaction in sensitized individuals, and induration develops 24 to 72 hours after injection. Purified protein derivative (PPD), which is standardized and without sensitizing properties, is superior to the old tuberculin that is a crude nonstandardized product containing extraneous antigens. In the Mantoux test, 0.1 mL of PPD is injected just under the skin of the volar forearm. Tests should be read between 48 and 72 hours after injection, but the induration usually persists for up to 1 week (Table 14.7). Induration is determined by palpation and inspection. Erythema is unimportant and should not be considered. Drawing a line with a ballpoint pen toward the margin of the skin test reaction and stopping when resistance is met is the best technique. Interpretation of the Mantoux skin test depends on risk factors. Many foreign-born individuals have a history of vaccination with bacille Calmette-Guerin (BCG). Because skin test reactivity from BCG usually declines within a few years, current guidelines are to ignore a history of BCG vaccination when interpreting tuberculin skin test results (42).

False-negative skin test reactions occur in the absence of intact cell-mediated immunity such as in women with concurrent infections, recent or overwhelming infection with M. tuberculosis, live virus immunization, chronic illnesses (e.g., renal failure, protein malnutrition, immunosuppressive drugs (e.g., corticosteroids), disease of the lymphoid organs (e.g., sarcoidosis, lymphoma), HIV infection, young or old age, and severe stress. In groups in which regular tuberculosis testing is done, the booster phenomenon should be considered. In some tuber-

Table 14.7. Interpretation of PPD Skin Test Results

0–4 mm	Negative
>or= 5 mm	Positive for contacts to persons with tuberculosis, suspected cases, or immunodeficient
>or= 10 mm	Positive for foreign-born persons or persons with expected high prevalence of tuberculosis infection, intravenous drug users, medically underserved, and patients with medical conditions that increase risk of tuberculosis Positive for persons who are in health care institutions, schools, or day care centers without other risk factors
>or=15 mm	Positive for all others

culin reactors, especially the elderly, there may be waning of the delayed hypersensitivity to tuberculin, resulting in a negative skin test response. Administration of the skin test itself boosts immunologic memory, so that a second tuberculin skin test up to 2 years later will be positive. This is known as the booster effect. In women being tested annually, the positive second response and negative first response will erroneously be thought to represent recent infection requiring treatment. To avoid this problem, women with initial negative tests should be retested 1 to 4 weeks later to assess the boosted response. The size of the second skin test can be used as a baseline to compare with future skin test results. Currently, regular tuberculin skin testing is indicated in populations at high risk for infection. Other candidates for regular testing include women who are in close contact with a person with infectious tuberculosis or those who work in a health care setting, school, or day care center (43).

Diagnosis of active disease is usually based on a positive TB test, suspicious chest radiograph and positive acid fast stain of sputum. Confirmatory culture and sensitivity should be obtained through first-morning sputums. New diagnostic techniques currently under study include polymerase chain reaction (PCR) (44), and immunoassay for mycobacterium tuberculosis antigens (45). DNA fingerprinting is used to delineate patterns of tuberculosis transmission (46).

Treatment

For active tuberculosis, pulmonary and extrapulmonary, the most commonly used regimen in the United States is isoniazid, rifampin, and pyrazinamide for 2 months, then isoniazid and rifampin for 4 months. This regimen appears to prevent drug resistance. Treatment of HIV-infected individuals includes a longer regimen with isoniazid and rifampin, usually 7 months. Drug susceptibility testing is recommended on all M. *tuberculosis* isolates because of increasing drug resistance in many parts of the United

States (47). Treatment can be started prior to obtaining cultures.

Treatment of latent or inactive tuberculosis (positive skin test, no evidence of active disease) is recommended for individuals who are under 35 years of age or who have converted their skin test to positive within the last two years. These individuals should take isoniazid for 6 to 12 months (48).

Pregnancy and Tuberculosis

Because pregnancy is a time when many women receive complete care, and because it is important to treat the mother before the infant is born and can be exposed, this may be an opportune time for skin testing for TB, especially if the woman has risk factors or possible exposure. The risk of untreated TB to the pregnant woman and child is much greater than the risk of problems from any of the TB drugs. If the pregnant woman has a history of PPD conversion with no or incomplete treatment, or her PPD tests positive during pregnancy, antibiotics should be started. As with other individuals under age 35 years with a PPD conversion, they should take isoniazid (INH) for at least 6 months. INH has little risk of teratogenicity (49). If the woman has clinical disease, treatment with rifampin and ethambutol can be added as indicated.

Obstructive Lung Disease

Because asthma and COPD overlap clinically and in diagnostic test results, they are often grouped together under the heading of obstructive lung disease. The clinical condition of chronic bronchitis and the pathologic entity of emphysema usually occur together and are included under the heading of COPD. It has been reported that there is a bias in diagnosing asthma in women and COPD in men (23). Differentiation between these two is usually based on risk factors, historical data, and information from PFTs.

PFTs can help diagnose a patient's disease and predict the course and prognosis of these diseases. PFTs are also used to assess the reversibility of airway obstruction and to evaluate work impairment. Basic spirometry includes forced expiratory volume in one second (FEV_1) and forced vital capacity, or the total volume that can be exhaled after a maximal inspiration (FVC). Airway obstruction is often found in patients with asthma and COPD. Reversible obstruction is considered diagnostic of asthma, yet it can also occur in COPD. The ratio of FEV_1 to FVC is used to evaluate airway obstruction. With airflow obstruction, FEV_1 is reduced, FVC is stable or increased, and a reduction of the ratio below 0.75 is seen. Pure restrictive ventilatory defects cause an equal reduction in both FEV_1 and vital capacity, and the ratio will be normal. Severe obstruction is usually present when the FEV_1 is less than 1.0 L, less than 25% predicted, or less than 25 to 40% of the FVC. Comprehensive pulmonary function testing includes measurement of lung volumes and is indicated when restrictive disease is suspected (50).

Both COPD and asthma may be treated with bronchodilators, theophylline, and steroids. Medications used in the treatment of these disorders are listed in Table 14.8.

Table 14.8. Medications Used in Treatment of Asthma and COPD[*]

Beta$_2$-Agonists
Inhaled - metered dose inhalers (MDI)

Albuterol (Proventil, Ventolin)	2 puffs q 4–6 hours
Metaproterenol (Metaprel, Alupent)	2 puffs q 4–6 hours
Bitolterol (Tornalate)	2 puffs q 4–8 hours
Terbutaline (Brethaire)	2 puffs q 4–6 hours
Pirbuteral (Maxair)	2 puffs q 4–6 hours

Cromolyn sodium
  MDI - 1 mg/puff; 2 puffs bid-qid
  Dry powder inhaler - 20 mg/capsule; 1 capsule bid-qid
  Nebulizer solution - 20 mg/2 Ml ampule; 1 ampule bid-qid
Theophylline
  Tablets, capsules: 100 mg, 200 mg, 300 mg
  Sustained-release tablets, capsules: 100 mg, 125 mg, 200 mg, 250 mg, 300 mg, 450 mg, 500 mg
Dosage to achieve serum concentration of 5–15 μg/Ml
Corticosteroids
Inhaled metered dose inhalers

Beclomethasone (Beclovent, Beconase, Vanceril)	2–4 puffs bid-qid
Triamcinolone (Azmacort)	2–4 puffs bid-qid
Flunisolide (AeroBid)	2–4 puffs bid

Oral

Tablets Prednisone	For acute exacerbations
Prednisolone	1–2 mg/kg a day for 3–5 days
Methylprednisolone	

Anticholinergic agents

Ipratropium-MDI (Atrovent)	2–4 puffs qid

[*](note - not all medications recommended for both, see text for recommendations)

Asthma

Asthma is characterized by reversible airway obstruction, inflammation, and increased responsiveness to a variety of stimuli. It is common, estimated to affect 4 to 5% of the population in the United States, and mortality has been increasing (51). Risk factors for asthma include a personal or family history of asthma, allergies, and atopy.

Presenting symptoms include any combination of cough, dyspnea, chest tightness, and wheezing. These often occur after exercise or other stimulus (e.g., respiratory infection, allergen, cold). The differential diagnosis includes lower respiratory tract infections that can cause transient airway hyperresponsiveness in otherwise healthy individuals (52), and congestive heart failure, COPD, hyperventilation syndrome, pulmonary infarction or embolism, and cystic fibrosis (53). Nocturnal symptoms are so common that some experts question the diagnosis of asthma in their absence. Wheezing has always been a classic sign establishing the diagnosis of asthma. Cough-variant asthma is described as a persistent cough without wheezing (54). Cough in the absence of wheezing, especially in older patients with bronchodilator-responsive PFTs, is often mistaken as a symptom of chronic bronchitis or congestive heart failure.

The diagnosis of asthma depends on the presence of either PFTs demonstrating reversibility of obstruction with a bronchodilator (if the FEV_1 increases by at least 15%), or hyperresponsiveness of airways on PFTs with histamine or methacholine challenge (55). When PFTs are normal, bronchoprovocation pulmonary function testing with methacholine may be required to make the diagnosis. Some investigators suggest that PFTs are not always required to diagnose asthma. Instead, the patient's history and response of symptoms to bronchodilator are used to make a diagnosis. This approach is acceptable for mild asthma that responds to once daily (or less) bronchodilator use. In moderate asthma requiring additional treatment, PFTs are indicated both to confirm the diagnosis and monitor treatment. A recent study demonstrated that experienced pulmonologists had difficulty diagnosing asthma using clinical information alone (56). The clinician should also determine the severity of asthma to tailor treatment and prevent serious sequelae. This is done initially with pulmonary function testing. Hand-held mini-peak-flow meters provide a measurement of peak expiratory flow rate (PEFR). This has been shown to closely correlate with FEV_1 and can be used to monitor the asthmatic patient's clinical condition and response to treatment (57).

Many classifications of types of asthma have been suggested (53). The provider should determine any precipitating factors that can be controlled or eliminated (58). Common allergens include ragweed, grass, pollens, animal dander, house dust, mites, and molds. Common irritants include tobacco smoke and smoke from wood burning stoves.

Occupational asthma should be suspected in any adult with new onset asthma (see Chapter 6.3). Over 200 agents in the workplace have been implicated in causing asthma. In occupational asthma, there is evidence that permanent airway hyperreactivity can be prevented if the inciting agent can be identified and the exposure stopped.

Standard therapy for asthma consists of allergen removal, inhaled steroids to reduce inflammation, and inhaled β-agonists for bronchodilatation. Treatment of asthma has changed in the 1990s. With the addition of inflammation to the definition of asthma, new guidelines for treatment emphasize the use of inhaled glucocorticoid therapy (59). Inhaled β-agonists are a good first line therapy in acute settings and may help to confirm the diagnosis. Metered dose inhalers have been demonstrated to be equal in efficacy to aerosolized treatments (60).

However, inhaled glucocorticoids are now

recommended for patients who need inhalation therapy with β-agonist more than once a day. A treatment algorithm based on peak flow measurements is listed in Figure 14.2. Numerous studies of inhaled glucocorticoids have shown minimal systemic effects at doses of up to 800 μg/day for adults. Because most of inhaled steroids (80 to 90%) is deposited in the oropharynx, systemic absorption can be reduced with the use of spacer devices and mouth rinsing. With high dosing, such measures should be routine (61). Acute episodes are frequently managed by adding a short course of an oral steroid (e.g., prednisone), usually 1 mg/kg daily for 5 days. Recent studies have determined there is no need to taper the dose of steroids when they are given for short courses of up to 10 days (62).

Asthma in Pregnancy

In any practice there will be women with asthma who become pregnant. Although medication in pregnancy should be carefully ex-

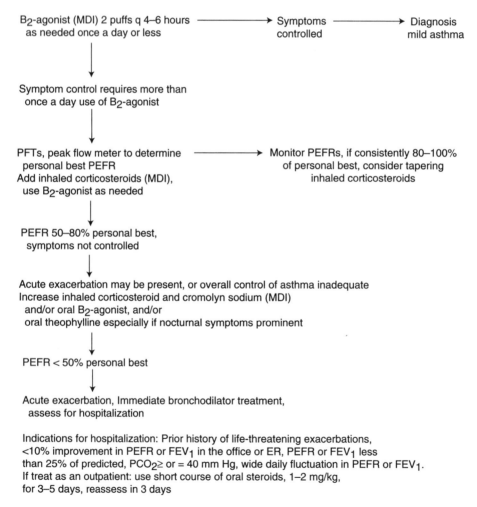

Figure 14.2. Treatment algorithm for asthma. (Data from Guidelines for the diagnosis and management of asthma: National Heart, Lung, and Blood Institute, National Asthma Education Program Expert Panel Report. J Allergy Clin Immunol 1991;88(Suppl):425–534.)

amined, making sure the woman is well oxygenated is important. Almost any medication used in nonpregnant asthmatics can be used in pregnant asthmatics, and it is often advisable to treat prophylactically to prevent emergencies and hospitalizations.

Inhaled β-agonists or steroid preparations can be continued in pregnancy. Oral beta-agonists, such as terbutaline, metoproterenol, or albuterol, can be used if needed. Theophylline preparations can be given, but with the changing volume of distribution, levels may need to be determined and dosages changed. In severe or emergency situations, oxygen and parenteral or oral steroids can also be used.

Chonic Obstructive Pulmonary Disease

COPD is a spectrum of chronic respiratory diseases characterized by cough, sputum production, dyspnea, airflow limitation, and impaired gas exchange (63). The term COPD includes emphysema and chronic bronchitis. Emphysema is defined pathologically as "a condition of the lung characterized by abnormal permanent enlargement of the air spaces distal to the terminal bronchioles accompanied by destruction of their walls and without obvious fibrosis (64). Chronic bronchitis is a clinical condition defined as the presence of chronic productive cough occurring on most days for at least 3 months in each of two successive years (65).

Estimates of the prevalence of COPD in the United States range from 8% of adult women to 14% of adult men. It is a leading cause of death in the United States in persons over the age of 55 years. COPD mortality rates are similar for men and women before age 55 years. After age 55 years, men develop appreciably higher mortality rates, and this disparity increases with age. Because of a change in smoking rates, the prevalence among women has increased by more than one third between 1979 and 1985, with a prevalence of 119/1000 in 1985. Most population studies have reported a higher prevalence of respiratory

symptoms in men than in women, even when the data are controlled for smoking (64).

The major etiologic factor in the development of COPD is chronic irritation by inhaled substances. Cigarette smoking is firmly established as the most important risk factor for COPD, yet only a minority (10 to 15%) of smokers develop clinically significant COPD. Tobacco smoking accounts for 80 to 90% of the risk of developing COPD in the United States. The role of environmental air pollution is unclear, yet appears small compared to that of cigarette smoking. The only other risk factor as important in alpha$_1$-protease inhibitor deficiency (API). In the United States, the latter accounts for approximately 2% of people with COPD. Asthma and atopy are not risk factors for COPD (66).

Alpha$_1$ antitrypsin deficiency is now known as API. Estimates of frequency range from 1 in 1600 to 1 in 4000 in North America and Europe. Homozygous deficiency of API is characterized by the premature development of severe COPD at a median age of 40 years in smokers and 53 years in nonsmokers. More than half these patients die of pulmonary disease. The serum API level should be tested in patients presenting with COPD at a young age, especially if they have affected siblings or parents and have minimal or no smoking history. Recently, replacement therapy with alpha$_1$-antitrypsin has been proposed (67).

Symptoms and Diagnosis

Clinical features of COPD include dyspnea, chronic cough, expectoration, and wheezing. Decreased exercise tolerance is commonly seen. The typical patient with COPD is 60 to 70 years of age and has been smoking more than 20 cigarettes a day for over 25 years. Often, there is a history of acute exacerbations occurring once or twice a year. These are characterized by increased cough, increased sputum with altered color or tenacity, wheeze, dyspnea, and chest tightness. During such acute exacerbations, most patients do not have symptoms or signs suggesting a systemic infection such as fever or leukocytosis. Hemoptysis can occur in chronic bronchitis, usually associated with purulent sputum during the exacerbation.

Pathologically, emphysema develops slowly, and involvement of the peripheral airways must be widespread before obvious generalized airway obstruction and dyspnea occur. Late in the disease, cyanosis, insomnia, somnolence, personality changes, and morning headache are indications of severe disruptions of blood-gas exchange and acid-base balance (68).

In COPD, the physical exam may be normal or there may be wheezes on auscultation. The forced expiratory time is prolonged beyond the normal 4 seconds. Accessory muscles of breathing may be used. Chest radiograph changes of COPD include significant and persistent overdistention of the lungs and excessively rapid tapering of the vascular shadows. Radiograph findings are neither sensitive nor specific for COPD. Bullae provide proof of emphysema but do not occur until end-stage or severe disease is present.

All patients with suspected COPD should have PFTs. Women with COPD will show a decreased FEV_1 and a reduction in the ratio of FEV_1/FVC. Because of an increase in residual volume, the total lung capacity is increased and the vital capacity is decreased. The normal rate of decline in FEV_1 over time is less than 30 mL per year; if the decline is greater, the woman is at risk for COPD.

Although most patients with COPD do not display bronchial hyperreactivity, 15 to 20% of patients will improve after bronchodilator treatment. A single trial of inhaled bronchodilators will not identify all patients with reversible defects in airflow limitation, nor will it always predict the response to long-term bronchodilator therapy.

Arterial blood gases should be checked in all patients with moderately severe airflow limitation, defined as those with an FEV_1 below 1.5 L. In COPD, patients can have varying degrees of hypoxemia and hypercapnia, depending on the severity of disease. The presence of erythrocytosis suggests chronic hypoxemia and is an indication to check arterial blood gases (64).

Treatment

Treatment of COPD should be directed at minimizing airflow limitation through reduction of secretions and bronchodilatation, correction of severe hypoxemia, and optimizing functional capability.

Eliminating airway irritants and preventing infections should reduce secretions. Smoking and occupational exposures are common irritants that should be eliminated, if possible. Pneumococcal and flu vaccinations help prevent infections. Acute exacerbations of bronchitis are often viral in etiology; studies differ over the benefit of antibiotics in acute exacerbations of bronchitis or emphysema (69). Most experts advocate treating with antibiotics. Trimethoprim-sulfamethisoxazole is the drug of choice. As discussed above, expectorants have no proven beneficial effects, although iodinated glycerol has been shown to significantly improve total condition during acute exacerbations of COPD.

Bronchodilation is a mainstay of treatment in COPD. Regardless of whether PFTs show reversibility of airflow limitation, sympathomimetics, anticholinergics, and theophylline have been shown to increase airflow and reduce dyspnea in patients with COPD. Inhaled B_2-agonists and anticholinergic agonists are recommended as first-line treatments. These agents appear to have equal efficacy in the treatment of acute exacerbations of COPD. For use regularly, ipratropium, an anticholinergic agonist, is preferred by some investigators because of its slower onset and longer duration of action (70). Theophylline was once the most prescribed medication for COPD, but its use declined following reports of poor efficacy and high toxicity. Nevertheless, theophylline treatment has been associated with physiologic improvement, and it continues to be recommended if there is suboptimal response to first-line treatments.

Corticosteroid therapy should be considered only if a combination of bronchodilators at maximum doses fails to control symptoms. There should be documented improvement in airflow or exercise performance with the use of corticosteroids. A 2- to 3-week trial of 0.5 to 1 mg/kg of prednisone should be followed by spirometry. If the baseline FEV_1 has not increased by 20 to 25%, the drug should be rapidly tapered and stopped. Some investigators believe that failure to improve airway obstruction with a short course of oral glucocorticoids serves to distinguish COPD from asthma. Inhaled corticosteroids have proven to be relatively ineffective in the treatment of COPD.

Long-term oxygen therapy is indicated for correction of hypoxemia when, regardless of activity, the PaO_2 is $\leq$ 55 mm Hg or SaO_2 is $\leq$ 89%. If there is evidence of cor pulmonale, polycythemia, or congestive heart failure, PaO_2 values of 56 to 59 mm Hg and SaO_2 of 89% are used. The goal of therapy is to maintain oxygen saturation above 90%. Medicare criterion for oxygen therapy is an SaO_2 of 88% or less.

Functional capacity in patients with COPD can be optimized by programs that provide respiratory, physical, and occupational therapy, as well as exercise conditioning, nutritional assistance, and psychosocial and vocational rehabilitation. Undernutrition, or weight less than 90% of ideal body weight, is estimated to be present in 25% of patients with COPD. It is associated with decreased respiratory muscle function and increased mortality, and is usually attributed to insufficient caloric intake (63). The provider will need to develop a complete and long-term continuing approach to the woman with COPD.

Interstitial Lung Disease (ILD)

These are a group of over 100 disease entities that infiltrate and scar the gas exchange units of the lungs. Table 14.9 includes a partial listing of these.

Table 14.9. Some Common Causes of Interstitial Lung Disease

Connective tissue diseases: systemic lupus erythematosus, rheumatoid arthritis, polymyositis-dermatomyositis, ankylosing spondylitis, mixed connective tissue

Pharmaceuticals: antibiotics (nitrofurantoin, sulfasalazine, penicillin), antiarrythmics (amiodorone, tocainide, propranolol), anti-inflammatory (gold, pencillamine), anticonvulsants (dilantin), chemotherapeutic agents, vitamins (L-tryptophan)

Occupational: silicosis, asbestosis, hard metal pneumoconiosis, coal worker's pneumoconiosis, Berylliosis, hypersensitivity pneumonitis (any organic chemical including farmer's lung and pigeon breeder's lung)

Other: therapeutic radiation, oxygen, paraquat, crack cocaine inhalation, postinfectious interstitial lung disease, Wegener's granulomatosis

Unclassified Diseases: sarcoidosis, eosinophilic granuloma, amyloidosis, adult respiratory distress syndrome, acquired immunodeficiency syndrome (AIDS), Bone marrow transplantation, Eosinophilic pneumonia, pulmonary lymphoma, bronchoalveolar carcinoma

Idiopathic pulmonary fibrosis

(Data from Coultas DB, Zumwalt RE, Black WC, Sobonya RE. The epidemiology of interstitial lung diseases. Am J Respir Crit Care Med 1994;150:967–972.)

Epidemiology

A recent study showed the prevalence of ILDs in women to be 67.2 per 100,000, or approximately 20% lower than the prevalence in men. The incidence is 26.1 per 100,000 in women compared with 31.5 per 100,000 in men. Autopsy studies suggest that the prevalence of undiagnosed ILDs could be as high as 1.8%, which is much more common than clinically recognized. However, data from hospital discharges and vital statistics suggest that pulmonary fibrosis is much less common. Pulmonary fibrosis and idiopathic pulmonary fibrosis together account for 44.2% of ILD in women, followed by sarcoidosis. The incidence and prevalence of ILD increases significantly with age; the median age for ILD is 69 years. The prevalence of ILD secondary to connective tissue disorders is 30% greater in women than in men (71).

Clinical Features

The presenting symptoms of interstitial lung disease are progressive dyspnea and cough. Chest pain is unusual, but it can occur in patients with sarcoidosis and other connective tissue disease also drug-related diseases. ILD is usually found in patients with established cases of connective tissue disease. Rarely, ILD will be the initial manifestation of connective tissue disease. The occupational history is essential; many inhaled substances found in the workplace can cause ILD. The provider must take a lifelong history in patients with ILD because there is a prolonged latency period for many causes of ILD.

Sarcoidosis typically occurs in younger women between age 20 and 40 years. It is characterized by granulomatous inflammation in a variety of organs, most commonly the lung. Women can be asymptomatic or have generalized constitutional symptoms, or symptoms attributable to the specific organ involved. It is treated with corticosteroids in symptomatic patients and in those with involvement of eyes, CNS, and heart. Sarcoidosis generally responds to steroids, but it is unclear if treatment alters the natural course of the disease.

On physical exam, bibasilar inspiratory, dry rales, or crackles are common findings. Clubbing of the digits indicates far-advanced fibrotic disease and is common in certain processes such as idiopathic pulmonary fibrosis, rheumatoid arthritis-associated ILD, and asbestosis. Clubbing is quite unusual in hypersensitivity pneumonitis, silicosis, and idiopathic bronchiolitis obliterans organizing pneumonia. Extrapulmonary findings can assist in diagnosing the etiology of the ILD.

Diagnosis

Diagnosis is often difficult. The chest radiograph is abnormal in 90 to 95% of cases, and the patterns and anatomic locations of infiltrates may provide clues to the etiology of ILD. PFTs usually show a reduction in lung volumes and spirometry, with no change in the FEV_1/FVC ratio. Sometimes, a combination of interstitial and obstructive changes can be found in ILDs. Cigarette smoking can significantly increase lung volumes in patients with IPF, falsely suggesting less severe ILD. The most sensitive indicator of the severity of ILD is exercise testing (72).

Bronchoalveolar lavage can be used to determine the etiology of an ILD. It is also useful in diagnosing the presence of ILD in patients with normal chest radiographs and PFTs. High-resolution computed tomographic scans are increasingly employed before going to the gold standard of open lung biopsy, but its usefulness with regards to diagnosis or change in treatment is questionable (73).

Treatment

End-stage fibrosis, whatever the cause, is irreversible and untreatable. Corticosteroids are often used in women with ILD. However, although 50% of patients experience subjective improvement, only 15 to 20% improve by objective measures. In certain disease processes, such as IPF, Wegener's granulomatosis, and collagen vascular disease-related ILD, immunosuppressive agents have been combined with lower doses of corticosteroids.

Lung Cancer

Epidemiology

Lung cancer is the leading cause of cancer deaths for women in the United States. Cancer mortality for women in the United States is increasing, and most of this increase is attributed to lung cancer. Cancer is the leading cause of death in women over 60 years of age, and lung cancer is responsible for over 25% of cancer deaths in women. Lung cancer mortality correlates closely with the use of cigarettes. Over 90% of all cancers of the lung, trachea, and bronchus are attributable to tobacco (74). The lifetime risk for lung cancer for a nonsmoker in the United States has been estimated at approximately 1 in 357, compared with 1 in 8 for a heavy smoker. Estimates of the male/female ratio for lung cancer range from 1.5:1 to 3:1; this is attributed to the higher historical smoking rates among men. Susceptibility to the carcinogenic effects of cigarette smoke for men and women is similar.

Lung cancer has the lowest 5-year survival rate of any cancer. Despite intense investigation into early detection, and trials of new approaches to treatment, over 90% of patients die of the disease. Reduction in smoking prevalence remains the best strategy to decrease the mortality of lung cancer. Interventions in this direction made in the last two decades will take 10 to 30 years to show any effect. Because of the long latency period of lung cancer, the rate in women can peak no sooner than the year 2010 before it starts to decline (75).

Other risk factors for lung disease include occupational causes, radon, and second-hand smoke. The most frequent occupational cause of lung cancer today is past exposure to asbestos. Approximately 85% of all lung cancers that occurred in the United States in 1981 were caused by tobacco smoking, and 5% were caused by occupational asbestos exposure. A synergistic relationship between asbestos and smoking has been observed in men; those with both exposures have 50 times the risk for lung cancer compared to nonexposed men. Asbestos exposure, which increases the risk for lung cancer, is usually substantial and associated with past work experience. There is no evidence of harm to the public from small amounts of asbestos exposure. No measurable effect is found when the total cumulative exposure is less than 10 fibers/mL air (76). Mesothelioma is a rare tumor associated with exposure to chrysotile asbestos.

Radon gas is a decay product of naturally occurring uranium in the earth. High levels of radon gas observed in uranium miners are known risk factors for lung cancer and are also synergistic with smoking. The level of radon exposure in most homes, as a result of radon decay products in foundations or groundwater, is at a relatively low level. The Environmental Protection Agency (EPA), based on extrapolation from higher occupational exposures, has recommended remedial measures for homes that consistently test above 4 pCi/L. The EPA attributes 5 to 10% of new lung cancer cases to environmental radon exposure. Reliable home-testing kits are available, and according to the EPA, a typical radon problem can be solved for under $2000 (77). Smokers and people who spend much of their time in their basements are at the highest risk. Many experts believe that the contribution from radon is negligible, and they advocate that when the exposure rate in individual houses approaches the rate found in mines (20 pCi/L), corrective action should be taken (78).

With environmental tobacco smoke, a small increase in the risk of lung cancer has been observed. The average lifetime passive exposure to a smoking spouse increases a nonsmoker's risk by 35%, as compared with the risk increase of 1000% for a lifetime of active smoking. Genetic factors seem to play a role in risk for lung cancer; six families of activated oncogenes have been associated with lung cancer.

Classification

Most oncologists prefer to classify lung cancer as either small cell lung cancer (SCLC) or nonsmall cell lung cancer (NSCLC); SCLC responds better to therapy. NSCLCs comprise approximately 70% of lung cancers and include squamous cell cancer, adenocarcinoma, and large cell carcinoma. Lung cancer is staged based on the size and location of the tumor, nodal involvement, and distant metastases (79).

Clinical Presentation

Chronic cough occurs in up to 90% of all lung cancer patients. Other common symptoms include weight loss, dyspnea, chest pain, and hemoptysis. Some patients will present with metastatic complications such as superior vena cava syndrome or Horner's syndrome. Approximately 15% of patients with lung cancer present with a paraneoplastic syndromes, such as inappropriate antidiuretic hormone syndrome, Cushing's disease, hypercalcemia, and hyperthyroidism (80).

Treatment

Whatever the treatment, the overall 5-year survival for lung cancer ranges from 5 to 10%. Patients with nonsmall cell carcinoma should be evaluated for resectability based on size and stage of the tumor. Consultation with a pulmonary physician or thoracic surgeon is advised. Women with an FEV_1 less than 1 L and a PCO_2 greater than 50 mm Hg are poor candidates for surgical resection and can be spared a work-up for staging (81). In certain cases, nonresectable tumors can be palliatively irradiated. Chemotherapy may be considered for small cell carcinomas (82).

Solitary Pulmonary Nodules

A solitary, pulmonary nodule discovered on chest radiographs is a common finding (Figure 14.3). These must be taken seriously, because studies indicate that up to 40% can be malignant. "Benign" nodules can be followed over time with repeat radiographs. The criterion for a benign nodule includes (a) size less than 3 cm, (b) no growth over 2 years after a review of previous radiographs, (c) a benign pattern of calcification, (d) age less than 35 years and (e) nonsmoker. Benign patterns of calcification include dense central, "popcorn," laminated (concentric), or diffuse calcification. Computerized tomographic (CT) scanning is used for indeterminate nodules. Twenty-two to 50% of solitary pulmonary nodules that appear noncalcified on plain radiographs have been shown to contain benign calcification on CT. CT densitometry is a procedure used to quantify calcification, but it is not standardized for different machines. The use of a reference phantom gives more reliable results, but these are expensive and not yet widely used. A suggested protocol for pulmonary nodules is outlined in Figure 14.3.

In cases where prospective observation is advised, repeat radiographs should be done at 1½ months, 3 months, 6 months, 12 months, 18 months, and 24 months (83). Pulmonary nodules that are 3 cm or greater in diameter should be regarded as malignant and resection is recommended (84).

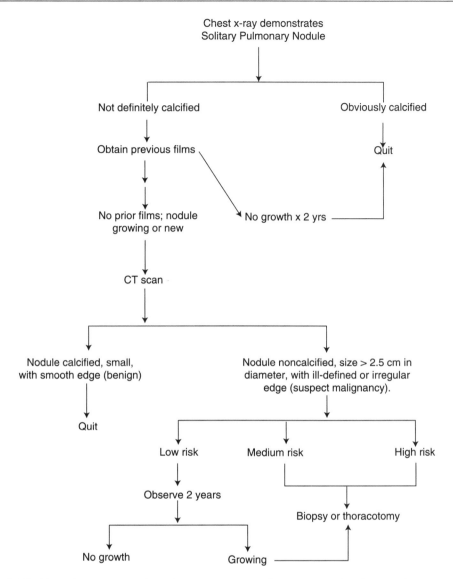

Figure 14.3. Algorithmic approach to the management of a patient with solitary pulmonary nodule. (Reprinted with permission from Howard TA, Woodring JH. Clinical and imaging evaluation of the solitary pulmonary nodule. Am Fam Physician 1992;46:1753–1759.)

Screening for Lung Cancer

There is a consensus that screening asymptomatic smokers for lung cancer with routine chest radiographs or sputum cytology is not recommended. This is because four randomized controlled studies on lung cancer screening have been conducted in men cigarette smokers and none of the studies has demonstrated reduced mortality. Recently there has been renewed debate on this issue. Two randomized trials have shown an association between radiograph screening and both early detection and improved survival (85).

Special Considerations in the Elderly

The lung diseases, except for asthma, have a much higher prevalence in the elderly. Many of these are attributable to toxins that often require years of exposure and a long latency before disease develops. Older people have an increased incidence of serious infectious diseases of the lung. This increased risk is attributed to alterations in immune function, significant underlying diseases, and age-related changes in pulmonary function and local defense mechanism efficiency.

Pneumonia is the single most important infectious cause of death in the elderly. A major factor is colonization of the pharynx with potential pathogens such as gram-negative bacteria, typically by retrograde spread from the patient's gastrointestinal tract (86). In elderly or debilitated patients with pneumonia, fever may be absent and atypical symptoms of weakness, confusion, and disorientation can be present. To prevent pneumonia in the elderly, pneumococcal vaccines and yearly influenzae vaccines should be offered to all patients over age 65 years. Increased rates of tuberculosis occur in elderly patients, especially those residing in nursing homes. Regular screening for tuberculosis is recommended.

Special Considerations for Nurse Practitioners and Physician Assistants

Primary, secondary, and tertiary prevention strategies will be used by nurse practitioners and physician assistants whether a respiratory problem is acute or chronic. In nearly all situations, interventions will include (a) smoking cessation, (b) identification and avoidance of airway irritants, (c) infection protection such as prophylactic vaccinations, (d) avoidance of risk situations such as crowds and handwashing, (e) adequate hydration to thin secretions and facilitate expectoration, and (f) recognition of signs and symptoms of impending infection or worsening of a chronic process (87). In addition, TB testing guidelines for all women should be established and implemented.

When caring for women with chronic pulmonary diseases, providers must evaluate the extent to which the disease process and other factors affect day-to-day activities. Individuals with COPD perceive greater functional difficulty with sleep and rest, home management, and recreation and pastime activities. Although dyspnea and disease severity has been related to functional state, psychosocial (e.g., depression, anxiety), economic support and other factors also appear to influence the woman's functional performance. It is difficult to determine if the disease process itself or the woman's emotional state is the predominate effect on her quality of life. Women have been underrepresented in these studies, so little is known through research how women experience chronic illnesses such as COPD, how they adapt, and how health care providers can assist them (88). Providers must, therefore, take time to ask women about their perception of daily difficulties and needs so that individualized plans of care can be developed.

Especially for women with chronic respiratory problems, treatment regimens, daily adjustments in activities, and performance of expected roles make successful adaptation a complex process. Women with chronic asthma may be measuring daily peak flows, using two or three different medications, working to eliminate allergens in the home, and worrying about exposure to irritants such as second-hand smoke or cold air. Keeping a daily diary for several weeks may assist the woman and her health care provider in understanding how these factors and others influence her adaptation. Aggravating conditions as well as patterns and efficiency of treatments might be identified through the diary (89).

How and when referrals and consultations need to be done depend on the protocols under which the provider functions, the availability of referral resources, and the setting for practice. Physician referral/consultation is indicated for moderate to severe respiratory distress, significant medication side effects or nonresponsiveness to medications, and atypical symptoms and when women have a poor history, e.g., multiple hospitalizations, concomitant debilitating diseases. Referral to specialists is often needed for chronic, severe asthma or COPD and treatment of tuberculosis (90). Nutritional referrals should be considered for women who continue to lose weight or experience nutritional deficiencies. Pulmonary rehabilitation can teach women with chronic pulmonary diseases how to control dyspnea and breathe and cough more effectively, as well as the need for exercise, proper use of medications, and the safe, correct use of oxygen. Psychosocial support and relaxation techniques may be part of a holistic program. The success of a rehabilitation program will depend on the woman's motivation and the support of her family or other significant relationships (87, 91).

All providers must be aware of the risk of seeing women who have undetected infectious diseases such as TB. Control plans for protection of employees and other women should be established, including baseline and periodic skin testing of employees, education about the transmission of infectious diseases, recognition of women at risk, and a high risk of suspicion for any woman who has persistent symptoms (92).

References

1. Zervanos NJ, Shute KM. Acute, disruptive cough. Symptomatic therapy for a nagging problem. Postgrad Med 1994;95:153–164.
2. Pratter MR, Bartter T, Akers S, et al. An algorithmic approach to chronic cough. Ann Intern Med 1993;119:977–9832.
3. Irwin RS, Zawacki JK, Curley FJ, French CL, Hoffman PJ. Chronic cough as the sole presenting manifestation of gastroesophageal reflux. Am Rev Respir Dis 1989;140:1294–300.
4. Krzyzanowski M, Robbins DR, Lebowitz MD. Smoking cessation and changes in respiratory symptoms in two populations followed for 13 years. Int J Epidemiol 1993;22:666–673.
5. Karlberg BE. Cough and inhibition of the renin-angiotensin system. J Hypertens 1993;11(suppl):S49–S52.
6. Hyde L, Hyde CI. Clinical manifestations of lung cancer. Chest 1974;65:299–306.
7. Irwin RS, Curley FJ. The treatment of cough. A comprehensive review. Chest 1991;99:1477–1484.
8. Fuller RW, Jackson DM. Physiology and treatment of cough. Thorax 1990;45:425–430.
9. Taylor JA, Novack AH, Almquist JR, Rogers JE. Efficacy of cough suppressants in children. J Pediatr 1993;122:799–802.
10. Kuhn JJ, Hendley JO, Adams KF, et al. Antitussive effect of guaifenesin in young adults with natural colds. Chest 1982;82:713–718.
11. Petty TL. The National Mucolytic Study: results of a randomized, double-blind, placebo-controlled study of iodinated glycerol in chronic obstructive bronchitis. Chest 1990;97:75–83.
12. Sen RP, Walsh TE, Bode FR. Hemoptysis: a manifestation of pulmonary disease confidently managed by military physicians. Military Med 1990;155:502–508.
13. Set PA, Flower CD, Smith IE, Chan AP, Twentyman OP, Shneerson JM. Hemoptysis: comparative study of the role of CT and fiberoptic bronchoscopy. Radiology 1993;189:677–680.
14. O'Neil KM, Lazarus AA. Hemoptysis. Indications for bronchoscopy. Arch Intern Med 1991;151:171–174.
15. Haponik EF, Chin R. Hemoptysis: clinicians' perspectives. Chest 1990;97:469–475.
16. Stulberg MS, Adams L. Dyspnea. In: Murray JF, Nadel JA, eds. Textbook of Respiratory Medicine. Philadelphia: WB Saunders,1994:519–528.
17. Simon PM, Schwartzstein RM, Weiss JW, et al. Distinguishable types of dyspnea in patients with shortness of breath. Am Rev Respir Dis 1990;142:1009–1014.
18. Schmitt BP, Kushner MS, Weiner SL. The diagnostic usefulness of the history of the patient with dyspnea. J Gen Intern Med 1986;1:389.

19. Zema MJ, Masters AP, Margouleff D. Dyspnea: the heart or the lungs. Chest 1984;85:59.

20. Murray JF, Basbaum AI. Chest pain. In: Murray JF, Nadel JA, eds. Textbook of respiratory medicine. Philadelphia: WB Saunders, 1994:552–561.

21. Cohen S. Tyrrell DAJ, Smith AP. Psychological stress and susceptibility to the common cold. N Engl J Med 1991;325:606–612.

22. Garibaldi RA. Epidemiology of community-acquired respiratory tract infections in adults. Incidence, etiology, and impact. Am J Med 1985;78:32– 37.

23. Rodnick JE, Gude JK. The use of antibiotics in acute bronchitis and acute exacerbations of chronic bronchitis. West J Med 1988;149:347–351.

24. Hahn DL, Dodge RW, Golubjatnikov R. Association of Chlamydia pneumoniae infection with wheezing, asthmatic bronchitis, and adult-onset asthma. JAMA 1991;266:225–230.

25. Rodnick JE, Gude JK. Diagnosis and antibiotic treatment of community-acquired pneumonia. West J Med 1991;154:405–409.

26. Heckerling PS, Tape TG, Wigton RS, et al. Clinical prediction rule for pulmonary infiltrates. Ann Intern Med 1990;113:664.

27. Gerberding JL, Sande MA. Infectious disease of the lungs. General principles and diagnostic approach. In: Murray JF, Nadel JA, eds. Textbook of Respiratory Medicine. Philadelphia: WB Saunders, 1994: 963–976.

28. Jenson PS, Halber MD, Putnam CE. Mycoplasma pneumonia. CRC Crit Rev Imagn Imaging 1980; 12:385–415.

29. Dietrich PA, Johnson RD, Fairbank JT, Walde JS. The chest xray in legionnaires disease. Radiology 1978;127:577–582.

30. Fang GD, Fine M, Orloff J, et al. New and emerging etiologies for community-acquired pneumonia with implications for therapy: a prospective multicenter study of 359 cases. Medicine 1990;69:307–316.

31. Macfarlane JT, Miller AC, Smith WH, Morris AH, Rose DH. Comparative radiologic features of community acquired legionnaires' disease, pneumococcal pneumonia, Mycoplasma pneumonia, and psittacosis. Thorax 1984;39:28–33.

32. Pomilla PV, Brown RB. Outpatient treatment of community-acquired pneumonia in adults. Arch Intern Med 1994;154:1793–1802.

33. Marrie TJ, Durant H, Yates L. Community-acquired pneumonia requiring hospitalization: 5-year prospective study. Rev Infect Dis 1989;11:586.

34. American Thoracic Society. Guidelines for the initial management of adults with community-acquired pneumonia: diagnosis, assessment of severity, and initial antimicrobial therapy. Am Rev Respir Dis 1993;148:1418–1426.

35. Fine MJ, Smith DN, Singer DE. Hospitalization decision in patients with community-acquired pneumonia: a prospective cohort study. Am J Med 1990;89:713–721.

36. Jareb JA, Kelly GD, Dooley Jr SW, et al. Tuberculo-sis morbidity in the U.S.: final data, 1990. In: CDC Surveillance Summaries, December 1991. MMWR 1991;40(No.SS-3):23–27.

37. American Thoracic Society. Control of tuberculosis in the U.S. Am Rev Respir Dis 1992;146:1623–1633.

38. Leads from the MMWR. Tuberculosis control among homeless populations. JAMA 1987;257:2886–2888.

39. Tuberculosis and human immunodeficiency virus infection: recommendations of the Advisory Committee for the Elimination of Tuberculosis. MMWR 1989;38:236–238.

40. Centers for Disease Control. The use of preventive therapy for tuberculosis infection in the U.S.: recommendations of the Advisory Committee for Elimination of Tuberculosis. MMWR 1990;39(No.RR8): 9–12.

41. Kissner DG. Tuberculosis. In: Victor LD, ed. Clinical Pulmonary Medicine. Boston: Little, Brown & Co, 1992:384–388.

42. American Thoracic Society. Diagnostic standards and classifications of tuberculosis. Am Rev Respir Dis 1990;142:725–735.

43. U.S. Preventive Services Task Force. Guide to clinical preventive services: an assessment of the effectiveness of 169 interventions. Report of the U.S. Preventive Services Task Force. Baltimore, MD: Williams & Wilkins, 1989:125–129.

44. Brisson-Noel A, Aznar C, Chureau C, et al. Diagnosis of tuberculosis by DNA amplification in clinical practice evaluation. Lancet 1991;338:364–366.

45. Al-Orainey IO, El Rab MOG, Al-Hajjaj MS, Saeed ES. Detection of mycobacterial antigens in sputum by an enzyme immunoassay. Eur J Clin Microbiol Infect Dis 1992;11:58–61.

46. Mazurek GH, Cave MD, Eisenach KD, Wallace RJ Jr, Bates JH, Crawford JT. Chromosomal DNA fingerprint patterns produced with IS6110 as strain-specific markers for epidemiologic study of tuberculosis. J Clin Microbiol 1991;29:2030–2033.

47. Barnes PF, Barrows SA. Tuberculosis in the 1990s. Ann Intern Med 1993;119:400–410.

48. Drugs for tuberculosis. Med Lett 1995;37: 67–70.

49. Benson CA. Mycobacterial infections. In: Gleicher N, ed. Medical Therapy in Pregnancy. Norwalk, CT: Appleton & Lange, 1992:579.

50. Clausen JL. The diagnosis of emphysema, chronic bronchitis, and asthma. Clin Chest Med 1990;11: 405–416.

51. McFadden Jr ER, Gilbert IA. Asthma. N Engl J Med 1992;327:1928–1937.

52. Laitenen LA, Elkin RB, Empey DW, et al. Bronchial hyperresponsiveness in normal subjects during attenuated influenza virus infection. Am Rev Respir Dis 1991;143:358–361.

53. Grammer LC, Greenberger PA. Diagnosis and classification of asthma. Chest 1992;101(suppl):393S–395S.

54. Patrick H, Patrick F. Chronic cough. Med Clin North Am 1995:79:361–372.

55. Hargreave FE, Ryan G, Thomson NC, et al. Bronchial responsiveness to histamine and methacholine in asthma: measurement and clinical significance. J Allergy Clin Immunol 1981;68:347–355.

56. Adelroth E, Hargreave FE, Ramsdale HE. Do physicians need objective measurements to diagnose asthma? Am Rev Respir Dis 1986;134:704–707.

57. Nowak RM, Pensler MI, Sarkar DD. Comparison of peak expiratory flow and FEV$_1$ admission criteria for acute bronchial asthma. Ann Emerg Med 1982;11:64–69.

58. American Thoracic Society. Environmental control and lung disease. Am Rev Respir Dis 1990;142:915–939.

59. Guidelines for the diagnosis and management of asthma: National Heart, Lung, and Blood Institute, national Asthma Education Program Expert Panel Report. J Allergy Clin Immunol 1991;88(suppl):425–534.

60. Summer W, Elston R, Tharpe L, Nelson S, Haponik EF. Aerosol bronchodilator delivery methods. Relative impact on pulmonary function and cost of respiratory care. Arch Intern Med 1989;149:618–623.

61. Barnes PJ. Inhaled glucocorticoids for asthma. N Engl J Med 1995;332:868–875.

62. O'Driscoll BR, Kalra S, Wilson M, Pickering CA, Carroll KB, Wookcock AA. Double-blind trial of steroid tapering in acute asthma. Lancet 1993;341:324–327.

63. Ferguson GT, Cherniack RM. Management of chronic obstructive pulmonary disease. N Engl J Med 1993;328:1017–1022.

64. Feinleib M, Rosenberg HM, Collins JG, et al. Trends in COPD morbidity and mortality in the U.S. Am Rev Respir Dis 1989;140:S9–S18.

65. American Thoracic Society. Standards for the diagnosis and care of patients with chronic obstructive pulmonary disease (COPD) and asthma. Am Rev Respir Dis 1987;136:225–244.

66. Sherill DL, Lebowitz MD, Burrows B. Epidemiology of chronic obstructive pulmonary disease. Clin Chest Med 1990;11:375–388.

67. Wewers MD, Casolaro MA, Sellers SE, et al. Replacement therapy for alpha$_1$-antitrypsin deficiency associated with emphysema. N Engl J Med 1987;316:1055–1062.

68. Snider GL, Faling LJ, Rennard SI. Chronic bronchitis and emphysema. In: Murray JF, Nadel JA. Textbook of Respiratory Medicine. Philadelphia: WB Saunders, 1994:1331–1397.

69. Anthonisen NR, Manfreda J, Warren CPW, Hershfield ES, Harding GKM, Nelson NA. Antibiotic therapy in exacerbations of chronic obstructive pulmonary disease. Ann Intern Med 1987;106:196–204.

70. Ghafouri MA, Patil KD, Kass I. Sputum changes associated with the use of ipratropium bromide. Chest 1984;86:387–393.

71. Coultas DB, Zumwalt RE, Black WC, Sobonya RE. The epidemiology of interstitial lung diseases. Am J Respir Crit Care Med 1994;150:967–972.

72. Wade JF, King TE. Infiltrative and interstitial lung disease in the elderly patient. Clin Chest Med 1993;14:501–521.

73. Raghu G. Interstitial lung disease: a diagnostic approach. Are CT scan and lung biopsy indicated in every patient? Am J Respir Crit Care Med 1995;151:909–914.

74. US Preventive Services Task Force. Guide to clinical preventive services: an assessment of the effectiveness of 169 interventions. Report of the U.S. Preventive Services Task Force. Baltimore, MD: Williams & Wilkins, 1989:67.

75. Beckett WS. Epidemiology and etiology of lung cancer. Clin Chest Med 1993;14:1–15.

76. Yesner R. Lung cancer: pathogenesis and pathology. Clin Chest Med 1993;14:17–27.

77. Radon: Worth learning about. Consumer Reports 1995;July:464–465.

78. Harley HH, Harley JH. Potential lung cancer risk from indoor radon exposure. CA 1990;40:265–275.

79. Mountain CF. A new international staging system for lung cancer. Chest 1986;89:225S–233S.

80. Chia MM, Gazdar AF, Carbone DP, Minna JD. Biology of lung cancer: In: Murray JF, Nadel JA. Textbook of respiratory medicine. Philadelphia: WB Saunders; 1994:1485–1503.

81. Shields TW. Surgical therapy for carcinoma of the lung. Clin Chest Med 1993;14:121–148.

82. Murren JR, Buzaid AC. Chemotherapy and radiation for the treatment of non-small-cell lung cancer: a critical review. Clin Chest Med 1993;14:161–172.

83. Howard TA, Woodring JH. Clinical and imaging evaluation of the solitary pulmonary nodule. Am Fam Physician 1992;46:1753–1759.

84. Lillington GA, Caskey CI. Evaluation and management of solitary and multiple pulmonary nodules. Clin Chest Med 1993;14:111–119.

85. Strauss GM, Gleason RE, Sugarbaker DJ. Chest X-ray screening improves outcome in lung cancer. A reappraisal of randomized trials on lung cancer screening. Chest 1995;107(6 Suppl):270S–279S.

86. Raju L, Khan F. Pneumonia in the elderly: a review. Geriatrics 1988;43:51–62.

87. Johannsen JM. Chronic obstructive pulmonary disease. Nurse Pract 1994;19:59–67.

88. Leidy NK. Functional performance in people with chronic obstructive pulmonary disease. IMAGE: J Nurs Scholarship 1995;27:23–33.

89. Uphold CR, Graham MV. Clinical Guidelines in Family Practice. Gainesville, FL: Barmarrae Books, 1993:381–385.

90. Shannon M. Respiratory/otorhinolaryngological disorders. In: Star WL, Lommel LL, Shannon MT, eds. Women's Primary Health Care. Washington, DC: American Nurses' Association, 1995;5:1–5-66.

91. Lewis D, Bell SK. Pulmonary rehabilitation, psychosocial adjustment, and use of health care services. Rehabilitation Nurs 1995;20:102–107.

92. Wolf L. A tuberculosis control plan for ambulatory care centers. Nurse Pract 1995;20:34–40.

15.1

Diabetes: Prevention, Treatment, and Follow-up

Ann J. Brown

Introduction

Although good blood glucose control avoids some long-term and costly complications of diabetes (1), achieving this remains an elusive goal for most patients. Some reasons for the inability of many women to achieve this goal include insufficient patient education, financial

constraints, lifestyle factors, availability of resources, and variability of provider's knowledge and emphasis on diabetes care. The primary care providers, who manage the vast
majority of patients with diabetes, have the
greatest opportunity to implement strategies
that will improve care and outcomes (2).

This chapter focuses on the care of women
with diabetes. Although treatment goals do
not differ significantly between the genders,
special considerations for the prevention, treatment, and follow-up of diabetes in women
arise from hormonal, psychological, and social
differences between women and men.

Epidemiology

Approximately 11 million people in the United
States have diabetes (3). Approximately 90% of
these have non–insulin-dependent diabetes mellitus (NIDDM). This figure may underestimate
the total number because screening programs
have determined that only half the individuals
with NIDDM are actually identified; the rest are
undiagnosed, and may remain so for years.

Insulin-dependent diabetes mellitus (IDDM),
on the other hand, does not have a prolonged
preclinical period and is easily diagnosed, so
prevalence rates are more easily determined.
Six percent of the population carries a diagnosis of diabetes (either NIDDM or IDDM), so a
practice of 3000 patients may include approximately 200 patients with diabetes, 20 of whom
will have IDDM. If this hypothetical practice
accurately reflects the population, minorities
will be well represented because NIDDM is
more common among African-American, Hispanic, and Native-American people than
among whites (3). Prevalence rates do not differ significantly between the sexes. However,
because the prevalence of diabetes increases
with age, and because women live longer than
men, the number of women affected as the population ages far surpasses the number of men.

The United States spends approximately
$90 billion caring for people with diabetes an-
nually (4). Most of these dollars are used to
treat the complications of diabetes, including
renal failure caused by nephropathy, amputations caused by neuropathy, and visual impairment because of retinopathy. If good glycemic
control can prevent or delay the complications
of both IDDM and NIDDM, an assumption
supported by the results of the Diabetes Control and Complications Trial (DCCT) (1, 5),
then early diagnosis and aggressive treatment
represent an excellent opportunity for providers
to help patients maintain good health, even in
the setting of a chronic disease, and to decrease the economic burden of diabetes.

Classification and Pathophysiology

Insulin-Dependent Diabetes Mellitus

Hyperglycemia may result from several different processes. In IDDM, or type I diabetes, autoimmune destruction of the pancreatic islet
cells results in absolute insulin deficiency (6).
As a result, glucose transport into insulin-
sensitive tissues fails to occur, and both fatty acid
breakdown within adipose tissue and hepatic
glucose production accelerate. The outcome of
these processes is hyperglycemia and ketosis.
Patients are usually under 30 years of age at diagnosis, but pancreatic destruction may occur
at any age and result in IDDM. Besides the autoimmune destruction of insulin-producing
islet cells, loss of islet cell function may result
from other causes including trauma, chronic
pancreatitis, or viral insults.

Non–Insulin-Dependent Diabetes Mellitus

In NIDDM, or type II diabetes, hyperglycemia
arises from resistance to the action of insulin
(7). In the liver, this results in excessive hepatic glucose production. In insulin-sensitive
tissues such as muscle, insulin resistance impairs glucose use. Inhibition of insulin's activity may occur at a number of cellular locations

in NIDDM, and the sites may vary from individual to individual. Examples of these defects include impaired insulin binding to cell surface receptors, decreased number of available glucose transporter molecules to move glucose across the cell membrane, and ineffective post receptor signal transduction.

Although NIDDM is a heterogeneous disorder at the cellular level, the clinical expression of these defects is similar. In the preclinical phase of NIDDM, maintenance of normoglycemia requires increased pancreatic insulin production. When insulin secretion fails to overcome cellular resistance to insulin action, hyperglycemia develops and the clinical phase of diabetes begins. Though blood glucoses are elevated at this point, years may pass before hyperglycemia produces symptoms significant enough to prompt medical consultation. Insulin levels measured during these early phases of the disease will be high. This prolonged hyperinsulinemia may contribute to the macrovascular morbidity (e.g., coronary artery disease) associated with NIDDM. With persistent hyperglycemia pancreatic insulin production eventually diminishes, and later in the disease process, insulin levels may be inappropriately normal or low.

NIDDM typically occurs in patients over 40 years of age. However, a group of children and young adults with NIDDM has recently been described (8). In this variant of diabetes, formerly called maturity onset diabetes of youth, a specific defect in the enzyme glucokinase causes hyperglycemia. This diagnosis must be distinguished from IDDM that more commonly affects this age group, as the treatment is quite different.

Gestational Diabetes Mellitus

Pregnancy can induce an insulin-resistant state that may ultimately result in gestational diabetes mellitus (GDM). Rising human placental lactogen levels exert the most profound inhibitory effect on insulin action, but high basal progesterone, estrogen, prolactin, and cortisol levels also contribute (9). GDM affects approximately 3% of pregnant women. Although it resolves after delivery of the fetus, as many as 60% of women with GDM will develop overt NIDDM within the next 20 years, and 90% will have GDM with a subsequent pregnancy (9). Affected women, then, represent a population of young people at high risk for future disease development, and, thus, are good candidates for health measures aimed at reducing that risk.

Drug-Exacerbated Diabetes Mellitus

Certain drugs exacerbate insulin resistance and may unmask NIDDM in patients with impaired glucose tolerance or asymptomatic diabetes. Among the most common offenders are the glucocorticoids, beta-blockers, diuretics, and nicotinic acid (niacin). Oral contraceptives have variable effects on glucose tolerance, depending on composition.

Impaired Glucose Tolerance

Patients with impaired glucose tolerance (IGT) have high blood glucose levels, but do not meet the diagnostic criteria for NIDDM. Approximately 25% of patients with IGT will go on to develop NIDDM (10), and this conversion may occur with the development of other risk factors such as advancing age, obesity, or pregnancy. Early recognition of this metabolic derangement is important because it has been identified as a risk factor for coronary heart disease (CHD) (11). Because IGT produces no symptoms, and screening for it is impractical, most cases will remain undiagnosed. Detection, then, will depend on vigilance for the conditions commonly associated with IGT, and an awareness of their potential link.

Like patients with early NIDDM, patients with IGT have insulin resistance and hyperinsulinemia. In addition, many patients with IGT have risk factors for coronary heart disease (CHD), including hypertension, hypertriglyceridemia, and decreased high-density lipoprotein (HDL) levels (12). Some investigators have proposed a causal link between the elevated insulin levels and these CHD risk factors, and have called the collection of findings "Syndrome X" (13), whether insulin induces the metabolic derangements, the syndrome does identify a subgroup of patients for whom preventive therapy aimed at reducing CHD risk may prove particularly useful. Viewed from another perspective, hypertension and dyslipidemia suggest the possibility that IGT and hyperinsulinemia may be present, and the presence of these can be used to identify patients who may benefit from interventions to reduce the risk of developing diabetes and CHD.

Polycystic Ovary Syndrome: An Insulin Resistant State

Recent work by Andrea Dunaif's group has identified a group of young women in whom there is an unexpectedly high prevalence of insulin resistance and undiagnosed diabetes. These women have polycystic ovary syndrome (PCOS), a syndrome characterized by chronic anovulation and hyperandrogenemia. Clinically, patients have irregular menses and hirsutism. Dunaif has shown that women with PCOS exhibit the hallmarks of insulin resistance when subjected to metabolic studies (14, 15). Specifically, they require more insulin to dispose of a glucose load and have increased hepatic glucose output (15). This pattern occurs in both lean and obese subjects, suggesting a defect beyond that conferred by obesity alone. Obesity compounds the insulin resistance of PCOS, as demonstrated in Dunaif's screening studies in which she discovered that 20% of obese women with PCOS have undiagnosed NIDDM when subjected to standard glucose tolerance testing (14).

Although the etiology of PCOS is unknown, some evidence suggests a relationship between hyperinsulinemia and hyperandrogenemia. In vitro insulin can stimulate androgen production by ovarian stroma (16), suggesting a plausible and possibly causal link between the two phenomena. Some studies have indicated that these patients are more likely to develop gestational diabetes (17), and as they age, overt diabetes, hypertension, and dyslipidemia (18).

Patients should receive appropriate preventive counseling regarding diet and exercise.

Diagnosis

The diagnostic criteria for diabetes mellitus have recently been published by the American Diabetes Association (ADA) in their Clinical Practice Recommendations 1995 (19).

Diagnosis of Insulin-Dependent Diabetes Mellitus

IDDM usually presents abruptly, with symptoms developing over a period of days to weeks. Polyuria, polydipsia, polyphagia, fatigue, weight loss, and blurry vision develop because of persistent hyperglycemia. Ketosis does not develop because the pancreas can produce even small amounts of insulin. Thus, hyperglycemia without ketosis may occur initially, providing a window in which a diagnosis can be made and treatment initiated before the development of ketoacidosis. Once absolute insulin deficiency develops, however, lipolysis is no longer inhibited. Ketone body production proceeds unabated, and ketoacidosis results.

Symptoms of diabetic ketoacidosis include nausea, vomiting, and abdominal pain besides the symptoms of hyperglycemia. IDDM most commonly affects people under 30 years of age. The diagnosis can be made in the presence of the classic symptoms of diabetes and a random plasma glucose over 200 mg/dL (19). Alternatively, a fasting plasma glucose greater than 140 mg/dL twice and two oral glucose tolerance tests showing a two-hour plasma glucose over 200 mg/dL, and at least one intervening glucose over 200 mg/dL, will secure the diagnosis.

In the presence of even mild ketosis, urine ketones will be present and should prompt immediate therapy. The presence of anti-insulin and anti-islet cell antibodies is not required for the diagnosis, but may be useful in predicting whether a new diagnosis of diabetes in a young adult will evolve into IDDM or NIDDM.

Diagnosis of Non–Insulin-Dependent Diabetes Mellitus

In contrast to IDDM, NIDDM may develop over a long period of time and may remain asymptomatic for years. However, once blood glucose rises consistently above the renal threshold for glycosuria (approximately 180 mg/dL), polyuria, polydipsia, and polyphagia develop. Blurry vision occurs when the chronically hyperosmolar state induces reversible shape changes in the lens. A random blood glucose over 200 mg/dL in the presence of the classic symptoms of diabetes will secure the diagnosis (19). A fasting plasma glucose over 140 mg/dL twice may also be used. Alternatively, a single fasting plasma glucose greater that 140 mg/dL *and* two oral glucose tolerance tests showing a 2-hour value greater than 200 mg/dL and one intervening value over 200 mg/dL will make the diagnosis. These criteria apply to all age groups, and therefore pertain to the diagnosis of NIDDM in children.

Diagnosis of Gestational Diabetes Mellitus

Because hyperglycemia may exert a toxic effect on the fetus before producing symptoms in the mother, screening for gestational diabetes is a routine part of prenatal care (9). Screening usually takes place at 24 to 28 weeks of gestation (9), although earlier screening may be justified in high-risk patients, such as those with PCOS, a prior history of GDM, or delivery of an infant weighing greater than 9 lbs. The screening test consists of a 50-g oral glucose load followed by a 1-hour plasma glucose determination. This value should be less than 140 mg/dL. Patients with values exceeding this

Table 15.1.1. Diagnosis of Diabetes

IDDM	> 200 mg/dL in a random plasmaglucose
	or
	FPG >140 mg/dL two times
	OGTT 2-hour PG >200 mg/dL and random PG>200 mg/dL
NIDDM	random PG > 200 mg/dL in a patient with symptoms
	or
	FPG > 149 mg/dL twice
	or
	FPG >140 mg/dL once and
	OGTT 2-hour PG >200 mg/dL and
	Random PG >200 mg/dL
Gestational	>140 mg/dL Screening: one-hour plasma glucose after a 50 g oral glucose load Diagnosis: oral glucose tolerance test
	Fasting (FPG)> 105 mg/dL
	1-hour PG > 190 mg/dL
	2-hour PG > 165 mg/dL
	3-hour PG > 145 mg/dL
Impaired glucose tolerance	FPG < 140 mg/dL and
	2-hour PG is between 140 mg/dL and 200 mg/dL
	and one random >200 mg/dL

FPG-fasting plasma glucose; PG = plasma glucose; OGTT = oral glucose tolerance test.

should undergo a formal oral glucose tolerance test (OGTT). If the glucose at any time during the OGTT exceeds the following normals, a diagnosis of GDM can be made: fasting plasma glucose (FPG) 105 mg/dL, 1-hour PG 190 mg/dL, 2-hour PG 165 mg/dL, and 3-hour PG 145 mg/dL (Table 15.1.1) (9, 19).

Impaired Glucose Tolerance

An OGTT, usually done to rule out diabetes, provides the parameters for the diagnosis of impaired glucose tolerance. When the FPG is less than 140 mg/dL, the 2-hour PG is between 140 mg/dL and 200 mg/dL and one intervening value exceeds 200 mg/dL, IGT is diagnosed (19).

Screening

Except for pregnant women, few people in clinical practice undergo true screening for diabetes. Most cases are discovered during an investigation of symptoms, or on blood work done for another reason. However, the staggering estimates for the number of undiagnosed cases of NIDDM call for a reconsideration of these practices. The ADA recommends that the following patients undergo screening with a fasting plasma glucose: individuals at high risk for developing diabetes, patients with disorders such as retinopathy, nephropathy, or neuropathy that might be a consequence of undiagnosed diabetes, and patients with the classic symptoms of diabetes (19).

In addition, pregnant women should undergo screening as described above. Markers of risk for the development of diabetes include (a) a family history of NIDDM, (b) body weight over 120% of ideal, (c) previous delivery of an infant weighing over 9 lbs, (d) a history of GDM, (e) impaired glucose tolerance, (f) being Native American, Hispanic or African-American, (g) hypertension, or (h) hyperlipidemia. Because of its association with insulin resistance, PCOS may ultimately be added to the list of risk factors for diabetes. In addition, because some patients with diabetes give a history of reactive hypoglycemia years prior to diagnosis (an early indication of impaired insulin secretory kinetics), this condition should prompt early vigilance for NIDDM.

Oral glucose tolerance testing is rarely required, but is useful in a few circumstances. First, when fasting or random plasma sampling gives variable results, as may occur early in the disease, an OGTT can clarify the diagnosis. Second, a 5-hour OGTT, measuring glucose *and* insulin levels can be used to document hyperinsulinemia in young women with PCOS. Occasionally, diabetes will be diagnosed. However, even a study showing normal glucose levels and elevated insulin levels is useful, because it establishes the urgency of intervention with diet and exercise, and illustrates to the patient the nature of her condition.

For optimum accuracy, an OGTT must be done after an overnight fast and in a healthy, "nonstressed" state. Intercurrent illness or the inactivity and stress associated with hospitalization may temporarily raise blood glucose.

Recent efforts to develop strategies for the prevention of IDDM have resulted in the development of screening tests for the presymptomatic phase of the disease. Anti-islet cell antibodies (ICA), present years before clinical IDDM, can identify patients who may be at risk for IDDM and are currently used as an initial screening tool in research studies (20). However, although the presence of the antibody increases the likelihood that IDDM will develop, it does not ensure it nor does it predict the timing of disease progression. In addition, an ICA-positive individual may revert to ICA-negative status over time. Despite these ambiguities, the blood test does have a place in clinical practice. First-degree relatives of patients with IDDM who may wish to participate in clinical trials should be tested. Those who screen positive should be referred to study centers for further testing and possible inclusion in IDDM prevention trials (21).

Therapy

Treatment Goals

The Diabetes Control and Complications Trial (DCCT), completed in 1993, provides clear and compelling evidence that the long-term microvascular complications of IDDM can be delayed or prevented by tight glucose control (1). In this study, intensive diabetes management resulted in a reduction in hemoglobin AIC, a measure of average blood glucose over the preceding 8 to 12 weeks, from approximately 9 to 7%. This drop in hemoglobin AIC reflected a decrease in average blood glucose from approximately 230 to 155 mg/dL. Over the 10-year course of the study, this degree of improvement in glycemic control resulted in a 76% reduction in the incidence of retinopathy, a 34% drop in the appearance of microalbuminuria, an indicator of nephropathy, and a 69% fall in the incidence of clinical neuropathy. If patients had mild retinopathy at the beginning of the study, intensive therapy reduced the risk of progression by 54%.

Further analysis of the findings showed that there was not a threshold below which benefits did not accrue. That is, the lower the average blood glucose, the greater the benefit. The study supports the hypothesis that high blood glucoses are responsible for the microvascular complications of diabetes, and argues for the application of the results to the far more prevalent disease, NIDDM. Insufficient data exist to determine whether improved glycemic control will result in a reduced risk for the macrovascular complications of diabetes, CHD, PVD, and stroke (22). Studies are underway to answer this important question (23, 24).

Thus, based on the available data, all patients with diabetes should aim for blood glucose as close to normal as possible to prevent or delay the microvascular complications of diabetes. However, coexisting medical conditions and lifestyle factors will influence an individual's goal blood glucose range. In the DCCT, for instance, hypoglycemia occurred with increasing frequency as the average blood glucose decreased (1). Thus, patients with hypoglycemic unawareness, use of beta-blockers, CHD, CVD, or a seizure disorder may want to adjust their target blood glucose range upward. Similarly, patients whose access to food is erratic, either by physiology (e.g., gastroparesis) or lifestyle (e.g., adolescence, demanding or rotating work schedule), may do poorly with strict attempts to normalize blood glucose. Thus, the therapeutic goals must adapt to an individual's physiology and lifestyle, with the aim of achieving the best glycemic control possible in the face of those limitations.

In clinical practice, achieving good blood glucose control depends only partially on the prescribed regimen. How that prescription is carried out in the women's everyday life will significantly determine the outcome. Consequently, it is particularly important to include education in the care plan of all women with diabetes. A multidisciplinary team, which can include a nurse, a nurse-educator, nutritionist, social worker and exercise physiologist, provides a useful mechanism to both educate and uncover lifestyle factors that may be preventing optimal glucose control.

Treatment Strategies

Diet, exercise, and medication form the basis of all treatment plans for people with diabetes. Although providers may feel most comfortable with their knowledge of medications, an understanding of each element of the triad expands the options for overcoming barriers to better glycemic control. Further, informed reiteration of the principles and their importance by the provider can contribute greatly to a woman's willingness to follow through with difficult lifestyle adjustments.

Nutritional Principles
In its most recent position statement outlining nutritional guidelines for people with IDDM

and NIDDM (25), the ADA made the following recommendations. First, women should achieve and maintain ideal body weight. However, recognizing the high failure rates in "curing" obesity and the negative psychological consequences of repeated failures to lose weight, modest weight reduction in obese women with diabetes can be encouraged with the expectation that blood glucose and lipids will improve. Second, 20 to 35 g of fiber should be included in the daily diet. Third, sucrose may be incorporated into the diet without a dramatic deterioration in blood glucoses. This is especially true for women who maintain good glycemic control.

Finally, the caloric composition of the diet should be structured around the following guidelines (see Table 15.1.2), with individual diets being tailored to meet additional goals of weight loss or cholesterol reduction. Of the total daily calories, saturated fat should provide less than 10%, polyunsaturated fats less than 10%, protein sources 10 to 20%, and carbohydrates and monounsaturated fats together should provide 60 to 70%. These differ from the prior ADA guidelines published in 1986 and allow for more variability in the amount of carbohydrate and monounsaturated fats. The previous guidelines called for 60% of calories in carbohydrates. The changes reflect recent research showing that diets higher in monounsaturated fats do not raise plasma cholesterol, and may have a beneficial effect on serum triglycerides and glucoses when compared to high carbohydrate diets (26). The new guidelines allow for

flexibility. Limiting fat intake to less than 30% of the total daily calories with fewer than 10% being saturated fats, as recommended in the 1986 ADA guidelines and by the National Cholesterol Education Program (27) and in Dietary Guidelines for Americans (28), remains useful for women with elevated LDL cholesterol and obesity. Women with hypertriglyceridemia may benefit from addition of monounsaturated fats to the diet.

Exercise and Diabetes

The benefits of exercise for women with IDDM and NIDDM include improved cardiovascular fitness and psychological well-being. In addition, exercise reduces insulin resistance, aids weight loss, and reduces blood sugar in women with NIDDM. It does not generally improve glycemic control in women with IDDM. However, the increased caloric demands may result in a decrease in blood glucose if not anticipated by increasing food consumption, decreasing insulin dose, or both (29). After appropriate screening for participation in an exercise program, which will include an evaluation for heart disease, neuropathy, uncontrolled hypertension, retinopathy, and other conditions requiring treatment prior to exercise, women should be encouraged to perform 20 to 45 minutes of moderate aerobic exercise at least 3 days a week. Walking is an excellent form of exercise and a relatively easy one to initiate and sustain. For safety and year-round convenience, walking in a mall provides a good location for many people. Blood glucose

Table 15.1.2. Nutritional Guidelines for People with IDDM and NIDDM

Food Source	Total Daily Caloric Intake (%)
Protein (mixture of animal and vegetable source)	10 to 20
Saturated fat	<10
Polyunsaturated fat	<10
Carbohydrate + monounsaturated fat	60 to 70
Total	100

* Adapted from ADA Clinical Practice Recommendations 1995

monitoring prior to and after exercise gives women confidence that they will not experience hypoglycemia during exercise, and provides critical positive reinforcement when blood glucoses are observed to decrease. Blood glucoses should be greater than 100 mg/dL and less than 300 mg/dL prior to beginning exercise.

Medical Therapies

IDDM. Women with IDDM require insulin to sustain life. No other hypoglycemic agent, including the sulfonylureas and metformin, currently has a place in the treatment of IDDM. Thus, therapeutic choices revolve around the kind of insulin, the timing and frequency of dosing, and the mode of delivery. Human insulin has essentially replaced the use of beef, pork, and beef-pork insulins. The antigenicity of the latter preparations can make absorption from subcutaneous tissue unpredictable (30).

Human insulin is produced through recombinant DNA technology (Humulin) or by substituting a single amino acid on the B chain of purified pork insulin so that its sequence matches that of human insulin (Novolin). Regular insulin has a rapid onset of action, with peak effect 2 to 5 hours after injection. NPH insulin, modified by the addition of protamine to prolong its action, has a peak effect at 4 to 12 hours. Lente insulin, to which zinc has been added to slow its effect, peaks in 6 to 15 hours. It is essentially interchangeable with NPH, with the important exception that mixtures of Lente and regular are unstable and must be used immediately after mixing. Ultralente human insulin consists of slowly dissociating zinc-insulin crystals and has the longest time-to-peak, 8 to 20 hours. However, because this does not differ greatly from Lente insulin and absorption may be more unpredictable, its use is limited (31). Novolin 70/30 is a premixed insulin that contains 70% NPH and 30% regular; it is useful for women who cannot mix their own insulin or require this specific distribution of rapid and long acting insulin. The insulin pump requires the use of a stabilized, buffered insulin (Velosulin insulin).

Most women with IDDM require between 0.3 and 0.6 U/kg of insulin daily. Dosing regimens can be tailored based on blood glucose responses and lifestyle. Single-shot regimens rarely provide adequate control, and at least two shots per day are recommended. Regimens entailing multiple daily injections offer flexibility in timing of meals, may allow for better glycemic control, and are usually well tolerated by women. The insulin pump, which provides a continuous infusion of buffered regular insulin and meal boluses on demand, offers the most flexibility. Suggested regimens are in Table 15.1.3.

Table 15.1.3. Suggested Regimens for Insulin Use in IDDM

1. Split-mix: regular+NPH (or Lente) ac breakfast and ac supper, with 2/3 of the total daily dose given in the am and 1/3 given in the pm. As an initial estimate, 1/3 of the am dose can be given as regular and 2/3 as NPH. In the evening, the dose can be divided the same way, or, if the evening meal is large, 1/2 regular and 1/2 NPH.
2. Regular+NPH (or Lente) ac breakfast, regular ac supper, NPH (or Lente) at bedtime. Two thirds of the total daily dose is given in the morning, and the remaining 1/3 is split as in #1 above, i.e., 1/3 to 1/2 as Regular ac supper, 1/2 to 2/3 as NPH (or Lente) at bedtime.
3. Regular ac meals (breakfast, lunch and dinner), NPH (or Lente) at bedtime.
4. Regular buffered insulin administered continuously via an insulin pump with premeal boluses of Regular delivered via the pump.

Injections should be given 30 minutes prior to meals and may be given in a rotating pattern in the abdomen. Injection in the arms, thighs, or buttocks may also be used; absorption from these sites is slower, and duration of effect may be longer. Adjustments in insulin dose or meal plan should be based on home blood glucose monitoring results.

NIDDM. Effective treatment of NIDDM may not require insulin use. With creative and concomitant use of diet, exercise, and oral agents, a need for exogenous insulin may never arise. However, if a trial of these therapies fails to adequately control blood glucoses, insulin therapy should be promptly initiated. The dosing schedules described above may be used for both IDDM and NIDDM, with the exception that insulin pump is rarely used in NIDDM.

Initial and ongoing therapy for NIDDM should include efforts to reduce insulin resistance using diet and exercise. If glycemic control remains poor, as indicated by symptoms of hyperglycemia or, somewhat arbitrarily, by fasting blood glucoses greater than 160 to 180 mg/dL or a hemoglobin AlC greater than 8%, an oral agent should be started. The available agents now include glipizide and glyburide (sulfonylureas) metformin, and acarbose. Each of these is acceptable as initial drug therapy. Metformin (Glucophage), introduced in the United States in 1995, improves insulin sensitivity, decreases hepatic glucose output, and may reduce triglyceride levels. Acarbose (Precose) became available in the United States in January 1996. It reversibly inhibits alpha-glucosidases in the brush border of the small intestine. This delays absorption of carbohydrates from the small intestine and blunts the postprandial rise in blood glucose. Trials of a related agent, Miglitol, are underway in the United States at the present time. Both metformin and acarbose may be used in combination with sulfonylureas. When used alone, these agents do not precipitate hypoglycemia. Preparations and dosing information for the oral agents are shown in Table 15.1.4.

If the use of a single agent at maximal dose fails to bring blood glucoses into goal range, combination therapy may be used. Sulfonylureas (SFUs) may be combined with metformin or acarbose in standard doses. Alternatively, insulin may be added to a sulfonylurea regimen. A particularly effective strategy is to add bedtime NPH or Lente, with the goal of decreasing fasting hyperglycemia (32). If this proves inadequate, the sulfonylurea should be stopped and insulin given in one or more daily shots. Metformin and acarbose are not currently approved for use with insulin in the United States.

Monitoring Guidelines and Preventive Care

Many factors influence an individual's target blood glucose range. These include ability to tolerate hypoglycemia, likelihood that microvascular complications will develop during the remaining life span, willingness to monitor blood glucoses at home, and anticipation of pregnancy. Whatever the established level of glycemic control, some general guidelines for routine care are listed below:

1. Establish individual target range for blood glucoses. "Tight" control guidelines (used in the DCCT): ac glucoses 70 to 120 mg/dL, pc glucoses less than 180 mg/dL, and 3 am glucoses greater than 65 mg/dL. Minimally acceptable goals: ac glucoses less than 200 mg/dL

2. Eradicate the symptoms of hyperglycemia, such as blurry vision, polyuria, and polydipsia.

3. Prescribe use of a blood glucose meter. Other methods such as color test strips (BG chemstrips) or urine test strips provide useful but less accurate data.

4. Measure hemoglobin AlC every 3 to 6 months as an indicator of average glycemic control over the previous 8 to 12 weeks.

5. Refer to an ophthalmologist for yearly dilated eye exams to detect early retinopathy and prevent blindness. More frequent

Table 15.1.4. Oral Agents for the Treatment of NIDDM

Generic Name	Brand Name	Dosing range	Comments
Glipizide	Glucotrol	5.0 mg po qam to 20 mg po bid ac	Take 30 minutes before meals.
Glipizide	Glucotrol XL	5.0–20 mg po qam	Pills release drug slowly through laser-drilled hole in capsule. Therefore, capsules should not be broken. Long duration of action may decrease fasting hyperglycemia more effectively than non-XL formulation.
Glyburide	Micronase	2.5 mg po qam-10 mg po bid ac	Take 30 minutes before meals.
Glyburide	Diabeta	same as Micronase	Take 30 minutes before meals.
Glyburide	Glynase	3–6 mg po bid ac	
Acarbose	Precose	100 mg po tid is maximum dose	Start low (e.g., 25 mg po tid) and increase dose slowly. This minimizes side effects of loose stools and flatulence. Take pill with first bite of meal for best effect. May be used in combination with sulfonylureas.
Metformin	Glucophage	500–1000 mg po bid ac usual dose. Maximum dose 2500 mg/day.	Do not use if Cr>1.6 in men or 1.4 in women, if LFTs elevated, or in chronically hypoxic conditions such as COPD. Side effects of intestinal gas and loose stools usually resolve in 2–4 weeks. May be used with sulfonylureas, but not insulin. Discontinue before procedures requiring IV contrast and during hospitalizations (conditions predisposing to dehydrated state).

Data from 1995 Physician's Desk Reference

exams may be recommended by the ophthalmologist if retinopathy is seen.

6. Obtain yearly 24-hour urine microalbumin determination for all women with IDDM to detect early nephropathy.

7. Obtain 24-hour urine protein determination for women with NIDDM who have greater than 1+ protein on urine dipstick testing.

8. Refer to diabetes education program for self-management skills and nutritional counseling.

9. Control blood pressure.

10. Encourage lifestyle modifications that will make self-care easier with attention to establishing routine eating and exercise patterns, stress reduction, and family support.

Diabetes and Pregnancy

Because hyperglycemia and hypoglycemia at the time of conception and in the first trimester of pregnancy are associated with an increased risk of spontaneous abortion and congenital malformations (33), normalization of blood glucose must be achieved and sustained prior to conception, i.e., the hemoglobin AlC for women with IDDM and NIDDM should be in the normal nondiabetic range before attempting to conceive. This observation has special relevance for primary care providers. Effective patient education, provided during usual care, can alert women to the critical importance of anticipating pregnancy. Achieving blood glucose in the normal range may require intensive insulin therapy, using multiple daily injections or the insulin pump as described for IDDM. The currently available oral agents are contraindicated in pregnancy.

Maternal hyperglycemia during pregnancy correlates with fetal macrosomia (33), perhaps reflecting the influence of high fetal insulin levels, secreted in response to high ambient blood glucose, on fat deposition. Thus, women with IDDM, NIDDM, and GDM should maintain tight blood glucose control during pregnancy to minimize the risk of diabetic fetopathy. The optimal blood glucose range is actively debated. The ADA recommends initiating insulin therapy if FBG is greater than 105 mg/dL or 2-hr postprandial BG is greater than 120 mg/dL. However, at this level of control, the rates of fetal macrosomia remain as high as 20 to 50% (34, 35). Some groups recommend aggressively lowering the average blood glucose to 95 mg/dL based on the observation that this level of control produces fewer large for gestational age babies than conventional control (36).

Following delivery, most women with gestational diabetes regain normoglycemia. However, in subsequent pregnancies, about 90% will develop gestational diabetes. In addition, as many as 50% will go on to develop overt NIDDM in the next 15 to 20 years (37). For these reasons, efforts to achieve or maintain ideal body weight and healthy exercise and eating habits should continue after pregnancy. Women should undergo postpartum screening for diabetes approximately 6 weeks after delivery and subsequently receive regular follow-up for early detection of diabetes (38).

Diabetes in Elderly Women

Although the prevention of long-term microvascular complications of diabetes may wane in priority as women age, glycemic control remains important. As women age, prevention of symptomatic hyperglycemia and hypoglycemia becomes the management focus. This is especially true for women with other medical conditions such as heart disease, transient ischemic attacks, stroke, or dementia, whose symptoms may worsen with extremes of glycemia.

However, even among healthy older women, hypoglycemia is dangerous. The adrenergic "warning signs" of hypoglycemia become less pronounced with age, so that the debilitating neuroglycopenic symptoms become the predominant expression of low blood glucose. Hypoglycemia may present with confusion, seizure, change in personality, or even coma, making early treatment difficult. Generally, blood glucose should be maintained between 100 and 200 mg/dL, with individual goals based on the medical profile (39).

In addition, strategies for management should accommodate disability. For instance, women with poor vision may have difficulty seeing the insulin syringe markings well enough to accurately dose their insulin. Such women might benefit from having their weekly supply of insulin drawn up in individual syringes by a family member or home health nurse and stored in well-marked containers in the refrigerator. Arthritis may make it difficult to manipulate the syringe, necessitating the same sort of intervention. Women with cognitive or physical barriers to adequate fluid intake are at increased risk for developing a hyperglycemic hyperosmolar state. Regular blood glucose monitoring provides a mechanism for early detection and treatment.

Diabetes accelerates the development of coronary artery disease, cerebrovascular disease, and peripheral vascular disease. Management of the conditions that contribute to the risk of development or progression of these conditions continues to be important as a woman ages. Many experts recommend aggressive treatment of hyperlipidemia even in the elderly (39). Physical activity, smoking, obesity, and hypertension should also be addressed.

Diabetes and Heart Disease in Women

Cardiovascular heart disease is the leading cause of death in American women, as it is in men. Of the nearly 1 million people who will die this year from cardiovascular disease, half will be women (40, 41). Despite a commonalty between the sexes in these sobering statistics, interesting gender differences exist in CHD. For instance, women manifest the disease 10 to 15 years later than men, with a dramatic rise in incidence after menopause. Although the risk of dying from CHD steadily increases after the age of 35 for men, women continue to have a relatively low risk until menopause (42).

The female advantage disappears in the presence of diabetes. The age-adjusted relative risk for developing CHD is 2:3 in diabetic men, whereas for women the relative risk escalates to 3 to 7 (11). The reasons diabetes poses a greater threat to the cardiovascular health of diabetic women remains unclear. Data from the Rancho Bernardo study show that diabetic women have higher triglyceride levels and lower HDL cholesterol levels than nondiabetic women (43). This discrepancy is greater than that found between diabetic and nondiabetic men. Further studies are needed to clarify the unique effect of hypertriglyceridemia on CHD in women.

Strategies for Heart Disease Prevention in Diabetes

Although diabetes is a risk factor for ischemic heart disease, there is currently no data to suggest that tight blood glucose control can prevent heart disease (24). Efforts to prevent heart disease in women with diabetes must focus on the traditional modifiable risk factors, including smoking cessation, weight control, blood pressure control, and cholesterol reduction. The strategies for women and men differ only slightly. In determining goal cholesterol levels, women with diabetes should be designated "high risk," because diabetes eliminates the benefit of gender. In the National Cholesterol Education Program (NCEP) classification of risk, men and women with diabetes may be considered equal in the gender category, and assigned the higher risk associated with being male (27). Therefore, in the absence of known CHD, the goal of LDL is < 130 mg/dL for both sexes. A history of CHD drops the goal LDL to < 100 mg/dL.

In women, hormone replacement therapy (HRT) reduces LDL, and may have salutary effects on other CHD risk factors, including a reduction in blood pressure and insulin levels, and a rise in HDL cholesterol. For obese women, weight reduction should be encouraged, both for its effect on glucose control and for its beneficial effects on CHD. However, a recent study showing that weight cycling may actually increase the risk for fatal and nonfatal CHD emphasizes the prudence of recommending methods for moderate and sustained weight loss (44).

Influence of Sex Steroids on Diabetes

Postmenopausal Hormone Replacement Therapy

The "female advantage" in heart disease remains incompletely explained and has generated interest in understanding the metabolic effects of estrogen. Salutary effects of estrogen have been observed on lipoprotein metabolism, vascular wall responsiveness, and coagulation parameters. In addition, recent studies exploring the effect of estrogen on carbohydrate metabolism suggest that at postmenopausal doses HRT may improve insulin resistance and lower fasting insulin levels. If hyperinsulinemia contributes to vascular and metabolic changes that raise CHD risk, lowering insulin levels may prove to be an important benefit of HRT.

Population-based studies support a beneficial role for HRT in improving insulin resistance. Because the fasting insulin level correlates well with more formal indices of insulin resistance, it serves as a useful indicator of insulin resistance in epidemiological studies. In the Rancho Bernardo cohort, postmenopausal women on HRT had lower fasting insulin levels than either men or postmenopausal women who were not on HRT (45). During the metabolic testing for the Rancho Bernardo study, some women were found to have impaired glucose tolerance or newly detected NIDDM. Analyzing these groups separately did not change the association between HRT and improved insulin sensitivity. In Nabulsi's cross-sectional analysis, current users of HRT had lower fasting insulin and glucose concentrations than nonusers (46).

Prospective studies investigating the effect of HRT on insulin resistance have yielded similar results. In a study comparing the effects of oral versus transdermal estrogen in postmenopausal women, there were lower fasting insulin levels during treatment with both preparations when compared with levels prior to treatment (47). However, this difference only reached statistical significance in those women using transdermal estrogen. Oral conjugated equine estrogen users had a nonsignificant decrement in insulin (97.1 vs 87.5 pmol/L), but a significant decrease in fasting glucose. In the recently completed PEPI trial in which estrogen-progesterone combinations were used,

fasting insulin levels tended to be lower in women receiving active treatment with estrogen or estrogen and progesterone in combination than in women receiving placebo, but the effect did not reach statistical significance (48). Lobo et al. studied 525 women on various HRT regimens, including Premarin alone, Premarin and Provera continuously, or in a cyclic fashion. All groups had slightly lower fasting insulin and glucose levels during the treatment phase than at baseline (49). In contrast to these studies, when O'Sullivan studied nine women before and after 10 weeks of treatment with either oral or transdermal estrogen, he found that insulin sensitivity was not altered by either regimen (50).

Further studies are needed to clarify the effects of estrogen and progesterone on carbohydrate metabolism, and to establish whether the type of agent or mode of delivery significantly influence these effects. Although studies have yielded conflicting results, epidemiological data and some prospective trials suggest that HRT may actually improve insulin sensitivity in women with normal glucose metabolism, impaired glucose tolerance, and NIDDM. These data support the speculation that HRT may exert its cardioprotective effect, in part, by reducing insulin levels or decreasing insulin resistance. The Rancho Bernardo cohort of women with IGT or NIDDM provides preliminary data that glucose control may not deteriorate under the influence of HRT (as was seen with early high-dose birth control pills) and may show modest improvement (45).

Oral Contraceptive Pills

Decreased glucose tolerance occurred frequently with use of the early high-dose oral contraceptive pills (51, 52). Newer preparations contain lower doses of ethinyl estradiol and progestins, with fewer adverse effects on carbohydrate metabolism (e.g., gestodene, desogestrel, norgestimate). Long-term follow-up studies of OCP users show that they have no greater risk of developing diabetes than nonusers (53). Further, women with diabetes generally do not require higher insulin doses during pill usage, although variable clinical experiences have been reported. Although alterations in glucose homeostasis may occur in some women using OCPs, these effects are usually minor with the low-dose combination pills. Usually, women with IGT, IDDM, or NIDDM can use them without significant worsening of glycemic control.

Living with a Chronic Illness

Diabetes is a chronic condition with potentially devastating consequences. Women understand this and, not surprisingly, perceive the entire experience of living with diabetes negatively. Not only do they face the possibility of acute illness, they must also cope on a daily basis with the inconveniences and frustrations of attending to their condition. Diabetes limits flexibility. It imposes restrictions in food choices, timing of meals, exercise regimen, timing of pregnancy, and daily schedule. For many women with family obligations, there is the added burden of balancing one's own needs against those of children, a spouse, or a sick relative. The sacrifice of "personal time" that comes with parenting takes on the added specter of sacrificing personal health to keep the family functioning smoothly. Effectively dealing with these issues and translating the negative messages into positive strategies for health maintenance, can profoundly influence a woman's ability to stay healthy with diabetes. For this reason, coping strategies and barriers to self-care should be the subjects of an ongoing dialogue between provider and patient. Toward this end, it is useful to determine whether an individual responds more to a participative style ("what do you think you will realistically be able to do to solve this problem?") or an authoritative style ("you need to monitor your blood glucoses more frequently"). Encouraging active participation in problem

solving will help to create a valuable sense of control and will increase the likelihood that strategies discussed in the office will be carried out at home. Developing appropriate decision-making abilities requires extensive and thoughtful patient education, and is best accomplished with a team of providers, including nurse educators, social workers, nutritionists, and exercise physiologists, who can provide follow-up and feedback to the primary care provider.

Although diabetes is a chronic illness, the experience of living with it does have positive elements. It may baffle a patient to ask her to describe her illness in positive terms, but the exercise may provide interesting insights. The answer may be that it makes good nutrition mandatory, it encourages her to exercise when she otherwise might neglect it, or it provides a reason to take herself out of a stressful situation. Reinforcing these positive elements of diabetes can contribute greatly to a woman's ongoing health, sense of well-being, and participation in her health care.

Conclusions

Although diabetes mellitus is a chronic illness, most of the woman's longitudinal care will focus on maintaining health. This means achieving the best glycemic control possible with medication, good nutrition, appropriate exercise, psychological support, and regular screening for complications. In the primary care setting, it also means vigilance for new cases of diabetes. Women with PCOS and a history of GDM represent a group of women with increased risk at a relatively young age and should undergo close monitoring and preventive counseling. Women with diabetes should receive counseling about birth control (including OCPs) and the importance of meticulous preconception glycemic control. In women with impaired glucose tolerance or diabetes, the gender-associated protection from heart disease is lost. Prevention of heart disease should include strategies to lower LDL cholesterol below 130 (or below 100 in the presence of known CHD) and initiation of postmenopausal HRT in women without contraindications. Finally, ongoing efforts to maintain health demand psychological health and intact coping mechanisms. Psychological stresses should be evaluated and treated thoughtfully, with emphasis, wherever possible, on the positive challenges of living with diabetes.

Special Considerations for Nurse Practitioners and Physician Assistants

Understanding of diabetes as a disease process must include an understanding of the concerns of those who live with diabetes. A summary of research reveals that chronic illnesses, including diabetes, can impinge on all aspects of a woman's life, including relationships, work, and marriage, and can lead to feelings of fear, anxiety, uncertainty, and decreased self-esteem. To cope, women may try to limit the effect of diabetes on their lives so that they can live more "normally" (54). In-depth interviews of adults with IDDM revealed that having to make a conscious effort to control what is normally an automatic, unseen process (blood sugar regulation) leads to a loss of spontaneity and the presence of uncertainty about their future. Individuals with diabetes may be relaxed to vigilant in their attempts to control blood sugar and to balance their need to keep blood sugar within the normal range with their desire to avoid hypoglycemia (54).

Dietary measures are an essential component of a treatment plan and must be approached in an individualized manner. There is no single diet for diabetes. Dietary goals are tailored to the woman's lifestyle, her type of diabetes, and her previous dietary intake, which might be affected by cultural background, economic, and other resources or family preferences. Appropriate goals will match the woman's primary needs, including normalizing blood sugar, improving lipid profiles, and/or reducing weight. Women with diabetes should not have to buy specially prepared "dietetic" food or pay more for food than other people. Referring the woman to a dietician who will plan a diet that is appropriate and meshes with her needs is a wise investment of time and money. Women should know in advance if their insurance will reimburse them for the consultation (55). Social support systems can affect the outcome of dietary management, and a woman will often have to consider how her family will react to dietary changes. It is possible that some women may sacrifice their own health needs to avoid family conflict or the increased work of preparing different foods for herself (56).

Exercise programs can positively affect blood glucose levels and reduce insulin resistance. Appropriate cardiac assessment is conducted before identifying with the woman a program that meets her needs. Vigorous exercise is undertaken only if the blood glucose is 100 to 200 mg/dL and there is no ketosis, eye, or foot complications (57). Referral to an exercise physiologist is optimal.

All the details of patient education about insulin therapy cannot be presented here. If available, a diabetic educator can assist women to manage this and other aspects of care. Women and their providers will need to decide about use of reusable versus disposable syringes and proper disposal of syringes. Contingency plans should be in place for hypoglycemic episodes and the management of diabetes during illness (57).

Prevention of complications such as foot problems can be accomplished with simple techniques of systematically identifying women at risk before serious conditions occur, examining feet every 1 to 12 months depending on risks, and educating them about foot care and glucose control (58). Additionally, women and their primary care providers must realize that eye disease can be present even with good vision. Regular screening with fundal examinations in the primary care setting, and referral for screenings and care by ophthalmologists, can help prevent retinopathy. Diabetic women, who often are seeing many different providers, may need help understanding the importance of vision screening (59).

Consultation with a physician is recommended for all newly diagnosed diabetes, when switching from oral hypoglycemics to insulin, and when the woman is seriously out of control, not responding to conventional insulin therapy, or experiencing increased problems and complications (58). Referral to appropriate specialists is made when indicated. Social services may also be needed, as well as support from local community groups (60).

The woman with diabetes has to be the main manager of her illness and must be an active participant in decisions made about care. Providers who go beyond a biomedical perspective of the disease to understanding the woman's experience in living with it will ultimately be more successful (54).

References

1. The Diabetes Control and Complications Trial Research Group. The effect of intensive treatment of diabetes on the development and progression of long-term complications in insulin-dependent diabetes mellitus. N Engl J Med 1993;329:977–986.
2. Mazze RS, Etzwiler DD, Strock E, et al. Staged diabetes management. Diabetes Care 1994;17:56–66.
3. Bennett RH. Epidemiology of diabetes mellitus. In: Rifkin H, Porte D, eds. Ellenburg and Rifkin's Diabetes Mellitus: Theory and Practice. New York: Elsevier, 1990:357–377.
4. Rubin RJ, Altman WM, Mendelson DN. Health care expenditures for people with diabetes mellitus, 1992. J Clin Endocrinol Metab 1994;78:809A–809F.
5. Nathan D. Do results from the diabetes control and complications trial apply in NIDDM? Diabetes Care 1995;18:251–257.
6. Palmer JP, Lernmark A. Pathophysiology of type I (insulin dependent) diabetes. In: Rifkin H, Porte D, eds. Ellenburg and Rifkin's Diabetes Mellitus: Theory and Practice. New York: Elsevier, 1990:414–435.
7. Kahn SE, Porte D. Pathophysiology of type II (non-insulin-dependent) diabetes mellitus: implications for treatment. In: Rifkin H, Porte D, eds. Ellenburg and Rifkin's Diabetes Mellitus: Theory and Practice. New York: Elsevier, 1990:436–456.
8. Winter WE, Maclaren NK, Riley WJ, et al. Maturity-onset diabetes of youth in black Americans. N Engl J Med 1987;316:285–291.
9. Jovanovic-Peterson L, Peterson C. Pregnancy in the diabetic woman: guidelines for a successful outcome. Endocrinol Metab Clin North Am 1992;21:433–456.
10. Lebovitz H, ed. Physician's Guide to Non-Insulin Dependent (Type II) Diabetes; Diagnosis and Treatment. 2nd ed. Alexandria, VA: American Diabetes Association, 1988.
11. Manson JE, Tosteson H, Ridker PM, Satterfield S, Herbert P, O'Connor GT, et al. The primary prevention of myocardial infarction. N Engl J Med 326:1406–1416.
12. Donahue RP. The insulin resistance syndrome (syndrome X) and risk factors for coronary heart disease: an epidemiologic overview. Endocrinologist 1994; 4112–4116.
13. Karam JH. Type II diabetes and syndrome X: pathogenesis and glycemic management. Endocrinol Metab Clin North Am 1992;21:329–350.
14. Dunaif A, Graf M, Mandel J, Laumas V, et al. Characterization of groups of hyperandrogenic women with acanthosis nigricans, impaired glucose tolerance and/or hyperinsulinemia. J Clin Endocrinol Metab 1987;65:499–507.
15. Dunaif A, Segal KR, Futterweit W, Dobrjansky A. Profound peripheral insulin resistance, independent of obesity, in polycystic ovary syndrome. Diabetes 1989;38:1165–1174.
16. Barbieri RL, Makris A, Randall RW, et al. Insulin stimulates androgen accumulation in incubations of ovarian stroma obtained from women with hyperandrogenism. J Clin Endocrinol Metab 1986;62:904–910.
17. Lanzone A, Caruso A, Di Simone N, et al. Polycystic ovary disease: a risk factor for gestational diabetes? J Reprod Med 1995;40:312–316.
18. Dahlgren E, Johansson S, Lindstedt G, et al. Women with polycystic ovary syndrome wedge resected in 1956 to 1965: a long-term follow-up focusing on natural history and circulating hormones. Fertil Steril 1992;57:505–513.
19. American Diabetes Association. Office guide to diagnosis and classification of diabetes mellitus and other categories of glucose intolerance. Diabetes Care 1995;18(suppl 1):4.
20. Muir A, Schatz DA, Maclaren NK. The pathogenesis, prediction, and prevention of insulin-dependent diabetes mellitus. Endocrinol Metab Clin North Am 1992;21:199–220.
21. American Diabetes Association. Prevention of type I diabetes mellitus. Diabetes Care 1995;18(suppl 1):42.

22. Klein R. Hyperglycemia and microvascular and macrovascular disease in diabetes. Diabetes Care 1995;18:258–268.

23. Abraira C, Colwell JA, Nuttall FQ, et al. Veteran's Affairs cooperative study on glycemic control and complications in type II diabetes (VA CSDM): results of the completed feasibility trial. Diabetes Care 1995;18:1113–1123.

24. UKPDS Group: UK Prospective Diabetes Study. Complications in newly diagnosed type 2 diabetic patients and their association with clinical and biochemical risk factors. Diabetes Research 1990;13:1–11.

25. American Diabetes Association. Nutrition recommendations and principles for people with diabetes mellitus. Diabetes Care 1995;18(suppl 1):16–19.

26. Bantle J. Current recommendations regarding the dietary treatment of diabetes mellitus. Endocrinologist 1994;4:189–195.

27. Expert Panel on Detection, Evaluation, and Treatment of High Blood Cholesterol in Adults. Summary of the second report of the National Cholesterol Education Program (NCEP) expert panel on detection, evaluation, and treatment of high blood cholesterol in adults (adult treatment panel II). JAMA 1993;269:3015–3023.

28. U.S. Department of Agriculture, U.S. Department of Health and Human Services. Nutrition and your health: dietary guidelines for Americans. 3rd ed. Hyattsville, MD: USDA's Human Nutrition Information Service, 1990.

29. American Diabetes Association. Diabetes mellitus and exercise. Diabetes Care 1995:18(suppl 1):28.

30. Galloway JA, deShazo RD. Insulin chemistry and pharmacology: insulin allergy, resistance, and lipodystrophy. In: Rifkin H, Porte D, eds. Diabetes Mellitus: Theory and Practice. 4th ed. New York: Elsevier, 1990:497–513.

31. Nolte M. Insulin therapy in insulin-dependent (type-I) diabetes mellitus. Endocrinol Metab Clin North Am 1992;21:281–305.

32. Yki-Järvinen H, Kauppila M, Kujansuu E, et al. Comparison of insulin regimens in patients with non-insulin dependent diabetes mellitus. N Engl J Med 1992;327:1426–1433.

33. Healy K, Jovanovic-Peterson L, Peterson CM. Pancreatic disorders of pregnancy. Endocrinol Metab Clin North Am 1995;24:73–101.

34. Jacobson JD, Cousins L. A population-based study of maternal and perinatal outcome in patients with gestational diabetes. Am J Obstet Gynecol 1989;161:981.

35. Philipson EH, Kalhan SC, Rosen MG, et al. Gestational diabetes mellitus: is further improvement necessary? Diabetes 1985;34(suppl 2):55.

36. Langer O, Berkus J, Brustman L, et al. Glycemic control in gestational diabetes mellitus. How tight is tight enough: small for gestational age versus large for gestational age? Am J Obstet Gynecol 1989;161:646

37. Jovanovic-Peterson L, Peterson CM. Pregnancy in the diabetic woman. Guidelines for a successful outcome. Endocrinol Metab Clin North Am 1992;21:433–456.

38. American Diabetes Association. Gestational diabetes mellitus. Diabetes Care 1995;18(suppl 1):24–25.

39. Singh I, Marshall MC. Diabetes mellitus in the elderly. Endocrinol Metab Clin North Am 1995;24:255–272.

40. Gura T. Estrogen: key player in heart disease among women. Science 1995;269:771–773.

41. National Center for Health Statistics. Monthly Vital Statistics Report 1992;40:1–47.

42. Gorodeski GI, Utian WH. Epidemiology and risk factors of cardiovascular disease in postmenopausal women. In: Lobo RA, ed. Treatment of the Postmenopausal Woman: Basic and Clinical Aspects. New York: Raven.

43. Barrett-Connor E. Diabetes mellitus, hypertriglyceridemia, and heart disease risk in women. Int J Fertil 1992;37(suppl 2):72–82.

44. Lissner L, Odell PM, D'Agostino RB, et al. Variability of body weight and health outcomes in the Framingham population. N Engl J Med 1991;324:1839–1844.

45. Ferrara A, Barrett-Connor E, Wingard DL, et al. Sex differences in insulin levels in older adults and the effect of body size, estrogen replacement therapy, and glucose tolerance status: the Rancho Bernardo Study, 1984–1987. Diabetes Care 1995;18:220–225.

46. Nabulsi AA, Folsom AR, White A, et al. Association of hormone-replacement therapy with various cardiovascular risk factors in postmenopausal women. N Engl J Med 1993;328:1069–1075.

47. Cagnacci A, Soldani R, Luigi P, et al. Effects of low doses of transdermal 17β estradiol on carbohydrate metabolism in postmenopausal women. J Clin Endocrinol Metab 1992;74:1396–1400.

48. The Writing Group for the PEPI Trial. Effects of estrogen or estrogen/progestin regimens on heart disease risk factors in postmenopausal women. JAMA 1995;273:199–208.

49. Lobo RA, Pickar JH, Wild RA, et al. Metabolic impact of adding medroxyprogesterone acetate to conjugated estrogen therapy in postmenopausal women. Obstet Gynecol 1994;84:987–995.

50. O'Sullivan AJ, Ho KKY. A comparison of the effects of oral and transdermal estrogen replacement on insulin sensitivity in postmenopausal women. J Clin Endocrinol Metab 1995;80:1783–1788.

51. Sondheimer SJ. Metabolic effects of the birth control pill. Clin Obstet Gynecol 1981;24:927–941.

52. Sondheimer SJ. Update on the metabolic effects of steroidal contraceptives. Endocrinol Metab Clin North Am 1991;20:911–923.

53. Duffy TJ, Ray R. Oral contraceptive use: prospective follow-up of women with suspected glucose intolerance. Contraception 1984;30:197–208.

54. Callaghan DC, Williams A. Living with diabetes: issues for nursing practice. J Advanced Nurs 1994;20:132–139.

55. Friesin J, Pi-Sunyer FX, Thom SL, Wishner K. Questions and answers on diets for diabetics. Contemp Nurse Pract 1995;1:44–46, 48–50.

56. Eriksson BS, Rosenquist U. Social support and glycemic control in non-insulin dependent diabetes mellitus patients: gender differences. Women Health 1993;20:59–70.

57. Uphold CR, Graham MV. Clinical Guidelines in Family Practice. Gainesville, FL: Barmarrae, 1993: 115–128.

58. Dorgan MB, Birke JA, Moretto JA, Patout CA, Rehm KB. Performing foot screening for diabetic patients. Am J Nurs 1995;95:32–37.

59. Beinkowski J. An overview of the progression of diabetic retinopathy with treatment recommendations. Nurse Practitioner 1994;19:50–58.

60. O'Mara E. Type I diabetes mellitus. In: Star WL, Lommell LL, Shannon MT, eds. Women's Primary Health Care. Washington, DC: American Nurses' Association, 1995:10-25–10-32.

15.2

Thyroid Disease

William J. Hueston

Introduction

Thyroid disorders are among the more common endocrine abnormalities in women. Thyroid disorders can affect many elements of a woman's life, including altering menstruation and fertility, mimicking depression or other psychiatric disorders, and complicating pregnancy and the postpartum state. The development of a clear understanding of the differential diagnosis of thyroid disorders, the evaluation of

thyroid diseases, management options for thyroid problems, and the role of thyroid diseases in pregnancy are important when offering care to women.

Epidemiology

Thyroid diseases affect 0.5% of adults (1). The prevalence of disease increases with age; 2 to 5% of patients are admitted to geriatric units having evidence of thyroid disease. Between 4 and 7% of the adults in the United States have thyroid nodules (2).

Thyroid disorders are approximately 10 times more common in women. Hyperthyroidism affect approximately 2% of all women and 0.2% of men. The risk of hypothyroidism in women is 2 to 12 times greater than in men (3). Enlargement of the thyroid in the absence of overt thyroid disease occurs in 4% of individuals (4) and occurs more commonly in women than men (5).

Evaluation of Thyroid Function

Serum Thyroid Tests

There are several different approaches to the evaluation of thyroid function (Table 15.2.1). The most straightforward test of thyroid function is the direct measurement of thyroxine (T4) and triiodothyronine (T3). Most thyroid hormone is protein bound. Over 99% of T4 and 97% of T3 are bound to albumin, thyroid-binding globulin (TBG), and other serum proteins. Pregnancy, adolescence, and use of medication such as OCPs and clofibrate influence the serum levels of TBG but not free thyroid hormone levels. Decreases in the level of TBG can occur with the use of corticosteroids or anabolic steroids, or in conditions causing loss of serum proteins such as nephrotic syndrome. Because direct levels of T4 and T3 are dependent on the changing levels of binding proteins, other more sensitive measurements are needed.

Two alternatives allow the estimation of free thyroid hormone. The first method is to measure an indirect evaluation of thyroid-binding capacity, and then combine it with total thyroid hormone measurements. This test, the T3 resin uptake (T3RU), measures the amount of exogenous radiolabeled T3 that remains after serum-binding sites have been occupied. The amount of remaining T3 decreases as the number of free binding sites increases. The value of T3RU is inversely proportional to the number of binding sites available. Thus, for euthyroid patients, when total T4 levels rise, because of increased binding capacity, the

Table 15.2.1. Thyroid Function Tests

Test			Interpretation	Comments
T4	T3RU	FTI		
NL	NL	NL	Euthyroid	Normal condition
High	Low	NL	Euthyroid	Seen with increased TBG such as with estrogen use and pregnancy
Low	High	NL	Euthyroid	Decreased TBG present as seen with anabolic steroids, steroid use, or protein deficient states
High	High	High	Hyperthyroidism	Suspect Graves' disease, hyperfunctioning nodule acute thyroiditis
Low	Low	Low	Hypothyroid	Suspect chronic thyroiditis, secondary hypothyroidism, congenital hypothyroidism
TSH— High			Decreased circulating free thyroid hormone	Primary hypothyroidism
TSH— Low			Increased circulating	Seen in hypothyroid free thyroid hormone states, secondary hypothyroidism

T4 = thyroxine; T3RU = triiodothyronine resin uptake; TSH = sensitive thyroid stimulating hormone assay; NL = normal.

T3RU drops; likewise, when T4 levels decrease as the amount of binding hormones declines, the T3RU will rise. Often the values of the total T4 and the T3RU tests are combined to form the free thyroid index (FTI) to represent normal and abnormal levels of active T4.

A second approach to evaluation of thyroid function is the measurement of a sensitive thyroid-stimulating hormone (TSH) level. TSH production by the pituitary is under negative feedback by free thyroid levels. As free thyroid levels fall, pituitary TSH production increases, and when excessive levels of free thyroid hormone are present, TSH production falls. Sensitive TSH levels can serve as a marker for hyperthyroid or hypothyroid states in patients with normal pituitary function. However, in cases of secondary or pituitary hypothyroidism (when thyroid function is depressed because of a lack of TSH), TSH levels will be low despite a hypothyroid state. Therefore, when using TSH levels as a tool to evaluate thyroid function, correlation with the patient's clinical state is necessary to avoid misdiagnosis in patient's with unsuspected pituitary dysfunction.

Thyroid Imaging

Several imaging studies are available to assess thyroid function. Some measure overall function (thyroid uptake) or offer an anatomical assessment of thyroid activity (thyroid scan), whereas others measure and define thyroid anatomy (ultrasound) (Table 15.2.2).

Thyroid scans depend upon the uptake of radioactive isotopes, usually ^{123}I or $^{99m}T_c$, by an active thyroid gland. Imaging of the uptake pattern will produce a diffusely overactive or underactive gland or produce local areas of altered activities. Areas of the gland where radioisotope uptake is decreased by 20% or more will appear "cold" or less active. Areas in

Table 15.2.2. Thyroid Imaging Studies

Test	Indications	Advantages/Limitations
Radiolabeled scans		
$^{99m}T_c$	Evaluation of hyper-thyroidism	Low absorbed radiation dose; can be used in presence of antithyroid drugs; poor choice for evaluation of thyroid masses
^{123}I	Evaluation of hyper-thyroidism or nodules	
Ultrasound	Evaluation of thyroid mass	Can distinguish cystic from solid structures; uniform solid masses most often nodule or normal tissue while hypoechoic mass more likely to be carcinoma
Fluorescent roentgenographic scanning	Evaluation of cold nodule	Measures the content of iodine in nodule; iodine content over 0.60 generally represents a benign nodule
CT scanning	Evaluation of malignant disease	Also can assess thyroid size and evaluation masses but no clear advantage over ultrasound and has greater radiation
MRI scanning	Evaluation of neck masses	Offers good resolution between thyroid, lymph nodes, and muscle; good choice for evaluation of tumor size and spread or differentiation of poorly defined neck mass

which there is increased uptake of 25% of more will appear "hot."

Localized cold lesions are typical of nonfunctioning nodules such as thyroid cancer, thyroid cysts, and localized ares of thyroiditis. Hot nodules generally are hyperfunctioning thyroid adenomas. Diffusely decreased uptake of the thyroid can be seen in thyroiditis, secondary hypothyroidism, and following radioactive ablation of the thyroid gland.

Ultrasounds may localize thyroid lesions and determine whether the lesions are solid or cystic. It is most useful in the evaluation of a cold nodule in which ultrasound can help decide whether to perform a biopsy. A solid cold hypoechoic structure has an increased likelihood of malignancy and necessitates biopsy, whereas a cystic cold structure has low malignant potential.

Thyroid Disorders

Hyperthyroidism

Clinical Symptoms and Diagnosis

In most cases of hyperthyroidism, patients will report tremulousness, anxiety, weight loss, sweats and/or heat intolerance, and possibly palpitations. Patients may also complain of dyspnea on exertion from a failure to provide adequate oxygenation to meet the demands of the high metabolic state (high-output heart failure). Physical findings can include a resting tachycardia or cardiac dysrhythmia, especially atrial fibrillation, and a fine tremor. The thyroid gland may be enlarged or normal size and can be tender. A tachycardia or atrial fibrillation on electrocardiograms may be found. Laboratory tests will be normal except for elevated thyroid functions, elevated T4, T3, and FTI, and a decrease in TSH levels.

There are various causes of hyperthyroidism. The most common of these are Graves' disease, thyroiditis, and an autonomous thyroid nodule. Because hyperthyroidism can arise from these three distinct clinical problems and the

treatment is different, a definitive cause for the hyperthyroid state should be established. The most useful tools in determining the etiology for the thyroid dysfunction is a radioactive thyroid scan and thyroid uptake.

Graves' Disease

Graves' disease is a disorder in which antithyroid antibodies are produced that stimulate production of thyroid hormone. Individuals affected by Graves' disease report gradual worsening of symptoms that include anxiety or nervousness, tremor, palpitations, weight loss, and sweats. Physical findings often include a resting tachycardia, fine tremor, and a possibly slightly enlarged and mildly tender thyroid gland. Later findings include the development of exophthalmos and, less commonly, alopecia.

The diagnosis of Graves' disease is made by the identification of circulating antithyroid antibodies in a woman with increased thyroid uptake and a normal appearing thyroid scan. Initial treatment should be aimed at minimizing the symptoms of hyperthyroidism and reducing the risk of complications from the hypermetabolic state such as myocardial infarction. Administration of propranolol or other betablockers can be useful in reducing symptoms and protecting patients from complications from thyrotoxicosis.

For the long-term treatment of Graves' disease, patients have three potential options (Table 15.2.3). These include (*a*) surgical removal of the thyroid gland, (*b*) radioactive thyroid ablation, and (*c*) antithyroid drugs, such as propylthiouracil (PTU) and methimazole that block thyroid hormone production and conversion of T4 to T3. Since the development of antithyroid agents and radioactive iodine therapy, surgical thyroidectomy is infrequently performed for Graves' disease.

For the majority of patients, radioactive iodine thyroid ablation is the treatment of choice. Radioactive iodine treatment is safe in all age groups, although it should not be used in pregnant women or in potentially fertile women

Table 15.2.3. Treatment Options for Graves' Disease

Treatment	Adult Dosage	Indications	Side Effects/Complications	Contraindications
Beta-blockers				
Propanolol	40–160 mg/d	Tachycardia Other symptoms	Wheezing, lethargy Depressed LV function	Asthma, LV dysfunction
Calcium channel				
Blockers: verapamil	240–360 mg/d	Tachycardia	Depressed LV function Constipation	LV dysfunction
Propylthiouracil (PTU) Methimazole (MTU)	100–600 mg/d 10–40 mg/d	Graves' disease (especially in children)	Rash, itching Arthralgias Hepatic dysfunction (rare), agranulocytosis (rare)	PTU preferred in pregnancy
Radioactive iodine	Varies	Nonpregnant adults with Graves'	Hypothyroidism	Pregnancy Breast-feeding
Surgery		Pregnant women allergic to antithyroid medications Graves' disease with nodular disease Patients allergic to anti- thyroid medications and unwilling to use radioactive iodine	Hypoparathyroidism (if parathyroid glands inad- vertently removed) Injury to recurrent laryngeal nerve Hypothyroidism	

who have been having unprotected intercourse. Women who are breast-feeding should also discontinue breast-feeding for 8 weeks following radioactive iodine treatment. Most patients respond to radioactive iodine treatment with a return to normal thyroid function and reduction in goiter size within 2 months of therapy. Although there are no immediate side effects of radioactive iodine treatment, hypothyroidism develops in a significant number of patients treated with this modality. Because radioactive iodine destroys thyroid tissue and may cause the release of stored thyroid hormone, patients who are susceptible to thyrotoxicosis, such as the elderly, should be pretreated with PTU or MMI to reduce the thyroid hormone levels in the gland prior to radioactive iodine treatment.

In children, there is some evidence that remission of Graves' disease is common. Up to 25% of pediatric patients enter remission every 2 years as the production of thyrotropin receptor antibodies naturally decreases. Once remission has occurred, evidence suggests that thyroid supplementation can prolong the remission. Because a significant number of patients will achieve a long-lasting remission within a short time after diagnosis, many pediatric endocrinologists prefer treatment with antithyroid agents and reserve radioactive iodine treatment for patients who do not achieve a remission after several years.

Thyroiditis

The term thyroiditis refers to several clinical conditions that involve inflammatory changes to the thyroid gland (Table 15.2.4). These include conditions related to a variety of etiologic conditions including infectious agents such as suppurative thyroiditis and subacute granulomatous (deQuervain's) thyroiditis, and autoimmune processes such as chronic lymphocytic (Hashimoto's) thyroiditis. Most conditions cause a brief and sometimes symptomatic hyperthyroid state, as the inflammatory condition causes breakdown of thyroid tissue and release of stored thyroid hormone into the circulation, followed by either transient hypothyroidism with a return to the euthyroid state or permanent hypothyroidism.

Depending on the etiology of the thyroiditis, patients may present with rather sudden onset of hyperthyroid symptoms or symptoms of hypothyroidism from chronic thyroid damage that results in a scarred underactive gland. Symptoms of hyperthyroidism may include all of the symptoms of thyrotoxicosis, although often symptoms are milder. Evaluation of thyroid hormone levels should confirm excessive free thyroid hormone. Thyroid imaging studies will demonstrate a gland with diffuse decreased activity, and uptake studies will confirm decreased thyroid activity. The profile of an underactive thyroid gland in the presence of excessive amounts of free thyroid hormone is the hallmark of early thyroiditis.

Treatment of thyroiditis depends on its etiology. In most conditions, no useful therapy has been identified. For suppurative thyroiditis, treatment with antibiotics and antiinflammatory agents is useful. The most common bacteria causing suppurative thyroiditis are *Staphylococcus aureus*, *Streptococcus pyogenes*, and *Strep pneumoniae*.

For subacute granulomatous thyroiditis, aspirin or other nonsteroidal anti-inflammatory agents may decrease the period of inflammation. Corticosteroids may be helpful for patients who do not respond to anti-inflammatory treatment, or those with acute lymphocytic (painless) thyroiditis. However, in most instances, simple reassurance and observation is all that is needed while the thyroiditis resolves spontaneously.

In cases of invasive fibrous thyroiditis (Riedel's struma), no effective intervention is available to halt the progressive fibrotic changes seen in the gland. Usually, therapy is directed toward surgical removal of the end-stage gland if it causes compression of the esophagus or trachea or cosmetic problems.

Pharmacological therapy is also not needed in chronic lymphocytic (Hashimoto's)

Table 15.2.4. **Causes of Thyroiditis**

Disease	Presumed Etiology	Symptoms/Signs	Thyroid Function	Treatment
Suppurative thyroiditis	Bacterial, fungal or parasitic	Painful, red thyroid, fever dysphagia, high WBC count, often preceded by pharyngitis or URI	Normal	Antimicrobials
Subacute granulomatous (DeQuervain's)	Viral, associated with HLA Bw35	Variable symptoms, may have severe or mild tenderness, fever, chills, myalgia, fatigue	Normal to hyperthyroid	Aspirin or anti-inflammatory including steroids
Subacute lymphocytic painless	Unknown	Hyperthyroid symptoms; nontender thyroid enlargement	Hyperthyroid	Beta-blockers for severe symptoms
Invasive fibrous (Reidel's)	Unknown	Enlarging firm nontender goiter and/or compression symptoms	Normal to late hypothyroid	Surgical removal; may need hormone replacement
Chronic lymphocytic (Hashimoto's)	Autoimmune production of anti-thyroid antibodies	Gradually enlarging thyroid, sometimes mild tenderness	Early hyper, late hypothy-roidism	Beta-blockers for hyper symptoms, late thyroid replacement

thyroiditis. Instead, the provider should monitor thyroid functions; if hypothyroidism develops later in the course of the disease, the provider should begin replacement of thyroid hormone.

In all cases of hyperthyroidism caused by thyroiditis, symptomatic treatment of the hyperthyroid state should be considered. Propranolol or other beta-blockers in low doses are usually adequate to relieve symptoms. Over time, the high levels that accompanied initial gland destruction clear and decrease, and then propranolol can be discontinued. Then a period of hypothyroidism may occur, so it is important to monitor thyroid hormone levels and provide thyroid replacement if hypothyroid states become symptomatic or persist.

Solitary Active Nodules (Hot Nodules)

The "hot" nodule usually is a thyroid adenoma that produces thyroid hormone either under the influence of TSH or autonomously. Patients often present with gradual onset of hyperthyroid symptoms and a nontender firm nodule present on thyroid examination. Serum thyroid studies confirm the hyperthyroid state and imaging studies show a localized area of increased thyroid activity with increased uptake.

Some thyroid adenomas may be treated using thyroid hormone suppression. These adenomas, thought to be partially dependent on TSH, will have reduced activity when TSH levels are suppressed by exogenous thyroid. In these situations, thyroid supplementation causes the paradoxical correction of hyperthyroidism.

Autonomous thyroid nodules are not dependent on TSH, and thyroid replacement will not result in reduced activity of the adenoma or decrease circulating hormone levels. These nodules must be excised to correct the hyperthyroidism.

Thyrotoxicosis

In patients with severe hyperthyroidism, thyrotoxicosis, the physiologic responses to the hypermetabolic state, can cause severe illness. Tachycardia can precipitate cardiac ischemia and high-output heart failure. Atrial fibrillation with a rapid ventricular response may also cause ischemic changes to the heart as well as low-output failure from decreased cardiac filling time. These complications are more common in the elderly who may already have some underlying coronary artery insufficiency or diminished left ventricular dysfunction. Prompt recognition of thyrotoxicosis and institution of appropriate management is essential to avoid these possible sequelae. For patients who are having cardiac symptoms or who are at high risk for vascular decompensation, hospitalization is necessary for stabilization. In patients who are mildly symptomatic and low risk for cardiac problems, outpatient therapy may be considered. In either case, treatment should be started with propranolol or other beta-blockers, which can decrease the heart rate either in sinus tachycardia or atrial fibrillation with a rapid ventricular response. Propranolol should be continued until the etiology of the hyperthyroid condition is determined and appropriate therapy has been instituted and is effective.

Hypothyroidism

Hypothyroidism, more common than hyperthyroidism, may be seen in up to 15% of older women (6). Hypothyroidism is most commonly caused by primary thyroid gland dysfunction, or by secondary hypothalamic or pituitary dysfunction.

Clinical Symptoms and Diagnosis

Signs and symptoms of hypothyroidism may be insidious and mimic other disorders. Lethargy, weight gain, depressed mood, and hair loss are frequent symptoms. Clinical signs include amenorrhea, dry skin, alopecia of head hair and the lateral two thirds of the eyebrows, bradycardia, and nonpitting edema. Galactorrhea may also be present and results from increases in prolactin released in response to increased production of thyroid-releasing hormone (TRH) by the hypothalamus. Later signs may include the development of significant myxedema including pericardial effusions with a rub or signs of decreased cardiac output, altered mental status including coma, and hypotension. Because hypothyroidism may mimic the symptoms of depression or chronic fatigue, new-onset hypothyroidism should be considered in the evaluation of any woman presenting for depression with other symptoms potentially suggestive of low thyroid.

In addition to abnormal thyroid studies, hyponatremia may also be found on serum studies. Other laboratory tests may be normal. TSH levels will be elevated in primary hypothyroidism and low in pituitary or hypothalamic dysfunction.

Especially in older individuals who may not exhibit the signs of hypothyroidism, a TSH is needed to confirm the diagnosis of hypothyroidism in women with depression or Alzheimer's-like senile dementia.

Primary Hypothyroidism

Among the causes of primary hypothyroidism, chronic lymphocytic thyroiditis, known as Hashimoto's thyroiditis, is the most common. Chronic lymphocytic thyroiditis usually begins in younger aged women and may exhibit a brief and usually asymptomatic hyperthyroid state before resulting in diminished thyroid production and clinical hypothyroidism. Other common causes for primary hypothyroidism are noted in Table 15.2.5.

Table 15.2.5. Common Causes of Acquired Hypothyroidism

Primary hypothyroidism
  Postthyroid irradiation
  Postsurgical
  Hashimoto's thyroiditis
  Late-stage invasive fibrous thyroiditis (Riedel's struma)
  Iodine deficiency
  Idiopathic
Secondary hypothyroidism
  Pituitary necrosis (Sheehan's syndrome)
  Congenital hypopituitarism
  Pituitary or hypothalamic neoplasms

The evaluation of hypothyroidism is relatively straightforward. Because treatment is not dependent on the etiology of the hypothyroid state, extensive evaluation with antithyroid antibodies or imaging studies is not cost-efficient. The diagnosis of hypothyroidism can be confirmed by finding decreased free thyroid levels in the blood along with an elevated TSH. Because elevation of the TSH is an indication of underproduction of thyroxine by the thyroid gland, this test alone may be a good screening tool for patients who are suspected of hypothyroidism. A low TSH level in the presence of clinical signs may be an indication of secondary hypothyroidism and requires further evaluation.

The treatment of hypothyroidism is thyroid hormone replacement. For older patients or those with risk for cardiac disease, replacement should begin with low doses of thyroid hormone (0.025 mg/day) with determination of TSH levels or thyroid hormone levels every 6 to 8 weeks. Medication should be adjusted on the basis of TSH levels. Increasing the dosage of replacement hormone too rapidly could result in tachycardia with cardiac ischemia or cardiac dysrhythmias such as atrial fibrillation.

For younger patients who are not at risk for cardiac complications for thyroid replacement, the initial thyroxine dose should approximate the daily thyroid requirement, 1.7 g/kg/day in adults and higher amounts in children.

Secondary Hypothyroidism

Secondary hypothyroidism is caused by pituitary and hypothalamic dysfunction that underproduce TSH. In this situation, both serum thyroid levels and TSH levels are reduced, showing inadequate stimulation of the thyroid gland. A TRH stimulation test can confirm a pituitary cause. In pituitary dysfunction, TSH levels will fail to rise or have a blunted response to the administration of TRH. In hypothalamic dysfunction, administration of TRH will cause a normal or exaggerated rise in TSH.

Secondary hypothyroidism is uncommon, affecting only a small percentage of patients who have hypothyroidism. The most common causes of secondary hypothyroidism include Sheehan's syndrome and pituitary adenomas. Sheehan's syndrome is caused by pituitary necrosis secondary to ischemia. It is rare today and was caused by ischemia after a hypotensive episode. In women it was commonly caused by postpartum hemorrhage with severe and prolonged hypotension. These women usually exhibit signs and symptoms of panhypopituitarism with antidiuretic hormone deficiency, galactorrhea, and amenorrhea.

Pituitary adenomas may cause hypothyroidism from local compression on the cells that produce TSH, or from excessive tissue removal associated with the excision of an adenoma. Signs or symptoms of endocrine dysfunction such as Cushing's disease or galactorrhea may also be present.

Although the treatment of secondary hypothyroidism does not differ from primary hypothyroidism, further evaluation is indicated in these patients to determine if other anterior pituitary hormones are also affected. Measurement of morning and evening serum cortisol levels, prolactin levels, and levels of gonadotropins may be useful to diagnose the extent of pituitary dysfunction. MRI or CT scanning of the pituitary may diagnose adenomas.

Nodular Thyroid Disease

Thyroid nodules are present in a wide spectrum of disease. Nodules may be associated with hyperthyroidism, or may have normal function. Several functioning adenomas may develop in the same thyroid giving rise to a multinodular goiter as discussed below. Nodules may have no thyroid activity. These represent either nonfunctional adenomas, thyroid cysts, or thyroid cancers.

Nonfunctional thyroid nodules do not take up radioactive iodine on thyroid scans and appear as radiolabel deficient areas or "cold" on radionucleotide scans. Radioactive iodine is the preferred radioisotope when performing a scan to evaluate a thyroid nodule. Because thyroid cancers can sometimes concentrate $^{99m}T_C$ and thus look hot rather than cold, technetium scans should be avoided when investigating cold nodules.

Because cold nodules present the risk of carcinoma, further evaluation is indicated when a nonfunctional nodule is identified. Ultrasound can be useful to distinguish a fluid-filled cystic mass from a solid mass. Cysts have little cancer potential and can be drained with needle aspiration or observed over time. For solid nonfunctioning nodules, a biopsy should be performed. This is most often performed using fine needle techniques that minimize trauma to the gland and discomfort to patients.

Multinodular goiter is a benign condition of uncertain etiology. The thyroid develops several nodules that are generally nontender, but can cause symptoms from compression of adjacent structures. Thyroid function tests are not altered by the nodules, and thyroid scans show diffuse decreased uptake in the nodules. Treatment is aimed at suppressing nodule thy-

roid activity by providing thyroid replacement. Rarely, the nodular thyroid may require surgical intervention to relieve compression or improve the patient's appearance.

Thyroid Function and Dysfunction under Special Circumstances

Pregnancy

Estrogen production in pregnancy causes a rise in circulating TBG levels, especially during the first 3 months of pregnancy. This results in an increase in the amount of bound thyroid hormone and a higher production of hormone by the thyroid, caused both by increased TSH production and by some degree of intrinsic thyroid stimulating activity of beta-HCG (human chorionic gonadotropin). There is a slight enlargement in the thyroid gland during pregnancy, especially in the first 2 months of pregnancy.

Following the first 2 months of pregnancy, TBG levels plateau and thyroid production can reach a new steady state. Although the thyroid gland may remain larger, compared to the prepregnancy size, no further enlargement should occur throughout the remainder of pregnancy.

When estrogen levels drop in the postpartum period, TBG levels will begin to decline. As a result, the total requirement for thyroid production will also fall and thyroid size will decrease. The thyroid should return to its prepregnancy size by the sixth week postpartum.

Hypothyroidism in Pregnancy

Pregnancy does not usually occur in patients who are severely hypothyroid. However, up to two thirds of pregnant hypothyroid patients who are on a stable dose of thyroid replacement may experience hypothyroid symptoms if the dosage of replacement hormones is not adjusted for new levels of binding hormones. For women who are taking thyroid replacement, it is recommended that free T4 or TSH levels be measured frequently in the first 3 months of pregnancy and then periodically for the remainder of pregnancy. Failure to adequately replace thyroid hormone during pregnancy may result in an increased risk of gestational hypertension, including preeclampsia. For patients with overt hypothyroidism, the risk of gestational hypertension nearly triples, whereas for subclinical conditions the risk is double. Following delivery, reassessment of thyroid supplement levels should be performed to determine how the replacement dosage should be adjusted as binding hormone levels fall.

Hyperthyroidism in Pregnancy

Thyroid dysfunction may be altered by other mechanisms during pregnancy as well. There is some evidence that thyroid levels increase with hyperemesis gravidarum, perhaps mediated by abnormally high levels of beta-HCG seen with hyperemesis. In addition, pregnancy may reduce the severity of Graves' disease. Monitoring of thyroid antibody activity and a reduction of thyroid suppressive medications may be needed to maintain euthyroid state for patients with preexisting Graves' disease. Postpartum exacerbation of Graves' is common, however, as the relative immunosuppression associated with pregnancy abates. Furthermore, because thyrotropin receptor antibodies associated with Graves' and Hashimoto's diseases cross the placenta, assessing levels of thyrotropin receptor antibody in the third trimester may be helpful in anticipating neonates who may exhibit thyrotoxicosis early in life.

For patients with Graves' disease who become pregnant, treatment should be instituted with propylthiouracil (PTU). PTU does cross the placenta, but does not appear to have any teratogenic effects. However, PTU does suppress fetal thyroid hormone production. Overly aggressive treatment of Graves' disease can result in transient neonatal hypothyroidism. The

risk of neonatal hypothyroidism is related to the dosage of PTU used. In women whose thyroid levels are maintained in the upper third of normal, the chance of neonatal hypothyroidism is approximately 10%; however, if maternal thyroid levels are maintained in the lower third of the normal range, the frequency of neonatal hypothyroidism rises to over 60%. Therefore, the minimum dose of PTU should be used to keep thyroid levels suppressed to normal levels, but in the higher range of normal. The other antithyroid drug available in the United States, methimazole (MMI), has been associated with aplasia cutis congenita (i.e., the congenital absence of skin) and should only be used if patients cannot take PTU. PTU also can be found in breast milk, but levels are extremely low and pose no threat to infant neonatal function.

Postpartum Thyroid Dysfunction

As mentioned above, immunologic function is usually suppressed during pregnancy, which can result in improvements in conditions such as Graves' disease. Following pregnancy, a rebound in immunologic function occurs. This hypervigilant immune state in postpartum women can lead to the development of postpartum thyroiditis. Various studies attempting to estimate the frequency of postpartum thyroid dysfunction range from under 2% to nearly 17%, depending on the ethnic group screened. In general, the overall prevalence of postpartum thyroiditis is believed to be approximately 5% in the first year after delivery (8).

Postpartum thyroiditis follows the clinical pattern of thyroiditis noted above, with an initial hyperthyroid state followed by a hypothyroid state that is usually transient, but can result in permanent thyroid dysfunction in up to 40% of women afflicted with postpartum thyroiditis (9). Early in the course of postpartum thyroiditis, the hyperthyroid condition can be confused with Graves' disease. The absence of thyrotropin-releasing antibody and a diffuse decreased uptake of radioisotope on the thyroid scan should confirm the diagnosis of postpartum thyroiditis. Radioactive isotope scans of the thyroid are safe in the postpartum period including those who are breast-feeding.

Postpartum thyroiditis appears to be related to the production of thyroid peroxidase antibodies, once known as antimicrosomal antibodies. The condition is usually painless and characterized by a brief period of hyperthyroidism lasting 1 to 3 months that occurs between 1 and 4 months postpartum, followed by a hypothyroid state lasting between 1 to 4 months somewhere between 4 and 8 months postpartum. Although the hyperthyroid state is often asymptomatic, the hypothyroidism is symptomatic in many women, and up to one-third may require thyroid replacement for symptoms of lethargy or depression. Because the symptoms of hypothyroidism may mimic several other problems encountered following pregnancy, such as depression, clinicians should be aware of the possibility of thyroid dysfunction in the postpartum period.

Adolescents

Thyroid disorders are the most common endocrine problem developed during adolescence. The most frequent thyroid abnormality is a goiter. Goiter occurs in between 1 and 3% of all healthy adolescents affecting young women more commonly than young men (10).

The most common etiology of goiter in adolescents is chronic lymphocytic (Hashimoto's) thyroiditis. In most cases, patients are not symptomatic. Antimicrosomal antibodies are usually positive in these patients, but patients infrequently develop symptoms of hyperthyroidism or hypothyroidism. Generally, the production of antibodies abates in approximately 2 years. Although thyroid hormone replacement is usually not needed for symptom control, hormone replacement may help reduce the size of the goiter and can be used if there are obstructive symptoms or cosmetic reasons. Most other instances of thyroid enlargement during adolescence represents colloidal goiter, a benign enlargement of the thyroid.

The need for further evaluation of a goiter in the adolescent woman depends on the physical presentation of the gland, clinical history, and family history of thyroid disease, especially autoimmune thyroid disorders and medullary carcinoma of the thyroid. A diffusely enlarged, nontender gland without any associated lymphadenopathy in a healthy young woman who has no family history of thyroid disorders requires no further investigation. Localized enlargement such as nodular disease, a tender gland suggestive of an underlying thyroiditis, and symptoms consistent with hypothyroidism or hyperthyroidism should prompt further evaluation. In addition, a history of neck irradiation, cervical adenopathy, or a family history of thyroid cancer are other factors that should lead to additional investigation.

Older Women

The diagnosis of thyroid disease in the elderly may be complicated by several factors. First, signs and symptoms may be absent, vague, or mimic other common clinical conditions such as depression, congestive heart failure, atrial fibrillation from other causes, and early dementia. Likewise, worsening of symptoms in patients with congestive heart failure or mild dementia may be caused by the development of thyroid disease rather than the natural progression of their underlying illness. In these cases, the diagnosis of thyroid disorder may be missed.

Secondly, older patients with thyroid dysfunction may not exhibit the classic signs of thyroid disease. For example, patients with hyperthyroidism may complain of lethargy or confusion and may resemble patients with hypothyroidism. This has been called apathetic hyperthyroidism. Patients with hypothyroidism may be ataxic or confused or present with hoarseness from thyroid enlargement. A high index of suspicion is needed to diagnosis thyroid disorders early and institute prompt therapy.

Finally, older patients may use a number of medications that alter thyroid function or mask the early signs and symptoms of thyroid disease. Beta-blockers and calcium channel blockers may prevent the tachycardia associated with hyperthyroidism.

Thyroid dysfunction becomes more common as women age. It is estimated that between 8 and 12% of older women have overt hypothyroidism (11). Although screening for thyroid disease is not cost-effective in younger populations, screening for hypothyroidism appears to be cost-effective in older women over age 60 years.

Special consideration should be given to a large group of older women who present with normal thyroid hormone levels but increased TSH. This is seen in up to 15% of women over the age of 60 (12). Because most often these women are asymptomatic, replacement thyroid hormone in these women is controversial. If thyroid hormone replacement is not used, the patient should have periodic monitoring of TSH levels and attention to possible cognitive impairment or other subtle signs of hypothyroidism every 6 to 12 months.

Medication Use

Several medications frequently used by women may affect thyroid levels, especially in patients with inactive glands who are taking thyroid replacement (Table 15.2.6). In addition, the use of thyroid hormone may have metabolic effects that alter other conditions that are common in women.

Oral contraceptives and estrogen replacement therapy may affect thyroid levels by changing the amount of thyroid-binding globulin. Patients who are taking stable doses of thyroid replacement and start oral contraceptives or

Table 15.2.6. Thyroid Drug Interactions

Drug Involved	Effect
Coumadin	Increased thyroid increases effect of coumadin; decrease in thyroid decreases coumadin effect
Insulin/oral hypoglycemic	Increasing thyroid increases need for insulin or hypoglycemic agent
Estrogens	Estrogen use increases need for thyroid replacement
Clofibrate or cholestyramine	May bind thyroid and impair absorption

estrogen replacement should have thyroid levels monitored 4 to 6 weeks later.

Thyroid replacement may also be affected by the administration of clofibrate or cholestryamine. These resins, used for the treatment of hyperlipidemias, also bind T4 and T3 and may impair absorption of thyroid replacement. To protect against impairments of absorption, cholestyramine or clofibrate should not be administered within 4 hours of the thyroid dose.

Administration of thyroid hormone may also alter other conditions. Thyroid hormone accelerates the metabolism of vitamin K-dependent clotting factors. Therefore, for patients who are anticoagulated with warfarin compounds, treatment of hypothyroidism with thyroid replacement may augment anticoagulation. Similarly, decreases in thyroid doses may be associated with decreased prothrombin time. Thus, whenever thyroid medication is adjusted in patients who are anticoagulated, close attention should be paid to prothrombin times. Alterations in thyroid function may also affect glycemic control. Increasing thyroid replacement may cause increased need for insulin or oral hypoglycemic agents in diabetic patients.

Special Considerations for Nurse Practitioners and Physician Assistants

A woman's complaints that may indicate thyroid disease are common, nonspecific, and often first attributed to emotional or other health problems. Signs and symptoms of thyroid disorders may emanate from almost any organ system and are largely independent of the etiology of the disorders. Women themselves may not be aware that they are sick because of the often insidious nature of the disease process (13). In the elderly, for example, unexplained weight loss, tachycardia, and failure to thrive may be the only manifestations of thyrotoxicosis. Signs of hyperthyroidism in pregnancy, such as tachycardia, may be missed because they are consistent with the pregnancy itself. Complaints of fatigue or sleeplessness postpartum, which might indicate thyroid disorders, can be attributed to the new mother's responsibilities for child care.

Because manifestations of thyroid diseases are subtle and involve nearly every system of the body, a complete review of systems must be done that includes characteristics of menstrual cycles (14). Consider the possibility of iodine-deficient diet, especially in new immigrants from regions in which there is iodine-deficient soil, e.g., some areas in South America. In addition, consider the possibility of these women having a diet relatively high in iodine after living in the United States. Ask also about the possibility of work-related exposure to radiation or radioactive iodine (15). Assessment of the woman's mental function is important. Symptoms of hypothyroidism such as sleep disturbances, crying spells, apathy, and reduced concentration can be confused with a depressive mood state and treated inappropriately (13). In addition to using tests specific to diagnosis of thyroid dysfunction, providers should obtain a CBC and serum cholesterol since anemia and hypercholesterolemia are frequently associated with hypothyroidism (13).

Consultation and/or referral resources must be available. Women with severe illness, unusual disorders, and confusing laboratory findings should be referred to a physician or endocrinologist. Consultation and referral are needed if there is myxedema, significant cardiac or respiratory compromise, secondary hypothyroidism, the need for antithyroid agents, or thyroid nodules. Referral to a pediatric endocrinologist for definitive diagnosis and treatment of thyroid diseases in children is recommended (14, 15). Women who have decreased visual acuity, diplopia, or other indications of orbitopathy should be referred to an ophthalmologist.

The woman must be involved in her treatment, especially when it is long-term, e.g., for hypothyroidism. The ability to concentrate or remember can be affected, making it necessary to give simple, repeated, and written instructions. Lifestyle changes may include rest periods, daily medications, and high-fiber diet for constipation. If there are associated psychomotor symptoms, the woman should be cautioned not to operate equipment until they have resolved. The woman's family and other supportive persons can assist her in making lifestyle changes, keeping appointments, and monitoring herself for signs of hypothyroidism and hyperthyroidism (13). The woman being treated with pharmacologic agents for thyroid diseases should understand that it may take weeks for her to reach the euthyroid state, and she will need reevaluation and laboratory monitoring as long as she takes the drugs (15).

References

1. Sakiayama R. Common thyroid disorders. Am Fam Physician 1988;38:227–238.
2. Bander JB, Gaston EA, Dawber TR. The significance of non-toxic thyroid nodules. Final report of a

15 year study of the incidence of thyroid malignancy. Ann Intern Med 1985;145:1386–1388.

3. Franklyn JA. The management of hyperthyroidism. N Engl J Med 1994;330:1731–1737.

4. Sofianides T. Thyroid gland disorders. In: Noble J., ed. General Medicine and Primary Care. Boston: Little Brown & Co, 1987:2046–2047.

5. Ladenson PW. Disorders of the thyroid gland. In: Harvey AG, Johns RJ, McKusick VA, et al., eds. The Principles and Practice of Medicine. Norwalk, CT: Appleton & Lange, 1988:916–917.

6. Sawin CT. Thyroid dysfunction in older persons. Adv Intern Med 1991;37:223–248.

7. Lueng AS, Millar LK, Koonings PP, Montoro M, Mestman JH. Perinatal outcome in hypothyroid pregnancies. Obstet Gynecol 1993;81:349–353.

8. Learoyd DL, Fung HY, McGregor AM. Postpartum thyroid dysfunction. Thyroid 1992;2:73–80.

9. Lazarus JH, Othman S. Review: thyroid disease in relation to pregnancy. Clin Endocrinol 1991;34:91–98.

10. Foley TP. Goiter in adolescents. Adolesc Endocrinol 1993;22:593–606.

11. Francis T, Wartofsky L. Common thyroid disorders in the elderly. Postgrad Med 1992;92:225–236.

12. Singer PA, Cooper DS, Levy EG, et al. Treatment guidelines for patients with hyperthyroidism and hypothyroidism. JAMA 1995;273:808–812.

13. Heitman B, Irizarry A. Hypothyroidism: common complaints, perplexing diagnosis. Nurse Pract 1995; 20:54–56, 58–60.

14. Uphold DR, Graham MV. Clinical guidelines in family practice. Gainesville, FL: Barmarrae, 1993: 140–155.

15. Saxe JM. Thyroid disorders. In: Star WL, Lommel LL, Shannon MT, eds. Women's Primary Health Care. Washington, DC: American Nurses Association, 1995:10-18–10-24.

Suggested Readings

Foley TP. Goiter in adolescence. Adolesc Endocrinol 1993;22:593–606.

Hall R, Richards CJ, Lazarus JH. The thyroid and pregnancy. Br J Obstet Gynecol 1993;100:512–515.

Hay ID. Thyroiditis: a clinical update. Mayo Clin Proc 1985;60:836–843.

Learyd DL, Fung HY, McGregor AM. Postpartum thyroid dysfunction. Thyroid 1992;2:73–80.

Mandel SJ, Larsen PR, Seely EW, Brent GA. Increased need for thyroxine during pregnancy in women with primary hypothyroidism. N Engl J Med 1990;323:91–96.

Shamma FN, Abrahams JJ. Imaging in endocrine disorders. J Reprod Med 1992;39:39–45.

Singer PA, Cooper DS, Levy EG, et al. Treatment guidelines for patients with hyperthyroidism and hypothyroidism. JAMA 1995;273:808–812.

Gastrointestinal Problems Including Colon Cancer

Jo Ann Rosenfeld

Introduction

The gastrointestinal (GI) tract and its functions are fundamental parts of every individual's life. Everyone eats at joyful and sorrowful occasions, alone and in company, to celebrate, or to work. Whether it is a hot dog grabbed in an airport, a wedding feast, or an intimate laboriously cooked meal for two, eating is an important ingredient of daily life. GI complaints are common in all offices. GI diseases are a continuing challenge. Knowledge of the woman, her family, surroundings, and her susceptibility to pain and illness will be invaluable to the provider caring for her.

Although the GI tract of women is not inherently different from men's, some GI diseases occur only seldom in women like gastric cancer, whereas others occur almost only in women such as biliary cirrhosis, gallstones and irritable bowel syndrome (IBS). Some diseases such as alcoholic liver disease affect women differently. Women have had fewer habits that cause or worsen GI disease, such as cigarette and alcohol abuse, or have practiced them for shorter periods. Some GI diseases occur more often and with greater severity in the elderly; because most of the elderly are women, providers see older women more often for diseases such as peptic ulcer disease.

Upper GI Tract: Esophagus, Stomach, Duodenum

Gastroesophageal Reflux Disease (GERD)

GERD is a common event. It is the most prevalent acid-related disease, and heartburn is a common symptom (1). Ten to 20% of individuals with heartburn will develop GERD and chronic reflux (2).

Some women are predisposed to develop GERD. It is common in pregnancy and may be more likely with use of progesterone. Several diseases that are more common in women can include GERD such as rheumatoid arthritis, Sjogren's syndrome, CREST syndrome (e.g., calcinosis, Raynaud's phenomena, esophageal strictures and telangiectasia), and scleroderma.

The main symptom is heartburn, but other symptoms include chest pain, a "bad taste" in mouth, and nausea and vomiting. Diagnosis can be made by a therapeutic trial, or upper gastrointestinal barium radiograph (UGI), barium swallow, or esophagoscopy.

Treatment starts with lifestyle modifications. Small, frequent low-fat meals and refraining from eating before bed improve the symptoms, as does raising the head of the bed. The woman should avoid drugs that decrease sphincter tone such as anticholinergics, calcium channel blockers, and theophylline, and those that injure the esophagus such as nonsteroidal anti-inflammatory agents (NSAIDs), aspirin, and tetracycline. Cessation of smoking and alcohol will improve the symptoms. Antacids, 15 mL 1 to 3 hours after meals and before bedtime, can be used.

The next steps in treatment include use of the histamine-2 blockers and sucralfate in doses similar to antiulcer dosages. Bethanecol (25 mg qac and qhs), metoclopramide (10 mg qac and qhs), and cisapride (10 mg qid or 20 mg bid) are prokinetic agents and speed healing. Finally, high-dose H_2 blockers or omeprazole (20 mg qd) may be needed (1). GERD is a chronic disease, and maintenance of lifestyle changes will be necessary.

Peptic Ulcer Disease

Incidence

The stomach and its acid production are inherently similar in women and men, although there have been few studies on basic GI physiology comparing women and men. One study found that fasting gastric pH and duodenal pH did not differ in women or men. Younger individuals had a lower pH after meals than older individuals, but this was not statistically significant and it did not affect drug absorption (3).

There have been few studies into the natural history of PUD comparing women and men. It is even uncertain whether women or men develop PUD more often. The rate of PUD for women is age-dependent: in one study it was 0.3 per 1000 women-years (WY) for women age 25 to 29, 0.62/1000 WY for women age 35 to 39, and 0.84/1000 WY for women over age 50 (4). In a prospective study, 4.9% of women developed PUD over an average of 12.5 years (5). In one study of Seventh-Day Adventists, lifetime prevalence of PUD was 11% in women and 13.5% in men. The annual incidence of PUD was 1.8/1000 women and 1.5/1000 men (6). A Swedish study showed that the risk of PUD was lower in women among nonsmokers, but there was no difference between women and men smokers (7).

The incidence of PUD increases with age in both women and men, but it occurs more often in older women. Younger women, perhaps because of fewer risk factors, have less PUD than young men. The elderly are more likely to develop PUD and its complications, and with greater severity. Among the elderly, there is an increasing prevalence for PUD in women with increasing age (8). Sixty-two percent of patients seen for PUD in one gastroenterologist's office were women (9), but this may not generalize to primary care practices.

In the Oxford Family Planning Association Contraceptive Study of adult younger women, PUD severe enough to require hospitalization occurred less frequently in women than men. Only 175 women (out of approximately 17,000) over more than 12 years were hospitalized for PUD (4). The incidence of PUD increased with the women's age, parity, and cigarette smoking history. The incidence was low in pregnancy and nonexistent in postpartum women. Oral contraceptive pill (OCP) use did not predispose toward PUD; current users of OCPs had the lowest incidence of hospitalization for PUD (11).

Risk Factors

There are several risk factors for PUD; most of these occur more often in men than women. *Cigarette smoking.* Cigarette smoking contributes to the development of PUD in women and men. Although few studies have included women, use of data from the First National Health and Nutrition Examination survey found that women who smoked were at increased risk of PUD. Although 4.9% of nonsmoking women developed PUD, 10% of current smokers and 6.4% of former smokers did (5). After adjusting for aspirin, coffee, and alcohol use, current women smokers were 1.8 times more likely and former smokers were 1.3 times more likely to develop PUD than women who never smoked. Twenty percent of PUD in women was attributable to smoking (5). Twenty-five percent of women's first time ulcers and 42% of recurrent ulcers were estimated to be caused by smoking (7).

The relative risk of developing PUD increases as the number of cigarettes smoked per day increase (5). With increasing smoking rates in younger and older women, decreased quitting rates, and longer histories of smoking greater amounts, the PUD rate in women may increase over the next years.
Use of nonsteroidal anti-inflammatory drugs (NSAIDs). NSAIDs are one of the most commonly used groups of drugs in the United States. Over 13 million individuals take NSAIDS (10), and the consumption of

NSAIDs increased during the 1980s (11). One hundred million prescriptions for NSAIDs are written yearly in the United States (12). The use of NSAIDs increased most in elderly populations, especially in women; women over age 65 years doubled their use of NSAIDs from 1979 to 1988 (11).

Because NSAIDS damage gastric and duodenal mucosa, common side effects include gastritis, dyspepsia, and increased risk of PUD (13). Ten to 30% of patients on NSAIDs have PUD, and 20 to 40% have gastritis (12). The risk of developing PUD is increased by 2.8 to 8.0 times by use of NSAIDS (13, 14), and is increased even more with use of multiple NSAIDs (10). Twenty-nine to 38% of PUD is caused by NSAID use (13, 15). NSAIDs probably cause 20% of all cases of peptic ulcers in those over age 60 (16).

NSAID use is also associated with an increased risk of developing severe complications of PUD, especially in the elderly. Women, because they comprise more of the elderly population or because they visit providers more often for complaints concerning joints and arthritis, take more NSAIDs, and are thus more likely to develop PUD and its complications. The rate of perforation of peptic ulcers in individuals taking NSAIDs has declined in all populations and in the elderly in the United Kingdom, but the rate has increased in women (16). Elderly women are more likely to be hospitalized for PUD caused by NSAIDs than men or younger individuals (11). Elderly patients taking NSAIDs are at four times greater risk of dying from a GI bleed than those not taking NSAIDs (8).

The analgesic effects of NSAIDs may modify symptoms of peptic ulcer, leading to delay in diagnosis, more serious presentations, and poorer prognosis. NSAIDs mask dyspepsia symptoms, especially in the elderly (8, 17). Elderly individuals using NSAIDs are more likely to present with major complication of PUD without any warning symptoms.

One study of over 9000 autopsies found 154 individuals who died of undiagnosed PUD complications (18). Two-thirds were over age 70 years. NSAIDs were used by nearly 60% of those who died of PUD complications, and women were more likely to be using these drugs than men (18).

Older NSAIDs such as naproxen, indomethacin, diclofenac, ketoprofen, prioxicam, and flurbirprofen are more likely to produce ulcers than newer ones such as fenbufen, nabumetone, ibuprofen, etodolac, azapropapazone, and tiaprofenic acid (19).

Elderly. The elderly, especially elderly women, are more likely to develop PUD, to develop bleeding and perforation without warning symptoms, and to develop severe and life-threatening complications than younger individuals. Peptic ulcers are more frequent and more serious in the elderly (8). The elderly develop larger ulcers and require more blood transfusions (8). In the United Kingdom, rates for hospital admission for PUD declined in all groups except older women (13). Older individuals, especially women, are more likely to die of complications of PUD. Eighty percent of mortality in PUD is in those over age 65 (8).

Infection with H. Pylori. Helicobacter pylori is a Gram-negative flagellated rod that infects and remains in the stomach by creating a vacuole. It is associated with the development of PUD, especially with chronic and recurrent disease, and gastric carcinoma. When it is eradicated by antibiotics, the risk of PUD decreases. However, whether it should or must be treated to cure PUD is disputed.

More than 95% of patients with duodenal ulcers (DU) and 75% with gastric ulcers (GU) are infected with this organism. Prevalence of infection with *H. pylori* increases with age; more than 80% of the individuals over age 60 years are infected. Women are more likely to be infected with *H. pylori* (8).

When the infection is treated and eradicated by antibiotics, such as tetracycline, amoxicillin, clarithromycin, or metronidazole, recurrence rates of ulcers fall from 75 to 90% to 9 to 25% (20). It is diagnosed by testing for the enzyme it produces, urease, by biopsy or on the patient's breath, by serological indicator, or by identification or culture from a biopsy specimen. Treatment with bismuth and two antibiotics usually eradicates the organism. Use of tetracycline and metronidazole is effective, eradicating it in 90%, but their side effects are significant and they are not well tolerated. Other regimens of amoxicillin or clarithromycin are better tolerated but have lower cure rates. Even after eradication, reinfection, and ulcers may recur.

Estrogen use and pregnancy. One study found no worsening of PUD symptoms or risk with estrogen use, concluding estrogen alone does not increase the risk of PUD (21).

In pregnancy, peptic ulcer disease is uncommon, although heartburn, GERD, and even dyspepsia are common because of mechanical displacement and hormone effects. If PUD is suspected, esophagogastroduodenoscopy (EGD) must be used for diagnosis, and H_2 blockers and misoprostol avoided in medical treatment (Table 16.1).

Table 16.1. Oral Treatment of PUD

Medication Generic Name	Trade Names	Oral Dose
H_2 blockers		
Cimetadine*	Tagamet	400 mg bid or 800 mg qhs
Ranitidine*	Zantac	150 mg bid or 300 mg qhs
Nizatidine*	Axid	300 mg qhs
Famotidine*	Pepcid	40 mg qhs (or 20 mg bid)
Others		
Misoprostol*	Cytotec	100–200 mg bid
Sucralfate	Carafate	2 g qid
Omeprazole*	Prilosec	20 mg qd

*Should not be used in pregnant women or women at risk for pregnancy.

Clinical Symptoms and Diagnosis

The symptoms of PUD can vary from none to life-threatening ones. The elderly, perhaps because of conconminant NSAID use, and those with communication problems may have no complaints until a life-threatening complication occurs such as massive hematemesis, perforation, or obstruction.

Abdominal pain is common; it can be intermittent, colicky, or constant, related to eating or worse between meals, and can be abdominal or radiate to the back. Belching, early satiety, heartburn, nausea, vomiting, and abdominal distention may be other symptoms. In severe situations, hematemesis, fainting, signs of dehydration from vomiting, or abdominal signs of perforation such as severe pain, paleness, and shock are possible.

Physical examination may be totally normal. The patient may be pale from blood loss. Abdominal examination may be normal or show epigastric or right upper quadrant (RUQ) tenderness. Bowel sounds are usually normal; decreased bowel sounds suggest diseases that affect the peritoneum such as pancreatitis or perforation. In cases of perforation, a rigid tender abdomen with no bowel signs and signs of rebound tenderness can be found.

Laboratory tests are normal. Liver function test abnormalities or bilirubin level elevations will suggest another diagnosis such as gallbladder or liver disease. Sometimes, amylase and lipase levels, and viral hepatitis antibody screens may be helpful in diagnosing other diseases.

Diagnosis is made either by UGI or EGD. The former is less expensive and possibly more comfortable, whereas EGD allows visualization of a greater surface area and the chance for biopsy.

Differential diagnosis should include cholelithiasis or cholecystitis, hepatitis (e.g., alcoholic, toxic, viral), other liver diseases, esophagitis, GERD, pancreatitis, and gastritis. An oral cholecystogram (OCG) or gallbladder ultrasound will diagnose gallbladder disease and stones. Liver function tests will be elevated in liver disease, viral antibodies should be present in viral hepatitis, and ultrasounds of the liver may help differentiate the presence and variety of liver disease. The UGI with a barium swallow and the EGD can diagnose GERD, gastritis, and esophagitis. A normal amylase and lipase serum and/or urine levels will eliminate pancreatitis.

Gastric versus Duodenal Ulcers

Although it may be difficult to differentiate between gastric versus duodenal ulcers, clinical and primary treatment is the same, follow-up is different because of the possibility that gastric cancer will present as a gastric ulcer (Table 16.2).

Gastric ulcers occur in the same frequency in men and women, mostly in individuals age 50 to 70 years. Gastric ulcer pain is epigastric and can radiate to the back, whereas duodenal ulcer pain is more likely to be in the RUQ. Gastric ulcer pain increases with meals, whereas duodenal pain is increased between meals. Duodenal ulcers are much more common and may

Table 16.2. Gastric Versus Duodenal Ulcer

	Gastric Ulcer	Duodenal Ulcer
Symptoms	Epigastric pain	RUQ pain
	Back pain	Pain worse be-
	Pain worsened	tween meals
	by meals	
Familial		
tendency	No	Yes
Infection with	95%	75%
H. pylori		
Diagnosis	UGI or EGD	UGI or EGD
Treatment	Diet, H$_2$	Diet, H$_2$
	blockers	blockers
Treatment	Antibiotics,	H$_2$ blockers,
for recur-	biopsy	antibiotics
rent ulcers		
Cancer	Yes	No
possibility		

have a familial tendency. Both are linked with H. pylori infections. Gastric ulcers must be considered possible carcinomas until proven otherwise, either by UGI-proven healing, EGD, or by endoscopic biopsy. Gastric ulcers are associated with a history of H. pylori infections and aspirin use, whereas duodenal ulcers are associated with H. pylori infections, male sex, bleeding, and pain on presentation, but not alcohol use (22).

Both are treated similarly. Gastric ulcers should heal with treatment within 6 weeks, or culture for H. pylori and biopsy for cancer are necessary. Recurrent or persistent duodenal ulcers can be retreated with other medical treatments because cancer is unlikely (Fig. 16.1).

Treatment

Over the last 20 years, treatment for PUD has radically changed, eliminating the need for surgery except in cases of severe bleeding or perforation.

Nonpharmacological treatment is primary. Although special diets are not used, the avoidance of alcohol, caffeine, and all coffee products is recommended. Cessation of NSAID and aspirin use and cigarette smoking is also necessary. Small frequent meals and low-fat diets may reduce acid production and improve symptoms.

Medical therapy is effective in relieving symptoms and healing the ulcers. Antacids can be used. However, in order to be effective, the equivalent of 30 mL of liquid antacids must be taken every 2 hours. Besides the inconvenience of the large quantities of medications needed, the magnesium antacids can cause diarrhea.

H$_2$ blockers are the backbone of treatment. Any one of the H$_2$ blockers is effective for symptom relief and treatment. All but nizatidine can be given IV and PO, and some are available over the counter. They are metabolized in the liver. Cimetadine and ranitidine interfere with the normal clearance of drugs through the P-450 system. All can cause diarrhea, mastodynia, flushing, sweating, and granulocytopenia, and, in men, gynecomastia and impotence. Memory loss and confusion can occur in the elderly. There are reports of teratogenecity and they should not be used in pregnant women.

There are a variety of other drugs that can be used instead of, in addition to, or as a second-line drug after H_2 blockers. Misoprostol, a prostaglandin E_1 analog, can also be used to protect the mucosa, especially in patients who are taking NSAIDs. However, it is a potent abortifacient and should not be used in women who are unprotected from pregnancy or are pregnant. Sucralfate, an aluminum-hydroxide compound that binds to the ulcer base, is as effective as H_2 blockers, and may be useful in smokers and in pregnancy. Omeprazole inhibits the proton pump, resulting in a 90% or greater reduction in gastric acid. It is effective, but because of concerns about complete acid suppression, it should not be used as maintenance therapy for more than 4 weeks.

The need for surgical therapy has decreased tremendously. The indications for surgery include hemorrhage unresponsive to medication, obstruction, perforation, and malignancy. Occasionally, patients unresponsive to medical therapy may need surgery, either partial or total gastrectomies, usually with vagotomies.

Comparison of Treatments

There are many effective ways to treat PUD and no one way. Some individuals with symptoms are treated before or without UGI or endoscopic proof of an ulcer; some experts require proof before therapy is started. Some authorities prefer a stepped-care approach starting with nonpharmacological methods, mucosal agents, H_2 blockers, and antibiotics, followed by omeprazole and finally surgery. Starting therapy with nonpharmacology methods and either H_2 blockers, mucosal agents, or antacids, then using another is acceptable. Use of omeprazole, testing for *H. pylori* and treating, if present, and surgery should

be kept for recurrent or persistent disease (Fig. 16.1).

Gastric Carcinoma

Gastric cancer is uncommon and occurs far more often in men than women (23), probably because women have fewer risk factors. The rate of incidence of women to men is 1:2 (24). However, when gastric carcinoma occurs in women, it presents with far more advanced disease and has a poorer survival rate. Adenocarcinomas are 95% of the gastric cancers with lymphomas, carcinoid tumors and sarcomas making up the last 5% (1).

Risk Factors

Gastric carcinoma is associated with alcohol abuse, cigarette smoking, deficiency in particular vitamins, chronic *H. pylori* infection, high intake of carcinogens, and a diet high in highly salted, pickled, or smoked foods, especially beans or fish (24). Studies have not found any particular nutrients, diet, or vitamins that might improve the mortality of gastric cancer (25).

In women, only multiparity greater than four was a risk factor for gastric cancer. Previous use of OCPs only slightly increase the risk. Women with a history of late menopause or longer fertile life are less likely to have gastric carcinoma. Estrogen, whether endogenous or exogenous, was not a factor in the development of gastric carcinoma (23). Women with short durations of fertility and early menopause had a higher risk of gastric cancer (26).

Survival Rate

In Japan, where endoscopic screening is common and gastric cancer is eight times more common than in the United States, the survival time had increased in the 1980s, but the survival rate and survival time for women, especially those less than age 50, was much lower than that of men. The 10-year survival for men was 39.2% and women 29.3% (24). In the United States, 5-year survival rate for men

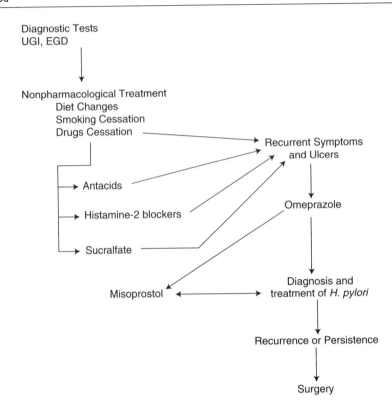

Figure 16.1. Treatment for PUD.

and women is only 10%, and the disease is usually metastatic at the time of diagnosis (1). Women were much more likely to have advanced disease, lymph node metastases, liver metastases, diffuse forms of cancer, and deeper invasion at diagnosis (24).

Clinical Symptoms and Diagnosis

Symptoms can be similar to those of PUD (e.g., nausea, vomiting, abdominal pain) but obstruction and hematamesis are more common. Gastric carcinoma often presents with only nonspecific symptoms such as anemia and weight loss until the apperance of obstruction, such as early satiety or an ulcer that bleeds or does not heal. Physical examination and laboratory tests are noncontributory.

Diagnosis is made by UGI or EGD with subsequent biopsy. Evaluation of patients with gastric cancer involves liver function tests, chest radiographs, and CT scans of chest and abdomen to look for metastases.

Treatment and Screening

The only treatment for gastric carcinoma is surgical. If the disease is diagnosed early, the surgery can give a 90 to 95% 5-year survival rate (1). Radiation can be used. Sometimes surgical palliation for relief of obstruction is necessary. Gastric lymphoma has a better cure rate.

Screening for gastric cancer in the United States is not suggested, except in high-risk populations. The diagnosis can rarely be made while the lesion is curable. Because more women are smoking greater amounts for longer periods of time and more women are abusing alcohol, this diagnosis must be considered in women with nonhealing ulcers, gastric ulcers, or severe PUD bleeding.

Gallstones

Incidence

Gallbladder disease and gallstones are particularly women's diseases, especially during childbearing years. Women of childbearing age have a three times greater risk of developing gallstones as men; the risk for women of all ages is twice that of the men (27). In one English study, the women under age 30 years were 9.7 times more likely and women of all ages were 2.3 times more likely to have a cholecystectomy for gallstones than men (28). In a Dutch hospital study, women under age 30 years were 7.0 times more likely to have a cholecystectomy.

Risk Factors

Risk factors for women developing gallstones include certain ages and ethnic groups, obesity, low daily energy output, and special diets including diets low daily calcium intake (29). "Fat, fertile, flatulent and forty" has been the disparaging way to remember these, but these risk factors may not be all accurate. Whether certain diets, estrogen use in OCPs or estrogen as replacement therapy (ERT), and cigarette smoking cause gallstones is disputed. Use of alcohol may be protective (30).

Age

As mentioned above, the peak incidence of gallstones is age 30 to 39 years, although all women under age 30 years had a 7 to 10 times greater risk of developing gallstones (29).

Ethnic Groups

Native American populations, Mexican-Americans, and other groups have higher rates of gallstone disease, whereas African-Americans had a lower rate than white Americans (31). Native American women had a higher cholecystectomy rate and a higher complication rate than non-native Americans, with a peak incidence at age 30 to 39 years. Native American women had a three times higher

cholecystectomy rate than Native-American men (32). One prevalence study of rural Canadian women found a rate of 167/1000 women; this was higher than the rate for women in the Framingham study of 59/1000 but not significantly different from the incidence than in Native American women (29).

Obesity

There is a significant increase in risk with obesity. A large body mass index (BMI) is the strongest predictor of gallstones of all risk factors (30). Women with BMI over 45 kg/m² had a sevenfold excess risk. Those with BMI greater than 30 kg/m² had a gallstone incidence of greater than 1% per year, whereas those with BMI greater than 45 kg/m² had a risk of developing gallstones of approximately 2% per year (27, 33).

Diet

There have been several large studies of women's diets and their effects on certain diseases. Neither coffee, tea, sucrose consumption, dietary fats, nor frequent attendance at fast food restaurants were found to cause gallstones (34). Long overnight fasts, dieting, and low-fiber diets may increase risk of gallbladder disease (38).

Pregnancy

Coexistent gallstones were noted by ultrasound in 3.9 to 11.3% of pregnant women (35). None of the following factors, however, could predict which pregnant women had gallstones: parity, age at menarche, early pregnancies, level of education, excessive coffee, tea, or sugar ingestion, cigarette smoking, alcohol use, or physical activity (34). However, being older, having a history of dysmenorrhea or previous breast-feeding, or a maternal history of gallstones increased the risk for gallstones during pregnancy (35).

Hormone Use

Hormones, specifically estrogen, affect the biliary metabolism; estrogen increases the cholesterol-to-bile ratio and biliary cholesterol levels by enhancing hepatic lipoprotein uptake and inhibiting bile acid synthesis (36). Estrogens have a cholestatic effect. However, whether physiologic periods of endogenous high estrogen, OCPs, and ERT cause gallstones is disputed.

One study found that women on HRT are at twice greater risk of developing gallstones (37). Gallstones occur more often in women with higher parity and lower age at first birth, those with greater exposure to endogenous estrogen (30, 38).

There have been a few long-term European studies on the effect of OCPs on gallstones and those study studied had large variations in findings. Most long-term studies found little or no increased incidence (35, 39, 40). An English study found the relative risk of gallstones for current OCP users as only 1.12, whereas an American study of OCPs found that the relative risk of coexistent gallbladder disease was 2.0 (38). A prospective study of over 96,000 women found little relationship between symptomatic gallstones and ever-use of OCPs. The relative risk was 1.2 for OCP "ever-users," 1.5 for use of 10 to 14 years, and 1.6 for current users (41). Other studies put the relative risk at no greater than 1.2 (38, 42).

Cigarette Smoking

Cigarette smoking has been linked with increased likelihood of developing gallstones in women in some studies (38, 33). Current cigarette smokers had a slightly higher risk than nonsmokers (30).

Clinical Symptoms and Diagnosis

Gallstones can be asymptomatic. Patients may complain of fatty food intolerance, nausea, vomiting, pain on eating, and RUQ pain that is constant or colicky and severe when a gallstone passes. The symptoms may be difficult to differentiate from PUD or pancreatitis. Complications include (a) cholecystitis with fever, (b) abdominal pain and vomiting, (c) bacterial infection, (d) pancreatitis, (e) ileus, (f) biliary obstruction, (g) biliary cirrhosis, (h) hepatic injury, (i) and perforation. Acute cholecystitis is the most common severe complication of gallstones.

Diagnosis is made which may be negative in patients with biliary obstruction, or ultrasound of the gallbladder. It made be made accidentally. HIDA scans of the gallbladder may be used to define gallbladder function if the OCG is noncontributory. Liver function tests, amylase, lipase, and bilirubin levels may help define degree of obstruction, although the alkaline phosphatase is the most sensitive indicator of biliary tract obstruction. If elevated, obstructive disease must be considered most likely.

Treatment

The treatment has historically been surgical, but lately conservative observation, medical treatment, and lithotripsy have provided new alternatives. Even the "gold standard of surgery," the open cholecystectomy, has been largely replaced by the laparoscopic cholecystectomy that has fewer days of hospitalization and fewer complications.

Although obesity is definitely linked to the formation of gallstones, there is no evidence that weight loss or low-fat diets will alter gallstone disease; dieting may increase gallstone incidence and colic. However, a high-fiber, high-calcium diet, ingestion of meals at regular times, and vigorous exercise may reduce the formation of further stones (43).

The natural history of gallstones is not well known, and whether asymptomatic gallstones can be left alone is disputed. Serious complications occur in 1 to 2% of patients with asymptomatic gallstones per year, with fewer complications occurring the longer gallstones are present. In patients with mild symptoms, the rates of complications are 1 to 3%

per year (44). There is no one factor that can predict who will get complications. There is no increase in life expectancy in performing surgery over watching asymptomatic gallstones (45).

In selected patients, cautious observation may be suggested. Patients with asymptomatic gallstones, those with preferences against surgery, or those who have contraindications to surgery such as pregnancy or respiratory problems may be observed. There is some evidence that observation does not carry an increased risk of mortality, only the possibility of future attacks of colic or cholecystitis (45).

Patients who do not wish surgery may be candidates for stone dissolution by medical means. For medical therapy, the gallstones should be less than 2 cm, cholesterol stones and the gallbladder should function, as seen by an OCG. Ursodiol (ursodeoxycholic acid), a naturally occurring bile acid, can be used to dissolve cholesterol stones directly and desaturate the cholesterol content of the bile. Although expensive, it is free of many serious side effects such as diarrhea, liver injury, and cholesterol (low-density) elevation, which were associated with previous bile acids such as chenodiol. Approximately half the patients have good dissolution of their stones within 2 years, more with small or cholesterol stones, and many patients are pain free before complete dissolution (46). Good candidates are women who are thin and who have stones less than 15 mm in size. Contact dissolution of stones with methyl tertbutyl ether is rapid and more often effective, but an interventional radiologist is needed (4).

Extracorporeal lithotripsy can be considered in those patients with calcium stones and a functioning gallbladder. It will shatter 95% of such stones and works best if there are fewer than three stones that are less than 3 cm in diameter. Ursodiol treatment should follow. This should not be considered in women with acute cholecystitis and can cause cardiac arrhythmias, bacteremia, hematuria, and liver

injury. The lithotripsy equipment and service may be difficult to locate.

However, if the gallstones are symptomatic, causing acute colic or cholecystitis, or perforate or obstruct the biliary system, then surgery is indicated. The surgery of choice is often the laparoscopic cholecystectomy (LC). The LC has a shorter duration of hospitalization and convalescence with lower complication rate that the traditional open cholecystectomy (47).

Special Situations: Pregnancy and the Elderly
Gallstone disease in pregnancy is often asymptomatic. If symptomatic, acute cholecystitis or colic can be watched, treated with IV fluids, bowel rest, pain medications, and antibiotics. Surgery may be contraindicated or ill-advised, such as in the first or third trimester. Surgery should be postponed if possible until after delivery.

In older women, gallstones can be treated the same way as in younger women, unless surgery is contraindicated or not desired. Then, ursodiol can be used first.

Liver Diseases

All common liver diseases affect both women and men, but some of these affect women differently (Table 16.3). Although there are many liver diseases that can be discussed, this chapter will discuss four. Primary biliary cirrhosis, autoimmune liver disease, and drug-induced liver disease occur more often in women. Alcoholic liver disease has different consequences in women than men.

Primary Biliary Cirrhosis

Primary biliary cirrhosis is an uncommon disease with an unknown etiology. There is an immunological injury to the bile ducts with resulting destruction of the small intrahepatic bile ducts. Ninety percent of cases occur in women between ages 40 and 60 years (37, 48).

Table 16.3. Risk Factors and Rates for Gallstone Disease in Women

Risk Factor	Known Relative Risk
Age	7.0 to 9.7 (under age 30)
Ethnic group	
Native Americans	3.0
Obesity	7.0 (BMI >45 kg/m^2)
Fatty diet	
Hormone replacement	2.0
Oral contraceptives	1.12 to 1.5
Cigarette smoking	
Alcohol use	
Obstetrical history	
More than 4 births	2.0

Clinical Symptoms and Diagnosis

The primary symptom is the insidious onset of pruritus and finally liver failure. It may be asymptomatic, discovered by an elevated alkaline phosphatase (AP) level on a routine chemistry panel. Associated symptoms include arthralgias, jaundice, fatigue, and dark urine (49).

Physical examination may show diffuse pigmentations, hepatomegaly, splenomegaly, and skin xanthomas. Jaundice is usually a late finding.

Over two thirds of the patients have an associated extrahepatic disease. Biliary cirrhosis is associated with (a) pernicious anemia, (b) Sjogren's disease, (c) lupus, (d) mixed connective tissue disease, (e) peripheral neuropathies, (f) scleroderma, (g) autoimmune thyroid disease, (h) lichen planus, (i) celiac disease, (j) renal tubular acidosis, (k) IgM glomerulonephritis, (l) thyroiditis, (m) rheumatoid arthritis, (n) and fat-soluble vitamin deficiencies.

Laboratory examination will show an elevated AP, and often serum gamma-glutamyl transpeptidase and low albumin and cholesterol. Serum IgM levels can be elevated. The disease has significant abnormal cellular immune regulation and T-suppressor cell depression (50). All patients will have antimitochondrial antibodies against M$_2$, an antigen of the inner mitochondrial membrane (48). Liver biopsy, which can be nonspecific, may show damaged intralobular ducts surrounded by a dense inflammatory infiltrate, which is full of plasma cells and histocytes with granuloma formation (48). Retrograde cholangiography shows no biliary obstruction or sclerosis that would be the sign of sclerosing cholangitis (Table 16.4).

Clinical Course and Prognosis

The course and prognosis of the disease are variable. Patients can be asymptomatic for over 10 years. Eventually, the disease progresses to cirrhosis with patients complaining of jaundice. After symptoms occur, the average life expectancy is 5 to 7 years, during which periods patients may feel well except for jaundice, malaise, fat-soluble vitamin deficiency resulting in night blindness and bone density loss, and weight loss. Osteomalacia, portal hypertension with ascites, esophageal varices, hepatic encephalopathy, and hemorrhage are late complications. The course can be painful and disabling with pathological fractures caused by the disease itself and corticosteroid therapy (37). Thus, although it has been used, many experts say that corticosteroids are contraindicated because of its effects on bone. Chlorambucil decreases hepatic inflammation and retards the hyperbilirubinemia, but its long-term effects are unknown. Penicillamine has been investigated but actually worsens late disease (49).

There has been an association with malignancy. In one study of 208 women, there was a 4.4 relative risk of extrahepatic malignancies, most of these breast cancers (50).

Treatment

There is no effective cure except liver transplantation. Therapy is aimed at maintaining nutrition and relieving pruritus. The diet should include adequate calories with reduced

Table 16.4 Elevated Liver Function Tests—Differential Diagnosis

	Biliary Cirrhosis	Viral Hepatitis	Autoimmune Hepatitis	Drug-induced Hepatitis	Alcoholic Hepatitis	Wilson's Disease
Clinical picture	Pruritus	Fever, malaise, wt. loss, poss. exposure history	Fever, malaise, wt. loss, autoimmune dis family history	Fever, malaise, drug use	Alcohol consumption	Family history, psychiatric problems
Important history	Age 40–59	Any age but usually young	Age 11–30	Middle age and older women	Middle age and older, but occurring younger	Young adult and older
SGOT	Often normal	High	High	High	High	High
SGPT	Often normal	High	High	High	High	High
Alk. phos.	Elevated	Often normal	Often normal	Often normal	Often normal	Often normal
Bilirubin	Elevated	Normal or elevated	Normal or elevated	Normal or elevated	Normal or late elevated	Normal or elevated
ANA	Normal	Normal	Elevated > 1/160	Normal	Normal	Normal
Antimitochondrial antibodies	100% positive	Negative	Often positive	Negative	Negative	Negative
Physical findings	HSMEG*	HSMEG	HSMEG	HSMEG	HSMEG, jaundice, wt loss, cirrhosis	HSMEG, Keiser-Fleischman rings
Associated diseases	Rheumatoid arthritis, thyroiditis, pernicious anemia, RTA, fat-soluble vitamin deficiency	None	Rheumatoid arthritis, thyroiditis, pernicious anemia, CREST	None	None	None

Table 16.4—Continued

	Biliary Cirrhosis	Viral Hepatitis	Autoimmune Hepatitis	Drug-induced Hepatitis	Alcoholic Hepatitis	Wilson's Disease
Course	Chronic, progressive	Either acute, can progress or be fatal	Chronic, progressive, may be treated with steroids	Usually acute	Progressive often, especially if chronic alcohol use	Progressive without treatment, chronic
Treatment	Symptomatic, liver transplant	Symptomatic, supportive	Steroids	Supportive; cessation of drug use	Supportive; cessation of alcohol use	***

Alk. phos. - Alkaline phosphatase
*HSMEG - Hepatosplenomegalys

fats (approximately one third). Supplemental vitamin A and D and 6 to 8 g of calcium a day should be given. Additional vitamin K is usually not needed unless bleeding occurs.

The pruritus can be treated with bile-salt binders in those patients whose stool is still pigmented, showing that bile is still passing into the intestine. Cholestyramine (one packet) before and after breakfast or 12 to 16 g per day is adequate.

Those without pigmented stool can take methyltestosterone 10 mg sublingual three times a day or neorethandrolone 10 mg orally twice daily. Phenobarbital that has been used to stimulate bile flow should be avoided because it aggravates bone disease.

Autoimmune Liver Disease

Like all autoimmune diseases, autoimmune liver disease or lupoid hepatitis occurs more often in women. Seventy percent of cases occur in women, over half in ages 11 to 30 (48). There is a strong familial association; individuals with this disease often have HLA-B8 and Drw3 histocompatibility loci. In this disease, cytotoxic antibodies are produced to an unknown antigen on hepatocyte, which initiates the liver cell destruction. It is associated with rheumatoid arthritis, thyroiditis, diabetes, pleuritis, and amenorrhea.

Clinical Symptoms and Diagnosis
The patient presents with chronic fatigue, malaise, anorexia, jaundice, hirsutism, stria, and acne. Physical examination may show jaundice and hepatosplenomegaly. The laboratory examination shows elevated liver function tests (e.g., SGOT, SGPT, GGT), elevated ANA levels (>1/160), and positive smooth muscle and antimitochondrial antibodies. Differential diagnosis includes viral hepatitis, drug-induced hepatitis, and other autoimmune diseases, and chronic active hepatitis. Liver biopsy shows signs of chronic active hepatitis and cirrhosis.

Clinical Course and Therapy
This disease is usually chronic and relapsing. Prognosis depends on the development of cirrhosis and its complications. Treatment with corticosteroids prolongs survival and usually has a good response.

Drug-induced Liver Disease

Drug-induced liver disease (DILD) is predominantly a disease of middle-aged and elderly women. Drugs cause approximately 27% of acute hepatitis (51). Many drugs can cause liver disease, but some hepatotoxic drugs such as oral contraceptives are used only for women; others such as nitrofuradantoin and other antibiotics or low-dose methotrexate are more often used to treat women for UTI prophylaxis or rheumatoid arthritis, or are more likely to be toxic in women such as halothane. There are several drugs that are well known to be hepatotoxic; the more common are phenytoin, sulfonamides, erythromycin, isoniazid, and alpha-methyldopa (51, 52). (Table 16.5) The risk of developing DILD increases with age, and there is a familial tendency.

Estrogen
Oral contraceptives can cause several forms of liver disease. Elevated liver function tests and hepatic disease are absolute contraindications to use of OCPs.

OCPs cause hepatomas, hepatitis, and cholestasis. However, estrogen use may be protective for hepatocellular carcinoma. One study of women on estrogen replacement therapy showed a possible protective effect of cancer of the liver or biliary tract (53).

Hepatic adenomas. Hepatomas are caused by OCPs, but are rare; the risk in long-term users is 3 to 4 per 100,000 women. The risk increases with duration of use and use over age 30 years. The mechanism is unknown. However, because hepatomas and hepatocarcinomas do not have estrogen receptors, direct toxicity is unlikely as the cause (48).

Table 16.5. Drugs Well Known for Hepatotoxicity

Antibiotics

Erythromycin
Isoniazid
Nitrofuradantoin
Sulfonamides
Tetracyclin
Trimethoprim-sulfamethoxasole

Anticonvulsants

Phenytoin

Hormones

Oral Contraceptives

Other

Alpha-methyldopa
Chlorpromazine
Chlorpropamide
Halothane
Lipid-lowering agents
Methotrexate

The patient is usually asymptomatic and liver function tests are normal. Diagnosis is made by CT scan or ultrasound. The adenomas are usually single encapsulated subcapsular tumors located in right lobe of liver. Biopsy shows normal-appearing hepatocytes without portal areas.

Asymptomatic tumors can be followed by ultrasound unless they are painful or bleed. If OCPs are stopped, the adenoma often regresses. There may be emergency complications of spontaneous hemorrhage or infarction that require surgery.

Nodular hyperplasia of liver. OCPs have been known to cause nodular hyperplasia, an unencapsulated parenchymal mass. This lesion on biopsy shows scarred areas that look like cir-

rhosis and fade with discontinuation of OCPs (48).

Cholestasis. The most common liver injury caused by OCPs is cholestasis. Withdrawal of OCPs usually resolves the problem.

Other Drugs

Halothane causes hepatitis in 1 of 10,000 anesthesia exposures. The risk of hepatitis increases with age, multiple exposures, older age, and obesity. The symptoms are fever and jaundice after exposure; liver function tests are significantly elevated, especially SGOT. The biopsy shows a picture similar to viral hepatitis. The mortality is over 40% (48). Individuals who have this reaction should never again be exposed to halothane. There is cross reactivity to methoxyflurane or enflurane as well.

Erythromycin esterate can cause a cholestatic hepatitis, especially in adults. Taking any erythromycin preparations gives an individual a 5.2 greater risk of developing acute hepatitis than one who takes no antibiotics. Other antibiotics, such as tetracycline and sulfonamides, also give the individual an increased risk of developing hepatitis (52). However, this risk is small; there are only 2.28 cases of erythromycin-induced hepatitis for 1 million 10-day treatments of erythromycin.

Nitrofuradantoin can cause cholestasis and chronic active hepatitis, which appears insidiously after weeks or years of therapy. This happens most often in women who are receiving prophylaxis for UTIs. It is associated with lupus-like syndrome, and may proceed to cirrhosis. Discontinuation of antibiotics usually resolves the injury.

Methotrexate causes liver damage when it is given in low pulse doses used to treat rheumatoid arthritis; thus, it is more likely to occur in women. Cirrhosis is possible.

Any drug that is metabolized in the liver can cause hepatitis. Anticonvulsants such as phenytoin, alpha-methyldopa, procainamide, and antipsychotics such as chlorpromazine are well-known hepatotoxins.

Clinical Diagnosis and Treatment

Drug-induced liver disease presents similarly to viral hepatitis with fatigue, fever, weight loss, malaise, jaundice, dark urine, and tan stools. Physical examination may be normal, or there may be hepatomegaly, RUQ tenderness, jaundice, and splenomegaly. Laboratory evaluation will show elevated liver function tests. Often bilirubin elevations are late or minimal, and alkaline phosphatase levels normal, but SGOT, SGPT, and SGGT are significantly elevated. Liver biopsy may be necessary for diagnosis. Differential diagnosis includes viral, autoimmune, and alcoholic hepatitis, Wilson's disease, and sclerosing cholangitis.

Usually conservative therapy of hydration, rest, and discontinuation of the medication should allow recovery. However, there is a 4% fatality rate (54).

Alcoholic Liver Disease

Alcoholic liver disease is more common in men, as is alcohol abuse. However, in women who abuse alcohol, its effect on the liver is much worse. Women develop alcoholic liver disease earlier, with greater severity, and after consuming less alcohol than men. The incidence of alcoholic liver disease is increasing in young people and in women.

Gender Differences

Liver damage is dose-dependent; women can develop liver damage at amounts of less than 20 g per day, whereas men usually develop liver disease at dosages above 60 g per day. In women, higher blood alcohol concentrations occur with the same amount of alcohol, and there is a slower rate of alcohol metabolism in the stomach (55).

Women present with more severe alcohol-related liver disease than men. Progression of disease in women occurs more rapidly, even if women abstain from alcohol. Women present with worse liver function, with lower serum albumin concentrations, and more severe hep-atic histologic changes (56, 57). Women develop alcoholic liver disease after shorter periods of excess drinking with less alcohol (58).

This increased severity in women may occur because women may develop higher blood ethanol levels after same dose, or because of a reduced volume of distribution. Experts disagree whether there are any differences between women and men in the activities of alcohol dehydrogenase.

Clinical Symptoms and Diagnosis

Alcoholic liver disease may be asymptomatic at first. It may present as episodes of acute alcoholic hepatitis that may appear similar to acute viral hepatitis. The woman complains of nausea, diarrhea, anorexia, weight loss, RUQ pain, or with social and work problems attributable to alcoholism. The physical exam may be normal, or it may show signs of liver disease such as jaundice, hepatomegaly, RUQ tenderness, and muscle wasting. There can be fever as well.

After repeated episodes and continued alcohol abuse, cirrhosis, portal hypertension, liver failure, and encephalopathy can occur. There will be signs of (a) chronic liver failure such as telangiectasias, (b) jaundice, (c) ascites, (d) muscle wasting, (e) cachexia, (f) pruritus, (g) hepatomegaly or a small liver, (h) splenomegaly, and an altered mental status, often fluctuating from confusion to coma. There may be UGI bleeding from esophageal varices caused by portal hypertension, or bleeding caused by lack of clotting factors.

Laboratory examination shows leukocytosis, transaminase liver function elevations especially SGGT and elevation of mean corpuscular volume (MCV). In liver failure, besides liver function test abnormalities, there can be signs of hypersplenism with thrombocytopenia and scarcity of clotting factors with an elevated prothrombin time. Ultrasound of liver and spleen may show hepatosplenomegaly. Upper GI radiograph may show gastritis, hepatomegaly, and esophageal varices.

Clinical Course and Treatment

Treatment of alcoholism and hepatic encephalopathy is beyond the scope of this discussion. Cessation of alcohol abuse, good nutrition, rest, and a low-protein, high-calorie diet may allow for reversal of some liver damage. Close follow-up is essential. Without cessation of alcohol use, progression to failure is probable.

Lower GI Disease: Colorectal Disease

Irritable Bowel Disease

Irritable bowel disease (IBS), described since 1919, is a syndrome of chronic intestinal stasis that is usually confined to women under age 35 years and associated with abdominal pain and bloating, alternating constipation and diarrhea or both, and possibly associated with infertility, amenorrhea, and ovarian cysts (59). "Functional" distressing colon complaints are common, affecting up to 30% of the US population and causing up to 70% of visits to gastroenterologists (60). These are the most common chronic GI disorders seen in primary care practices (61).

IBS is much more common in women, occurring twice as often as in men, especially between 20 and 40 years. A survey of workers at a factory revealed that 7/655 women and 0/400 men had bowel frequency of two stools weekly or less, making constipation usual in approximately 1% of women (59).

The defect or abnormality that causes IBS is not known. Some experts believe IBS arises from disturbances in the neurohormonal control of the GI tract with motility disturbances and without overt pathology. Often the colon, small intestine, or both are described as hyperactive. IBS may be precipitated by stress, psychological factors, a low-fiber diet, or an anticholinergic medication (37). Other studies found a lack of dietary fiber correlated well with IBS symptoms (60).

Symptoms and Associated Problems

Women with IBS complain of severe constipation, diarrhea, or a combination of the two, colicky abdominal pain, gas, eructation, bloating, nausea, and malaise. Nausea and vomiting occur in over 50%, dyspepsia in 25%, chronic headaches in 60%, and urinary symptoms in up to 60% of women. These symptoms have usually impaired the individual's life socially and economically.

Diagnosis is clinical; physical and laboratory examination are normal, except for possible mild abdominal tenderness. Barium enema radiograph is normal. The diagnosis is one of exclusion—there should be no demonstrable bowel pathology. Differential diagnosis includes inflammatory bowel disease and infectious diarrheas.

In women, IBS has been associated with a history of family deprivation and disrupted relationships. In one referral practice, 44% of women with IBS reported a history of sexual or physical abuse and forced intercourse (61). It has also been associated with infertility, dysmenorrhea, anorgasmia, and dyspareunia (63). In one study, 60% of women with dysmenorrhea had associated IBS as compared with 20% of controls (64). Women with IBS were three times more likely to have had gynecological or any type of surgery, especially a hysterectomy. In women with IBS, a hysterectomy was less likely to relieve pelvic pain than women without IBS who had a hysterectomy (59, 64).

Psychological traits associated with IBS include personality disturbances such as orderliness, over-conscientiousness, indecision, worry, rigidity, emotional overcontrol, and depression (37). One small but intensive study that compared volunteers with women with GERD or IBS found that almost three times more women with GERD or IBS reported sexual or physical abuse than volunteers. These women had lower pain thresholds and a significantly greater number of psychiatric disorders and pain syndromes (65).

Clinical Course and Treatment

Although the exact cause is not known, the prognosis is good. IBS usually has an intermittent course. However, when it worsens, it has a high deleterious effect on education, work, and interpersonal relationships.

Treatment is increased ingestion of dietary fiber. Twenty to 30 g dietary fiber should be added by adding bran, fiber additives, vegetables, and psyllium preparations daily. The individual should start adding fiber to their diet slowly and increase the amounts over a 2- to 4-week period.

Inflammatory Bowel Disease

Inflammatory bowel disease, Crohn's disease (CD), or ulcerative colitis (UC) is more common in women and young people, with 35,000 new cases in the United States per year (37). The yearly incidence of UC in women is 0.15 per 1000, and for CD 0.09 per 1000. Smoking increases the incidence of CD, but decreases the incidence of UC. Use of OCPs increased the incidence of both (4). There is also a familial tendency.

The diagnosis, treatment, and follow-up of both these diseases are extensive and may require more study.

Clinical Symptoms and Diagnosis

The primary symptom for both diseases is acute or intermittent diarrhea, often bloody especially in CD. Abdominal pain is common in both; in UC, the pain is often crampy in both lower quadrants and relieved by bowel movements, whereas in CD the pain is often right-sided, postprandial, and accompanied by vomiting. In UC, urgency of defecation and hematochezia often occurs. Anal complaints such as fissures, hemorrhoids, abscesses, and inflammation are more common with CD; 90% of individuals with CD have abnormal anal regions.

Differential diagnosis includes infectious diarrheas (66). Barium enema will often sug-gest the diagnosis. Diagnosis can be made after negative stool cultures, with a sigmoidoscopy or colonoscopy with biopsy. UC always has rectal involvement and proceeds continuously, uninterruptedly, and universally proximal, whereas CD has skip regions, areas of normality between areas of inflammation with "cobblestoning," and areas of deep ulceration crossed by furrows. However, there is a 20 to 25% overlap between the diseases (67).

Both diseases have associated manifestations outside the colon including arthritis, arthralgias, thrombotic complications, and ocular inflammatory diseases. Cholesterol gallstones and calcium oxide kidney stones are more common in CD, whereas cholangitis is more common in UC.

Clinical Course and Treatment

Both diseases have chronic, relapsing courses. UC carries the threat of colon cancer. However, when the colon is removed, the GI symptoms resolve. Although CD carries no increased risk of cancer, because it skips throughout the GI tract, colectomy does not resolve the disease.

Medical treatment is the primary therapy in both diseases. Corticosteroids, sulfazalazine, and immunosuppressants are used. Vitamin supplements and good nutrition are important. When the diarrhea and weight loss are unresponsive to medical therapy, surgical removal of the colon in UC or worse areas in CD are contemplated.

Effect on Women

These diseases certainly have the possibility of affecting sexual function and body image. Fertility is unaffected by UC, but is slightly decreased in CD. During pregnancy, the activity of both diseases can be highly variable. Most women with either CD or UC have no increased risks during pregnancy (37). However, active UC or CD at the time of conception carries an increased risk of spontaneous abortion. UC and CD are more likely to flare up in the first trimester and 6 weeks after delivery.

Colon Cancer

Incidence

In women, colorectal cancer is the third most common malignancy and the second most common cause of cancer death (68). In 1985 72,000 women had colorectal cancer diagnosed, and 30,900 died. The individual risk for women is 6%, only slightly less than the 7% risk in men. The male-to-female ratio for 1995 was 1.29 for rectal cancer and 0.98 for colon cancer (37, 69).

The risk of colon cancer increases after age 40 years with 90% of cases in individuals over age 50 years. The total mortality, which has not decreased, is 60%. Only 50% of individuals will have curable disease on presentation (70).

Trends

Survival rates are better for women under age 65 years. However, more advanced disease is reported in women, at younger ages, and those of lower socioeconomic status (69).

Over the last 20 years the rate of colon cancer in women has increased slowly as the rate for rectal cancer has declined, possibly caused by an increase of colon cancer in women over age 75 years. As well, colon cancer has become increasingly more proximal; more right and transverse colon cancers have occurred, whereas fewer left and rectal cancers have been detected (69).

Risk Factors (Table 16.6)

Age. Age over 40 years is a definite risk factor for colon cancer. The risk increases slowly to age 50 years and then rates rise sharply.

Race. There is no association with development of colon cancer and race in women. However, racial differences exist in mortality; the mortality rate for colon cancer for white women and men decreased over the last 20 years, although it remained unchanged among African-American women and increased in black men (68).

Table 16.6. Risk Factors for Colon Cancer

Age over 40

Other colon disease: ulcerative colitis; familial polyposis, including inherited polyposis of colon and rectum and Gardner and Turcot syndromes

Other cancers: multiple cancer syndromes, breast, endometrial

Environment: living in the United States

Family history of colon cancer

Industrial and occupational exposures: asbestos, mineral oil, and metal

Diet: possibly diets high in fat or meat

Alcohol: increased risk of rectal cancer

Smoking: more than 35 years duration

Other colon disease. There is an increased risk of colon cancer in individuals with UC and familial polyposis, including inherited polyposis of colon and rectum and Gardner and Turcot syndromes (68). In familial polyposis, which is inherited as autosomal dominant, the individual develops adenomas that have an almost 100% malignant potential.

Other cancers. There is an increased risk of colon cancer in families who have multiple cancer syndromes. As well, women with a history of breast, endometrial, or ovarian cancer may be at a higher risk for colorectal cancer (71, 72).

Environment. There is some evidence, based on different colon cancer rates between immigrants to the United States and their children, that environmental factors can increase the risk of colon cancer. Migrating populations assume the colon cancer risk of their new country; Puerto-Rico-born New Yorkers have a twice greater risk of colon cancer than Puerto-Ricans living in Puerto Rico, whereas Japanese immigrants to the United States have a 2.5 greater risk than Japanese living in Japan (68).

Industrial and occupational exposures. Some occupational exposures increase the risk of colon cancer. This includes workers exposed to asbestos, mineral oil, and some metals.

Family history. A family history of colon cancer increases an individual's risk. Having a first-degree relative with colon cancer increases the risk fourfold (68).

Smoking. Smoking is not a risk factor for colon cancer, until the individual has smoked over 35 years. In a study of 12 years duration, women who were both active and passive smokers, especially older women smokers, had a decreased risk of colon cancer (73). Another study showed that women who smoked 20 years or more had a higher risk of small adenomas and a lower risk of large adenomas (74). In women who had smoked more than 35 years, smoking was a definite risk factor for cancer and became a stronger risk factor the longer the women smoked. Smoking 35 to 39 years gave the women a relative risk of 1.47 of developing colon cancer, increasing to a relative risk of 1.63 in years 40 to 45 of smoking, and 2.00 after 45 years of smoking (74).

Diet. There have been several large studies on women's health examining the effect of diet on various diseases that have produced conflicting results. Some showed that diets high in total fat were associated with some increased risk of colon cancer (75). One analysis of 23 studies found that 10 studies showed a direct association with colon cancer of high-fat diets, and 13 studies showed an association with high-meat diets with colon cancer, whereas six found no association with fat and 10 found no association with meat (76). The Iowa Women's Health Study of over 41,000 women over 4 years found that diets high in garlic, vegetables, and dietary fiber decreased the risk of colon cancer (77). There is no consensus, but many experts believe that although diets high in fat may increase the risk, diets high in fiber, especially vegetable fiber, decrease the risk of colon cancer (68, 78).

Alcohol. In the Iowa's Women's Health Study, the relative risk of developing rectal cancer for women drinking more than 4 g of alcohol per day was 1.27, whereas the risk of distal colon cancer decreased with increased alcohol intake (79).

Estrogen. It is unlikely that either endogenous or exogenous estrogen is a risk factor for colon cancer. Certainly women of childbearing age do not develop colon cancer more often. A study of over 118,000 nurses found that there was no association between colon cancer and parity, early menarche, early first birth, and use of oral contraceptives (80). A prospective study of over 63,000 women in Norway found no association with colon cancer and any reproductive factors, except multiple therapeutic abortions (81). Use of ERT was associated with a decreased risk of colon cancer (82).

Clinical Symptoms and Diagnosis

The woman with colon cancer may be asymptomatic for a long time, making screening important. A change in bowel habits, rectal bleeding, and abdominal pain are possible symptoms. Anemia (63%) and bowel obstruction are signs of right-sided cancers, whereas change in bowel habits, rectal bleeding, and abdominal pain were more common in left-sided cancers (68). Rectal bleeding has a variety of causes. In patients with rectal bleeding over age 60 years, only 10% had colon cancer, whereas 25% had noncancerous polyps (78).

The physical exam may be normal, or it may show weight loss, an abdominal mass, paleness, hepatomegaly, and rectal blood or positive stool guiacs. Laboratory examination may show anemia, an elevated sedimentation rate, abnormal liver function tests (with metastases), or may be normal. A carcioembryonic antigen (CEA) level is not a good screening or diagnostic tool. It is elevated in many situations including liver disease and smoking, but can be used to detect residual or metastatic disease. Diagnosis is made by barium enema, especially a double-contrast barium enema, or colonoscopy with biopsy. An abdominal CT scan may be indicated to evaluate for metastases, especially in the liver, and lymph node involvement.

Clinical Course and Treatment

Colon cancer is curable surgically, if found before spread through the serosa. Prognosis is directly related to stage at diagnosis and treatment. Colorectal cancer spreads locally first through the mucosa and muscle, and then through the serosa into the peritoneum and surrounding tissues and lymph nodes. Common metastatic sites are the lung and liver. Colorectal cancers are staged either by the Duke's stages (A to D) or the TNM staging dependent on degree of spread. There is a 5-year survival rate of 89.4% for localized cancer, 58.2% 5-year survival rate for cancer with regional spread, and 5.9% for cancer with distant metastases (68). (Table 16.7)

Surgery is the treatment of choice, but is not always benign. In patients with signs of obstruction or impending obstruction, it may be necessary on an emergent basis. In one study, 86% of surgeries were able to resect the primary tumor by wide resection, but almost half the patients had a complication, and 8% died in the postoperative period (68). Surgery is contraindicated in patients with hepatic metastases or ascites, unless obstruction, perforation, or uncontrolled bleeding make palliation necessary (78).

There are some studies investigating adjuvant chemotherapy and radiation that found some advantage to adding fluorouracil (5FU) and semustine to postoperative radiation for rectal cancer with regional or deep local spread. Adjuvant radiation for colon cancer may decrease pelvic metastases. For metastatic

Table 16.7. Prognosis for Colorectal Cancer

Stage	5-Year Survival (%)	10-Year Survival (%)
Stage I	90 to 97	74
Stage II	38 to 48	36
Stage III	26 to 56	5

disease, therapy with 5FU and levamisole HCL reduced the risk of recurrence by 41% and overall mortality by 33% (83). However, more than half of patients with colon cancer die from its complications.

The 1991 NIH consensus conference concluded that for stage I colon cancer, surgery was the choice without adjuvant therapy. Adjuvant therapy is not recommended for stage II, although treatment with 5FU and levamisole was suggested for stage III. For rectal cancer, radiation and chemotherapy were suggested for stage II and III only in ongoing clinical trials (78).

Follow-up for colon cancer or cancerous polyps includes colonoscopy annually for 2 years and then every 3 to 5 years. CEA levels should be normal after a complete resection, and followed yearly. Persistent or new CEA elevations suggest metastatic disease.

The most important factor in reducing colorectal cancer is primary prevention (i.e., change in diet), and secondary prevention (i.e., adequate screening). This is as important in women as men.

Special Considerations for Nurse Practitioners and Physician Assistants

The key to evaluation and diagnosis for the woman with GI complaints is listening. Woman often come to practitioners with vague complaints involving several body systems that health care providers might dismiss

as stress; yet, symptoms such as fatigue, nausea, or feelings of fullness after eating can be the result of serious, potentially life-threatening illnesses. Whether or not a serious disease process is diagnosed, the symptoms are affect-

Table 16.8. Lifestyle Modifications and GI Diseases

Disease	Dietary Changes	OTC Drugs/Alcohol	Caffeine	Tobacco	Other
GERD	Small frequent meals with fluids taken between meals to decrease volume; avoid large meals in evening; avoid food for 2–4 hours before bedtime; avoid symptom-producing food (frequent offenders are peppermint and chocolate; esophageal irritants such as red peppers, citrus juices and tomato products; acid secretion stimulators such as cola and milk; foods that decrease LES pressure and delay emptying such as high-fat foods)	Avoid NSAIDS; avoid alcohol (gastric acid stimulator)	Avoid (decaffeinated coffee may also irritate esophagus)	Avoid	Raise HOB up to 6" or use wedge-shaped bolster; avoid supine position or bending over after meals; avoid heavy lifting; avoid tight belts, girdles; weight loss; stress reduction; avoid use of straws or chewing gum if they increase flatus
PUD	Small, frequent meals to buffer acidity during acute stages; avoid aggravating foods (individualized), e.g., carbonated beverages, gas-forming foods, black pepper and chili powder which cause gastric irritation; eat slowly and chew food thoroughly	Avoid NSAIDS; avoid alcohol or use only moderate amounts with food	Avoid (decaffeinated coffee may also stimulate acid secretion)	Avoid	Stress management, moderate exercise program
Gallbladder disease	Avoid extreme dieting; increase fiber; avoid long overnight fasts (90)			Avoid	Exercise

Table 16.8.—Continued

Disease	Dietary Changes	OTC Drugs/Alcohol	Caffeine	Tobacco	Other
IBS	Limit problem foods on *individualized* basis, (e.g., discontinue fiber, especially popcorn, seeds, nuts, fruit peels, broccoli, dried beans; restrict lactose; restrict fatty foods); increase fiber slowly; high-calorie, high-protein diet; multivitamins including folic acids and minerals; supplemental formulas if needed; small frequent meals to increase intake	Avoid alcohol	Avoid	Avoid tobacco, especially with CD	Counseling
Liver disease (cirrhosis)	Balanced high-calorie diet; restrict fat if steatorrhea present; protein intake may be increased or decreased depending on liver function; vitamin and mineral supplements; avoid hypervitaminosis; restricted sodium (if ascites); avoid spices, pepper, coarse food if esophageal varices present	Avoid alcohol	Avoid especially if esophageal varices present		Rest; behavioral or other therapy

Data from Lommel LL (87), Uphold DR, Graham MV (88), and Davis JR, Sherer K (89).

ing the woman's quality of life on a daily basis.

After a woman has had time to describe her concerns, directed questions assist the practitioner to obtain a clear, complete, and accurate history. Careful documentation of drug use is critical. Use common brand names and symptoms to explore further, e.g., by asking the woman if she takes aspirin for headache, antibiotics for acne or urinary tract infections, or oral contraceptives for birth control. Especially for the woman with a possible liver abnormality, ask specifically about the use of vitamins and herbal agents, some of which can harm the liver. Because GI symptoms can be nonspecific and indicative of many diseases, practitioners must recognize women who are at risk as a result of smoking, drugs, alcohol abuse, diet, age, or other factors.

When the initial physical examination is normal, observation may be appropriate for women with milder symptoms of GI distress. During this time, a symptom log is maintained by the woman, and subsequent follow-up visits can aid decision making. Providers must be willing to re-evaluate and change the initial impression of the problem. For example, continuing complaints of heartburn by a pregnant woman might indicate gallbladder disease or other problems. All complaints during pregnancy (or at other stages of a woman's life) are not normal and caused by hormonal changes.

Interventions for GI problems must be planned with the woman. For many GI diseases, a cornerstone of treatment is lifestyle modification (Table 16.8). Help the woman identify specific goals for weight loss, smoking cessation, or other lifestyle changes. Assist her to locate resources such as support groups or health clubs and realistically evaluate whether she has the time, money, and other resources to use these services. Ask the woman if there are barriers to her goal achievement. Will family or coworkers resist or support her changes in lifestyle? If she anticipates lack of support, work with her to plan specific strategies for

such encounters. Plan for continuing contact and support.

Before referring a woman to any support group, the provider must ensure that there is a match between the woman's needs and the group's goals. Women's satisfaction with local groups must be continually evaluated, as well as the current status of the group. Some self-help groups may be active for only a short period of time; others may have problems with leadership (85).

An interdisciplinary approach is often needed for GI disorders. Nutritional counseling for weight loss or management of IBS for some women may be beyond the scope of the primary care practitioner. The woman who abuses alcohol or tobacco may need specialized help, as may the woman with body image disturbance, sexual functioning problems, or chronic progressive disease. Providers should consult for decisions regarding surgical versus nonsurgical treatment (e.g., for cholecystitis), management of problems with early or complicated cirrhosis, persistent, worsening or atypical symptoms, GI bleeding, the management of IBS, or extensive diagnostic testing (86).

References

1. Norris, TE. Upper gastrointestinal problems. Monograph, Edition No. 190. Home Study Self-Assessment program. Kansas City, MO: American Academy of Family Physicians, 1995.
2. Wolfe MM. What is intensive therapy for gastroesophageal reflux? Gastroenterology 1992;103:1696–1698.
3. Russell TL, Berardi RR, Barnett JL, et al. Upper gastrointestinal pH in seventy-nine healthy elderly North American men and women. Pharmaceut Res 1993;10:187–196.
4. Vessey, MP, Villiard-Mackintosh L, Painter R. Oral contraceptives and pregnancy in relation to peptic ulcer disease. Contraception 1992;46:349–357.
5. Anda RF, Williamson DR, Escobedo LG, Remington PL. Smoking and the risk of peptic ulcer disease among women in the United States. Arch Intern Med 1990;150:1437–1441.
6. Kurata JH, Nogawa AN, Abbey DE, Peterson F. A prospective study of risk for peptic ulcer disease in

Seventh-Day Adventists. Gastroenterology 1992; 102:902–909.

7. Schoon IN, Mellstrom D, Ytterberg BO, Oden A. Peptic ulcer disease in older age groups in Gothenburg in 1985. Age Ageing 1991;20:371–376.

8. Miller DK, Burton FR, Burton MS, Ireland GA. Acute upper gastrointestinal bleeding in elderly person. JAGS 1991;39:409–422.

9. Brazer SR, Tyor MP, Pancotto FS, et al. Studies of gastric ulcer by community based gastroenterologists. Am J Gastroenterol 1990;85:824–828.

10. Agrawal N. Risk factors for gastrointestinal ulcers caused by nonsteroidal anti-inflammatory drugs (NSAIDS). J Fam Pract 1991;32:619–624.

11. Henry D, Robertson J. Alimentary tract: nonsteroidal anti-inflammatory drugs and peptic ulcer hospitalization rates in New South Wales. Gastroenterology 1993;104:1083–1091.

12. Bjarnason I, Hayllar J, MacPherson AJ, Russell AS. Side effects of nonsteroidal antiinflammatory drugs on the small and large intestine in humans. Gastroenterology 1993;104:1832–1847.

13. Walt R, Katschinski B, Logan R, Ashley J. Rising frequency of ulcer perforation in elderly people in the United Kingdom. Lancet 1986;I(8479):489–492.

14. Griffin MR, Piper JM, Daugherty JR, Snowden M, Ray WA. Nonsteroidal anti-inflammatory drug use and increased risk for peptic ulcer in elderly persons. Ann Intern Med 1991;114:257–263.

15. Taha AS, Capell HA, Sturrock RD, Russell RI. Nonsteroidal peptic damage in rheumatoid patients receiving second line drugs. Am J Gastroenterol 1991;86:1588–1591.

16. Faulkner G, Prichard P. Somerville K, Lanman MJ. Aspirin and bleeding peptic ulcers in the elderly. Br Med J 1988;297:1311–1313.

17. Skander MP, Ryan FP. Non-steroidal anti-inflammatory drugs and pain free peptic ulceration in the elderly. Br Med J 1988;297:833–834.

18. Armstrong CP, Whitelaw S. Death from undiagnosed peptic ulcer complications: a continuing challenge. Br J Surg 1988;75:1112–1114.

19. Taha AS, Dahill S, Sturrock RD, Lee RD, Russell RI. Predicting NSAID related ulcers—assessment of clinical and pathological risk factors and importance of differences in NSAID. Gut 1994;35:891–895.

20. Fennerty MB. Helicobacter pylori. Arch Intern Med 1994;154:721–727.

21. Scavone JM, Ochs HF, Greenblatt DJ, Matlis R. Pharmacokinetics of oxaprozin in women receiving conjugated estrogen. Eur J Clin Pharmacol 1988;35: 105–108.

22. Schubert TT, Bologna SD, Nensey Y, et al. Ulcer risk factors: interactions between Helicobacter pylori infections, non-steroidal use and age. Am J Med 1993;94:413–418.

23. LaVecchia C, D'avanzo B, Franceschi S, et al. Menstrual and reproductive factor and gastric cancer risk in women. Int J Cancer 1994;59:761–764.

24. Maehara Y, Watanabe A, Kakeji Y, et al. Prognosis for surgically treated gastric cancer patients is poorer for women than men in all patients under age 50. Br J Surg 1992;65:417–420.

25. Raiha IH, Impivaara O, Seppala M, Sourander LB. Prevalence and characteristics of symptomatic gastroesophageal reflux disease in the elderly. JAGS 1992;40:1209–1211.

26. Palli D, Cipriani F, Decarli A, et al. Reproductive history and gastric cancer among post-menopausal women. Int J Cancer 1994;56:812–815.

27. Hoover EL, Jaffe BM, Webb H, England DW. Effects of female sex hormones and pregnancy on gallbladder prostaglandin synthesis. Arch Surg 1988;123: 705–708.

28. Van Beek EJ, Farmer KC, Millar DM, Brummelkamp WH. Gallstone disease in women younger than 30 years. Neth J Surg 1991;43:60–62.

29. Williams CN, Johnson JL. Prevalence of gallstones and risk factors in Caucasian women in a rural Canadian community. Can Med Assoc J 1980;122: 664–668.

30. Ransohoff DF, Gracie WA, Ransohoff DF. Treatment of gallstones. Ann Int Med 1993;119:606–619.

31. Diehl AK, Stern MP, Ostrower VS, Friedman PC. Prevalence of clinical gallbladder disease in Mexican-American, Anglo and black women. South Med J 1980;73:438–441,443.

32. Cohen MM, Young TK, Hammarstrand KM. Ethnic variation in cholecystectomy rates and outcomes. Manitoba, Canada 1972–1984. Am J Pub Health 1989;79:751–566.

33. Stampfer MJ, Maclure KM, Coliditz GA, Manson JA, Willett WC. Risk of symptomatic gallstones in women with severe obesity. Am J Clin Nutr 1992;55:652–658.

34. Basso L, McCollum PT, Darling MR, Tocchi A, Tanner WA. A descriptive study of pregnant women with gallstones. Relation to dietary and social habits, education, physical activity, height, and weight. Eur J Epidemiol 1992;8:629–633.

35. Basso L, McCollum PT, Darling MR, Tocchi A, Tanner WA. A study of cholelithiasis during pregnancy and its relationship with age, parity, menarche, breast-feeding, dysmenorrhea, oral contraception and a maternal history of cholelithiasis. Surg Gynecol Obstet 1992;175:41–46.

36. Everson GT, McKinley C, Kern F Jr. Mechanism of gallstone formation in women. Effects of exogenous estrogen and dietary cholesterol hepatic lipid metabolism. J Clin Invest 1991;87:237–246.

37. Bjorkman DJ, Burt RW, Tolman KG. Primary care for women with gastrointestinal disorders. Clin Obstet Gynecol 1988;31:974–987.

38. Vessey M, Painter R. Oral contraceptive use and benign gallbladder disease; revisited. Contraception 1994;50:167–173.

39. Jorgensen T. Gallstones in a Danish population: fertility period, pregnancies and exogenous female sex hormones. Gut 1988;29:433–439.

40. Rome Group for the epidemiology and prevention

of cholelithiasis. Prevalence of gallstone disease in an Italian adult female population. Am J Epidemiol 1984;119:796–805.

41. Grodstein F, Colditz GA, Hunter DJ, et al. A prospective study of symptomatic gallstones in women: relation with oral contraceptives and other risk factors. Obstet Gynecol 1994;84:207–214.

42. Gholson CF, Sittig K, McDonald JC. Recent advances in the management of gallstones. Am J Med Sci 1994;307:293–304.

43. Hofmann, AF. Future of laparoscopic chylecystectomy. Primary and secondary prevention of gallstone disease: implications for patient management and research priorities. Am J Surg 1993;165:541–548.

44. Friedman GD. Natural history of asymptomatic and symptomatic gallstones. Am J Surg 1993;165:399–404.

45. Ransohoff DF, Gracie WA, Ransohoff DF. Treatment of gallstones. Ann Intern Med 1993;119:606–619.

46. Schoenfield LJ, Marks JW. Oral and contact dissolution of gallstones. Am J Surg 1993;164:427–430.

47. Barkun JS, Barkun AN, Meakins JL. Laparoscopic versus open cholecystectomy: the Canadian experience. The McGill Gallstone Treatment Group. Am J Surg 1993;165:455–458.

48. Sherlock S. Liver disease in women: alcohol, autoimmunity and gallstones. West J Med 1988;149:683–686.

49. James SP. Primary biliary cirrhosis. N Engl J Med 1985;312:1055–1057.

50. Wolke AM, Schaffner E, Kapelman B, Sacks HS. Malignancy in primary biliary cirrhosis. High incidence of breast cancer in affected women. Am J Med 1984;76:1075–78.

51. Carson JL, Stom BL, Duff A, et al. The feasibility of studying drug-induced acute hepatitis with use of medicaid data. Clin Pharmacol Ther 1992;52:214–219.

52. Carson JL, Strom BL, Duff A, et al. Acute liver disease associated with erythromycins, sulfonamides, and tetracycline. Ann Intern Med 1993;119:576–583.

53. Adami HO, Persson I, Hoover R, Schairer C, Bergkvist L. Risk of cancer in women receiving hormone replacement therapy. Int J Cancer 1989;44:833–939.

54. Lee MG, Hanchard B, Williams NP. Drug-induced acute liver disease. Postgrad Med J 1989;65:367–370.

55. Sherlock S. Alcoholic liver disease. Lancet 1995;345:227–229.

56. Morgan MY, Sherlock S. Sex related differences among 100 patients with alcoholic liver disease. Br Med J 1977;1:939–941.

57. Loft S, Oleson KL, Dossing GM. Increased susceptibility to liver disease in relation to alcohol consumption in women. Scan J Gastroenterol 1987;22:1251

58. Saunders JB, Davis M, Williams R. Do women develop alcoholic liver disease more readily than men? Br Med J (Clin Res Ed). 1981;282:1140–1143.

59. Preston DM, Lennart-Jones JE. Severe chronic constipation of young women: "idiopathic slow transit constipation." Gut 1986;27:41–48.

60. Georges JM, Heitkemper MM. Dietary fiber and distressing gastrointestinal symptoms in midlife women. Nurs Res 1994;43:357–361.

61. Drossman DA, Leserman J, Nachman G, et al. Sexual and physical abuse in women with functional or organic gastrointestinal disorders. Ann Intern Med 1990;113:828–833.

62. Sandler RS. Epidemiology of the irritable bowel syndrome in the United States. Gastroenterology 1990;99:409–415.

63. Hogston P. Irritable bowel syndrome as a cause of chronic pain in women attending a gynecology clinic. Br Med J 1987;294:934–935.

64. Crowell MD, Dubin NH, Robinson JC, et al. Functional bowel disorders in women with dysmenorrhea. Am J Gastroenterol 1994;89:1973–1977.

65. Scarinici IC, McDonald-Hale J, Bradley LA, Richter JE. Altered pain perception and psychosocial features among women with GI disorders and history of abuse: a preliminary model. Am J Med 1994;97:108–118.

66. Ogorek CP, Fisher RS. Differentiation between chron's disease and ulcerative colitis. Med Clin North Am 1994;78:1249–1259.

67. Katz J. The course of inflammatory bowel disease. Med Clin North Am 1994;78:1275–1280.

68. Wayne MS, Cath A, Pamies RJ. Colorectal cancer: a practical review for the primary care physician. Arch Fam Med 1994;4:357–367.

69. Steele GC, Jessup LM, Winchester DP, Murphy GP, Menck HR. Clinical highlights from the national cancer data base: 1995; Can J Clinicians 1995;45:102–113.

70. Barnes J. Early diagnosis of colorectal cancer. Practitioner 1991;235:908–911.

71. Furner SE. Large bowel cancer and hormone exposure in women. Diss Abstr Int 1988;48:2942.

72. Rex DK, Sledge GW, Harper PA, et al. Colonic adenomas in asymptomatic women with a history of breast cancer. Am J Gastroenterol 1993;88:2009–2014.

73. Sandler RS, Sandler DP, Comstock GW, Helsing KJ, Shore DL. Cigarette smoking and the risk of colorectal cancer in women. J Natl Cancer Inst 1988;80:1329–1333.

74. Schoen RE, Weissfeld JL, Kuller LH. Are women with breast, endometrial or ovarian cancer at increased risk for colorectal cancer? Am J Gastroenterol 1994;89:835–842.

75. Holtsman D. The relationship between dietary fat consumption and breast cancer mortality in American women. Diss Abst Int (Sci) 1985;46:812b.

76. Bostick RM, Potter JD, Kushi LH, et al. Sugar, meat and fat intake and non-dietary risk factors for colon cancer incidence in Iowa women (United States). Cancer Causes and Control 1994;5:38–52.

77. Steinmetz KA, Kushi LH, Bostick RM, Folson AR, Potter JD. Vegetables, fruit, and colon cancer in the

Iowa's women's health study. Am J Epidemiol 1994;139:1–15.

78. Herold AH, Warner EA, Oldenski RJ, Perchalski JE. Oncology III. Monograph Edition #170. Home Study Self-Assessment program. Kansas City, MO: Am Acad Fam Physicians, July 1993.

79. Gapstur SM, Potter JD, Folsom AR. Alcohol consumption and colon and rectal cancer in postmenopausal women. Int J Epidemiol 1994;23:50–57.

80. Chute CG, Willet WC, Colditz GA, et al. A prospective study of reproductive history and exogeneous estrogens on the risk of colorectal cancer. Epidemiology 1991;2:201–207.

81. Kvale G, Heuch I. Is the incidence of colorectal cancer related to reproduction? A prospective study of 63,000 women. Int J Cancer 1991;47:390–395.

82. Jacobs EJ, White E, Weiss NS. Exogenous hormones, reproductive history, and colon cancer. Cancer Causes Control 1994;5:359–366.

83. Moertel CB, Fleming TR, MacDonald JS, et al. Levamisole and fluorouracil for adjuvant therapy of resected colon cancer. N Engl J Med 1990;322:352–358.

84. Bredfeldt JE. Liver disease. In: Lemcke DP, Pattison J, Marshall LA, Cowley DS, eds. Primary Care of Women. Norwalk, CT: Appleton & Lange 1995;241–150.

85. Dudley SL, Starin RB. Cholelithiasis: diagnosis and current therapeutic options. Nurse Pract 1991;16:12, 14, 16, 18, 23–24.

86. Alley NM, Foster MC. Using self-help groups: a framework for nursing practice and research. J Adv Nurs 1990;15:1383–1388.

87. Lommel LL. Gastrointestinal disorders. In: Star WL, Lommel LL, Shannon MT, eds. Women's Primary Health Care. Washington, DC: American Nurses Association, 1995;7-1–7-67.

88. Uphold DR, Graham MV. Clinical Guidelines in Family Practice. Gainesville, FL: Barmarrae Books, 1993, pp. 506–555.

89. Davis JR, Sherer K. Applied Nutrition and Diet Therapy for Nurses. 2nd ed. Philadelphia: WB Saunders, 1994:805–853.

90. Sichieri R, Everhart JE, Roth H. A prospective study of hospitalization with gallstone disease among women: role of dietary factors, fasting period, and dieting. Am J Pub Health 1991;81:880–883.

17.1

Lactation

Joy Melnikow

Introduction

The physiologic and nutritional function of the female breast is lactation. Although "natural," it often takes encouragement, role-modeling, and support to perform, and it has cultural and social meanings. Breast-feeding may have significant medical and psychological consequences.

Unfortunately, breast-feeding has declined in the United States. The percentage of women breast-feeding at discharge from the hospital after a delivery decreased from 60% in 1984 to 52% in 1989 (1). Providers have an important role in reversing this trend. They can provide support for breast-feeding during the prenatal and postpartum periods, they can provide accurate information to pregnant women and breast-feeding mothers, and they can manage clinical problems that may arise in ways that facilitate continued breast-feeding. This chapter will review normal anatomy and physiology of lactation, methods for promotion of successful breast-feeding, and management of common maternal problems related to lactation.

Reasons to Breast-feed

Breast-feeding reduces morbidity from lower respiratory infections, gastroenteritis, and otitis media for infants in developed countries (2–4). Breast milk contains immunoglobulins and white blood cells that will help the infant fight infections. Iron found in breast milk has greater bioavailability than that in high-iron formulas, and breast milk is low-phosphate. It has been recognized by a wide range of authorities as the ideal, and preferably the only, food for newborns and infants up to age 4 to 6 months (5–7). Because of these benefits, *Healthy People 2000* set a goal of 75% of women breast-feeding at hospital discharge (8).

Breast-feeding has maternal benefits as well: convenience because of the lack of need for preparation of formula and bottles, facilitation of maternal-infant bonding, and facilitation of maternal weight loss postpartum (9). Feeding the mother more calories may be less expensive than buying formula.

Anatomy and Physiology of Lactation

When pregnancy commences, breast development is stimulated by pituitary, luteal, and placental hormones. Although breast size is not a determinant of successful lactation, hormonally stimulated breast development does lead to breast enlargement during pregnancy. From the second trimester until after delivery, colostrum is produced in the radial array of breast lobes. These lobes drain toward the nipple through the lactiferous ducts. The lactiferous ducts converge into wider lactiferous sinuses, generally found below the border of the areola. When the lactiferous sinuses are massaged by the gums of the nursing infant, by manual expression, or by mechanical pumping, milk is expressed through a series of 15 to 25 openings on the nipple (Fig. 17.1.1). Each

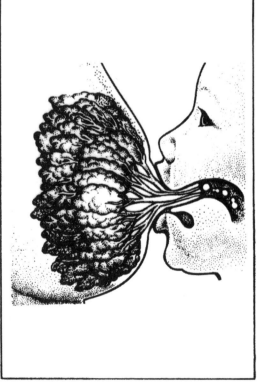

Figure 17.1.1. Anatomy of the lactating breast *(right)*, showing positioning of the infant's gums over the lactiferous sinuses. *(Left)* Good latch-on position. (Courtesy of Childbirth Graphics, Waco, TX).

opening drains a single lactiferous sinus. Understanding this anatomical arrangement is key to correct positioning of the infant on the breast, and for the management of problems such as blocked ducts.

After delivery, the rapid decline in placental hormones combined with nipple stimulation from suckling of the newborn results in the establishment of lactation. In the neuroendocrine cycle of lactation, stimulation of afferent sensory neurons in the nipple by the nursing infant results in release of prolactin and oxytocin from the pituitary. Prolactin acts to increase milk synthesis, whereas oxytocin stimulates the contraction of myoepithelial cells surrounding the breast alveoli, resulting in the let-down or milk ejection reflex.

Supporting Lactation: The Role of the Provider

Decisions about method of infant feeding are made before pregnancy or during the prenatal period, usually before the third trimester (10).

Family and cultural beliefs have a large effect on whether a woman breast-feeds. Family members of friends who have successfully breast-fed increase the chance that the woman will. The woman's expectations also play a large role. The father's feelings about breast-feeding exert an important influence on the decision to breast-feed; fathers who believe breast-feeding is healthier for the baby are more likely to be supportive of breast-feeding (11).

Both clinician support and organized programs of breast-feeding promotion during the prenatal period have been shown to be effective in increasing the proportion of mothers choosing to breast-feed their infants (12, 13). Providers of prenatal care should encourage their patients, first, by asking what their experiences of breast-feeding have been, and then by emphasizing the many benefits to mother and infant. Free patient education pamphlets on infant feeding provided by infant formula companies may contain biased information on breast-feeding. Independently developed patient education materials, at appropriate reading levels, are preferable (Table 17.1.1).

During the postpartum period in the hospital, both breast-feeding in the delivery room as soon as possible after delivery and infant rooming-in have been shown to improve the rate of successful breast-feeding (14). Most infants are alert and ready to feed in the first hour after birth. Following this, they often become sleepy and disinterested in feeding for a prolonged period. During the first and subsequent feedings, the provider should work with the nursing staff to assist new mothers with positioning their infants.

Infants' mouths should open widely, and their head is brought forward onto the nipple so that as much of the areola as possible is taken into their mouth. This position ensures that the infant's gums are massaging the lactiferous sinuses. The infant and mother should be positioned chest to chest. The infant can be held in one of several alternative positions, including the cradle hold, the football hold, and side-lying (Fig. 17.1.2). These last two positions are particularly useful for women who have undergone a cesarean section. Alternating feeding positions at each feed will reduce repeated friction to one portion of the nipple and may reduce nipple trauma.

Postpartum hospital policies are important for ensuring successful breast-feeding. Rooming-in and demand feeding (usually every 1 to 3 hours) have been shown to increase successful breast-feeding (14). Conversely, formula supplements, pacifiers, and discharge packs of formula have all been demonstrated to reduce the rate of successful breast-feeding (14–16). Providers should work with nursing staff and hospital administration to implement hospital policies that foster successful breast-feeding. Continuing education on breast-feeding may be needed for clinicians, resident physicians, and nursing staff. A curriculum has been designed to meet these edu-

Table 17.1.1 Breast-feeding Patient Education Materials

Books
- Dana N, Price A. *Successful Breastfeeding: A Practical Guide for Nursing Mothers.* New York: Meadowbrook Press, 1989.
- Dana N, Price A. *The Working Woman's Guide to Breastfeeding.* New York: Meadowbrook Press, 1987.
- Gaskin IM. *Babies, Breastfeeding, and Bonding.* South Hadley, MA: Bergin & Garvey Publishers, 1987.
- Huggins K. *The Nursing Mother's Companion.* Harvard, MA: Harvard Common Press, 1990.
- Mason D, Ingersoll D. *Breastfeeding and the Working Mother.* New York: St. Martin's Press, 1986.
- Reukauf DM, Trause MA. *Commonsense Breastfeeding: A Practical Guide to the Pleasures, Problems, and Solutions.* New York: Atheneum, 1988.
- Worth C. *Breastfeeding Basics: Easy-to-Read, Easy-to-Use Directions for the Breastfeeding Mother.* New York: McGraw-Hill, 1983.

Pamphlets
- Childbirth Graphics, Ltd, P.O. Box 21207, Waco, TX 76702 (800) 299-3366
    Danner SC, Cerrutti E. *Nursing Your Baby for the First Time*
    Danner SC, Cerrutti E. *Nursing Your Baby Beyond the First Days*
    Danner SC, Cerrutti E. *Expressing Breastmilk*
    *Breastfeeding—Getting Started in 5 Easy Steps**
    *20 Great Reasons to Breastfeed Your Baby**
    *Helpful Hints on Breastfeeding**
    Breastfeeding and Returning to the Workplace
- Nancy Bryant/Fuentes Productions 1721 Dayton Rd., Chico, CA 95928
    *Simple Supplemental Aids to Breastfeeding: A Copy Book**
    (1 page handouts can be copied for distribution to patients)
- Krames Communications 1100 Grundy Lane, San Bruno, CA 94066 (800) 333-3032

Videos
- *A Healthier Baby by Breastfeeding.* Smith L. Television Innovation Company, 8349-N Arrowridge Blvd., Charlotte, NC 28273. Available from Childbirth Graphics.
- *Breastfeeding: The Art of Mothering.* Alive Productions, Ltd., Port Washington, NY. Available from American Academy of Pediatrics 141 Northwest Point Blvd., P.O. Box 927 Elk Grove Village, IL 60009 (800) 433-9016.

*Available in English and Spanish.

cational needs (17). Hospitals can apply to UNICEF for a "Baby Friendly Hospital" designation if they can document that their policies meet UNICEF requirements for breast-feeding promotion (Table 17.1.2).

As hospital stays following delivery have shortened, the need for short-term postpartum follow-up has increased. Follow-up by phone within a few days of discharge should be supplemented by a brief postpartum office or home visit within the first 2 weeks after delivery. Problems or questions related to breastfeeding can be addressed, the importance of frequent nursing and avoiding formula supplements during the first few weeks can be reemphasized, and the weight of the infant checked. The first 2 weeks are critical. If the woman has someone (e.g., family members, sister, nurse, friend, mother, mother-in-law, someone from a nursing support group, physi-

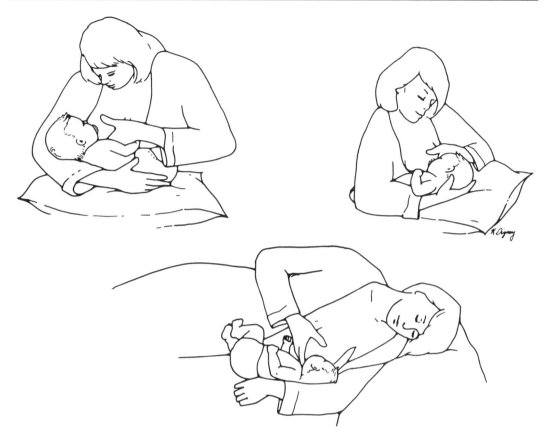

Figure 17.1.2. Positions for breast-feeding: cradle hold *(top left),* football hold *(top right),* side lying *(bottom).* (Reprinted with permission from Melnikow J, Bedinghaus JM. Management of common breastfeeding problems. J Fam Pract 1994;39:56–64.)

Table 17.1.2. Hospital Policies Required to Qualify as a "Baby Friendly Hospital" (From World Health Organization/UNICEF)

Ten Steps to Successful Breastfeeding

Every facility providing maternity services and care for newborn infants should foster the following:

1. Have a written breast-feeding policy that is routinely communicated to all health care staff.
2. Train all health care staff in skills necessary to implement this policy.
3. Inform all pregnant women about the benefits and management of breast-feeding.
4. Help mothers initiate breast-feeding within 30 minutes of birth.
5. Show mothers how to breast-feed, and how to maintain lactation even if they should be separated from their infants.
6. Give newborn infants no food or drink other than breast milk, unless *medically* indicated.
7. Practice rooming-in: allow mothers and infants to remain together 24 hours a day.
8. Encourage breast-feeding on demand.
9. Give no artificial teats or pacifiers (also called dummies or soothers) to breast-feeding infants.
10. Foster the establishment of breast-feeding support groups and refer mothers to them on discharge from the hospital or clinic.

cian) to whom to turn with her questions and from whom to receive support, successful and rewarding breast-feeding is much more likely.

Lactation increases daily maternal caloric requirements by 300 to 700 kcal (18). Adequate fluid intake is critical, although pushing large volumes of fluid will not increase the milk supply. Many clinicians advise lactating women to continue prenatal vitamins during lactation. Bone mineralization in the spine appears to decrease during lactation but returns to baseline when lactation ends (19), emphasizing the importance of adequate calcium intake during lactation (1200 mg/day). Moderate exercise has no adverse effects on breast-feeding (20).

Maternal Problems during Lactation (Table 17.1.3)

Sore Nipples

Sore nipples are a common complaint of breast-feeding mothers and are frequently cited as a reason to discontinue breast-feeding (21–23). Transient pain when the infant latches onto the breast is a normal discomfort that usually subsides after the first few weeks. Continuous pain throughout feeding, or cracked, bruised, or bleeding nipples require clinical attention, or preferably, prevention.

Sore nipples may be prevented by prenatal nipple rolling, starting at 35 to 36 weeks gestation (24). Nipple rolling is performed by grasping the areola behind the nipple between the thumb and finger, pulling gently but firmly outward, and rolling the nipple back and forth. The position of the thumb and finger are then shifted around to another position on the areola and the exercise is repeated. After birth, close attention to proper positioning of the infant's mouth on the breast and alteration of nursing positions at each feeding (Fig. 17.1.2) may serve to prevent nipple trauma. Hand expression or pumping to soften engorged breasts before the infant is put to the breast is also important for prevention of nipple trauma.

Once nipple trauma has occurred, observation of nursing and correction of any factors caused by poor positioning or engorgement are the first steps. Ensuring adequate let-down and nursing on the less sore breast until let-down occurs are also helpful. Allowing a small amount of breast milk to dry on the nipple after feedings is thought to be helpful. Acetaminophen may be taken for pain relief. Application of commercial creams, lanolin, antibiotic ointment, and antiseptic spray are ineffective (25–28). Alcohol and soap solutions will increase nipple soreness (26). Limiting the length of time for breast-feeding or limiting the frequency of feeds are sometimes recommended to reduce nipple soreness, but are not effective and are likely to decrease the percentage of women continuing to breast-feed (29, 30).

Problems with the Milk-Ejection Reflex

The release of oxytocin from the pituitary at the initiation of suckling results in a significant increase in milk flowing from the breast. It is identified in several ways: the infant will suddenly begin to get much more milk with each compression of the nipple and will swallow more frequently, a tingling sensation in the nipple with an increased heaviness or fullness in the breasts may be noted, or milk may leak from the opposite breast. Because of the effects of oxytocin on the uterus, uterine cramping is often noted simultaneously in the first postpartum days.

The milk-ejection, or let-down reflex, often takes several days to become well established. It is inhibited by psychological stress (31), pain, anxiety, and cold (32). If it does not occur, the infant may not get sufficient milk, and the nipples may be traumatized by longer and more vigorous nursing. The reflex can be enhanced by attention to the comfort, privacy, and relaxation of the mother. A warm bath or shower prior to nursing, or use of a heating pad or hot water bottle to the breasts, may assist with let-down. Oxytocin can be prescribed as a

Table 17.1.3. Common Problems in Lactation

Problem	Symptoms	Signs	Treatment
Sore nipples	Transient or continuous pain	Cracked or bleeding nipples, or no physical signs	Prevention by nipple rolling starting at 36 weeks pregnant; proper positioning of infant; ensuring adequate let-down; nursing on the less sore breast until let-down occurs; allowing a small amount of breast milk to dry on the nipple after feedings; Acetaminophen
Problems with the milk-ejection reflex	No Let-down during nursing	If continues, cracked and sore nipples and frustration may occur	Often takes several days to become well established and is inhibited by psychological stress, pain, anxiety, and cold
			Attention to the comfort, privacy, and relaxation of the mother; a warm bath or shower prior to nursing, or use of a heating pad or hot water bottle; use of prescription oxytocin nasal spray
Engorgement	Pain, difficulty feeding	Hard, swollen, and tender breasts; low-grade fever <38.5°	Milk should be hand-expressed or pumped before nursing; cool compresses
			Longer duration
Insufficient milk supply	Difficulty feeding	Infant feeds often, seems unsatisfied	Describe supply-demand cycle; reassure, supplement only as last resort
			Increase frequency of feeds to every 2 hours including night
Blocked ducts	Lump	Smooth, slightly tender or nontender lump in the breast that does not change in size with nursing.	Heat, massage of the area toward the nipple during and after nursing, and varying the infant's nursing position

Table 17.1.3.—Continued

Problem	Symptoms	Signs	Treatment
Puerperal mastitis	Flu-like symptoms; pain, fever, breast swelling, redness, heat	Red, wedge-shaped area on the breast Red, hot, tender, swollen breast	Frequent nursing, antibiotics directed against *S. aureus* such as cephalothin, or dicloxacillin, fluids, analgesics such as acetaminophen or ibuprofen
Breast abscess	Redness, heat, local swelling, palpable mass	Redness, heat, fever, local fluctuance	Incision and drainage, PO or IV antibiotics covering Staph
Maternal illness	Decreased milk supply	No signs	Push fluids and analgesics, rest, supplementation only if absolutely necessary Feed baby every 2 hours

nasal spray (Syntocinon, Sandoz Pharmaceuticals, East Hanover, NJ) to enhance let-down within 1 or 2 minutes after use. It is contraindicated in pregnancy and may cause uterine cramping or headache (33). Use of prescription oxytocin can generally be discontinued after a few days as the reflex becomes established.

Engorgement

Breast engorgement occurs when the milk supply "comes in," usually after hospital discharge, on the third or fourth postpartum day. The breasts fill with milk and become hard, swollen, and tender. Engorgement may be accompanied by a low-grade fever (<38.5°C). The infant has difficulty latching on to the engorged breast, because it is swollen and distended. Milk should be hand expressed or pumped before nursing to soften the breast and increase the mother's comfort. Cool compresses placed over the breasts may relieve discomfort (34). Longer duration of nursing in the early postpartum period may reduce the severity of engorgement (35). Engorgement is self-limited and generally resolves within a few days.

Insufficient Milk Supply

Although an insufficient supply of breast milk creates a risk for the infant, not the mother, it is one of the most common causes for cessation of breast-feeding. Understanding the demand-supply basis of the neuroendocrine stimulation of the breast is critical in addressing this problem. More frequent nursing results in greater release of prolactin, and milk production will respond within 24 to 48 hours. Formula supplementation will reduce breast stimulation and further decrease the breast milk supply. Advising the mother to go to bed with her baby and nurse on demand at a minimum of every 2 to 3 hours through the night will often succeed in resolving the problem. The infant may need to be awakened to nurse. If supplemental formula is considered necessary, a supplemental feeding device that allows the infant to obtain additional formula through a thin plastic tube while suckling the breast is recommended (24). Metaclopromide stimulates prolactin release and has been used to increase milk production in doses of 10 mg three times a day (36, 37).

Usually within the first 2 weeks, and again in the second month, there are "growth spurts" when the infant feeds frequently and seems constantly hungry. The mother may fear she lacks sufficient milk. Explanation of the demand-supply cycle, with emphasis on frequent nursing and reassurance by the provider, or other individual support for the woman through this period of increased need may support the continuation of breast-feeding. Breast milk supply will increase within 48 hours to match demand. Anticipatory guidance of these episodes at the early or 2-week office visit may decrease anxiety and emergency calls or visits.

Blocked Ducts

A blocked milk duct results in a smooth, slightly tender or nontender lump in the breast that does not change in size with nursing. It may result from failure to vary infant position for nursing, incomplete emptying of the breast, an overly copious milk supply, or an overly tight bra. Treatment consists of heat, massage of the area toward the nipple during and after nursing, and varying the infant's nursing position. A blocked duct in the presence of mastitis may result in a breast abscess.

Puerperal Mastitis

Mastitis occurs most frequently in the first 2 months postpartum. A recent study found the incidence in Canadian breast-feeding women was 2.9% in the first 7 weeks (38). Mastitis most often presents with flulike symptoms of fever and myalgias, and a red, wedge-shaped area on the breast. In some women, the entire breast becomes hot, bright red, tender, swollen, and hot. Systemic symptoms are often prominent, and breast pain may only be noted later in the course of the illness. It is most often caused by *Staphylococcus aureus*, but may result from *Escherichia coli* or Streptococcus species as well (39).

Treatment includes frequent nursing, antibiotics directed against *S. aureus* (such as a

first-generation cephalosporin such as cefalex-ien 500 mg or dicloxicillin 500 mg four times a day), rest, fluids, and analgesics such as acetaminophen or ibuprofen. Continued nursing is essential to drain the breast, and because the causative organisms are also found in the infant's mouth flora, nursing is not considered harmful to the infant (40). Bilateral mastitis, a rare problem, has been associated with group B streptococcus and may require treatment of the infant as well (41). If the symptoms and fever do not respond to oral antibiotics, rest, fluids, and parenteral antibiotics may be necessary.

Monilial Infection

Monilial infection of the nipple is described as causing an intense burning or stabbing pain in the breast when nursing. The nipple may show the typical erythematous rash with papular satellite lesions, or may appear normal. This problem is best treated by topical nystatin to the nipple and oral nystatin to the infant, even if there is no evidence of thrush (42).

Breast Abscess

Breast abscess occurs in 5 to 10% of cases of mastitis, resulting from untreated mastitis or mastitis complicating a blocked duct (38). It presents as a tender, hard breast mass with erythema of the overlying skin; needle aspiration of the mass yields pus, generally containing organisms similar to those seen in mastitis. Treatment consists of incision and drainage, antistaphylococcal antibiotics, and analgesics. Continued drainage of milk from the affected breast is essential. This may be accomplished in the first few days by gentle mechanical pumping with continued nursing on the opposite side; then nursing on the affected side can be resumed.

For women who insist on stopping breast-feeding, an alternative approach to treatment is incision and drainage with primary closure and drain placement, and antistaphylococcal antibiotics (43).

Maternal Illness

Maternal illness is only rarely a reason to recommend against breast-feeding. Exceptions are HIV infection, which may be transmitted through breast milk, and untreated, active tuberculosis (44). Infants of women with active or chronic hepatitis B infection should be immunized as soon as possible after birth and should receive hepatitis B immunoglobulin, but there has not been documented transmission of hepatitis B through breast-feeding (45). Diabetic women can safely breast-feed, although attention must be paid to increased caloric requirements with lactation and the possibility of reduced insulin requirements. Common medical problems in women of reproductive age (e.g., hypertension, many infectious diseases) can usually be treated with medications that are compatible with breast-feeding.

Maternal Medications and Contraception

Many maternal medications are compatible with continued breast-feeding. Excellent, up-to-date references are available (46, 47), and providers should always consult these before advising a woman to stop breast-feeding because of a required maternal medication. Often consideration of possible alternative medications will permit selection of a drug entirely compatible with continued breast-feeding. Concentration of a drug in breast milk depends on many factors, including lipid solubility, serum drug levels, and whether active transport occurs or not. Women with untreated active alcohol or other abuse or addiction problems should not breast-feed.

Whether a drug should be used must be considered individually. Usually, a less dangerous medication can be used. For example, for antibiotics, chloramphenicol and tetracyclines should be avoided, whereas the penicillins,

cephalosporins, and macrolides are relatively safe. For antihypertensive medications, beta-blockers should probably be avoided, and calcium channel blockers or alpha-methyldopa are better choices (Tables 17.1.4 and 17.1.5).

Breast-feeding is not a reliable contraceptive method. Although the duration of lactational amenorrhea averages 8 months in women exclusively breast-feeding, the timing of ovulation in an individual lactating woman is unpredictable. Barrier contraceptives, intrauterine devices, and progesterone-only contraceptives, including the progesterone-only oral contraceptive pill, levonorgestrel implants

Table 17.1.4. Some Commonly Used Drugs Considered Compatible with Breast-feeding

Antibiotics	**Anticonvulsants**
Penicillins	Carbamezipine
Cephalosporins	Phenytoin
Erythromycin	
Clindamycin	**Other**
Trimethoprim-sulfa*	Digoxin
	Heparin
Analgesics	Warfarin
Acetaminophen	Magnesium sulfate
Ibuprofen	Rubella vaccine
Naproxen	Rhogam
Codeine	
Contraceptives	
Progestin-only	
oral contraceptives	
Depo-Provera	
Norplant	
Antihypertensives	
Alpha-methyldopa	
Captopril	
Hydrochlorothiazide	
Calcium channel blockers	

*Avoid sulfonamides in mothers with infants < 2 months, premature, stressed, or ill infants or those with G6PD deficiency.

Table 17.1.5. Drugs Not Recommended during Breast-feeding

Prescription drugs contraindicated during breast-feeding	Prescription drugs of concern
Bromocriptine	HMG-CoA reductase inhibitors
Cyclophosphamide	Quinolone antibiotics
Cyclosporin	
Doxorubicin	Chloramphenicol
Ergotamine	Metronidazole
Lithium	Benzodiazapines
Methotrexate	Tricyclic antidepressants
Radionucleotides for diagnostic studies	Antipsychotics
	Phenothiazines

Drugs of abuse	Drugs to be used with caution
Alcohol	Aspirin
Amphetamines	Clemastine
Heroin	Phenobarbital
Marihuana	Primidone
Nicotine	Sulfasalazine
Phencyclidine	

(Norplant), and injectable depot medroxyprogesterone acetate (Depo-Provera) are all compatible with breast-feeding (48). Combination oral contraceptives may result in a reduced milk supply if used in first 6 weeks postpartum (49).

Maternal Employment and Breast-feeding

Fifty-three percent of mothers age 18 to 44 years return to work within the first year after giving birth, and both providers and mothers often assume that returning to work requires cessation of breast-feeding. If fact, with some advance planning, breast-feeding can readily be continued (50). Given the many benefits to the infant of maintaining breast-feeding for a minimum of 6 months, providers should support and encourage continued breast-feeding after the mother returns to work. Alternative approaches to continued nursing include pumping or expressing while at work, reverse cycle feeding, feeding the infant on work breaks, and minimal nursing.

Breast pumps come in manual, battery operated, and electric models. Manual pumps are smaller and less expensive, whereas electric pumps are bulky and expensive but highly efficient. Electric pumps are often available for short- or long-term rental. Manual expression requires no equipment, but may be more time-consuming. Patient education resources are available (Table 17.1). Breast milk can be safely stored in a clean container in the refrigerator for up to 48 hours and frozen in a standard deep freezer for up to 6 months (51). Many mothers who are not employed outside the home find that pumping or expressing milk so that another caregiver can feed the baby enables them to have occasional time away from the baby. For women employed outside the home, if the mother can return home during breaks, if on-site day care is available, or if the infant can be brought to work, full breast-feeding without pumping can be maintained. Unfortunately, these options are not available to many women.

Reverse cycle feeding involves more frequent breast-feeding (every 1 to 2 hours) in the early morning and evening, with fewer feedings in the middle of the day. It is helpful in maintaining the milk supply, which may decline somewhat if pumping is frequently substituted for nursing. It can be combined with pumping or manual expression, or may be combined with formula supplementation. Minimal breast-feeding consists of limiting feeds to a few when the mother is with her infant, generally combined with formula supplementation while the mother is at work. Although abrupt change from full-time nursing to minimal nursing will lead to engorgement, with gradual institution many women can maintain a limited milk supply for many months (52).

Conclusion

Breast-feeding can be enhanced and supported by the primary care provider, working with the woman, her family, and the hospital. Most breast-feeding problems have straightforward solutions that are readily taught or discussed and can permit continued breast-feeding. Using these, the provider can increase the likelihood that the woman will continue to breast-feed.

Breast Pain/Nonlactational Mastitis

Nonlactating women complaining of breast pain are best assessed by clinical history and examination. History will reveal whether the pain is cyclic or constant in nature. Physical exam will detect chest wall tenderness, breast masses, or inflammatory changes.

Mastitis is characterized by localized breast tenderness with redness of the overlying skin that responds to antibiotics. It must also be distinguished from fat necrosis, in which there is usually a history of trauma to the breast. Nonpuerperal mastitis is frequently related to duct ectasia, and is more often caused by mixed anaerobic/aerobic infections than is puerperal mastitis (53). Clindamycin or a first-generation cephalosporin provides adequate coverage for *S. aureus* and metronidazole and anaerobes. Nonpuerperal mastitis not responding to a trial of antibiotics requires further evaluation for inflammatory breast cancer (54).

Breast pain that is related to the menstrual cycle, without abnormal findings on physical exam, is extremely common and does not represent a pathologic process. Generalized fibronodular breast tissue is a normal variant. Most women with this problem respond well to reassurance. Use of a supportive bra and analgesics such as acetaminophen or nonsteroidal anti-inflammatory drugs or diuretics during the premenstrual period may offer relief with minimal side effects. Hormonal treatments such as danazol, bromocriptine, oral contraceptives, progestins, tamoxifen, and gonadotropin-releasing hormone agonists have been advocated for cyclic mastalgia. Abstinence from caffeine has also been recommended, but evidence to support their effectiveness has not been demonstrated in controlled trials. Evidence of efficacy is strongest for oral contraceptives, danazol, bromocriptine, and tamoxifen. Danazol, bromocriptine, and tamoxifen are all expensive and may have significant side effects (55, 56). If physical exam reveals a discrete breast mass that is cystic in nature, needle aspiration or fine needle aspiration (FNA) in the office can be both a diagnostic and a therapeutic procedure. Cyst fluid that is clear and nonbloody can be discarded. If the cyst does not resolve completely with aspiration or recurs on follow-up exam, further evaluation with mammography, breast ultrasound, and/or FNA is indicated.

Tender breast masses that are not clearly cystic or do not resolve with aspiration require further evaluation to rule out malignancy. Normal mammography in the presence of a palpable mass does not rule out malignancy, and further work-up by biopsy or fine needle aspiration for cytology is required (56).

Special Considerations for Nurse Practitioners and Physician Assistants

Choices in infant feeding should be explored during pregnancy and mentioned in preconception counseling when common myths and beliefs about breast-feeding can be explored. Verbal messages, posters, and printed materials in the provider's setting should make it clear that breast-feeding is encouraged and supported (57).

Prenatal education for the woman who is considering breast-feeding is individualized and focuses on the basics, e.g., how the breast functions, initiation of feeding, evaluation of success, positioning. If, instead, complications and their treatment are emphasized, the woman may lose her confidence for successful feeding (58). Mothers are assured that the provider will work with them to answer questions and deal with any problems. Including fathers or partners in discussion helps elicit their support and provides opportunities to talk about their specific roles in the infant's care. Although most women will not need special physical preparation of the breasts during pregnancy, use of breast shells have been recommended for inverted nipples (59). However, no research studies have supported the efficacy of any antenatal strategies to toughen nipples or make them more protractile (60). If a woman has decided against breast-feeding, misconceptions and emotional reasons should be determined and addressed (57). Low-income women who planned to bottle-feed have reported barriers to breast-feeding, including lack of confidence, dietary concerns, loss of freedom, embarrassment, and influence of family and friends. Even the advice and materials distributed by professions can act as barriers by reinforcing the perception of low-income women that successful lactation is limited to more affluent women (61).

Teaching for the new mother, as well as interventions for common problems, is based on current knowledge and approached in a consistent manner by all concerned, including consultants and support groups. Postpartum women who are inexperienced, sensitive, and vulnerable should not be confused and discouraged by conflicting advice about techniques of feeding. Information given through videos, pamphlets, posters, and individual and group teaching should be evaluated for consistency and accuracy (62). Many previously common approaches to breast-feeding, such as rigid time periods to prevent nipple soreness, have not proven beneficial and often hinder the success of feeding.

Other problems such as insufficient milk supply have no single correct answer and must be approached by assessing the individual woman. Observation of a feeding experience can often give the best information through a systematic assessment made by observing for correct body alignment, areolar grasp, areolar compression, and audible swallowing (62). Women with special-needs infants (e.g., infants who are premature or neurologically impaired, have cleft lip, palate defects) or women who have more than one infant to feed can benefit from referral to breast-feeding specialists (64).

Telephone contact should be made with a new mother within a few days after birth for assessment of the infant's feedings and the mother's perception and concerns. In addition, names and numbers of local support groups, lactation consultants, and breast pump rental depot's familiar to the clinician can be provided. During the early postpartum period, issues surrounding birth control and sexual relationships can be explored. Fatigue, engorgement, breast soreness, and vaginal dryness may contribute to a decreased libido (59), leading to more dissatisfaction with breast-feeding.

Breast-feeding is more than a feeding method. The complexities of this dynamic process must be considered as well as the vulnerability of the relationships involved. Mothers and infants are both critical players in a process that many women fear they will fail, perhaps because of in part to providers' lack of interest, misinformation, and inadequate support (65).

References

1. Ryan AS, Rush D, Krieger FW, Lewandowski GE. Recent declines in breast feeding in the United States, 1984 through 1989. Pediatrics 1991;4:719–27.
2. Wright AL, Holberg CJ, Martinez FD, Morgan WJ, Taussig LM. Breast feeding and lower respiratory

tract illness in the first year of life. Br Med J 1989;299:946–949.

3. Howie PW, Forsyth JS, Ogston SA, Clark A, du V Florey C. Protective effect of breast feeding against infection. Br Med J 1990;300:11–16.

4. Cunningham AS, Jelliffe DB, Jelliffe EFP. Breastfeeding and health in the 1980s: a global epidemiologic review. J Pediatr 1991;118:659–66.

5. Nutrition Committee of the Canadian Paediatric Society and the Committee on Nutrition of the American Academy of Pediatrics. Breast-feeding. Pediatrics 197862:591–600.

6. American Academy of Pediatrics. The promotion of breast-feeding. Pediatrics 1982;69:654–661.

7. American Public Health Association. Infant feeding in the United States. Am J Public Health 1981;71:207–211.

8. U.S. Department of Health and Human Services. Public Health Service. Healthy People 2000. Washington, DC: US Government Printing Office; DHHS Publication No. (PHS) 91-50212, 1990:379.

9. Dewey KG, Heining MJ, Nommsen LA. Maternal weight loss patterns during prolonged lactation. Am J Clin Nutr 1993;58:162–166.

10. Ryan AS, Rush D, Krieger FW, Lewandowski GE. Recent declines in breast feeding in the United States, 1984 through 1989. Pediatrics 1991;4:719–727.

11. Littman H, Medendorp SV, Goldfarb J. The decision to breastfeed. The importance of father's approval. Clin Pediatr 1994;33:214–219.

12. Winlkoff B, Baer EC. The obstetrician's opportunity: translating "breast is best" from theory to practice. Am J Obstet Gynecol 1980;138:105–117.

13. Brent NB, Redd B, Dworetz A, D'amico F, Greenberg JJ. Breastfeeding in a low-income population: program to increase incidence and duration. Arch Ped Adolesc Med 1995;149:798–803.

14. Perez-Escamilla R, Pollitt E, Lonnerdal B, Dewey KG. Infant feeding policies in maternity wards and their effect on breast-feeding success: an analytical overview. Am J Public Health 1994;84:89–97.

15. Kurinij N, Shiono PH. Early formula supplementation of breast-feeding. Pediatrics 1991;88:745–50.

16. Barros FC, Victoria CG, Semer TC, Tonidi Filho S, Tomasi E, Weiderpass E. Use of pacifiers is associated with decreased breast-feeding duration. Pediatrics 1995;95:497–99.

17. Woodward-Lopez G, Creer AE, eds. Lactation Management Curriculum. A Faculty Guide for Schools of Medicine, Nursing and Nutrition. San Diego: Wellstart International, 1994.

18. Institute of Medicine. Committee on Nutritional Status During Pregnancy and Lactation, Food and Nutrition Board. Nutrition During Lactation. Report of the Subcommittee on Nutrition During Lactation. Washington, DC: 1991; National Academy Press.

19. Kalworf HJ, Specker BL. Bone mineral loss and recovery after weaning. Obstet Gynecol 1995;86:26–32.

20 Dewey KG, Lovelady CA, Nommsen-Rivers LA, McRory MA, Lonnerdal B. A randomized study of the effects of aerobic exercise by lactating women on breast milk volume and composition. N Engl J Med 1994;330:449–453.

21. West CP. Factors influencing the duration of breastfeeding. J Biosoc Sci 1980;12:325–331.

22. Loughlin HH, Clapp-Channing NE, Gehlbach SH, et al. Early termination of breast-feeding: identifying those at risk. Pediatrics 1985;75:508–513.

23. Yeung DL, Pennell MD, Leung M, et al. Breastfeeding: prevalence and influencing factors. Can J Public Health 1981;72:323–330.

24. Melnikow J, Bedinghaus J. Management of common breast-feeding problems. J Fam Pract 1994;39:56–64.

25. Storr GB. Prevention of nipple tenderness and breast engorgement in the postpartal period. J Obstet Gynecol Neonatal Nurs 1988;17:203–209.

26. Newton N. Nipple pain and nipple damage. Problems in the management of breast feeding. J Pediatr 1952;41:411–423.

27. Hewat RJ, Ellis DJ. A comparison of the effectiveness of two methods of nipple care. Birth 1987;14:41–45.

28. Inch S. Antiseptic sprays and nipple trauma. Practitioner 1986;230:1037–1038.

29. Slaven S, Harvey D. Unlimited suckling time improves breast feeding. Lancet 1981;1:392–393.

30. De Carvalho N, Robertson S, Klaus MH. Does the duration and frequency of early breastfeeding affect nipple pain? Birth 1984;11:81–580.

31. Veda T, Yokoyama Y, Irahara M, Aono T. Influence of psychological stress on sucking induced pulsatile oxytocin release. Obstet Gynecol 1994;84:259–62.

32. Newton M, Newton NR. The let-down reflex in human lactation. J Pediatr 1948;33:698–704.

33. Goldfarb J, Tibbetts E. Breast Feeding Handbook. Hillside, NJ: Enslow, 1980:138.

34. Gaskin IM. Babies, Breastfeeding and Bonding. South Hadley, MA: Bergin & Garvey, 1987;67.

35. Moon JL, Humenick SS. Breast engorgement: contributing variables and variables amendable to nursing intervention. J Obstet Gynecol Neonatal Nurs 1989;18:309–315.

36. Ehrenkranz RA, Ackerman BA. Metoclopramide effect on faltering milk production by mothers of premature infants. Pediatrics 1986;78:614–620.

37. Kauppita A, Kivinen S, Ylikorkala O. A dose-response relationship between improved lactation and metoclapramide. Lancet 1981;1:1175–1177.

38. Kaufman R, Foxman B. Mastitis among lactating women: occurrence and risk factors. Soc Sci Med 1991;33:701–705.

39. Olsen CG, Gorden RE Jr. Breast disorders in nursing mothers. Am Fam Physician 1990;41:1509–1516.

40. Marshall BR, Hepper JK, Zirbel CC. Sporadic puerperal mastitis. JAMA 1975;233:1377–1379.

41. Lawrence RA. The puerperium, breastfeeding, and breast milk. Curr Opin Obstet Gynecol 1990;2: 23–30.

42. Johnstone HA, Marcinak JF. Candidiasis in the breastfeeding mother and infant. J Obstet Gynecol Neonatal Nurs 1990;19:171–173.

43. Khanna YK, Khanna A, Arora YK, et al. Primary closure of lactational breast abscess. J Indian Med Assoc 1989;87:118–120.
44. Goldfarb J. Breastfeeding: AIDS and other infectious diseases. Clin Perinatol 1993;20:225–243.
45. Ghaffar YA, Elsobky MK, Raouf AAM, Dorgham LS. Maternal-to-child transmission of hepatitis B virus in a semirural population in Egypt. J Trop Med 1989;92:20–26.
46. Committee on Drugs. The transfer of drugs and other chemicals into human breast milk. Pediatrics 1994;93:137–150.
47. Briggs CG, Freeman RK, Yaffe SJ. Drugs in Pregnancy and Lactation. 3rd ed. Baltimore: Williams & Wilkins, 1990:309–317.
48. Hatcher RA, Trussell J, Stewart F, et al. Contraceptive Technology. 16th ed. New York: Irvington, 1994:441–444.
49. Nilsson S, Mellbin T, Hofvander Y, et al. Long-term follow-up of children breast-fed by mothers using oral contraceptives. Contraception 1986;34:443–447.
50. Auerbach KG. Assisting the employed breastfeeding mother. J Nurse Midwifery 1990;35:26–34.
51. Larson E, Zuill R, Zier V, Berg B. Storage of human breast milk. Infect Control 1984;5:127–130.
52. Morse JM, Harrison MJ, Prorose M. Minimal breastfeeding. J Obstet Gynecol Neonatal Nurs 1986;15:333.
53. Edmiston CE Jr, Walker AP, Krepal CJ, Gohr C. The nonpuerperal breast infection: aerobic and anaerobic recovery from acute and chronic disease. J Infect Dis 1990;162:695–699.
54. Dahlbect SW, Donnelly JF, Theriault RL. Differentiating inflammatory breast cancer from acute mastitis. Am Fam Physician 1995;52:929–934.
55. Belieu RM. Mastodynia. Obstet Gynecol Clin North Am 1994;21:461–477.
56. Grady LF. The painful breast. In: O'Grady LF, Kindfors KK, Howell LP, Rippon MB, eds. A Practical Approach to Breast Disease. Boston: Little, Brown & Co. 1995:119–130.
57. Chute GE. Promoting breastfeeding success: an overview of basic management. NAACOG's Clin Issues Perinatal Women's Health Nurs 1992;3:570–582.
58. Janke JR. The incidence, benefits and variables associated with breastfeeding: implications for practice. Nurse Practitioner 1993;18:22–23, 28, 31–32.
59. Bear K, Tigges BB. Management strategies for promoting successful breastfeeding. Nurse Pract 1993;18:50–59.
60. Enkin M, Keirse MJ, Renfrew M, Neilson J. A Guide to Effective Care in Pregnancy and Childbirth. 2nd ed. Oxford: Oxford University Press, 1995:349–363.
61. Bryant CA, Coriel J, D'Angelo SL, Bailey DFC, Lazarov M. A strategy for promoting breastfeeding among economically disadvantaged women and adolescents. NAACOG's Clin Issues Perinatal Women's Health Nurs 1992;3:723–730.
62. Ellis DJ. The impact of agency policies and protocols on breastfeeding. NAACOG's Clin Issues Perinatal Women's Health Nursing 1992;3:553–559.
63. Shrago L, Bocar D. The infant's contribution to breastfeeding. JOGNN 1990;19:209–215.
64. Chute GE, ed. NAACOG's Clin Issues Perinatal Women's Health Nurs 1992;3.
65. Driscoll JW. Breastfeeding success and failure: implications for nurses. NAACOG's Clin Issues Perinatal Women's Health Nurs 1992;3:565–569.

17.2

Nipple Discharge

Jo Ann Rosenfeld

Introduction

A complaint of a nipple discharge (ND) is not uncommon. However, there are few certainties in the work-up and treatment. The etiologies of most NDs are benign. Yet, the possibility of cancer with the chance of accompanying disfigurement is significant. Eight to 14% of NDs are caused by cancer (1, 2).

Epidemiology

ND ranks third after "lump" and "breast pain" as the presenting breast complaint in surgical practices and as the second most common symptom in women requiring breast surgery (3, 4, 5). ND was the presenting symptom in 3 to 10% of women with breast complaints (1, 6). In a review of presenting complaints in over 200 general practices in Edinburgh, the average general practitioner only saw 13 women a year with a breast complaint; ND was rare (7). How frequently it occurs in general practice in the United States is unknown.

Most ND occurs in women between age 30 and 50 years (8), but can present in women of all ages. The most common cause is fibrocystic disease in women under age 40 years, whereas in women over age 50 years, cancer is more likely (5). In one study, malignancy was discovered in 7% of those women with nipple discharge under age 60 years, but in 32% of those over age 60 years (1).

Evaluation

History

The history of the ND must be determined (Fig. 17.2.1). First, the discharge can be intermittent or continuous and persistent. Intermittent discharges can be irritative, and are more common with oral contraceptive use and in pregnancy and lactation. If the discharge is persistent, investigation for possible cancer is necessary.

Second, use of concurrent medications should be obtained. Medication use, especially phenothiazines and other psychotropic medications, can cause bilateral galactorrhea but seldom causes pathological discharges. Third, the location of the discharge is important. Malignancy is more likely if the discharge comes from a single duct, because it is usually caused by a localized lesion (6).

Finally, the color of the discharge may be predictive. The probability of cancer is thought to be related to the color of the discharge. Seven types of discharges have been described: (*a*) milky, (*b*) purulent, (*c*) multicolored and sticky, (*d*) clear (watery), (*e*) yellow (serous), (*f*) pink (serosanguineous), and (*g*) bloody (sanguine) (Table 17.2.1) (9). Galactorrhea or milky discharges are often physiological.

Bacterial infection, usually caused by staphylococcus or streptococcus, usually causes purulent discharges. These are most often from multiple ducts, spontaneous, and are accompanied by tenderness, heat, redness, and pain. These are most common in lactating women.

A multicolored discharge often is caused by ductal ectasia; it is usually nonbloody and can be white, grey, yellow, green, brown, and/or reddish brown. It may be bilateral and sticky. The breast produces an irritating lipid fluid that becomes a nipple discharge and can cause nipple eversion, nipple and areolar thickening, periductal inflammation, and even an abscess (9). It occurs most often in multiparous women between the ages of 35 and 55 years. Some women have elevated prolactin levels, and one-half of these have pituitary adenomas (8).

Clear, yellow, pink, and bloody discharges are serious and require investigation. Although most are caused by benign etiologies, the risk of cancer is significant. In almost 6% of women with yellow discharges, cancer was the cause; 12.9% of pink discharges, 27% of bloody discharges, and 33.3 to 45% of watery discharges were caused by malignancy (5, 8). An intraductal papilloma or carcinoma typically causes a straw-colored, bloody, or blood-stained discharge from a single duct (10).

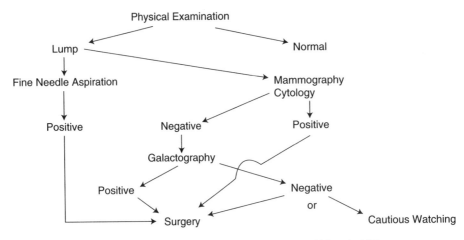

Figure 17.2.1. Evaluation and treatment of bloody NDs.

Table 17.2.1. Types of NDs

Color	Other names	Most Common Causes	Frequency of Occurrence (%)	Caused by Cancer (%)
Milky	Galactorrhea	Physiologic: breast-feeding, pregnancy, postpartum Prolactin excess Pituitary adenomas	—	Unknown
Multicolored	Sticky, green, yellow, serous	Ductal ectasia	—	Rare
Purulent	Infected	Bacterial infection	—	Rare
Clear	Watery	Ductal carcinoma	2.2	33.3–45
Yellow	Serous	Fibrocystic disease Ductal papillomas	41.1	5.9
Pink	Serosanguineous	Fibrocystic disease Ductal papillomas	31.8	12.9
Bloody	Sanguineous	Fibrocystic disease Ductal papillomas	24.9	27

Most experts believe bloody discharges are significant and pathological, and although rare, a profuse crystal clear discharge is associated with multiple intraductal papillomas and often carcinoma (3, 5, 9).

Physical Examination

Most women with nipple discharges have normal physical examinations. A few will have a mass. In one study, less than 13% of women with an ND caused by malignancy had a palpable mass (8), but a palpable lump increases the likelihood of malignancy (3).

Radiological and Cytological Examination

Mammography and cytology of the discharge should always be performed. If the discharge is bloody and a lump or a cyst is present, fine needle aspiration or biopsy is also suggested.

In women with discharges, the most common mammographic findings are intraductal papillomas and fibrocystic changes. Mammograms diagnosed intraductal papillomas in 48.1%, fibrocystic changes in 32.9%, precancerous lesions in 7.3%, and cancer in 14.3% in one study (8).

Although they can be helpful if positive, mammography and cytology can be normal in the presence of cancer. Further investigation by galactography is necessary in women with bloody, watery, or multicolored discharges.

There are some investigational chemical tests to increase the sensitivity and specificity of cancer in the diagnosis of ND. Elevated serum levels of c-erbB-2 oncoprotein, elevated in women with intraductal breast cancer, identified 25 to 50% of women with nonpalpable cancer in one study. All patients with ErbB levels over 100 ng/mL had carcinomas (11).

Galactography

Galactography is suggested for all pathological NDs, and it is a method of displaying ducts using contrast medium (2). Although galactography can detect intraductal pathology such as papillomas or carcinomas, it cannot differentiate benign from malignant disease conclusively. Positive tests, although alarming, are helpful, whereas, negative tests do not rule out malignancy. This method is also time-consuming and can be painful.

In one large study, in over half the women, galactography could identify cancer or ductal papilloma as the cause of a single duct ND (2). Thirteen percent had invasive cancer or ductal carcinoma in situ (DCIS), 40% had a single ductal papilloma, and 13% had intraductal solid papillary or adenomatous growths (2, 9). Galactography had a false-negative rate of 38% in one study (9).

Treatment

Because little research has been done except surgical and pathological studies in the United Kingdom or Japan by surgeons on referral populations, it is difficult to advise what treatments are best for US primary care populations. Besides, the conservative traditional approach for treatment of many breast discharges has been total mastectomy, a treatment not always acceptable today. Mastectomy relieves the fear of missing a cancer while treating any cancer or intraductal papillomas found. However, the more recent preferences for more conservative, breast-sparing surgery as treatment for pathological breast discharges must be considered, and these have had no long-term studies.

Antibiotics and incision and drainage are the treatment of purulent discharges. If the infection recurs or persists, biopsy of the area is suggested to rule out cancer. Ductal ectasia is treated by bed rest, ice packs, and nonsteroidal anti-inflammatory drugs. If the discharge persists or an inflammatory mass develops, surgical excision may be needed (9).

The treatment of bloody discharges is disputed. Any positives found by mammography,

cytology, or galactography necessitate biopsy and perhaps lump excision or mastectomy. However, some experts suggest in a woman with single duct intermittent bloody ND with normal mammography and cytology and a normal galactogram (no papillomas or carcinomas), cautious observation can be recommended. The woman's preferences for either preservation of her breast or surgery (e.g., microdochectomy, lumpectomy, mastectomy) with the definitive diagnosis of benign or malignant disease must be discussed. The psychological consequences of either course of therapy are significant for the woman (9).

If a papilloma is identified by mammography or galactography, surgery is recommended; the potential risk of degeneration of a single ductal papilloma to cancer is 5 to 35% (2). If an intraductal carcinoma is identified, surgery is necessary. However, the physician and woman must explore the decision to proceed with microdochectomy (surgery just beneath the nipple), with possible mastectomy, later, if widespread carcinoma or DCIS is discovered, or mastectomy immediately (9). Customarily, the management of single-duct bloody ND was surgery, and often mastectomy. These surgeries result in poor cosmetic appearances, difficulties in breast-feeding, and altered sensation (3, 9).

DCIS is a multifocal disease that often spreads intraductally (9, 12). Microdochectomy is not considered curative, although the natural history of DCIS has not been well studied. In one study of women who had mastectomies after microdochectomy for DCIS, residual DCIS was present in 6 and atypical ductal hyperplasia in 4 of 16 mastectomy specimens. Intraductal spreading was present in 8. Among 12 women with DCIS who did not have a mastectomy, invasive carcinoma developed in 3. This one study suggests that even with clear margins, DCIS is multifocal and malignant, and a woman with this diagnosis may need mastectomy. If a lumpectomy or microdochectomy only is performed, recent evidence shows that the woman needs subsequent radiation for improved survival (13). A recent review of several studies suggested, however, that breast-conserving surgery with radiation may give good local treatment and a good chance at cure (14).

Conclusion

An ND is an uncommon but potentially serious complaint, possibly heralding intraductal carcinoma. If persistent and bloody, multicolored, pink, or watery nipple discharge occurs, mammography and cytology, and, if these are negative, galactography are necessary. Surgery is the treatment for papillomas or carcinomas. However, breast-conserving surgery with radiation may be a reasonable alternative to mastectomy sometimes. More long-term primary care studies are needed.

Special Considerations for Nurse Practitioners and Physician Assistants

The female breasts may have many symbolic meanings including nuturance and sexuality. They are the external signs of femaleness, identifying the female body throughout history from primitive paintings to contemporary advertisements (15). Because of the importance of the breasts to most women in their body image and feelings of attractiveness, any changes or problems can cause extreme anxiety and fear.

When the woman is concerned about nipple discharge, a complete history includes (*a*) age, (*b*) presence of lumps, (*c*) any related symptoms at onset (such as pain or itching), (*d*) nature of discharge (color, bilateral vs. unilateral, spontaneous vs. induced), (*e*) menstrual history noting in particular regularity of cycles, (*f*) parity, (*g*) previous lactation and when, (*h*) method of contraception and possibility of pregnancy, (*i*) history of breast manipulation or trauma, (*j*) medications, (*k*) family history of breast disease, and (*l*) general health status (16). In addition, information should be elicited about the presence of headaches or visual changes indicative of increased intracranial pressure.

During the physical examination, symmetry and skin changes should be assessed, including superficial lesions of the periareolar region that could be the source of a discharge. The provider should note any dimpling, dominant lumps, associated lymphadenopathy, and whether the discharge appears to come from single or multiple ducts. Referrals and consultations should be initiated when there is any indication of intracranial lesions (e.g., restriction in visual fields, deterioration in visual acuity, papilledema, progressive headache, nausea, vomiting), signs suggestive of breast pathology, persistent discharge with no breast manipulation, abnormal mammograms, severe inflammation or abscesses, or for confirmation and management for certain problems such as galactorrhea (16–18).

The diagnostic process will likely cause anxiety and perhaps additional fears related to testing procedures. Continuing support, explanation, prompt scheduling, and interpretation of findings are essential roles in the primary care setting. Because the etiology of most nipple discharges is benign, women are often relieved when diagnostic and testing procedures are completed. Providers can use this time as an opportunity to emphasize health practices such as breast self-examination and clinical examinations and mammograms as recommended.

References

1. Conry C. Evaluation of breast complaint: is it cancer? Am Fam Physician 1994;49:445–450.
2. Paterok EM, Rosenthal H, Sabel M. Nipple dis-

charge and abnormal galactogram. Results of a long-term study (1964–1990). Eur J Obstet Gynecol Reprod Biol 1993;50:227–234.

3. Carpenter R, Adamson A, Royle GT. A prospective study of nipple discharge. Br J Clin Pract Symp Suppl 1989;68:54–57.

4. State D. Nipple discharge in women: is it cause for concern? Postgrad Med 1991;89:65–68.

5. Leis HP, Greene FL, Cammarata A, Hilfer SE. Nipple discharge: surgical significance. South Med J 1988;81:20–26.

6. Fung A, Rayter Z, Fisher C, King DM, Trott P. Preoperative cytology and mammography in patients with single-duct nipple discharge treated by surgery. Br J Surg 1990;77:1211–1212.

7. Roberts MM, Elton RA, Robinson SE, French K. Consultations for breast disease in general practice and hospital referral patterns. Br J Surg 1987;74:1020–1022.

8. Leis HP. Management of nipple discharge. World J Surg 1989;13:736–742.

9. Rosenfeld JA. Evaluation of non-lactational nipple discharges. Female Patient 1995;20:39–49.

10. Sanghera M. Breast ductography in the investigation of nipple discharge. Radiogr Today 1991; 57:15–16.

11. Inaji H, Kayoma H, et al. ErB-2 protein levels in nipple discharge: role in diagnosis of early breast cancer. Tumor Biol 1991;14:271–278.

12. Ohuchi N, Furata A, Mori S. Management of ductal carcinoma in situ with nipple discharge. Cancer 1994;74:1294–1302.

13. Fisher B, Costatino J, et al. Lumpectomy compared with lumpectomy and radiation therapy for the treatment of intraductal breast cancer. N Engl J Med 1993;328:1581–1586.

14. Schnitt SJ, Silen W, Sadowsky NL, Connolly JL, Harris JR. Ductal carcinoma in situ of the breast. N Engl J Med 1988;318:898–902.

15. Nettles-Carlson B. Problems of the breast. In: Fogel CI, Woods NF, eds. Women's Health Care. Thousand Oaks, CA: Sage, 1995:673–700.

16. D'Epiro JH. Evaluating nipple discharge in the primary care setting. J Am Acad Physician Assist 1993; 6:253–260.

17. Lommell LL. Breast disorders. In: Star WL, Lommell LL, Shannon MT, eds. Women's Primary Health Care. Washington, DC: American Nurses Association, 1995:4-3-4-36.

18. Edge DS, Segatore M. Assessment and management of galactorrhea. Nurse Pract 1993; 18:35–48.

17.3

Breast Cancer and Prevention

Rima J. Couzi and Nancy E. Davidson

Introduction

Magnitude of the Problem

In 1995, nearly 182,000 women will be diagnosed with breast cancer, and 46,000 women will die of the disease (1). Excluding skin cancer, it is the most common malignancy in women, and it is second to lung cancer as a cause of cancer mortality in women; it accounts for 32% of new cancer diagnoses and 18% of cancer deaths annually (1). Based on current incidence rates, the lifetime probability of a woman receiving a diagnosis of invasive breast cancer in the United States is 12.9% for a white woman and 8.8% for an African-American woman (2).

Although these statistics have increased public awareness about breast cancer, they do not adequately convey age-related differences in risk. The incidence of breast cancer increases with age, with median ages at diagnosis and death of 64 and 68 years, respectively (2). Information about breast cancer risk may be better relayed by accounting for current age and providing risk estimates over shorter periods of time. For example, a 50-year-old woman with no previous diagnosis of breast cancer has a 5.5% chance of developing the disease by age 70 years and an 8.7% chance by age 80 years (2).

Trends in Breast Cancer Incidence and Mortality

Age-adjusted breast cancer incidence rates have been rising steadily since the 1940s, although breast cancer mortality rates have remained relatively constant. Between 1940 and 1982, incidence rates rose by approximately 1% per year based on data from the Connecticut Tumor Registry (3). The National Cancer Institute's Surveillance, Epidemiology and End Results (SEER) program started collecting cancer statistics in 1973 from eight geographical areas in the United States. Between 1980 and 1987, the incidence of breast cancer rose by 32.5% from 85.2 cases per 100,000 cancers in 1980 to

a peak of 112.4 cases per 100,000 cancers in 1987 (2). This sharp rise in incidence rates has been largely attributed to the increasing use of screening mammography (4–6). Most of the excess breast cancers seen during that period were either preinvasive or small ($<$ 2 cm) invasive tumors, which is consistent with the ability of mammography to detect disease at an early stage (6). Breast cancer incidence rates have started to decline, with 108.8 cases per 100,000 reported in 1990 (2). Improvements in breast cancer mortality rates are not yet fully apparent, but they have started to be seen in areas of high mammography use (4).

Risk Factors and Risk Assessment

The etiology of breast cancer is multifactorial; multiple interactions between genetic and environmental factors occur during carcinogenesis (7). Although several factors are associated with an increased risk of breast cancer (8), 70% of patients have no identifiable risk factors other than age (9). Yet, most women with one or more risk factors never develop breast cancer. A woman's risk for breast cancer is likely to be influenced by a number of factors, including her age, family history, hormonal milieu, and environmental exposures. Most of the known risk factors are associated with only mild or moderate increases in risk, but exceptions include a family history of premenopausal or bilateral breast cancer or a personal history of atypical hyperplasia or carcinoma in situ in breast tissue (Table 17.3.1).

Family History and Inherited Susceptibility

Breast cancer has long been known to cluster in families. Estimates of the proportion of breast cancers that are associated with family history vary between 5 and 20% (10–12). Women who have one first-degree relative

Table 17.3.1. Risk Factors for Breast Cancer

Increasing age
Family history of breast cancer
Personal history of atypical hyperplasia or CIS
    of breast
Menstrual characteristics
    Early menarche
    Late menopause
    Short menstrual cycles
    Nulliparity
    Late age at first childbirth
Hormone replacement therapy use
Oral contraceptive pill use
Alcohol use
Increased dietary fat intake

(i.e., sister or mother) with a history of breast cancer are at 1.5 to 3 times greater risk for the disease compared to women without such a family history. The risk is 4 to 6 times greater when two first-degree relatives have had breast cancer (13). These risks increase even further if the family members had premenopausal or bilateral breast cancer.

Approximately 5% of patients have a family pedigree consistent with hereditary breast cancer in which the disease is often diagnosed at an early age (younger than age 45 years) and affects at least three family members (14). Familial breast cancers also aggregate with a variety of other cancers as in the breast-ovary cancer syndrome and the Li-Fraumeni syndrome (i.e., soft tissue and bony sarcomas, brain tumors, leukemia, adrenocortical carcinomas, breast cancers) (15). In these cancer syndromes, predisposing genes are inherited in an autosomal dominant pattern.

BRCA1 and BRCA2 are the first two genes to be implicated in hereditary breast and breast-ovarian cancer syndromes (16, 17). A woman who has a germline BRCA1 mutation has a greater than 50% chance of developing breast cancer before age 50 years and an 85% lifetime probability (18); acquired mutations of BRCA1 have not been seen in breast cancers to date. Germline mutations of the p53 gene occur in the Li-Fraumeni syndrome (15), and acquired mutations of the gene are also frequently associated with sporadic breast cancer (18).

Benign Breast Disease

Fibrocystic disease of the breast comprises a heterogeneous group of lesions associated with varying degrees of breast cancer risk. Dupont and Page have categorized benign breast disease by histology into nonproliferative and proliferative lesions (19–21). Nonproliferative lesions such as breast cysts, fibrosis, and mild epithelial hyperplasia are not associated with any increase in breast cancer risk. Proliferative disease without atypia such as papilloma, sclerosing adenosis, and moderate hyperplasia of usual types is associated with a slight increase in breast cancer risk (1.5 to 2 times). The presence of atypical ductal or lobular hyperplasia on a breast biopsy moderately increases (4 to 5 times) a woman's risk for breast cancer compared with women with no history of breast biopsies.

There is, however, a strong interaction between the presence of atypical hyperplasia and a positive family history of breast cancer (22). Women with both of these risk factors have 11 times greater risk for breast cancer than women with nonproliferative disease.

Reproductive Factors

Many studies have identified early age at menarche, late age at menopause, a short menstrual cycle length, nulliparity, and late age at first childbirth as factors that moderately increase the risk of breast cancer (8, 23 ,24). The risk associated with some of these variables is thought to be related to the total number of ovulatory cycles during the reproductive years (25). Large numbers of ovulatory cycles may result in greater breast tissue exposure to endogenous hormones. Women in whom menarche occurs at age 12 years or younger have a 30% increase in risk of breast cancer (RR 1.3), compared with women who start menstruating at age 15 years or older. A shorter menstrual cycle length between age 29 and 39 years may also increase breast cancer risk. Natural menopause at or after age 55 years is associated with a doubling of breast cancer risk (RR 2.0) relative to women whose menopause occurs before age 45 years. In comparison, women who have had bilateral oophorectomies before age 40 years have a 50% reduction in the lifetime risk of breast cancer.

Nulliparity and late age at first childbirth also increase breast cancer risk. Nulliparous women are at 20 to 70% increased risk for breast cancer compared with parous women. The risk of breast cancer increases up to twofold (RR 1.4 to 2.0) in women who have their first child after age 30 years compared with those giving birth before age 20 years. However, women who have their first child after age 35 years have a higher breast cancer risk than nulliparous women for up to 15 years after childbirth (26). Reports of the effects of infertility and spontaneous and induced abortions on breast cancer risk have been inconsistent (23).

Breast feeding is associated with approximately 30% reduction in the risk of premenopausal breast cancer, with the protective effect noted to occur mostly after 2 or more years of lactation (27). However, a recent large case-control study reported a significant reduction in the risk of premenopausal breast cancer after 4 or more months of breast-feeding (28).

Oral Contraceptives and Hormone Replacement Therapy

Many studies, including two meta-analyses, have explored the relationship between oral contraceptive use and the risk of breast cancer (29, 30). In most studies, long-term use has not been associated with an increase in either the overall risk or the risk of breast cancer after age 45 years (31). However, oral contraceptive use for 10 or more years increases the risk of premenopausal breast cancer (RR 1.46, $P = 0.001$) (29). In addition, women who take oral contraceptives for 4 or more years before their first term pregnancy may also be at slight increased risk compared with nonusers (RR 1.72, 95% confidence interval 1.36 to 2.19) (29).

The Cancer and Steroid Hormone Study, the largest case-control study in the United States on the relationship between oral contraceptive use and breast cancer risk, reported age-specific differences in risk (32). A positive association was confined to women on OCPs diagnosed with breast cancer between age 20 and 34 years (32).

The association between hormone replacement therapy and breast cancer risk has been studied even more extensively. At least 40 case-control and cohort studies and six meta-analyses have been published with conflicting results (33–38). Most studies find little or no associations with any use or short-term use (5 years or less). However, there is less agreement on the effect of long-term use. In a meta-analysis of case-control studies performed in North America, use of conjugated estrogen for 10 or more years was associated with slight increases in breast cancer risk ranging between 15 to 29% (38). A report from the Nurses' Health Study shows that the increased risk is also present with combination estrogen and progesterone therapy and is greater among older women (39). However, hormone replacement therapy has many proven benefits that should be considered when counseling patients about its use (40).

Alcohol

Many epidemiological studies have shown that alcohol use modestly increases the risk of breast cancer (8). The mechanism underlying this association is unknown, but alcohol-induced hormonal changes have been implicated (41).

There is strong evidence for a dose-response relationship between alcoholic beverage consumption and breast cancer risk (42). For example, daily consumption of one alcoholic beverage is associated with an 11% increase in breast cancer risk compared with nondrinkers, whereas three drinks a day increase the risk by 38% (42).

Diet and Obesity

Dietary fat has long been implicated as a risk factor for breast cancer. The evidence is derived mostly from animal models of breast carcinogenesis (43), or deduced from the international differences seen in breast cancer incidence (44). However, most studies have found either no associations or weak associations between fat intake and breast cancer (45, 46). This relationship is being assessed by the Women's Health Initiative, a large prospective randomized clinical trial evaluating the effects of dietary modification and hormone replacement therapy on cancer and heart disease (47).

Obesity is not a risk factor for premenopausal breast cancer, but has a weak association with postmenopausal breast cancer (8). However, obese women have a worse prognosis that may be related to delayed diagnosis.

Risk Assessment and Counseling

Risk assessment provides the opportunity to identify and adequately counsel women at moderate or high risk for breast cancer. For most women seeking advice about their breast cancer risk, statistical models such as the Gail and Claus models may be used to provide reasonable risk estimates (13, 48). However, these models are not appropriate for women with a family history suggesting an inherited breast cancer syndrome. Screening for genetic mutations in these families is currently under study and offered only at selected centers (49). All women at increased risk for breast cancer should be counseled about increased breast cancer surveillance and encouraged to participate in breast cancer prevention clinical trials (50, 51).

Screening for Breast Cancer

The aim of breast cancer screening is to detect the disease at the earliest stage possible, hopefully, when effective treatment confers the greatest chance for cure. Three methods of breast cancer detection are often used concurrently: mammography, clinical breast examination (CBE), and breast self-examination (BSE). A main endpoint in evaluating any cancer screening modality is its impact on cancer-related mortality, with the most reliable and unbiased data coming from randomized clinical trials.

Several cohort and case-control studies, and eight large randomized clinical trials of breast cancer screening have been conducted since the 1960s (52–63). Nearly 500,000 women have been enrolled into the randomized clinical trials, which are summarized in Table 17.3.2. Breast cancer screening is effective in decreasing breast cancer mortality. However, direct comparisons among the various screening studies are difficult to make because of differences in study design and the type and frequency of the screening modalities. A recent meta-analysis of 13 studies (9 randomized clinical trials and 4 case-control studies) showed an overall 25% reduction in breast cancer deaths among women who underwent screening mammography compared with those who did not (RR 0.75, 95% CI, 0.68 to 0.83) (64). Women who were between age 50 and 74 years at the start of screening had a significant reduction in breast cancer mortality after 7 to 9 years of follow-up (RR 0.74, 95% CI 0.66 to 0.83), regardless of the screening interval or the number of mammographic views per screen. However, in women age 40 to 49 years at the start of screening, no significant reduction in breast cancer mortality was seen at 7 to 9 years

Table 17.3.2. Relative Risk for Death Caused by Breast Cancer According to Age at Entry, Screening Modality, and Duration of Follow-up

Study (Ref)	Age at Entry (yr)	Screening Modality	Frequency (months)	Follow-up (yr)	Relative Risk (95% Confidence Intervals)		
					All Ages	<50 years	>50 years
HIP (54, 55)	40–64	M + CBE	12	9–18	0.71 (0.55–0.93)	0.77 (0.50–1.16)	0.68 (0.49–0.96)
					0.77 (0.61–0.97)	0.76 (0.59–0.97)	0.79 (0.65–0.97)
Two-county (56–58)	40–74	M	24 (<50 yrs) 33 (≥50 yrs)	6–13	0.69 (0.51–0.92)	1.26 (0.56–2.84)	0.61 (0.44–0.84)
					0.70 (0.58–0.85)	0.87 (0.54–1.41)	0.66 (0.54–0.81)
					0.69 (0.57–0.84)		
Malmo (59)	45–69	M	18–24	8.8	0.96 (0.68–1.35)	Age <55 years 1.29 (0.74–2.25)	Age ≥55 years 0.79 (0.51–1.24)
Stockholm (60)	40–64	M	28	7.4	0.71 (0.40–1.20)	1.09 (0.40–3.0)	0.57 (0.3–1.1)
Gothenberg (62)	40–59	M	18	7	0.86 (0.54–1.37)	0.73 (0.27–1.97)	NS
Edinburgh (62, 63)	45–64	M + CBE	12 (for CBE) 24 (for M)	7–10	0.83 (0.58–1.18)	NS	NS 0.85 (0.62–1.15)
					0.82 (0.61–1.11)	0.78 (0.46–1.31)	
NBSSI (64)	40–49	M + CBE	12	7	NA	1.36 (0.84–2.21)	NA

M = mammography; CBE = clinical breast examination; NS = not stated; NA = not applicable.

(RR 1.01, 95% CI 0.81 to 1.34) and 10 to 12 years of follow-up (RR 0.83, 95% CI, 0.65 to 1.06). These results confirm those obtained from an overview of five Swedish randomized breast cancer screening trials (59).

Controversies about Screening Women Younger than Age 50 Years

Although all organizations agree that women age 50 years or older should be screened, the recommended age for starting screening mammography has been a source of much controversy. The debate has intensified since the publication of the Canadian National Breast Screening Study (62, 65, 66). The International Workshop on Screening for Breast Cancer sponsored by the National Cancer Institute (NCI) reviewed the effectiveness of mammography in February 1993 (67). The NCI replaced its previous guidelines on screening mammography in women age 40 to 49 years by a statement acknowledging the disagreement among experts on the role of routine screening mammography for women in this age group (68). The NCI now recommends that these women discuss the issue with their physician. The ACS continues to recommend that women age 40 to 49 years be screened every other year by mammography, citing results from the Breast Cancer Detection Demonstration Project (BCDDP) (69).

Screening Modalities

Mammography

Mammography usually detects breast cancer before a mass becomes palpable, but can miss up to 10% of lesions. The sensitivity of mammography varies according to the patient's age, breast density, and size of the mass. In the randomized clinical trials, the sensitivity and specificity of mammography ranged between 63 to 88% and 96 to 99%, respectively (67). In the United States, the positive predictive value (PPV) of mammography has ranged between 15 and 30% (70). The PPV increases with age and in patients with a family history of breast cancer (71).

Approximately 25% of all mammographically detected masses are benign cysts (72). Breast sonography is a useful adjunct to mammography in evaluating breast masses because it can differentiate simple cysts from solid masses with 98 to 100% accuracy (72). However, breast sonography is not a useful screening modality because it cannot detect microcalcifications and is unreliable in detecting masses smaller than 1 cm (73).

Clinical Breast Examination

The sensitivity and specificity of CBE are highly dependent on the skills of the examiner. The average provider unfortunately has limited experience in CBE (74), although skilled providers can sometimes palpate lesions 1 cm or less in diameter. In the BCDDP, clinical breast exam alone detected 9% of cancers in women age 50 to 74 years, and 17% of breast cancers were detected by SBE in the intervals between screening (74). The Canadian National Breast Screening Study, which randomized women age 50 to 59 years to yearly mammography and CBE versus CBE alone, found no added benefit of annual mammography to CBE after a mean follow-up of 8.3 years (63).

Breast Self-Examination

Breast self-examination is advocated as a low-cost method for breast cancer detection. However, BSE has not been specifically evaluated in randomized clinical trials. Some observational studies suggest that women who perform BSE have lower breast cancer mortality rate than those who do not (75). The survival advantage may, however, be partly related to other differences between self-examiners and nonexaminers. BSE is a useful adjunct to CBE and screening mammography, although conclusions about its impact on breast cancer mortality cannot be made at this time. One sixth of the incident cases in the Breast Cancer Detection

Demonstration Project were discovered by patients in the intervals between CBEs (76).

Breast Cancer Screening Guidelines

Breast cancer screening guidelines are updated as new data become available (77, 78). The most current guidelines from selected North American organizations are grouped according to age (Table 17.3.3).

Women Younger than Age 50 Years

The American Cancer Society recommends monthly BSE beginning at age 20 years and CBE every three years between age 20 to 40 years. For women age 40 years and older, annual CBE is recommended by the American Cancer Society (ACS), American Academy of Family Physicians (AAFP), American College of Obstetricians and Gynecologists (ACOG), and American College of Physicians (ACP).

For women age 40 to 49, the ACS and the ACOG recommend annual CBE and mammography every 1 to 2 years. Baseline mammography at age 35 years is no longer felt to be necessary. The NCI states that there is disagreement among experts on the role of mammography in this age group, but recommends that women discuss the issue with their physicians.

Women Older than Age 50 Years

All major professional bodies agree that women age 50 years or older should be screened for breast cancer, but they vary in their recommendations on the frequency of screening and the age at which screening can be stopped. The ACS, ACP, AAFP, ACOG, and Canadian Task Force on the Periodic Health Examination advocate annual CBE and annual mammography for women age 50 years or older, whereas the NCI recommends CBE and mammography every 1 to 2 years. No upper age limit for mammography is given by these organizations. The US Preventive Services Task

Table 17.3.3. Breast Cancer Screening Guidelines for Women without High-Risk Family History for Breast Cancer

Age	Organization	Recommendations
<40	American Cancer Society	Monthly BSE beginning at age 20 CBE every 3 years between age 20–40
40–50	American Cancer Society American Academy of Family Physicians	Annual CBE
	American College of Obstetricians and Gynecologists	Annual CBE and mammography
	American College of Physicians	
>50	ACS, ACP, AAFP, ACOG, Canadian Task Force on the Periodic Health Examination	Annual CBE and mammography
	National Cancer Institute	CBE and mammography every 1–2 years.
	US Preventive Services Task Force	Annual CBE and mammography every 1 to 2 years until age 75
65–74	National Institutes of Health Breast Screening Forum American Geriatrics Society	Annual CBE and mammography
>75	American Geriatrics Society	CBE and mammography q 2 years

Force recommends annual CBE and mammography every 1 to 2 years until age 75 years. Data from the screening studies are inadequate to make conclusions about the benefit of mammography in older women because no study included women older than 75 years.

Decisions regarding screening older women should be based on the woman's general health and should consider comorbid diseases or other medical conditions. The National Institutes of Health Breast Screening Forum and the American Geriatrics Society recommend annual CBE and mammography every 2 years for women age 65 to 74 years (78). For those women older than 75 years with a good general health life expectancy, CBE and mammography are encouraged at approximately 2-year intervals (78).

Special Surveillance for High-Risk Women

Most professional bodies do not provide specific recommendations for screening women at high risk for breast cancer. At present, it is not known whether increased surveillance decreases breast cancer mortality in high-risk patients. High-risk women with a family history of premenopausal breast cancer in a first-degree relative are often advised to start screening earlier than the earliest age of onset of breast cancer in the family. The recommended age for starting screening mammography varies between age 25 and 35 years, and the screening interval between 6 and 12 months (50).

New Breast Imaging Techniques

Several new breast imaging techniques are under development and evaluation. These include digital mammography, magnetic resonance imaging of the breast (MRI), positron emission tomography (PET), and computer-aided diagnosis (79). The exact role for these techniques is still being defined, but they hold promise as adjuncts to mammography in difficult cases. Digital mammography provides several advantages over conventional mammography including the ability to better detect subtle tissue contrast and

the decrease in time needed for mammographically guided needle localization procedures (80). In patients with a history of breast cancer treated with lumpectomy and radiation, MRI may be helpful in identifying local recurrences. PET scanning may help in evaluating mammographically dense breasts and is being evaluated as a noninvasive early indicator of treatment efficacy for breast cancer. All of these approaches are investigational at the present time.

Management of in-situ Breast Cancer

Noninvasive breast lesions are divided into two types: ductal carcinoma in situ (DCIS, intraductal carcinoma) and lobular carcinoma in situ (LCIS). Light microscopy reveals malignant proliferation of ducts, lobules, or both, without invasion through the basement membrane (81). The distinction between DCIS and LCIS is important because of the different therapeutic options available for each lesion.

Ductal Carcinoma in situ

The natural history of DCIS is not fully understood, because most patients were treated with mastectomy in the past. DCIS is generally believed to be a precursor of invasive carcinoma, although the progression to invasive disease is not absolute. The incidence of DCIS has risen in the last 10 to 15 years with the increasing use of screening mammography (6). Most DCIS lesions are now discovered with mammography, appearing as cluster microcalcifications.

Histologically, DCIS comprises a heterogeneous group of lesions; the most frequent histologic subtypes are comedo, cribriform, micropapillary, and solid. These lesions can be broadly divided into comedo and noncomedo subtypes, although there is overlap between the two groups. Comedo lesions are characterized by large plesiomorphic cells with high-grade nuclei, numerous mitoses, and cell necrosis. These cells often overexpress the c-erbB-2 oncogene, and show accumulation of p53 tumor suppressor gene products in the surrounding stroma (82).

Noncomedo lesions generally appear less aggressive histologically, with lower grade cells, few mitoses, and minimal or no necrosis. If noncomedo DCIS is left untreated, the likelihood of progression to invasive cancer is estimated at 30% after 6 to 10 years (83). Comedo lesions are likely to show higher rates of progression.

The management of DCIS is controversial. In the past, mastectomy was the treatment of choice with cure rates of 98 to 99% (83). Mastectomy remains the treatment of choice for patients in whom DCIS is too extensive for adequate local excision. However, the routine use of mastectomy has been questioned, especially because breast conservation is an acceptable alternative to mastectomy for early stage breast cancer (84). At present, no prospective information is available comparing mastectomy with lumpectomy and radiation therapy in the treatment of DCIS. With close monitoring, the risk of dying from invasive breast cancer is estimated at 1 to 2% for the former treatment modality compared with 2 to 3% for the latter (82). In a prospective randomized study comparing lumpectomy followed by radiation therapy to lumpectomy alone in the treatment of DCIS, the combined modality arm was associated with fewer ipsilateral invasive breast cancer recurrences after a median follow-up of 43 months (7 vs. 16%) (85).

Because in situ disease carries a minimal risk of disseminated disease, women with DCIS do not require axillary lymph node dissection and no adjuvant systemic therapy is routinely indicated. However, the role of tamoxifen in the prevention of local recurrences and contralateral breast cancers after treatment of DCIS is currently under study.

Lobular Carcinoma in situ

Lobular carcinoma in situ has no distinctive clinical or mammographic features and often presents as an incidental finding in breast biopsies performed for presumed benign lesions. It is most commonly identified in premenopausal women, with an average age at diagnosis of 44 to 46 years (86). LCIS is found in approximately 3% of biopsies for fibrocystic disease and 10% of mammographically generated biopsies (86). Histologically, the lesion is characterized by proliferation of cells with small, round, and monotonous nuclei within the breast lobules. However, the distinction between LCIS, atypical lobular hyperplasia, and even DCIS is sometimes difficult to make. Lobular carcinoma in situ is multicentric in approximately two thirds of cases and bilateral in at least 30% of patients (87).

A diagnosis of LCIS is associated with an increased risk for subsequent invasive breast cancer, estimated at 20% after 20 years of follow-up (87). The increased risk is equal for both ipsilateral and contralateral breast cancer, and the invasive lesions can be either lobular or ductal in origin (83). These important observations have led researchers to believe that LCIS is a marker rather than a precursor of invasive cancer, and they have also influenced the treatment recommendations. The two treatment recommendations are diametrically opposed and consist of either careful observation or bilateral simple mastectomies. The majority of women are currently managed with close surveillance with yearly mammography, monthly BSE and CBE every 3 to 4 months. A few women remain uncomfortable with the former option and opt for bilateral prophylactic mastectomies.

Invasive Breast Cancer

Staging of Breast Cancer

Breast cancer is most commonly staged using the TNM staging system. Disease stage depends on the size of the primary tumor, the presence or absence of diseased lymph nodes, and distant metastasis (Table 17.3.4). However, TNM staging alone may not be adequate

Table 17.3.4. American Joint Committee on Cancer (1992)—TNM Staging

Primary Tumor (T)

TX	Primary tumor cannot be assessed
TO	No evidence of primary tumor
Tis	Carcinoma in situ, intraductal carcinoma, lobular carcinoma in situ, or Paget's disease of the nipple with no tumor
TI	Tumor 2 cm or less in greatest dimension
TIa	0.5 cm or less in greatest dimension
TIb	More than 0.5 cm but not more than I cm in greatest dimension
TIc	More than I cm but not more than 2 cm in greatest dimension
T2	Tumor more than 2 cm but not more than 5 cm in greatest dimension
T3	Tumor more than 5 cm in greatest dimension
T4	Tumor of any size with direct extension to the chest wall or skin
T4a	Extension to chest wall
T4b	Edema (including peau d'orange) or ulceration of the skin of breast or satellite nodules confined to same breast
T4c	Both T4a and T4b
T4d	Inflammatory carcinoma

Lymph Node (N)

NX	Regional lymph nodes cannot be assessed
NO	No regional lymph node metastasis
NI	Metastasis to movable ipsilateral axillary lymph node(s)
N2	Metastasis to ipsilateral axillary lymph node(s) fixed to one another or to other structures
N3	Metastasis to ipsilateral internal mammary lymph node(s)

Distant Metastasis (M)

MX	Presence of distant metastasis cannot be assessed
MO	No distant metastasis
MI	Distant metastasis (including metastasis to ipsilateral supraclavicular lymph nodes)

Stage Grouping

Stage	T	T	N	N	M	M
O	Tis		NO		MO	
I	TI		NO		MO	
IIA	TO		NI		MO	
		TI		NI		MO
		T2		NI		MO
IIB	T2		NI		MO	
		T3		NO		MO
IIIA	TO		N2		MO	
		TI		N2		MO
		T2		N2		MO
		T3		NI		MO
		T3		N2		MO
IIIB	T4		Any N		MO	
		Any T		N3		MO
IV	Any T		Any N		MI	

Adapted with permission from Fisher B, Redmond D, Poisson R, et al. Eighty-year results of a randomized clinical trial comparing total masectomy and lumpectomy with or without irradiation in the treatment of breast cancer. N Engl J Med 1989; 320; 822–828.

in distinguishing patients at increased risk of recurrence. For example, prognosis has been shown to be related to the extent of axillary lymph nodes involvement. As a result, patients are often categorized according to the number of involved lymph nodes: no positive nodes, 1 to 3 positive nodes, 4 to 9, or 10 or more positive lymph nodes.

Treatment of Breast Cancer

The major goal of treatment of breast cancer is to obtain long-term control of the disease whenever possible. The primary determinant of whether this goal can be achieved is the stage of the tumor at diagnosis, because long-term control is generally possible only when the surgeon is able to remove all evidence of tumor present in the breast and draining lymph nodes. According to the staging criteria listed above, women with clinical stages I, II, and III breast cancer are considered potentially curable, and the therapeutic approach for such women should be tailored appropriately toward this goal. Fortunately, the trend to diagnosis of breast cancer at earlier stages means that more women can achieve long-term, disease-free survival. For instance, among women receiving a new diagnosis of breast cancer, the percentage of women with stage I disease has increased significantly, and a high percentage of such patients can have long-term disease control with modern therapy (88).

Unfortunately, the prognosis of women with metastatic breast cancer has not improved substantially, and no study to date has conclusively shown a major benefit in either overall or progression-free survival resulting from chemotherapy or radiation therapy. Therefore, in the group of women with stage IV breast cancer, treatment should be reserved only for cosmetic considerations or for relief of symptoms directly attributable to the cancer.

The first steps in the treatment of breast cancer should be confirmation of the diagnosis and evaluation of the clinical extent of the disease. All women presenting with a persistent palpable breast mass or suspicious lesions on mammography should have a biopsy of the suspicious lesion performed promptly. If cancer is found in the biopsy specimen, the extent of disease should be evaluated with a history and physical examination with special attention to the presence of enlarged axillary or supraclavicular lymph nodes, bilateral mammography, complete blood count, liver function tests, and a PA and lateral chest radiograph. CT scans of the chest and liver and scintigraphic bone scanning are necessary only to evaluate symptoms or abnormal laboratory tests, or in the case of stage III breast cancer, as such women have a high incidence of occult metastases. The conclusion of the clinical staging evaluation is an appropriate time for the woman with newly diagnosed breast cancer to discuss treatment options with each member of a multidisciplinary team which consists of primary care provider, surgical oncologist, radiation therapist, and medical oncologist, so that a treatment decision that is both appropriate to the stage of disease and acceptable to the patient can be made.

The mainstay of treatment of early breast cancer is surgery. Appropriate therapy of women with early breast cancer must include removal of the primary breast mass and an adequate margin of surrounding normal tissue, and determination of the pathologic status of ipsilateral axillary lymph nodes. Furthermore, a sample of the primary breast mass must be submitted for estrogen and progesterone receptor determination. Women with early stage breast cancer may choose between modified radical mastectomy, which involves removal of the entire breast and some or all of the axillary nodes, and breast conserving surgery ("lumpectomy") with a separate axillary dissection, followed by radiation therapy of the conserved breast to prevent local recurrence. Six randomized trials have compared breast conservation therapy with more radical surgery, and each has shown the two approaches to yield equivalent overall and distant disease-free survival (89–94). Although the rate of local recurrence is higher among women receiving conservative surgery, most of these women can be salvaged by mastectomy at the time of recurrence. The need for systemic therapy following definitive local treatment of women with early stage breast cancer then depends on the pathologic status of the axillary nodes, the quantity of hormone receptors expressed by the tumor, and the age and menopausal status of the patient.

Management of Early-stage, Node-negative Breast Cancer

Although most women with early-stage, node-negative breast cancer are cured by surgery with or without radiation therapy, 10- to 20-year follow-up of such women indicates that as many as 21% of patients relapse (95). The ability to accurately predict which women will relapse is therefore extremely important in guiding further therapy. Many prognostic factors have been evaluated for their usefulness in predicting the risk of recurrence and guiding the choice of treatment (96, 97). The most commonly used and validated prognostic factors in this setting are tumor size, estrogen and progesterone receptor status, histologic subtype, and histologic grading. Other markers, such as flow cytometry, cathepsin D, HER-2/neu oncogene, epidermal growth factor, angiogenesis, and p53 mutations are currently being investigated for their prognostic significance but have not been validated for routine clinical practice.

The ability of adjuvant therapy to reduce the risk of relapse and enhance overall survival in such women has been confirmed by the Early Breast Cancer Trialists' Collaborative Group (EBCTCG), who compiled an overview analysis of 133 randomized trials involving 75,000 women receiving therapy between 1957 and 1985 (98). The results of this trial were used at the Fifth International Conference of Adjuvant Therapy of Breast Cancer to formulate recommendations for women with node-negative breast cancer (99). Women were divided into low-, good-, and high-risk categories. The low-risk group included women with < 1-cm lesions discovered incidentally on screening mammography and women with tumors < 2 cm and favorable histology. Such women were felt to have a relapse risk of < 10%, and no systemic treatment of any type was recommended. Good-risk women were those with tumors between 1 and 2 cm in diameter, estrogen receptor (ER)-positive, and of low histologic grade; tamoxifen treatment was recommended for this population. Women with ER-negative tumors > 1 cm, ER-positive tumors > 2 cm, and poorly differentiated tumors were judged to have a high risk of relapse. Adjuvant chemotherapy was recommended for all premenopausal women and for postmenopausal women less than age 70 years with ER-negative tumors. Tamoxifen was recommended for high-risk women with ER-positive tumors or for those women over age 70 years.

Management of Early-stage, Node-positive Breast Cancer

Breast cancer patients with disease present in the axillary nodes have a 40 to 80% risk of relapse; therefore, some form of adjuvant therapy should be considered (100, 101). Results of the EBCTCG overview analysis indicate that premenopausal, node-positive women benefit from adjuvant chemotherapy; the addition of tamoxifen may be considered. Postmenopausal women with ER-positive tumors should receive tamoxifen with or without chemotherapy. Those women with tumors lacking estrogen receptors should receive chemotherapy, with or without tamoxifen.

Breast cancer patients with 4 or more involved lymph nodes are at especially high risk of relapse. Such women should be particularly encouraged to consider entry into clinical trials of newer therapies, such as those studying the addition of new agents or high-dose chemotherapy with autologous stem cell support.

Treatment of Locally Advanced Stage III Breast Cancer

Patients with stage IIIA breast cancer usually receive "triple therapy"—radical surgery, post-operative irradiation therapy to the chest wall, and chemotherapy with or without hormonal manipulation. More recently, multiagent chemotherapy has been given prior to surgery ("primary" chemotherapy) to achieve tumor shrinkage, allowing the use of breast-conserving surgery followed by local and regional radiotherapy. The results of this approach appear promising, but its use is currently restricted to clinical trials (102, 103).

Patients with stage IIIB disease generally receive primary chemotherapy in an attempt to achieve tumor shrinkage to allow complete surgical removal of the primary tumor. Whether surgery is performed, radiotherapy is delivered subsequently to improve locoregional control of disease. All patients with stage III disease are at extremely high risk of disease recurrence and, thus, should be considered as candidates for trials of aggressive therapy, including high-dose chemotherapy with autologous stem cell support.

Treatment of Metastatic (Stage IV) Breast Cancer

Although patients diagnosed with metastatic breast cancer are often responsive to initial treatment, complete remission occurs in only 5 to 25% of patients, and cure of the disease or even substantial improvement in survival with therapy has not yet been achieved. For this reason, therapy should be contemplated only when the benefits of treatment outweigh the toxicities, for instance when palliation of symptoms is required. Approximately one third of all patients with metastatic disease respond to hormonal manipulation, with the figure rising to 65 to 75% if the tumor expresses both estrogen and progesterone receptors. Such women may benefit from endocrine therapy such as tamoxifen, but tumor shrinkage may be too slow for effective symptom palliation.

Multiagent chemotherapy may be preferable in the treatment of patients with rapidly progressive disease or for treatment of lung or liver metastases. Symptomatic bone pain or brain metastasis may best be relieved by radiation therapy, and intrathecal chemotherapy may be required to treat carcinomatous meningitis. Patients with metastatic breast cancer who receive high-dose chemotherapy and autologous stem cell support have a higher percentage of partial and complete tumor responses than patients receiving standard multiagent chemotherapy; whether this improved response rate will mean improved overall or disease-free survival is not yet proven.

Special Considerations in Breast Cancer

Breast Cancer and Pregnancy

Pregnancy-associated breast cancer and the safety of pregnancy after successful treatment of breast cancer have become more important topics as more women are delaying childbirth until later in their reproductive years. Although the diagnosis of pregnancy-associated breast cancer is uncommon, it nevertheless presents special management challenges. First, mammography is not useful in the evaluation of breast masses during pregnancy because of the increase in breast density. Second, radiation therapy is contraindicated during pregnancy because it is not possible to completely shield the fetus from the delivered radiation. In these situations, mastectomy is an alternative to conservative surgical management. However, if breast cancer is diagnosed in the third trimester, lumpectomy can be performed and radiation therapy can be withheld until after delivery. Finally, although chemotherapy during pregnancy is not absolutely contraindicated, the long-term effects of such treatment on the fetus are not well defined. Despite all these caveats, when adjusted for stage and age at presentation, pregnancy does not worsen the prognosis of breast cancer (104).

Some young women who have received definitive treatment for breast cancer ask about the advisability of subsequent pregnancy. Because the risk of recurrence is highest within the first 2 years after breast cancer treatment, these women may wish to delay conception (105). Although based on small and possibly highly selected groups of women, the available evidence appears to indicate that pregnancy after treatment of breast cancer does not worsen its prognosis (105).

Screening and Treatment of Breast Cancer in the Elderly

Women older than age 65 years are at the highest risk for developing breast cancer, but have the lowest rates of participation in breast cancer screening (106, 107). They are also more likely to present with advanced disease (108) and to have a worse outcome, mostly caused by comorbid illnesses (109). Barriers to screening in older women include (1) lack of knowledge that screening is needed, (2) lack of physician recommendation, (3) cost, (4) not having a regular health care provider, (5) poor access, (6) lower income, and (7) lower educational level (106). Attempts to overcome these barriers are needed to improve screening rates among older women.

Breast cancer treatment decisions for older women are usually extrapolated from results of clinical trials in younger patients, as few studies have included older women. Elderly women are, however, less likely than younger women to receive standard surgical procedures (110) or adjuvant therapy (111, 112). The differences in the way younger and older women are treated may reflect concerns that surgery, radiation therapy, or chemotherapy may be less efficacious or more toxic in the elderly, or that these women may not live long enough to realize a benefit from aggressive therapy.

However, there is evidence that, in the absence of comorbid diseases, older women tolerate surgery and chemotherapy well, with only mild increases in toxicity (112). Given the higher incidence of breast cancer in elderly women, appropriate management and inclusion of these women in clinical trials of breast cancer therapy will be a critical influence on improving both survival and quality of life for women with this disease.

Special Considerations for Nurse Practitioners and Physician Assistants

In American culture, the female breast is closely linked with womanhood, so that the potential loss of a breast can be psychologically devastating to a woman. In addition, loss of a breast during childbearing years may threaten a woman's ability to nourish her offspring.

Women react to breast problems within a sociocultural context that will also affect their care (113). Psychological barriers to breast cancer screening for African-American women may include higher levels of cancer anxiety. Such findings indicate that campaigns designed to scare women into mammography may not be appropriate for these women (114). Older women, the group most likely to benefit from mammography, is the group least likely to get mammograms for many reasons, including lack of referrals (115). When focus groups were conducted with women living in a retirement community, investigators found that 94% of the women did not know that the risk of breast cancer increased with age, and many felt that a mammogram was not needed if they felt well or had no family history of breast cancer. Concerns regarding radiation, cost, and pain were also barriers to mammogram use. When findings from the focus groups were used to develop targeted educational programs, a significant number of women obtained screening (116). Barriers to seeking care for breast changes include conflicting commitments (e.g., work, family), finances, fears, and avoidance of the possibility of cancer (117).

Some women will seek advice from a lay referral system before seeing a health care provider. Providers who are involved in educational programs must recognize the importance of family, friends, and other community networks if they are to be successful in distributing information. Accessibility barriers to screenings may also be reduced by the use of a mobile van at work or community sites.

To adequately examine the breasts, providers must allow sufficient time and follow a specific technique, observing and palpating each breast with the woman sitting and lying down. A thorough examination of the axillary, supraclavicular, and cervical lymph nodes should be performed (119). Different patterns of palpation (i.e., concentric circles, stripping, spokes or wedges) are acceptable as long as all breast tissue is covered with variable degrees of pressure. The same technique should be taught to the woman so that she can perform thorough BSE and potentially detect even small lumps. Women should be taught to use the pads, not tips, of their fingers for palpation and to examine all quadrants of their breasts and the axillary tail. Providers should emphasize to the women that the purpose of BSE is not for them to make a diagnosis, but for them to become familiar with their own breasts and thus be able to recognize changes. Written information can supplement the provider's teaching, but not substitute for it (113).

Abnormal or suspicious finding must be carefully documented using descriptive terms. Masses should be described assuming a clock position or by marking them on a breast diagram and indicating the distance from the base of the nipple. Dimensions of masses should be measured and noted, as should the consistency, shape, mobility, presence of tenderness, and any associated skin changes. The presence or absence of any nipple discharge and lymphadenopathy should be described. Some suggest that a second examiner corroborate breast findings. Consultation and referral is needed for any suspicious masses or other findings (120). A full evaluation of a breast mass must be done, even in the presence of a normal mammogram (121).

Women undergoing treatment for breast cancer will have ongoing primary care needs. Primary care providers should establish open communication with the specialists who are managing cancer therapy. Prevention and early detection of communicable diseases may be care objectives for the primary provider (119). When breast cancer is diagnosed, the woman and her family will have many difficult decisions to make in a short period of time. After surgery, they may benefit from referral to support groups such as Reach to Recovery and books written by and about women who have experienced breast cancer (113).

References

1. Wingo PA, Tong T, Bolden S. Cancer statistics, 1995. CA Cancer J Clin 1995;45:8–30
2. Ries LAG, Miller BA, Hankey BF, Kosary CL, Harras A, Edwards BK(eds). SEER Cancer Statistics Review, 1973–1991: Tables and Graphs, National Cancer Institute. NIH Pub. No. 94-2789. Bethesda, MD, 1994.
3. Miller BA, Feuer EJ, Hankey BF. The significance of the rising incidence of breast cancer in the United States. In: DeVita VT, Hellman S, Rosenberg SA, eds. Important Advances in Oncology. Philadelphia: JB Lippincott, 1994:193–207.
4. Newcomb PA, Lantz PM. Recent trends in breast cancer incidence, mortality, and mammography. Br Cancer Res Treat 1993;28:97–106.
5. Wun LM, Feuer EJ, Miller BA. Are increases in mammographic screening still a valid explanation for trends in breast cancer incidence in the United States? Cancer Causes Control 1995;6:135:144.
6. Miller BA, Feuer EJ, Hankey BF. Recent incidence trends for breast cancer in women and the relevance of early detection: an update. CA Cancer J Clin 1993;43:27–41.

7. Helzlsouer KJ. Early detection and prevention of breast cancer. In: Greenwald P, Kramer BS, Weed DL, eds. Cancer prevention and control. New York: Marcel Dekker, 1995:509–535.

8. Kelsey JL, Gammon MD. The epidemiology of breast cancer. CA Cancer J Clin 1991;41:146–165.

9. Skolnick MH, Cannon-Albright LA. Genetic predisposition to breast cancer. Cancer 1992:70:1747–1754.

10. Colditz GA, Willett WC, Hunter DJ, et al. Family history, age, and risk of breast cancer: prospective data from the Nurses' Health Study. JAMA 1993; 270:338–343.

11. Slattery ML, Kerber RA. A comprehensive evaluation of family history and breast cancer risk. JAMA 1993;270:1563–1568.

12. Sattin RW, Rubin GL, Webster LA, et al. Family history and the risk of breast cancer. JAMA 1985; 253:1908–1913.

13. Gail MH, Brinton LA, Byar DP, et al. Projecting individualized probabilities of developing breast cancer for white females who are being examined annually. J Natl Cancer Inst 1989;81:1879–1886.

14. Claus EB, Risch N, Thompson WD. Genetic analysis of breast cancer in the Cancer and Steroid Hormone Study. Am J Hum Genet 1991;48:232–242.

15. Malkin D, Li FP, Strong LC, et al. Germ line P53 mutations in a familial syndrome of breast cancer, sarcomas and other neoplasms. Science 1990;250: 1233–1238.

16. Miki Y, Swensen J, Shattuck-Eidens D, et al. A strong candidate for the breast and ovarian cancer susceptibility gene BRCA1. Science 1994;266:66–71.

17. Wooster R, Neuhausen S, Mangion J, et al. Localization of a breast cancer susceptibility gene, BRCA2, to chromosome 13q12–13. Science 1994;265:2088–2090.

18. Easton DF, Bishop DT, Ford D, Crockford GP. Genetic linkage analysis in familial breast and ovarian cancer: results from 214 families. Am J Hum Genet 1993:53:678–701.

19. Page DL, Dupont WD. Benign breast disease: indicators of increased breast cancer risk. Cancer Detect Prev 1992;16:93–97.

20. Page DL, Dupont WD. Anatomic indicators (histologic and cytologic) of increased breast cancer risk. Breast Cancer Res Treat 1993;28:157–166.

21. Dupont WD, Parl FF, Hartmann WH, et al. Breast cancer risk associated with proliferative breast disease and atypical hyperplasia. Cancer 1993;71: 1258–1265.

22. Dupont WD, Page DL. Risk factors for breast cancer in women with proliferative breast disease. N Engl J Med 1985;312:146–151.

23. Kelsey JL, Gammon MD, John EM. Reproductive factors and breast cancer. Epidemiol Rev 1993;15: 36–47.

24. Colditz GA. Epidemiology of breast cancer: findings from the Nurses' Health Study. Cancer 1993;71: 1480–1489.

25. Henderson BE, Ross RK, Judd HL, et al. Do regular ovulatory cycles increase breast cancer risk? Cancer 1985;56:1206–1208.

26. Lambe M, Hsieh CC, Trichopoulos D, Ekbom A, Pavia M, Adami HO. Transient increase in the risk of breast cancer after giving birth. N Engl J Med 1994;331:5–9.

27. Byers T, Graham S, Rzepka T, Marshall J. Lactation and breast cancer: evidence for a negative association in premenopausal women. Am J Epidemiol 1985;12:664–674.

28. Newcomb PA, Storer BE, Longnecker MP, et al. Lactation and a reduced risk of premenopausal breast cancer. N Engl J Med 1994;330:81–87.

29. Romieu I, Berlin JA, Colditz G. Oral contraceptives and breast cancer: review and meta-analysis. Cancer 1990;66:2253–2263.

30. Rushton L, Jones DR. Oral contraceptive use and breast cancer risk: a meta-analysis of variations with age at diagnosis, parity and total duration of oral contraceptive use. Br J Obstet Gynecol 1992;99: 239–246.

31. Malone KE, Daling JR, Weiss NS. Oral contraceptives and relation to breast cancer. Epidemiol Rev 1993;15:80–97.

32. Wingo PA, Lee NC, Ory HW, Beral V, Peterson HB, Rhodes P. Age-specific differences in the relationship between oral contraceptives use and breast cancer. Obstet Gynecol 1991;78:161–170.

33. Grady D, Rubin SM, Petitti DB, et al. Hormone therapy to prevent disease and prolong life in postmenopausal women. Ann Intern Med 1992;117: 1016–1037.

34. Steinberg KK, Thacker SB, Smith SJ, et al. A meta-analysis of the effect of estrogen replacement on the risk of breast cancer. JAMA 1991;265:1985–1990.

35. Dupont WD, Page DL. Menopausal estrogen replacement therapy and breast cancer. Arch Intern Med 1991;151:67–72.

36. Colditz GA, Egan KM, Stamper MJ. Hormone replacement therapy and risk of breast cancer: results from epidemiologic studies. Am J Obstet Gynecol 1993;168:1473–1480.

37. Sillero-Aernas M, Delagado-Rodriguez, Rodrigues-Canteras, Buemo-Cavanillas A, Galvez-Vargas R. Menopausal hormone replacement therapy and breast cancer: a meta-analysis. Obstet Gynecol 1992;79: 268–294.

38. Steinberg KK, Smith SJ, Thacker SB, Stroup DF. Breast cancer risk and duration of estrogen use: the role of study design in meta-analysis. Epidemiology 1994;5:415–421.

39. Colditz GA, Hankinson SE, Hunter D, et al. The use of estrogens and progestins and the risk of breast cancer in postmenopausal women. N Engl J Med 1995; 332:1589–1593.

40. Davidson NE. Hormone-replacement therapy—breast versus heart versus bone. N Engl J Med 1995;332: 1638–1639.

41. Dorgan JF, Reichman ME, Judd JT, et al. The relation between reported alcohol ingestion to plasma levels of estrogens and androgens in premenopausal

women (Maryland, United States). Cancer Causes Control 1994;5:53–60.

42. Longnecker MP. Alcoholic beverage consumption in relation to risk of breast cancer: meta-analysis and review. Cancer Causes Control 1994;5:73–82.

43. Welsch CW. Relationship between dietary fat and experimental mammary tumorigenesis: a review and critique. Cancer Res (Suppl) 1992;52:2040–2048.

44. Prentice RL, Sheppard L. Dietary fat and cancer: consistency of the epidemiological data, and disease prevention that may come from a practical reduction in fat consumption. Cancer Causes Control 1990;1:81–97.

45. Howe GR, Hirohata T, Hislop TG, et al. Dietary factors and risk of breast cancer: combined analysis of 12 case-control studies. J Natl Cancer Inst 1990;82:561–569.

46. Prentice RL, Pepe M, Self SG. Dietary fat and breast cancer: a quantitative assessment of the epidemiological literature and a discussion of methodological issues. Cancer Res 1989;49:3147–3156.

47. Eaker E, Hahn RA. Women's Health Initiative. N Engl J Med 1994;330:70–71.

48. Claus EB, Risch N, Thompson WD. Autosomal dominant inheritance of early-onset breast cancer: implications for risk prediction. Cancer 1994;73:643–651.

49. Hoskins KF, Stopfer JE, Calzone KA, et al. Assessment and counselling for women with a family history of breast cancer: a guide for clinicians. JAMA 1995;273:577–585.

50. Vogel VG, Yeomans A, Higginbotham E. Clinical management of women at increased risk of breast cancer. Breast Cancer Res Treat 1993;28:195–210.

51. Morrow M. Identification and management of the woman at increased risk for breast cancer development. Breast Cancer Res Treat 1994;31:53–60.

52. Habbema JDF, van Oortmarssen GJ, van Putten DJ, Lubbe JT, van der Maas PJ. Age-specific reduction in breast cancer mortality by screening: an analysis of the results of the Health Insurance Plan of Greater New York study. J Natl Cancer Inst 1986;77:317–320.

53. Chu KC, Smart CR, Tarone RE. Analysis of breast cancer mortality and stage distribution by age for the Health Insurance Plan clinical trial. J Natl Cancer Inst 1988;80:1125–1132.

54. Tabar L, Fagerberg CJG, Gad A, et al. Reduction in mortality from breast cancer after mass screening with mammography. Lancet 1985;1:829–832.

55. Tabar L, Fagerberg G, Duffy S, Day NE, Gad A, Grontoft O. Update on the Swedish two-county program of mammographic screening for breast cancer. Radiol Clin North Am 1992;30:187–210.

56. Tabar L, Fagerberg G, Chen HH, et al. Efficacy of breast cancer screening by age. New results from the Swedish two-county trial. Cancer 1995;75:2507–2517.

57. Andersson I, Aspergen K, Janzon L, et al. Mammographic screening and mortality from breast cancer: the Malmo mammographic screening trial. Br Med J 1988;297:943–948.

58. Frisell J, Eklund G, Hellstrom L, Lidbrink E, Rutqvist L-E, Somell A. Randomized study of mammography screening—preliminary report on mortality in the Stockholm trial. Breast Cancer Res Treat 1991;18:49–56.

59. Nystrom L, Rutqvist LE, Wall S, et al. Breast cancer screening with mammography: overview of Swedish randomized trials. Lancet 1993;341:973–978.

60. Roberts MM, Alexander FE, Anderson TJ, et al. Edinburgh trial of screening for breast cancer: mortality at seven years. Lancet 1990;335:241–246.

61. Alexander FE, Anderson TJ, Brown HK, et al. The Edinburgh randomized trial of breast cancer screening: results after 10 years of follow-up. Br J Cancer 1994;70:542–548.

62. Miller AB, Baines CJ, To T, Wall C. Canadian National Breast Screening study: 1. Breast cancer detection and death rates among women aged 40 to 49 years. Can Med Assoc J 1992;147:1459–1476.

63. Miller AB, Baines CJ, To T, Wall C. Canadian National Breast Screening study: 1. Breast cancer detection and death rates among women aged 50 to 59 years. Can Med Assoc J 1992;147:1477–1488.

64. Kerlikowske K, Grady D, Rubin S, Sandrock C, Ernster VL. Efficacy of screening mammography: a meta-analysis. JAMA 1995;273:149–154.

65. Eckhardt S, Badellino F, Murphy GP. UICC meeting on breast-cancer screening in premenopausal women in developed countries. Int J Cancer 1994;56:1–5.

66. Sickles EA, Kopans DB. Mammographic screening for women aged 40 to 49 years: the primary care practitioner's dilemma. Ann Intern Med 1995;122:534–538.

67. Fletcher SW, Black W, Harris R, Rimer BK, Shapiro S. Report of the international workshop on screening for breast cancer. J Natl Cancer Inst 1993;85:1644–1656.

68. Kaluzny AD, Rimer B, Harris R. The National Cancer Institute and guideline development: lessons from the breast cancer screening controversy. J Natl Cancer Inst 1994;86:901–903.

69. Smart CR, Hartmann WH, Beahrs OH, Garfinkel L. Insight into breast cancer screening of younger women: evidence from the 14-year follow-up of the Breast Cancer Detection Demonstration Project. Cancer 1993;72:1449–1456.

70. Kopans DB. The positive predictive value of mammography. AJR 1992;158:521–526.

71. Kerlikowske K. Grady D, Barclay J, et al. Positive predictive value of screening mammography by age and family history of breast cancer. JAMA 1993;270:2444–2450.

72. Jokich PM, Monticciolo DL, Adlwe YL. Breast ultrasonography. Radiol Clin North Am 1992;30:993–1009.

73. Bassett L, Kimme-Smith C. Breast sonography. AJR 1991;156:449–455.

74. Foster RS, Worden JK, Costanza MC, Solomon LJ. Clinical breast examination and breast self-examination: past and present effect on breast cancer survival. Cancer 1992;69:1992–1998.

75. Huguley CM, Brown RL, Greenberg RS, Clark W. Breast self-examination and survival from breast cancer. Cancer 1998;62:1389–1396.

76. Baker LH. Breast Cancer Detection Demonstration Project: Five year summary report. CA 1982;32:194–225.

77. US Preventive Task Force. Guide to Clinical Preventive Services: an assessment of the effectiveness of 169 interventions. Report of the U.S. Preventive Services Task Force. Baltimore: Wilkins & Wilkins, 1989.

78. Anonymous. Screening recommendations of the Forum Panel. J Gerentol 1992;47:5.

79. Adler DD, Wahl RL. New methods for imaging the breast: techniques, findings and potential. AJR 1995;165:19–30.

80. Dershaw DD, Fleischman RC, Liberman L, Deutch B, Abramson AF, Hann L. Use of digital mammography in needle localization procedures. AJR 1993;161:559–562.

81. Silverstein MJ. Noninvasive breast cancer. The dilemma of the 1990s. Obstet Gynecol Clin North Am 1994;21:639–658.

82. Hetelekidis S, Schnitt SJ, Morrow M, Harris JR. Management of ductal carcinoma in situ. CA Cancer J Clin 1995;45:244–253.

83. Harris JR, Lippman ME, Veronesi U, Willett W. Breast cancer. N Engl J Med 1992;327:390–398.

84. Jacobson JA, Danforth DN, Cowan KH. Ten-year results of a comparison of conservation with mastectomy in the treatment of stage I and II breast cancer. N Engl J Med 1995;332:907–911.

85. Fisher B, Costantino J, Redmond C, et al. Lumpectomy compared with lumpectomy and radiation therapy for the treatment of intraductal breast cancer. N Engl J Med 1993;328:1581–1586.

86. Osborne MP, Hoda SA. Current management of lobular carcinoma in situ of the breast. Oncology 1994;8:45–49.

87. Posner MC, Wolmark N. Non-invasive breast carcinoma. Br Cancer Res Treat 1992;21:155–164.

88. Roberge AE, Erban JK. Today's adjuvant therapy in breast cancer: who should receive what? Cancer Control 1995;2:209–217.

89. van Dongen JA, Bartelink H, Fentiman IS, et al. Randomized clinical trial to assess the value of breast-conserving therapy in stage I and II breast cancer: EORTC 10801 trial. Monogr Natl Cancer Inst 1992;11:15–18.

90. Veronesi U, Banfi A, Salvadori B, et al. Breast conservation is the treatment of choice in small breast cancer: long-term results of a randomized trial. Eur J Cancer 1990;26:668–670.

91. Sarrazin D, Le MG, Arriagada R, et al. Ten-year results of a randomized trial comparing a conservative treatment to mastectomy in early breast cancer. Radiother Oncol 1989;14:177–184.

92. Blichert-Toft M, Rose C, Andersen JA, et al. Danish randomized trial comparing breast conservation therapy with mastectomy: six years of life-table analysis. Monogr Natl Cancer Inst 1992;11:19–25.

93. Fisher B, Redmond D, Poisson R, et al. Eight-year results of a randomized clinical trial comparing total mastectomy and lumpectomy with or without irradiation in the treatment of breast cancer. N Engl J Med 1989;320:822–828.

94. Jacobson JA, Danforth DN, Cowan KH, et al. Ten-year results of a comparison of conservation with mastectomy in the treatment of stage I and II breast cancer. N Engl J Med 1995;332:907–911.

95. Rosen PP, Groshen S, Saigo PE, et al. Pathological prognostic factors in stage I (T1 N0 M0) and stage II (T1 N1 M0) breast carcinoma: a study of 644 patients with median follow-up of 18 years. J Clin Oncol 1989;7:1239–1251.

96. Elledge RM, McGuire WL, Osborne CK. Prognostic factors in breast cancer. Semin Oncol 1992;19:244–253.

97. Ravdin PM. A practical view of prognostic factors for staging, adjuvant treatment planning, and as baseline studies for possible future therapy. Hematol Oncol Clin North Am 1994;8:197–211

98. Early Breast Cancer Trialists' Collaborative Group: Systemic treatment of early breast cancer by hormonal, cytotoxic, or immune therapy: 133 randomized trials involving 31,000 recurrences and 24,000 deaths among 75,000 women. Lancet 1992;339:1–15,71–85.

99. Goldhirsch A, Wood WC, Senn H-J, Glick J, Gelber RD. Meeting highlights: international consensus panel on the treatment of primary breast cancer. J Natl Cancer Inst 1995;87:1441–1445.

100. Valagussa P, Bonadonna G, Veronesi U. Patterns of relapse and survival following radical mastectomy: analysis of 716 consecutive patients. Cancer 1978;41:1170–1178.

101. Nemoto T, Vana J, Bedwani R. Management and survival of female breast cancer. Cancer 1980;45:2917–2924.

102. Bonadonna G, Veronesi U, Brambilla C. Primary chemotherapy to avoid mastectomy in tumors with diameters of three centimeters or more. J Natl Cancer Inst 1990;82:1539–1545.

103. Mauriac L, Durnad M, Avril A. Effects of primary chemotherapy in conservative treatment of breast cancer patients with operable tumors larger than 3 cm. Results of a randomized trial. Ann Oncol 1991;2:347–354.

104. Von Schoultz, Johansson H, Wilking N, et al. Influence of prior and subsequent pregnancy on breast cancer prognosis. J Clin Oncol 1995;13:430–434.

105. Petrek JA. Pregnancy safety after breast cancer. Cancer 1994;74:528–531.

106. Costanza ME. The extent of breast cancer screening in older women. Cancer 1994;74:2046–2050.

107. Smith RA, Haynes S. Barriers to screening for breast cancer. Cancer 1992;69:1968–1978.

108. Yanick R, Ries LG, Yates JW. Breast cancer in aging women: a population-based study of contrasts in stage, surgery, and survival. Cancer 1989;63; 978–981.

109. Satarino WA, Ragland DR. The effect of comorbidity on 3-year survival of women with primary breast cancer. Ann Intern Med 1994;120:104–110.

110. August DA, Rea T, Sondack VK. Age-related differences in breast cancer treatment. Am Surg Onc 1994;1:15–52.

111. Fleming ID, Fleming MD. Breast cancer in the elderly. Cancer 1994;74:2160–2164.

112. Muss HB. Chemotherapy of breast cancer in the older patient. Semin Ocol 1995;22:14–16.

113. Nettles-Carlson B. Problems of the breast. In: Fogel CI, Woods NF. Women's Health Care. Thousand Oaks: Sage, 1995:673–700.

114. Miller LY, Hailey BJ. Cancer anxiety and breast cancer screening in African-American women: a preliminary study. Women's Health Issues 1994;2: 170–174.

115. Sutton SM, Doner LD. Insights into the physician's role in mammography utilization among older women. Women's Health Issues 1992;2:175–179.

116. Rimer BK, King E. Why aren't older women getting mammograms and clinical breast exams? Women's Health Issues 1992;2:94–101.

117. Lauver D, Coyle M, Panchmatia B. Women's reasons for and barriers to seeking care for breast cancer symptoms. Women's Health Issues 1995;5:27–35.

118. Brown LW, Williams RD. Culturally sensitive breast cancer programs for older black women. Nurse Pract 1994;19:21–35.

119. Shapiro TJ, Clark PM. Breast cancer: what the primary care provider needs to know. Nurse Pract 1995;20:36–53.

120. Lommell LL. Breast cancer screening. In: Star WL, Lommell LL, Shannon MT, eds. Women's Primary Health Care. Washington, DC: American Nurses Association, 1995:4–8–4-11.

121. Ellis GK. Breast cancer. Primary Care OB/Gyns 1994;1:17–25.

Suggested Readings

Harris JR, Lippman ME, Veronesi U, Willett W. Breast cancer (1). N Engl J Med 1992;327:319–328.

Harris JR, Lippman ME, Veronesi U, Willett W. Breast cancer (2). N Engl J Med 1992;327:390–398.

Harris JR, Lippman ME, Veronesi U, Willett W. Breast cancer (3). N Engl J Med 1992;327:473–480.

Hoskins KF, Stopfer JE, Calzone KA, et al. Assessment and counselling for women with a family history of breast cancer: a guide for clinicians. JAMA 1995; 273:577–585.

18.1

Urinary Tract Infection

Kathleen L. B. Beine

Introduction and Epidemiology

Urinary tract infections (UTI) are among the most common bacterial infections seen by physicians (1). Adult women are 30 times more likely to develop a UTI than men. Ten to 20% of American women will have a UTI sometime in their life (2). Up to 35% of women age 20 to 40 years have had UTIs. Ap-

proximately 20% of women have frequent recurrences of infections, ranging from three to six episodes per year (3). For these women with recurrent UTIs, most will be urinary tract reinfections rather than unresolved urinary tract infections.

Acute urinary conditions resulted in an estimated 6.5 million physician visits in 1993 in the United States (4). Outpatient expenditures approach 1 billion dollars yearly (5), and additional millions of dollars are spent annually on patients hospitalized caused by UTIs (6). Total economic expenditures significantly exceed this amount if all costs are considered, including medical visits, laboratory tests, hospital costs, prescriptions, time off from work, transportation expenses, and childcare, in addition to pain and suffering (7).

Additionally, urinary tract infections are the most common hospital-acquired infections. The nosocomial infection rate for hospitalized patients is estimated to be 5.7%, and 42% of these infections originate from the urinary tract. In the mid-1970s in US hospitals, there were an estimated 902,732 nosocomial urinary tract infections (8).

Normal Defenses

The urinary tract has inherent defenses against infection: physiologic acid pH, extremes of osmolality, urea, and organic acids in the urine, in addition to antiadherent qualities of the mucin layer of the bladder (9). The flow of urine dilutes and flushes bacteria out of the bladder.

The renal medulla, with its high osmolality and ammonia content, is much more susceptible to infection. As few as 10 organisms are needed to infect the renal medulla, as compared to 100,000 organisms needed to infect the cortex. Additionally, conditions in the medulla favor cell wall-deficient bacterial variants that are resistant to antimicrobials (10).

Microbiology

Normal flora of the distal urethra and skin include *Staphylococcus epidermidis*, diphtheroids, lactobacilli, *Gardnerella vaginalis*, and anaerobes. Generally, isolation of these organisms suggests contamination; however, they may also be infectious (11).

In an acute uncomplicated UTI, there is rarely more than one bacterial species (Table 18.1.1). For uncomplicated lower and upper UTIs, usual causative uropathogens are *Es-*

Table 18.1.1. Bacterial Organisms Causing UTIs

	Uncomplicated UTI (%)	Complicated UTI (%)
Gram-negative pathogens		
Escherichia coli	80 to 95	30 to 40
Proteus mirabilis	< 1	10 to 15
Klebsiella species	< 1	7
Pseudomonas aeruginosa	< 1	4 to 5
Enterobacter species	< 1	2 to 5
Acinetobacter species	< 1	2
Citrobacter species	< 1	1 to 2
Providencia, Morganella species	< 1	1 to 2
Serratia marcescens	< 1	1 to 2
Gram-positive pathogens		
Enterococcus faecalis	< 1	10 to 15
Staphylococcus epidermidis	5 to 10	5 to 10
Staphylococcus aureus	1 to 5	5
Staphylococcus saprophyticus	5 to 10	2 to 5

Modified from Neu HC. Urinary tract infections. Am J Med 1992;92(suppl 4A): 63S–70S.

cherichia coli in 80 to 95%, *Staphylococcus saprophyticus* in 5 to 10%, occasionally *Proteus mirabilis*, Klebsiella species, or enterococci. Six serotypes of *E. coli* account for 85% of acute UTIs. Rectal flora is the primary source of pathogens for community-acquired UTIs in women.

Unless the patient is at risk for complicated UTI, multiple organisms often represent a contaminated urine specimen (12). However, in as many as 10 to 15% of symptomatic patients, bacteriuria cannot be detected with routine methods (13).

Pathogens such as *Chlamydia trachomatis*, *Neisseria gonorrhea*, or herpes simplex virus may result in sexually transmitted urethritis. Vaginitis may mimic acute urethritis or UTI and is often caused by *Trichomonas vaginalis* and/or Candida species (14).

Use of the Laboratory

Because the clinical diagnosis of UTI is often inaccurate, laboratory data are important to confirm the diagnosis, especially in women with symptoms of frequency and dysuria (15). No difference has been demonstrated clinically between women with high versus low urine colony counts. A presumptive diagnosis can be made based on a patient's presenting symptoms, physical exam findings, urinalysis, and, if indicated, examination of vaginal discharge. However, it is inappropriate to use bacteriuria as the single criterion to establish the diagnosis of UTI.

Urinalysis

The standard urinalysis should include a description of urine color, specific gravity, pH, glucose, protein, ketones, blood, and bilirubin. Dipstick test results are available within 1 minute.

Proper and consistent handling of the urine specimen is essential in order to have consistently reliable results. Typically, pyuria is quantified on the basis of direct microscopic examination of urinary sediment from a centrifuged specimen. This method often is inaccurate because of (a) improper specimen collection, (b) not examining fresh urine, (c) variable or unmeasured initial urine volume, (d) variable or imprecise time and speed of centrifugation, (e) inconsistent resuspension volume following centrifugation, (f) variable amounts of urine placed on the slide for microscopic examination, (g) counting inaccuracy caused by not having reference grid lines on the slide, (h) incomplete examination of the urinary sediment and/or (i) observer bias in favor of areas on the slide where leukocytes are seen more easily (16).

The presence of pyuria and bacteriuria, two major indicators of UTI, can be determined by direct microscopic examination of urine (centrifuged or uncentrifuged) or by rapid assays using the dipstick method. Leukocytes represent an inflammatory response and are present in almost all symptomatic urinary tract infections. However, leukocytes are present with vaginitis, urethritis, and leukorrhea of pregnancy. If leukocytes are absent, another etiology may be responsible for the patient's symptoms. The centrifuged sediment of properly collected and processed midstream clean catch normal urine should have less than 5 to 10 WBC/hpf, that represents 50 to 100 WBCs/mm^3 of urine. The presence of white blood cell casts strongly suggests pyelonephritis; however, their absence does not rule this out.

Leukocyte esterase test, used to detect pyuria, has sensitivity of 75 to 96% and specificity of 94 to 98% for detecting more than 10 WBCs/mm^3. Nitrate reductase is produced by Gram-negative bacilli. A positive test indicating their presence has sensitivity ranging from 35 to 85% and a specificity of 92 to 100%. False-negative tests may occur when the infection is caused by *Staphylococcus* spp, *Enterococcus* spp, or *Pseudomonas* spp.

Microscopic or gross hematuria may be

present in urinary tract infections. Other causes of hematuria include calculi, tumor, vasculitis, glomerulonephritis, and renal tuberculosis. Proteinuria is a common nonspecific finding with UTI. Women with UTI usually excrete less than 2 g of protein in 24 hours. Women with glomerular disease typically excrete 3 g or more.

Bacteriuria, the presence of bacteria in the urine, may occur with or without pyuria and is detected by quantitative urine culture. Microscopically, in uncentrifuged Gram-stained urine, the presence of at least one organism per oil immersion field correlates with $\geq 10^5$ colony-forming units per mL (cfu/mL), with a sensitivity and specificity rate of almost 90%; if there is no pyuria, bacteriuria may represent colonization, as in women with indwelling catheters (17).

Urine Culture

Traditionally, a positive culture has $\geq 10^5$ cfu/mL in a culture of freshly voided urine or any growth in urine obtained by suprapubic aspiration (18). Urine is sterile under normal circumstances. The definition of $\geq 10^5$ cfu/mL has a low sensitivity; up to 50% of women with UTI do not meet this criterion (19). Quantitative urine cultures are especially important in situations in which the patient has symptoms of acute uncomplicated cystitis, but does not have pyuria, bacteriuria, or hematuria, or when the patient's symptoms are not characteristic of a UTI (20). Use of a dipslide culture technique is simple and reliable for office use (21).

Low colony counts of $\geq 10^2$ cfu/mL are difficult to verify. In a student health center study of asymptomatic women, low colony counts (10^2 to 10^4 cfu/mL) of E. coli and S. saprophyticus were observed in 10% of the women (22). If these women with low colony counts were not treated within 2 days, half developed high urinary colony counts (23). Other studies have found that approximately one third of

women with acute lower UTI caused by E. coli, S. saprophyticus, and Proteus have colony counts in midstream urine between 10^2 and 10^4 cfu/mL (24). The correlation between number of organisms and symptoms increased as the bacterial count increased. Thus, low counts may represent early stages of UTIs. Consequently, some physicians recommend antibiotic treatment in symptomatic patients with acute dysuria, frequency, urgency, and pyuria on urinalysis, or treatment without obtaining a pretreatment urine culture (25).

Others report $\geq 10^3$ cfu/mL in the urine culture as indication for treatment (26). Because of the multitude of interpretations, the definition of significant bacteriuria has been revised from $\geq 10^5$ cfu/mL to $\geq 10^3$ cfu/mL in midstream clean catch urine specimens of patients with lower tract symptoms. In most clinical laboratories, detecting 10^2 cfu/mL may be difficult; thus, the suggested minimum colony count of 10^3 cfu/mL provides higher specificity without much loss of sensitivity (27). In bacteremic patients with UTI as the only identifiable source, approximately 80% will have 10^5 cfu/mL, 10 to 15% will have 10^4 to 10^5 cfu/mL and the remaining 5 to 10% will have $< 10^4$ cfu/mL in a midstream urine culture (28).

Negative cultures occur in up to 15% of patients with uncomplicated urinary tract symptoms; these patients should be evaluated for Chlamydia trachomatis, Ureaplasma urealyticum, or Mycoplasma hominis. Cultures may also be falsely negative because of residual soap contaminating the specimen collection, antimicrobial usage, total obstruction below the infection, infection with a fastidious organism or renal tuberculosis, and/or diuresis. Cultures should be obtained when symptoms of acute uncomplicated pyetonephritis or complicated infection are present. In the elderly, urine cultures should guide antibiotic treatment (29).

Polymicrobial UTI does occur, especially in association with risk factors such as elderly patients, diabetics, long-term catheterization, and nosocomially acquired infection. Although the frequency of true mixed infections is unknown, recovering the same combination of microorganisms from blood and urine, or identifying on sequential urine cultures the same assortment of bacteria, may indicate its significance. This is especially true in situations of long-term catheterization, which primarily results in polymicrobial infections. In properly collected urine samples, polymicrobial growth often represents true mixed infection and should be completely evaluated (30).

Risk Factors (Table 18.1.2)

Sexual intercourse is one of the most important risk factors for urinary tract infections, presumably from the mechanical effect of introducing uropathogens into the bladder (31). Following intercourse, in approximately one third of women, pathogenic and nonpathogenic urine bacterial counts increase, typically beginning 1 hour afterward and resolving in the majority of study participants within 48 hours (32). Typically, urinating within l hour following intercourse has a protective effect against *E. coli* bacteriuria (33).

Contraceptive methods can predispose to UTIs also. A prospective study evaluating the effects of contraceptive method on the occurrence of bacteriuria and vaginal colonization

Table 18.1.2. Risk Factors for UTI

Sexual intercourse
Spermicides, diaphragms, condoms with
  Nonoxynol-9
Pregnancy
Pelvic masses—uterine fibroids, tumors
Being postmenopausal
Age > 65 years
Chronic catheterization
Abnormalities of the urinary tract
Nephrolithiasis
Intrarenal obstruction

found a strong association between UTIs and sexual intercourse, but only when either a spermicide, a diaphragm plus spermicide, or a condom with spermicidal foam was used. These data suggest that spermicides, specifically the commonly used surfactant-detergent nonoxynol-9, increase vaginal colonization with uropathogens, presumably by eradicating normal lactobacilli vaginal flora and enhancing adherence of *E. coli* vaginal epithelial cells (34). *E. coli* bacteriuria and vaginal colonization was not associated with patients' ages, history of prior UTI, coital position, duration of coitus, number of ejaculations by the patient's partner, interval between intercourse and clinic visit, or for diaphragm users, the length of time the diaphragm was in place. In some patients with a prior history of UTI, a diaphragm can cause a relatively small amount of urinary outlet obstruction, but this does not correlate with developing a UTI (35).

Abnormalities of the urinary tract that result in obstruction to urine flow increase the risk of UTI. Pregnancy is one of the most common causes. Almost every pregnant woman develops right-sided, and often bilateral hydroureter, and hydronephrosis. This makes pregnancy a high-risk situation in which asymptomatic bacteriuria may develop rapidly into a UTI or pyelonephritis, requiring treatment sooner than with nonpregnant women.

Additional extrarenal causes of obstruction include congenital anomalies of the ureter or urethra, calculi, or other extrinsic ureteral compression. Causes of intrarenal obstruction include nephrocalcinosis, uric acid nephropathy, analgesic nephropathy, polycystic kidney disease, hypokalemic nephropathy, and renal lesions of sickle cell tract or disease. Also predisposing to UTI are conditions that result in incomplete emptying of the bladder, such as diabetic neuropathy or other neurogenic malfunction.

Contradictory results have been reported for the following factors causing UTIs; some investigators report no risk (36), and others report increased risk (37). These factors include wearing slacks, especially tight jeans, wearing pantyhose, using tampons or sanitary napkins, or drinking coffee or tea. No increased risk has been demonstrated for the following: wiping back-to-front after defecation, number of times urinating during the day or night, or masturbation. No protective effect has been demonstrated for drinking more than 3 glasses of fluids per day or for wearing cotton underwear, but increased risk has been associated with usage of deodorant soap and bubble bath.

It is possible that in the individual patient, one or more of these factors may be significant. Thus, for women with recurrent UTIs, in an effort to decrease the risk of infection, it is reasonable to recommend good hydration, regular bladder emptying, and front-to-back wiping after defecation.

Postmenopausal women, because of changes in vaginal pH and altered endogenous flora may be prone to developing UTIs (38). Up to 20% of elderly women have UTIs; in women 80 years of age and older, there is a 20 to 50% incidence of bacteriuria (39). In institutionalized elderly patients and those with debilitating disease, UTIs are even more common (40). An indwelling urinary catheter is the leading cause of nosocomial-induced UTIs, and the most common predisposing factor in fatal Gram-negative sepsis in hospitals (41).

Classification of UTIs

UTIs range from asymptomatic bacteriuria to complicated UTIs with perinephric abscesses to overwhelming sepsis. Symptoms vary depending on the age and health status of the patient, location and extensiveness of the infection, and concomitant neurologic disease. Clinical symptoms frequently do not correlate well with the site of infection (42).

Uropathogens gain access to the urinary tract by ascending and hematogenous routes (43). In women, the ascending route occurs

more commonly. Because a woman's urethra is short in length and located near the rectum, there is increased likelihood of colonization of bacteria from the vaginal introitus and fecal flora. The colonization of the vaginal introitus with uropathogens precedes most UTI (44).

UTI in adults can be categorized into five groups (Table 18.1.3): (*a*) young women with acute uncomplicated cystitis, (*b*) young women with recurrent cystitis, (*c*) young women with acute uncomplicated pyelonephritis, (*d*) all adult women with complicated UTI, and (*e*) all adult women with asymptomatic bacteriuria (45).

Acute Uncomplicated UTI

An *acute uncomplicated UTI*, which includes the categories of acute dysuria, acute cystitis, and acute urethral syndrome, occurs in otherwise healthy women with structurally and functionally normal urinary tracts. In approximately 70% of women, an acute UTI affects only the bladder and/or urethra. Symptoms include urinary frequency, burning, urgency, and often suprapubic discomfort; flank pain and fever are rare (46).

Table 18.1.3. Categories of Urinary Tract Infections in Women

1. Acute, uncomplicated cystitis
2. Unresolved or recurrent UTI
3. Acute, uncomplicated pyelonephritis
4. Complicated UTI
   Acute complicated cystitis and/or pyelonephritis
   Anatomic or functional abnormality of the urinary tract
   Bacteriuria and/or pyelonephritis in pregnancy
   Indwelling catheter-related infection
   Fungal UTI
5. Asymptomatic bacteriuria

Modified from Kim ED, Schaeffer AJ. Antimicrobial therapy for urinary tract infections. Semin Nephrol 1994;14:551–569.

Acute dysuria in young women usually is caused by one of three types of infection: (*a*) acute bacterial cystitis, (*b*) acute urethritis caused by *Chlamydia trachomatis*, *Neisseria gonorrhoeae*, or herpes simplex virus, or (*c*) vaginitis caused by Candida or trichomonas. Acute dysuria may also be caused by physical or chemical agents, urethral trauma, or symptoms without any recognized cause (47).

A urine culture can confirm acute cystitis. In symptomatic young women with acute dysuria, frequency, urgency and pyuria on urinalysis, a urine culture of $\geq 10^2$ cfu/mL of a uropathogenic species usually indicates infection. This is a significant difference from the traditional standard for the diagnosis of UTI as $\geq 10^5$ cfu/mL of a single pathogenic bacterium cultured from urine as being indicative of infection (48, 49). The criterion of $\geq 10^5$ cfu/mL fails to identify almost 50% of truly infected symptomatic women.

Recurrent UTI

Reinfection or relapse most frequently occurs soon after the treatment of the inital UTI. Relapse, caused by the original infecting organism, usually occurs within 6 weeks, but may occur within 1 to 2 weeks of cessation of antibiotic therapy. Typically, relapse is associated with renal infection and/or structural abnormalities of the urinary tract. Reinfection with a different organism occurs in 2 to 10% of patients and is attributed to contamination from the fecal flora reservoir. Reinfection is the primary cause of recurrent UTI in women; therefore, successful treatment occurs with antimicrobial prophylaxis (50).

Uncomplicated Pyelonephritis

An *acute uncomplicated pyelonephritis* occurs when the soft tissues of the kidney are infected. Women may present with systemic symptoms of fever, rigors, sweats, headache, nausea, vomiting, malaise prostration, and localized flank, low back or abdominal pain, in addition to lower tract symptoms. Approximately one third of patients with an occult acute uncomplicated pyelonephritis may present with only lower tract symptoms of acute cystitis. In elderly and neurologically impaired patients, atypical presentations may occur, such as changes in mentation, appetite reduction, abdominal pain, incontinence, urgency, nocturia, decreased social interaction, and/or inattention to personal hygiene. These symptoms may be present in any combination; additional clinical evidence is required to evaluate the seriousness of infection.

Complicated UTIs

A *complicated UTI* implies the presence of host conditions in the patient that may promote or account for the persistence or recurrence of infection. This often occurs where the urinary tract has sustained repeated infections, leaving residual inflammatory changes, or when obstruction, stones, or neurological lesions interfere with drainage of urine in some part of the urinary tract. Such underlying conditions include pregnancy, diabetes, structural or functional urinary tract anomaly, a hospital-acquired infection, recent urinary tract instrumentation, immunosuppressed state, polycystic kidney disease, and/or recent antibiotic use. Extremes of patient age, either very young or very elderly, are also factors. Addressing the underlying disorder, is often essential.

Asymptomatic Bacteriuria

Asymptomatic or covert bacteriuria refers to the presence of significant bacteriuria in a patient who lacks symptoms requiring medical consultation. Typically, this condition is detected when screening apparently healthy populations. More rigid criteria are required for diagnosis: two consecutive clean catch midstream urine cultures with the same organism at $\geq 10^5$ cfu/mL has a sensitivity and specificity of $> 95\%$ (51). In women, the prevalence of bacteriuria during the first decade of life is approximately 1% and increases approximately 1% with every decade (52). Because of significant economic cost, it is probably beneficial only to screen routinely high-risk populations such as pregnant women and patients scheduled to undergo urologic surgery.

Approximately 40% of elderly patients have asymptomatic bacteriuria, especially those in nursing homes. Routine screening and/or use of antimicrobial agents for the prevention or treatment of asymptomatic bacteriuria is not recommended, despite occasional symptomatic infections including their complications.

Definitions of Response to Therapy

Resolution of symptoms is the clinical goal. Clinical cure is the relief of symptoms and pyuria. Bacterial cure with the eradication of the organism and prevention of recurrence are additional goals.

"Cure" is the disappearance of bacteriuria after treatment, with negative urine cultures although the patient is receiving therapy and 1 to 2 weeks following treatment. Bacterial counts should decrease within 48 hours after appropriate therapy is started (53).

"Persistence" is bacteriuria persisting during and after treatment, either significant bacteriuria after 48 hours of treatment or the presence of low numbers of the infecting organism after 48 hours. This may be caused by drug resistance, subtherapeutic urinary concentrations, or the presence of a bacterial nidus within the soft tissues of the urinary tract or calculi.

"Relapse" is posttreatment recurrence of bacteriuria caused by the same organism as was originally isolated and results from persistence of the organism in the urinary tract. Approximately 20% of women with acute UTIs have frequent relapses and account for a great deal of morbidity, increased health care expenditures, and time lost from work (54).

"Reinfection" is the recurrence of bacteri-uria after treatment caused by an organism different from that originally isolated, occurring after initial sterilization of the urine and usually involving a different bacterial species or a different serotype of the same species (55).

"Superinfections," the presence of a new organism resistant to current antibiotics, develop although patients are receiving therapy. "Therapeutic failures" occur in asymptomatic patients with $\geq 10^5$ cfu/mL of a uropathogen or symptomatic patients with $\geq 10^3$ cfu/mL and pyuria for 5 to 9 days and/or 4 to 6 weeks following treatment (56).

Criteria for "cure" include that the urine specimens are collected at specified times after completion of treatment over a defined period (not usually less than 6 weeks). If follow-up specimens show no evidence of infection, or if reinfection with a different organism is found, the subject is considered cured of the original infection. If the posttreatment specimens show a relapse with the original organism, or if the bacteriuria persists, treatment is considered to have failed.

Treatment

Methods of treatment include antibiotics, increasing oral fluid intake to flush the urinary tract system, and, if needed, urinary analgesics such as phenazopyridine hydrochloride (Pyridium). The latter should not be taken for more than 2 days; otherwise, it may mask symptoms of worsening infection, and it should not be used in patients with renal dysfunction. If flank pain or dysuria are severe, systemic analgesics can be used.

Forcing fluids results in increased urine production, rapid dilution of bacteria, and removal of infected urine by frequent bladder emptying; generally, bacterial counts return to original levels overnight when hydration is stopped. Additional potential problems may result from diuresis, such as dilution of antibacterial substances that are normally present in the urine, dilution of administered antimicrobial agents, and decreased urinary acidification. Thus, forcing fluids is not recommended.

Urinary acidification by administration of ascorbic acid or methionine is frequently difficult to achieve, and is rarely, if ever, necessary. Acidification of the urine can result in the precipitation of urate stones or the formation of oxalate stones.

Juice from cranberries and blueberries has been found to contain potent inhibitors of bacterial adherence by *E. coli*. The antiadhesive agents contained in these juices may act in the gut, in the bladder, or both, by preventing colonization of these sites; they may be particularly beneficial in the management of patients who suffer recurrent infections (57, 58).

Choice of Antibiotics

Preferred characteristics for the antibiotic chosen include (*a*) having appropriate antimicrobial susceptibility spectrum, (*b*) achieving adequate duration and high concentration in the urine, (*c*) minimal effect on vaginal and fecal flora, (*d*) low potential for undesirable side effects, (*e*) acceptable patient tolerance, and (*f*) low expense. Antimicrobial selection and length of treatment is guided by epidemiological factors such as the patient's age, infecting organism, site of infection, prior UTI history, underlying disease, and institutionalization, if present. Bactericidal agents have not been shown to be superior to bacteriostatic drugs in treating UTIs. For treating relapsing UTI, however, bactericidal antimicrobials may be preferred for theoretical reasons.

The complete eradication of pathogenic organisms, while preventing recurrence and minimizing drug toxicity, is the goal of treatment. Antimicrobial agents that have little effect on anaerobic vaginal and fecal flora, but eradicate aerobic Gram-negative rods, are preferred. High drug levels in the renal medulla are thought to be more closely correlated with cure in upper tract UTIs than either serum or urinary

levels. Thus, in treating presumptive uncomplicated pyelonephritis, agents should be used that provide high kidney tissue levels. With longer duration of therapy, the most frequent and severe side effects are primarily gastrointestinal symptoms (diarrhea and nausea), skin reactions, and vulvovaginal candidiasis (59).

Acute Uncomplicated UTI

It is generally safe to assume that a young, sexually active, nonpregnant woman with recent onset of dysuria, frequency, or urgency who has not been recently instrumented, has not been treated with antimicrobials, and has no history of a genitourinary tract abnormality has an uncomplicated lower (cystitis) or upper (pyelonephritis) UTI.

The acutely symptomatic woman rarely needs a pretreatment culture. If a culture is done, sensitivity testing is not necessary unless the patient has received antibiotics within the preceding 3 months. Performing a vulvovaginal exam, examining the urine for leukocytes and bacteriuria, and obtaining dip slide cultures are adequate for initial evaluation. Uncomplicated infections virtually never cause end-stage renal disease. Uncomplicated infections have not been demonstrated to cause any permanent damage to the urethra or bladder, or to predispose the bladder epithelium to neoplastic changes.

Good initial choice of antibiotics for these nonpregnant women include amoxicillin, sulfisoxazole, sulfamethoxazole, trimethoprim/sulfa, cephalexin, or nitrofuradantoin, taking into account woman drug sensitivities, allergies, and local bacterial resistances (Table 18.1.4). A fixed combination of Pyridium (50 mg) and sulfisoxazole (500 mg Azogantrisin) or sulfamethoxazole (500 mg Azogantanol), usually prescribed two tablets four times a day, is a good first choice because of the anesthetic properties of the Pyridium. However, there are a great many tablets to take and the Pyridium stains sweat and urine bright orange.

Traditionally, acute uncomplicated UTI

Table 18.1.4. Multi-Day Oral Antibiotic Regimens for Acute Uncomplicated Cystitis

Drug	Dose/Frequency	Efficacy
Penicillins		
Ampicillin*	250 to 500 mg q 6 h	Resistance rates of up to 25% have been reported
Amoxicillin*	250 to 500 mg q 8 h	Similar increasing resistance has been noted
Amoxicillin/clavulanate	250 to 500 mg q 8 h	Not effective against most Enterobacter and Pseudomonas species; protects against beta-lactamase resistance
Carbenicillin indanyl sodium*	1 to 2 tablets q 6 h	Only recommended for *Pseudomonas aeruginosa*
Cephalosporins		
Cephalexin	250 to 500 mg q 6 h	These first-generation cephalosporins have generally no advantages over TMP/SMX and are less effective as single dose therapy
Cefaclor*	250 mg q 8 h	
Cefactor	500 mg q 6 h	
Cefadroxil	1 g q 12–24	
Cefuroxime axetil	125 mg q 12 h	Second-generation
Cefixime*	400 mg q 24 h	Third generation, no antistaphylococcal and antipseudomonas activity
Nitrofurantoin (macrocrystalline)	50 to 100 mg q 6 to 12 h	Not effective against *Pseudomonas* and some *Klebsiella, Enterobacter* and *Proteus* species
Sulfisoxazole*	1 g, then 500 mg q 6 h	Resistance patterns similar to ampicillin
Trimethoprim	100 mg q 12 h	Low 5 to 15% resistance in uncomplicated acute cystitis
Trimethoprim/ sulfamethoxazole	1 double-strength tablet q 12 h (160 mg/800 mg)	Not effective against *Pseudomonas aeruginosa* and Enterococci, but highly effective against most uropathogens

*Not recommended for empiric treatment.

has been treated with 7- to 14-day regimens of oral antibiotics. However, shorter 3-day antibiotic regimens have been proven effective and are desirable because of improved compliance, lower costs, and lower frequency of adverse reactions (Table 18.1.5). In a woman with a first or infrequent UTI, who has not been on antibiotics has no risk factors for complicated UTI and no symptoms of upper tract disease, single-dose regimens may be acceptable. However, follow-up with repeat cultures is essential within 7 to 14 days in these women.

Although more convenient for the patient, single-dose regimens have been found to be less effective than traditional multiday regimens. Also, single-dose treatment is less effective in eradicating rectovaginal *E. coli*, resulting in more frequent same-strain recurrent

Table 18.1.5. Single-Dose Oral Antibiotic Treatment Options for Urinary Tract Infections in Women

Drug	Dose
Amoxicillin	3 g
Cefaclor	2 g
Cefadroxil	1 g
Cefuroxime	1000 mg
Cephalexin	3 g
Ciprofloxacin	250 mg, 500 mg
Enoxacin	600 mg
Fleroxacin	200 mg, 400 mg
Nitrofurantoin	400 mg
Norfloxacin	400 mg, 800 mg
Ofloxacin	200 mg, 400 mg
Sulfisoxazole	2 g
TMP/SMX	2 double-strength tablets
Trimethoprim	400 to 600 mg

TMP/SMX = trimethoprim-sulfamethoxazole in a 1:5 ratio by weight.

infections within 2 weeks of treatment; thus, relapse is caused by rectovaginal organisms rather than a nidus of infection in the upper urinary tract (60). Single-dose regimens are less effective in treatment of infections when an unrecognized complicating factor is present, such as pregnancy, diabetes, an anatomic or functional abnormality of the urinary tract, or occult UTI. Relapse following single-dose treatment suggests the presence of an upper UTI, and can serve as an indicator for further urinary tract evaluation (61).

Acute Dysuria/Pyuria Syndrome

This condition, formerly referred to as urethritis or acute urethral syndrome, is defined as having symptoms suggestive of a lower UTI, but in the absence of significant bacteriuria with a conventional pathogen (62). This syndrome is common and accounts for up to 50% of women presenting with acute dysuria. The physical examination is not helpful in differen-

tiating this condition from typical cystitis, nor in distinguishing among possible etiologies.

In these women, 71% had pyuria, and the most common infectious agents identified are *E. coli* and *Chlamydia trachomatis*, with *Staphylococcus saprophyticus*, herpes simplex virus, and *Neisseria gonorrhea* less frequently identified (45). However, the urine was sterile in 37% of the women in this study. Stamm et al. speculate that bacteriuria with $< 10^5$ cfu/mL may represent an early stage of cystourethritis or a balance in the interaction between invading microorganisms and host-defense mechanisms. Women who have urinary symptoms, pyuria, and urine cultures $< 10^5$ cfu/mL can benefit from treatment with doxycycline 100 mg bid for 10 days (63).

Occasionally, urethritis can be caused by *Neisseria gonorrhea*, *Trichomonas vaginalis*, *Candida albicans*, or herpes simplex, and treatment would be accordingly prescribed. Women with symptoms caused by chlamydial infection were more often active with a new sexual partner in the month prior to onset of symptoms. However, in symptomatic women without pyuria, no benefit was seen with antibiotic therapy. Noninfectious causes of urethritis include trauma, possible allergies to chemical dyes and perfumes, estrogen deficiency, and psychological factors.

Acute Uncomplicated Pyelonephritis

Strains of *E. coli* that cause pyelonephritis in otherwise normal hosts belong to a small number of groups as defined by O, H, and K serotyping. These strains are more likely to have *P. fimbriae* and produce aerobactin and hemolysin than strains that cause cystitis or that infect hosts with known upper tract abnormalities. Also commonly cultured from the urine are Gram-negative bacteria (e.g., Klebsiella, Proteus, Enterobacter, Pseudomonas, Serratia, Citrobacter) and Gram-positive bacteria (*S. saprophyticus*, *Streptococcus fecalis*, *Staphylococcus aureus*).

Symptoms include flank pain and/or tenderness, fever, often associated with dysuria, urgency, and frequency, and significant bacteriuria, occurring in an otherwise healthy host and is caused by an acute infection of the kidney, with invasion of the renal interstitium. One third of patients with pyelonephritis present with only symptoms of acute cystitis.

Many women with acute uncomplicated pyelonephritis can be treated with outpatient oral therapy if the diagnosis is secure, if they do not have nausea or vomiting, are willing to comply with the treatment regimen, and have no known structural abnormality of the urinary tract (64).

For women with nausea, vomiting, or moderate to severe illness, other measures include hospitalization, rehydration, pain medications, and parenteral antimicrobial treatment (Table 18.1.6). Women generally respond in 24 to 48 hours and are able to take oral medications. Duration of hospitalization should be based on the patient's rate of improvement and results of the susceptibility testing of the urinary pathogen.

Recommendations for length of antimicrobial treatment are traditionally 2 weeks (65), although others recommend 10 days. Bailey had good results in a number of prospective studies using aminoglycosides and quinolone/β-lactam combinations and only hospitalizing women for 5 days (66). The combination of ampicillin and an aminoglycoside has been traditionally used as initial therapy for patients hospitalized with uncomplicated acute pyelonephritis. However, with increasing resistance to ampicillin in *E. coli* strains, use of ampicillin is less attractive unless indicated by urine culture and sensitivity patterns. Ampicillin/sublactam, trimethoprim/sulfa, or a third-generation cephalosporin with gentamycin intravenously may be used instead.

Urinalysis and urine cultures should always be obtained in patients with symptoms of upper tract disease. A Gram stain of the urine is often helpful in choosing initial therapy. Therapy can be modified after 24 to 48 hours when susceptibility test results are available. Follow-up urine cultures should be obtained at 2 and 4

Table 18.1.6. Indications for Hospital Admission for Pyelonephritis

Inability to maintain oral hydration and/or
    medications
Known or suspected complicated pyelonephritis
Severe illness with high fevers, severe pain or
    significant debility
Uncertainty about diagnosis
Concern about compliance
Uncertain social situation

Modified from Hooton TM, Stamm WE. Management of acute uncomplicated urinary tract infection in adults. Med Clin North Am 1991;75:339–357.

weeks after completion of therapy. In adults, uncomplicated pyelonephritis only rarely leads to permanent renal damage with scarring.

Complicated Pyelonephritis

Complications occur in patients with anatomic or neurologic lesions that slow urine flow, have host factors that compromise resistance, or have uropathogens resistant to antimicrobials (Table 18.1.7). These may include anatomic obstructions, congenital anomalies, polycystic renal disease, foreign bodies or stones, infection with *Proteus mirabilis* (caused by calculus formation), analgesic nephropathy, hemoglobinopathy, diabetes mellitus, immunodeficiency, renal transplant, and pregnancy. The clinical spectrum ranges from mild cystitis to life-threatening urosepsis.

Urine cultures, obtained before, during, and after treatment, with susceptibility testing are essential for accurate diagnosis and treatment. If fever persist after 72 hours of antimicrobial therapy, a complicating factor, such as abscess, calculi, or obstruction may be present. However, few natural history or treatment studies of complicated UTIs have been performed; consequently, there are few standards of therapy and most regimens are empirical (67). These patients are often infected with unusual and multiply resistant uropathogens

Table 18.1.7. Factors that Suggest the Presence of an Occult Renal Infection or a Complicated UTI in Women

Symptoms >7 days

Temperature >38°C

Episode of UTI in the last month

Recent antibiotic usage for any reason

Symptoms of upper tract UTI

Functional or anatomic abnormality of the urinary
   tract

History of urinary stones

History of childhood UTI

Pregnancy

Diabetes

Hospital-acquired infection

Indwelling urinary catheter

Immunosuppression

Presentation in an urban emergency department

Modified from Hooton TM, Stamm WE. Management of acute uncomplicated urinary tract infection in adults. Med Clin North Am 1991;75:339–357.

that are difficult to eradicate. Unless the underlying anatomical, functional, or metabolic defect is corrected, infection usually recurs. Surgery may be indicated in management of these patients (68). Diagnosis is assisted with new developments in imaging, especially renal ultrasound and computed tomography (CT) scans (69).

In more seriously ill, hospitalized patients, initial empirical therapy of ampicillin plus gentamicin or imipenem plus cilastatin provides coverage against most expected uropathogens, including *Pseudomonas aeruginosa* and most enterococci. Antimicrobial treatment, usually begun as parenteral therapy, can be adjusted as appropriate to culture sensitivities, may be changed to oral medications, and is generally continued for at least 10 to 14 days if patients improve clinically.

Papillary necrosis, which may occur in the presence of diabetes mellitus, urinary tract ob-

struction, sickle cell disease, or analgesic abuse, results in necrotic papillae sloughing and causing unilateral or bilateral ureteral obstruction. Bacteria persist in the necrotic papillae, requiring partial nephrectomy for cure (70).

Intrarenal abscess secondary to bacteremia or complications of severe pyelonephritis may occur. Women present with symptoms of acute pyelonephritis, with high fever, severe flank pain, and tenderness. CT scan will reveal intense inflammation and necrosis in a lobe of the kidney, which will often develop into an intrarenal abscess. Most patients respond slowly to antibiotic therapy, but occasionally drainage is necessary.

Perinephric abscess, an uncommon complication of UTI, occurs when microorganisms from either the renal parenchyma or blood are deposited in the soft tissues surrounding the kidneys. Urinary calculi and diabetes mellitus, common predisposing factors, often are associated with obstruction. Women may have either nonspecific symptoms or a more classic appearance of acute pyelonephritis, but they generally have been ill for 2 or more weeks. If the patient does not respond to antimicrobial therapy for acute pyelonephritis, the possibility of an abscess must be explored, preferably using CT scan technology. The abscess may be confined to the perinephric space or extend throughout the retroperitoneum. Using ultrasound or CT scan guidance, diagnostic needle aspiration and placement of drains can be safely performed. Cultures should be obtained of any drainage and antimicrobial therapy adjusted accordingly.

Bacterial Resistance

The major identifiable risk factor for bacterial resistance to antibiotics is a history of recent antibiotic usage, inducing high numbers of resistant fecal organisms. This is especially true for ampicillin and its derivatives, sulfonamides, tetracyclines, and cephalexin.

E. coli strains from uncomplicated UTI patients are almost always susceptible to one or more of the commonly used oral agents. However, as many as 25 to 35% of isolates demonstrate in vitro resistance to ampicillin, amoxicillin, and sulfonamides (71), thus decreasing their desirability as therapeutic agents. Resistance has also been increasing to cephalexin, cephradine, and trimethoprim (72).

Nitrofurantoin, despite being ineffective against *Proteus mirabilis*, is useful for treating UTIs. However, efficacy and minimal adverse side effects can be obtained with 50 mg q 8 h dosage and using the macrocrystalline formulation to lessen adverse gastrointestinal effects (73).

In women with uncomplicated UTI, fluoroquinolones should not be used for initial empiric therapy and are recommended primarily for patients who are allergic to other antimicrobials, recurrent infections, treatment failures, or infections that are resistant to other antimicrobials. Fluoroquinolones must be used judiciously because of emergence of resistant organisms (73a). Newer quinolones are believed by some investigators to be the oral agents of choice for uncomplicated UTI, but they should be reserved for use when they have definite advantages over other antimicrobials (73b).

Recurrent UTI and Prophylaxis

Women with recurrent UTI have increased susceptibility to vaginal colonization by uropathogens. The period of greatest risk for acquiring a recurrent infection was found to be immediately after treatment of the initial infection (74). *E. coli* is the predominant cause of both symptomatic and asymptomatic infections, with *Klebsiella* species, Enterococci, *and Enterobacter* species also causing infections. *Proteus mirabilis* and coagulase-negative *Staphylococcus* species are uncommon causes of infection.

In sexually active, premenopausal women with histories of recurrent UTI, most infections are intercourse-related, with 75% beginning within 24 hours following intercourse

(31). The use of either a spermicide, a diaphragm plus spermicide, or a condom with spermicidal foam has been associated with increased recurrence of UTI, probably caused by alteration of the vaginal flora resulting in increased colonization with *E. coli*. Urination within 1 hour following intercourse had a protective effect against *E. coli* bacteriuria (33).

Antimicrobial prophylaxis is recommended for women who experience two or more symptomatic UTIs over a 6-month period, or three or more over a 12-month period, using a 6-month trial of medication, followed by close observation after discontinuation. Prophylaxis has been used successfully for years in some women. However, once prophylaxis is discontinued, most women return to their prior pattern of recurrent infections unless other factors, such as sexual activity or diaphragm-spermicide use, are modified (20).

For women who have recurrent UTIs, first their urine must be sterilized before beginning a prophylaxis regimen. Prophylaxis can be taken continuously nightly, alternate nights, 3 nights per week, intermittently self-administered single dose treatment (75), or postcoital antibiotics (76, 77) (Tables 18.1.8 and 18.1.9).

Trimethoprim-sulfamethoxazole, given at 40 mg/200 mg daily has been effective, usually reducing the number of infections to between 0 to 0.15 per patient year. Postcoital trimethoprim-sulfamethoxazole, 40 mg/200 mg, is also effective in preventing UTI, but has no effect on vaginal and urethral colonization with *E. coli*. Both trimethoprim and trimethoprim-sulfamethoxazole prophylaxis regimens have been effective with patients over several years, and the patients have been free of side effects. Resistance, unfortunately, is increasing to trimethoprim.

Nitrofurantoin does not alter perineal or fecal flora; resistant bacterial strains do not develop and it is believed that its effectiveness results from direct antimicrobial activity in the urine. Frequent side effects reported in women receiving low-dose continuous nitrofurantoin

Table 18.1.8. Continuous Antibiotic Prophylaxis Regimens

Drug	Dose*
Cephalexin	125 or 250 mg
Methenamine	1 g
Nitrofurantoin	50 or 100 mg
Norfloxacin	200 mg
Sulfamethoxazole	500 mg
Trimethoprim/ sulfamethoxazole 80 mg/400 mg	1/2 or 1 single-strength tablet
Trimethoprim	100 mg

*Dosage may be nightly, alternate nights, or 3 nights per week.

Table 18.1.9. Postcoital Single-Dose Antibiotic Prophylaxis Regimens

Drug	Dose
Cephalexin	250 mg
Cinoxacin	250 mg
Nitrofurantoin	50 or 100 mg
Trimethoprim/ sulfamethoxazole	1/2 or 1 single strength tablet 80 mg/400 mg

include interstitial pneumonia, allergic pneumonitis, hepatitis, and other complications, so its usage should be monitored carefully.

Elderly women may also be at risk for recurrent UTI, because of increased postvoiding residual urine. Postmenopausal women with atrophic vaginitis and recurrent symptomatic UTIs have been successfully treated with intravaginal estrogen creams (38, 78). These women experienced a significant decrease in the incidence of UTI and a similar decrease in antimicrobial use. Minimal side effects of localized pruritus or burning occurred in a small percentage of patients. Use of intravaginal estrogen may be especially useful to avoid antibiotic side effects, allergic reactions, drug interactions, or emergence of antimicrobial-resistant uropathogens.

Urinary Tract Investigations

The majority of women with recurrent uncomplicated UTI do not have an anatomic or functional abnormality of the urinary tract. Less than 5% of women who have recurrent UTIs demonstrate any abnormalities on excretory urography or cystoscopy, and few of these identified lesions are correctable.

With acute pyelonephritis, some experts suggest that investigations are not recommended unless there is a delayed response to therapy (> 72 hours), that may suggest an underlying, complicating factor such as obstruction, calculi, or development of a perinephric or renal abscess. Investigation may also be recommended when there is a history of (a) persistent hematuria, (b) childhood UTI, (c) diabetes mellitus, (d) increased serum creatinine levels, (e) bladder dysfunction, (f) prior genitourinary surgery, or (g) an unusual uropathogen (69). One study found that with one episode of pyelonephritis requiring hospitalization, 70 to 100% of women already had structural abnormalities such as hydroureter or hydronephrosis, 20% had previously unsuspected kidney stones, and 10% had abnormalities in kidney structure such as double collecting systems or a horseshoe kidney. This would suggest that a woman with one episode of hospital-requiring pyelonephritis deserves radiologic evaluation (79).

Evaluation would consist first of ultrasonography, then as indicated intravenous pyelogram (IVP), and to a lesser extent renal scan, voiding cystourethrogram (VCUG), cystoscopy, or CT scan of abdomen. Ultrasound allows identification of structural abnormalities (e.g., hydronephrosis, ureteric dilation, bladder lesions), but does not assess renal function. Ultrasound combined with a plain radiograph of the abdomen can replace IVP for evaluating some young women with UTI.

An IVP provides detailed information on the pelvicalyceal system and renal excretion of contrast material, making possible the detection of structural abnormalities, delayed excretion, vesicoureteric reflux, and bladder pathology. CT is valuable in evaluating for perirenal and intrarenal abscesses; magnetic resonance imaging (MRI) offers no advantage over CT in these situations.

VCUG may be indicated if hydroureters or hydronephrosis are noted without an obvious obstruction; they are normal in up to 70% of patients with UTI. Cystoscopy in younger women rarely influences management. This procedure should be reserved for use in older women or in the examination of the urine or the response to treatment is unusual (80).

Special Situations

UTIs in Pregnancy

Pregnancy is an independent risk factor for UTI. Pregnancy causes a physiologic obstruction of the female urinary tract, with dilation of the ureters and renal pelves and significantly decreased ureteral peristalsis. Two important issues include unsuspected upper tract infection and possible antimicrobial resistance unknown at initiation of treatment.

Bacteriuria occurs in 4 to 10% of pregnant women and 25 to 30% of postpartum women. The prevalence of bacteriuria is higher in women of lower socioeconomic class, increased parity, age, sexual activity, diabetes mellitus, sickle cell trait, and prior history of UTI (81).

The risk of developing bacteriuria increases over the course of the pregnancy, from 0.8% in the 12th week of gestation to 1.93% at term, with the risk of onset of bacteriuria being the highest between the 9th and 17th weeks of gestation. The 16th week of gestation appears to be the optimal time to obtain a single screening for bacteriuria in order to maximize the number of infection-free weeks during the pregnancy (82).

Pregnant women with asymptomatic bacteriuria should be treated, because if left un-

treated, up to 60% will develop symptomatic pyelonephritis and subsequent potential serious sequelae. Both preterm labor and prematurity have been correlated with symptomatic UTI. However, the relationship between UTI and low birth weight, intrauterine growth retardation, preeclampsia, and hypertension are debated (83).

Recommendations include an initial screening dipslide culture of a midstream clean catch urine for all patients at their first prenatal visit. For women with negative screening cultures, routine prenatal care is provided. If a woman has an initial negative screening culture, but also has a history of frequent UTIs or other factors that may place her at higher risk, the urine is routinely recultured at the beginning of the third trimester. A positive dipslide culture should be confirmed with a quantitative method, allowing for identification and antimicrobial sensitivity testing of the organism. In asymptomatic women, bacterial levels of $\geq 10^5$ cfu/mL cultured from midstream specimens distinguished contaminated urine from significant bacteriuria. The significance of 10^2 to 10^4 Gram-positive or fastidious organisms (many of which are present in the vaginal flora) in midstream urine specimens of asymptomatic pregnant women is less well understood (83).

While treating bacteriuria during pregnancy, one should be mindful of potential toxicities to mother and/or fetus (Table 18.1.10). Short-course regimens (7 to 10 days) have been effective on initial treatment of 70 to 80% of patients with bacteriuria (81). Treatment should be based on antimicrobial sensitivity. A follow-up urine culture should be obtained approximately 1 week after completing initial therapy. If the urine is sterile, monthly cultures should be obtained until delivery. If the bacteriuria did not resolve after the initial course of antimicrobials, a second 7- to 10-day course, using a different agent based on sensitivity testing, should be given. In approximately half of these patients, the bacteriuria will persist or they will have a recurrence with the same organism, indicating the likely presence of an upper UTI or a structural abnormality (83).

In pregnant women that have persistent or recurrent bacteriuria, a short course of an antibiotic, based upon sensitivities, is given to suppress infection, followed immediately by nitrofurantoin, 50 to 100 mg nightly until delivery, for prophylaxis. Frequent urine cultures

should be obtained to evaluate for possible re-infection by a resistant organism. Also, follow-up cultures should be obtained after delivery, and urologic evaluation of the urinary tract should be performed within 3 to 6 months after delivery (81).

Pregnant women who develop pyelonephritis can become quite ill. Recommendations include hospitalization for parenteral antimicrobials, usually initial empiric therapy with

Table 18.1.10. Antimicrobial Agents Used in Pregnancy

Drug	Dose/Frequency	Safety of Usage
Agents considered safe		
Penicillins		
Ampicillin	500 mg q 6 h	Extensively used
Amoxicillin	250 mg q 8 h	Safe and effective
Penicillin V	500 mg q 6 h	Used less frequently, but achieves excellent urinary levels
Unasyn	1.5–3 g q 6 h	
Cephalosporins		
Cephalexin	500 mg q 6 h	Extensively used
Rocephin	250 mg q 6 h	Somewhat more effective against gram negatives
Agents to be used with caution		
Gentamicin	2.0 mg/kg IV or IM loading dose; 1.7 mg/kg q 8 h maintaining dose	May be toxic to 8th cranial nerve development in the fetus
Nitrofurantoin	100 mg q 6 h	May result in hemolytic anemia in patients with G6PD deficiency
Sulfisoxazole	1 g, then 500 mg q 6 h	May cause kernicterus in the newborn. Also may cause hemolytic anemia when G6PD deficiency is present
Agents that should be avoided		
Chloramphenicol		Associated with "gray baby syndrome"
Erythromycin		Associated with maternal cholestatic jaundice
Fluoroquinolones		Possible damage to immature cartilage
Tetracyclines		May cause acute liver decompensation in the mother and inhibition of new bone growth in the fetus
Trimethoprim		May cause megaloblastic anemia because of antifolic action

Modified from Kim ED, Schaeffer AJ. Antimicrobial therapy for urinary tract infections. Semin Nephrol 1994;14:551–569.

ampicillin and an aminoglycoside. Within 72 hours, 95% of patients improve and can be changed to an oral antimicrobial to complete a 2-week course, followed by suppressive therapy until delivery. If the patient does not improve within 72 hours, other etiologies or possible urinary tract complicating factors may be present (83).

UTIs during Lactation

All of the following antibiotics can be used during lactation to treat a UTI: (*a*) β-lactams (e.g., penicillin), (*b*) penicillins with β-lactamase inhibitor activity, (*c*) cephalosporins, and (*d*) aztreonam, aminoglycosides, and trimethoprim. Sulfonamides should be avoided in the first 2 months of the infant's life. Antibiotics that are contraindicated include fluoroquinolones, nitrofurantoin, and tetracyclines (83a).

UTIs in the Elderly

Bacteriuria occurs in 15 to 20% of elderly women living in the community and 30 to 50% of elderly hospitalized patients (84). Contributing factors include loss of the estrogen effect on the genitourinary mucosa, increased postvoiding residual urine, genitourinary abnormalities (e.g., cystoceles, rectoceles, bladder diverticula), chronic medical diseases (e.g., diabetes mellitus), and neurological diseases (e.g., Alzheimer's disease, Parkinson's disease, cerebrovascular disease) that frequently lead to altered bladder control (73a).

The causative organisms of UTIs in the elderly depend on where the infection was acquired. Noninstitutionalized elderly women have a similar spectrum of uropathogens as younger noninstitutionalized individuals (85). For institutionalized women, the distribution of uropathogens change. Forty-seven percent of UTIs are caused by *E. coli*, 22% by Proteus spp, 8% by *Klebsiella pneumoniae*, 3% by *Pseudomonas aeruginosa*, and 3% by Gram-positive organisms. Mixed infections accounted

for 11% of UTIs in institutionalized elderly women. Many of these identified organisms exhibit multiple antimicrobial resistance (86).

Asymptomatic bacteriuria is generally believed to not require antimicrobial therapy in elderly patients. Treatment of bacteriuria results in transient clearing, but with increased incidence of adverse drug effects, emergence of resistant organisms, and early recurrence of UTI, either by reinfection or relapse. An exception to this philosophy of nontreatment occurs when asymptomatic bacteriuric patients are scheduled to undergo an invasive genitourinary procedure; then antimicrobial therapy, specific to the infecting organism, should be administered prior to the procedure. If treatment does not occur, there is a high incidence of subsequent bacteremia and occasionally death from septic shock (73a).

Elderly patients with symptomatic UTIs often have atypical presentations including (*a*) unexplained fever, (*b*) delirium, (*c*) confusion, (*d*) lethargy, (*e*) loss of interest in eating, drinking, social activities, and self-care, and (*f*) lower urinary tract symptoms of incontinence, urgency, or nocturia (87). These patients should be evaluated with a urinalysis, urine culture, and, most importantly, a Gram stain of the urine specimen.

Because of the frequency of resistant uropathogens in up to 25% of UTIs, antibiotics selected must have a broad spectrum of activity. Because enterococci and *Staphylococcus aureus* cause approximately 3% of UTIs, if Gram-positive organisms are seen on the urine Gram stain, vancomycin should be used for empiric therapy. For Gram-negative infection, either a third-generation cephalosporin, β-lactam (ticarcillin-clavulanate), trimethoprim-sulfa, or ciprofloxacin are good initial choices. Women at high risk of resistant organisms should be treated initially with a broad spectrum β-lactam or imipenem-cilastatin and an aminoglycoside. If symptoms fail to resolve, or if back pain or positive urine cultures persist, the patient should be further evaluated for possible obstruction or perinephric abscess. Antimicrobial therapy for symptomatic cystitis should continue for 7 days and for pyelonephritis 14 days (1).

Urinary Catheterization

To prevent catheter-associated UTI, unnecessary use of catheters should be avoided and the catheter promptly removed when it is no longer needed. The risk of an infection from a single catheterization in healthy patients in an outpatient setting is 0.5 to 1%, whereas in a hospital setting the risk for healthy women is 10 to 20% (88). Indwelling catheters produce infection at the rate of 4 to 7.5% per day (89). The prevalence of long-term indwelling catheters in long- term care of elderly patients approaches 10%, with nearly all the catheters being placed because of chronic urinary incontinence.

Virtually all patients with indwelling catheters become bacteriuric, but only a small percentage develop symptomatic infection. In order to decrease the incidence of infection, catheterization should be restricted to a scrupulously maintained closed drainage system and continued for a limited time.

Bacteria, especially Proteus and Pseudomonas, proliferate in a biofilm on the inner surface of the catheters, promoting encrustation and shielding the bacteria from antimicrobial agents. Urine cultures obtained from the catheter may not reflect bladder bacteriuria in patients who have organisms in a biofilm on the inner surface of the catheter. Frequently, bacteriuria is polymicrobial; 85% of patients have more than two strains, and 10% have more than five strains. Some bacterial strains will persist, although others cycle in and out of the urinary tract (90).

Antibacterial prophylaxis only provides protection for 3 to 4 days; long-term use of antibiotics produces bacterial resistance. As an alternative to long-term catheterization, intermittent catheterization appears to reduce occurrences of bacteriuria.

Procedures such as percutaneous endoscopy, urethral dilation, retrograde studies, ureteropyeloscopy, and stone manipulation may increase the risk of bacteremia to the patient. Preferred antibacterial prophylactic agents prior to procedures include broad-spectrum cephalosporins and penicillins; the fluoroquinolones are being evaluated for this purpose.

Conclusion

UTIs are common problems seen by primary care providers. UTIs may range from mild, uncomplicated presentations that can resolve spontaneously to overwhelming sepsis leading to death. The manifestations and implications of UTI vary according to the woman's age, medical histories, and potential complicating factors. Thus, treatment and interventions for this common problem have great potential variety and must be evaluated and applied appropriately to each patient individually.

Special Considerations for Nurse Practitioners and Physician Assistants

When a woman presents with symptoms of UTI, a thorough history related to her complaint is obtained, including onset and duration of symptoms, strength and character of the urine stream, when dysuria occurs (during or after urination), and associated symptoms such as fever, GI symptoms, hematuria, and vaginal or urethral discharge. If appropriate, the woman is asked about her method of birth control, last menstrual period, and changes in sexual practices or partners. She should be asked about the number of previous UTIs and the successes and failures of previous treatments (91).

Diagnosis of UTI is not always easy, especially in the young child or the elderly patient. Characteristic symptoms of frequency, urgency, dysuria, and lower abdominal pain may not be present. UTI is considered in the differential diagnosis when a child has unexplained fever, vomiting, diarrhea, poor feeding, or failure to gain weight (92). In the elderly woman, abdominal pain, sudden incontinence, nocturia, recent-onset falling, and changes in appetite, mentation, or respiration may result from a UTI (93).

Urine collected for microscopy and culture should be the first voided specimen of the day, if possible, or urine that has been in the bladder for at least 2 hours. Noting the patient's fluid intake or urine-specific gravity helps determine whether the specimen is diluted, thus affecting the bacteria and leukocyte count (92).

Because antimicrobial therapy can take 24 to 48 hours to reduce symptoms, the woman's level of discomfort needs to be addressed. A local analgesic agent (Pyridium) can be prescribed for short-term relief of symptoms, while therapeutic levels of the antibiotic are being reached or laboratory results are awaited in more questionable cases (92). Specific instructions are given regarding antibiotics, any needed follow-up after antibiotics, and the need for the patient to call if there is no improvement or worsening of symptoms within 1 to 2 days.

Consultation and/or referral is indicated if there are (a) indications of urinary stones, other obstructions, or hydronephrosis; (b) abnormal cystogram, IVP, or other findings; (c) diagnosis of pyelonephritis; and (d) gross hematuria with negative urine cultures. High-risk women (e.g., wheelchair-confined) with recurrent infections and women with a history of childhood infections need specialist evaluation (94).

Women can learn methods to support their own bodies' defense mechanisms and help prevent not only the discomfort of UTIs but also the need for antibiotics (92). Predisposing factors may be either intrinsic/host or extrinsic/behavioral factors (95). The contradictory results of research on these factor (as previously discussed) make it difficult for the provider to know what preventive methods to teach. Instead of overwhelming the woman with a long list of risk factors, providers would serve a woman better by determining her potential individual risk factors and addressing those factors in management.

Many of the common recommendations are unsubstantiated and the advice given may be contradictory to that given by other providers, leaving the woman confused. Behavior modifications related to sexual activity (e.g., voiding after intercourse) should be presented in such a way that the woman does not think of a UTI as a sexually transmitted disease (95). Yet, sexual practices and positions, as well as hygiene practices (of the woman and her partner) may deserve exploration if there are recurrent UTIs (96).

Women who have interstitial cystitis, in which there is no evidence of bacterial infection, report using hundreds of self-care measures in an attempt to increase comfort (97). Their attempts to deal with this problem, as well as the lack of scientific basis for many commonly taught prevention strategies for UTIs, shows the need for interdisciplinary research in these areas.

References

1. Hooton TM. Epidemiology, definitions and terminology in urinary tract infections. In: Neu HC, Williams JD, eds. New Trends in Urinary Tract Infections. Basel: Karger, 1988;1–8.
2. Kass EH, Savage WD, Santamarina BAG. The significance of bacteriuria in preventative medicine. In: EH Kass, ed. Progress in Pyelonephritis. Philadelphia: FA Davis, 1964;3.
3. Stamm WE, Hooton TM, Johnson JR, Johnson C, Stapleton A, Roberts PL, et al. Urinary tract infec-

tions: from pathogenesis to treatment. J Infect Dis 1989;159:400–406.

4. Kovar M. Data systems of the national center for health statistics through the 1980s. National Center for Health Statistics, United States Department of Health and Human Services, DHHS publication number PHS 89–1325, Government Printing Office accession number 89016133, Hyattsville, MD.

5. Johnson JR, Stamm WE. Diagnosis and treatment of acute urinary tract infections. Infect Dis Clin North Am 1987;1:773–791. [Erratum, Infect Dis Clin North Am 1990;4:xii.]

6. Powers RD. New directions in the diagnosis and therapy of urinary tract infections. Am J Obstet Gynecol 1991;164:1387–1389.

7. Patton JP, Nash DB, Abrutyn E. Urinary tract infection: economic considerations. Med Clin North Am 1991;75:495–513.

8. Meares EM. Current patterns in nosocomial urinary tract infections. Urology 1991;37(suppl):S9–S12.

9. Measley RE Jr, Levison ME. Host defense mechanisms in the pathogenesis of urinary tract infection. Med Clin North Am 1991;75:275–286.

10. Childs S. Current diagnosis and treatment of urinary tract infections. Urology 1992;40:295–299.

11. Maskell R, Pead L, Sanderson RA. Fastidious bacteria and the urethral syndrome: a 2 year clinical and bacteriological study of 51 women. Lancet 1983;2:1277–1283.

12. Sobel JD, Kaye D. Urinary tract infections. In: Mandell GL, Bennett JE, Dolin R, eds. Principles and Practices of Infectious Disease. 4th ed. New York: Churchill Livingstone, 1995.

13. Ronald AR, Conway B. An approach to urinary tract infections in ambulatory women. Curr Clin Top Infect Dis 1988;9:76–125.

14. Berg AO. Establishing a cause of genitourinary symptoms in women in a family practice. JAMA 1984;251:620–623.

15. Pappas PG. Laboratory in the diagnosis and management of urinary tract infections. Med Clin North Am 1991;75:313–325.

16. Stamm WE. Measurement of pyuria and its relation to bacteriuria. Am J Med 1983;75(suppl):53–58.

17. Kim ED, Schaeffer AJ. Antimicrobial therapy for urinary tract infections. Semin Nephrol 1994;14:551–569.

18. A Report by the Members of the Medical Research Council Bacteriuria Committee. Recommended terminology of urinary-tract infection. Br Med J 1979;2:717–719.

19. Stamm WE, Counts GW, Running KR, Fihn S, Turck M, Holmes KK. Diagnosis of coliform infection in acutely dysuric women. N Engl J Med 1982;307:463–468.

20. Hooton TM, Stamm WE. Management of acute uncomplicated urinary tract infection in adults. Med Clin North Am 1991;75:339–357.

21. Cohen SN, Kass EH. A simple method for quantitative urine culture. N Engl J Med 1967;277:176–180.

22. Kunin CM, White LV, Hua TH. A reassessment of the importance of "low-count" bacteriuria in young women with acute urinary symptoms. Ann Intern Med 1993;119:454–460.

23. Arav-Boger R, Leibovici L, Danon YL. Urinary tract infections with low and high colony counts in young women: spontaneous remission and single-dose vs multiple-day treatment. Arch Intern Med 1994;154:300–304.

24. Stamm WE, Wagner KF, Amsel R, Alexander ER, Turck M, Counts GW, et al. Causes of the acute urethral syndrome in women. N Engl J Med 1980;303:409–415.

25. Komaroff AL. Urinalysis and urine culture in women with dysuria. Ann Intern Med 1986;104:212–218.

26. Neu HC. Urinary tract infections. Am J Med 1992;92(suppl 4A):63S–70S.

27. Johnson JR, Stamm WE. Urinary tract infections in women: diagnosis and treatment. Ann Intern Med 1989;111:906–917.

28. Roberts FJ. Quantitative urine culture in patients with urinary tract infection and bacterenia. Am J Clin Pathol 1986;85:616–618.

29. Baldassarre JS, Kaye D. Special problems of urinary tract infection in the elderly. Med Clin North Am 1991;75:375–390.

30. Siegman-Ingra Y. The significance of urine culture with mixed flora. Curr Opin Nephrol Hypertens 1994;3:656–659.

31. Nicolle LE, Harding GKM, Preiksaitis J, Ronald AR. The association of urinary tract infection with sexual intercourse. J Infect Dis 1982;146:579–583.

32. Buckley RM Jr, McGuckin M, MacGregor RR. Urine bacterial counts after sexual intercourse. N Engl J Med 1978;298:321–324.

33. Hooton TM, Hillier S, Johnson C, Roberts PL, Stamm WE. *Escherichia coli* bacteriuria and contraceptive method. JAMA 1991;265:64–69.

34. Hooton TM, Fennell CL, Clark AM. Nonoxynol-9: differential antibacterial activity and enhancement of bacterial adherence to vaginal epithelial cells. J Infect Dis 1991;164:1216–1219.

35. Fihn SD, Johnson C, Pinkstaff C, Stamm WE. Diaphragm use and urinary tract infections: analysis of urodynamic and microbiological factors. J Urol 1986;136:853–856.

36. Remis RS, Gurwith MJ, Gurwith D, Hargrett-Bean NT, Layde PM. Risk factors for urinary tract infection. Am J Epidemiol 1987;126:685–694.

37. Foxman B, Frerichs RR. Epidemiology of urinary tract infection: II. Diet, clothing and urination habits. Am J Pub Health 1985;75:1314–1317.

38. Raz R, Stamm WE. A controlled trial of intravaginal estriol in postmenopausal women with recurrent urinary tract infections. N Engl J Med 1993;329:753–756.

39. Boscia JA, Abrutyn E, Kaye D. Asymptomatic bacteriuria in elderly persons: treat or do not treat? Ann Intern Med 1987;106:764–766.

40. Nicolle LE. Urinary tract infection in the institutionalized elderly. Infect Dis Clin Pract 1992;1:68–72.

41. Kunin CM. Genitourinary infections in the patient

at risk: extrinsic risk factors. Am J Med 1984;76: 131–139.

42. Busch R, Huland H. Correlation of symptoms and results of direct bacterial localization in patients with urinary tract infections. J Urol 1984;132:282–285.

43. Kunin CM. Detection, Prevention and Management of Urinary Tract Infections. 3rd ed. Philadelphia: Lea & Febiger, 1979:9–10.

44. Stamey TA, ed. Pathogenesis and Treatment of Urinary Tract Infections. Baltimore: Williams & Wilkins, 1980:131.

45. Stamm WE, Hooton TM. Management of urinary tract infections in adults. N Engl J Med 1993;18: 1328–1334.

46. Stamey TA, ed. Pathogenesis and Treatment of Urinary Tract Infections. Baltimore: Williams & Wilkins, 1980:125.

47. Komaroff AL. Acute dysuria in women. N Engl J Med 1984;310:368–375.

48. Kass EH. Asymptomatic infections of the urinary tract. Trans Assoc Am Physicians 1956;69:56–64.

49. Kass EH. Bacteriuria and the diagnosis of infections of the urinary tract. Arch Intern Med 1957;100: 709–714.

50. Stamey TA. Recurrent urinary tract infections in female patients: an overview of management and treatment. Rev Infect Dis 1987;9(suppl 2):S195–S210.

51. Zhanel GG, Harding GKM, Guay DRP. Asymptomatic bacteriuria: which patients should be treated? Arch Intern Med 1990;150:1389–1396.

52. Ronald AR, Patullo ALS. The natural history of urinary infection in adults. Med Clin North Am 1991; 75:299–312.

53. Parsons CL, Protocol for treatment of typical urinary tract infection: criteria for antimicrobial selection. Urology 1988;(suppl 32):S22–S27.

54. Kreiger TN. Urinary tract infections in women: causes, classification, and differential diagnosis. Urology 1990;(suppl 35):S4–S7.

55. Johnson CC. Definitions, classification and clinical presentation of urinary tract infections. Med Clin North Am 1991;75:241–252.

56. Hatton J, Hughes M, Raymond CH. Management of bacterial urinary tract infections in adults. Ann Pharmcother 1994;28:1264–1272.

57. Sobota AE. Inhibition of bacterial adherence by cranberry juice: potential use for the treatment of urinary tract infections. J Urol 1984;131:1013–1016.

58. Ofek I, Goldhar J, Zafriri D, Lis H, Adar R, Sharon N. Anti-*Escherichia coli* adhesin activity of cranberry and blueberry juices. N Engl J Med 1991;324:1599.

59. Bump RC. Urinary tract infection in women: current role of single-dose therapy. J Reprod Med 1990; 35:785–791.

60. Fihn SD, Johnson C, Roberts PL, Running K, Stamm WE. Trimethoprim-sulfamethoxazole for acute dysuria in women: a single-dose or 10-day course. Ann Intern Med 1988;108:350–357.

61. Nicolle LE, Ronald AR. Recurrent urinary tract in-

fection in adult women: diagnosis and treatment. Infect Dis Clin North Am 1987;1:793–806.

62. Hamilton-Miller JMT. The urethral syndrome and its management. J Antimicrobial Chemother 1994; 33(suppl A):63–73.

63. Stamm WE, Running K, McKevitt M, Counts GW, Turck M, Holmes KK. Treatment of the acute urethral syndrome. N Engl J Med 1981;304:956–958.

64. Safrin S, Siegel D, Black D. Pyelonephritis in adult women: inpatient versus outpatient therapy. Am J Med 1988;85:793–798.

65. Stamm WE, McKevitt M, Counts GW. Acute renal infection in women. Treatment with trimethoprim-sulfamethoxazole or ampicillin for two or six weeks: a randomized trial. Ann Intern Med 1987;106:341–345.

66. Bailey RR. Duration of antimicrobial treatment and the use of drug combinations for the treatment of uncomplicated acute pyelonephritis. Infection 1994;22(suppl 1):S50–S52.

67. Ronald AR, Nicolle LE, Harding GKM. Standards of therapy for urinary tract infections in adults. Infection 1992;20(suppl 3):S164–S170.

68. Bishop MC. Urosurgical management of urinary tract infection. J Antimicrobial Chemother 1994; 33(suppl A):75–91.

69. James JM, Testa HJ. Imaging techniques in the diagnosis of urinary tract infection. Curr Opin Nephrol Hyperten 1994;3:660–664.

70. Conrad S, Busch R, Huland H. Complicated urinary tract infections. Eur Urol 1991;19(suppl 1):16–22.

71. Fowler JE. Urinary tract infections in women. Urol Clin North Am 1986;13:673–683.

72. Neu HC. Optimal characteristics of agents to treat uncomplicated urinary tract infections. Infection 1992;20(suppl 4):S266–S271.

73. Bailey RR. Management of lower urinary tract infections. Drugs 1993;45(3 Suppl):139–144.

73a. Nicolle LE. Urinary tract infection in the elderly. J Antimicrobial Chemother 1994;33(suppl A):99–109.

73b. Sable CA, Scheld WM. Fluoroquinolones: how to use (but not overuse) these antibiotics. Geriatrics 1993;48:41–51.

74. Stamm WE, McKevitt M, Roberts PL, White, NJ. Natural history of recurrent urinary tract infections in women. Rev Infect Dis 1991;13:77–84.

75. Wong ES, McKevitt M, Running K, Counts, GW, Turck M, Stamm WE. Management of recurrent urinary tract infections with patient-administered single-dose therapy. Ann Intern Med 1985;102:302–307.

76. Stapleton A, Latham RH, Johnson C, Stamm WE. Postcoital antimicrobial prophylaxis for recurrent urinary tract infection: a randomized, double-blind, placebo-controlled trial. JAMA 1990;264:703–706.

77. Stamm WE. Prevention of urinary tract infections. Am J Med 1984;5:148–154.

78. Privette M, Cade R, Peterson J, Mars D. Prevention

of recurrent urinary tract infection in post-menopausal women. Nephron 1988;50:24–27.

79. Rosenfeld JA. Radiological abnormalities in women admitted with pyelonephritis. Del Med J 1987;59:717–719.

80. Fowler JE, Pulaski, ET. Excretory urography, cystography, and cystoscopy in the evaluation of women with urinary-tract infection: a prospective study. N Engl J Med 1981;304:462–465.

81. Rosenfeld JA. Renal disease in pregnancy. Am Fam Physician 1989;39:209–212.

82. Stenqvist K, Dahlén-Nilsson I, Lidin-Janson G, Lincoln K, Odén A, Rignell S, et al. Bacteriuria and pregnancy: frequency and risk of acquisition. Am J Epidemiol 1989;129:372–379.

83. Andriole VA, Patterson TF. Epidemiology, natural history and management of urinary tract infections in pregnancy. Med Clin North Am 1991;75:359– 373.

83a. Sanford JP, Gilbert DN, Gerberding JL, Sande MA. Guide to Antimicrobial Therapy. Dallas: Antimicrobial Therapy, 1994.

84. Sant GR, Waimstein M. Therapy of urinary tract infections in the elderly. Urology 1990;35:19–21.

85. Crossley KB, Peterson PK. Infections in the elderly. In: Mandell GL, Bennett JE, Dolin R, eds. Principles and Practices of Infectious Disease. 4th ed. New York: Churchill Livingstone, 1995.

86. Nicolle LE. Urinary tract infections in the elderly: how to treat and when? Infection 1992;20(suppl 4):S261–S264.

87. McCue JD. Urinary tract infections in the elderly. Pharmacotherapy 1993;13:51S–53S.

88. Amin M. Antibacterial prophylaxis in urology: a review. Am J Med 1992;92(suppl 4A):114S–117S.

89. Larson EH, Gasser TC, Madsen PO. Antibacterial prophylaxis in urologic surgery. Urol Clin North Am 1986;13:591–604.

90. Stamm WE. Catheter-associated urinary tract infections: epidemiology, pathogenesis, and prevention. Am J Med 1991;91(suppl 3B):65S–71S.

91. Uphold CR, Graham MV. Clinical Guidelines in Family Practice. Gainesville, FL: Barmarrae, 1993: 574–581.

92. Hassay KA. Effective management of urinary discomfort. Nurse Pract 1995;20:36, 39–40, 42– 44, 47.

93. French M. UTI in the elderly. Advance Nurse Pract 1995;3:25–26, 28.

94. Norman SL. Urinary tract infection. In: Star WL, Lommel LL, Shannon MT, eds. Women's Primary Health Care. Washington, DC: American Nurses'Association, 1995:12-177–12-182.

95. Leiner S. Recurrent urinary tract infections in otherwise healthy adult women. Nurse Pract 1995;20: 48, 51–56.

96. Griffith CJ. Urinary tract infection in young women. Physician Assist 1993;17:21–23, 27–28, 31, 34.

97. Webster DC, Brennan T. Use and effectiveness of physical self-care strategies for interstitial cystitis. Nurse Pract 1994;19:55–61.

18.2

Urinary Incontinence

Jo Ann Rosenfeld

Introduction

Urinary incontinence (UI) is common in women. Yet, women seldom discuss it with their providers. Women fail to complain about UI, and providers are uncomfortable dealing with it, perhaps because of the difficulty in defining and treating the problem. Although its medical and economic costs are high, as much as over 10 billion dollars in the United States annually (1), its psychological costs are even higher for the individual woman. The specter of disability, diapers, loss of independence and privacy, and social problems resulting from UI, including inconvenience, shame, embarrassment, and total isolation, make its discussion necessary and important, even if the answers are incomplete and difficult.

Epidemiology

UI is common and its incidence increases with age (2). In some surveys, up to 31.4% of all women over age 18 years had some degree of incontinence, whereas 16% had incontinence regularly, and 5% had daily incontinence (3, 4). Ten to 20% of community-living elderly women and up to 50% of nursing home women are incontinent. Stress incontinence increases up to age 55 years after which its incidence declines, whereas urge incontinence increased after age 65 years (4). Up to half of young nulliparous women report occasional stress incontinence (1). In a population survey of over 10,000 Swedish women, 12.1% of women in their 50s said they had UI, whereas 24.6% of women in their 80s and 90s said they had UI (2).

To be continent takes more than a bladder that works well. The woman must have an intact central nervous system (CNS) to be able to recognize the sensation of the need to urinate, to act on that recognition, and to get up and find a toilet. She must have the motor coordination and capacity and peripheral sensation and balance to walk to the toilet and sit down, ready to urinate, within a reasonable amount of time. Then, she must have an intact, coordinated sympathetic and parasympathetic nervous system under good control, as well as a functioning bladder. It is almost a wonder that anyone is continent.

Pathophysiology and Classification

The bladder has a maximum volume of 350 to 550 mL of urine, and the urge to urinate should occur at approximately 150 mL. Over 500 to 600 mL, the bladder will overflow. Diabetes mellitus or insipidus, renal failure with poor concentrating ability, or diuretics may increase the urinary volume remarkably, stressing a poorly functioning system and creating overflow incontinence.

The bladder consists of three layers of smooth muscle enervated by sympathetic and parasympathetic nerves. The parasympathetic nerves from the sacral plexus (S2-S4) control contraction, whereas the sympathetic (T11-L2) alpha-adrenergic nerves maintain external sphincter tone and the beta-adrenergic nerves relax the internal sphincter during

voiding. Many medications interfere with the normal functioning of these nerves.

There are five types of UI: (*a*) stress, (*b*) urge, (*c*) overflow, (*d*) functional, and (*e*) mixed. Stress incontinence, leakage of urine with straining, laughing, or coughing, is the most common. Urge incontinence, or detrusor instability, is the most common type in the elderly. Overflow incontinence is caused by a neurological problem or a urethral obstruction. Functional incontinence is cause by psychological problems that make remembering to urinate difficult, like dementia, depression, or delirium, or mechanical or motor problems that makes getting to the toilet or using it difficult.

Risk Factors

In women, the greatest risk factor for incontinence is parity. The percentage of women with UI increases linearly with age and parity (4). The prevalence of UI in 60-year-old nulliparous women in the Swedish study was 7.7%, whereas it was 11.1% in women age 60 to 70 years who had had one vaginal delivery and 14.0% in women age 60 to 70 years with three or more vaginal deliveries. The greatest prevalence occurred after the birth of the first child. Women who had a hysterectomy were more likely to have UI (2). Previous use of oral contraceptives did not increase the likelihood of UI in any age woman (2).

Cigarette smoking is linked to both stress and motor incontinence in women. Current smokers were 2.5 times more likely to have stress incontinence than nonsmokers (5).

Medications can cause UI (Table 18.2.1). Urinary retention with subsequent overflow can occur with any drug with anticholinergic side effects, including antipsychotics, antidepressants, anticholinergics, and narcotics and alpha- or beta-adrenergic agonists. Use of alcohol, coffee, caffeinated drinks, or diuretics can increase the urinary output causing

Table 18.2.1. Medications that can Commonly Cause Incontinence

Anticholinergic drugs: Bentyl, Donnatal
Antipsychotics: phenothiazines, Haldol
Antidepressants: tricyclic antidepressants,
  MAO inhibitors
Antihypertensive drugs: prazosin
Narcotics
Alpha- or beta-adrenergic agonists: terbutaline
Diuretics: hydrochlorothiazide, furosemide
Alcohol
Coffee and caffeinated drinks

polyuria and UI. Sedatives can relax urethral control causing UI.

Effects on Quality of Life

Incontinence can have profound effects on a woman's life. Medically, incontinence can lead to urinary tract infections, urinary sepsis, and decubitus ulcers. Socially, it can have consequential effects. Incontinence can keep women from leaving their homes for fear of embarrassment. At a time when an elderly woman may need to get out and meet others, she may be kept in the house, isolated and secluded, and may worsen her psychological ability to cope. Inability to shop or visit providers' offices may imperil health. At times, incontinence can cause loss of independence, privacy, and even living in her own home in the community. Incontinence may require the woman to ask for help in changing beds and keeping clean. Embarrassment and the loss of privacy occur. Family members who may be willing to help or keep an elderly relative in their home, may balk at changing diapers. Sons may not want to care for their mothers in this most private of areas, and the woman may lose her home and end up in a nursing home.

In an elderly group of over 400 British women, women with urge or mixed UI had higher scores in symptoms of emotions disturbance and social isolation than women without UI (6).

History and Evaluation

Few women actually seek help for UI. In one study, only one third of women actually asked providers for help (4). Reasons for delay included accepting incontinence as normal or having little expectation that there would be any effective treatment.

All providers should ask about urinary incontinence. The incidence, frequency, inciting factors, and how much urine is lost at a time should be determined. The duration and variations of symptoms and body position in which UI occurs is important. Has she had an increase in urinary symptoms, e.g., polyuria, nocturia, or dysuria? The woman's obstetrical and gynecologic and back surgery history, if any, should be obtained. If she had any episiotomies or complications of repair of vaginal deliveries, these should be noted. Menstrual and menopausal history are important. A medication history should be obtained (Tables 18.2.1 and 18.2.2).

Analysis of central and peripheral neurologic function should also be obtained. Does the woman have any signs of CNS dysfunction, dementia, or delirium? Does she have any motor impairment or any difficulty with motor function? Does she have any problems with stooling, soiling, or stool incontinence? Are her reflexes and sensory and motor function of her lower extremities intact including vibration and touch? Does she have dysesthesias or paresthesias? Other medical problems should be noted, especially neurological problems, dementia, psychological problems, or vascular problems such as diabetes, Berger's disease, syphilis, or giant cell arteritis. Gastrointestinal diseases especially Crohn's that can cause fistulas should be noted.

Physical examination includes, first, evaluation of CNS function. A mental status exam is reasonable. Examination of peripheral neurologic function in the legs is important. Can she walk, does she have a gait problem, can she coordinate a trip to the toilet, or is it difficult? The woman with a hemiparesis from a stroke, or with severe Parkinson's disease, may have trouble with these.

Next, a complete abdominal exam is vital, looking for masses or tenderness. An evaluation to discover signs of vasculitis or diabetes, including fundal exam should be performed. Then a genital/anal examination should occur. The vaginal exam should note degree of atrophy, and bimanual exam should note the presence of masses or tenderness, especially suprapubic or in front of the uterus. There may be a vaginal discharge or vaginitis caused by the chronic leakage. Examination of the urethra, especially with cough or bearing down, is necessary with a full bladder. Examination of the anus for tone and strength,

anal wink, and presence of fecal impaction is important.

Neurological examination is important. Look for signs of myelopathy such as spasticity and hyperreflexia. The examination of the anal reflex will help eliminate early neurological disease, after examination of patellar, ankle, and plantar reflexes. The anal reflex is elicited by stroking the skin next to the anus causing contraction of the external anal sphincter, "the anal wink."

Laboratory evaluation should always include a urine analysis to detect urinary concentrating ability, signs of infections or renal disease, and culture. Electrolytes and fasting blood sugars are also indicated. In some cases, an erythrocyte sedimentation rate may be helpful.

A pelvic (and/or transvaginal) ultrasound may be necessary to investigate pelvic masses or tenderness in some cases. Other studies such as barium enema, CT scan of abdomen, or electromyograms of the legs may be needed, only if physical examination points to abnormalities.

Table 18.2.2. Causes of Urinary Incontinence

Medications

Delirium, depression, dementia

Gastrointestinal disorders: Crohn's disease, fecal impaction, colon cancer

Gynecological disorders: uterine masses, fibroids, cancer

Neuromotor impairment: paralysis, myasthenia gravis, muscular dystrophy

Neurological disorders: cord lesions, syphilis, peripheral neurological diseases

Endocrine disorders: diabetes, thyroid disease, diabetes insipidus

Renal failure: high-output failure

Urinary tract infection or tumors

Bladder dysfunction

Differential Diagnosis

When a woman has UI, certain medical and psychological problems may be a major cause and need to be considered first. Initially, medication use should be eliminated as a cause. Often, the medication cannot be stopped because the medical problem is more serious than the UI. However, if possible, those medications mentioned earlier should be stopped and the effects on the UI observed. Use of alcohol, coffee, tea, and caffeinated beverages should be minimized.

Secondly, the examination should give the provider an impression of the woman's mental and motor abilities. Motor instability or paralysis or balance disorders should be obvious causes of UI. UI often coexists with dementia, delirium, or psychosis. If the state is reversible, the provider must wait until her condition is stable before attempting to work on continence. Although other causes of UI may coexist with dementia, treatment may be difficult when dementia is present. Depending on the degree of dementia, cooperation with family and caretakers may or may not bring improvement.

Next, physical examination (and lab and radiologic studies, if needed) should be able to eliminate pelvic or rectal masses that may be causing urethral obstruction or increased bladder pressure. Stool impaction should be easily eliminated as a cause. Postmenopausal vaginal atrophy should be obvious. Asking the woman to strain while in the lithotomy position should cause leakage, if she has stress incontinence, or make a cystocoele obvious.

Peripheral neurological disease or vasculitides that present as neurological disease such as diabetes or syphilis should be discovered by examination. EMGs may be necessary to document the extent of disease. Diabetes, multiple sclerosis, B_{12} deficiency, syphilis, or stroke can cause incontinence.

Urinary infections may be the cause and the result of the urinary incontinence, especially if detrusor instability or diabetes is present. Once the urinary infection is treated and cured, the woman should be re-evaluated for distressing urinary incontinence.

Once these diseases and conditions are eliminated, the woman and the provider are left with a chronic condition that often can be improved.

Treatment

Urinary incontinence is not a disease that can be cured, but if viewed as a chronic problem in which small but steady gains are possible, improvement is definitely reasonable. Even partial improvement in symptoms may give the woman a great improvement in her quality of life. For example, if her stress incontinence goes from often to occasional, she may be able to get out of the house by using a pad or liner, decreasing her isolation and embarrassment tremendously, although she is still left with stress incontinence (Table 18.2.3).

The first step is to eliminate medications, especially diuretics, and decrease, if not stop, use of alcohol, coffee, tea, and caffeinated drinks.

Stress Incontinence

Stress incontinence, the most common of UI, is loss of small volumes of urine with increased abdominal pressure such as cough, sneezing, exercise, or straining. It is rare at night, and more common in multiparous, menopausal, and overweight women. Rarely is it caused by surgery, trauma, a cystocoele, or a prolapsed uterus. It may be caused by relaxation of the control of the urethra along its length. Its symptoms usually can be improved easily in over 80% of women (1).

Although the cotton swab test has been used, history and elimination of other causes should be sufficient for diagnosis. First, the woman can attempt to strengthen her perineal muscles with Kegel's exercises. In one small study, Kegel pelvic muscle exercises improved over half the women's symptoms (7). Regular urinating may help. If there is evidence of atrophic vaginitis, a trial of intravaginal estrogen cream, three times a week for 2 to 4 weeks and then weekly for several months, can be used. Estrogen has been showed to increase urethral pressure in up to 30% of women with stress incontinence (8). Unopposed use of estrogen is not suggested in women with intact uteruses, and long-term oral ERT with progesterone should be considered.

If these do not work, a trial of phenylpropanolamine 50 to 100 mg per day divided bid can be tried. Added to estrogens, this drug significantly improves stress incontinence symptoms in 60 to 70% of women with stress incontinence (1, 8). If there is a suspicion of a mixed form of UI, or if these methods have not worked, a trial of imipramine 10 to 100 mg per day divided bid can be attempted.

Surgery is not indicated for stress incontinence, and has a poor cure rate. Complications of surgery include increased incontinence, detrusor instability, fistulas, uterine prolapse, and infections. If the woman has a grade III or IV cystocoele, or a cystocoele that is causing chronic and recurrent UTIs, a pessary often works and can be tried first (1) (see Chapter 21). Only if chronic and persistent disability occurs, should surgery be considered. Various surgical techniques that supports the bladder neck and urethra have been used with varying success; up to half of women who have surgery have continued stress incontinence afterwards.

Detrusor Instability or Urge Incontinence

Detrusor instability is reduced bladder capacity caused by excessive and inappropriate muscle contractions. This may be caused by decreased cortical inhibition of detrusor contraction, caused by strokes, dementias, and Parkinson's disease, or by bladder irritation from chronic cystitis or hypertrophy caused by outflow tract obstruction. The woman will have frequent, unpredictable, and sudden losses of moderate to large amounts of urine, including during the night while sleeping. Many women also have incomplete and frequent voiding.

First, the woman should have "bladder retraining," that consists of having the woman void

Table 18.2.3. Treatments of Urinary Incontinence

Avoid medications that might affect urinary system
Avoid alcohol, coffee, tea, caffeinated beverages
Avoid diuretics

Type	First Steps	Pharmacological Therapy
Stress incontinence	Strengthen perineal muscles with Kegel's exercises	Phenylpropanolamine 50–100 mg/d divided bid or
	If there is evidence of atrophic vaginitis, try intravaginal estrogen cream	Imipramine 10–100 mg/d divided bid
Detrusor instability	Have woman void regularly, and increase intervals slowly	Tricyclic antidepressants such as imipramine 10–25 mg qd to qid
	Consider bedside commode for elderly or disabled	Oxybutynin (Ditropan) 2.5–5 mg qd to qid
		Calcium channel blocker such as nifedipine 10 mg tid or 30 mg SR
Overflow incontinence	Rule out and treat any mechanical obstruction or curable neurologic deficit	Bethanechol 5–25 mg bid to qid
	Teach patient to void while Valsalva or pushing on bladder	Antibiotic prophylaxis
Functional incontinence	Treat mechanically: move bed, add bedside commode, etc.	

regularly, every 30 to 60 minutes, and then over the next few weeks have her increase intervals slowly. Consider a bedside commode for elderly or disabled women who may have difficulty getting to the toilet quickly. Obviously, UTIs, if present, should be treated and cure proven; chronic suppression may be needed. If a pelvic mass is found, evaluation of this should be rigorously pursued.

Pharmacological treatments include tricyclic antidepressants such as imipramine 10 to 25 mg qd to qid, or oxybutynin (Ditropan) 2.5 to 5 mg qd to qid. Estrogen therapy can reduce urgency but not incontinence (1). Calcium channel blocker such as nifedipine (10 mg tid or 30 to 60 mg SR) may be better tolerated in women with hypertension or heart disease.

Overflow Incontinence

Overflow incontinence comes from either long-standing outlet obstruction or impaired sensation. The bladder becomes large and flaccid, and urination consists of overflowing urine. Renal failure can result. This can occur from urethral obstruction, lower motor neuron damage, such as with a peripheral neuropathy or diabetes, or medications.

Treatment is first, relief of any obstruction, or treatment of reversible neurological problems such as B_{12} deficiency if possible. Obstruction, of course, is more common in men than women. Peripheral neurological diseases should show signs in the legs as well, and many, such as alcohol or diabetic neuropathy, are not reversible. Then, teach patient to void while Valsalva or pushing on bladder. Bethanechol 5 to 25 mg bid to qid can be added and may improve regular urination. Monitor the woman's postvoid residual. If she has over 100 mL, consider chronic antibiotic prophylaxis to prevent UTIs, chronic pyelonephritis, and renal failure.

Functional Incontinence

This occurs when a woman cannot get to the toilet, either because of balance problems, motor incoordination, paralysis, arthritis and arthralgias, or other reasons. The treatment is mechanical; moving the bed, adding a bedside commode, or otherwise improving the physical situation is the treatment. Often this occurs with other forms of UI and worsens a marginally tolerable situation. A home visit by a provider or home health nurse may produce some helpful suggestions for the woman and her family.

Use of Chronic Indwelling Catheters

The use of chronic indwelling catheters should be avoided, because they cause chronic colonization, UTIs, renal infections, and sepsis. Acutely, they are often needed in the hospital for monitoring of urinary function. However, often medications started in the hospital may prevent the return of continence on returning home, and a catheter is continued. Every effort should be made to remove it, including removal of medications, if possible, bladder training, regular urinating, and the medications listed in Table 18.2.1 for urge and/or overflow incontinence.

Catheters can be considered on a short-term basis for women who have developed decubitus ulcers or other rashes until the lesions heal. At times, women with overflow incontinence develop renal failure that requires chronic catheterizations. Occasionally there is a social situation in which a woman may be able to live either alone or still in her home and cared for by her family, if a catheter is placed. Each situation must be decided individually between family and provider.

Conclusion

Urinary incontinence is a condition that can sometimes be cured and often improved. Continued cooperation between the provider, the woman, and the woman's family may produce significant results.

Special Considerations for Nurse Practitioners and Physician Assistants

A woman may be reluctant to admit that she is incontinent and may have already resorted to the use of perineal pads or absorbent underwear, thinking that nothing else can be done for her. Women who deny having urinary leakage may later tell the provider that they are having problems with their bladders (9). Especially with the woman at risk, e.g., the postmenopausal woman or the woman with impaired mental status, providers must ask specifically about problems with incontinence (10). In addition to the history and physical previously discussed, providers might ask the woman to keep a diary of intake and output, urinary patterns, and incontinent episodes, noting any activity associated with incontinence (9, 11). The provider should acknowledge to the woman that incontinence does affect the quality of her life and assure her that efforts will be made to help her. Referral to a support group may be helpful for some women.

It is possible using the history, physical examination, and office tests for the primary care practitioner to get a good idea of the type of incontinence the woman is experiencing. However, UI is a symptom, not a disease (12). If the woman's incontinence does not respond to initial therapies or if a more absolute diagnosis is needed, referral should be made to a urogynecologic specialist for urodynamic testing, more in-depth diagnosis, and treatment (10, 11). When corrective treatment is not possible, continence specialists (e.g., nurses) may be available to help women through behavioral training and or assistive devices have optimum quality of life, independence, and personal dignity (9).

Behavioral training might focus on bladder retraining by teaching the woman to increase bladder stability. One method used to control the urge sensation is slow, deep breathing until the urge is reduced. Especially for the cognitively impaired woman, a planned schedule for voiding (habit training) can be tried. Based on the woman's voiding/incontinence pattern, the provider may work with her to develop a schedule for voiding whether or not the woman experiences an urge to void. If Kegel exercises are recommended, the woman can be helped to identify the muscle group that should be contracted, for example by having her squeeze or pull in and up the muscles around the provider's finger. Women can also be advised that the muscle group to be exercised is the same muscles used to stop urinary flow (9, 11). The woman should identify intervals and times that she can do the exercise, e.g., with each voiding or for longer periods morning and night. Measures to prevent UTI should be emphasized if needed, including an adequate fluid intake, a recommendation that the incontinent woman may have difficulty understanding unless time is taken to explain the rationale (11).

Absorbent products should not be used long-term, unless a basic evaluation has been done by a health professional, correction of the woman's problem is not possible, and behavioral training is not successful (9, 13). Early dependency on absorbent pads may deter continence and, when improperly used, can contribute to skin breakdown and UTI (13). The type of incontinent aid that is best for the woman is based on the type of incontinence (i.e., urinary, fecal, or both), the volume lost at any one time, and the frequency of loss (14). Consideration should also be given to the woman's functional ability, availability of caretakers, and preference (13). A woman who needs to purchase incontinent products (which are being advertised heavily) should be advised to find a type that meets her needs and to compare prices. Because of the long-term nature of use, the financial burden can be great.

Primary prevention is not often considered for incontinence. Maintaining normal functioning of the genitourinary tract may decrease the likelihood of incontinence. Postmenopausal women should be educated about the signs and symptoms of atrophic vaginitis, perineal hygiene, weight management, fluid intake (while avoiding caffeine and alcohol), exercises such as Kegel's, and avoidance of constricting undergarments or clothes (15). Continence should be the expected norm in all health care settings.

Primary care providers have a responsibility to raise public awareness of continence difficulties so that women will seek help and support. "The message that incontinence may be prevented and can be treated should be disseminated through aggressive public education by health care professionals during routine health care visits, in the lay press, at health fairs, health spas, beauty salons, libraries, community centers, and schools" (15).

References

1. Walters MD, Realini JP. The evaluation and treatment of urinary incontinence in women: A primary care approach. J Am Board Fam Pract 1992; 5:289–301.
2. Milsom I, Ekelund P, Molander U, Arvidsson L, Areskoug B. The influence of age, parity, oral contraception, hysterectomy and menopause on the prevalence of urinary incontinence in women. J Urol 1993;149:1459–1462.
3. Holst K, Wilson PD. The prevalence of female urinary incontinence and reasons for not seeking treatment. NZ Med J 1988;101:756–758.
4. Rekers H, Drogendijk AC, Valkenburg H, Riphagen F. Urinary incontinence in women from 35 to 79 years of age: Prevalence and consequences. Eur J Obstet Gynecol Reprod Biol 1992;43:229–234.
5. Smith RJ. Cigarette smoking and urinary incontinence in women. Am J Obstet Gynecol 1992;167: 1213–1218.
6. Grimby A, Molander U, Ekelun P, Milsom I, Wiklund I. The influence of urinary incontinence on the quality of life of elderly women. Age Ageing 1993; 22:82–89.
7. Elia G, Bergman A. Pelvic muscle exercises: When do they work? Obstet Gynecol 1993;81:283–286.
8. Elia G, Bergman A. Estrogen effects on the urethra: Beneficial effects in women with genuine stress incontinence. Obstet Gynecol Survey 1993;48:509–517.
9. Newman DK. Strategies for managing urinary incontinence in home-bound patients. Adv Nurse Pract 1994;2:11–14.
10. Stenchever MA. Office evaluation of incontinence and nonsurgical management options. Primary care update OB/GYNS 1995;2:30–34.
11. Garner CH. The climacteric, menopause, and the process of aging. In: Youngkin EQ, Davis MS, eds. Women's Health. Norwalk, CT: Appleton & Lange, 1994:309–343.
12. Qualey TL. An approach to elderly incontinence. Nursing Management 1995;26:48Q–48T.
13. Urinary Incontinence Guideline Panel. Urinary incontinence in adults: clinical practice guidelines. AHCPR Pub. No. 92-0038. Rockville, MD: Agency for Health Care Policy and Research, Public Health Service, U.S. Department of Health and Human Services. March 1992.
14. Promoting continence (professional development). Nurs Times 1994;90:9–12.
15. Palmer MH. A health-promoting perspective of urinary incontinence. Nurs Outlook 1994;42:163–169.

IV

PERIMENOPAUSAL YEARS

19

Preventive Health Care

Ellen L. Sakornbut

Introduction

Preventive health care requires two critical components for its success. The provider must be aware of the likelihood of preventable or modifiable health problems that may arise in an individual, and the individual must be motivated to take ownership of her responsibilities to herself, including the promotion of her own well-being. Experiences and perspectives acquired by mature women influence their interest and receptiveness to preventive care. Chronic medical conditions are much more commonly seen in this age group than in younger women. Chronic conditions do not negate the ability of a woman to achieve a state of health or well-being despite the alterations that the condition makes in her state of function or the increased need for maintenance care. The partnership of the provider and the woman to achieve the best possible state of well-being can become the focus of all ongoing medical care, preventive or otherwise. Many items that will be mentioned in this chapter do not fall under the category of formal screening tests or interventions, but are based on the relationship and communication between an individual provider and a woman.

There are concerns and opportunities for preventive health care unique to the middle-aged woman because her focus is increasingly directed at preservation of function. This chapter will address general approaches and ways to individualize care. Topics covered will include prevention and screening of cardiovascular disease, metabolic and endocrine conditions, musculoskeletal problems, and cancer. Cancer screening for uterine, cervical, colon, and breast cancer are addressed in other chapters. The provider-woman partnership will be emphasized as it relates to the promotion of healthy lifestyles.

Preventive health care can be conceptualized as components of general promotion of healthy lifestyle, specific preventive measures that some women may need because of increased risk, generalized screening measures in which all women should have as part of their health care, increased or specialized screening that is indicated in women with high risks for disease, and case-finding of disease as a part of preventive care in a woman with minimal symptoms or findings.

The issues encountered in preventive care entail many questions that are value and philosophy-centered or that pertain to individual perspective. Thus, different panels of experts have arrived at varying conclusions regarding indicated or justifiable measures of screening and prevention. The United States Preventive Health Services Task Force (USPHS) and the Canadian Task Force represent structured approaches to determining appropriate preventive services, often with the use of evidence-based criteria. The American Cancer Society (ACS), the American Heart Association (AHA), and medical specialty groups such as American Academy of Family Physicians (AAFP) American College of Obstetrics and Gynecology (ACOG) have also developed consensus guidelines and recommendations that reflect the specific concerns and perspectives relative to their area of focus.

The use of clinical guidelines as a basis for the individual provider's care of an individual woman carries with it many questions of ethics, judgement, the art of medicine, and the role of the provider. Nonetheless, clinical guidelines are being adopted by third-party payers and other key organizations. This produces enormous impact on the individual practice of medicine and the patients served.

At best, there exists limited time in the average medical office to convey meaningful information to a woman about preventive health care. Areas of controversy may surface as the woman explores concerns she may have encountered through the lay media or personal experience. Previous personal and family medical experiences influence the manner in that a woman approaches or avoids discussion of her concerns.

Although the issues surrounding preventive care may be complex, adequate communication between provider and woman is the most important step in providing preventive health care, regardless of screening strategy or intervention chosen. Supporting systems, community resources, and a reliable method of information documentation and monitoring provides crucial structure to a successful program in preventive care.

Assessment of Risk and Preventive Services

Any part of a standard medical encounter including the medical and social history, the physical examination, laboratory evaluations, and even the acquisition of demographic and insurance information) has a role in the assessment of risk and the provision of preventive services.

Besides traditional methods of assessment, standardized health assessment tools have been developed that address issues such as health risk and health and functional status. Health risk screens are available that can be filled out by the woman before the physician encounter. These can be scored and used as a formal feedback mechanism to direct patient education in health habits. The Medical Outcomes Study Short-Form General Health Survey (SF-20) uses six scales of health and functional status that includes physical functioning, role functioning, bodily pain, general health perception, social functioning, and mental health (1). This instrument has been widely used in an effort to evaluate health-related quality of life. Self-reporting scales such as the SF-20 may not be used with every patient, but should be considered with women seen with specific diagnoses (such as chronic or recurrent pain), frequent visits, or other red flags of underlying problems (see section on Mental Health Screening).

Even if formal risk scoring systems are not used, the health maintenance flow sheet should have prompters to the physician to inquire about issues such as the use of seat belts. The use of orientation brochures or practice newsletters can convey information on common health risks or health questionnaire devices.

Social History

Life Cycle and Preventive Health Care

Women age 45 to 65 years are, in most cases, beyond the childbearing age. Nonetheless, they are frequently still caring for their own children or their grandchildren. Their roles and tasks, both individually and in families, may be strongly derived from circumstances of childrearing. Often, they are motivated by health measures that they perceive to be important for the whole family, including their children and spouse. Therefore, information about the prudent diet, genetic and environmental transmission of susceptibility to diseases, and other preventive woman education is often well-received. However, a woman may spend so much time and energy providing care to her family that she deprioritizes her own well-being. This is an opportunity for the provider to encourage her to meet her own needs by pursuing neglected physical concerns, incorporating exercise, or stress-reduction measures.

Women also frequently assume another caregiver role as they assume responsibilities with aging parents and other family members. Widowhood becomes more common in middle-age. The substantial time and financial pressures generated by the role of the caregiver can overshadow other needs (2).

Changes in a woman's social role often occur simultaneously with a change in her perception of her body. Most women appreciate anticipatory guidance about the bodily changes of menopause and aging, what can be done to relieve symptoms, and what can be done to prevent unnecessary alteration in function. They may also have concerns about sexuality and the continued opportunity to participate in satisfactory relationships with a partner. Further discussion about the menopause may be found in Chapter 21. It is important for the provider to recognize the patient's concerns about her role as a woman as her social and biologic function is altered. This presents an opportunity to discuss intimacy and sexual function (3).

Employment, Preventive Services, and Health Insurance

A two-earner family is encountered in many marriages; many women have been in the work force for most of their adult life, and others have returned to income-producing work as their children grow-up. Other women must return to work when their husband is laid off, becomes disabled, retires, or dies. Current and past employment may suggest occupational hazards such as hepatitis A or B, cumulative trauma disorders, and environmental exposures including chemical and noise exposure (see Chapter 6.3). Although less common with current precautions, women may also have past exposures to hazards encountered by themselves or their spouses at work, such as lead and asbestos contamination brought home on clothing.

The work history and the spouse's work history may have additional impact in medical care, because the majority of health insurance coverage is tied to employment. Women age 45 to 65 years and their partners frequently have concerns about changing or losing employment because of the potential lack of opportunity for them in the job market and because of difficulty with insurance coverage related to preexisting conditions. Prevention of disability and sick days and the availability of convenient care is of practical interest to patients.

The changing health care market has altered the types of health care delivery available to a large number of patients, with a shift towards managed care and away from fee-for-service. Some surveys of patient satisfaction showed decreased satisfaction with managed care over traditional fee-for-service. Managed care has traditionally covered preventive care as a fully covered service, although some indemnity insurance plans have not. One study demonstrated a reduction in breast cancers cervical cancer, melanoma, and colon cancer diagnosed at a later stage in patients enrolled in a health maintenance organization as compared to patients seeking care under fee-for-service arrangements (4). Screening methods with some degree of demonstrated effectiveness exist for all these malignancies. Current trends in health care delivery include quality monitors for implementation of screening, and quality indicators are being used as employers decide how to spend health care funds on their employees.

Substance Use

The use of tobacco, caffeine, alcohol, and nonprescription drugs should be noted in all patients, both past and present use. A more accurate alcohol history can sometimes be obtained by observing the quality of the response to questioning and by asking questions that pertain to consequences of drinking.

Medical and Family History

The medical history will help the provider concentrate on possible problems. A list of important problems are included in Table 19.1.

The family history is important in middle-aged women, because many of the diseases that have affected their family members will surface during this time period. Family history will often determine that women need more inten-

Table 19.1. Important Personal Past Medical History

1. Reproductive history	Operative and vaginal deliveries; a history of pregnancy-induced hypertension or gestational diabetes; a history of infants with growth retardation; onset of childbearing after age 30
2. Gynecologic history	Surgical or premature menopause without hormonal therapy, abnormal menses; a history of abnormal Pap smears, any hormonal therapy
3. Cardiopulmonary disease	A history of asthma or recurrent bronchitis; a history of valvular heart disease, heart murmurs, or mitral valve prolapse; any history of elevated blood pressures
4. Gastrointestinal disease	Inflammatory bowel disease; irritable bowel syndrome or "spastic colitis;" a history of hepatitis B, C, or transfusion-associated, or chronic carriage of Hepatitis B surface antigen; gallbladder disease; pancreatitis, cirrhosis, and peptic ulcer disease
5. Renal disease	Recurrent urinary tract infections; kidney stones
6. Mental health history	Panic attacks; previous episodes of depression; "nerve problems" or a "nervous breakdown;" history of manic or hypomanic spells; prolonged use of tranquilizers or other psychoactive substances; a history of abuse (either physical or sexual)
7. Musculoskeletal disease	Soft-tissue rheumatic syndromes; specific joints affected by arthritis; lower back problems
8. Nervous system disease	Seizure disorders; migraine headaches, diabetic neuropathy or unexplained neuropathy
9. Endocrine disease	Diabetes mellitus; any thyroid disease; head and neck irradiation; autoimmune disorders
10. Skin disease	The geographic area and overall sun exposure; actinic keratoses, skin cancers, dysplastic nevi, or severe blistering sunburns; northern European ancestry
11. Infectious disease	HIV disease
12. Personal history of neoplasia	Cancers of the breast, colon, endometrium, upper respiratory tract, lung, tumors of endocrine glands, and previous radiation and chemotherapy
13. Medication history	All current meds and chronic or recurrent use of medications in the past with attention to the following issues: corticosteroids; estrogen and other female hormone medications; over-the-counter analgesics; thyroid replacement; psychoactive and potentially addictive medications; allergic reactions and adverse drug reactions

Table 19.2. Important Family History Indicating Increased Risk for the Woman

Cerebrovascular disease	Myocardial infarction, heart failure; hypertension
Type II diabetes	Especially in first-degree relatives; hyper- or hypothyroidism; multiple endocrine neoplasia
Cancers with genetic links	Colon and familial polyposis; breast cancer, ovarian (especially in families with both breast and ovarian cancer); melanoma
Environmental cancers	Tobacco; other chemical exposures
Mental health disorders	Alcoholism and other addictions; depression, unipolar or bipolar; "nervous breakdowns;" patterns of familial abuse and domestic violence, somatoform disorders
Osteoporosis	Connective-tissue disease and auto-immune disorders

sive screening or special interventions. Causes of mortality and ages at the time of death are valuable as medical information, and this information can be helpful in understanding the patient's experience and motivation. Especially important topics in the family history are included in Table 19.2.

Review of Systems

Questions that are routinely pertinent to women age 45 to 65 years include (*a*) the presence or absence and normality of menses or hormonal-therapy–related vaginal bleeding, (*b*) vasomotor flushes or "hot flashes," (*c*) general questions of bowel or urinary complaints, (*d*) problems with weight gain or diet, (*e*) and problems with sexual function.

Physical Examination

The routine yearly physical examination has largely been proven to be ineffective as a means of prevention. It has been replaced by the process of risk assessment, screening, and targeted interventions. However, patients often expect the physician to examine them and feel that something has been missed if they are not examined. Some portions of the physical

exam may be more useful as a means of screening or case-finding. The process of examination also prompts both physician and woman to address specific issues. Common findings pertinent to preventive services are covered by system.

Vital Signs

The patient's weight should be recorded at the time of any visit to the primary care provider's office. Obesity is considered to be a body weight 20% or greater than the ideal body weight. Weight-to-height proportion are crucial, because many serious disorders, including breast, colon, and endometrial cancers, cardiovascular disease, diabetes (3 times increase), hypertension (3 times increase), and degenerative joint disease of the knees, have been linked to obesity.

The waist-hip ratio (WHR) has been used as a means of targeting truncal obesity, especially linked to cardiovascular disease, diabetes, hypertension, and cerebrovascular accidents (5–7). WHR is calculated by measuring the waist circumference at the level of the umbilicus or greatest anterior protrusion of the abdomen and measuring the hips at the level of the buttocks in the greatest dimension. The formula for the WHR is waist circumference/hip circumference. Values greater than

0.8 are considered elevated in women and are associated with increased risk of the diseases described earlier.

Blood pressure should be screened at any visit to the provider's office. Minimum intervals for blood pressure screening in middle-aged women range from 1 to 2 years, with yearly blood pressures for women with diastolics in the 85 to 89 mm range. The American College of Physicians also recommends yearly screening in patients who are moderately or extremely obese, African-Americans, and those with first-degree relatives with hypertension or a personal history of hypertension (8).

Head, Eyes, Ears, Nose, Throat

The retinal examination will be unrevealing in most healthy women. Most women in this age group will not need hearing screening other than ability to discern the whispered voice, but women who have worked in high-noise industries should be encouraged at this time to wear protective equipment and should have regular audiometric screening, which is usually offered in their workplace. Women who use tobacco or who have dentures should have periodic examinations of the oral cavity. Periodontal disease is the leading cause of adult tooth loss and can affect nutritional status. Medications that cause an increased incidence of gingival disease include phenytoin. Dental referral and instructions about proper brushing and flossing may take place if gingival disease is noted.

Endocrine

The palpation of the thyroid is indicated in well-person exams, because thyroid disease are encountered on a regular basis.

Cardiopulmonary

The presence of cardiac murmurs may indicate the need for SBE prophylaxis or diagnostic studies. Functional murmurs are encountered in mature adults, but not with the frequency that they are seen in children and young pregnant women. Signs of asthma, cardiac rhythm irregularities, and gallops are all important evidence of disease.

Breasts

The breasts should be examined on a yearly basis in this age group while educating the woman in breast self-examination. The breasts should be palpated in a systematic fashion that allows deep and shallow palpation of all areas of the breast (like the spokes of a wheel) in the supine and upright position, examination of the nipples for discharge, fixed inversion, or eczematous changes, palpation of the axillary tail of the breast, and the axillary nodes. Observation for fixation of the skin to underlying structures can be noted as the woman leans forward or dimpling of the skin when the woman presses downward on her hips.

Pelvic

A Pap smear is indicated on a periodic basis in middle-aged women, with greater frequency of screening indicated in women who have had previous abnormal smears or who have known risk factors for cervical cancer. Although cervical cancer screening may not be indicated on a yearly basis in low-risk women, there are a number of other benefits associated with the pelvic exam in women during the perimenopausal decades. The general condition of tissues in the vulvar area and introitus should be noted, and whether there is any evidence of atrophic change or vulvar lesions. The vaginal mucosa should be inspected for evidence or lack of estrogen effect. The uterus is palpated for size, tenderness, position, texture, and irregularity of contours suggestive of fibroids. The examination detects signs of estrogen deficiency and any factors that may make the issue of hormonal therapy more complex (fibroids or an enlarged uterus). The adnexa are palpated for masses and tenderness; postmenopausal ovaries are generally not palpable.

A rectovaginal exam completes the examination, but should be completed with a clean glove, allowing the provider to perform a fecal occult blood test at the same time with an uncontaminated glove. The rectal exam is ineffective in detecting any except a small percentage of colorectal cancers, but serves as well to prompt the provider to provide the woman with an additional fecal occult blood testing kit and instructions about cancer screening.

Extremities

The gait and general mobility are probably of greatest interest in asymptomatic women. The provider may wish to direct additional attention to the knee exam in obese women, looking for crepitus with flexion and ligamentous instability.

Neurologic

A basic mental status assessment and assessment of mood can be obtained throughout the process of the interview.

Nutrition

Obesity Prevention

Over one fourth of all women are considered overweight, with a trend toward increasing weight with aging. A sedentary lifestyle and failure to adopt a reduction in calories as metabolism slows is the most common reason for this nutritional problem. Patients should be made aware of what constitutes a range of ideal body weight for them and encouraged to pursue a healthier weight goal.

Screening for dietary problems may be accomplished by asking for a 24-hour dietary recall and by asking about likely problems with obtaining a healthy diet (such as the tendency to skip meals, dine out frequently, or eat "fast food" or "junk food" frequently).

Nutrition counseling should be offered to all obese women. Counseling by the provider, an office nurse, or by a nutritionist should emphasize balanced diets without the use of fads, fasting, diet pills, or other unproven methods. The woman will often have tried some of these methods to lose and regain the weight. An educational approach directed at long-term alteration in diet with reduction in fats is medically appropriate for the vast majority of patients. Commercially available liquid diet supplements may not contain sufficient fiber to promote good bowel function and do not engender adequate long-term dietary habits. Very low-calorie diets require strict medical supervision and are not appropriate for most patients for the same reason. Weight loss can only be sustained and beneficial if the woman decides to alter her approach to eating and exercise by a lifestyle change.

Metabolic evaluation of the obese woman will not be fruitful in the majority of cases. However, because hypothyroidism is common in this age group, it may be worthwhile to check thyroid values on obese women who are age 50 years or older.

Fat and Cholesterol

A typical diet in the United States consists of approximately 40 to 50% of calories in fat. Targeted ranges for fat consumption are less than 30%, with 10% or less in saturated fat. Women should be a primary target for nutrition education regarding fat content to decrease their risk of heart disease and other vascular disease. Women are the individuals buying and preparing foods in a majority of households. The introduction of a healthier diet to this individual can have consequences for the rest of the family.

Although protein needs are in the 15 to 20% range, a typical diet uses more meat than is necessary to meet protein needs and thus contains excessive amounts of saturated fat and cholesterol. Protein sources that are lower in saturated fat and cholesterol include chicken and turkey (especially with skin removed), fish, dried beans and other legumes, other grains, and low-fat dairy sources, especially if fixed by a method that does not involve cooking fat.

Dietary components that may affect cholesterol levels have been the subject of many investigations. The quality of information about Omega-3 fatty acids and oat bran is variable. Certainly, in principle, both of these food items should be a part of a prudent and well-balanced diet. Multiple studies have suggested that individuals with moderate alcohol intake have lower cholesterol levels. Again, this information should be balanced with individual risk factors.

Fiber

Alteration of the diet structure by decreasing fat requires replacement with other nutrients. A diet that is composed of 50 to 60% carbohydrate with the majority of this as complex carbohydrates should include a number of fiber-containing foods. Fiber is found in two major types: soluble and insoluble. Soluble fiber is found in fruits and vegetables (pectin) and in oat bran. Insoluble fiber is most commonly found in the outer covering of grains such as wheat bran. A high-fiber diet, low in saturated fats, has been associated with reduced risk of cancer of the colon, diverticular disease, and chronic constipation. It can be safely advocated for the vast majority of patients in this age group, although individual patients may experience increase in bowel gas production or complaints of intolerance of certain types of roughage (seeds, popcorn) with diverticular disease.

Calcium

Adult women may have stopped or decreased milk consumption because of some degree of lactose intolerance, substitution of caffeine-containing beverages, or avoidance of calories associated with whole milk. Generally, women in this age group should be encouraged to ingest 1000 to 1500 mg of calcium daily, either by dietary means or with mineral supplements. In-

creased fat consumption can be avoided by the use of skim or low-fat milk. Lactose intolerance is often not a problem if the calcium-rich food is cheese or yogurt. Lactase additives may also be helpful. It is difficult to obtain sufficient calcium by dietary means alone if no dairy foods are used, because calcium-rich vegetables like spinach do not contain as much absorbable calcium as a dairy source. A typical serving of a dairy product, such as an 8-oz carton of yogurt, contains approximately 300 mg of calcium.

Vitamins and Minerals

Women age 45 to 65 years usually require less iron need than during the premenopausal time period. Unless they are still menstruating or are chronically iron-deficient, they should not need supplementation to maintain adequate hemoglobin. Most women in these ages should be able to meet their nutrition requirements for vitamins without supplementation with a balanced diet. Exceptions may be vitamin D supplementation in women with low amounts of dairy products in their diet, nursing home patients (9), those on phenytoin therapy, and multivitamin supplementation for women with overall malnutrition or chronic illness producing a catabolic state.

Exercise and Activity

Exercise as a prescription can be used effectively for concerns ranging from hypertension to depression to low back pain. Adherence to exercise as a lifestyle change requires the woman to prioritize her own well-being and organize time to meet her needs. This change in priorities can be positive and empowering for women, adding to the benefits of relief of symptoms, improved tone and appearance, and improvement in health status.

The basis for a successful exercise prescription is a motivated woman who is assisted in finding a program to which she can adhere.

General well-being is enhanced in all women by the institution of aerobic exercise targeting 70% of maximal heart rate lasting 20 to 30 minutes at least 4 or 5 days per week. This should be an activity that the woman can find enjoyable, perhaps by involving social contact such as joining an exercise class, walking with a companion in her neighborhood, or square-dancing with a partner. Other women enjoy solitary activities because of the promotion of time for their own internal focus.

Specific prescriptions of targeted exercises (such as those for low-back conditioning) must be discussed in complete enough detail so that the woman will know how to perform the exercise and why it is useful. The use of physical therapy training, videos, or other educational or audiovisual materials can be reinforcing.

Many forms of exercise can be safely pursued by mature women, but prudent exercise programs should include adequate protection of feet and joints and a warm-up stretching period in exercise sessions involving jogging and more intensive activities. Women should be counseled to use proper footwear and report problems such as recurrent foot pain. Strength and flexibility exercises will assist in preventing musculoskeletal injury.

Low-impact aerobics, walking, exercise in water (e.g., arthritis programs or swimming), stationary bicycles, and treadmills or similar equipment can generally be undertaken without any special preparation as long as the woman starts slow and increases with tolerance. More vigorous exercise programs such as running and long-distance cycling can be undertaken by women in this age group, but individual evaluation may be of benefit for the woman who has previously been sedentary, especially if risk factors for heart disease are present.

Exercise for Women with Special Needs

Arthritis
Patients with arthritis will find that exercise is vital to preservation of optimal joint function and general well-being, but they should be prepared to follow careful guidelines. Patients with rheumatoid arthritis should pursue a deliberate program of active range-of-motion exercise for each joint group each day, especially for affected joints. They need to moderate their activities with rest periods. Range-of-motion, general mobility, and strengthening exercises can be taught by a physical therapist and are helpful in preventing fixed joint deformity. Occupational and physical therapists often can provide specific orthotic devices or procedures that protect the impaired joints with activity. Patients with degenerative joint disease will also find exercise to be beneficial, especially programs of moderate walking coupled with weight loss in patients with knee disease. Many Arthritis Foundation chapters and exercise centers provide exercise programs in water, using the benefits of resistance to movement with decreased gravitational stress.

Cardiovascular Disease
Women with known cardiovascular disease or significant risk factors for coronary artery disease should be targeted for aerobic exercise that provides the opportunity to build collateral circulation. Most patients can begin on a program of daily walking or similar activity with slow increase, using cardiac rehabilitation programs for the patients with greater risk and self-supervised programs for those with lesser risk. Walking has also been found to be helpful in building collateral circulation in patients with peripheral arterial vascular disease.

Substance Use and Abuse

Smoking cessation counseling by their provider has been found to be a modality that women acknowledge as an effective influence. Counseling should be a recurrent part of the medical care of any smoker. It may be helpful to concentrate on this issue when the woman presents with her yearly wintertime attack of bronchitis, but other opportunities include well-woman visits and presentation for hormonal therapy. Smoking cessation is covered in more depth in Chapter 6.2. Combined approaches that include behavior modification, pharmacologic relief of withdrawal symptoms or nicotine substitute therapy, and other motivational techniques (e.g., stop-smoking classes) are needed by many women. Women, in general, display greater effects of alcohol, both intoxication and long-term physical consequences to heavy drinking, because of a smaller proportion of muscle than men. The provider's advice about alcohol intake should be individualized to the patient.

Osteoporosis Prevention

Prevention of osteoporosis in women age 45 to 65 years has become increasingly important as the average life expectancy increases. Fractures are responsible for a large proportion of morbidity and mortality in the elderly, with the emphasis being placed on morbidity. The elderly woman who has lost her mobility and sense of well-being because of chronic pain or acute injury is vulnerable to loss of function in other systems and loss of independence (10). The woman may voluntarily limit her activity because of fear of the consequences of falls, again altering quality of life.

There are two major types of osteoporosis. Type I with fractures occurs in the axillary skeleton (that is primarily composed of trabecular bone) include vertebral compression fractures and distal forearm. These are generally seen in postmenopausal women. Type II is seen in elderly women and men with fractures of the femoral neck, humerus, and pelvis.

Besides acute fracture-associated pain, other problems seen with vertebral fractures include kyphoscoliosis with loss of height in the vertebral column, restriction of the "bucket-handle" motion at the costovertebral junction, and resultant restrictive lung disease

and loss of chest volume. Women experience decreased exercise tolerance despite normal myocardial function, airway movement, and diffusion capacity. Some women experience prolonged and chronic pain with fractures, resulting again in loss of function.

Risk factors for osteoporosis include the following: (*a*) female, (*b*) white or oriental race, (*c*) thin habitus, (*d*) cigarette smoking, (*e*) alcohol intake, (*f*) positive family history, (*g*) lack of estrogen, (*h*) chronic or prolonged corticosteroid therapy (11), and (*i*) over-replacement of thyroid hormone or hyperthyroidism (12). Osteoporosis is less common in African-American women because of denser initial bone mass. It is seen less commonly in obese women because of higher circulating levels of estrone (E3), caused by the peripheral conversion of endogenous steroid hormones in fat.

Bone densitometry has been used as a means of predicting risk of osteoporosis. Techniques include radiographic absorbiometry of the hand; dual-energy photon absorbiometry of the spine, hip, or total body; and dual-energy roentgenographic absorbiometry (DXA) of the spine, hip, or total body. There is no evidence at the current time that low or normal risk women need bone densitometry as a screening test. The World Health Organization recommends bone densitometry studies as a means only of directing nonhormonal therapy for osteoporosis (13). Other screening measures that are under investigation currently include the use of urinary magnesium and calcium-creatinine ratio (14). Although these tests may provide information about efficacy of treatment regimens, their use for the general population has yet to be demonstrated. There are women who do need special screening.

The components of osteoporosis prevention include adequate calcium intake for bone mineralization, weight-bearing exercise to stimulate maintenance of bone mass, and maintenance of a favorable milieu, either hormonal or by other pharmacologic means to promote a favorable balance between osteoclastic and osteoblastic activity.

Weight-bearing exercise is important to maintenance of healthy bone mass. Many women are not compliant with regular, sustained exercise programs, limiting its efficacy as a preventive measure (15). Immobilization during illness leads to rapid loss of bone mass. Despite the positive influence of exercise in women athletes, women who engage in heavy training via running, cycling, or other forms of exercise resulting in a lean body mass often encounter amenorrhea and decreased bone mass. Swimming does not appear to be associated as commonly with amenorrhea. The provider should obtain a history from women who have been active athletically to ascertain increased risk of osteoporosis, such as prolonged amenorrhea-oligomenorrhea, frequent stress fractures, and heavy training.

Hormonal replacement therapy (HRT) is discussed in Chapter 20, but certainly forms the mainstay of pharmacologic therapeutic measures at this time to prevent osteoporosis. Education of women about the risks and benefits of estrogen, medication adjustment for side effects, and other components of osteoporosis prevention should be provided to all women.

Women who may need further evaluation with bone densitometry to evaluate their current status include those with multiple risk factors and evidence of current osteoporosis, those with metabolic bone disease (such as renal osteomalacia or hyperparathyroidism), and others in whom nonhormonal therapy may be indicated as a substitute or in addition to HRT. Bone densitometry may be useful as additional information when a woman is hesitant to use HRT (16).

Additional measures to prevent or treat osteoporosis include biphosphonates, fluoride supplementation, calcitonin, and vitamin D. Nonhormonal pharmacologic measures to prevent osteoporosis are summarized in Table 19.3.

Table 19.3. Nonhormonal Therapy for Osteoporosis

Medication	Mechanism of Action	Side Effects
Salmon calcitonin (injectable) 100 IU sq or IM qd, use limited to 2 yrs	Inhib. bone resorbtion, GI, renal effects use w/Ca++, Vitamin D	Nausea, vomiting, dermatologic,
Salmon calcitonin nasal spray 200 I.U. intranasal qd	Same as above use w/Ca++, Vitamin D	Rhinitis, epistaxis, sinusitis
Etidronate sodium 5mg/kg/d or 400 mg qd × 14 d every 3 mos	Suppresses bone turnover	Nausea, diarrhea
Vitamin D 400 IU qd, adjunctive and important in women with metabolic abnl	Multiple sites: renal, GI for women in cold climates w/poor sunlight exposure, anticonvulsants	None significant in therapeutic dosage
Fluoride, slow release, 25 mg bid × 12 mos, 2 mos off + 800 mg Ca++/d	Stimulates osteoblast formation, new bone, bone denser but not stronger in absence of adequate Ca++	Increased fractures in early studies, gastric irritation reduced in slow-release

Ca++ = calcium

Occupational Health Issues

Women working in numerous occupations are at risk for repetitive strain injuries or cumulative-trauma disorders, especially those related to the upper extremities (see Chapter 6.3). Repetitive activities in the workplace may cause chronic tendonitis, carpal tunnel syndrome, and other chronic low-grade disorders that can result in significant disability.

Well-designed work environments are designed using principles of ergonomics to modify work stations or procedures for minimization of recurrent stresses or injury. Providers may become involved with prevention of recurrent injuries by assisting the woman in requesting training or equipment modification to avoid recurrence. Proper instruction in back care will be of benefit to many women who work in nursing, personal care, childcare, industry, and food service. The use of protective clothing, gloves, hearing protection, respirators, and eyewear is crucial to safety in the workplace and long-term well-being. Providers should reinforce safety training with their women when obtaining an occupational history.

Infectious Disease Prevention

Immunizations (Table 19.4)

Influenza Vaccination
Influenza vaccination is indicated in the following occupations: (*a*) health care workers, particularly nursing home personnel and others having contact with elderly, (*b*) immunocompromised or chronically ill patients, (*c*) employees of any custodial institution (including penal), (*d*) childcare workers, and (*e*) military workers in combat-ready or barracks situations. Less crucial but advisable may be anyone employed in settings in which large numbers of individuals are enclosed in a small

Table 19.4. Immunizations Required

Influenza vaccination	Health care workers, employees of nursing homes, any custodial institution, childcare workers, and military workers
	Chronic conditions: lung, renal, heart and neurologic disorders, diabetes, autoimmune dysfunction or chronic corticosteroid use, or immunocompromised status (including HIV disease)
	Women who live in a household with another individual having these conditions
Pneumococcal vaccination	Same chronic medical conditions as influenza vaccination in specific conditions in which splenic function may be compromised
Hepatitis B vaccination	Any health care, environmental, or custodial worker who may be exposed to body fluids, dental workers, and workers or clients in institutions or educational/vocational programs and group homes for the mentally-retarded, mentally-ill, or incarcerated
	Household situations with known carriers or acutely-infected individuals. Adults with HIV disease
Tetanus	In occupations with significant risk of injuries, soil exposures, farming, and construction

space (such as teachers) and anyone whose continued function is necessary within the context of their employment.

Chronic conditions that warrant influenza vaccination include any type of chronic lung disease (e.g., asthma), heart disease, neurologic disorders that may affect respiratory status, diabetes, chronic renal insufficiency, significant autoimmune dysfunction or chronic corticosteroid use, or immunocompromised status (including HIV disease). Women who live in a household with another individual having these conditions may also merit influenza vaccination as a protective measure.

Pneumococcal Vaccination

Pneumococcal vaccination is warranted in essentially the same list of chronic medical conditions as influenza vaccination and in specific conditions in which splenic function may be compromised, such as myeloproliferative disorders, chronic immune thrombocytopenia purpura, or other disorders with splenic sequestration, and in individuals with surgical splenectomy.

Hepatitis B Vaccination

Hepatitis B is indicated in the following occupational exposures—any health care worker, environmental, or custodial worker who may be exposed to body fluids, dental workers, and workers or clients in institutions or educational/vocational programs and group homes for the mentally retarded, mentally ill, or incarcerated.

Additional indications for hepatitis B vaccination are encountered in household situations with known carriers or acutely infected individuals. Theoretically, hepatitis B is transmitted by blood products and sexual contact, but there are instances in which transmission has occurred through the oral-fecal route. Hepatitis B vaccination is indicated in adults with HIV disease who have no evidence of previous hepatitis B exposure (neg HBsAb or Ag) and in women whose sexual contacts make hepatitis B exposure likely.

Hepatitis A Vaccination

Hepatitis A vaccination is indicated in the following occupational exposures: (a) childcare workers, health care workers, and others who may be exposed to fecal-oral contamination of women with acute hepatitis A, (b) food service workers, and (c) custodial and environmental waste workers who may have potential exposure.

Tetanus

Tetanus immunization is frequently neglected by women and providers alike as a primary preventive measure. It is required in a number of employment situations and is specifically indicated in occupations with significant risk of injuries, soil exposures, farming, and construction. A diphtheria-tetanus booster (dT) is indicated every 10 years for individuals with a primary immunization series.

Prevention of Blood-borne Pathogens

Women exposed through occupational risk or as caregivers in the home to blood-borne pathogens should be counseled in the observance of universal precautions. Most nursing staff will be familiar with these precautions, but custodial workers, sitters with the elderly or mental health patients, and other nonmedical personnel may have little or no training in these concepts. Although sexually transmitted diseases are less commonly encountered in middle-aged women than in younger women, individual women will have counseling needs about protective measures for safe sex. Women who are planning elective surgeries in which there is some likelihood of significant blood loss should be counseled about the benefits of autotransfusion of stored units.

Screening for Tuberculosis

Health care workers, especially those who work with the elderly, immunocompromised, and HIV women, should receive regular, generally yearly, screening for tuberculosis via the Mantoux test using purified protein derivative. Other women who should be screened include food service and childcare workers. Recent contacts (within 3 months) of active tuberculosis cases need screening, as well as women with HIV infection and women who are institutionalized.

Preventive Care for Cardiovascular Diseases

Although most research that has been performed in the prevention of coronary artery disease has been targeted at middle-aged men, heart disease remains the leading cause of death in women (see Chapter 13.1). A preventive approach to heart disease in middle-aged women includes the following: hormonal therapy (see Chapter 20), cholesterol screening and lipid-lowering therapy, weight loss, and hypertension control.

Lipid-Lowering Therapy

Cholesterol screening is recommended every 5 years during adulthood and the National Cholesterol Education Program recommends obtaining HDL levels. Lipoprotein analysis has been recommended in all adults with coronary heart disease (CHD) and in all adults with total cholesterol levels > 240 mg/dL or in individuals with levels 200 to 239 mg/dL and 2 or more risk factors for CHD, or in individuals with an HDL < 35 mg/dL (17). HDL levels appear to be most reflective of cardiovascular risk status in women (18).

A step I diet, using NCEP guidelines, can be recommended in women with elevated cholesterol. This diet derives less than 10% of calories from saturated fat and contains less than 300 mg of cholesterol per day. The NCEP recommends the use of hormonal replacement therapy to lower LDL levels and raise HDL levels before considering using cholesterol-lowering medication (19). Because of the low rate of coronary heart disease in women less than age 65 years, the use of cholesterol-lowering medication has not been demonstrated to result in reduced cardiovascular mortality among healthy women (20). Women who may benefit from cholesterol-lowering medication include those with known coronary artery disease (33), diabetics (21), and smokers who will not quit.

When using HRT to treat hyperlipemia, estrogen alone produces the most elevation in HDL and decrease in LDL, but all forms of combination HRT with progestins have been demonstrated to have an overall beneficial effect on lipids, with the most favorable combined regimen for lipid-lowering to be cyclic estrogen and micronized progesterone (22).

Hypertriglyceridemia in women diabetics has been associated with a proportionately greater increase in mortality than in men (23). Presumably, diabetic women with elevated triglycerides fall into a risk group, justifying antilipid therapy if good glucose control does not improve lipid levels.

Postmenopausal women with regular strenuous physical activity will experience decreases in LDL levels, as have been observed in men (24). Goals for exercise should include an aerobic activity with stimulation of the heart rate to 70% of maximum for 30 minutes 4 to 5 times per week.

Weight Loss

Even mild to moderate weight gains (5 to 20 kg) have been associated with increased risk of cardiac disease and related conditions (e.g., diabetes, hypertension) (25). Women should be encouraged to maintain ideal body weight.

Hypertension

Women with a strong family history of hypertension, those who are obese, diabetic, or who otherwise have increased risk for coronary artery disease should be screened yearly for hypertension and encouraged to maintain normal body weight. A decrease in sodium intake may not be helpful in all women to prevent hypertension, but should be particularly beneficial in African-American women and others with increased risk to develop low-renin hypertension.

Women with Special Concerns

CHD

Women with known CHD should be on a program to lower LDL cholesterol, cardiac rehabilitation with supervision individualized, smoking cessation (if applicable), and regular monitoring for symptoms and function. Influenza vaccination is indicated.

Valvular and Congenital Heart Disease

Women with mitral valve prolapse without audible regurgitant murmur, and those with ASD, do not require SBE prophylaxis and can be treated symptomatically. Women with mitral regurgitation, idiopathic hypertrophic subaortic stenosis, ventricular septal defect, and aortic valvular disease should receive SBE prophylaxis. Women with a history of rheumatic heart disease should receive continued penicillin prophylaxis if they work in an occupation with widespread contact with young children (e.g., teaching). Influenza vaccination is indicated.

Women Receiving Androgenic Medication

The provider must individualize each patient's therapy to balance the risks and benefits of androgenic medication used for other conditions, such as endometriosis, and risk of cardiovascular disease.

Diabetic Women

There is increasing evidence that good control decreases the risk of end-organ disease. The provider must be aware of the increased incidence of silent ischemia and myocardial infarction. A screening electrocardiogram is useful in diabetic women in assessing the presence of end-organ disease and as a screen for coronary artery disease. Diabetics are more likely to have small vessel disease than nondiabetics.

Preventive Services for Metabolic and Endocrine Disorders

Thyroid Disease

Laboratory evidence of thyroid dysfunction is found in up to 10% of women over the age of 60 years. Hypo- and hyperthyroidism are more commonly seen in women, older adults, and those with a family history of thyroid disease, as well as individuals with type I diabetes, other autoimmune disorders, Down's Syndrome, and a history of head and neck irradiation. There is some evidence that thyroid function tests should be performed in individuals with depression, weight loss, atrial fibrillation, and congestive heart failure (case-finding).

Routine screening is not recommended in the general population, but the American College of Providers recommends screening with thyroid function tests, including TSH, in women over the age of 50 years who have symptoms that may be a result of thyroid disease, and ACOG recommends thyroid screening every 3 to 5 years for women over age 65 years and in younger women with autoimmune disorders or a strong family history of thyroid disease (26).

Screening of thyroid function in women 45 to 65 years is best performed with a panel including the T4, T3RU, and TSH. This allows the provider to assess thyroid values within the context of the patient's individual hormonal status.

Diabetes Mellitus (DM)

DM is the leading cause of blindness in adults, the seventh leading cause of mortality in the United States, and the cause of one third of the cases of end-stage renal disease (see Chapter 15.1). Diabetes is found in approximately 5% of the general population; 95% of diabetics are type II diabetics. Diabetes is increased in some groups of Native Americans, Hispanics, and African-Americans, and is seen more frequently in adults over age 40 years, obese individuals, those with a family history, and women with a history of gestational diabetes (approximately 35 to 40%). Diabetes may be present for years in an asymptomatic or minimally symptomatic state.

Primary prevention of type II diabetes includes education about proper diet, exercise, and weight reduction in individuals at greater risk for diabetes. Secondary prevention of diabetes includes the same measures implemented in individuals with a diagnosis of type II diabetes or glucose intolerance who may be able to resume normal glucose metabolism if they are successful in changing their habits. Screening is not recommended in the asymptomatic population without an increased risk of diabetes.

In women with increased risk, screening is recommended (with some minor variations) in obese adults, women with a personal history of gestational diabetes, history of diabetes in a first-degree relative, family history of diabetes, and membership in an ethnic group with high prevalence of DM (27). The American Diabetes Association also recommends screening in women who have given birth to one or more infants weighing 9 lbs or more at birth, adults with hyperlipidemia or hypercholesterolemia, and hypertensive individuals.

Screening is usually accomplished by performing a fasting plasma glucose with a value of greater than or equal to 140 mg/dL considered as elevated and values 115 to 140 mg/dL generally meriting further evaluation. Fasting overnight is preferable, but a minimum of 3 hours is absolutely necessary. A random value greater than 200 mg/dL also merits further evaluation.

Preventive Services for Cancer

Cervical, uterine and other gynecological cancers, colon, and breast cancer are covered elsewhere (see Chapters 12.3, 12.4, 16, and 17.3 respectively). This section will discuss an overall approach to cancer screening and prevention, as well as skin and colon cancer screening. Table 19.5 lists cancer screening tests that have been used for women age 45 to 65 years.

Concepts and Techniques in Cancer Screening

Cancer screening is generally well-accepted by the public because of the clear recognition of cancer as a feared cause of morbidity and mortality. Nonetheless, there are individuals, notably women who are afraid of disfigurement, who avoid cancer screening such as in breast cancer, not wanting to face the prospects of loss of a body part that is intimately associated with gender, appearance, and feelings about one's sexuality. To submit to possibly embarrassing examinations and tolerate procedures that are perceived as invasive or uncomfortable necessitates a great deal of education. The campaign to raise provider and woman awareness about the value of Pap smears was a successful initiative on the part of numerous medical organizations.

Nonetheless, campaigns to promote awareness about Pap smears have not been wholly successful. There are still a large number of older, rural, and poor women who have not received proper screening. In addition,

Table 19.5. Cancer Screening Tests for Women Age 45 to 65 Years

Site of Cancer	Test	Clinical Application
Breast	Mammography	Yearly ages 50–70; use in women <50 and elderly women undecided
Cervical	Pap smears	Frequency in ages 45 to 65 determined by risk status and h/o previous disease, q 2–3 yrs in low-risk women
Uterine	Endrometrial Bx	Use in monitoring w/HRT controversial, indicated in some high-risk women, e.g. tamoxifen
Ovarian	CA-125	Transvaginal U/S use in monitoring w/HRT controversial use not well-defined and experimental
		High-risk; postmenopausal transvaginal U/S use not well-defined and experimental
Colorectal	FOBT	High-risk; postmenopausal yearly ages 50 and above
	Flexible sigmoidoscopy	Every 3–5 yrs starting age 50, somewhat controversial
	Colonoscopy	Very high-risk only
Lung	CXR, sputum cytology	Not recommended for use as a screen

many other forms of cancer screening methods that are at least partially effective remain underused. Even when properly used as screening measures, a medical system may fail to serve its women if clear provisions are lacking for follow-up of results.

Methods that can be used to increase awareness of cancer screening include information and screening availability at community health fairs, screening for cervical cancer as part of sexually transmitted disease clinics, presentations before lay organizations, and media coverage. The communication between the provider and woman, and the process of providing screening care through the provider's auspices, remains a mainstay of cancer screening, because the woman can receive education about screening and prevention, examinations or other more invasive procedures, discussion of findings, and coordination of therapeutic measures all in one source. Effective provider and woman reminder systems for periodic screening are in-

creasingly available and contribute substantially to effective primary care. Most clinical laboratories have developed systems to track abnormal Pap smears and other tests that they anticipate will be followed up with biopsies.

Cancer as a Familial Pattern

Distinct patterns of familial association have been found with breast, colon, and ovarian cancers. Family history of breast cancer appears to account for approximately 5 to 20% of breast cancer in the population (28). A small subset of families has been noted to demonstrate multiple cases of breast cancer, particularly occurring in premenopausal women, and ovarian cancer. Women with a first degree-relative with colon cancer have been found to have increased risk of breast cancer (29). A family history of dysplastic nevi is also seen in a small subset of women with malignant melanoma.

Cancer of the Skin

There are four major types of malignant neoplastic lesions of the skin and two premalignant conditions. These include the following:

1. Actinic keratoses (premalignant)
2. Dysplastic nevi (premalignant)
3. Basal cell carcinoma
4. Squamous cell carcinoma
5. Malignant melanoma
6. Keratoacanthoma (locally invasive and destructive)

Primary prevention of skin cancer can be affected most by limitation of skin exposure to ultraviolet radiation from the sun. Skin exposure is generally more crucial in fair skinned and light-eyed individuals, but skin cancers that are sun-related can occur in those with dark skin. In the southern latitudes of the United States, individuals should be advised to wear sunblock preparations daily from mid-spring until mid-fall. The sunblock should be at least sun-protection factor (SPF) 15, worn all day long on sun-exposed surfaces with reapplication as needed as a result of perspiration or swimming. Even this measure will not eliminate all ultraviolet exposure, and other devices to limit exposure such as hats are useful. "Sun-worship" and use of tanning beds should be avoided. Individuals who work outside all day long be informed that sun exposure is also accumulated through clothing that is thin and light colored.

Secondary prevention of skin cancer becomes more important in middle-aged women, as this is the time period when actinic keratoses and skin cancers are likely to begin appearing. All women should have a skin examination on a periodic basis, with individuals who have been noted to have sun-related malignant or premalignant lesions screened at least yearly. Areas of particular interest include the face, back of the neck, upper shoulders and forearms, and the ears. Lesions can also be found in the scalp, on the legs, and other areas on the trunk in women who have tanned frequently.

Actinic keratoses should be treated to prevent progression to carcinomas, either by cryosurgery or with 5-FU or other topical modality. Unusual or irregular appearing moles should be removed along with any nevi or other skin lesions that show the warning signs of cancer (e.g., pain, bleeding, enlargement). An ABCDE system has been used to evaluate dysplastic nevi and potential melanomas (Table 19.6).

Other preventive measures include the removal of any sore that will not heal, because chronic inflamed tissues can be the initial focus for a squamous cell carcinoma. Squamous carcinoma of the vulva and Bowen's disease (squamous carcinoma-in-situ) are uncommon, but unusual or ulcerating genital lesions that are persistent should be biopsied.

Colorectal Cancer

Primary prevention of cancer of the colon includes the following: eating a low-fat, high-fiber diet, and possibly ingestion of aspirin on a daily basis. Information in support of the former has been derived from multiple sources (30). Regular aspirin users were less to develop cancer of the colon than nonusers. This effect

Table 19.6. A System to Evaluate Dysplastic Nevi

A = appearance consistent vs. irregular in nature
B = border smooth vs. irregular
C = color consistent vs. variable
D = diameter < 5mm or > 5mm
E = elevation flat vs. thickened

appears to be present, even accounting for more frequent diagnostic investigations that may have been performed in aspirin-users for fecal occult blood. There are other studies that have noted that regular aspirin ingestion for other disease states, such as rheumatoid arthritis, was associated with a lower incidence of cancer of the colon.

Investigations at this time do not support the use of antioxidant vitamins for primary prevention of cancer of the colon. A limited number of individuals may choose primary prevention of cancer of the colon through total colectomy (those with long-standing ulcerative colitis and those with multiple, recurrent polyps as in familial polyposis).

Individuals at increased risk for cancer of the colon include those with long-standing ulcerative colitis, familial polyposis, a personal history of previous adenomatous polyps or carcinomas, a personal history of breast, endometrial, or ovarian cancer, and a first-degree family member with carcinoma of the colon or adenomatous polyps.

The focus of screening in colon of the cancer is the detection of lesions that may be premalignant, such as adenomatous polyps, and the detection of early-stage, localized carcinomas. Five-year survival is approximately 90% in this instance. Screening for cancer of the colon includes the following modalities: digital rectal exam (DRE), fecal occult blood testing (FOBT), flexible sigmoidoscopy, and colonoscopy. Each modality has its limits, but two of the screening modalities can be performed in an inexpensive and reasonably noninvasive manner. Cancer of the colon is covered in more depth in Chapter 16.

Digital Rectal Exam

DRE is unlikely to detect only a small proportion of all colorectal cancer of itself. Nonetheless, it is inexpensive combined with other periodic examinations and provides the provider an opportunity to instruct the woman on fecal occult blood testing. Fecal occult blood testing performed on a specimen obtained from DRE is not more likely to produce false-positive results and can therefore be included in FOBT screens. DRE is recommended yearly starting at the age of 40 by the American Cancer Society and the AAFP.

Fecal Occult Blood Testing

FOBT is performed using one of two types of available products, guaiac-impregnated cards that rely on peroxidase-like activity of hemoglobin or quantitative tests that use the conversion of heme to fluorescent porphyrins. Guaiac-impregnated cards can produce false-positive results with items in the patient's diet such as red meat, raw fruits and vegetables such as citrus, and nonsteroidal anti-inflammatory medications. Women being evaluated with guaiac-impregnated cards should follow dietary precautions for 48 hours before obtaining specimens, but may take iron supplements. The cards are easily read by providers.

The quantitative porphyrin tests do not require special dietary precautions but are not specific for lower GI tract bleeding and must be processed through a laboratory. Women using either method are instructed to obtain two samplings of each of 3 separate stool specimens.

Although FOBT has been associated with a low sensitivity (approximately 25 to 40%) and a high false-positive rate (over 90%), there is evidence that its use has been associated with a reduction in late-stage colorectal cancer (31). It is more sensitive at picking up colon cancer than adenomatous polyps. FOBT is recommended starting at age 50 years in low-risk individuals by most organizations.

Sigmoidoscopy and Colonoscopy

Flexible sigmoidoscopic exam (FSE) is recommended by the ACS to be performed on all women on or after the age of 50 years followed by a second examination 3 to 5 years later if the first exam is negative. Its use in the United States at this time certainly does not approach these recommended guidelines. The test involves specific preparation and some expense, depending on the procedural charge generated, the amount of time a woman takes off from work to prepare or undergo the test, and whether or not a consultation was performed or the test performed by the primary care provider.

FSE as a screening test has been shown to pick up adenomatous polyps, villous adenomas, and cancers that were missed in asymptomatic women with negative FOBT (32). The risks of the procedure are low; approximately 1 in 10,000 or less experience bowel perforation. The procedure is usually minimally to mildly uncomfortable, but women may believe it to be more uncomfortable, invasive, or embarrassing than they wish to endure. Nonetheless, all women should be informed of the potential benefits of this procedure for cancer screening and those with a family history of cancer of the colon should be encouraged to undergo endoscopic screening.

Colonoscopy is more expensive, invasive, and requires more training than flexible sigmoidoscopy to perform. It requires conscious sedation, but can be safely performed by primary care providers in the office setting, lessening some expense (charges for facilities and consultation) (33). Its use as a screening tool is recommended by most organizations for individuals with the highest risk of colon cancer. These include women with a long history of ulcerative colitis, familial polyposis, personal history of previous adenomatous polyps, family cancer syndrome, or previous carcinoma of the colon.

Summary of Preventive Care

Chronic illness is seen more frequently in the middle-aged woman than in younger women. Much of the illness that is encountered or developing during this period in life is caused by lifestyle-related choices, genetic risk, and common stresses of living. Women need information in order to be proactive in their own health-associated behaviors, and the provider has a key role in educating and empowering the woman to make choices that reflect her best interest. The emphasis of preventive care in middle age begins to shift increasingly towards prevention of function as well as prevention of disease.

Special Considerations for Nurse Practitioners and Physician Assistants

Midlife should viewed as more than a transition or preparation for old age and death. For most women, it is, or can be, a dynamic period of generativity, growth, and satisfaction. Providers must guard against stereotyping midlife women as dysfunctional because of menopause, devastated because of "empty nest" syndrome, or overwhelmed because of multiple roles associated with the sandwich generation. In actuality, most of these women are not providing extensive parent care or saddened by their children leaving home. In fact, midlife is a quality time, the prime of life for many women (34).

Many transitions will occur during these years, some of which the woman expects and for which the provider can help her plan (e.g., menopause). Other disruptions in her life occur because of changes in the lives of others, e.g., a parent's illness or an adult child's moving back home. Some transitions are more subtle and gradual, including gaining weight or slipping into unhealthy habits. At times, it may be the provider who helps women realize the potential impact of these changes on her overall health (35).

The disagreement among experts about

screening recommendations makes it difficult for providers to make some decisions about screening of asymptomatic women. In addition, associated risks, costs, time involved, and the possibility of false-positive results have to be considered. Clinicians are obligated to provide women with information about screening tests, leaving the decision about having the test in the woman's control (36).

Midlife is a complex time, making it necessary for providers and their women patients to fit health promotion practices into the context of women's multiple roles and relationships. An exercise program, for example, is not likely to be sustained if it requires a complete reordering of daily activities (34). Likewise, needed nutritional changes become difficult if the woman perceives lack of family support or if her work habits are not considered.

Promoting health for midlife women can take place through one-on-one contact in the primary care setting. Grouping of patients for a comprehensive screening and education program is also a possibility. Community education and screening programs are often available, but not all are aimed at lower-income groups. Because some of the community programs are marketing ventures for hospitals or pharmaceutical products, providers must be informed about the program to be sure it meets patient needs (37). Community workshops enable providers to share knowledge with large groups of women in civic clubs, volunteer group settings, and church groups (38).

References

1. Wells KB, Stewart A, Hays RD, et al. The functioning and well-being of depressed patients: results from the Medical Outcomes Study. JAMA 1989;262:914–919.
2. Butler RN, Collins KS, Meier DE, Muller CF, Pinn VW. Older women's health; "taking the pulse" reveals gender gap in medical care. Geriatrics 1995;50:39–40.
3. Bachmann GA. Sexuality in older women. Menopausal Women 1995;3:1–5.
4. Riley GF, Potosky AL, Lubitz JD, Brown ML. Stage of cancer at diagnosis for Medicare HMO and fee-for-service enrollees. Am J Public Health 1994;84:1598–1604.
5. Ostlund RE, Staten M, Kort WM, Schultz J, Malley M. The ratio of waist-to-hip circumference, plasma insulin level, and glucose intolerance as independent predictors of HDL2 cholesterol level in older adults. N Engl J Med 1990;322:229–334.
6. Egger G. The case of using waist to hip ratio measurements in routine medical checks. Med J Aust 1992;156:280–285.
7. Folsom AR, Kaye S, Sellers TA, et al. Body fat distribution and 5-year risk of death in older women. JAMA 1993;269:483–487.
8. Clinician's Handbook of Preventive Services. US Department of Health and Human Services, Public Health Service, 1994:135–140.
9. Chapuy MC, Arlot ME, Duboeuf F, et al. Vitamin D$_3$ and calcium to prevent hip fractures in elderly women. N Engl J Med 1992;327:1637–1642.
10. Galindo-Ciocon D, Ciocon JO, Galindo D. Functional impairment among elderly women with osteoporotic vertebral fractures. Rehabil Nurs 1995;20:79–83.
11. Adler RA, Rosen CJ. Glucocorticoids and osteoporosis. Endocrinol Metab Clin North Am 1994;23:641–654.
12. Nuovo J, Ellsworth, Christensen DB, Reynolds R. Excessive thyroid hormone replacement therapy. J Am Board Fam Pract 1995;8:435–439.
13. Kanis JA. Assessment of fracture risk and its application to screening for post-menopausal osteoporosis:synopsis of a WHO report. Osteoporosis Int 1994;4:368–381.
14. Kaplan B, Neri A, Kitai E, Pardo Y, Blum M, Friedman J. Low-does estrogen replacement therapy in early post-menopausal women. Effect on urinary magnesium and calcium:creatinine ratios. Clin Exp Obstet Gynecol 1994;21:170–172.
15. Preisinger E, Alacamliogu Y, Pils K, Saradeth T, Schneider B. Therapeutic exercise in the prevention of bone loss. A controlled trial with women after menopause. Am J Phys Med Rehabil 1995;74:120–123.
16. Ringa V, Durieux P, Breart G. Bone mass measurements around menopause and prevention of osteoporotic fractures. Eur J Obstet Gynecol Reprod Biol 1994;54:205–213.
17. National Cholesterol Education Program. Second Report of the National Cholesterol Education Program Panel on Detection, Evaluation, and Treatment of High Blood Cholesterol in Adults (Adult Treatment Panel II). Bethesda, MD: National Institutes of Heart, Lung, and Blood Institute. USDHHS Pub. No. NIH 93-3095, 1993.
18. Bass KM, Newshaffer CJ, Klag MJ, Bush TL. Plasma lipoprotein levels as predictors of cardiovascular death in women. Arch Intern Med 1993;153:2209–2216.
19. Expert Panel on Detection, Evaluation, and Treatment of High Blood Cholesterol in Adults. Sum-

mary of the Second Report of the National Cholesterol Education Program (NCEP) Expert Panel on Detection, Evaluation, and Treatmentof High Blood Cholesterol in Adults (Adult Treatment Panel II). JAMA 1993;269:3015–3023.

20. Walsh JME, Grady D.Treatment of hyperlipidemia in women. JAMA 1995;274:1152–1158.
21. Krowlewski AS, Warren JH, Valsania P, et al. Evolving natural history of coronary artery disease in diabetes mellitus. Am J Med 1991;90(suppl 2A):56S–61S.
22. The Writing Group for the PEPI trial. Effects of estrogens or estrogen/progestin regimens on heart disease in postmenopausal women. JAMA 1995;273:199–208.
23. Goldschmidlt MG. Dyslipidemia and ischemic heart disease mortality in men and women with diabetes. Circulation 1994;89:991–997.
24. Hartung GH, Moore CE, Mitchell R, Kappus CM. Relationship of menopausal status and exercise levels to HDL cholesterol in women. Exp Aging Res 1987;10:13–18.
25. Willet WC, Manson JE, Stampfer MJ, et al. Weight, weight change, and coronary heart disease in women: risk within the "normal" weight range. JAMA 1995;273:461–465.
26. Clinician's Handbook of Preventive Services. US Department of Health and Human Services, Public Health Service, 1994:223–226.
27. Clinician's Handbook of Preventive Services. US Department of Health and Human Services, Public Health Service, 1994:201–205.
28. Hoskins KF, Stopfer JE, Calzone KA, et al. Assessment and counseling for women with a family his-tory of breast cancer. A guide for clinicians. JAMA 1995;273:577–585.
29. Slattery ML, Kerber RA. A comprehensive evaluation of family history and breast cancer risk. The Utah population database. JAMA 1993;1563–1568.
30. Giovannucci E, Rimm ER, Stampfer MJ, Colditz GA, Ascherio A, Willett WC. Aspirin use and the risk of colorectal carcinoma and adenoma in male health professionals. Ann Intern Med 1994:121:241–246.
31. Mandel JS, Bond JH, et al. Reducing cancer mortality from colorectal cancer by screening for fecal occult blood. N Engl J Med 1993;328:1365–1371.
32. Cauffman JG, Hara JH, Rasgon IM, Clark VA. Flexible sigmoidoscopy in asymptomatic women with negative fecal occult blood tests. J Fam Pract 1993;34:281–286.
33. Rodney WM, Dabov G, Chronic C. Evolving colonoscopy skills in a rural family practice: the first 293 cases. Fam Pract Res J 1993;13:43–52.
34. Fogel CI, Woods NF. Midlife women's health. In: Fogel CI, Woods NF, eds. Women's Health Care. Thousand Oaks, CA: Sage, 1995:79–100.
35. Frank MEV. Transition into midlife. NAACOG's Clin Issues Perinatal Women's Health Nurs 1991;2:421–428.
36. Murphy PA. Primary care for women: screening tests and preventive services recommendations. J Nurse Midwifery 1995;40:74–87.
37. Garner CH. Midlife women's health. NAACOG's Clin Issues Perinatal Women's Health Nurs 1992;2:473–481.
38. Lowdermilk DL. Preventive health care for mid-life women. Capsule Comments Perinatal Women's Health Nurs 1995;1:25–34.

Estrogen Replacement Therapy

Mindy Smith and Leslie A. Shimp

Introduction

Women approach menopause with varying degrees of comfort and concern. As with many life transitions, health care providers can play a pivotal role in anticipatory guidance by raising questions about a woman's understanding and expectations of menopause and her knowledge and interest in hormone replacement therapy (HRT). This chapter will provide an overview of the evidence on the dual role of HRT, the relief of potential menopausal symptoms and the prevention of disease. Risks of HRT and many concerns of women will be discussed in decision making. Alternate approaches for managing symptoms will be presented. If treatment is selected, information on pretreatment assessment, choice of medication, dosing schedule, duration of hormone therapy, and the management of common side effects is presented.

Estrogen Replacement Therapy (ERT)

As women age, ovarian secretion of estrogen decreases until there is no significant contribution by the ovaries to circulating estrogen. The rate and degree of decline in circulating estrogen vary from woman to woman, but levels decrease in all women to 30% or less of the levels present before menopause. The decline in circulating estrogen may be associated with early symptoms of menopause and the long-term potential adverse effects of osteoporosis and cardiovascular disease.

Osteoporosis

Over 90% of patients affected by osteoporosis are postmenopausal women. Between 25 and 44% of postmenopausal women develop osteoporosis-related fractures, most commonly fractures of the vertebrae, hip, and distal forearm. Among white women, the rate of osteoporotic fractures is approximately 8 per 1000 woman-years, whereas for African-American women the rate is 3 per 1000 (1). Although the white and Asian races have an increased risk for osteoporosis-related fractures, African-American women have higher rates of death within the first 6 months after a hip fracture compared to white women (2).

Estrogen therapy can slow the development of osteoporosis and decrease the risk for osteoporosis-related fractures. In 1984, an NIH conference on osteoporosis recommended estrogen therapy as the best measure for preventing and treating osteoporosis (3). Studies suggest that women who have ever taken estrogen have a relative risk of 0.75 for hip fractures compared to nonusers. Fractures of the distal forearm are decreased by approxi-

mately 50% among women who have taken estrogen for 10 or more years and decreased rates of vertebral fractures were reported in three prospective studies (4, 5). A large study by Riggs and colleagues showed the impressive protective effect of estrogen (6). Compared to a placebo group that experienced 834 vertebral fractures per 1000 patient years, and the calcium alone group that experienced 419 fractures per 1000 patient years, the estrogen plus calcium (and fluoride, which is no longer recommended) group experienced only 53 vertebral fractures per 1000 patient years. Similarly, Lindsay et al. reported that after 10 years of therapy, spinal bone mass was 29% greater in women taking estrogen than in the placebo group (7).

Ideally, for maximal inhibition of bone loss, therapy would begin at menopause and continue at least until age 70 years, and perhaps lifelong, because most bone fractures occur after 75 years of age (7). Recent data suggest that at least 5 to 7 years of estrogen therapy is required for persistent long-term effects on bone density and a corresponding decrease in fractures (5, 8). Limiting estrogen exposure to only 5 to 10 years of therapy at the time of menopause is unlikely to have an effect that will persist to age 75 years. Furthermore, there is evidence that suggests after age 70 to 75 years, estrogen is less influential in preventing bone loss (8). Estrogen also appears to be effective in protecting against further bone loss if therapy is initiated many years (10 to 15 or more) postmenopause (9, 10). However, if estrogen therapy is discontinued, bone loss occurs, usually at a rate similar to that seen at menopause (7, 9).

Cardiovascular and Cerebrovascular Disease

Cardiovascular (CV) disease is the leading cause of death for women in the United States, and the incidence of cardiovascular disease increases significantly after menopause (11).

Many studies have shown a cardioprotective effect of estrogen. The cardiovascular benefits of estrogen include a decreased rate of coronary heart disease (CHD), a decreased death rate from both CHD and CV disease, reduced coronary artery occlusion, improved survival of women with coronary stenosis, decreased risk of myocardial infarction (MI), and a decrease in all-cause mortality (12). Most studies reported a 50% reduction in CHD; a recent meta-analysis reported the relative risk for users for MI was 0.56 (CI, 0.5 to 0.61)(11, 13).

The recent International Consensus Conference on Postmenopausal Hormone Therapy and the Cardiovascular System concluded that unopposed estrogen therapy may have a place in primary prevention of CV disease in "selected" postmenopausal women (14). Given the prevalence of CV disease and its associated morbidity and mortality, the use of estrogen for primary prevention was felt to outweigh its potential risks in almost all women; no subgroup of women could be identified in which the risk was greater than the benefit. However, women with significant CV disease are the most likely to benefit from estrogen therapy; death from coronary artery disease was reduced to a greater extent for women with severe coronary occlusion compared to women with mild disease (12, 14).

Most of the studies showing a cardioprotective effect of estrogen used oral estrogens. Oral estrogens are known to have the most favorable effect on lipids. The International Consensus Conference concluded that there were not enough long-term data to show a cardioprotective effect from nonoral estrogen. However, this group did suggest that in women with elevated triglycerides, nonoral estrogen might be considered (14). Schwartz et al., echoing the International Consensus Conference, have recommended oral conjugated equine estrogen (CEE) in a daily dose of 0.625 mg for a cardioprotective effect (12).

Concerning stroke, the data are inconclusive. The pooled estimate of relative risk of stroke for HRT users in a meta-analysis of 15 studies was 0.96 (95% confidence index, 0.65 to 1.45) (15).

Cancer

Most studies agree that ERT given to a woman with an intact uterus increases the risk for endometrial cancer. The risk is estimated to increase between three- to sixfold with relatively short duration of use, as little as 3 to 10 years, and to increase 10-fold after a decade or more of therapy. The risk for this cancer increases with both increasing dose and duration of therapy and, unfortunately, persists for years after estrogen therapy is discontinued (16–18). Both continuous daily therapy and regimens in which estrogen use is stopped for 5 to 7 days per month carry a similar risk (18).

The association between estrogen use and ovarian cancer is less clear. Of 10 case-control studies in the United States, none showed a significant association (17).

One of the most significant unanswered questions regarding postmenopausal hormone therapy is the possible association with breast cancer. Early data from individual studies and several meta-analyses indicated that estrogen therapy did little to increase the risk for breast cancer (17, 19). However, these studies were limited by their inability to address the risk of long-term therapy and the differential in risk for ever-users compared with current users. Currently, the consensus opinion suggests (*a*) less than 5 years of use is associated with little increase in risk; (*b*) with a longer duration of use such as 10 to 15 years or more, the risk is increased by approximately 30 to 50%; (*c*) previous use seems to cause little increased risk, after therapy is discontinued for several years; (*d*) older women, women who had a late menopause, and women with a previous history of breast cancer are at highest risk; and (*e*) doses greater than 1.25 mg CEE are associated with a higher risk than are lower doses (16, 17, 19–21).

Hormone Replacement Therapy (HRT): The Impact of the Addition of Progestin Therapy to ERT

Osteoporosis

Estrogen has been documented to increase calcium absorption from the GI tract, decrease bone resorption, and retard postmenopausal bone loss. It has been suggested that the addition of progesterone may increase the production of new bone (22). However, this effect has not been uniformly demonstrated and it is uncertain whether the newer progesterones or different dosing regimens will confirm this effect.

Cardiovascular Disease

With respect to cardiovascular disease, the effect of progestins on lipids has received the most attention to date. The impact again depends on both the type of progestin used and the regimen (sequential/cyclic or continuous) (23). Using sequential HRT, most studies show a significant decrease in LDL and small decreases of cyclic changes in HDL. Triglycerides are reported to be unchanged. This may represent an improvement in lipid profile, because ERT alone results in elevations of triglycerides. For continuous regimens, most studies show a decrease in LDL and cholesterol. Because only 30 to 50% of cardiovascular risk is attributed to lipoproteins, and some studies of HRT have shown a return of lipid levels to baseline over time, longer follow-up periods are needed to assess the potential benefits on lipids and on patient outcome.

One of the largest randomized trials of HRT, the Postmenopausal Estrogen/Progestin Intervention Trial (PEPI), measured four endpoints relevant to cardiovascular disease: HDL-C, systolic blood pressure (SBP), serum insulin, and fibrinogen (24). Eight hundred and seventy-five healthy women were randomized to placebo, ERT, or three different regimens of HRT (two cyclic and one continuous regimen) and were followed for 3 years. Women on the placebo treatment had a slight lowering of HDL-C over time (1.2 mg/dL), increases in SBP (1.2 mm Hg), a decreased postchallenge insulin level, and a slight increase in fibrinogen level. All treatment groups showed significant increases in HDL-C, with the most favorable change seen with either women on unopposed estrogen (5.6 mg/dL) or estrogen with cyclic microprogesterone (4.1 mg/dL). Active treatment (all groups) resulted in decreased LDL (14.5 to 17.7 mg/dL) and increased triglycerides (11.4 to 13.7 mg/dL) compared to placebo. There was no effect on SBP or postchallenge insulin level between groups. Fibrinogen increased significantly less with all of the active treatment groups compared with placebo. As expected, unopposed estrogen therapy resulted in increased risks of adenomatous or atypical hyperplasia (34% vs. 1 %) and of hysterectomy (6% vs. 1 %). This study confirms that both ERT and HRT improve HDL-C (the best predictor of heart disease in women).

Cancer

Progestins were added to ERT in the late 1970s after studies found an increased risk of endometrial hyperplasia and carcinoma with use of ERT alone. Gambrel et al. were among the first to demonstrate an endometrial protective effect of a progestin (25). The addition of progestin for 12 days to ERT lowered the rates of endometrial hyperplasia from > 20% among users of ERT to < 1% among users of HRT, with a concomitant rate reduction of endometrial cancer from 248/100,000 women years found in the general population to approximately 56/100,000. The effects of progestin on other organ systems is less certain, in part because the different types of progestogens possess different binding capacities on progesterone and androgen receptors.

The effect of HRT on the risk of breast cancer is still controversial. Although some studies report a protective (26) or no effect (27), others report a deleterious one (28). Endogenous progesterone appears to act synergistically with estrogen on breast mitotic activity. High doses of oral synthetic progestins have been used effectively in the treatment of breast cancer, but little can be implied about the lower doses used in HRT. Long-term studies of HRT are clearly needed.

Decision-Making

Risk-Benefit Analysis

The topic of long-term HRT is commonly approached as a risk-benefit analysis. Despite studies, there is still significant controversy regarding many aspects of HRT, including the optimal types and doses of these hormones, the extent of risk and degree of benefit, appropriate duration of therapy and even whether women should avoid or be encouraged to take HRT. Clearly, however, until more data are available, the decision to use postmenopausal hormone therapy must be made with incomplete information. Women should be educated about the potential risks and benefits of hormone therapy and that the individual's health goals, risk profile, and concerns are weighed, particularly when long-term therapy is considered.

Risk-benefit analysis is designed to provide insight into the consequences of long-term therapy by estimating the effect of therapy on longevity and the likelihood that patients will develop or avoid certain medical conditions. When this type of analysis is applied to postmenopausal hormone therapy, the analysis usually includes possible increased risks for endometrial and breast cancer and possible decreased risks for CHD and osteoporosis. In addition, some analyses include other risks or benefits, such as the risk of stroke, gynecologic procedures and hysterectomy, colon cancer, and myocardial infarction.

The basis for the analyses is estimates of alteration in risk because of exposure to hormone therapy. These analyses are population-based and generally provide little guidance to individual women, although recent reports have attempted to address which women would benefit to the greatest extent (4, 29). Still, the concern that remains is that published benefits may be overestimated if generally healthier women are more likely to be prescribed estrogen therapy and risks may be underestimated if higher risk women (e.g., family history of breast cancer) are excluded from therapy.

The most commonly cited risks of postmenopausal hormone therapy are endometrial cancer and breast cancer (Table 20.1). The two benefits of postmenopausal estrogen routinely cited in risk-benefit analyses are a decreased risk for osteoporosis-related fractures and coronary heart disease. Although there is disagreement in the risk-benefit estimates, the figures presented in the table reflect consensus from the literature. Because CHD is the most common cause of death for postmenopausal women and these analyses measure risk-benefit in terms of mortality, estrogen's benefit on decreasing cardiovascular mortality overshadows the number of deaths attributed to cancer, even if a 30% increase in the risk for breast cancer is included in the analysis. This has led many investigators to conclude that HRT should be prescribed for almost all women. Although heart disease is a common condition, the percentage of women affected by osteoporosis is only 10 to 20% (30), so many women may not develop either condition. In addition, the benefit of ERT/HRT is often not differentiated from the benefits of other concurrent health behaviors (e.g., exercise, dietary changes). Healthier women with good health behaviors may be more likely to continue to

Table 20.1. Risks and Benefits of Hormone Replacement Therapy

	Risk for Untreated Women	Risk with ERT	Risks with HRT
Endometrial cancer	Lifetime risk 2.6%	Risk is increased 4–11 fold	Little added risk if progestin is added for at least 10 days per month
		Higher dose and longer duration associated with greater risk	
		5-year survival for low grade–early stage cancers 92% in one study	Some regimens may provide greater protection than others
Breast cancer	Lifetime risk 10%	No increased risk short-term (<5 years) therapy may be a 15–30% risk for longterm therapy	Most data suggests the risk is similar to that for ERT; it has been suggested that progestins increase or decrease the risk
Osteoporosis	15% lifetime probability of hip fracture (white women)	Estrogens reduce the incidence of fractures of hip, spine, and wrist by 50% after 6–10 years of therapy	Progestins do not negate estrogen's effect on bone
	10–20% of women develop osteoporosis	The benefit of therapy related to both dose and duration; a dose of 0.625 mg of CEE is the minimal dose required; 5–7 years the minimum length of therapy for long-term effect.	
Coronary heart	46% lifetime probability of developing—31% dying from CHD	Estrogen (current use) reduces risk of CHD by 50%; ever-users have two-thirds risk of non-controversial users	Progestins may reduce benefit up to 50%—data
	By age 60, one in 17 women have had a coronary event	Benefit is greatest for women with diagnosed CHD	Progestins vary in the extent of lipid alterations
	After age 60, CHD is the primary cause of death for women, for women age 50 or older the average annual CHD mortality rate is 3.8%		MPA has little lipid effect

take ERT. However, some data suggest that estrogen can offer cardiovascular benefits even when variables known to increase the risk for CHD (e.g., HTN, DM, tobacco use, elevated cholesterol, obesity) are considered (31). Consistent with this idea is the recommendation that ERT or HRT is most appropriately prescribed for certain subgroups of women, particularly women with CHD (29, 32).

The use of ERT or HRT provides a magnitude of benefits similar to other common preventive interventions such as treatment of high blood pressure or elevated cholesterol, or recommending a patient stop smoking (29, 32). In addition, the extent of benefit is likely to be related to duration of use; decreased mortality or life years gained is most likely to be seen after at least 10 to 15 years of therapy (32). Furthermore, ERT/HRT may provide benefits that improve the quality of life and decrease mortality.

At this time, the data from the risk-benefit analysis can be a starting point for discussion but risk factors for a particular individual should be carefully considered. Not all women are likely to benefit from ERT/HRT. Women with CHD appear likely to benefit, whereas women with a family or individual history of breast cancer may be at particular risk from therapy; for many women, the optimal course of action will be unclear (4, 29).

Women's Concerns

Menopause is an important transition in a woman's life. Over the past decade, the medical literature has virtually been flooded with reports of the many adverse health events following menopause, events that need to be prevented and/or treated with hormonal therapy. This view of menopause, as an estrogen-deficient state that heralds the onset of aging and illness, has many consequences for women in this country—in the way they view themselves, in the information that they receive, and in their willingness to consider ERT/HRT.

In truth, there is significant disagreement about which health consequences can be attributed to aging, which are particular to the individual woman and her life situation, and which are specific to the lowered serum estrogen concentration and absence of menses that defines menopause. For example, despite lower serum estrogen levels, Japanese women have lower rates of cardiovascular disease than white women (33). It is difficult to ascribe symptoms to menopause when few studies have attempted to correlate symptoms with hormonal status in population samples. One of the few studies examining this issue, a survey of 850 British women age 45 to 65 years, found that vasomotor symptoms (hot flushes and night sweats), difficulty falling asleep, decreased sexual interest, and vaginal dryness were significantly associated with cessation of menses, after controlling for the effects of age (34). Sexual satisfaction, however, did not change with menopausal status, and other symptoms commonly attributed to menopause, such as cognitive difficulties, depression, irritability, and various somatic symptoms, were more strongly predicted by social class and employment status (see Chapter 23).

Even the presence of vasomotor symptoms is highly variable and strongly influenced by culture. Population surveys of women age 45 to 55 years performed in different countries demonstrated significant differences in reported rates of symptoms with 12.3, 31, and 34.8% of Japanese, Canadian, and US women reporting vasomotor symptoms (35). Severity of vasomotor symptoms appears to have a major impact on the perception of other "menopausal" symptoms such as tenseness and irritability, with women with severe vasomotor complaints reporting higher percentages of somatic and psychological symptoms and poorer overall well-being regardless of whether or not they were still menstruating (36). Although menopause is a universal biologic phenomenon among women of all racial and ethnic groups, its meaning, and even the associated symptoms, appear to be highly individual and influenced by both race and culture.

Although many providers appropriately consider the potential health risks and benefits listed above in counseling women about HRT, women primarily come to medical attention seeking relief of symptoms (often depression), and for education and support (37). The fact that less than 20% of postmenopausal women in the United States have ever had ERT or HRT prescribed, and less than 40% of those women will continue it after 1 year (38), signals a need to understand and address the concerns of women when approaching treatment decisions.

How then do women view menopause? In a 1994 report of a random population sample of women from the Netherlands (n = 234, age 45 to 65 years), nearly all women regarded the absence of menstruation with relief and most preferred a natural approach to the problems encountered (39). Only one of three peri- and postmenopausal women were troubled enough by the symptoms to have consulted a provider, and only 12% of the women were current users of HRT. Attitudes towards the use of HRT were neutral, but the level of knowledge about menopause was judged by the investigators to be poor, and most women obtained their information from the media.

There are many reported reasons for poor medication compliance, including lack of understanding of the reasons for taking hormones, fear of breast cancer, reactivation of uterine bleeding, and concern about side effects. In a survey of women graduates of Stanford, respondents indicated a much greater concern about breast cancer than heart disease, with 65% rating the risk of breast cancer as the most important concern compared to 27% rating the benefit on heart disease to be most important. In general, women perceived their risk of heart disease as low (73% rated risk of developing heart disease by age 70 as < 1%) and their risk of breast cancer high (52% perceived risk of developing breast can-

cer by age 70 years as > 10 %) (40). Although more accurate information on actual risk may be useful to women considering HRT, women are likely indicating value judgments and personal preferences that may more strongly inform treatment choices than population prevalence rates and risks.

In an attempt to understand women's decision making, Schmitt et al. studied 265 women who estimated their likelihood of taking ERT/HRT to alleviate menopausal symptoms when faced with hypothetical cases (41). They identified four groups with respect to their approach to this decision: (1) one group (n = 120) for whom the predominant factor was severity of hot flashes, (2) a second group (n = 83), the most highly educated women, who were influenced by both vasomotor symptoms and osteoporosis risk, (3) a third group (n = 40) influenced both by severity of hot flashes and by concern about resumption of menses, and (4) a fourth group (n = 9) for whom cancer risk most influenced choice. It should be noted that 14 women were removed from the analysis because most of them gave consistent responses indicating no probability of taking ERT under any circumstances. Addressing a woman's predominant concerns may result in greater success in assisting women with this decision.

Different aspects of ERT/HRT may be more appropriate to discuss at different times. For example, a lengthy discussion of risks and benefits of HRT is inappropriate for a women currently highly distressed with hot flashes, but becomes more important later in assessing her need and willingness to continue with treatment.

Side effects, often termed nuisance effects, of ERT and HRT are not a trivial matter for patients. In the Scottish study noted earlier, side effects were reported in 38% of the 101 current and previous users of hormones and included weight gain, nausea, depression, headache, and breast tenderness (regardless of hormone preparation) (42). Information on rates of individual side effects was difficult to find and primarily came from older studies. With respect to breast tenderness, 9 of 31 women (27%) taking hormones (but no control subjects) had mammographic evidence of increased breast density, and 7 of these women had moderate or severe breast pain following treatment (43). A paradoxical improvement in breast pain has also been reported following initiation of HRT among women with frequent tenderness at baseline (44). Women should be counseled about the likelihood of some breast tenderness (13 to 32%), but those with current breast tenderness may actually note some improvement.

Premenstrual symptoms of bloating, headache, irritability, and fluid retention were reported by one investigator to be the most common side effects of HRT, occurring in 15% of women; however, no data to support this estimate were provided. The issue of weight gain could not be substantiated from the literature reviewed: a prospective study showed no increase over a 2-year period in central body fat among estrogen users compared to an increase among women in the matched control group (45).

Women who have not undergone hysterectomy should also be advised that with HRT they may experience more difficulty with bleeding. In a study of cyclic HRT, the incidence of abnormal vaginal bleeding necessitating gynecologic procedures for evaluation was significantly higher (RR 3.1, 95% CI, 2.1–4.5), as was the rate of endometrial biopsy (RR 3.4, CI 2.3–5.1), and dilation and curettage (RR 1.5, CI 0.7–3.3) among women receiving HRT (46).

In summary, approximately one third of population samples and the majority of clinic samples of women in this country experience symptoms at the time of menopause (most often vasomotor), but most do not seek medical attention. Of those who do, symptom control is the primary motivation, and ERT/HRT is often prescribed. In deciding about whether to use ERT/HRT, knowledge about actual risks and benefits of treatment is often poor. Health care providers are encouraged to engage women in discussions about menopause and HRT early in the perimenopausal period. As women may vary in predominant concerns about HRT, soliciting this information and seeking to understand the individual woman's viewpoint is critical to imparting information and supporting her decision.

Once a treatment is prescribed, approximately one third of women experience troublesome side effects, and many do not appear to tolerate them, particularly the reactivation of menstrual bleeding. Rather than advising women that side effects such as breast tenderness are not life-threatening and should not be of concern, acknowledging the possibility of side effects and offering strategies for managing them should they be encountered (as outlined in the final section of this chapter) will likely improve compliance. Greater attention to women's desire for a natural progression through menopause and a better understanding of their perceptions of risk, vulnerability, and values will likely improve both treatment choices and compliance.

Pretreatment Assessment

History
In assessing the risks and benefits of ERT/HRT for the individual woman, several aspects of the history and physical examination are important (Table 20.2). Cancer risk is perhaps the most concerning feature of prescribing ERT/HRT. A case-control study of women who developed breast cancer during HRT, however, is reassuring (47). The investigators found that these women had fewer locally advanced tumors and more well-differentiated cancers. Unfortunately, available data, although demonstrating no association, are from case series (Wile) and case-control studies (Bonnier). Therefore little can be concluded about the safety of subsequent hormone therapy on cancer recurrence.

Table 20.2. Pretreatment Assessment for HRT

Parameter	Consideration
History	
Cancer	
(breast, endometrium)*	Uncertain risk of worsening or recurrence of cancer
Cholelithiasis	Estrogen increases the risk of gallstones
Diabetes mellitus	Estrogen may slow progression of atherosclerosis
Hypertension	Estrogen in OCP+ raises blood pressure
Hyperlipidemia	Estrogen may precipitate pancreatitis
Ischemic heart disease	HRT lowers risk of MI+ and stroke
Liver disease	Estrogen is metabolized by the liver, levels increase
Migraine headache	Possible increase in headache
Reactive airway disease	Potential exacerbation of disease
Smoking	Earlier menopause, predisposes to OP+ and IHD+
Thrombosis (DVT/PE)+	High-dose estrogen predisposes to clotting
Vaginal bleeding*	If undiagnosed, may represent endometrial CA+
Family history	
Breast cancer	Estrogen increases risk of breast cancer*
Heart disease	Estrogen decreases risk of heart disease
Osteoporosis	Estrogen decreases risk of bone loss
Physical examination	
Height and weight	Obesity predisposes to endometrial/breast CA
Blood pressure	Theoretically, ERT/HRT may raise blood pressure
Breast examination	Estrogen may stimulate the growth of breast CA
Pelvic examination	Uterine fibroids predispose to excessive bleeding
Laboratory tests (optional)	
Clotting factors	Estrogen may have unfavorable effects
Lipid profile	Preexisting hypertriglyceridemia, pancreatitis risk
Liver function tests	As above
Procedures	
Endometrial biopsy	ERT or continuous HRT may not prevent hyperplasia
Bone densitometry	This may be a deciding factor in initiating HRT

*Considered contraindications to HRT
+CA = cancer, DVT = deep vein thrombosis, IHD = ischemic heart disease, MI = myocardial infarction, OCP = oral contraceptive pill, OP = osteoporosis, PE = pulmonary embolis
*data primarily for ERT

Theoretically, breast cancers that are hormone-receptor negative, presumably unresponsive to estrogen, should not be considered contraindications to HRT. The question remains as to whether women, following removal of estrogen-receptor positive tumors of the breast or endometrium, will undergo progression of disease with HRT. The answer at present is unknown. If HRT is initiated and there is a recurrence of breast cancer, withdrawal from HRT has been shown in some cases to result in a temporary regression of metastatic disease (48). The use of ERT/HRT for women with other types of cancer does not appear to be an added risk.

Although the use of oral contraceptives

typically results in a small rise in blood pressure, the use of estrogen almost never raises blood pressure (49). In addition, because the presence of hypertension increases the risk of cardiovascular disease, ERT/HRT may be even more important to consider for this group of women. The same is true for women with ischemic heart disease and a history of a previous MI. Although there are no data directly addressing the benefit of HRT among women with previous stroke, there is no reason to believe that there would be a detrimental effect.

Estrogen is metabolized by the liver, and oral estrogen produces a pronounced hepatic response that alters bile composition and appears to lower the cholesterol saturation index (50). For women with existing gallstones, estrogen administered by transdermal route should be considered. Estrogen administered to women with active liver disease may result in increased circulating estrogen causing profound vasodilation. Caution should be exercised when considering ERT/HRT for these women.

Migraine headaches have been considered a relative contraindication to HRT because estrogens participate in the regulation of cerebral vasomotor tone and have been found to trigger or increase these headaches in approximately 3% of women initiating ERT (51). Although migraines have been implicated in stroke, this association does not appear to be valid, and ERT/HRT may be considered on an individual basis for these women. Because estrogen withdrawal can trigger migraine, continuous estrogen treatment is recommended. It may also be prudent to wait 4 to 12 weeks before initiating progesterone, so that it can be determined which, if any, hormone is affecting the headaches (50).

Reactive airway disease may be another relative contraindication for prescribing HRT. Although it is well known that bronchospasm can be exacerbated during the luteal phase of the menstrual cycle, it had not previously been reported with the administration of exogenous estrogen. A more recent report of ERT use among postmenopausal women with mild to moderate asthma found a subclinical worsening of disease activity measured by peak expiratory flow and use of inhalers (52). In this study, general feeling of well-being did not change during ERT.

In addition to the well-known adverse health effects of smoking on lipids, coagulation factors, and the risk of ischemic heart disease and osteoporosis, smoking tobacco alters the metabolism and lowers the serum concentration of estrogen. Because of this, women who smoke, despite being in greater need of the preventive aspects of ERT/HRT, may not receive the same benefit as women who do not smoke. Smokers also have an earlier onset of menopause. These facts may provide additional motivation for women to stop smoking.

The relative contraindication of thrombophlebitis has been questioned because evidence to support the association of ERT with increased venous thrombosis is lacking. The International Consensus Conference concluded that postmenopausal estrogen therapy does not increase the risk for thrombosis and, in low doses, ERT is not contraindicated in most women with a prior history of thrombosis or for women with collagen vascular diseases, such as lupus (14, 53). They also concluded that ERT does not have to be stopped prior to surgery. However, there is some evidence that high-dose estrogen may be thrombogenic in daily doses of 1.25 mg or more CEE (13).

Additional factors of importance include a family or personal history of heart disease or osteoporosis and conditions such as hyperlipidemia or diabetes mellitus that predispose a woman to accelerated ischemic heart disease. Inquiry into lifestyle factors is also important. Although preventive strategies in this area are covered elsewhere in this book, specific attention to dietary calcium, fat content, and food sources rich in phytoestrogens (e.g., soybeans, legumes), and exercise and smoking may influence the perceived need for preventive treatment with HRT.

Physical and Laboratory Examination

Physical examination factors of importance in the decision to begin ERT/HRT include the height and weight, blood pressure, breast examination, and pelvic examination. A clinical breast examination also provides an opportunity to review self breast-examination and encourage women to perform these checks monthly. Pelvic examination is performed both for cancer screening (cervical/ovarian) and for the presence of an enlarged uterus that may indicate the presence of myomas. The latter may predispose women to excessive or irregular bleeding on HRT.

If not previously assessed, a lipid profile should be considered prior to the prescription of ERT/HRT, especially if the woman is on a medication known to alter lipid profiles such as noncardioselective beta-blockers or thiazide diuretics. In women with severe hypertriglyceridemia, the precipitation of pancreatitis has been reported with ERT (54).

The need for and usefulness of measurements of bone density is still a subject of debate. A recent overview on bone mineral density (BMD) measurement suggested its use, using dual-energy radiograph absorptiometry, in two situations: (*a*) when a woman's decision to begin HRT rests only on her risk for osteoporosis, and (*b*) for purposes of follow-up, perhaps to increase medication compliance (55). Women at highest risk of osteoporosis are those with low baseline bone density and those experiencing high rates of bone loss, up to 30% of women (56).

No conclusions can be drawn, at present, about the best site for BMD measurement. Rozenberg et al. suggest that a vertebral site be considered for assessment in early menopause and the wrist or femur for older women (55). Although the relationship between initial BMD and fracture incidence is consistently

demonstrated (RR of between 1.4 and 2.6 per standard deviation decrease in BMD), the ability to estimate higher rates of bone loss is limited by poor precision in estimates of BMD.

The question of pretreatment endometrial biopsy is also a controversial one. For women selecting cyclic HRT, pretreatment biopsy is unwarranted because of the low prevalence of hyperplasia in otherwise healthy postmenopausal women. As well, HRT with at least 12 days of progestin has been shown to reverse preexisting hyperplasia in 98 to 99% of cases (57). Among women selecting continuous treatment, some investigators do recommend pretreatment biopsy, because endometrial hyperplasia may persist and there appears to be a poor correlation between endometrial histology and bleeding pattern; the presence of amenorrhea may not exclude endometrial pathology (58). Some investigators suggest use of a progestogen challenge test (12- to 13-day course of medroxyprogesterone acetate [Provera] 10 mg a day or norethindrone [Norlutin] 2.5 to 5 mg per day) for all menopausal women being considered for ERT/HRT to identify the presence of estrogen-primed endometrium, reserving biopsy for women who have withdrawal bleeding.

For women selecting ERT, a pretreatment biopsy and yearly biopsies thereafter has been suggested because the risk of endometrial cancer on this regimen increases fourfold. A diagnostic endometrial biopsy (or vaginal sonography) should be performed with any heavy, irregular, or mistimed bleeding once started on hormone replacement.

Routine screening for breast and cervical cancer is encouraged before initiating ERT/HRT. Although the rationale for the former is clear, the recommendation for the latter, particularly if HRT is selected, is not justified beyond the prevention guidelines for cervical cancer screening in the general population. After age 65 years, regular Pap smears may be discontinued. HRT is not contraindicated for women with cervical, epithelial ovarian, vulvar, or vaginal carcinomas (59).

Posttreatment Surveillance

Posttreatment surveillance of women on ERT/HRT, with the exception of endometrial biopsy, does not differ from the recommended preventive strategies for the general population. It should be remembered, however, that HRT may increase breast parenchymal density and lower mammography sensitivity making self- and clinical breast examination even more important.

Alternative Therapy

Alternatives to hormone therapy can be useful when a woman is reluctant to use hormone therapy or if she has a contraindication or intolerance to either estrogen or progestin. Estrogen is intolerable or unsafe for approximately 10% of women (60). Alternative therapy is generally not well studied and may not be as efficacious as hormone therapy.

There are many preventive therapies for cancer, osteoporosis, and heart disease that can be considered either general preventive therapies (e.g., exercise, avoiding tobacco, diet modification, ingestion of adequate amounts of calcium, maintaining lean weight, environmental modifications to decrease the risk of falls) or specific for medical conditions (e.g., treatment of hypertension or hypercholesteremia for prevention of heart disease). These therapies should be considered regardless of the decision to proceed with HRT.

Treatment of Hot Flashes

Progestin therapy can be used alone to treat hot flashes. The progestin best studied is MPA; it has been used as both the oral form (10 to 20 mg per day) and the injectable, depo-medroxyprogesterone acetate (DMPA), in doses of 50 to 150 mg monthly. In a number of studies MPA or DMPA was found to be superior to placebo in relieving hot flushes (60). One trial comparing 150 mg DMPA to 0.625 mg CEE found the two drugs to be equally effective; the percentage of patients who initially experienced a decrease in the number of hot flushes on CEE or DMPA was 62 and 69%, respectively (61).

The efficacy of DMPA therapy appears to increase with increasing doses. One study of 50-mg, 100-mg, and 150-mg doses found that hot flushes were relieved in 65 to 80%, 80 to 95%, and 85 to 100%, of patients, respectively (62). It may be appropriate to try a lower dose initially and titrate upward, because effects usually appear after 2 weeks and maximal benefit is seen at 4 weeks. Common side effects from progestin therapy are irregular bleeding, headache, and vaginal dryness. One study also reported a 10% incidence of depression in women treated with DMPA, but it was unclear how strongly this symptom was related to the drug therapy (60).

Clonidine has also been studied for the treatment of hot flashes, but its efficacy, both in oral and transdermal forms, is disputed (60, 63). Effective doses were in the range of 0.1 to 0.2 mg twice a day. However, it is recommended that a woman initially be treated orally with 0.05 mg twice daily and the dose titrated upward. The maximum daily dose is 2.4 mg. Side effects including orthostatic hypotension, sedation, fatigue, dizziness, and weakness are common. These symptoms may prompt many patients to discontinue therapy, so it is important to warn patients on clonidine not to suddenly stop the drug to prevent rebound hypertension. Transdermal clonidine is likely to be much better tolerated.

Bellergal-S (40 mg phenobarbital, 0.6 mg ergotamine, 0.2 mg belladonna alkaloids) is another agent that has been studied. There is little evidence supporting it use and, given the potential adverse effects (habituation to phenobarbital, sedation, contraindications to ergots such as peripheral or coronary vascular disease, and clinically significant drug-drug interactions) the use of this agent is rarely indicated (60, 64).

Some natural products have been suggested for relieving hot flashes. Many of the agents suggested anecdotally to be helpful contain natural estrogenic substances. These agents include ginseng, fenugreek, sarsaparilla, licorice root, and wild yam root (60).

Urogenital Atrophy

Dyspareunia and related vaginal symptoms may cause sexual intercourse to be uncomfortable for 8 to 25% of postmenopausal women. Continued sexual activity may lessen the severity of urogenital atrophy (60). Vaginal water-soluble lubricant products may offer some relief for both dyspareunia and other symptoms of urogenital atrophy such as vaginal dryness, itching, and burning. Lubricant products can be applied just at the time of sexual intercourse if dyspareunia is the primary symptom, or they can be used regularly to manage other symptoms. Judicious use of the lubricant products (initially 2 tablespoons can be applied several times daily; the dose can then be titrated in quantity and frequency to comfort) may provide relief of atrophic vaginitis. The effect of water-soluble lubricants may not be long-lasting, and products containing polycarbophil may provide a longer duration of benefit.

Osteoporosis

There is some limited evidence that progestins used alone may provide some protection against osteoporosis (61, 65). Progesterone may have an independent effect on bone, promoting bone formation, and may play a role in coupling bone resorption to bone formation as part of the normal bone cycle (66). Limited animal and human data suggest that progesterone stimulates the formation of bone and may decrease bone loss; various progestins have been used in the trials (66).

Management Guidelines

Selection of therapy for an individual woman is based on the goals of therapy and the woman's medical history. Duration of therapy is determined by whether the goal is to relieve symptoms such as hot flashes and insomnia or to prevent cardiovascular disease or osteoporosis. Similarly, the route of administration and dose are determined partially by the goal of therapy. For example, symptoms associated with urogenital atrophy can often be managed with intermittent low-dose topical therapy, although relieving hot flashes or preventing osteoporosis is generally treated with oral or transdermal therapy and higher doses of estrogen. The woman's personal medical history (e.g., blood pressure, history of venous thrombosis during pregnancy or while on an oral contraceptive), family history (e.g., breast cancer, heart disease, osteoporosis) and a pretreatment assessment (e.g., lipid profile, bone density measurement) will also provide a useful framework for determining optimal therapy.

Initiating Therapy

Selection of Estrogen Therapy

Both synthetic and natural estrogens are available. Although synthetic estrogens (e.g., ethinyl estradiol) are most commonly used in oral contraceptives, the natural estrogens (e.g., conjugated equine estrogen, 1 7–13-estradiol) are preferred for ERT because they have lower potency in stimulating liver proteins and fewer metabolic effects (67). Ethinyl estradiol is estimated to be 1000 times more potent in stimulating liver proteins as conjugated equine estrogen (CEE).

The estrogen with the strongest receptor affinity at the cellular level is estradiol. Transdermal estrogen (~ estradiol) produces the most

Errata for *Women's Health in Primary Care*, edited by Jo Ann Rosenfeld

Page 448, column 2, line 33 should read "causes for loss of flow and ovulation are." The full sentence should read "By definition, hypothalamic causes for loss of flow and ovulation are adaptive and reversible."

Page 449, column 1, lines 41-43 should read "progesterone 300 mg/d) for 14 days (days 14 through 27 of the calendar month). Continuous dosing of progesterone every day and cyclic estrogen as." The corrected sentences should read "Medroxyprogesterone or progesterone should be prescribed in physiological doses (MPA 10 mg/d or oral micronized progesterone 300 mg/d) for 14 days (days 14 through 27 of the calendar month). Continuous dosing of progesterone every day and cyclic estrogen as described will cause, in 85% of women, amenorrhea without risk of osteoporosis."

physiologic ratio of estradiol to estrone, while oral CEE results in higher estrone levels than estradiol levels. The clinical implications of these differences are unclear.

The ability of estrogen to relieve menopausal symptoms and to maintain bone density is dependent on achieving an adequate serum concentration. The estradiol level achieved by a dose of 0.625 mg CEE is able to relieve menopausal symptoms in most women, and is the lowest dose that is adequate to prevent osteoporosis in 90% of women. This is also the dose commonly employed by studies in which a cardiovascular benefit was demonstrated for women taking estrogen. Therefore, it is recommended that estrogen therapy be initiated with a daily dose 0.625 mg of CEE or an equivalent (70). Reevaluation of the dose should be done only after 3 months of therapy, because it takes this long for the maximum effect to occur (71).

If menopausal symptoms continue, the estrogen dose can be increased to 0.9 to 1.25 mg CEE. Higher doses of estrogen are rarely required to manage menopausal symptoms. However, higher doses (e.g., 1.25 mg CEE) might be needed to relieve symptoms in women just after surgical menopause or to treat a woman with osteoporosis-related fractures. If higher doses are initially required for relief of menopausal symptoms, the estrogen dose can often be decreased after 1 to 2 years of therapy (72).

If therapy is begun solely to treat menopausal symptoms, it can be discontinued after several years when symptoms decrease. Tapering off of estrogen therapy is recommended to avoid provoking symptoms from a sudden decrease in estrogen levels (73). In contrast, the treatment of symptoms associated with urogenital atrophy can generally be accomplished with topical therapy administered only twice a week. However, topical therapy should be initiated with 3 to 4 weeks of daily administration (71).

Estrogen is usually administered orally or transdermally. In general, oral therapy is pre-

ferred (70). However, transdermal therapy may be more appropriate for certain subgroups of patients (74). Oral therapy is preferred because of the controversy about whether the transdermal preparations will have the same cardioprotective effect as has been demonstrated for oral therapy (67). Transdermal estrogen avoids the "first-pass effect" of liver metabolism and serum levels are more consistent. This may be useful for patients who notice estrogenic side effects at times of peak serum concentrations or menopausal symptoms when trough serum concentrations occur. However, some patients using the transdermal patch may notice an increase in vasomotor symptoms at the end of the dosing interval for the patch as estradiol levels begins to decline (68). Similarly, because tobacco stimulates liver metabolism, it has been suggested that tobacco smokers may benefit from transdermal delivery of estrogen (74). Exposure of the liver to oral estrogen may cause greater effects on clotting factors and lipids (68). Women with a history of thromboembolism, migraine headaches, isolated hypertriglyceridemia, or gall stones may be better candidates for transdermal therapy, although women with elevated cholesterol levels should receive oral therapy. Transdermal therapy, because it provides lower serum levels of estrone, may be less likely to promote cystic breast changes (74).

Selection of Progestin Therapy

Progestins are categorized into three types by the parent chemical compound: progesterone derivatives (e.g., micronized progesterone), 17-hydroxy-progesterone derivatives (e.g., medroxyprogesterone acetate), and 19-nortestosterone derivatives (e.g., norethindrone, norgestrel) (Table 20.3). Micronized progesterone is a natural progesterone, but because of variability in absorption and metabolism between women, the synthetic progestins are more widely used in the United States (68). MPA has properties similar to natural progesterone and a lesser potential for adverse lipid effects

Table 20.3. Estrogens and Progestins Available

ESTROGENS	Tradename	Dosage Form	Doses Available
Estrones			
Conjugated equine estrogen	Premarin and generics	Oral	0.3, 0.625, 0.9, 1.25, 2.5 mg
		Vaginal cream	0.0625%
Esterified estrogens	Estratab, Menest	Oral	0.3, 0.625, 1.25, 2.5 mg
Estropipate	Ogen, generic	Oral	0.625, 1.25, 2.5, 5 mg
		Vaginal cream	0.15%
Estradiols			
Estradiol (micronized)	Estrace	Oral	1 or 2 mg
		Vaginal cream	0.01%
(17-B-estradiol)	Estraderm, Climara	Transdermal	0.05, 0.1 mg/24 h
Ethinyl estradiol	Estinyl, Feminone	Oral	0.02, 0.05 mg
Nonsteroidal Estrogen			
Dienestrol	Ortho-Dienestrol, DV	Vaginal	0.01%
PROGESTINS			
17-hydroxyprogesterone derivative			
Medroxyprogesterone acetate	Provera, generic	Oral	2.5–10 mg
19-nortestosterone derivative			
Norethindrone	Micronor, Norlutin	Oral	5 mg
Norgestrel	Ovrette	Oral	0.075 mg
Progesterone derivative			
Micronized progesterone	Only bulk powder for compounding available in the United States		300–400 mg

Abstracted from Jones KP. Estrogens and Progestins: What to use and how to use it. Clin Obstet Gynecol 1992;35:871–883.

and androgenic side effects than the 19-nor-testosterone derivatives (67, 68).

Gambrell has suggested that previous menstrual symptoms might help guide selection of a progestin (75). The 19-nor-testosterone derivatives might be a better choice for women who experience dysmenorrhea or heavy menstrual bleeding, because menstrual flow is generally lighter and shorter with these androgenic progestins. Conversely, if a woman had previously experienced breast symptoms, such as tenderness, or had a history of fibrocystic disease, a 17-hydroxyprogesterone derivative would be more suitable.

Progestin therapy is indicated for women who have not had a hysterectomy and need endometrial protection (70). Progestin therapy is protective by converting the proliferative endometrium created by estrogen therapy to a secretory endometrium. This conversion requires 10 to 14 days of progestin therapy (68); 12 days of therapy are preferred by many providers. For cyclic therapy with oral estrogen, it has been thought that early bleeding (on day 10 or earlier) represents a proliferative endometrium, and the progestin dose should be increased until bleeding begins regularly on or after day 11 (71, 76). A small increase is often adequate (e.g., increase the daily dose of MPA from 10 mg to 15 mg). For a symptomatic perimenopausal woman being treated with hormone replacement therapy synchronizing the addition of progestin to her normal cycle avoids irregular bleeding (71).

The protective effect of sequential HRT on the endometrium has recently been questioned. In a study of 413 women using sequential HRT for greater than 6 months (mean duration 2.7 years), endometrial biopsies were performed prior to initiating continuous HRT (77). Most women had bleeding starting around day 13 after starting progestogen. There was no correlation between endometrial histology and the time of onset of bleeding. Complex hyperplasia was found in 2.7% of women. The investigators believe that although preexisting cystic and adenomatous hyperplasia has been found to revert to normal under the influence of progestogen, patients who progress to complex or atypical hyperplasia may not revert to normal. Consequently it would be expected that 3 to 4% of these cases would progress to malignancy over the subsequent 13 years compared to a rate of endometrial cancer of approximately 5% among untreated postmenopausal women.

Selection of a Regimen

Patients who require only ERT should be provided daily dosing without interruption (70). Uninterrupted therapy has the advantages of avoiding estrogen deficiency symptoms, providing a continuous cardioprotective effect and creating an easy regimen that promotes woman compliance.

If the combination of ERT and HRT is used, there are four possible regimens that might be prescribed. Selection of an HRT regimen for an individual woman can be accomplished by evaluating the potential benefits of each regimen and considering the woman's ability to tolerate both estrogen and progestins. Regimens can be either cyclic or continuous; cyclic regimens have hormone-free

days (5 days) in the cycle. Regimens can also be referred to as sequential or combined indicating whether the progestin is given intermittently (sequential) or daily with the estrogen. The regimens are shown in Figure 20.1.

Cyclic sequential therapy is the regimen with the longest history in the United States. This regimen provides estrogen for 25 days a month; progestin is added for the last 12 days of the month, and from day 25 to 30 the woman does not receive any hormones. With this regimen almost all women (97%) have withdrawal bleeding, usually light and painless, until at least age 60 years; after age 65 years only 60% continue to bleed. This regimen has a low incidence of hormone-related side effects; 8% of patients experience side effects such as headache, irritability, depression, or lethargy compared to 14% of women on a continuous sequential regimen (75).

The continuous sequential regimen (continuous estrogen-sequential progestin) adds estrogen on the 5 days that were previously hormone-free. This regimen was designed to avoid estrogen deficiency symptoms for those women who experience them on the days off estrogen. Progestins are then administered on the first 12 to 14 days of the cycle.

Continuous estrogen and progestin therapy regimens were designed to promote amenorrhea in order to address one of the commonest objections to HRT, continued menses. The most common continuous regimen and the one recommended by the American College of Physicians is estrogen 0.625 mg CEE daily plus MPA 2.5 mg daily (70). During the first 4 to 6 months of this regimen, approximately 35% of women often experience unpredictable spotting and bleeding, but by 6 months, 60 to 65% of women are amenorrheic (68, 75). Unfortunately, there is a concern about the ability of this regimen to protect against endometrial cancer. At least 19 cases of endometrial cancer have been reported among women on this regimen (75). Rosenfeld suggests that a dose of 5 mg of MPA is necessary to achieve endome-

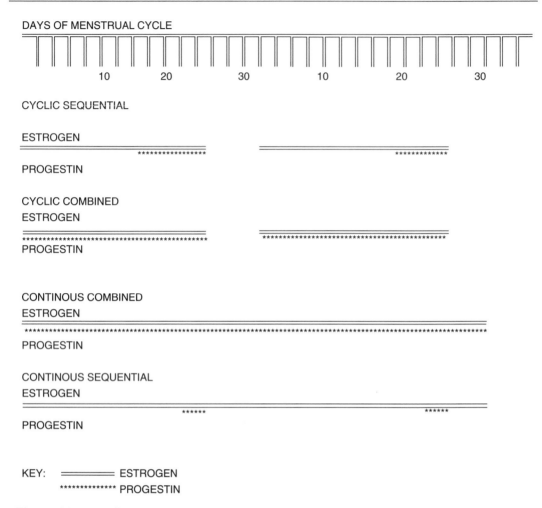

DAYS OF MENSTRUAL CYCLE

CYCLIC SEQUENTIAL

ESTROGEN

PROGESTIN

CYCLIC COMBINED
ESTROGEN

PROGESTIN

CONTINOUS COMBINED
ESTROGEN

PROGESTIN

CONTINOUS SEQUENTIAL
ESTROGEN

PROGESTIN

KEY: ═══════ ESTROGEN
************* PROGESTIN

Figure 20.1. Different treatment regimens for Hormone Replacement Therapy. (Adapted with permission from Gambrell RD. Update on hormone replacement therapy. Am Fam Pract 1992;46:878–968.)

trial atrophy for the majority of women on a continuous combined regimen (78). She suggests that women start on 2.5 mg MPA but, if bleeding is still present after 3 months, increase the dose to 5 mg daily. If bleeding is present at 6 months, the dose should again be increased to 10 mg daily. This approach achieves amenorrhea in 85 to 95% of women by 9 months of therapy.

The final type of regimen is the cyclic combined (both estrogen and progestin every day in same doses but only for 25 days per month). This regimen provides both estrogen and progestin for 25 days a month in the same doses used for continuous combined but there is a 5 day hormone-free period in the cycle. The potential advantage of this regimen is greater endometrial protection because stopping the progestin allows for shedding of the endometrium. In addition, there is less breakthrough bleeding after the first month of this regimen than is seen with the continuous combined regimen and a greater percentage of women are amenorrheic by 4 months (75% of women on cyclic combined vs. 60 to 65 % on continuous combined). However, there is less amenorrhea with this regimen in younger women (less than age 55 years) (75).

Another approach to reducing the side effect of bleeding with cyclic therapy is to use a progestin only every third to fourth month. The potential benefits cited for this approach are a lower annual dose of progestin, resulting in decreased progestin-type side effects, and the avoidance of more frequent withdrawal bleeding. The dose and duration of MPA employed for these widely spaced progestin regimens is 10 to 20 mg MPA for 14 days. The withdrawal bleeding associated with these regimens is longer and heavier than that seen with more frequent dosing of progestins (5 to 8 days; heavy bleeding in 12 to 30% of women) (79, 80). Despite this, the widely spaced regimen was preferred by 60% of women in one study (79). These women preferred less frequent bleeding, even if bleeding, when it occurred, was heavier and lasted longer. Unscheduled bleeding was experienced by some women and the recommended management was to shorten the time between MPA administration or to use the widely spaced regimen only for women who were menopausal for greater than 3 years (79, 80). Both studies reported a low incidence of endometrial hyperplasia (1.5 to 3%), a rate consistent with the rate of hyperplasia seen with monthly cyclic MPA.

Management of Common Side Effects

The management of reported side effects of HRT was recently reviewed by Evans et al. (81) and is summarized in Table 20.4. Similar to advice with oral contraceptive pills, nausea can be managed by taking the medication with food or at bedtime. Because nausea is attributed to initial sensitivity to estrogen, a gradual increase of dose to normal maintenance over the first 2 to 4 weeks may be useful. If nausea persists beyond the first few months, a different brand or formulation of estrogen may be better tolerated or transdermal patches may be offered.

Breast tenderness may improve through employing strategies of reducing the estrogen dose (by administering estrogen on a schedule of days 1 to 25 of each month or Monday through Friday) or trying a different progestin. Other avenues include limiting caffeine intake, adding a mild diuretic or daily vitamin E (200 to 400 IU/d) (82). Underlying breast disease should be considered.

The progestational side effects of mood alterations and bloating are thought to occur in 15% of patients. Bloating may be managed by

Table 20.4. How to Manage Side Effects of HRT

Symptom	Suggested Treatment
Rash, skin irritation	Rotate site of application if using transdermal. Use a fresh patch after bath or swimming. Air-dry skin before applying
Migraine headaches	Relatively contraindicated to use HRT. Try a transdermal patch. Stop HRT if continues, evaluate a new headache
Nausea	Often decreases in time. Take medication with food or at bedtime. Try lower doses and transdermal patches.
Abdominal bloating	Try lower or different progestin. Try HCTZ 25 mg qd during progestin therapy
Breast tenderness	Use lower estrogen dose, or give a break. Change progestin. Consider use of HCTZ, avoid caffeine, evaluate if persists.

Data from Evans MP, Fleming KC, Evans JM. Hormone replacement therapy: management of common problems. Mayo Clin Proc 1995;70:800–805.

switching to a different progestational agent or by decreasing the dose. A strategy of limiting progestin therapy to once every 3 months should also be considered.

Complaints of continued vasomotor symptoms can be managed by increasing the estrogen dose, changing to a different estrogen, or trying a different delivery system. For women who report difficulties with decreased libido, a combined androgen-estrogen hormone replacement can be considered, but may be associated with elevated serum testosterone, hirsutism, and virilism (82).

Bleeding problems can often be managed by changes in dosing. Regular bleeding at the time of progesterone withdrawal should be expected with cyclic HRT, although 3% of younger women and 40% of women over the age of 65 years develop amenorrhea. The number of women with regular bleeding, however, may be overestimated. Based on information obtained from menstrual diaries of women on HRT, Al-Azzawi and Habiba (using a variability in onset of bleeding of 2 days and in duration of bleeding of 1 day) were able to predict the bleeding patterns of less than one-third of their patients on various regimens (82).

Heavy withdrawal bleeding can be diminished by decreasing the estrogen dose, if possible, or by switching to continuous dosing. Any irregular bleeding in a woman on cyclic HRT requires evaluation. The standard is to obtain an endometrial biopsy. Transvaginal ultrasound is considered an option, especially for women with cervical stenosis in which biopsy may be difficult.

In a review of the use of vaginal sonography in assessing the endometrium in postmenopausal women, the investigators concluded that an endometrial thickness of < 5 mm almost excludes the diagnosis of endometrial cancer (83). Although the expected number of endometrial cancers among women who have irregular bleeding on HRT is unknown, biopsy data from women with postmenopausal bleeding show that approximately 10% have endometrial cancer (see Chapter 12.4).

Among women on continuous-combined regiments, evaluation for irregular bleeding should be considered if it is heavy (heavier than a normal menstrual period), prolonged (longer than 10 days at a time), or persists beyond the first 10 months of therapy. Unpredictable uterine bleeding occurs in 35 to 40% of women with a uterus who are on ERT (70). All women on ERT who have bleeding should be evaluated.

Conclusions

There are a variety of good reasons to take ERT/HRT. Each woman and her provider must address the decision individually. However, with the variety of regimens and possibilities of minimizing symptoms, HRT should be strongly considered, if the provider and woman can work together.

Special Considerations for Nurse Practitioners and Physician Assistants

The use of hormones, especially for preventive reasons, remains controversial. At one end of the spectrum, some health care providers recommend hormones for all postmenopausal women, whereas others (85) insist that hormones are never indicated for menopausal symptoms. Many issues about HRT are unresolved, making it impossible for the health care provider to give clear-cut answers (86). The woman is often caught up in this controversy and uncertainty about HRT. The provider should be honest in telling a woman what is known (and not known) about HRT and then trust the woman to make the decision (87).

Most women will get their information about HRT from the mass media and may have distorted perceptions of the risks involved with using hormones. Ideally, education about HRT should begin before menopause so that a discussion of possible benefits and risks can start prior to any menopausal symptoms. In addition, the risks and benefits of preventive, long-term therapy can be mentioned in the broader context of other health teaching about nutrition, exercise, and health screening (88).

Before HRT is begun, a complete history is obtained, noting especially symptoms of hypoestrogenism and any family history of osteoporosis, heart disease, or hypertension. The provider should note the baseline values for cholesterol and lipid profile, urinalysis, CBC, blood chemistry profile, colorectal cancer screen, cervical screening, and mammogram. If the ovaries are nonpalpable because of obesity, there is suspected enlargement or mass, or a family history of ovarian cancer, ovarian/pelvic ultrasound may be indicated. A menstrual diary and accurate record of other bleeding episodes can assist the provider in diagnosis and treatment (89). After HRT is begun, the woman should be encouraged to continue to keep a diary of symptoms, noting especially bleeding and its relationship to her HRT schedule.

Many factors can influence a woman's compliance with prescribed HRT. Fears, especially of cancer, may lead her to stop HRT, as may withdrawal bleeding, endometrial monitoring by biopsy (if recommended), and common side effects such as breast tenderness, breakthrough bleeding or local skin irritation with the patch. Women should be asked what concerns them about taking hormones and also provided with written instructions, pamphlets, and videos if available. Providers should tell women to call them if they have questions and let patients know that they will work with them to find the right combination of hormones and schedule to alleviate side effects (88, 90). Side effects (e.g., menses, bloating,

weight gain) can affect compliance. If a woman understands when she should expect bleeding and when to call the provider, her ability to stay on HRT is enhanced (91).

When oral hormones are prescribed, the provider should help the woman plan ways to remember her medication, e.g., by associating it with another daily habit. When the patch is used, women need to be taught measures that may prevent skin irritation, e.g., rotating sites of application and applying the patch to skin that is clean, dry, and free of oil, powder, lotion, perfume, or soap. Leaving the patch open to air, with the protective cover off, for 10 to 15 minutes before application, (or waving the patch to air dry it) allows some of the alcohol to evaporate (89, 90).

Some women who are still ovulating may have indications for supplemental hormonal therapy, e.g., to control irregular or breakthrough bleeding. These women need to understand that HRT does not provide contraception (89).

After the initiation of HRT, a woman is usually evaluated at 3 months unless she has problems in the interim, and then every 6 to 12 months. A woman who decides not to continue HRT (or not to start it at all) may still need help in coping with distressing symptoms and there are other medications which may be helpful (92).

Providers should consult with a physician regarding the need for an endometrial biopsy or if the woman on HRT experiences irregular uterine bleeding or a suspicious or abnormal mammogram. Consultation is also indicated when considering less commonly used routes of administration or less well-established regimens (93).

References

1. Jacobsen SJ, Goldberg J, Miles TP, et al. Hip fracture incidence among the old and very-old: a population-based study of 745,435 cases. Am J Public Health 1990;80:871–873.

2. Jacobsen SJ, Goldberg J, Miles TP, et al. Race and sex difference in mortality following fracture of the hip. Am J Public Health 1992;82:1–4.

3. Consensus Conference: Osteoporosis. JAMA 1984; 252:799–802

4. Grady D, Rubin SM, Petitti DB, et al. Hormone therapy to prevent disease and prolong life in postmenopausal women. Ann Intern Med 1992;117: 1016–1037.

5. Compston JE. HRT and osteoporosis. Br Med Bull 1992;48:309–344.

6. Riggs BL, Seeman E, Hodgson SF, et al. Effect of the fluoride/calcium regimen on vertebral fracture occurrence in postmenopausal osteoporosis. N Engl J Med 1982;306:446–450.

7. Lindsay R, Cosman F. Estrogen and osteoporosis. In: Hajj SN, Evans WJ, eds. Clinical Postreproductive Gynecology. Norwalk, CT: Appleton & Lange, 1993.

8. Felson DT, Zhang Y, Hannan MT, et al. The effect of postmenopausal estrogen therapy on bone density in elderly women. N Engl J Med 1993;329:1141–1146.

9. Quigley MET, Martin BL, Burnier AM, Brooks P. Estrogen therapy corrects bone loss in elderly women. Am J Obstet Gynecol 1987;156:1516–1523.

10. Marx CW, Dailey III GE, Cheney C, Vint II VC, Muchmore DB. Does estrogen improve bone mineral density in osteoporotic women over age 65? J Bone Mineral Res 1992;7:1275–1279.

11. Lobo RA. Cardiovascular implications of estrogen replacement therapy. Obstet Gynecol 1990;75:18S–24S.

12. Schwartz J, Freeman R, Frishman W. Clinical pharmacology of estrogens: cardiovascular actions and cardioprotective benefits of replacement therapy in postmenopausal women. J Clin Pharmacol 1995;35: 1–16.

13. Psaty BM, Heckbert SR, Atkins D, et al. A review of the association of estrogens and progestins with cardiovascular disease in postmenopausal women. Arch Intern Med 1993;153:1421–1427.

14. Lobo RA, Speroff L. International consensus conference on postmenopausal hormone therapy and the cardiovascular system. Fertil Steril 1994;62 (suppl 2):176S–179S.

15. Manson JE. Postmenopausal hormone therapy and atherosclerotic disease. Am Heart J 1994;128:1337–1343.

16. Hulka BS. Links betwen hormone replacement therapy and neoplasia. Fertil Steril 1994;62(suppl 2): 168S–175S.

17. Barrett-Connor E. Hormone replacement and cancer. Br Med Bull 1992;48:345–355.

18. Grady D, Gebretsadik T, Kerlikowske K, et al. Hormone replacement therapy and endometrial cancer risk: a meta-analysis. Obstet Gynecol 1995;85:304–313.

19. Colditz GA, Stampfer MJ, Willett WC, et al. Prospective study of estrogen replacement therapy and risk of breast cancer in postmenopausal women. JAMA 1990;264:2648–2653.

20. Mann RD. Breast cancer risk and the administration of human hormones Part I: Hormone replacement therapy. Adverse Drug React Toxicol Rev 1992;11: 149–172.

21. Colditz GA, Hankinson SE, Hunter DJ, et al. The use of estrogens and progestins and the risk of breast cancer in postmenopausal women. N Engl J Med 1995;332:1589–1593.

22. Gambrell RD. Update on hormone replacement therapy. AFP 1992;46:87S–96S.

23. Soble NB. Progestins in preventive hormone therapy. Obstet Gynecol Clin North Am 1994;21:299–319.

24. The Writing Group for the PEPI Trial. Effects of estrogen or estrogen/progestin regimens on heart disease risk factors in postmenopausal women. The Postmenopausal Estrogen/Progestin Interventions Trial. JAMA 1995;273:199–208

25. Gambrell RD Jr, Massey FM, Castaneda TA, et al. Use of the progestogen challenge to reduce the risk of endometrial cancer. Obstet Gynecol 1980;55: 732–738.

26. Gambrell RD. Role of progestogens in the prevention of breast cancer. Maturitas 1986;8:169–176.

27. Stanford JL, Weiss NS, Voigt LF, et al. Combined estrogen and progestin hormone replacement therapy in relation to risk of breast cancer in middle-aged women. JAMA 1995;274:137–142.

28. Colditz GA, Stampfer MJ, Willett WC, et al. Type of postmenopausal hormone use and risk of breast cancer: 12-year follow-up from the Nurses' Health Study. Cancer Causes Control 1992;3:433–439.

29. Zubialde JP, Lawler F, Clemenson N. Estimated gains in life expectancy with use of postmenopausal estrogen therapy: a decision analysis. J Fam Pract 1993;36:271–280.

30. Breslau NA. Calcium, estrogen, and progestin in the treatment of osteoporosis. Rheum Dis Clin North Am 1994;20:691–716.

31. Gambrell RD. The menopause: benefits and risks of hormone replacement therapy. Comprehensive Therapy 1994;20:580–585.

32. Daly E, Roche M, Barlow D, et al. HRT: an analysis of benefits, risks and costs. Br Med Bull 1992;48: 368–400.

33. Khaw KT. Epidemiology of the menopause. Br Med Bull 1992;48:249–261.

34. Hunter M, Battersby R, Whitehead M. Relationships between psychological symptoms, somatic complaints and menopausal status. Maturitas 1986;8: 217–228.

35. Lock M. Menopause in cultural context. Exp Gerontol 1994;29:307–317.

36. Oldenhave A, Jasmann LJB, Haspels AA, Everaerd W. Impact of climacteric on well-being. Am J Obstet Gynecol 1993;168:772–780.

37. Anderson E, Hamburger S, Liu JH, Rebar RW. Characteristics of menopausal women seeking assistance. Am J Obstet Gynecol 1987;156:428

38. Hammond CB. Women's concerns with hormone

replacement therapy—compliance issues. Fertil Steril 1994;62(6 Suppl 2):157S–160S.

39. Barentsen R, Foekema HA, Bezemer W, van Stiphout FL. The view of women aged 45–65 and their partners on aspects of the climacteric phase of life. Eur J Obstet Gynecol Reprod Biol 1994;57:95–101.

40. Pilote L, Hlatky MA. Attitudes of women toward hormone therapy and prevention of heart disease. Am Heart J 1995;129:1237–1238.

41. Schmitt N, Gogate J, Rothert M, et al. Capturing and clustering women's judgement policies: the case of hormonal therapy for menopause. J Gerontol 1991;46:92–101.

42. Garton M, Reid D, Rennie E. The climacteric, osteoporosis and hormone replacement; views of women aged 45–49. Maturitas 1995;21:7–15.

43. McNicholas MM, Heneghan JP, Milner MH, et al. Pain and increased mammographic density in women receiving hormone replacement therapy: a prospective study. Am J Roentgenol 1994;163:311–315.

44. Marsh MS, Whitcroft S, Whitehead MI. Paradoxical effects of hormone replacement therapy on breast tenderness in postmenopausal women. Maturitas 1994;19:97–102.

45. Haarbo J, Marslew U, Gotfredsen A, Christiansen C. Postmenopausal hormone replacement therapy prevents central distribution of body fat after menopause. Metabolism 1991;40:1323–1326.

46. Ettinger B, Selby JV, Citron JT, et al. Gynecologic complications of cyclic estrogen progestin therapy. Maturitas 1993;17:197–204.

47. Bonnier P, Romain S, Giacalone PL, et al. Clinical and biologic prognostic factors in breast cancer diagnosed during postmenopausal hormone replacement therapy. Obstet Gynecol 1995;85:11–17.

48. Dhodapkar MV, Ingle JN, Ahmann DL. Estrogen replacement therapy withdrawal and regression of metastatic breast cancer. Cancer 1995;75:43–46.

49. Kaplan NM. The treatment of hypertension in women. Arch Intern Med 1995;155:563–567.

50. Berga SL. Hormonal management of the sick menopausal woman. Obstet Gynecol Clin N Am 1994;21:231–244.

51. Kaiser HJ, Meienberg O. Deterioration or onset of migraine under estrogen replacement therapy in the menopause. J Neurol 1993;240:195–197.

52. Lieberman D, Kopernik G, Porath A, et al. Sub-clinical worsening of bronchial asthma during estrogen replacement therapy in asthmatic post-menopausal women. Maturitas 1995;21:153–157.

53. Arden NK, Lloyd ME, Spector TD, Hughes GR. Safety of hormone replacement therapy (HRT) in systemic lupus erythematosus (SLE). Lupus 1994;3:11–13.

54. Glueck CJ, Lang J, Hamer T, Tracy T. Severe hypertriglyceridemia and pancreatitis when estrogen replacement therapy is given to hypertriglyceridemic women. J Lab Clin Med 1994;123:59–64.

55. Rozenberg S, Vandromme J, Kroll M, et al. Overview of the clinical usefulness of bone mineral measure-ments in the prevention of postmenopausal osteoporosis. Int J Fertil 1995;40:12–24.

56. Christiansen C. Selection of postmenopausal women for estrogen therapy. Postgrad Med 1989;85:10–12.

57. Gambrell RD. Prevention of endometrial cancer with progestogens. Maturitas 1986;8:159–168.

58. Whitehead MI, Hillard TC, Crook D. The role and use of progestogens. Obstet Gynecol 1990;75:59S–76S.

59. Buller RE. Hormone replacement therapy following gynecologic cancer. Postgrad Obstet Gynecol 1993;13:1–6.

60. Miller KL. Alternatives to Estrogen for Menopausal Symptoms. Clin Obstet Gynecol 1992;35:884–893.

61. Lobo RA, McCormick W, Singer F, et al. Depo-medroxyprogesterone acetate compared with conjugated estrogens for the treatment of postmenopausal women. Obstet Gynecol 1984;63:1–5.

62. Morrison JC, Martin DC, Blair RA, et al. The use of medroxyprogesterone acetate for relief of climacteric symptoms. Am J Obstet Gynecol 1980;138:99–104.

63. Lomax P, Schonbaum E. Postmenopausal hot flashes and their management. Pharmacol Ther 1993;57:347–58.

64. Ginsberg ES. Hot flashes—Physiology, hormonal therapy and alternative therapies. Obstet Gynecol Clin North Am 1994;21:381–390.

65. Lee JR. Is natural progesterone the missing link in osteoporosis prevention and treatment? Med Hypotheses 1991;35:316–318.

66. Prior JC. Progesterone as a bone-trophic hormone. Endocr Rev 1990;11:386–398.

67. Sitruk-Ware R. Hormonal replacement therapy: what to prescribe, how and for how long. In: Sitruk-Ware R, Utian WH, eds. The Menopause and Hormone Replacement Therapy. New York: Marcel Dekker, 1991.

68. Jones KP. Estrogens and progestins: What to use and how to use it. Clin Obstet Gynaecol 1992;35:871–883.

69. Stenchever M. Hormone replacement. In: Stenchever MA, Aagaard G, eds. Current Topics in Obstetrics and Gynecology: Caring for the Older Woman. New York: Elsevier, 1991.

70. American College of Physicians. Guidelines for counseling postmenopausal women about preventive hormone therapy. Ann Intern Med 1992;117:1038–1041.

71. Marsh MS, Whitehead MI. Management of the menopause. Br Med Bull 1992;48:435–457.

72. Gambrell RD. Estrogen replacement therapy. Drug Therapy 1987;17:68–69, 71–72, 77–78, 80–81.

73. Birkenfeld A, Kase NG. The management of the postmenopausal woman. In: Glass RH, ed. Office Gynecology. 4th ed. Baltimore: Williams & Wilkins, 1993.

74. Lufkin E, Ory S. Relative value of transdermal and oral estrogen therapy in various clinical situations. Mayo Clin Proc 1994;69:131–135.

75. Gambrell RD. Guidelines for choosing the regimen—managing attending problems. Consultant 1994;34:1047–1049, 1054, 1056–1057.

76. Padwick ML, Pryse-Davies J, Whitehead MI. A simple method for determining the optimal dosage of progestin in postmenopausal women receiving estrogen. N Engl J Med 1986;315:930–934.

77. Sturdee DW, Barlow DH, Ulrich LG, et al. Is the timing of withdrawal bleeding a guide to endometrial safety during sequential oestrogen-progestogen replacement therapy? Lancet 1994;344:979–982.

78. Rosenfeld J. Update on continuous estrogen-progestin replacement therapy. Am Fam Physician 1994;50:1519–1523.

79. Ettinger B, Selby J, Citron JT, et al. Cyclic hormone replacement therapy using quarterly progestin. Obstet Gynecol 1994;83:693–700.

80. Hirvonen E, Salmi T, Puolakka J, et al. Can progestin be limited to every third month only in postmenopausal women taking estrogen? Maturitas 1995;21;39–44.

81. Evans MP, Fleming KC, Evans JM. Hormone replacement therapy: management of common problems. Mayo Clin Proc 1995;70:800–805.

82. Al-Azzawi F, Habiba M. Regular bleeding on hormone replacement therapy: a myth. Br J Obstet Gynaecol 1994;101:661–662.

83. Wikland M, Granberg S, Karlsson B. Assessment of the endometrium in the postmenopausal woman by vaginal sonography. Ultrasound Quarterly 1992;10:15–27.

84. Akkad AA, Habiba MA, Ismail N, et al. Abnormal bleeding on hormone replacement: the importance of intrauterine structural abnormalities. Obstet Gynecol 1995;86:330–334.

85. Voda AM. Risks and benefits associated with hormonal and surgical therapies for healthy midlife women. West J Nurs Res 1994;16:507–523.

86. Fogel CI, Woods NF. Midlife women's health. In: Fogel CI, Woods NF, eds. Women's Health Care. Thousand Oaks, CA: Sage, 1995:70–100.

87. Oestreich S. A closer look at hormone replacement therapy. Advance Nurse Practitioners 1995;3:11–14.

88. Grimes DA, ed. Weighing the benefits and risks of hormone replacement therapy after menopause. Contraceptive Report 1995;6:4–11, 14.

89. Garner CH. The climacteric, menopause, and the process of aging. In: Youngkin EQ, Davis MS, eds. Women's Health Care. Norwalk, CT: Appleton & Lange, 1994:309–343.

90. Scharbo-Dehann M. Management strategies for hormonal replacement therapy. Nurse Pract 1994;19:47–57.

91. Ravnikar VA. Compliance with hormone replacement therapy: are women receiving the full impact of hormone replacement therapy preventive health benefits? Women's Health Issues 1992;2:75–82.

92. McKeon VA. Hormone replacement therapy: evaluating the risks and benefits. JOGNN 1994;23:647–657.

93. Taylor D. Perimenopausal symptoms and hormone therapy. In: Star WL, Lommell LL, Shannon MT. Women's primary health care. Washington, DC: American Nurses Association, 1995:12–123–12–140.

Menopause

21

Jo Ann Rosenfeld

Introduction

What is menopause? Although it means much more, it is definitely the cessation of menses and the production of endogenous female hormones. Women live much longer. Continuing to provide hormones exogenously prolongs the hormones' beneficial effects on morbidity, mortality, bones, coronary arteries, lipid profiles, and skin and genitourinary systems (1). How should postmenopausal life in women be considered? Is menopause, or life after the age of endogenous hormone production, a disease that needs treatment? Is the postmenopausal period a pathological state? Does the woman, ceasing menses, devolve into an asexual non-person who has something "wrong" with her? With the medicalization of much of women's normal life-cycles, such as pregnancy, and the assertion that some medical diseases of women are psychological or functional and thus, not needing "real medicine," such as menstrual cramps and labor pain, where should menopause be placed? This is not a trivial question; in one study of 48 British practices, the consultation rate for menopausal symptoms was 88.2/1000 women, one of the highest for any complaint (2). Women and society have come to consider menopause a problem requiring medical intervention.

Certainly menopause marks a physiological change. Whether this change heralds as much physical or psychological alteration as adolescence or parenthood (neither of which has yet been declared a disease requiring treatment) deserves discussion. Much of what menopause means to a woman may be cultural. If a woman's sexual and personal identity is based on childbearing and childrearing, it may truly mean an end to productive life. If a woman's identity is based on sexual appeal to man, aging and decreased hormones may be catastrophic. In a society that views youth, thinness, and beauty as the ideal, menopause is a definite marker for aging, perhaps with visions of weight gain and flabbiness. In US society, it has typically meant a change of life-cycle to "empty nest"—children grown and leaving.

However, today's women and families are much more varied. More women work outside the home, more women have children at different times, and families are changing in composition. The cultural, occupational, personal, and family changes affecting women from age 45 to 65 years must also be examined (Table 21.1). Menopause is definitely a change and must be viewed in the context of all these changes.

Cultural Expectations

The way society views women, middle-aged and older women specifically, and how it honors or dishonors age may explain some personal and societal changes that come upon women as they reach middle-age and menopause. It has been typically said that, in the United States and United Kingdom, older age and old women are not venerated, and sexual activity into old age is unexpected. One study of preindustrial and traditional societies found that older women were much more sexually active than older men or younger women; they were less inhibited about sexual conversations, humor, and gestures, and were less censured (3). A study of five Israeli subcultures found that all women "emphatically welcomed the cessation of their fertility" (4). However, the women in the two most traditional groups, those in which women were viewed primarily as childbearers, had some negative expectations of menopause (5). In a study comparing Canadian and Japanese women, 78% of the Canadian but only 55% of the Japanese felt that menopause did not change a woman (6). However, a cross sectional study of Japanese middle-aged women found that few women complained of hotflashes (and cessation of menses had little significance in the aging process). Menopausal syndrome in Japan has been considered a "luxury" disease of women who have too much time on their hands, who are not properly occupied in caring for the elderly (7).

Table 21.1. Some Possible Psychological Tasks for the Woman Age 45 to 65 Years

- Maintaining independence either as single person or in relationship
- Participating as member of a partnership or marriage
- Taking responsibility for one's own health and life circumstances
- Continuing to be self-supportive and creating a satisfying work situation
- Establishing and maintaining a nurturing and secure family structure for raising children
- Participating as a responsible member of extended family: grandparenting, caregiving
- Balancing role demands: those of family, work, society

Anatomical and Physiological Changes

Menopause and the cessation of production of endogenous female hormones cause certain physiological changes, most of which are discussed in Chapter 24.

Genito-urinary Changes

Vaginal Changes
Vaginal atrophy and dryness are definite changes of menopause. Symptoms can range from none to dyspareunia, pain on penetration, burning, pruritus, discharge, and urinary symptoms. These symptoms respond well to estrogen treatment, either topically or orally.

Hysterectomy
Hysterectomy is the second most frequent major operation in the United States (after cesarean section), with up to 590,000 performed annually (8). Approximately 33% of women over age 60 years in the United States (8) and up to 50% in some populations have had hysterectomies (9, 10). In Europe the hysterectomy rate is only 9 to 13% of women over age 60 years (10). The rate dropped slightly in the 1980s, but there is still considerable variation in hysterectomy rates between regions, physicians, and countries. Because there are new techniques both for performing hysterectomies and for curing the problems previously treated by hysterectomy, previous indications and methods must be examined.

Ninety percent of hysterectomies are performed for nonmalignant conditions. Indications for hysterectomy include uterine leiomyomas, dysfunctional uterine bleeding, endometriosis, chronic pelvic pain, endometrial hyperplasia, cancer, PID, and obstetrical complications (Table 21.2).

Fibroids or uterine leiomyomas are the most frequent reason for hysterectomy. There is little proof supporting hysterectomy in women with asymptomatic fibroids, and no proof that removal of uteruses with fibroids less than 12-week size, prophylactically, will decrease future operative complications or hemorrhage. Hysterectomy may be suggested in women with asymptomatic fibroids with

Table 21.2. Indications for Hysterectomy

Indication	Percent
Uterine leiomyomas	30
Dysfunctional uterine bleeding	20
Endometriosis	20
Chronic pelvic pain	10
Endometrial hyperplasia	6
Cancer	combined 14
Pelvic inflammatory disease	
Obstetrical complications	

ureteral obstruction or with uterine growth not caused by hormones. In women with fibroids with symptoms of menometrorrhagia, vaginal bleeding, pelvic pain, and anemia hysterectomy may be indicated if further fertility is not desired (8). Hemorrhage should be evaluated and medical treatments tried before hysterectomy is indicated. Alternatives to hysterectomy for fibroids include myomectomy and gonadotropin-releasing hormone agonists.

Hysterectomy is also performed for dysfunctional uterine bleeding unresponsive to medical therapy. Estrogen, progesterone, or a combination of both can now be comfortably prescribed to older women than previously was suggested; this has decreased the need for surgery. When surgery is indicated, hysteroscopic endometrial ablation may be used because it has less postoperative complications and fewer hospital-days and recovery days required; it has become an accepted alternative to hysterectomy for control of bleeding (8).

Genital prolapse has been an indication for hysterectomy. Each woman should be evaluated individually. Estrogen cream, pessaries, and pelvic exercises may provide considerable relief; they are the first treatments for women with both nonprolapsing and prolapsing uteruses. Although hysterectomy may be suggested for women with uteruses that prolapse beyond the introitus, the surgery for strengthening pelvic musculature for a nonprolapsing uterus does not require hysterectomy.

Hysterectomy is only indicated in endometriosis when medical therapy and conservative surgical techniques fail to control symptoms or large endometriomas are present. Hysterectomy has been performed for endometrial hyperplasia. However, because less than 1% progress to endometrial cancer, hysterectomy is not the indicated treatment (8). Hysterectomy is indicated for cervical intraepithelial neoplasia class III that cannot be excised by conization, early invasive cervical cancer, or adenocarcinoma.

Although hysterectomy has been performed for pelvic pain, the evaluation and treatment of this complaint are much more complicated. Pelvic pain (see Chapter 12.7) should not be considered either totally anatomical or completely psychological. Because up to 40% of women with pelvic pain have histories of significant psychopathology and sexual abuse, combined medical and psychological evaluation and treatment are suggested, and medical therapy should always be considered first. Many hysterectomies for pelvic pain do not relieve the pain.

Hysterectomy, although often performed and usually benign medically, has complications medically and psychologically. The mortality rate is 6 to 11 per 10,000 hysterectomies performed on nonpregnant women without cancer. From 24 to 43% of women who have abdominal hysterectomy have postoperative complications including fever, infection, and hemorrhage, whereas morbidity rates as low as 3% are associated with vaginal hysterectomy (8). Most women have good outcomes. However, changes in body image and sexual relations are possible.

Other Changes

Mood Changes
Menopause has been linked with depression and feeling "badly." Whether estrogen is nec-

essary for a woman's well-being and whether menopause itself causes ill-feeling and estrogen improves it is disputed. Researchers in gynecological and psychiatric fields have argued that menopause is completely natural and any difficulties a woman has is caused by her stage of life and that it is totally an estrogen-deficiency state requiring treatment. The idea that each woman has an individual response to the physical, emotional, and life changes has received only a small notice (11). Analysis of incidence is difficult because referral populations and those who attend special "menopause" clinics are not representational. Analysis of studies is difficult because most are retrospective and both menopause and depression are seldom diagnosed, defined, or measured similarly in different studies.

Certainly there is a variety of the level of disturbance and severity of symptoms experienced by women during menopause from none to substantial. Systemic symptoms attributed to menopause that may bring women to the physician include psychological symptoms, forgetfulness, difficulty concentrating, insomnia, dizziness, backache, headaches, depression, myalgias, fluid retention, and tiredness (11).

Some studies have shown that women "felt better" and had a better "quality of life" on estrogen replacement therapy (ERT). One US randomized double-blind study compared the effect of estrogen on psychological function of 36 asymptomatic menopausal, well-adjusted women over 3 months. The women on ERT had significant improvements in income-management in the Profile of Adaptation to life and in depression symptoms in the Beck Depression Inventory, whereas they had no improvement in memory (12). However, this study examined only a few women. Another mail survey studied 682 asymptomatic women, who were not seeking treatment. It found that there was a significant association between depressed mood, sexual problems, vasomotor symptoms, and sleep problems and menopause (13). However, when 36 of these women were followed over 3 years, although depression, vasomotor symptoms and sleep disturbances continued, the incidence of depression was most likely predicted by a previous history of depression or unemployment than by the menopause alone (14). One British study of over 400 women found that 42% felt the "need for (some) treatment" concerning menopause (2).

Several studies in each of four countries— Canada, Norway, the United Kingdom, and the United States—have shown that women may be menopausal and depressed, but there is no statistical relationship between the two (15). Depression was more likely linked to responsibilities, stresses, and work and money problems than to menopause alone. An Australian telephone survey of 1500 women age 45 to 55 years, using a well-being scale, found that well-being was related to current health status and attitudes toward aging and menopause. However, healthy lifestyle behaviors such as smoking cessation, exercise, and good marital relations were significantly related to well-being, whereas menopause alone was not (16). Specifically, anxious attitudes about menopause and aging predicted ill-health more than menopause; women who felt that menopause led to reduced physical attractiveness and income and were worried about deaths of family and friends scored low on the positive affect scale and on overall well-being. Women who believed menopause was related to depression were more likely to be depressed (16). Many researchers who have examined normal general populations of women have found emotional disturbances related more to ill health, previous history of depression or psychiatric disturbances, lower social class, lack of social supports, unemployment, or social stresses rather than menopause (11). Some studies found no improvement in mood ratings or sexual behavior with treatment with ERT (17).

As well, few women consistently take or stay on ERT. If it worked very well, made women feel good, and was the "cure" to the problem of menopause, women would most likely continue it spontaneously. One study of a general population of women showed that although 42% of women wanted some treatment and 72% had taken some course of ERT, only 1% were long-term users (2). Many women stop ERT within the first year (15). One study showed that estrogen levels rose spontaneously in depressed women as they recovered, suggesting that depression may cause decreased estrogen levels (18). This discussion may be inconsequential, however, if ERT is prescribed to many women for its cardiovascular effects.

Some women were prescribed psychotropic medication for their symptoms. In the Glasgow study, 8% of women had received psychotropic medication (2). Women are twice as likely as men to be prescribed psychotropic medication, and middle-aged women are often typified as depressed, worried, and drug-seeking (19). High use of psychotropic drugs in middle-aged women was more associated with high numbers of major life events and stress and problems with interpersonal relationships than the event of menopause. Increasing age and poor health status rather than menopause were significantly related to use of psychotropic medication (19).

Hot Flashes

Hot flashes occur perimenopausally, caused by decreasing endogenous estrogen. Approximately 50% of women have flushing and 30% night-sweats (2). Their effect on a woman's life and health varies from none to mild disturbances to substantial interruption of normal life, especially sleep. It was the most common reason (68%) menopausal women sought help from physicians (2).

Treatment is estrogen replacement and/or reassurance. Use of estrogen or estrogen and progesterone significantly reduces hot flashes (17).

Insomnia

Disruptions in sleep are common problems. Sleep is less efficient and there is decreased

REM sleep (11). Estrogen is known to have effects on the hypothalamus.

Some experts attribute women's psychological changes such as irritability and depression to hot flashes causing disturbed sleep patterns or disturbed sleep patterns alone (20). The sleep disturbances caused by hot flashes can lead to fatigue, irritability, and disturbed concentration.

Treatment should first include a thorough evaluation of the nature, duration, patterns, and possible causes of sleep disturbances. Estrogen can be offered if the symptoms are coincident with decreasing or cessation of menses, are associated with hot-flashes, and are not long-standing (11).

Other Health Problems

As mentioned throughout this book, most studies specifically excluded women. There have been few studies directly examining menopausal status and its effects on medical problems. One US study of 468 women that examined determinants of blood pressure changes in middle-aged women found that menopausal status and ERT were unrelated to changes in blood pressure, whereas high-anxiety levels, parental history of hypertension, high baseline fasting insulin, increased alcohol use, and high baseline body mass index did predict later onset of hypertension (21).

Personal Changes

Employment

Many women are employed outside the home and are finding satisfaction there. Women comprise 45% of the employed population and three fourths of these women work full time (22). Forty-eight percent of women age 35 to 54 years, and 29.3% of women age 55 to 64 years are employed full-time. Another 23 to 30% of women age 34 to 65 years work part-time (23). In rural areas, women are often not just "house-wives" but co-workers on the family farm (15).

Just as it is for men, women in their 40s and 50s should be reaching the peak of their employment, productivity, and careers. This is especially true for women who may have taken time off, worked part time, or worked more slowly during either their 20s or 30s to bear and raise children. The 40s and 50s may be decades in which these women are "reaching their stride."

There have been few studies of working midlife women, perhaps because the crest of the increasing wave of employed women is now just reaching age 40 years. There was speculation that when women worked outside the home they would get "men's" disease, especially coronary artery disease. Employment does not increase a woman's chance for heart disease, and when the women feels in control of her job environment, employment actually lowers the risk of heart disease (22).

Multiple social roles may also enhance health. In the Framingham study, women who worked more than half their adult lives did not have an increased incidence in heart disease over women at home (24). Women who work, especially at midlife and older ages, enjoy better physical and mental health than those not employed (25). Working women reported better physical health than housewives, fewer psychosomatic symptoms, and a better self-image (19, 26). One US study of middle-aged working women found that employed women had less depressive symptoms (27). Middle-aged women who are not employed are more likely to take psychotropic drugs (19). The reasons for working, the satisfaction, challenges, rewards and stresses of work are more predictive of its effects on a woman's health than the actuality of working (19, 28). For women, working protects against psychological illness (4).

However, employed women also maintain a home and provide childcare. Having two full-time jobs, they have less free-time and less time available for education leading to job advancement.

Involvement with Providers

Only one third of the women get their information about menopause from their providers (29). Two-thirds of the providers reported discussing it with their patients (30). In one British study, most women who had problems with menopause had seen their general physician and felt comfortable with his/her approach (2), whereas in a Gallup poll, only 44% of US women felt satisfied with care they received (1). One third never consulted a physician. Of those who did, 84% of women said that their physician focused completely on ERT, whereas less than 5% discussed activity or diet (1). Many women have not had adequate preventive care; in one survey over half the women over age 50 years had not had a mammogram and more than one third had not had a Pap smear or pelvic examination within the last year (29).

Insurance
Insurance status may change at this time, perhaps just when women need it more. Twenty-three to 30% of women work part-time, 10% live below the poverty level (as compared to 7.5% of men) and approximately 14% are not covered by any type of medical insurance (23). Part-time work or divorce at these ages may make obtaining medical insurance difficult or impossible. Women who are uninsured are less likely to have a regular provider, less likely to have had a mammogram or breast exam (31).

Lifestyle: Habits, Abuse, and Exercise
As the menopausal woman ages, lifestyle changes or improvements are even more necessary and important. Women may become more sedentary because of job and home and have less time to exercise or less impetus to change with the demands of work, home, and

caretaking. Along with ERT, the physician should emphasize good lifestyle habits at these ages. Smoking cessation (see Chapter 6.2) is of continuing and increasing importance as women have smoked 20 to 30 years. Cessation of smoking any time, but especially before fatal or progressively worsening lung or heart disease occurs, improves the health. A healthy heart-smart (moderate cholesterol) diet, realization of ideal body weight, and an adequate intake of calcium is important for health in these and later years. Moderate exercise, easy to avoid with busy lives, must become a definite goal.

Sexuality

Change in Sexual Life
The normal sexual life of middle-aged women has been poorly researched. Sexual life may or may not change during menopause. One study of over 600 Danish women found that most had no change in sexual desire between age 40 and 51 years, and that any change in sexual desire had no relation to menopause (32). Frequency of sexual desire was correlated with previous and present health status, former sexual activity, and partner availability (32). Studies of older women showed that nearly all married people in their mid-50s are sexually active, and 36% of women at age 70 years still have regular coitus (11). Some women have increased sexual interest with age. Continuing sexual activity is correlated to active sexual life throughout life, physical exercise, social activities, and lack of disability (32, 33).

Sexual life may slow down for several reasons, many of which have little to do with desire. The five most commonly reported changes or symptoms associated with menopause include, (a) diminished sexual responsiveness, (b) decline in sexual desire, (c) dyspareunia, (d) decreased sexual activity, and (e) a dysfunctional male partner. However, studies have shown that sexual functioning in many normal physically and sexually healthy women is not affected by lack of estrogen or improved by starting ERT (17).

Vaginal atrophy and dryness can cause dyspareunia and are discussed earlier. Estrogen, topical or oral, or lubricant use will improve these symptoms. There is proof that there is less vaginal atrophy and dryness in sexually active women than women who are not sexually active (34).

Changes in sexual life may be caused by marital changes or partner's health changes. Women may divorce or their husbands may die, making finding a partner more difficult. Women outnumber men and this increases with age. Husband's death is the main reason for cessation of intercourse. The incidence of male sexual dysfunction and disabilities increases with age. The male partner is usually older and may be on medications that inhibit sexual functioning (35). In one study of women age 60 to 70 years, half-reported partner impairment and/or partner's difficulty achieving erection (36). Disabilities in women such as arthritis or heart or lung failure may also limit sexual activity.

Women should be advised that they can continue to enjoy sexual activity with advancing age. Sexual advice for individuals with disabilities and dysfunction, such as different positions for arthritic patients or expressions of intimacy that may not involve penetrative sex, may be needed and offered by the provider. Therapy with couples is important.

Contraceptives

Although many women over 45 years are menopausal, many still need contraception. Most use sterilization, either by tubal ligation or hysterectomy; sterilization was the choice of 60.5% of women age 35 to 39 years and 67% of women age 40 to 44 years (37). In one rural area, 40% of women over age 30 had a tubal ligation (38), and 50% of women over age 50 had had a hysterectomy (9). However, if a permanent surgical form of contraception has not been used, oral contraception and barrier methods should be considered.

Oral contraceptive pills (OCPs) are used by only 3 to 5% of women over age 35 years (37). Previously avoided in women over 35 years, new data and lower estrogen products have caused the Food and Drug Administration to modify the oral contraceptive labeling to include women over age 40 years as possible users. In nonsmoking healthy women, OCP may improve the perimenopausal menstrual changes and provide efficacious contraception. Injectable hormonal contraception (Depoprovera) may also be used in this age group (37).

Family Changes

Traditionally, the menopausal time has been considered a time of change for the family. Children were supposed to grow up and leave home, leaving the woman and her husband alone. In reality, both conventionally and with the increasing changes in the US household, this is seldom true. First, many women are single heads of household. Twenty-six percent of family groups with children, over 17 million families, and 85% of all single-parent households are headed by women (39). In 40% of these families headed by single women, the women are age 40 to 64 years. Sixteen percent of women age 45 to 54 years and 12.2% of women age 55 to 64 years are divorced (39).

In a study of over 1300 Canadian middle-aged women, only one fourth lived in homes without children (15). In one North American study, 58% of middle-aged women still had children at home (19). Another study found that the failure of adult children to leave home produced more stress than leaving (40), although another study found that having children at home reduces the likelihood of use of psychotropic medication (19). Psychotropic medication used in middle-aged women was more related to whether the children and husband were causing problems rather than absence or presence in home (19).

Different patterns of childbearing and childrearing have changed the traditional family make-up at the woman's menopause. Many women are having children at older ages. A woman who has had children after age 35 or 40 years is unlikely to be worrying about an empty nest while her children are still in school. In 1989, 29% of births (over 1,100,000 births) were to women older than age 30, and 8% (340,000) were to women over age 35 years. By the year 2000, 10% of all births will be to mothers over age 35 years (37). Over seven million women, 10% of women age 40 to 64 years have children aged less than 18 in the home (39).

Desire for pregnancy may still be a continuing issue and frustration. The birth rate for women age 45 to 49 years is 2 per 10,000 women (41). Women who were concerned about being too old to have children had the highest rating on a negative affect scale (16).

Alternatively, women who bore their children in their teens and 20s may be finding that these children are returning home with the grandchildren. The middle-age woman may be left to raise her grandchildren on her own. Total divorce rates of 50%, blended families, and single mothers all contribute to the phenomenon of grandmothers raising or significantly contributing to the raising of grandchildren. Studies of Mexican-American and African-American families in which up to 65% of women over 45 are raising grandchildren found that those with children are more likely to feel "sadness" than households without children (42–44).

Marital Changes

Changes in work or family demands of one or both spouses can strain the marriage. As the woman is reaching her prime, or still working full time, her husband, who is often older, may be slowing down or even retiring. The hus-

band may still be working while the woman has to slow-down or cease working to care for a parent.

There is an increase of marital breakdown both in the 45 to 65 age range and with retirement. This rate is increasing. Between 1975 and 1985 the number of divorces involving women over age 40 years increased from 19% in 1980 to 23% in 1985 (45). Approximately one woman in eight can anticipate a first marriage ending in divorce after age 40 years, and by 2025 only approximately 37% of women age 65 to 69 years will still be in their first marriage (45). However, divorce rates decrease with increasing age from 13.1 per 1000 married persons at age 45 to 49 years to 2.7 per 1000 married persons at ages 60 to 65 years (46). Predictably, in the Australian telephone survey, women who lived with a partner scored better in well-being (16). Divorced women are more likely to live alone, be unemployed, live in homes they do not own, and have reduced financial resources (45).

Caregivers

As is described in Chapter 22, women are traditionally and continually the caregivers of the old. As they age, their parents age, and the stress and strain of caring for the aged falls to the daughter or daughter-in-law. This can be a strain on the marriage and career.

Conclusion

Menopause should be viewed as an event or signal post that can affect different women differently. Even if a physiological basis for mood or emotional changes exists, it does not mean all women or even most women will experience the changes or experience them similarly. The provider must view each woman individually and expect that her experience will be individual. Just as early parenthood comes to different individuals at different times, so will the changes (physical, personal, familial) be different for each woman. The provider must be willing to cast aside preconceptions and listen to the needs of the whole woman.

Special Considerations for Nurse Practitioners and Physician Assistants

Although the perimenopausal period is a time of normal transitions, it is often viewed negatively by women and providers alike. The words providers use to describe changes can add to the negativity associated with this time in a woman's life. Telling a woman about "failed" functions, organs that "wither, shrink, or atrophy," and "senile" ovaries may leave her with negative feelings about her own body. Women's concerns about how long "menopause" will last might be alleviated if providers used a more positive approach when teaching about this period of time.

Women can cope with life changes by planning for the change, rehearsing the transition mentally, and acknowledging personal strengths and supports. Such planning can help a woman control a situation and, thus, manage it better (47). During the health care of women aged in their 40s, providers should initiate discussions of expected normal perimenopausal changes and ask the woman what she expects to happen during this period of time. The provider can address any fears or myths that the woman expresses and also leave the woman with an invitation to ask questions about future concerns.

Menopause is not pathological or unhealthy, but some women will experience disabling symptoms. Some women find themselves torn between the feminist and medical approaches to the process. If they seek medical attention, they feel they are rejecting the normalcy of the process; yet, they may suffer needlessly if self-management is not helping their individual problems (48). Health care providers must work with each woman to find an individualized, balanced approach to care that neither medicalizes a normal process nor ignores her needs for intervention.

Providers should not automatically suggest treatment for symptoms that a woman describes. One group of generally well-educated women age 43 to 58 years who perceived themselves to be in good health, reported a wide range of perimenopausal symptoms, but did not worry about most of them. Many used self-care measures such as "throw myself into my work" and "accept changes in my body" to manage their symptoms and their general health (49).

If a woman's symptoms are worrisome to her and she desires help, providers should have specific suggestions. If, for example, a woman has difficulty sleeping, the provider can evaluate napping patterns and use of caffeine and alcohol. Lack of exercise as well as exercise immediately before bedtime can interfere with rest. Suggestions can be made regarding a comfortable sleep environment, quiet activities before bedtime, and relaxation techniques (50). For sleep disturbances and most other symptoms that worry the woman, she can learn techniques to help herself and thus feel empowered and in control during this transition.

At no time should a provider automatically attribute any complaints of a midlife woman to "just menopause." Mood changes, sleep disturbances, changes in sexual functioning, and other symptoms can have many causes. Consultation with a physician and even referral to mental health, sleep therapy, or other specialists may be indicated for these women just as they might be for any other age group.

References

1. Andrews WC. The transitional years and beyond. Obstet Gynecol 1995;85:1–5.
2. Barlow DH, Grossett KA, Hart H, Hart DM. A study of Glasgow women in the climacteric years. Br J Obstet Gynecol 1989;96:1192–1197.
3. Goldstein MK, Teng NN. Gynecologic factors in sexual dysfunction of the older woman. Clin Geriatr Med 1991;7:41–61.
4. Freidan B. The Fountain of Aging. New York: Simon & Schuster, 1993:142.
5. Datan N, Ontonovsky A, Maoz B. A Time to Keep: The Middle-age of Women in Five Israeli Subcultures. Baltimore: Johns Hopkins University Press, 1981.
6. Lock M. Ambiguities of aging: Japanese menopause in culture. Med Psychiatry 1986;10:343–359.
7. Lock M. Menopause: contested meanings of the menopause. Obstet Gynecol Survey 1991;46:783–784.
8. Carlson KJ, Nichols DH, Schiff I. Indication for hysterectomy. N Engl J Med 1993;328:856–860.
9. Rosenfeld JA, Everett K, Woodside J, Zahorik PM. Cigarette Smoking Behaviors in Rural Appalachian Elderly Women. Submitted for publication, 1995.
10. Morely JE, Kaiser FE. Sexual function with advancing age. Med Clin North Am 1989;73:1483–1495.
11. Stone AB, Pearlstein TB. Evaluation and treatment of changes in mood, sleep and sexual functioning associated with menopause. Obstet Gynecol Clin North Am 1994;21:391–403.
12. Ditkoff EC, Crary WG, Cristo M, Lobo RA. Estrogen improves psychological function in asymptomatic postmenopausal women. Obstet Gynecol 1991;78:991–997.
13. Hunter MS, Whitehead MI. Psychological experience of the climacteric and postmenopause. In: Hammond CB, Haseltine FP, Schiff I, eds. Menopause: Evaluation, Treatment and Health Concerns. New York: Alan R Liss, 1989:211.
14. Hunter MS. Somatic experience of the menopause. A prospective study. Psychosom Med 1990;52:357–367.
15. Kaufert PA. A health and social profile of the menopausal woman. Exper Gerontol 1994;29:343–350.
16. Dennerstein L, Smith AM, Morse C. Psychological well-being, mid-life and the menopause. Maturitas 1994;20:1–11.
17. Myers LS, Dixen J, Morrissette D, Carmichael M, Davidson JM. Effects of estrogen, androgen and progestin on sexual psychophysiology and behavior in post-menopausal women. J Clin Endocrin Metabol 1990;70:1124–1131.
18. Morse CA. Menopausal mood disorders. Compr Ther 1989;15:22–28.
19. Kaufert PA, Gilbert P. The context of menopause; psychotropic drug use and menopausal status. Soc Sci Med 1986;23:747–755.
20. Ballinger CB. Psychiatric aspects of menopause. Br J Psychiatry 1990;156:773–777.
21. Markovitz JH, Matthews KA, Wing RR, Kuller LH, Meilahn EN. Psychological, biological, and health behavior predictors of blood pressure changes in middle-aged women. J Hypertension 1991;9:399–406.
22. La Rosa JH. Prevention and management of cardiovascular risk in women. Women, work and health: employment as a risk factor for heart disease. Am J Obstet Gynecol 1988;158:1597–1602.
23. US Department of Commerce. Economics and Statistics Administration, Bureau of the Census. Consumer Income Series. Poverty in the United States. Washington, DC: 1992.
24. Haynes SG, Feinleib M. Women, work and coronary heart disease: prospective findings from the Framingham heart study. Am J Pub Health 1980;70:133–141.
25. Wheeler AP, Lee ES, Loe HD. Employment, sense of well-being, and use of professional services among women. Am J Pub Health 1983;73:908–911.
26. Nye FI. Effects on mother. In: Hoffman LW, Nye FI, eds. Working Mothers. San Francisco: Jossey Bass Publishers, 1974:207–225.
27. Bromberger JT, Matthews KA. Mental Health/Substance Abuse: Employment status and depressive symptoms in middle-aged women: A longitudinal investigation. Am J Pub Health 1994;84:202–206.
28. Rosenfeld JA. Impact of maternal employment on health of the family. Curr Prob Pediatr 1995;25:1–10.
29. Andrews WC. The transitional years and beyond. Obstet Gynecol 1995;85:1–3.
30. Quantum sufficit. Am Fam Physician 1994;1:21.
31. Center for Disease Control and Prevention. Leads from the MMWR: Health Insurance coverage and receipt of preventive health services—United States, 1993. JAMA 1995;273:1083–1084.
32. Koster A, Garde K. Sexual desire and menopausal development. A prospective study of Danish women born in 1936. Maturitas 1993;16:49–60.
33. George LK, Weiler SJ. Sexuality in middle and later life. Arch Gen Psychiatry 1981;38:919–923.
34. Leiblum S, Bachmann G, Kemmann E, Colburn D, Swarsman L. Vaginal atrophy in postmenopausal women: The importance of sexual activity and hormones. JAMA 1983;248:2195–2198.
35. Bachmann GA. Sexual function in the perimenopause. Obstet Gynecol Clin North Am 1993;20:379–389.
36. Bachmann GA, Lieblum SR: Sexuality in sexagenarian women. Maturitas 1991;13:43–47.
37. Sulak PJ, Haney AF. Contraceptive choices for women with medical problems. Unwanted pregnancies: Understanding contraceptive use and benefits in adolescents and older women. Am J Obstet Gynecol 1993;168:2042–2048.
38. Rosenfeld JA, Zahorik PM, Saint W, Murphy G. Women's satisfaction with birth control. J Fam Pract 1993;36:169–173.
39. U.S. Department of Commerce. Economics and

Statistics Administration. Bureau of the Census. Household and family characteristics. March 1993.

40. Cooke DJ. A psychosocial study of the climacteric. In: Broome A, Wallace L, eds. Psychology and Gynaecology Problems. London: Tavistock Publication, 1984:243–265.

41. Vital Statistics of the United States. Vol 1—Natality. U.S. Department of Health and Human Services. 1990.

42. Friedan B. The Fountain of Age. New York: Simon & Schuster, 1993.

43. Brenner T, Ragan P. The effects of the empty nest on the morale of Mexican American and white women. Presented at Gerontological Society, San Francisco, CA, 1977.

44. Burton L, Bengston V. Black grandmothers: issues of timing and continuity of roles. In: Bengtson V, Robertson J, eds. Grandparenthood. Thousand Oaks, CA: Sage, 1985.

45. Uhlenberg P, Cooney T, Boyd R. Divorce for women after midlife. J Gerontol 1990;45:S3–S11.

46. Vital Statistics of the United States. Volume II—Marriage and Divorce. U.S. Department of Health and Human Services, 1987.

47. Frank MEV. Transition into midlife. NAACOG's Clin Issues Perinatal and Women's Health Nurs 1991; 2:421–428.

48. Quinn AA. Menopause: plight or passage. NAACOG's Clin Issues Perinatal Women's Health Nurs 1991;2: 304–311.

49. Bernhard LA, Sheppard L. Health, symptoms, self-care, and dyadic adjustment in menopausal women. JOGNN 1993;22:456–461.

50. Garner CH. The climacteric, menopause, and the process of aging. In: Youngkin EQ, Davis MS, eds. Women's Health. Norwalk, CT: Appleton & Lange, 1994:309–343.

V

OLDER WOMEN

Preventive Health Care and Medical Problems of Older Women

Gail S. Marion

Introduction

Medicine is a mirror of the culture. The increasing visible presence of able and older women explains the current intense focus on older women's health issues. The view of woman as a young pelvis, whose value is mostly as a reproductive unit, is anachronistic. A male model of disease, based on research done largely, and often exclusively, on men is now unacceptable as a basis for caring for older women. There must be a shift from disease intervention toward prevention and health promotion. Life must not just be extended; instead, there must be ways found to facilitate optimal function and well-being during the later years of women's lives (1).

At the turn of the 20th century, women who did not die in childbirth had a life expectancy of 51 years—the same age that women, on average, reach menopause today (2, 3). Today, a woman born in the middle of the baby-boom generation can expect to live to age 74, whereas women born in 1989 have a life expectancy of 79. By 2015, 45% of American women will be age 45 years or older. One third of women's lives will be lived after cessation of menses (3, 4).

To care for older women, providers must learn to listen to what women perceive to be their most important health concerns, what they believe about the care they receive, and how they care for themselves. Proper attention to issues of prevention, health promotion, and medication management, and appropriate evaluation of the older woman (which includes addressing issues of sexuality for heterosexual and homosexual women) are critical to gain the trust and respect of women. Providers must be sensitive to common-place problems in the lives of older women such as physical and emotional abuse and caregiver stress. The challenge is to recognize that whereas culture sees this group as homogenous, older women are the most heterogenous group in the society. Caring for them means not only tending to the frail, but also working with many healthy, dynamic, and powerful people.

Special Concerns in Evaluating the Older Woman

Few aspects of primary care are as challenging as comprehensive evaluation of the older person. Lack of adequate training about older women, the "busy"-ness of practice, and the complex, atypical, and subtle presentation of disease and disability in this age group make evaluation difficult. The important elements of high-quality evaluation of the older woman are respect, patience, and a thorough approach that can be tailored to fit each woman.

Most important is respect for the older woman. Older women are traditionally the least valued segment of the population. They must be respected as valuable individuals. They need to be addressed by their last names, avoiding "hon" and "sweetie." Providers should ask the woman how they prefer to be addressed (e.g., Ms, Miss, Mrs, Dr, Professor).

When examining the patient, settings should be free of distracting noises. The provider should talk to the older woman herself and not just to the caregiver/family member, unless it is obvious that the older woman cannot answer for herself. Some time alone with the woman is crucial to allow confidential discussion. Modesty must be respected during exams, and providers should insist on respectful patient treatment from the office staff, students, residents, and consultants.

Obtaining a history, often of 80 years or more, will take longer than in a person half this age. Vision, hearing, language, and cultural differences may contribute to decreased efficiency and effectiveness in evaluation. Providers must be aware of background noise, poor lighting, and interruptions. Even by sitting at eye level and maintaining an unhurried approach, providers may not obtain a complete history and a thorough physical in one visit. Several closely spaced visits may be used for follow-up of initially identified problems. Family providers and those who have relationship with the woman, over time, can produce both a better relationship and a more accurate picture of the older woman. Both will enhance quality care.

Multidimensional Evaluation in the Older Woman

A traditional medical evaluation may miss critical information, leave the provider feeling frustrated, and may harm the woman. Medical, functional, psychologic, social, economic, and environmental domains need to be considered when evaluating the older woman.

History

Obtaining a traditional medical history in the older woman is insufficient. The provider must consider life concerns, cultural influences and spiritual family health experience, and social situation. Although these suggestions may seem time-consuming, many of them can be performed by different members of the health care team over several visits in the home or office. Some ways to maximize information gathering include the following:

1. Request medical records and have the woman or family complete a health questionnaire at home or before the office visit; the questionnaire should be in print that is a readable size.
2. Avoid asking the woman to tell her story more than once.
3. Pace the interview to fit the patient's abilities, while avoiding interruption.
4. If open-ended questions are too difficult, use simple yes/no type questions.

The provider should remember that the initial interview is therapeutic in itself and sets the stage for the relationship. The information is not the most important part of the visit, but instead the relationship developed. The provider may be one of the most important individuals in this person's life (5).

Older women more often underreport than overreport illness. Fear of loss of independence and expectations that their symptoms are a normal part of aging are reasons for underreporting. Older women have altered physiological response to disease that can result in absent or subtle presentations, such as myocardial infarctions presenting as confusion or nonsteroidal anti-inflammatory agents masking the "typical presentation" of peptic ulcer disease. Symptoms may be vague and/or nonspecific and may be distorted by other disease or medication effect. Dementia and depression can impair the ability to articulate symptoms.

Overreporting is equally frustrating, but is often related to emotional, not physical, disease. Knowing the patient over time allows the provider critical insight to detect subtle changes and decreased function. Understanding how the woman fits into her family and how well or poorly the patient and caregiver function together is imperative.

Past medical history is critical to place symptoms in perspective, particularly when the current picture may be vague and confusing. Reviewing family history may be the time when a woman says, for example, "I never want to be on a feeding tube like my mother was."

A detailed medication record should include the names of those providers who administer medications and from how many sources those medications are prescribed.

Review of Systems

Questions related to general symptoms such as fatigue, weight loss, insomnia, falling, and incontinence may elicit treatable underlying disease (Table 22.1). Older women who may be limiting activity to minimize symptoms need to be asked questions such as "What is the most strenuous activity you do and how far do

Table 22.1. Important Elements of Historical Evaluation

Social History
   Who provides the social support?
   What is the environmental and financial situation?
   With whom do you live?
   Are you a caregiver/carereceiver?
   Are you able to perform activities of daily living?
   What hobbies, social activities or work give you pleasure?
   Does a religious or spiritual faith provide comfort for you?
   Who provides transportation for you?
   What formal education did you receive?
   Do you have a current sexual partner?
   What exercise do you do/how often?
   How much alcohol/tobacco do you use daily?
   What is a typical day for you?
Past medical history
   What major illnesses, hospitalizations, previous surgeries?
   Immunization status
   Testing/exposure to tuberculosis
Medication history
   What medications are you currently taking (e.g., prescription, nonprescription, herbal preparations)?
   Allergies to medication
   Do you know why you take each medication?
   Do you take it as prescribed?
   What prevents you from taking medications as prescribed?
   Do you believe the medications help you/produce side effects?
   How do you pay for the medications?
Review of Systems

Before an organized systems review, determine if generalized symptoms exist such as fatigue, insomnia, or anorexia.

HEENT	Visual/hearing/taste changes
	Dentures well-fitting
	Dizziness/vertigo
Cardiopulmonary	Shortness of breath
	Tightness of heaviness in chest (pain usually not anginal symptom)
	Cough
	Orthopnea
	Syncope
	Palpitations
	Lower extremity edema
	Claudication
Gastrointestinal	Dysphagia
	Abdominal pain
	Weight change
	Changes in bowel habits

Table 22.1.—Continued

Genitourinary	Frequency
	Urgency
	Dysuria (usually absent with infection)
	Nocturia
	Hesitancy
	Incontinence
	Hematuria
	Vaginal bleeding, itching, discharge
	Dyspareunia
Musculoskeletal	Diffuse or focal pain
	Diffuse of focal weakness
Neurological	Falling
	Unsteadiness
	Transient focal changes
	Tingling, burning or decreased sensation in lower extremities
Cognitive/affective	Forgetfulness/confusion
	Anxiety/agitation
	Depression
	Grief
	Paranoia

you walk most days?" Providers need to ask how a woman manages the instrumental activities of daily living (IADLs) and activities of daily living (ADLs).

Physical Exam

Multiple pathological and physical findings intermix with age related changes. For example, changes in skin and postural reflexes affect hydration evaluation (Table 22.2). It is important to know age related changes before determining pathology. As previously stressed, the heterogeneity of this group is unparalleled.

Gait evaluation is not routinely performed in adults populations, but it can be a valuable tool in this age group. Providers typically walk into the room and see the woman seated, then leave as she dresses and undresses, missing opportunities for functional assessment. Besides

watching the woman walk and get onto the exam table, Tinetti's gait assessment may be useful (6). This tool can be used to determine both disability and help define etiology. Components of this assessment include observation of gait initiation, step height length and symmetry, path delineation, trunk stability, walking stance, and turning ability.

In older women with well-honed social skills, significant dementia can be missed in routine medical care. A formal mental status exam is required to determine the level of cognitive ability (Fig. 22.1). This exam is a useful tool to help differentiate between depression and dementia in the older woman. This may be done initially, and at 1- to 2-year intervals if no deficits are detected. A mental status exam can elicit mild to moderate cognitive loss that can go undetected for long periods and increase risks of inappropriate med-

Table 22.2. Physical Findings That Often Require Further Evaluation

Vital Signs	Elevated or postural changes in blood pressure
	Irregular pulse
	Bradycardia/tachycardia
	Tachypnea
	Weight changes
General Appearance and Behavior	Grooming/hygiene changes
	Slowed thinking or speaking
	General state of conditioning
Eyes	Visual loss
	Dryness
	Cataracts
	Fundoscopic exam difficult
Ears	Hearing loss
	Cerumen impactions
Mouth	Missing teeth/poor repair
	Dentures ill fitting
	Caries
	Lesions
Skin	Decreased turgor (most accurate over anterior trunk)
	Ulcerations
	Pressure ulcers
	Multiple skin lesions
	Seborrheic keratoses
	Actinic keratoses
	Basal cell carcinoma
	Squamous cell
	Melanoma
Chest	Kyphosis
	Vertebral fractures (Focal tenderness)
	Rales (Without cardiopulmonary disease indicates age-related fibrosis or atelectasis)
Cardiovascular	Asymptomatic arrhythmias common
	Systolic murmurs common, usually benign
	Extra heart sounds
	Vascular bruits
	Decreased lower extremity pulses
Abdomen	Prominent aortic pulsation
	Renal bruits
	Mass

Table 22.2.—Continued

Genitourinary	Vaginal atrophy/infection
	Cystocele
	Rectocele
Extremities	Periarticular pain
	Decreased range of motion
	Edema (If unilateral, look for proximal obstruction)
	Skin breakdown
	Foot deformities (Long-term use of women's dress foot wear)
Neurological	Mental status changes
	Depression, confusion, slow thinking
	Unilateral or bilateral weakness
	Subtle peripheral neuropathy
	Decreased vibratory sensation in toes common without other detectable pathology
	Decreased or absent ankle jerks common without other pathology
	Pathologic reflexes without other pathology evident
	Wide-based stooped, short-stepped gait (may not represent Parkinson's disease)
	Gait assessment (see Tinetti)
	Unsteadiness

ication use, accidents, and poor financial decision making. Use of this scale requires knowledge of the person's age and level of formal education. Crum found a median score for individuals over age 80 years was 25 out of a possible 30 on Folstein's mini-mental status exam (7).

Laboratory Assessment

Few abnormal laboratory values are true aging changes. Table 22.3 shows unchanged and common abnormal laboratory parameters. Fifty percent of older people have glucose intolerance with normal fasting blood sugar levels of 140 mg/dL or less, making glucose tolerance testing less helpful (8). Al-

though the therapeutic goals for older diabetics are the same as those for younger ones, the goals must be balanced with increased risks associated with hypoglycemia in this group. Those older women with short life expectancies will likely fare better if hypoglycemic symptom control is the goal rather than strict adherence to normal fasting glucose levels (Chapter 19).

Functional Ability

Several assessment techniques designed to assess function provide a structure to the evaluation process. Although every woman is not in need of functional assessment, a systematic approach with the belief that improvement is

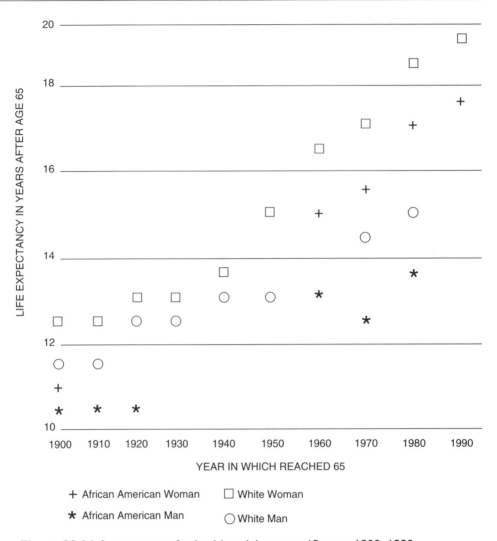

Figure 22.1 Life expectancy for healthy adults at age 65 years 1900–1990.

feasible is helpful. A team approach provides the most practical way of evaluation.

A common and easy-to-use test in outpatient settings is Katz's ADLs and IADLs (9) (Table 22.4). The ability to complete basic activities of daily living both affects and reflects a woman's health and well-being, and helps to determine suitable treatment regimens. Sudden losses in functional ability provide invaluable diagnostic information. For example, infection, myocardial infarction, or depression may present with a functional decline rather than with fever, chills, pain, or frank sadness.

Those people most concerned about the older woman may restrict activity in the name of protecting the patient. Teaching rehabilitative skills is more time-consuming than providing the service. It is helpful to counsel family members and caregivers that doing this breeds dependence and deterioration. Through better geriatric training and recognition of the role stereotype plays in the care of older women, providers can offer more satisfying care.

Table 22.3. Laboratory Assessment

Common Abnormal Laboratory Values
  Sedimentation rate may be increased 10–20
    mm/hr (slightly higher for older women)
  Decreased glucose tolerance
    (fasting levels increase 2 mg/dL for each
      decade after age 60)
  Renal function reduced with high normal or
    mildly elevated values
  Slight alkaline phosphatase elevation
  Albumin values mildly decrease with age
    (<0.5 g/mL) greater decreases indicate
      nutritional deficiency
  Urinalysis (asymptomatic bacteriuria and
    pyuria common, hematuria is abnormal)
  Chest radiographs
    Age-related interstitial changes
    Widely diminished bone density
  Electrocardiogram
    ST segment and T waves changes
    Atrial and ventricular arrhythmias (often
      asymptomatic)

Laboratory Values Unchanged With
Advancing Age
  Hemoglobin and hematocrit
  White blood cell count
  Platelet count
  Serum iron and iron binding capacity
  Electrolytes
  Blood urea nitrogen
  Liver function studies
  Free thyroxine (T4) and thyroid-stimulating
    hormone (TSH)
  Calcium
  Phosphorus

Table 22.4. Activities of Daily Living and Instrumental Activities of Daily Living

Basic Activities of Daily Living
  Feeding
  Toileting
  Ambulation
  Continence
  Communication
  Dressing
  Bathing
  Transfer
  Grooming

Instrumental Activies of Daily Living
  Writing
  Reading
  Cooking
  Cleaning
  Shopping
  Laundry
  Stair climbing
  Telephone use
  Medication use
  Manage finances
  Provide or access transportation
  Perform paid work outside the home

For each activity score 1, 2, or 3: (1) can perform alone, (2) can perform with some assistance, (3) cannot perform. Adapted from Katz S, Ford A, Moskowitz R, et al. The index of ADL: A standardized measure of biological and psychosocial function. JAMA 1963; 185:914–919.

Prevention and Health Promotion Concerns

Care of the older woman often occurs haphazardly. The reasons for this are many. Many older women receive care from several sources. In addition, different authorities conflict in their recommendations for care (Table 22.5). Prospective trial data that includes women is virtually nonexistent for the 65 years and older age population, the fastest growing segment of the population. Reimbursement for screening studies and lifestyle issues counseling is scarce (10, 11). This section will address preventive care including screening recommendations (and lack thereof for the over 65 years age group), immunizations, and lifestyle counseling.

Clinicians typically see the most ill women. In addition to the cultural stereotypes

Table 22.5. American Academy of Family Physicians, Periodic Health Examination,* Ages: 65 Years and Over, Schedule: Every Year†*(See Preamble)*

	Screening	
History	Physical Examination	Laboratory/Diagnostic Procedures
Interval medical and family history[1]	Height and weight	Nonfasting *or fasting[5]* total blood cholesterol
Medication use (prescription and non-prescription)	Blood pressure[2]	Dipstick urinalysis
Prior symptoms of transient ischemic attack	Visual acuity	Mammogram[6]
	Hearing and hearing aids	Thyroid function tests[7]
Dietary intake	Clinical breast exam[3]	High-Risk Groups
Physical activity	*Pelvic exam*	Fasting plasma glucose (HR5)
Tobacco/alcohol/drug use	*Cardiac auscultation*	Tuberculin skin test (PPD) (HR6)
Functional status at home	*Digital rectal exam[4]*	Electrocardiogram (HR7)
	High-Risk Groups	Papanicolaou smear[8] (HR8)
	Auscultation for carotid bruits (HR1)	Fecal occult blood/sigmoidoscopy (HR9)
	Complete skin exam (HR2)	Fecal occult blood/colonoscopy (HR10)
	Complete oral cavity exam (HR3)	
	Palpation of thyroid nodule (HR4)	

	Counseling	
Diet and Exercise	Substance Use	Sexual Practices
Fat (especially saturated fat), cholesterol, complex carbohydrates, fiber, sodium, calcium[9]	Tobacco cessation	*Sexuality*
Nutritional assessment	Alcohol and other drugs:	
Selection of exercise program	Limiting alcohol consumption	
	Driving/other dangerous activities while under the influence	
	Treatment for abuse	

Injury Prevention	Dental Health	Other Primary Preventive Measures
Prevention of falls	Regular tooth brushing, flossing, dental visits	Glaucoma testing
Safety belts		*Advance directives/living will/durable power of attorney*
Smoke detector		Discussion of hormone replacement therapy in women
Smoking near bedding or upholstery		High-Risk Groups
Hot water heater temperature (≤120°F)		Discussion of aspirin therapy (HR13)
Safety helmets		Skin protection from ultraviolet light (HR14)
High-Risk Groups		
Prevention of childhood injuries (HR12)		

Table 22.5.—*continued*

Immunizations and Chemoprophylaxis

Tetanus-diphtheria (Td) booster[10]
Influenza vaccine[11]
Pneumococcal vaccine
High-Risk Groups
Hepatitis B vaccine (HR15)

Additional Notes

Leading Causes of Death:	Heart disease	Remain Alert For:	Depression symptoms
	Cerebrovascular disease		Suicide risk factors (HR11)
	Obstructive lung disease		Abnormal bereavement
	Pneumonia/influenza		Changes in cognitive function
	Lung cancer		Medications that increase risk of falls
	Colorectal cancer		Signs of physical abuse or neglect
			Malignant skin lesions
			Peripheral arterial disease
			Tooth decay, gingivitis, loose teeth

*This list of preventive services is not exhaustive. It reflects only those topics reviewed by the U.S. Preventive Services Task Force *and the AAFP Commission on Public Health and Scientific Affairs.* Clinicians may wish to add other preventive services on a routine basis and after considering the patient's medical history and other individual circumstances. Examples of target conditions not specifically examined by the Task Force include:

Chronic obstructive pulmonary disease	Travel-related illness
Hepatobiliary disease	Prescription drug abuse
Bladder cancer	Occupational illness and injuries
Endometrial disease	

†The recommended schedule applies only to the periodic visit itself. The frequency of the individual preventive services listed in this table is left to clinical discretion, except as indicated in other footnotes.
[1]An updating of the previously obtained medical and family medical history is recommended by the subcommittee.
[2]At every physician visit with a minimum of every two years.
[3]Annually
[4]The subcommittee recommends this procedure but recognizes the scientific evidence supporting it may not be conclusive.
[5]At least every five years
[6]It is recommended that mammography be performed annually for all women beginning at age 50.
[7]For women
[8]Every 1–3 years
[9]For women
[10]Every 10 years
[11]Annually

High-Risk Categories

HR1 = Recent divorce, separation, unemployment, depression, alcohol or other drug abuse, serious medical illnesses, living alone, or recent bereavement.

HR2 = Persons with risk factors for cerebrovascular or cardiovascular disease (e.g., hypertension, smoking, CAD, atrial fibrillation, diabetes) or those with neurologic symptoms (e.g., transient ischemic attacks) or a history of cerebrovascular disease.

HR3 = Persons with a family or personal history of skin cancer, increased occupational or reacttional exposure to sunlight, or clinical evidence of precursor lesions (e.g., dysplastic nevi, certain congenital nevi).

Table 22.5.—continued

HR4 = Persons with exposure to tobacco or excessive amounts of alcohol, or those with suspicious symptoms or lesions detected through self-examination.

HR5 = Persons with a history of upper-body irradiation.

HR6 = The markedly obese, persons with a family history of diabetes, or women with a history of gestational diabetes.

HR7 = Household members of persons with tuberculosis or others at risk for close contact with the disease (e.g., staff of tuberculosis clinics, shelters for the homeless, nursing homes, substance abuse treatment facilities, dialysis units, correctional institutions); recent immigrants or refugees from countries in which tuberculosis is common (e.g., Asia, Africa, Central and South America, Pacific Islands); migrant workers; residents of nursing homes, correctional institutions, or homeless shelters; or persons with certain underlying medical disorders (e.g., HIV infection).

HR8 = Men with two or more cardiac risk factors (high blood cholesterol, hypertension, cigarette smoking, diabetes mellitis, family history of CAD); men who would endanger public safety were they to experience sudden cardiac events (e.g., commercial airline pilots); or sedentary or high-risk males planning to begin a vigorous exercise program.

HR9 = Women who have not had previous documented screening in which smears have been consistently negative.

HR10 = Persons who have first-degree relatives with colorectal cancer; a personal history of endometrial, ovarian, or breast cancer; or a previous diagnosis of inflammatory bowel disease, adenomatous polyps, or colorectal cancer.

HR11 = Persons with a family history of familial polyposis coli or cancer family syndrome.

HR12 = Persons with children in the home or automobile.

HR13 = Men who have risk factors for myocardial infarction (e.g., high blood cholesterol, smoking, diabetes mellitus, family history of early-onset CAD) and who lack a history of gastrointestinal or other bleeding problems, and other risk factors for bleeding or cerebral hemorrhage.

HR14 = Persons with increased exposure to sunlight.

HR15 = Homosexually and bisexually active men, intravenous drug users, recipients of some blood products, persons in health-related jobs with frequent exposure to blood or blood products, household and sexual contacts of HBV carriers, sexually active heterosexual persons with multiple sexual partners diagnosed as having recently acquired sexually transmitted disease, prostitutes, and persons who have a history of sexual activity with multiple partners in the previous six months.

*These recommendations are provided only as an assistance for physicians making clinical decisions regarding the care of their patients. As such, they cannnot substitute for the individual judgment brought to each clinical situation by the patient's family physician. As with all clinical reference resources, they reflect the best understanding of the science of medicine at the time of publication, but they should be used with the clear understanding that continued research may result in new knowledge and recommendations.

that equate frailty with aging, the frequency with which providers care for the sickest causes them to see old age as a less vital time than it often is. For instance, at age 80 years only 20% of women need help with an activity of daily living (Table 22.6) (12).

Although basic agreement exists among authorities for many types of preventive care

Table 22.6. Prevalence of ADL and IADL Limitations Among Community-Dwelling Women

Women	≥1 ADL Limitation (%)	≥1 ADL or IADL Limitation (%)
65–69	6	14
70–74	8	16
75–79	14	25
80–84	20	38
85+	40	62

ADL = Activity of Daily Living; IADL = Instrumental Activity of Daily Living.
Data from U.S. Senate Subcommittee on Aging, American Association of Retired Persons, Federal Council on Aging, and U.S. Administration on Aging. *Aging America: Trends and Projections*. DHHS Publication No. (FCoA) 91-28001. U.S. Department of Health and Human Services, 1991.

guidelines, these guidelines often apply only to those under age 65 years. It is important to maintain adequate screening procedures for older women, because they are often quite healthy and have life expectancies of 10 to 20 more years (13, 14). Statistically, the older a healthy woman becomes, the greater her life expectancy. For example, a healthy 65-year-old woman can expect to live another 19 years—a full 10 years beyond her peers' average age. Women at the same age can expect to live longer than men the same age; a 65-year-old man can expect to live only another 15 years. At age 85 years, a healthy woman can expect to live another 5 years (14).

Lifestyle Counseling

Counseling interventions are information and advice given to reduce the risk of illness and injury. To be considered effective, an intervention should influence personal behavior, such as smoking cessation counseling techniques. US Preventive Services Task Force (USPSTF), American College of Physicians (ACP), and Canadian Task Force (CTF) recommend that clinicians encourage seat belt use and recommend limited alcohol intake.

Providers should ask women about the safety of their homes and neighborhoods. They should learn about the woman's home, e.g., whether stairs and bathrooms are equipped with adequate railings, about the presence of smoke alarms, carpet and throw rugs, and air conditioning, and if heating and lighting are adequate. Although not possible for every or even many patients, a home visit may give invaluable information.

Women need to be counseled about reducing dietary fat and sodium and increasing fiber. The 1994 NIH Consensus Conference on Optimal Calcium Intake recommends that postmenopausal women on estrogen replacement therapy take 1000 milligrams of calcium daily and 1500 mg each day for those women not on estrogen therapy (15).

Older adults are often motivated to change lifestyle behaviors for many reasons. They want to remain independent, they want to maintain their emotional, physical, and monetary resources, and many older people have more discretionary time and resources to participate in lifestyle changes.

Advance Directives

Most older women have thought about what they do and do not want regarding end-of-life care and welcome the opportunity to discuss their wishes. Arrangements for a living will and a durable power of attorney need to be made. These documents are best completed by the primary care provider and the woman herself. Include advance directive discussions at the time of annual visits and revisit these discussions periodically. Documents for completion of the directives should be kept in clinic offices to facilitate completion.

Screening

Screening Criteria

Screening is performed to detect a disease that causes specific morbidity or mortality before symptoms are evident. The natural history must include an asymptomatic period in which the disease can be diagnosed. The results of early treatment must be superior to those obtained after symptoms appear. The screening test has to be sensitive and specific, and the condition must be prevalent enough in the population to justify screening. The patient must have sufficient life expectancy to warrant intervention, and must be willing to undergo the screening and potential treatment (16).

Because screening programs are expensive, time-consuming, and anxiety-producing to the patient, individual providers are often slow to embrace such programs, especially for older adults, even when those providers are philosophically supportive of preventive measures. The US Public Health Service, in partnership with the American Academy of Family Physicians and other national organizations, recently developed the "Put Prevention Into Practice" (PPIP) campaign that targets not only the primary provider but nursing, office staff, and the patient herself (17). Office tools are available through the campaign to facilitate delivery of preventive care. The core tools are similar to those recommended by the 1989 USPSTF guidelines for clinical preventive services. Figure 22.2 shows the adapted version of the adult preventive care timeline. This version excludes a second set of recommendations made by some authorities. Figure 22.3 is a sample preventive care flow sheet that has been tailored to an older woman.

Key steps for improving preventive care services in clinical practice include the following: (1) establishing a protocol; (2) using office tools such as tracking devices, reminder postcards, charts and posters, and prevention prescription pads; (3) involving office staff; (4) activating patients; (5) performing preventive care correctly; and (6) monitoring progress. For more detailed information, the Clinician's Handbook of Preventive Services may be ordered as an individual item from the PPIP kit by calling 1-800-944-0000 and request product #1980.

Some issues not fully addressed by the adult preventive care timeline require thoughtful individual attention for each older woman. Screening for hypothyroidism, mental status changes, skin disease, sensory impairment, and colon cancer should be completed periodically.

Hypothyroidism

At least 4% of women over age 65 years become hypothyroidal. Therefore, USPSTF recommends one-time screening at age 65 years by obtaining a thyroid-stimulating hormone study (TSH) (10). Hypothyroidism typically begins with gradual fatigue that is often mistaken for normal aging change by the woman, her family, and providers. It is not uncommon for many more classic symptoms of hypothyroidism to be absent (Chapter 18.2).

Mental Status Screening

Studies of demented and depressed older patients in hospital settings found that providers were often unaware of these mental status changes (18). Well-honed social skills and advanced education level of the older woman, the tendency for social skills to be affected last, and busy office practices often contribute to the lack of awareness of these important changes. A formal screening mental status exam should be considered at annual exams after the age of 75 years (19).

Skin Examination

Epidemiologic studies confirm a continuing annual increase in the number of basal cell, squamous cell, and melanoma cancers. Most of the 600,000 basal cells found annually occur in the fair-skinned older adult around the head and neck. Squamous cell carcinoma is the second most common skin cancer in Caucasians and the most common among African-American older adults. This cancer is related to sun exposure.

Melanoma is increasing especially among older adults. Half of the melanomas found occur after age 55 years (20). Older women at

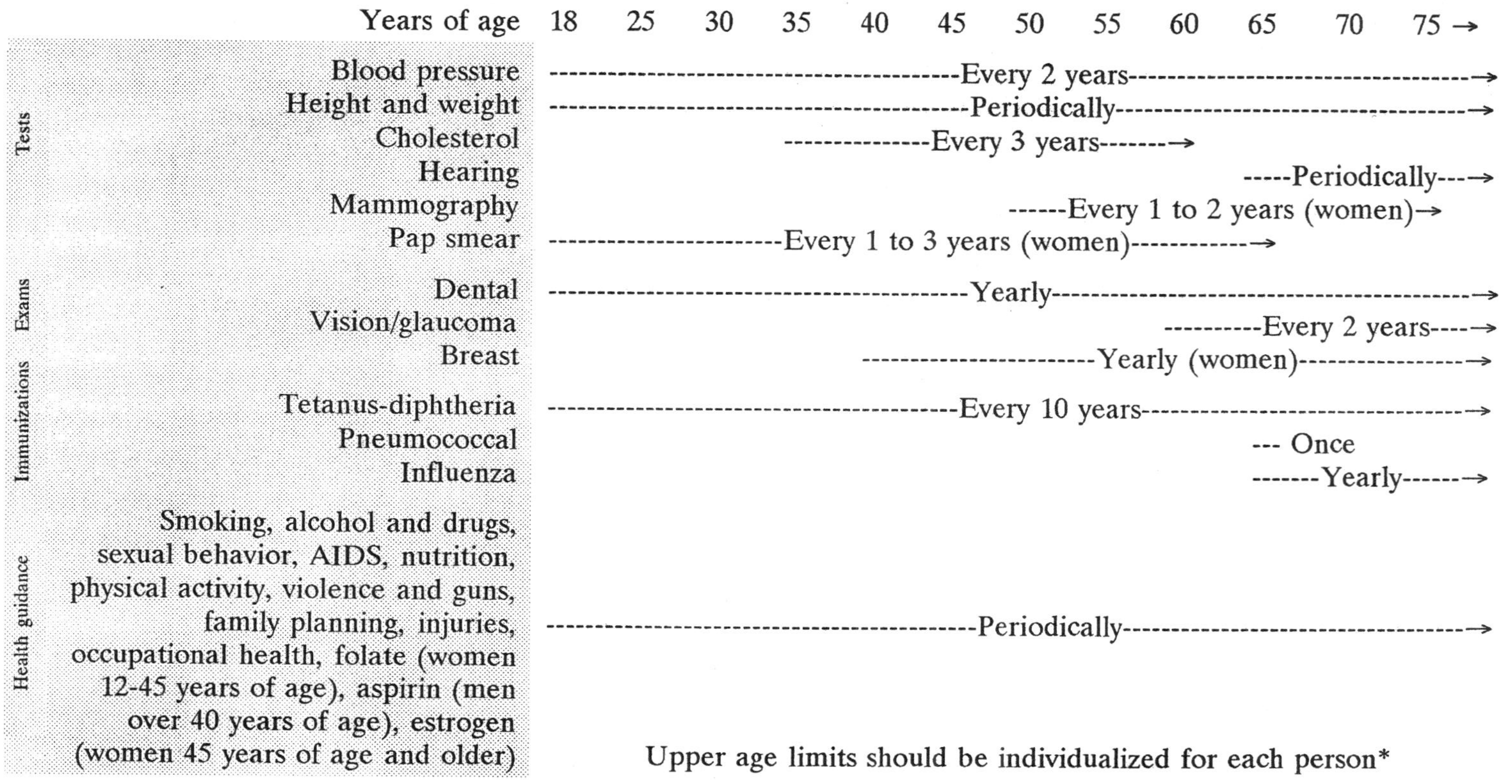

Years of age	18	25	30	35	40	45	50	55	60	65	70	75 →

Tests

Blood pressure --------------------Every 2 years-------------------→
Height and weight --------------------Periodically-------------------→
Cholesterol --------Every 3 years-------→
Hearing   ----Periodically--->
Mammography   -----Every 1 to 2 years (women)-→
Pap smear --------Every 1 to 3 years (women)------→

Exams

Dental ------Yearly------→
Vision/glaucoma   -----Every 2 years----→
Breast ------Yearly (women)----→

Immunizations

Tetanus-diphtheria --------Every 10 years-------→
Pneumococcal   --- Once
Influenza   ------Yearly------→

Health guidance

Smoking, alcohol and drugs,
sexual behavior, AIDS, nutrition,
physical activity, violence and guns,
family planning, injuries,
occupational health, folate (women
12-45 years of age), aspirin (men
over 40 years of age), estrogen
(women 45 years of age and older) --------Periodically-------→

Upper age limits should be individualized for each person*

Figure 22.2 Adult preventive care timeline. (Reprinted with permission from U.S. Public Health Service: Put Prevention Into Practice Campaign, Spring, 1995.)

Circle if appropriate		Year	'96	'97	'98	'99	'00	'01	'02
Drugs/Alcohol Physical Activity		Age							
Estrogen Tobacco Folate UV exposure		Date/ Type							
HIV/AIDS Violence Injuries		Date/ Type							
Nutrition		Date/ Type							
Occupational Health		Date/ Type							

Check-up Visit	Frequency	Date/ Result												
Blood Pressure	Every 2 yrs													
Cholesterol	Every 2 yrs													
Fecal Occult Blood	Every 5 yrs													
Vision	Every 2 yrs 60													
Hearing	Every 2 yrs >65													
Breast Exam	Every 1-3 yrs													
Mammography	Every yr > 50													
Pap Smear	q 1 yr x 3 then q 3 yrs													
Sigmoidoscopy	Every 5 yrs > 50													
Skin Exam	Every 6-12 mos													
Tetanus/diphth	q 10 yrs													
Pneumococcus	once													
Influenza	Yearly > 65													

Adapted from Put Prevention into Practice.

Figure 22.3 Adult preventive care flow sheet.

risk include those with fair skin, light eye and hair color, those exposed to occasional intense sunlight, and those with blistering burns during childhood or adolescence. In women with previous skin disease, fair skin, or "busy" skin, twice yearly exams are suggested. Women with companions who see well should be encouraged to regularly examine each other's skin. This increases the likelihood of finding lesions, particularly on ear tips and on the back, while they are highly treatable.

Sensory Impairment Screening

Seventy-five percent of older people have significant visual and auditory dysfunction they do not report to their physicians (21). Treating remedial conditions greatly improves the ability to perform activities of daily living, decreases accident rates, and prevents social isolation and depression. As with many other problems of old age, vision and hearing problems occur so gradually that a woman may not recognize that she has a deficit until an accident occurs or a relative or health care provider detects the loss.

Vision. Decreases in visual acuity from morphological changes in all parts of the eye. Intraocular pressure slowly rises with increasing age. Tear secretion diminishes in older adults. This can lead to dryness of the eyes and can cause discomfort and endanger the intactness of the corneal surface. This is especially true for postmenopausal women. Substitution therapy with artificial tears is recommended (21). Ophthalmologic screening is recommended every other year after age 65 for acuity examination, evaluation of intraocular pressure, and visual field testing (22).

Hearing. Hearing problems are common in the elderly, particularly in a society in which high noise levels and age interact to cause hearing losses. Most often the loss in sensorineural (23). Common problems that are correctable in the offices include hearing loss caused by cerumen occluding the external auditory canal and medication side effects. The cerumen affects low-frequency sounds and worsens pre-existing hearing impairment. Women who routinely over-clean often use cotton-swabs or hairpins to attempt to remove wax; this pushes the cerumen against the tympanic membrane. Women who are taking aspirin in several different over-the-counter preparations may have a reversible hearing impairment. Providers need to encourage older women to get a hearing evaluation, although these women may be reluctant to wear hearing aids for a variety of reasons. Audiological referral for treatable hearing loss is recommended every 2 to 3 years after age 65 (24).

Taste and smell. With advanced aging, there is significant loss of lingual papillae and subsequent decrease in ability to taste. Salivary secretion diminishes with aging and decreases the solubilization of flavoring agents. Secondary taste sites may be covered by upper dentures and decrease taste acuity. In addition, olfactory bulbs atrophy (25). Anticholinergics, antihistamines, antidepressants, and other medications decrease salivary secretion and cause further problems (26, 27). Taste and olfactory changes can contribute to diminished interest in food. Providers should periodically evaluate for loss of ability to taste to prevent weight loss and other nutritionally related conditions.

Cancer Screening

Colon Cancer

Colorectal cancer is the third leading cause of death in American women. In 1994, 70,000 new cases and 28,000 deaths were reported (28). Because it is thought that most colorectal cancers develop from polyps, screening strategies to identify localized cancers and find polyps for removal may decrease mortality (Chapter 20) (29). These methods include fecal occult blood testing and sigmoidoscopy. Colon cancer screening is not included in the PPIP. There has been no consensus on whether, or how, to screen people at average risk for colorectal cancer, because until recently there have been no studies showing a mortality benefit. Special screening is recommended for those at high risk; risk factors include colorectal cancer in a first-degree family member, familial polyposis coli, personal history of endometrial, ovarian, or breast cancers, ulcerative colitis, and prior colon cancer.

Fecal occult blood testing. The American College of Physicians (ACP) recommends annual fecal occult blood testing (FOBT) after age 50 years (30). The CTF and the USPSTF found insufficient evidence for or against FOBT to make a recommendation (31). Of five large, randomized controlled trials, Mandel et al. recently published their results. This study (on equal numbers of women and men) compared FOBT using six guaiac-impregnated rehydrated slides performed every year, every 2 years, or not at all. After 13 years, a 3.3% reduction in mortality in colorectal cancer was found in the screened group compared with the unscreened group. No difference was found in mortality between the annually and the biannually screened groups. The positive predictive value of FOBT for cancer was 2.2%. The FOBT for colorectal cancer has poor sensitivity, only 30%. A modest mortality benefit, poor positive predictive value, and low sensitivity makes FOBT a poor method for screening (32).

Sigmoidoscopy. Randomized trials of sigmoidoscopy do not exist. Selby et al., however, conducted a well-designed, case-controlled study suggesting strong evidence for decreased mortality for colorectal cancer by periodic screening with rigid sigmoidoscopy. Patients who died of cancer of the rectum and distal colon within the view of the 20-cm rigid scope were less likely than matched controls to have had a screening sigmoidoscopy within the previous 10 years. Mortality from distal tumors was 59%. Interestingly, the mortality benefit for screening within 10 years was the same as that for screening within 2 years. For those at average risk, ACP recommends screening intervals of 3 to 5 years (33). USPSTF and CTF have not recommended screening (new guidelines are forthcoming) (10, 31).

Colonoscopy. Colonoscopy screening for those at high risk for colorectal cancer is recommended by all three groups (10, 31). Although indications and timing of screening vary, all recommend that colonoscopy begin at age 40 years for those with a first-degree family member with colorectal cancer. The ACP recommends a frequency of every 3 to 5 years (an air contrast barium enema may be substituted for colonoscopy) (31).

Breast Cancer

In the United States, only lung cancer causes more deaths among older women than breast cancer (Chapter 17.3). In 1994, breast cancer cause 46,000 deaths, and 182,000 new cases were detected (29). Breast cancer found early is highly treatable and should be treated more aggressively, in the older population than it has been previously.

Breast self-examination. No randomized trial evidence supports breast self-examination as a useful screening test. Retrospective studies showing greater detection of early stage tumors may be biased by the increased tendency to seek medical care in the people who regularly practice self-examination (34, 35). USPSTF, ACP, and CTF do not recommend this practice.

Mammography. Many randomized trials have shown significant reductions in breast cancer mortality in women over 50 who regularly received mammography (29). USPSTF, CTF, and ACP recommend annual or biannual screening for this age group. USPSTF recommends screening be stopped at age 75 years (10). The American Geriatrics Society recommends age 85 years as the age to stop mammograms. For a healthy older woman, a clinician should consider continued mammography every 2 to 3 years after age 85 years along with clinical breast exams.

Cervical Cancer

Sixty thousand cases of cervical cancer are diagnosed each year in the United States (Chapter 15.3). Although women over age 65 account for 14% of the women population, this group comprises 25% of new annual cervical cancer cases and 41% of deaths from this highly treatable disease (36). This alarming statistic is thought to be related chiefly to inadequate screening over the course of women's adult lives.

For those women age 65 years or older, decisions regarding cervical cancer screening should consider sexual activity, previous numbers of normal Papanicolaou tests since last sexual activity, and other risk factors including the number of lifetime partners (over three), intercourse before age 21, evidence of human papilloma virus (HPV), history of cigarette smoking, and previous history of cervical cancer or dysplasia (36).

The American Cancer Society and the National Cancer Institute revised their guidelines in 1988; in a consensus statement with the American College of Obstetricians and Gynecologists, they recommended screening throughout a woman's lifetime with no age cessation (37, 38). The CTF continues to recommend age 70 years as a last age for Pap tests, provided a patient has a history of two recent satisfactory Pap smears and no abnormal Pap smears within the last 9 years before screening ceases (39). If a woman is at low risk, with regular screenings, and two consecutive normal Pap tests up to age 65 years, additional screening may not be necessary, if she is no longer sexually active. A woman who continues regular sexual activity should have Pap testing after age 65 years every 3 years, if she has no risk factors other than continued sexual activity. Since 1990, Medicare reimburses for triennial screening with no upper age limit.

Uterine and Ovarian Cancers

Older woman are more likely than younger women to have any of the gynecologic cancers (Chapters 15.4 and 15.6). Endometrial ovarian and cervical cancers are usually more advanced at time of diagnosis. Studies show higher morbidity and mortality rates from late stage tumors and comorbidities. One to two yearly bimanual exams in healthy older women could reduce the incidence of many cancers being found late. Older women with decreased life expectancy, unwillingness or inability to accept treatment, or unwillingness to accept pelvic examinations represent groups for whom these recommendations are not applicable. The American College of Gynecology recommends cytologic exams of the vagina at 3- to 5-year intervals.

Lung Cancer

Lung cancer is the leading cause of cancer death in women in the United States. No current effective screening tests exist. Eighty percent of all lung cancers in women are a result of cigarette use. Chronic exposure to passive smoke causes additional numbers of lung cancers in nonsmoking women. All women should be counseled at each visit to stop smoking (Chapter 17).

Immunizations

Providers should examine their practice styles for efficiency of providing universal coverage of immunizations to the patients. Using personal immunization records might help to improve older women's immunization status as it has for children. Providing printed guidelines concerning anticipated immunization requirements by age may also be helpful. It is beneficial to time older patient's health maintenance exams or routine blood pressure rechecks to mid or late fall when all immunizations (i.e., influenza, pneumococcus, tetanus, and diphtheria) can be given at once as needed.

Tetanus and Diphtheria

Almost all cases of tetanus reported in the United States occur in persons over age 65 (40). Many older women have never received the primary series of tetanus and diphtheria immunizations. Immunization screening must include asking a woman if she has had her primary series of three injections (41). Most cases of diphtheria and tetanus occur in those who have never completed the immunization series. Women who have not received a tetanus-diphtheria toxoid series should be given the primary series of two doses, 4 weeks apart of 0.5 mL Td toxoids intramuscularly, with a third dose 6 months later. A booster should be given every 10 years.

Influenza

Influenza vaccines should be given to those at high risk within several weeks of the usual time for influenza outbreak in your region. Giving the vaccination too early in the year decreases its efficacy, which already may be as low as 30 to 40% in the frail elderly. Persons exposed to an outbreak of influenza A benefit from amantadine if given within 24 to 48 hours of the clinical symptoms. A dose of 100 mg per day in the elderly is recommended with further reductions if renal failure is present (42).

Pneumococcus Vaccination

Pneumococcus accounts for 40,000 deaths annually in the United States. Only 14% of persons age 65 and older have received the 23-valent pneumococcal vaccine. The vaccine is to be given at age 65 and again 6 years later in those patients who are considered at high risk, such as those with diabetes mellitus, chronic renal failure or lung disease, and congestive heart failure. The effectiveness is estimated at 50%; however, the 23 serotypes covered by the vaccine represent nearly 90% of the documented pneumococcal infections in the elderly. While the incidence of pneumonia is not affected, the vaccine is effective in decreasing the rates of bacteremia and subsequent mortality (43).

Modifying Risks of Cardiovascular Disease

Cardiovascular disease is the number one cause of death in women of all ages in the United States. Fifty percent of all people who die of this disease are women (29). After age 60 years, coronary artery disease is the number one cause of death in women (44). Primary prevention through modification of risk factors is the most effective way to reduce disease (Chapter 16.1). The modifiable risk factors are tobacco use, hypertension, hypercholesterolemia, and sedentary lifestyle (45). The Nurses Health Study, a nonrandomized trial, reports that women over the age of 50 with known coronary heart disease who take up to six aspirin each week may benefit from this precaution or practice as a secondary preventive measure (46). Vitamin E intake has been found to be inversely associated with risk of death from coronary artery disease, whereas intake of vitamins A and C were not related (46a).

Smoking Cessation

Twenty-nine percent of adult American women smoke (29). Consensus exists among the three panels (i.e., USPSTF, CTF, and ACP) that patients who smoke should be counseled to stop smoking at each visit. Brief office interventions were effective in reducing smoking rates. Considerable evidence exists that risk of myocardial infarction is reduced by smoking cessation in women as well as men, with benefits realized almost immediately. Smoking cessation reduces the risk for head and neck, esophageal, lung, bladder, and other cancers, as well as coronary artery disease, stroke, and chronic lung disease. There is a greater opportunity for smoking cessation to be effective in women because coronary artery disease develops in women at a later age than men. Within just 2 years, a woman who stops smoking before the onset of disease experiences a one-fourth reduction in mortality from all causes (47) (Chapter 6.2).

Hypercholesterolemia

Controversy exists regarding the benefits of screening cholesterol levels in older women. Information on cholesterol treatment to prevent heart disease is limited in women. Most studies have had no women or few women as participants. Two trials that did have women as participants showed no benefit from intervention (48, 49).

Older women chosen for hypercholesterolemia screening should be those in whom the benefits outweigh the risks. These include those with known heart or peripheral vascular disease, diabetes, smoking history, hypertension, and family history of premature heart disease (29).

Hypertension

USPSTF, ACP and CTF recommend blood pressure measurement at every office visit (every 2 years in those with normal blood pressure; annually if diastolic pressure is 85 to 90 mm Hg). A diagnosis of hypertension is made if on three separate office visits with two or more readings at each visit the blood pressure is elevated (Chapter 16.2) (50).

Studies in men have shown definite benefits from early detection. There has also been shown that treatment of hypertension in women creates a 40% decrease in stroke incidence. Hypertension treatment should be offered as vigorously as in men by the guidelines established by the Joint National Committee on Detection Evaluation and Treatment of High Blood Pressure.

Exercise

Nearly half the older adults are sedentary. There are established relationships between several chronic diseases and lack of physical activity, including glucose intolerance, obesity, hypertension, reduced HDL levels, and osteoporosis. Regular physical activity is beneficial to older women. Counseling to change exercise behavior is unproved.

Principles of Medication Management

Principles of Prescribing for the Older Woman

Complex dosage schedules are often unnecessary and costly, and predispose the older woman to nonadherent behavior and, worse, to adverse drug reactions. The greatest cause of iatrogenic illness is adverse drug reactions (51). Annual review of all prescription and nonprescription medications should be done; medications should be brought to the visit. A personal medical record will simplify communication for all participants. More medication problems occur in this age group from misuse than abuse. Routine clarification is critical, especially as the number of prescriptions increases.

Pharmacologic and nonpharmacologic considerations influence the effectiveness and safety of drug therapy. Table 22.7 outlines critical nonpharmacologic factors that may hin-

Table 22.7. Factors Influencing Proper Drug Therapy

- Incorrect diagnoses due to
  Under-reporting of symptoms
  Vague, low grade and multiple complaints when they do occur
  Physical symptoms that overlap with psychological symptoms
  Atypical presentation of disease
  Health care providers may treat symptoms with drugs rather than determine origin of symptoms
- Older women with several problems may consult with several providers
- Family members may exert pressure on health care providers to provide medications
- Lack of a personal record and routine gathering up of all medications, including OTCs, for office visits increases misuse problems
- Adherence to therapy can be impaired by
  The nature of chronic illness requiring ongoing therapy
  Decreased hearing, vision, taste, and short-term memory loss
  Transportation
  Prescriptions not covered by Medicare
  Child-proof bottles

der success when prescribing for this population.

Strategies to increase adherence include (1) simplifying drug regimens in keeping with daily routine, once daily if possible; (2) educating caregivers using personal medical records and prescription bottles during clinic visit, and (3) facilitating older persons' ability to obtain and open medication packaging.

Adverse Drug Reactions and Interactions

Adverse drug reactions account for nearly 10% of hospital admissions and several billion dollars annually in health care expenditures. Most adverse reactions mimic other illnesses and are not recognized to be medication-related (or worse, are treated with another medication). Drug displacement from protein-building sites by other highly protein-bound drugs, inductions or suppression of the metabolites of other drugs, and additive effects of drugs on blood pressure and mental function are the most common types of potential adverse drug reactions.

Age-Related Changes

Although changes related to renal function can be predicted with some certainty, the effects of other age-related changes are difficult to predict and are variable. Hydration, nutrition, and cardiac output are more important than age-related changes. Absorption, distribution, metabolism, excretion, and tissue sensitivity are factors that may affect the way in which an older woman responds to a medication. Age-related changes related to absorption are caused by decreases in absorptive surface, increased gastric pH, and altered gastrointestinal motility. Decreases in total body water, lean body mass, serum albumin, and increased fat and altered protein-binding alter the volume of distribution.

The effects of aging on drug metabolism are difficult to predict depending on the pathway of drug metabolism in the liver and other factors such as gender and the amount of smoking. Smoking (and to a lesser extent other environmental factors) decreases induction of drug-metabolizing enzymes with advancing age. Older women, even with normal liver function tests, may not metabolize drugs as efficiently as younger women.

Many factors are related to the effects of aging on renal function and drug elimination. Renal function declines with age; pharmacokinetics of several drugs that are eliminated predominantly by the kidney are adversely affected. The half-life and duration of action are prolonged, and there is a tendency to accumulate potentially toxic drug concentrations in their steady state. There is wide individual variation in the rate of decline of renal function with increasing age. There is an average of a 50% decline in renal function between ages 20 and 90 years.

Muscle mass declines with age and daily endogenous creatinine production decreases. Serum creatinine may be normal at a time when renal function is substantially reduced. Serum creatinine does not reflect renal function as accurately in the older woman as it does in the younger woman. Creatinine clearance, rather than serum creatinine, should be used to determine renal function.

Older adults must be thoroughly evaluated to determine conditions that can benefit from drug therapy, be adversely affected by pharmacological interventions, or influence the efficacy of these treatments. Drug interactions should be avoided. Providers should know the pharmacology of drugs, and should use nomograms to determine proper dosages, obtain drug levels if needed, and help adherence to drug therapy by helping to maintain optimal function and by frequent monitoring to assure opportunities for communication.

Special Considerations

Facilitating Sexual Health and Well-Being

Cultural bias against older women's sexuality is strong. This bias can make a woman unwilling to discuss sexual function with her health care provider who often has little training for such dialogue. Few studies address sexual function in older women (52).

Physiological Factors Influencing Sexuality

There is a decrease in frequency of sexual activity from age 35 years. Reasons for this include life stressors and partner disinterest. Individual response accounts for wide variation. Table 22.8 shows factors that can negatively

Table 22.8. Issues Affecting Sexual Function in the Older Woman

Social factors
   Cultural bias related to sexuality of older women
   Increased prevalence of anxiety and depression
   Lack of satisfactory sexual partner
   Religious devoutness
   Lack of privacy: living with adult children or in long-term care facilities
Biological factors
   Anatomic changes
      Genitalia: smaller vaginal size, thinning of walls, decreased lubrication, and blood flow, thinning
         of labia majora and labia minora, increased exposure of clitoris, decreased sensitivity, vagi-
         nal infection
      Breast: decreased engorgement during arousal, sensory changes in nipple and areola
      Perineal muscle tone diminished
   Hormonal changes
      Decreased plasma levels of estrogen and androstenedione
      Increased plasma levels of follicle-stimulating hormone, luteinizing hormone, and testosterone
   Comorbid illness: diabetes mellitus, thyroid disease, congestive heart failure, angina, arthritis,
      dementia, cancer, urinary disease, gynecological surgery, ostomies
   Drug use: alcohol, antihypertensive, antidepressants and antihistamine use
   Medication use

impact sexual behavior in older women. These issues need to be addressed as part of routine health maintenance to help support the process of healthy sexual function in later years.

Dialogue Designed to Elicit Sexual Problems

Identifying sexual problems and answering questions related to sexual concerns is a good first step to help a woman ensure a healthy mid- and late life (Table 22.9). A medical history that covers the spectrum of biopsychosocial factors lays the foundation for learning what issues or conditions may be affecting sexual function. Information obtained during the review of systems will identify problems such as vaginal atrophy, arthritis, or orthopnea which may hinder sexual relations. This conversation may take extra time and subtlety, because it is not considered culturally acceptable for a 60 year old woman to seek advice about

decreased libido. The provider should open the door by asking general open-ended questions like, "Are you having any problems with sexual relations?" This will give the message that such topics are health-related and that help may be possible.

Medical Conditions That May Interfere with Sexual Function

Endocrine disorders increase with age. One third of diabetic women have secondary anorgasmy about 5 years after the disease is diagnosed. These women often have problems with vaginal lubrication secondary to frequent vaginitis. Sexual dysfunction related to endocrine disease is usually caused by peripheral nerve damage, or less commonly from circulatory insufficiency, and is usually treatable (53).

With mild heart disease, there is usually no associated sexual dysfunction, although anxiety over the effect sexual excitement has

Table 22.9. Ways Providers Can Facilitate Sexual Function in Older Women

Educate regarding the biology of aging
   How aging alone usually does not negatively impact sexual function
   Changes in sexual function related to medications, alcohol abuse and disease
Educate regarding the psychosocial factors of aging
   Wide variation in interest "norms" which is life long
   Postsurgical changes are variable
Correct physiological conditions
   Estrogen/testosterone
   Vaginal dryness
   Pelvic scarring
Suggest alternate noncoital activity
   With a partner
   Without a partner
Support need for privacy in long-term care facility
Refer for sex therapy

on the heart can prompt avoidance. Ability to participate in sexual activity is limited with severe heart disease. After a myocardial infarction, women seem to have less anxiety about sexual relations than men do (54). As women age, treatment for heart disease and hypertension increases. Some women on antihypertensives describe decreased libido, altered sexual arousal, and anorgasmy (55). Tranquilizers and antidepressants can also cause anorgasmy (56).

Women with chronic obstructive lung disease who use high dose glucocorticoids may negatively impact the hypothalamic-pituitary-gonadal axis (57). Since shortness of breath with minimal exertion would certainly contribute to the avoidance of sexual activity, it is critical to maximize pulmonary function.

Osteoarthritis or rheumatoid arthritis may prevent sexual pleasure. Analgesics, taken properly and timed to the sexual act, may improve sexual function. Exploring alternative coital positions may also be helpful. In one study, 27 of 53 women who underwent total hip replacement reported that the operation alleviated sexual difficulties that had been caused by pain (58).

Women who have breast cancer and undergo surgery experience a variety of sexual responses. Approximately one fourth of the women report lack of orgasm after mastectomy. The psychological effects of loss of a breast on sexual and body imagery can range from mild to serious (59). The additional burden of being advised not to take estrogen replacement can be quite difficult.

Large numbers of older women have had gynecologic surgery. Old wives' tales of hysterectomy decreasing femininity may cause women to respond with decreased sexual interest. Women who had once felt positively about their bodies may feel a distinct loss after hysterectomy that can affect sexual pleasure (60). Secondary pelvic scarring and adhesions may also cause problems.

In exploring problems, providers should consider drugs that both they and others may have prescribed, such as antihistamines that can cause decreased vaginal lubrication. Providers should routinely question alcohol intake, which decreases sexual arousal in 40% of women and anorgasmy in 15%. Adverse effects of narcotics are well known. Sixty percent of those women studied had low sexual interest, and 30% reported lack of orgasm. Marijuana also slows reflexes and causes vaginal dryness.

With advancing age many women find themselves without a sexual partner. Those who remarry are often faced with new problems such as stepchildren and financial concerns that can cause strain. Women who have managed to stay married and develop a positive sexual relationship by late adulthood may discover an opportunity to focus on their own responses and create opportunities for more relaxed sexual activity. Couples often enjoy sex more fully as they know each other better and as children move away from home.

Sexual issues are somewhat different for lesbians. The available literature suggests that lesbians make easier transitions into middle and late adulthood because most of these women are in lasting monogamous relationships. They may also have fewer worries stemming from the culture's definitions of physical attractiveness; they have explored other ways of sexual expression as they have not been and will not be dependent on coital sex. However, a lesbian woman who has been poorly treated by health care professionals in the past may require more time before trust is established. She may not mention her sexual orientation or sexual concerns until she is certain that she will be respected (Chapter 10.7).

Providers of care of older women in nursing homes should consider how their psychological needs for intimacy and privacy in these environments can be supported. Acting as advocates for women in institutional settings and for women who live with families who are nonsupportive of an older woman's need for ongoing intimacy will be important. Masturbation, oral sex, and manual stimulation are useful alternatives for couples where erection is not possible. Couples often need resource materials on how to develop creative ways of expressing their closeness. Table 22.9 shows how older women can be aided in maintenance of their sexual function and be supported in this important, ongoing pleasure and need. Satisfying sexual function remains a reasonable and important goal throughout the life cycle.

Caregiver Stress

Nearly three fourths of the care provided at home for older persons is provided by women. Most of the day-to-day care in acute and long-term care facilities is provided by women. Women care for themselves, their children, grandchildren, spouses, parents, and sometimes their grandparents (Table 22.10). Most also work outside the homes and are nonetheless expected to perform this caregiving. Their own health and well-being often suffers in the process.

Table 22.10 Caregivers for Older Persons

Women	Percentage	Men	Percentage
Daughters	29	Husbands	13
Wives	23	Sons	8
Other Women	20	Other Men	7
Total	72	Total	28

Data from U.S. Senate Subcommittee on Aging, American Association of Retired Persons, Federal Council on Aging, and U.S. Administration on Aging. *Aging America: Trends and Projections.* DHHS Publication No. (FCoA) 91-28001. U.S. Department of Health and Human Services, 1991.

Health care providers to older women play a vital role in providing education and support to older women as they care for disabled family members. Frequently, providers may be the only person who understands that this caregiving is overwhelming, isolating, dangerous to well-being, and virtually impossible to maintain in a healthy way. Providers must be vigorous advocates for these women. Table 22.11 outlines ways in which providers can support women patients who function as caregivers.

Emotional and Physical Abuse of the Older Woman

Older women are seen as vulnerable and frail targets for many abuses, both by family and by strangers. They are often afraid or unable to speak about the abuse to anyone, including their health care provider. Annually an estimated 1 million older adults experience abuse or neglect. Nearly 90% of older women who are abused are abused by a relative; of these, 40% are abused by a spouse (61).

Table 22.11. Ways in Which Providers Can Facilitate Caregiver Health and Well-being

Recognize that each caregiver faces emotional, physical and/or economic stress. They feel frustrated, isolated and overwhelmed.

Remind caregivers of these needs for self-care:
Keep regular appointments for their own care.
Find daily ways to create time for self.
Remember to take medications properly.
Enlist services or family and friends who offer to help, e.g., make a list and when someone asks what they can do, tell them specifically what is needed.
Use respite care as often as possible.

Educate office staff to help women seek self-help and support groups who can create insight and a sense of connectedness.

Be knowledgeable regarding community services for assisting these caregivers

Be prepared to make home visits to prevent older women from transporting a disabled family member in an ambulance for which Medicare often will not pay. The provider team can share this responsibility to decrease stress on one provider.

Encourage the woman to plan ahead by consulting with an attorney to plan for crises, long-term care issues and possible division of assets.

Schedule a family conference to help other family members know what needs to be done and how the family can work together.

Routinely formalize advance directive discussions with older women patients and those for whom they care to prevent unnecessary hardship related to end-of-life decisions.

Encourage the caregiver not to promise that she will not place a loved one in a long-term care facility as this may be beyond her control.

Let caregiver know you understand some of what is required to maintain their loved one as well as they do.

Although it is easy to say that providers should routinely screen for signs and symptoms of abuse, to do so means that providers must be knowledgeable in what steps to take when evidence of this common problem is found. Although some providers feel poorly trained or uncomfortable in providing appropriate counseling, there are several ways in which providers can build a bridge between the woman who has been abused and the help she needs. Providers routinely need to question her about fears for her physical or emotional safety. If a positive response, verbal or nonverbal, is given, providers can gently proceed to more supportive, focused questions. It is critical to have an excellent knowledge of the psychotherapeutic, support group, and protective service organizations in the communities, and to have ongoing relationships with someone in each of these organizations. Often, several groups need to be coordinated around a problem and the provider may initially serve as the case manager.

Evaluating or re-evaluating an older woman's medical problems in light of this information may provide clues to unexplained headache, abdominal pain, pelvic pain, or failure to thrive (62, 63). Certainly a more detailed physical examination is required after such a history.

If the provider encounters a woman who is experiencing abuse, the first thing to do is to determine if she is in immediate danger in her present environment and assure her that her safety is the most important step. Next, is the coordination appropriate investigative/therapeutic services and provision of comprehensive ongoing health care with opportunities to discuss her emotions/concerns related to this difficult situation. This is likely to create some uncomfortable moments for both the woman (who may be feeling fear, shame, guilt, anger, and frustration) and the provider.

Some older women will leave a dangerous home environment the first time the problem is discussed with them. Others cannot and will stay through years of abuse. Women are often afraid to leave for fear of being maimed or killed or for reasons related to economics, family pressures, or religious convictions. Accurate documentation is critical, because these problems may lead to civil or criminal action. As providers are sometimes the only person the abused person sees regularly or can trust, the attention to this problem is the victim's only potentially safe road to a healthy life free of abuse.

Team Care of the Older Woman

The subtle and complex presentations of illness in a woman of advancing age combined with the need to assess health in a multidimensional fashion and provide a wide range of resources makes team care a necessity. Physical, psychological, functional, environmental, economic, and social parameters need to be assessed in older women for whom primary care is provided.

As the need for home care, multiple office visits, consultant communication, and longer clinical encounters increase, shared clinical responsibilities between physician assistants, nurse practitioners, social workers, and physicians will increase the chance that a woman will see someone with whom she is familiar and that care will be provided in a timely, efficient manner.

Conclusion

Providers are not intentionally ageist, but rather mirror those negative stereotypes in the culture. These attitudes and practices are not accurate reflections of this heterogeneous population and can negatively impact the care. Taking more time for each visit and using more visits to assess an older woman may seem difficult when one considers possible reimbursement barriers. However, a patient, comprehensive, and respectful approach to evaluation results in more efficient and satisfying relationships for the older woman patient.

Providers need to think less of "managing" problems and more about facilitating health and well-being. Providers need to replace the language of "failed production," "withering," and "shutting down," with language that de-scribes the process of menopause and aging as a normal, healthy, and vibrant time of life. Older women have much to teach the culture. It may be helpful to think of the term "saging" (from "sage") than "aging."

Special Considerations for Nurse Practitioners and Physician Assistants

When an older woman seeks health care, the provider can easily be so overwhelmed with many concurrent chronic diseases that health promotion issues are forgotten. Sometimes the more acute or health-threatening problems will use all the time available for a woman's visit. In that case, nurse practitioners and physician assistants should tell the woman that a review of her health screening and promotion needs will be done on the next visit. Use of protocols, chart stickers, posters, and tracking devices will help. Providers who believe in the value of health promotion activities for older women will take extra measures, when necessary, to provide the comprehensive care previously discussed.

Not enough is known about what keeps older women healthy and adjusted, but it is not likely that older women want to leave their health to chance. In a sample of 477 subjects age 65 years and over, those who reported their current health as good, had high self-esteem, and believed their health was under their own control were more likely to engage in frequent or routine nutrition, stress management, interpersonal support, and exercise health promotion activities. Even women whose health was not good were more likely than men to engage in exercise and nutrition behaviors (64). Many older women have faced difficult losses and adjusted successfully, continuing to participate in activities and maintain a good morale (65). Other frail older women have been able to maintain their independence and reside in the community (66). Additional research on resilient, adjusted healthy women must be done to identify factors that help older women function to their fullest capacity.

All health care providers must become more aware of ageist attitudes and behaviors they or their staff may exhibit. Overprotective behaviors by providers or family members can prevent the older woman from having a voice in health care decisions. If the older woman's concerns are ignored and she is continually treated as a child, then she may internalize others' ageist attitudes, creating a self-fulfilling prophecy. If she does express herself assertively, she may face the risk of being labeled as a difficult patient (67).

As the women age who lived through and participated in the activism of the 1960s, it is likely they will confront governmental bureaucracy about the past sexism in research and demand that action be taken to keep women from dying of breast cancer, heart disease, ovarian cancer, and other tragedies. These women will likely use computer technology to network support groups for action (68). Older women should not have to demand a comprehensive, compassionate, and respectful approach to health care. All providers should be offering that care on a routine basis.

Acknowledgment

The author wished to thank Ms. Barbara Sale for her patience and expertise in the preparation of the manuscript. She also wished to thank Davis Miller and Elizabeth Marion Thomas for their kind and wise readings.

Appendix I

Resource List

Organization	*Phone Number*
Administration on Aging	1-202-401-4541
Alzheimer's Association	1-800-272-3900
Alzheimer's Disease Education and Referral Center	1-800-438-4380
American Association of Retired Persons	1-202-434-2277
Children of Aging Parents	1-215-945-6900
Elder Care Locator	1-800-677-1116
Help for Incontinent People	1-800-BLADDER
National Aging Resource Center on Elder Abuse	1-202-682-2470
National Cancer Institute	1-800-4CANCER
National Hospice Organization	1-800-658-8898
NIMH Depression Awareness, Recognition and Treatment Program	1-800-421-4211
National Institute on Aging Information Center	1-800-222-2225
National Stroke Association	1-800-367-1990
Sex Information and Education Council of the U.S.	1-212-819-9770

References

1. Legato M. Health Care in the United States: The new focus on women. Physician Assistant. Special supplement to February, 1995:33–39.
2. Bureau of Labor Statistics. Working Women. A Chart Book. Washington, DC: U.S. Department of Labor: 1991. Bulletin 2385.
3. U.S. Senate Special Committee on Aging. Aging America: Trends and Projections. Washington, DC: U.S. Department of Health and Human Services; 1988.
4. The Menopause, Hormone Therapy in Women's Health. Washington, DC: Congressional Office of Technology Assessment, 1992.
5. Mader SL, Ford AB. History and physical examination of the geriatric patient. In: Calkins E, Ford AB, Katz PR, eds. Practice of Geriatrics. 2nd ed. Philadelphia: WB Saunders, 1992:101–109.
6. Tinetti M. Performance oriented assessment of mobility problems in elderly patients. J Am Ger Soc 1986;34:199.
7. Crum RM, Anthony JC, Bassett SS, Folstein MS. Population based norms for the mini-mental state examination by age and educational level. JAMA 1993;269:2386–2391.
8. Kane RL, Ouslander JG, Abrass IB. Essentials of Clinical Geriatrics. 3rd ed. New York: McGraw-Hill, 1994:280–281.
9. Katz S, Ford A, Moskowitz R, et al. The index of ADL: A standardized measure of biological and psychosocial function. JAMA 1963;185:914–919.
10. Preventive Services Task Force. Guide to Clinical Preventive Services: Report of the United States Preventive Services Task Force. Baltimore: Williams & Wilkins, 1989.
11. Sox HC Jr. Preventive health services in adults. N Engl J Med 1994;330:1589.
12. Kane RL, Ouslander JG, Abrass IB. Essentials of Clinical Geriatrics. 3rd ed. McGraw-Hill, 1994:29–30.
13. U.S. Senate Special Committee on Aging America. Trends and Projections, 1987–1988.
14. Kane RL, Ouslander JG, Abrass IB. Essentials of Clinical Geriatrics. 3rd ed. New York: McGraw-Hill, 1994:24.
15. Optimal Calcium Intake, NIH Consensus Statement 1994, June 6–8;12(4):1–31.
16. Fetherston DS, Althouse L. Geriatric medicine, In: Lemcke DP, ed. Primary care of women. Norwalk, CT: Appleton & Lange, 1995:26–30.
17. U.S. Public Health Service. Put Prevention Into Practice Campaign, Spring, 1995.
18. Roca RP, Klein LE, Kirby SM, et al. Recognition of dementia among medical patients. Arch Intern Med 1984;144:73–75.
19. Folstein MF, Folstein SE, McHugh PR. "Mini-Mental State": A practical method for grading the cognitive state of patients for the clinician. J Psychiatric Res 1975;12:189–198.
20. Yoshikawa TT, Cobbs EL, Brummel-Smith K. Ambulatory Geriatric Medicine. St Louis: Mosby, 1993:277–287.
21. Kane RL, Ouslander JG, Abrass IB. Essentials of Clinical Geriatrics. 3rd ed. New York: McGraw-Hill, 1994:308–311.
22. Marmor MF. Normal age-related vision changes and their effects on vision. In: Faye EE, Stuen CS, eds.

The Aging Eye and Low Vision. New York: Light-house, 1992.

23. Kane RL, Ouslander JG, Abrass IB. Essentials of Clincial Geriatrics. 3rd ed. New York: McGraw-Hill, 1994:319–326.

24. Mulrow CD, Lichtenstein MJ. Screening for hearing impairment in the elderly: rationale and strategy. J Gen Intern Med 1991;6:249–258.

25. Kane RL, Ouslander JG, Abrass IB. Essentials of Clincial Geriatrics. 3rd ed. New York: McGraw-Hill, 1994:327.

26. Anand KB, Eschmann E. Systemic effects of ophthalmic medication in the elderly. NY State J Med 1988;88:134–136.

27. Williamson J, Chopin JM. Adverse reactions to prescribed drugs in the elderly: A multi-centre investigation. Ageing 1980;9:73–80.

28. Boring CC, et al. Cancer statistics, 1994. CA 1994; 44:7.

29. Smith GD, Song F, Sheldon TA. Cholesterol lowering and mortality: The importance of considering initial level of risk. Br Med J 1993;306:1367.

30. American College of Physicians' Guidelines. In: Eddy DM, ed. Common Screening Tests. Philadelphia, PA: American College of Physicians, 1992:415–416.

31. Canadian Task Force on the Periodic Health Examination: The periodic health examination. Vol. 2. 1987 Update. Can Med Assoc J 1988;138:618.

32. Mandel JS, et al. Reducing mortality from colorectal cancer by screening for fecal occult blood. N Engl J Med 1993;328:1365.

33. Selby JV, et al. A case control study of screening sigmoidoscopy and mortality from colorectal cancer. N Engl J Med 1992;326:653.

34. Eddy DM. Screening for breast cancer. Ann Intern Med 1989;111:389.

35. Baker LH. Breast Cancer Detection Demonstration Project: five year summary report. CA 1982;32: 194.

36. Fahs MC, Mandelblatt J, Schechter C, Muller C. Cost-effectiveness of cervical cancer screening for the elderly. Ann Intern Med 1992;117:520–527.

37. National Institute of Health. Press release. Bethesda, MD: January 1988.

38. Fink DJ. Change in American Cancer Society check-up guidelines for detection of cervical cancer. CA 1988;38:127–128.

39. Miller AB, Anderson G, Brisson J, et al. Report of a national workshop on screening for cancer of the cervix. Can Med Assoc J 1991;145:(suppl)1301–1325.

40. Williams WW, et al. Immunization policies and vaccines coverage among adults: the risk for missed opportunities. Ann Intern Med 1988;108:616.

41. Gardner P, Schaffner W. Immunization of adults. N Engl J Med 1993;328:1252.

42. Prevention and Control of Influenza: Recommendations of the Immunization Practice Advisory Committee. MMWR 1992;41[RR-9].

43. Shapiro ED, et al. The protective efficacy of polyvalent pneumococcal polysaccharide vaccine. N Engl J Med 1991;325:1453.

44. Rich-Edwards JW, Manson JE, Hennekens CH, Buring JE. The primary prevention of coronary heart disease in women. N Engl J Med 1995;332:1758–1765.

45. Lerner D, Kannel W. Patterns of coronary heart disease morbidity and mortality in the sexes: A 26 year follow-up of the Framingham population. Am Heart J 1986;111:383.

46. Manson JE, Stampher MH, Colditz GA, et al. A prospective Study of Aspirin Uses and Primary prevention of cardiovascular disease in women. JAMA 1991;266:521–527.

46a. Kushi LH, Folsom AR, Prineas RJ, Mink PJ, Wu Y, Bostick RM. Dietary antioxidant vitamins and death from coronary heart disease in postmenopausal women. N Engl J Med 1996;334:1156–1162.

47. Centers for Disease Control and Prevention: Cigarette smoking among adults—United States, 1991. MMWR 1993;42:230.

48. Dorr AE, et al. Colestipol hydrochloride in hypercholesterolemia patients: Effect on serum cholesterol and mortality. J Chronic Dis 1978;31:5.

49. Frantz ID, et al. Test of effect of lipid lowering by diet on cardiovascular risk. The Minnesota Coronary Study. Atherosclerosis 1989;9:129.

50. Joint National Committee on Detection, Evaluation, and Treatment of High Blood Pressure: The Fifth Report of the Joint National Committee on Detection, Evaluation, and Treatment of High Blood Pressure. Arch Intern Med 1993;153:154.

51. Lamy P. The elderly and drug interactions. J Am Geriatr Soc 1986;34:586.

52. Nachtigall LE. Sexual function. In: Lobo RA, ed. The treatment of the postmenopausal woman. New York: Raven Press, 1994:301–306.

53. Mooradian A, Greiff V. Sexuality in older women. Arch Intern Med 1990;150:1033–1038.

54. Baggs JG, Karch AM. Sexual counseling of women with coronary heart disease. Heart Lung. 1987;16:154–159.

55. Papadopoulos C. Cardiovascular drugs and sexuality: a cardiologist's review. Arch Intern Med 1980; 140:1341–1345.

56. Buffum J. Pharmacosexology update: prescription drugs and sexual function. J Psychoactive Drugs 1986;18:97–106.

57. Thompson WL. Sexual problems in chronic respiratory disease: achieving and maintaining intimacy. Postgrad Med 1986;79:41–52.

58. Baldursson H, Brattstrom H. Sexual difficulties and total hip replacement in rheumatoid arthritis. Scand J Rheumatol 1979;8:214–216.

59. Silberfarb PM, Maurer H, Crouthamel CS. Psychosocial aspects of neoplastic disease, I: Functional status of breast cancer patients during differ

ent treatment regimens. Am J Psychiatry 1980; 137:450–455.

60. Northrup C. Menopause. In: Women's Bodies, Women's Wisdom. New York: Bantam, 1994:430–478.

61. Benton D, Marshall M. Elder abuse. Clin Geriatr Med 1991;7:831.

62. Drossman D. Sexual and physical abuse in women with functional or organic gastrointestinal disorder. Ann Intern Med 1990;113:828.

63. Rapkin A, et al. History of physical and sexual abuse in women with chronic pelvic pain. Obstet Gynecol 1990;76:92.

64. Duffy ME. Determinants of health-promoting lifestyles in older persons. IMAGE: J Nurs Scholarship 1993;25:23–28.

65. Wagnild G, Young HM. Resilience among older women. IMAGE: J Nurs Scholarship 1990;22:252–255.

66. Schrank MJ, Lough MA. Profile: frail elderly women, maintaining independence. J Advanced Nurs 1990;15:674–682.

67. Sharpe PA. Older women and health services: moving from ageism toward impowerment. Women Health 1995;22:9–20.

68. Freda MC. Childbearing, reproductive control, ag-

ing women, and health care: the projected ethical debates. JOGNN 1994;23:144–152.

Suggested Readings

Anderson EG. How not to talk with elderly patients. Geriatrics 1990;45:84–85.

Besdine RW. Clinical evaluation of the elderly patient. In: Hazzard WR, Andres R, Bierman EL, Blass JP, eds. Principles of Geriatric Medicine and Gerontology, 2nd ed. New York: McGraw-Hill, 1990, 175–183.

Bloom JS, Ansell P, Bloom MN. Detecting elder abuse: a guide for physicians. Geriatrics 1989, June;44:40–44, 56.

Doress PB, Siegal DL. Ourselves, Growing Older. New York: Touchstone, 1987:198–212.

Kane RL, Ouslander JG, Abrass IB. Essentials of Clincial Geriatrics. 3rd ed. New York: McGraw-Hill, 1994.

Mooradian A, Greiff V. Sexuality in older women. Arch Intern Med 1990;150:1033–1038.

Northrup C. Women's Bodies, Women's wisdom. New York: Bantam, 1994:430–478.

Root MJ. Communication barriers between older women and physicians. Public Health Report 1987; July–August (Suppl):152–155.

23

Psychosocial Issues of Older Women: Independence and Interdependence

Mary Elizabeth Roth

Independence and Interdependence of the Older Woman

As women start the transition from middle age (around age 55 years) into the physical and psychological work of aging within society, they experience profound changes. Issues that faced them earlier, such as menopause, and choices they made, such as medical choices of hormone replacement, impact their health the rest of their life (see Chapters 20, 21). For example, the crisis of fractures and dependency in old age may be the direct result of choosing not to take hormone replacement in middle age (1, 2). Further, middle-age women carry multiple evolv-

Table 23.1. Sociologic Tasks of Older Women

- Adjusting to declining physical strength and health
- Adjusting to retirement and its reduced income
- Adjusting to changes in the health of one's spouse
- Establishing an explicit affiliation with one's age group
- Adopting and adapting social roles in a flexible way
- Establishing satisfactory physical living arrangements

ing responsibilities of the sandwich generation; these are passed along from their shoulders to their daughters as they age. Yet, the women in this last third of their lives are personally unique. Neither providers nor society can make sweeping generalizations. Although many may face increasing disability, many others find new challenges, independence, new relationships, and interconnections as they age. The provider will be challenged to work with each older woman and forge a relationship that will be to both of their benefits.

In sociologic terms, women have developmental tasks for this last dimension of personal growth and development (Table 23.1) (3). These tasks include the preparation for grief, dying and death of spouse, friends, family, and self. The provider needs to assess and support the ability of the older woman to maintain self-acceptance, self-esteem, and a positive self-concept (4).

This chapter explores these developmental tasks in clinical terms for clinical assessment, support, and care of the older woman.

Family Life Cycle Expectations

Completion of Childrearing

Customary Expectations
In planning for "old age," most women expect to raise their children to independence outside

their own household. Family life cycle theories place an expectation that mothers become grandmothers and that older women have a spouse to share retirement and time for all the avocations and delayed gratifications of the American middle class lifestyle (5). The concept of the family life cycle is part of the socialization of what it means to be part of a family, to grow old, and to die. It creates an expectation of birthing and regeneration of family traditions.

Women aspire to the role of supportive grandparent and knowing elder. Further, the role of rest and respite from drudgery of mothering small children, while enjoying small children's growing curiosity and play time, is a promised, and many times accomplished, reward for raising one's own children. Children are expected to become self-supporting adults with interests and energy of their own. Mature parents expect their children to bring resources and activity to them, and not in their later decades of life to support and entertain their own middle-age children.

Exceptions to Customary Expectations

There are some circumstances that do not allow an older woman the chance of attaining customary expectations. Women who have mothered children who have failed to develop mentally past childhood face the frustrating dilemma of entering old age with a child who is still dependent (6). This problem becomes serious when women of such children age and watch their peers enjoying adult children raising grandchildren. These mothers face the role of motherhood perpetually. Children with severe cerebral palsy, the amino-acid urias, mental retardation, autism, and Down's syndrome may become dependent adults on their aging mothers. Women with children with Down's syndrome face the additional burden and threat that their child may develop Alzheimer's dementia in their 40s to create permanent dependency. Medical and psychological problems of a child that seemed heavy to a woman age 25 years can become overwhelming to the same mother at age 65 years. The promise of independence in middle life is denied, and depression and fatigue are high risk for these aging mothers.

There are other circumstances that may interfere with a woman's completion of child-rearing. After a young adult has a catastrophic accident or disease, his mother often resumes the parental and nursing role. Many adults with the debilitating problems of AIDS return to their mothers' care. These women accept the medical and psychological burdens of caring for their child. Providers need to attend to the elderly mother caregivers of distressed or mentally impaired adult children as women at higher physiologic and psychologic risk. Physically caring for a child heavier than themselves causes risk of back pain and regurgitation dyspepsias. Older women caregivers have more hypertension, angina, sleep problems, anxiety, depression, and substance abuse.

Schizophrenia as a chronic and debilitating illness frequently returns a child to their mother's house. The risk of violence and battering to an aging parent from adult mental health patients must be assessed. Women with adult underemployed children in the household need to be asked about the present risk for violence. Sociopathic, drug-using adult children have impulse control problems that may endanger their frail mother. Elder abuse can happen to cognitively competent elderly with physically dangerous mentally impaired children and relatives (7).

Caring for one's grandchildren as primary caretaker is an assumed role often in inner-city and extended families. The physical burdens of caring for toddlers and adolescents complicate the lives of many economically burdened older women. Raising one's grandchildren is more than a social burden and raises most health risks.

Planning for Retirement

Customary Expectations

Another life-cycle expectation is choice of retirement at a planned age with pension and ability to live in a comfortable environment with leisure time (8). Marriage to a healthy spouse allows greater economic possibilities. Other life-cycle expectations include a marriage that survives the changing social demands of middle-age and alteration of family needs.

Exceptions to Customary Expectations

The most profound risk for women entering the retirement cycle is loss of spouse by death or divorce prior to attaining the reward of retirement, pension, and leisure. However, an older husband may have a lower expected life expectancy and may develop an illness or die. Often death of a spouse while the women are in their late 50s leaves a major economic crisis; the woman may have partial social security or pension survivor benefits that produce inadequate income to maintain lifestyle. She faces returning to work, moving in with adult children or other family, subsidized apartments, or other downturns in lifestyle. If the spouse dies prematurely and unexpectedly, the woman faces widowhood with growing or dependent children requiring adaptation and realignment of roles (8). After her caregiving years to possibly a sick spouse, sick in-laws, and adult children, the early widow faces her old age in a home alone. Her need to create new adult relationships that will last into her old age are critical to her survival emotionally.

Women facing divorce in late life also have changes in their plans for retirement and how leisure life will be experienced. Depression and prolonged grief reactions may complicate the ability to adapt to these problems of aging relations.

Statistically, women outlive men by 7 to 8 years. In American heterosexual couples, a man usually marries a woman 4 to 5 years younger than him. This presents the routine developmental task for women to accept the death of their spouse. Society presumes women will survive a spouse, and social security and social convention supports this premise. Women normally will adjust and precede with adaptive relationships after a grief period.

With the restructuring of corporate America, many couples face early retirement with less than expected income or loss of one or both incomes prematurely. The loss of cash flow during the years of maximal preretirement saving causes major stressors on attaining old-age independence. The failure of investments and late life bankruptcy has a high suicide and depression risk.

Caring for older women includes helping her plan lifelong exercise and pleasurable activities into old age. Many women who initiate aerobic exercise programs in midlife become increasingly frustrated when chronic pain, arthritis, and osteoarthritis limit their pleasure and possible fulfillment of leisure plans. The expectation that spouses will share similar hobbies often is matched by an ever widening differentiation in leisure pleasures as a couple ages. The "fantasy" that a spouse will find pleasure in like interests must be clinically addressed. The developmental task to find others of like interest is critically important for older women who find pleasure in activities that have little interest or are not physically possible for an ill spouse. As women return to a household that contains solely their marital partner, they need to realign their life priorities without children. This can be a major adjustment. Marriages strengthen and break as the couple face each other without childraising interruptions or priorities. Couples often find their personal interests and hobbies quite divergent by old age. This requires separate but equal time for development of both partners with other relationships and opportunities.

Many women save all their adult lives to change lifestyles with retirement. However, often older women face the inability to convince adult children to support their plan, they can't move an elderly sick spouse, they can't find the desired lifestyle or locale, it is no longer attainable or reasonable, or they find their planned (radical) change in their lifestyle frightening and threatening to their own supports. The failure of many couples or older women in living in Arizona, Palm Springs, or rural Michigan rests on the lost adaptability of the plan to the reality of the health and mental capability of an aging person. What appeared an idealistic retirement choice at age 52 years can become a catastrophe at age 68 years.

The best laid plans of couples can be crippled by "premature" chronic or terminal illness (9). The debility of routine illness in a woman or her spouse can alter drastically their plans for leisure in late life. For example, the need for chronic dialysis ties a couple to being near organized medical resources and to schedule vacations near dialysis units. Too old for a possible renal transplant, a stable older patient with renal failure finds herself scheduling the couple's life around dialysis. Rafting down the Colorado for 5 days may be as impossible as a Caribbean cruise or canoeing the Great Lakes with the grandchildren. Cancer risk increases risk with age, with 60% of cancers in individuals over age 60. A woman with cancer discovers that treatment requires regular appointments and possible residence near a center for chemo-therapy. The older person seeking cure must often postpone leisure distractions (10).

Progressively, the older woman will need assistance in maintaining a secure and enjoyable lifestyle (11). This includes awareness that external services and agencies may be needed to help an older woman maintain her home of origin. This might be the acceptance of help in maintaining the household such as the plumber, roofer, lawn maintenance, and gradual assistance in cleaning and shopping. The review most valuable for the provider to understand these issues are the Instrumental Activities of Daily Living (IADLs). (Table 23.2) After age 65, 50% of women will need assistance with at least one IADL, and by age 80, 50% will need assistance with another intimate Activities of Daily Living (ADLs) (13). There may be developed services that are active in outreach to the elderly. Women may be able to stay in their own homes until death or extreme disability because local resources make home a real comfort of old age.

However, large parts of rural America and remote counties do not have organized resources to help the elderly in their own homes.

Table 23.2. Activities of Daily Living (ADLs)—Physical Self-Maintenance

Each rated on a 5-point scale ranging from fully self-sufficient and independent to "requires assistance and prompting to do or is incompetent/incontinent"

- Toileting: continence and ability to use toilet alone
- Feeding: able to feed self without resistance or soilage
- Dressing: selects and dresses and undresses self appropriately
- Grooming: neatness of clothes, hair and body
- Transfers/ambulation: walks independent or with device alone
- Bathing: cleanses self without assistance

Instrumental Activities of Daily Living (IADLs)—Environmental competence scales, ability on dealing with the patient's social skills of survival

Tasks to be considered vary by author but are summarized here

- Uses telephone independently (in and out home)
- Prepares meals: plans, fixes, and times
- Personal laundry: able to wash all clothes
- Housekeeping: keeps home clean with minimal assistance with heavy work
- Takes own medicine to schedule appropriately
- Ambulates beyond home safely and independently
- Shops for groceries and needs independently
- Transportation: negotiates car or mass transport alone
- Finances: budgets money, pays bills, and timed payments including taxes and rent

Consequently, women with developing disabilities need to consider moving themselves or an impaired spouse in with others, into situations including retirement communities, relatives and adult children, just to assure a safe environment, regular meals, and help if it is needed (14). Fears of most older women include becoming dependent and disabled, and leaving their home, and placing physical, emotional, and economic burdens on others (15).

The acceptance of others working within one's home is a sociocultural difficulty for many women (16). Cultural value may be attached to a woman maintaining a household for herself, her spouse, or her impaired adult children. Providers need to review the family's and the woman's cultural values of her role before recommending services. Pride and self-worth may prevent using federally qualified programs to aid some elderly women. Racial, religious, and ethnic biases may impose barriers of who, how, and what are possible in an elderly woman's home to help her maintain her independence. Some would rather die than break tradition. Awareness by the provider of concerns and creative planning often solves problems. As an example, Kosher Meals-on-Wheels meet both the Jewish, Muslim, and Seventh Day Adventist food preparation guidelines.

As a developmental step, adapting to one's own age group is important. Senior centers, "Mature Minglers," and widows/widowers social clubs have enlivened the activities of older Americans. Yet, many older women lack the access to this. Transportation to a senior center frustrates many older women who may have never learned to drive, lost driving with vision or other medical problems, or are limited to mass transportation access problems. Getting out during the day for activities is only an ideal reached by small numbers of community-based older urban women. This may be because of lack of adequate socialization skills, transportation, and economic ability to pay for trips or extra activities by many economically strapped elderly (17). The federal support of lunches for the elderly makes it possible for many older women to experience the socialization and quality of a warm meal weekdays at a senior center. Distribution of these federal programs allow small communities to support senior activities.

With the increasingly obvious physical limits of aging on women in their 70s and 80s, the family frequently chooses one of two major pathways (14). Healthy families become increasingly involved in the planning and support of the older woman in her lifestyle. Adult children join their parents' discussion of choices, options, and decisions about finances, living arrangement, and medical care. In healthy families, adult children respect their parents' need for autonomy and the need for support by their children of their decisions, especially as it may create new dependence on their children. Decisions about selling houses, securities and businesses, signing of advanced directives, choosing for aggressive treatment of a malignancy or hospice, moving to a retirement community, and other major decisions of old age are comfortably discussed across the generations of a healthy family.

Dysfunctional individuals and families extend their pathology into old age. Women who have been victims of spousal abuse often develop abusive relationships with adult children (18, 19). Alcoholic parents who generated hate from their children reap these feelings in old age. Women with Axis I and II mental health disorders often manifest the product of years of dysfunctional family relationships when they age. Women with borderline or narcissistic personalities usually are alone, as they feared. Chronic mental health problems frequently manifest themselves as dysfunctional family function around the problems of old age. The provider needs to take a good mental health history to understand dysfunctional behaviors of a family, when crises arise around an elderly woman in distress. Often there are roots of a lifetime of psychiatric disorder that preceded the dysfunction the provider witnesses.

Choices for Living and Dying

To plan a graceful dying, an elderly woman has to be mentally competent and unconfused

emotionally. Depression occurs in 20% of the elderly, and is often undertreated by primary care providers. Depressed women are indecisive, feel guilty about the past, fail to focus, and have difficulty making decisions. Some depression in the elderly presents as "pseudodementia."

In the follow-up care for a woman who cares for a failing spouse or has lost a spouse the provider should discuss what the woman wants for herself when she faces life's end. This is the most opportune time to discuss what the patient felt about the decisions made for her husband, and how she would want decisions made for herself. In the situation of feeling powerless in the face of a recent death, the provider can empower a woman to make decisions for her future of how she wants her own end of life decisions made (20). The introduction of advance directives or living will, consistent with state laws, focuses the woman on choosing how things will be done if she is not able to state her preferences (21). It further requires her to reach out and identify other important people in her life to serve as her advocate. In many ways, this simple act in continuity care may bond the provider and woman (22). Further, adult children, relatives, and neighbors may not agree with the choices for the end of life a mother chooses. Often a widow will share her advance directives with her providers and friends only to be contradicted by adult children living elsewhere. Family members remote to daily routines may misjudge the quality of life of the elderly woman, or have unresolved issues that impede acceptance of her wishes. They may place unreasonable expectations on a woman in her choices for her end of life.

Dignity and independence as priorities are often disrupted for older women by simple problems like incontinence, frequent falls, decreased vision, and chronic diarrhea. The intervention by a geriatric assessment team may be the difference between continued independence at home and the decision to become dependent on others.

Changing Needs from Sandwich Generation Responsibilities to the Golden Years

Customary Expectations

As women give up their responsibilities as caregiver to the youth, disabled, and elderly of the family, they face the reality of surrendering the powerful position of family decision member (8). As women see their children become independent, they see less-encumbered years as possible. They look to the health of their husband, partner, parents, and/or in-laws as a warning of how much longer these older family members will not need them on an intense level. Sandwiched between the generations, women look both ways as they cross the street of life as they can get hit from any direction to be a caregiver.

The social needs of a woman in this transition zone are to address, with her life partner, her priorities for the second half of her life after childrearing. The provider needs to work with women in this age group on a preventive medicine protocol, because the highest risks for disease developing occur in the fifth decade. Heart disease and cancer are the two highest death risks for women over age 50 years. The need to design a health plan including exercise, diet, and leisure pleasure with a life partner is important parts of the provider's role in this age group (23).

The provider needs to update the social activities of women after the sixth decade regularly along with the Review of Systems to assure there are reasonable expectations in light of physiological aging and disease. For example, driving for Meals on Wheels and mowing the lawn at age 70 years may be safe for most women, but roofing for Habitat for Humanity, supervising 20 preschoolers alone, or driving a snow plow for the church may not. Just as an exercise plan needs to be encouraged to reduce disease, a reasonable expectation should be set about physical demands with an aging body considering the patient's known diseases and risks (12).

The provider often needs to assess the health of the older woman as the competent adult caregiver for her spouse, her parents, friends, and ultimately herself. The physical needs and body mechanics of the tasks required of the caregiver and the physiologic conditioning of the elderly woman needs to be assessed (10). The willingness to care for a dying spouse may blind a woman to her physical inability to do his ADLs and IADLs. For example, there may need to be a discussion of capabilities when an 80-year-old mother with COPD accepted daily care of her agitate 54-year-old son with end-stage AIDS, who despite wasting, weighed more than she. Counseling the woman about her realistic skills and her need to invite others to help her were a priority. She can become the decision-maker and coordinator of his home based care with many younger care givers included in his care.

Lastly, in the transition issues of surrendering the job of family caregiver is acceptance of an earned respite from burden. To be a respected matriarch is an earned and desirable role for an aging woman. In some societies, women perceive their lives as always burden and work and there is no imagined earned rest. Most of Christian society accepts the earned "day of rest" as an image of old age, even for women. Providers need to ask women about their cultural beliefs. For women from cultural norms that place a woman always as a focus of generated family work, aging has no attraction and becomes stressful as they become less competent to contribute to the family well-being. This loss of ultimate worth to their family with aging needs to be recognized as a high risk for depression and apathy in old age.

Widowhood and Singlehood in Old Age

Noah's Ark had the animals marching aboard two-by-two for survival. In aging, partnered couples fare better physiologically, economically, and psychologically. Single life has no advantage in old age. However, as women age, they fall into this undesired state increasingly each decade. Approximately 35% of women age 65 to 74 years live alone; 50% of women over age 75 years live alone, and 77% of the elderly who live alone are women (4).

Each woman's situation is different. Seventy percent of older women have adult children (17). Single women in old age often have shallow supports. Women in religious life are dependent on their adopted families for support in old age. Community-living never-married childless women need to plan their support systems in old age because there are limited social supports and no routinized outreach to help them. Divorced childless women frequently face the same dilemma. Providers need to assess the support situation of older women.

Statistically, women die in their late 70s after 10 years of widowhood. As women enter their 80s and 90s, among their hardest adaptive moments are facing the decline and possible death of their adult children. The burden of staying healthy as younger family members fail in health may overshadow the disappointment of outliving friends and siblings. The depression, loneliness, and isolation of the lone survivor of a generation or a family are often missed by the observer's delight in a healthy nonagenarian. Reaching age 100 years can be lonely without family or social supports.

Unique social and clinical dilemmas face the single childless woman as she faces retirement years and old age (17). She must be self-sufficient in her financial and resource planning for old age. Traditionally, the maiden old aunt school teacher or nurse put in her 45 years and had savings and a pension. However, many women who worked as domestics or in service industry jobs have little pension protection and they carry great fears for their old age. Women make 70% (at a full-time occupation) of what a man worker makes. Women fill most of the entrance level and service industry jobs. As primary income jobs, these lack salary, benefits, and security. Many women face the possibility they may need to work well into their seventies or until they fail by disability. Lesbian couples may have the advantage of combined two-person income to build retirement possibilities, but they may not be able to share couples' benefits in old age; they are considered single in federal and other pension programs, although this may be changing.

Older women do not only live alone, but they live in poverty. The state of living alone and in poverty is associated with 43% of single women, whereas only 4% of couples are considered poor (16). Financial independence as a goal is rarely reached by unmarried, unpartnered women over 70 years.

Social independence for the widowed or single woman is threatened as well. Couples are the common method of socialization in senior centers, churches, and other institutions. Older women as single adults become increasingly isolated. Most never married women have created social circles of support by old age. For many women, the imposed social isolation of widowhood and divorce is painful and illness-inducing. Lacking the financial means to initiate social life outside traditional subsidized senior activities further limits women.

A major burden of living alone in late life is establishing safe and supportive health routines (17). Sleep, diet, and exercise need to be planned. To make sure that regular nutritious meals are shopped for, prepared, and eaten, an elderly woman living alone needs several intact IADLs ranging over finances, transportation, shopping, cooking, cleaning, and reading labels and recipes. The need to assure care for such simple issues of how food gets to an apartment for a woman living alone is the difference of survival or loss of home and possibly life.

Any childless older woman living alone who is sick enough to be admitted to the hospital has a social and a medical crisis. There are no obvious resources to support her return to her home. The greater the illness, the greater the possibility she will need an alternative living arrangement upon discharge (16).

The provider needs to identify "living alone" as a problem on the office chart's problem list. The use of LOLLA is no longer as an intern's pejorative ("little old lady living alone"), but as an accurate prediction of mortal risk. Elderly women with osteoporosis risks are physically small for many tasks of managing a household, and falls can be life-threatening if lighting and railings aren't provided. These women have little reserve physiologically and small bones. Any falls or accidents need to be taken seriously.

Loss and Grief Counseling of Older Women

Lone survivors of great catastrophes and sole family survivors are at great risk of guilt, depression, loneliness, and potential suicide. Therefore, in caring for the oldest old who may survive past their spouse, siblings, friends and children, the provider needs to elicit feelings of possible guilt, anger, depression, and suicide (17). Prolonged grief reactions may interfere with nutrition, medication compliance and survival. There are no realistic time limits in the DSM IV guidelines for grief for loss of a life partner/spouse of 50 or 65 years (24). Six months appears a trivial interval. Therefore, pathologic grief needs to be diagnosed when it impairs the function and health of the woman such that her survival may be limited or shortened.

For women who have outlived family and friends, adaptation may be difficult, and the provider needs to explore her choice of equilibrium and refocusing of life relationships (25). For some women, other foci easily appear, such as pets, great grandchildren, church, garden, radio-television serials, or sports. For others, the inability to adapt and flexibly find a "reason for living" is associated with high morbidity and mortality (8). The ethical dilemma for the provider is that some women prefer to die than go on without family. Others will accept the provider's concern and involvement as temporary surrogate family as they relegate their love relationships to new persons or activities. The complexity of end-of-life decisions emphasizes the need for a continued dialogue with all older women about their values and choices for their resolution of their life's journey (26).

Interdependence of Older Women

As women age, they have opportunity to engage in establishing new coalitions with other older adults (3). This may start as the social enjoyment of senior travel discounts and trips, retirement clubs going to the theater, and other pleasurable activities. This becomes more important as women are alone. Travel and the arts become possible for many newly retired women through the senior coalitions available in communities, churches, and corporate retirement clubs. Local senior centers may offer the safest low-impact aerobic exercise program and create an antiosteoporosis attitude in an older woman while getting her socially engaged.

The well-developed senior center will include more than just a hot lunch program, such as concerts, field trips, exercise classes, nature walks, sports and arts classes. Senior centers can serve as centers for local political action for better nursing homes and senior housing, and safer codes for fire in apartments. Senior centers can reach many elderly women who have never spoken out on an issue to become empowered to make their home community a better place to live out their last days.

The community college systems have found an extended daytime tuition-paying audience in their senior students. Computer classes, arts and crafts, finances, and great books are some activities that keep older women intellectually engaged outside the home and increase social interaction safely. The crafts of many older women support local charities, while valuing the contribution of time and talent of the women.

Older women can put to good use their good health and skills as community volunteers. The range of tasks open has expanded well beyond hospital flower delivery ladies of the 1970s to include patient resource library technicians, drivers for cancer patients and Meals on Wheels, and coaches for sports. The ability to read can be recorded for the blind so that local newspapers are available to neighbors. Senior volunteers serve as home inspectors for the Area Agency on Aging for housebound elderly from their local church. The isolated elderly trust another older woman from their own church to enter their home more than someone hired by a federal agency. Women who may have difficulty seeing their self-worth can focus on their community's needs for volunteers.

For women with little means, many programs carry small stipends to help financially. As an example, there are federal programs for older woman companions to keep the frail elderly company and assist with IADLs including meal preparation; it has assured small supplemental income without physical demands. For centuries, older women have baby-sat to support themselves. Older women can be paid day care workers into their seventies. Working in senior services for pay often is self-fulfilling. The foster grandparent program for mentally impaired and psychologically at risk inner-city children has paid low-income older women to spend time each day with an assigned "grandchild." This program provided a stable older adult to visit and focus attention on an unwanted child. This program valued elderly women as loving and stable yet provided income.

Older women choose new coalitions and living arrangements as they age. Sharing living space with others lowers the risk of economic and psychologic isolation. Many older women will share space by renting rooms in their homes, sharing apartments and expenses with nonmarital partners and even seeking live-in relationships with alternative relationships.

This includes friends who are both widowed who consolidate households for financial and social reasons. Brothers and sisters will create households for survival in old age. Old relationships are renewed and realigned along ability to support and survive as one household. Living with others lowers the risk of poverty.

For a multitude of reasons and of many options, many older women accept living with their adult children. The use of "mother-in-law units" heralds the use and need for women to have separate but attached status to the household of their children. The need for communities to have special temporary zoning variances for aggregate housing of non-nuclear families heralds an era of parents choosing their adult children as an accepted option instead of institutionalization, retirement communities, or other senior-only living arrangements. The interdependence born of a physically independent older woman living near another woman's household (daughter or daughter-in-law) creates positive and negative alliances. Shared family moments may be overshadowed by family turmoil. Easy access for babysitting may be balanced by need for companionship and trips to the store for a non-driving older woman. The positive aspects of the interdependence of an older mentally competent woman joining a child's household is supported by the continued custom and the documented better health of women.

Women with serious illnesses living with adult children have better survival than women living in nursing homes or other institutions. If a woman can continue to live alone, she has better survival than all living arrangements except in a marital living arrangement, which has the highest survival for the frail elderly.

Dependence in Functional Support

With aging, there is a decline in function. Both the rate and nature of that decline very radically between individuals. Except those with severe mental retardation, psychiatric disease, and catastrophic medical illness, most American-born women at age 60 years have intact ADLs and IADLs (Fig. 23.1).

For individuals, the decline in ADL and IADLs is directly related to acute medical crises, progression of chronic disease, and acute accidents and injuries. Therefore, the provider is most intimately able to anticipate with a woman her changing needs for support.

The early IADL that competent women have problems with is finances. The relevance of warning elderly women to seek reasonable and competent financial advice and avoid scams and fraud is obvious. Poverty produces a higher risk for noncompliance with medical protocols. Poverty lurks for most older women as they age, so finances need to be reinforced as an instrument for survival and health in old age. Women need empowerment to learn late in life self-protective IADLs.

The next IADLs require physical competence such as house maintenance, gardens, mowing lawns, house cleaning, grocery shopping, and putting up storm windows. Each woman needs realistic review of her competence to do it in her chosen household. Climbing poorly lit wobbly basement steps with a full laundry basket at age 80 years can be deadly. Yet, the task of doing the laundry is not. The need for family to join in the review becomes critical when there are accidents and poor health.

Malnutrition (e.g., loss of weight, anemia, low cholesterol and albumin) may be the late herald of failure to shop for groceries or inability to cook any longer (27). It is a priority for the provider to assure nutritional integrity of the elderly person, especially those who are community-based and living alone (28). The importance of inquiring to each person over age 65 years whether they have two or more meals a day, multiple food groups and if they have awareness of necessary nutrients and access to them. As women age past 80 years, their interest and abilities to prepare meals diminish.

External support to assure adequate nutrition includes grocery shopping services, meal delivery, family stocking the freezer with prepared meals, going to a central dining room, and lastly having someone come and present a meal. When living alone can't work, assisted living centers offer a safe option. Meals are available as contracted for one to three meals a day.

Additional nursing services can be added as the older woman can't do for herself. A lone woman may only need help with a bath, hair washing, and preparing dinner. Assisted-living can provide these. Ultimately the board and care aspect of assisted living helps as dependency becomes deeper in areas of clothes, laundry, meal-preparation, medication monitoring, and transportation to providers.

Adult children may alert the provider to their perceived concern re IADLs. Often children request the doctor to stop a mother from driving a car after "a few accidents" with no explained reason.

The independent elderly woman who has had some problems with her IADLs needs to be reassured the provider might be a problem solver to find alternative sources. The provider needs to avoid the role of "executioner" for the patient who perceives the doctor as pushing them to leave their home. Case managers from the hospital, Area Agency for Aging, social workers in home care can help the provider find grocery buying services, home cooking services, Meals on Wheels, companions, and many other services that keep the dependent elderly in their own home. The provider needs to work for a win-win situation when an elderly woman is found to have had decline in her function. Microwave ovens have kept many fire-starting elderly in their own homes a few more years. Brighter light bulbs, louder door bells, and bathroom railings also help.

Humans are identified by communication skills through voice and visual reproductions. For the elderly who have hearing and/or vision problems, the risk of social and psychologic isolation is high. The provider needs to assess

Percentage of Individuals over 70

Unable to perform certain tasks

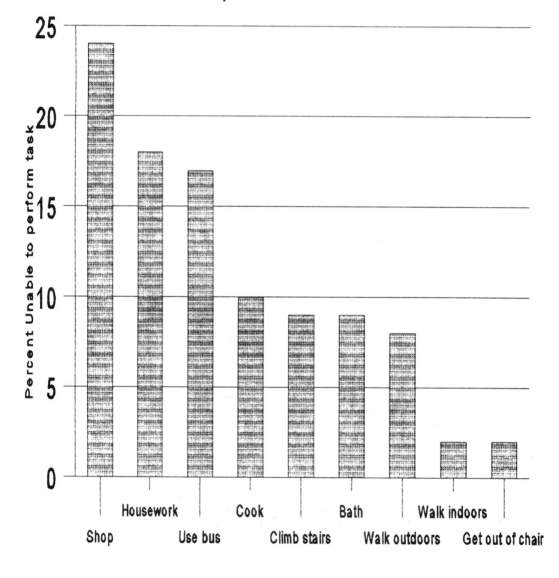

Figure 23.1. Percentage of individuals over age 70 years unable to perform certain tasks.

all persons over age 70 yearly for visual and hearing acuity. Accidents, family disagreements, medication-errors, and poor self-care accelerate in light of visual or hearing loss. Communication is more important as a functional capacity than locomotion because the telephone brings friends and family into the home of any isolated elderly (29).

With acute or chronic decline in sensory competence, the provider should anticipate dependence. The most common problem is progressive vision loss after age 80 years. Driving a car allows independence; loss of vision heralds dependence. The tasks of daily clothing, bathing, shopping and preparing a meal, cleaning, and socializing require eyesight in an untrained person. The most critical skill required for safety is using a telephone; a voice magnifier for hearing and loud bells or lights attached to the telephone helps the hearing impaired. Hearing loss may be occult and present as communication or alleged memory deficits (30). Automatic dialers help the visually impaired to reach out for family, friends, and doctor.

As decline in function occurs, the greatest fear of many elders occurs, they lose their privacy. Their problems become more public. As family outsiders, support agencies, providers become aware of the problem; each professional needs to limit their discussion with professional confidentiality and objectivity. These "ladies" may be profoundly stressed that anyone know they can't keep their home clean, safely take a bath, or cook an organized meal to survive. Self-esteem and ego must be protected while intervening for elderly women in danger living alone.

The other boundary providers need to monitor lies between generations and sexes. In the helping of a failing parent, adult sons may be bathing and dressing a mother, or a middle-aged woman may be intimately caring for a father. This boundary of privacy may have been sacrosanct for 60 years and been broken for crisis. Providers need to anticipate the distress of patient and caregiver this may accrue. Family boundaries in healthy families were established

for teleologic reasons. They need to be adaptable but not sacrificed for care of the elderly woman.

In historically dysfunctional families, boundary maintenance is more important. The elderly patient can be violated in many spheres in their dependency—physically, financially, psychologically, and socially. Elder abuse will arise when previously dependent and often abused relatives now assume power over a dependent elder. The protection of dependent older women in their families' care lies with the objective provider aware of family dynamics and possible history of dysfunction. All children and relatives should not be presumed loving and competent to care for a dependent elder. The provider needs to evaluate their skills as directly as the skills of an outside agency or hired caregiver. Often the "paranoid" ravings of the elderly that their money or belongings have been taken by family members have truth. To every accusation there is a unique two-sided story. Each statement of "she's just a frightened old woman" may need investigation.

Screening for the Problems of the Frail Elderly

For all women over age 70 years, the provider needs to consider a protocol for screening for risks of dependency and decline in function. Yearly, every woman over age 50 years needs to see her provider. Screens for functional decline should be applied at earlier ages for the medically impaired, and a short battery of tests should be considered as routine after age 70 years. Sensory and mental competence are critical to negotiate the environment alone. Therefore, the first important screening tests are visual and hearing acuity and mental status exams. The second inexpensive monitor, height and weight, screen for malnutrition and osteoporotic loss of height (31). Also associated with survival in the elderly are standardized "Quality of Life" scales. These self-administered tests seek the patient's internal sense of well being, depression, and hopelessness and have high correlation with mortality and morbidity. One example is the SPS-36 used in HEDIS monitoring of ambulatory care.

In addition, older women have high morbidity and mortality from falls; every provider should plan a risk assessment of falling for all osteoporotic patients and all women over age 80 years. Osteoporosis may be secondary to estrogen deficiency or corticosteroid use and occur in the fifties and sixties (32, 33). These patients need safe transfers and activity to not fracture. Hip fractures after the age 80 years still carries a mortality of approximately 20% in the first 6 months, and causes greater than 50% of elderly women to lose their ability to go to their own home and remain independently in the community. The provider needs to see older women walk, turn, stretch overhead, and seat themselves each year (34). Seeing how a woman negotiates a hallway, chair, and bathroom will alert the provider to which women are unstable and high risk (35).

There should be time for an open-ended agenda to assess mental status, functional competence, and communication skills. This requires a provider to talk to the patient in concrete and abstract terms to test details of memory, abstraction, calculation, relationships, and language. For older patients this may be the only time that anyone confronts their information for accuracy and competence. The provider needs to test but also to individualize the routinized mental status testing so that the woman is not insulted, embarrassed, or overwhelmed (31, 35). The older the woman, the more varied will be competence in functional testing. For example, a woman age 80 years who has driven herself alone to the office on time and has dressed in a gown, provided a urine sample, filled out insurance forms without confusion or errors needs a different test than the 80-year-old woman brought into the office by a family member (or spouse) who assists them with the gown, gets flustered about whether she needs to go to the bathroom or not, and doesn't know the name of the family member sitting in the room

with her. The former needs focused screening for untested areas, whereas the latter needs gross screening for probable cognitive loss.

The provider should talk to the woman about her lifestyle. This can be a time efficient functional status inventory: (a) Now, do you cook for yourself? (b) What type of things? (c) Where do you get the ingredients? (d) What's the hardest part of cleaning your house? (e) Who does it? (f) What was your most interesting trip since I last saw you? (g) Who drove? (h) Do you handle your own money and bills? (i) Do you mail your bills or use the telephone service? Talk to an elderly woman and learn her accommodation to her aging body so she can stay independent, which allows the provider to spot check for problems and, if respectfully considered, contribute suggestions for additional supports and ways to achieve a full life despite aging limitations. Exercise, nutrition, loving relationships, and control of chronic medical problems are the highest priorities of health maintenance for elderly women. To achieve these she must have adequate functional capacity to do the IADLs and ADLs to survive.

Finally, there should be an assessment of depression as a frequent treatable disease. The formal use of a depression scale confirms for the less experienced provider the diagnosis of depression. The 15 question geriatric depression scale is validated, easy, and direct. One third of patients suffering a stroke or acute myocardial infarction will have a major depressive episode in the year afterwards that is diagnosable and treatable with antidepressants.

Each provider needs to develop their own style with older patients. For an effective doctor-patient relationship, a provider may need to ask the woman how she wants the doctor-patient relationship to be developed. The relationship over time should include intimate discussion of end-of-life decisions, family secrets, and financial details. Each woman will have her own sensitivity and needs for the depth of such discussion. Intimacy and confidentiality are required for success. Trust must be developed.

Confidentiality

Just as with the adolescent, the relationship of the elderly woman with her provider must be protected from the interventions possibly offered by family, agencies, and/or senior centers. Each woman needs her own active advocate for her well-being and maintenance of independence in the community. The provider must first view the woman as his patient, then her context in the family. Then the provider can hopefully act as objective arbiter for the patient when she no longer can safely negotiate her home. The provider may need to intervene for a safer environment.

Issues for the Provider

For the provider working with a population of older adults, much pleasure accrues from several aspects of practicing comprehensive geriatrics. The priorities in the care of the elderly frequently lie less in winning the battle against a disease and fall into surviving some battles to enjoy the peace after the battle. The provider often plans with a patient how medicine and therapy can make the distractions of pain and an aging body work for an independent self-directed life outside institutions (36). Global function and quality of life are the foci of caring for older women. No other area of medicine spends as much energy evaluating and supporting mind, body, and spirit of the patient with evaluation scales devoted to tasks of daily living in society and possible inquiring to the patient's ability to shop, drive a car, walk

to the bathroom, and handle their finances. The depth and breadth of concerns concern the impact of ethnicity, personal values, and cultural experience on patient decisions is expressed as a component of quality care. The outcome parameters of care are life satisfaction rather than pure survival (37).

Personalized care over time is the priority. Continuity is required; this makes the care of older women an extended exchange between the patient, her family, and the health care team. Comprehensive care takes precedence. Preventive medicine follows cost-benefit analysis and avoids a knee-jerk routine and adjusts to the individual patients risks and clinical history.

Certainly, much of the provider's pleasure working with older women comes from the cohort's hardy survival. These women in their last third of life tend to be flexible and adaptable. Each woman uniquely finds ways to navigate the vicissitudes of life and come back for more. The quitters rarely survive to old age.

Lastly, lies the concern for ageism that permeates much of health care services. To surrender to ageism is to surrender to racism, discrimination, bigotry, and malice. To presume to know better the needs of older women without asking relegates them to nonentities. Therefore, the power of care for older women is to empower each woman her choices, options, and alternatives in her health care. Functioning is the sentinel assessment to survival of an elderly woman, the health care provider needs to allow women access to the information and the science of their own bodies to make informed decisions about their futures.

Special Considerations for Nurse Practitioners and Physician Assistants

All health care providers must be aware of their potential for stereotyping the older woman. The combined forces of ageism and sexism (and racism for women of color) can

lead to subtle humiliation during health care encounters and compromises in the quality of care. In an excellent review of the literature, Sharp summarizes how stereotyped attitudes can affect the care of elderly women. Interactions may be paternalistic, with joking that trivializes the woman's experiences. Complaints (e.g., arthritis, incontinence) may be dismissed as normal to aging and, thus, not receive further attention. Speech may be modified ("baby talk") during encounters, which can be demoralizing, and along with overprotective behaviors, create dependency. Although older women may have more complex health problems, providers may spend less time with them and use fewer diagnostic tests than with younger clients (38).

In addition, because of negative stereotypes of the elderly, health care providers may not recognize the strengths that older women possess, perhaps because health care providers most often encounter older women in the sick role. Despite the presence of health problems, frail older women who continued to live in the community rated their health positively. These same women did not feel dependent, even though they had to rely on others for services such as transportation (39). It is likely that physical health is not global in its effects on the self-concept of elderly women. Instead, it seems important to have a multidimensional understanding of self-concept in order to assess overall psychological well-being (40).

Despite many difficulties and losses, an older woman may adjust successfully with inner strengths, including a balanced perspective of the joys and sorrows in her life, a positive comparison with others, belief in self, determination and perseverance, a sense of humor, and faith in God. Asking a woman how she copes with problems will help providers determine the woman's inner resources. Providers must also ascertain the older woman's external sources of support, such as family, friends, meaningful work, and other activities (41).

The sexual nature of the older woman must not be ignored. Taking a sexual history encourages her to express her personal concerns, and it conveys to her the importance of the sexual role. The provider will have to determine the woman's needs, capabilities, and individual concerns before proceeding with a detailed sexual history. Correcting myths about sexuality and aging women is important, because these myths may become self-fulfilling prophecies (42). Older women who become celibate because of lack of a partner retain their needs for closeness and intimacy with another person.

Behavioral changes, for example, ceasing tobacco use and increasing activity, can benefit health and quality of life even in old age (43). Health promotion programs for older women have the potential to encourage skill-building and behavior changes that lead to empowerment to make decisions about health (38). Older women who report their current health as good, have high self-esteem and believe that they have control of their health are more likely to report health promotion activities (44).

An encounter with an older woman will be unsatisfactory if the provider focuses the history on only what the provider considers important, hurries through the examination, and reassures the woman as the provider goes through the door (45). It is unlikely that the next generation of older women will accept this type of care. The baby boom generation that originated the wellness movement will demand a health care system that assists them in keeping healthy as they age. Health care services must move away from a model of sickness care to a more holistic model of person-centered wellness care for the older woman (46). If health care providers are to meet these women's needs, they must be willing to look beyond the treatment of biological disorders to a partnership with the older woman for comprehensive, health-focused physical and psychological care.

References

1. Greendale GA, Barrett-Connor E, Ingles S, Haile R. Late physical and functional effects of osteoporotic fracture in women: the Rancho Bernardo Study JAGS 1995;43:955–961.
2. Vogt MT, Cauley JA, Kuller LH, Nevitt MC. Functional status and mobility among elderly women with lower extremity arterial disease: the Study of Osteoporotic Fractures JAGS 1994;42:923–929.

3. Havighurst RJ. Developmental Tasks and Education, David McKay New York 1972.

4. Brown AS. The Social Processes of Aging and Old Age. Englewood Cliffs, NJ: Prentice Hall, 1990.

5. Baber KM, Allen KR. Women and families: feminist reconstructions. New York: Guilford Press, 1992: 143–175.

6. Stephens MA, Franks MM, Townsend AL. Stress and rewards in women's multiple roles: the case of the women in the middle. Psychol Aging 1994; 9:45–52.

7. Lachs MS, Pillemer K. Abuse and neglect of elderly persons. N Engl J Med 1995;332:437–443

8. Hansson RO, Carpenter BN. Relationships in old age: Coping with the challenge of transition. New York: Guilford Press, 1994:15–27.

9. Silliman RA. Predictors of family caregivers' physical and psychological health following hospitalization of their elders. JAGS 1993;41:1039–1046.

10. Karmilovoch SE. Burden and stress associated with spousal caregiving for individuals with heart failure. Prog Cardiovascular Nurs 1994;9:33–38.

11. Hunter GR, Treuth MS, Weinsier RL, et al. The Effects of Strength Conditioning on Older Women's Ability to Perform Daily Tasks JAGS 1995;43:756–760.

12. Langlois JA, Smith GS, Nelson DE, Sattin RW, Stevens JA, DeVito CA. Dependence in activities in daily living as a risk factor for fall injury events among older people living in the community. JAGS 1995;43:275–278.

13. Rozzini R, Frisoni GR, Bianchetti A, Zanetti O, Trabucchi M. Physical Performance Test and Activities of Daily Living Scales in the Assessment of Health Status in Elderly People. JAGS 1993;41:1109–1113.

14. DeBettignies BH, Mahurin RK. Assessment of independent living skills in geriatric populations. Clin Geriatric Med 1989;5:461–475.

15. Gill TM, Williams CS, Tinetti ME. Assessing risk for the onset of functional dependence among older adults: the role of physical performance. JAGS 1995; 43:603–609.

16. Rubenstein RL, Kilbride JC, Nagy S. Elders Living Alone: Frailty and the Perception of Choice Aldine de Gruyter. New York; Hawthorne, 1992;12–49.

17. Suzman RM, Willis DP, Manton KG, eds. The Oldest Old. New York: Oxford University Press, 1992:341–380.

18. Lachs MS, Pillemer K. Abuse and neglect of elderly persons. N Engl J Med 1995;332:437–443.

19. Costa AJ. Elder abuse. Primary Care 1993; 20:375–390.

20. Fins JJ, ed. Futility in clinical practice series. JAGS 1994;42:861–905.

21. Silberfeld M, Nash C, Singer PA. Capacity to complete an advance directive. JAGS 1993;41:1141–1143.

22. Fried TR, Rosenberg RR, Lipsitz LA. Older community dwelling adults' attitudes toward and practices of health promotion and advance planning activities. JAGS 1995;43:645–649.

23. Wolinsky MA. A Heart of Wisdom: Marital Counseling with Older and Elderly Couples. New York: Brunner/Mazel, 1990:14–70.

24. Hays JC, Kasl S, Jacobs S. Past personal history of dysphoria, social support and psychological distress following conjugal bereavement. JAGS 1994;42: 712–718.

25. Zisook S, Shuchter SR. Early psychological reaction to the stress of widowhood. Psychiatry 1991;54:320–333.

26. Dula A. The life and death of Miss Mildred: an elderly black woman. Clin Geriatr Med 1994;10:419–430.

27. Wallace JI, Schwartz RS, LaCroix AZ, Uhlmann RF, Pearlman RA. Involuntary weight loss in older outpatients: incidence and clinical significance. JAGS 1995;43:329–337.

28. Dwyer JT, Gallo JJ, Reichel W. Assessing nutritional status in elderly patients. AFP 1993;47:613–620.

29. Lichtenstein MJ. Hearing and visual impairments. Clin Geriatric Med 1992; 8:173–182.

30. Jerger J, Chmiel R, Wilson N, Luchi R. Hearing impairment in older adults: new concepts. JAGS 1995; 43:928–935.

31. Reuben DB, Greendale GA, Harrison GG. Nutrition screening in older persons. JAGS 1995;43:415–425.

32. Reid IR, Ames RW, Evans MC, Gamble GD, Sharpe SJ. Effect of calcium supplementation on bone loss in postmenopausal women. N Engl J Med 1993; 328:460–464.

33. Felson DT, Zhang Y, Hannan MT, Kiel DP, Wilson PWF, Anderson JJ. The effect of postmenopausal estrogen therapy on bone density in elderly women. N Engl J Med 1993;329:1141–1146.

34. Fiatarone MA, O'Neill EF, Ryan ND, et al. Exercise training and nutritional supplements for physical frailty in very elderly people. N Engl J Med 1994; 330:1769–1775.

35. Reuben DB, Valle LA, Hays RD, Siu AL. Measuring physical function in community dwelling older persons: a comparison of self administered, interviewer-administered and performance based measures. JAGS 1995;43:17–23.

36. Reuben DB, Bradley TB, Zwanziger J, Beck JC. Projecting the need for physicians to care for older persons: effects of changes in demography, utilization patterns and physician productivity. JAGS 1993; 41:1033–1038.

37. Miller DK, Coe RM, Romeis JC, Morley JE. Improving quality of geriatric health care in four delivery sites: suggestions from practitioners and experts. JAGS 1995;43:60–65.

38. Sharpe PA. Older women and health services: moving from ageism toward empowerment. Women Health 1995;22:9–20.

39. Schrank MJ, Lough MA. Profile: frail elderly women, maintaining independence. J Advanced Nurs 1990;15:674–682.

40. Heidrich S. The self, health, and depression in elderly women. Western J Nurs res 1994;16:544–555.

41. Wagnild G, Young HM. Resilience among older women. IMAGE 1990;22:252–255.

42. Morrison-Beedy D, Robbins L. Sexual assessment and the aging female. Nurse Practitioner 1989;14:35–45.

43. Guinn B. Modifying influences on serum lipids among postmenopausal women. Women's Health Issues 1994;4:156–161.

44. Duffy ME. Determinants of health-promoting lifestyles in older persons. IMAGE 1993;25:23–28.

45. Willson R. The older woman: what are the physician's concerns? Primary care update for OB/Gyns 1995;2:35–36.

46. Freda MC. Childbearing, reproductive control, aging women, and health care. JOGNN 1994;23:144–152.

Osteoarthritis

Louise S. Acheson and Abby Goulder Abelson

Introduction

Almost all types of arthritis are more common in women than in men. However, by far the most prevalent type of arthritis is osteoarthritis. In population-based studies, 75% of symptomatic arthritis and over 90% of radiographically identified arthritis is osteoarthritis (1). This chapter will focus on how osteoarthritis affects women.

Diagnosis and Classification of Osteoarthritis

Osteoarthritis (OA) occurs almost universally with aging. It is as much a source of disability for women as cardiovascular disease, yet rigorous criteria for the diagnosis of OA have only recently been developed. The features of OA are captured in this World Health Organization definition: "Osteoarthritis is the result of both mechanical and biologic events that destabilize the normal coupling of degradation and synthesis of articular cartilage and subchondral bone. Although it may be initiated by multiple factors including genetic, developmental, metabolic, and traumatic, OA involves all of the tissues of the joint . . . " (2).

Part of the difficulty with diagnosis and study of OA is that the disease develops over a period of many years and is not significant by specific symptoms or findings early in the course. Cartilage changes precede radiologic changes, which may precede joint symptoms. Soft-tissue inflammation is sporadic. Furthermore, clinical manifestations such as joint pain and limited movement do not correlate well with the severity of radiologic abnormalities; symptoms are more common in women than in men for a given radiologic grade of disease (3).

OA affects fingers, the spine, and weight-bearing joints such as the first metatarsal-phalangeal (MTP) joint, hips, and knees. Each body site has its own clinical features and epidemiology. Generalized OA, predominantly a disease of older women, is more likely than localized disease to be severe and progressive. Standard clinical, skeletal, and radiographic criteria are available for establishing the diagnosis and grading the severity of OA in the hands, hips, and knees (2, 4, 5).

Hand Osteoarthritis

The most common form of OA involves the distal interphalangeal (DIP) joints (Heberden nodes), proximal interphalangeal (PIP) joints (Bouchard nodes), and base of the thumb (6). Hereditary, "nodular," polyarticular, or generalized, OA is 10 times more common in middle-aged women than in men. The enlarged DIP and PIP joints are often painless (although sometimes accompanied by synovitis), and exhibit mild stiffness and eventually mild bony deformities or ankylosis. OA at the base of the thumb is often painful and can interfere with grip. Primary OA does not usually involve the metacarpal and wrist joints, thus distinguishing it from rheumatoid arthritis (RA), and rarely produces as much disability to the hands as RA.

Knee Osteoarthritis

OA of the knee is approximately twice as common in women as in men. It is the major source of functional disability from OA caused primarily by interference with walking. OA can involve the tibiofemoral joint, especially the medial compartment that experiences higher mechanical stresses, and/or the patellofemoral joint. Knees with previous fractures into the joint, meniscus injuries, or mechanical instability are prone to develop OA prematurely. In addition to knee pain, patients experience increased stiffness after inactivity (the "gel" phenomenon). Joint-line tenderness, crepitus, effusion, popliteal cysts, and eventually limitation of movement, bony deformity, quadriceps atrophy, and ligament instability are clinical features of knee OA (6). Radiographically, the formation of osteophytes and asymmetric joint space narrowing are diagnostic of OA in the knee (2).

Hip Osteoarthritis

OA of the hip is equally common in women and men. The primary radiographic feature is narrowing of the joint space, especially superiorly, with osteophyte formation. Premature OA of the hip results from underlying anatomic abnormalities, such as acetabular dysplasia, slipped capital-femoral epiphyses, Legg-Perthes disease, and possibly epiphyseal and chondrodysplasias, but hip arthritis, often bilateral, is also a feature of generalized idiopathic OA (6). Patients with hip OA complain of stiffness and pain with standing and walking; pain may be referred to the groin, buttock, knee, or distal thigh. The most sensitive physical sign is limited internal rotation of the flexed hip (2). Other signs include painful range of motion, limping, flexion contracture, and abductor weakness (Trendelenburg sign) (6).

Osteoarthritis of the Foot

OA often involves the first MTP joint of the foot. The joint enlarges, and dorsiflexion is limited by osteophyte formation ("hallux rigidus"). Examination of joint fluid for crystals may be needed for differential diagnosis if the joint is acutely inflamed. Diabetics may have neuropathic joint degeneration (Charcot's joints), typically in the midfoot.

Spine Osteoarthritis

Although the joints between vertebral bodies are fibrocartilagenous not synovial, both these and the facet joints are commonly affected by OA. Marginal osteophyte formation (spondylosis) characteristically occurs at the peaks of the cervical and thoracic curves (C5–6, T10–11) and in the lumbar vertebrae (5). Most spinal OA is probably asymptomatic. Lateral osteophytes can impinge on nerve roots and spinal stenosis can cause cervical myelopathy or cauda equina syndrome (so-called "spinal claudication" in which symptoms are worse with extension of the lumbar spine). The relationship between exceedingly common symptoms of back pain and OA of the spine has yet to be defined.

Other Joints

Other joints are affected by osteoarthritis as a result of anatomic abnormalities, injuries, or repetitive stresses: e.g., the elbows of Inuit kayakers (5), the elbows and shoulders of base-ball pitchers (7), or joints of individuals with epiphyseal dysplasia.

Hereditary and Secondary Osteoarthritis

Osteoarthritis is often further classified as idiopathic ("primary"), or as "secondary" to another disease process, injury, or anatomic abnormality (2). Primary generalized OA, symmetrically involving multiple joints with Heberden's and Bouchard's nodes, has long been known to be hereditary with a strong female preponderance. Autosomal dominant inheritance of primary generalized OA has recently been shown to be associated in one kindred with a point mutation in the type 2 procollagen gene (8).

Secondary OA should be suspected when OA occurs before age 45 years or involves unusual joints. Hereditary forms of degenerative joint disease include calcium pyrophosphate and hydroxyapatite deposition diseases affecting articular cartilage matrix: (a) Stickler syndrome, in which premature OA occurs in conjunction with ocular vitreous degeneration and retinal detachment, (b) chondrodysplasias, in which joint laxity may lead to OA, and (c) multiple epiphyseal dysplasias, which lead to OA through distortion of the subchondral bone (8). Other secondary causes of OA include hemochromatosis (characteristically affecting the second and third MCP joints), sequelae of joint infection (more common in developing countries) (9), neuropathic joint damage, Wilson's disease, and acromegaly (3). Rheumatoid arthritis or gout can coexist with OA. A late-onset form of gout may be fairly common in elderly women taking diuretics.

Epidemiology

Archaeological and fossil specimens show that OA has been common throughout human history; it has been observed in animals from primates to dinosaurs (5). The prevalence of OA increases with age; symptomatic OA is uncommon before age 45 years, but radiographic signs of OA are present in the hands of almost everyone who lives to age 80 years, and arthritis is diagnosed in the majority of people by their mid-70s (1, 10–12). In the United States, 12.3% of people aged 24 to 74 years had OA confirmed by physical examination (1). In a population-based sample from Ontario, the prevalence of self-reported arthritis increased from 6.3% of those aged 16 to 24 years to 51% of people age 75 and older. The overall prevalence of arthritis was 34% higher in women than men (1).

Disability and Cost Attributable to Osteoarthritis

On a population basis, OA, which persists for years without causing mortality, results in more chronic limitation of activity than any other condition (1). There are 68 million days of work lost per year in the United States because of OA. Individuals with OA are more likely than other individuals their age to have additional chronic medical conditions and to be poor (10–12). Many retire early because of disability from OA (12). Most incur substantial medical costs, and a large fraction of these costs are in categories not completely reimbursed by Medicare (12). For example, in Ontario one fourth of people with arthritis had taken prescription medication for it during the preceding 2 weeks (1). In Olmstead County, Minnesota, a population-based retrospective cohort with physician-diagnosed OA (mean age = 67 years; 62% women; 20% of county residents over 35) was compared with the somewhat younger, nonarthritic population (12). Those with OA experienced 28% higher age-sex–adjusted medical care charges ($2,044 per person) and 500% higher nonmedical expenses ($282 per person) in 1987. A population-based interview study of women over 65 (mean age = 75 years) in the Baltimore area

showed that 58% reported having been diagnosed with arthritis by a physician (11).

Arthritis was more frequently associated with comorbidities such as coronary artery disease, diabetes, stroke, hypertension, and lung disease in these women. After adjustment for age, race, education, marital status, and other chronic conditions, women with arthritis were more likely than other elderly women to have difficulty with a wide variety of daily activities involving movement. A higher mortality rate observed among women with OA may be caused by associated comorbid conditions (13).

Risk Factors for Osteoarthritis

Occupation

Besides age and gender, there are biomechanical risk factors for OA. In addition to overt injuries, joint malalignment, and instability, there is some evidence that repetitive stresses on a normal joint can be associated with the development of OA. Occupations that require heavy lifting and frequent knee bending (e.g., squatting, kneeling, stair climbing) are associated with OA of the knees. Occupations with the most squatting and kneeling include teaching, nursing, janitorial, and construction work (14). Household work and childcare were not studied. Among men, farmers are consistently found to have a higher prevalence of hip OA than other men whose occupations involve prolonged walking and heavy lifting, who themselves have more hip OA than men in sedentary occupations. Most hip OA in women is idiopathic and associated with OA in multiple joints.

Obesity

Both cross-sectional and prospective studies show that obesity is a potent risk factor for OA of the knee in women and men (15). Obese individuals also have an increased risk of OA in the hips and the hands. Because mechanical stresses on the hands are not increased by obesity, other unknown systemic effects of being overweight may predispose to arthritis. One mediating factor could be that people who are overweight have higher bone mineral density than others. Individuals with higher bone density are more likely to have OA than those with osteoporosis, when body weight is controlled (16). Denser subchondral bone may be stiffer (i.e., less deformable), thus transmitting more force to the joint cartilage.

Data from the Framingham Osteoarthritis Study suggest that for women whose baseline body mass index (BMI) was above the median, weight loss (an average of 11 lbs) reduced by more than 50% their odds of developing knee OA later, whereas gaining the same amount of weight somewhat increased the odds of developing OA (15). OA was not related to weight gain or loss in women with below average BMI. Thus, maintaining an optimal body weight may be a promising measure for preventing OA, as well as associated chronic problems such as hypertension and diabetes. Framingham study data also suggest that current and past users of postmenopausal estrogen therapy have a lower incidence and less progression of knee OA than nonusers, but the reasons for this association are not known (16).

Pathophysiology of Osteoarthritis

Most theories about the etiology of OA hypothesize that joint tissues, especially the cartilage, are repeatedly subjected to mechanical forces that can cause "wear and tear." Biochemical or immunologic insults might also occur. Adaptive responses early in the course of OA lead to hypertrophy and limited repair of bone and cartilage, and to protection of the joint (17).

Over time, joint cartilage in OA wears down. The joint capsule, ligaments, tendons,

and muscles absorb more of the forces around the joint (13). Inflammation of the synovium, contractures of the joint capsule, or joint effusion and stretching of the joint capsule and ligaments cause pain. Pain also results from microfractures in the subchondral bone, from periosteal irritation by impingement of osteophytes, and from muscle spasm (18). The roles of growth factors, cytokines, and peripheral innervation in modulating joint pain and inflammation are active areas for research (19).

Ordinarily, patterned reflex muscle contractions protect the joint from extreme movements and forces. Proprioceptive feedback may not be essential once these patterns are established. A change in gait or in the biomechanics of the joint results in revised reflex patterns, unless joint innervation or other parts of the reflex arc are impaired. Joints that are both unstable and denervated are prone to severe degeneration (Charcot's joints).

Diagnosis

Symptoms and Physical Examination: Differential Diagnosis

Clinical features of OA in various joints have been described above. The MCP joints, wrists, and ankles are usually spared by OA. Typically, morning stiffness in OA lasts less than 30 minutes. A deep, aching pain can occur at first with joint use, peaking by the end of the day; later, nocturnal pain may become more prominent. Deconditioning and atrophy of muscles around the affected joint are common as a result of disuse. Tendonitis is also common near joints affected by OA. Point tenderness may be found over the supraspinatus and subscapularis tendons of the shoulder, trochanteric or gluteal bursae near the hip, the pes anserine bursa medial to the knee, and De Quervain's tenosynovitis near the first carpometacarpal joint (18). Patients with anserine bursitis may complain that when they lie in bed it is painful for their knees to touch each other without a pillow between.

The clinical significance of painful bursitis and tendonitis is that a simple treatment, e.g., local injection of a corticosteroid, can give long lasting relief.

In the differential diagnosis of knee pain, hip problems and L4–5 radiculopathy should be considered (18). A sudden worsening of pain with knee OA, significant variation in symptoms from one day to the next, locking or giving way, or a persistent effusion without radiologic changes of OA may indicate mechanical problems such as damage to a meniscus, impingement by folds of synovium, or a loose piece of articular cartilage in the joint space. In such cases, arthroscopy with "debridement" may be indicated, although long- lasting improvement has not been demonstrated in controlled trials (20).

Examination of Joint Fluid

The synovial fluid in OA is typically clear or serous, and noninflammatory with less than 2000 cells per mL. Examination of joint fluid is helpful when the joint is painful and appears inflamed, and where there is a monarticular or acute arthritis. Aspiration of synovial fluid is worthwhile in order to examine it for crystals diagnostic of gout or pseudogout and for cultures to exclude infection. Although various products of cartilage breakdown pass into synovial fluid with OA, currently no biochemical tests of synovial fluid are clinically useful for diagnosis or staging the progression of OA.

Serological Tests

In OA the erythrocyte sedimentation rate is usually normal, and the rheumatoid factor is less than 1:40. Serum markers of collagen turnover, such as keratin sulfate, hyaluranon, or cartilage oligomeric matrix protein (COMP), are being investigated to find markers of early OA and/or prognostic factors for disease progression, but they are not in clinical use (21–23).

Radiographic Imaging

The radiographic features of OA are reactive changes of subchondral bone (e.g., osteophyte formation, subchondral sclerosis, cysts) and joint space narrowing owing to loss of articular cartilage (19). Knee and hip radiographs should, if possible, be taken in a weight-bearing position standing. MRI can image cartilage and soft tissues, e.g., demonstrating meniscal damage in the knee joint, but it has limited resolution for detecting early changes of OA (24–25).

Arthroscopy

Arthroscopy, with the development of smaller scopes that can be inserted under local anesthesia, may in the future offer a way to observe OA in its earlier stages.

Guidelines for Management of Osteoarthritis

The goals of management of patients with OA should be to reduce pain, to maintain or improve joint mobility, and to limit functional disability. After determining that the patient's pain is indeed a result of OA, an individualized treatment program must be formulated, taking into account the patient's coexisting medical conditions and activities of daily living. Education of the patient, family, and caregivers, and encouraging their participation in arthritis self-help groups is beneficial; studies show that patients experience decreased pain, decreased frequency of physician visits, and overall improvement in the quality of life after attending these programs (26). Because individuals with OA may have limitation on their ADL, consultation with physical and occupational therapists is crucial. These therapists will evaluate the patient's strength, mobility, and functional abilities, and recommend a variety of appropriate modalities and assistive devices to improve the patient's quality of life.

Pharmacotherapy

There is some controversy, but little evidence, that OA progression depends on joint inflammation or that antiinflammatory treatments modify the progression of OA (27). All drugs used to treat OA today are used for relief of pain, not specifically directed to the pathologic processes within the joint (28). Oral analgesics can be given as needed, rather than on a fixed dosing schedule; this results in lower overall doses and less opportunity for toxicity.

Acetaminophen

Acetaminophen, up to 4 g/day, is recommended as the first-line analgesic for OA pain. Recent controlled clinical trials have shown that it is as effective as various NSAIDs in relieving OA symptoms and improving function,

both acutely and during 2 years of chronic use (28, 29). Long-term use of acetaminophen has been linked to renal failure, but renal impairment is much more likely (16 times) with nonsteroidal anti-inflammatory drugs (NSAIDs), which can decrease glomerular blood flow by eliminating the regulatory effects of prostaglandins. Hepatotoxicity is a concern with doses of acetaminophen above 4 g/day (usually above 10 g), especially in conjunction with alcoholic liver damage or fasting, but does not usually occur at the dose recommended for long-term use (3 to 4 g/day) (27).

Nonsteriodal Anti-inflammatory Drugs

NSAIDs can be useful as "rescue" medications for short-term exacerbations of pain, or may be preferred by some individuals for chronic use (Table 24.1). No consistent differences in the

Table 24.1. Non-hormonal Therapy for Osteoporosis

Medication	Mechanism of Action	Side Effects
Salmon calcitonin (injectable) 100 I.U. sq or IM q d, use limited to 2 yrs	Inhib. bone resorbtion, GI, renal effects; use w/Ca++, Vitamin D	N, V, dermatologic, flushing, hypersensitivity rxn
Salmon calcitonin nasal spray 200 I.U. intranasal qd	Same as above; use w/Ca++, Vitamin D	Rhinitis, epistaxis, sinusitis
Etidronate sodium 5 mg/kg/d or 400 mg qd × 14 d every 3 mos	Suppresses bone turnover	Nausea, diarrhea
Alendronate sodium 10 mg q AM with water 30 min before eating or drinking juice, not w/Ca++ or Fe products	Same as etidronate but does not need to be pulsed, need adequate Ca++ and Vitamin D	Avoid in UGI dx, creatinine clearance < 35, avoid recumbency post dosage, GI upset, HA, Musculoskeletal pain
Vitamin D 400 I.U. qd, not Rx of itself but adjunctive and important in women w/metabolic abnl	Multiple sites: renal, GI for women in cold climates w/poor sunlight exposure, anticonvulsants	None significant in therapeutic dosage
Fluoride, slow release, 25 mg BID × 12 mos, 2 mos off + 800 mg Ca++/d	Stimulates osteoblast formation, new bone, bone denser but not stronger in absence of adequate Ca++	Increased fractures in early studies, gastric irritation reduced in slow-release

efficacy of various NSAIDs for arthritis pain have been observed; a drug-like ibuprofen may be chosen because of its low cost, or a drug like naproxen for the convenience of its twice daily dosing (27). The toxicity of NSAIDs increases dramatically with the dose, whereas pain relief probably does not; the lowest effective dose is the best. Adverse effects of NSAIDs include renal impairment, hypertension, hepatotoxicity, and most important, gastritis, peptic ulcers, and upper GI bleeding. Among elderly people using NSAIDs, two thirds of peptic ulcer-related hospitalizations and deaths are caused by NSAIDs (27). Studies underway may determine whether prophylactic treatment of elderly patients with misoprostol can be cost-effective and acceptable.

Narcotics

It is wise to avoid the use of oral narcotics such as codeine in OA, because the condition is chronic and addiction can be a major problem (28). Tolerance to the analgesic effect often develops after several days of use. Further, the side effects of sedation, light-headedness, constipation, and nausea make them intolerable to approximately one fourth to half of elderly patients (27). Narcotic therapy in OA is only appropriate when used in short-term treatment of acute pain exacerbations or for an injury to a joint already afflicted with OA.

Capsaicin and Rubefacients

Capsaicin, 0.025% cream applied topically to the painful area three or four times a day for several weeks, has been shown in one randomized controlled trial to improve the pain of knee arthritis; it is also efficacious for other types of chronic pain (30). A higher strength, 0.25% capsaicin cream applied only twice a day, may have more rapid onset of action and more effective pain relief (31). This drug, extracted from hot peppers, stimulates fibers responsible for pain sensation, depleting them of substance P and rendering them unable to transmit pain signals. It is expensive and im-

practical for use on large body areas such as the hip. Many patients experience burning initially, which disappears with continued use of capsaicin cream.

Counterirritants that produce mild skin inflammation can temporarily reduce perceived pain from a nearby joint. Those approved by the FDA include allyl isothiocyanate, methyl salicylate, turpentine oil, ammonia, and menthol, camphor, histamine dihydrochloride, and methyl nicotinate (32).

Corticosteroids

Systemic corticosteroids are to be avoided in the treatment of OA, but the judicious use of intraarticular corticosteroids is appropriate in patients who have joint effusions and local signs of inflammation, especially in the knee (33). For these patients, aspiration of fluid followed by intraarticular injection of a corticosteroid preparation is an effective short-term mode of pain relief. Corticosteroids should not be injected into a given joint more frequently than three to four times per year because of concerns about possible development of cartilage damage. Joint aspirations and injections should be done using aseptic technique and the fluid sent for cell counts, culture, and crystal examination unless there is no sign of inflammation. Although the efficacy of intraarticular corticosteroid therapy of the hip is controversial, this technically difficult procedure should be performed by an orthopedist, radiologist, or rheumatologist under fluoroscopic guidance.

Nonpharmacologic Management

Exercise

Except during acute exacerbations of OA, exercise is likely to be beneficial for general aerobic conditioning (7, 34). This can be accomplished by walking, swimming, pool exercises, cycling, or other low-impact aerobic exercise regimens three times a week. An 8-week controlled trial of supervised walking in moderate knee OA showed increased mobility and improved functional status and was well tolerated (7). Specific isometric exercises are beneficial for strengthening muscles that will stabilize the joint. For patellofemoral or knee OA, isometric quadriceps exercises (straight leg raising) 100 sets every other day are recommended, perhaps progressing to isotonic exercise against mild resistance and accompanied by mild stretching exercises. The goals of an exercise program in OA of the hip are to preserve at least 30° of flexion and full extension of the hip, and to strengthen hip abductors and extensors (26).

Rest and Joint Protection

All patients with symptomatic OA can benefit from measures to rest and protect the affected joints, often instituted in consultation with physical and occupational therapists. Simple measures include use of a cane or forearm crutch contralateral to an affected hip or knee, temporary support, or bracing of the joint for short periods of time (e.g., with a soft cervical collar, lumbosacral support, knee brace), avoiding movements that exacerbate pain (such as kneeling, stair-climbing for knee OA, gripping for thumb OA), and arranging the environment to minimize stress on the joints (e.g., raised toilet seats to minimize knee flexion, shower or bath chair for hip OA). An observational study has shown good long-term symptomatic relief of medial compartment knee OA by lateral shoe wedges (orthotics) that distribute more stresses toward the lateral compartment of the knee. The use of lightweight knee braces is particularly useful in patients with tibiofemoral arthritis with lateral instability. Taping the medial knee can benefit those with patellofemoral OA until a program for strengthening the vastus medialis has taken effect (35).

Heat and Cold: Physical Stimuli

Although not supported by scientific evidence, local applications of heat, especially before exercise, are considered helpful by the majority of arthritis sufferers (36). Local heat does not affect the deep structures, except in the hands. Moist heat will raise the tissue temperature more than dry heat. Paraffin baths are not more effective than warm water for hand OA. There is little evidence that diathermy (deep heat) is better than superficial heat. Cold applications (cold compresses or a spray) may decrease pain and swelling after exercise or overuse. Inconsistent results have been obtained in controlled trials of acupuncture, acupressure, and "cold" laser light.

Psychological Support

For a given severity of OA by radiographic criteria, divorced people have more symptoms and limitations than married people. Psychological support, such as telephone contact with a lay person or group information sessions, has been demonstrated to improve functional status and well-being in patients with OA (34). The placebo effect is quite strong in many studies of treatments for OA.

Arthroscopic Treatments

Arthroscopic or needle lavage of the joint space is hypothesized to act by removing inflammatory mediators and breakdown products of cartilage from the synovial fluid. Some patients with persistent synovitis in the knee appear to obtain long-lasting relief from joint lavage. As noted above, patients with OA and signs of meniscus injury or a loose body in the knee may benefit from arthroscopic debridement. Abrasion of the joint surface adds no benefit compared to debridement alone.

Surgical Treatments

Patients with severe, intractable pain and disability from OA of the hip or knee can obtain dramatic pain relief with arthroplasty (total knee or hip prostheses). There are potential immediate and late complications of this major surgery. An intense rehabilitation period is essential. Sometimes arthrodesis or osteotomy is performed first as a temporizing measure.

Summary

Osteoarthritis is a chronic disease that affects many individuals. A continuing relationship between provider and woman will improve symptoms over time.

References

1. Badley EM. The effect of osteoarthritis on disability and health care use in Canada. Rheumatol 1995;22 (suppl 43):19–22.

2. Hart DJ, Spector TD. The classification and assessment of osteoarthritis. Ballieres Clin Rheumatol 1995;9:407–432.

3. Jones A, Doherty M. ABC of rheumatology: Osteoarthritis. BMT 1995;310:457–460.

4. Lane NE, Kremer LB. Radiographic indices for osteoarthritis. Rheum Dis Clin North Am 1995;21: 379–394.

5. Jurmain RD, Kilgore L. Skeletal evidence of osteoarthritis: a paleopathological perspective. Ann Rheum Dis 1995;54:443–450.

6. Michet CJ. Osteoarthritis. Primary Care 1993;20: 815–826.

7. Lane NE, Buckwalter JA. Exercise: A cause of osteoarthritis? Rheum Dis Clin North Am 1993;19: 617–633.

8. Williams CJ, Jimenez SA. Heredity, genes, and osteoarthritis. Rheum Dis Clin North Am 1993;19: 523–541.

9. Adebajo AO. Osteoarthritis. Baillieres Clin Rheumatol 1995;9:65–74.

10. Hamerman D. Clinical implications of osteoarthritis and ageing. Ann Rheum Dis 1995;54:82–85.

11. Hochberg MC, Kasper J, Williamson J, Skinner A, Fried LP. The contribution of osteoarthritis to disability: preliminary data from the Women's Health and Aging study. Rheumatol 1995;22(suppl 43):16–18.

12. Gabriel SE, Crowson CS, O'Fallon WM. Costs of osteoarthritis: estimates from a geographically defined population. J Rheumatol 1995;22(suppl 43):23–25.

13. Felson DT. The course of osteoarthritis and factors that affect it. Rheum Dis Clin North Am 1993;19:607–615.

14. Cooper C. Occupational activity and the risk of osteoarthritis. J Rheumatol 1995;22(suppl 43):10–12.

15. Felson D. Weight and osteoarthritis. J Rheumatol 1995;22(suppl 43):7–9.

16. DeQueker J, Mokassa L, Aerssens J. Bone density and osteoarthritis. J Rheumatol 1995;22(suppl 43): 98–100.

17. Zhang YQ. Presentation at the American College of Rheumatology annual meeting 1995, quoted in Brown SJ. Estrogen therapy reduces knee osteoarthritis risk. Family Practice News, December 1, 1995:32.

18. Mandell BF, Lipani J. Refractory osteoarthritis: differential diagnosis and therapy. Rheum Dis Clin North Am 1995;21:163–178.

19. Malemud C. The role of growth factors in cartilage metabolism. Rheum Dis Clin North Am 1993;19: 569–580.

20. Ike RW. The role of arthroscopy in the differential diagnosis of osteoarthritis of the knee. Rheum Dis Clin North Am 1993;19:673–687.

21. Thonar EJ-MA, Shinmei M, Lohmander LS. Body fluid markers of cartilage changes in osteoarthritis. Rheum Dis Clin North Am 1993;19:635–657.

22. Thonar EJ-MA, Masuda K, Lenz ME, Hauselmann HJ, Kuettner KE, Manicourt DH. Serum markers of systemic disease processes in osteoarthritis. Rheumatol 1995;22(suppl 43):68–70.

23. Saxne T, Heinegard D. Matrix proteins: potentials as body fluid markers of changes in the metabolism of cartilage and bone in arthritis. J Rheumatol 1995;22(suppl 43):71–74.

24. Kaye JJ. Radiologic assessment of osteoarthritis: New Techniques. Rheum Dis Clin North Am 1993;19: 659–672.

25. Hutton CW, Vennart W. Osteoarthritis and magnetic resonance imaging: potential and problems. Ann Rheum Dis 1995;54:237–243.

26. Lorig KR, Mazonson PD, Holman HR. Evidence suggesting that health education for self-management in patients with chronic arthritis has sustained health benefits while reducing health care costs. Arthritis Rheum 1993;36:439–446.

27. Griffin MR, Brandt KD, Liang MH, Pincus T, Ray WA. Practical management of osteoarthritis. Arch Fam Med 1995;4:1049–1055.

28. Batchelor EE, Paulus HE. Principles of drug therapy. In: Moskowitz RW, Howell DS, Goldberg VM, Mankin HJ, eds. Osteoarthritis: Diagnosis and Medical/Surgical Management. 2nd ed. Philadelphia: WB Saunders, 1992.

29. Bradley JD, Brandt KD, Katz BP, Kalasinski LA, Ryan S. Comparison of an antiinflammatory dose of ibuprofen, an analgesic dose of ibuprofen, and acetaminophen in the treatment of patients with osteoarthritis in the knee. N Engl J Med 1991;325: 87–91.

30. Deal Cl, Schnitzer TJ, Lipstein E, Seibold JR, Stevens RM, Levy MD, et al. Treatment of arthritis with topical capsaicin: a double blind trial. Clin Ther 1991;13:383–395.

31. Schnitzer TJ, Posner M, Lawrence ID. High strength capsaicin cream for osteoarthritis pain: rapid onset

of action and improved efficacy with twice daily dos-ing. J Clin Rheumatol 1995;1:268–273.

32. Flynn BL. Rheumatoid arthritis and osteoarthritis: current and future therapies. Am Pharm 1994;NS34: 31–37, 41–42.

33. Neustadt DH. Intraarticular steroid therapy. In: Moskowitz RW, Howell DS, Goldberg VM, Mankin HJ, eds. Osteoarthritis: Diagnosis and Medical/Sur-gical Management. 2nd ed. Philadelphia: WB Saun-ders, 1992

34. Brandt KD. Nonsurgical management of os-teoarthritis, with an emphasis on nonpharmacologic measures. Arch Fam Med 1995;4:1057–1064.

35. Cushnagen J, McCarthy C, Dieppe P. Taping the patella medially: a new treatment for osteoarthritis of the knee joint? BMT 1994;308:753–755.

36. Puett DW, Griffin MR. Published trials of non-medicinal and noninvasive therapies for hip and knee osteoarthritis. Ann Intern Med 1994;121: 133–140.

Appendix B. United States Preventive Services Task Force Recommendations

Table 1. Ages 11–24 Years

Interventions Considered and Recommended for the Periodic Health Examination	Leading Causes of Death, Motor vehicle/other unintentional injuries, Homicide, Suicide, Malignant neoplasms, Heart diseases

Interventions for the General Population

Screening
Height & weight
Blood pressure[1]
Papanicolaou (Pap) test[2] (females)
Chlamydia screen[3] (females <20 yr)
Rubella serology or vaccination hx[4]
   (females >12 yr)
Assess for problem drinking

Counseling
Injury Prevention
   Lap/shoulder belts
   Bicycle/motorcycle/ATV helmets*
   Smoke detector*
   Safe storage/removal of firearms*
Substance Use
   Avoid tobacco use
   Avoid underage drinking & illicit drug use*
   Avoid alcohol/drug use while driving,
      swimming, boating, etc.*
Sexual Behavior
   STD prevention: abstinence*; avoid high-risk
      behavior*; condoms/female barrier with
      spermicide
   Unintended pregnancy: contraception

Diet and Exercise
   Limit fat & cholesterol; maintain caloric
      balance; emphasize grains, fruits, vegeta-
      bles
   Adequate calcium intake (females)
   Regular physical activity*
Dental Health
   Regular visits to dental care provider*
   Floss, brush with fluoride toothpaste daily*

Immunizations
Tetanus-diphtheria (Td) boosters (11–16 yr)
Hepatitis B[5]
MMR (11–12 yr)[6]
Varicella (11–12 yr)[7]
Rubella[4] (females >12 yr)

Chemoprophylaxis
Multivitamin with folic acid (females planning/
   capable of pregnancy)

Interventions for High-Risk Populations

Population	Potential Interventions (see detailed high-risk definitions)
High-risk sexual behavior	RPR/VDRL (HR1); screen for gonorrhea (female) (HR2), HIV (HR3), chlamydia (female) (HR4); hepatitis A vaccine (HR5)
Injection or street drug use	RPR/VDRL (HR1); HIV screen (HR3); hepatitis A vaccine (HR5); PPD (HR6); advice to reduce infection risk (HR7)
TB contacts; immigrants; low income	PPD (HR6)
Native Americans/Alaska Natives	Hepatitis A vaccine (HR5); PPD (HR6); pneumococcal vaccine (HR8)
Travelers to developing countries	Hepatitis A vaccine (HR5)
Certain chronic medical conditions	PPD (HR6); pneumococcal vaccine (HR8); influenza vaccine (HR9)
Settings where adolescents and young adults congregate	Second MMR (HR10)
Susceptible to varicella, measles, mumps	Varicella vaccine (HR11); MMR (HR12)
Blood transfusion between 1975–1985	HIV screen (HR3)
Institutionalized persons; health care/lab workers	Hepatitis A vaccine (HR5); PPD (HR6); influenza vaccine (HR9)
Family h/o skin cancer; nevi; fair skin, eyes, hair	Avoid excess/midday sun, use protective clothing[*] (HR13)
Prior pregnancy with neural tube defect	Folic acid 4.0 mg (HR14)
Inadequate water fluoridation	Daily fluoride supplement (HR15)

[1]Periodic BP for persons aged ≥21 yr. [2]If sexually active at present or in the past: q≤3 yr. If sexual history is unreliable, begin Pap test at age 18 yr. [3]If sexually active. [4]Serologic testing, documented vaccination history, and routine vaccination against rubella (preferably with MMR) are equally acceptable alternatives. [5]If not previously immunized: current visit, 1 and 6 mo later. [6]If no previous second dose of MMR. [7]If susceptible to chickenpox.
[*]The ability of clinical counseling to influence this behavior is unproven.
From U.S. Preventive Services Task Force Guide to clinical preventive services, 2nd ed. Baltimore: Williams & Wilkins, 1996. Format and design © 1996 Williams & Wilkins. Pages xiv and xv.

HR1 = Persons who exchange sex for money or drugs, and their sex partners; persons with other STDs (including HIV); and sexual contacts of persons with active syphilis. Clinicians should also consider local epidemiology

HR2 = Females who have: two or more sex partners in the last year; a sex partner with multiple sexual contacts; exchanged sex for money or drugs; or a history of repeated episodes of gonorrhea. Clinicians should also consider local epidemiology

HR3 = Males who had sex with males after 1975; past or present injection drug use; persons who exchange sex for money or drugs, and their sex partners; injection drug-using, bisexual, or HIV-positive sex partner currently or in the past; blood transfusion during 1978–1985; persons seeking treatment for STDs. Clinicians should also consider local epidemiology

HR4 = Sexually active females with multiple risk factors including: history of prior STD; new or multiple sex partners; age under 25; nonuse or inconsistent use of barrier contraceptives; cervical ectopy. Clinicians should consider local epidemiology of the disease in identifying other high-risk groups

HR5 = Persons living in, traveling to, or working in areas where the disease is endemic and where periodic outbreaks occur (e.g., countries with high or intermediate endemicity; certain Alaska Native, Pacific Island, Native American, and religious communities); men who have sex with men; injection or street drug users. Vaccine may be considered for institutionalized persons and workers in these institutions, military personnel, and day-care hospital, and laboratory workers. Clinicians should also consider local epidemiology

HR6 = HIV positive, close contacts of persons with known or suspected TB, health care workers, persons with medical risk factors associated with TB, immigrants from countries with high TB prevalence, medically underserved low-income populations (including homeless), alcoholics, injection drug users, and residents of long-term facilities

HR7 = Persons who continue to inject drugs

HR8 = Immunocompetent persons with certain medical conditions, including chronic cardiac or pulmonary disease, diabetes mellitus, and anatomic asplenia. Immunocompetent persons who live in high-risk environments or social settings (e.g., certain Native American and Alaska Native populations)

HR9 = Annual vaccination of: residents of chronic care facilities; persons with chronic cardiopulmonary disorders, metabolic diseases (including diabetes mellitus), hemoglobinopathies, immunosuppression, or renal dysfunction; and health care providers for high-risk patients

HR10 = Adolescents and young adults in settings where such individuals congregate (e.g., high schools and colleges), if they have not previously received a second dose

HR11 = Healthy persons aged $\geq$13 yr without a history of chickenpox or previous immunization. Consider serologic testing for presumed susceptible persons aged $\geq$13 yr

HR12 = Persons born after 1956 who lack evidence of immunity to measles or mumps (e.g., documented receipt of live vaccine on or after the first birthday, laboratory evidence of immunity, or a history of physician-diagnosed measles or mumps)

HR13 = Persons with a family or personal history of skin cancer, a large number of moles, atypical moles, poor tanning ability, or light skin, hair, and eye color

HR14 = Women with prior pregnancy affected by neural tube defect who are planning pregnancy

HR15 = Persons aged >17 yr living in areas with inadequate water fluoridation (<0.6 ppm)

Table 2. Ages 25–64 Years

Interventions Considered and Recommended for the Periodic Health Examination	Leading Causes of Death, Malignant neoplasms, Heart diseases, Motor vehicle and other unintentional injuries, Human immunodeficiency virus (HIV) infection, Suicide and homicide

Interventions for the General Population

Screening

Blood pressure
Height and weight
Total blood cholesterol (men age 35–64, women age 45–64)
Papanicolaou (Pap) test (women)[1]
Fecal occult blood test[2] and/or sigmoidoscopy (≥50 yr)
Mammogram ± clinical breast exam[3] (women 50–69 yr)
Assess for problem drinking
Rubella serology or vaccination hx[4] (women of childbearing age)

Counseling

Substance Use
    Tobacco cessation
    Avoid alcohol/drug use while driving, swimming, boating, etc.[*]
Diet and Exercise
    Limit fat & cholesterol; maintain caloric balance; emphasize grains, fruits, vegetables
    Adequate calcium intake (women)
    Regular physical activity[*]
Injury Prevention
    Lap/shoulder belts
    Motorcycle/bicycle/ATV helmets[*]
    Smoke detector[*]
    Safe storage/removal of firearms[*]
Sexual Behavior
    STD prevention: avoid high-risk behavior[*]; condoms/female barrier with spermicide[*]
    Unintended pregnancy: contraception
Dental Health
    Regular visits to dental care provider[*]
    Floss, brush with fluoride toothpaste daily[*]

Immunizations

Tetanus-diphtheria (Td) boosters
Rubella[4] (women of childbearing age)

Chemoprophylaxis

Multivitamin with folic acid (women planning or capable of pregnancy)
Discuss hormone prophylaxis (peri- and postmenopausal women)

Interventions for High-Risk Populations

Population	Potential Interventions (See detailed high risk definitions)
High-risk sexual behavior	RPR/VDRL (HR1); screen for gonorrhea (female) (HR2), HIV (HR3), chlamydia (female) (HR4); hepatitis B vaccine (HR5); hepatitis A vaccine (HR6)
Injection or street drug use	RPR/VDRL (HR1); HIV screen (HR3); hepatitis B vaccine (HR5); hepatitis A vaccine (HR6); PPD (HR7); advice to reduce infection risk (HR8)
Low income; TB contacts; immigrants; alcoholics	PPD (HR7)
Native American/Alaska Natives	Hepatitis A vaccine (HR6); PPD (HR7); pneumococcal vaccine (HR9)
Travelers to developing countries	Hepatitis B vaccine (HR5); hepatitis A vaccine (HR6)
Certain chronic medical conditions	PPD (HR7); pneumococcal vaccine (HR9); influenza vaccine (HR10)
Blood product recipients	HIV screen (HR3); hepatitis B vaccine (HR5)
Susceptible to measles, mumps, or varicella	MMR (HR11); varicella vaccine (HR12)
Institutionalized persons	Hepatitis A vaccine (HR6); PPD (HR7); pneumococcal vaccine (HR9); influenza vaccine (HR10)
Health care/lab workers	Hepatitis B vaccine (HR5); hepatitis A vaccine (HR6); PPD (HR7); influenza vaccine (HR10)
Family h/o skin cancer; fair skin, eyes, hair	Avoid excess/midday sun, use protective clothing* (HR13)
Previous pregnancy with neural tube defect	Folic acid 4.0 mg (HR14)

[1]Women who are or have been sexually active and who have a cervix: q≤3 yr. [2]Annually. [3]Mammogram q1–2 yr. or mammogram q1–2 yr with annual clinical breast examination. [4]Serologic testing, documented vaccination history, and routine vaccination (preferably with MMR) are equally acceptable.
*The ability of clinician counseling to influence this behavior is unproven.
From U.S. Preventive Services Task Force Guide to clinical preventive services, 2nd ed. Baltimore: Williams & Wilkins, 1996. Format and design © Williams & Wilkins. Pages xvi and xvii

HR1 = Persons who exchange sex for money or drugs, and their sex partners; persons with other STDs (including HIV); and sexual contacts of persons with active syphilis. Clinicians should also consider local epidemiology

HR2 = Women who exchange sex for money or drugs; or who have had repeated episodes of gonorrhea. Clinicians should also consider local epidemiology

HR3 = Men who had sex with men after 1975; past or present injection drug use; persons who exchange sex for money or drugs, and their sex partners; injection drug-using, bisexual, or HIV-positive sex partner currently or in the past; blood transfusion during 1978–1985; persons seeking treatment for STDs. Clinicians should also consider local epidemiology

HR4 = Sexually active women with multiple risk factors including: history of prior STD; new or multiple sex partners; nonuse or inconsistent use of barrier contraceptives; cervical ectopy. Clinicians should consider local epidemiology

HR5 = Blood product recipients (including hemodialysis patients), persons with frequent occupational exposure to blood or blood products, men who have sex with men, injection drug users and their sex partners, persons with multiple recent sex partners, persons with other STDs (including HIV), travelers to countries with endemic hepatitis B

HR6 = Persons living in, traveling to, or working in areas where the disease is endemic and where periodic outbreaks occur (e.g., countries with high or intermediate endemicity; certain Alaska Native, Pacific Island, Native American, and religious communities); men who have sex with men; injection or street drug users. Consider for institutionalized persons and workers in these institutions, military personnel, and day-care hospital, and laboratory workers. Clinicians should also consider local epidemiology

HR7 = HIV positive, close contacts of persons with known or suspected TB, health care workers, persons with medical risk factors associated with TB, immigrants from countries with high TB prevalence, medically underserved low-income populations (including homeless), alcoholics, injection drug users, and residents of long-term facilities

HR8 = Persons who continue to inject drugs

HR9 = Immunocompetent institutionalized persons aged $\geq$50 yr and immunocompetent persons with certain medical conditions, including chronic cardiac or pulmonary disease, diabetes mellitus, and anatomic asplenia. Immunocompetent persons who live in high-risk environments or social settings (e.g., certain Native American and Alaska Native populations)

HR10 = Annual vaccination of: residents of chronic care facilities; persons with chronic cardiopulmonary disorders, metabolic diseases (including diabetes mellitus), hemoglobinopathies, immunosuppression, or renal dysfunction; and health care providers for high-risk patients.

HR11 = Persons born after 1956 who lack evidence of immunity to measles or mumps (e.g., documented receipt of live vaccine on or after the first birthday, laboratory evidence of immunity, or a history of physician-diagnosed measles or mumps)

HR12 = Healthy adults without a history of chickenpox or previous immunization. Consider serologic testing for presumed susceptible adults

HR13 = Persons with a family or personal history of skin cancer, a large number of moles, atypical moles, poor tanning ability, or light skin, hair, and eye color

HR14 = Women with prior pregnancy affected by neural tube defect who are planning pregnancy

Table 3. Age 65 and Older

Interventions Considered and Recommended for the Periodic Health Examination	Leading Cause of Death, Heart diseases, Malignant neoplasms (lung, colorectal, breast), Cerebrovascular disease, Chronic obstructive pulmonary disease, Pneumonia and influenza

Interventions for the General Population

Screening

Blood pressure
Height and weight
Fecal occult blood test[1] and/or sigmoidoscopy
Mammogram ± clinical breast exam[2] (women ≤69 yr)
Papanicolaou (Pap) test (women)[3]
Vision screening
Assess for hearing impairment
Assess for problem drinking

Counseling

Substance Use
  Tobacco cessation
  Avoid alcohol/drug use while driving, swimming, boating, etc.[*]
Diet and Exercise
  Limit fat & cholesterol; maintain caloric balance; emphasize grains, fruits, vegetables
  Adequate calcium intake (women)
  Regular physical activity[*]
Injury Prevention
  Lap/shoulder belts
  Motorcycle and bicycle helmets[*]
  Fall prevention[*]
  Safe storage/removal of firearms[*]
  Smoke detector[*]
  Set hot water heater to <120–130°F[*]
  CPR training for household members

Dental Health

Regular visits to dental care provider[*]
Floss, brush with fluoride toothpaste daily[*]
Sexual Behavior
  STD prevention: avoid high-risk sexual behavior[*]; use condoms

Immunizations

Pneumococcal vaccine
Influenza[1]
Tetanus-diphtheria (Td) boosters

Chemoprophylaxis

Discuss hormone prophylaxis (peri- & postmenopausal women)

Interventions for High-Risk Populations

Population	Potential Interventions (See detailed high-risk definitions)
Institutionalized persons	PPD (HR1); hepatitis A vaccine (HR2); amantadine/ rimantadine (HR4)
Chronic medical conditions; TB contacts; low income; immigrants; alcoholics	PPD (HR1)
Persons ≥75 yr; or ≥70 yr with risk factors for falls	Fall prevention intervention (HR5)
Cardiovascular disease risk factors	Consider cholesterol screening (HR6)
Family h/o skin cancer; nevi; fair skin, eyes, hair	Avoid excess/midday sun, use protective clothing* (HR7)
Native Americans/Alaska Natives	PPD (HR1); hepatitis A vaccine (HR2)
Travelers to developing countries	Hepatitis A vaccine (HR2); hepatitis B vaccine (HR8)
Blood products recipients	HIV screen (HR3); hepatitis B vaccine (HR8)
High-risk sexual behavior	Hepatitis A vaccine (HR2); HIV screen (HR3); hepatitis B vaccine (HR8); RPR/VDRL (HR9)
Injection or street drug use	PPD (HR1); hepatitis A vaccine (HR2); HIV screen (HR3); hepatitis B vaccine (HR8); RPR/VDRL (HR9); advice to reduce infection risk (HR10)
Health care/lab workers	PPD (HR1); hepatitis A vaccine (HR2); amantadine/ rimantadine (HR4); hepatitis B vaccine (HR8)
Persons susceptible to varicella	Varicella vaccine (HR11)

[1]Annually. [2]Mammogram q1–2 yr, or mammogram q1–2 yr with annual clinical breast exam. [3]All women who are or have been sexually active and who have a cervix. Consider discontinuation of testing after age 65 yr if previous regular screening with consistently normal results.
*The ability of clinician counseling to influence this behavior is unproven.
From U.S. Preventive Services Task Force Guide to clinical preventive services, 2nd ed. Baltimore: Williams & Wilkins, 1996. Format and design © 1996, Williams & Wilkins. Pages xviii and xix.

HR1 = HIV positive, close contacts of persons with known or suspected TB, health care workers, persons with medical risk factors associated with TB, immigrants from countries with high TB prevalence, medically underserved low-income populations (including homeless), alcoholics, injection drug users, and residents of long-term facilities.

HR2 = Persons living in, traveling to, or working in areas where the disease is endemic and where periodic outbreaks occur (e.g., countries with high or intermediate endemicity; certain Alaska Native, Pacific Island, Native American, and religious communities); men who have sex with men; injection or street drug users. Consider for institutionalized persons and workers in these institutions and day-care, hospital, and laboratory workers. Clinicians should also consider local epidemiology

HR3 = Men who had sex with men after 1975; past or present injection drug use; persons who exchange sex for money or drugs, and their sex partners; injection drug-using, bisexual, or HIV-positive sex partner currently or in the past; blood transfusion during 1978–1985; persons seeking treatment for STDs. Clinicians should also consider local epidemiology

HR4 = Consider for persons who have not received influenza vaccines or are vaccinated late; when the vaccine may be ineffective due to major antigenic changes in the virus; for unvaccinated persons who provide home care for high-risk persons; to supplement protection provided by vaccine in persons who are expected to have a poor antibody response; and for high-risk persons in whom the vaccine is contraindicated

HR5 = Persons aged 75 years and older; or aged 70–74 with one or more additional risk factors including: use of certain psychoactive and cardiac medications (e.g., benzodiazepines, antihypertensives); use of ≥4 prescription medications; impaired cognition, strength, balance, or gait. Intensive individualized home-based multifactorial fall prevention intervention is recommended in settings where adequate resources are available to deliver such services

HR6 = Although evidence is insufficient to recommend routine screening in elderly persons, clinicians should consider cholesterol screening on a case-by-case basis for persons ages 65–75 with additional risk factors (e.g., smoking, diabetes, or hypertension)

HR7 = Persons with a family or personal history of skin cancer, a large number of moles, atypical moles, poor tanning ability, or light skin, hair, and eye color

HR8 = Blood product recipients (including hemodialysis patients), persons with frequent occupational exposure to blood or blood products, men who have sex with men, injection drug users and their sex partners, persons with multiple recent sex partners, persons with other STDs (including HIV), travelers to countries with endemic hepatitis B

HR9 = Persons who exchange sex for money or drugs and their sex partners; persons with other STDs (including HIV); and sexual contacts of persons with active syphilis. Clinicians should also consider local epidemiology

HR10 = Persons who continue to inject drugs

HR11 = Healthy adults without a history of chickenpox or previous immunization. Consider serologic testing for presumed susceptible adults

Table 4. Pregnant Women**

Interventions Considered and Recommended for the Periodic Health Examination

Interventions for the General Population

Screening
First Visit
Blood pressure
Hemoglobin/hematocrit
Hepatitis B surface antigen (HBsAg)
RPR/VDRL
Chlamydia screen (<25 yr)
Rubella serology or vaccination history
D (Rh) typing, antibody screen
Offer CVS (<13 wk)[1] or amniocentesis
  (15–18 wk)[1] (age ≥35 yr)
Offer hemoglobinopathy screening
Assess for problem or risk drinking
Offer HIV screening[2]
Follow-up visits
Blood pressure
Urine culture
Offer amniocentesis (15–18 wk)[1]
  (age ≥35 yr)

Offer multiple marker testing[1] (15–18 wk)
Offer serum α-fetoprotein[1] (16–18 wk)

Counseling
Tobacco cessation; effects of passive
  smoking
Alcohol/other drug use
Nutrition, including adequate calcium intake
Encourage breastfeeding
Lap/shoulder belts
Infant safety car seats
STD prevention: avoid high-risk sexual behav-
  ior*; use condoms*

Chemoprophylaxis
Multivitamin with folic acid[3]

Interventions for High-Risk Populations

Population	Potential Interventions (See detailed high-risk definitions)
High-risk sexual behavior	Screen for chlamydia (1st visit) (HR1), gonorrhea (1st visit) (HR2); HIV (1st visit) (HR3); HBsAg (3rd trimester) (HR4); RPR/VDRL (3rd trimester) (HR5)
Blood transfusion 1978–1985	HIV screen (1st visit) (HR3)
Injection drug use	HIV screen (HR3); HBsAg (3rd trimester) (HR4); advice to reduce infection risk (HR6)
Unsensitized D-negative women	D (Rh) antibody testing (24–28 wk) (HR7)
Risk factors for Down syndrome	Offer CVS[1] (1st trimester), amniocentesis[1] (15–18 wk) (HR8)
Prior pregnancy with neural tube defect	Offer amniocentesis[1] (15–18 wk), folic acid 4.0 mg[3] (HR9)

[1]Women with access to counseling and follow-up services, reliable standardized laboratories, skilled high-resolution ultrasound, and, for those receiving serum marker testing, amniocentesis capabilities. [2]Universal screening is recommended for areas (states, counties, or cities) with an increased prevalence of HIV infection among pregnant women. In low-prevalence areas, the choice between universal and targeted screening may depend on other considerations (see Ch. 28). [3]Beginning at least 1 mo before conception and continuing through the first trimester.
*The ability of clinician counseling to influence this behavior is unproven.
**See Tables 2 and 3 for other preventive services recommended for women of this age group.

HR1 = Women with history of STD or new or multiple sex partners. Clinicians should also consider local epidemiology. Chlamydia screen should be repeated in 3rd trimester if at continued risk

HR2 = Women under age 25 with two or more sex partners in the last year, or whose sex partner has multiple sexual contacts; women who exchange sex for money or drugs; and women with a history of repeated episodes of gonorrhea. Clinicians should also consider local epidemiology. Gonorrhea screen should be repeated in the 3rd trimester if at continued risk

HR3 = In areas where universal screening is not performed due to low prevalence of HIV infection, pregnant women with the following individual risk factors should be screened: past or present injection drug use; women who exchange sex for money or drugs; injection drug-using bisexual, or HIV-positive sex partner currently or in the past; blood transfusion during 1978–1985; persons seeking treatment for STDs

HR4 = Women who are initially HBsAg negative who are at high risk due to injection drug use, suspected exposure to hepatitis B during pregnancy, multiple sex partners

HR5 = Women who exchange sex for money or drugs, women with other STDs (including HIV), and sexual contacts of persons with active syphilis. Clinicians should also consider local epidemiology

HR6 = Women who continue to inject drugs

HR7 = Unsensitized D-negative women

HR8 = Prior pregnancy affected by Down syndrome, advanced maternal age (≥35 yr), known carriage of chromosome rearrangement

HR9 = Women with previous pregnancy affected by neural tube defect

Appendix C. Age Charts For Periodic Health Examination

American Academy of Family Physicians
November 1995

These Age Charts contain recommendations based on the *First Edition of the Guide to Clinical Preventive Services* (1989) and other outcomes-based recommendations, as well as the CDC Advisory Committee on Immunization Practices and the AAFP Commission on Public Health and Scientific Affairs through September 1995. A second revision of these age charts is anticipated in 1996 because of publication of the *Second Edition of the Guide to Clinical Preventive Services*, December 1995. There are Age Charts for all age groups.

Other charts available include

- 510   Preamble
- 510A   Ages Birth–18 Months
- 510B   Ages 19 Months–6 Years
- 510C   Ages 7–12 Years
- 510D   Ages 13–18 Years
- 510E   Ages 19–39 Years
- 510F   Ages 40–64 Years
- 510G   Ages 65 Years and Older

Preamble to Age Charts for Periodic Health Examination

Periodic health examination, including immunizations, counseling, and other preventive services, are a part of continuing, comprehensive care in family practice. The content and frequency of these health examinations should be tailored to the patient's age, sex, and risk factors. Delivery of clinical preventive services should not be limited only to visits for health maintenance but also should be provided as a part of visits for other reasons such as acute and chronic care. For many patients, these visits provide the only opportunity to receive preventive services.

The following age-specific charts for periodic health examination are recommended by the Subcommittee on Periodic Health Intervention of the Commission on Public Health and Scientific Affairs as the minimum clinical preventive services to be provided for asymptomatic patients. They are based on the *First Edition of the Guide to Clinical Preventive Services: Report of the U.S. Preventive Services Task Force*, the American College of Physicians outcomes-based recommendations on hormone replacement therapy and recommendations of the Commission on Public Health and Scientific Affairs. In making these recommendations, the subcommittee notes:

A) That all patients new to a medical practice should be urged to receive a comprehensive history and physical as well as the screening, laboratory and diagnostic procedures, counseling, immunizations and chemoprophylaxis appropriate for the patient's age, sex, and risk. Subsequent visits may be used in completion of workup.

B) That former health records should be obtained for review and avoidance of duplications of laboratory testing.

C) That the charts are not exhaustive and that physicians may add other preventive services either routinely or for individual patients based on clinical judgement.

D) That as new scientific findings become available, the subcommittee anticipates changes in the recommendations.

E) That the subcommittee has added interventions beyond the recommendations of the U.S. Preventive Services Task Force and other explicitly developed guidelines that it feels are necessary. These are noted with footnotes on the charts and shown in italics.

F) The date in the lower left hand corner identifies the most recent update of these charts. The date in the lower right hand corner is the most recent printing. This document is updated annually.

Index

References in italics denote figures; "t" denotes tables